THE NATURE OF TEN

LANDLORD AND TENANT LAW
The Nature of Tenancies

BY

SUSAN BRIGHT

and

DR GEOFF GILBERT

CLARENDON PRESS · OXFORD

1995

Oxford University Press, Walton Street, Oxford OX2 6DP

Oxford New York
Athens Auckland Bangkok Bombay
Calcutta Cape Town Dar es Salaam Delhi
Florence Hong Kong Istanbul Karachi
Kuala Lumpur Madras Madrid Melbourne
Mexico City Nairobi Paris Singapore
Taipei Tokyo Toronto
and associated companies in
Berlin Ibadan

Oxford is a trade mark of Oxford University Press

Published in the United States
by Oxford University Press Inc., New York

British Library Cataloguing in Publication Data
Data available

Library of Congress Cataloging in Publication Data
Data available
ISBN 0–19–876348–4
ISBN 0–19–876349–2(Pbk)

1 3 5 7 9 10 8 6 4 2

Set by Hope Services (Abingdon) Ltd.
Printed in Great Britain
on acid-free paper by
Biddles Ltd., Guildford and King's Lynn

PREFACE

The genesis of this book stemmed from our joint teaching of a course on landlord and tenant law in which we sought to explore not only the law, but the policies and concerns underlying it, and to trace common themes of regulation across all sectors. None of the existing books took this approach to the subject and we have written this book in the hope that it will fill this gap. The book therefore covers all types of residential tenancy, commercial tenancies and agricultural tenancies— and we have drawn on legal and non-legal matters that help to explain how the landlord and tenant relationship works in practice. It should also be noted that an underlying problem with trying to set landlord and tenant law in context is that information on housing policies and practice often applies to the whole of the United Kingdom, while Scotland, for instance, has a separate legal system. The book is intended as an analytical study of landlord and tenant law for academics, students, practising lawyers, surveyors and property specialists generally. Selected materials are included: some, in particular statutory material, were selected because of the need to ensure that the reader is able to read the precise wording of the section (rather than our summary of it) and to have key statutory controls available within the book as a source of reference. Some statutory material has been included because it is not readily accessible to lawyers from statute books which generally omit the particular provisions—this is especially true of the sections dealing with rent to mortgage. Other material, such as extracts from law reports and articles, have been included where it is better to quote the original rather than to paraphrase points made by others. Given the confines of space, the book cannot be fully comprehensive in treatment of detailed issues of landlord and tenant law—for this there are specialist looseleaf books available. What this book seeks to do is to help the reader understand the way in which the landlord and tenant relationship works and the ways in which the law regulates this relationship.

Writing a legal textbook is complicated by the rapid changes that occur in the law. The law is stated as at 1 January 1995, although some developments have been incorporated since that date. Most notable are the changes to agricultural tenancy law. The government has recently announced its intention to exempt tenanted agricultural land from inheritance tax so that this sector will be treated on a par with owner occupied land (see Inland Revenue Press Release, 27 January 1995). In addition, the Agricultural Tenancies Bill 1995 has, at the time of writing, just received its Third Reading in the House of Commons, having already been considered in the House of Lords. The main provisions of this Bill were well flagged by various government announcements and are referred to in the text of the book. In addition, the Annex sets out the most important sections of the Bill. Reform of continuing liability in leases, somewhat misleadingly labelled privity of contract, has been high on the agenda in recent years and although no legislation on this was announced in the Queen's Speech in the Autumn of 1994, there are signs that early reform on this is still possible—a further consultation paper has been issued with the possibility of legislation during the Parliamentary session 1995–96 (Lord Chancellor's Department, *Rights and Duties of Landlords and Tenants: A Consultation Paper*, March 1995). Privity may even be reformed by the summer of 1995 as the government has announced its support for a private member's bill (see Financial Times, 22 April 1995). The lines of reform are outlined in the text of the book but it may be that landlords will be given stronger rights to vet proposed assignees than suggested by the earlier proposals. The revised Tenant's Guarantee, 1994, was finalised at the very end of 1994 and the book refers to the anticipated changes between the earlier, 1991, version and the 1994 revision. The duties of local authorities towards the homeless have been further reduced by a recent decision of Blom-Cooper J (*R v Wandsworth LBC, exparte Crooks*, The Times 12 April 1995). It enables local authorities to satisfy their duty to homeless applicants with priority need who are not intentionally homeless to provide settled accomodation by securing the provision of short-term lets in the private sector. Finally, the Prime Minister, John Major, announced a new government White Paper on housing in April 1995 which would encourage homeownership, give the Right To Buy to all housing association tenants, prevent single mothers from obtaining priority on council waiting lists and seek to attract private investment into social housing (The *Sunday Times* pp 1 and 2, 2 April 1995).

While our backgrounds to this subject are very different, it is very much a jointly written book. Geoff has experience of advising mostly on the public law side of housing stemming from advice work in clinics; Sue has experience mainly of private housing and commercial property having practised as a solicitor in London. Notwithstanding these differing backgrounds, large sections of the book have effectively been written by us together—and the remaining sections we have both read and tinkered with quite freely.

As is usual with a project of this size, we have received a great deal of help from others, especially in our Departments at Essex and Oxford. In particular, we would like to thank various people who have commented on the structure of the book, suggested reading and looked at individual chapters. For this, we are indebted to Professor Mike Harloe of the Department of Sociology at Essex, Christopher Coombe of Linklaters & Paines, Jonathan Turton of Boodle Hatfield, Simon Gardner of Lincoln College, Oxford, John Dewar of Hertford College, Oxford, Peter Luther and Maurice Sunkin at Essex and Eddie Veitch, University of New Brunswick. Particular mention must be made of Ruth Gladden whose services in typing (and correcting many of our errors) were invaluable following Sue's unexpected incapacity in the aftermath of a car crash—Ruth was truly wonderful. Our thanks also go to John Whelan, Richard Hart, Sandra Sinden and

Kristin Clayton at Oxford University Press for all their help. Lastly, but by no means least, we would like to thank our partners for their encouragement and patience: in particular, Sue would like to thank Chris for many helpful discussions, while Geoff received many useful ideas from Clare on aspects of Chapter 2, *Policy.*

And finally, we especially mention Geoff's girls, *Sarah and Mary-Ann,* and Sue's boys, *Samuel and Thomas.*

Susan Bright
Geoff Gilbert
1995

CONTENTS

ACKNOWLEDGEMENTS

Grateful acknowledgement is made to all the authors and publishers of extract material which appears in this book, and in particular to the following for permission to reprint material from the sources indicated:

ASI Research: Burton, J., *Retail Rents: Fair and Free Market?*, (1992), pp 82–3.

Boston College Law Review: Glendon, 'The Transformation of American Landlord–Tenant Law', (1982), 23 Bos C LR 503, pp 503–5, 555–6.

Butterworth & Co. (Publishers) Ltd.: Extracts from the *All England Reports*; Rodgers, C.P., *Agricultural Law*, (1991), pp 2, 151; Bright, 'Uncertainty in Leases—Is it a Vice?', (1993) 13 *Leg Stud* 38, pp 44–5, 47.

Campaign for Bedsit Rights: Jew, P., 'Law and Order in Private Rented Housing: Tackling Harassment and Illegal Eviction', (1994), pp 14, 33, 79.

Greenwood Press: van Vliet, W., *International Handbook of Housing Policies and Practices*, (1990), pp 91, 94, 96, 117, 121–2, 138–9, 148–9, 300, 311, 320, 321, 337, 342, 355, 728, 730–1.

HMSO Publications: 'Approval of Short Term Lettings and Licences: Joint Announcement of the Agricultural Departments: 10 August 1989', (extracted in Rodgers, *Agricultural Law*, (1991), pp 384–5); 'Housing the Homeless: the Local Authority Role', Audit Commission, (1989); 'Developing Local Authority Housing Strategies', (1992), para 13; 'Landlord and Tenant, Distress for Rent', Law Com No 194, (1991), para 1, Part III 3.2; 'Landlord and Tenant: Reform of the Law', Law Com No 162, (1987); 'Landlord and Tenant: Responsibility for State and Condition of Property', Consultation Paper, Law Com No 123, (1992), paras 2.19, 2.22, 2.25, 2.27, 3.15, 3.1, 3.31, 4.14, 4.8, 4.9, 5.7; 'Covenants Restricting Dispositions, Alterations and Change of User', Law Com No 141, (1985), paras 3.61, 4.15, 7.2.

Joseph Rowntree Foundation, and Wilcox, S.: *Housing Finance Review 1994/95*, (1994), p 82, and Tables 13b, 56, 75, 101b.

Macmillan Education: Gibb, K., and Munro, M., *Housing Finance in the United Kingdom: An Introduction*, (1991), pp 143–4, 210, 219.

Macmillan Press Ltd.: Malpass, P., and Murie, A., *Housing Policy and Practice*, 3rd edn. (1990), pp 6–7, 88, 92–4, 133, 142, 143, 150–1; 4th edn, (1994), pp 4, 10, 26, 32, 37, 61, 62, 71, 98–105, 115–16, 126, 140–1, 172–7, 209, 282–3, 286–7, 309, 299–300, 301.

Monash University Law Review: Effron, 'The Contractualisation of the Law of Leasehold', (1988), 14 Monash Univ Law Rev 83, at 98.

Oxford University Press: Atiyah, P.S., *The Rise and Fall of Freedom of Contract*, (1979), pp 184, 428, 634, 636, 317, 636–7; Bright, 'Beyond Sham and Into Pretence', (1991) 11 *OJLS* 136, pp 140–1, 142.

Pitman Publishing: Ginsburg, 'Home Ownership and Socialism in Britian: A Bulwark Against Bolshevism', (1983) 3:1 Critical Social Policy 34, p 47; Jacobs, 'The Sale of Council Houses: Does It Matter?', (1981) 1:2 Critical Social Policy 35, pp 37, 41–2, 44.

Roof: Blake, 'Whose Future Is It Anyway?', (September/ October 1994), pp 20, 22; 'Selected Housing Associations', (March/April, 1993), Table; (May/June 1994), p 13, Tables 54(a) and (b); Forrest and Murie, 'The Right To Buy', in Grant, C., *Built to Last?: Reflections on British Housing Policy—A Collection of Articles from 'Roof' magazine*, (1992), pp 139, 141, 145.

Shelter (National Campaign for the Homeless): Butler, Carlisle, and Lloyd, *Homelessness in the 1990s: Local Authority Practice*, (1994), pp 20, 21, Table 15 on p 27.

The Estate Gazette Group: Brett, M., *Property and Money*, (1990), pp 11–12.

The Incorporated Council of Law Reporting for England & Wales for permission to reproduce extracts from the *Weekly Law Reports* and *Official Law Reports*.

Sweet and Maxwell Ltd.: Extracts from the *Housing Law Reports*; Yates, D., and Hawkins, A.J., *Landlord and Tenant Law*, 2nd edn., (1988), pp 6, 7, 162, 801, 810.

The Yale Law Journal Company and Fred B. Rothman & Co.: Ackerman, 'Regulating Slum Housing Markets on Behalf of the Poor: Of Housing Codes, Housing Subsidies and Income Redistribution Policy', (1971), *Yale Law Journal*, vol. 80, pp 1095, 1096–7.

* Every effort was made to contact copyright holders.

TABLE OF CASES

UK

AUSTRALIA

CANADA

EUROPEAN COURT OF HUMAN RIGHTS

IRELAND

TABLE OF UNITED KINGDOM LEGISLATION

TABLE OF LEGISLATION FROM OTHER JURISDICTIONS

IRELAND

US

TABLE OF INTERNATIONAL INSTRUMENTS

1

Introduction

1.1 EXAMINING THE NATURE OF TENANCIES

This book takes a fresh look at the principles which provide the foundation of the landlord and tenant relationship. The dynamics of this relationship are shaped not only by law, but also by a variety of social, political and economic factors. A study of the law alone does not give a complete picture of the landlord and tenant relationship. An exclusive concentration upon the legal aspects of the relationship makes it difficult to understand the role that letting property plays within our society, and the social, political and economic goals that the legislation in this area is seeking to promote and protect.

The landlord and tenant relationship gives rise to a number of issues that are common to all types of tenancies, whether they be residential, commercial or agricultural. For tenants, the tenancy is important not simply because it is a property asset but because of the particular and special significance of that asset, whether it be a home or a commercial base. In all sectors, security of tenure and affordable rents may be important to the tenant. The reasons why security is important to him may differ: for the retailer it may be essential to the success of his business as security protects the goodwill built up over the years, whereas for the home-dweller it provides shelter and protects him from the psychological trauma, disruption and economic consequences of having to move. Nor is a lease simply a right to occupy premises—in many situations, the tenant is entitled, by contract or statute, to receive a package of services from the landlord, such as the right to have the property well maintained and heated.

For landlords, although the lease will generally be a source of wealth, there may be other considerations that influence the landlord's behaviour. While some landlords seek to observe good management practices, whether for welfarist or commercial motives, others may be more ruthless in their treatment of tenants, seeking to maximize profit and minimize management costs. In some situations the law has, therefore, had to intervene to promote minimum standards of behaviour and to protect tenants from exploitation and eviction.

In writing this book we have decided to break with the more traditional 'black letter' law sector-by-sector analysis and, instead, to examine issues that arise in the landlord and tenant relationship across the different sectors. The book will therefore be divided up by reference to these issues rather than by sector. There are many occasions when it is necessary to look at the regulation of each sector individually, but whenever possible the sectors are dealt with collectively to examine the common features of regulation. In exploring these issues, the book draws upon legal materials from other jurisdictions where appropriate and upon studies from other disciplines.

1.2 THE VARIETY OF LETTING ARRANGEMENTS

The relationship of landlord and tenant arises when one person, the tenant, has the right to exclusive possession of the land of another, the landlord, for a length of time. Usually, but not always, this will be in return for some kind of monetary payment, the rent. This relationship can be described as either a tenancy or a lease—while there is no difference between a tenancy and a lease, the expression tenancy is more often used in the case of short term lettings.

There is wide variety within the landlord and tenant relationship. Some may be intended to last for only a short period, such as a let of holiday accommodation, and some may be for extremely long periods, such as a 999 year lease. Some may be granted in return for a substantial capital payment and only a nominal rent, others for no premium, but for a market rent. It is helpful to set out the characteristics of some of the more standard relationships that occur to highlight the major issues facing landlords and tenants in each sector.

1.2.1 The Public Sector

Before 1989, the public sector would have comprised residential properties let by local authorities and similar public institutions, such as New Towns, along with residential accommodation let by housing associations. The public sector was synonymous with social housing, where the landlord was not trying to make a profit out of renting accommodation. It was assumed to be low-rent housing for low-income households, although the picture was somewhat more complex—see ch 2 generally. The Housing Act 1988 took subsequent housing association lets into the private sector, although safeguards for new tenants found in the Tenants' Guarantee put them in a better position than standard private sector 'assured' tenants (Housing Corporation Circulars 28 and 29/91; in addition, a 1994 Housing Corporation Consultation Document includes a revised Draft Tenants' Guarantee). Nevertheless, housing associations are now receiving less grant aid from central government than in the past, and have adopted two strategies to try to continue to meet need. First, deals are reached with local authorities to acquire land or properties on favourable terms, with local authorities then having rights to allocate many of the new housing association tenants (§A3,

Tenants' Guarantee, *op. cit.*; see also, Langstaff, 'Housing Associations: A Move to Centre Stage', in Johnston Birchall (ed.) *Housing Policy in the 1990s*, 1992, p 29, and esp. at pp 40–41). Secondly, housing associations have to borrow ever larger sums from private financial institutions, putting up rents and creating conflict between their social roots and their present commercial needs (Blake, *Whose Future Is It Anyway?* ROOF, September/October 1994, pp 20 *et seq.*). Thus, with housing associations granting only private sector tenancies now, the public sector is predominantly local authority lettings.

Local authority lettings were negligible before the end of World War I, but by 1979 they comprised 32 per cent of all households in England and Wales. The Right To Buy, giving council tenants the right to become owner-occupiers or long leaseholders of their home at a discounted price, was introduced in the Housing Act 1980 and led to a dramatic move to owner-occupation in the early part of the 1980s. Nevertheless, local authorities remain the biggest residential landlord (approximately 4 million dwellings) with a somewhat reduced share of the total rented stock to that which they had in 1979. Local authorities, by their very size, tend to be impersonal and remote from their tenants. To combat this, many have established decentralized housing offices within council estates.

From 1918 onwards, it was common policy between the political parties that local authorities fulfilled a necessary housing role, although the precise nature of that role differed somewhat. However, Conservative Party policy since 1979 has been to residualize the role of the local authorities as much as possible in all fields, and housing has been similarly constrained, with transfers of assets, reduced autonomy, restricted funding and compulsory contracting out. Whether local authorities will remain providers of housing in the future, as opposed to regulators and co-ordinators, is not yet finally resolved. Nevertheless, no other landlord has the experience to manage such large quantities of housing and meet housing need on such a scale—to dispense with that experience would render what limited overall housing policy (as opposed to tenure policy) that exists in England and Wales even more unco-ordinated and, necessarily, ineffective.

Local authority tenants tend to hold on short term (weekly or monthly) periodic tenancies. The idea, though, used to be that once a person became a council tenant, then the household had a home for life. Several things have changed that: the Right To Buy, council estate transfers of various sorts, the deteriorating standard of some council properties and government proposals to use council housing for emergency cases only while tenants are eventually housed in the private sector. Council tenants are a changing community, too. The role of local authorities as a provider of homes has been subject to debate ever since the 1920s: are they general landlords or are they landlords for the poor only? This debate forms part of a wider discussion of housing policy as a whole and its impact upon local authorities. (This discussion is dealt with in greater detail at ch 2.6.3—see also,

Malpass and Murie, *Housing Policy and Practice*, 4th edn, 1994, pp 44–95.) In brief, the condition of private rented properties was very poor before 1914, whereas local authority building after World War I was of a higher standard, leading to councils becoming the landlord of choice. Given that they were building good quality homes, particularly up to the mid-1950s, local authorities charged rents that were beyond the reach of the very poor—council housing provided homes for the skilled, better-off working class households. Nevertheless, central government, especially when the Conservatives were in power, sought to push local authorities to a more welfare-oriented role. Several individual policies contributed to this change, including the emphasis on tenant subsidies (presently, housing benefit) rather than a general housing subsidy for the local authority, but the current position where two-thirds of all council tenants are in receipt of housing benefit and where many have economically inactive heads of household (unemployed, single parents, elderly) can in large measure be attributed to the pre-eminence given to owner-occupation as the solution to housing problems in the 1980s. Wherever possible, council tenants bought their own homes under the Right To Buy. The better-off tenants left the local authority sector and took the better quality housing with them—local authorities were prevented from building to replace this lost housing. Yet, for the remaining tenants, local authorities are still the landlord of choice, as can be seen from the fact that Tenants' Choice, where tenants could vote to oust the local authority and accept a new (private or housing association) landlord, was such an abysmal failure—(see further, ch 10.6).

1.2.2 The Private Sector

There has been a dramatic decline in the size of the private rental sector this century: from representing about 90 per cent of housing in 1914, to around 10 per cent in the 1990s. Whereas in the nineteenth century the majority of housing was privately rented, the sector now largely houses those who are unable to gain access to the other tenures; those who do not have the resources for owner-occupation and are not in priority categories for public housing. It no longer represents the generally preferred form of tenure, and housing standards and conditions in this sector are generally worse than in the other two tenure types. In consequence, the private sector tends to house the economically weak or those who wish to remain mobile, for example, students, people who frequently move jobs or who are settling into a new area. Lettings tend to be either short term periodic lettings (weekly or monthly)—which may in practice be continued for many years—or lettings for fixed term periods. It is difficult to obtain accurate statistics on private renting, and numerous surveys have been conducted with differing results, depending in part upon methodology, sample size and geographical area surveyed. Nevertheless, it is clear that much of the private sector is owned by small landlords (that is, landlords with relatively few holdings). A recent survey showed that 63 per cent of private rented stock was owned by individual landlords (3 per cent of whom were resident), 21 per cent by employer landlords, 9 per cent by property companies and the remaining 7 per cent were non-identified (Rauta and Pickering, *Private Renting in England 1990*, 1992, p 9). This survey excluded property rented from housing associations and charitable trusts. The survey also excluded a group that is felt to be a potentially significant sub-group, that is, tenants of owner-occupiers who would count as members of the landlord's household. An earlier survey of densely populated areas in England and Wales conducted by Paley adopted a slightly different classification of landlords which makes direct comparison with the survey by Rauta and Pickering difficult. Nevertheless, it is interesting that Paley found that about one-quarter of individual landlords lived on the same premises as their tenants (see Paley, *Attitudes to Letting in 1976*, 1978, p 9; see also ch 2). During the 1990s' property slump, a significant proportion of landlords were property owners unable or unwilling to sell their properties (almost one-fifth of landlords in one survey: Joseph Rowntree Foundation, Housing Research Findings No. 90, May 1993).

As demand for rented housing generally outstrips supply, the landlord is usually in the stronger bargaining position and this inequality has led to government intervention in the relationship, in particular to protect the tenant from rising rents and eviction. As Scarman LJ said in *Horford Investments Ltd v Lambert* [1976] Ch 39 at 52:

The policy of the Rent Acts was and is to protect the tenant in his home, whether the threat be to exhort a premium for the grant or renewal of his tenancy, to increase his rent, or to evict him . . . The Rent Acts have throughout their history constituted an interference with contract and property rights for a specific purpose—the redress of the balance of advantage enjoyed in a world of housing shortage by the landlord over those who have to rent their homes.

While the pattern of legislation since 1915 has been to strengthen tenants' rights, this policy has recently been reversed. The Housing Act 1988 makes dramatic inroads on the protection previously given to tenants, in the belief that it is necessary to return to free market principles in order to revitalize this sector. However, different landlord-types will have different priorities and goals in letting property—legislation that is designed to revitalize the private rented sector may have an impact on certain groups of landlord, but not others.

Notwithstanding the 1988 reforms, investment in the private rental market remains generally unattractive for a variety of reasons. In economic terms, rental residential property often provides a relatively low return on investment: one report in the early 1980s found that, on average, net returns on *registered* rents were of the order of 1–2 per cent once the costs of providing the accommodation were taken into consideration but before any tax liability (House of Commons Environment Committee, *The Private Rented Housing Sector*, 1981/2, Vol 1, para 36). Average yields have improved since the passing of the Housing Act 1988 which enabled landlords to charge market rents: the Rowntree Research Findings No. 90, *op. cit.*, found that net returns were in excess of 6 per cent (but found also that a net return in excess of 10 per cent was required to attract new investment). Tax is payable on the capital gains when the property is sold, and bad tenants can mean landlords suffering the effects of arrears or costly eviction proceedings. Property also has a low liquidity: unlike shares, for example, property takes considerable time to sell, and to realize its full potential it needs to be sold with vacant possession. Day-to-day management—rent collection, repairs and so on—can be costly and time consuming. In addition to these factors, there are various negative images associated with private landlordism. Landlords as a class have often been perceived as profiteers, exploiting the vulnerable in society.

Many feel that in order to revitalize the private rented sector it is necessary to attract institutional investors. Until private rented housing is able to provide a competitive and secure return on investment, institutional funds are, however, unlikely to invest significantly in this sector. In the absence of reform of the housing finance system, including the taxation treatment of money invested in housing, there is unlikely to be any significant change in the level of institutional investment.

This pattern of decline has also been found in the United States. A study by Sternlieb and Hughes shows that as the private rental market has increasingly become the tenure of low income groups this, coupled with rent control and more onerous management duties, has placed constraints on the attraction of investment in rental housing (see Sternlieb and Hughes, *The Future of Rental Housing*, 1981, esp. pp 87–9, 93–4).

1.2.3 Long Leases of Residential Property

Long leases have been used for selling sometimes both houses and flats. Historically, long leasehold sales were used for housing developments, originally under the building lease system (see 1.2.6), and more recently by landlords with a long term perspective on investment. Since the Leasehold Reform Act 1967 gave long leaseholders of houses the right to buy the freehold, few new housing developments were sold on a leasehold basis.

Since the 1950s it has been increasingly common for flats and maisonettes to be purpose-built for sale on long leases and for existing buildings to be converted into flats. Blocks built for rental in earlier times have been 'broken-up' for long leasehold sales and many of these buildings now contain flats of mixed tenure, some rental and some long leasehold. The Report of the

Committee of Enquiry on the Management of Privately Owned Blocks of Flats, 1985 (The Nugee Committee Report), traced several reasons for this development: the restriction on rents imposed by the Rent Acts made renting less attractive to landlords, there was rapid escalation in the capital values of flats with vacant possession, owner-occupation was of growing popularity, and financial institutions were more willing to lend on the security of long leasehold flats.

Typically, these leases will be granted for terms of 99, sometimes 999, years and sold at a substantial premium (close to an equivalent freehold value), with a low ground rent being reserved. The major reason why these flats are sold on a leasehold, rather than freehold, basis is due to the problems of enforcing freehold covenants. For the purchaser, the premium will often be partially funded by mortgage monies and, while he may appreciate that he owns only a leasehold interest rather than a freehold, he will essentially regard himself as an 'owner' rather than a tenant. Nevertheless, as a tenant, the long leaseholder is subject to the contractual restrictions placed upon him by the lease and has an asset which diminishes in value over time. In 1993, long leaseholders of flats were given the collective right to purchase the freehold to the block—but given the complexities of the legislation it may be that relatively few flat-owners will be able to buy the freehold (see ch 12).

1.2.4 Commercial Property

The commercial property market is normally divided into three discrete sectors: office, retail (shops, shopping complexes) and industrial (factories etc.). Within each sector, properties tend to display similar characteristics in terms of letting arrangements and trends in performance and value. This threefold division is not, however, comprehensive. In recent years there has, for example, been a growth in the number of business parks—an expression which covers a variety of developments such as science parks, technology parks, parks with mixed industrial and office premises, and trading parks. These parks tend to include well designed infrastructure such as access routes, landscaping and parking, as well as providing continual maintenance as part of the overall estate management. Most units on business parks will be occupied on a leasehold basis—both for the commercial reasons discussed below but also due to the difficulties of enforcing schemes of management on freehold sites (*cf.* the reason for granting long leases of residential flats). There are also other types of commercial property that do not fall into any of the usual classifications, such as public houses, petrol stations, hotels, and sports centres.

Whereas in the residential market the majority of properties are owner-occupied, it is more common for businesses to rent than purchase—the British Property Federation has described commercial property markets as 60 per cent rented (P. Turnham MP, Hansard, HC Deb., 1 July 1994, Vol 245, col.1106). The popularity of letting is accounted for by a variety of reasons. Renting provides greater flexibility than outright purchase—both in terms of the amount of property occupied and of the opportunities for financing land acquisition and business expansion:

The ability of a tenant to transfer his entire interest, or to carve out lesser ones, has significant commercial consequences. It facilitates large-scale commercial or domestic developments, producing smaller occupational units which are readily marketable. For example, a landowner whose site is ripe for commercial development might grant a long lease, at a nominal rent, to the developer. The lease will contain a break clause or rent revision clause which can be implemented when the development is complete. The developer will agree to build a substantial block, comprising offices, shops and possibly some residential units. On completion of the development the site owner will receive a larger rent. The head tenant or developer will, at the same time, let off the several units, often in as large a block as possible, to sub-tenants. For example, all the office accommodation may be let off to one entrepreneurial tenant, such as a bank, which has no immediate need for such extensive accommodation for its own use. Consequently it will occupy only such parts as it needs, reducing its own overall financial liabilities, and making a small profit by subletting the rest to a company which, possibly for commercial reasons, does not want to acquire a long-term interest in the property. As these short leases come to an end, the bank has the choice of taking over more office accommodation itself for its own expanding business, or re-letting on further short terms. The several shops will ultimately be let to non-competing traders. So a development is carried out that neither the landowner nor the individual traders could have mounted, and smaller units which enjoy greater market flexibility have been created. A further commercial result of the use of tenancies in connection with large-scale development is that the estate owner can control the management of the whole development over a period of years. This will be done not only in his own best financial interests but also for the preservation of adequate standards of maintenance, repair and control over the use of individual units.

Conversely, the device of a tenancy may be used to raise a lump sum rather than annual income. A trader running a business on his own fully developed property or farm may sell his own premises and take a lease back to himself as tenant. He may find that the advantages in releasing his own capital outweigh the benefits of owning the premises. (Yates and Hawkins, *Landlord and Tenant Law*, 2nd edn, 1986, pp 6, 7)

This latter kind of sale and leaseback arrangement is, in fact, not an unusual way of raising capital.

There are other commercial reasons for renting. Many businesses do not have the kind of capital needed for outright purchase of premises, and renting means that capital can be used for investment in business development instead of being tied up in property. In addition, whereas the rent payable will be deductible from profits in computing income and corporation tax charges, the purchase cost of a land and building would not normally be tax deductible (although some capital allowance may be available).

Unlike residential property, commercial property has been seen as an attractive medium for investment. It provides both income flow from the rent (at a reasonable, and increasing, rate of return) and the potential for capital gain. Over the 25 years to 1991, rental growth in each of the three main sectors (office, retail and industrial) exceeded the growth in the Retail Prices Index. The risks involved in commercial property can be reduced in ways not generally available in the residential market, for example, by passing on all repairing and management costs to the tenant, taking guarantees and by granting long leases. In consequence, most landlords in the commercial property market are investors; the main groups being institutions (including insurance companies and pension funds), property companies, private investors (often through indirect methods) and, more recently, overseas buyers.

What has perhaps been most significant in shaping the landlord and tenant relationship in the commercial sector is the dominance of institutional investors until 1980. These investors play an important role in financing property development. When a developer selects a site for property development, for example, to become a major shopping arcade, it is necessary to find financial backing for the project. The developer itself is unlikely to be able to provide more than a small proportion of the costs. Two forms of finance are required: short term development finance (the costs of constructing the development, such as land purchase, building costs, professional fees and marketing costs), and long term investment finance (enabling the developer to repay the short term borrowing and to either retain an interest in the completed development—an investor developer—or realise the profit from the development—a trader developer).

Traditionally the short term finance has been provided by clearing and merchant banks whereas institutional investors have provided long term finance. Sometimes the institutional investor is willing to 'forward-fund' the project, that is, to pay the short term development costs as well as to provide the long term finance for the development.

The main institutional investors are pension funds and insurance companies: in 1990 it was estimated that insurance companies had holdings of £42 billion in commercial property and pension funds £22 billion. Both have large funds of money available for long term investment and advantageous tax positions as regards investment in property. Their dominance over the market and the desire to avoid risk led to the development of the 'institutional lease', a form of occupational lease (the lease granted to the occupier of the premises) that is acceptable to institutional investor landlords. Thus the occupational lease would be for a long period, typically 25 years, and would ensure that the rent payable increased at regular intervals and that all uncertain costs, such as repair, insurance and maintenance, were borne by the tenant. The investor was therefore in receipt of a rent net of all expenses. The institutional or occupational lease will be discussed in greater detail below (see ch 5.3.3).

Since 1980 the market has undergone various changes. First, an increase in property investment from banks and overseas investors and a decline in new investment by the pension funds and insurance companies have decreased the share of the commercial property sector held by the institutional investors. Investment in the 1990s is likely to be marked by increasing diversification in landlords. Secondly, the recession of the early 1990s and oversupply of new commercial property space has effected a change in the bargaining relationship between investor landlords and prospective tenants. To some extent these changes have meant that leases are now less standardized. Nevertheless the institutional lease continues to play a very significant role in the commercial sector.

1.2.5 Agricultural Leases

Historically, most agricultural land was farmed by tenants but, as with the private residential sector, this century has witnessed a move away from renting to owner-occupation. In 1979 it was thought that only 35–40 per cent of agricultural land was tenanted as against 88 per cent in 1914 (Report of the Committee of Inquiry into the Acquisition and Occupancy of Agricultural Land, Cmnd 7599, 1979 (the Northfield Committee)). The Northfield Committee predicted that this downward trend would continue but felt that as it is important to the agricultural community to maintain a variety of tenure types, the government should try to ensure that by 2020 the overall percentage of tenanted land should not have fallen below 20–25 per cent. By 1994, only 24 per cent of agricultural holdings were tenanted and the transfer of land from the rented sector into owner occupation was continuing (see Kerr, *Farm Business Tenancies: New Farms and Land 1995–97*, Royal Institution of Chartered Surveyors, 1994, at paras 2.1 and 5.2).

The position of agricultural tenants has been strengthened by statute as a matter of deliberate public policy—maintaining an efficient and competitive agricultural industry is important to the national economy and well-being. To this end it is clearly important to promote principles of good husbandry and to look after the long term productivity of the land. As part of this overall policy, tenants have been given a degree of security of tenure and may get compensation for improvements they carry out on the land in order to encourage them to invest capital in the production process. During 1995, legislation will be passed to deregulate the agricultural sector for future lettings, while retaining certain minimal safeguards for tenant farmers (see MAFF, *Agricultural Tenancy Law,*

Proposals for Reform, February 1991; MAFF, *Reform of Agricultural Holdings Legislation: Detailed Proposals*, September 1992; News Release, *Agricultural Tenancy Law Reform*, 6 October 1993). The idea behind this deregulation is to revitalize the rented sector. The Northfield Committee was keen to preserve the strength of this sector, because it saw tenanted agricultural land as providing opportunities that were not available through a system of owner-occupation; in particular in terms of entry into the farming profession as the start up costs of owner-occupation farming would be prohibitive to young farmers. In addition, the Committee examined the role played by landlords and found that renting farm land allowed for the sharing of expertise, with the landlord able to concentrate on land management policies and financing land purchase and the tenant able to concentrate on farming skills and the provision of working capital.

One of the concerns that the Northfield Committee was asked to investigate was the increasing purchase of agricultural land by financial institutions. In overall terms, these institutions owned a very small proportion of agricultural land (1.2 per cent of agricultural land in Great Britain) but this represented a more significant proportion of tenanted land and was increasing. Institutions were attracted to agricultural land by historically good rental growth, expectations of capital growth and the fact that it enabled them to diversify their portfolios. The Committee, however, found no cause for concern in this trend. It was not expected that financial institutions would ever own an undue proportion of agricultural land and the evidence did not support fears that they were motivated by solely financial considerations but showed that they did effect good social and environmental policies even when there was no expectation of direct financial return.

1.2.6 The Building Lease

In a building lease, typically for 99 years, the tenant is granted an estate in vacant land at a low (ground) rent and puts up a building at his own expense. For the landlord this represents a long term investment, because at the end of the lease the building will become his. The tenant may well be a developer who in turn lets the completed building to an occupational tenant.

1.3 INTERVENTION IN THE LANDLORD AND TENANT RELATIONSHIP

One of the key issues in the area of landlord and tenant law is the extent to which it is proper for the state to intervene in this relationship in order to regulate the supply of decent affordable housing, economic production and to secure the tenant's interests, be they economic or social.

In the commercial sphere, the farm, shop, office or factory clearly represents an important asset to the tenant's business. In the housing sector, the property has a significance far beyond its economic value: for the tenant the property is his *home*. Poor, insanitary, insecure and overcrowded accommodation will have an adverse effect on every aspect of the tenant's life, including his ability to be a productive member of society. It is also widely accepted that the right to shelter is a basic human right, and yet in this country there are large numbers of homeless people, a significant proportion of whom are young or mentally handicapped.

1.3.1 Historical Dimension

The landlord and tenant relationship was historically governed by the notion of freedom of contract. It was in the agricultural sector that the first major statutory reforms of the landlord and tenant relationship were implemented in recognition that the *laissez-faire* model led to inefficient farming methods, as explained by Lord Hailsham LC in *Johnson v Moreton* [1978] 3 WLR 538 (at 551–2):

At least since the 1880s successive Parliaments have considered the fertility of the land and soil of England and the proper farming of it as something more than a private interest. Fertility is not something built up as the result of a mere six months' activity on the part of the cultivator, which was all the period of notice given by the common law to the individual farming tenant, by whom in the main the land was cultivated then, as now, mainly under a yearly tenancy. It takes years (sometimes generations) of patient and self-abnegating toil and investment to put heart into soil, to develop and gain the advantage of suitable rotations of crops, and to provide proper drains, hedges and ditches. Even to build up a herd of dairy cattle, between whose conception and first lactation at least three years must elapse, takes time and planning, while to disperse the work of a lifetime of careful breeding is but the task of an afternoon by a qualified auctioneer. Even within the space of a single year the interval between seed time and harvest, between expenditure and return, with all the divers dangers and chances of weather, pest or benignity of climate is sufficient to put an impecunious but honest cultivator at risk without adding to his problems any uncertainty as to his next year's tenure. At first Parliament was concerned simply with compensation for cultivation, manuring and improvement. But it never regarded these as matters simply for private contract, or something wholly unconnected with any public interest. From the first, Parliament was concerned with the management of the soil, the land of England which had grown gradually into its present fertility by the toil of centuries of husbandmen and estate owners. By the 1920s Parliament similarly concerned itself with the length of notice to which the yearly tenant was entitled. Such provisions are now to be found in ss 23 and 24 of the 1948 Act. But they date from this time. In 1947 a new and momentous step was taken. The landlord's notice to quit, save in certain specified instances, was at the option of the tenant to be subject to consent, at first of the Minister, but latterly of a quasi-judicial tribunal, the agricultural land tribunal. Even the consent of the agricultural land tribunal is carefully regulated by s 25 of the 1948 Act (consolidating and amending the 1947 provisions). The circumstances in which its consent may be accorded are thus defined and limited by objective and justiciable criteria . . . It is a public interest introduced for the sake of the soil and husbandry of which both landlord and tenant are in a moral, though not of course a legal sense, the trustees for posterity.

The *laissez-faire* model also came under pressure in relation to housing with the rapid industrialisation and urbanisation of Britain during the nineteenth century. Rapid population growth in urban centres and inadequate supplies of pure water and systems of waste disposal led to conditions of squalor and overcrowding. These public health risks paved the way for state intervention in the provision of housing. Initially this took the form of giving local authorities a regulatory role with powers to remove unfit property. Even these earliest forms of intervention were resisted as representing an unfair interference with the rights of private property and it was argued that they would damage the housing market—specification of minimum standards would cause costs to rise, and thus rents. Unless wages rose similarly, the situation would actually be made worse for the poor rather than better as the supply of affordable housing would diminish.

Direct state provision of housing to remedy the problems of overcrowding and insanitary conditions was never seriously on the agenda in the nineteenth century. The political ideology favoured a free market: state intervention would both distort the market and encourage a 'dependency culture'. Nevertheless, pressure for reform built up. The working classes became more politically active and a Royal Commission reporting in the 1880s highlighted the slum conditions that the poor were living in (Royal Commission on the Housing of the Working Classes, 1885).

By the Housing of the Working Classes Act 1890, local authorities were empowered to build housing for rental, but the absence of financial assistance meant that few authorities took up the opportunity. By World War I there was still relatively little state housing, with some authorities proving the exception. Within the private sector, there were problems with overcrowding and poor conditions.

With the outbreak of war the housing shortage put landlords in a position where they could demand increasingly higher rents; those tenants employed in the munitions industry were able to pay them but ordinary working class families could not. The consequent frequent evictions and profiteering by landlords generated civil unrest on such a scale that the government was forced to intervene and introduced the first measure aimed at rent control, the Increase of Rent and Mortgage Interest (War Restrictions) Act 1915. This statute was intended as a temporary measure but ever since the 1915 Act there has been state regulation of some sort in the private residential sector. The current principal legislation in the private sector, the Housing Act 1988, represents a swing away from close state regulation towards regeneration of a freer market in housing. Even with this recent shift in political thinking, landlords' powers in letting property are heavily constrained by the legislation and it is clear that the 1915 legislation marked a highly significant break from the *laissez-faire* model, which has never since been recaptured.

The end of World War I also marked an important turning point in direct state involvement in housing. The shortage of housing in the private sector, exacerbated by the effects of the war on new building programmes and the imposition of rent control making new private investment uneconomic, led to a large scale programme of subsidized municipal house building. Eventually council housing outstripped the private rental sector.

Whereas there has been some protection for tenants in the private sector dating from World War I, legislation to regulate social landlords in the public sector is a recent innovation. The idea, at least in respect of local authorities, was that housing was but part of a wider frame of local autonomy: the change in the relationship between central and local government during the 1980s has equally led to a diminution in the absolute nature of local authority control, although there had been some whittling away even before 1979. The Housing (Homeless Persons) Act 1977 provided that unintentionally homeless persons with priority need would be able to sidestep the local authority's own allocation procedures. Nevertheless, it was the Housing Act 1980 (now consolidated into the Housing Act 1985) which introduced a wholesale change in the nature of the landlord and tenant relationship in the public sector. The so-called Tenants' Charter provided local authority and housing association tenants with legally enforceable rights for the first time.

In the commercial property sector the picture is very different. The landlord and tenant relationship is still dominated by the *laissez-faire* model. Statutory intervention has been kept to a minimum, with the main areas of regulation being compensation payable to tenants at the end of a lease and the tenant's right to renew the lease. There has been no interference in the level of rents payable (apart from a brief foray in the 1970s when rents were frozen in an attempt to curb inflation). Save for the few areas where there is statutory regulation, the relationship between landlord and tenant will be dominated by the terms of the lease agreed between them.

In each sector, the landlord and tenant relationship is therefore now governed by a mixture of common law, statutory provision and the contractual obligations agreed between the parties. In the residential sectors this interplay is the product of complex issues of housing policy—incorporating attempts to alleviate overcrowding, ensure certain minimal standards of housing, reduce the shortfall of dwellings in relation to households, provide affordable homes, protect tenants from unfair eviction and so on. In the public sector, the housing issue has also been a focal point of the tensions between central and local government autonomy. Housing has also been a key area within political debate, and policies have received different emphases according to the politics of the governing party. In the commercial sector, the landlord and tenant relationship has never been as politically sensitive as in housing. Yet even here it would be wrong to think of their relationship as purely contractual, as both common law obligations and statutory provisions impinge on particular aspects.

(Policy will be discussed further in ch 2. There are a number of books examining housing policy and responses up to 1914: Gauldie, *Cruel Habitations*, 1974; Malpass and Murie, 1994, *op. cit.*; Burnett, *A Social History of Housing 1815-1970*, 2nd edn, 1985.)

1.3.2 The Limits of Legal Process

1.3.2.1 Legislation and Housing Policy

While the focus of this book will be upon the legal regulation of the landlord and tenant relationship, it is important to appreciate that the law is only one of the tools used to influence housing provision. It is frequently claimed that rent control and security of tenure have made investment in housing for rental unattractive and thereby caused the dramatic decline in the private rental sector this century. Indeed, one of the planks of the government reforms implemented in the Housing Act 1988 was effectively to remove rent control from new lettings, enabling landlords to charge a market rent, in the hope that this would stimulate the revival of the private rental sector. This is, however, an oversimplistic analysis of the way that the housing market works. While protective legislation may have contributed to the decline, it is only one factor amongst many. Balchin identifies numerous factors that explain the decline in this sector: slum clearance; policies aimed at dealing with overcrowding; housing rehabilitation (with finance available for upgrading property many were sold for owner occupation); the unattractiveness of investing in private rented housing (high construction costs and rent control); the cost of repair and maintenance; the desire to own one's own house; and subsidies and tax allowances (favouring owner occupation and public housing) (Balchin, *Housing Policy: an Introduction*, 2nd edn, 1989, pp 108-9).

Indeed, legislative reform of landlord and tenant law is often accompanied by exaggerated claims about its expected impact. This is not to deny that some changes can have a substantial effect upon the pattern of housing provision, as for instance in the conferral of the Right To Buy on council tenants by the Housing Act 1980. Nevertheless, as Donnison and Ungerson have pointed out,

[past] experience in the housing field—with the Rent Act 1957, the half-million housing programme of 1966 and the Housing Finance Act 1972, for example—

suggests that the impact of new policies is rarely as dramatic as either their advocates hope or their critics fear. (Donnison and Ungerson, *Housing Policy*, 1982, at p
161)

What is important to bear in mind, therefore, is that while the law is an important mechanism it will seldom, by itself, be pivotal to change. Instead, it should
be seen as playing a part, alongside other economic and social factors, of the
process of change within the housing system.

1.3.2.2 Legislation and Tenancies

While some legislation has a 'macro-policy', in the sense that it is intended to
impact on patterns of housing provision, much legislation is directed at regulation of behaviour and conduct within individual landlord and tenant relationships. Examples are the anti-harassment and anti-eviction laws in the private
rental sector, the imposition of repairing obligations on landlords and the rights
of the homeless to be rehoused by the local authority if within priority categories.
There is, however, often a gap between the legislative goal (the officially sanc-
tioned behaviour) and actual practice.

In part this gap is due to the vulnerability of the tenant and ignorance of legal
rights. In his study of the private rental sector in six countries Harloe observed:

Each country had complex legal provisions which aimed to regulate landlord/
tenant relations. These laws could, in principle, be analysed without too much
difficulty. But in so personal a matter as the relationship between a landlord and
a tenant, the ability of the law to govern actual conduct was severely limited.
These limitations were probably most often experienced at the bottom end of the
market. The private rental sector was contracting yet it still provided the main
source of housing to many who were effectively barred from access to owner
occupation or social rented housing. In these circumstances landlords were often
able to pick and choose tenants and to control the terms of their tenancies in
ways which had little regard to the law. Tenants who might protest at the unfair
burdens which this placed on them knew that it could cost them their tenancy. In
some cases disregard for the law was also the product of the widespread
ignorance of its provisions which both landlords and tenants frequently displayed. (Harloe, *Private Rented Housing in the United States and Europe*, 1985, p 266)

The situation is worsened by the generally poor level of provision of advisory
services for tenants and lack of legal representation, due in part to the cost of
seeking a court-based remedy and ignorance of the availability of legal aid. The
Civil Justice Review in 1988 found a large unmet legal need in the housing field
and found clear evidence of minimal take-up of legal remedies (Civil Justice
Review, *Report of the Review Body on Civil Justice*, Cm 394, 1988, esp. ch 10). This
is part of a wider problem of access to justice.

This shortfall between legislative aims and practice is visible in several areas. One example is the Landlord and Tenant Act 1987, which was passed in order to cure some of the management problems that arise in private blocks of residential flats. The legislation aimed to strengthen tenants' powers in relation to management and to give them a right of pre-emption when a landlord decides to sell the reversion, thus enabling them to assume a management role themselves. However, a report published in 1991 showed that the Act's effectiveness in practice was seriously impaired. There was widescale ignorance of its provisions and the pursuit of the remedies made available was seen as costly, lengthy and restrictive. (Thomas *et al.*, *The Landlord and Tenant Act 1987: Awareness, Experience and Impact*, 1991)

Similarly, a study conducted by Shelter into harassment and illegal eviction following the implementation of the Housing Act 1988 found widespread ignorance of the law by landlords, tenants and solicitors. But the efficacy of the law was also reduced in other ways. The effectiveness of the legislation as a deterrent depends upon the willingness of authorities to prosecute landlords acting improperly and on the willingness of tenants to bring civil proceedings. Shelter found, however, that tenants' fear of reprisal made them reluctant to pursue landlords and made obtaining evidence difficult. On top of this, there were difficulties in obtaining legal aid to bring proceedings and those tenants not eligible for legal aid were concerned about the costs of going to court. Local authority response to harasssment also varied a lot—with some authorities according very low priority to it—and there was a large gap between the number of cases of harassment reported and the number of prosecutions brought. (Burrows and Hunter, *Forced Out*, 1990; see also ch 11)

1.3.2.3 Avoiding Statutory Control

In addition to the problems caused by ignorance and non-enforcement of legal remedies, it is not uncommon for landlords to arrange their affairs so as to escape effective regulation. The land owner may do this by structuring the occupation agreement in a way that avoids the legislative controls, for example, by entering into a partnership agreement with a farmer rather than granting him a tenancy. He may also avoid legislative control by taking advantage of statutory exceptions, such as the ability to 'contract out' of the business tenancy legislation (see the Landlord and Tenant Act 1954, s 38). The land owner may also seek to avoid controls artificially, for instance, granting licences rather than leases (see further, ch 6).

1.4 EXPLAINING THE STRUCTURE OF THE BOOK

The remainder of this book will look at issues common to tenancy relationships, with particular reference to public housing, private housing and commercial property. In the private sector, all tenancies entered into after 15 January 1989 are regulated by the Housing Act 1988—although pre-1989 lettings are still governed by the law contained in the Rent Act 1977 this book will focus upon the more recent legislation. Agricultural tenancies will be referred to mainly as a point of contrast—to illustrate where a different approach has been adopted towards the relevant issue. In order to understand the impact of legislative control, it is important to be aware of the wider policy concerns—this is dealt with in ch 2. Chapters 3 and 4 examine the nature of tenancies, showing tenancy law as a product of the interplay of several legal doctrines (property law, contract, public law and statutory intervention, ch 3) and how tenancies differ from other occupancy arrangements (ch 4). The remaining chapters of the book explore the different stages of tenancy relationships.

Entering into Tenancies

Chapters 5 and 6 look at how property is allocated to tenants, the form and content of tenancy agreements (ch 5) and which forms of agreement are regulated by legislation (ch 6).

Managing the Tenancy Relationship

During the tenancy relationship, management issues are at the fore. Chapter 7 looks at the ways in which these issues are dealt with, including the repair of the property, and ch 8 examines the mechanisms for fixing rent levels and securing payment of the rent.

Changing the Parties to the Relationship

As leases are often long term property interests, the lease may be transferred by either the tenant or the landlord. Chapters 9 (tenant) and 10 (landlord) look at the controls on such dispositions and the effect that a disposition has on the contractual promises contained in the lease.

Ending the Relationship

Chapter 11 describes the circumstances in which the landlord is able to end the tenancy, including material often considered under the heading 'Security of Tenure'. The chapter also shows how the landlord's behaviour is constrained to protect the tenant from being unfairly and improperly evicted from the property. Finally, in the last 40 years, certain categories of tenants have been given the right to 'upgrade' their leasehold interests—either into longer leases or freeholds. These rights are dealt with in ch 12.

2

Policy

[The] crucial and ultimate test of the effectiveness of housing policy is the condition of the worst-housed families in our communities . . . [Ultimately], the solution to this central problem of housing lies in the formation of a philosophy concerning the rights and equities within our society. (Carver, 'Houses for Canadians', 1948, pp 123 and 128; cited in van Vliet, *International Handbook of Housing Policies and Practices*, 1990 pp 320 and 321)

Provided that the majority of the population remains reasonably well housed, the living conditions of the poor—increasingly marginal to the labour market and with little organized political voice—may remain a topic of limited governmental concern. In this respect Britain's housing future may now be converging with that of the United States and other postindustrial societies. (Harloe in van Vliet, *op. cit.*, at p 122)

2.1 INTRODUCTION

The central aim of this chapter is to examine the housing policies which help shape the law relating to the residential landlord and tenant sector for those with a background in legal analysis and who are not familiar with social science terminology or structure. Certain ideas and themes recur throughout the chapter. This re-emphasis is deliberate. This chapter is designed for lawyers who are not familiar with arguments on housing policy. Establishing the links between policy, practice and the law requires novel frames of reference for lawyers. This chapter discusses housing policy itself, and provides a context for analysis of the law considered in subsequent chapters.

Since the commercial sector is subject to less intervention and has been left to free market principles, policy is less formalized and formulated. Therefore, there is only limited consideration of commercial policy. Whereas in the residential sector the major concern has been to ensure a sufficient supply of homes, this has not been an issue in the commercial sector. Planning and development restrictions have, at times, had the effect of increasing demand for existing buildings, but on the whole the 'market' has been left to regulate supply and has been felt to work satisfactorily. What has been a critical factor in this sector is the continued willingness of institutions to invest.

Most of the rest of this chapter will focus on residential tenancies, questioning whether private and public sectors are influenced by the same policies and examining those policies specific to each sector. At the end of the chapter, sections on commercial and agricultural policy have been included to look at their specific, discrete areas of interest.

2.2 HOUSING IN THE UNITED KINGDOM

One of the major misconceptions with housing in the United Kingdom is that there is a private sector that is wholly dependent on the market, while alongside it, and competing with it, there is a public sector wholly dependent on state intervention. In reality, both private and public sectors receive state support and use private institutions to meet their needs. Local authorities can seek funding from the financial institutions to cover the costs of private building firms building houses for them to let: the private sector, on the other hand, receives subsidies for loan capital for private buyers and for improvements, has its rents effectively underwritten by housing benefit in many cases and is dependent on overall urban planning. The government stated in its *Expenditure Plans 1991–92 to 1992–93* that its policies towards the provision of private sector rental property included

... **deregulation of rents and tax relief under the Business Expansion Scheme** ... (Chapter 8, Environment, p 3, Cm 1008, 1990; the BES has since been abolished)

Studies in the United States have revealed a similar interplay between private and public influences on the housing market.

Private **is hardly an accurate term to describe the system of housing provision in the United States, even though more than 97 per cent of all housing is privately owned [including accommodation let to tenants: 3 per cent is publicly owned by Federal or State government] and an even higher percentage privately built. A private housing industry indeed exists and is the dominant force in the housing supply system, but it operates within, and is dependent on, government action at every step of the housing-provision process. The laying out and the paving of streets; the supply of water; sewage disposal; utility provision (sometimes directly public, more often publicly regulated); building codes; zoning restrictions; health, fire and safety codes; standards for materials; ... mortgage insurance; the financing and regulation of financial institutions; direct research and development; ... the provision of those public services and facilities without** which most persons would not be able to remain in occupancy of housing (schools, fire protection, sanitation, . . ., and so on); the regulation of tenancy, including eviction controls, requirements, or prohibitions, as to relations between landlord and tenant; mortgage foreclosure laws—all of these are public activities. (van Vliet, *op. cit.*, p 342)

As will be considered below, British housing policy has consisted primarily of encouraging or limiting local authority building developments and encouraging home ownership; the preference seen since 1979 for private sector rental growth has been achieved by restricting the powers of local authorities to build new houses and by deregulating new housing association lets so that they are closer to the private rather than public model.

In another sense it is reasonable to see the entire rented sector as one unit, for it is all part of the provision of housing within the United Kingdom. In allocating appropriate housing for the intending occupant, there is not necessarily any distinction to be made between the private and public sectors, although the allocation systems are very different (see ch 5). This understanding is clearly demonstrated, despite the smallness of the programme, by the government's encouragement to local authorities to rent private sector properties for up to three years to provide short-term dwellings for homeless persons.

Further, it is clear that the Department of the Environment does not divide up its responsibilities wholly by reference to whether it is a private or public housing matter, but, in part, takes an administrative rather than sectoral approach. As Malpass and Murie showed in *Housing Policy and Practice*, 3rd edn, 1990, the Department was reorganized after 1979 into three directorates. In 1990, these three divisions were concerned with the following matters:

1. Public Housing Management and Resources including estate action division, local authority housing finance, housing management (homelessness and related policy issues; housing management policy, housing services advisory unit, specialist management and renewal, gypsy sites), housing defects and mortgageability, new towns, *private sector renewal policy*.
2. Housing Associations and Private Sector including private finance for housing, private rented sector, housing corporation sponsorship and finance, *Tenants' Choice*, housing associations generally, *Right To Buy*.
3. Housing Monitoring and Analysis including housing group secretariat (responsible for Public Expenditure Survey, Housing Consultative Council, ministerial visits, research strategy, etc.), *household surveys, housing economics unit, housing data and statistics, stock condition, architectural policy, housebuilding practice, land and general statistics, social research division*.

(Malpass and Murie, 1990, *op. cit.* p 133; emphasis added to reveal overlapping sectoral issues.)

However, in 1991 the Department again underwent re-organization. Housing became part of the housing and urban group. This group comprised, *inter alia*, owner-occupiers, private renting, housing associations and local authorities— Malpass and Murie, *Housing Policy and Practice*, 4th edn, 1994, p 161. While the frequent changes cannot assist policy making, the practice of treating all resi- dential rented sectors as part of a single structure should be noted.

Nevertheless, despite this overlap which indicates the rental sector should be considered as a source of housing without regard to whether it is private or pub- lic stock, there are other elements of the housing system in the United Kingdom that demonstrate that there are different issues affecting these sectors. There are different types of landlord, more or less willing to fulfil their legal obligations, ranging from the exploitative in the private sector to quasi-tenant co-operatives in the public sector. The legal nature of the relationship may be similar in both cases, but the day-to-day experience of those two relationships will be very dis- similar.

Even given the restrictions placed upon local authority housing since 1979, it is still the case that there is a much greater supply of council housing than private sector and housing association properties and that because of perceived prob- lems with private sector landlords, at least, the demand on council housing far outstrips that supply. The figures in Table 2.1 reveal the relative sizes of rental stock in England and Wales in 1981 and 1994.

Table 2.1 Rental stock by sector, 1981 & 1994

	April 1981		March 1994	
	000's	%	000's	%
Local Authority	5416	67.76	3953	57.22
Housing Association	421	5.27	816	11.81
Private Landlord	2156	26.97	2140	30.97
All Rented Dwellings	7993		6909	

Source: Housing and Construction Statistics, March Qtr 1994, Pt II.

2.3 HOUSING POLICY

While tenure division will form the basis of our analysis of housing policy, there are housing policy specialists who would approach this topic differently and would argue that this is too narrow a focus; distinctions drawn between owner-occupiers and tenants and between tenants in different sectors merely place a label on the legal nature of the occupation which hides a diverse series of relationships.

The . . . problem inherent in a tenure analysis is that tenure is a mere consumption label: it tells us something about the terms on which households occupy their homes, but beyond that its utility is limited. There is no necessary link, for instance, between tenure and methods of financing and producing housing: although in practice owner-occupied housing in Britain is normally produced by speculative builders, this is not exclusively the case and both local authorities and housing associations are also increasingly involved in building for sale. (Malpass and Murie, 1990, *op. cit.*, pp 6–7; see also 4th edn, 1994, p 4)

Ball, in *Housing Policy and Economic Power*, 1983, suggested at p 158 that, as well as consumption, it is essential in developed economies to have regard to Production, Distribution/Exchange and Reproduction. Nevertheless, since the law and the political debate surrounding it are centred on systems of tenure, it is intended to look at policy towards housing in the light of the recognized tenure divisions and the sectoral divisions within rented property.

2.3.1 What is Policy?

[The] crucial and ultimate test of the effectiveness of housing policy is the condition of the worst-housed families in our communities . . . [Ultimately], the solution to this central problem of housing lies in the formation of a philosophy concerning the rights and equities within our society. (Carver cited in van Vliet, *op. cit.*, pp 320 and 321)

The first issue to be answered is how policy is to be understood. It would be ingenuous to expect that there is a single policy for housing in the United Kingdom, but a policy can range from the particular approach to be taken towards the obligation to repair, for example, through to the general attitude of government in encouraging owner-occupation over renting. It is this latter sense of policy which is under consideration in this chapter.

The philosophy/[ideology] prevailing in a given society at any particular time profoundly influences its social objectives. These objectives are, in turn, a determinant of social policy. The law is one of the chief instruments whereby social policies are implemented. (Calvert, *Social Security Law*, 1978, p 1)

Of course, to think that a complex, pluralistic society would have simply one prevailing philosophy/ideology is naive, while a social objective, on the other hand, may be achieved via a variety of policies. Housing for all can be achieved through a policy of encouraging cheap owner-occupation through subsidies directed at the consumer in the form of mortgage interest tax relief (MITR), or by allowing social landlords to build dwellings and then subsidizing those landlords. It should also be noted that objectives are often phrased in very vague terms, making it difficult to assess with any precision how successful any implementation through specific policies has been. Furthermore, there will be a range of objectives connected with housing, not just one, and their related policies may well conflict.

A policy of housing those in most urgent need may conflict with a policy of replacing the worst houses, and both may conflict with a policy for stimulating demand through subsidies directed to those who are most likely to be persuaded by such help to build or buy homes for themselves: different people will benefit from the pursuit of each of these objectives . . . A policy designed to eliminate rent controls and create a 'free market' in housing may conflict with the need to avoid inflation of living costs and wages. Every country's housing policies contain the seeds of several such conflicts, for housing is so central a feature of the economy and the way of life it supports that many of the competing aspirations at work in a society gain some expression in this field. (Cullingworth, *Problems of an Urban Society*, 1973, Vol 2, p 40)

If a policy is a method of achieving an objective, what constitutes a housing policy? Partly this answer is dependent on how inclusive a description of housing matters is adopted; the government's policies on tax and unemployment can have a decisive effect on the state of housing in the nation, but only tangentially. Yet, without this context, housing policy is seen in a vacuum and its relative insignificance compared, for instance, with health, education or trade and industry in terms of public funding goes unnoticed. Additionally, but from the opposite perspective, housing policies can have profound influences on the rest of the economy. The collapse of the housing market in the South-East of England from about 1988 onwards led to unemployment in building and related industries, immobility of workers in all industries because homes could not be sold, even if those workers were looking to move to new jobs, and a deeper general recession as a result of unrealisable equity being tied up in bricks and mortar—see Muellbauer, *Housing's Economic Hangover*, ROOF, May/June 1993, p 16. And, finally, even if an accepted definition of policy could be contrived by which to assess the scope of British government intervention in the housing market, there is the further problem that housing policies can fail to achieve the intended objective.

2.3.2 British Housing Policy

Reporter: 'Mr Ghandi, what do you think of Western Civilization?'
Mahatma Ghandi: 'I think it would be a good idea.'
It is arguable that you could substitute British housing policy for Western Civilization.

Given that housing policy is, in general, understood to have the various shades of meaning discussed above, then British government practice should be the principal influence both reflecting and shaping such policies and concomitant laws. However, it is arguable that British governments have never had a housing policy as such, but instead have focused on promoting particular forms of tenure rather than ensuring an adequate supply of housing (*cf.* Goodlad and Gibb, *Housing and Social Justice*, 1994—part of the independent Commission on Social Justice established by the late Labour leader, John Smith). If there is a policy of encouraging home ownership, it cannot be a housing policy, for the issues faced in relation to housing have little to do with the type of tenure of the occupant. The major problem is an inadequate supply of low-cost housing.

The doctrinaire theories of the [1980s] have put the emphasis on ownership of homes rather than provision of homes. (Des Wilson, a founder of the housing charity Shelter, quoted in the *Guardian* p 5, 3 December 1991)

Harloe (ch 2 in van Vliet, *op. cit.* pp 114–16) sees the problem as more long-term, less to do with a particular ideology than with a failure to have firm housing policies; governments reactively deal with issues as they arise. Indeed, Conservative and Labour approaches to housing have tended to be similar over the decades since 1945, indicating that rather than having entrenched policies, the parties have reacted to the circumstances. The role of the local authority in the provision of housing in England and Wales will be considered below, but council housing has grown in this country to meet needs after the two World Wars. In 1914 there were approximately 20,000 council owned properties for renting, less than one per cent of the total housing stock. The two big building sprees occurred during the inter-war period and immediately after 1945 when Labour were, in part, elected on a promise to expand council housing: 80 per cent of housing built between 1945 and 1951 was for public authorities (see, English, *Built to Last*, ROOF, November/December 1991, pp 34 *et seq.*). The Conservative election victory of 1951, based partly on an election promise to improve on the Labour government's record on housing completions, led very briefly to an even greater council house building programme. At the same time, the speculative building industry was preparing itself to take over the lead role and develop housing for owner-occupation, which it succeeded in doing by the early 1960s; simply put, once the private suppliers of housing were ready, the Conservative government restricted growth in council house funding in order to let the private sector fill the gap thereby created. The almost full employment that existed in Britain during that period also helped the change of emphasis to owner-occupation. Up to 1979, though, there was no question but that council housing was seen by both parties as having a major role to play. Furthermore, as more Labour party supporters turned to owner-occupation during the 1960s, the party changed its policies for fear of electoral damage—

Ginsburg, *Home Ownership and Socialism in Britain: A Bulwark Against Bolshevism*, (1983) 3:1 Critical Social Policy 43. For the most part, therefore, housing policy has not been driven by housing need, but by the needs of a building industry, including the building finance sector, that has been left to fill a gap where governments have been loath to tread. The private sector was left to create the system of housing in Britain much as it wanted, with council housing being either encouraged or marginalized depending on which party was in power. Pre-1979, however, the Conservative Party did not actively seek the end of local authority participation in the provision of housing, it merely placed emphasis on owner-occupation through fiscal subsidies. It was only in the 1980s that an approach was adopted that challenged the role of the councils in the provision of housing. In Germany, the question of party political ideology shaping housing policy has also been raised and the dividing line is more pronounced—the parties have different policies.

In addition to the free-market stance, the Christian Democrats have been staunch protagonists of the idea that as many households as possible should live in their own homes . . . As time went on, this strategy [of encouraging home ownership] was guided by the political calculation that homeowners would develop a political leaning toward the conservative and liberal cause. Thus one of the main goals of the subsidy system that was developed in the 1950s and 1960s under Christian Democratic leadership was to stimulate and financially assist owner-occupied housing. To promote this goal quantitatively, the homeowner-oriented subsidies were designed in an across-the-board fashion, indiscriminately granting the subsidy also to the well-to-do who could have afforded to acquire a home without the subsidy . . .
　　On the other hand, from the concept of an active welfare state propagated and shared particularly by the Social Democrats, it was concluded that the state should intervene in the market, not only in a temporary but in a permanent fashion, to correct malfunctions. The basic assumptions underlying this position are that, taking the specific features of the 'commodity' housing and dwelling, the market will not be able to provide the population, particularly low-income groups, with adequate housing, certainly not in the short run and probably not even in the long run. So it is a crucial task and responsibility of an active welfare state to counteract the 'social blindness' of the market forces. (van Vliet, *op. cit.*, pp 148–9)

The 1980s in Britain will go down as the decade of privatization, with many public utilities being sold via the stock market into private hands. However, the most financially lucrative 'privatization' was the sale of council houses under the Right To Buy to sitting tenants. The details will be looked at below (ch 12), but whereas there were 5.5 million local authority dwellings in December 1979, there were only approximately 4 million in 1994. This deconstruction of the council sector could not initially be supported by the Labour Party, but before the 1987 election it had come out in favour of the Right To Buy simply because of the electoral damage its negative attitude was causing. For political reasons, the housing policies of the two main parties have been reasonably similar for the last 50 years. Since 1987 policy differences have been minimal. The Conservative government's White Paper on Housing (Cm 214) stated in para 1.11:

There are other reasons too why it is not healthy for the public sector to dominate provision of rented housing. At the national level, investment in housing has to compete with other public sector spending programmes; and private investment has not been available to supplement limited public sector resources, in order to provide alternative forms of renting on a sufficient scale. At the local level, short term political factors can override efficient and economic management of housing in the long term, leading to unrealistically low rents and wholly inadequate standards of maintenance. Local authority housing allocation methods can all too easily result in inefficiencies and bureaucracy, producing queuing and lack of choice for the tenant. A more pluralist and more market-oriented system will ensure that housing supply can respond more flexibly to demand, will give the tenant wider choice over his housing and will allow greater scope for private investment and more effective use of public sector money.

The resulting Housing Act 1988 was the subject of only weak parliamentary opposition from the Labour Party according to Harloe (van Vliet, *op. cit.,* p 115). Moreover, Labour's pre-1992 election housing document would have given tenants the right to transfer the management and ownership of their homes if they were dissatisfied with the level of service from their current landlord, although the emphasis was still on local authorities as providers (A Welcome Home, September 1991, p 13; see also Goodlab and Gibb, *op. cit.,* pp 17–18). In 1992, shortly after the Conservatives' election victory, the *Guardian* could write that

[apart] from the fundamental question of how much money should be spent on housing, Labour and the Conservatives are moving closer together on detailed policy. Local compromises between Labour councils (in Hull, Liverpool and most recently Birmingham) and the government over housing action trusts softened the party's national opposition just before the election began. (17 July 1992, p 32)

In many ways, housing policy in Great Britain has become housing ideology, and the ideologies of the two main parties are drawing closer, although the means for effecting those similar ends are different. However, before moving on to consider policies towards the various tenures and sectors, it may be worth noting the remaining, most noticeable difference. It concerns Labour's plan to build through the social landlord sector with funding coming from a housing investment bank financed, in part, by the national and international capital markets (see also, Goodlad and Gibb, *op. cit.*, pp 49 *et seq.*, esp. p 59). Labour party intervention is no longer centred on building programmes in the council sector, but rather on improved methods of financing social housing. The issue is not so much about landlords any more, as it is about the funding for growth in the number of dwellings available for occupation. The Conservative government is still relying solely on the Housing Corporation to attract private sector funds for the housing associations alone. Still, as the *Guardian* put it,

... if that failed, it would not be out of character for the Conservatives to rename the bank the Housing Investment Agency, appoint an ex-Cabinet minister to run it and say 'even Labour think it's a good idea'. (17 July 1992, p 32)

Housing policy at the end of the twentieth century will not be shaped by party politics, but by the growing belief that owner-occupation has reached saturation point and that homes for renting have to be revived (see Dwelly, *Labour's Bank Job*, ROOF, November/December 1991, p 26 at p 29). It is necessary to look, therefore, at the state of the different tenures and sectors.

2.3.2.1 The Position up to 1995

England and Wales are amongst the European Union States with the highest proportion of owner-occupied housing. However, apart from Ireland, it has the smallest private rented sector if housing association lets are excluded (Oxley and Smith, *Private Rented Housing in the European Community*, 1993, p 2; *cf.* Goodlad and Gibb, *op. cit.*, p 50).

It is the continued growth in owner-occupation since 1979 that makes England and Wales stand out from their European counterparts. Therefore, it would take a very brave person to predict how housing in Britain will look in even ten years' time. However, an examination of those factors that have shaped the present position may reveal the internal constraints which affect that balance of tenures. Before examining the various policies in relation to each sector within the rental market, the overall position of rented properties *vis-à-vis* owner-occupied housing needs to be considered—rented housing needs to be seen in the context of overall housing provision.

As can be seen from Table 2.2, (see next page) even as late as 1951, the majority of people lived in privately rented accommodation. Since then, owner-occupation has expanded, first at the expense of the private rented market and, when that had dwindled to a level where no further increase was possible, the public sector was encroached upon. The goal of owner-occupation has been part of Conservative Party policy for over 40 years and 1980s Thatcherism saw a 'property-owning democracy' as an article of faith. However, Sternlieb and Hughes, in commenting

Table 2.2 Housing stock by tenure

(Figures as a percentage of all housing in England and Wales)	Owner-occupied	Local authority/ new town	Private rented/ housing association	
1914	10	>1	90	
1951	31	17	52	
1961	43	27	31	
1971	52	29	19	
1979	55	32	13	
			Private	H.A.
1981	58	28	11	2
1986	63.5	24	10	2.5
1989	67	21	9	3
1991	67.5	19.5	10	3
1994	67.5	18.5	10	4

Sources: Housing and Construction Statistics, March Qtr 1994, and Boddy, *The Building Societies*, 1980.

on the American housing market, have shown that owner-occupation is dependent on house price inflation in order to satisfy householders' desires to trade-in 'their investment' and trade-up—it is not a matter of having a housing policy to meet the demand for accommodation, but rather to protect 'the premier middle-class collectible' (Sternlieb and Hughes, *The Future of Rental Housing*, 1981, pp 1–2). Rental property is left, therefore, for those whose income cannot cover the cost of purchasing a home and it assumes a second class status. Such a proposition has been borne out by the experience in the United Kingdom during the property crash of the early 1990s, when owner-occupiers trying to deal with excessive housing debts preferred to reschedule their repayments over a longer period rather than turn to 'mortgage to rent' schemes; although such schemes were never heavily promoted and were not readily available. This perception of housing as a latent investment is due to several factors which skew the true position—housing has not been and still is not fiscally neutral.

UK markets for residential land and housing are riddled with distortions. On the supply side, planning controls are very tight, especially in the South-East. On the demand side, housing demand, and so demand for the underlying land, is subsidised on all sides. For low income households there is housing benefit and subsidies to housing associations. For landlords, there is the Business Expansion

Scheme. And for owner-occupiers, there is mortgage interest tax relief, the absence of [Capital Gains Tax] on main residences and, where employers such as banks choose to subsidize mortgages, no national insurance on such payments. (Muellbauer, *The Great British Housing Disaster and Economic Policy*, 1990, at p 16)

Owner-occupation may be the predominant tenure, but that may well be due to fiscal incentives, primarily seen in MITR. The Joseph Rowntree Foundation sponsored Inquiry into British Housing, Second Report, 1991 (see p 31) found that while in 1980 council tenants received more than 50 per cent of all housing subsidies, the position had so fundamentally changed by 1989 that owner-occupiers now received nearly twice as much by way of subsidy as council tenants and that even on a salary as low as £7,500 p a. (1988–89 figures), owner-occupiers received more support than tenants on the same income. Changes in subsidy since 1989 have reduced general subsidies to owner-occupiers, but they still receive more overall subsidy than council tenants.

Table 2.3 Assistance with housing costs for owner-occupiers and tenants

(£ million at 1993 prices)	1980/81	1983/84	1989/90	1993/94
General Subsidies				
Owner-Occupiers	4122	4603	8424	4300
Council Tenants	4480	1388	988	120
Total	8602	5991	9412	4420
Means-tested Assistance				
Owner-Occupiers	149	248	431	1222
Council Tenants	1769	3279	3597	5004
Private Tenants	385	888	1631	3817
Total	2303	4415	5659	10043
All Assistance				
Owner-Occupiers	4272	4852	8855	5522
Council Tenants	6249	4666	4584	5124
Private Tenants	385	888	1631	3817
Total	10905	10406	15070	14463

Source: Wilcox, *Housing Finance Review 1994/95*, 1994, Table 101b

With the government in the mid-1990s seeking to cut back on public expenditure, the budget for housing and for housing subsidies is likely to be reduced even more—see Wilcox, *op. cit.*, Table 13b. Nevertheless, the preference for owner-occupiers is likely to continue, even if on a smaller scale (Dwelly, *Eyes on the Prize*, ROOF, March/April 1994, p 20; the *Guardian* 2 p 12, 12 August 1994; Walter, *Open Door, Open Mind?*, ROOF, November/ December 1994, p 20).

Apart from there being those for whom owner-occupation is financially impossible, it may have other deleterious consequences, such as restricting job mobility—Joseph Rowntree Foundation, *A Competitive Economy: the Challenge for Housing Policy*, 1994. Most other European and North American countries with similar economies have a much higher percentage of people in privately rented accommodation: in most of western Europe it is 20 per cent, in what was the old West Germany that figure rises to 45 per cent and in Canada and the United States it is approximately 30 per cent (see Joseph Rowntree Foundation, Housing Research Findings No. 129, October 1994). For young people and those seeking work in general during a recession, renting may be better for the economy, allowing people to move more readily to take up jobs. Making owner-occupation almost as cheap as renting through tax incentives and the added bonus of a capital gain, however, renders renting unattractive.

The principal issue, though, is that owner-occupation cannot meet the housing needs of all existing and prospective households, yet it receives the dominant share of government subsidy. In the United States, according to Sternlieb and Hughes, *op. cit.*, only those who cannot afford to buy now rent, predominantly households headed by a black female in the inner city whose income was, on average, less than 40 per cent of that of owner-occupiers in 1978 (at pp 17–35). Furthermore, in Australia both Left and Right have attacked the preference given to owner-occupation, partly because of the fiscal distortions and partly because the majority of those in housing need are not people who could afford to buy— van Vliet, *op. cit.*, pp 728, 731–2. The same is true to a certain extent in this country, especially having regard to the number of people declared homeless following the repossession of their home for failure to keep up their mortgage payments. Thus, an alleged housing policy has been adopted and brought into play via generous fiscal benefits, yet those who need housing derive no accommodation as a result of it and do not benefit from the associated fiscal advantages.

Yet it is growing increasingly clear that a mono-tenurial system does have its negative implications for certain sections of the population. High entry costs are precluding substantial numbers of special needs groups, including single-income families, sole-parent families [and] the disabled . . . from the benefits that attach to ownership.

In sharp contrast, the public sector serves the less-skilled working class and contains a high proportion of economically inactive heads of household, some of them are elderly, but public housing concentrations of the unemployed, single-parent families, and others dependent on social security benefits . . . [The] expansion of home ownership, together with the collapse of private renting (which housed many on the lowest incomes), has resulted in a growing polarization, in terms of incomes and socio-economic composition, between the two main tenures. It is this trend that has given rise to recent concern about the 'marginalization' or 'residualization' of public housing and its possible reduction to welfare housing on the US model. (van Vliet, *op. cit.*, p 728 on Australia, and p 91 on the United Kingdom, respectively)

Owner-occupation is not bad in and of itself, but the over-emphasis on it as the sole means of meeting housing need has meant that the possibility of an increased rented sector has been ignored for too long by government to the detriment of those in need of accommodation. The position may be changing, as will be seen below, but there is no evidence that this is as a result of a comprehensive and coherent plan for housing, rather than as a stop-gap until a general recovery in the housing market is under way.

Despite this criticism, it has to be recognized that owner-occupation is treated preferentially in most Western European, Australasian and North American countries and the phenomenon is not confined just to the United Kingdom. In the Netherlands, while the growth in expenditure on all housing increased steadily between 1977 and 1986, tax relief to owner-occupiers far outstripped rent subsidies and 'since 1982 housing costs for renters have increased considerably more quickly than those of owner-occupiers' (Priemus in van Vliet, *op. cit.*, pp 180–1). In the former West Germany, the problems of reconstruction after 1945 meant that housing policies took a somewhat different path. This led, in part, to producer subsidies taking priority rather than consumer incentives. However, owner-occupation has always been promoted and while the majority of people still rent their homes (Oxley and Smith, *op. cit.*, pp 2, 10 *et seq.*), since 1976 the largest share of housing being constructed in the social sector was for owner-occupaton. While there is no equivalent of MITR, 5 per cent of the construction/purchase costs can be deducted from taxable income as can all payments, up to a maximum level, into 'saving for building' accounts run by banks—the equivalent in Britain of saving with the building society specifically to buy a house (Jaedicke and Wollmann in van Vliet, *op. cit.*, pp 129–35). In Australia, housing receives little by way of public support by comparison with other industrialised countries, but 73 per cent of what is given, primarily through tax reductions, goes to owner-occupiers (Burke, Newton and Wulff in van Vliet, *op. cit.*, pp 731–5). The tax relief in the United States for owner-occupiers in 1985 totalled over $40 billion; it was proposed that social housing in 1986 would receive less than $5 billion. The tax benefits are also regressive, favouring the rich; a household earning less than $10,000 received $125 by way of housing subsidy (of whatever form), while one earning in excess of $50,000 received $1,860. (Marcuse in van Vliet, *op. cit.*, at pp 356–7 and 337–9, respectively). United Kingdom tax structures are also regressive, but the withdrawal of MITR is 'levelling the playing field'. At present, in the tax year 1995/96, MITR will only be available at the lower rate of 15 per cent when the basic rate of income tax is 25 per cent. Whether the government will reduce it further is unknown, but Goodlad and Gibb, *op. cit.*, suggest it could be phased out before the end of the century without causing major harm to the owner-occupied sector (at pp 42–7; see also, Blake, *Housing's High Noon*, ROOF, January/February 1994, p 23).

Some would suggest that favouring home ownership has an ideological base deeper than mere party politics. There is a popular belief that owner-occupiers are more likely to vote Conservative, but some of the writings on home ownership make it almost a symbol of democracy in and of itself and, in the United States at least, provide an explanation of the support it receives from government.

[Political] as well as business leaders have long seen home ownership buttressing stability, allegiance, thrift, hard work and patriotism . . . 'Tenancy is unfavourable to freedom . . . It should be the policy of republics to multiply their freeholders, . . .' '[All] observers agree that measured by the old standards, the [renter] shows a loosening of moral fibre . . .'. (van Vliet, *op. cit.*, p 337)

The Secretary of State for the Environment in 1979 could complement such sentiments as follows.

We propose to create a climate in which those who are able can prosper, choose their own priorities and seek the rewards and satisfactions that relate to themselves, their families and communities . . . (cited in Malpass and Murie, 1990, op. cit., at p 88; cf. Saunders, *A Nation of Home Owners*, 1990)

Such remarks are unsubstantiated by any research, and what empirical research that has been undertaken suggests the contrary.

[Conversely, at] a local level in Britain, too, it is not always true that the more conservative an area, the greater the preponderance of owner occupiers. We have already mentioned Coventry's very high level of working class owner occupation in a city famous for wage militancy and its shop stewards movement. Coventry has four parliamentary constituencies, of which three returned Labour MPs in 1979 and one a Tory. Yet the constituency with the highest proportion of owner-occupiers voted Labour. Even in Dennis Skinner's Bolsover constituency where two-thirds of the vote went to Labour, owner-occupiers outnumber council tenants. At the extremes of course, tenure and electoral preference go hand in hand, but in general housing tenure is reflected in voting even less clearly than trade union membership, and 35% of trade unionists voted Tory in 1979! (Ginsburg, *op. cit.*, p 47; see ch 12.5, below)

Nevertheless, owner-occupation in Britain has embedded itself in the popular culture as a goal for which to strive, almost as part of being British. Partly as a result of the residualization of the other secure form of accommodation, council housing, people are being forced to consider only home ownership, private renting still bearing the stigma of high costs, lack of security and, indeed, Rachmanism (see ch 11.5). Given the financial incentives that are also available to owner-occupiers, the rental sector is going to remain secondary, but it ought not to be second-class since it meets the housing needs of 30 per cent of house-holds and can allow for greater mobility where this is important. In conclusion, the subsequent study of rental housing has to be understood against a back-ground of almost 70 per cent owner-occupation, but it plays not an insignificant role in the housing needs of the United Kingdom.

Future overall housing policy is unclear. The government instituted a housing review in the early 1990s which was due to report in Spring 1994, but the report date has been put back and it is not certain that the Secretary of State for the Environment will make it public when it has been completed. The Labour Party instituted its Commission on Social Justice at about the same time. The Commission considered housing policy and finance. However, it is not guaran-teed that the Commission's recommendations will become Labour Party policy. Moreover, the Labour Party has issued its own policy documents in the same period. Such a state of indecision in both main parties is not helpful for anyone, whether he be a consumer of housing or, indeed, involved in its production or finance—Dwelly 1994, *op. cit.*; Borrie, *Think Tank Rolls into Action*, ROOF, May/June 1994, p 8; Goodlad and Gibb, *op. cit.*; Smith, *Backdoor*, ROOF, May/June 1994; Battle, *How to Bridge the Funding Gap*, ROOF, July/August 1994, p 9; Walter, *op. cit.*

2.4 POLICY TOWARDS PRIVATE RENTING

The emphasis in this section will be on recent policy developments that have affected the private rental sector, which does not include housing associations which are dealt with below—see Crook, Private Rented Housing and the Impact of Deregulation, in Johnston Birchall, *Housing Policy in the 1990s*, 1992, at p 91; Harloe, *Private Rented Housing in the United States and Europe*, 1985; Birch, Dwelly and Kemp, *The Point of Low Return*, ROOF, March/April 1993, p 22; McManus, *Renting's Long Goodbye*, ROOF, May/June 1993, p 28. In March 1994 privately rented homes accounted for just over 2.1 million dwellings or 31 per cent of the rental market. The main problem for private renting is that it is in direct competition with owner-occupation for properties. Given the preferential tax treatment that owner-occupation receives, there is no incentive to rent for prospective householders. Each year during the 1980s, about 80,000 previously privately rented properties were either left empty, demolished or sold. The increase in the private rented sector in the early 1990s was the result of the house price crash and the inability of owner-occupiers to sell. Those who had to move could only do so by letting out their present house. Once any recovery occurs in house prices, then such properties will cease to be rented. The most apposite solution to this tenure distortion would be to phase out MITR to create a level playing field and there are suggestions that the Treasury has not entirely ruled this out. As things stand, in the 1995/96 tax year, the rate of MITR will only be 15 per cent, as pointed out above (2.3.2.1). It would be a political gamble to phase out MITR completely, but Goodlad and Gibb, *op. cit.*, p 47, show that it could be achieved with little pain for the mortgagor. (Figures are based on a £40,000 mortgage repayable over 25 years at a compound interest rate of 12.5 per cent.)

Table 2.4

Year	Relief at: (%)	Nominal monthly repayment (£)	Percentage change
0	15	398	
1	12	407	2.3
2	9	416	2.2
3	6	424	1.9
4	3	431	1.6
5	0	440	2.0

If renting is uneconomic for householders, it is one of the worst possible investments for potential landlords. MITR, as the Rowntree Inquiry, *op. cit.*, pointed out, also pushes up house prices because if people have more disposable finance as a result of tax relief, they will spend it on more expensive housing. It is available to purchasers who use the property as their principal or only home, but there is no equivalent for the rented sector. Thus, landlords have to cover the cost of their unsubsidized mortgage through very much higher rents, to be paid in theory by people who cannot afford to buy, or by limiting their profit margins. As such, the large institutional investors have not put their funds into private renting. The chairman of Quality Street, a company providing homes for rent, suggested in 1992 that there was a 30 per cent shortfall 'between the returns we can earn and what the investor wants' (*Financial Times*, 8 September 1992). Research in 1993 suggested a 10 per cent return was needed for landlords—Joseph Rowntree Foundation Housing Research Findings No. 90, May 1993, and No. 95, July 1993; Birch, Dwelly and Kemp, *op. cit.* According to Holman's *Housing Policy in Britain*, 1987, the decline in the private sector is as much to do with tax relief for owner-occupation as rent and tenure controls. To remedy this imbalance between owner-occupation and renting, given that the phasing out of MITR is still in a state of flux, Muellbauer, *op. cit.*, suggested that owner-occupiers ought to be taxed on the imputed rental value of their properties (no matter that housing policy in Britain would benefit from tenure neutrality).

There are also very important 'microeconomic' or resource allocation arguments which favour a tax on residential property or land values. First such values give rise to higher real spending power to owner-occupiers in the form of imputed rent income. It is distortionary to tax wage and salary income and indeed rents received by landlords and not to tax such imputed rents. A similar neutrality argument applies to small businesses who at the margin may face a choice between investing funds in the business or in owner-occupied property, or in supplying rented accommodation . . . Removing this would help regenerate the private rented sector . . . (p.17)

The government indicated at the end of 1992 that it would instead give tax relief or capital grants to encourage new private landlords, adopting the Joseph Rowntree Foundation Inquiry's 1991 proposal, *op. cit.*—see also, the *Guardian* p 33, 15 May 1993.

To stimulate supply, in the face of regulation, we recommend *a choice for land-lords of tax exemption or capital allowances*, for all privately rented property subject to 4 per cent capital-value rents (subject to 'approval' . . .). Either landlords would be exempt from payment of income tax on rent/Capital Gains Tax, and for companies, Corporation Tax; or 100 per cent of capital costs of the property would be offset against the landlord's tax liabilities achieving a similar result . . . The arrangement would be for new lettings only (of existing as well as new properties) . . .

   With one or other of these concessions, the return on capital from rents and appreciation is enhanced to a point where, we hope, more investors will be attracted into this sector. We see this measure as placing renting on a more even footing with owner-occupation. And we feel that this balance between tax concessions and rent regulation should achieve the political consensus which a long-term investment demands. (Rowntree Inquiry, *op. cit.*, p 62)

The new government proposals, which are along the lines of the Rowntree Inquiry recommendation, recognise the failure of the measures taken towards the end of the 1980s to stimulate the private rented sector without attacking the inequities to which MITR gives rise. There were two main strands to this encouragement of private landlords—the Business Expansion Scheme and partial deregulation.

   The Business Expansion Scheme was extended to the provision of rental property in the Finance Act 1988. An investor was allowed to put up to £40,000 p.a. into shares in a company providing approved renting and set that sum against taxable income; further there was no Capital Gains Tax on the subsequent sale of those shares. However, the tax concessions were limited to a five-year period, after which the properties could be sold to owner-occupiers—hardly a long-term solution to the malaise in the private rental sector, rather a stop-gap. The Joseph Rowntree Foundation found that BES produced £2 billion for investment and 40,000 homes as against a decline in private rental properties throughout the 1980s of 80,000 per year (Joseph Rowntree Foundation, Housing Research Summary, December 1993). As Will Hutton in the *Guardian* put it,

The Government's solution, allowing BES schemes scandalously high 15 per cent returns to build homes for rent that when the tax exemptions cease are then sold back into home ownership, is an expensive and futile means of achieving little. (23 December 1991, p 10; see also, Wilcox, *op. cit.*, Table 42)

Moreover, as Muellbauer explains, by making more money available through these tax concessions, the price of land and property is forced up, giving rise to higher rents for the eventual tenants. Indeed, BES properties were not generally aimed at the poorest sections of the community.

In the longer term BES cannot be the saviour of the private rented sector although it will, in all probability, have a major role in the short to medium run. If we acknowledge the need for a thriving quality rental sector catering for a wide range of demands, then generous tax concessions to individual investors is no answer. (Gibb and Munro, *Housing Finance in the UK*, 1991, p 219)

The government ended the BES in 1993 and nothing took its place in the rental sector. Furthermore, the recession in the property market meant that final profits for investors were nowhere near as substantial as had been predicted: in the gamble on BES, no one emerged as a winner, neither the tenants, the investors, nor the Treasury—the *Guardian* p 35, 19 November 1994.

Deregulation of the private rental sector took place throughout the 1980s, but it reached its zenith (or nadir, depending on your outlook) in the Housing Act 1988. There is a view held by some that the decline in the private rental sector was due to the fact that the tenant had been given too many rights with respect to security of tenure and rent control. New private lets after 15 January 1989 are either assured or assured shorthold tenancies: assured tenancies have security, but there is no rent control other than what the market will bear; assured shorthold tenancies are for a fixed period, with no security beyond that period and no effective rent control. The first Rowntree Inquiry report in 1985 had recommended some deregulation in favour of the private landlord (possibly because, as Harloe points out, private landlord interests were very strongly represented on the Inquiry team—van Vliet, *op. cit.*, p 119), but the government's 1988 reforms went even further. Nevertheless, while tenants' rights might have deterred some from becoming private landlords, it is more likely that the financial disincentives were the major cause, especially when it is remembered that it was relatively straightforward to avoid the Rent Act 1977 safeguards. This opinion is borne out by the Australian experience of the collapse of its rental market, even though there are very few State regulations giving tenants security of tenure or rent control.

The 1988 Act had one other major consequence. The effective deregulation of rent led to massive increases over and above the rate of inflation—the *Guardian* p 6, 16 March 1994. These increases were funded in part by housing benefit—see Wilcox, *op. cit.*, pp 46 *et seq.*, and Table 93. The government is now reviewing the housing benefit scheme as a whole (the *Guardian* 2 p 19 9 September 1994), but given that private landlords want an adequate return and that rents are now deregulated, restricting housing benefit alone will not reduce rents and tenants will simply not be able to afford them. The result will be increased homelessness and previously privately rented properties standing empty once again.

The future of the private rental sector is in a state of flux but it is clear that there is all party agreement on an expanded and diverse rental sector. There was even an acknowledgement in Labour Party documents prior to the 1992 election that there was 'clearly a need for a 'market' sector which serves people at the top end of the market . . .' (A Welcome Home, September 1991, p 15; see also Goodlad and Gibb, *op. cit.*). Small scale measures from the Conservative government include trying to encourage shop owners to rent out rooms above the shop and the rent-a-room provisions in the Finance Act 1992—householders letting a room in their homes can receive rent up to a specified amount, £3,250 in 1994, tax free ((1994) 144 NLJ 1520). In the longer term, the issues will revolve around the related concepts of encouraging increased investment in the private rental sector and improving its image. Taking the latter point first, the Rowntree Inquiry recommended the establishment of a system of approved landlords who would have to provide accommodation to the appropriate statutory standard, have no past conviction for harassment nor be an undischarged bankrupt and charge the Rowntree approved rent of 4 per cent of capital-value. One aim of this approved status for landlords is to 'give confidence to investment institutions who will see these landlords as free from political controversy' (Rowntree Inquiry, *op. cit.*, 1991, p 77). The major factor, though, in promoting the growth of the private sector will be, as discussed above, how much money the government is prepared to give to landlords, directly or indirectly, to balance out the preferential treatment currently enjoyed by owner-occupiers. Gibb and Munro, *op. cit.*, make the further suggestion that since private renting is now equated with a business, that landlords should be able to set off against tax the depreciating value of their asset. However, they see little growth in the private sector, anyway, apart from possibly the furnished let—see also, Down, Holmans and Small, *Trends in the Size of the Private Rented Sector in England*, Housing Finance No. 22, May 1994, at p 7. In conclusion, the private rental sector has been in decline since 1914 and unless the government's proposals at the end of 1992 on tax changes bear fruit with the Treasury, there is little reason to believe that it will do more than stabilise at about 30 per cent of the rental market.

2.5 POLICY TOWARDS HOUSING ASSOCIATIONS

Housing associations provide the least amount of rental housing in Britain and always have done.

In 1989, there were 2672 associations registered with the Housing Corporation . . . The Housing Corporation's returns indicate some 500,000 fair rent units . . . in England in 1989 . . . Nearly half of all registered housing associations had less than 25 units and almost three-quarters have less than 100. The seven associations with more than 10,000 units owned over 20 per cent of the stock and the 97 associations with more than 1,000 controlled two-thirds of the stock. (Malpass and Murie, 1990, op. cit., pp 150-1; see also, Malpass and Murie, 1994, *op. cit.*, pp 172–7)

Fewer than 600 of those housing associations carry out development work that qualifies under the Housing Act 1988, ss 50-53 for grant aid from the government's Housing Corporation; the rest are less active (Hanson, *How Affordable Can Social Housing Be?*, (1993) 11 EG 104). Nevertheless, housing associations are set to be the largest provider in the twenty-first century because of the popular distrust of private landlords and government aversion to local authorities as landlords—Cope, *Housing Associations: Policy and Practice*, 1990.

The Thatcher legacy has some surprising beneficiaries. Who would have thought a decade ago, that housing associations, worthy but dull, would be given the job of solving the country's housing crisis? . . . In the late 1980s the government decided that housing associations were to take over from councils as the social housing providers of the future . . . They didn't ask for this job. The reason they've got it is more to do with Thatcher's hatred of local authorities than any fondness for housing associations, despite their reputation as capable and trusted landlords. (Kate Miller in the *Guardian* p 23, 14 October 1991)

Housing associations first appeared in the middle of the nineteenth century, partly as a response to the appalling conditions the working class had to live in and partly to try and show that there was no need for state intervention in the housing market—see Malpass and Murie, 1994, *op. cit.*, pp 89 *et seq.*; Spicker, 'Victorian Values', and White, 'Business Out Of Charity', both in Grant, *Built To Last*, 1992, p 8 and p 1, respectively. Similar bodies grew up in the former Federal Republic of Germany (*gemeinnützige Wohnungsunternehmen*—see van Vliet, *op. cit.*, pp 131–2) and the Netherlands where they are today the largest force in the rental sector with 64 per cent of the stock (see van Vliet, *op. cit.*, pp 168–9). The rent the working class could pay on nineteenth-century wages in Britain was too low for private landlords to make a commercial return on their investment and housing associations, among other schemes, provided cheaper accommodation, though even that was too high for many. The Peabody Trust, one of the largest housing associations in existence today, was founded in 1862. In trying to maintain public health standards and prevent overcrowding, however, it could not provide housing cheaply enough for the poorest of those looking for accommodation, according to Malpass and Murie, 1994, *op. cit.* Moreover, all the initiatives in the nineteenth century tended to help the better-off working class, due, to some extent, to views about deserving and undeserving poor—see Clapham, 'A Woman of Her Time', in Grant, *op. cit.*, p 15.

In the Victorian era, under the influence of *laissez-faire*, the impulse was, and to an extent still is, directed towards self-improvement and the prevailing, paternalist, forces tended towards the provision of opportunities for self-help . . . Voluntary service was not only good for the bodies of its beneficiaries; it was also good for the souls of those who offered it.

The bubble burst. A fact which had throughout been obvious became, with the changing philosophy, worth stating. 'In helping those only who help themselves, or who can get others to help them, we have left unhelped those who need help' said a Member of Parliament in 1870. (Calvert, *op. cit.*, pp 4–5)

The scale and intensity of the housing problem in Victorian Britain was such that these various approaches were overwhelmed and, instead of demonstrating that enlightened private enterprise could cope with the situation, their failure tended to enhance the case for municipal intervention. (Malpass and Murie, 1994, *op. cit.*, p 37)

By the beginning of the twentieth century, it was clear that housing associations could not meet the need for adequate housing for all of the working class at affordable rents, and attention shifted to municipal housing until the mid-1970s.

Housing associations are now defined in the Housing Act 1974 as societies, companies or bodies of trustees the objective of which is to build, improve or manage houses on a non-profit making basis—Malpass and Murie, 1994, *op. cit.*, pp 172–7. It is only since 1974 that they have been resuscitated from a somewhat moribund state. Before 1960, public housing development was placed firmly in the hands of local authorities and new towns, despite initiatives in the Housing Acts 1935 and 1936 whereby the government made small grants to the National Federation of Housing Societies. Although some moves were made in the 1960s to encourage housing association activity, including the creation of the Housing Corporation (see Birch, *For the Defence*, ROOF, July/August 1994, p 30) and a greater willingness on the part of councils to co-operate in renovations especially, it was the Housing Finance Act 1972 and the Housing Act 1974 which revitalized their efforts. They were also later assisted by the Thatcher administration's dislike of local authorities acting as landlords—housing associations were a convenient replacement in the social rental sector. By means of deficit subsidies and grants, channelled through the Housing Corporation to registered housing associations, housing associations' share of the rental sector rose from 5 to almost 12 per cent between 1981 and 1994 (see Table 2.1 above). However, this increase in percentage terms has to be set against the background of a reduction in rented properties in that period from just under 8 million to under 7 million. Nevertheless, housing associations were the only sector to increase their stock in this period, and this despite selling off 90,000 properties under the Right To Buy.

In 1979, local authorities in Great Britain had completed 85049 new dwellings. In 1992 they completed 4044. The expansion of housing association activity in the 1990s raised their completions to 25094 in 1992 compared with 17835 in 1979 and the low point of 11215 in 1988. (Malpass and Murie, 1994, *op. cit.*, pp 115–6)

The Right To Buy provisions were part of the Housing Act 1980 and placed housing associations firmly in the public sector along with local authority lets, although not all were bound by the RTB provisions—see ch 12. However, as indicated by Malpass and Murie, by 1986 the government was looking for ways to reduce central government subsidy to associations, including encouraging private funding from financial institutions. The 1987 Housing White Paper (Cm 214) recommended this way of providing additional funds should be turned into the main source of housing association development.

For new lettings all housing associations will let on an assured tenancy basis in the same way as the private rented sector. This should give them the essential freedom and flexibility in setting their rents to enable them to meet the requirements of private sector finance instead of relying on funding from public sources. (at para 4.6)

The Housing Act 1988, therefore, adopted an approach which may, over a long period, change the very nature of association lets. Instead of them being part of the public sector, new tenants after 15 January 1989 are granted assured tenancies as though it was a private sector landlord providing the lease (see generally, Cope, *op. cit.*; Langstaff, 'Housing Associations: A Move to Centre Stage', in Johnston Birchall, *op. cit.*, p 29; Hanson, *op. cit.*). Moreover, the Housing Association Grant (HAG), which dates from the 1970s, is no longer assessed on the basis of development costs that cannot be met through the low rents charged. Rather, it is set by government on a regional basis and, therefore, it requires associations to establish rents to meet their remaining costs—withdrawal of subsidy, as suggested in the 1992 Economic Statement from the Chancellor, is leading to greater reliance on financial institutions and consequent increased rents. Against that has to be set the Housing Corporation's Tenants' Guarantee: Guidance on the Management of Accommodation Let on Assured Tenancies by Registered Housing Associations (Housing Corporation Circulars 28 and 29/91; other versions of the Guidance apply to tenancies other than assured ones), issued under the Housing Associations Act 1985 s 36A, which is intended to guide housing associations in the terms of these new assured tenancies. Section D refers to rents.

§D2 Associations are . . . expected to set and maintain their rents at levels which are within the reach of those in low paid employment. This will usually entail setting rents below market level. Associations should not discriminate in their rent setting between those who are eligible for housing benefit and others.

Despite the fact that this guidance received the Secretary of State's *imprimatur* as recently as 1991, cuts in government subsidies to housing associations have meant that fulfilling it has proved extremely difficult. Indeed, rather than approve this 'stick with which to beat its own back', the proposed re-draft of the Tenants' Guarantee (Housing Corporation 1994 Consultation Document, including a revised Draft Tenants' Guarantee) states that housing associations should only 'endeavour' to set rents which low-paid workers could afford. The National Federation of Housing Associations' Formal Response to §D2 stated its total opposition to this watering down of the Housing Corporation's and government's commitment to affordable rented housing. And the above has not even touched on problems arising from the potential rent differentials between neighbours where one has a pre-15 January 1989 lease and so still benefits from a registered fair rent—Randolph, 'The Reprivatisation of Housing Associations', in Malpass and Means, *Implementing Housing Policy*, 1993, pp 45–6. Indeed, new housing association rents are only 20 per cent lower than market rents or the cost of a mortgage to a first-time buyer—Joseph Rowntree Foundation Housing Research Findings No. 126, September 1994. The 1988 Act could prove to be the greatest obstacle in trying to turn housing associations into the major social landlord, yet another aim of the Conservative government. The two policies of replacing local authorities with housing associations in the social rental sector and of funding those same associations increasingly through the commercial financial markets seem to be incompatible.

[All] costs have to be met out of the association's own resources, which effectively means rent or reserves. . . . HAG is paid as a percentage of development costs at a level which is set annually, and which has been subject to downward pressure since the start of the new regime; in 1989/90 the rate was set at 75 per cent [of development costs], but by 1993/94 it had been reduced to 67 per cent (reflecting lower long-term interest rates and reduced procurement costs in the recession), with the prospect of 60 per cent in 1994/95 and 55 per cent in 1995/96. In practice the grant for 1994/95, announced in August 1993, was 62 per cent (*Inside Housing*, 6 August 1993), but it was increasingly clear that associations were encouraged to bid competitively for grant, and associations which could bid at less than the nominal grant rate could expect to receive higher allocations. To do so they would have to increase efficiency and/or contribute from their own reserves or from new capital receipts. (Malpass and Murie, 1994, *op. cit.*, p 209)

But we may have reached a point at which the [private sector financial institutions] *themselves* feel unease, and may not want to extend their own commitment. The assumption until now has been that, provided there is reasonable security, lenders will be comfortable with the share they fund. This is changing. As the servicing of the debt is increasingly dependent on continuing high levels of housing benefit payment, lenders are listening *very* carefully to the words of [the Secretary of State for Social Security], and his commitment to cut back spending on a housing benefit bill which, by any standards, is spiralling out of control. For financial institutions, property—any property—is currently an investment viewed with some suspicion, for obvious reasons. How does an association start to explain to a banking credit appraisal expert that higher amounts of loans are needed, payments on which are serviced primarily by people on housing benefit, who pay rents which are increasingly viewed as unaffordable? (Edmonds, *How to Score a Classic Own Goal*, ROOF, November/December 1992, p 15)

Moreover, taking into account the Chancellor's 1992 Autumn Statement that the grant to housing associations will be cut, associations are going to be ever more dependent on these financial institutions which will start to fund only those associations which look likely to be able to repay such large amounts—*Financial Times* p 16, 11 July 1994; the *Guardian* 2—Society p 8, 19 October 1994. Housing Corporation research shows that only about a quarter of existing associations would qualify. There is also the danger, as the Rowntree Inquiry suggests, that smaller, specialized housing associations, catering for the needs of particularly vulnerable groups, will be taken over by bigger, more impersonal and more remote ones which will soon assume the bureaucratic tendencies of the worst elements of local authority provision to which this change to housing associations was meant to put an end.

Housing associations are undergoing a period of change and whether they survive in their current form is not at all clear.

Margaret Mervis, Conservative Chair of Housing at Wandsworth Council: 'Associations should not see themselves remaining the same in ten years' time – but that doesn't mean that they are going to disappear off the face of the map. There are big associations who will tell you with great pride that they are doing things better and more efficiently than [private] developers. My question then is: why should they have the cushion of [government] subsidy? Alternatively, why shouldn't the developers have some of the subsidy as well? . . . It may turn out that some housing associations *do* become only managers, so they can acquire better skills and avoid diluting their energies by trying to be developers as well.'
Jim Coulter, Chief Executive of the NFHA: 'If the trends in the [Housing] Corporation priorities continue, it's true there can't conceivably be the same

number of associations remaining viable as businesses long term. There will be some changes in structure as some associations merge to increase efficiency. But I don't think there will be a sudden big bang with only a few associations left standing.' (both in Blake, *Whose Future Is It Anyway?*, ROOF, September/October 1994, pp 20 and 22, respectively; see also, Dwelly, *Kilburn's High Road*, ROOF, March/April 1993, p 29)

Furthermore, the cuts seem to be forcing some associations to build poorer quality housing, creating ghettoes of housing association tenants dependent on housing benefit and living in substandard accommodation—Page, *Housing for the Have-Nots*, ROOF, July/August 1993, p 10; Karn and Sheridan, *New Homes in the 1990s*, 1994; *cf.* Lomax, *Corporation Woes in Perspective*, ROOF, July/August 1994, p 8. Added to all that, new accounting practices required by the National Federation of Housing Associations at the behest of the Housing Corporation and the Department of the Environment, may, according to one commentator, also affect the ability of housing associations to provide low-cost rental accommodation—Hill, *In the Land of the Rising Sums*, ROOF, November/December 1994, p 10. If the government wants housing associations to replace local authorities as the major social landlord, then they are going an odd way about it.

Another problem is that the scale of the change envisaged in making housing associations the major social landlord is just too great. The figures cited above show that very few associations have any experience of renting to large numbers of tenants and, indeed, much of the success of the associations in the past has been due to the close relationship they could develop with their tenants.

Only ten per cent of association chiefs think that they can fulfil the 'main provider' role nationally under current policies. The remaining 90 per cent are clear that this is not possible. [In the view of one housing association director], 'associations simply don't have the expertise to deal with the management problems of large scale estates. We're not up to it'. (Dwelly, *No Sign of Movement*, ROOF, November/December 1992 p 21 at p 22; see also, the *Guardian* 2—Society p 8, 26 October 1994)

Possibly the best solution in line with government commitment to increase housing association involvement would be for greater co-operation between local authorities and housing associations. Such proposals were put forward by the Institute of Housing.

In the climate of expenditure cuts and complex political compromises, social housing itself has to continue to strive towards greater economy, efficiency and effectiveness. The prospect of large numbers of housing organizations all working independently in one area makes little sense . . . Unless the social housing sector seizes the opportunities to develop a much stronger collaborative framework, it runs a major risk of being replaced altogether. Too many people depend

on the services that councils and housing associations provide for that to happen. (Williams, *Allies or Adversaries*, ROOF, January/February 1993, p 28, at p 29)

The revised Draft Tenants' Guarantee, *op. cit.*, provides in §A3 that housing associations must 'consult and co-operate with the local housing authority' and they 'must also make available at least 50 per cent [of] nominations to local authorities on all housing which has received public subsidy for development and repair'—see also, the *Guardian* 2 p 21, 8 April 1994.

If housing associations are to take the sole role in social housing, though, then new building completions alone will not be sufficient to effect this change of principal provider. Even though there were more association than local authority completions in 1991/92, it would take over a hundred years for housing associations to become the larger provider on those figures alone—according to ROOF, it is 'like a plankton swallowing a whale'. Four routes other than building are available to housing associations if they are to become the largest landlord:

1   Taking over existing local authority properties, either following a voluntary transfer by the council or through the Tenant's Choice initiative—both are examined below in ch 10.

2   Becoming managers for private institutional investors who have put funds into property, but which they have no interest in personally operating (Housing Associations as Managing Agents—HAMA schemes). This is more to do with trying to encourage financial institutions to invest in private sector landlordism, but given that the housing association will be the operating landlord, effectively it increases association stock.

3   Similar to the last proposal, the government wishes to encourage HAMA schemes where an owner-occupier has an empty property suitable for letting. There are meant to be 600,000 such potential homes. However, research has shown

    that disappointingly few private sector empty houses are likely to be available for short term leasing by housing associations. Owners of property in poor condition or awaiting sale were those most likely to express an interest. However, repairs required tended to extend beyond the resources available . . . Owners of property in good condition wanted higher rents than those on offer from housing associations. (Prosser, *An Offer They Can Refuse*, ROOF January/February 1993, p 15)

4   As a result of the housing crash in the early 1990s, the Chancellor's Autumn 1992 Economic Statement gave associations £750 million to buy up empty houses, either those repossessed by building societies from defaulting mortgagors or those built by developers and originally intended for owner-occupiers. This decision in itself re-emphasizes the government's preference for housing associations over local authorities and its attempt to turn the former

into the main social landlord. At the beginning of January 1993, the Housing Corporation had approved the purchase of 6,500 houses under this scheme, predominantly from developers.

Only the first option promises to turn housing associations into the major social landlord. And there have to be questions about the depth of that social commitment from the government when it is probable that 42 per cent of funding in 1995/96 will come from the financial markets looking for a commercial return on their investment.

Richard Gregory of the Margaret Blackwood housing association: 'Should we allow rents to be raised to any level to suit the available [Housing Association Grant]? This will erode the character of the [housing association] movement, which is both idealistic and caring. The movement will not be destroyed by a lack of resources, it will be destroyed by the dilution of our moral authority.' (Robertson, *You take the high rents, and I'll take the low rents*, ROOF, November/ December 1992, p 12)

Bill Payne, Chief Executive of Yorkshire Metropolitan housing association: 'We have waiting rooms full of people who need homes, who are in desperate circumstances. Our motivation for borrowing isn't about being large commercial businesses, it's about housing *people*. [Private development companies] don't tend to share this aspiration. The bottom line is that we are not for profit. We combine good management skills, commercial skills with a not-for-profit approach.' (Blake, *Whose Future Is It Anyway?, op. cit.*)

2.6 POLICY TOWARDS LOCAL AUTHORITIES

In 1914 council housing accounted for less than one per cent of housing in Britain; by 1979 32 per cent of housing stock was owned by local authorities. This rise began immediately after World War I, with central government providing a subsidy to local authorities in the Housing and Town Planning Act 1919. That subsidy lasted only until 1921, but was reintroduced in the Housing Financial Provisions Act 1924, although after 1933 the subsidy only attached to slum clearance and the relief of overcrowding. The 1920s and 1930s were a period when rent control was maintained in the private sector and the public sector was allowed to grow. Nevertheless, by the beginning of World War II Conservatives were seeking to residualize the role of local authorities.

[It] was a Conservative rebate scheme that in Birmingham in 1939 caused the largest and most successful council tenants' rent strike in the inter-war years. Here the intention was to raise basic rents, to induce better-off tenants to leave the public sector, and to provide rebates for the poor. The rent strike and the approach of the war resulted in postponement and ultimate abandonment of the scheme. (Malpass and Murie, 1994, *op. cit.*, p 62)

The immediate post-war years saw another period of growth in the public sector to cope with the loss of housing caused by the war. It continued past the 1951 general election which brought the Conservatives to power, but from about the mid-1950s priority was given to building for owner-occupation. The period up to 1979 saw ever increasing constraints on the public sector, especially in relation to housing finance. Moreover, through schemes such as the Inner City Policy and Comprehensive Community Programme, central government started to take a more direct involvement in local authority provision. The 1980s merely increased the pace at which these changes were taking place—greater emphasis on home ownership, reduced autonomy for local authorities whose overall role was residualized to that of a welfare-landlord and, subsequently, simply as an enabler of private sector provision—Malpass, 'Housing Policy and the Disabling of Local Authorities', in Johnston Birchall, *op. cit.*, p 10; Audit Commission, *Developing Local Authority Housing Strategies*, 1992. It is these three topics that will form the basis of this analysis of policy towards local authorities.

2.6.1 Local Authorities and Owner-Occupation

A first point to note is that the communist principle 'from each according to his abilities, to each according to his needs' can be satisfied by either public or private housing. So far as consumer goods, as opposed to the means of production, are concerned, the issue is a pragmatic one. No socialist seriously wants collective, socially-owned toothbrushes; collective, socially-owned museums and parks make obvious sense; and between these extremes there is a wide area open to debate. Thus, . . . there is nothing *theoretically* wrong with universal home ownership as a strategy. (Cowling and Smith, '*Home Ownership, Socialism and Realistic Socialist Policy*', (1984) 3:3 CSP 64 at p 65)

The sale of council housing and the cuts in new building reduced the share of public housing in the total stock by about 5 percent between 1979 and 1987. But, as already noted, even with the extensive discounts for tenant purchasers, sales decreased after 1983. The problem for the government was that there was a limit to how far its privatization strategy could be pushed, given that fewer and fewer of the remaining tenants could afford to buy even with the discounts. So in [1988] the government introduced [the Housing Act 1988] that aims at a far more radical alteration of the rental housing market. Now it seems to be accepted that *some* households will always want or need to rent (perhaps around 30 percent). So the basic objective of the new policy is to replace the [local authority] as the houser of lower-income households by a combination of the private rental sector, housing associations, tenant 'co-operatives' and private 'housing trusts'. (Harloe in van Vliet, *op. cit.*, p 117)

The law student coming to landlord and tenant law has traditionally focused on the private sector for that was where the case law was to be found. It is only truly since 1980 that local authority leases were given a similar system of statutory protection. Nevertheless, local authorities have been the main provider of rented housing for nearly 30 years; most leases were for council houses as against private sector accommodation. Further, despite over a decade of Conservative government which has sought to residualize the role of the local authority as a landlord, councils still have almost 60 per cent of the rental sector. Although its overall share of housing in Britain has fallen from its peak of 32 per cent in 1979, local authorities are still overwhelmingly the principal landlord. In 1992, the biggest housing association in Birmingham had 5,500 homes; Birmingham city council had 114,000. As a provider of accommodation, local authority housing should properly be compared with owner-occupation, not private landlords or housing associations. A comparison of its position with respect to owner-occupation, especially in terms of finance, will assist in understanding overall housing provision in Britain.

The Conservative government starved local authorities of cash for their housing programmes during the 1980s. Before 1979 council tenants received more by way of subsidy than owner-occupiers, but that position was drastically reversed by 1989.

The disparity between levels of support for council tenants and owner-occupiers increased. The judgement that the country could not afford public investment, general subsidy to council housing or a 'no losers' introduction of housing benefits, but could afford a rising level of tax relief associated with housing is a political rather than an economic one. (Malpass and Murie, 1994, *op. cit.*, p 126)

Harloe presents figures indicating that in the tax year 1985/86, tax relief on mortgage interest and on capital gains made at time of sale cost the government £6.5 billion (van Vliet, *op. cit.*, pp 110–11); at the same time, subsidy to local authorities and housing benefit, paid to between 60 and 70 per cent of tenants to help with the cost of rent, were both cut. The government provided additional funds in order to promote owner-occupation through the discounts under the Right To Buy. Harloe states that the discount scheme cost £2.9 billion between just 1980 and 1983. The encouragement to owner-occupation was such that 1.2 million council houses were sold during the 1980s alone—the figure up to 1994 is over 1.5 million council properties. That type of sale has slowed down, but as well as fostering the transfer of entire council estates, the government has introduced rent-to-mortgage schemes in Part II of the Leasehold Reform, Housing and Urban Development Act 1993 whereby tenants buy part of the equity in their home; the quest for ever increasing levels of home ownership goes on despite the signal failure of pilot rent-to-mortgage schemes in Scotland, Wales, Basildon and Milton Keynes. The government speaks of cutting the cost of public sector housing, but it has simply fudged the distinction between the public sector and owner-occupation.

State-subsidized home ownership has become the dominant form of public support for housing. The level of tax expenditure has grown with home ownership, high interest rates and house price increases. (Malpass and Murie, 1990, *op. cit.*, pp 92–4; see also, Malpass and Murie, 1994, *op. cit.*, pp 98–105)

Yet, it should be borne in mind that while the local authority sector is allowed to wither and be eaten into, those people left who cannot afford to buy, a high proportion of the 30 per cent who still rent, will not be able to afford market rents—they will still need social rented housing and there have to be doubts as to whether the housing associations, increasingly dependent on financial institutions, will be able to meet that need. Canadian experience casts doubt on whether a market-led housing system can meet all needs.

Since the market responds to effective market demand rather than social need, the reliance of Canadian housing policy on market forces has led to huge disparity between the quality and the quantity of housing consumed by the poor and the rich. The poor simply cannot generate effective market demand in the rental sector. In 1986 about 500,000 families and 800,000 single-person households in the rental sector lived below the official poverty line. About 37 percent of all renter households live in poverty compared with 9 percent of homeowners. (van Vliet, *op. cit.*, p 311)

In Britain, the last fifteen years have seen a remarkable change in the structure of society, to the extent that Margaret Thatcher called into question the very existence of 'society'. Unemployment and poverty have reached levels unseen since 1945, while house prices at first attained new peaks and then fell sharply back. The number of homes to rent, taking into account all sectors, decreased—such a fall should not have been unexpected given that the main provider for over 30 years, the local authority, was restrained until 1993 from building new properties, despite having very large capital receipts generated by council house sales. Homelessness also achieved record levels. The almost total reliance on the market and owner-occupation may, on this evidence, prove to be fundamentally flawed, calling into question whether anything justifying the term 'housing policy' has been in place since 1979.

Having examined the interplay of owner-occupation and council housing, the role of local authorities in the provision of housing has to be considered from the point of view of the conflict between central and local government and that of local authorities and tenants. Some of this analysis is necessarily historical to provide framework for current theory and practice.

2.6.2 Local Authority Housing and the Central-Local Debate

As stated earlier, prediction of the details of housing trends in the future is fraught with difficulty, but Harloe has produced an analysis of the likely evolution of local authority housing in the light of central government policies and tenant-need.

[During] the next few years, the key developments to follow will undoubtedly be those that are linked to the government's current attempt to replace social housing by forms of private sector renting. In several respects these initiatives mark a reversion to late-Victorian 'solutions' to the problem of lower-income housing, in the era before public housing was politically acceptable. Then much (misplaced) reliance was put on the ability of the private rental market and of '5 percent philanthropy' to solve the 'housing question'. The government's proposals for the breakup of public housing and its disposal to a mix of commercial and limited profit landlords, non-profit housing associations and co-operatives looks familiar to those with a long view of British housing history. Moreover, the proposed new role for local housing authorities, regulating but not intervening directly in the lower-income housing provision, also has nineteenth century parallels. From the 1840s to the early 1900s the major emphasis in British housing legislation was on just such a regulative role. Although the limitations of this approach were evident well before 1914, it took the social, economic and political crisis of the war years to bring about a definitive shift in policy direction. This process was sustained by the exigencies of the interwar period and then World War II and the postwar housing shortages. Further housing historians may identify the 1970s and 1980s as a period when a new social and economic crisis led to a radical shift away from the politics of a mixed economy and the welfare state, and with it the onset of a new Victorian age in housing . . . Alternatively, the ability of the private market to deliver lower-income housing without massive and continuing state support may be tested and found wanting, as it was in Victorian Britain. (van Vliet, *op. cit.*, pp 121–2)

In some respects, until very recently the only housing policy, if such is taken to mean a policy designed to provide dwellings for those in need, that any British government has ever had has been concerned with how much by way of central government resources would be devoted to local authority house building and how much freedom local government would enjoy in the exercise of its role as landlord. By contrast, owner-occupation and private sector landlordism were subsidized to some extent by central government, but were left to find their own levels subject to certain regulations, while housing associations were too insignificant to have that much effect on supply and demand. Central and local government were, therefore, dependent on each other for the provision of state housing. Since both central and local government were separately democratically elected, there was an in-built tendency to conflict.

With rents set and housing capital programmes agreed, councils are ready to start again on the annual cycle of bidding for capital resources. Once again they will prepare to submit a housing investment programme bid to the government and to revise their agreed needs statements with the Housing Corporation . . .

The most urgent priority might be for new rented housing, but it would be a foolish council that made that the centre of its strategy, let alone proposed to build such housing itself. That would be to invite condemnation of the strategy as unrealistic . . .

Another area to avoid is affordability. An important bit of 'realism' is the willingness to put up rents ahead of inflation! . . . Having forced up rents, ministers then feign horror at the size of the housing benefit bill and at the welfare ghettoes they have created – and blame those wicked councils again. (Singh, Chair of the Association of District Councils, *Backdoor*, ROOF, March/April 1994)

In the former Federal Republic of Germany similar strains existed between the central government and the *Länder* as the latter sought to assert its autonomy with respect to centrally devised housing policies and centrally provided funding. Central-local clashes are an inevitable part of issues of subsidiarity within the state. It was not possible for central government to direct local authorities to carry out its housing policies without undermining local democracy—it could only influence their decisions by either providing a framework for growth or by restricting the amount of resources available for building. However, the 1980s saw an approach by central government to local authorities in general that questioned the latter's independent role as a provider.

Central and local government have different aims, objectives and preoccupations in relation to housing, because the centre is concerned with economic regulation, capital accumulation, investment and taxation consequences; local government, on the other hand, is concerned with need, territorial defence, local political pressure, management of the stock and costs (rent and Council tax) falling on local residents. Several significant policy developments [during the 1980s] affecting council rents, rebates, sales, new building and homelessness, all involving reduction in local autonomy, can be explained against this background. From the point of view of local councillors, a residualized public sector has little appeal and few political advantages, though at the same time it carries political risks. (Malpass and Murie, 1994, *op. cit.*, p 10)

To try and instil such a change in the nature of the rental sector while there was a boom in owner-occupation would have been possible, but the concomitant collapse of the housing market at the beginning of the 1990s has meant that the private sector and housing associations have been given too little time to take over the role of local authorities as the main provider of rented accommodation when people are unable to buy their own home.

The Conservative government of the 1980s sought from the outset to residualize the role of local authorities as providers of homes. However, it would be a mistake to think that this process of residualization only started in 1979. Council housing was seen as the only solution that would meet the need for housing after

World War I; indeed, Orbach has argued that the government of the day feared a revolution similar to that in Russia in 1917 if it failed to provide proper homes for the returning soldiers (see Swenarton, *Homes Fit for Heroes*, 1981, p 49). As such, it started off as general housing available to the whole community, much as the private rental sector had been up to 1914. Nevertheless, given that both the major political parties were also encouraging owner-occupation, times of economic prosperity would inevitably lead to the better-off opting to buy their homes; by the 1950s and 1960s, the government was also giving generous tax concessions to people buying on a mortgage, which provided a further incentive. Thus, while local authority housing replaced private sector renting as homes previously rented out were sold off, it was destined to be housing for the least well-off in society, welfare housing. The 1980s merely speeded up this process because the government was trying generally to cut back on expenditure and such policies limit the funds available for new homes and inevitably reduce the scope of local autonomy. To control local authority costs relating to housing matters, the government had to take greater control of the detail of providing housing—rents, repairs, management. In the end, the ultimate consequence of wishing to restrain local authority expenditure is to reduce its role. The corollary, though, should be that for the first time central government is in a position to lay down housing policies that should be implemented without there being any question of usurping the function of another democratically elected institution. Unfortunately, while residualizing the role of local authorities in the housing system, the government failed to take adequate steps to enhance the roles of private landlords and housing associations sufficiently to fill the ensuing gap. It was also hindered in its aims by rising unemployment and the recession that started at the end of the 1980s.

Having given an overview of the decline in the position of local authorities, it is necessary to examine some of the issues in more detail. The first of these concerns the financing of council housing by central government. Central government has always provided a subsidy to local government for the building of housing—see generally, The Government's Expenditure Plans: Department of the Environment, 1994-95 to 1996-97, Cm 2507, 1994. Between 1920 and 1972 the subsidy was used to determine the type of public housing policy that central government wanted; would it allow general housing that would be available to any applicant or would it be limited to slum clearances and special needs housing? After 1972, though, the subsidy was used as a crude tool to influence rent levels in local authorities. Since 1979, there have been a series of statutes trying to impose a greater share of the funding on local sources, namely council rents: under the latest, the Local Government and Housing Act 1989, the subsidy represents the difference between local authority costs (interest rate charges, repairs, maintenance, housing benefit for council tenants) and what can be raised by rents—reducing subsidy results in either reduced services or higher rents, usually the latter.

[Housing] is not only the welfare programme suffering the largest cuts, it is also the only programme where cuts have been over-achieved: by 1981/82 the estimated out-turn cut was one-and-a-half times the size the government had planned in 1980. (O'Higgins, cited in Malpass and Murie, 1990, *op. cit.*, p 104; see also, Malpass and Murie, 1994, *op. cit.*, pp 107–13)

In 1977 rents and subsidy contributed about 40 per cent each to the local authority housing costs; by 1983, according to Leather and Murie ('The Decline in Public Expenditure', in Malpass, ed., *The Housing Crisis*, 1986, p 51), rents covered 55 per cent of costs, while central government subsidy only amounted to 16 per cent. 'Spending on new buildings by local authorities fell from £4.7 billion in 1976/77 to £0.6 billion in 1988/89' (Rowntree Inquiry, *op. cit.*, p 13). Before 1989 local authorities could subsidise rents through the transfer of funds raised from ratepayers, but the 1989 Act 'ring-fenced' the housing revenue account to prevent unauthorised payments in or out. Further, by including housing benefit payments for council tenants as a charge on the housing revenue account, this Act placed an unavoidable cost which cannot be deferred, as, for instance, repairs might have been in the past, on local authorities and on better-off tenants whose rents help meet housing benefit costs. Nevertheless, local authority housing as a whole was, for the most part, self-financing as regards basic housing costs in 1993—the *Guardian* 2 p 21, 15 October 1993; Joseph Rowntree Foundation Housing Research Findings No. 126, September 1994.

One consequence of [the 1993/94] rent increases is that English council housing will cease to be a net recipient of 'basic' housing subsidy. The [Department of the Environment] forecast for 1994/95 is that those authorities still in receipt of basic housing subsidy will get £832 million. Against that 'negative entitlements', which are set against rent rebate subsidy, are forecast at £898 million. In other words, English council housing as a whole will move £66 million into surplus in 1994/95. That surplus is expected to grow substantially in future years. (Wilcox, *op. cit.*, p 82, and see Table 56)

Somewhere between 60 and 70 per cent of council tenants receive housing benefit, a proportion in the public sector that is likely to rise as rents increase and purchasing becomes ever more attractive for the better-off tenant. Since the beginning of the 1970s, during which time the Conservatives were in power for most of the time, the financing of local authorities' housing accounts has been one major tool used by central government to increase rents so as to cut central costs and encourage council tenants to become owner-occupiers. However, the current failure to provide sufficient new housing has prompted many to suggest that there must be changes in the way local authorities are funded with respect to housing costs, which suggestions would reduce central government control. First, the restriction on the use of capital receipts from sales under the RTB could be changed—it would seem only ever to have been a Treasury-led measure, not one that was originally intended by the framers of the Right To Buy (Sir Hugh Rossi, quoted in the *Guardian 2*—Society p 8, 5 October 1994). Rowntree (1991 Inquiry, *op. cit.*, pp 72–3) proposed that local authorities should be able to borrow freely from the private financial institutions, for instance, and Gibb and Munro (*op. cit.*, pp 248–52) generally concur. However, the policy director of the Institute of Housing took this analysis a step further, coming up with two ideas to break the central-local impasse.

The first is to change accounting definitions so that only the *subsidy* received by councils counts as public spending. Their private borrowing would then be outside government control. Social housing bodies in France and Germany have this freedom . . . The second idea is to allow councils to set up local housing companies to take over part of the council stock and raise private finance for improvement or new building. (John Perry in the *Guardian*, p 21, 10 June 1992)

Both ideas have been taken up—Wilcox, Bramley *et al.*, *Local Housing Companies: New Opportunities for Council Housing*, 1993; Dwelly, *Nothing Ruled Out*, ROOF, September/October 1993, p 22. Indeed, given that the government's view on local authority private borrowing still having to be within the public borrowing limits has been endorsed by the Maastricht Protocols, the two have to go hand in hand. Only if local authorities divest themselves of their housing to local housing companies can there be expansion in this sector—Goodlad and Gibb, *op. cit.*, at pp 49–52. The conclusion must be that the government's use of financial restrictions as part of a process of residualizing the role of local authorities has run into serious opposition. The opponents of further reductions in local authority autonomy are putting the provision of accommodation before Conservative party inflexible dogma that social housing can only improve without councils.

As well as trying to control local authorities through the system of housing finance, central government has increasingly interfered in the functioning and management of local authority housing. Again, some of this restraint on autonomy started before 1979. The 1977 Housing (Homeless Persons) Act shows that sometimes this interference in the local decision making processes, regarding allocation in this case, can be for welfare reasons rather than to try and obtain greater influence over the implementation of housing policy. On the other hand, the legislation reflected the fact that many authorities were not following centrally recommended advice and guidance concerning homeless persons and that it had proved necessary to impose statutory duties—without, it may be noted though, any additional funding. However, the 1980s saw legislation which was intended to erode local authority autonomy with regard to housing. The Housing Act 1980 did this in two ways—through the Tenant's Charter and through the Right To Buy. The Tenants' Charter primarily gave council tenants similar rights to those enjoyed by private sector tenants under the then Rent Act 1977. In so doing, however, it fettered local authority discretion as regards succession and the grounds for eviction, although in many ways it simply mirrored previous council practice. In terms, though, of direct interference in local authority housing, the Right To Buy cannot be dismissed as the codification of existing practice—only 42,000 local authority dwellings were sold in 1979, at that time on a voluntary basis. The Right To Buy gave secure tenants of, then, three years' standing the right to purchase their council property at a substantial discount. Furthermore, central government prohibited local authorities from using the capital receipts for new building. The effect was to take over 200,000 council houses into the owner-occupied sector without replacement in 1982 alone. The figures then declined, reflecting the fact that richer tenants had already bought their properties, but almost 180,000 were bought in 1988 and over 190,000 in 1989. By 1993, in the midst of a recession, only 68,504 council homes were sold in Great Britain (source, Housing and Construction Statistics, March Qtr 1994, Table 2.14). The simultaneous changes in subsidy calculation meant that rents rose faster than inflation, making buying even more attractive, especially in the house price spiral of the 1980s. Even where a local authority attempted to restrict sales, possibly as part of an election commitment to reduce council house waiting lists or to ensure a sufficient supply for the elderly, the Secretary of State could intervene to force through Right To Buy applications (Housing Act 1980, s 23; see now Housing Act 1985, ss 164-6). In Norwich, council house sales between December 1981 and May 1985 were handled by a government appointed administrator after the Secretary of State found there were unreasonable delays in processing applications. The combined effect of all those developments was to limit local authority autonomy over an ever-dwindling supply of housing, with the threat of direct intervention if central policy was not followed. Furthermore, Australian experience would suggest that central government policies might erode the local authority role in housing to such a point that it becomes unviable.

Because of the privatizing of so much of the public housing stock, State housing authorities in Australia have created many of the negative outcomes predicted by researchers in those overseas countries that more recently embarked on a similar policy. Much high-quality and better-located stock has been sold, leaving behind a residual of low-status, often high-rise, dwellings. Moreover, public authorities still have years to wait for purchasers to repay their loans, yet are hard pressed to find public funds to meet the increasing demand for rental rebates to the predominantly welfare tenants left in the wake of privatization . . . [It] may be that Australian public housing authorities will be unable to meet their . . . current financial commitments, let alone provide for future need. (van Vliet, *op. cit.,* p 731)

Table 2.5

Expenditure (£ billion) per year	Housing	Law, order and protective services
1980–81	11.3	8.0
1981–82	7.7	8.5
1982–83	6.5	8.8
1983–84	7.2	9.4
1984–85	6.9	9.9
1985–86	6.0	9.7
1986–87	5.7	10.3
1987–88	5.6	10.9
1988–89	4.1	11.4
1989–90	6.0	12.2
1990–91	5.3	12.7
1991–92	5.8	13.5
1992–93	6.2	14.2
1992–93	5.3	14.4
Real growth 1980–81 to 1992–93	–52.7%	79.4%

(*Source*: Wilcox, *op. cit.*, Table 13b; see also Hills, *Unravelling Housing Finance*, 1991)

A further residualization policy, accompanying the change in local authority housing finance and the Right To Buy, was the restriction placed on new building. Central government has used its subsidy leverage to control the quantity of local authority housing since 1919, but it had always been the case before the International Monetary Fund crisis in the mid-1970s that an increase in stock was to be expected. The financial cuts made to the housing budget again provide evidence of a concerted attempt to marginalize centrally funded housing.

The November 1994 Budget provided such inadequate funding for new buildings that, in fact, the fewest number of new council homes for 50 years will be built—at the same time, rents will rise by over 7 per cent, almost three times the rate of inflation. Furthermore, whereas during the 1980s local authorities had unprecedented capital receipts generated by the Right To Buy, those monies were directed by central government to be used for debt repayment rather than replacement homes. The effect of this restraint on new building was an 11 per cent rise in homeless families and the absurd result that it cost local authorities £174 million p a. more to house those families in Bed and Breakfast hotels and short-term private sector lets than it would to have built new homes for them. In

1991 it seemed that the only new money for the public sector up to 1993–94 would be £150 million and that via Housing Action Trusts (see p 15, LAG Bull., Sept 1991). The homelessness crisis, in part, led to a relaxation in government rules and any capital housing receipts generated between November 1992 and December 1993 could be used by local authorities, if they so wished, to build new homes. It is notable that a similar housing crisis in Australia has led by contrast to an obligation on public housing authorities to replace any house sold, to widen its eligibility criteria to include young, single homeless applicants and a move away from market rents to the much cheaper historic-cost rents (van Vliet, *op. cit.*, p 731).

Two other changes reflect the marginalisation of local authorities in the provision of housing: Compulsory Competitive Tendering and Local Housing Companies. Compulsory Competitive Tendering was extended to housing matters by the Leasehold Reform, Housing and Urban Development Act 1993. It requires local authorities to put the provision of housing services out to tender—see ch 7 and ch 10, below. Undoubtedly, it will have an effect on the council staff who manage housing, but whether any benefits trickle down to the tenants is less clear—Robertson, *Backdoor*, ROOF, March/April 1993, and McIntosh, *Tender Moments*, ROOF, March/April 1993, p 38. Local Housing Companies in one way seek to emulate the methods used in the rest of Europe to manage social housing. By transferring housing stock to such companies, but retaining an influence through representation, local authorities are marginalized, but it may well be the best way forward given the attitude of central government to funding council housing; Local Housing Companies could borrow from the private financial institutions without affecting the PSBR—see Goodlad and Gibb, *op. cit.*, pp 17–19 and 50–2; Warburton, *Backdoor*, ROOF, September/ October 1994.

To conclude with respect to this section on how the struggle between central and local government has affected housing policy, Malpass and Murie (1994, *op. cit.*, p 53) suggest that the existence of the subsidy from central government inevitably leads to attempts at greater control. '[No] government has ever been, nor could ever be, content *merely* to provide financial support, leaving the authorities free to make all the decisions about what sort of service municipal housing was actually going to be.' Part of the problem is that central and local government view council housing from different perspectives. For local government it is part of its activities in meeting local needs: central government, though, sees it as social expenditure to be controlled like any other element of government spending. Housing policies devised by central and local government cannot, therefore, be expected to have the same designs and what has been seen since 1979 is simply the increased centralisation of all expenditure programmes, including housing. Given this increasing residualization, what role is there for local authority housing in the future?

2.6.3 The Role of Local Authority Housing

Para 2–3. One of the most important functions of local government is housing. The government believe that the accurate assessment of housing requirements and the provision of housing and housing advice to the individual is of such paramount importance that the service should be operated as close to the citizen as possible. (1971 White Paper on Local Government in England, Cmnd 4584)

Objectives for the Future- Para 1.16 . . . the Government will encourage local authorities to change and develop their housing role. Provision of housing by local authorities as landlords should gradually be diminished, and alternative forms of tenure and tenant choice should increase . . . Local authorities should increasingly see themselves as enablers who ensure that everyone in their area is adequately housed; but not necessarily by them. (1987 White Paper on Housing, Cm 214)

Sixteen years of Conservative thought on housing.

There is no statutory obligation on local authorities to have any housing stock to let (Housing Act 1985, s 9(5)) and all their duties to provide housing for certain specific groups, such as the non-intentionally homeless with priority need (Housing Act 1985, Pt III) and people living in a clearance area (Housing Act 1985, s 289), can be properly carried out by third parties (for example, Housing Act 1985, s 69). However, for the time being at least, local authorities will continue to act as landlords and the issue is whether they have a role to play in meeting general housing need or are they to be confined to a welfare role similar to that of public housing in the United States.

In the nineteenth century, local authorities were limited to a regulatory role, checking on the quality of housing provided by private landlords. However, as has been noted above, the rate of return on housing the poor rendered private sector landlordism an uncommercial venture and, following the failure of housing associations and the like to fill the gap, local authorities were promoted after World War I as the principal social landlord. Even between the Wars, though, central government policy varied between providing general subsidies and simply funding to allow slum clearance. Was the local authority to have a generalist role in housing provision or was it to be limited to providing for the poor—those who could not afford private sector rents or the costs of owner occupation? Immediately after 1945, the need for housing to replace that damaged during World War II meant that local authorities were again encouraged to adopt a generalist role, but by the mid-1950s Conservative governments were favouring owner-occupation. Thus, it was only briefly at the end of each of the World Wars that council housing enjoyed a period of unrestricted growth. Even when local authorities were in the ascendancy, they tended to allocate not to the poorest members of society, but to the better-off working class.

There is really no doubt about how rent policy worked out in practice. The market for local authority houses was largely confined to a limited range of income groups, that is, in practice, the better-off families, the small clerks, the artisans, the better-off semi-skilled workers with small families and fairly safe jobs. (Bowley, *Housing and the State*, 1945, p 129, cited in Malpass and Murie, 1994, op. cit., p 61)

Thus, a purely welfarist role has always been forced on local authorities who have resisted by favouring better-off tenants. Back in 1933, the Housing (Financial Provisions) Act removed the general subsidy available to local authorities on the basis that, in the eyes of central government, council housing was only for the poor: local authorities, on the other hand, preferred tenants with secure wages who could pay the rent.

[The] underlying philosophy seemed to be that council tenancies were to be given only to those who 'deserved' them, and that the 'most deserving' should get them. Thus, unmarried mothers, cohabitees, 'dirty' families and 'transients' tended to be grouped together as 'undesirables'. Moral rectitude, social conformity, clean living and a 'clean' rent book on occasion seemed to be essential qualifications for eligibility—at least for new houses. (Cullingworth Report, Council Housing Purposes, Procedures and Priorities, 1969, cited in Malpass and Murie, 1994, *op. cit.*, p 282)

Central government, in its desire to keep down expenditure, prefers, and has always preferred, means-tested rent rebates, such as housing benefit. These means-tested benefits allow the poor to afford council rents, while they make private sector rents and owner-occupation not such a costly alternative in relative terms to better-off council tenants.

However, there are non-monetary factors to be considered which result from residualizing local authorities to a mere welfare role, such as the type of housing available from councils. The direct and intended consequence of some legislation has been that local authorities have in the past concentrated on clearing slums in the inner city and moving the occupiers to high-rises in overspill estates. The Housing Subsidies Act 1956 reduced general subsidy, but left in place the subsidy for dwellings built to replace those lost in slum clearance; this slum clearance subsidy was set at a higher rate if the household's new dwelling was in a block of flats more than three storeys high. Such properties are not the choice of any family that can afford to find a house elsewhere.

Around the perimeter of Liverpool huge public developments of corporation housing estates have been built since 1945 . . . When I first visited one large outer estate, I brought with me the eyes of a Londoner. There we used to feel that, if only the suburbs would allow land for building, the housing problems of a crowded city would be solved. Now I was seeing plenty of space; yet every empty

house or flat has all its windows broken. In several streets empty houses have
their roofs smashed in. Most shops don't go in for glass, but have metal shutters.
Blocks of maisonettes . . . stand boarded up and totally empty. Some of the walk-
up blocks have been demolished. In some other estates *four-storey blocks have had
the top two floors removed, to make smaller houses again;* some very large blocks . . .
are to be demolished. The dream of green fields development seems in a number
of instances to have been smashed. (David Sheppard, Bishop of Liverpool, *Bias to the
Poor*, 1984, p 20; emphasis added)

Thus, given the residualization referred to in the previous section, the welfare
role envisaged for the rump of the local authority sector by central government
will lead to council tenants being much poorer than the rest of society, ever more
dependent on housing benefit and living in the worst housing. The future consequences are likely to include the following matters, having regard in some
instances to experience in other countries. First, although the government has
taken steps to curtail local authorities' role as providers, the housing associations
and private sector landlords have not filled the gap. The result may be that while
there is a surplus of housing with respect to the number of households at present,
given the trend towards smaller household units and the increasing break-up of
families through divorce, there may be insufficient appropriate housing to rent
unless the housing associations can replace the role of the local authorities. And
even then, it may not be affordable if housing associations have had to fund the
development through borrowing from financial institutions. Local authorities
can only enable people to find housing if it has been built by housing associations and private landlords.

Secondly, those tenants still in council housing will be more likely to be
unskilled or dependent on social security. Table 2.6 shows, as might have been
expected, that there are no professional heads of household in local authority
housing, but also that the proportion of unskilled heads of household is highest
in that sector. Economically inactive heads of household are found in large number owning their own home outright, reflecting those retired persons who have
paid off any mortgage. However, they are also present in substantial numbers in
local authority lets, some of whom will be retired, but including, as well, a sizeable proportion of single parent heads of household; there are, in addition, many
temporarily inactive heads of household who are currently unemployed. The
most telling statistic, though, relates to the average weekly income of heads of
household in the local authority sector—the figure for a council tenant is less
than 50 per cent of that for an owner-occupier with a mortgage.

[Until] the fifties there was a far less skewed distribution of households in public
housing, but the expansion of home ownership, together with the collapse of private renting (which housed many on the lowest incomes), has resulted in a grow-

Table 2.6 Head of household tenure profile

| | Owner-occupied | | Rented | | | | | % of Total Households |
	Owned outright	With mortgage	With job/ business	L.A./New Town	H.A./Co-operative	Unfurnished private	Furnished private	
Age (%) Base figure 9987								
<25	Ø	3	4	5	6	9	37	4
25–29	Ø	11	7	9	12	10	25	8
30–44	5	45	46	20	21	20	26	27
45–59	23	33	30	19	15	13	8	25
60–64	14	4	8	8	7	5	1	8
65–69	17	2	2	10	8	7	Ø	8
70–79	28	2	2	19	23	20	2	13
80+	13	Ø	Ø	10	10	16	2	6
SEG (%) Base figure 9829								
A	3	9	15	Ø	1	3	9	5
B	6	24	31	2	3	5	10	13
C	3	13	12	3	4	6	16	8
D	3	7	4	3	5	6	9	5
E	11	28	15	15	12	15	14	19
F	4	8	19	10	12	10	10	8
G	2	2	1	5	5	2	2	3
H	67	9	4	62	59	53	31	39
Avg. Gross Income (£) Base figure 9437								
Mean	194	320	288	110	120	149	170	£225
Median	140	280	246	85	88	98	115	£168

Source: OPCS, 1992 *General Household Survey,* Tables 10.7, 10.9 and 10.13; see also, Forrest and Murie, 'The Right to Buy', in Grant, *op. cit.,* pp 139 *et seq.*

Ø = less than one per cent.

Socio-Economic Group: A = Professional; B = Employers and managers; C = Intermediate non-manual; D = Junior non-manual; E = Skilled manual and own account non-professional; F = Semi-skilled manual and personal service; G = Unskilled manual; H = Economically inactive heads of household. Members of the armed forces, economically active full-time students and those unemployed persons who had never worked were excluded.

ing polarization, in terms of incomes and socio-economic composition, between the two main tenures. (van Vliet, *op. cit.*, p 91)

That local authority housing is drifting towards the marginalised position of public housing in the United States is borne out by comparable data which suggests that in the United States couples are leaving the rented sector for owner-occupation, while inner-city rental stock is let to households headed by a low-paid black woman (Sternlieb and Hughes, *op. cit.*, pp 4–5). Public housing in the United States was established to cater specifically for the poor of the community. The qualifying households must earn no more than 80 per cent of the median income for the area and the rent is set as a percentage (now thirty per cent) of that wage. According to Marcuse (van Vliet, *op. cit.*, pp 357–8), the principle of public housing has always been unpopular amongst those not dependent upon it and so the quality of the accommodation has been kept low. In Japan, on the other hand, (see Hayakawa in van Vliet, *op. cit.*, p 681) although centrally subsidized public housing is reserved for low income families whose wage is less than a set level, the standard of the housing is not kept deliberately poor. Indeed, one of the objectives of the public housing programme would appear to be to improve the conditions of the qualifying tenants when they cannot do so in the private sector because of their low pay. In the United Kingdom, central government has used local authority housing on occasions to meet general housing need, so the quality of the accommodation was in some cases very high, but as a result of the Right To Buy this better accommodation has been sold off leaving only the poorer housing (including a substantial proportion of high rise tower blocks) to let to those who cannot afford to buy or rent from a housing association. The policy has not been open as in the United States, but the effect has been to create welfare landlordism via general residualization of housing stock. The problem is that where housing is only for welfare tenants, then those living there become dissatisfied but are offered no way out. In Canada, the government, both Federal and Provincial, has taken steps to ensure a social mix in its public housing developments, but the consequence of unrestrained residualization in the United States has been the creation of 'ghettoes' with more than just housing problems.

[By the 1980s, those] groups that had protested massively in the 1960s, awakening fear and concern among both private and governmental leaders, were now seen as defeated, no longer to be feared. The type of individualized resistance represented by street crime, drugs and vandalism, could be seen, and dealt with, as 'social problems', rather than as societal problems—or, more callously, simply allowed to run rampant but confined to inner cities, areas of no interest to a business leadership whose basis for power lay elsewhere. (van Vliet, *op. cit.*, p 355; see also, Croftin, *Tales of Lost Regeneration*, ROOF, November/December 1994, p 30)

In conclusion, local authorities have never acted as wholly welfare landlords and have no interest in doing so. However, central government, through a host of measures, is seeking to play a minimal role in housing provision: the result is that in the foreseeable future, unless owner-occupation is open to the household, they will be housed in a shrinking rental market where the largest provider, the local authorities, is starved of funds.

2.7 COMMERCIAL PROPERTY

Arguably, there is no co-ordinated policy in the commercial sector, but practices have developed which have shaped the structure of leasing and the pattern of commercial property ownership. Most commercial property is now occupied on a rental basis rather than under freehold ownership (see ch 1.2.4). For the tenant, leasing generally offers greater flexibility in terms of business development plans than outright ownership, but renting may also be necessitated by financial constraints on outright purchase. The current picture is one that has emerged as a result of commercial and investment decisions rather than direct state intervention. On the whole, the attitude of government has been to allow market forces to regulate the supply and to determine the tenure of commercial property, although planning laws will also have an impact on supply. The market in 'prime property' (property most in demand) is dominated by the amount of such property owned by institutional investors, such as pension funds and insurance companies, and the control exerted by them over the content and structure of leases, requiring long term (25 year) leases with a guaranteed and rising rental income (see generally, ch 5.3.3). This dominance is the product of the changing investment climate during the twentieth century, leading to investment in commercial property becoming more attractive, especially to institutions.

In a thesis examining the growth of investment in commercial property, Scott identifies five conditions which need to be met in order for a significant volume of institutional property investment to take place:

1 A substantial number of commercial property transactions, providing a steady stream of investment opportunities.
2 The growth of an efficient and integrated property investment market, covering the geographical area in which the investments were situated.
3 The development of a 'scarcity premium'; the scarcity of prime property sites ensuring that investment property was likely to maintain, or increase, its value over time.
4 A financial climate in which commercial enterprises had considerable incentives to rent, rather than own, their business premises, or to dispose of some property rights to their premises in return for an immediate capital sum.
5 The emergence of a significant differential between the performance of prop-

erty and alternative assets, property performing sufficiently better than other investments to overcome its inherent disadvantages of lack of marketability, uncertainty of value, indivisibility and higher management costs. (Scott, *Financial Institutions and the British Property Investment Market 1850–1980*, D.Phil Thesis, 1992, Oxford University)

Scott's thesis explores how these factors explain the level of investment in commercial property. The first three criteria relate to market conditions. It was not until the inter-war period that a strong market began to develop in commercial property, particularly in the retail sector. The rapid expansion of retailing chains generated a vibrant market and demand for high street sites grew. With this came a growth in the number of firms of commercial estate agents, the acquisition of more detailed market information and improvements in quantitative techniques for evaluating property investments—all important factors in developing a more efficient market. In order to finance expansion plans, businesses found that sale and leaseback arrangements provided an easily available and inexpensive source of finance, compared to alternative sources of funds (thus meeting Scott's fourth condition, above). Various post-war office development restrictions served only to enhance the demand for property and thus to increase property values.

A number of factors have contributed to Scott's fifth condition being met, that is that property has a high investment performance over other possible investments. First, there are taxation advantages to property as an investment medium for institutional funds, rather than shares. There are particular advantages in direct ownership of property, rather than ownership via property companies, as this avoids the payment of corporation tax. This is particularly important for institutions which pay no tax, such as pension funds, or pay tax at a preferential rate, such as life assurance companies. Property is also advantageous over shares in other ways: rent is payable gross, quarterly in advance, and tax can be deferred for up to twelve months, whereas shares have interest paid net of tax, half yearly in arrears. Secondly, perception changed from seeing property as a form of fixed interest investment (for example, letting property on long leases of 99 or even 999 years in return for a fixed rental return), to seeing it as a form of investment with variable returns on the investment. This led to two major changes: institutions began to participate in funding the development process as equity investors, sharing in the profits of the development, and, perhaps more significantly, upwards only rent review clauses were included in leases which provide for the rent to be increased at periodic intervals, but not decreased, even in a falling market. Until the mid-1950s review clauses were rare but review clauses gradually became more common, first with rent reviews at the thirty-third and sixty-sixth years of the lease, and later at progressively shorter intervals as the practice became more widespread and the effects of inflation more widely appreciated. This meant that investors would see steady income growth throughout the lease, which more than compensated for property's greater risk, lower marketability, indivisibility, higher management costs, and other disadvantages compared to gilts. Five yearly rent review is now standard. A third factor in the growth of investment in property was that as investment managers gained increased expertise in property transactions, they developed a bias towards investment in this sector, feeling they had a greater knowledge of its workings than of the stock market. Lastly, high demand for property coupled with inelastic supply led to rapid growth in market rents (and thus capital values).

A further factor important in attracting institutional investment nowadays is the security of income provided by the almost-standard structure of occupational leases of prime property. This security stems from the fact that the investor is assured of a rising income over a long term clear of possible deductions, due to a variety of factors: upwards only rent review, the length of the standard lease (25 years), the fact that the original tenant remains liable under the lease even after assigning, and the fact that the cost of all repairs, servicing and insurance (unknown quantities) has to be borne by the tenant in addition to the rent and not by the landlord out of its rental income (a 'clear' lease). In financial terms, this structure makes a significant difference to the value of the landlord's investment. The impact of a clear lease is shown in the case of *O'May v City of London Real Property Co Ltd* [1983] 2 AC 726, where the House of Lords was determining what the terms of a new (renewed) tenancy would be. The tenant had the right to a new lease under Part II of the Landlord and Tenant Act 1954 (see ch 6.4) and the dispute was over the form that this lease would take. The landlord argued that it should be a clear lease. The importance of the clear lease to the landlord is shown in the speech of Lord Hailsham (at 737):

The effect of giving [a clear lease] . . . would, according to the evidence, be to enhance the value of the appellants' reversion by a sum somewhere between one and two million pounds, and at the same time to render it more readily marketable partly owing to the increasing part played (amongst others) by pension funds and life insurance companies in purchasing office property as an investment. The purpose of a 'clear lease' is to render the income derived from the rent payable by the tenants as little subject to fluctuation in respect of outgoings as may be possible.

The government has been content to leave the structure of commercial leases to market forces and the historic strength of the landlord in the negotiating process has ensured that leases provide the level of certainty about future income required by institutional investors.

In other European countries the leasehold systems make investment less attractive, so much so that English commercial property has attracted a lot of overseas investors. Letting practices in other parts of Europe differ significantly from English practices:

1 Leases are generally shorter. In the Netherlands, leases are typically granted for five years; in France, for nine years.
2 Many countries give tenants an unlimited right to break the lease at periodic intervals. In the French nine-year lease, the tenant has the right to end the lease after each three-year period.
3 In some jurisdictions, tenants have much stronger security of tenure than in England (for the English position, see ch 6.4). In Belgium, a tenant with a commercial lease (a lease for retail purposes, or other purposes involving direct contact with the public) is absolutely entitled to three renewals, each for the same term as the original term. This is not, however, universally the case. In Germany, the tenant has no statutory right to renewal.
4 Rents are generally adjusted by indexation, increases being based upon the retail price index or on a construction cost index. Over time, the rents can therefore become quite out of line with open market rental values (contrast the English position, see ch 8.3.2).
5 The original tenant will not remain liable after assignment.
6 Landlords generally have greater liability for repair and maintenance. So, for example, in Belgium the landlord must accept responsibility for substantial repairs unless they are due to the tenant's negligence in maintaining the property. Landlords are generally responsible for insurance. It is, therefore, hard for investors to find a 'clear' lease with a certain net income.

(On European lease structures, see Bernstein, Lewis, *UK lease structures in the melting pot*, (1992) 45 EG 108; Ryland, *EC Leasing Practices*, (1992) 26 EG 110; Shone, *EC leasehold regimes: a comparison*, (1992) 11 EG 92; Royal Institution of Chartered Surveyors, *International Leasing Structures*, Paper No. 26, 1993.)

In terms of the theme of this book, the significance of such strong institutional investment in the United Kingdom commercial property market is that it is investment criteria that have largely shaped the leasehold structure and the consequent rights and obligations of landlord and tenant. Government intervention has been minimal, save in so far as the tenant may have renewal rights so as to provide security for his trading location.

2.8 AGRICULTURAL LAND

The government's policy towards the agricultural sector reflects concerns that are evident both in the residential and commercial sectors. Early controls implemented in relation to tenancies of agricultural holdings were largely concerned with promoting good husbandry and designed to ensure that the tenant farmer was given sufficient security to think about the long-term productivity of the land. The motivation behind this was not so much the need to protect the tenant's business, as seen in the commercial property sector, but to protect the public interest in efficient long term food production:

[The] Acts of 1947 and 1948 were passed on the morrow of the second occasion within a half-century when this country faced mortal peril through its dependence on imports of food in consequence of the long agricultural decline when an unprotected farming interest had to face the competition of cheap food from abroad.

. . . The security of tenure which tenant farmers were accorded by the Act of 1947 was not only for their own protection as an important section of the public, nor only for the protection of the weak against the strong; it was for the protection of the nation itself. (*Johnson v Moreton* [1980] AC 37, *per* Lord Simon at 68, and Lord Salmon at 52 respectively)

In recent years, the policy focus has had some parallels with the residential sector. This stems from concern over the decline in the size of the agricultural rented sector. The Northfield Committee (*Report to the Committee of Inquiry into the Acquisition and Occupancy of Agricultural Land*, Cmnd 7599, 1979) was concerned that a sizeable proportion of farmland should remain as tenanted land—it was important to retain variety in tenure (see ch 1.2.5). The statutory restrictions on the landlord's freedom of management and, in particular, the freedom to re-let land when and to whom they choose were perceived to be contributing factors to the decline of the tenanted sector. The Committee's recommendations were subsequently enacted and were designed to lead to a greater supply of farms to let and greater efficiency on those that are let. Again, there are analogies with the deregulation of the private residential sector at the end of the 1980s. This process of deregulation of agricultural tenancies is set to be carried further (see ch 6.5.2.3), in order to encourage a larger rental sector:

Without [the deregulating reforms] . . . landowners will not let land. The freer availability of land is the key to the attraction of a greater diversity of entrepreneurial talent into the countryside and to the realisation of all our hopes for a revival of the fortunes of our rural world. (MAFF, News Release, *Agricultural Tenancy Law Reform*, 6 October 1993).

3

The Lease as Property, as a Contract and as a Public Law Relationship

3.1 THE HYBRID NATURE OF LEASES

The law regulating the landlord and tenant relationship is a blend of property law, contract law, statutory regulation and, particularly in the public sector, administrative law. The lease itself, although now one of the two legal estates in land permitted by the 1925 legislation, has historical roots in the law of contract and not the law of property. Prior to the thirteenth century, leases for a term of years were generally given by landowners as security for borrowing, in order to circumvent the church's prohibition on usury. The rights given to the lessee were then solely contractual. Over time, the lease was increasingly used to grant rights over agricultural land for farming purposes and with this change of function it became necessary to provide remedies to protect the tenant's possession of land—remedies in personam (damages) were no longer adequate, what the tenant needed now was a right in rem. During the fifteenth century, the action of ejectment became available to tenants so that, if dispossessed, they could recover the land itself and not just claim damages. The extension of real remedies to tenants meant that they were now seen as having 'property' interests (*cf.* the transition in Roman law, see Stein, *Legal Institutions*, 1984, p 153. For the historical development of English law, see Megarry and Wade, *The Law of Real Property*, 5th edn, 1984, App.1, *Actions for Recovery of Land*). Nevertheless, the lease is still classified as personal property rather than 'real property'.

The modern tenancy relationship reflects the contractual agreement between landlord and tenant, the proprietary nature of the lease and public regulation of leases. The fact that a lease is property as well as a contractual relationship has shaped the development of landlord and tenant law. Various aspects of leases, outlined below, have contributed to the fact that leases are often treated differently from other contracts.

The Lease as an Estate

On entering into the lease, the tenant is granted an estate in land (Law of Property Act 1925, s1(1)(b) and see ch 4), usually in return for payment by the tenant in the form of a premium or rent. This estate gives the grantee (the tenant) the right to exclusive control over the land (see further, ch 4.3.1) and, in the absence of contractual or statutory restriction, is capable of being disposed of and of being enforced against third parties.

The Lease as an Executory Contract

The grant of the estate to the tenant is only the beginning of the landlord and tenant relationship. After that, many obligations remain to be performed, for example, the landlord's continuing obligation to insure and repair the premises and the tenant's obligation to pay rent.

The Lease as a Long Term Relationship

Although leases may be only short term arrangements, many leases continue for considerable periods of time. This, coupled with the fact that leases are regularly assigned (disposed of to another party), affects the way in which the relationship is regulated.

The Lease as a Disposition of Property

The land owner who enters into the lease is disposing of a limited interest in his property. One of the claims frequently made in relation to ownership of property is that the owner has the right to dispose (or not) of the property in the manner he chooses, free from external control. Although there are differing political views of property, it is generally accepted that interference with the landlord's property rights should be justified in some manner (see further, 3.9 below, ch 12.7.2—enfranchisement, ch 8.4.4—rent control).

The Lease as a Right of Property

The tenant owns a property asset, bringing with it a bundle of rights. Indeed, one of the defining features of leases is the right to exclude others from the land (see ch 4.3). Other rights generally associated with the ownership of property include the right to use the property (in the case of leases this right is often restricted by contract, see ch 7.3), and the right to dispose of the property at will (again, this right is often restricted, see ch 9).

The Lease as a Statutory Right

Statutory codes of protection sometimes provide security for tenants while, at the same time, restricting their rights. The limited nature of the tenant's rights in this situation may mean that the tenant can only be said to have a statutory right to occupy, and not a property right (see 3.10 below).

The Lease as an Interest in Land

The fact that there is a finite supply of land has a considerable impact upon the rules applicable to leases. The limited supply of land suitable for different kinds of property developments creates situations of shortage and puts landlords in a quasi-monopolistic position. This enables landlords to exploit those seeking to rent the property—pushing up rents and generating insecurity as, in the absence of external constraint, landlords are free to evict tenants in order to replace them with higher paying tenants. The inequality of bargaining power generated by this imbalance has been an important strand in justifying intervention in the land-lord and tenant contract.

The Lease as a Source of Wealth

For most landlords the lease is a source of wealth. This is especially true of com-mercial property where the letting market is dominated by the demands of insti-tutional investors, leading to the creation of the 'institutional lease' which is structured to provide a clear income stream to investors (see ch 2.7). For many non-commercial landlords also, the return on the investment is an important part of the decision to become or remain a landlord. Local authority landlords and housing associations are motivated by additional concerns—fulfilment of a political function and a welfare role. The removal of housing associations from the public sector into the private sector and the need to raise private capital to fund new developments means that housing associations must now also take account of the investment returns, and this will affect the way that they manage their properties.

The Lease as a Home

This aspect focuses on the fact that the lease provides a very special form of prop-erty which is important for the 'particular thing' it represents, whether a residen-tial home or the home of a business. In the residential context, the lease meets a basic human need for 'shelter' and 'security'. In addition, many people develop a strong emotional bond to their home. In a commercial context, security may be important because of the property's own unique combination of location, size and layout and in order to protect the goodwill of the business and avoid the disruption and expense of relocation. In the agricultural context, security is important to encourage long term efficiency in farming methods. The uniqueness of this property interest is often seen as needing special protection above that afforded to the tenant through the express contractual agreement. This century has seen varying degrees of statutory regulation of the landlord and tenant relationship, much of which has been concerned to protect the tenant in his 'home'—not because of the proprietary nature of his interest but because of the importance of the particular asset to him. It is, therefore, misleading to see the lease only as a private law relationship between two individuals—it is also subject to a considerable amount of public regulation.

The remainder of this chapter will look at some of the ways in which leases are given special treatment in law and discuss the reasons for this differential treatment. The areas examined in this chapter are also dealt with elsewhere in the book, the purpose of this chapter being to explore the underlying conceptual nature of leasehold law.

3.2 REMEDIES AVAILABLE FOR BREACH

3.2.1 Remedies Peculiar to the Landlord and Tenant Relationship

Some of the remedies available for breach of leasehold obligations are peculiar to the landlord and tenant relationship and are not available to other forms of contract, although it is sometimes hard to support this differential treatment. Nevertheless, it highlights the hybrid nature of the landlord and tenant relationship.

3.2.1.1 Distress for Rent

The remedy of distress for rent is an incident of the landlord and tenant relationship under the common law.

The essence of the law of distress for rent can be expressed with deceptive simplicity. It enables a landlord who is owed rent to take goods from the demised premises and sell them, retaining for himself sufficient of the proceeds of sale to satisfy the arrears of rent, plus the cost of using the remedy. (Law Commission, *Distress for Rent*, Working Paper No. 97, 1986, para 2.1)

The essence of distress may be simple, but the rules on distress are complex and arbitrary (see Law Commission, *Landlord and Tenant, Distress for Rent*, Law Com. No. 194, 1991, Part II; see also, ch 8.7.2).

Historically, this self-help remedy arose from the feudal system:

[The landlord's right to distrain] may be a survival from the days when lords of tenants kept a court for those tenants, and distrained by the judgement of that court . . . However . . . the right continued to be the right of the landlord after he had ceased to possess or hold a court . . . As happened in other cases, what had at first been the right of lords high in the feudal scale became the right of all landlords. Thus it becomes to be merely an incident of the relationship of landlord and tenant. (Holdsworth, *History of English Law*, 3rd edn, 1923, Vol III, pp 281–2)

The contemporary justification for distress lies in the special position that landlords are in as a consequence of the proprietary nature of leases. It is argued that landlords are peculiarly vulnerable creditors and therefore deserve the extra protection afforded by special remedies such as distress (see Law Com. Working Paper No. 97, *op. cit.*, para 3.6). Unlike a supplier of other goods or services, a landlord who is owed money cannot simply halt all future supplies. In order to do this the landlord may have to bring possession proceedings, which takes both time and money. Distress is said to provide a fast and efficient remedy to the landlord. Against this, it is argued that distress gives landlords unfair priority over other creditors and the very fact that it is a self-help remedy, not subject to judicial control, runs counter to the direction of modern legislation concerned to protect tenants and debtors from harassment. The Law Commission have recommended that distress be abolished (Law Com. No. 194, *op. cit.*). Nevertheless, for present purposes it is interesting to note that the major remaining justification for it lies in the 'peculiar' position of a landlord, namely that a lease is indeed a special form of contract as it confers a proprietary estate on the tenant that cannot be simply and immediately terminated as to the future following a breach (subject, perhaps, to the further development of repudiatory breach of leases, see 3.2.2.1 below).

3.2.1.2 Relief Against Forfeiture

In contract law, termination provisions in a contract are strictly applied. If there is express provision for termination on a particular event happening and that event occurs, then the non-defaulting party is entitled to end the contract even though he has suffered little, if any, prejudice and the breach is only minor (see Treitel, *The Law of Contract*, 8th edn, 1991, pp 680-1).

In landlord and tenant law a different approach is followed. Leases will usually be drafted in such a way that the landlord has a right of 're-entry' in the event of breach of any covenants on the tenant's part (see ch 11.2.3). If this were an ordinary contract, the fact that a tenant is in breach, however technical a breach, would give rise to a right in the landlord to determine the contract. This is not, however, the case in relation to leases. While this breach provides the landlord with a ground to forfeit the lease, both equity and statute have intervened so as to provide tenants with possible relief against forfeiture which would allow them to keep their tenancies. In addition, the landlord is required, in the case of breach of any covenant apart from a covenant to pay rent, to comply with certain procedural requirements set out in the Law of Property Act 1925, s 146 before proceeding to enforce the right to forfeit. In outline, the landlord must serve notice on the tenant, give him the opportunity to remedy the breach (if this is possible) and it must normally require that the tenant make compensation in money for the breach. Even where the landlord has complied with these procedural requirements, the court has power to grant the tenant relief from forfeiture, to enable him to keep his leasehold interest. Whether or not relief is actually given is a discretionary matter for the court.

Why does this jurisdiction to relieve from forfeiture exist for leases? The usual explanation is that the reservation of the right of re-entry is intended to be of deterrent value—it is inserted into the lease not because the landlord wants to forfeit but because he wants to ensure that the tenant will comply with the terms of the lease. In *Chandless-Chandless v Nicholson* [1942] 2 KB 321 at 323, Lord Greene MR said that:

[the] court, in exercising its jurisdiction to grant relief in cases of non-payment of rent is, of course, proceeding on the old principles of the court of equity which always regarded the condition of re-entry as being merely security of payment of the rent and gave relief if the landlord could get his rent.

Thus, where the breach is non payment of rent, the right to forfeit is seen as providing security for payment. It is, however, usual for the landlord also to have a right to forfeit for breach of other covenants. The reason why relief from forfeiture is available then is because of the injustice that may otherwise arise:

In 1881 Parliament interfered to supplement equity and to enable any tenant to be relieved from forfeiture. The need for such intervention was and is manifest because otherwise a tenant who had paid a large premium for a 999-year lease at a low rent could lose his asset by a breach of covenant which was remediable or which caused the landlord no damage. The forfeiture of any lease, however short, may unjustly enrich the landlord at the expense of the tenant. In creating a power to relieve against forfeiture for breach of covenant Parliament protected the landlord by conferring on the court a wide discretion to grant relief on terms or to refuse relief altogether. In practice this discretion is exercised with the object of ensuring that the landlord is not substantially prejudiced or damaged by the revival of the lease. (*per* Lord Templeman, *Billson v Residential Apartments Ltd* [1992] 2 WLR 15 at 18–19)

These arguments would seem to apply equally to any contract where the exercise of the right to determine the contract would give a windfall to the innocent party. The courts have not, however, been willing to grant equitable relief from forfeiture to *all* contracts, only to those involving possessory or proprietary rights. Why is this?

In several charterparty cases, the charterer has sought to argue that the similarities between a contract for the hire of a ship (a charterparty) and a contract for the hire of land (a lease) require the court to extend the availability of equitable relief from forfeiture beyond leases to contracts generally. A time charterparty has been defined as

one by which the shipowner agrees with the time charterer that during a certain named period he will render services by his servants and crew to carry the goods which are put on board his ship by the time charterer. (per Mackinnon LJ, *Sea and Land Securities Ltd v William Dickson and Co. Ltd* [1942] 2 KB 65 at 69)

The charterer pays for the hire of the ship in much the same way as the tenant pays for the hire of land and the shipowner will generally have power to determine the charterparty upon non-payment in much the same way as a landlord will have a right to forfeit the lease for non payment of rent. The charterparty does not, however, result in the charterer having any proprietary interest in the ship, unlike a tenant who acquires a legal estate in the land. It has been argued that these similarities support the concept of equitable relief from forfeiture being extended to charterparties. The House of Lords has rejected this argument and held that relief from forfeiture is not available to charterparties. In *Barton Thompson and Co Ltd v Stapling Machines Co* [1966] Ch 499, Pennycuick J felt that a charterparty is 'a different kind of contract from an ordinary lease' (at 509). But on what grounds have leases been distinguished from other contracts?

In *The Scaptrade (Scandinavian Trading Tanker Co. A.B. v Flota Petrolera Ecuatoriana* [1983] 2 AC 694), the owners of the Scaptrade withdrew the vessel in accordance with the terms of the charterparty following non punctual payment by the charterers. The case had been brought by the charterers in the hope that the court might follow the lead given by Lord Simon in an earlier case, *The Laconia* [1977] AC 850, where he saw an analogy between the charterparty cases and leases. The point on relief had not been properly argued in *The Laconia* and although the House of Lords declined to take the point on appeal, Lord Simon hinted (at 873–4) that the differences between a lease of land or buildings and the hire of a ship under a time charter were not material. In *The Scaptrade*, the House of Lords firmly rejected this view. In the first place it was held that relief from forfeiture is available only to contracts 'involving any transfer of proprietary or possessory rights' (*per* Lord Diplock at 702). This restriction has been adhered to in subsequent cases with the result that relief from forfeiture was given in a case involving forfeiture of patent rights as these were personal property (*BICC plc v Burndy Corp and another* [1985] 1 All ER 417), but not in a case giving only a contractual licence to use trademarks, contractual licences not being property rights (*Sport International Bussum BV and others v Inter-Footwear Ltd* [1984] 1 WLR 776; see also *Crittall Windows Ltd v Stormseal (UPVC) Window Systems Ltd* [1991] RPC 265). The line drawn between these cases has been criticised as not justifiable in commercial terms (see *Chitty on Contracts*, 27th edn, 1994, para 26–070, fn.92).

Without more, this explanation as to why lease contracts are treated differently from most other forms of contract is inadequate as it does not draw out what is so special about proprietary and possessory rights that they merit separate treatment. Why *should* the proprietary nature of leases make them stand apart? There is a sense in which property rights have always been accorded special treatment. Atiyah refers to this when he discusses the increase in the protection of the expectation interest in contract law during the nineteenth century:

Hume, Adam Smith, and Bentham, were all agreed on the importance of expectations in justifying the binding nature of promises, they all agreed also that bare expectations were less important than expectations allied to present rights, especially rights of property. Hume and Adam Smith, for example, both said that expectations arising out of property deserved greater protection than expectations to something which had never been possessed. To deprive somebody of something which he merely expects to receive is a less serious wrong, deserving less protection, than to deprive somebody of the expectation of continuing to hold something which he already possesses. (Atiyah, *The Rise and Fall of Freedom of Contract*, 1979, p 428, footnotes omitted)

Another reason given by Lord Diplock in *The Scaptrade* for not making relief available in charterparty cases was that to grant relief from forfeiture would be tantamount to an order of specific performance, a remedy which is not available where the contract includes the provision of services. As a charterparty involves the provision to the charterer of not only the vessel but also the services of the crew, it is not the kind of contract capable of specific performance:

To grant an injunction restraining the shipowner from exercising his right of withdrawal of the vessel from the service of the charterer, though negative in form, is pregnant with an affirmative order to the shipowner to perform the contract; juristically it is indistinguishable from a decree for specific performance of a contract to render services; and in respect of that English courts have always disclaimed any jurisdiction to grant. This is, in my view, sufficient reason in itself to compel rejection of the suggestion that the equitable principle of relief from forfeiture is juristically capable of extension so as to grant to the court a discretion to prevent a shipowner from exercising his strict contractual rights under a withdrawal clause in a time charter which is not a charter by demise. (*The Scaptrade, op. cit.*, at 701)

Yet this objection could also be raised in relation to many leases. While the lease is proprietary, it is also partly executory and in most leases the landlord will be under repairing and maintenance obligations, either express or implied. Is this not then equally a contract in part for the use of the thing (the premises) but also for the provision of services? It is true to say that the courts have not shown the same reluctance to award specific performance in relation to enforcement of landlords' covenants as in relation to other contracts for services (for example, an order for the landlord to restore a balcony was given in *Jeune v Queens Cross Properties Ltd* [1974]

1 Ch 97, and the Landlord and Tenant Act 1985, s 17 expressly provides that the court may order specific performance of a landlord's repairing covenant in relation to dwellings). To base the distinction between charterparties and leases on this ground is, however, unconvincing. While specific performance may be available for some breaches by landlords, it is not generally available (*Jeune v Queens Cross Properties Ltd, op. cit.*; *Gordon v Selico Ltd* [1985] 2 EGLR 79).

Another feature that was important in *The Scaptrade* was that it was a commercial contract with the parties bargaining on equal terms. Lord Diplock stressed that parties to a commercial contract bargaining on equal terms can make 'time of the essence' in relation to performance of any primary obligation under the contract. But could this not also be true of some leases? While in residential leases there is seldom equality of bargaining power, the balance of power between commercial landlords and tenants may be not dissimilar from that between the owner of a ship and its hirer. The relative strength of the parties will depend on the buoyancy of the relevant market at the particular time (the freight market/commercial property market) and the identity and needs of the particular parties. Does this mean that a commercial landlord can make the time that rent is paid 'of the essence' of the contract and treat any late payments as a repudiatory breach by the tenant?

The most convincing distinction between leases and charterparties is the commercial context in which they operate. For charterparties there needs to be certainty of result whenever there is a breach:

... when a shipowner becomes entitled, under the terms of his contract, to withdraw a ship from the service of a time charterer, he may well wish to act swiftly and irrevocably ... He may wish to refix his ship elsewhere as soon as possible, to take advantage of a favourable market ... (I)f the question to be decided is whether the tribunal is to grant equitable relief, investigation of the relevant circumstances, and the collection of evidence for that purpose, cannot ordinarily be carried out in a very short period of time. (*per* Robert Goff LJ in the Court of Appeal [1983] QB 529 at 540–1, cited with approval in the House of Lords)

The same considerations are not present in the property market. Property is not usually quickly let—in addition to the difficulties in finding a new tenant, the legal formalities take some time to complete.

In practice it was probably not the proprietary nature of leases *per se* that led to the intervention of equity but the desire to prevent an injustice, due to a landlord taking advantage of a trivial or easily remedied breach. In the case of commercial contracts, the courts have generally been more concerned to uphold freedom of contract and encourage certainty (see *Legione v Hateley* (1983) 46 ALR 1 at 31 in support). If this is the case, then it does leave two questions. First, can the limitation on the jurisdiction to relieve still be restricted, with justification, to contracts involving possessory or proprietary rights? Secondly, should commercial and residential leases continue to be treated in the same manner?

For further reading on this, see Harpum, *Relief Against Forfeiture and the Purchaser of Land*, [1984] CLJ 134; JMT, 99 LQR 489; Mitchell, *The Equitable Doctrine of Relief against Forfeiture*, (1987) 11 Sydney Law Rev 387.

3.2.1.3 Landlords' Termination Orders

The Law Commission have recommended replacing the system of forfeiture with a scheme for landlord termination of leases by court order (Law Commission, *Forfeiture of Tenancies*, Law Com. No. 142, 1985; Law Commission, *Termination of Tenancies Bill*, Law Com. No. 221, 1994; and see 3.2.2.1 below, and ch 11.2.3.3). The object of this is not to fundamentally affect the relationship between landlord and tenant but to remedy defects in the existing law. This scheme will reinforce the differential treatment of leases—requiring a court order in all cases of termination, something not required for most contracts:

This seems to be right: the loss of his tenancy is usually a serious matter for a tenant whether he is in occupation or not, and we do not think it should ever occur except by consent or with the authority of the court. (Law Com. No. 142, *op. cit.*, para 3.8)

In addition, the court will always have a 'primary discretion' as to whether the tenancy shall end or not, similar in effect to the jurisdiction to relieve from forfeiture.

3.2.2 Are Contractual Remedies Available for Breach?

The fact that a tenant is granted a legal estate upon entering into the contract has led the courts in the past to view the contract as if it were completed at the time of grant, in many ways as if it were analogous to a sale contract under which the seller's obligation is discharged once the transfer of title is complete, with the risk falling on the purchaser thereafter. Under this view, the land owner is seen as simply providing the land, and not as providing any services during the relationship. This view of leases was strengthened by the fact that most early leases were agrarian: a skilled tenant farmer was well able to assess the quality of land for himself and the most important element of the lease was the land itself.

The fact that the lease was viewed as simply the grant of an estate in land had important consequences. It followed from this that normal contractual remedies were frequently not allowed following breach. Once the lease had been executed the tenant was seen to have received what was bargained for, the law would protect the tenant's possession of the land to ensure that the grant was not denied but beyond this the law did little to recognize that the tenant might lose other aspects of the bargain. Under the common law there are, for example, very few covenants implied into a lease—the two main implied covenants being the covenant for quiet enjoyment and not to derogate from grant (see ch 5.3.2). The covenant for quiet enjoyment is an undertaking that the tenant will enjoy quiet possession without interruption, and so protects his possession of the land. The obligation not to derogate from grant means that the landlord cannot do anything which is inconsistent with the purposes for which the property is let. Quinn and Phillips refer to the law's preoccupation with the 'possession-rent relationship' under which the two elements of the relationship that were important were the payment of rent in return for the possession of land:

The landlord's primary obligation was to turn over possession of the land to the tenant and to agree to leave him in peaceful possession. The tenant, in turn, was expected to pay the 'rent'. In technical terms, the tenant 'covenanted' to pay the rent while the landlord 'covenanted' to keep him in quiet possession.

Significantly, the landlord was not being paid to do anything. He was turning over the land to the tenant with the rent serving as continuous compensation for the transfer. The landlord was *not* expected to assist in the operation of the land. Quite the reverse, he was expected to stay as far away as possible. In other words, for the term of the lease, the lands were subject to the tenant's, not the landlord's care and concern. Should the landlord interfere, he risked violating real property law . . .

The point that emerges and which bears emphasis is that the basic remedies peculiar to landlord-tenant law are possession oriented. The tenant who failed to pay rent was evicted from possession [provided the landlord had reserved the power to terminate in this event]. In turn, the landlord violated the law when he deprived the tenant of possession. (Quinn and Phillips, *The Law of Landlord-Tenant: A Critical Evaluation of the Past with Guidelines for the Future*, (1969) 38 Fordham L Rev 225 at pp 227–30, footnotes omitted)

This pre-occupation with the possession-rent relationship is illustrated by the fact that the tenant was denied remedies that would have been available for breach of any other type of contract. Until recently, repudiation was thought to be inapplicable to leases: see *Total Oil Great Britain Ltd v Thompson Garages (Biggin Hill) Ltd* [1972] 1 QB 318, esp. at 324. The thinking behind this was, presumably, that repudiation depends upon breach of a fundamental term of the contract—as the essence of a lease was the conveyance of an estate, and this term or expectation was fulfilled at the time of completion of the grant, repudiation could not occur. Frustration was, until 1980, also felt to be inapplicable to leases: see *Leighton's Investment Trust Ltd v Cricklewood Property and Investment Trust Ltd* [1943] KB 493, where, although the application of frustration to leases was left open by some members of the House of Lords, Lords Russell and Goddard emphatically denied that frustration could apply to leases.

This general denial of contractual remedies stemmed from the perception that leases operated at 'one-level': the grant of an estate/possession in return for rent. Any breach which did not disturb possession was not serious enough to justify termination. This view was argued in earlier editions of Megarry and Wade:

In general, the doctrine [of frustration] does not apply to executed leases: for a lease creates an estate which vests in a lessee . . . In other words, the lessor's principal obligation is executed when he grants the lease and puts the tenant into possession. The doctrine of frustration can apply to obligations which are executory and which can therefore be rendered impossible of performance by later events. (Megarry and Wade, *The Law of Real Property*, 4th edn, 1975, p 673)

This denial was not confined to English law. An example taken from the United States relates to the rule of independent covenants that applied to leases but not to other contracts. The general rule for bilateral contracts is that the promises are seen as mutually dependent: breach of the promise on one side deprives the party in default from enforcing performance by the other. This doctrine of mutual dependency of covenants did not, however, apply generally to leases (with some exceptions) because leases were seen primarily as conveyances, the covenants being merely incidental. This has been referred to in several cases:

This theory of independent covenants in leases was established in early property law prior to the development of the concept of mutually dependent covenants in contract law. At common law, the lease was traditionally regarded as a conveyance of an interest in land, subject to the doctrine of *caveat emptor*. The landlord was required only to deliver the right of possession to the tenant; the tenant, in return, was required to pay rent to the landlord. Once the landlord delivered the right of possession, his part of the agreement was completed. The tenant's duty to pay rent continued as long as he retained possession, even if the buildings on the leasehold were destroyed or became uninhabitable. The landlord's breach of a lease covenant did not relieve the tenant of his duty to pay rent for the remainder of the term because the tenant still retained everything he was entitled to under the lease—the right of possession. All lease covenants were therefore considered independent. (*per* Spears J, *Davidow v Inwood North Professional Group* 747 SW 2d 373 (Tex 1988) at 375)

So, for example, if the landlord was in breach of a covenant to repair this did not mean that the tenant had a right to stop paying rent, although it may give rise to an action for damages (see further, Hicks, *The Contractual Nature of Real Property Leases*, (1972) 24 Baylor LR 443, esp. at pp 453–69).

This 'one-level' view of leases developed in an era when most leases were of agricultural land. The land itself was the most important aspect of the lease and there were relatively few covenants in the lease. This century has seen the lease increasingly used in an urban and industrial context where the detailed covenants in the lease form an important part of the bargain and the ongoing obligations of the landlord to supply services and amenities to the tenant are often as important as the possession of the land. This has led to the lease being now seen as a 'two-level relationship': the first level being the 'possession-rent relationship', and the second level being the provision of services. Recognition of this second level did not, however, significantly impact upon the remedies available for breach for some time. In 1969, Quinn and Phillips explained that the second level had not then attained equal significance:

On level two, the newer and less important legally, he had a right to heat, light and other services from the landlord. Level two constituted a separate agreement . . .

Significantly, the two levels were separate and distinct. A failure to perform on one level generated a remedy on that level, but in no way affected the other level. In technical terms, the covenants on one level were not reciprocal with the covenants on the other. What it actually meant was that the tenant had to pay the full rent so long as he had possession of the premises (level one), even though the landlord failed miserably in the delivery of services (level two). The sophisticated legal structure was a velvet glove which concealed an iron fist. (Quinn and Phillips, *op. cit.*, at p 234)

In practical terms, this meant that if the tenant had a flat in a tower block which the landlord had covenanted to heat but failed to, the tenant had no right to withhold rent. Even if the lack of heat forced the tenant to move out, he was still liable for the rent, though he may be able to claim damages. If, instead, this could be looked at as a purely contractual matter, breach of such an important term of the contract might well lead to the court finding that there was a breach of a condition by the landlord, entitling the tenant to simply walk away and accept that the contract is at an end.

Since Quinn and Phillips wrote, the courts have begun to make contractual remedies available to tenants (and landlords) in order to protect the second level expectations (although, as English contract law does not have a doctrine of dependent covenants, it still remains true in English law that a tenant is not able to withhold rent for breach of second level duties). The need for adaptation of the law to meet the changing use of leases is recorded in judgments in several American states. One instance is given here:

Since 16th century feudal England a lease has been considered a conveyance of an interest in land, carrying with it the doctrine of *caveat emptor* . . .

[The landlord] made a conveyance which ordinarily involved no covenants or warranties, express or implied (except a right to convey and quiet enjoyment), leaving the tenant to the tender mercy of *caveat emptor*. However, the tenant in that agrarian feudal society was likely to be an artisan capable of shifting for himself in inspecting the land and relatively simple improvements. The improvements were incidental; it was the land that was sought . . .

During and following the Industrial revolution, the population migration from rural to urban areas accentuated the importance of the structural improvements on the premises, and a corresponding decrease in the significance of the land itself. Leases often developed into complex transactions. The typical lease began to look more like a contract than a conveyance of real estate, often containing numerous express covenants . . .

Re-evaluation of the lessor-lessee relationship was inevitable for various reasons. Probably the single most important reason was recognition that the lease had been gradually transformed from essentially a conveyance to a contract, ie, that its essential nature is contractual.

Additional factors prompting re-evaluation included widespread enactment of housing codes, shortage of low-cost housing (creating a disparity in bargaining power between landlords and residential tenants), organization of tenant unions, development of legal services for the poor, and the growing similarity between the merchant-consumer and landlord-tenant transactions. (*per* Buchanan, Court of Appeals Indiana, *Old Town Development Company v Langford* 349 N E 2d 744 (1976) at 753–6, footnotes omitted)

Recognition of the importance of the second level of the relationship, the ongoing contractual obligations, accounts for many of the developments that have occurred recently. In the United States, the rule on independent covenants has been abandoned in many States, at least in relation to residential leases:

Under contract principles . . . the tenant's obligation to pay rent is dependent upon the landlord's performance of his obligations, including his warranty to maintain the premises in habitable condition. (*per* Judge Skelly Wright, *Javins v First National Realty Corporation* 428 F 2d 1071 (1970) at 1082)

3.2.2.1 Frustration and Repudiation

Growing recognition of the contractual nature of leases has led English courts to accept that leases can be ended by frustration and by repudiation. In *National Carriers Ltd v Panalpina (Northern) Ltd* [1981] 1 All ER 161, the House of Lords held that the doctrine of frustration applies to leases. The speech of Lord Simon dispels the view that there is something special about property rights which means that the rules of contract should not apply and also recognizes that ongoing contractual promises in the lease may be important to the parties:

I can for myself see nothing about the fact of creation of an estate or interest in land which repels the doctrine of frustration . . . It cannot be because a lease operates in rem; so, for example, does a contract for seaman's wages, since that gives rise to a maritime lien, yet can presumably like other contracts for personal services be frustrated by ill-health or death . . . Nor . . . is it realistic to argue that on execution of the lease the lessee got all that he bargained for. The reality is that this lessee, for example, bargained, not for a term of years, but for the use of a warehouse owned by the lessor, just as a demise charterer bargains for the use of this ship.

I turn, then, to the second main contention, namely, that the risk of unforeseen mischance passes irrevocably to the lessee at the moment of conveyance . . . [The] sale of land is a false analogy. A fully executed contract cannot be frustrated; and a sale of land is characteristically such a contract. But a lease is partly executory; rights and obligations remain outstanding on both sides throughout its currency. (*Panalpina, op. cit.*, at 179)

The House of Lords decided that a lease could be frustrated, the point being that it would be wrong to compartmentalise the law of contract and apply general contractual principles to some contracts but not others. Nevertheless, the fact that a lease is an estate and may be a long term relationship are special qualities that need to be taken account of when considering whether frustration has occurred:

[Though the cases in which leases are frustrated] may be rare, the doctrine of frustration is capable of application to leases of land. It must so be applied with proper regard to the fact that a lease, ie a grant of a legal estate, is involved. The court must consider whether any term is to be implied which would determine the lease in the event which has happened and/or ascertain the foundation of the agreement and decide whether this still exists in the light of the terms of the lease, the surrounding circumstances and any special rules which apply to leases or to the particular lease in question. (*per* Lord Wilberforce, *Panalpina, op. cit.*, at 173)

On the facts of *Panalpina*, a ten-year lease of a warehouse was not frustrated by a twenty-month road closure which prevented the warehouse being used for the intended purpose.

Similarly, in the Australian case of *Progressive Mailing House Pty Ltd v Tabali Pty Ltd* (1985) 57 ALR 609, Deane J said, at 635–6,

. . . it should be accepted that, as a general matter and subject to one qualification, the ordinary principles of contract law are applicable to contractual leases. The qualification is that the further one moves away from the case where the rights of the parties are, as a matter of substance, essentially defined by executory covenant or contractual promise to the case where the tenant's rights are, as a matter of substance, more properly to be viewed by reference to their character as an estate (albeit a chattel one) in land with a root of title in the executed demise, the more difficult it will be to establish that the lease has been avoided or terminated pursuant to the operation of the ordinary principles of frustration or fundamental breach. Indeed, one may reach the case where it would be quite artificial to regard the tenant's rights as anything other than an estate or interest in land (eg, a 99 year lease of unimproved land on payment of a premium and with no rent, or only a nominal rent, reserved). (See also Mason J at 621, Brennan J at 626 *et seq*.)

Deane J is effectively distinguishing here between leases which are probably correctly still viewed as primarily proprietary in nature and those in which the on going contractual obligations are paramount. The former would occur where a long estate has been granted and this grant, coupled with the payment of a capital sum to purchase the estate, forms the substance of the transaction—the contract then is largely executed and there are minimal outstanding obligations on either party still to be performed. The latter would be typified by a modern commercial lease under which the tenant is paying a market rent at periodic intervals and the landlord assumes management and repairing obligations. The bulk of the obligations remain to be performed after the initial grant and the contract is essentially executory. These examples are at opposite ends of the spectrum and there are examples that shade between the two. Nevertheless, it is in the case of the largely executory leases that the courts are likely to be most willing to develop the contractual rules on termination.

There is also recent English authority that the doctrine of repudiation applies to leases. In *Hussein v Mehlman* [1992] 2 EGLR 87 ([1993] Conv 71; [1993] CLJ 212), Stephen Sedley QC acknowledged the 'tide of the general law' recognizing that the foundation of a lease is contractual and held that the landlord's conduct constituted a repudiatory breach, which the tenant could accept by vacating the premises and returning the keys without incurring further rent liability. The landlord's breach involved a consistent failure to comply with the statutory repairing obligation set out in the Landlord and Tenant Act 1985, s 11 (see ch 7.2.4.5(b)(i)): there was no heating, the ceiling of one bedroom had collapsed, water pipes had burst, a flat roof extension was leaking and there was damp in the hall.

Courts in other jurisdictions have also accepted that leases can be repudiated, again drawing on the desire to harmonize leasehold law with other areas of contract. In the Australian case of *Progressive Mailing House Pty Ltd v Tabali Pty Ltd*, *op. cit.*, Mason J reviewed the authorities, including *Panalpina*, and concluded that

... **as the law of landlord and tenant had outgrown its origins in feudal tenure, it was more appropriate in the light of the essential elements of the bargain, the modern money economy and the modern development of contract law that leases should be regulated by the principles of contract law.**

Accordingly ... the balance of authority ... supports the proposition that the ordinary principles of contract law, including that of termination for repudiation or fundamental breach, apply to leases. (at 618)

Similarly, in Canada it is accepted that leases can be ended by repudiation: see the seminal case of *Highway Properties Ltd v Kelly, Douglas & Co Ltd* (1971) 17 DLR (3d) 710. In the United States it is also recognized that a tenant can end a lease and avoid further rent liability when the landlord is in breach of a warranty of habitability, although the cases frequently talk of the tenant 'rescinding' rather than accepting a repudiatory breach. So, for example, in *Pugh v Holmes* 405 A 2d 897 (Pa 1979), Larsen J said, at 907, that the tenant may vacate the premises where the landlord materially breaches the implied warranty of habitability . . . Surrender of possession by the tenant would terminate his obligation to pay rent under the lease. (See also *Steele v Latimer* 521 P 2d 304 (Kan 1974); *Teller v McCoy* 253 SE 2d 114 (1978))

In *Hussein v Mehlman, op. cit.*, repudiation added another weapon to the tenant's armoury against the landlord. This is a significant development as the other remedies available to a tenant when a landlord is in breach of covenant are of limited effect, apart from an action for damages. As the Law Commission noted in 1985:

Where the fault is that of the landlord, the tenant almost invariably has now no means of terminating the tenancy, because tenancy agreements rarely if ever contain a right to terminate, although such a right would be effective if included. (Law Commission, *Forfeiture of Tenancies*, Law Com. No. 142, 1985, at para 1.4; see also paras 17.6–17.9 for a commentary on other remedies available to tenants)

The decision in *Hussein v Mehlman* changes this as it enables the tenant to end the lease when there is a serious breach by the landlord.

In other jurisdictions, accepting a repudiatory breach of the lease has been more commonly used by the landlord against the tenant: in *Nai Pty Ltd v Hassoun Nominees Pty Ltd* [1985–1986] Aust and NZ Conv Rep 349, it was used against a tenant who had attempted to sublet in violation of the lease and had failed to pay costs and taxes due under the lease; and in *Wood Factory Pty Ltd v Kiritos Pty Ltd* (1985) 2 NSWLR 105, it was used against a tenant who had abandoned the premises and stopped paying rent.

The impact of *Hussein v Mehlman, op. cit.*, will be restricted if the Law Commission's report on Forfeiture of Tenancies is implemented. The 1985 Law Commission report recommended that the introduction of a scheme for termination of tenancies by court order instead of by forfeiture should be available to tenants as well as landlords, in the belief that both the landlord and the tenant should be exposed to the same consequences if they are in breach (Law Com. No. 142, *op. cit.*, at para 17.5). When the subsequent report was produced in 1994, it pushed for implementation of the landlords' termination order scheme but did not propose implementing the tenants' termination order scheme at that stage (Law Commission, *Termination of Tenancies Bill*, Law Com. No. 221, 1994; and see ch 11.2.3.3).

For landlords, if the 1994 recommendations are implemented, it will no longer be possible to end the lease by accepting a repudiatory breach by the tenant but only by obtaining a court order. Clause 2 of the draft Bill provides:

(1) Subject–
     (a) to section 41 below [which relates to abandoned premises]; and
     (b) to Schedule 1 to the Sexual Offences Act 1956 (rights of landlord where tenant convicted of permitting use of premises as brothel),

the only way in which a landlord may procure the termination of a tenancy by reason of the occurrence of a termination order event is by obtaining an order of the court for its termination.

Clause 5 then states what constitutes a 'termination order event':

(1) Subject to the provisions of this Act, a breach of any of the tenant's obligations is a termination order event.
(2) It is immaterial whether a breach is an act or omission and whether it is repudiatory.

The explanatory note to subsection (2) reads:

This makes it clear that the tenant's breach of obligation will be a termination order event, even though the breach is repudiatory in character, and whether or not it is an act or omission. It has recently been held that the doctrine of repudiatory breach applies to tenancies: *Hussein v Mehlman* [1992] 2 EGLR 87. Accordingly, a breach of this kind by the tenant, and its acceptance by the landlord, would serve of itself to end the tenancy. The subsection ensures that the scheme for termination orders cannot be by-passed in this way. (Law Com. No. 221, *op. cit.*)

The doctrine of repudiatory breach will, however, remain important to the tenant as it will be the only way by which the tenant can end the tenancy when the landlord is in serious breach. Further, when the Law Commission discussed extending the termination order scheme to tenants it was felt important that the tenant should also be given a right to damages upon termination, otherwise the right to end the lease would be little used in practice (see Law Com. No. 142, *op. cit.*, at paras 17.13–17.17). Application of the doctrine of repudiatory breach achieves much the same result as the Law Commission proposal's would have done and, arguably, the need to obtain the protection of using the court as the means of ending a lease is unnecessary when it is the tenant rather than the landlord ending the lease (see also, ch 11.2.4).

3.2.2.2 Award of Contractual Damages following a Repudiatory Breach of Lease

The *Hussein v Mehlman* decision, *op. cit.*, may have a significance beyond the doctrine of repudiation. Prior to *Hussein*, the position was that

a landlord who forfeits a tenancy for breach of covenant can get a judgment for any damages caused by that breach (eg for the cost of undone repairs) but he cannot claim damages for any loss suffered by reason of the termination of the tenancy, eg because the rental value of the premises has gone down or because he is unable to let the premises for a period of time. (Law Com. No. 142, *op. cit.*, para 1.10)

However, once the principle of repudiating leases is accepted, it should follow that the full range of contractual remedies should be available to the innocent party. This was held to be the case in the Canadian decision of *Highway Properties Ltd v Kelly, Douglas & Co Ltd, op. cit.* A major tenant in an unsuccessful shopping centre moved out of its supermarket premises and later wrote repudiating the lease. The tenant's departure had an adverse effect on the whole centre and other tenants moved out. In this situation, a landlord would traditionally have a choice between either refusing to accept the abandonment by the tenant and continuing to sue for the rent as it falls due, or accepting the abandonment and taking possession in lieu of rent. The landlord in *Highway Properties* did not want to do either and instead sought damages for the losses caused. Laskin J in the Supreme Court referred to the transformation of the 'estate' concept by the 'social and economic aspects . . . [of] urban living conditions and . . . commercial practice' but observed that this new contractual emphasis had 'stopped short of full recognition of its remedial concomitants'. Until *Highway Properties*, it had not been accepted that a landlord could obtain damages for post-repudiation losses:

The developed case law has recognized three mutually exclusive courses that a landlord may take where a tenant is in fundamental breach of the lease or has repudiated it entirely, as was the case here. He may do nothing to alter the relationship of landlord and tenant, but simply insist on performance of the terms and sue for rent or damages on the footing that the lease remains in force. Second, he may elect to terminate the lease, retaining, of course, the right to sue for rent accrued due, or for damages to the date of termination for previous breaches of covenant. Third, he may advise the tenant that he proposes to relet the property on the tenant's account and enter into possession on that basis. [*Nb*. With this route, the lease continues and the new rental is credited to the tenant.] Counsel . . . suggests a fourth alternative, namely, that the landlord may elect to terminate the lease but with notice to the defaulting tenant that damages will be claimed on the footing of a present recovery of damages for losing the benefit of the lease over its unexpired term. (*per* Laskin J, Highway Properties, *op. cit.*, at 716)

In the event, Laskin J held that damages for prospective losses were available:

It is no longer sensible to pretend that a commercial lease, such as the one before this Court, is simply a conveyance and not also a contract. It is equally untenable to persist in denying resort to the full armoury of remedies ordinarily available to redress repudiation of covenants, merely because the covenants may be associated with an estate in land. (at 721)

Similarly, in the landmark Australian case of *Progressive Mailing House Pty Ltd v Tabali Pty Ltd, op. cit.*, the damages awarded to the landlord included the cost of delay in reletting following a repudiatory breach, and in *Wood Factory Pty Ltd v*

Kiritos Pty Ltd, op. cit., damages included the net loss of rent on reletting (for criticism of the *Wood Factory* case, see Effron, *The Contractualisation of the Law of Leasehold,* (1988) 14 Monash Univ Law Rev 83 at pp 96-8).

If the landlord does pursue contractual damages, both Canadian and Australian authorities have stated that a duty to mitigate arises, for example, by the landlord trying to relet the premises and recoup some of his losses rather than simply leaving the premises empty and suing for unpaid rent and other losses (*B G Preeco 3 Ltd v Universal Explorations Ltd* (1988) 42 DLR (4th) 673; *George Kosiadis v First Pioneer Petroleums (Quinte) Ltd,* 2 July 1993, Ont. Crt, unreported; *Tall-Bennet & Co Pty Ltd v Sadot Holdings Pty Ltd* (1988) NSW Conv R 57,881).

3.2.2.3 The Relationship between Contractual Remedies and Proprietary Remedies

In Canada, cases since *Highway Properties, op. cit.,* have had to determine whether the effect of the decision was that *only* contractual remedies were available, so that a landlord *had* to accept a repudiatory breach and mitigate, or whether the contractual remedies co-exist alongside traditional property remedies (see Lem, *The Landlord's Duty to Mitigate Upon a Tenant's Repudiation of a Commercial Lease,* (1993) 30 RPR (2d) 33). Some critics felt that the 'contractualization of leases' had now gone so far that it was no longer appropriate to regard a lease as a conveyance and to apply traditional property remedies to it (see, for example, Sternberg, *The Commercial Landlord's Duty to Mitigate Upon a Tenant's Abandonment of the Premises,* (1984–85) 5 Advocates' Q 385). Several cases, though, support the view that the traditional property remedies remain available, whereby a landlord can chose to do nothing following a repudiatory breach by the tenant and sue for rent arrears as they fall due: *607190 Ontario Inc v First Consolidated Holdings Corp* (1992) 26 RPR (2d) 298 (a decision of Then J in the Ontario Divisional Court); see also the Australian case of *Tall-Bennet & Co Pty Ltd v Sadot Holdings Pty Ltd, op. cit.* The option of electing to treat the lease as continuing and suing for rent as it falls due (effectively, instalment litigation), may be subject to qualification. In one Australian case, *J and S Chan Pty Ltd v McKenzie and McKenzie,* 1993, No SCA 65, unreported, the court viewed this option as simply an application of the normal contractual rule that the innocent party is entitled to elect to treat a contract as continuing following a repudiatory breach and to sue in debt. According to *Chan v McKenzie, op. cit.,* the option to treat the lease as continuing would be subject to the same qualifications as apply in contract law and which were set out by Lord Reid in *White & Carter (Council) Ltd v McGregor* [1962] AC 413. The first qualification is that where the innocent party (the landlord in the tenant abandonment cases) cannot continue with performance without co-operation of the party in breach, he must accept the breach. This does not apply in the tenant abandonment cases as the landlord is able to make possession available to the tenant without the tenant's co-operation. The second qualification is that 'if it can be shown that a person has no legitimate interest, financial or otherwise, in performing the contract rather than claiming damages, he ought not to be allowed to saddle the other party with an additional burden with no benefit to himself' (Lord Reid, *White & Carter, op. cit.*, at 431). The exact scope of this exception is unclear but it seems that it does not require the landlord of abandoned premises to accept that the lease is at an end and sue for damages (subject to the duty to mitigate) instead of suing for rent (with no duty to mitigate) (see *Chan v McKenzie, op. cit.*).

This property approach can be criticised on the grounds that it is economically inefficient (see Bradbrook (1977) 8 SLR 15 at p 17). Why should the landlord be able to sit back and claim rent rather than seek to reduce his losses? For these reasons, some jurisdictions have restricted the landlord's options. In Ontario, the option of doing nothing and seeking rent instead of damages has been prohibited for residential leases (see Landlord and Tenant Act RSO 1990, c L7, s 90). Similarly, in British Columbia the landlord of residential premises has a duty to relet 'at a reasonably economic rent' when a tenant has terminated the lease or vacated or abandoned the premises (Residential Tenancy Act, S.B.C. 1984, c 15, s 48(b)).

3.2.2.4 Can Contract Circumvent Property Legislation?

A further difficulty is whether contractual remedies can be used to circumvent landlord and tenant legislation which is designed to protect the tenant from hasty and unconscionable repossession by the landlord (see generally, ch 11). The problems are illustrated by two Australian cases which adopt different approaches:

Nai [*Nai Pty Ltd v Hassoun Nominees Pty Ltd, op. cit.,*] and *Gallic* [*Gallic Pty Ltd v Cynayne Pty Ltd* (1986) 83 FLR 31] present disturbing examples of how the contractualisation of lease law can be used to manipulate statutes regulating tenancy and rights. In *Nai*, Zelling J accepted a submission that s 10 of the Landlord and Tenant Act (S.A.) 1936 (providing a duty on the lessor to give notice before re-entry) did not apply because the termination of a lease for repudiation or fundamental breach was not a 're-entry'. The act of the lessor in taking possession was simply renamed to take the lessor's conduct outside the name for such conduct referred to in the statute. In *Gallic*, the reverse exercise was performed with regard to 'forfeiture'. The Northern Territory's *Real Property Act* s 192(IV) allowed 'any lessor where . . . the lease became forfeited . . .' to summon a person before a judge in chambers to show cause why the person summoned should not give up possession to such a lessor. Kearney J held that acceptance by the lessor of repudiation by the lessee constituted a 'forfeiture' and thus s 192(IV) applied.

If the statute is drafted in the language of land law, the court now has a choice whether to address the case in land law terms and apply the statute or to address the case in contract law language and hold that the statute does not apply. (Effron, *The Contractualisation of the Law of Leasehold, op. cit.,* at p 98, footnotes omitted)

As Effron observes, this opens up the possibility of landlords circumventing protective legislation by resorting to contract remedies rather than proprietary ones (see also ch 11.2.3.3 and 11.2.4; Harpum, *Leases as Contracts,* [1993] CLJ 212, esp. at p 214).

In *Hussein v Mehlman, op. cit.,* Sedley QC recognized that the decision would have significant implications but seemed to suggest that repudiation would have to work within the existing statutory framework for ending leases:

I recognize that the proposition that a contract of tenancy can be repudiated like any other contract has a number of important implications . . . It will have effect subject not only to all the statutory provisions which now hedge the right to recover possession but also, I would think, to the provisions contained in the contract of letting itself in relation to forfeiture (where there is a term certain): in other words, the right to terminate by acceptance of repudiatory conduct may itself be modified by further contractual provisions which lay down conditions, supported by statute, for the exercise of the right. (at 90)

In England, many of these further questions have not yet begun to be explored. As we have seen, other jurisdictions have already begun to tackle the questions of what follows once the principle of repudiation of leases is accepted. It is hard to imagine that *Hussein v Mehlman, op. cit.,* will not be followed here even though it is only a first instance judgment. As we have seen, it is entirely in line with developments occurring in other jurisdictions.

3.3 THE APPLICATION OF CONTRACT LAW TO LEASES

The extension of contractual remedies for breach to leases seen above is significant not only for its own sake but also as part of a larger move towards applying general contractual rules to leases. The decision in *Hussein v Mehlman, op. cit.,* was based on the fact that a lease is in essence a contract and there is a tide of cases giving pre-eminence to the contractual nature of leases and playing down their proprietary aspects. This is not to say that the proprietary nature of leases is unimportant but that, unless one of the dimensions of leases discussed in 3.1 above requires the lease to be given differential treatment, leases should be treated in the same manner as other contracts.

3.3.1 Ending a Joint Tenancy by Notice

The general process of treating leases as contracts can be seen in the House of Lords decision in *Hammersmith and Fulham London BC v Monk* [1992] 1 All ER 1. Mr Monk and Mrs Powell had a weekly tenancy of a flat which they held as joint tenants. After their relationship broke down, Mrs Powell served a notice to quit on the landlord without Mr Monk's knowledge or concurrence. The question before the court was whether one joint tenant acting alone could determine the joint tenancy. The House of Lords saw the case as requiring the solution to be found in either contract law or property law. Looked at from a contractual perspective, the notice to quit would be effective. For renewal of the contract (the periodic tenancy), the consent of both parties is required (Lord Bridge at 3), and the fact that one party had served a notice to quit showed that there was not joint consent for renewal. Looked at from a property perspective, which emphasises the unity of joint tenants, it would seem to follow that the notice would not be effective as both parties would need to participate in order to end the tenancy. However, the law had not developed along the lines of the property law approach: Lords Bridge and Browne-Wilkinson refer to authority for the view that joint *lessors* of a periodic tenancy had *all* to agree individually to *renew* (*Doe d Aslin v Summersett* (1830) 1 B & Ad 135) and that joint *tenants* of a periodic tenancy had *all* to agree individually to *renew* (*Greenwich London BC v McGrady* (1982) 46 P & CR 223). Accordingly, the House of Lords in *Hammersmith, op. cit.*, took the contractual approach, Lord Bridge stating at 3:

As a matter of principle I see no reason why this question should receive any different answer in the context of the contractual relationship of landlord and tenant than that which it would receive in any other contractual context . . .

[In] any ordinary agreement for an initial term which is to continue for successive terms unless determined by notice, the obvious inference is that the agreement is intended to continue beyond the initial term only if so long as all parties to the agreement are willing that it should do so . . .

Thus the application of ordinary contractual principles leads me to expect that a periodic tenancy granted to two or more joint tenants must be terminable at common law by an appropriate notice to quit given by any one of them whether or not the others are prepared to concur.

Thus, Mrs Powell's notice was effective to end the tenancy.

The problem with the *Hammersmith* case is that, according to the analysis of the House of Lords, neither a property nor a contractual approach could give a satisfactory result. The contract approach gives insufficient account to the importance of the lease as a home. Lord Browne-Wilkinson observes in *Hammersmith, op. cit.*, at 10:

. . . the flat in question was the joint home of Mr Monk and Mrs Powell: it therefore cannot be right that one of them unilaterally can join with the landlords to
put an end to the other's rights in the home.

In addition, the result undermines the security provided by statutory codes—the
local authority landlord would have been unable to get Mr Monk to leave, but the
co-tenant is able to do so simply by serving notice. Indeed, it is now relatively
simple to defeat the statutory rights of co-owners, particularly in the case of a
family breakdown, either by the co-tenant simply electing to end the tenancy or
by the landlord suggesting that the co-tenant serves a notice, possibly, where the
landlord is a local authority, refusing to rehouse the departing co-tenant unless a
notice to quit is served (see further, ch 9.8). The property approach did not, however, provide any better solution; by requiring joint action to end the lease, the
result would be that all co-tenants are bound indefinitely and one individual may
never be able to get released from the contractual obligations:

Mr Monk and Mrs Powell undertook joint liabilities as tenants for the purpose of
providing themselves with a joint home and . . ., once the desire to live together has
ended, it is impossible to require that the one who quits the home should continue
indefinitely to be liable for the discharge of the obligations to the landlord under
the tenancy agreement. (*per* Lord Browne-Wilkinson, *Hammersmith, op. cit.*, at 10)

An alternative approach to the *Hammersmith v Monk* problem is to say that
the periodic tenancy, although strictly a series of renewed contracts which retro-
spectively form a single term (see Lord Bridge at 9), is continued not by actual
consent to renewal but automatically, by an implied consent. It therefore needs
to be ended (non-renewed) by serving a 'proper notice' withdrawing that consent and a proper notice requires the agreement of all owners. This reinforces the
unity traditionally associated with joint tenancies and which was referred to by
Lord Browne-Wilkinson. The contrary authorities relied on have been subjected
to forceful criticism (see Webb, *Notices to Quit by One Joint Tenant*, [1983] Conv
211) and are an unnecessary and undesirable departure from the normal rules
on joint ownership. When one co-tenant alone serves notice to quit on the landlord this is not a 'proper notice' but will, if accepted by the landlord, operate to
release that co-tenant, leaving the remaining co-tenant liable for the entirety of
the obligations under the tenancy (see Webb, *op. cit.*, at p 206; Tee, *The Negative
Nature of a Notice to Quit*, [1992] CLJ 218; Dewar, *When Joint Tenants Part*, (1992)
108 LQR 375).

3.3.2 General Contractual Doctrines

In many areas the courts have applied general contract rules without question.
In *United Scientific Holdings Ltd v Burnley Borough Council* [1978] AC 904, the

House of Lords had to decide whether time was of the essence in relation to rent review clauses, to see whether a landlord who had failed to keep strictly to the timetable laid down in the lease for agreeing the new rent would be unable to receive an increased rent until the next review date. The House of Lords decided that, in accordance with general contractual principles, there was a presumption that time was not of the essence:

I see no relevant difference between the obligation undertaken by a tenant under a rent review clause in a lease and any other obligation in a synallagmatic contract that is expressed to arise upon the occurrence of a described event, where a postponement of that event beyond the time stipulated in the contract is not so prolonged as to deprive the obligor of substantially the whole benefit that it was intended he should obtain by accepting the obligation. (*per* Lord Diplock at 930)

In the classic case of common mistake, *Solle v Butcher* [1950] 1 KB 671, the Court of Appeal ordered that a lease be set aside because the landlord had let the flat at a yearly rent of £250 without serving a notice of increase as required by the Rent Act 1938. The landlord had done this in the mistaken belief that he was free to do so but under the law then, the failure to serve the notice meant that he could only let it at the previous controlled rent of £140 a year. The Court of Appeal rescinded the lease on terms, developing the doctrine of mistake in equity but unconcerned with the fact that the particular contract was a lease. In *Killick v Roberts* [1991] 1 WLR 1146 ((1992) 51 CLJ 21; [1992] Conv 269), the Court of Appeal applied the contractual doctrine of rescission for fraudulent misrepresentation to a lease without question, and in *Boustany v Piggott* [1993] EGCS 85 ((1993) 109 LQR 530), the Privy Council set aside a lease on the grounds of unconscionability (see also, ch 5.2.3)

3.4 CERTAINTY OF LEASE TERMS

Under general contract law, the contractual terms must be sufficiently certain in order for the courts to be able to enforce the contract. This means that the contract must neither be vague nor incomplete (see Treitel, *op. cit.*, pp 48-58). Nevertheless, the courts are reluctant not to give effect to the parties' intentions and will do their best to uphold the contract, especially where it has been acted upon by the parties. This principle is particularly strong in the case of leases where the lease has been partly executed (by the grant of an estate) and also represents a long term relationship. This is illustrated by remarks made in *Beer v Bowden* [1981] 1 All ER 1070, where the lease provided for the rent to be increased at intervals but neglected to state what assumption was to be made about the amount of the new rent:

Had this been a contract of sale or an ordinary commercial contract of some sort, there would be a great deal to be said for the view that from the date of the first

rent review in March 1973 the contract was void for uncertainty, the parties having failed to agree on a vital term of the contract. But here there is a subsisting estate, and a subsisting estate in land, the lease, which is to continue until 1982, 14 years from the date of the lease itself. (*per* Geoffrey Lane LJ at 1075-6)

The court was, therefore, willing to imply a term that the rent should be the fair market rent excluding tenant's improvements.

The need for certainty in leases goes beyond the need for linguistic certainty and completeness. As will be seen in ch 4.4, the duration of a lease must also be certain in the sense that it can be predicted what the maximum duration of the lease is (*Lace v Chantler* [1944] KB 368; *Prudential Assurance Company Limited v London Residuary Body* [1992] 3 All ER 504). The need for this degree of certainty is said to follow from the proprietary nature of leases. The policy of the 1925 property legislation is to require leases to have a predictable end-date: hence the reference in the definition of a 'term of years absolute' to a term 'either certain or liable to determination by notice, etc' (Law of Property Act 1925, s 205(xxvii)); the statutory conversion of leases for life or until marriage into leases for 90 years (Law of Property Act 1925, s 149(6)) and the conversion of perpetually renewable leases into leases for 2,000 years (Law of Property Act 1922, s 145). Smith supports the outcome in the *Prudential* case:

If Parliament has required the parties to all but the shortest terms to execute a deed, in order to pass a legal (and thus secure) leasehold title to the tenant, it may be because it wishes the parties to take care in the drafting of the terms of any agreement for the grant of a fixed term lease . . . There is little to condemn in a rule of certainty which encourages parties in this process and which punishes carelessness at the time of drafting the lease . . .

[There] is much to commend a certainty rule which is simple and which penalises carelessness in drafting of leasehold agreements, especially since the policy of the 1925 legislation is to favour security of titles. (Smith, *What is Wrong with Certainty in Leases?*, [1993] Conv 461 at p 465)

Notwithstanding Smith's arguments, it is hard to find any persuasive reasons for requiring predictability if this requires striking down otherwise valid agreements between landlord and tenant. Predictability of termination dates is not required for contracts generally and it is hard to see why leases need to be treated differently. Lord Browne-Wilkinson comments on the injustice of the outcome in *Prudential*:

It is difficult to think of a more unsatisfactory outcome or one further away from what the parties to the 1930 agreement can ever have contemplated. Certainly it was not a result which their contract, if given effect to, could ever have produced. If the 1930 agreement had taken effect fully, there could never have come a time when the freehold to the remainder of Nos 263-265 would be left without a road frontage.

This bizarre outcome results from the application of an ancient and technical rule of law which requires the maximum duration of a term of years to be ascertainable from the outset. No one has produced any satisfactory rationale for the genesis of this rule. No one has been able to point to any useful purpose that it serves at the present day. (*Prudential Assurance Company Limited v London Residuary Body, op. cit.*, at 511–2)

3.5 ENFORCEABILITY AGAINST THIRD PARTIES

The fact that a lease is a legal estate in land means that it can be enforced against a third party. This is clearly of vital importance to the commercial, economic and social value of leases. If the original landlord sells his reversion, the tenant will be able to remain in occupation of the premises and enforce the term of the lease against the new reversioner.

This enforceability stems from the proprietary nature of the lease and is one of the features that makes a lease of much more value than other, lesser, interests in land. There has, for example, been much debate in recent years as to whether a contractual licence—founded (as the lease is) in contract but not at the same time conferring a proprietary interest—is capable of binding a third party. While the precise position on contractual licences remains unclear and there may be circumstances in which they can be enforced against third parties, the general rule is that they are personal interests only, enforceable against the grantor and only exceptionally against a third party—*Ashburn Anstalt v Arnold* [1988] 2 All ER 147. There is extensive academic literature on the effect of licences on third parties: see, for example, Briggs, *Licences: Back to Basics*, [1981] Conv 212, *Contractual Licences: A Reply*, [1983] Conv 285; Thompson, *Licences: Questioning the Basics*, [1983] Conv 50, *Correspondence*, [1983] Conv 471; Moriarty, *Licences and Land Law: Legal Principles and Public Policies*, (1984) 100 LQR 376; Dewar, *Licences and Land Law: An Alternative View*, (1986) 49 MLR 741; Battersby, *Contractual and estoppel licences as proprietary interests in land*, [1991] Conv 36.

3.6 LEASE OR LICENCE

As we shall see in the next chapter, the courts can have great difficulty in determining whether an occupation agreement is a lease or a licence. The distinction between them is important for many reasons. A lease is a proprietary interest, whereas a licence is at most contractual (subject to the debate on enforceability against third parties referred to at 3.5 above). In most of the cases the distinction has been important for a different reason—to determine whether or not statutory protection is available to the occupant. In the private residential and commercial sectors protection is only available to tenants, in the public and agricultural sectors protection is available to tenants and only certain categories of licensee (see ch 6). It is clear, following the landmark case of *Street v Mountford* [1985] 2 All ER 289, that the key question to be asked to see if an occupation agreement is a lease is whether there is exclusive possession for a term (see ch 4.3). Exclusive possession exists when the occupant has the right to exclude all others from the premises. The difficulty that the courts have faced is in deciding to what extent the parties themselves are free to define the existence or non-existence of this right in the contract. In many cases, the parties have stated in the contract that the occupant does not have exclusive possession and yet, in practice, the facts indicate that it would be a physical impossibility for anyone else to share the premises with the occupant. Which prevails? The contractually expressed intention of the parties; or the fact of exclusive possession being enjoyed in practice? Is the classification of the occupation agreement a question of contract law or of property law?

Although many areas of leasehold law appear to be giving greater recognition to the contractual nature of leases, in the lease/licence arena many of the cases appear to be moving in the opposite direction, stressing that it is the fact of exclusive possession that is pivotal to the classification of the relationship and not the contractually expressed intention of the parties. The reason for this trend is clearly policy-based—the legislation is directed at conferring statutory protection on those who have the status of tenants and who occupy the premises as a home or as a place of business. In the case of *AG Securities v Vaughan, Antoniades v Villiers* [1988] 3 All ER 1058, a couple taking a small flat were asked to sign two separate 'licence' agreements denying that they had exclusive possession. The House of Lords held that there was a lease, not mere licences: the denial of exclusive possession and the use of two agreements was a pretence to avoid statutory protection (see ch 4.3.3). Nevertheless, even with the adoption of the pretence doctrine in *AG Securities v Vaughan, op. cit.*, it must not be forgotten that the starting point for analysis of the relationship is the contract. The courts will only override the contractual intention of the parties where it is clear that terms inserted were 'artificial' and 'wholly unrealistic'. So the contractual nature of leases is still central, it is simply that it cannot be manipulated to hide the grant of proprietary rights to the occupier.

Even where the occupant does have exclusive possession, it does not necessarily follow that he has a lease. In *Street v Mountford, op. cit.*, Lord Templeman accepted that where it appeared 'from the surrounding circumstances that there was no intention to create legal relationships there would be no lease' (at 300). The logic of this distinction is questionable: in most cases where it is agreed that someone is to occupy property on terms (which will generally include payment of rent), there is surely an intention to create legal relations, that is to have an enforceable agreement (see further, ch 4.3.4.1). Nevertheless, there are several cases in which accommodation has been provided, seemingly with exclusive possession, and yet the courts have held that there is no lease. Although it may be true of some cases that there is no contractual intention, the more convincing explanation of the outcomes is that the courts will strain to find that there is no tenancy when it would be unfair on the owner to confer statutory protection on the occupant. *Marcroft Wagons v Smith* [1951] 2 KB 496 is an example. As an act of kindness, the tenant's daughter was allowed to remain in the property after her mother's death. The Court of Appeal held that she was a licensee even though she had exclusive possession and was paying rent.

Throughout the lease/licence debate, the courts continue to base their decisions on the contractual terms agreed between the parties. What seems to happen is that where the courts are anxious to say that there is a lease (notwithstanding the contract), they will place paramount emphasis on the fact of exclusive possession and the clear artificiality of leasehold terms denying that, thus emphasising the lease's proprietary characteristics. In other cases, where they are anxious to avoid finding a lease (with the statutory protection that entails), they will play down the proprietary features (exclusive possession) and deny that there was any contractual intention, presumably leaving the occupant with a bare licence. To what extent the earlier cases, such as *Marcroft Wagons, op. cit.*, and *Facchini v Bryson* [1952] 1 TLR 1386, can logically survive in the light of the paramountcy of exclusive possession following *Street v Mountford* is open to question. This line of cases illustrates the scope for manipulation of factual situations in judicial reasoning, supporting the view put forward by Atiyah that the requirement of an intention to create legal relations can be seen as a device to support a just result. Atiyah talks of the

relatively modern device of refusing to enforce a promise which the courts think, for one reason or another, it is unjust or impolitic to enforce. (Atiyah, *Essays on Contract*, 1988, p 184)

His argument appears to be borne out in the lease/licence arena.

3.7 LIABILITY UNDER THE LEASE

3.7.1 Privity of Estate

Under the law of contract, it is possible to assign the benefit, but not the burden, of a contract (see Megarry VC in *Tito v Waddell (No 2)* [1977] Ch 106 at 291; Treitel, *op. cit.*, pp 604-6). In the case of leasehold contracts, different rules apply. Whenever there is privity of estate, that is the legal relationship of landlord and tenant, covenants which relate to the land are enforceable by and against the landlord and the tenant for the time being, even though there may be no relationship of contract between the parties (*Spencer's Case* (1583) 5 Co Rep 16a). The tenant is able to assign the lease, the landlord is able to assign the reversion, and the new owner/assignee will both be liable under the covenants in the lease and able to enforce covenants against the other party so long as they 'touch and concern the land' (see further, ch 9.6). Thus, for example, a purchaser of the reversion from the original landlord can enforce the tenant's covenant to pay rent but will also be bound to perform the landlord's covenants, such as to insure and repair the property. The landlord and tenant for the time being will continue to be liable even if the original parties have been released from liability (*City of London Corp v Fell* [1993] 4 All ER 968).

Why is it possible to assign contractual obligations and make non-contracting parties liable with leases but not other contracts? In *City of London Corp v Fell, op. cit.*, at 972-3, Lord Templeman spoke of the running of covenants as being necessary 'for the effective operation of the law of landlord and tenant':

Common law, and statute following the common law, were faced with the problem of rendering effective the obligations under a lease which might endure for a period of 999 years or more beyond the control of any covenantor. The solution was to annex to the term and the reversion the benefit and burden of covenants which touch and concern the land. The covenants having been annexed, every legal owner of the term granted by the lease and every legal owner of the reversion from time to time holds his estate with the benefit of and subject to the covenants which touch and concern the land. The system of leasehold tenure requires that the obligations in the lease shall be enforceable throughout the term, whether those obligations are affirmative or negative. The owner of a reversion must be able to enforce the positive covenants to pay rent and keep in repair against an assignee who in turn must be able to enforce any positive covenants entered into by the original landlord . . .

The effect of common law and statute on a lease is to create rights and obligations which are independent of the parallel rights and obligations of the original human covenantor who and whose heirs may fail or the parallel rights and obligations of a corporate covenantor which may be dissolved. Common law and statute achieve that effect by annexing those rights and obligations so far as they touch and concern the land to the term and to the reversion. Nourse LJ neatly summarized the position when he said in an impeccable judgment ([1993] 2 All ER 449 at 454, [1993] 2 WLR 710 at 716):

'The contractual obligations which touch and concern the land having become imprinted on the estate, the tenancy is capable of existence as a species of property independently of the contract.'

Similar views are expressed by Cheshire and Burn:

[I]t was early seen that to enforce this doctrine of privity of contract was highly undesirable in the case of leases, since both parties had transmissible interests the value of which depended largely upon the obligations that each had assumed. Thus the medieval land law, although it never lost sight of the general principle that a stranger to a contract cannot sue or be sued upon it, did recognize that

covenants contained in a lease might have a wider operation than ordinary contracts. (Cheshire and Burn, *Modern Law of Real Property*, 15th edn, 1994, p 444–5)

It is hard to see why these considerations do not apply equally to other long term contracts. In general contract law, the rule that no one is bound by a contract to which he is not a party has been found at times to be an inconvenient rule and there have been various attempts to avoid the effects of privity of contract. Indeed, in the case of *De Mattos v Gibson* (1858) 4 De G & J 276, an observation by Knight Bruce LJ suggested that whenever a person acquired property from another with knowledge of a previous contract he could not use the property in a manner inconsistent with the prior contract. This approach was adopted in *Lord Strathcona SS Co v Dominion Coal Co* [1926] AC 108, where an owner of a ship was refusing to honour a charterparty granted to Dominion by the previous owner, even though the current owner bought the ship expressly subject to the rights of Dominion under the charterparty. The Privy Council restrained him from using the ship in a manner inconsistent with the prior charterparty. In the later case of *Port Line Ltd v Ben Line Steamers Ltd* [1958] 2 QB 146, Diplock J felt that the *Strathcona* case was not good law. In *Swiss Bank Corpn v Lloyds Bank Ltd* [1979] Ch 548, Browne-Wilkinson J felt that both *De Mattos v Gibson* and *Strathcona* were good decisions, but not on the basis that as a general proposition contractual obligations can bind successors with notice. Instead, the imposition of liability stemmed either from constructive trust principles or from the tort of inducing breach of contract. These are both of limited and restricted application. In a leasehold situation, the purchaser of the reversionary interest will be bound by prior leases.

In a note in 1958, Wade explored why the approach of property law should not apply to contracts generally:

Perhaps the theoretical answer is that purchasers have a right to expect that the incumbrances to which they may be liable shall be few and familiar. In the land law they are strictly defined—leases, easements, restrictive covenants, etc—but in the law of contract the possible obligations are limited only by the imagination of the contracting parties. If any sort of contractual obligation could run with property the distinction between contractual and proprietary rights would virtually disappear. Another and more practical answer is that the plaintiff has a sufficient remedy in damages by suing the original owner, who contracted with him, and who by parting with the property has put it out of his power to perform the contract. (Wade [1958] *CLJ* 169 at p 170)

A similar explanation is offered by Gardner who argues that only obligations meeting certain policy criteria should be capable of having proprietary effect:

The criterion for identifying objects meriting proprietary treatment is apparently the strength of the covenantee's interest in obtaining a remedy going specifically to the user of the chattel, rather than being confined to compensation by an

action for breach of contract against the original covenantor. (Gardner, *The Proprietary Effect of Contractual Obligations under Tulk v Moxhay and De Mattos v Gibson,* (1982) 98 LQR 279 at p 320)

3.7.2 Continuing Liability

The fact that leases are treated differently from other contracts, enabling the benefit and burden of leasehold covenants to be passed to third parties as seen in the previous section, means that leases are regularly assigned. Following assignment, though, the position of the original contracting parties continues to be regulated by general contract law even though there are strong arguments as to why contract law should cease to apply to the liability of the original parties post assignment. The rule within contract law is that contracting parties remain liable for contractual promises for the duration of the contract. In practice, however, because the burden of a contract cannot be assigned, where long term contracts contain ongoing benefits and burdens they are not generally sold to third parties in an analogous manner to leases. The ability to pass the burden of leases means that they are regularly sold, yet the fact that the burden passes to the new assignee does not mean that the original contracting party is thereby released from liability. Instead, stemming from contract doctrine, the original landlord and the original tenant remain liable under the lease after assignment, even though they no longer retain an interest in the property, have ceased to benefit from the contract and have no control over the current use of the property.

The burden of continuing liability falls more heavily on the original tenant than on the original landlord as it is the tenant who will generally have more onerous obligations within the lease. This liability can cover increased rents payable as a result of rent reviews conducted with later tenants, even though the original tenant has no opportunity of influencing the amount by participating in the rent review (*Centrovincial Estates plc v Bulk Storage Ltd* (1983) 46 P & CR 393, see ch 9.6.1) or as a result of improvements made to the property by later tenants, even when the lease had forbidden the making of such improvements (*Selous Street Properties v Oronel Fabrics Ltd* (1984) 270 EG 643, 743).

In leasehold law, this continuing liability is commonly known as 'privity of contract', but is more accurately described as original tenant or original landlord liability. Strictly speaking, privity of contract is the contractual doctrine whereby only parties to the contract can benefit from and be burdened by the contract— in leasehold law, *Spencer's case* enables covenants to be enforceable by and against non-contracting parties because of the lease's proprietary nature. To talk of privity of contract is therefore misleading, what is meant is that, because the original parties to the lease are in a contractual relationship, they remain liable throughout the term of the lease. Both the contractual and proprietary nature of the lease are therefore necessary to explain the liability for leasehold covenants—contractual doctrine leads to the original parties remaining liable after assignment, proprietary rules account for the liability of later assignees.

The Law Commission have recommended a move away from normal contractual rules in the context of the liability of the original parties. In 1986, the Law Commission issued a Working Paper examining this and set out some of the arguments for and against continuing liability:

3.1 Some people see the continuing liability of the privity of contract principle as intrinsically unfair. They regard the contractual obligations undertaken in a lease as only properly regulating the terms on which the owner for the time being of a property permits the tenant for the time being to occupy and use it, or as the case may be, to sublet and profit from it. They see no reason why responsibility should last longer than ownership of the particular interest in the property. Furthermore, as the facts seem to indicate that the continuing responsibility in practice falls more on tenants than on landlords, those of this view see the principle as operating in an unfair way, being biased against tenants . . .
3.3 The contrary view is that the obligations contained in a lease are freely entered into, and if the parties wish to limit their liability in any particular way, they are perfectly at liberty to do so. Freedom of contract is a basic principle of our law, and it should only be modified when it can be demonstrated that it is important or necessary to do so. (The Law Commission, *Landlord and Tenant, Privity of Contract and Estate, Duration of Liability of Parties to Leases,* Working Paper No. 95, 1986)

The response to the Working Paper elicited many examples of the difficulties and injustices of continuing liability (for which see Law Commission, *Landlord and Tenant, Privity of Contract and Estate,* Law Com. No. 174, 1988, at paras 3.5–3.23). This persuaded the Law Commission to recommend reform, accepting that 'the purpose of a lease should be to create temporary property ownership' [and obligations?] (para 3.26). The proposed reform is prefaced on the principle that

a landlord or a tenant of property should not continue to enjoy rights nor be under any obligations arising from a lease once he has parted with all interest in the property. (para 4.1)

This principle, is not, however, fully translated into the detailed recommendations. In outline, the position of the tenant will be that a tenant will not generally remain liable after assignment. Where the lease contains a covenant against assignment (as is usual), the landlord may, however, require the tenant to 'guarantee' the performance of the leasehold covenants (in whole or part) by the tenant's immediate successor. The position of the landlord would be different. The landlord will remain liable following assignment unless he is released from liability either by the tenant or, if the tenant objects, by the court if the landlord can establish that it is reasonable for him to be released. In 1993, the government announced that these proposals would be implemented in relation to future, but not existing, leases. Legislation has still to be introduced.

The tenor of the Law Commission reports and much public opinion is therefore to limit contractual liability. The reason for the proposed change, however, is partially based on the perception that a lease regulates property ownership and that a person should be liable under the lease only for the duration of their ownership of the property. The outcome would be similar to the general position under contract law where, although the contracting parties are liable throughout the contract, they will, in practice, be benefitting simultaneously from the contract.

3.8 PUBLIC REGULATION OF LEASES

Until this century, the landlord and tenant relationship was largely a matter for private regulation between the two parties. Throughout this century, however, there has at various times been statutory intervention in a number of areas: to ensure minimal standards of repair, to give tenants the right to remain in the property once the contractual lease has expired (security of tenure), to control the amount of rent that can be charged, to protect the tenant from harassment, to compensate the tenant for improvements that he has made to the property, and even to give certain tenants the right to buy the freehold or an extended lease.

Underlying much of this legislation has been the perceived need to provide the tenant with security in his home or business base and to protect him from unfair exploitation by the landlord. The importance of the lease as a home or business base is seen in the security of tenure legislation in the residential and agricultural sectors and the rights of renewal given to tenants of business property. It also explains the need to serve a formal notice on tenants in the private residential sector who are being granted tenancies with only limited (or no) security of tenure, the purpose of the notice being to forewarn the tenant of the limited protection available to him so that he does not have a false expectation of long term security (see ch 5.2.4.2). The fundamental nature of the home concept can also be seen in the huge public outcry over the government's plans to reform the homelessness legislation so that homeless persons will no longer have a right to permanent housing but will, instead, face the prospect of a series of temporary housing (see ch 5.1.4.1(b)). Notwithstanding the strength of the home concept, it does, however, have to be weighed against other factors. The partial deregulation of private residential and agricultural tenancies in the 1980s and 1990s (see ch 6) is explained not by a weakening in the perceived importance of a secure base but by the policy factors explored in ch 2, including the need to increase the supply of property for renting.

In the United States, the public regulation of tenancies has occurred more recently, and more rapidly. Many commentators talk of a 'revolution' in landlord and tenant law since the late 1960s. Ways in which the law has changed are manifold: many States have imposed a duty on landlords to maintain residential premises in habitable condition; rent control has been introduced in many States; there have been controls on the eviction of tenants; an expansion of landlords' tort liability; the rule on dependant covenants has been applied to residential leases; and landlords' abilities to choose or reject new tenants have been limited. What is different about the position in the United States is the pace of change and also the role that the judiciary have played within this. In England, most of the intervention in the leasehold relationship has been by statute and has been more gradual. In America many of the developments have stemmed from judicial intervention. This is illustrated vividly in the case of *Javins v First National Realty Corporation, op. cit.* A landlord was seeking possession from tenants who had not paid their rent. The tenants claimed that there were approximately 1500 violations of Housing Regulations at the premises (housing codes laying down minimum standards), and were withholding the rent as a protest against the defective state of the apartments. Although there had been a few earlier cases eroding the caveat lessee rule and imposing a warranty of habitability on the landlord (see *Delameter v Foreman* 239 NW 148 (Minn 1931) at 149; *Pines v Perssion* 14 Wis 2d 590 (1961)), these had received relatively little publicity. It was the *Javins* decision that had the greatest impact upon future legal development. The case was important for changing several common law rules. First, Judge Skelly Wright (for the District of Columbia Court of Appeals) held that a warranty of habitability was implied into the lease of urban dwellings covered by the Housing Regulations. Secondly, breach of this warranty gave rise to 'the usual remedies for breach of contract'. This means that a tenant's obligation to pay rent may be suspended if the landlord has broken a repairing obligation.

In addition to the actual decision in *Javins*, the case is interesting for the reasoning followed. Judge Skelly Wright traced the change from the lease being seen primarily as a conveyance to greater recognition of its contractual elements. In addition, the urban tenant was not simply buying land but

'shelter' . . . **a well known package of goods and services—a package which includes not merely walls and ceilings, but also adequate heat, light and ventilation, serviceable plumbing facilities, secure windows and doors, proper sanitation, and proper maintenance.** (at 1074, footnotes omitted)

The court saw tenancy law as having been constrained by viewing the lease as a proprietary interest. Recognition of its contractual nature, and comparison with other consumer contracts, provided the route for development:

In order to reach results more in accord with the legitimate expectations of the parties and the standards of the community, courts have been gradually introducing more modern precepts of contract law in interpreting leases . . .

In interpreting most contracts, courts have sought to protect the legitimate expectations of the buyer and have steadily widened the seller's responsibility for the quality of goods and services through implied warranties of fitness and merchantability . . .

The rigid doctrines of real property law have tended to inhibit the application of implied warranties to transactions involving real estate. Now, however, courts have begun to hold sellers and developers of real property responsible for the quality of their product. For example, builders of new homes have recently been held liable to purchasers for improper construction on the ground that the builders had breached an implied warranty of fitness . . .

Despite this trend in the sale of real estate, many courts have been unwilling to imply warranties of quality, specifically a warranty of habitability, into leases of apartments. Recent decisions have offered no convincing explanation for their refusal; rather they have relied without discussion upon the old common law rule that the lessor is not obligated to repair unless he covenants to do so in the written lease contract . . . In our judgment, the old no-repair rule cannot coexist with the obligations imposed on the landlord by a typical modern housing code, and must be abandoned in favour of an implied warranty of habitability . . .

In our judgment the common law itself must recognize the landlord's obligation to keep his premises in a habitable condition. This conclusion is compelled by three separate considerations. First, we believe that the old rule was based on certain factual assumptions which are no longer true; on its own terms, it can no longer be justified. Second, we believe that the consumer protection cases discussed above require that the old rule be abandoned in order to bring residential landlord-tenant law into harmony with the principles on which those cases rest. Third, we think that the nature of today's urban housing market also dictates abandonment of the old rule . . .

Today's urban tenants, the vast majority of whom live in multiple dwelling houses, are interested, not in the land, but solely in a 'house suitable for occupation'. Furthermore, today's city dweller usually has a single specialized skill unrelated to maintenance work; he is unable to make repairs like the 'jack-of-all-trades' farmer who was the common law's model of the lessee . . . In addition, the increasing complexity of today's dwellings renders them much more difficult to repair than the structures of earlier times. In a multiple dwelling repair may require access to equipment and areas in the control of the landlord . . .

Our approach to the common law of landlord and tenant ought to be aided by principles derived from the consumer protection cases referred to above. In a lease contract, a tenant seeks to purchase from his landlord shelter for a specified period of time. The landlord sells housing as a commercial business-man and has much greater opportunity, incentive and capacity to inspect and maintain the condition of his building. Moreover, the tenant must rely upon the skill and *bona fides* of his landlord at least as much as a car buyer must rely upon the car manufacturer. In dealing with major problems, such as heating, plumbing, electrical or structural defects, the tenant's position corresponds precisely with the 'ordinary consumer who cannot be expected to have the knowledge or capacity or even the opportunity to make adequate inspection of mechanical instrumentalities, like automobiles, and to decide for himself whether they are reasonably fit for the designed purpose'. *Henningsen v Bloomfield Motors, Inc.*, 32 NJ 358, 375, 161 A 2d 69, 78 (1960).

. . . Contract principles established in other areas of the law provide a . . . framework for the apportionment of landlord-tenant responsibilities; they strongly suggest that a warranty of habitability be implied into all contracts for urban dwellings. (*per* Skelly Wright J, *Javins, op. cit.*, at 1075–9, footnotes omitted)

From the above extract it seems that Judge Skelly Wright saw the implied warranty as an aspect of the contract between the parties; presumably this was a term implied by law ('. . . the housing code must be read into housing contracts' at 1081). Several factors were important in the line of reasoning: the analogy with consumer law, the recognition of the contractual nature of leases, inequality within the bargaining relationship and the fact that the legislature had made a policy judgment about housing standards through the housing codes. It is remarkable that the court was happy to create private law rights out of the statutory codes; taking a much more pro-active part in legal development than English courts have generally done.

As mentioned before, the warranty of habitability in *Javins* is not an isolated development. Over forty jurisdictions now give private law rights and remedies to tenants whose homes do not meet minimum standards of habitability. There have also been significant judicial developments in other areas: see *Whetzel v Jess Fisher Management Co* 282 F 2d 943 (DC Cir 1960) (tenant tort action based on landlord's violation of housing code); and *Edwards v Habib* 397 F 2d 687 (DC Cir 1968) (tenant action for retaliatory eviction by landlord).

Collectively, the changes in American landlord and tenant law have transformed the nature of the law. Various explanations have been offered for this 'revolution':

To many, the essence of the change has seemed to be a shift of the basis of lease law from principles of property to principles of contract. This view is particularly noticeable in the opinions of judges who have been instrumental in bringing about fundamental alterations in the common law of landlord-tenant, . . . In fact, however, landlord-tenant case law was already deeply pervaded by contract notions by the end of the nineteenth century. Awareness of this earlier contractualization of lease law has led one writer to interpret the recent changes as primarily involving a movement from traditional contract law to modern commercial law. Where leases of dwellings are concerned, some scholars have seen in recent movements a transition from contract to status . . .

Over the twentieth century, the elimination of certain anomalies within lease law brought it into closer harmony with modern principles of contract, tort, civil procedure and commercial law.

What is new, if not revolutionary, in the past twenty years, is that residential and commercial landlord-tenant law have gradually diverged, the former more influenced by developments in consumer law, the latter by commercial law. The decisive element in the transformation of the residential landlord-tenant relationship has been its subjection to pervasive, mostly statutory, regulation of its incidents . . . Together, legislative and judicial treatment of leases of dwellings now make it plain that the movement in residential lease law has not been from one area of private law to another, but from private ordering to public regulation. In this process of transition from private to public law, the habitability issue, which has dominated residential landlord-tenant law for the past two decades, is now yielding center stage to developments even more far-reaching in their implications: rent regulation, security of tenure for the tenant, and the qualification of the landlord's traditional rights to alienate the freehold or to convert it to another use . . .

Underlying these . . . changes is the idea that shelter is a basic human necessity, and that public regulation of the terms and conditions on which it is offered and held is therefore appropriate. (Glendon, *The Transformation of American Landlord-Tenant Law*, (1982) 23 Bos C LR 503 at pp 503-5, footnotes omitted)

The distinction drawn above by Glendon between the residential and commercial sectors may be crumbling. In the Supreme Court of Texas, it has been held that in a commercial lease there is an implied warranty that the premises are suitable for their intended commercial purpose, and that the tenant's obligation to pay rent is dependent on the landlord's compliance with this warranty. Referring to the reasoning used in the residential cases, Spears J stated:

It cannot be assumed that a commercial tenant is more knowledgeable about the quality of the structure than a residential tenant. A businessman cannot be expected to possess the expertise necessary to adequately inspect and repair the premises, and many commercial tenants lack the financial resources to hire inspectors and repairmen to assure the suitability of the premises . . . Additionally, because commercial tenants often enter into short-term leases, the tenants have limited economic incentive to make any extensive repair to their premises . . .

Although minor distinctions can be drawn between residential and commercial tenants, those differences do not justify limiting the warranty to residential leaseholds. Therefore, we hold there is an implied warranty of suitability by the landlord in a commercial lease that the premises are suitable for their intended commercial purpose. (*Davidow v Inwood North Professional Group, op. cit.*, at 376-7)

In Massachusetts and Hawaii, the State courts, while leaving open the possibility of extending the warranty to commercial leases, have expressed reservations about whether such an extension is appropriate: *Chausse v Coz* 540 NE 2d 667 (Mass 1989) at 669; *Cho Mark Oriental Food v Intern* 868 P 2d 1057 (Hawaii 1992) at 1061 n1.

Whatever route is taken for implementing change—whether it be through the implication of contractual terms, extension of tort liability, or statute—the shift in landlord-tenant law is due to a shift in public policy. Meyers describes the changes in American landlord and tenant law as stemming neither from its proprietary nor its contractual status but 'the moral principle of redistribution of wealth from landlord to tenant' (Meyers, *The Covenant of Habitability and the American Law Institute*, (1975) 27 Stan L Rev 879 at p 882). This view can be supported by looking at the way that the courts have developed the implied warranty since the *Javins* decision. The warranty cannot be waived by the parties (contrary to general contract principles), and has developed in some States so as to impose a strict obligation on a landlord, thus he can be liable even though the breach was caused by his maintenance employees being on strike (*Park West Management Corp v Mitchell* 418 NY S 2d 310 (1979)), and rent will start abating immediately upon breach even though the landlord has had no time to begin to remedy the defect (*Berman & Sons, Inc v Jefferson* 396 NE 2d 981 (1979)). Such a strict duty goes beyond contractual concerns with reliance and expectation and becomes a matter of public regulation. In the *Berman* case, *op. cit.*, the court recognized this:

[W]e note that the landlord's liability without fault is merely an economic burden; the tenant living in an uninhabitable building suffers a loss of shelter, a necessity. (at 984–5)

Indeed, in one case the dissenting judge said that the majority decision proceeded on the theory that

if not an outlaw a landlord is at least a public utility, subject to regulation by the court in conformity with its concept of public convenience and necessity. (Judge Robb in *Robinson v Diamond Housing Corp* 463 F 2d 853 (1972) at 871)

The tenant is perceived to be unequal in the bargaining relationship, not skilled or sufficiently informed to evaluate the risk of defects, and, as the economically weaker of the parties, not in a position to bear the economic burden of repair. As Glendon states

The landlord is treated as controlling a resource of such central importance in society that it must be regulated, and the courts start borrowing analogies, not from sales law, but from public utility law . . .

With increased regulation, the landlord-tenant relationship takes on some characteristics of a status, with its terms and conditions fixed by law. The movement in residential landlord-tenant law turns out not to have been a movement from one field of private law to another, but a movement from private law to public law. (Glendon, *op. cit.*, at pp 555–6, footnotes omitted)

In England, the picture cannot be painted as clearly. While there is intervention in the private law relationship, the level of control fluctuates. In periods of greater intervention, as under the Rent Act 1977, the motivation is, in part, a reflection of the idea that a tenant in an unequal bargaining situation needs protection. As shelter is a basic human need, the tenant is given security in his home.

This basic protection is also a partial explanation of the enfranchisement laws, giving the tenant of a house or a flat the right to buy the freehold. This is, however, only a partial explanation. As with regulation of the tenancy relationship itself, the level of control is related to wider political goals and issues of policy. To ask who should bear the responsibility for repair as between two individuals (as has been done in the American habitability cases) is to see the issue too narrowly; the wider ramifications of allocation of risk also need to be borne in mind, in particular the consequence that this will have on the amount of rent and the supply of housing for rental. Similarly, the partial de-regulation of private renting in the Housing Act 1988 was brought about by the perceived need to stimulate investment in housing for rental; tight controls on landlords (treating them like public utilities) was a disincentive and would, in the long term, have an adverse effect on the size of the rental sector.

For further reading on the American position see Hicks, *The Contractual Nature of Real Property Leases*, (1972) 24 Baylor L Rev 443; Cunningham, *The New Implied and Statutory Warranties of Habitability in Residential Leases: From Contract to Status*, (1979) 16 Urb L Ann 6; Berger, *The New Residential Tenancy Law—Are Landlords Public Utilities?*, (1981) 60 Neb L Rev 707; Glendon, *The Transformation of American Landlord-Tenant Law*, (1982) 23 Bos C L R 503; Rabin, *The Revolution in Residential Landlord-Tenant Law: Causes and Consequences*, (1984) 69 Cornell LR 517 (and the following symposium responses).

3.9 INTERVENTION—A DENIAL OF PROPERTY RIGHTS?

The extensive public regulation of tenancies challenges our understanding of rights associated with the ownership of property: any intervention in the landlord and tenant relationship represents a restriction on the landlord's rights of ownership. This strong sense of property underlay much of the early resistance to housing reform:

Private property stood as a defence between the state and the individual, giving the English the kind of strength which had in the past defeated attempts at despotic monarchy and ambitious parliaments. Thus the very idea of the creation of the inspectorate which would have been necessary to enforce building standards was interpreted as an intolerable attack on private property. (Gauldie, *Cruel Habitations*, 1974, at p 117)

In a number of jurisdictions the right to own private property is constitutionally recognised. This is illustrated by the provisions of the French Civil Code:

The general law of landlord and tenant is contained in articles 1713 through 1779 of the French Civil Code. The underlying principle which gave birth to these articles almost two hundred years ago is the assumption that the right of the landlord over his property should be virtually absolute, and that the relationship between

landlord and tenant should constitute a contract which is best left unconstrained by legislation. (De Moor, *Landlord and tenant in French law: a recent statute*, (1983) 3 OJLS 425 at p 425)

Yet even in France, as in most jurisdictions, it has been found necessary to erode these rights in relation to commercial, agricultural and residential leases. Nevertheless, although the right to own property free from interference has not been treated as inviolate, the importance attached to 'property' is such that any interference with it requires explanation and justification:

Property is a legal institution the essence of which is the creation and protection of certain private rights in wealth of any kind. The institution performs many different functions. One of these functions is to draw a boundary between public and private power. Property draws a circle around the activities of each private individual or organization. Within that circle, the owner has a greater degree of freedom than without. Outside, he must justify or explain his actions, and show his authority. Within, he is master, and the state must explain and justify any interference. It is as if property has shifted the burden of proof; outside, the individual has the burden; inside, the burden is on government to demonstrate that something the owner wishes to do should not be done. (Reich, *The New Property*, (1964) 73 Yale LJ 733 at p 771)

The major justifications given for intervention are summarised in the Law Commission Report on Reform of Landlord and Tenant Law:

2.6 One major concern has been to protect tenants against the oppressive use of the landlord's power. This is a classic interference with apparent freedom of contract, in the belief that the position of the parties when they negotiate is so unequal that the freedom is illusory ...

Agricultural land

2.8 The problems of an agricultural tenant of arable land are unique in one way. Unless he is allowed to occupy the land let to him for long enough to harvest any crop he has sown, he may not be able to obtain any return at all from his use of the property. This is balanced by the fact that unless he observes the tenets of good husbandry, he can seriously prejudice the future productivity of the soil, and therefore the value of the land. Again, good farming may require the provision of permanent improvements, which will benefit the landlord after the tenancy ceases ... In agriculture, more than in any other field, landlord and tenant legislation emphasises the partnership between the two parties, each of whom should appropriately contribute to what is in a sense a joint enterprise.

2.9 Security of tenure was given to farm tenants to protect their farming business, and it is in effect conditional on their conducting that business properly. The influence of parallel legislation covering residential properties, where the motive is to provide tenants with a permanent home, led to an extension of the security of agricultural tenants, allowing members of the family to succeed them on death or retirement. Because this dramatically reduced the number of farms offered for letting, this policy was reversed.

Business property

2.10 Similar influences affected legislative intervention into the law governing commercial tenancies, although it came later. A business established on leasehold property can be put at risk when the lease expires, if the landlord does not wish to renew it or demands exorbitant terms. Also, a tenant may wish to make an improvement to increase the efficiency of the business. If there is residual value in that improvement when the lease ends, he might simply have provided a greater incentive to the landlord to decline to renew it.

2.11 . . . In the first instance, the emphasis was on ensuring that tenants were not unjustly deprived of the residual value of improvements they had made: they were given the option of compensation or a new lease. Later, the emphasis was placed on renewal of the tenancy, and, with certain exceptions, tenants now have the right to a new lease when their current one ends.

Residential property

2.12 Three separate strands of policy can be detected in the considerable volume of legislation which has been passed to protect residential tenants. First, there is a desire to ensure that the properties they occupy are suitable, properly repaired and with reasonable facilities. Secondly, statue provides a guarantee that tenants can remain in their home indefinitely. Thirdly, tenants who paid a capital sum for a long lease are protected against the consequences of that lease expiring. These elements overlap . . . (Law Commission, *Landlord and Tenant: Reform of the Law*, Law Com. No. 162, 1987)

These kinds of restrictions on the landlord's property rights have not gone unchallenged. In both the United States and Ireland there have been constitutional challenges to protective legislation. The absence of a written constitution in England and Wales means that the only challenge that can be made is that the legislation violates the rights secured by the European Convention on Human Rights. These challenges will be looked at in the appropriate subject chapters (see ch 8.4.4—rent, ch 11.1—eviction, ch 12.7—enfranchisement).

3.10 PUBLIC LAW ATTRIBUTES OF A LEASE

Rather than as a mere source of regulatory codes for 'private contracts dealing with property rights', public law can have a more direct impact on the landlord and tenant relationship. Where a local authority exercises control over housing, whether remotely through environmental health officers or more directly through planning agreements with developers or as landlord, a public law relationship is created. The relationship between central and local government also has implications for the local authority's role as landlord. That local authorities are the biggest residential landlord means that issues for many tenants and prospective tenants are within the purview of judicial review and associated administrative law remedies rather than a common law action—Rules of the Supreme Court, Order 53; see also, Law Commission, *Administrative Law: Judicial Review and Statutory Appeals*, Law Com. No. 226, 1994; Partington, *Reforming Judicial Review: the Impact on Homeless Persons Cases*, [1994] JSW&FL 47. Thus, there is this further sense in which a lease can give rise to a public law relationship which itself has two facets. First the proceedings themselves distinguish the relationship as being one of public law, secondly the types of challenge that might be raised also reflect a specifically public law nature to an action; for example, a tenant might question the local authority's overall policy on rent across the borough in order to challenge his personal rent increase.

The aim of this section is to look at those areas where the landlord and tenant relationship is subject to public law and to consider the overlap with common law actions. While landlords and tenants in the private residential, commercial and agricultural sectors rely on property and contract rights, local authority tenants have to fit many of their similar claims into public law actions.

3.10.1 Questioning the Decisions of Public Authorities

The fact that a local authority rather than a private sector landlord has taken a decision that affects the landlord and tenant relationship should, on the face of things, make no difference to the ability of the tenant to challenge it. Nevertheless, the courts have laid down that where a public law remedy is available, then judicial review should usually be the route taken by an aggrieved tenant or prospective tenant rather than through issuing a writ at common law.

Now that . . . all remedies for infringements of rights protected by public law can be obtained on an application for judicial review, as can also remedies for infringements of rights under private law if such infringements should also be involved, it would in my view as a general rule be contrary to public policy, and as such an abuse of the process of the court, to permit a person seeking to establish that a decision of a public authority infringed rights to which he was entitled to protection under public law to proceed by way of an ordinary action and by this means to evade the provisions of Ord 53 for the protection of such authorities. (*O'Reilly v Mackman* [1982] 3 All ER 1124, *per* Lord Diplock at 1134; see also, Law Com. No. 226, *op. cit.*, para 3.13)

The protection referred to is that the applicant must seek leave of the court to bring an action for judicial review within 3 months of the decision that is being challenged. A speedy response is, therefore, available to both parties and the courts act as a filter to prevent frivolous claims against local authorities which have no hope of success—*Cocks v Thanet DC* [1982] 3 All ER 1135 at 1139. The three months, though, can prove to be a very short time limit and even if the action for judicial review is successful, the courts can only quash the initial decision and ask the local authority to reconsider on proper grounds—once the appropriate factors are taken into account, there is nothing to stop the local authority reaching the same decision unless it would be unreasonable within *Wednesbury* principles (*Associated Provincial Picture Houses v Wednesbury Corporation* [1948] 1 KB 223, *per* Lord Greene MR at 230). Lord Diplock continued, however, that there may be exceptions to this general rule,

particularly where the invalidity of the decision arises as a collateral issue in a claim for infringement of a right of the plaintiff arising under private law . . .
(*O'Reilly, op. cit.*, at 1134)

The House of Lords applied *O'Reilly* to a housing case, namely an application for rehousing under the homelessness legislation, in the very next reported decision, *Cocks v Thanet DC, op. cit.* Lord Bridge divided a local authority's functions into two, decision-making and executive. Decision-making referred to the local authority's obligation to investigate a genuine claim for homelessness to see if a duty to rehouse had arisen. Since statute conferred exclusive jurisdiction on the local authority to reach the decision, its decision was of a public law nature and could only be challenged by judicial review.

On the other hand, the housing authority are charged with executive functions. Once a decision has been reached by the housing authority which gives rise to the temporary, the limited or the full housing duty, rights and obligations are immediately created in the field of private law. Each of the duties referred to, once established, is capable of being enforced by injunction and breach of it will give rise to a liability in damages. But it is inherent in the scheme of the [homelessness legislation] that an appropriate public law decision of the housing authority is a condition precedent to the establishment of the private law duty.
(*Cocks v Thanet DC, op. cit.*, at 1138)

One of the initial reasons for favouring judicial review was that it gave the parties quick access to the courts. Unfortunately, the explosion in the number of applications to the courts has clogged the system—see Sunkin, Bridges and Mészáros, *Judicial Review in Perspective*, 1993, at p 13. Lord Brightman went so far as to say that there was overuse of review in homelessness cases, a questionable remark once it has been decided that the only way to challenge a local authority's decision is by that means. According to Lord Brightman, only if a local authority decision were perverse should the courts intervene:

My Lords, I am troubled at the prolific use of judicial review for the purpose of challenging the performance by local authorities of their functions under the [homelessness legislation]. Parliament intended the local authority to be the judge of fact. The Act abounds with the formula when, or if, the housing authority are satisfied as to this, or that, or have reason to believe this, or that. Although the action or inaction of a local authority is clearly susceptible to judicial review where they have misconstrued the Act, or abused their powers or

otherwise acted perversely, I think that great restraint should be exercised in giving leave to proceed by judicial review. The plight of the homeless is a desperate one, and the plight of the applicants in the present case commands the deepest sympathy. But it is not, in my opinion, appropriate that the remedy of judicial review, which is a discretionary remedy, should be made use of to monitor the actions of local authorities under the Act save in the exceptional case. The ground on which the courts will review the exercise of an administrative discretion is abuse of power, *eg.* bad faith, a mistake in construing the limits of the power, a procedural irregularity or unreasonableness in the *Wednesbury* sense (see *Associated Provincial Picture Houses Ltd v Wednesbury Corp.* [1947] 2 All ER 680, [1948] 1 KB 223), ie. unreasonableness verging on an absurdity: see the speech of Lord Scarman in *Nottinghamshire CC v Secretary of State for the Environment* [1986] 1 All ER 199 at 202, [1986] 2 WLR 1 at 5. Where the existence or non-existence of a fact is left to the judgment and discretion of a public body and that fact involves a broad spectrum ranging from the obvious to the debatable to the just conceivable, it is the duty of the court to leave the decision of that fact to the public body to whom Parliament has entrusted the decision-making power save in a case where it is obvious that the public body, consciously or unconsciously, are acting perversely. My Lords, I would dismiss this appeal. And I express the hope that there will be a lessening in the number of challenges which are mounted against local authorities who are endeavouring, in extremely difficult circumstances, to perform their duties under the 1977 Act with due regard for all their other housing problems. (*Puhlhofer v Hillingdon LBC* [1986] 1 All ER 467, *per* Lord Brightman at 474)

The goose that laid the golden egg, swift and declaratory applications for judicial review, had become, and still is, egg bound. The government seem confused on judicial review and dispute resolution. The new proposals on homelessness indicate that there will be a separate, independent appeal system for all applicants for housing—the *Guardian* p 2, 19 July 1994. Furthermore, the Law Commission (Law Com. No. 226, *op. cit.*) recommended that a right of appeal to a court or independent tribunal be created for homelessness cases rather than the applicant having to seek judicial review (see para 1.12): such a change is still some years away, however. Regardless, there are several areas of the landlord and tenant relationship which can only be challenged through judicial review where the landlord is a local authority, a public institution exercising statutory obligations.

3.10.2 Questioning the Decisions of Local Authorities on Landlord and Tenant Matters

Lest it be thought that public law only impinges in the case of public sector residential lettings, in *R v Welwyn Hatfield DC, ex parte Slough Estates plc* [1991]

EGCS 38, a commercial developer used public law to challenge a variation in a lease between a local authority and one of its commercial tenants which was developing a competing site. The case focussed on a 'Tenant Mix Agreement' between the council and the developers of a site within its area, A1 Gallerias, which was intended for use, *inter alia*, for leisure activities. The local authority, as owner of the site, granted a lease to A1 Gallerias Investment Corporation Ltd which incorporated the Tenant Mix Agreement. Slough Estates plc were developing another site within the local authority area and feared that this council owned development would take trade away. At the planning hearing for the A1 Gallerias development, the Tenant Mix Agreement formed part of the basis of Welwyn Hatfield DC's and A1 Gallerias Investment Corporation Ltd's joint defence, that is, that their development would be materially different from that undertaken by Slough Estates plc. After obtaining planning consent, the council relaxed the Tenant Mix Agreement by a side-letter and Slough Estates plc sought judicial review to quash this relaxation of a term of the lease and to force a choice of tenants for A1 Gallerias in line with that original Agreement. The availability of judicial review *vis-à-vis* public bodies gave Slough Estates plc, in this particular case, an additional remedy.

Even where a decision of the local authority as landlord of its housing stock is in issue, the public law nature of this landlord and tenant relationship may be further reflected in the fact that the local authority challenges a decision of central government. In *R v Secretary of State for the Environment, ex parte Greenwich LBC* (1990) 22 HLR 543, the local authority sought judicial review of their housing subsidy allocation under the Local Government and Housing Act 1989. The decision was grounded in an application for judicial review of the Secretary of State's decisions in relation to the allocation of grant to all local authorities, but, since the 1989 Act ring-fenced the Housing Revenue Account (see below, ch 8), the Secretary of State's decision had a direct effect on the rent paid by Greenwich's tenants. The public law nature of the landlord and tenant relationship is brought out in this conflict between central and local government.

Nevertheless, it is where tenants or prospective tenants seek to challenge a decision of the local authority and have to rely on judicial review that the public law nature of the relationship is most prominently presented. In *R v Canterbury CC, ex parte Gillespie* (1987) 19 HLR 7, Simon Brown J. dealt with a case concerning whether a person could be excluded from the housing waiting list. Unlike the private sector, local authorities are obliged to give a reasonable preference to certain groups for housing, including those living in insanitary conditions or where there is overcrowding and to those deemed homeless—Housing Act 1985, s 22 (see ch 5). In exercising this preference, the applicant argued that the council had a blanket rule which fettered its discretion. The judge agreed, *op. cit.*, at 14–15, making it clear that the courts can judicially review any decision by the local authority in the exercise of their statutory powers—*op. cit.*, at 12. Because local authorities have a series of statutory responsibilities pertaining to housing matters, such duties can be reviewed through the courts under principles of public law in cases where a tenant or prospective tenant of any other sort of landlord would have no justiciable action whatsoever. To that extent, at least, the public law nature of the relationship is beneficial to tenants.

In addition to *Gillespie*, there are any number of cases where the applicant has asked the courts to review a decision about their status as a homeless person under the Housing Act 1985, Part III and, indeed, *Cocks v Thanet, op. cit.*, was a case in point. That local authorities have to meet housing need according to statutory rules and that housing the homeless is a public law issue open to review before the courts cannot be gainsaid, but the practical limits of subjecting these decisions to judicial scrutiny and the functionality of doing so can be doubted given the extent of political and economic factors that form part of any housing question. For instance, judicial review is no substitute for good working relationships between local authorities.

I would also quash the referral [to Tower Hamlets from Newham] on a ground which is not very different from that relied upon by Nolan J. Section 60(4) [Housing Act 1985] does not, as such, impinge upon any question of referral, as distinct from a finding of intended homelessness. But good administration and comity between local authorities demand that in exercising a power, such as that contained in s 67, the authority should take full account of the general circumstances prevailing in relation to housing in both their areas and should give serious consideration to whether, notwithstanding that the conditions of referral [under local connection principles] are satisfied (in the absence of which no question of referral arises), the public interest requires that the rehousing should be undertaken by it rather than by the other authority. This was not done and it is not for the court to do it and indirectly to decide what Newham's decision should have been. (*R v Newham LBC, ex parte Tower Hamlets LBC* [1992] 2 All ER 767, *per* Lord Donaldson MR at 778; see also, *Puhlhofer, op. cit.*, at 474)

Allocating a scarce resource such as social rented housing is a political and economic decision influenced by a variety of factors. Although many questions before the courts have political and economic ramifications, decisions on unfair redundancies under labour laws or whether a duty of care should be extended to encompass a new form of damage or new class of plaintiff, for example, are dealt with through private law actions. However, where the landlord is a local authority, the question has to be skewed to fit within the confines of an application for judicial review. On the other hand, since a decision to quash by the courts merely remands the question back to the local authority for reconsideration taking into account all relevant factors, it does not require the courts to substitute their own political and economic views. Such matters come to the fore in cases concerning rent rises in the local authority sector. There is no equivalent to Rent Tribunals or Rent Assessment Committees for council tenants. Direct action through the courts will normally have to be undertaken on the ground that the rent rise agreed by the council is unreasonable and, therefore, *ultra vires*. Very few cases succeeded in the past because the courts felt that rent rises were partly a matter of social policy (*Hemsted v Lees & Norwich CC* (1986) 18 HLR 424, *per* McCowan J at 430), but the attempt to specify in more detail what might be debited from the Housing Revenue Account in the Local Government and Housing Act 1989, Sch 4 may lead to the courts being more willing to intervene to require the local authority to reconsider a rise where extraneous items are included— *R v LB of Ealing, ex parte Jennifer Lewis* (1992) 24 HLR 484. Nevertheless, the court's reluctance to interfere with rent rises on public law principles, rather than in terms of rent review seen in the private residential and commercial sectors, can be garnered from the judgment of Woolf LJ in *Ex parte Jennifer Lewis*, *op. cit.*, at 494.

In general, I have no doubt that it is inappropriate and undesirable for a court on an application for judicial review to become involved in the detail as to how individual authorities draw up their respective HRAs. If the court were to become so involved it would lead to an undesirable increase in litigation which could interfere, as this case threatens to interfere, with the budgetary process of an authority. In general it is preferable to leave the supervision in the hands of the Secretary of State and the District Auditor and for the courts, if they are to become involved, to defer that involvement until the matter has been canvassed before other bodies. If this is not done, problems may arise because in relation to the auditing process which is conducted under the Local Government Finance Act 1982, the Secretary of State has the power to sanction an item in an account although it appears to the auditor when carrying out the audit that the item is contrary to law. Furthermore, on an application to the court by the auditor where it appears to the auditor that an item of account is contrary to law, the court's power to grant a declaration is limited 'if the court is satisfied that for example the person authorising an expenditure acted reasonably'. The undesirability of the court becoming involved is underlined where the consequences of possible illegality involve calculations which the court is not in a position to make and where the amount at issue is small.

In *Lewis*, the Court of Appeal, having found in favour of the applicant tenant, went on to defer a decision on the sort of relief to grant in order that the parties might take the opportunity to consider the court's judgment (*per* Lord Woolf at 499). Once again, not only does the public law nature of the relationship determine the type of court proceedings available, it requires the courts to tread carefully lest they usurp the functions of elected bodies. The courts are wary of interfering in public law relationships (see again, *Puhlhofer, op. cit.*, at 474).

It was a matter of real concern that the divisional court, exercising the power of judicial review, was increasingly, and particularly in this part of the case, being

used for political purposes superficially dressed up as points of law. (*R v Greater London Council, ex parte Royal Borough of Kensington & Chelsea,* The Times, 7 April, 1982)

Even though the tenant must usually challenge a local authority decision through judicial review which will lead to the court remanding the decision back to the local authority, the tenant can also seek damages for the harm done by the inappropriate initial decision—*Cocks v Thanet, op. cit.,* and *R v London Borough of Lambeth, ex parte Barnes* (1993) 25 HLR 140. Even where the administrative element of a claim for judicial review is settled, the tenant can continue a claim for damages through the Order 53 procedure by seeking a declaration; to do otherwise would deny the applicant justice since a writ will not issue—*R v Northavon District Council, ex parte Palmer* (1993) 25 HLR 674. Furthermore, while a lease from a local authority does create a public law relationship which can ordinarily only be reviewed through an application for judicial review, it may be possible to question whether a local authority has exercised its statutory duties properly in a private action, either as an *O'Reilly-Cocks* exception or on a more flexible interpretation of the exclusivity principle—see Law Com. No. 226, *op. cit.,* paras 3.8 *et seq.* In *Wandsworth LBC v Winder* [1985] 1 AC 461, the local authority had issued notices of rent increases which the tenant had felt were excessive and so he had continued to pay the old rent. Wandsworth LBC sued for possession and for the arrears. Winder's defence was that he was not liable for arrears since the rent increases were *ultra vires* and counterclaimed for a declaration to that effect. At first instance the counterclaim and defence were struck out as an abuse of process since a challenge to the council's policies should be initiated by judicial review. The judgment, however, was reversed by the Court of Appeal and the House of Lords. Lord Fraser held that a local authority could be challenged on its policies in a private, as opposed to public, action, at least by way of defence where there is 'a pre-existing private law right' (*op. cit.,* at 508; *cf. London Borough of Tower Hamlets v Abdi* (1993) 25 HLR 80, citing *Avon County Council v Buscott* [1988] QB 656 at 663).

It would in my opinion be a very strange use of language to describe the respondent's behaviour in relation to this litigation as an abuse or misuse by him of the process of the court. He did not select the procedure to be adopted. He is merely seeking to defend proceedings brought against him by the appellants. In so doing he is seeking only to exercise the ordinary right of any individual to defend an action against him on the ground that he is not liable for the whole sum claimed by the plaintiff. Moreover, he puts forward his defence as a matter of right, whereas in an application for judicial review, success would require an exercise of the court's discretion in his favour. Apart from the provisions of Order 53 and section 31 of the Supreme Court Act 1981, he would certainly be entitled to defend the action on the ground that the plaintiff's claim arises from a resolution which (on his views) is invalid . . . I find it impossible to accept that the right to

challenge the decision of a local authority in the course of defending an action for non-payment can have been swept away by Order 53, which was directed to introducing a procedural reform (*per* Lord Fraser, *Winder, op. cit.*, at 509)

Adopting the broad approach to *O'Reilly*, Lord Lowry in *Roy v Kensington & Chelsea and Westminster Family Practitioner Committee* [1992] 1 All ER 705 at 728–9, went further and was prepared to accept that a public institution could be sued for breach of statutory duty rather than be challenged by judicial review, although, on the facts, Roy could also have brought his claim as a private action on his contract with the FPC—see also, Law Com. No. 226, *op. cit.*, at paras 3.9 *et seq.* The only constraint is that the private law rights must dominate the proceedings when seeking to enforce performance of a public law duty in an action commenced by writ. That this whole area of law is somewhat unsettled, however, is brought out by three decisions of the Court of Appeal each dealing with a refusal by a homeless family to accept accommodation offered as permanent rehousing on the ground that it was not suitable—*Ali v Tower Hamlets LBC* [1992] 3 All ER 512; *Abdi, op. cit.*; *London Borough of Hackney v Lambourne* (1993) 25 HLR 172. In *Ali*, the plaintiff had tried to force the council to provide suitable housing by initiating an action for breach of statutory duty (*cf. Roy, op. cit.*), while *Abdi* and *Lambourne* attempted to use the unsuitability of the permanent accommodation offered as a defence when challenged over their right to remain in temporary accommodation once that offer of permanent accommodation had been refused; the defence was rejected. *Abdi* and *Lambourne*, especially, must be incorrect, otherwise procedural rules, particularly that judicial review must be sought within three months, will deprive people of their rights. Moreover, the only distinction from *Winder, op cit.*, is that the latter was already a tenant, but he too could have challenged Wandsworth's rent rises through judicial review rather than waiting until the council sought to evict him. Cowan, *The Public/Private Dichotomy and 'Suitable ccommodation' under s 69(1) of the Housing Act 1985*, [1993] JSW&FL 236, criticizes the reasoning displayed in the three cases by the Court of Appeal as being too narrow and leading to a proliferation of proceedings on the ground that the Court of Appeal requires tenants to seek relief through judicial review—*cf.* Law Com. No. 226.

In conclusion, however, the problem, as Cowan's title makes clear, is that there is a dichotomy between public and private law which may not always be appropriate or sensible when dealing with the landlord and tenant relationship—procedural niceties must not stand in the way of housing need or enforcement of rights. It is a difficult balancing act to ensure that local authorities can exercise relevant political and economic discretions and carry out their duties, while giving prospective and existing tenants a ready ability to protect their rights.

It was a matter of real concern that the divisional court, exercising the power of judicial review, was increasingly . . . being used for political purposes superficially dressed up as points of law . . . The impropriety of coming to court when political capital was sought to be made could not be over stressed. It was perhaps even worse when public servants were or felt constrained to file affidavits which demonstrated a political purpose. (*R v GLC, ex parte Royal Borough of Kensington and Chelsea*, The Times, 7 April 1982, *per* McNeill J)

3.11 STATUTORY RIGHTS —A KIND OF PROPERTY?

Under the Rent Act 1977, and earlier legislation, there was some confusion over the precise status of the occupier of private rented property after the termination of his lease. This arose because of the way that statute sought to provide the occupier with security of tenure. Unlike in the commercial code of protection where the tenant has the right to renew his lease (and thus acquire a further proprietary interest), the private sector tenant was given a 'statutory tenancy' which gave him 'no estate or property as tenant at all, but . . . a purely personal right to retain possession of the property' (*Roe v Russell* [1928] 2 KB 117 at 131), a 'statutory right of irremovability' (*Marcroft Wagons Ltd v Smith, op. cit.*, at 501). Megarry described the nature of the statutory tenant's interest as 'something of a jurisprudential curiosity' (Megarry, *The Rent Acts*, 11th edn, 1988, p 255). It had been argued that the extent of the statutory tenant's powers, such as rights to dispose of the property (albeit limited), were such that his interest should be recognised as a proprietary interest (Hands, *The Statutory Tenancy: An Unrecognised Proprietary Interest?*, [1980] Conv 351). Nevertheless, the general view is that the statutory tenancy is a purely personal right: 'a statutory tenancy is not a tenancy properly so called' (*per* Balcombe LJ, *Johnson v Felton*, 20 July 1994, CA, unreported).

A similar confusion exists over the precise status of a public sector 'secure tenancy'. The protected public sector tenancy (a secure tenancy) can only be brought to an end by court order; if a fixed term expires it is statutorily continued (ch 11.2.5); and the secure tenancy is not capable of being assigned other than in certain exceptional cases (ch 9.2.3). This has led the Court of Appeal to conclude that the secure tenancy is, like a Rent Act tenancy, only a personal right (*City of London Corporation v Bown* (1989) 22 HLR 32 at 38–39). Other features of secure tenancies suggest, however, that they do have proprietary characteristics (see ch 9.9).

In the Housing Act 1988, the status of the tenant has been made clear and he will at all times have a lease and thus a proprietary interest. In principle this should therefore be freely alienable and capable of devise by will or transmission on intestacy. The Housing Act 1988 also therefore had to introduce rules modifying these effects; thus the tenant's rights on alienation may be limited (see ch 9.9) and, while the tenancy is capable of being inherited, the landlord has been given powers to terminate the tenancy following the tenant's death (see ch 11.4.13).

4

The Essential Elements of a Lease

4.1 INTRODUCTION

The focus of this book is on the relationship of landlord and tenant and it is there-fore necessary to discuss the distinctions between leases and other occupancy arrangements. It is not always easy to determine whether the occupancy is on a leasehold basis or on some other basis such as licensor/licensee, or even as a squatter. In order to determine this, it may be necessary to look to both the form and substance of the agreement. The outcome of this enquiry may be important for a number of reasons, including to find out whether the occupant is within a code of statutory protection. In the private residential and commercial sectors, protection is only available for tenants (for details, see ch 6). In the public and agricultural sectors, protection may be available to some licensees—but not to all—and a further question that needs to be asked is whether there is in fact a valid distinction that can be drawn between these protected licences and leases.

In addition, a letting for a term of years absolute (a lease) is one of the two legal estates in land permitted under the 1925 legislation (Law of Property Act 1925, s1(1)(b))—the other being the fee simple absolute in possession (the freehold). As a legal estate a lease is a property right and so can be sold or sublet (unless these rights are cut down by contractual terms). Further consequences of its pro-prietary nature were examined in the previous chapter.

4.2 DIFFERENT TYPES OF TENANCY

As was seen in ch 1, leases are used in a variety of different situations, from the sale of long term interests in property to the weekly renting of accommodation. In this section we shall briefly outline the different types of tenancy recognized in law. In the following section we shall examine the elements essential to the exis-tence of all leases.

4.2.1 Fixed Term Lease

This is a lease for a fixed period of time—say 'for five months', 'for 99 years'. It is within the definition of a term of years absolute, defined in the Law of Property Act 1925, s 205(1)(xxvii) as meaning

a term of years (taking effect either in possession or in reversion whether or not at a rent). . . and either certain or liable to determination by notice, re-entry, operation of law, or by a provision for cesser on redemption, or in any other event (other than the dropping of a life, or the determination of a determinable life interest) . . .; and in this definition the expression 'term of years' includes a term for less than a year, or for a year or years and a fraction of a year or from year to year.

It follows from this definition that it does not matter that the lease might be brought to an end before the expiry of the fixed term; for example, where the landlord has the right to forfeit the lease if the tenant fails to pay rent, or if the tenant has the benefit of a 'break clause' by which he is given the right in a 25-year lease to 'break' it at the end of five years. Nor does the fixed term have to be a single continuous period. Thus, 'time-share' arrangements can be leases, as in *Cottage Holiday Associates Ltd v Customs and Excise Commissioners* [1983] QB 735, where Woolf J accepted as a lease a document which granted the lessee a right to occupy a holiday cottage for one week a year for 80 years (see also *Smallwoods v Sheppards* [1964] 1 WLR 1064, upholding a lease for three successive bank holidays).

As there is no need for the lease to be 'in possession' (that is, currently enjoyed by the tenant), it is possible to have 'reversionary leases' that take effect at a future date. By the Law of Property Act 1925, s 149(3) however, it must take effect within 21 years otherwise it is void.

What is essential, however, is that the maximum duration of the term should be known from the outset (*Prudential Assurance Co Ltd v London Residuary Body* [1992] 3 All ER 504). This need for certainty of maximum duration will be discussed later in this chapter.

The fixed term will automatically end when the term finishes and there is no need to serve any notice to end the lease.

4.2.2 Periodic Tenancies

A periodic tenancy is one which is for a period and which automatically continues from period to period until ended by the appropriate notice. A person could have, say, a weekly tenancy which continues week by week for fifty years. The law perceives periodic tenancies not to be a series of separate and new tenancies but as one continuing tenancy, 'not a reletting at the commencement of every year [week/month/quarter, etc.] but . . . a springing interest.' (*Gaudy v Jubber* (1865) 9 B & S 15; see also *Queen's Club Garden Estates v Bignell* [1924] 1 KB 117 at 125, 130).

There is no doubt that periodic tenancies are within the definition of a term of years absolute. Section 205(1)(xxvii) states that the

expression 'term of years' includes a term for less than a year, or for a year or years and a fraction of a year or from year to year.

While it may be created expressly, a periodic tenancy will often arise informally where a person occupies land with consent and pays rent by reference to a certain period, for example, £100 monthly. Indeed, until recently it was generally felt that there was a presumption that when someone entered into exclusive possession of property and started paying rent there would be a periodic tenancy: in *Doe d Lord v Crago* (1848) 6 CB 90 at 99, Wilde CJ referred to

the principle, that, from the payment of rent, unexplained, the law will imply a tenancy from year to year, with the incidents attached to it, namely, the necessity of a regular notice to quit, before the defendant's possession could be disturbed.

In *Javad v Aqil* [1991] 1 All ER 243 at 248 ([1991] CLJ 232), however, Nicholls LJ stressed that this presumption only applies where there is nothing more in the surrounding facts to indicate what the parties' intentions are:

As with other consensually-based arrangements, parties frequently proceed with an arrangement whereby one person takes possession of another's land for payment without having agreed or directed their minds to one or more fundamental aspects of their transaction. In such cases the law, where appropriate, has to step in and fill the gaps in a way which is sensible and reasonable. The law will imply, from what was agreed and all the surrounding circumstances, the terms the parties are to be taken to have intended to apply. Thus if one party permits another to go into possession of his land on payment of a rent of so much per week or month, failing more the inference sensibly and reasonably to be drawn is that the parties intended that there should be a weekly or monthly tenancy. Likewise, if one party permits another to remain in possession after the expiration of his tenancy. But I emphasise the qualification: 'failing more'. Frequently there will be more. Indeed, nowadays there normally will be other material surrounding circumstances. The simple situation is unlikely to arise often, not least because of the extent to which statute has intervened in landlord-tenant relationships. Where there is more than the simple situation, the inference sensibly and reasonably to be drawn will depend on a fair consideration of all the circumstances, of which the payment of rent on a periodical basis is only one, albeit a very important one.

The search is therefore to elicit the intention of the parties and the presumption of periodic tenancy will only apply where there are no other factors to be taken into account. In *Javad v Aqil* itself, the occupier had entered into possession while negotiating for a long lease of the property and this indicated that the parties did not intend a periodic tenancy to arise—on the facts Aqil was held to be only a tenant at will (see further 4.2.3). From what was said in *Sopwith v Stutchbury* (1983) 17 HLR 50, it seems that the courts will be slightly less ready to infer a periodic tenancy in a case where a tenant is holding over at the end of a fixed term lease than when he is first entering into the property (see Stephenson LJ at 74).

Where a periodic tenancy is presumed, the period of the tenancy is calculated by reference not to how often the rent is paid but the period by reference to which it is calculated, for example, a rent of £12,000 per annum payable in £1,000 monthly instalments would be a yearly tenancy.

4.2.3 Tenancies at Will

A tenancy at will arises whenever a tenant, with the consent of the owner, occupies land as tenant 'at the will' of the landlord, that is, on terms that either party can bring the tenancy to an end at any time. It is a hybrid kind of interest, for although the occupier has exclusive possession there is no 'term of years' as it can be brought to an end at any time by the owner. For this reason it is not a legal estate:

A tenancy at will, though called a tenancy, is unlike any other tenancy except a tenancy at sufferance, to which it is next-of-kin. It has been properly described as a personal relation between the landlord and his tenant: it is determined by the death of either of them or by any one of a variety of acts, even by an involuntary alienation, which would not affect the subsistence of any other tenancy. (*per* Viscount Simonds, *Wheeler v Mercer* [1957] AC 416 at 427)

The personal nature of this interest means that the tenant cannot assign or sublet his interest. Nevertheless, as the tenant has 'possession' he is able to bring an action in trespass against a stranger (unlike a licensee). The tenancy at will lies somewhere between the periodic tenancy and the licence and the cases illustrate that the courts often have difficulty analysing the legal position when a person simply moves into possession and commences paying rent—the relationship may be construed as one of licence only (as in *Sharp v McArthur and Sharp* (1987) 19 HLR 364; see 4.3.4.2(a)), or as a tenancy at will (as in *Javad v Aqil, op. cit.*) or as a periodic tenancy (as in *Bretherton v Paton* [1986] 1 EGLR 172, see 4.3.4.2(a)).

4.2.4 Perpetually Renewable Leases

A perpetually renewable lease is one for which the tenant can demand renewal on the same terms, that is, including the clause for renewal. These are converted by the Law of Property Act 1922, s 145 and Sch 15 into leases for 2,000 years determinable earlier by the tenant but not by the landlord (Sch 15, para 10(1)).

Such a long lease is usually the last thing that either party would have intended and so the courts tend to lean against a construction that would result in a perpetually renewable lease. Before the courts find a perpetually renewable lease they require very clear wording that the renewed lease was intended to include the right to renewal as well as all the other covenants. For example, in *Marjorie Burnett Ltd v Barclay* (1980) 258 EG 642, a seven-year lease contained a covenant for renewal for a further seven years, the renewed lease to 'contain a like covenant for renewal for a further term of seven years on the expiration of the term thereby granted'. Nourse J held that this was not an obligation for perpetual renewal, only for double renewal. Nevertheless, the use of certain words has become a 'formula' for indicating a perpetually renewable lease. In *Caerphilly Concrete Products Ltd v Owen* [1972] 1 WLR 372, this formula was used: the new lease to contain 'the like covenants and provisos as are herein contained (including an option to renew such lease for the further term of five years at the expiration thereof)'. Sachs LJ referred to the fact that a 2,000-year lease would be at odds with the parties' intentions and went on to refer to 'judicial unease' at this result. While the parties had been talking in terms of five-year leases, it became a lease for 2,000 years.

Furthermore, it may well be the case that the parties have not built into the lease the kinds of terms and conditions that one would normally expect to see in long leases—for example, provision for rent increase, repair and decoration and so on. A result closer to the parties' expectations would be to permit only a limited number of renewals—although the number selected would be somewhat arbitrary, it would create less injustice. As put forward by Lord FitzGerald in *Swinburne v Milburn* (1884) 9 App Cas 844, only in cases where the parties have clearly intended a perpetual lease by using words such as 'for ever' or 'from time to time hereafter' should a 2,000-year lease be imposed.

4.2.5 Tenancies at Sufferance

These arise where a tenant who has enjoyed a term of years holds over at the end of the term without the consent of the landlord:

such a tenant is said to be in possession without either the agreement or disagreement of the landlord. (*per* Viscount Simonds, *Wheeler v Mercer, op. cit.*, at 426)

It is not a tenancy in any meaningful sense and is a device to avoid the occupier being regarded as a trespasser. As Megarry and Wade write:

. . . it is strictly incorrect to call it 'tenancy' at all, for there is no 'privity', ie. tenure, between the parties. But since it normally arises between parties who have been landlord and tenant it has acquired the title of tenancy. (*The Law of Real Property*, 5th edn, 1984, at pp 655–6)

No rent is paid in a tenancy at sufferance (if rent is accepted this would imply consent from the landlord). But the landlord is able to sue for damages for use and occupation of the property, seemingly on the basis of an implied contract (see further *Gibson v Kirk* (1841) 1 QB 850; Yates and Hawkins, *Landlord and Tenant Law*, 2nd edn, 1986, at pp 192–3). The claim for use and occupation is different from the right to recover mesne profits from a trespasser.

Tenancies at sufferance are now rare, the position of tenants holding over at the end of a lease being generally governed by statute (see ch 6).

4.3 THE NEED FOR EXCLUSIVE POSSESSION

What is it then that distinguishes the lease from other agreements to occupy land?

In the leading case of *Street v Mountford* [1985] 2 All ER 289 ([1985] Conv 328; [1986] Conv 39; [1985] CLJ 351), Lord Templeman set out the three hallmarks of a lease: exclusive possession at a rent for a term. Only two of these are, however, *necessary* for a lease; in *Ashburn Anstalt v Arnold* [1988] 2 All ER 147, the Court of Appeal said that there was no need for the payment of rent for there to be a lease—although in most leases there is in fact a periodic rental payment, this is not essential (see also, Australian authority that rent is not essential: *Commonwealth Life (Amalgamated) Assurance Ltd v Anderson* (1946) 46 SR (NSW) 47 at 49). *Ashburn Anstalt* has since been overturned—but on a different point. The view that rent is not essential to a lease is also supported by s 205(1)(xxvii) Law of Property Act 1925:

'Term of years absolute' means a term of years (taking effect either in possession or in reversion *whether or not at a rent*) . . . (emphasis added)

The other two features (exclusive possession for a term) remain necessary for a lease—but even where they are present, there may be a relationship other than a leasehold one (see 4.3.4).

4.3.1 The Nature of Exclusive Possession

Exclusive possession is the legal right to exclude others from the property. A distinction is sometimes drawn between exclusive possession and exclusive occupation—the latter being descriptive of the fact that someone has the sole right to occupy property, but not a right which carries with it the right to exclude others from the property. An example would be a lodging arrangement, where the lodger may well have exclusive occupation but will not have exclusive possession as the owner will have unrestricted rights of access. Lord Templeman recognized this in *Street v Mountford*:

An occupier of residential accommodation at a rent for a term is either a lodger or a tenant. The occupier is a lodger if the landlord provides attendance or services which require the landlord or his servants to exercise unrestricted access to and use of the premises. A lodger is entitled to live in the premises but cannot call the place his own. (*op. cit.*, at 293; see also *Luganda v Service Hotels Ltd* [1969] 2 Ch 209 at 219)

In *Marchant v Charters* [1977] 1 WLR 1181, a person lived in a bed-sit and the owner cleaned the rooms daily and provided clean linen. The absence of exclusive possession meant that the occupier was not a tenant.

These phrases, 'exclusive possession' and 'exclusive occupation', are increasingly being used interchangeably (see, for example, Lord Templeman in *AG Securities v Vaughan*; *Antoniades v Villiers* [1988] 3 All ER 1058; Lord Donaldson MR in *Aslan v Murphy (Nos 1 and 2)* [1989] 3 All ER 130). Notwithstanding somewhat loose use of these phrases, it remains the case that unless there is exclusive possession there cannot be a tenancy:

What then is the fundamental right which a tenant has that distinguishes his position from that of a licensee? It is an interest in land as distinct from a personal permission to enter the land and use it for some stipulated purpose or purposes. And how is to be ascertained whether such an interest in land has been given? By seeing whether the grantee was given a *legal right of exclusive possession* of the land for a term or from year to year or for a life or lives. If he was, he is a tenant. And he cannot be other than a tenant, because a legal right of exclusive possession is a tenancy and the creation of such a right is a demise. . . A right of exclusive possession is secured by the right of a lessee to maintain ejectment and, after his entry, trespass. A reservation to the landlord, either by contract or statute, of a limited right of entry, as for example to view or repair, is, of course, not inconsistent with the grant of exclusive possession. Subject to such reservations, a tenant for a term or from year to year or for a life or lives can exclude his landlord as well as strangers from the demised premises. All this is long-established law: see Cole on *Ejectment* ((1857) pp 72, 73, 287, 485). (*per* Windeyer J, *Radaich v Smith* (1959) 101 CLR 209 at 222; adopted by Lord Templeman in *Street v Mountford*, op. cit., at 300)

It does not follow, though, that if there is exclusive possession there must always be a tenancy, see 4.3.4.

The reason why exclusive possession is necessary for a lease is presumably linked into the traditional idea that 'private property' is to do with the rights to exclude others from the use and benefit of a thing:

. . . that is property to which the following label can be attached:
To the world:
Keep off X unless you have my permission, which I may grant or withhold.
Signed: Private citizen.
Endorsed: The State. (Cohen, *Dialogue on Private Property*, (1954) 9 Rutgers L. Rev. 357 at p 374)

The tenant possessing exclusive possession can keep out strangers and keep out the landlord unless the landlord is exercising limited rights reserved to him by the tenancy agreement to enter and view and repair. A licensee lacking exclusive possession can in no sense call the land his own and cannot be said to own any estate in the land. (*per* Lord Templeman, *Street v Mountford, op. cit.*, at 292)

There are many differing philosophical and political views on what constitutes 'private property', but central to most is this notion of exclusivity—without this, rights to occupy land remain personal in the sense that the right is only held against a particular person and not against subsequent owners of the land. (See Gray, *Property in Thin Air*, [1991] CLJ 252 at p 268 *et seq*. for a discussion of 'excludability' as an essential quality of property.)

4.3.2 Finding Exclusive Possession—the Factual Matrix

Whether or not exclusive possession exists on the facts of any case will not always be easy to determine. In some cases, the difficulty lies in deciding whether rights reserved to the owner are so extensive that the occupier is effectively denied the degree of territorial control necessary to the finding of a lease.

Where the occupier can be required to share the accommodation with another, or with the owner, this will mean that there cannot be exclusive posses-sion (so long as this reflects the genuine intention of the parties).

Where the owner reserves the right to move the occupier to another part of the property, this will also usually negate the existence of a tenancy. In *Dresden Estates v Collinson* (1988) 55 P & CR 47, a workshop and store were occupied under an agreement called a licence. The agreement contained the following provisions:

4 This licence is personal to the Licensees and the Licensees shall not transfer this interest in the same in any manner whatsoever. . .

(b) This Licence confers no exclusive right for the Licensees to use and occupy the
Premises. . . and [the Licensors] shall be entitled from time to time. . . to require [the Licensees] to transfer this occupation to other premises within the Licensor's adjoining property.

These provisions were important to the Court of Appeal's finding that there was a licence and not a lease. Glidewell LJ stated at 53:

You cannot have a tenancy granting exclusive possession of particular premises, subject to a provision that the landlord can require the tenant to move to some-where else. (For criticism of the case, see [1987] Conv 220; (1987) 50 MLR 655)

This kind of workshop-type accommodation is fairly common, particularly with buildings intended to provide the type of accommodation required by small businesses at their start-up. The occupier takes space which may be serviced with, for example, heating and secretarial help, and the owner retains considerable control over the use of the building. Mobility clauses can also be found in residential and agricultural contexts. In *Westminster CC v Clarke* [1992] 1 All ER 695 ([1992] Conv 285), Mr Clarke was a homeless person and was given accommodation in a hostel by the local authority, 'designed to be a halfway house for rehabilitation and treatment en route to an independent home'. The Licence stated that Mr Clarke did not have exclusive occupation and that the accommodation allocated to him could be changed from time to time. Mr Clarke caused disturbance to the neighbours and the Council wanted to get possession quickly. Construing the Housing Act 1985, s 79 the House of Lords held that Mr Clarke would be a secure tenant (and thus it would be a slower process to evict him) if he either had a lease or a licence with exclusive possession (see further ch 6 on the meaning of secure tenant). Either way, exclusive possession was critical—did he have exclusive possession? The House of Lords paid particular attention to the council's object of providing 'temporary accommodation for vulnerable homeless persons' and its need to retain possession of every room. It was held that Mr Clarke did not have exclusive possession:

By the terms of the licence to occupy Mr Clarke was not entitled to any particular room, he could be required to share with any other person as required by the council and he was only entitled to 'occupy accommodation in common with the Council whose representative may enter the accommodation at any time' . . . The conditions of occupancy support the view that Mr Clarke was not in exclusive possession of room E. He was expressly limited in his enjoyment of any accommodation provided for him. He was forbidden to entertain visitors without the approval of the council staff and was bound to comply with the council's warden or other staff in charge of the hostel. These limitations confirmed that the council retained possession of all the rooms of the hostel in order to supervise and control the activities of the occupiers, including Mr Clarke. Although Mr Clarke physically occupied room E he did not enjoy possession exclusively of the council. (*per* Lord Templeman at 703)

In the agricultural case of *McCarthy v Bence* [1990] 17 EG 78 ([1991] Conv 58, [1991] Conv 207), there was a 'share milking' agreement under which the landowner was to supply the land and buildings, and the milk farmer to provide the herd and labour. The agreement provided, *inter alia*, that the fields to be made available could be changed from time to time. The Court of Appeal found that the farmer did not have exclusive possession, again placing much emphasis on the mobility clause.

Another factor in determining whether or not there is exclusive possession is whether the owner retains keys. What matters is not the fact that keys have been kept, but the reason why the owner wants them:

A landlord may well need a key, in order that he may be able to enter quickly in the event of emergency, fire, burst pipes or whatever. He may need a key to enable him or those authorized by him to read meters or to do repairs which are his responsibility. None of these underlying reasons would of themselves indicate that the true bargain between the parties was such that the occupier was in law a lodger. On the other hand, if the true bargain is that the owner will provide genuine services which can only be done by having keys, such as frequent cleaning, daily bed-making, the provision of clean linen at regular intervals and the like, there are materials from which it is possible to infer that the occupier is a lodger rather than a tenant. (*per* Lord Donaldson MR, *Aslan v Murphy (Nos 1 and 2)*, *op. cit.*, at 135–6)

What the court has to decide is whether the totality of the occupancy agreement reveals that the occupier has such extensive use and control of the property that there is exclusive possession:

. . . there is a spectrum of exclusivity ranging from the occupier of a detached property under a full repairing lease, who is without doubt a tenant, to the overnight occupier of a hotel bedroom who, however up-market the hotel, is without doubt a lodger. The dividing line, the sorting of the forks from the spades, will not necessarily or even usually depend on a single factor, but on a combination of factors. (*per* Lord Donaldson MR, *Aslan v Murphy, op. cit.*, at 133)

4.3.3 Finding Exclusive Possession—The Significance of the Parties' Intentions

Determining whether a lease or licence has been granted has been complicated by owners of property attempting to 'dress up' agreements to include all the clothing of a licence, as a means for avoiding security of tenure legislation. One common form of dressing up is to describe the agreement as a 'licence', while granting extensive rights of control to the occupier, rights more usually associated with leases. Another form is to state in the 'licence' that the occupier does not have exclusive possession, even though in practice both parties understand that the occupier will enjoy exclusive possession. Given that exclusive possession is the touchstone of a lease, it must be seen whether the occupier has exclusive possession and it is impossible to determine this without looking to the agreement between the parties. For example, the fact that the owner retains a right to move the occupier to another part of the property can only be seen by looking to the agreed contract.

When the courts look to the agreement they must, however, look to the substance of the agreement and not the form. This is evident from *Street v Mountford, op. cit.* Mrs Mountford had been granted the right to occupy some rooms and signed an agreement clearly purporting to be a licence. It was, however, conceded by the owner that she had exclusive possession and the issue was therefore whether the parties were free to ascribe their own label to this agreed bundle of rights, or whether the label to be attached must be determined by law. The House of Lords held there was a lease, not a licence:

... the consequences in law of the agreement, once concluded, can only be determined by consideration of the effect of the agreement. If the agreement satisfied all the requirements of a tenancy, then the agreement produced a tenancy and the parties cannot alter the effect of the agreement by insisting that they only created a licence. The manufacture of a five-pronged implement for manual digging results in a fork even if the manufacturer, unfamiliar with the English language, insists that he intended to make and has made a spade. (*per* Lord Templeman, *Street v Mountford, op. cit.*, at 294)

Street v Mountford was an extremely significant decision. Notwithstanding the fact that Mrs Mountford had clearly signed an agreement calling itself a licence, the House of Lords was prepared to override the contractual agreement of the parties and hold that there was a lease.

The full significance of *Street v Mountford* has only become apparent in later cases. In *Street v Mountford* itself the agreement contained all the indicia of exclusive possession—it was simply that the parties had given the wrong label to the agreement:

Unless these three hallmarks [exclusive possession at a rent for a term] are decisive, it really becomes impossible to distinguish a contractual tenancy from a contractual licence save by reference to the professed intention of the parties or by the judge awarding marks for drafting. (*per* Lord Templeman, *Street v Mountford, op. cit.*, at 299-300)

The more difficult cases are where the agreement itself contains terms that indicate that a licence was intended (for example, by expressly stating that the occupant does not have exclusive possession), but it is argued that these provisions were inserted in order to avoid statutory protection and that, in practice, the occupier is enjoying the rights usually associated with leases. This raises very complex issues. How can the court decide if there is exclusive possession without looking to the agreement defining the respective rights of the parties? In *Street v Mountford*, Lord Templeman said:

... in order to ascertain the nature and quality of the occupancy and to see whether the occupier has or has not a stake in the room or only permission for himself personally to occupy, the court must decide whether on its true construction the agreement confers on the occupier exclusive possession. (*op. cit.*, at 299)

In looking for the 'true construction', is the court bound to look simply at the face of the agreement or can it take account of the fact that terms have been inserted to avoid statutory protection?

Until *Street v Mountford* there were a number of cases supporting the view that it was the contractual intention of the parties as evidenced on the face of the agreement that was paramount. The high water mark of this is shown by *Somma v Hazelhurst* [1978] 1 WLR 1014, where a double bed-sit was let to an unmarried couple by two separate agreements, both of which contained clauses denying the grant of exclusive possession. The couple enjoyed exclusive possession in practice. The Court of Appeal looked at the face of the agreements and said that it was not prepared to rewrite them—as the agreements said that the couple did not have exclusive possession, they had personal licences and not leases:

We can see no reason why an ordinary landlord. . . should not be able to grant a licence to occupy an ordinary house. If that is what both he and the licensee intend and if they can frame any written agreement in such a way as to demonstrate that it is not really an agreement for a lease masquerading as a licence, we can see no reason in law or justice why they should be prevented from achieving that object. (*per* Cumming-Bruce LJ at 1024–5; see also *Shell-Mex and BP Ltd v Manchester Garages Ltd* [1971] 1 All ER 841; *Buchmann v May* [1978] 2 All ER 993)

There has for some time been an exception to this strict contract-based approach where the document was a 'sham'. The classic legal definition of sham was given in *Snook v London & West Riding Investments Ltd* [1967] 2 QB 786. It requires that the relationship between the parties, as understood by them, be different from the relationship reflected in the written agreements (see Diplock LJ at 802). This is very narrow—it effectively means that the parties must have agreed outside of the written document that, for example, exclusive possession is in fact given whereas the agreement says it is not.

In *Street v Mountford, op. cit.*, the concept of sham was referred to by Lord Templeman:

Although the Rent Acts must not be allowed to alter or influence the construction of an agreement, the court should, in my opinion, be astute to detect and frustrate sham devices and artificial transactions whose only object is to disguise the grant of a tenancy and to evade the Rents Acts. (at 299)

The reference to 'sham' in this quote was not intended to be construed in the narrow and technical manner found in *Snook, op. cit.*, and, in *AG Securities v Vaughan, op. cit.* (Hoath [1989] JSWL 246; Harpum [1989] CLJ 19; Smith [1989] Conv 128), Lord Templeman made clear that he had a much wider and more flexible doctrine in mind. This case was a joint hearing of two appeals. In the second of these appeals, *Antoniades v Villiers*, an unmarried couple had signed two separate 'licence' agreements, each denying the 'licensee' exclusive possession. Clause 16 provided:

The licensor shall be entitled at any time to use the rooms together with the licensee and permit other persons to use all of the rooms together with the licensee.

It was clear that the couple intended to live together as man and wife. Indeed, the flat was totally unsuitable for two persons to live in unless they were 'a couple'. There had been no discussion as to how the sharing clause could have been operated and no attempt had been made to exercise the right. The House of Lords held that the sharing clause was a pretence and could be disregarded:

In *Somma v Hazelhurst*. . . and other cases considered in *Street v Mountford* the owner wished to let residential accommodation but to avoid the Rent Acts. The occupiers wished to take a letting of residential accommodation. The owner stipulated for the execution of agreements which pretended that exclusive possession was not to be enjoyed by the occupiers. The occupiers were obliged to acquiesce with this pretence in order to obtain the accommodation. In my opinion the occupiers either did not understand the language of the agreements or assumed, justifiably, that in practice the owner would not violate their privacy. The owner's real intention was to rely on the language of the agreement to escape the Rent Acts. The owner allowed the occupiers to enjoy jointly exclusive occupation and accepted rent. A tenancy was created. *Street v Mountford* reasserted three principles. First, parties to an agreement cannot contract out of the Rent Acts. Second, in the absence of special circumstances, not here relevant, the enjoyment of exclusive occupation for a term in consideration of periodic payments creates a tenancy. Third, where the language of licence contradicts the reality of lease, the facts must prevail. The facts must prevail over the language in order that the parties may not contract out of the Rent Acts. In the present case cl 16 was a pretence. (*per* Lord Templeman, *AG Securities v Vaughan, op. cit.*, at 1068)

The true nature of the agreement was therefore held to be a joint tenancy.

This new approach, focusing on pretence rather than a restricted definition of sham, enables the court to ignore terms of an agreement that are inserted solely to avoid the application of statutory codes of protection. In the light of *Antoniades v Villiers*, the pretence doctrine can be seen as a three stage process:

1 The courts must establish a valid consensus ad idem, if any [the *Snook* concept of sham will enter in at this stage].
2 Given this consensus ad idem, does it contain a term which is inserted *for the purpose of avoiding statutory protection? If so the term is struck out.*
3 The agreement minus the struck out clause is then construed to see if it is a lease.

This approach is much more based on consumer protection than a belief in contractual freedom, as argued by one of the authors elsewhere: Bright, *Beyond Sham and Into Pretence*, (1991) 11 OJLS 136 at pp 140–1:

Whereas the *Snook* doctrine is easy to reconcile with contractual theory, the pretence doctrine appears more at odds. Notwithstanding the terms actually agreed between the parties, the court will disregard any provision inserted for avoidance purposes. This flies in the face of the principle of sanctity of contract.

Freedom of contract has not, however, always been paramount and is a particularly inappropriate model when dealing with the consumer as a contracting party. The whole focus of the housing legislation is to provide protection based on status as a residential occupier and not to allow market place forces to dominate. Lord Simon has observed that

'(t)here was one economic and social relationship where it was claimed that there were palpably lacking the prerequisites for the beneficent operation of *laissez-faire*, that of landlord and tenant. The market was limited and sluggish: the supply of land could not expand immediately and flexibly in response to demand. . . It was to counteract this descried constriction of the market and to redress this descried inequality of bargaining power that the law, specifically, in the shape of legislation, came to intervene repeatedly to modify freedom of contract between landlord and tenant.' [*Johnson v Moreton* [1980] AC 37 at 66–7]

It is clear from Lord Templeman's speech in *Antoniades v Villiers* that his decision is policy driven:

'. . . Parties to an agreement cannot contract out of the Rent Acts; if they were able to do so the Acts would be a dead letter because in a state of housing shortage a person seeking residential accommodation may agree to anything to obtain shelter. . . Since parties to an agreement cannot contract out of the Rent Acts, a document expressed in the language of a licence must nevertheless be examined and construed by the court in order to decide whether the rights and obligations enjoyed and imposed create a licence or a tenancy.' [at 1064]

This is not the first time that the House of Lords has given clear pre-eminence to policy over contractual terms. In *Johnson v Moreton*, an agricultural tenant covenanted not to serve a counter notice on his landlord, which effectively denied him security of tenure. The House of Lords held the covenant was ineffective as there was a public interest in tenants having security:

'. . . it can no longer be treated as axiomatic that, in the absence of explicit language, the courts will permit contracting out of the provisions of an Act of Parliament where that Act, though silent as to the possibility of contracting out, nevertheless is manifestly passed for the protection of a class of persons who do not negotiate from a position of equal strength.' [*op. cit.*, at 60]

Translated into the lease/licence arena, Lord Templeman is saying that, if a non-exclusive occupation clause is inserted as a pretence and is not intended to be relied upon, then this is an attempt to contract out of the Rent Acts and so cannot be allowed. (footnotes omitted)

The difficulty with the pretence doctrine is determining whether or not a term has been inserted 'for the purpose' of avoiding statutory protection. Simply because a right, for example, to introduce another occupant, has not yet been exercised, it does not follow that it is not a genuine clause or that it may not be intended to exercise it in the future: see *Crancour Ltd v Da Silvaesa* (1986) 52 P & CR 204 at 230. How are the courts to decide whether or not to read the agreement at its face value? In *AG Securities v Vaughan, op. cit.*, Lord Oliver said, at 1072:

. . . though subsequent conduct is irrelevant as an aid to construction, it is certainly admissible as evidence on the question of whether the documents were or
were not genuine documents giving effect to the parties' true intentions.

In the cases where the pretence doctrine has been used, the artificiality of the
clause has been evident from the factual matrix: the pre-existing relationship
between the occupiers, the negotiations, the fact that no attempt has been made
to exercise the right and the physical layout and size of the accommodation. In
Aslan v Murphy, op. cit., Mr Murphy occupied a small room (4ft 3in by 12ft 6in),
and yet the agreement denied him exclusive possession. The agreement also
stated that he only had a licence to use it from midnight to 10.30am and from
noon to midnight every day (that is, minus ninety minutes daily). Lord
Donaldson MR described these provisions as 'wholly unrealistic' and 'clearly
pretences', with the result that Mr Murphy had a lease. In *Duke v Wynne* (being
heard with the appeal on *Aslan v Murphy, op. cit.*), a three-bedroomed house had
been 'let' to the Wynne family, which included two children. The agreement
stated that the owner wanted to be able to get vacant possession on short notice,
and denied the occupier exclusive possession. The owner made no attempt to
introduce a third party and took no steps at all towards trying to fill the vacancy.
Lord Donaldson MR found the 'true bargain' to be

that the Wynnes should be entitled to exclusive occupation unless and until Mrs
Duke wanted to exercise her right to authorize someone else to move in as a
lodger, and she never suggested that this was a serious possibility. (at 137)

In *Antoniades v Villiers, op. cit.*, the flat was too small to introduce a third person.
   This doctrine of pretence has to date only been used in three situations:
1 Where joint occupiers have been made to sign two separate agreements

   There is an air of total unreality about these documents read as separate and
   individual licences in the light of the circumstance that the appellants were
   together seeking a flat as a quasi-matrimonial home, *per* Lord Oliver, *AG
   Securities v Vaughan, op. cit.*, at 1071;

2 Where the agreement includes an artificial non-exclusive possession or sharing clause

   It cannot realistically have been contemplated that the respondent would
   either himself use or occupy any part of the flat or put some other person in to
   share accommodation specifically adapted for the occupation by a couple living together, *per* Lord Oliver, *AG Securities v Vaughan, op. cit.*, at 1071; the idea that
   the first defendants might choose to sleep at the flat or take their meals there or
   put their guests up there overnight is simply fanciful, *Skipton Building Society v
   Clayton* (1993) 66 P & CR 223, finding of first instance judge referred to by Sir
   Christopher Slade at 231;

3 Where the occupant is artificially denied access for part of the day (as in *Aslan v Murphy, op. cit.*).

It has also been implicity accepted that a mobility clause could be struck out as a pretence. In *Westminster v Clarke, op. cit.*, Lord Templeman—in finding that there was a licence—stressed the special nature of the case and that because the mobility clause was important to the council to enable it to provide temporary accommodation to the homeless, there was no pretence involved.

The doctrine should not, however, be regarded as limited to these examples. Given the policy-led nature of the doctrine, it should be applied whenever a pretence is being used to circumvent protective legislation. This view is supported by the parallel development that has taken place towards tax-avoidance, the 'artificial transaction' doctrine.

A line of cases in the early 1980's, culminating with the House of Lords decision in *Furniss v Dawson* [*Ramsay (WT) Ltd v IRC, Eilbeck (Inspector of Taxes) v Rawling* [1982] AC 300; *IRC v Burmah Oil Ltd* [1982] STC 30; *Furniss (Inspector of Taxes) v Dawson* [1984] 1 All ER 530], decided that when there is a preordained series of transactions with one or more steps inserted with no independent commercial objective other than the avoidance of tax the court is permitted to disregard the intermediate artificial steps and look at the overall end result in order to determine the taxation consequences of the transactions. There is judicial authority for applying the artificial transaction doctrine to property cases. In *Gisborne v Burton* [[1989] QB 390], a landlord sought to avoid the security of tenure provision of the agricultural holdings legislation. To achieve this he proposed to grant the tenancy not directly to the proposed occupant but to his (the owner's) wife who would then sublet to the occupant. As a subtenant has no security against the superior landlord in the event of the superior lease being determined the landlord would be able to control the occupancy. The Court of Appeal held that this scheme was ineffective: '. . . a similar principle [*ie.* similar to the tax artificial transaction principle] must be applicable wherever there is a preordained series of transactions which is intended to avoid some mandatory statutory provision, even if not of a fiscal nature'. (at 399) (Bright, 1991, *op. cit.*, at p 142, footnotes omitted)

It has also been argued that the pretence doctrine should be applied when the owner insists on a letting to a company instead of an individual solely to avoid the application of the statutory codes and for no independent commercial purpose (see Bright, 1991, *op. cit.*). The courts have, however, tended to take a pre-*Vaughan* approach to sham in these cases and upheld the lettings as genuine: see *Hilton v Plustitle* [1988] 3 All ER 1051; *Kaye v Massbetter* [1991] 39 EG 129 ([1992] Conv 58). The difficulty with applying the pretence doctrine to these cases would be that it is much harder to prove that the identity of the tenant is *clearly artificial*—in most of the exclusive possession cases, the artificiality was evident from the fact that it would have been physically impracticable to implement the disputed term (*Duke v Wynne, op. cit.*, being a possible exception).

It is generally accepted that the approach in *Street v Mountford* applies equally to commercial agreements: see *University of Reading v Johnson-Houghton* [1985] 2 EGLR 113; *London & Associated Investment Trust plc v Calow* (1987) 53 P & CR 340; *Esso Petroleum Co Ltd v Fumegage* [1994] 46 EG 199 (business tenancies); and *Colchester BC v Smith* [1991] 2 All ER 29 (at first instance) (agricultural tenancy). In principle, the doctrine of pretence as used in *Vaughan* should also be applicable to commercial cases. As mentioned earlier, the related 'artificial transaction' doctrine developed in revenue cases has been applied to agricultural lettings (see *Gisborne v Burton* [1989] QB 390). Although, historically, the policy towards business lettings has been less interventionist than for the other sectors, it is now possible effectively to contract out of protection in all of the sectors—with Ministry approval (agricultural), court approval (commercial), and through use of the shorthold tenancy (residential) (see ch 6). The doctrine of pretence exists to ensure that the vulnerable are not exploited and this should apply to all sectors—if the owner wishes to avoid legislative control, he should do so by invoking the statutory methods for doing so which contain in-built protection for occupiers (through notice requirements or third party approval of the arrangement), not through clever drafting and dressing up agreements. There will, though, be fewer commercial cases in which the factual matrix reveals arrangements that are 'wholly unrealistic' or 'clearly pretences':

The decisions in both *Dresden Estates v Collinson* and *McCarthy v Bence* seem to indicate that the courts are willing to use the different factual matrix, within which business arrangements of this sort are entered into, to dictate the manner in which the documents are construed—not least, one suspects, because an intention to exercise clauses denying exclusivity can more readily be inferred than in the context of a residential letting, even if those rights have not actually been exercised. (Rodgers, *Share Farming, Joint Ventures and Problems of Exclusive Possession*, [1991] Conv 58 at p 63)

4.3.4 Exclusions from the Concept of Tenancy

In *Street v Mountford, op. cit.*, Lord Templeman recognized that, while exclusive possession is necessary for a lease, it is not decisive. The exclusive possession may be explained by something other than a lease:

. . . an occupier who enjoys exclusive possession is not necessarily a tenant. He may be owner in fee simple, a trespasser, a mortgagee in possession, an object of charity or a service occupier. (*Street v Mountford, op. cit.*, at 294)

. . . the only intention which is relevant is the intention demonstrated by the agreement to grant exclusive possession for a term at a rent. Sometimes it may be difficult to discover whether, on the true construction of an agreement, exclusive possession is conferred. Sometimes it may appear from the surrounding circumstances that there was no intention to create legal relationships. Sometimes it may appear from the surrounding circumstances that the right to exclusive possession is referable to a legal relationship other than a tenancy. Legal relationships to which the grant of exclusive possession might be referable and which would or might negative the grant of an estate or interest in the land include occupancy under a contract for the sale of the land, occupancy pursuant to a contract of employment or occupancy referable to the holding of an office. (*Street v Mountford, op. cit.*, at 300)

The intention to create a tenancy was negatived if the parties did not intend to enter into legal relationships at all, or where the relationship between the parties was that of vendor and purchaser, master and service occupier, or where the owner, a requisitioning authority, had no power to grant a tenancy. (*Street v Mountford, op. cit.*, at 295–6)

The three exceptional categories referred to by Lord Templeman are discussed below.

4.3.4.1 No Intention to Create Legal Relations

Lord Templeman's statement that there would be no lease where it appeared 'from the surrounding circumstances that there was no intention to create legal relationships' is consistent with the 'generosity factor' cases. In these cases, occupation was granted to someone as an act of friendship or generosity and was held to create a licence, not a lease. In *Facchini v Bryson* [1952] 1 TLR 1386, Denning LJ said at 1389:

In all the cases where an occupier has been held to be a licensee there has been something in the circumstances, such as a family arrangement, an act of friendship or of generosity, or such like to negative any intention to create a tenancy . . .

It is, however, difficult to accept Lord Templeman's analysis of this exception. From what he says elsewhere we would expect it to be the fact of exclusive possession that is important in determining whether there is a lease, not the motivation underlying the arrangement—as observed by Taylor J in *Radaich v Smith, op. cit.*, at 220:

. . . if, as Denning LJ himself agreed [in *Facchini v Bryson*], the relationship created between the parties by a particular transaction is to be determined by its substance and not by its mere form, I am unable to see that the fact that a particular transaction may have been induced by ties of kinship, or by friendship or generosity could operate to bring it within this exceptional class. Such considerations cannot operate to transmute a lease into a licence or a licence into a lease.

Indeed, it seems that many of these cases can in fact be explained by an absence of exclusive possession (as observed by Windeyer J in *Radaich v Smith, op. cit.*, at 223). An example is *Heslop v Burns* [1974] 1 WLR 1241. In *Street v Mountford, op.*

cit., Lord Templeman cites *Heslop* as an example of 'no intention to create legal relations' but it can also be explained on the ground that the occupiers did not have exclusive possession. In this case, the owner had formed an emotional bond with a family and provided them with free accommodation, in a separate house, until his death. The owner visited the family daily. Given the relationship between them, the Court of Appeal found it impossible to infer that the couple had the right to exclude the owner (see Stamp LJ at 1247).

In *Heslop v Burns*, the accommodation was provided on an entirely gratuitous basis. Given this, it may therefore also be correct to say (as the Court of Appeal did) that there was no intention to create any legal relations. (This could also explain other cases where the occupancy was rent free: *Booker v Palmer* [1942] 2 All ER 673; *Cobb v Lane* [1952] 1 All ER 1199.) It is more usual, though, to find some consideration being provided for the accommodation and in these cases it is hard to accept that the circumstances do negate any intention to enter into legal relations. Would the parties really not have intended any agreed obligations between them to be binding? What if the friend agreed to pay £30 per week— would the owner not be able to sue for this if the friend refused to pay? In several of the earlier cases, the courts were not denying *any contractual intention*, but an intention to create a *tenancy*—what both parties wanted was a licence. For example, in *Marcroft Wagons v Smith* [1951] 2 KB 496, Roxburgh J said at 508:

. . . the plaintiffs intended the defendant to remain for the time being in occupation of the premises for a consideration, but without becoming a tenant.

In *Errington v Errington & Woods* [1952] 1 KB 290, a father had bought a house for his son and wife and told them that if they lived there and paid the mortgage instalments, he would transfer the house to them when the mortgage was repaid. The Court of Appeal held that the couple were licensees, not tenants, Denning LJ stating at 298:

. . . although a person who is let into exclusive possession is *prima facie* to be considered to be a tenant, nevertheless he will not be held to be so if the circumstances negative any intention to create a tenancy . . . [If] the circumstances and the conduct of the parties show that all that was intended was that the occupier should be granted a personal privilege, with no interest in the land, he will be held to be a licensee only . . .

Again, more recently, in *Monmouth BC v Marlog* [1994] 44 EG 240, the first instance judge had said that there had been no intention to create any legal relationship. In the Court of Appeal, Nourse LJ said:

What the judge was really saying . . . was that there was no evidence that there was ever any intention . . . to create a sub-tenancy. (at 241)

In two recent cases it has been held that the existence of a family relationship did not prevent the creation of a tenancy: *Nunn v Dalrymple* (1989)

21 HLR 569 (although it was admitted that this factor *could* negate the existence of a tenancy); and *Ward v Warnke* (1990) 22 HLR 496 ('If the facts constitute a tenancy the relationship of the parties does not displace that' at 500). This is the more correct approach—if exclusive possession is granted, then the motive behind the occupancy agreement should not affect its interpretation.

The tendency has been for the courts to use the 'absence of contractual intention' as a tool to avoid the housing legislation in cases where the element of generosity would make its application unfair. In *Marcroft Wagons v Smith, op. cit.*, for example, the landlord allowed the tenant's daughter to remain in the property after the tenant's (her mother's) death to give her time to recover from her bereavement. She stayed for six months, paying rent weekly. When the landlord sought possession, the Court of Appeal held that the daughter was only a licensee. The Court was clearly influenced by the fact that it would be unfair to penalize the landlord with an irremovable tenant simply because he had acted with decency towards the daughter. Evershed MR said at 501:

I should be extremely sorry if anything which fell from this court were to have the effect that a landlord could never grant to a person in the position of the defendant any kind of indulgence. . . (Compare the comments of Denning LJ in *Facchini v Bryson, op. cit.*, at 1388: 'In such circumstances it would obviously be unjust to saddle the owner with a tenancy, with all the momentous consequences that that entails nowadays.'; see also Windeyer J in *Radaich v Smith, op. cit.*, at 222-3: 'These decisions are largely a by-product of rent restriction statutes and other legislation here and in England.' For further discussion, see Street [1985] Conv 328 at pp 331–2; Clarke [1986] Conv 39 at p 43.)

4.3.4.2 Possession Referable to a Legal Relationship other than a Tenancy

In *Street v Mountford*, Lord Templeman also accepted that there may be situations in which even though there is exclusive possession, there is still no lease as that exclusive possession is explained by there being some other relationship between the parties apart from a lease. This could be because the occupier is a trespasser or a mortgagee-in-possession. It is also long-established that a service occupancy is only a licence, although this is somewhat harder to rationalize as an exception. A still more difficult question is determining the status of a person allowed into occupation pending a sale or long term letting of the property, or holding-over at the end of a fixed term lease pending negotiations for a renewal. These are fairly common situations in practice, yet the courts have failed to adopt a consistent approach to these cases.

(a) *Occupation prior to sale or letting and holding-over*

In *Street v Mountford*, Lord Templeman included within his exceptional categories 'occupancy under a contract for the sale of the land'. The explanation provided by Hoffman J in *Essex Plan Ltd v Broadminster* (1988) 56 P & CR 353 ([1989]

Conv 55), as to why there is an exception in this situation, is that the exclusive possession is referable not to there being a tenancy but to the equitable interest which the purchaser has in the property pending completion:

[Counsel] drew attention to the fact that contracts for the sale of land commonly provide for the purchaser to be allowed into occupation as a licensee pending completion on terms that he is to pay all outgoings together with interest on the purchase money and is to keep the premises in good repair. The purchaser's possession is ancillary and referable to his interest in the land created by his contractual right to a conveyance and Lord Templeman acknowledges that such a relationship, although exhibiting the ordinary badges of a tenancy, does not create one. (at 355–6)

There is further support for this view in the judgment of Millet J in *Camden LBC v Shortlife Community Housing* (1993) 25 HLR 330, where he makes clear that the exception only applies where there is some other legal relationship between the parties:

Where, however, the *only* legal relationship between the parties is the relationship between the grantor and the grantee of a legal right of exclusive possession, a tenancy is created . . .

It follows, in my judgment that in the absence of some other legal relationship to which it can be attributed, the grant of a legal right of exclusive possession by a body with power to grant it to a body with power to take it creates the relationship of landlord and tenant. There is no room for 'special circumstances' to negative the legal consequences of the transaction. That is not to say that 'special circumstances' in the wider sense are irrelevant. They may negative an intention to create legal relations, or an intention to grant a right to exclusive possession; but that is all. Were it otherwise, there would be no standard by which 'exceptional circumstances' could be evaluated, and no workable test to enable those which lead to the creation of a licence only to be distinguished from those which lead to the creation of a tenancy. (at 341)

In the *Essex Plan* case, *op. cit.*, the exception was extended to cover occupancy under a licence agreement pending the exercise of an option to take a long lease of the property:

The option gave Essex Plan the right to call for the grant of the lease and therefore gave it in equity an immediate interest in the land. Its entry into occupation pending the exercise or expiry of the option was ancillary and referable to that interest. There is therefore no need to infer the creation of a tenancy which would give Essex Plan a different interest in the same land. (at 356)

The idea that the exception is limited to cases where the occupier has some other interest in the land (usually an equitable interest arising from an estate contract) is theoretically attractive and would explain some decisions. Thus the exception did not apply in *Bretherton v Paton, op. cit.*, where the occupier was given exclusive possession of property on the understanding that she would do it up with a view to buying it when it was in good enough condition for her to be able to obtain mortgage finance. There was no enforceable sale agreement and therefore no other interest in the land to which exclusive possession could be referred apart from a tenancy.

While it is possible to argue that Hoffman J's explanation should mark the limits of the exception, the courts' approach has varied. In some cases, there has been held to be a tenancy even though exclusive possession could be referred to some other interest in the land—thus casting doubt on whether there is in fact an exception in these cases. These are the cases in which a purchaser allowed into occupation pending completion has been held to be a tenant at will and not a licensee—see *Chamberlain v Farr* [1942] 2 All ER 567; *Wheeler v Mercer, op. cit.* On the other hand, there are numerous cases which have held that a person in exclusive possession is only a licensee, even though the occupant has no larger interest in the property to which the exclusive possession could be referred. The exception in these cases is being made much wider than suggested by Lord Templeman and Hoffman J. The explanation of these cases appears to be that the courts are being heavily influenced by the impact that statutory protection has upon the relationship, depending on whether it is placed into the tenancy or licence pigeonhole. In the business letting context, designation as either a tenancy at will or a licence will not attract statutory protection. In the residential context, however, it is only the licence arrangement that is outside the statutory code. Thus, the tendency has been for the courts to construe the relationship as one of tenancy at will in the business letting context and as a licence in the residential context. As Millet J feared in *Camden v Shortlife, op. cit.*, there appears to be no standard by which to judge 'exceptional circumstances' apart from a notion of whether it is 'right to infer a tenancy'.

In *Javad v Aqil, op. cit.*, Aqil was let into business premises while negotiating for a ten-year lease. The lease was never agreed and the Court of Appeal held that he was a tenant at will. It had not, however, been argued in *Javad* that Aqil might be a licensee; the alternative interpretation of the events put forward (and rejected) was that he was a periodic tenant. Nicholls LJ pointed out the need for caution in cases where the occupancy was 'subject to contract' for a larger interest:

Where parties are negotiating the terms of a proposed lease, and the prospective tenant is let into possession or permitted to remain in possession in advance of, and in anticipation of, terms being agreed, the fact that the parties have not yet agreed terms will be a factor to be taken into account in ascertaining their intention . . . They cannot sensibly be taken to have agreed that he shall have a periodic tenancy, with all the consequences flowing from that, at a time when they are still not agreed about the terms on which the prospective tenant shall have possession under the proposed lease, and when he has been permitted to go into

possession or remain in possession merely as an interim measure in the expectation that all will be regulated and regularised in due course when terms are agreed and a formal lease granted.

Of course, when one party permits another to enter or remain on his land on payment of a sum of money, and that other has no statutory entitlement to be there, almost inevitably there will be some consensual relationship between them. It may be no more than a licence determinable at any time, or a tenancy at will. But when and so long as such parties are in the throes of negotiating larger terms, caution must be exercised before inferring or imputing to the parties an intention to give to the occupant more than a very limited interest, be it licence or tenancy. Otherwise the court would be in danger of inferring or imputing from conduct, such as payment of rent and the carrying out of repairs, whose explanation lies in the parties' expectation that they will be able to reach agreement on the larger terms, an intention to grant a lesser interest, such as a periodic tenancy, which the parties never had in contemplation at all. (at 248)

In another commercial case, the tenant was holding-over at the end of a lease that had been excluded from statutory protection and was paying a periodic rent pending the agreement of a longer lease. It was held that he was a tenant at will. This meant that he did not now gain statutory protection which he had not previously had (*Cardiothoracic Institute v Shredcrest Ltd* [1986] 3 All ER 633). In a residential holding-over case, however, the Court of Appeal rejected the view that any contractual tenancy had been created (*Longrigg Burrough & Trouson v Smith* (1979) 251 EG 847). Indeed there was fairly open recognition of the impact of statutory control on the construction of the agreement:

The old common law presumption of a tenancy from the payment and acceptance of a sum in the nature of rent dies very hard. But I think the authorities make it quite clear that in these days of statutory control over the landlord's rights of possession, this presumption is unsound and no longer holds. The question now is a purely open question; it is simply: is it right and proper to infer from all the circumstances of the case, including the payments, that the parties had reached an agreement for a tenancy? (*per* Ormrod LJ in *Longrigg Burrough & Trouson v Smith, op. cit.,* at 849)

Similarly, in a residential case involving entering into occupation prior to agreement (as against holding-over), the Court of Appeal found that there was a licence only: *Sopwith v Stuchbury* (1983) 17 HLR 50, see especially the comments of Stephenson LJ at 74 and Kerr LJ at 78. Again, in *Sharp v McArthur and Sharp, op. cit.,* the Court of Appeal held that a person allowed to occupy property as a favour (but for consideration) pending sale to a third party was only a licensee. It was felt there were 'exceptional circumstances', but it is hard to see what these were, apart from the harshness of the vendor being unable to evict the occupant so that he could sell with vacant possession.

(b) *Service occupancy*

Where an employee is required to occupy his employer's accommodation in order to perform his job, he will generally be regarded as a licensee and not as a tenant. The reason for this is that the employee is seen not as occupying for himself but on behalf of his employer:

As Lord Templeman observed, 'the possession of the servant is treated as the possession and occupation of the master and the relationship of landlord and tenant is not created.' [*Street v Mountford, op. cit.*]. It may be questioned whether this attribution of 'possession' to the master as distinct from the 'servant' unduly echoes, in both terminology and ideology, a bygone age when the personality of the 'servant' was virtually suspended for the duration of his service. There is, however, surprisingly modern judicial support for the old view that the occupancy granted to an employee results in a mere licence provided that the occupancy is 'strictly ancillary to the performance of the duties which the occupier has to perform' within the employment relationship. [*Smith v Seghill Overseers* (1875) LR 10 QB 422 at 428]. (Gray, *Elements of Land Law*, 2nd edn, 1993, at p 714 (footnotes omitted))

The test is not simply whether it is a condition of his employment to live there, but whether this required occupation will enable him to perform his job better, as in the case of a caretaker. The test set out by Lord Reid in *Glasgow Corporation v Johnstone* [1965] AC 609 is whether it is *necessary or of material assistance* in carrying out his employment duties. Examples of licences include where a mechanic, also employed to drive coaches, was required to live at the premises so that he would be available in an emergency (*Norris v Checksfield* [1991] 1 WLR 1241), and where a surgeon was required to live at the hospital (*Dobson v Jones* (1844) 5 Man & G 112).

(c) *Local authority lettings of temporary accommodation*

There is some uncertainty over the status of lettings to homeless persons by local authorities in discharge of their obligations under the Housing Act 1985 (see ch 5). In *Ogwr Borough Council v Dykes* [1989] 2 All ER 880 ([1989] Conv 194), a homeless person was granted a licence for a period of thirteen weeks. She stayed beyond this period and eventually the local authority sought possession. The Court of Appeal held that, even though she had exclusive possession of the property, there was only a licence. The occupation was referable to the legal relationship arising from the authority's duties under the homeless persons' legislation and the occupant's acknowledgement of her situation negatived any inference of a tenancy. This decision was seriously doubted by the Court of Appeal in *Family Housing Association v Jones* [1990] 1 All ER 385. In this case, the temporary accommodation to a homeless person had been provided not by the local authority itself but by a housing association. This factor enabled Balcombe LJ to

distinguish the earlier case and to find that a lease existed—the exclusive possession could no longer be explained by reference to discharging statutory duties.
He also thought, however, that *Ogwr* was inconsistent with the decision in *AG
Securities v Vaughan, op. cit. Ogwr* was overruled by the Court of Appeal in *City of
Westminster v Clarke* (1991) 23 HLR 506. When *Clarke* went to the House of Lords
as *Westminster City Council v Clarke, op. cit.*, the earlier Court of Appeal decision
was reversed but *Ogwr* was not cited. Their Lordships also overturned other
aspects of the *Family Housing Association* decision.

In practice the issue is now unlikely to be of any significance. In view of the
interpretation given by the House of Lords to the Housing Act 1985, s 79(3) in the
Westminster case (see ch 6.3.2.1(c)), secure status turns not on whether a lease or
licence exists, but on whether there is exclusive possession—so whichever of the
cases is followed on this point, the occupier may still have protected status. In
addition, tenancies and licences granted to homeless persons by local authorities, housing associations or private landlords are not initially secure but only
become so if not determined within twelve months from the date upon which the
tenant is notified of the authority's decision on his status as a homeless person
(Housing Act 1985, Sch 1, para 4; Housing Act 1988, s 1(6)).

4.3.4.3 No Power to Grant a Tenancy

There can not be a tenancy if the grantor has no power to create a tenancy: see
Torbett v Faulkner [1952] 2 TLR 659; *Camden v Shortlife, op. cit.*. Yates and
Hawkins suggest this might provide a way to create a 'judge proof' licence. This
would be done by arranging matters so that the grantor lacks the legal capacity to
create a lease, perhaps by setting up a company with no capacity to licence or
lease the land (*op. cit.*, at pp 14–15).

4.3.5 Multiple Occupancy Arrangements

Flat and house sharing agreements can be particularly difficult to analyse where
accommodation is shared and there are separate occupancy agreements with
each person. Although most sharing households have a single tenancy agreement, in about 4 per cent of cases there are separate tenancy agreements: Down,
Holmans, Small, *Trends in the Size of the Private Rented Sector in England*,
Housing Finance No. 22, May 1994, p 7 at p 8 (although the article does not make
it clear if 'tenancy' is being used in a technical sense or as a synonym for occupancy agreement). The courts have considered three ways of looking at the relationship under separate occupancy agreements. First, that there is a series of
licences. No individual occupier has exclusive possession of any part, nor do the
occupants collectively have exclusive possession. Therefore, no individual has

security of tenure under the housing legislation. This was the result reached by the House of Lords in the first of the two appeals under consideration in *AG Securities v Vaughan, op. cit.* A large flat was let to four occupants who moved in at different times, were paying different rents, and signed separate licence agreements denying exclusive possession. As one left, the owner would find a replacement (with the agreement of the others). In practice, the occupiers agreed amongst themselves who would have which room and when one left those remaining might exchange rooms and leave a different room for the new occupant to have. The House of Lords held that they were licensees—there had been no question of pretence. As Lord Bridge said at 1061, the arrangement was

a sensible and realistic one to provide accommodation for a shifting population of individuals who were genuinely prepared to share the flat with others introduced from time to time who would, at least initially, be strangers to them.

Of the four unities required for there to be a joint tenancy, three were missing in *Vaughan*—time, title and interest. Only unity of possession existed. Nor could it be said that the occupants collectively had exclusive possession:

. . . if the licence agreement is what it purports to be, that is to say merely an agreement for permissive enjoyment as the invitee of the landlord, then each shares the use of the premises with other invitees of the same landlord. The landlord is not excluded for he continues to enjoy the premises through his invitees, even though he may for the time being have precluded himself by contract with each from withdrawing the invitation. (*per* Lord Oliver at 1074)

This result was also found in *Mikeover v Brady* [1989] 3 All ER 618, where a couple had signed two separate licence agreements, each containing an obligation to pay one half of the total rent for the flat. When the woman left, the man offered to pay the whole amount of the rent but the owner refused to accept it and continued to receive only the man's half of the rent. Slade LJ found, as a matter of construction of the agreements, that the owner had no right to introduce a new occupant to the flat during either agreement. This meant that the

effect was to confer on the defendant and Miss Guile together, so long as Miss Guile remained, a right of joint exclusive occupation of the property. (at 625)

Nevertheless, as the monetary obligations were not joint, there could not be a joint tenancy as one of the four unities, unity of interest, was absent. There was no pretence involved as the owner had, in fact, refused to accept the whole rent from the man. From this,

[it] follows that there was no joint tenancy. Since inter se Miss Guile and the defendant have no power to exclude each other from occupation of any part of the premises, it also follows that their respective several rights can never have been greater than those of licensees during the period of their joint occupation. (*per* Slade LJ, at 627)

In effect, Slade LJ found that even when the *Street v Mountford* conditions for a lease are met, there can be no lease in the case of co-occupation with separate agreements unless the four unities—time, title, interest and possession—exist. It has been argued that the court should have considered whether there was a lease in this situation taking effect (in equity) as a tenancy in common:

Where occupiers collectively have exclusive possession of accommodation for a term this fulfils the hallmarks of a lease. This will be the case where there are multiple sharing arrangements and the co-occupants take the accommodation as a group. The fact that the four unities are absent is unimportant provided that there is unity of possession, for there can still be co-ownership through a tenancy in common. There are arguments for saying that the result should be extended to cover any situation where the co-occupants enjoy de facto exclusive occupation of a dwelling, which is what the Court of Appeal tried to do in *Vaughan*. To reach this result would require a re-examination of the hallmarks of a lease. To reach the result that Mr Brady and Miss Guile [in *Mikeover v Brady*] were lessees requires no more than for the courts to admit that there is another method of co-ownership apart from the joint tenancy. (Bright, *Protecting multiple occupancy— Brady revisited*, (1992) 142 NLJ 575 at p 578. See also, Sparkes, *Co-Tenants, Joint Tenants and Tenants in Common*, (1989) 18 Anglo-Amer. L Rev. 151)

The second possible analysis in multi-occupancy situations is that each individual has exclusive possession of part of the premises—his bedroom—and shares the other facilities. This means that he has a lease of part, which is sufficient to provide security of tenure (Housing Act 1988, s 3).

The third analysis is that there is a joint tenancy of the whole, as was found in *Antoniades v Villiers, op. cit..* Here an unmarried couple had signed separate licence agreements, each of which stated that each occupier was liable for only half of the rent—this absence of unity of interest would usually prevent there being a joint tenancy. Nevertheless, the House of Lords said that the factual matrix, in particular the smallness of the flat, showed that it was a pretence to have two separate agreements and, so, they should be read together as a joint agreement. Once this was done it was possible to say that all four unities existed and there was no difficulty in finding a joint tenancy. (See Sparkes, *Breaking Flat Sharing Agreements*, (1989) 5 JSWL 295.)

It is also possible to have multi-occupancy when the owner has let accommodation to a tenant, who in turn allows in other occupiers, paying rent to the tenant. This occurred in *Monmouth BC v Marlog, op. cit..* Here, a council tenant, Mr Roberts, shared accommodation with Mrs Marlog and her children. They had separate bedrooms, but shared the living accommodation, and Mrs Marlog paid £20 a week to Mr Roberts. The Court of Appeal upheld the finding that Mrs Marlog was only a licensee, not a tenant:

Where two persons move into residential premises together under a tenancy granted to one but not the other of them, each occupying a bedroom or bedrooms and the remainder of the premises being shared between them, the court will be slow to infer a common intention that the one who is not the tenant shall be the subtenant of the one who is. The natural inference is that what is intended is a contractual house sharing arrangement under the tenancy of one of them. The inference is greater strengthened where, as here, there is a written agreement between the landlord and the tenant and none between the tenant and the other occupant. (*per* Nourse LJ at 241)

4.4 THE NEED FOR CERTAINTY

In order to be a lease, there must be a 'term certain', which means that the beginning, the duration and the end-date of the lease must be ascertainable as at the commencement of the lease. The need for certainty is long established in English law; in *Say v Smith* (1530) 1 Plowden 269 at 272, Anthony Brown, Justice, said:

... **every contract sufficient to make a lease for years ought to have certainty in three limitations, *viz*. in the commencement of the term, in the continuance of it, and in the end of it: so that all three ought to be known at the commencement of the lease.** (See also Sparkes, *Certainty of Leasehold Terms*, (1993) 109 LQR 93 for an account of judicial support for this rule.)

This requirement was recently re-affirmed by the House of Lords in *Prudential Assurance Company Limited v London Residuary Body* [1992] 3 All ER 504.

4.4.1 Types of Lease and Satisfying the Certainty Requirement

How this certainty requirement applies to leases is seen more easily when we look at the different types of lease that there are.

4.4.1.1 Fixed Term Leases

Due to requirements of certainty, the maximum duration of a fixed term lease must be known from the outset. So, in *Lace v Chantler* [1944] KB 368, a lease for the 'duration of the war' was held void for uncertainty. In the *Prudential Assurance* case, *op. cit.*, the London County Council granted a lease of a strip of land adjoining a road 'until the ... land is required for the purposes of the widening of Walworth Road and the street paving works rendered necessary thereby'. This was also void for uncertainty.

In both cases the desired result could have been achieved by a different route. In *Prudential Assurance, op. cit.*, Lord Templeman said, at 506:

The agreement was clearly intended to be of short duration and could have been secured by a lease for a fixed term, say five or ten years, with power for the land-

lord to determine before the expiry of that period for the purposes of road widening.

No reason is given why it is permissible to arrange the letting this way, save for the fact that it no longer offends the rule requiring a certain maximum duration. As Russell LJ observes in *Re Midland Railway* [1971] Ch 725 at 732, this distinction 'has an air of artificiality, of remoteness from practical considerations'.

Indeed, it is hard to find any justification for the rules on certainty. The certainty required in the cases appears to be not only linguistic certainty (that is, a sufficiently clear definition of the end-date), but also predictability (that is being able to predict when the end-date will occur). Why predictability is so important is not clear. In part, it may be a concern over potential perpetuity—if the end-date cannot be predicted, it may never occur. The dislike of perpetuity is evident from the Law of Property Act 1922, s 145, which converts perpetually renewable leases into leases for 2,000 years (see 4.2.4). In addition, the open-ended nature of such leases offends the tidiness of the 1925 legislation:

. . . the perpetual lease was a conceptual nonsense in that it postulated a term without a *terminus*. Such a lease struck at the heart of the doctrine of estates by threatening to confound the distinction between the term of years and the one perpetual estate recognised by the common law, the estate in fee simple. The perpetual lease offended against the intrinsic orderliness of the common law arrangement of estates. (Gray, 1993, *op. cit.*, p 689)

If perpetuity were the real concern, however, it could be met by statutory conversion of uncertain leases into, say, ninety-year leases determinable upon the earlier happening of the end-event (as Gray, 1993, *op. cit.*, suggests at p 692, and following the model of the Validation of War Time Leases Act 1944, which converted leases for 'the war' into leases for ten years determinable upon the earlier ending of the war). A similar solution has been proposed in New Zealand, in that a lease will be valid if the event upon which it is to end is adequately defined so as to be identifiable when it occurs (so complying with the need for linguistic certainty) and, if that event does not occur within ten years of the commencement of the lease, it will end on the tenth anniversary or on any later date specified in the lease (so meeting concerns over perpetuity)—see Wilkinson, *Fresh Thoughts from Abroad*, [1994] Conv 428.

The underlying concern in many of the cases is that these 'uncertain leases' have become grossly unfair over time:

In most of the arrangements to come before the courts the parties only ever envisaged a short term letting. In these cases it is not perpetuity *per se* that forms the basis of the objection but the fact that this was not part of the bargain envisaged by the parties.

Contractual Imbalance
The fact that the letting was intended by the parties to be fairly short term and

was drafted on that basis means that the arrangement, initially evenly balanced, becomes heavily slanted against the landlord over time. What was initially a reasonable rent for the premises becomes an unreasonable one. . . In the *Prudential Assurance* case, Lord Templeman refers to the fact that the agreement purported to grant a term of uncertain duration which, if valid, now entitles the tenant to stay there for ever and a day at the 1930 rent of £30; valuers acting for both parties have agreed that the annual current commercial rent exceeds £10,000 [at 506] . . . . (Bright, *Uncertainty in Leases—Is it a Vice?*, (1993) 13 Leg. Stud. 38 at pp 44–5)

Contract law doctrine does not, however, permit renegotiation of long term relational contracts. By applying the certainty rule the courts are, in effect, able to open up the relationship to enable the parties to renegotiate the lease on new and fairer terms:

. . . given the restrictive approach of contract law, the courts have in fact been able to achieve relatively sensible (and reasonably fair) results by resorting to the ancient rule in property law requiring certainty in relation to leasehold terms. By declaring the lease void or terminable upon service of common law notice it is, in fact, opening up the relationship to be renegotiated to reflect current property values. The outcome is the same as would have been achieved through application of the frustration doctrine—but has been achieved by using the language of property law rather than contract. (Bright, 1993, *op. cit.*, at p 47)

An alternative, more flexible, approach would be for contract law to be changed so as to additionally permit renegotiation where the parties had contracted on the joint assumption that the terminating event would occur within a short period and allocated risks on this basis, but in fact the event does not occur and the lease becomes imbalanced over time (see Bright, 1993, *op. cit.*, pp 49–end). In cases such as *Lace v Chantler, op. cit.*, where the lease has not run for a long time, the parties should be held to their bargains. To strike down the contractual agreement because it offends the certainty rule defeats the parties' intentions without good justification. In the *Prudential Assurance* case, *op. cit.*, Lord Browne-Wilkinson invited the Law Commission to review the basis of the rule requiring a term certain, in effect inviting its abolition:

No one has produced any satisfactory rationale for the genesis of this rule. No one has ever been able to point to any useful purpose that it serves in the present day. (at 512)

The views argued here are not universally accepted. There are some who defend the certainty rule on the grounds that it promotes care in drafting the terms of agreements:

. . . there is much to commend a certainty rule which is simple and which penalises carelessness in drafting of leasehold agreements, especially since the policy of the 1925 legislation is to favour the security of titles. (Smith, *What is Wrong with Certainty in Leases?*, [1993] Conv 461 at p 465)

It is also seen as a necessary concomitant of the fact that leases are estates and that there are sound legislative-policy reasons for requiring certainty (Smith, 1993, *op. cit.*, at pp 464–5). Why the fact that a lease is an estate requires predictable certainty is not, however, made clear. Sparkes also defends the certainty rule, fearing that any relaxation would

be to allow the creation by accident of an incumbrance against property of indefinite duration at what may become a derisory rent. (Sparkes, 1993, *op. cit.*, at p 113)

These fears could, however, be met by either adopting the solution proposed in New Zealand or by a development of rules permitting renegotiation as suggested above.

4.4.1.2 Leases for Life

Under the certainty rule a lease granted for someone's life, or until they marry, would be void. However, by the Law of Property Act 1925, s 149(6), a lease at a rent or for a premium which is granted for someone's life or until a person marries, or granted for a term which will end on death or marriage, is converted to a lease for 90 years. After the person's death or marriage, either party can end the lease by serving notice.

4.4.1.3 Periodic Tenancies with No Restriction on the Right of Either Party to Terminate

Lord Templeman made clear in *Prudential Assurance, op. cit.*, that the rule on certainty applies equally to periodic as to fixed leases. Nevertheless, it is not clear how (or why) the certainty rules apply to periodic tenancies. At the beginning of a periodic tenancy, it is not known what the maximum duration will be. As Russell LJ pointed out in *Re Midland Railway, op. cit.*, at 732:

. . . It cannot be predicated that in no circumstances will it exceed, for example, 50 years; there is no previously ascertained maximum duration for the term; its duration will depend on the time that will elapse before either party gives notice of determination.

Yet the juristic nature and legal quality of periodic tenancies is not doubted. The most common explanation as to how they satisfy the requirements of certainty is that each separate period is of known maximum duration:

A tenancy from year to year is saved from being uncertain because each party has power by notice to determine at the end of any year. . . (*per* Lord Templeman, *Prudential Assurance, op. cit.*, at 510)

But this is highly unsatisfactory as an explanation. It ignores the fact that periodic tenancies are not seen as a series of separate and new tenancies but as one continuing tenancy (see Lord Bridge, *Hammersmith and Fulham LBC v Monk* [1992] 1 All ER 1 at 9).

A preferable approach would be to say that the rule on certainty does not apply to periodic tenancies. There is no reason why it should: it is not necessitated by the definition of 'term of years absolute' in the Law of Property Act 1925, s 205, which refers to terms 'for a fraction of a year or from year to year' quite separately from the reference to certainty earlier in the definition. Nor are periodic tenancies objectionable in principle. Either party can serve notice ending the relationship. Ability to predict the overall maximum duration is not important. They do not tend to perpetuity, in that they can be ended at any time on notice. The fairness of the bargain is achieved by the power to end the relationship—in effect, a renegotiation tool. The tenant's position, in so far as it is perceived to need protection, is protected through the relevant statutory codes (see ch 6).

4.4.1.4 Periodic Tenancies with a Contractual Fetter on the Right to Terminate

By confirming in *Prudential Assurance, op. cit.*, that the certainty rule applies with equal force to periodic tenancies as to fixed leases, Lord Templeman overruled several inconsistent Court of Appeal decisions (some were directly overruled, others implicitly). Most of these cases were concerned with the effectiveness of a contractual fetter on the common law right to serve a notice to quit—for example, where the landlord agrees not to serve a notice to quit unless he wants the premises for his own occupation. Many of these cases talked in terms of 'repugnancy' as invalidating periodic tenancies rather than 'uncertainty', but the courts have not shown a consistent approach.

In both *Re Midland Railway, op. cit.*, and *Breams Property Investment Co Ltd v Strougler* [1948] 2 KB 1, the Court of Appeal upheld periodic tenancies that contained provisos preventing the landlord from ending the tenancy unless the premises were required for the landlord's own use. Yet in other cases, the courts have said that restrictions on the right to determine the lease are repugnant to the nature of periodic tenancies. In *Cheshire Lines Committee v Lewis & Co* (1880) 50 LJQB 121, the Court of Appeal held a lease invalid where the landlord agreed not to serve a notice to quit until the landlord wanted the premises 'to pull them down'. In *Centaploy v Matlodge* [1974] Ch 1, a tenancy of garages terminable only by the tenants was held void. In the *Prudential Assurance* case, *op. cit.*, Lord Templeman considered the possibility that the lease, being void as an attempted fixed term, nevertheless took effect as a yearly tenancy subject to a restriction that the landlord would not end the lease unless the property was required for the road widening. He firmly rejected this idea on the grounds that this

would make a nonsense of the rule that a grant for an uncertain term does not create a lease and would make nonsense of the concept of a tenancy from year to year because it is of the essence of a tenancy from year to year that both the land-

lord and the tenant shall be entitled to give notice determining the tenancy. (at 508)

Re Midland Railway, op. cit., was disapproved.

Following *Prudential Assurance, op. cit.*, it seems that a distinction needs to be drawn between three kinds of fetters:

1 *Total restrictions*—where one party has no right to end the lease (as in *Centaploy v Matlodge, op. cit.*). In this case, the lease will be void.

2 *Partial restrictions*—where one party cannot end the lease 'unless a defined event happens', as in *Cheshire Lines Committee v Lewis & Co, op. cit..* Such leases will also be invalid—hence in *Prudential Assurance, op. cit.*, the House of Lords overruled *Re Midland Railway, op. cit.* (but see Wilde (1994) 57 MLR 117, who argues that these leases are not uncertain).

3 *Restrictions limited to a fixed time*—where one party cannot end the lease for a set period 'unless a defined event happens' (as in *Breams Property Investment Co Ltd v Strougler, op. cit.*, where the restriction on the landlord serving notice only applied for the first three years). These leases would still be valid: in *Prudential Assurance, op. cit.*, Lord Templeman said that

[a] lease can be made from year to year subject to a fetter on the right of the landlord to determine the lease before the expiry of five years unless the war ends. (at 510)

In any of the cases where the lease is said to be invalid, it may still take effect as a periodic tenancy, but without the restriction.

Most of the cases have approached the problem from a property perspective, starting with the premise that it is inherent to the nature of a periodic tenancy that either party should be able to end the lease by serving the appropriate notice, although Lord Templeman in *Prudential Assurance, op. cit.*, spoke in terms of uncertainty rather than repugnancy. However, in *Re Midland Railway, op. cit.*, Russell LJ approached the problem differently. Instead of adopting a property analysis, he looked at periodic tenancies as a contractual agreement between two parties. This meant that instead of simply stating that certain matters are inconsistent with the nature of periodic tenancies (without offering any explanation as to why they should be), he saw the tenancy as a contract between two people and then asked if there were any reasons in property law why effect should not be given to this bargain:

Our instinct . . . is to give effect if possible to the bargain made by the parties . . . [We] see no reason why an express curb on the power to determine which the common law would confer upon the lessor should be rejected as repugnant to the nature of the leasehold interest granted. (at 733; see also Fox LJ in *Ashburn Anstalt v Arnold, op. cit.*, at 156: '. . . there is no reason why the court should not hold the parties to their agreement'. This was overturned by *Prudential Assurance, op. cit.*)

To approach the matter from a contractual perspective would mean that these periodic tenancies would be upheld. There is no good reason why the parties should not be able to agree that one of them can fetter his common law right to end the lease. Nor should it matter if the restriction is total or partial. In *Centaploy, op. cit.*, why should the landlord not be free to agree that only the tenant can end the lease? Again, in *Cheshire Lines, op. cit.*, why should the landlord not be able to agree that the tenant could have the premises until the landlord wanted to pull them down? In each of these cases it may be that some would say that the landlord is making an imprudent bargain, but this in itself is surely not sufficient to justify the courts interfering with the contractual relationship. So long as we respect contractual freedom, there are no grounds to interfere with the initial bargain. If the contract has become grossly imbalanced over time, for instance, because it was jointly envisaged that the trigger event permitting service of a notice would happen within a short period but this has not occurred, then the parties should be free to renegotiate the lease—as argued earlier in relation to fixed term leases. (For further discussion, see Bright, 1993, *op. cit.*, at pp 50–2.)

The present law, as applied in *Prudential Assurance, op. cit.*, would result in the 'tenant' not having a lease which is secure until the triggering event occurs (void for a repugnant fetter), and hence no real security from day one and no compensation for being evicted. The landlord could simply change his mind, and serve a notice to quit, notwithstanding the contractual arrangement. While some would argue that the fact that a periodic tenancy is an estate should make all the difference, it is hard to understand why this is so (see Smith, 1993, *op. cit.*).

5

Entering into the Lease

This chapter will look at issues that arise when the parties are entering into a lease—from selecting a tenant, to the form that a lease will take.

5.1 ALLOCATION

5.1.1 Introduction

The first issue is to ask how the landlord selects tenants, and *vice versa*. Is it commercial or social considerations that are important, or a combination of these? In the social sector, the landlord's choice on allocation of empty property is heavily circumscribed by statute with the intention of giving housing to those in the greatest need of it.

The tenant seldom chooses property because of who the landlord is; more important are the characteristics of the property itself. The choice of property is generally governed by considerations of availability, affordability and the standard of accommodation and service provision. Within the residential sector, the shortage of public sector and housing association accommodation means that many potential occupants are excluded from this sector and are forced into the lower end of the private residential sector (or onto the streets). For superior quality housing, the only choice is the private sector.

Table 5.1 Households and dwellings in England and Wales 1951–91 (millions)

	1951	1961	1971	1976	1991
Total dwellings	12.53	14.65	17.02	18.1	20.81
Total households	13.26	14.72	16.78	17.6	19.86
Difference	(0.729)	(0.078)	0.245	0.5	0.95

Sources: Malpass & Murie, *Housing Policy and Practice*, 4th ed. 1994, at p 71; LRC Housing Update at p 3, ROOF, November/December 1992

Housing statistics, therefore, can paint a misleading picture. As Table 5.1 shows, there was a surplus of approximately one million homes by 1991. Nevertheless, it does not follow that there is adequate housing provision. Many homes remain empty, despite the fact that they are owned by public bodies. In 1994 there were 864,000 empty properties owned by such bodies as the Ministry of Defence, police authorities and local authorities, although the latter will often have obtained the house only in order to knock it down in line with a road widening plan under the Conservative government's transport policy—the *Guardian* p 4, 31 January 1994; the *Guardian* 2—Society pp 8–9, 28 September 1994. Allocation of housing remains an issue because not all of this residential accommodation is of the appropriate size or in the appropriate places. If people lived in appropriate sized units in those places where there was sufficient capacity and if cost factors were to be ignored, then, subject to renovation, there would again be less of a problem in allocating housing (see Audit Commission, *Developing Local Authority Housing Strategies*, 1992, Exhibit 7, p 12). However, . . .

The private market alone [private-rented and owner-occupation] is unable without subsidies to meet the objective of providing a decent home for every family. So the provision of social housing for those households who cannot afford the cost of housing of an acceptable standard in the private sector remains important in national policy. Currently the total demand for social housing is not being met and so 'need' has to be prioritized. Definitions of need are value judgements, but a family with children without secure accommodation would usually be included. In contrast, single young people living at home with their parents and with no serious family difficulties would probably not be included, even if they wished to find a home of their own. The point on the spectrum at which the definition of need is drawn is a matter of judgement and is partly conditioned by the available resources. But defining the level of need which is to be met and therefore the demand for social housing is essential to the determination of housing programmes at a national and local level. (Audit Commission, 1992, *op. cit.*, at para 13)

The Audit Commission predicted that about 740,000 new units of social housing will be required by 2001 (1992, *op. cit.*, Exhibit 3, p 7, and Appendix 1). The shortage of homes in the 'right place' has led to calls for empty office space in the major cities, which became free in the recession of the late 1980s and 1990s, to be converted for housing—Hendry, *Taking Back the Empties*, ROOF, September/October 1993, p 17; Joseph Rowntree Foundation Housing Research Findings No. 102, December 1993, and No. 111, March 1994.

Other things being equal, such as price, location and quality, a tenant may make a choice between landlords on the basis of their reputation for fair treatment of tenants. In the commercial sector it is property related considerations that tend to dominate the decision of which premises to take; such as location, the standard of the accommodation and services, and the leasehold terms.

Whereas for a residential tenant the rent payable under a lease and the length of the letting are quite likely to be the only terms discussed between the parties prior to the letting, a commercial tenant will generally take a much keener interest in other terms of the lease as these will impact upon the tenant's business and the ability to dispose of the lease during its life. A residential tenant will not usually be tied into the lease for a substantial period.

Allocation in the residential and commercial sectors is predicated on three criteria: commercial matters, personal factors and formal/mechanical rules. The latter has most bearing on the social sector. For all landlords, the likelihood that the prospective tenant will be able to pay the rent is an issue bearing on whether the lease should be granted. In the commercial sector it will be the most pressing of matters—but other commercially oriented decisions will also be taken by the landlord. In some developments, in particular shopping complexes, the long term success depends heavily on a carefully planned tenant mix. For instance, there is little point allocating all retail units in a shopping centre to one type of store, so a variety of retailers will be granted leases to encourage more shoppers and only healthy competition. In office blocks the issues are not as clear cut, for there may be less of a problem with having three firms of solicitors, for example, in one block; the landlord may prefer to have complementary professions, though, in order to improve the business accessibility of the tenants.

The factors determining the appropriate tenant mix in any one development are complex. They are an amalgamation of investment criteria as to the financial standing of tenants, planning criteria as to the most desirable range of goods and services for the locality, and management criteria as to the compatibility of deliveries, waste, opening hours and clientele between the range of tenants envisaged.

The managing surveyor will be seeking to satisfy customer needs . . ., to maximize turnover and enable tenants to pay top rents. (Arnison, Bibby and Mulquiney, *Commercial Property Management*, 1990, at para 10.3.1.2)

In the private residential sector, depending on the type of landlord, payment of rent will always be important, but certain other matters might impinge. To be dealt with in detail below with respect to the local authority sector, it has been shown that racist attitudes sometimes shape the landlord's decision—even in the 1950s, it was common to see signs in houses with rooms to let stating that Irish people need not apply, and the non-white community has more recently suffered much the same sort of discrimination, although more covertly. Further, the landlord may have a certain tenant-type in mind when putting the property out to let—if only a short-term commitment is desired, then students looking for accommodation during the academic year will appeal, while another landlord may want to avoid the hassle of continually finding 'safe' new tenants and may see the lease as a long-term investment. The extension of the Business Expansion

Scheme to include private sector residential tenancies added another twist, since the investors expected to be able to regain their capital after five years—the result was that during the period when Business Expansion Schemes extended to private sector leases, they tended to target the naturally mobile sector of the population, such as young professionals. Apart from legislation to prevent unlawful discrimination, however, the private landlord is under no formal obligations when allocating a lease.

Social sector landlords will have regard to commercial and personal factors, but also have to allocate in line with some formal rules. For some housing associations, the type of tenant they are to choose is laid down in their foundation instrument—for example, single parents or recently released prisoners; see Cope, *Housing Associations: Policy and Practice*, 1990, at pp 221–71. In *Re Gardom* [1914] 1 Ch 662, a charitable trust was established to provide housing to 'ladies of limited means'. Most of the larger housing associations, however, seek to provide general housing.

B3.1 Associations are expected to have allocation policies which are clear. They should be based upon the severity of an applicant's housing needs. Associations are expected to pay special attention to the specific housing difficulties experienced by particular groups. These will vary from time to time and from place to place. They may include—subject to the association's specific objects—elderly people, single people, families with young children, single parent families, people from ethnic minorities, young people without family support, women suffering domestic violence, disabled people and those who care for people who would otherwise be unable to remain in their own home, but this list is not intended to be exhaustive. (The Tenants' Guarantee, issued by the Housing Corporation under s 36A Housing Act 1985; Housing Corporation Circular 29/91, 1991. The new revised Tenants' Guarantee, provides similarly in §B5, but under §B1 associations should provide for open and equal access from all sections of the community—[*cf.* National Federation of Housing Associations' Formal Response, p 3])

Before 1988 the tenants of housing associations tended to be poorer than those renting from local authorities if the proportion of those claiming housing benefit provides any accurate guide. Since 1988, though, housing associations have had to find more of their income from the private sector and rents for new tenants have risen accordingly (see below, ch 8). On the other hand, where the housing has been obtained through a deal with the local authority, it may be that the agreement includes provision for the local authority to nominate prospective tenants—see revised Tenants' Guarantee, *op. cit.*, at §A3, which stipulates that local authorities should have 50 per cent of nominations; and Langstaff, 'Housing Associations: A Move to Centre Stage', in Johnston Birchall, *Housing Policy in the 1990s*, 1992, at pp 29 *et seq.*. In 1992/93, 45 per cent of all housing association new lets were made to local authority nominees—FactFile Figure 2, ROOF, July/August 1994.

Turning to local authorities, surprisingly, they are under no general obligation to provide housing.

Housing Act 1985 (as amended)
s 9(5) **Nothing in this Act shall be taken to require (or to have at any time required) a local housing authority itself to acquire any houses or other land for the purposes of this Part.** (Inserted by the Housing Act 1988, s 161(1))

This is not to ignore any specific duties in certain cases nor those duties to provide accommodation to some applicants, even if this is effected through a different landlord. By way of example, local authorities have obligations to those in need of care and attention by reason of age or infirmity, to those whose homes have been included in a designated slum clearance area and, most notably, to the homeless. Nevertheless, most local authorities retain some properties which they let to applicants on the general waiting list. The effect of the restrictions in the 1980s on new building and the loss of existing stock through the Right To Buy, though, has had several consequences for allocation policies. The first point to note is that the council properties which were sold tended to be family houses on the better estates, not the flats in tower blocks (see Malpass & Murie, 1994, *op. cit.*, pp 300–1; and see, 3rd edn, 1990, at p 273). Thus, the homes that are most sought by council tenants have become least available. Whereas in the 1970s local authorities, on the advice of the then government, ended the practice of putting families with children into tower blocks, there is now little option but to house them there for want of anywhere else—an estimated 40,000 children live in tower blocks, a dramatic increase on the figure for 1988 (see the *Guardian* p 9, 13 February 1993; and Prince Charles in the *Guardian* p 1, 27 October 1993, p 25, 29 October 1993): Tower Hamlets LBC has ended up making 'unfair and irrational' decisions in its allocation of properties to homeless applicants—a family of six, among other cases, were offered a flat on the twelfth floor of a tower block (see Rose LJ in *R v London Borough of Tower Hamlets, ex parte Mohib Ali et al.* (1993) 25 HLR 218 at 228—the policy itself was not declared unlawful). Furthermore, given that local authorities do possess certain specific duties to some particular applicants, fewer of those on the general waiting list can be given any accommodation. The government proposals, discussed below, 5.1.4.1(c), which will abolish priority for the homeless are premised on this argument.

The overall position for those seeking to rent has also been worsened by the decline in the number of private sector rentals available. This lack of availability is partly due to sales into the owner-occupied sector, but also as a result of disrepair. It is estimated that 864,000 homes are empty, mostly due to the need for repairs, with 100,000 of them owned by local authorities and over 700,000 empty units owned by private landlords or other public bodies (see the *Guardian* p 5, 8

June 1992; the *Guardian* p 4, 31 January 1994; the *Guardian* 2—Society pp 8–9, 28 September 1994). However, the most influential factor on allocation of residential dwellings in the rental sector is the state of the local authority sector since it still accounts for almost 60 per cent of the pool.

5.1.1.1 Policy towards Local Authority Allocations

Central government did little to intervene in the allocation policies of local authorities before 1988. In the words of Lord Porter in *Shelley v L.C.C.* [1948] 2 All ER 898 at 900, councils could 'pick and choose their tenants at will'. When the Cullingworth Report was published in 1969, (*Council Housing: Purposes, Procedures and Priorities*, 9th Report of the Housing Management Sub-Committee on the Central Housing Advisory Committee), it merely encouraged local authorities to adopt its recommendations. The most direct interference pre-1988 was seen in the Housing (Homeless Persons) Act 1977 (see now, Part III Housing Act 1985). The 1977 Act was, in part, passed to deal with the problem that local authorities were not, on the whole, taking measures to meet the needs of homeless people: legislation was necessary to impose an obligation, although government plans would severely curtail the rights of homeless applicants. The Housing Act 1980, while it introduced the Tenants' Charter, did little for the prospective tenant. The 1985 Act, though, made a slight inroad into local authority autonomy in this area. Section 21 reaffirmed the general powers of local authorities, but s 22 required them to grant a reasonable preference when allocating to a variety of applicants, including those living in insanitary conditions or where there is overcrowding and to those deemed homeless. This reasonable preference was found, despite its vagueness, to be justiciable in *R v Canterbury CC, ex parte Gillespie* (1987) 19 HLR 7. However, the position was completely changed by the Conservative government's 1987 White Paper on Housing (Cm 214).

1.16 Third, the Government will encourage local authorities to change and develop their housing role. Provision of housing by local authorities as landlords should gradually be diminished, and alternative forms of tenure and tenant choice should increase. Some authorities will want to move in this direction themselves, and the government will assist them. Some tenants will want to take the initiative and the Government will give them new rights to do so because this will enable them to improve their housing conditions and to have a say in their own future. Local authorities should increasingly see themselves as enablers who ensure that everyone in their area is adequately housed; but not necessarily by them.

Rather than trying to impose conditions on how local authorities ought to allocate, which would presume for them a role in the provision of accommodation, the government decided to provide the means whereby their housing stock would be transferred to other landlords (see, for example, Parts III and IV Housing Act 1988). The government sought to reduce local authorities to a role more akin to that they played in the nineteenth century of regulating the quality of housing, existing and proposed (see Harloe in van Vliet, *International Handbook of Housing Policies and Practices*, 1990, pp 121–2), and of pointing applicants for housing in the right direction. Such a drastic change, however, required private sector landlords and housing associations to be ready to step in and fill the gap lest the rented sector in general contract still further—they were not fully prepared and the Audit Commission stated in 1992 (*op. cit.*) that 740,000 new units of social housing alone would have to be built by 2001.

5.1.2 Landlords and Tenants

5.1.2.1 Landlords

In setting the laws on allocation in context, it is helpful to be aware that there are different types of landlord within each sector and that they may apply different preferences, priorities and prejudices when selecting their 'perfect tenant'.

Commercial landlords of prime properties tend to be investors. Often, short-term costs, such as development, will be met by banks, while long-term investment will be by the large institutions, for instance, pension funds or insurance companies, letting on 'clear' leases for 25 years (see 5.3.3, below). These institutional investors have large funds of money available for long-term investment and advantageous tax positions as regards investment in property. The clear lease passes on all unknown cost elements, such as the cost of repair and insurance, to the tenants ensuring that the landlord's return is certain, without any worry of unexpected maintenance costs eating into its income. This certainty of rental income is a critical factor to most commercial landlords.

There is a tendency to assume that all residential landlords are much the same. Leaving aside the local authorities, who are pretty uniform, there is a wide variety of other types of landlord, especially in the private sector. Housing associations range from the small charity with only a few properties through to the very large organisations such as Anchor or North British—8 per cent of housing associations control 75 per cent of the properties (see Gibb & Munro, *Housing Finance in the United Kingdom*, 1991, at pp 109–10). The larger associations function much like a local authority with professional managers and other staff. The smaller ones, while they too will employ professional staff, have little in common with the bureaucratic nature of the local authority—Cope, *op. cit.*, at pp 22 and 51. As such, they may well be able to have a more personal relationship with their tenants, but they are not in a position to take over estates from councils—

indeed, they may well have to be subsumed within one of the larger associations as the operating costs increase.

Mike Lazenby, Nationwide Building Society Head of Housing: **I think there will also be a contraction of housing associations, not least because some will go bust under the current regime.**
Margaret Mervis, Conservative Councillor, Chair of Housing Committee, Wandsworth, **I think there will be amalgamation, there will be the big ones, and there will be those who can just manage and not develop—and I do think some of them will just fall by the wayside.** (Blake, *Whose Future Is It Anyway?*, ROOF, September/October 1994, p 20 at p 24)

While the range of housing association landlords looks set to narrow, private sector landlords continue to be a varied group. One can differentiate between them simply on grounds of the size of their holdings, but this is to ignore the underlying factors behind the various types of landlord and landlordism. The Joseph Rowntree Foundation (Housing Research Findings No. 90, May 1993, Table 2) found that the vast majority of private sector landlords were individuals (but note that the Rowntree Inquiry did not list a category of employer landlords):

Table 5.2

Individual Landlords	%
Temporarily absent landlords	41
Landlords unable/unwilling to sell	18
Other individual landlords	26
Property Companies	
BES Companies	3
Other property companies	7
Organizations	
Mortgage lenders	1
House builders	1
Other organisations	3

This diversity in the private sector stems from the landlords having entered the market for an assortment of reasons. Allen and McDowell performed a wide-ranging survey of landlords in Islington and Hackney in London in the late 1980s which analysed landlord-types by reference to their objectives. They concluded that there were several different varieties of private sector landlord (see, Allen and McDowell, *Landlords and Property*, 1989, in ch 3, 4 and 5; see also ch 1.2.2).

[We] distinguish between six types of residential landlordism in Britain: traditional landlords, employer landlords, informal landlords, investor landlords, commercial landlords and financial landlords. (p 48; the case studies can be found at pp 74 *et seq.*)

According to Allen and McDowell (pp 49–50), traditional landlords provide accommodation for its economic return, but 'modified by a service ideology'— examples include the church and the Crown Estate. The housing is an investment, but they see themselves as, in part, providing a social service to their tenants. This implicit intention may influence the choice of individual tenants. Employer landlords (Allen and McDowell, *op. cit.*, pp 50–1) represent a continuation of nineteenth century practices, where an industrialist would build housing for the workforce on the grounds that it would improve production if they did not live in unhealthy housing—for example, Port Sunlight on Merseyside was built by Lever Brothers to provide homes for the workers at the soap factory and their families, Cadburys built homes in Bournville outside Birmingham for their chocolate factory workers and Rowntrees built New Earswick by York for the workers in their cocoa factory. The aim of employers today is to ensure that workers who are needed outside working hours, such as park keepers or school caretakers, are available; the employers have little interest in making a profit from their employees, so rent may be minimal. 'Informal landlords' is the term used by Allen and McDowell (*op. cit.*, pp 51–3) to describe very small landlords, with only one property, and resident landlords. Unlike the types of landlord to be considered below, while the level of rent is important, it is not a sufficient criterion in making a decision on the selection of a tenant. If the tenant is to be sharing the same accommodation with the landlord, then personal factors play a large part, as does the ability to be rid of the tenant with as little delay as possible. Investor landlords may well also be informal landlords. Allen and McDowell (*op. cit.*, pp 53–4) define them in terms of the source of their properties, which is usually by way of a legacy. They then make a generalization, that while the historic costs will be low, the maintenance costs may well be high on old buildings. This categorisation is the least satisfactory of those made by Allen and McDowell and seems too much premised on the inner-city areas of North London chosen for the survey. This is not to say that there are not a certain number of landlords who have inherited their property and find it to involve high maintenance costs, but that they can probably be fitted into one of the other five categories. Commercial landlords let property for the profit (see Allen and McDowell, *op. cit.*, at pp 54–5). They seek to maximize their return, both in terms of rent received and in terms of capital outlay by selling the property. There are large areas of overlap between this sub-group and investor landlords and Allen and McDowell do not make clear the divide between the two. BES companies (companies established under the government's former Business Expansion Scheme) would probably fall under this heading. A report published in 1991 estimated that during the first two years of BES assured tenancies, approximately 9,700 rented properties were provided by BES companies (Crook, Kemp, Anderson, Bowman, *The Business Expansion Scheme and Rented Housing*, 1991); more recently it has been estimated that BES provided an extra 40,000 homes (Joseph Rowntree Housing Research Summary, December 1993). Finally, financial landlords, which term is meant to include public property companies and financial institutions such as insurance companies and pension funds, are again out to maximize their profits, but they have much greater capital assets to utilize and investment in rented housing is but a small part of their portfolio; BES companies may fall into this category, too. Rented housing does not provide sufficient guarantees for such landlords, according to Allen and McDowell (*op. cit.*, pp 55–7), especially in a time of recession in the housing market, so there seems to be a policy of disinvestment, but they still remain a significant proportion of all landlords.

Allen and McDowell's classifications are a useful analysis of landlord types and give greater insight than those based on mere size of holdings, although some of their own definitions do seem to hark back to the level of the landlord's investment. Better, however, is their analysis of what various landlord groups want out of their properties and, therefore, the types of tenant to whom they would allocate accommodation.

Having examined the types of landlord, it is now proper to consider what it is that those landlords look for in a tenant.

5.1.2.2 Tenants

If landlords are varied, tenants are positively disparate. Most of the research as to what residential landlords look for in a tenant has focussed on the public sector, partly because it is the largest landlord and partly because it is associated with certain types of tenant. In searching for the 'perfect' tenant, it seems to be part of the private sector landlord's property rights that he be able to choose whomsoever he wishes, as long as this is consonant with non-discrimination laws—as an example of this discretion, in the United States landlords of a quarter of all the rental units would not let to households with children (van Vliet, *op. cit.*, p 342). The different types of landlord enumerated above by Allen and McDowell will have different perceptions of the profile of the perfect tenant, but their choice is constrained by legislation or public views as to the role of private rented accommodation in only limited ways (*cf.* insurance companies have indicated that they might not provide cover if tenants are either students or are unemployed and claiming Housing Benefit—the *Guardian* p 33, 5 June 1993). In practice, however, with the growth in owner-occupation, private landlords have disproportionate numbers of the elderly, the young and poorly paid, non-vulnerable, single persons: the elderly because they were in secure, unfurnished accommodation before the start of the owner-occupation boom and could not afford to take on a mortgage late in their working lives, the young because they have yet to settle down and renting enhances mobility, and non-vulnerable, single people because they do not qualify for council housing and cannot afford to buy. The Joseph Rowntree Foundation (Housing Research Findings No. 90, *op. cit.*, Table 1, *Lettings Activity in 1992 Compared with 1991 by Employment Status and Household Type*) found that the private sector was becoming ever more directed towards certain social groups: the survey of members of the Association of Residential Letting Agents found that generally lettings were up, but that this was concentrated on unemployed people (54 per cent of ARLA members found an increase as opposed to only 4 per cent recording a decrease) and single people (52 per cent: 8 per cent).

Table 5.3 Lettings activity 1992 compared to 1991 by employment status and household

	Increased %	Unchanged %	Decreased %
Employment Status			
People in work	38	44	18
Unemployed people	54	42	4
Students	16	76	8
Retired people	18	70	12
Other	15	75	10
Household Type			
Single people	52	40	8
Childless couples	41	56	3
Families with children	44	44	12
Elderly people	15	70	15
Other	10	79	11

This situation, though, is the result of external factors rather than any systematic attempt by private sector landlords to attract such tenants. A similar situation has arisen in Australia.

[After] housing costs are considered, the percentage of private renting units who are 'very poor' rises to 12.7, while among all other income units the percentage falls to 5.1. This relationship can be seen another way: although only 21.4 per cent of all income units are private renters, 40.8 per cent of all income units which are 'very poor' after housing costs rent private accommodation . . .

The findings in *Poverty in Australia* also demonstrate that some of society's most vulnerable groups are likely to be tenants: 35.5 per cent of all migrants, Aboriginals and 'disability combination' income units, 27.4 per cent of all single

females, 25.7 per cent of all single parent families and 25.4 per cent of all sick, unemployed and invalids are private tenants, compared with a total community figure of 21.4 per cent. (Australian Poverty Commission 1975 Report, cited as still accurate by Sackville & Neave, *Property Law: Cases and Materials*, 5th edn, 1994, para 9.4 p 644; see also, van Vliet, *op. cit.*, pp 742 *et seq.*)

Public sector landlords, on the other hand, are meant, to some extent, to be providing a welfare service and it seems appropriate, therefore, to judge the allocation policies they adopt—there is a system that can be examined.

The social housing sector in Germany, which receives government subsidies, is contractually bound to accept only tenants whose income falls within specified limits.

In areas of urgent demand, for housing, the landlord is obliged to rent social housing units only to households that are proposed by the municipal housing agency. Furthermore, additional 'strings attached' may be agreed upon between the housing investor and the public agencies during the application and the allocation of the subsidy. In such cases, the municipal housing agency may have the right to nominate families with many children or with disabled persons as candidates for a rental contract. (see van Vliet, *op. cit.*, pp 138–9)

No such strict rules exist in Britain, though deals may be negotiated between local authorities and housing associations. Housing associations are having to reassess their image in the light of the increases in rent resulting from the changes wrought in the Housing Act 1988 and to try and improve the public view of renting.

In a number of visible locations, particularly in the inner city, housing association developments threaten to become synonymous with unemployment, social deprivation and, in the view of some, failure. (see Dow, *Move On Up*, ROOF, November /December 1992, p 18)

Dow argued that failure to attract those not dependent on state benefits into renting would trap the traditional type of tenant into ghettoes of poverty. The figures in Table 5.4 reveal the dramatic increase in the number of unemployed and single parent (At Home) tenants in housing association properties. On the other hand, housing associations are having to balance their welfare role with the need to be able to charge market rents and the desire to make renting generally attractive so as to prevent residualization of a particular housing sector and its tenants. The inherent contradiction in this position is evident in the Tenants' Guarantee, *op. cit.*, promulgated by the Housing Corporation, a government quango (see §§D2 and D3).

§D2 Where housing association accommodation has been provided with the help of public subsidy, . . . , it is intended to be accessible to people on low income, whether or not they are in paid employment or in receipt of housing benefit.

Table 5.4 Economic status of head of household (% to 31 March)

Status	1990/91	1991/92	1992/93
Working full-time	26	21	19
Working part-time	4	4	4
Govt. training scheme	1	1	1
Unemployed	24	29	33
Retired	30	27	23
At Home	9	11	13
Student	2	2	2
Sick/disabled	4	5	5
Child	0	0	0
Total	100	100	100

Source: FactFile, *op. cit.*, Figure 6

Associations are therefore expected to set and maintain their rents at levels which are within the reach of those in low paid employment. This will usually entail setting rents at below market level ...
§D3 In addition, associations are expected to take account of the need to cover the costs (after subsidy) of loan charges and of management and maintenance ... (The revised Tenants' Guarantee, *op. cit.*, amends §D2—housing associations would no longer be 'expected' to set rents within the reach of the low-paid, but should merely 'endeavour' so to do. The National Federation of Housing Associations' Formal Response is completely opposed to the change and the dilution of the government's commitment to affordable housing)

The role of the local authority is currently under debate again, although the discussion goes back to the beginnings of council housing in this country after World War I (see above, ch 2). However, local authorities have never been obliged to play solely a welfare role. Indeed, the Cullingworth Report (*op. cit.*) noted that

the underlying philosophy seemed to be that council tenancies were only to be given to those who 'deserved' them, and the 'most deserving' should get the best houses. Thus, unmarried mothers, cohabitees, 'dirty' families and 'transients' tended to be grouped together as 'undesirables'. Moral rectitude, social conformity, clean living and a 'clean' rent book on occasion seemed to be essential qualifications for eligibility—at least for new houses. (cited in Malpass & Murie, 1994, *op. cit.*, at pp 282-3)

Local authorities always preferred to let their properties to the better-off working class, the skilled labourers. Commercially this policy made sense, but the essence of allocation policies in the local authority sector should turn on the perceived nature and purpose of the housing. Regardless of local authority preferences however, since the early 1960s owner-occupation has become more popular and more accessible to a wider proportion of society. According to Harloe (van Vliet, *op. cit.*, pp 91–3), the percentage of skilled manual workers who were home owners rose from 37 per cent to 56 per cent between 1961 and 1981, and the 1980s then saw the biggest ever rise in owner-occupation in general. Concomitantly, local authority properties tended to serve the semi- and unskilled workers and an increasing number of economically inactive heads of households. While a fair proportion of the latter were elderly persons who missed out on the boom in owner-occupation, a position similar to that found in the private sector, many were unemployed or single parents: council housing is being allocated along welfare model lines by default.

So far the consideration of allocation policies has focussed on who should have priority for the grant of a lease, but the converse, which groups of applicant will be excluded, whether expressly or implicitly, also deserves attention. The limits of the present legislation on homelessness include the fact that it excludes the single, non-vulnerable applicant from the opportunity of using that route to obtain housing or rehousing; however, such matters are examined below. Here, the emphasis is on the prejudices of landlords. Discrimination occurs on the basis of race, gender and sexual orientation—see Handy, *Discrimination in Housing*, 1994; Johnson, *Untold Tales of the City*, ROOF, September/October 1994, p 13; *cf.* revised Tenants' Guarantee, *op. cit.*, §§B2(e) and B6. The Sex Discrimination Act 1975 and the Race Relations Act 1976 both provide that it is unlawful to discriminate on the stated grounds in the allocation of rented housing (see, SDA 1975, ss 1, 2 and 30(1) and RRA 1976, ss 1, 3 and 21(1)—the wording is almost identical).

Race Relations Act 1976

s 21(1) It is unlawful for a person, in relation to premises in Great Britain of which he has power to dispose, to discriminate against another -
   (a) in the terms on which he offers those premises; or
   (b) by refusing his application for those premises; or
   (c) in his treatment of him in relation to any list of persons in need of premises of that description.

(There is an exception in both statutes for resident landlords and small premises; see also, Handy, *op. cit.*)

Racism affects allocation in all tenures, although whether that is direct or merely a result of institutionalized racism in society in general cannot be gleaned from the empirical research. Nor is the quality of the housing in each tenure held by each ethnic group evident from these bald statistics—Asian families in Oldham are predominantly owner-occupiers, but they live in older, more run-down, substandard properties which are often overcrowded (Steele, *Unfair Shares*, ROOF, May/June 1994, p 17).

Table 5.5 Percentage of households in each tenure by ethnic group, Great Britain 1991

	Owner-occupiers	Private renters	Social renters
Indian	82	8	10
Pakistani	77	11	13
White	67	9	24
Chinese	62	21	17
Head born in Ireland	55	13	31
Black Caribbean	48	7	45
Bangladeshi	45	12	43
Black African	28	20	52

Taken from LRC Housing Update p 2, ROOF, May/June 1994—original source, Census Report for Great Britain 1991, OPCS, Crown Copyright

Nevertheless, several studies have found that landlords, especially local authorities (although this may merely reflect the ease with which data necessary for an empirical study can be garnered with respect to council housing), discriminate on grounds of race, giving the poorest quality housing to members of Afro-Caribbean and Asian ethnic minorities (Smith and Hill, 'An Unwelcome Home', in Grant, *Built to Last*, 1992, pp 101 *et seq.*; Ginsburg & Watson, 'Issues of Race and Gender Facing Housing Policy', in Johnston Birchall, *op. cit.*, pp 140 *et seq.*; Steele, *op. cit.*). In the late 1970s and early 1980s Henderson and Karn examined allocation policies in Birmingham (*Race, Class and State Housing: Inequality and the Allocation of Public Housing in Britain*, 1987, p 273) and found that ghetto-ization resulted as much from the desires of white applicants as it did from council policies—prospective white tenants wanted suburban estates and so strong was this desire that council officials tended not to offer them inner city properties, leaving them for Afro-Caribbean and Asian applicants (see, however, Jacobs, *Race, Empire and the Welfare State: Council Housing and Racism*, (1986) 5:1 Critical Social Policy 6, which suggests that racism and social control are central to any analysis of the British welfare state; see also, the *Guardian* p 9, 18 February 1994). Moreover, the pressures on local authorities to ensure that properties do not remain empty for very long reinforce this cycle of ghetto-ization, because housing officers see little point in offering poor quality inner city dwellings to white applicants knowing that they will reject them (see, Malpass and Murie, 3rd edn, 1990, *op. cit.*, at p 259; Black, *Waking Up To Racism*, ROOF, January/February 1994, p 20). In response to such practices, the Commission for Racial Equality (CRE) had to take Liverpool City Council to court over failure to comply with a non-discrimination notice—the *Guardian* p 6, 13 October 1993. Another response has been for the Housing Corporation to attempt to set up black Housing Associations (see, Todd, *Slow Train Coming*, ROOF, November/ December 1992, pp 16–17). The CRE has also issued guidance on positive action and racial equality in housing (1989) and a Code of Practice on rented housing (1991). Moreover, the Labour Party's pre-1992 election document, *A Welcome Home* (September 1991, at p 12), spoke of the need to enhance equal opportunities.

It should also be noted that the British experience is not isolated. In Germany's social housing, which is provided by the private sector but receives public subsidies, only where the municipal housing body could nominate 'needy families' did Turkish guest workers and single parents have any success in obtaining such accommodation (van Vliet, *op. cit.*, pp 141–2). In general, such groups were excluded. In the United States, the federal courts have had to strike down zoning plans which forbade the building of low-cost housing because the effect was to exclude black residents from the area—*U.S. v City of Black Jack, Missouri*, 508 F.2d 1179 (1974); *Metropolitan Housing Development Corp. v Village of Arlington Heights*, 558 F.2d 1283 (1977).

Finally, though, as suggested above, discrimination in the allocation of public sector housing in Britain is but one manifestation of a wider picture of institutionalized racism and sexism—until this more fundamental underlying failing in society is sorted out, discrimination in the allocation of housing will continue.

But the effects of direct housing-related discrimination are also bound up with the consequences of discrimination and disadvantage in education and employment that result in high levels of poverty among ethnic minorities. This in itself leads to restricted access to decent and affordable housing. (see van Vliet, *op. cit*, p 96)

5.1.3 Priorities in the Commercial Sector

In the commercial sector, the landlord's first interest is in a regular income and the second is in capital appreciation. Regular income is dependent on business success, so allocation is dependent to some extent on an assessment of the viability of the particular business. Similar factors are taken into account by agricultural landlords when they look for tenants who will farm in accordance with principles of good husbandry—Rodgers, *Agricultural Law*, 1991, pp 55 *et seq*. The primary consideration in the commercial sector in choosing a tenant is, therefore, the ability of the tenant to pay the rent and meet the other covenants. High returns are not the only factor, certainty of payment is also important:

... **[The] type of covenant can be critical to the investment value of a property. A small private company may go into liquidation, while a large public company is less likely to do so. A government department cannot go into liquidation. The stronger the tenant who covenants to pay the institution's rent, the more secure the income flow. Over the last two decades, the investing institutions have insisted upon secure tenant covenants. More than 20 years ago Galbraith stated that business men do not, in practice, aim to seek maximum profits and promote free enterprise. Instead they aim to reduce risk. Since that time, the investing institutions appear to have followed Galbraith's thesis. The risk averse institutions have a strong penchant for publicly quoted companies and government departments as lessees at the expense of small private companies which have a greater probability of falling into the hands of the receiver. This can be noted more clearly as far as property is concerned by looking at any major shopping high street where many of the shops are now owned by institutions. Relatively few private tenants remain ... The investing institutions, by seeking secure tenants, have not necessarily been the harbourers of free enterprise and a truly competitive market.** (McIntosh, Sykes, *A Guide to Institutional Property Investment*, 1985, p 34, footnotes omitted)

Other landlords, such as property companies and individuals, will be in a less strong position to insist on such 'blue-chip' covenants, as the properties they own will often not be prime properties and, so, will be in less demand. In order to let the property they will often have to accept lesser covenant strength; but in choosing between possible tenants, covenant strength will clearly be a vital determining factor.

In a new development it is important to try and 'pre-let' as much of the development as possible. This means that even before the development is completed, the landlord will be seeking to get tenants to enter into agreements to lease. These agreements will be legally enforceable contracts and mean that the tenants are committed to taking leases once the development is completed. If possible, the landlord will often try to get a major tenant signed up at a very early stage of the development process. Financing the development then becomes much easier, as lenders can foresee a reliable income flow. The most important pre-let to get is that of an 'anchor' or 'magnet' tenant as this will attract other lettings. A household name such as Marks and Spencer would, for example, be an anchor tenant in a new shopping development—it would provide a secure covenant and, due to the way it would draw customers into the centre, it will improve the likelihood of success for other retail outlets. In view of the importance of such an anchor tenant to the success of the development, the landlord will frequently require a covenant from the tenant to keep the shop open during normal business hours (see further ch 7). This covenant will not only require the tenant to trade during normal hours, but also means that the store cannot be closed altogether without there being a breach of covenant. In return, the anchor tenant may well be able to negotiate a lower rent and to negotiate more favourable lease terms generally. In *Transworld Land Co Ltd v J Sainsbury plc*, [1990] 2 EGLR 255, Sainsbury's was the anchor tenant in a development. The rent in the lease was initially fixed at a very favourable rate, and when the upwards only rent review provision came into operation it provided that, so long as Sainsbury's was still trading from the premises, the rent payable would be only 75 per cent of the reviewed rent. It is worth the landlord giving such favourable terms to the anchor tenant because the presence of an anchor tenant should increase the occupancy rate within the development and the level of rent expected of other tenants. Allocation is also a question of tenant mix, that is, the landlord will seek to ensure that the complex offers as much variety as is necessary for the type of development—*R v Welwyn Hatfield DC, ex parte Slough Estates plc*, [1991] EGCS 38.

During an economic recession, as experienced in the early 1990s, the high levels of tenant insolvency led to many voids in existing developments and made new developments (planned and built in the boom days) hard to let. In order to attract tenants, it became necessary for landlords to offer a range of inducements to tenants, such as rent-free periods (no rent payable during, for example, the first year of the lease) and financial contributions towards the tenant's costs of fitting out the premises ready for occupation.

Research conducted for the Royal Institution of Chartered Surveyors found that, in 1992, over 40 per cent of the rental value of units let in that year was subject to rent-free agreements, and that the average period of deferral of the start of rent payments was for seven months. (Cullen & McMillian, *Lease Structure Changes 1992*, RICS Paper Number 32, 1994)

Landlords did, however, resist making any changes to the basic structure of the institutional lease—short term reduction in rental income and one-off payments were more acceptable than any disruption of the long term certainty of income flow.

Nevertheless, some tenants were able to negotiate for break clauses to be included in the lease—giving the tenant the option to end the lease early. This could be particularly useful to the tenant setting up a new enterprise, who may find it difficult to predict future needs. If, for example, the tenant found that it needed to expand into new premises after five years, it would, under the conventional lease structure, have to assign the existing lease and remain liable under the covenants while, at the same time, taking on a commitment to new premises. If the lease contained a break clause, though, the tenant could end the existing lease and then take on the new premises.

5.1.4 Local Authorities and Allocation

Local authorities, unlike other landlords, have a highly formalised process for allocating their properties and bear duties established by statute to ensure that certain persons and groups are provided with rented accommodation. If there is law on allocation, then it is in these systems that it is to be found. While central government is whittling away at the direct responsibilities of local government, councils are still the biggest landlord and their 'heirs apparent', housing associations, seem set to have to adopt similar practices, if on a smaller scale. The revised Tenants' Guarantee, *op. cit.*, speaks of housing associations having to provide applicants with information on their policies and procedures for deciding priority in allocation so that applicants can take a reasonable view of their own priority—§B2(c). In some councils, the housing associations and the local authority are operating joint waiting lists—the *Guardian* 2 p 21, 8 April 1994; this is encouraged in paras 3.2(iii) and 22 of the Department of the Environment's 1994 Consultation Paper, *Access to Local Authority and Housing Association Tenancies.*

Local authorities have responsibilities to the sick and disabled, to children, to those whose homes are being compulsorily purchased and to the homeless. In addition, they operate waiting lists for prospective tenants and for those seeking an exchange within the authority or a transfer from a different authority (exchanges and transfers will be covered in full in ch 9.3, below). While the Housing Act 1985, s 21 gives local authorities control over allocation, s 22 provides generally that

s 22 A local housing authority shall secure that in the selection of their tenants a reasonable preference is given to -
(a) persons occupying insanitary or overcrowded houses,
(b) persons having large families,
(c) persons living under unsatisfactory housing conditions, and
(d) persons towards whom the authority are subject to a duty under section 65 or 68 (persons found to be homeless).

(The government's proposals on housing responsibility, paras.18–22 of the Department of the Environment's *Access to Local Authority and Housing Association Tenancies: A Consultation Paper*, *op. cit.*, 1994, are considered below. 5.1.4.1(c).)

Taking the general applicant first, local authorities that maintain a housing stock will regulate applicants for that housing by means of waiting lists. There will be several cross-referenced lists covering transfers, exchanges and the general waiting list and tying them in with lists of the type of housing the applicant wants. Thus, when a three bedroom house becomes available, the housing officers will look to see which applicants would find such accommodation suitable and then see where they lie on their respective lists. And therein lies one of the conflicts that housing officers have to resolve—if a house becomes available in a good area, should the authority grant it to the family at the top of the waiting list or should they give it to their existing tenant who is seeking a transfer and allocate the latter's current, usually inferior, home to the waiting list applicant? The system of keeping lists itself gives rise to further questions concerning the nature of the list and as to whom should be admitted on to the list. In Japan (see van Vliet, *op. cit.*, p 681) allocation of local authority housing is based on income levels, on the standard of the current accommodation and then there is a lottery for the qualifying pool of applicants. Hoath (*Public Sector Housing Law*, 1989, at pp 31–2) claims there are four types of list system operating in Britain—date order, which amounts to no more than 'first-come, first-served' and is only appropriate where there is an adequate supply of housing in the authority; points schemes; merit schemes, or case by case analysis; and, a combination of the first three. Cullingworth (1969, *op. cit.*, at paras 128–35) favoured points schemes with a residuary discretion for exceptional cases. Points would be allocated depending on various factors pertaining to the applicant—how many children are in the family, what is the standard of their present accommodation? Of course, points schemes also provide an opportunity for housing officers to impose their own personal prejudices. Jacobs (1986, *op. cit.*, pp 15–16), moreover, gives a radical critique of points schemes and of council housing generally.

[In *The Intelligent Man's Guide to the Post-War World*, 1947, p 447], Cole's vision of post-war Britain was of housing estates containing creches, communal restaurants and social centres . . . Instead, state housing sadly produced poorly designed, shoddy and cheaply built estates, commonly devoid of even basic amenities. Grading procedures, at the heart of the allocation system, rather than foster feelings of solidarity, served to alienate and individualise and, in the process, destroyed viable working-class communities. Indeed, housing policies, symbolized on the one hand by the bulldozer and on the other, by the grey uniformity of council estates, have been an integral part of capital's incessant assault on working class culture, values and independent institutions . . . It needs to be fully understood that equitable allocation policies are virtually impossible in conditions of acute housing shortage.

Given that a list system is the best that can reasonably be achieved, though, and that it is in place, how should a local authority go about admitting people on to such? Is it required to accept anyone on to its list? As a result of some homelessness cases, children, mentally incapacitated persons and illegal immigrants have no right to apply for housing under Part III Housing Act 1985 (see *R v Oldham MBC, ex parte G, R v Bexley LBC, ex parte B, R v Tower Hamlets LBC, ex parte Ferdous Begum* [1993] 2 WLR 609; *R v Secretary of State for the Environment, ex parte Tower Hamlets LBC*, [1993] QB 632), but that does not necessarily mean that, for instance, a child's name could not, in theory, be put down on a waiting list in the hope that by the time he reaches his majority he would be near the top thereof (indeed, the Housing Act 1985, s 22, may require admission on to the list). At the other extreme, could a local authority exclude certain undesirable persons from the list, such as known drug pushers (Brimacombe, *Weed Out the Undesirables*, ROOF, November/December 1993, p 24)?

The one common condition for acceptance on to a housing list is some form of residence qualification, often that the applicant has lived in the borough for six months. While Cullingworth (*op. cit.*, at para 169) argued against residence qualifications in order that a true assessment of full housing need could be made, they are still lawful so long as they do not constitute indirect discrimination for the purposes of the Race Relations Act 1976; on the other hand, they can leave an authority open to judicial review of its decisions. In *R v Canterbury CC, ex parte Gillespie, op. cit.*, a successful challenge to a local authority decision was made under the Housing Act 1985, s 22, in such a way as to call into question absolute residence bars. The *Gillespie* case concerned a woman who had broken up from her former partner but technically still had access to their former home, a secure tenancy in another borough. The local authority initially prohibited her from even being placed on the waiting list, but, at the institution of proceedings for judicial review, it relented. However, it then refused to consider her for accommodation because of that former secure tenancy. In the meantime, she had to live with her mother and one of her two children in overcrowded and unsatisfactory conditions.

I need cite only a very short passage from the judgment of Templeman LJ . . . in [*A-G, ex rel.Tilley v London Borough of Wandsworth*] reported at [1981] 1 WLR 854 at 858A:
'On well recognised principles public authorities are not entitled to fetter the exercise of discretion or to fetter the manner in which they are empowered to discharge the many duties that are thrust on them. They must at all times, in every particular case, consider how to exercise their discretion and how to perform their duties.'

The effect of [Canterbury] council's decision adopted in the instant case is, in my judgment, to exclude from consideration any applicant on the waiting list who has a secure tenancy of the kind referred to in the policy whether with another local authority or a housing association wholly irrespective of the circumstances of that tenancy and in particular of the availability of that tenancy to the applicant, . . .

That . . . is inconsistent with the proper exercise by the authority of their power accorded to them under section [21 of the 1985] Act and *a fortiori* constitutes a breach of their express duty to give reasonable preference to those in unsatisfactory housing conditions imposed by section [22]. . . .

In my judgment, this challenge succeeds not essentially because the policy is intrinsically irrational, but rather because it constitutes a rule which requires to

be followed slavishly rather than merely a stated general approach which is always subject to an exceptional case and which permits each application to be individually considered. (*per* Simon Brown J at 13–15)

This limited control on local authority allocation policies is the one general obligation owed to all applicants. For the most part, local authorities are free to allocate as they wish, subject only to the one overriding constraint, the limited, and ever-decreasing, quantity of housing stock. According to Malpass and Murie (1994, *op. cit.*, at pp 285–6), though, the applicant's greatest assistance in obtaining the accommodation required is not to be found in any piece of legislation, but, rather, it is possession of practically unending reserves of patience.

Before moving on to local authority duties to specific groups of applicant, one other factor affecting all applicants concerns illegal tenants (see generally, Miller, *Criminal Tenancies*, ROOF, November/December 1991, pp 20 *et seq.*; Kelly, *Knock, Knock. Who's There?*, ROOF, November/December 1993, p 16). Illegal tenants is an umbrella term to cover all those using properties who have not had the house officially allocated to them. Squatting is the most widely known example of an illegal tenancy and there are estimated to be 60,000 squats in England and Wales. The government has introduced legislation to criminalize squatting in the Criminal Justice and Public Order Act 1994, but there are fears this will just exacerbate the numbers sleeping rough (the *Guardian* p 3, 7 June 1993). With respect to council housing, key-selling and unauthorized transfers and exchanges meant that councils did not control the letting of their properties and, therefore, such homes were denied to those at the top of the waiting list. Figures for London in 1986/87 indicate 3.5 per cent of total housing stock had been allocated in an unauthorized manner. What is worse is that many of the illegal lettings were to single people who would not qualify for council housing. While moves to regain control of all local authority properties are obviously proper, thereby allowing those on the waiting lists and in temporary accommodation to be rehoused, the savings therefrom must be speculative. Some of the illegal tenants would qualify for council housing, anyway. Evicting the illegal tenant merely shifts one family from temporary accommodation into full housing and another from full housing into temporary accommodation. Nevertheless, to reassert local authority control of its own housing, illegal tenants must be evicted and those on the waiting list rehoused—the overall solution, though, requires more affordable accommodation to come on to the market in those areas where people need to live.

5.1.4.1 Specific Local Authority Housing Duties

(a) *Land Compensation Act 1973*

Somewhat discrete and a very specific part of the allocation process, local authorities owe a duty to those people who are caught by, *inter alia*, redevelopment schemes. The Land Compensation Act 1973, s 39 as amended, sets out the duty to a displaced person (see *Prasad v Wolverhampton BC* [1983] Ch 333) as follows.

s 39 (1) Where a person is displaced from residential accommodation on any land in consequence of–
    (a) the acquisition of the land by an authority possessing compulsory purchase powers;
    (b) the making . . . or acceptance of a housing order . . . or undertaking in respect of a house or building on the land [see s 29(7)];
    (c) where the land has been previously acquired by an authority possessing compulsory purchase powers or appropriated by a local authority and is for the time being held by the authority for the purposes for which it was acquired or appropriated, the carrying out of [any improvement to a house or building on the land or of] redevelopment on the land;
    and suitable alternative residential accommodation on reasonable terms is not otherwise available to that person, then, subject to the provisions of this section, it shall be the duty of the relevant authority to secure that he will be provided with such other accommodation.
(Caravan dwellers are dealt with in s 40; see also, Legal Action, September 1991, p 13)

Because of the distinctive nature of this obligation, many local authorities do not consider it appropriate to place such applicants on any notional waiting list, but deal with their claims forthwith as they arise. However, in practically the first case under the 1973 Act, Lord Denning MR held that

the local authority fulfil their duty when they do their best, as soon as practicable, to get him other accommodation. No doubt they can take into account the fact that he has been displaced under a closing order; but it does not mean that he takes priority over everybody else in the housing list. His circumstances must be considered along with the others and a fair decision made between them. (*R v Bristol Corporation, ex parte Hendy* [1974] 1 WLR 498 at 501)

Furthermore, the scope and extent of the obligation in s 39 is not transparently obvious and there is room for dispute between the local authority and the displaced person. The obligation arises when a local authority declares a clearance area when property is unfit (Housing Act 1985, s 289) and when an improvement notice is served under Part VII Housing Act 1985. Where a local authority makes a demolition or closing order with respect to unfit property under Part IX Housing Act 1985, then the duty again arises, but it should be noted that it does not cover council dwellings declared unfit. In *R v Corby DC, ex parte McLean* [1975] 1 WLR 735 at 738, a case dealing with compensation payments for the loss of one's home under s 29, Lord Widgery CJ, having previously held that s 39 deals with 'factually identical circumstances' to those set out in s 29, went on in the following terms.

Paragraph (b), it will be remembered, was the making, passing or acceptance of a housing order, resolution or undertaking in respect of the dwelling, and clearly in view of the definition in [s 29(7)] it relates to unfit privately owned housing where the local authority makes a clearance or associated order under the Housing Act because the houses are unfit for habitation. Section 29(1)(b), I think, is clearly making provision for a home loss payment in that extent, where one has a private landlord as the owner of the property, the property is unfit for habitation and the tenant is displaced by virtue of an order under the Housing Act.

In *R v Cardiff City Council, ex parte Cross* (1981) 1 HLR 54; (1982) 6 HLR 1, the issue arose again when a council tenant's home was declared unfit for human habitation. The case turned on whether the provisions in the Housing Act 1957 (now Part IX Housing Act 1985) applied to properties owned by the Council. If so, then the Land Compensation Act would also apply. The Court of Appeal, affirming the fuller judgment of Woolf J, held that, while it puts a council tenant in a disadvantageous position *vis-à-vis* occupants in all other sectors or forms of tenure, a local authority cannot serve an order on itself with regard to unfitness if it owns and controls the property in question (see Lord Lane CJ at 11–12) and, thus, if a council does find that its own properties are unfit, then no obligation arises under the Land Compensation Act 1973 to its tenants.

Section 39 has also come before the courts with respect to the meaning of 'suitable' and 'on reasonable terms' in these circumstances. In *Hendy, op. cit.*, at 502; followed by *Re Smith's Application*, The Times, 20 April 1990, Scarman LJ analyzed it in the following terms.

I think the word 'suitable' really means in the context no more and no less than suitable to the requirements of the person and his family in the circumstances in which they find themselves. It is a word of some flexibility, but I think that is what is covered in this section by that adjective. I think the words 'on reasonable terms' are of great importance, indicating that this is a duty to act reasonably. I do not think it is necessary in the context of this section to read the word 'terms' as necessarily meaning only covenants in a lease or tenancy agreement. I think the phrase is an indication that the duty to secure accommodation placed upon the local authority is a duty to act reasonably.' (See also, in a different context, *R v Brent LBC, ex parte Omar*, (1991) 23 HLR 446)

Under different legislation, the Court of Appeal has held that what is suitable depends, in part, on the neighbourhood of the new accommodation: a flat in Kilburn, London, that was in many ways internally superior to the former accommodation was not suitable as a replacement for a flat in the 'leafier suburb' of Hampstead (*Dawncar Investments Ltd v Plews* (1993) 25 HLR 639).

In conclusion, the Land Compensation Act 1973 is a very specific housing responsibility of local authorities that for most councils gives rise to a particular allocation regime.

(b) *Homeless Applicants*

The number of households accepted for permanent accommodation under Part III Housing Act 1985 fell by 2 per cent in England between 1991 and 1992 and by a further 6 per cent in the year to December 1993—LRC Housing Update p 4, ROOF, May/June 1994; see also, Wilcox, *Housing Finance Review 1994–95*, at p 178. The fall may be real or it may simply reflect a change in the way the statistics are collected and a harsher attitude from some local authorities towards applicants as the quantity of their available housing stock continues to decrease. The number of households in temporary accommodation, however, rose 24 per cent between 1990 and 1992. At the end of March 1993 there were 62,250 homeless households in temporary accommodation in England, with an estimated 87,150 children (see, LRC Housing Update p 6, ROOF, May/June 1993; Blake, *Playing the New Numbers Game*, ROOF, July/August 1993, p 9; and, the *Guardian* 2 p 20, 22 July 1993; *cf.* by the mid-1990s, the figures appeared to be slowly dropping—LRC Housing Update p 4, ROOF, May/June 1994). There is also a fear that homelessness will rise with the closure of hostels—the *Guardian* p 2, 30 May 1994. Furthermore, homelessness is a European wide issue, with 2.5 million officially homeless within the European Union. (See Table 5.6, next page)

The homelessness figures, may moreover, significantly underestimate the true figures—the *Guardian* p 6, 31 December 1993. In seeking to reduce this number of homeless, the most frequent causes behind losing secure accommodation need to be examined. (See Table 5.7, next page)

To understand the root causes of homelessness, though, requires deeper analysis examining overall housing policies. During the 1980s there was a steep increase in the number of households claiming to be homeless (see van Vliet, *op. cit.*, p 96, and Joseph Rowntree Foundation Inquiry into British Housing, Second Report, 1991, pp 12 & 13), although the peak had apparently passed by the mid-1990s—see Table 3, Butler, Carlisle & Lloyd, *Homelessness in the 1990s: Local Authority Practice*, 1994. The Rowntree Inquiry (*op. cit.*, pp 18 and 13) suggested that the galloping house-price inflation in the late 1980s put owner-occupation beyond the reach of many low-income families when there was a dearth of rented accommodation; indeed, the high cost of freeholds made private landlordism even less attractive as an economic investment. As a result of

Table 5.6

	Numbers of Homeless	Homeless per 1,000
Germany	1,030,000	12.8
United Kingdom	688,000	12.2
France	627,000	11.1
Belgium	26,000	2.6
Netherlands	30,000	2.0
Italy	90,000	1.6
Ireland	5,000	1.4
Luxembourg	500	1.3
Spain	30,000	0.8
Denmark	2,800	0.5
Portugal	2,500	0.2

The *Guardian* p 12, 25 September 1993.

Table 5.7 Reasons for homelessness (%)

	1987	1988	1989	1990	1991	1992	1993
Parents, relatives, friends no longer willing or able to accommodate	41	43	43	43	42	42	38
Breakdown of relationship with partner	18	19	17	27	16	17	19
Loss of private dwelling, including tied accommodation	15	15	16	14	14	15	17
Mortgage arrears	9	7	6	9	12	10	8
Rent arrears—local authority dwelling	2	2	3	2	1	1	1
Rent arrears—private dwelling	2	2	2	2	1	1	1
Other	13	12	13	13	13	15	16

Source: Department of Environment Homelessness Statistics. Reproduced in Wilcox, *op. cit.*, Table 75 at p 179

this shortage of affordable accommodation of either tenure, people were forced to live with family and friends, but, as the Department of Environment statistics show (Wilcox, *op. cit.*, Table 75 p 179), this proved to be no ideal solution. Government mishandling of the economy is only partly to blame for increased homelessness, however, because another cause noted by Rowntree is the emergence of the 'baby-boom' generation into the housing market as they reached the age 'at which they formed separate households' (this trend has now petered out, however—Blake, July/August, 1993, *op. cit.*). At the very time the number of households increased, there was a reduction in the availability of council housing and neither housing associations nor the private sector were able to step in and fill the gap (see Malpass and Murie, 1994, *op. cit.*, p 118). It was only in late 1992 that central government released sufficient funds to housing associations with the intention of providing an extra supply of housing to assist in rehousing the homeless (the *Guardian* p 33, 12 December 1992). The new policy, though, of replacing local authorities with housing associations as the main source of accommodation for homeless families may, until changes take effect towards the end of the century, be founded on a superficial knowledge and understanding of the housing association sector. Local authorities have always built for families and the homelessness legislation in its present form is geared towards rehousing families—see the Housing Act 1985, s 59 below. However, as Table 5.8 (see next page) partly indicates, several of the larger housing associations have a stock consisting primarily of properties which are wholly inappropriate for homeless families, otherwise more homeless applicants would have been housed—this is particularly true of Anchor. The type of accommodation housing associations such as Anchor offer would not be appropriate for many homeless applicants with priority need, that is families. That greater targeting of homeless families than is evidenced in Table 5.8 is the norm in the housing association sector, can be gleaned from the fact that the NFHA's Formal Response to the 1994 Revised Tenants' Guarantee, *op. cit.*, spoke of 50 per cent of nominations normally being given to local authorities for this purpose (para 1.2).

At first glance, the table might seem to indicate an inability on the part of housing associations to replace local authorities as the provider of accommodation for homeless applicants under Part III Housing Act 1985. Miller's analysis (*The Let Down*, ROOF, March/April 1993, pp 20 *et seq*: *cf.* Taylor, *Scottish Let Down*, ROOF, July/August 1993, p 17), though, shows that this is a period of transition as housing associations change from supplementing the role of local authorities towards homeless people and instead become the principal providers. In the past, housing associations saw their role as, in part, providing for those homeless people who did not qualify under the statute, for example, the able bodied, single person—*cf.* Kemp, Anderson & Quilgars, *Single Homelessness—What Lies Behind the Numbers*, ROOF, September/October 1993, p 18. The statistics do not include

Table 5.8

Housing Association	Stock total at 31/3/92	Lettings 1991/92	Statutory homeless households	% of lettings made to statutory homeless
London & Quadrant	12,368	1,403	479	34%
Circle 33	6,898	616	182	30%
Peabody	11,690	794	187	24%
North British	21,030	3,215	704	22%
Guinness	10,331	1,533	305	20%
English Churches	6,737	857	138	16%
Merseyside Improved Homes	14,776	1,561	87	6%
Anchor H.A.†	22,225	2,584	51	2%
All H.A.s	646,100	86,400	14,700	17%

Source: Selected H.A.s from ROOF, March/April 1993, at p 11: † ≈ 90% of the stock of Anchor consists of one bedroom properties.)

the 15 per cent of lettings London & Quadrant made to single persons. Nor do they allow for the people living with families who remain in overcrowded conditions without claiming to be homeless (the so-called 'hidden homeless'), but instead apply direct to the housing association, nor those living in hostels who are effectively homeless. London & Quadrant let a further 8 per cent of their properties to the hidden homeless and 6 per cent to those previously in hostels. Nor do the statistics deal with the position where there are not that many statutory homeless needing to be rehoused: according to Merseyside Improved Homes, in Liverpool it is not difficult to obtain a flat, the problem is the quality of that accommodation. Further, housing associations are dependent on local authorities referring homeless applicants to them until some form of unified waiting list can be drawn up. Nevertheless, while housing associations account for such a small proportion of the rented sector and while a good deal of their stock is not suitable for families, local authorities will continue to provide the housing in fulfilment of their statutory duty under the Housing Act 1985, Part III.

Local authorities have not always carried out their obligations to homeless applicants as well as might have been hoped, but the circumstances militated against a straightforward and smooth running of this part of the allocation process. The duty, initially imposed in the Housing (Homeless Persons) Act 1977, never attracted additional funding from central government: so much so, that the Association of District Councils lobbied Parliament to make the Housing

(Homeless Persons) Act 1977 more restrictive, arguing that homeless applicants were 'queue jumpers' (see, Richards, *The Housing (Homeless Persons) Act 1977— A Study in Policymaking*, Working Paper 22, SAUS University of Bristol, 1981; Richards, 'A Sense of Duty', in Grant 1992, *op. cit.*, at p 129). When local authorities were restricted during the 1980s in the amount they could spend on new housing and had to sell off existing stock under the Right To Buy, then the obligations to homeless applicants under the 1985 Act imposed an overwhelming strain on resources.

The 'right to buy', one of the most persuasive populist slogans coined for the Conservatives' 1979 election manifesto, has meant 1.527 million council homes being purchased by former tenants. But the chief architect of the programme, Sir Hugh Rossi, now admits the scheme did not function as planned. The surge in the number of homeless in the eighties, he insists, might have been avoided if legislation had been implemented as originally intended.

'As sales progressed and borrowings were paid off, the remainder [of the capital receipts] would have been used to put houses into good repair. What was left over would be spent on constructing new properties, which would again become subject to the right to buy . . . The Treasury mucked around with the scheme and [the Chancellor] first froze the proceeds of sale in the hands of local authorities, and wouldn't allow them to use them. Instead of treating it as old money coming back into the coffers, he treated it as new expenditure. It was these wretched Treasury conventions which distorted the policy.' (Sir Hugh Rossi, quoted in the *Guardian* 2—Society p 8, 5 October 1994)

However the [homelessness] legislation leaves substantial room for different interpretations and rates of acceptance. And, when accepted, homeless persons are treated in widely different ways . . . [The] homeless household is often treated in a less favourable way than other households seeking housing. It is common practice to deny homeless households more than one offer of accommodation. A refusal of accommodation can be regarded as evidence of intentional homelessness and as removing any obligation on the council to provide housing. The nature of the legislation makes such practices possible, and leaves the homeless with very little power to 'bargain' for better housing as well as little capacity to wait. The likelihood of their being offered and accepting properties which those with more bargaining power and capacity to wait have rejected is reflected in evidence about where the homeless are housed. While the likelihood of such outcomes is affected by the context of supply and demand, it is also affected by policy (and especially attempts to monitor and counter such tendencies) and by the practice of those involved in implementing policy. (Malpass & Murie, 1994, *op. cit.*, at pp 286–7. See generally pp 286 *et seq.*)

Before looking at the statutory provisions, it is worth noting Loveland's views (*Administrative Law, Administrative Processes and the Housing of Homeless Persons: A View from the Sharp End*, [1991] JSW & FL 4; see also, Butler, Carlisle and Lloyd, *op. cit.*). Loveland's analysis, based on a study of practice in a New

Town in Eastern England (known as Eastern in his article), shows that the detail of the legislation is not at the forefront when dealing with homeless applicants. The fact that it is so difficult to appeal from the decision of a local authority and that there is such a wide discretion in the making of a decision in the first place, means that housing officers have ample scope to reach the conclusion they want without worrying whether the courts might interfere—Butler, Carlisle and Lloyd, *op. cit.* pp 12–13.

But is it accurate to say that the 'law' relating to homelessness has not been made increasingly restrictive by the Thatcher governments?

That argument would at best be myopic, at worst entirely deceitful, depending entirely on interpreting 'law' without reference to the end product of the governmental process. That end product is not to be found in *Halsbury's Statutes* or the *All England Law Reports*, but in the several hundred local authority offices where untold thousands of Part III decisions are made every day. One conclusion supported by this limited data is that in studies of the 'law-in-context', it is the context, and not the law, that should occupy centre stage. This paper represents [and] tentatively suggests that lawyers might better understand the governmental process they seek to control if they *begin* their analyses by examining the relationships between the major actors involved, rather than just using speculative assertions or secondhand data to qualify the legal arguments that have gone before.

One might gain an enhanced empathy with this perspective simply by being in Eastern's [Homeless Persons Unit] at 9 o'clock one morning. When [housing] officers arrive . . . [they] may in passing curse their councillors' corporate indecisiveness, or despair at the ineptitude or harshness of another authority. But the first thing they do every day is telephone the area offices and the [Commission for New Towns] to see how many properties, and of what type, are available for immediate allocation to an ever growing list of homeless persons. The information thereby gleaned is the key informant of subsequent decision-making procedures: that is, in micro-terms, the 'context' within which the 'law' relating to homeless persons in Eastern is constructed . . .

The tangible long term product of 10 years of Thatcherism for Britain's homeless has been persistently high unemployment, rampant house price inflation in the owner-occupied and rented sectors, successive cuts in the purchasing power of housing benefit, almost complete removal of benefit from 16-18 year olds, a virtual end to public sector house building and pervasive deregulation of private rented housing. [Rising numbers of households accepted as homeless.] Additionally, households accepted as homeless comprise barely 50 per cent. of those that apply: in the 1986-87 financial year 109,000 applications were rejected (Audit Commission, *Housing the Homeless: the Local Authority Role*, 1988, p 8). How those people resolved their housing problems is unknown.

That is the context, in macro-terms, in which Part III of the Housing Act 1985 is applied across the country . . . Many more applicants, and much less affordable housing, necessarily means that a smaller percentage of the homeless population is housed, that people wait longer for that housing and that the quality of the homes eventually allocated continues to decline.

In those contexts, whether at the micro- or macro-level, legalistic perceptions of the 'law' will rarely be of more than minor significance. This is not to say that statute or case law has no hortatory role to play in structuring administrative behaviour. Even within the constraints of this (avowedly anti-legalistic) study it is clear that the threat of judicial review can have a marked short term effect on senior officers' perception of the way the administrative process should be controlled. But legalism is an intruder into the administrative arena. It does not prescribe administrative behaviour, but challenges it. It does not facilitate the decision making process, rather it gets in the way. It is not respected, but ignored. And if it cannot be ignored, it is grudgingly accepted as an unrealistic impediment to rational decision-making. (pp 20, 21 and 22)

There is force in Loveland's arguments that the day-to-day reality of homelessness applications has little to do with fine studies of the statute and of the decisions of the superior courts when considering judicial review. Homeless applicants will initially have their case decided by reference to the availability of housing stock, the length of waiting lists and some subjective assessment of their need. Nevertheless, when this initial decision is challenged, it will be on the basis of the law relating to homelessness, regardless of its appropriateness to every day practice.

The present law on homeless applicants is found in the Housing Act 1985, Part III. The government initiated a review of it in 1993-94—the proposed changes are considered below, 5.1.4.1(c). In addition to Part III of the 1985 Act, though, there is a Code of Guidance issued in accordance with s 71 and an inter-local authority agreement. Failure to follow the Code of Guidance may result in a decision under Part III being quashed—*R v Newham LBC, ex parte Barnes* (1993) 25 HLR 357. There will be no attempt here to provide a comprehensive analysis of the statutory provisions and case law. The topic is large and goes beyond the remit of a section on the allocation duties of local authorities (for fuller coverage see, Hoath, 1989, *op. cit.*, pp 47–156; Arden, *Homeless Persons*, 1988; or, Sweet & Maxwell's *Encyclopaedia of Housing*, vol 1). The principal elements of the obligation under Part III are:

1 The applicant is homeless or threatened with homelessness (s 58);
2 The applicant has priority need (s 59);
3 The applicant is not intentionally homeless (s 60); and
4 The applicant has a local connection or, if not, has no local connection with any other local authority (s 61).

The duty owed to an applicant is graded depending on the answers to those points (s 65).

(i) Homeless or threatened with homelessness. To apply for housing under Part III the applicant does not previously have to have been living in a cardboard box. Section 58 (as amended) sets out the requirement as follows.

s 58(1) A person is homeless if he has no accommodation in England, Wales or Scotland.

   (2) A person shall be treated as having no accommodation if there is no accommodation which he, together with any other person who normally resides with him as a member of his family or in circumstances in which it is reasonable for that person to reside with him–

   (a) is entitled to occupy by virtue of an interest in it or by virtue of an order of a court, or

   (b) has an express or implied licence to occupy, or in Scotland has a right or permission or an implied right or permission to occupy, or

   (c) occupies as a residence by virtue of any enactment or rule of law giving him the right to remain in occupation or restricting the right of another person to recover possession.

   (2A) A person shall not be treated as having accommodation unless it is accommodation which it would be reasonable for him to continue to occupy.

   (2B) Regard may be had, in determining whether it would be reasonable for a person to continue to occupy accommodation, to the general circumstances prevailing in relation to housing in the district of the local housing authority to whom he has applied for accommodation or for assistance in obtaining accommodation.

   (3) A person is also homeless if he has accommodation but–

   (a) he cannot secure entry to it, or

   (b) it is probable that occupation of it will lead to violence from some other person residing in it or to threats of violence from some other person residing in it and likely to carry out the threats, or

   (c) it consists of a movable structure, vehicle or vessel designed or adapted for human habitation and there is no place where he is entitled or permitted both to place it and to reside in it.

   (4) A person is threatened with homelessness if it is likely that he will become homeless within 28 days.

(Subss (2A) and (2B) added by s 14(2) Housing and Planning Act 1986)

The main factors to note are that the applicant applies for himself and any other person with whom he normally resides 'as a member of his family or in circumstances in which it is reasonable for that person to reside with him'—see, for example, *R v Kingswood BC, ex parte Smith-Morse*, The Times, 8 December 1994. Rarely for housing legislation, this phrase may encompass gay relationships (*cf. Harrogate BC v Simpson* (1986) 2 FLR 91; it can include cohabitees—*R v Wimbourne DC, ex parte Curtis* (1985) 1 FLR 486). The Housing and Planning Act 1986 amended s 58 to reverse the House of Lords' decision in *R v Hillingdon LBC, ex parte Puhlhofer* ([1985] JSWL 300; ROOF, September/October 1985, p 18; [1985] 3 All ER 734, CA; [1986] 1 All ER 467, HL), the closest landlord and tenant law in the public sector gets to a 'Barbara Cartland-esque' romance. The

Puhlhofers met in a bed and breakfast hotel and married while awaiting rehousing by Hillingdon LBC. Angela Puhlhofer had a three-year-old child by a former relationship and by the time of the first hearing she had had another baby by the applicant. After the marriage, Ricky Puhlhofer reapplied for rehousing because of a material change in circumstances. However, Hillingdon LBC retorted that the family was not homeless because it had accommodation which it was entitled to occupy—one bedroom with a double and single bed but no cooking or washing facilities, with a baby in nappies and the three-year-old having nightmares because of the inevitable family rows. Hillingdon also argued that it was proper to have regard to the general housing conditions and availability of accommodation in the area. At first instance, Hodgson J, following *Parr v Wyre BC* (1982) 2 HLR 71, held that accommodation had to be appropriate having regard to the size of the family (*per* Lord Denning MR at 78). Hodgson J had regard to the Code of Guidance which referred local authorities to the general housing and public health legislation. Having regard to those measures, the Puhlhofers did not have 'appropriate' accommodation and so were homeless for the purposes of what is now s 58, while the general conditions in the area were irrelevant to the question of homelessness. The Court of Appeal held that the Puhlhofers lived in intolerable conditions, but that the bedroom still counted as accommodation for the purposes of s 58. The question of reasonableness was not material; only if the premises were uninhabitable would an applicant be treated as homeless. The House of Lords affirmed the decision of the Court of Appeal, placing some emphasis on the imposition the original 1977 Act had made on local authorities (see Lord Brightman at 473). The words appropriate and reasonable were not to be imported into s 58 (Lord Brightman at 474). There were only two concessions. First, while the statutory definition of overcrowding has no part to play, if the dwelling was so small that it could not from an objective standpoint accommodate the applicant and those with whom he normally resided, then he would be homeless (at 474). Secondly, it probably cheered the Puhlhofers no end to know that their own failure did, even so, extend the obligations of local authorities to treat as homeless 'classical Greeks who lived in barrels' (at 474)! The decision in *Puhlhofer*, it should be noted, also had the effect of leaving the law on homelessness confused as between the definition of accommodation and intentional homelessness. Consequently, the Housing and Planning Act 1986, s 14(2), inserted subsections (2A) and (2B) into s 58. Under s 58(2A) a person will not be treated as having accommodation if it would not be reasonable for him to have to continue to occupy the dwelling in question. Nevertheless, there is still scope for different approaches to be taken under ss 58 and 60—compare *R v Croydon LBC, ex parte Jarvis* (1994) 26 HLR 194, with *R v Newham LBC, ex parte Ugbo* (1994) 26 HLR 263. Furthermore, under s 58(2B) [regard]may be had, in determining whether it would be reasonable for a person to continue to occupy accommodation [under s 58(2A)], to the general circumstances prevailing in relation to housing in the district of the local housing authority to whom he has applied for accommodation or for assistance in obtaining accommodation.

While reasonableness is once more an issue, the housing conditions of the area can be used as a defence by the local authority. What it would be reasonable for an occupier to leave in one area, might qualify as acceptable accommodation elsewhere. Further, a local authority which has sold off its better properties under the Right To Buy and which has not sought to build replacements could be in a better position *vis-à-vis* applicants under Part III (*cf.* District Auditor's Provisional Report on Westminster CC's policy of voluntary sales beyond the Right To Buy, which found that such sales led to a breach of the homelessness obligations owed by the council: see, the *Guardian* 2—Society p 6, 12 October 1994). It should finally be noted that this reversal of the *Puhlhofer* decision by Parliament to incorporate a test of reasonableness into the definition of homelessness, did not necessarily improve the lot of homeless applicants that much. Very few cases have found accommodation to be unreasonable. In *R v South Herefordshire CC, ex parte Miles* (1985) 17 HLR 82, it was held that a rat-infested hop-picker's hut with no mains services did not count as accommodation. In *R v Gloucester CC, ex parte Miles* (1985) 17 HLR 292, a badly vandalized flat did not count as accommodation. In *R v Westminster CC, ex parte Ali* (1983) 11 HLR 83, where a family of seven lived in a room ten feet by twelve feet, the judge was also prepared to hold the accommodation to be unreasonable. Nevertheless, in the unreported decision of *R v Blackpool BC, ex parte Smith*, cited in Hoath, *op. cit.*, p 62 n.4, the court held accommodation was not automatically unreasonable even if it was unfit and constituted a fire risk.

Section 58(3)(b) represents a continuous theme of the homelessness legislation, that a person should not be deemed to have accommodation if occupying it would

lead to violence from some other person residing in it or to threats of violence from some other person residing in it and likely to carry out the threats.

The primary objective of such a provision would be to protect battered women. Nevertheless, research by Bristol University (the *Guardian* p 6, 29 April 1993) indicates that many local authorities will not treat a woman as under threat of physical violence unless she institutes legal proceedings to have her partner evicted from the home—of course, if she were successful, she could return home and would not need assistance from the Homeless Persons Unit. In *R v Westminster CC, ex parte Bishop* (1993) 25 HLR 459, the local authority looked for confirmatory evidence from the police or the estate office when the applicant surrendered her tenancy because of violence from her former partner, and the lack thereof told against her claim not to be intentionally homeless. Regardless of the strain on a local authority's resources, no woman fearing violence should be put in a position of danger and she should be treated as having no accommodation without having to first take her partner to court.

(ii) Priority Need.   The second element in the legislation relates to priority need—Blake, *The Right to Act*, ROOF, September/October 1993, p 27.

s 59(1) The following have a priority need for accommodation –
    (a) a pregnant woman or a person with whom a pregnant woman resides or might reasonably be expected to reside;
    (b) a person with whom dependent children reside or might reasonably be expected to reside;
    (c) a person who is vulnerable as a result of old age, mental illness or handicap or physical disability or other special reason, or with whom such a person resides or might reasonably be expected to reside;
    (d) a person who is homeless or threatened with homelessness as a result of an emergency such as flood, fire or other disaster.
(2) The Secretary of State may by order made by statutory instrument -
    (a) specify further descriptions of persons as having a priority need for accommodation, and
    (b) amend or repeal any part of subsection (1).
(3) Before making such an order the Secretary of State shall consult such associations representing relevant authorities, and such other persons, as he considers appropriate.
(4) No order shall be made unless a draft of it has been approved by resolution of each House of Parliament.

The grounds for priority need are reasonably self-explanatory. For instance, under paragraph (b), an applicant with resident, dependent children will have priority need. For the purposes of making a hypothetical claim under Part III, though, can a child claim to be in priority need? The issue of who can apply for rehousing will be considered below when looking at intentional homelessness, but the House of Lords in *R v Oldham MBC, ex parte Garlick, R v Bexley LBC, ex parte Bentum, R v Tower Hamlets LBC, ex parte Ferdous Begum, op. cit.*, held that there could be no duty even to place dependent children at the front of the waiting-list queue, on the ground that a dependent child living with a parent or guardian could not have priority need under s 59(1) since there was no express provision in the section therefor (see Lord Griffiths at 614). The parents are expected to provide accommodation and their child gives them priority need under s 59(1)(b).

Excluded by s 59 are non-vulnerable, single homeless persons and couples without children—Butler, Carlisle and Lloyd, *op. cit.*, p 12; Kemp, Anderson and Quilgars, *op. cit.* Section 59 contributes to the numbers sleeping rough—Randall, *Out for the Count*, ROOF, September/October 1993, p 9. Indeed, Shelter claim half its caseload does not fall within Part III of the Housing Act 1985—the *Guardian* p 8, 16 November 1993.

(iii) Intentional Homelessness.   This limitation on access to housing is the area of greatest controversy in the homelessness legislation. The Housing (Homeless Persons) Bill 1977 was originally introduced in the House of Lords and Conservative support for it in the Commons would not have been forthcoming without such a provision. The fear during the its passage through Parliament was that the Bill would become a charter for 'scroungers and scrimshankers' and that the homeless would jump the queue in front of those on the waiting list (W.R. Rees-Davies MP, Hansard, HC Deb, 18 Feb 1977, 5th Series, vol 926, col. 905). The aim behind this particular limitation had been to catch those who became homeless intentionally in order to secure accommodation under the homelessness legislation (see, B. Douglas-Mann, Hansard, HC Deb, 27 July 1977, 5th Series, vol 936, col. 879). Nevertheless, the more general provision catching all those who become homeless intentionally was eventually enacted. The Housing Act 1985, s 60 provides that:

s 60(1) A person becomes homeless intentionally if he deliberately does or fails to do anything in consequence of which he ceases to occupy accommodation which is available for his occupation and which it would have been reasonable for him to continue to occupy.

(2) A person becomes threatened with homelessness intentionally if he deliberately does or fails to do anything the likely result of which is that he will be forced to leave accommodation which is available for his occupation and which it would have been reasonable for him to continue to occupy.

(3) For the purposes of subsection (1) or (2) an act or omission in good faith on the part of a person who was unaware of any relevant fact shall not be treated as deliberate.

(4) Regard may be had, in determining whether it would have been reasonable for a person to continue to occupy accommodation, to the general circumstances prevailing in relation to housing in the district of the local housing authority to whom he applied for accommodation or for assistance in obtaining accommodation.

(See Loveland, *The Politics, Law and Practice of 'Intentional Homelessness': 1—Housing Debt*, [1993] JSW&FL 113; *2—Abandonment of Existing Housing*, [1993] JSW&FL 185)

Where the homelessness could not have been avoided, then the local authority must consider this factor in assessing 'intentionality'. Since an assured shorthold tenancy can be terminated without a tenant having any effective challenge, its ending should not mean that the former assured shorthold tenant is intentionally homeless—compare *R v Croydon LBC, ex parte Jarvis, op. cit.*, with *R v Newham LBC, ex parte Ugbo, op. cit.* (see also ch 11.2.6).

It is not the act of becoming homeless that must be deliberate, but rather the act that causes homelessness which must be intentional. Very rarely will a person set out to become homeless, however failure to pay rent or mortgage payments will, in certain circumstances, render the former occupier liable to be deemed intentionally homeless (see *R v Salford CC, ex parte Devenport* (1984) 82 LGR 89). On the other hand, a local authority cannot have a fixed policy that certain behaviour always constitutes intentional homelessness. Every case must be viewed on its own facts and, for instance, simply because an applicant was evicted for rent arrears cannot mean that automatically this is a case of intentional homelessness—it could be that the applicant did not claim certain welfare state benefits of which they were unaware, but to which they were entitled and therefore the homelessness will not be deemed intentional since no deliberate act or omission gave rise to it (*Williams v Cynon Valley BC* [1980] LAG Bull.16; *R v Swansea CC, ex parte Thomas* [1983] JSWL 356, The Times, 14 April 1983; *R v Tower Hamlets LBC, ex parte Khalique*, The Times, 17 March 1994). The Court of Appeal showed the breadth of this limitation in *R v Wandsworth LBC, ex parte Hawthorne* [1994] 1 WLR 1442. Here, the local authority claimed that the applicant was intentionally homeless due to a second set of rent arrears: she claimed that her housing benefit was inadequate to cover her current rent plus a further £7 per week to meet the earlier assessment of arrears. The Court of Appeal held that the present arrears were not deliberate within the meaning of s 60 because of the applicant's 'poverty and inability to make ends meet'—she had chosen to spend her cash in hand on the maintenance of her children rather than on the rent. The local authority had failed to address whether her inability to meet both her rent and arrears and the maintenance of her children meant that the current arrears were deliberate. Many people in arrears might benefit from this decision—see also, the Irish Supreme Court cases of *Daniel Quirke v Folio Homes Ltd* [1988] ILRM 496, and *Dowd v Pierce* [1984] ILRM 653, both decided under Ireland's Housing (Private Rented Dwellings) (Amendment) Act 1983, s 13 which requires the rent tribunal to have regard to the means of the tenant in setting the rent.

Nevertheless, while local authorities cannot have a set, fixed policy that certain facts will inevitably lead to a finding of intentional homelessness, there are several normally accepted causes of intentional homelessness (see Table 5.9, following page).

Nor can a local authority look beyond the case of the individual applicant. The issue is whether the applicant has deliberately done or failed to do something as a consequence of which he has become homeless, not whether anyone else with whom he ordinarily resides has so done. In the *Puhlhofer* case, *op. cit.*, the application following the material change of circumstances was made by the husband because the wife had been deemed intentionally homeless. In *R v West Dorset DC, ex parte Phillips* (1985) 17 HLR 336, the wife was entitled to be treated as unintentionally homeless where she was shown not to have acquiesced in her husband's spending on alcohol. However, this is not to say that an applicant

Table 5.9 Local authority interpretations of intentional homelessness

	Yes %
Loss of tied accommodation through voluntary termination of employment	73
Rent arrears	49
Moved to area seeking employment	49
Applicant does not intend to pursue legal rights to family home	38
Expiry of holiday let or short-term lease	20
Mortgage arrears	16
Other	6
Loss of tied accommodation through involuntary termination of employment	3
Expiry of assured shorthold tenancy	2

Source: Butler, Carlisle and Lloyd, *op. cit.*, Table 15, p 27

cannot, in certain circumstances, become tainted by another member of the family unit's 'intentionality'. In *Lewis v North Devon DC* [1981] 1 All ER 27, the applicant's partner lost his job which attracted tied accommodation. Woolf J held that the applicant had acquiesced in her partner's conduct which led to the loss of job and was, thus, infected with his intentionality (see also, *Ex parte Thomas, op. cit.*). The consequence of treating the applicant in isolation is that even where one member of the family unit is intentionally homeless, with a judicious choice of applicant, the whole family can be rehoused regardless. In *R v Oldham MBC, ex parte Garlick, R v Bexley LBC, ex parte Bentum, op. cit.*, the applicants were both four years old; Garlick's mother had been previously deemed intentionally homeless because of her failure to pay rent while Bentum's parents were intentionally homeless because they had deliberately omitted to make mortgage payments—see Cowan & Fionda, *New Angles on Homelessness*, [1993] JSW&FL 403. Article 27 of the U.N. Convention on the Rights of the Child, 28 International Legal Materials 1457 (1989), provides that:

1 States parties recognize the right of every child to a standard of living adequate for the child's physical, mental, spiritual, moral and social development.
   . . .
3 States Parties, in accordance with national conditions and within their means, shall take appropriate measures to assist parents and others responsible for the child to implement this right and shall in case of need provide material assistance and support programmes, particularly with regard to . . . housing.
– Article 1 states that a child means anyone under the age of eighteen.

International understanding, therefore, is that a child needs a home for proper and full development. If a child is a member of a homeless family, what rights are owed to him? Before looking at Part III of the Housing Act 1985, it is worth considering the Children Act 1989. It provides in s 20(1) that a local authority must provide accommodation to a child in need (see Children Act 1989, ss 17(10) and 105(7)) if the child requires such accommodation as a result of

(c) **the person who has been caring for him being prevented (whether or not permanently, and for whatever reason) from providing him with suitable accommodation ...**

How far this provision might be of use where the family has been evicted from its former home will be considered below. Where the child is 16 or more, s 20(3) obliges the local authority to provide accommodation if it considers that otherwise his welfare 'is likely to be seriously prejudiced'. This measure is intended to assist those children leaving care as they approach their majority, but it is extremely limited since it requires the local authority to find that his welfare will be seriously prejudiced—the pressures on Social Services Departments also means that this obligation to young people does not necessarily receive the priority it deserves (see CHAR, *Reassessing Priorities*, 1993). Moreover, according to Butler, Carlisle and Lloyd, *op. cit.*, at Table 14, only 65 per cent, less than two-thirds, of local authorities treated children leaving care as in priority need for the purposes of the Housing Act 1985, s 59; according to the Campaign for the Homeless and Rootless (CHAR), *Acting in Isolation*, 1994, social services and housing departments are failing to work together as envisaged during the passage of the Children Act to protect children in general and 16–17 year olds in particular.

Thus, the Children Act 1989 may, in certain cases, supplement those local authority obligations found in the Housing Act 1985, Part III. Does the law, however, allow the child to apply for rehousing where his parents would not satisfy s 65(2) and qualify for permanent rehousing? The initial problem is to be found in the Law of Property Act 1925, s 19. It states that an attempt to convey the legal estate to a minor grants only an equitable lease (see also, the Law of Property Act 1925, s 1(6) and the Settled Land Act 1925, s 27; s 27(2) would take effect to make an adult hold the legal estate on trust for the child). Nevertheless, either by means of a licence or some adult acting as trustee of the legal estate for the child, an effective disposition of lease can take place. Moreover, while there are constraints on granting leases to minors, there are no restrictions on minors being applicants for rehousing under Part III of the Housing Act 1985. Section 65(2) provides only that if the applicant has priority need and is not intentionally homeless, then the local authority shall 'secure that accommodation becomes available for his occupation'. It is unlikely that children would be intentionally homeless and, under s 59(1)(c), they could have priority need as being vulnerable as a result of some other special reason, namely their youth. The question therefore turns on whether precedence should be given to protecting the child's needs or to preventing evasion of the Act by using the child to rehouse the intentionally homeless parents. Lord Griffiths in *Garlick* and *Bentum, op. cit*, articulated the question before the court in terms of what duty, if any, would be owed to a dependent child living with his parents (at 612). On a general note, Lord Griffiths set out the nature of the duty under Part III of the 1985 Housing Act as follows:

It is not a duty to take the homeless off the streets and to place them physically in accommodation. The duty is to give them and their families the first priority in the housing queue. (at 613)

Possibly putting the cart before the horse (at 618), Lord Griffiths went on to hold that there could be no duty even to place dependent children at the front of the queue: a dependent child living with a parent or guardian could not have priority need under s 59(1) on the ground that there was no express provision in the section referring to dependent children (at 614). According to Lord Griffiths, the parents are expected to provide accommodation and their child gives them priority need under s 59(1)(b).

Several supplementary questions are raised by Lord Griffiths' reasoning: who is a dependent child, what if the parents cannot provide accommodation and what if a dependent child is not living with his parents? A child is dependent according to the Code of Guidance for Local Authorities (3rd edn, 1991, at para 6.3—see s 71 Housing Act 1985, considered at 614) if he is under 16 or between 16 and 18 and still in full-time education. An under-16 year old will only be treated as independent, and even this case is not automatic, if he has left home and is deemed to be vulnerable (at 614—see also, *Kelly v Monklands DC* [1986] SLT 169). However, in the case of parents who are found to be intentionally homeless, they are incapable of providing permanent accommodation. The Housing Act 1985, s 65, grants applicants with priority need only temporary accommodation if they are intentionally homeless and, after a reasonable period, they are expected to make their own arrangements—given, though, that the rented sector has significantly contracted since 1979, the general availability of homes for the poorest in the community is substantially restricted. Thus, Lord Griffiths' premise for his denial of applicant status to dependent children is proved to be inadequate to meet all situations, even taking into account the Children Act 1989, s 20. On the other hand, Lord Griffiths was prepared to acknowledge that legally dependent children not living with their parents might have priority need. Moreover, Lord Griffiths' fundamental point that a dependent child's parents ought to make the application, for they are responsible for their child's accommodation, does not necessarily preclude a coexisting right in the child where he is not intentionally homeless and he has priority need through being vulnerable for whatever reason (see, for instance, the impediment to achievement at school that homelessness places in the way of the child—the *Guardian* 2 p 20, 20 July 1993).

A secondary theme in the judgment relates to notification duties (see the Housing Act 1985, ss 64, 74).

s 64(1) On completing their inquiries under section 62, the local housing authority shall notify the applicant of their decision on the question whether he
is homeless or threatened with homelessness.
(2) If they notify him that their decision is that he is homeless or threatened
with homelessness, they shall at the same time notify him of their decision on the question whether he has a priority need.
(3) If they notify him that their decision is that he has a priority need, they
shall at the same time notify him—
(a) of their decision whether he became homeless or threatened with
homelessness intentionally ...

Lord Griffiths relied on this provision and s 74, which might be interpreted to require the applicant to provide the local authority with full and truthful infor-
mation and to notify it of any change of circumstances, to claim that the duty under Part III is owed only to those homeless persons in priority need who can consciously decide whether or not to accept the offer and that this does not include dependent children (at 615; Lord Griffiths reached the same conclusion with respect to applicants who are so disabled that they are unable to compre-
hend or evaluate the offer—at 617). In other words, there is a competency test for applicants. This question of capacity can only be challenged by judicial review.

On the other hand, Lord Slynn, who concurred in the judgment of Lord Griffiths in so far as it applied to *Garlick* and *Bentum*, dissented with respect to *Ferdous Begum*, the disabled adult 'applicant' whose case was joined. He found that s 74 would allow an 'applicant' to apply through another and he rejected any test of capacity which was not explicit in the Act (at 619). He distinguished the children from the disabled adult on the ground that the latter was expressly listed in s 59 as having priority need. Nevertheless, his analysis of this issue of capacity can be read more widely.

I do not consider that the person making the application is to be excluded from the class of vulnerable persons who can establish a priority need because he or she is not capable of understanding the nature or details of a lease or contract.

It is all-embracing enough to include even four-year-old applicants, but it is more likely to be adopted with respect to applicants who are capable of making decisions for themselves, possibly those as young as fifteen still living with their parents. A child of fifteen, for example, living with his intentionally homeless parents, might be able to argue that, given some proof of priority need, he should be able to make an application. Such a result would be contrary to the majority judgment, but the idea that a hard and fast line can be drawn at the sixteenth birthday as to when a child is dependent or not ignores reality.

With regard to Part III of the Housing Act 1985, however, the decision in *Ex parte Garlick* and *Bentum* (at 615) is best summarized by Lord Griffiths.

If a family has lost its right to priority treatment through intentional homelessness, the parent cannot achieve the same result through the back door by an application in the name of a dependent child; if he could it would mean that the disqualification of intentional homelessness had no application to families with dependent children. If this had been the intention of Parliament it would surely have said so.

In a passing aside, though, Lord Griffiths went on to indicate that the Children Act 1989, ss 20 and 27, deal with the accommodation and care of children. Three responses can be put forward. First, as Lord Slynn pointed out with respect to Ferdous Begum, while other social welfare legislation might be applicable (in that case, the National Assistance Act 1948 and see now the National Health Service and Community Care Act 1990), this does not conclusively exclude the possibility that a further duty is owed under the homelessness legislation (at 619). Secondly, this other social welfare legislation does not provide that this accommodation shall be suitable for the child and anyone else with whom he normally resides. The Children Act 1989 is designed to deal with those children who need to go into care away from their family. Finally, Lord Griffiths seems to have ignored a pertinent authority, *R v Tower Hamlets LBC, ex parte Byas*, (1993) 25 HLR 105. In *Byas*, the Court of Appeal was faced with a claim for judicial review of a decision by Tower Hamlets housing authority not to provide accommodation to the applicant, a single parent with five dependent children, in pursuance of the Children Act 1989, ss 20 and 27, when requested so to do by Tower Hamlets social services department—the housing department had previously found her to be intentionally homeless and she was in temporary accommodation under the Housing Act 1985, s 65, when social services asked for assistance under ss 20 and 27 of the 1989 Act. Having held that s 27 only applies to inter-authority requests for help, not inter-department requests within a single local authority, Russell LJ went on, *obiter*, to quote May J from the first instance decision.

. . . The argument is that, if there is a child to whom s 20(1)(c) applies, the obligation to provide accommodation for that child, or those children, translates into an obligation to house that child or those children with their parents, and therefore an obligation to house their parents . . . I should find severe difficulties in reaching a conclusion that, where an adult has become intentionally homeless,

such that under the Housing Act the local authority ceases to be obliged to provide accommodation for him or her, the local authority nevertheless, by virtue of this argument under the Children Act, became obliged to provide accommodation for that adult. That in no way detracts from an obligation which the local authority may have under the Children Act in relation to children. (Byas, *op. cit.*, at 107)

In the subsequent case of *R v Northavon, ex parte Smith* [1994] 3 All ER 313, the House of Lords held that Part III of the 1985 Act is in no way subject to the Children Act 1989. Furthermore, fewer of these cases should be coming before the courts because the House also stated that judicial review was not the appropriate medium for getting the Housing and Social Services Departments to talk to each other under the Children Act 1989, s 27. In *R v Brent LBC, ex parte Sawyers* (1994) 26 HLR 44, the court stated that where an applicant was relying on Children Act 1989, s 23, then the appeal should primarily be to the Secretary of State under s 84 of the 1989 Act, not to the courts by way of judicial review.

Taking *Smith, Byas* and *Garlick* together, one is left with the position that, other than through taking a child into care, neither under the Housing Act 1985 nor the Children Act 1989 is a local authority required to provide a home to a dependent child, no matter how vulnerable, if he is still living with his parents. Indeed, where the family does become homeless, local authorities are threatening to take children into care as the 'solution' to the present dilemma.

'It's one of the most traumatic cases I've ever dealt with. A family forced first into homelessness and then threatened with break-up and children going into foster care. They couldn't believe that their lives might get worse.' Beryl Clarke, advice worker. (Summerskill, *Homebusters*, ROOF, September/October 1994, p 26)

And yet studies have shown that a stable home is one of the most important factors in a child's development (see, Kellmer-Pringle, *The Needs Of Children*, 2nd edn, 1980, at pp 110–13.). In conclusion, in balancing the needs of the child against the discretion of the local authority in its allocation processes, the House of Lords has come down firmly in favour of the local authority (see also, Davies & Molnar, *All Our Tomorrows*, National Housing Forum, 1993; Campbell, *Three's a Crowd*, ROOF, May/June 1993, p 13; Cowan & Fionda, 1993a, *op. cit.*). The result is that for the purposes of the Housing Act 1985, s 60, one of the adult applicants must not be contaminated by any other member of the family unit's intentionality.

If an applicant is intentionally homeless, for how long will this status attach? Is there a so-called 'chain of intentionality'? The reason that this is important is that a finding of intentionality effectively relieves the local authority of its obligations to allocate housing to the applicant. It may be that an application is made following the termination of a short-term lease; in those circumstances the applicant

has not done or failed to do anything as a consequence of which the accommodation was lost, the short-term let has simply come to a natural end—*Ugbo, op.
cit.* However, should a local authority have to entertain such an application
where prior to the short-term let the applicant was a secure council tenant and
he lost that tenancy through some act or failure to act? That was the case, more or
less, in *Dyson v Kerrier DC* [1980] 3 All ER 313, where the Court of Appeal held that
giving up a secure council tenancy to move into a 'winter let', a private sector tenancy lasting eight months at most (see now the Housing Act 1988, Sch 2, Pt I,
Ground 3), amounted to intentional homelessness and the fact the
winter let had now ended still left the applicant chained to her initial intentionality. Normally, only if a formerly intentional applicant obtains non-temporary
accommodation will the chain be broken—whether an assured shorthold tenancy under the Housing Act 1988, s 20, which might only last six months, would
suffice to break the chain is debateable. Once the intentionally homeless applicant has found non-temporary accommodation, the local authority must only
consider the most recent cause of homelessness. The case of *Krishnan v
Hillingdon LBC* [1981] LAG Bull.137, shows that moving in with relatives can
break the chain if there was an expectation that the applicant was going to live
there for at least twelve months, even if for reasons not connected with the applicant the stay is for a shorter period. The concept of the chain re-emphasizes the
idea that intentional homelessness was introduced into the Act to exclude self-
induced homelessness; after finding non-temporary accommodation by one-
self, subsequent homelessness is viewed in its own right, not as a continuation of
the earlier intentionality. It is in essence a nineteenth-century view of the poor as
deserving or undeserving and the Victorian tenet that self-help is to be rewarded.
It has little to do, however, with obtaining suitable accommodation at a time of
shortage in the social sector. It should be applied in conformity with the known
constraints faced by applicants.

The homelessness legislation raises further issues with respect to allocation
policies in the case where the applicant has just entered the United Kingdom.
Those issues concern illegal entrants, refugees and whether giving up accommodation abroad can result in a finding of intentional homelessness—see *R v Tower
Hamlets LBC, ex parte Khatun*, the *Guardian*, 4 October 1993. Paragraph 4.11 of
the Code of Guidance issued under the Housing Act 1985, s 71, states:

**Authorities cannot refuse to rehouse a family because they are immigrants.
Everyone admitted to this country is entitled to equal treatment under the law;
their rights under Part III of the [Housing Act 1985] are no different from those of
any other person. Authorities should remember to treat as confidential information received on an applicant's immigration status.**

Under the immigration rules, however, if leave to enter the United Kingdom is
obtained by means of a false statement about the availability of accommodation,

then that will result in illegal immigrant status. The question before the Court of Appeal in *R v Secretary of State for the Environment, ex parte Tower Hamlets LBC* [1993] QB 632, was whether the local authority should investigate this matter under its inquiries under the Housing Act 1985, s 62(1).

s 62(1)   If a person (an 'applicant') applies to a local housing authority for accommodation, or for assistance in obtaining accommodation, and the authority have reason to believe that he may be homeless or threatened with homelessness, they shall make such inquiries as are necessary to satisfy themselves as to whether he is homeless or threatened with homelessness.

The Court of Appeal found that it was appropriate despite the fact that housing officers are not trained in the complexities of immigration law. The people most likely to be caught are members of the family of a person already settled in the United Kingdom who claim they will place no burden on public funds, including public housing, when the settled person's accommodation is wholly unsuitable for an entire family. Bingham MR, though, stated the scope of this discretion more widely.

[Housing] authorities [owe] no duty to those, homeless or not, in priority need or not, who entered illegally. It would be an affront to common sense if those who stole into this country by subterfuge were then to be housed at public expense. There was no reason why those who entered by fraudulently obtaining leave to enter should be differentiated from the position of those who entered unlawfully by evading the requirement to obtain leave to enter altogether. (See also, Campbell, *New Borders to Cross,* ROOF, July/August 1993, p 11)

The government then picked up on this decision and issued advice to local authorities to check on the immigration status of applicants for council housing (the *Guardian* p 7, 26 May 1993). The fear expressed by housing and immigration organisations is that councils will target for investigation non-white applicants, creating a strain on race relations in an area of social policy where, as has been seen, there is already some tension. Nevertheless, the position is that there are no allocation duties owed to illegal immigrants.

The rights of asylum applicants have also been curtailed. The Asylum and Immigration Appeals Act 1993, ss 4 and 5 and Sch 1 reduce the rights of applicants for asylum and their dependants under the Housing Act 1985, Part III. In a similar vein to the decision in *Ex parte Tower Hamlets, op. cit.,* Sch 1(2) requires local authorities to make such inquiries so as to satisfy themselves that the applicant is an asylum-seeker or an asylum seeker's dependant—if immigration law is complex, the determination of refugee status is even more intricate and laden with discretion and once more there is doubt as to whether it is proper to assign this task to housing officers (*cf.* Sch 1(7) 1993 Act provides that the Secretary of State shall supply information to the housing authority, if requested, concerning whether the applicant is an asylum-seeker or an asylum seeker's dependant and when the applicant ceased to be such). Secondly, if a qualifying asylum-seeker has any accommodation available to him that is suitable for himself and anyone with whom he normally resides (s 5(7) 1993 Act) then, no matter how temporary its status, the local authority will owe no obligations under Part III (1993 Act, s 4(1)). If he has no accommodation for the purposes of s 4(1), then any offer made under the Housing Act 1985, Part III, is to be treated as only temporary while a decision is made on refugee status. Finally, Sch 1 adds one further hurdle to asylum-seekers attempts to obtain permanent housing under this modified allocation process.

para 6 (1) A tenancy granted in pursuance of any duty under Part III of the Act of
1985 to a person who is [an asylum-seeker or dependant of an asylum-
seeker] cannot be–
(a) a tenancy which is a secure tenancy for the purposes of that Act, or
(b) a tenancy which is an assured tenancy for the purposes of the
Housing Act 1988,
before the expiry of the period of twelve months beginning with the
date on which the landlord is supplied with written information given
by the Secretary of State . . . that the person has ceased to be [an asylum-seeker or dependant of an asylum-seeker], unless before the
expiry of that period the landlord notifies that person that the tenancy
is to be regarded as a secure tenancy or, as the case may be, an assured
tenancy.

The aim is to provide the landlord with time to reallocate housing to the asylum-seeker without the bother of dealing with security of tenure. Unfortunately, it might well add to the sense of insecurity of people who are already feeling displaced and vulnerable.

For non-refugees who legally enter the United Kingdom, there should be no discrimination in terms of the provisions of the Housing Act 1985, Part III, although institutionalised racism affects homeless applicants in the same way as all other non-white persons seeking the allocation of housing (5.1.2.2 above). Persons immigrating to the United Kingdom have to satisfy the law on homelessness in the same way as any other applicant, including the application of the intentional homelessness provision. In *De Falco v Crawley BC* [1980] QB 460, the Court of Appeal laid down that if it is to prove intentionality, the housing authority must show that the applicant arrived in the United Kingdom without permanent housing having deliberately left behind accommodation that was available for his occupation. The accommodation left behind must also have been a suitable size for the applicant and those who normally reside with him—*Islam v Hillingdon LBC* [1981] 3 All ER 901. In general, the local authority need to ascertain the true reason for leaving the foreign accommodation if a finding of intentional homelessness is not to be subject to judicial review—*Khatun, op. cit.*

The final issue surrounding intentional homelessness concerns accommodation 'which it would have been reasonable for him to continue to occupy'. Reasonableness has to be understood in terms of s 60(4).

s 60(4) Regard may be had, in determining whether it would have been reasonable for a person to continue to occupy accommodation, to the general circumstances prevailing in relation to housing in the district of the local housing authority to whom he applied for accommodation or for assistance in obtaining accommodation.

The question resolves itself into whether it was reasonable for the applicant to have left, although strictly speaking that is not what s 60 is dealing with—it might have been reasonable to leave even though it was also reasonable to continue to occupy the former accommodation and it is, in theory, only the latter concept that is within the Act.

The deliberate act of failing to pay rent cannot be divorced from the subsequent cessation of occupation due to sexual harassment and personal violence. (*R v Newham LBC, ex parte Campbell* (1994) 26 HLR 183 at 189-90)

Moreover, in deciding on this issue of reasonableness, the local authority has to have regard to all members of the family unit—*R v Westminster CC, ex parte Bishop, op. cit.*, where the medically evidenced needs of the applicant's daughter were ignored. *Prima facie*, the condition of the applicant's former housing will figure strongly in any assessment of whether it was reasonable to leave (discussed above with respect to s 58), but non-housing matters can also be taken into account, including the lack of employment opportunities in the area from which the applicant came—*R v Hammersmith & Fulham LBC, ex parte Duro-Rama* (1983) 81 LGR 702; *cf., R v Tower Hamlets LBC, ex parte Monaf* (1987) 19 HLR 577; (1988) 20 HLR 529.

(iv) The Duty. Having investigated whether the applicant is homeless (s 62), has priority need and is intentionally homeless, what duties does a local authority owe?

s 65(1) This section has effect as regards the duties owed by the local housing authority to an applicant where they are satisfied that he is homeless.
  (2) Where they are satisfied that he has a priority need and are not satisfied that he became homeless intentionally, they shall, unless they notify another local housing authority in accordance with section 67 (referral of application on grounds of local connection), secure that accommodation becomes available for his occupation.
  (3) Where they are satisfied that he has a priority need but are also satisfied that he became homeless intentionally, they shall—
    (a) secure that accommodation is made available for his occupation for such period as they consider will give him a reasonable opportunity of securing accommodation for his occupation, and

(b) furnish him with advice and such assistance as they consider appropriate in the circumstances in any attempts he may make to secure that accommodation becomes available for his occupation.

(4) Where they are not satisfied that he has a priority need, they shall furnish him with advice and such assistance as they consider appropriate in the circumstances in any attempts he may make to secure that accommodation becomes available for his occupation.

Section 65 provides a graduated scale of duties owed to homeless applicants. The primary duty is owed to an applicant with priority need who is not intentionally homeless. It is a duty to secure that accommodation becomes available and it can be satisfied by the local authority itself providing it or, under s 69(1)(b), 'by securing that he obtains suitable accommodation from some other person', such as a housing association or a private landlord or another local authority (see, *R v Bristol CC, ex parte Browne* [1979] 3 All ER 344), or by giving advice and assistance to the applicant so as to obtain a mortgage in order that he can buy his own home. On the other hand, if the applicant has priority need, but is intentionally homeless, then the local authority's obligation is reduced; only temporary accommodation for a reasonable period (see, *Lally v Kensington & Chelsea BC*, The Times, 27 March 1980) and advice and assistance on where to look for permanent accommodation need be offered. If applicants do not have priority need, regardless of whether they are intentionally homeless or not, then they are only entitled to the minimal duty, the provision of advice and assistance on where to look for permanent accommodation—the single homeless person and the childless couple fall into this last category.

What does the primary duty involve? First, the local authority only has to secure that accommodation becomes available. Normally, the local authority will only make one or two offers of accommodation to a homeless applicant. If they are 'unreasonably' rejected, then the authority will be treated as having discharged its s 65 duty—*Newham, ex parte Campbell, op. cit.*; *R v Brent LBC, ex parte Awua* (1994) 26 HLR 539. Since the applicant never occupied the rejected accommodation, however, he cannot have 'ceased' to occupy it for the purposes of s 60. Nevertheless, if, having fulfilled its duty under s 65 by making the offer, the authority then evict the applicant from any temporary accommodation, it is a mixed question of fact and law whether the temporary accommodation was a settled residence such that the applicant has ceased to occupy 'accommodation' for the purposes of s 60—*Din v Wandsworth LBC* [1983] AC 657; *R v City of Westminster, ex parte Chambers* (1982) 6 HLR 24; *R v Ealing LBC, ex parte McBain*, [1985] 1 WLR 1351; *R v Brent LBC, ex parte Macwan* (1994) 26 HLR 528; *Ex parte Awua, op. cit.*The only argument that an applicant can raise against a finding of intentionality after temporary accommodation has been lost following the rejection of an offer under s 65, is that the offered property was not suitable under the Housing Act 1985, s 69(1)(a)—*R v*

Lewisham LBC, ex parte Dolan (1993) 25 HLR 68; *cf. Ali v Tower Hamlets LBC* [1992] 3 All ER 512; *London Borough of Tower Hamlets v Abdi* (1993) 25 HLR 80; *London Borough of Hackney v Lambourne* (1993) 25 HLR 172; Cowan, *The Public/Private Dichotomy and 'Suitable Accommodation' under s 69(1) of the Housing Act 1985*, [1993] JSW&FL 236. The Court of Appeal in *R v Newham LBC, ex parte Dada* (1994) 26 HLR 531, however, held that the local authority is not obliged to take account of the future housing needs of an unborn child when allocating accommodation to a pregnant woman, reversing the first instance decision.

The full permanent rehousing duty owed to homeless applicants with priority need and who are not intentionally homeless can be fulfilled over a period of time—*Ex parte Awua, op. cit.* The local authority's duty does not exist in a vacuum and the general availability of suitable housing in the area has to be taken into account—*Ex parte Macwan, op. cit.* The question that remains, however, is whether offering a private sector let that can be ended under the Housing Act 1988, Sch 2, fulfils the duty to provide rehousing? An assured shorthold tenancy could hardly fulfil the s 65 obligation—Cowan, *op. cit.*; the *Guardian* 2 p 21, 22 October 1993. One reason that local authorities like using the private sector is that if the new accommodation is outside the borough, then, when the private sector let comes to an end, the local authority responsible for the area where the private sector let occurred would now be responsible for any rehousing under the homelessness legislation—the *Guardian* p 20, 2 February 1994. On the other hand, in *R v Tower Hamlets, ex parte Kaur*, unreported, QBD, February 1994, it was held that offering applicants private sector housing where the rent is so high that housing benefit will not cover it all does not fulfil the s 65 duty. Further, offering the applicant housing to which she cannot gain entry similarly fails to fulfil the s 65 duty—*R v Lambeth LBC, ex parte Campbell* [1994] New Property Cases 34.

The primary duty in s 65 is also subject to the local connection rule.

(v)Local Connection.   The local connection rule dates back to Tudor times when 'vagrants' could be returned to their own parish. The aim was to protect the parish in order to be in a position to 'look after one's own'. The modern-day equivalent of this particular application of the adage 'charity begins at home', is found in s 67.

s 67(1) If the local housing authority -
   (a) are satisfied that an applicant is homeless and has a priority need, and are not satisfied that he became homeless intentionally, but
   (b) are of opinion that the conditions are satisfied for referral of his application to another local housing authority in England, Wales or Scotland, they may notify that other authority of the fact that his application has been made and that they are of that opinion.
   (2) The conditions for referral of an application to another local housing authority are—

(a) that neither the applicant nor any person who might reasonably be expected to reside with him has a local connection with the district of the authority to whom his application was made,

(b) that the applicant or a person who might reasonably be expected to reside with him has a local connection with the district of that other authority, and

(c) that neither the applicant nor any person who might reasonably be expected to reside with him will run the risk of domestic violence in that other district.

(3) For this purpose a person runs the risk of domestic violence -

(a) if he runs the risk of violence from a person with whom, but for the risk of violence, he might reasonably be expected to reside, or from a person with whom he formerly resided, or

(b) if he runs the risk of threats of violence from such a person which are likely to be carried out.

In certain circumstances, having finished their investigations and having found the applicant to be homeless, in priority need and not intentionally homeless, the housing officers can pass the applicant on to be allocated housing by another local authority with whom he has a local connection. The rule is as follows:

1 If the applicant, or any other person with whom he normally resides, has no connection with any other local housing authority in Great Britain, then the authority to which the application is made must assume full responsibility. Such a situation might arise with persons immigrating—see, *Ex parte Browne*, *op. cit.*

2 If the applicant, or any other person with whom he normally resides, has a local connection with the local authority to which the application is made, it must assume full responsibility.

3 If the applicant, or any other person with whom he normally resides, has no connection with the local authority to which the application is made, but does have a connection with another housing authority in England, Wales or Scotland, then the case may be referred to that other authority, unless the applicant, or any other person with whom he normally resides, runs the risk of domestic violence.

Having examined the essence of the rule, how does one determine whether the applicant has any, or even several, local connections? Section 61 provides a list of factors to be taken into account.

s 61(1) References in this Part to a person having a local connection with the district of a local housing authority are to his having a connection with that district -

(a) because he is, or in the past was, normally resident in that district, and that residence is or was of his own choice, or

(b) because he is employed in that district, or

(c) because of family associations, or

(d) because of special circumstances.

Normal residence is taken to mean at least six months—*Eastleigh BC v Betts*, [1983] 2 All ER 1111.

In applying the rule, reference must be made to s 68 of the 1985 Act.

s 68(2) If it is determined that the conditions for referral are satisfied, the notified authority shall secure that accommodation becomes available for occupation by the applicant; if it is determined that the conditions are not satisfied, the notifying authority shall secure that accommodation becomes available for occupation by him.

Regard must also be had to the s 71 Code of Guidance and the unauthoritative but practically useful *Agreement on Procedures for Referrals of the Homeless—Revised*, drawn up in 1979 by the Association of District Councils, the Association of Metropolitan Authorities and the London Boroughs Association. Hoath, 1989, *op. cit.*, p 114, characterizes the 1979 Agreement in the following way.

The 1979 Agreement is not authorised by the 1985 Act: it does not form part of any 'arrangements' directed by Ministerial order to deal with the disputes between authorities pursuant to the Act, nor is it Ministerial guidance falling within section 71. Despite its lack of precise legal status, the 1979 Agreement is in practice a useful legal aid for councils in England and Wales to the interpretation of the sometimes rather vague 'local connection' provisions; the House of Lords [in *Betts, op. cit.*,] ... decided that a council is free to apply the 'eminently sensible and proper' guidelines in the 1979 Agreement, provided it does not close its mind to considerations as to the suitability or otherwise of the guidance to the particular facts of each case.

There are not that many referrals under s 67, but they do raise some interesting issues of discretion in the allocation process—see Thornton, *Who Houses? Homelessness, Local Connection and Inter-Authority Referrals under Section 67 of the Housing Act 1985*, [1994] JSW&FL 19. Section 67 is concerned only with referrals by one authority to another after the former has decided that a local connection exists with the latter. The review of a s 67 decision is concerned solely with whether the decision on the existence of a local connection is correct; it does not look to see if the referring authority properly assessed the applicant's status— that he is homeless, that he has priority need and that he is not intentionally homeless.

The unsatisfactory nature of this system of referral is highlighted where, . . ., the applicant has applied to and been refused by housing authority A and then applies to housing authority B which, in effect, reverses the decision of the first authority. However, this is not an essential feature. An applicant can apply to authority B in the first instance which, if the conditions for referral are satisfied, can then impose on authority A an obligation to accommodate him without that authority having had any opportunity of considering whether the applicant is homeless or has priority need or became homeless intentionally. The dispute resolution machinery contained in s 67(4) is limited to deciding whether 'the conditions of referral', namely those specified in sub-s (2) read with sub-s (3), are satisfied. They do not include the fundamental questions referred to in sub-s (1), which fall to be decided by the authority to which the applicant happens to apply or to be currently applying.

The vice of this system, which originated in the 1977 Act, was pointed out a decade ago in *R v Slough BC, ex parte Ealing London Borough*, [1981] 1 All ER 601, . . . This was not a case of the court criticising housing policy, which depends in large measure upon considerations which are not for the judiciary, but of criticising a dispute resolution system on the grounds that it offended against established concepts of fairness, a matter which is legitimately within the purview of the judiciary . . .

[Good] administration and comity between local authorities demand that in exercising a power, such as that contained in s 67(4), the authority should take full account of the general circumstances prevailing in relation to housing in both their areas and should give serious consideration to whether, notwithstanding that the conditions of referral are satisfied . . ., the public interest requires that the rehousing should be undertaken by it rather than by the other authority. (*R v Newham LBC, ex parte Tower Hamlets LBC*, [1992] 2 All ER 767 at 775–6 and 778)

The result of *Newham LBC, ex parte Tower Hamlets, op. cit.*, is that the local authority to which an application is made must, when assessing intentional homelessness, consider the housing conditions in any authority to which the first authority is intending to refer the case under s 67. Nevertheless, there is still no appeal on the primary facts from a decision to refer.

(c) Summary Having examined the present homelessness legislation with respect to allocation systems, it can readily be seen that it is imperfect in its operation. Part of the problem is economic. In 1989, the government's own Audit Commission, *Housing the Homeless: the Local Authority Role*, found that the use of bed and breakfast accommodation as temporary housing for the homeless was very expensive and that it would be economically more sensible to allocate a greater proportion of permanent housing to homeless applicants—para 128, p 41; the response has been to use temporary private sector lets rather than bed and breakfast hotels (Wilcox, *op. cit.*, Table 74, p 179), but it would be even cheaper for local and central government if funds were released to allow local authorities to provide permanent rehousing—Burrows and Walentowicz, *Homes Cost Less than Homelessness*, 1992. The Audit Commission, 1989, *op. cit.*, even suggested that local authorities should be allowed to buy family-sized accommodation from elderly owner-occupiers in exchange for the tenancy of a smaller

home—para 141, p 44. Finally, the Audit Commission recommended that central government should take greater account of homelessness when allocating capital resources to local authorities—paras 153–7, pp 49–50. Needless to add, the Conservative government ploughed a somewhat different furrow.

From a legal perspective, rather than merely tidying up some of the areas of imprecision, it may be necessary to institute some more fundamental reforms. Looking first at reforms to the present legislation, the very scope of the homelessness legislation may be too narrow in only recognising the needs of those categorised as having priority in s 59. The young, single homeless need to be seen as requiring assistance from local authorities, especially when their social security payments have been so severely curtailed such that they cannot afford private sector tenancies (see the *Guardian* 2 p 21, 23 July 1993, on the government's interest in the French *foyer* scheme for housing the young—'student hostels for non-students'). The housing associations, the traditional provider of homes to those not deemed to have priority need, are hard pressed to replace local authorities as the principal houser of the statutory homeless and so it is somewhat futile to expect them to continue their traditional role without a large increase in their available stock. The picture is so grim that commentators have suggested using empty buildings which were never designed for long-term occupation, such as hotels and hospitals—see the *Guardian* 2 p 19, 16 July 1993; the *Guardian*— Society pp 8-9, 28 September 1994. There is a fear being expressed, moreover, that homelessness among the young is creating an underclass where recidivism among ex-juvenile offenders is increasing (Cowan and Fionda, *Cause for Offence*, ROOF, May/June 1993, p 10) and where time spent in prison is seen as an improvement on life as a homeless person (the *Guardian* p 8, 3 June 1993). The Labour Party pre-1992 document on housing, *A Welcome Home, op. cit.*, at p 8, recommended that local authorities ought to take responsibility for single homeless people and some redrafting of s 59, especially in the light of *Garlick* and *Bentum*, [1993] 2 WLR 609, and the limited scope of 'vulnerable for some other special reason', seems to be required.

The second area within the present system where reformers seek to effect change is in relation to the means of reviewing decisions of the authority.

Furthermore, the principles of judicial review can appear unnecessarily restrictive . . . In *Dolan*, Sir Louis Blom-Cooper, Q.C., . . . , used the following test . . . to determine whether the offer of accommodation was 'reasonable' (The 'Wednesbury Test'):
'[Is the decision] so outrageous in its defiance of logic or of accepted moral standards that no sensible person who had applied his mind to the question to be decided could have arrived at it?' (Dolan, *op. cit.*, p 77)
Applicants for judicial review of a local authority's decision on this question thus have a difficult barrier to cross. (Cowan, *op. cit.*, p 238)

Arden thinks this criticism misses the point and that any change would be ineffectual anyway. He blames the problems the homeless face on the wording of the
Act and the difficulties in reviewing local authority decisions stem from that—
only if the statutory phraseology is amended will any sensible review be possible.

For Parliament chose, wholly gratuitously from a legal point of view, to preface
every duty under the Act with the magic words 'if the authority is of the opinion'
or 'if the authority has reason to believe'. Once an authority does this, Parliament
says to the courts: the decision is that of the authority. Even if you do not like the
decision, you cannot interfere; you may only interfere on well-established principles of administrative law—eg the authority has disregarded a relevant consideration or has taken one into account that is irrelevant, acted in bad faith or
contrary to the policy of the Act, misunderstood or misapplied its words, acted as
no reasonable authority could act or reached a decision which has no basis at all,
failed to act in accordance with the dictates of administrative fairness, or failed to
reach an individual decision where one is required. (*Bashing the Homeless*, ROOF,
March/April 1982, p 13 at p 15)

Nevertheless, judicial review is cumbersome and may not be appropriate to deal
with homelessness decisions whether the statute is amended or not. Some local
authorities have established internal appeal procedures (see Butler, Carlisle and
Lloyd, *op. cit.*, Table 13), but their decisions, too, are judicially reviewable—*R v
Newham LBC, ex parte Laronde*, The Times, 11 March 1994. Given the growth in
homelessness in the 1980s, it was inevitable that applications for judicial review
would spiral as well. It was not unexpected, therefore, when in *Puhlhofer*, [1986]
1 All ER 467, Lord Brightman expressed the hope that

there [would] be a lessening in the number of challenges which are mounted
against local authorities who are endeavouring, in extremely difficult circumstances, to perform their duties under the [1985] Act with due regard to all their
other housing problems.

After a brief drop in applications immediately after *Puhlhofer*, though, the number of cases regarding homelessness decisions has risen steadily. Along with
cases on immigration decisions, homelessness cases make up a substantial proportion of all applications for judicial review—Law Commission, *Administrative
Law: Judicial Review and Statutory Appeals*, Law Com. No. 226, 1994, para 1.11;
Partington, *Reforming Judicial Review: the Impact on Homelessness Cases*, [1994]
JSW&FL 47.

   The alternative to judicial review seems to be a choice between an appeal to
the County Court where facts could be reviewed or the establishment of a specialist tribunal to deal with homeless persons cases (McGrath & Hunter, *Time to
Get the Act Together*, ROOF, March/April 1993, p 15). Both have the merit of
allowing full appeals, rather then the limited procedure available on judicial
review, and greater ease of access. On the other hand, decisions in proceedings

Figure 5.1 Applications by homeless persons 1987–89

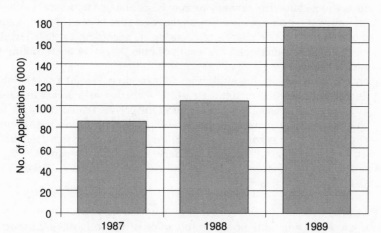

Source: Sunkin, Bridges and Mészáros, *Judicial Review in Perspective* 1993, at p.13, Preliminary figures for the first quarter of 1991 suggested this rate of increase was continuing.

for judicial review carry great weight and can have national effect, whereas a decision of the county court or some new tribunal may not carry as much weight. And there is always Arden's point that the Act is flawed and that as a result any change to the review procedures does not meet the real issues. The Law Commission (Law Com. No. 226, *op. cit.*) recommended in para 1.12 that a right of appeal to a court or independent tribunal should be established for homelessness cases.

More radically, however, than simply reforming the law on homelessness within the present system and structures, the government has looked at an alternative approach that turns its back on the 1977 Act blueprint. The starting point for this rethink was around the time of the Conservative Party conference in 1993 when, seeking to find ways to cut expenditure, single mothers were deemed to be queue-jumpers for housing through use of the homelessness legislation—the *Guardian* p 7, 8 October 1993; *cf.* Blake, September/October, 1993, *op. cit.*; the *Guardian* p 2, 6 October 1993 and p 7, 7 October 1993. The government eventually put forward its proposals on homelessness in January 1994.

The main elements of the proposal are:
(i) confine local authorities' duty to one of securing accommodation for a limited period for applicants who are in priority need, in an immediate crisis that has arisen through no fault of their own, and who have no alternative accommodation available to which they could reasonably be expected to go;

(ii) make waiting lists the sole route by which people may be allocated a secure local authority tenancy or may be nominated by a local authority for a similar housing association, so that everyone in need of such accommodation has a fair chance of securing it, according to their housing needs, their resources and the length of time they have been waiting for such housing;

(iii) encourage local housing authorities to help lower income households to find accommodation to suit their needs—whether as a tenant of a local authority or a housing association, or in the private rented sector, or in a shared home ownership scheme—by providing more user-friendly approaches such as common waiting lists and housing advice centres.

The first two elements will require primary legislation. (Department of the Environment, *Access to Local Authority and Housing Association Tenancies: A Consultation Paper*, 1994, at para 3.2)

This proposed new duty would originally only have been to provide emergency assistance to applicants with 'no accommodation of any sort available for occupation' through no fault of their own, and the duty would originally only have arisen after the investigation by the local authority had taken place—paras 5.1 and 5.2, *Access to Local Authority and Housing Association Tenancies: A Consultation Paper, op. cit.* Even this accommodation would only be provided for a limited period—para 6.1. For the first time, the government would make statutory provision setting out broad principles for allocating priority for access to social housing and such principles would apply to local authority and housing association tenancies—paras 20–22, *Access to Local Authority and Housing Association Tenancies: A Consultation Paper, op. cit.* The alleged justification for the changes was that the homeless were queue-jumpers, taking priority over those on the local authority waiting lists. Nevertheless, if the government's principles for allocating priority work on some form of points scheme related to housing need (para 20.3, *Consultation Paper*) akin to the lists currently operated by local authorities, then those who would have been given secure housing because they were homeless under the Housing Act 1985 will now be placed near the head of the queue because of their 'priority need'. There is no problem with the 1985 Act *per se*, the problem is that there is too little affordable, rented accommodation due to the government's own cutbacks on housing expenditure since 1979. This is a case of the government blaming the law for revealing a failure of policy.

The proposals met with widespread condemnation for their inadequacy, inappropriateness and harshness from, amongst others, church figures (the *Guardian* p 22, 29 March 1994 and the *Guardian* 2 p 19, 3 June 1994) and housing specialists (see, Loveland, *Cathy Sod Off! The End of Homelessness Legislation*, [1994] JSW&FL 367; Campbell, *Legal Eye: Cathy Comes Back*, ROOF, March/April 1994, p 14; Hendry, *Hysterical and Exaggerated*, p 18, Grant, *Don't Shoot the*

Messenger, p 19 and Blake, *Homeless All At Sea,* p 26, ROOF, May/June 1994). In all, 9,000 people responded to the *Consultation Paper.* Some saw the proposed legislation as a return to the position pre-1977 when the homeless had no exhaustive statutory guarantees—Grant 1994, *op. cit.* There were also some who saw it as a way to 'massage' the homelessness figures.

Perhaps we are witnessing an attempt to do to the homeless what has already been done to the unemployed and sick: introduce measures that alter the figures and do nothing about the real problem.

Consider this extract from the review: 'While the number of statutorily homeless households has shown a welcome decline over the last year, the underlying trend could continue upward unless steps are taken to alter the current legislation.' Think about it. (Campbell, *op. cit.*)

The government did not withdraw these proposals in the face of the criticism, but stated that they would only be proceeded with when parliamentary time allowed and watered down some of the provisions. The present position is summarized in Burns, *Notes,* ROOF, September/October 1994, p 8.

- **Homelessness will not now be legally redefined as rooflessness: people in refuges, hostels and B&B will still be regarded as homeless.**
- **Councils' duty to assist homeless people will still begin as soon as an applicant applies—not after enquiries are made.**
  Concessions? Maybe. But the core elements of the plans remain ominous:
- **No right to permanent housing for homeless people.**
- **Allocation of permanent housing from the waiting list only.**
- **A new definition of homelessness excluding those with access to suitable alternative accommodation.**
- **A time-limited duty, of a year, to provide temporary accommodation for the homeless.**

It is strange that the government is prepared to continue with such radical proposals on the basis of, *inter alia,* the cost of the present scheme without having costed out the proposed changes—see Argent, *A Worthwhile Price to Pay,* ROOF, November/December 1994, p 14.

There are many other points connected with the homelessness legislation which need to be reformed, but this overview of the topic, focusing on the implications for allocation, should highlight the pressures on social sector housing, the steps taken to diffuse the burden and the sweeping changes being planned. It also highlights how a book on the law relating to tenancies cannot ignore the political and economic context of housing policy.

5.2 FORMALITIES ON ENTERING INTO THE LANDLORD AND TENANT RELATIONSHIP

The formalities that are required when entering into a lease vary according to the length of the lease and the type of letting.

5.2.1 Statutory Requirements for All Leases

By the Law of Property Act 1925, s 52 a deed is required in order to create a legal estate, which includes a lease. There is, however, an exception for short leases. The Law of Property Act 1925, s 54(2) provides that no formality is required for a lease which takes 'effect in possession for a term not exceeding three years . . . at the best rent which can be reasonably obtained without taking a fine'. The effect of these provisions is that any lease for more than three years must be created by deed, whereas leases for three years or less can be created orally, by writing, or by deed. A periodic tenancy, such as a weekly or monthly tenancy, counts as a lease not exceeding three years even though it may, in practice, continue for more than three years (*In re Knight, ex p. Voisey* (1882) 21 Ch D 442). A lease which is initially for not more than three years will also be regarded as within s 54(2), even if it contains an option to renew beyond that period (*Hand v Hall* (1877) 2 Ex D 355). On the other hand, a lease for more than three years which can be determined earlier is not within the exception and will need to be created by deed (*Kushner v Law Society* [1952] 1 KB 264 at 274).

Some short leases are not within the s 54(2) exception, and therefore cannot be entered into informally. Reversionary leases, which take effect at some time in the future, are not within this exception as they are not 'in possession'. A lease can, however, be 'in possession' even if the tenant is not in physical occupation of the property—what the expression means is that the tenant must have the present right to possession of the property, which can include the right to receive rents from it (Law of Property Act 1925, s 205(xix)). The exception is intended to include leases for which the tenant is paying a rack rent (notwithstanding the wording of s 54(2), it is not necessary for the tenant to be paying the *best possible* rent) and which have not been purchased by a capital premium. In practice, it does tend to be short tenancies, such as weekly tenancies, which are created informally—often by the tenant simply moving into the property for an agreed rent.

With longer leases, especially of commercial property, the lease is likely to be the product of negotiations. The usual practice is for the landlord's solicitor to produce the first draft of the lease, which will then be amended by the tenant's solicitor, and so on until agreed upon. Once the parties have agreed upon the terms they may either proceed directly to the execution of the lease itself, or enter into a binding agreement to enter into a lease. Agreements for lease will be used, *inter alia*, where the tenant is undertaking a legal commitment to take a lease before the property is completed (as in pre-lets; see allocation, above). In order to be an enforceable contract, the agreement must comply with all the usual requirements of contract law (such as offer, acceptance, and considera-tion), and also with the Law of Property (Miscellaneous Provisions) Act 1989, s 2. Section 2 requires, *inter alia*, that all of the terms of a contract to lease must be contained in a single signed written document (or in two documents that are exchanged):

s 2(1) A contract for the sale or other disposition of an interest in land can only be made in writing and only by incorporating all the terms which the parties have expressly agreed in one document or, where contracts are exchanged, in each.

(2) The terms may be incorporated in a document either by being set out in it or by reference to some other document.

(3) The document incorporating the terms or, where contracts are exchanged, one of the documents incorporating them (but not necessarily the same one) must be signed by or on behalf of each party to the contract.

This section applies to contracts entered into after 27 September 1989 (for the previous position, see Law of Property Act 1925, s 40). Short leases (as referred to in Law of Property Act 1925, s 54(2)) are, again, exempted from these formalities requirements. Often the agreement for lease is not being entered into in isola-tion. In *Tootal Clothing Ltd v Guinea Properties Ltd* (1992) 64 P & CR 452, for example, the parties also entered into a separate agreement by which the land-lord agreed to pay £30,000 to the tenant towards the costs of fitting out works. In other situations, an agreement for lease may form part of a larger commercial transaction, such as a company takeover, and may therefore be simply one aspect of a complex web of agreements. Great care must be taken to ensure that the resulting agreement still complies with the s 2 requirement for all the terms which the parties have agreed upon to be incorporated into one document. In the *Tootal Clothing* case, the Court of Appeal held that the separate agreement to pay £30,000 was enforceable by the tenant. Although this is undoubtedly a sensi-ble outcome, the reasoning used to find that s 2 was complied with is somewhat questionable (see [1993] Conv 89).

Where the parties do enter into an agreement for lease before the lease itself is completed, it is usual for the agreed form of lease to be annexed to the agreement so that there can be no dispute over the agreed terms of the lease.

Where formalities are required, the lease must be properly executed as a deed (complying with Law of Property (Miscellaneous Provisions) Act 1989, s 1). Often, the lease is in two identical parts—one part, the original lease, is executed by the landlord and handed to the tenant on completion; the other part, the counterpart, is executed by the tenant and handed to the landlord on completion. After the lease has been formally completed, it may be necessary to pay stamp duty on it (see Stamp Act 1891; Ross, *Drafting and Negotiating Commercial Leases*, 3rd edn, 1989, para 15.10) and, if the lease is for more than 21 years, to register it under the Land Registration Act 1925 (see Gray, *Elements of Land Law*, 2nd edn, 1993, pp 174–5).

If either party refuses to complete the lease and there is an enforceable agreement for lease, an action for breach can be brought. This could be either an action for damages or, more usefully, an action for specific performance. Specific performance is a discretionary remedy and will not be granted where, for example, the party seeking enforcement has behaved badly or where enforcement would cause intolerable hardship (see Evans and Smith, *The Law of Landlord and Tenant*, 4th edn, 1993, pp 50–2). If the agreement that is being enforced failed to specify the terms of the lease, the court will imply into the agreement a term that the lease will include the 'usual covenants and provisos'. The usual covenants will include a covenant to pay rent, to pay rates and taxes, to keep and deliver up in repair, to allow the lessor to enter and view the state of repair, and a covenant by the landlord for quiet enjoyment (*Hampshire v Wickens* (1878) 7 Ch D 555). In addition, covenants that are in ordinary use for that kind of property, length of lease, *etc.*, may also be included as 'usual covenants' (see *Flexman v Corbett* [1930] 1 Ch 672; *Chester v Buckingham Travel Ltd* [1981] 1 All ER 386).

5.2.2 The Effect of Non-observance of the Formality Requirements

If the parties fail to comply with the formality requirements, the lease will not take effect as a legal estate. This does not mean, however, that it has no consequence. When the tenant moves into occupation it will, at law, take effect as a tenancy at will (Law of Property Act 1925, s 54(1); a tenancy at will may be protected if it is a private residential sector let, but not if in the business sector; see ch 6). If, for example, the landlord grants the tenant a ten year lease, but only in writing and not by deed, the lease will not be a legal estate (s 52). However, when the tenant moves in he will be a tenant at will. In addition, if the tenant starts paying rent, this may turn the tenancy at will into a periodic tenancy at law (subject to the cautionary words of Nicholls LJ in *Javad v Aqil* [1991] 1 All ER 243, where he said that a periodic tenancy will not arise where the surrounding circumstances reveal some other intention of the parties—see ch 4.2.2). Such a periodic tenancy will incorporate all of the terms of the abortive legal lease, so far as compatible with a periodic tenancy (*Martin v Smith* (1874) LR 9 Ex 50).

In equity, the effect of an informal lease may be much wider if there is an agreement for lease which is capable of specific performance. As equity looks on that as done which ought to be done, the tenant is regarded as having an equitable lease on the same terms as those in the 'abortive' legal lease (*Parker v Taswell* (1858) 2 De G & J 559). The extent of this is shown by *Walsh v Lonsdale* (1882) 21 Ch D 9. Here, the landlord granted a seven year lease in writing, one of the terms being that the tenant should pay the yearly rent in advance. At law, because there was no deed, the tenant would be a periodic tenant. The tenant paid rent in arrears—which under a legal periodic tenancy he was entitled to do. If, however, the tenant was seen as having an equitable lease on the same terms as the defective legal lease, he should pay rent in advance. The Court of Appeal decided that the rules of equity prevailed:

there are not two estates as there were formerly, one estate at common law by reason of the payment of rent from year to year, and an estate in equity under the agreement. There is only one Court, and the equity rules prevail in it. The tenant holds under an agreement for a lease. He holds, therefore, under the same terms in equity as if a lease had been granted . . . (*per* Jessell MR at 14)

The result was that the landlord was allowed to recover the rent due in advance.

When the doctrine of *Walsh v Lonsdale* does apply, there may be relatively little difference between having a properly executed legal lease and a mere contract (which will be seen as being an equitable lease on the same terms). There are, nevertheless, some remaining differences. The doctrine of *Walsh v Lonsdale* can only be used where the contract is one capable of specific performance. So, for example, it will not be used to assist a tenant who is in breach of a covenant (*Coatsworth v Johnson* (1886) 55 LJQB 220) or where specific performance would cause the tenant to be in breach, as in *Warmington v Miller* [1973] QB 877, where granting the lease would be in breach of a covenant against subletting. Also, as the tenant of an equitable lease does not have a legal estate, there is no privity of estate and, so, the landlord will not be able to enforce leasehold covenants against successors (see ch 9.6.2.4; for other differences, see Gray, 1993, *op. cit.*, pp 749–51).

5.2.3 Vitiating Factors and Leases

Although the hybrid nature of leases as both property interests and contracts has often led to a denial that general contract rules apply to leases (see ch 3), the courts are willing to find leases vitiated by the same factors that apply to contracts more generally. So, a lease can be rescinded for fraudulent misrepresentation (*Killick v Roberts* [1991] 1 WLR 1146). Again, in *Boustany v Piggott* [1993] EGCS 85, the Privy Council set aside a lease on the grounds of 'unconscionability'—the rent was one-sixth of the true value, fixed for ten years with an option to renew for a further ten years at the same rent, and the Privy Council held that the tenant 'must have taken advantage' of the landlord. There is no reason why other contract doctrines should not also apply, such as non est factum, undue influence and duress.

In addition, individual lease terms may be invalid. Clauses restricting the way in which the tenant can use the property may be found to be anti-competitive or, although less likely, in restraint of trade (see ch 7.3). While the Unfair Contract Terms Act 1977 does not apply to interests in land (Sch 1, para (1)(b)), it may be that new European Community legislation does apply to leases. The EC Directive on Unfair Terms in Consumer Contracts (93/13/EEC), implemented in the United Kingdom at the end of 1994 (The Unfair Terms in Consumer Contracts Regulations 1994, SI 1994 No. 3159), provides that any 'unfair term' in a contract concluded by a seller or supplier with a consumer will not be binding on the consumer. There is some doubt over whether this applies to a contract creating a property right, but if it is found to apply to the grant of a lease it could apply to any lease not individually negotiated, such as standard form leases, granted by local authorities and property companies, etc., so as to invalidate any clauses which 'contrary to the requirement of good faith' cause a significant imbalance in the parties' rights and obligations under the contract, to the detriment of the consumer.

5.2.4 Providing Information to Tenants

If a written lease has been entered into, the tenant is likely to have details of the terms of the tenancy (assuming that the tenant got a copy of the lease). However, as we have seen, there is no requirement for short leases to be in writing. Nor, even when the lease is in writing, will the tenant always have an adequate understanding of his position and rights. There are, therefore, various statutory provisions that are designed to provide information to tenants.

5.2.4.1 Information about the Terms of the Tenancy and the Identity of the Landlord

In the case of weekly residential tenancies, the landlord is under a duty to provide the tenant with a rent book. The Landlord and Tenant Act 1985, s 4 provides:

s 4(1) Where a tenant has a right to occupy premises as a residence in consideration of a rent payable weekly, the landlord shall provide a rent book or other similar document for use in respect of the premises.

(2) Subsection (1) does not apply to premises if the rent includes a payment in respect of board and the value of that board to the tenant forms a substantial proportion of the whole rent.

This applies to both contractual licensees and tenants (s 4(3)) unless the rent includes a substantial sum for board (subs (2), above). The rent book must contain information prescribed by regulation and includes the basic terms of the letting, such as the name and address of the landlord (s 5(1)), the address of the premises, the amount of rent payable, details of any other accommodation which the occupier has the right to share with other people, and a statement of the number of people permitted to use that dwelling (see the Housing Act 1985, s 332; Rent Book (Forms of Notice) Regulations 1982, SI 1982 No. 1474, as amended by SI 1988 No. 2198, SI 1990 No. 1067, and SI 1993 No. 656).

The rent book thus performs an evidentiary role, witnessing the main terms of the letting. Nevertheless, the scope of the legislation has been criticized as being too narrow. The Francis Committee felt that the duty to provide a rent book should apply to any residential letting where the rent is payable in intervals of not more than two months (not limited to weekly tenancies), and that the tenant should be entitled to keep the rent book (the existing duty is only to supply one). In addition, the Committee suggested that for furnished lettings the rent book should provide an inventory of the furniture supplied (see *Report of the Committee on the Rent Acts*, 1971, Cmnd 4609, pp 226–7). There have also been suggestions that the contents of the rent book should be more detailed:

First, it is not made clear whether the stated rent is payable in advance or in arrear. Secondly, no statement is required concerning the nature of any services to be provided by the landlord at his own or at the tenant's expense. And thirdly, no reference is made to the landlord's responsibility for structural and external repairs in the case of short leases . . . (Hoath, *Rent Books: The Law, Its Uses and Abuses*, [1978-9] JSWL 3 at p 12, footnotes omitted)

An additional flaw is that many landlords simply do not provide a rent book; and even though failure to do so constitutes a criminal offence (Landlord and Tenant Act 1985, s 7), it does not prevent the landlord from recovering rent from the tenant (*Shaw v Groom* [1970] 2 QB 504; for levels of disregard of these provisions, see Hoath, 1978–9, *op. cit.*, at p 12).

Weekly tenants who have been correctly supplied with a rent book will already have details of their landlord, but for other tenants of dwellings there is a right to request the landlord's identity in the Landlord and Tenant Act 1985, s 1.

s 1(1) If the tenant of premises occupied as a dwelling makes a written request for the landlord's name and address to—
    (a) any person who demands, or the last person who received, rent payable under the tenancy, or
    (b) any other person for the time being acting as agent for the landlord, in relation to the tenancy,
that person shall supply the tenant with a written statement of the landlord's name and address within the period of 21 days beginning with the day on which he receives the request.

Where the landlord is a body corporate, the tenant can also request the name and address of every director and secretary of the landlord (s 2). These sections apply only to tenants, not licensees. Failure to comply with the request is a criminal offence (s 1(2)). The Nugee Report found that although few tenants had difficulties in identifying their landlord, it was 'a serious issue when it did arise' (Report of the Committee of Inquiry on the Management of Privately Owned Blocks of Flats, 1985, para 7.1.2) and it felt that relatively few prosecutions were being brought under ss 121,122 Housing Act 1974 (the predecessor to the Landlord and Tenant Act 1985, s 1). Accordingly, following the Nugee Report, further provisions were introduced to help the residential tenant communicate with his landlord. The provisions apply to 'premises which consist of or include a dwelling and are not held under a tenancy to which Part II of the Landlord and Tenant Act 1954 applies' (s 46 Landlord and Tenant Act 1987). Section 47 Landlord and Tenant Act 1987 provides that all written demands for money due under the lease (whether rent or service charge), must contain the landlord's name and address; and if that address is outside the jurisdiction, an address for service in the jurisdiction must be given. Failure to include this information results in the tenant not having to pay any service charge element of the demand until the information is supplied. Section 48 requires the landlord to provide the tenant with an address within the jurisdiction for service of notices. The address must be supplied by notice in writing (s 54(1); *Rogan v Woodfield Building Services Ltd*, (1995) 27 HLR 78. However, neither section relieves the tenant of making payment if a manager or receiver has been appointed to receive rents and service charges (ss 47(3), 48(3)).

In the case of public sector tenants, there is an additional requirement to keep tenants informed. The Housing Act 1985, s 104 provides:

s 104(2) The landlord under a secure tenancy shall supply the tenant with . . .
> **(b) a written statement of the terms of the tenancy, so far as they are neither expressed in the lease or written tenancy agreement (if any) nor implied by law;**
> **and the statement required by paragraph (b) shall be supplied on the grant of the tenancy or as soon as practicable afterwards.**

The effect of s 104(2) is that even if the tenancy is made orally, the tenant should receive a written statement of the tenancy terms. In recent years it has, however, become the practice for local authorities to issue written tenancy agreements.

Housing association tenants should always have a written tenancy agreement, with a clear explanation of the terms (see the Tenants' Guarantee, *op. cit.*, §C; see below at 5.2.4.2).

In the agricultural sector, there is provision for a written tenancy agreement to be supplied on request. This applies if either there is no written agreement containing all the terms of the tenancy or if there is an agreement but it does not make provision for matters that are specified in Sch 1. The Sch 1 matters relate not only to information about the tenancy, such as the parties' names and the length of the letting, but also to various covenants (see 5.3.5). Either party can request a written agreement setting out these items (Agricultural Holdings Act 1986, s 6). If no agreement is entered into following such a request, the matter can be referred to arbitration (see Rodgers, *op. cit.*, pp 51–2).

5.2.4.2 Information about the Tenant's Rights

Various statutory provisions provide for the tenant to be advised not simply about the terms of the tenancy itself, but also about his rights. Where rent books are required by the Landlord and Tenant Act 1985, s 4, they must contain, in addition to information about the tenancy, information about the provisions on overcrowding contained in the Housing Act 1985, s332, and certain other information about the tenant's potential rights. In the case of assured tenancies, for example, the rent book must advise the tenant that he cannot be evicted without a court order and that he might have a right to remain in the property, that he may be able to claim housing benefit, and that it is a criminal offence for the landlord to force him to leave by harassing him. The Francis Committee, *op. cit.*, felt that rent books provide an important educational role:

> . . . rent books are perhaps the most important and effective vehicle for conveying information to tenants about their rights under the Rent Act. (p 216)

In the public sector, the information to be supplied under the Housing Act 1985, s 104 should include, in addition to the information on the terms of the tenancy, information about the rights given to public sector tenants (the Tenants' Charter, see ch 6.3.1).

s 104(1) Every body which lets dwelling-houses under secure tenancies shall from time to time publish information about its secure tenancies, in such form as it considers best suited to explain in simple terms, and so far as it considers it appropriate, the effect of–
    (a) the express terms of its secure tenancies,
    (b) the provisions of this Part [Part IV; the rights of secure tenants] and Part V (the right to buy), and
    (c) the provisions of sections 11 to 16 of the Landlord and Tenant Act 1985 (landlord's repairing obligations).

A copy of this information must also be supplied to every secure tenant (Housing Act 1985, s 104(2)(a)).

The most extensive provisions relating to information to be given to tenants are to be found in the Tenants' Guarantee: Guidance on the Management of Accommodation Let on Assured Tenancies by Registered Housing Associations (there are different versions of the Guidance for the various types of tenancy). Under the Housing Associations Act 1985, s 36(A) the Housing Corporation is empowered to issue guidance to registered housing associations relating to their management. The Guidance has been issued in the form of 'The Tenants' Guarantee' (see Housing Corporation, *op. cit.*; reissued in revised form at the end of 1994). There is an incentive for housing associations to comply with this guidance as s 36A(1) authorizes the Corporation to have regard to whether the Guidance is being followed in considering 'whether action needs to be taken to secure the proper management of an association's affairs or whether there has been mismanagement'. Indeed, the Introduction to the Guidance states:

. . . **the Corporation will take into account the extent to which an association complies with this Guidance when deciding:**
whether the association should receive Housing Association Grant,
whether the association can be approved to take part in 'Tenants' Choice'; and
whether a High Management Allowance is justified.
(The revised Guarantee refers, in this context, only to receipt of HAG and whether revenue funding of whatever kind should be made available).

The Guidance issued covers a wide range of matters and requires housing associations to inform tenants about their rights and the association's management policy and performance. More specifically, it requires tenants to be told about security of tenure and their spouse's right of succession (§C5); to be given details of the rent and service charge, and how they can be altered (§C7(c)); to be told about the repairing obligations of the landlord (§C7(d)); to be apprised of the initial rent, the procedure for altering it and the association's policy on arrears and eviction (§C8(c), (g)); to be told about the association's complaints procedure and the tenant's right to refer any complaint to the Housing Associations' Tenants' Ombudsman (§C8(e)); and to be told about the various policies and procedures of the housing association, relating to issues such as how tenant complaints are dealt with and the association's allocation policy (§§G1, B1). The aim of the Guarantee is to ensure that housing associations are good managers and follow good practice.

Both the Housing Act 1985, s 104, and the Landlord and Tenant Act 1985, s 4, are general provisions applying to all tenancies covered by the sections. In addition, there may be particular requirements because of the type of tenancy which the landlord is granting to the particular tenant. One example is the special notice requirement where a private sector tenant is being offered reduced security of tenure. Under the Housing Act 1988, a tenant within the legislation (an assured tenant) will generally have security of tenure (the right to remain in the property after the contractual term has expired) and the landlord will only be able to recover possession if he can prove that certain grounds for possession exist. Many grounds for recovery of possession are based on tenant default (see ch 11). It is, however, also possible to grant assured tenancies with more limited security of tenure, permitting recovery of possession on additional grounds. In order for the landlord to take advantage of this, he must serve a notice on the tenant prior to the grant of the tenancy so that the tenant is aware of the fact that he has a more limited form of security. One example is the Housing Act 1988, Ground 3, Sch 2. This ground is directed at landlords who let property to tourists for holidays during the summer months and who wish to be able to enter into a longer letting during the winter months, without that winter tenant acquiring security of tenure. Ground 3 provides:

The tenancy is a fixed term tenancy for a term not exceeding eight months and–
(a) not later than the beginning of the tenancy the landlord *gave notice in writing to the tenant that possession might be recovered on this ground*; and
(b) at some time within the period of twelve months ending with the beginning of the tenancy, the dwelling-house was occupied under a right to occupy it for a holiday.
(emphasis added)

Some of the grounds, for example Ground 1 (landlord occupation), enable the court to dispense with the requirement of notice where 'it is of the opinion that it is just and equitable' to do so. In many of the cases on this, an informal oral notice has been given, and when the courts consider what is just and equitable they look not only to the impact that the purported notice itself had on the tenant's expectations but also to whether or not it would, in the circumstances, be 'just and equitable' to order possession: *Bradshaw and Martyn v Baldwin-Wiseman* (1985) 17 HLR 260; *White v Jones* (1994) 26 HLR 477.

In *Panyai & Pyrkos v Roberts* (1993) 25 HLR 421, the Court of Appeal had to consider the adequacy of a notice given to an assured shorthold tenant prior to the tenancy. An assured shorthold tenancy must be for a fixed term of not less than six months. The shorthold tenant has very limited security of tenure after the fixed term expires as the landlord can recover possession on two months' notice (Housing Act 1988, s 21; see ch 6.2.1). The statutory provisions for creating an assured shorthold require a notice in a prescribed form, or a 'form substantially to the same effect', to be served on the tenant before entering into the tenancy (Housing Act 1988, s 20(2)). In *Panyai & Pyrkos* the letting was initially for twelve months but the notice referred only to a six-month letting. Counsel for the landlord argued that the notice was still effective because it still served the legislative purpose of warning the tenant that 'she was about to enter into a shorthold with limited rights of protection'. Mann LJ sets out the issue:

There is a statutory precondition that a notice should have been served in the prescribed form. The prescribed form requires for completion a specification of the date on which the tenancy in respect of which a notice is served both commences and ends. The narrow issue is whether a notice which gives a wrong date (here a termination) is 'substantially to the same effect' as one which gives the correct date. (at 424)

The Court of Appeal held that giving the wrong date was more than an irrelevant error and the notice was insufficient:

A notice with an incorrect date is not substantially to the same effect as a notice with the correct date and in this case the mistake was not obvious. The short answer to . . . [counsel's] submission is that although the legislative purpose of the primary legislation could perhaps be met without a specification of date, the legislative requirement of the secondary legislation is that there should be a date, and a correct one, in respect of the tenancy granted. (*per* Mann LJ at 425)

The result in this case was that, as an assured shorthold tenancy had not been created, the tenant was an assured tenant with greater rights as to security of tenure.

The aim of these prescribed notices is a limited one; in effect, adjusting the tenant's expectation of long term security so that he is aware that early possession may be required by the landlord:

The purpose of giving the written notice is obvious and important. It is of the utmost importance to a tenant that he should appreciate when he takes rented property whether or not he is obtaining a secure tenure. I can think of nothing likely to have a greater effect on the way people order their lives than the knowledge one way or the other whether or not they have a secure home . . . (*Bradshaw and Martyn v Baldwin-Wiseman, op. cit.*, per Griffiths LJ at 264)

Beyond this, the notices do little to advise tenants of their rights as tenants.

There are also notice requirements which have to be complied with in order to end residential tenancies. Before obtaining a court order for possession against a protected residential tenant, the landlord must serve a notice of intended proceedings in a prescribed form (Housing Act 1988, s 8; Housing Act 1985, s 83). There are also prescribed forms of notices to quit (see ch 11.2.5.7).

5.3 THE CONTENTS OF LEASES

There is no such thing as a standard lease. Nevertheless, within each sector, it·is possible to comment on the kind of things that tend to be covered by the lease. Within the residential sector, a lease will be a fairly short document, a few pages long. In the commercial sector, however, leases are often heavily negotiated by the parties, their lawyers and surveyors. The result is a lease of considerable length—50–80 pages. It is also the case that long residential leases, purchased with a large capital sum, tend to be fairly long documents.

5.3.1 The Structure of Leases

A lease is generally divided into five parts:

The premises

These include details such as the date, details of the parties to the lease, a description of the property let (the parcels clause), the grant of the estate (the operative words), and any exceptions and reservations (for example, reserving a right of way for the landlord).

The habendum

This states the length of the term.

The reddendum

This reserves the rent. Many leases will be at a 'rack rent'; including most short term or periodic residential tenancies, 25 year commercial leases and agricultural leases. This is a rent based on the full annual rental value of the premises, or near to it. Essentially, it is a market rent. Although some rent control measures may depress the level of rent recoverable below the market rent, the maximum legally recoverable rent will still be a rack rent. A rack rent may also be subject to periodic review. Long residential leases are likely to be purchased with a capital sum or premium, and to reserve only a 'ground rent'. This will be more than a peppercorn or nominal rent, but will be substantially less than the full market rental value of the property. In effect the rent has been capitalised. For a fuller discussion of the different types of rent, see Yates and Hawkins, *Landlord and Tenant Law*, 2nd edn, 1986, pp 166–73.

The covenants

These are the covenants undertaken by the landlord and the tenant, and will often form a large part of the lease. The covenants may cover diverse matters, ranging from a covenant by the tenant to pay the rent, to a covenant 'each morning to empty any rubbish of the previous day suitably wrapped into the refuse receptacles or other means of refuse disposal provided by the landlord'.

Leases will often contain covenants on the following matters:

1 To pay rent, service charges, rates and taxes.
2 User, regulating the manner in which the tenant can use the property (see ch 7.3).
3 Repair, stating which party is responsible for the repairs and decorations (see ch 7.2). It may well be that the landlord takes responsibility for external work, and the tenant for internal work. In addition, the clause may define the expected standard of work. An example of a decorating covenant in a commercial lease is for the tenant:

To decorate the Premises in a good and workmanlike manner with good quality materials at least once in every period of five years and in the last year of the Term to the landlord's reasonable satisfaction.

4 Alterations, stating whether or not the tenant is permitted to make any alterations to the premises. Often, the tenant is not allowed to make any structural
alterations, but is permitted to make internal, non-structural alterations with
the landlord's consent, which the landlord agrees not to withhold unreasonably.

5 Alienation, stating whether or not the tenant is able to sell, sublet, mortgage,
etc, his leasehold interest (see ch 9).

6 Insurance, stating which party is responsible for insuring the property (see ch
7.4).

7 Quiet enjoyment, whereby the landlord covenants that the tenant 'shall
peaceably hold and enjoy the Premises without any interruption by the landlord or any person claiming under or in trust for the landlord'. The
covenant for quiet enjoyment has a fairly technical meaning, as will be discussed below.

Provisos and options

The provisos will cover such things as what will happen if the rent is not paid on
time; generally, this failure by the tenant would give the landlord the right to forfeit the lease (see ch 11.2.3). The options will, *inter alia*, state whether the tenant
has the right to renew the lease.

5.3.2 Implied Covenants

In addition to the express covenants in the lease, there may be covenants that are
implied by common law and statute. Save in the case of agricultural leases (see
5.3.5), these covenants are relatively few. They include:

5.3.2.1 Covenant for Quiet Enjoyment

In the absence of an express covenant for quiet enjoyment, there will be a
covenant for quiet enjoyment implied from the landlord and tenant relationship. The effect of this covenant is that the landlord covenants that he has good
title and will deliver possession to the tenant, and that the tenant shall peace-
fully enjoy the premises. In effect, this is a covenant that the landlord will not
interfere with the tenant's *possession* of the premises; it is not, notwithstanding
the way it is phrased, a covenant that the tenant can enjoy peace and quiet at the
property:

**I think the word 'enjoy' used in this connexion is a translation of the Latin word
'fruror' and refers to the exercise and use of the right and having the full benefit of
it, rather than to deriving pleasure from it.** (*Kenny v Preen* [1963] 1 QB 499, *per*
Pearson LJ at 511; see also, *Browne v Flower* [1911] 1 Ch 219)

Although there is some authority for the view that there must be a *physical* interference in order for there to be a breach of this covenant (see esp. Parker LJ in *Browne v Flower, op. cit.*, at 228), more recent authority suggests that this is not necessary.

This covenant is not confined to direct physical interference by the landlord. It extends to any conduct of the landlord or his agents which interferes with the tenant's freedom of action in exercising his rights as tenant: see *Kenny v Preen* . . . [1963] 1 QB 499 at 513, *per* Pearson LJ. It covers, therefore, any acts calculated to interfere with the peace or comfort of the tenant, or his family. (*McCall v Abelesz* [1976] QB 585, *per* Lord Denning MR at 594)

So, in *Kenny v Preen, op. cit.*, Pearson LJ felt that there would be a breach if the tenant was persistently persecuted and threatened with physical eviction (at 513). The covenant was breached where the landlord removed doors and windows of the premises in order to force the tenant to leave (*Lavender v Betts* [1942] 2 All ER 72; this might also constitute the criminal offence of harassment, see ch 11.5); and where scaffolding was erected outside the tenant's shop, preventing the customers from getting to the shop window (*Owen v Gadd* [1956] 2 QB 99).

5.3.2.2 Non-Derogation from Grant

This is a covenant to the effect that the landlord will not, at the same time as granting a lease to the tenant, act in some way which effectively denies this lease to the tenant. The covenant will be broken when the landlord, or someone claiming under him, does something which makes the premises less fit for the purpose of the lease; but, if that purpose is unusual, there will only be a breach if the landlord knew of the proposed use. In *Harmer v Jumbil (Nigeria) Tin Areas Ltd* [1921] 1 Ch 200, the covenant was broken when the tenant had been let land specifically for storing explosives and the neighbouring land was used in a way that would prevent the tenant from legally using his land for that purpose. In this case, it was not even the landlord using the neighbouring land, but another tenant of the landlord. There is a degree of overlap between the implied covenant not to derogate from grant and the implied covenant for quiet enjoyment (see Woodfall, *Landlord and Tenant*, Vol 1, at para 11.301)

5.3.2.3 Disclaimer of Landlord's Title

This is a covenant not to deny the landlord's title or to act in a way inconsistent with the tenancy. In *W G Clark Ltd v Dupre Ltd* [1992] Ch 297, disclaimer of title was likened to the tenant repudiating the lease:

A tenant who repudiates the relationship of landlord and tenant should be in no different position from a party to a contract who repudiates or renounces it. It seems to me that the doctrine of disclaimer is analogous to the concept of

repudiation of a contract . . . *Hill and Redman's Law of Landlord and Tenant* (18th edn, 1991) vol. 1, para 2181 says:

'There is implied in every lease a condition that the lessee shall not do anything that may prejudice the title of the lessor; and that if this is done the lessor may re-enter for breach of this implied condition. The principle may be traced back to the reign of Henry II and appears to be founded on the oath of fealty given by a tenant of real property to his lord under the medieval system of tenure.'

. . . Where the disclaimer is by words . . . then whether there has been a repudiation of the relationship is to be determined by looking at the words used in the context in which they were used. The court must decide whether those words in that context evinced an intention on the part of the tenant no longer to be bound by the relationship of landlord and tenant. (*per* Morison QC at 302–3)

5.3.2.4 Miscellaneous Covenants

There are also some covenants that are implied by statute; as, for example, the repairing obligation that is placed on residential landlords of short leases by the Landlord and Tenant Act 1985, s 11 (see ch 7.2). Some covenants are implied by common law; for example, with a letting of a furnished house there is an implied covenant that the house is fit for habitation at the beginning of the tenancy (see ch 7.2). In addition, some covenants may be implied as a necessary incident of the landlord and tenant relationship in order to make the lease work—as in *Liverpool CC v Irwin* [1976] 2 All ER 39, where the House of Lords found the council landlord under an implied obligation to keep an essential means of access in reasonable repair (see ch 7.2). See also 5.3.4. and 5.3.5 below for terms implied into protected residential leases and agricultural leases.

The range of implied covenants is fairly limited. Apart from the repairing covenants, the implied covenants operate at what Quinn and Phillips describe as the possession-rent level of the relationship (*The Law of Landlord-Tenant: A Critical Evaluation of the Past with Guidelines for the Future*, (1969) 38 Fordham L Rev 225; see ch 3.2.2). At this level, the relationship is seen as being one whereby the tenant seeks possession of the land from the landlord in return for payment of the rent, but has no expectations of service from the landlord beyond this. So, for example, the covenant of quiet enjoyment protects the tenant's expectations of physical possession of the land. As shown in ch 3, this view of the landlord and tenant relationship was appropriate in an agrarian society but does not fit well with the modern use of leases for housing and commercial purposes, where on-going contractual obligations form an important part of the relationship. The landlord, in many cases, is not simply letting out land, but is letting out part of a building which needs servicing. In this country, the common law has been reluctant to imply new covenants to extend the range of obligations on the landlord—intervention has tended to be by statute, such as the Landlord and Tenant Act 1985, s 11. In the United States, the common law has been used much more extensively as a tool for expanding the obligations upon a landlord, as can be seen, for example, in the implied warranty of habitability (see ch 3.8).

5.3.3 The Content of Commercial Leases

Although there is no such thing as a standard form lease, many commercial leases follow a similar pattern, particularly where the lease is of 'prime' property and needs to be attractive to potential investor landlords. Most investors favour prime property which provides the best quality in terms of location (at a national and local level), design, size, lease terms and strength of tenant covenant. These features mean that the property is in high demand and, therefore, provides the safest form of long term investment. A prime property will often be owned by an investor on a freehold or long-leasehold basis, say on a 125 year lease. The investor will then sublet floors to occupational tenants on long leases—what the investor will be looking for is a secure long term lease with income growth. Hence, a common pattern of occupational leases of prime property is a 25 year lease, containing provisions for the rent to be reviewed upwards throughout the life of the lease, generally at five yearly intervals. All potential items of expenditure, such as the cost of repair and insurance, are passed onto the tenant(s) through a service charge (see ch 7.6). This is known as a 'clear' lease as the landlord receives a guaranteed rent clear of all deductions (see ch 7.2).

Although the standard length of an institutional lease is generally said to be 25 years, research conducted for the Royal Institution of Chartered Surveyors shows that there has in fact been a steady decline in the length of leases, from over fifty years for lettings in the early 1970s, to below twenty years in 1992. The 1992 figure is, however, misleading in terms of showing the pattern of the market, as it reflects the fact that, during the recession, many new lettings were short term lettings of up to five years. Even in 1992, however, most of the higher rental value lettings were still for 20-25 years (Cullen and McMillian, *op. cit.*). Another feature of the recession is that more tenants were able to negotiate to have break clauses in leases, giving them the option of ending the lease before the expiry of the fixed term.

While the financial institutions have played a central part in the commercial property market and shaping the occupational lease, there are other landlords who invest in the 'secondary' (non-prime) market. The leases granted by them will be less standardised, with greater variety in length, the degree of control given to the landlord and the extent of the obligations imposed upon the tenant.

5.3.4 The Content of Residential Leases

Apart from housing association lettings, most private sector terms are, in theory, negotiated between the parties. In practice, it is generally the landlord who will supply the tenancy agreement (if there is one) and the tenant will have to take it or leave it. A few terms are implied by statute: there are limited rights to assign (Housing Act 1988, s 15; see ch 9.2.4); limited succession rights (Housing Act 1988, s 17; see ch 9.9); and the landlord is given a right of access to carry out repairs (Housing Act 1988, s 16).

In the public sector, certain rights are implied into every secure tenancy. These include the right to take in lodgers (Housing Act 1985, s 93; see ch 9.2.3); limited rights to assign (Housing Act 1985, ss 91–94; see ch 9.2.3); succession rights (Housing Act 1985, ss 87-90; see ch 9.9); self-help rights to repair (Housing Act 1985, s 96; see ch 7.2.5.3); and qualified rights to improve the property (Housing Act 1985, ss 97–101; see ch 7.2.7).

Although housing association lets are now regulated by the private sector legislation, the relationship between housing associations and their tenants is strongly directed by the Tenants' Guarantee, *op. cit.* The idea underlying the Guarantee is to provide assured tenants with most of the rights enjoyed by secure tenants. The Guidance issued states that:

§C6. Associations are expected to give their assured tenants additional contractual rights within the terms of the tenancy agreement, which should include:
   (a) the right to exchange tenancies with tenants of other associations, New Towns or local authorities, subject to both landlords' agreement, which the associations should not unreasonably withhold;
   (b) the right to take in lodgers, or to sublet part of their accommodation, (provided it does not cause overcrowding and that the sub-letting attracts no security of tenure) subject to the association's permission which should not be unreasonably withheld;
   (c) the right to carry out improvements, with the association's permission which would not be unreasonably withheld;
   (d) the right to carry out repairs and have the cost refunded in certain circumstances where the association has failed to carry out its repairing obligations (see also Section E); and
   (e) the right to be consulted about housing management changes, (see also Section F), and to be informed about association management policies (see Section G). (annotations omitted)

The revised Tenants' Guarantee, *op. cit.*, replaces (d) and (e) by giving tenants two further rights: the right to compensation for improvements carried out by the tenant; and the right to get urgent repairs carried out, with compensation available for failure by the association. The Guidance also states that tenants should be given long term security of tenure wherever possible and that assured shorthold tenancies (giving much lesser security) should only be used in exceptional circumstances (§C3). The National Federation of Housing Associations (NFHA) has issued model forms of tenancy agreements which are widely used by housing associations, either as pro-forma letting agreements or subject to minor variations. In the NFHA tenancy agreement, the landlord limits its rights to recover possession, so that only some of the Housing Act 1988 specified grounds can be used. In addition, although under the Housing Act 1988 a spouse living with an assured tenant at the time of his death has a right to succeed to the tenancy (see ch 9.9), this right of succession is extended in the NFHA agreement to any member of the tenant's family who has been living with the tenant for a twelve-month period.

5.3.5 The Content of Agricultural Leases

Under the Agricultural Holdings Act 1986, there is considerable regulation of the content of leases. The parties can request a written agreement containing matters set out in Sch 1.

SCHEDULE 1: MATTERS FOR WHICH PROVISION IS TO BE MADE IN
WRITTEN TENANCY AGREEMENTS
1 The names of the parties.
2 Particulars of the holding with sufficient description, by reference to a map or plan, of the fields and other parcels of land comprised in the holding to identify its extent.
3 The term or terms for which the holding or different parts of it is or are agreed to be let.
4 The rent reserved and the dates on which it is payable.
5 The incidence of the liability for rates (including drainage rates).
6 A covenant by the tenant in the event of destruction by fire of harvested crops grown on the holding for consumption on it to return to the holding the full equivalent manurial value of the crops destroyed, in so far as the return of the value is required for the fulfilment of his responsibilities to farm in accordance with the rules of good husbandry.
7 A covenant by the tenant (except where the interest of the tenant is held for the purposes of a government department or where the tenant has made provision approved by the Minister in lieu of such insurance) to insure against damage by fire all dead stock on the holding and all harvested crops grown on the holding for consumption on it.
8 A power for the landlord to re-enter on the holding in the event of the tenant not performing his obligations under the agreement.
9 A covenant by the tenant not to assign, sub-let or part with possession of the holding or any part of it without the landlord's consent in writing.

In addition, there are model clauses relating to the maintenance, repair and insurance of fixed equipment which are 'deemed to be incorporated in every contract of tenancy of any agricultural holding except in so far as they would impose on one of the parties to an agreement in writing any liability which under the agreement is imposed on the other' (Agricultural Holdings Act 1986, s 7(3); for contents of the model clauses see Agricultural (Maintenance, Repair and Insurance of Fixed Equipment) Regulations 1973, SI 1973 No. 1473, as amended by SI 1988 No. 281). If there is a written tenancy agreement which has terms inconsistent with the model clauses, either party can refer the matter to arbitration and have the terms rewritten so as to incorporate the model clauses (Agricultural Holdings Act 1986, s 8; and see ch 7.2.4.5(b)(iv)).

Under the government's proposals for reform of agricultural tenancies, the parties will be free to negotiate their own terms and there will be no setting of minimum terms within the lease (MAFF, *Agricultural Tenancy Law—Proposals for Reform*, February 1991; MAFF, *Reform of Agricultural Holdings Legislation: Detailed Proposals*, September 1992; MAFF, *News Release, Agricultural Tenancy Law Reform*, 6 October 1993). This reform will be enacted for new leases during 1995.

5.3.6 Standard Form Leases

At various times, there have been discussions about introducing more standard leases. The Law Commission addressed this issue in 1987, observing that there were two objectives: to ensure that leases are comprehensive; and to make leases readily comprehensible to laymen, which requires clear language and for the lease not to be too long (Law Commission, *Landlord and Tenant: Reform of the Law*, Law Com. No. 162, 1987). These objectives may, however, turn out to be mutually incompatible (para 3.6).

One way of reducing the length of leases would be to use 'key words' which would have a statutory meaning. So, for example, the meaning of a covenant 'to repair' would be defined by statute (see Law Com. No. 162, *op. cit.*, paras 3.8–3.10). Another approach would be to extend the range of terms to be implied into leases (see Law Com. No. 162, *op. cit.*, paras 3.11–3.13). However, both approaches would require regular legislative changes to ensure that the meaning attributed to the key words reflected modern conditions. They would also defeat the objective of making the lease comprehensible as the face of the lease would not tell the parties what the full extent of their obligations is.

The other option considered by the Law Commission is standardizing leases (see Law Com. No. 162, *op. cit.*, paras 3.14–3.18). This would have the advantage that simple language could be used in the standard form, and leases could be more easily prepared. Leases are, however, highly individualized agreements and it is hard to envisage a standard form lease that could be used for a variety of transactions. Attempts at introducing standard forms in the past have not met with much success. In 1991, the Law Society introduced two standard form business leases aimed at 'high street' lettings for up to ten years; one for use with a whole building, and one for use with a letting of part of a building. In practice, these standard leases are little used. Practitioners are reluctant to depart from precedents which they are familiar with, and from phrases and clauses which may have been tested in the courts. In addition, whereas most leases tend to be biased in favour of the landlord (subject to his negotiating position), the Law Society's lease was intended to be 'fair, acceptable to both parties' (Anstey and Freedman, *A standard form of business lease*, (1991) 24 LS Gaz. 27). As it is the landlord's solicitor who produces the first draft, the inclination is to produce a precedent more favourable to the landlord. Some degree of standardization is almost achieved through the use made of precedent books by practitioners. Probably the most successful attempt at standardization was the joint publication by the Law Society and the Royal Institution of Chartered Surveyors of rent review clauses for commercial leases, although even these are not widely used and have had to be published in alternative versions (see ch 8.3.2.1).

5.3.7 Variation of Lease Terms

Generally, the terms of a lease can only be varied by consent of both parties. In the public sector there is, however, a statutory procedure for varying the lease terms. This provides three methods of varying the terms of a secure tenancy.

The first method is by agreement between the landlord and the tenant (Housing Act 1985, s 102(1)(a)). The second method applies only to a variation relating to 'rent or to payments in respect of rates or services'. These terms can be varied in accordance with any provision in the tenancy agreement, thus, for example permitting a clause whereby the landlord could unilaterally change the rent (Housing Act 1985, s 102(1)(b)). The third method applies to periodic tenancies and involves the landlord serving a notice of variation on the tenant. Before serving the notice of variation, the landlord must serve a preliminary notice on the tenant, enabling him to be consulted about the variation. Section 103 provides:

s 103(2) **Before serving a notice of variation on the tenant the landlord shall serve on him a preliminary notice–**
  (a) **informing the tenant of the landlord's intention to serve a notice of variation,**
  (b) **specifying the proposed variation and its effect, and**
  (c) **inviting the tenant to comment on the proposed variation within such time, specified in the notice, as the landlord considers reasonable;**
  and the landlord shall consider any comments made by the tenant within the specified time.
    . . .

(4) The notice of variation shall specify—
    (a) the variation effected by it, and
    (b) the date on which it takes effect;
    and the period between the date on which it is served and the date on which it takes effect must be at least four weeks or the rental period, whichever is the longer.
(5) The notice of variation, when served, shall be accompanied by such information as the landlord considers necessary to inform the tenant of the nature and effect of the variation.

Part IV of the Landlord and Tenant Act 1987 contains provisions to enable the variation of long leases where the lease fails to make satisfactory provision for repair and maintenance of the property (see ch 7.2.5.2).

6

Protecting the Relationship

6.1 INTRODUCTION

The tenancy relationship is protected by a variety of means. Some regulation is provided by the common law, for example, by the implication of covenants such as the tenant's obligation to use the premises in a tenant-like manner and the landlord's covenant for quiet enjoyment. In addition, the contractual documentation, if any, supporting the tenancy will often substantially determine the respective rights and obligations of the parties. Within each sector, there is also a statutory code of protection which will apply to a majority of tenancies in that sector. This chapter will set out the particular relationships to which this additional statutory protection applies, and will outline the main consequences of protection. Further details of how the protection operates will be covered in later chapters dealing with the relevant topics, for example, the detailed grounds on which a landlord is able to obtain possession from protected tenants will be examined in ch 11, *Ending the Relationship.* As the codes of statutory protection are mutually exclusive, and the form of protection given varies, each of the sectors will be dealt with separately in this chapter.

6.2 THE PRIVATE RENTED SECTOR

6.2.1 Legislative Controls in The Private Residential Sector

Since the first controls in the private sector, introduced in 1915 in response to the urgent crisis in war-time housing, there has been a stream of measures regulating private sector lettings, with varying degrees of control and de-control. The swings in the level of control reflect changes in the housing policy of different governments and renewed attempts to match restrictions to perceptions of the housing needs of the country. The first measure was intended to apply to poorer quality housing, but over the years the controls have been gradually extended so that most standard housing is within the legislation and only properties at the top end of the housing market are excluded. Several measures provided lesser protection for furnished premises, on the assumption that a tenant taking this kind of accommodation did not intend it as a permanent home. By the mid-1970s it was apparent that increasing numbers of landlords were choosing to let property furnished, often poorly, so as to avoid regulation. The introduction of controls on furnished lettings in 1974 was therefore an attempt to provide some kind of protection to this class of private sector tenant. The Rent Act 1974 also introduced a 'resident landlord' exception designed to encourage owner-occupiers to let part of their homes without the tenant gaining full protection—a policy that persists in the current legislation.

The principal legislation now is contained in the Housing Act 1988, which came into effect on 15 January 1989 in so far as it relates to the private sector. Tenancies entered into before that date are still governed by the Rent Act 1977.

The Rent Act 1977 was itself a consolidating statute. A tenancy falling within the Act is known as a 'protected tenancy' during the contractual term (Rent Act 1977, s 1). At the end of the contractual term, a 'statutory tenancy' comes into existence (Rent Act 1977, s 2). Protected and statutory tenancies are collectively known as 'regulated tenancies' (Rent Act 1977, s 18). Some residential lettings are excluded from protection (Rent Act 1977, ss 4–16A). Two principal consequences stem from regulated status: security of tenure and rent control, explained below.

Security of tenure is provided by the landlord being unable to end the tenancy unless he has obtained a court order, and the court is prohibited from making such an order unless the landlord can show that he has a good and sufficient reason in law for possession. These reasons are exclusively prescribed by statute. In outline, they fall into three broad categories:

1 Suitable alternative accommodation is available to the tenant (Rent Act 1977, s 98(1)(a)); or

2 The landlord is able to establish a 'ground for possession' (Rent Act 1977, s 98(1)(b), Sch 15) which can be either:
   (a) a discretionary ground based upon tenant default, such as non-payment of rent, or landlord management concerns, as where the premises are required for an employee (Part I, Sch 15); or
   (b) a mandatory ground, where the tenant was notified before the letting that possession may be required on this ground, for example, when the landlord wants to retire to the property (Part II, Sch 15).

Establishing a mandatory ground for possession gives the landlord an automatic right to recover the property, provided the contractual tenancy has come to an end. In contrast, a discretionary ground or the availability of suitable alternative accommodation gives no automatic right to possession, which will only be given if the court considers it reasonable (on grounds for possession under the Housing Act 1988, see ch 11).

As a result of these provisions the tenant has, during the statutory tenancy, what has been described as a 'status of irremovability', *per* Stephenson LJ, *Jessamine Investment Co v Schwartz* [1978] QB 264 at 277. The statutory tenancy is generally regarded as being a merely personal right rather than a proprietary right as the tenant is unable to assign or transfer the tenancy (except under limited provisions in Sch 1 to the Act) and it cannot be disposed of by will (see also, ch 3.11). The 1977 Act did, however, introduce succession rights whereby a tenancy may, following the tenant's death, be succeeded to by a resident surviving spouse or, if there is none, a member of the deceased's family able to show two years' residence (the residency requirement being extended from six months to two years by the Housing Act 1988). Under the Rent Act 1977 as originally enacted, there could be two such successions—one to the successor, and then again to qualified persons on that successor's death (this two succession rule has been modified by the Housing Act 1988). It has been argued that the succession rules, and certain other features of statutory tenancies, display proprietary characteristics and the statutory tenancy can therefore be seen as a kind of proprietary right (see Hands, *The Statutory Tenancy: An Unrecognised Proprietary Interest*, [1980] Conv 351). In any event, Gray has argued that the status of the tenant under the Rent Act 1977 has 'effectively become an informal version of title' (Gray, *Elements of Land Law*, 1st edn, 1987, p 13), a new kind of property:

In reality . . . the legislation confers on eligible residential tenants certain 'social rights of property' which prevail over strict legal entitlements as defined in the orthodox law of property or as fixed by private agreement between landlord and tenant. (Gray, 1987, *op. cit.*, p 966)

The Rent Act 1977 also provides a form of rent regulation, the 'fair rent' system, first introduced in 1965. This rent is intended to reflect the rent for the particular property that would be set in conditions in which there is no scarcity of accommodation to rent. Either party to the tenancy can apply for the registration of a fair rent (Rent Act 1977, Part IV). Once a fair rent is registered the landlord is unable to charge more, although there are provisions for reviewing the registered rent after two years. In the past, fair rents were generally considerably lower than market rents although with the reduction in levels of scarcity in recent years fair rents have more recently been set at levels approaching market rentals (see further, ch 8.4.1).

Under the Rent Act 1977, a different level of protection is given to tenancies known as 'restricted contracts'. These are contracts to occupy a dwelling as a residence which include as part of the arrangement 'payment for the use of furniture or for services' (Rent Act 1977, s 19) or involve the sharing of some accommodation with the landlord (Rent Act 1977, s 21). Most furnished tenancies are fully regulated under the Rent Act 1977 and the restricted contract category essentially catches arrangements involving substantial payments for attendance (services personal to the occupant) and lettings by resident landlords. Tenants under restricted contracts have less protection than other tenants: they are able to refer the contract to a rent tribunal, who judge the rent by the criterion of 'reasonableness' (see Rent Act

1977, s 78) but have no effective security of tenure, only limited rights to postpone the date upon which they could be made to leave (see Protection from Eviction Act 1977, s 5; Rent Act 1977, s 106A). Since the introduction of the Housing Act 1988, no new restricted contracts can be entered into (see Housing Act 1988, s 36) and this category of occupancy agreements will rapidly disappear—many are short term arrangements and a variation to them, including a change to the rent, may give rise to a new contract which will be governed by the regime in the 1988 Act (Housing Act 1988, s 36).

When the Conservatives came to power in 1979 they sought to reverse the decline of the private rented sector. The fair rent concept was retained, but new forms of letting were introduced in the Housing Act 1980. The two main categories were the 'protected shorthold' and the 'assured tenancy'. The idea underlying the protected shorthold tenancy was that landlords would be more willing to let property if they could be certain of regaining possession at the end of the term. Accordingly, the protected shorthold tenancy enabled a landlord who let property for a fixed term period of between one and five years to regain possession when the term expired. The protected shorthold was still subject to rent regulation, on the other hand, and either party was able to apply for a fair rent to be registered. The 1980 Act assured tenancy was designed to encourage new accommodation to be built for rental by enabling 'approved landlords' (such as pension funds, housing associations and building societies) to let property free from Rent Act control but subject to the business tenancy code of control contained in the Landlord and Tenant Act 1954, Part II (see 6.4). The effect was that the tenant had security for the contractual term and at the end of the term had a right to a new lease at a market rent.

These measures brought relatively little new property onto the market and in the 1987 White Paper on Housing the government took the view that a more radical change was necessary. In its opinion, it was rent control coupled with security of tenure that had contributed to both the shortage of housing and poor housing conditions:

1.3 Too much preoccupation since the War with controls in the private rented sector, and mass provision in the public rented sector, has resulted in substantial numbers of rented houses and flats which are badly designed and maintained and which fail to provide decent homes. The return to private sector landlords has been inadequate to persuade them to stay in the market or to keep property in repair . . . .
1.8 Rent controls have prevented property owners from getting an adequate return on their investment. People who might have been prepared to grant a temporary letting have also been deterred by laws on security of tenure which make it impossible to regain their property when necessary. These factors have contributed to shortages of supply and poor maintenance. (*Housing: The Government's Proposals*, 1987, Cm 214)

To reverse the decline in the private rental sector, the government felt it was necessary to encourage the letting of property by removing rent restrictions. The Housing Act 1988 therefore represents a move away from the interventionist policies of previous Rent Acts and lettings under the Act can be made at a market rent. In addition, there were changes to the security of tenure system which fell into three broad categories.

First, the shorthold tenancy concept was extended; secondly, new mandatory grounds for possession were introduced, making it easier for landlords to recover possession for their own management interests; and, thirdly, it was made easier to recover possession from a bad tenant. Fears were expressed that the move to market rents would lead to a new wave of Rachmanism—with landlords trying to force out existing Rent Act protected tenants (paying a fair rent) in order to replace them with new market rent tenants. To meet these concerns, the Housing Act 1988 also strengthened the pre-existing laws on harassment and unlawful eviction (see further, ch 11.5).

Under the Housing Act 1988 there are two types of tenancy: the assured tenancy and the assured shorthold tenancy. Despite, confusingly, the terminology being the same as that used in the Housing Act 1980, the assured tenancy in fact operates in a similar manner to the protected and statutory tenancies under the Rent Act 1977—save that there is no rent control and there are extended grounds for recovering possession. An assured periodic tenancy can only brought to an end by a court order and not, for example, by serving a notice to quit (Housing Act 1988, s 5(1)). The court order cannot be given unless one of the grounds for possession is proved. If the assured tenant has a fixed term tenancy the landlord's right to forfeit is limited by the Act, to prevent the landlord from ending the lease without having to prove that one of the statutory grounds exists. At the end of the fixed term, a statutory periodic assured tenancy comes into being (Housing Act 1988, s 5(2)) which will then be within s 5(1) and so can only be brought to an end by court order.

Unlike the statutory tenant under the Rent Act 1977, the assured tenant does at all times have a tenancy, and thus proprietary rights. These rights are, however, restricted by statute. So, for example, in the absence of contractually agreed alienation provisions, s 15 provides that it is an implied term of every periodic assured tenancy that the tenant will not sublet, assign or part with possession of the whole or any part of the dwelling without the landlord's consent (see further, ch 9). The 1988 Act also restricts the succession rights of assured tenants. Succession to an assured tenancy can now only occur once and only in favour of the tenant's spouse. Again, this reflects the desire of the government to remove disincentives to letting.

The assured shorthold tenancy represents an extension of the protected shorthold first introduced in the Housing Act 1980. It is, however, much more attractive to landlords as it can now be for even shorter fixed term lettings (the minimum being six months; Housing Act 1988, s 20(1)(a)), it is easier for the landlord to recover possession (see Housing Act 1988, s 21; ch 11.4.17), and the rent can effectively be a market rent, although there is limited regulation of the rent (Housing Act 1988, s 22; ch 8.4.2). The extension of the shorthold concept was perceived by the government as likely to help to revitalise the private sector—landlords would be attracted by the ease with which possession could be recovered. It was anticipated that rents under assured tenancies would be higher than under assured shortholds, tenants being willing to pay more for the security available under the former. This in turn would compensate landlords for the lower liquidity of their investment under the assured tenancy regime.

The other change aimed at encouraging increased private sector investment was the extension of the Business Expansion Scheme. Business Expansion Schemes provided tax incentives for individuals investing in companies which provided houses let on assured tenancies (see Finance Act 1983, s 26; Finance Act 1988, s 50). There were several qualifying conditions and the aim of the provisions was to promote the provision of accommodation of a reasonable standard to be used as a home. These tax incentives were, however, introduced only on a five-year temporary basis and ended in 1993. The government's aim was that the incentive of tax relief would 'kick-start' new investment in private rented housing and that new investment would continue at the end of the five-year period (see further, ch 2).

6.2.2 The Operation of the Housing Act 1988

This section will focus on the 1988 Act but it must be remembered that tenancies entered into before 15 January 1989 continue to be regulated by the Rent Act 1977. There will for some time, therefore, remain tenancies which are within the fair rent regime and subject to the stricter conditions for recovery of possession than contained in the Housing Act 1988.

6.2.2.1 The Meaning of Assured Tenancy

Protection under the Housing Act 1988 is given to 'assured tenancies'. Section 1 Housing Act 1988 provides:

s 1(1) A tenancy under which a dwelling-house is let as a separate dwelling is for the purposes of this Act an assured tenancy if and so long as—
  (a) the tenant or, as the case may be, each of the joint tenants is an individual; and
  (b) the tenant or, as the case may be, at least one of the joint tenants occupies the dwelling-house as his only or principal home; and
  (c) the tenancy is [not excluded by Part 1 of Sch 1 or subs(6)]

In order to be an assured tenancy five conditions must be satisfied:
1 There must be a lease and not a licence;
2 The dwelling-house must be let as a separate dwelling;
3 The tenant, or in the case of a joint tenancy, each of the tenants, must be an individual;
4 The tenant, or at least one of the joint tenants, must occupy the dwelling as his only or principal home; and
5 The tenancy must not be within any of the categories set out in Sch 1 (the excluded categories).

(a) There must be a Lease   The distinction between leases and licences was discussed in ch 4. Protection is available only to tenants—under previous Rent Acts this was taken to include all kinds of tenancies including fixed term tenancies, periodic tenancies, tenancies at will (*Francis Jackson Developments Ltd v Stemp* [1943] 2 All ER 601), tenancies at sufferance (*Artizans, Labourers and General Dwellings Co v Whitaker* [1919] 2 KB 301) and tenancies by estoppel. The same approach will presumably be taken under the 1988 Act.

Denial of protection to licensees appears to be based upon ideas of justice and pragmatism. Many licence arrangements arise as a personal favour and are intended to be short term. As Denning LJ said, in *Facchini v Bryson* [1952] 1 TLR 1386 at 1388,

In . . . circumstances [such as a family arrangement, an act of friendship or generosity] it would obviously be unjust to saddle the owner with a tenancy, with all the momentous consequences that that entails nowadays.

Again, in the public sector case of *Westminster v Clarke* [1992] 1 All ER 695, where the local authority had granted a homeless person a licence to occupy a 'half-way house', it would have severely hindered the work of the local authority in providing hostel accommodation had the licence not been exempt from the legislation (see also, ch 4.3.1.1; 6.3.2.1(c)).

Nevertheless, licences can be entered into as long term arrangements and it is in these cases that it is most difficult to distinguish between licences and tenancies. Given the developing doctrine of pretence and that exclusive possession is now likely to result in a tenancy (unless there are special circumstances; see ch 4), it may be that the legislation already catches all those cases where residential occupancy should be protected. This is the view that the government has taken (see Hansard, Standing Committee G, Second Sitting, 15 December 1987, cols 42 and 43). On the other hand, it is likely that the lease/licence debate will rumble on and the Law Commission question whether a person's rights should depend on a distinction which is so difficult to draw, and whether the tenant protection statutes should be amended so that all the benefits extend to licensees as well as to tenants (Law Commission, *Landlord and Tenant: Reform of the Law*, Law Com. No. 162, 1987, at paras 4.4–4.11).

In addition to the doubts surrounding the lease/licence distinction, the boundaries of protection are unclear in other situations. While it is generally accepted that statutory protection is available to tenants at will (see above), it has been argued that the authority on this is not conclusive (Sparkes, *Purchasers in Possession*, [1987] Conv 278). Indeed, the sense of this can be questioned. It can be very difficult to distinguish between licences and tenancies at will. In *Street v Mountford* [1985] 2 All ER 289, Lord Templeman stated that a purchaser in occupation pending completion would be a licensee. Other cases, at least where there is an open contract to purchase, support the view that the purchaser would be a tenant at will: *Chamberlain v Farr* [1942] 2 All ER 567; *Wheeler v Mercer* [1957] AC 416; see ch 4.3.4.2(a). In addition, the justice of a purchaser being protected in this situation can be questioned; in the context of business tenancies Viscount Simonds felt that to give the purchaser security would be 'manifestly unjust' (*Wheeler v Mercer, op. cit.*). Whether or not a person is protected under the legislation can, therefore, turn on some very fine distinctions.

(b) The dwelling house must be let as a separate dwelling   It is clear that a dwelling-house can be a house or part of a house (Housing Act 1988, s 45(1)) and, thus, lettings of flats can be protected. The intention is to provide protection when the property has been let to be used as an independent dwelling. This has several consequences:

(i)   Protection is only available if the property is let for the purpose of using it as *a single unit of habitation*. It will not cover the letting of a larger unit which is intended to be broken down into smaller units of occupation: see *St Catherine's College v Dorling* [1979] 3 All ER 253; *Horford Investments Ltd v Lambert* [1976] Ch 39. This interpretation promotes the purpose of providing protection to residential occupants and not, for example, to entrepreneurs who take a lease intending to profit from subletting parts.

(ii) The tenant must be able to carry on 'all the major activities of life, particularly sleeping, cooking and feeding' (*per* Scott LJ in *Wright v Howell* (1947) 204 LTJ 299 at 300). In *Wright v Howell*, the letting of an unfurnished room was not protected as the room had no cooking facilities or water and the tenant did not sleep there.

(iii) If the dwelling-house is let with other land, the entire letting can be protected provided that the 'main purpose of the letting is the provision of a home for the tenant' (Housing Act 1988, s 2).

(iv) If the tenant has exclusive possession of part of a larger unit, such as a bedroom, he can still be protected even though he only has a right to share other parts which provide necessary facilities, such as a kitchen and bathroom, and not exclusive possession of the whole (Housing Act 1988, s 3). He will not, however, be protected if he shares with the landlord:

s 3(1) Where a tenant has the exclusive occupation of any accommodation (in this section referred to as 'the separate accommodation') and—

    (a) the terms as between the tenant and his landlord on which he holds the separate accommodation include the use of other accommodation (in this section referred to as 'the shared accommodation') in common with another person or other persons, not being or including the landlord, and

    (b) by reason only of the circumstances mentioned in paragraph (a) above, the separate accommodation would not, apart from this section, be a dwelling-house let on an assured tenancy,

the separate accommodation shall be deemed to be a dwelling-house let on an assured tenancy and the following provisions of this section shall have effect.

    . . .

    (3) While the tenant is in possession of the separate accommodation, any term of the tenancy terminating or modifying, or providing for the termination or modification of, his right to the use of any of the shared accommodation which is living accommodation shall be of no effect.

    (4) Where the terms of the tenancy are such that, at any time during the tenancy, the persons in common with whom the tenant is entitled to the use of the shared accommodation could be varied or their number could be increased, nothing in subsection (3) above shall prevent those terms from having effect so far as they relate to any such variation or increase.

    (5) In this section 'living accommodation' means accommodation of such a nature that the fact that it constitutes or is included in the shared accommodation is sufficient, apart from this section, to prevent the tenancy from constituting an assured tenancy of a dwelling-house.

(v) In order to be a dwelling it seems there also needs to be some degree of permanency in the siting of the structure: *R v Rent Officer of Nottingham Registration Area, ex parte Allen* (1985) 17 HLR 481. There are around one quarter of a million people in the United Kingdom who live in mobile homes. Some of these will be protected by the Housing Act 1988 if the home itself is rented and can be shown to be permanent. Most, however, will own the home but rent the pitch that it is on. A separate code of protection applies to these mobile homes. All occupants have the benefit of the Caravan Sites Act 1968, but this offers only the limited protection of a minimum of four weeks' notice to quit and the site owner being unable to evict an occupier without making a court application. Persons who own their own home and rent the site have more extensive rights under the Mobile Homes Act 1983, including a substantial degree of security of occupation, the right to sell the home and to gift it. (See further, Letall, *Mobile Homes, An Occupiers Guide*, 1988, Shelter.) In the United States, mobile home ownership is increasingly popular as it is seen to be a way of providing affordable housing of reasonable quality (in 1992, two million dwelling units were mobile homes, see Baar, *The Right to Sell the 'Im'mobile Manufactured Home in its Rent*

Controlled Space in the 'Im'mobile Home Park: valid regulation or unconstitutional taking?, (1992) 24 The Urban Lawyer 157). Several states have introduced laws protecting mobile home tenancies, ranging in the protection offered from limits on rent increases and evictions through to granting tenants rights of first refusal on a sale of the park.

(c) The tenant, or each of joint tenants, must be an individual   This requirement clearly excludes bodies such as companies from being protected—even, it seems, if the company is inserted as a device to avoid the application of the Act: *Hilton v Plustitle* [1988] 3 All ER 1053; *Kaye v Massbetter* [1991] 39 EG 129 ([1992] Conv 58). It has been argued that denying protection to occupiers under artificial company lets is inconsistent both with the trend of recent case-law on the lease/licence distinction and also with the policy underlying the protective legislation (Bright, *Beyond Sham and into Pretence*, (1991) 11 OJLS 136; see also, ch 4.3.3).

(d) The tenant, or one of joint tenants, must occupy the dwelling as his only or principal home   This condition is aimed at ensuring that an individual can only claim protection for one home—under the Rent Act 1977, there was no such provision and it was possible to claim protection for two homes (*Langford Property Co Ltd v Tureman* [1949] 1 KB 29). While there is no definition of 'principal home' in the Act, it is an expression that is found in the public sector legislation (Housing Act 1985, s 81) where it has been taken to be a question of fact (*Crawley BC v Sawyer* (1988) 20 HLR 98). Factors that will be relevant are whether there are 'signs of occupation' and 'an intention, if not physically present, to return' (Parker LJ, in *Crawley, op. cit.*).

(e) If and so long as   If any of the above conditions cease to exist, then the tenancy will cease to be assured. The most likely event is that the tenant will cease to occupy it as his principal home. In *Gofor Investments v Roberts* (1975) 29 P & CR 366, it was said that when a tenant has left the property the tenancy will only remain protected if he can show both an intention to return and a physical state of affairs that makes this possible, for example, keeping furniture and clothing at the property (see also, *Crawley BC v Sawyer, op. cit.*).

(f) The excluded categories   Even if the foregoing conditions are met, a tenancy may still be incapable of being an assured tenancy. Most of the exceptions are contained in the Housing Act 1988, Sch 1, and are listed below.

(i) Pre-Housing Act 1988 tenancies and transitional cases (paras 1 and 13). The 1988 Act applies only to tenancies entered into after 15 January 1989.

(ii) Tenancies of dwelling houses with high values (para 2). Housing in the top bracket of the market is excluded from protection as the policies justifying intervention in the landlord and tenant relationship do not apply to this sector—

tenants who can afford to rent more expensive housing are generally better able to negotiate their own terms, there is no pressing shortage of accommodation and the renting of 'up-market' accommodation cannot be seen as any kind of fundamental right that needs protection. In relation to tenancies entered into on or after 1 April 1990, exclusion is by reference to the annual rental, which must not exceed £25,000 if the tenancy is to be protected. In relation to tenancies entered into before that date, exclusion is by reference to the rateable value of the house on 31 March 1990, which must not exceed £1,500 if in Greater London and £750 elsewhere, if the tenancy is to be protected. These limits are very high and exclude relatively little property.

(iii) Tenancies at a low rent. Para 3 excludes tenancies at no rent or at a low rent. In relation to tenancies entered into on or after 1 April 1990, a low rent is £1,000 or less a year in Greater London and £250 or less a year elsewhere. In relation to tenancies entered into before that date, a low rent is one which is less than two-thirds of the rateable value of the dwelling-house as at 31 March 1990. This excludes two types of situation. First, where the tenant has paid a premium for a long lease of the property and the rent being paid is a ground rent. These tenants may, however, have rights to stay in occupation at the end of the contractual term of the lease, or to extend the lease, or even to buy the freehold—see the Landlord and Tenant Act 1954, Part I, the Leasehold Reform Act 1967, the Local Government and Housing Act 1989, s 186, and the Leasehold Reform, Housing and Urban Development Act 1993 (ch 12). Secondly, where the tenant is being allowed to occupy the property for a nominal (or no) payment, as a favour.

Unlike the Rent Act 1977, the Housing Act 1988 does not prohibit the taking of a premium on letting property. There is a risk therefore that landlords may seek to avoid regulation by charging the tenant a large sum on entering into the tenancy while reserving only a low rent. If this does occur it could be viewed as a pretence and ineffective to exclude protection. The courts have in the past looked to the substance of a payment rather than its form and, in *Samrose Properties Ltd v Gibbard* [1958] 1 WLR 235, treated a premium payment as commuted rent.

(iv) Business tenancies. Where any part of the premises is used for business purposes the letting will come within the Landlord and Tenant Act 1954, Part II. Lettings within Part II of the 1954 Act are excluded from the Housing Act 1988 (para 4). This will be true even if the original letting was for residential purposes and the occupant later uses it for business purposes: *Cheryl Investments v Saldanha* [1978] 1 WLR 1329.

(v) Licensed premises (para 5). These have recently been brought within the business tenancy code.

(vi) Agricultural land. Tenancies which include agricultural land exceeding two acres with the dwelling (para 6) and tenancies of dwellings occupied by the person responsible for the farming of an agricultural holding (para 7) are excluded.

For the purposes of para 6, 'agricultural land' has the meaning set out in the General Rate Act 1967, s 26(3)(a).

(vii) Lettings to students. A letting to a student 'who is pursuing or intends to pursue a course of study provided by a specified educational institution' (including universities) (para 8) is exempt so long as the tenancy is granted by the educational institution itself and not, for example, by a private landlord. If the educational institution has taken a lease from another landlord in order to provide student accommodation, that landlord will not be subject to the statutory repairing obligations usually imposed by the Landlord and Tenant Act 1985, s 11 (Landlord and Tenant Act 1985, s 14(4)).

(viii) Holiday lets where the tenant has the right to occupy for a holiday (para 9). There is no statutory definition of holiday. In *Buchmann v May* [1978] 2 All ER 993, the Court of Appeal said that the dictionary definition of 'a period of cessation from work or a period of recreation' would be a workable definition provided the word recreation was not too narrowly construed. This has, however, been criticized as a definition as it would appear to exclude, for example, working holidays. The emphasis should be on whether it is being used as a *home* or not (see Lyons, *The Meaning of 'Holiday' under the Rent Acts*, [1984] Conv 286). In *Francke v Hackmi* [1984] CLY 1906, a wider view was taken and it was said that

a holiday is a temporary suspension of one's normal activity not necessarily implying a period of recreation. A temporary suspension involves such a period of time as would indicate that one intends to resume one's normal activity at its conclusion *and* that period is not so long as to imply that another activity had taken its place.

The intention behind this exception is clearly to enable owners to let out properties for holidays without the risk of the occupants claiming that they have a right to remain at the end of the holiday.

The holiday let has, however, frequently been used by landlords as a means of avoiding the protective legislation. Indeed, in 1982 the Labour Party announced that they would remove the holiday let exception as it was a loophole in the Rent Acts. The main case addressing the effectiveness of 'artificial' holiday lets was *Buchmann v May, op. cit*. In this case, a couple had occupied premises for two years under a series of agreements. The wife signed a tenancy which stated that it was 'solely for the purpose of the tenant's holiday in the London area'. At the end of the tenancy she refused to vacate, claiming that she had a protected tenancy. The Court of Appeal held that it was not protected. The reasoning is typical of pre-*Street* and pre-*Vaughan* reasoning. Several cases had laid down the principle that in determining the question of whether a house has been let as a separate dwelling (condition 2 above), any express provision in the lease as to the purpose of the letting is the primary consideration and subsequent events are not relevant (see, for example, *Horford Investments Ltd v Lambert* [1976] Ch 39). In the absence of sham or a false label, the court could not look beyond the actual agreement. In *Buchmann*, the statement of purpose in the agreement prevailed. Sir John Pennycuick did, however, state in *Buchmann v May, op. cit.*, at 999 that

the court would be astute to detect a sham where it appears that a provision has been inserted for the purpose of depriving the tenant of statutory protection under the Rent Acts. But it is for the tenant to establish this, and not for the landlord to establish affirmatively that the express purpose is the true purpose.

It is not clear that the letting was necessarily artificial on the facts of *Buchmann*: the tenant was in the country on a series of short resident permits, had been out of the country for several months before signing the disputed agreement and had told the landlord that she wished to stay in England for only two months more. In the light of subsequent decisions, in particular *Street v Mountford, op. cit.*, and *AG Securities v Vaughan, Antonades v Villiers* [1988] 3 All ER 1058 (see ch 4.3.3), the approach taken in the case (but not necessarily the result) must be challenged. While the doctrine of pretence is yet to be applied to terms of a tenancy not relating to exclusive possession, there is no justification for not applying it to holiday lets.

(ix) Resident landlords. Where the tenancy has been granted by a landlord who, at the time of the grant, and since, has had his or her only or principal home in the same building. There are fairly complex provisions in Sch 1, Part I, para 10 and Part III explaining when a landlord will be regarded as resident in the same building (see also, Pawlowski, *Residence and the resident landlord*, (1991) 11 EG 78).

para 10(1) A tenancy in respect of which the following conditions are fulfilled—
(a) that the dwelling-house forms part only of a building and, except in a case where the dwelling-house also forms part of a flat, the building is not a purpose-built block of flats; and
(b) that, subject to Part III of this Schedule, the tenancy was granted by an individual who, at the time when the tenancy was granted, occupied as his only or principal home another dwelling-house which,—
  (i) in the case mentioned in paragraph (a) above, also forms part of the flat; or
  (ii) in any other case, also forms part of the building; and
(c) that, subject to Part III of this Schedule, at all times since the tenancy was granted the interest of the landlord under the tenancy has belonged to an individual who, at the time he owned that interest, occupied as his only or principal home another dwelling-house which,—
  (i) in the case mentioned in paragraph (a) above, also formed part of the flat; or
  (ii) in any other case, also formed part of the building; and

     (d) that the tenancy is not one which is excluded from this sub-para-
graph by sub-paragraph (3) below.

(2) If a tenancy was granted by two or more persons jointly, the reference
in sub-paragraph (1)(b) above to an individual is a reference to any
one of those persons and if the interest of the landlord is for the time
being held by two or more persons jointly, the reference in sub-paragraph (1)(c) above to an individual is a reference to any one of those
persons.

(3) A tenancy (in this sub-paragraph referred to as 'the new tenancy') is
excluded from sub-paragraph (1) above if–

     (a) it is granted to a person (alone, or jointly with others) who, imme-
diately before it was granted, was a tenant under an assured tenancy (in this sub-paragraph referred to as 'the former tenancy') of
the same dwelling-house or of another dwelling-house which
forms part of the building in question; and

     (b) the landlord under the new tenancy and under the former tenancy
is the same person or, if either of those tenancies is or was granted
by two or more persons jointly, the same person is the landlord or
one of the landlords under each tenancy.

PART III
PROVISIONS FOR DETERMINING APPLICATION OF PARAGRAPH 10 (RESI-
DENT LANDLORDS)
para 17(1) In determining whether the condition in paragraph 10(1)(c) above is at
any time fulfilled with respect to a tenancy, there shall be disregarded–

     (a) any period of not more than twenty-eight days, beginning with the
date on which the interest of the landlord under the tenancy
becomes vested at law and in equity in an individual who, during
that period, does not occupy as his only or principal home another
dwelling-house which forms part of the building or, as the case
may be, flat concerned;

     (b) if, within a period falling within paragraph (a) above, the individual
concerned notifies the tenant in writing of his intention to occupy
as his only or principal home another dwelling-house in the building or, as the case may be, flat concerned, the period beginning
with the date on which the interest of the landlord under the tenancy becomes vested in that individual as mentioned in that paragraph and ending–

        (i) at the expiry of the period of six months beginning on that
date, or

       (ii) on the date on which that interest ceases to be so vested, or

      (iii) on the date on which that interest becomes again vested in
such an individual as is mentioned in paragraph 10(1)(c) or
the condition in that paragraph becomes deemed to be fulfilled by virtue of paragraph 18(1) or paragraph 20 below,

whichever is the earlier; and

(c) any period of not more than two years beginning with the date on which the interest of the landlord under the tenancy becomes, and during which it remains, vested–

   (i) in trustees as such; or

   (ii) by virtue of section 9 of the Administration of Estates Act 1925, in the Probate Judge, within the meaning of that Act.

(2) Where the interest of the landlord under a tenancy becomes vested at law and in equity in two or more persons jointly, of whom at least one was an individual, sub-paragraph (1) above shall have effect subject to the following modifications–

(a) in paragraph (a) for the words from 'an individual' to 'occupy' there shall be substituted 'the joint landlords if, during that period none of them occupies'; and

(b) in paragraph (b) for the words 'the individual concerned' there shall be substituted 'any of the joint landlords who is an individual' and for the words 'that individual' there shall be substituted 'the joint landlords'.

para 18(1) During any period when–

(a) the interest of the landlord under the tenancy referred to in paragraph 10 above is vested in trustees as such, and

(b) that interest is or, if it is held on trust for sale, the proceeds of its sale are held on trust for any person who or for two or more persons of whom at least one occupies as his only or principal home a dwelling-house which forms part of the building or, as the case may be, flat referred to in paragraph 10(1)(a),

the condition in paragraph 10(1)(c) shall be deemed to be fulfilled and accordingly, no part of that period shall be disregarded by virtue of paragraph 17 above.

(2) If a period during which the condition in paragraph 10(1)(c) is deemed to be fulfilled by virtue of sub-paragraph (1) above comes to an end on the death of a person who was in occupation of a dwelling-house as mentioned in paragraph (b) of that sub-paragraph, then, in determining whether that condition is at any time thereafter fulfilled, there shall be disregarded any period–

(a) which begins on the date of the death;

(b) during which the interest of the landlord remains vested as mentioned in sub-paragraph (1)(a) above; and

(c) which ends at the expiry of the period of two years beginning on the date of the death or on any earlier date on which the condition in paragraph 10(1)(c) becomes again deemed to be fulfilled by virtue of sub-paragraph (1) above.

para 19 In any case where–

(a) immediately before a tenancy comes to an end the condition in paragraph 10(1)(c) is deemed to be fulfilled by virtue of paragraph 18(1) above, and

(b) on the coming to an end of that tenancy the trustees in whom the interest of the landlord is vested grant a new tenancy of the same or substantially the same dwelling-house to a person (alone or jointly with others) who was the tenant or one of the tenants under the previous tenancy, the condition in paragraph 10(1)(b) above shall be deemed to be fulfilled with respect to the new tenancy.

para 20(1) The tenancy referred to in paragraph 10 above falls within this paragraph if the interest of the landlord under the tenancy becomes vested in the pesonal representatives of a deceased person acting in that capacity.

(2) If the tenancy falls within this paragraph, the condition in paragraph 10(1)(c) shall be deemed to be fulfilled for any period, beginning with the date on which the interest becomes vested in the personal representatives and not exceeding two years, during which the interest of the landlord remains so vested.

para 21 Throughout any period which, by virtue of paragraph 17 or paragraph 18(2) above, falls to be disregarded for the purpose of determining whether the condition in paragraph 10(1)(c) is fulfilled with respect to a tenancy, no order shall be made for possession of the dwelling-house subject to that tenancy, other than an order which might be made if that tenancy were or, as the case may be, had been an assured tenancy.

para 22 For the purposes of paragraph 10 above, a building is a purpose-built block of flats if as constructed it contained, and it contains, two or more flats; and for this purpose 'flat' means a dwelling-house which–
(a) forms part only of a building; and
(b) is separated horizontally from another dwelling-house which forms part of the same building.

The exception will not apply if the building is a purpose built block of flats, unless the landlord is sharing the actual flat. In *Bardrick v Haycock* (1976) 31 P & CR 420, it was said that what constitutes a building is a question of fact for the trial judge—in *Bardrick*, the landlord lived in an extension which had been built with its own entrance and he was held not to be a resident landlord.

Under the Rent Act 1977, resident landlord lettings were not capable of being protected tenancies (Rent Act 1977, s 12) but were not totally exempt from control—they fell into the 'restricted contract' category (Rent Act 1977, s 20), which essentially meant there was some form of rent control but very limited security of tenure (see 6.2.1). Scarman LJ referred to the purpose behind this exception in *Bardrick, op. cit.*, at 424:

the mischief at which the section was aimed was the mischief of that sort of social embarrassment arising out of close proximity which the landlord had accepted in the belief that he could bring it to an end at any time allowed by the contract of tenancy.

There is also a clear housing policy objective in encouraging home-owners to rent out spare rooms. Commenting on the resident landlord exemption in the Rent Act 1977, Hirst LJ stated in *Barnett v O'Sullivan* [1995] 4 EG 141 at 143:

The purpose of s 12 is manifest, namely to encourage resident owners of houses with rooms to spare to let them, with the assurance that they will be able to recover possession at the end of the contractual tenancy (as they may very understandably wish to do so should the tenant prove incompatible), and also to enable them to sell what is probably their major asset with vacant possession . . .

The 1988 Act aimed to remove all restrictions on resident landlords—not only is there no rent control or security of tenure, but the resident landlord does not have to serve four weeks' notice to quit under the Protection from Eviction Act 1977 to evict a tenant (Protection from Eviction Act 1977, s 5(1B)) or obtain a court order to recover possession (Protection from Eviction Act 1977, s 3A).

(x) Crown tenancies and local authority tenancies. Where the landlord is the Crown or a government department (para 11) or certain local authority or other public bodies (para 12). Most of the latter tenancies will be secure tenancies governed by the Housing Act 1985 (see 6.3.2). Sch 1 excludes:

para 11(1) A tenancy under which the interest of the landlord belongs to Her Majesty in right of the Crown or to a government department or is held in trust for Her Majesty for the purposes of a government department.

(2) The reference in sub-paragraph (1) above to the case where the interest of the landlord belongs to Her Majesty in right of the Crown does not include the case where that interest is under the management of the Crown Estate Commissioners.

para 12(1) A tenancy under which the interest of the landlord belongs to–
(a) a local authority, as defined in sub-paragraph (2) below;
(b) the Commission for the New Towns;
(c) the Development Board for Rural Wales;
(d) an urban development corporation established by an order under section 135 of the Local Government, Planning and Land Act 1980;
(e) a development corporation, within the meaning of the New Towns Act 1981;
(f) an authority established under section 10 of the Local Government Act 1985 (waste disposal authorities);
(g) a residuary body, within the meaning of the Local Government Act 1985;
(h) a fully mutual housing association; or
(i) a housing action trust established under Part III of this Act.
(2) The following are local authorities for the purposes of sub-paragraph (1)(a) above–

(a) the council of a county, district or London borough;

(b) the Common Council of the City of London;

(c) the Council of the Isles of Scilly;

(d) the Broads Authority;

(e) the Inner London Education Authority; and

(f) a joint authority, within the meaning of the Local Government Act 1985.

(xi) Lettings to homeless persons. If a private landlord or housing association helps a local authority to discharge its homelessness obligations under the Housing Act 1985 by agreeing to grant tenancies to homeless people in priority need, the tenancy granted cannot be an assured tenancy:

s 1(6) If, in pursuance of its duty under–

(a) section 63 of the Housing Act 1985 (duty to house pending inquiries in case of apparent priority need),

(b) section 65(3) of that Act (duty to house temporarily person found to have priority need but to have become homeless intentionally), or

(c) section 68(1) of that Act (duty to house pending determination whether conditions for referral of application are satisfied),

a local housing authority have made arrangements with another person to provide accommodation, a tenancy granted by that other person in pursuance of the arrangements to a person specified by the authority cannot be an assured tenancy before the expiry of the period of twelve months beginning with the date specified in subsection (7) below unless, before the expiry of that period, the tenant is notified by the landlord (or, in the case of joint landlords, at least one of them) that the tenancy is to be regarded as an assured tenancy.

(7) The date referred to in subsection (6) above is the date on which the tenant received the notification required by section 64(1) of the Housing Act 1985 (notification of decision on question of homelessness or threatened homelessness) or, if he received a notification under section 68(3) of that Act (notification of which authority has duty to house), the date on which he received that notification.

The tenancy will become assured twelve months after the local authority notifies the applicant for housing of its decision, provided that the other assured tenancy conditions are satisfied.

The aim is to help local authorities to meet local housing needs by encouraging landlords to enter into temporary lettings which will not attract security of tenure. The other way of enabling local authorities to make greater use of private sector accommodation is by providing that the local authority can take a lease or licence from the private landlord and grant a right to occupy to the homeless applicant without it attracting security under the public sector legislation—see 6.3.2.3(f).

(xii) Transitional cases. Certain transitional cases are excluded under Sch 1, Part I:

para 3(1) A protected tenancy, within the meaning of the Rent Act 1977.

    (2) A housing association tenancy, within the meaning of Part VI of that Act.

    (3) A secure tenancy.

    (4) Where a person is a protected occupier of a dwelling-house, within the meaning of the Rent (Agriculture) Act 1976, the relevant tenancy, within the meaning of that Act, by virtue of which he occupies the dwelling-house.

If any of the exceptions in Sch 1 or s 1(6) apply, the tenant has no security of tenure. Once a notice to quit has been served and expired, the tenant has no statutory protection (save where it is necessary to take court proceedings under the Protection from Eviction Act 1977). All the landlord has to show is that the contractual tenancy has come to an end. Nor has the tenant any right to challenge the rent.

The position of an assured tenant is discussed later in the book: security of tenure is examined in ch 11 and the rental provisions in the Housing Act 1988 are examined in ch 8.

6.2.2.2 The Meaning of Assured Shorthold Tenancy

The 1988 Act extended the concept of the shorthold tenancy which had first been introduced in 1980. The Housing Act 1988, s 20 sets out the requirements for an assured shorthold tenancy.

s 20 Assured shorthold tenancies

(1) Subject to subsection (3) below, an assured shorthold tenancy is an assured tenancy–

    (a) which is a fixed term tenancy granted for a term certain of not less than six months; and

    (b) in respect of which there is no power for the landlord to determine the tenancy at any time earlier than six months from the beginning of the tenancy; and

    (c) in respect of which a notice is served as mentioned in subsection (2) below.

(2) The notice referred to in subsection (1)(c) above is one which–

    (a) is in such form as may be prescribed;

    (b) is served before the assured tenancy is entered into;

    (c) is served by the person who is to be the landlord under the assured tenancy on the person who is to be the tenant under that tenancy; and

    (d) states that the assured tenancy to which it relates is to be a shorthold tenancy.

(3) Notwithstanding anything in subsection (1) above, where–

> (a) immediately before a tenancy (in this subsection referred to as 'the new tenancy') is granted, the person to whom it is granted or, as the case may be, at least one of the persons to whom it is granted was a tenant under an assured tenancy which was not a shorthold tenancy, and
> (b) the new tenancy is granted by the person who, immediately before the beginning of the tenancy, was the landlord under the assured tenancy referred to in paragraph (a) above,
>
> the new tenancy cannot be an assured shorthold tenancy.

The conditions for an assured shorthold are therefore:

1 It must be for a fixed term of not less than six months (the previous minimum was one year);
2 There is no maximum length (under the 1980 Act there was a five-year maximum);
3 The landlord cannot have power to determine the tenancy for the first six months, which effectively means that there must not be a landlord's break clause for six months—a right to forfeit is allowed (s 45(4)). The effect of this is to ensure the tenant a minimum term of fixed security, unless he is in default so as to trigger the landlord's right to forfeit.
4 There must have been prior notice given to the tenant that it was to be an assured shorthold tenancy. The aim of this is to ensure that the tenant is made aware of the fact that he will not be fully protected. The Court of Appeal have stressed the need for any notice to be, if not in the exact prescribed form, then 'substantially to the same effect': *Panyai & Pyrkes v Roberts* (1993) 25 HLR 421 (see ch 5.2.4.2; such a strict approach is taken generally in relation to Rent and Housing Act notices: *Ridenhalgh v Horsefield* (1992) 24 HLR 453; *Mountain v Hastings* (1993) 25 HLR 427).
5 But for the above, it would otherwise be an assured tenancy, and so it must satisfy all the usual requirements for protection.

Assured shorthold tenancies offer no long term security of tenancy: at the end of the fixed term a new assured tenancy arises which is deemed to be an assured shorthold (s 20(4)), but the landlord is able to recover possession on two months' notice (see ch 11). They are also subject to minimal rent control (see ch 8.4.2). It is therefore somewhat misleading to think of them as 'assured'.

6.2.3 The Impact of the Housing Act 1988

It is premature to judge the full impact of the changes introduced by the Housing Act 1988 on the size of the private rental market. Nevertheless, it is unlikely to have a significant impact.

Historical attempts at revitalizing this sector by deregulation have not been a success. The 1957 Rent Act introduced major rent deregulation. Nevertheless, the sector continued to decline (and at an increased rate of decline): between

June 1956 and December 1961 the number of privately rented dwellings in Great Britain fell from 5.4 million to 4.1 million (from 36 per cent of the total housing stock to 25 per cent). Further, the impact was more severe in areas of greatest shortage (such as Inner London) and at the bottom end of the market (see Kemp, 'The Ghost of Rachman', in Grant, *Built to Last*, 1992, ch 14).

Apart from historical comparisons, it seems that a significant number of lettings were in any event unregulated, even before the 1988 Act deregulations. Within the furnished sub-sector, up to one half of new lettings in the 1980s were not regulated, as landlords used various devices to avoid the statutory codes, such as granting licences rather than leases and making sham use of genuine exclusions, such as holiday lettings. In addition, most rents were privately agreed and were not registered as fair rents. The furnished sub-sector accounted for 49 per cent of privately rented homes in 1991 (*LRC Housing Update*, ROOF, May/June 1993) and is the sub-sector which tends to provide short-stay, ready access housing—the kind of housing provision that the government has been most concerned to encourage. Given this relatively high proportion of *de facto* deregulated lettings, the impact that *de jure* deregulation will have on the furnished sub-sector is limited. The unfurnished sub-sector tends to house long stay, elderly households, usually at less competitive rates of return, although there are signs that an increasing number of unfurnished lettings are being entered into on an annual letting basis—see *The Times* p 19, 7 September 1994. In relation to the unfurnished sub-sector, many tenants are still protected under the 1977 Rent Act and the uneconomic nature of returns means that upon a vacancy occurring landlords frequently sell homes into owner-occupation in preference to reletting (see Crook, 'Private rented housing and the impact of deregulation', in Johnston Birchall, *Housing Policy in the 1990s*, 1992, ch 5; Kemp, *op. cit.*; Todd and Foxon, *Recent Private Lettings 1982–84*, 1987).

In addition, it must not be forgotten that the impact of the legislation is likely to vary between types of landlord or 'potential' landlord. Some landlord types are not primarily concerned with investment returns. A 1976 study showed that a relatively high proportion of resident landlords were satisfied with the rent they received as they were not letting the property primarily for financial reasons and an overwhelming majority stated that the laws on repossession had made no difference to their letting policies—total deregulation of resident landlords by removing them from even the 'restricted contract' category of lettings found in the 1977 Rent Act is, therefore, unlikely to have much impact, even coupled with the 'rent-a-room' tax allowances (see ch 2). Similarly, charities and housing associations were often letting property for some special purpose, such as providing housing for certain categories of people in need, and, again, financial return was not, generally, important although this picture has probably changed since 1976 as regards rent, given the new financial regime for housing associations. Nor had the repossession laws had any impact on letting practices for the majority of charities and housing associations. It was in the case of lettings by non-resident individuals, companies, non-charitable trusts and executors and some public bodies that the level of financial return was of most importance—and in these cases less than one-third of the landlords were satisfied with the rent received. Repossession laws have also affected the letting policies of this group much more than the other two groups previously mentioned. The 1988 Act changes are, therefore, most likely to influence this group. Further, the last-mentioned categories represent the majority of private sector landlords (Paley, *Attitudes to Letting in 1976*, 1978, pp 21–6, esp. Table 3.15, and p 30).

Early evidence suggested that the decline in the private rental sector has continued since the 1988 Act, from representing 8.8 per cent of all households in 1988 to 8.5 per cent in 1990 (Rauta and Pickering, *Private renting in England 1990*, 1992, p 1; the General Household Survey showed a similar decline from 8.6 per cent in 1988 to 8.4 per cent in 1990). The greatest decline is in resident landlord lettings—from 102,000 lettings in 1988, to 68,000 in 1990 (Rauta and Pickering, *op. cit.*, p 1). Other figures suggest that there has been an increase in the number of privately rented dwellings since 1988—an additional 270,000 dwellings by 1993 (see Down *et al.*, *Trends in the Size of the Private Rented Sector in England*, Housing Finance No. 22, May 1994, p 7). It is likely, however, that the increases have not been in the mainstream private rented sector but in particular sub-sectors—secondary residences, such as holiday homes, employment related accommodation, and accommodation leased to local authorities by private owners (see Down *et al.*, *op. cit.*, Table 4).

When looking at these figures, it must also be borne in mind that there have been two temporary boosts to the sector since 1988, without which the overall rate of decline in the mainstream private rental sector would probably have been greater. First, the introduction of the Act coincided with the collapse of the home ownership market. This will have given an artificial boost to the private rental sector as home owners, needing to move yet unable to sell their properties, are forced to rent out their properties and to rent homes in the area to which they have moved. Indeed, a survey of members of the Association of Residential Letting Agents found that, in 1992, about 20 per cent of new lettings were by private individuals who were unable or unwilling to sell their properties—although the survey is not fully representative of the private rented sector as ARLA members tend to be involved in the middle and upper end of the market (see Joseph Rowntree Foundation Housing Research Findings No. 90, May 1993). A second temporary boost was the result of the tax incentives to let on assured tenancies provided by the Business Expansion Scheme. While Business Expansion Schemes did bring new investment in private rental housing (estimated at 40,000 extra rented homes, Joseph Rowntree Foundation, Housing Research Summary, December 1993), most of this was only short term rental housing—many BES companies targeted 'naturally mobile' occupants, such as young professionals, with the aim of selling the properties at the end of the five-year period. A study of the first two years of BES assured tenancies showed that had the government channelled the equivalent of the tax foregone into housing association development instead, the number of rented dwellings produced would have been at least 60 per cent of the number produced through the BES, and this would have been housing available for rental on a more permanent basis (see Crook, Kemp, Anderson and Bowman, *The Business Expansion Scheme and Rented Housing*, May 1991, at p 34).

It was hoped that the assured shorthold tenancy would also encourage new investment and there are signs that it is a very popular form of letting: the Joseph Rowntree Foundation Housing Research Findings No. 90, *op. cit.*, found that 70 per cent of all new lettings were assured shorthold tenancies, although the professional awareness of ARLA members of the advantages of assured shorthold lettings may mean that this figure is higher than for the sector as a whole. It is questionable, however, whether it is bringing much new property into the market. Instead, it is usually used as a preferred route of letting to the assured tenancy: the landlord can be certain of both recovering possession and of obtaining a market rent. While it had been thought that there would be differential rents for assured shortholds and assured tenancies, rents being higher for the latter to reflect the more secure status, there is some evidence that it is shorthold tenants that do in fact pay more (18 per cent more according to Sharp, *Problems assured—private renting after the 1988 Act*; 8 per cent according to Rauta and Pickering, *op. cit.*, at p 1 and p 25, Figure 5.1). There is often no reason for a well-advised landlord to choose the assured tenancy as an alternative.

Many housing policy commentators believe that the decline in this sector cannot be reversed unless there is a more fundamental change in the housing finance system. While the legislative changes may help provide the right legal framework for promoting investment they cannot achieve this alone. Crook sets out four conditions that are generally considered necessary to sustain and attract investment (Crook, Private rented housing and the impact of deregulation, *op. cit.*, p 104):

First, the rate of return must be competitive with alternative investments of similar risk and liquidity The Joseph Rowntree Foundation Inquiry into British Housing, Second Report, 1991, felt that a minimum return of 7–8 per cent is needed to attract investment (at p 58); others feel that even higher returns would be needed (over 10 per cent net according to members of the Association of Residential Letting Agents; Housing Research Findings No. 90, *op. cit.*; and see Crook, *Private Rented Housing, op. cit.*, at p 97). In the unfurnished sub-sector, pre-1988 rates of return were typically 3 per cent net of management and maintenance (see Crook, *Private Rented Housing, op. cit.*, at p 94). In the furnished sub-sector, rates of return were much more competitive, but housing conditions were generally poor and these rates were dependant upon the landlords avoiding Rent

Act control. In relation to post-1988 assured tenancies and assured shorthold tenancies, there is less difference in average rents between furnished and unfurnished lettings (Rauta and Pickering, *op. cit.*, p 26). In addition, market rents are,
of course, now permissible on new lettings and Rauta and Pickering found that
the mean weekly rent in privately rented accommodation had increased by 43 per
cent between 1988 and 1990, *op. cit.*, p 24. There remains, however, an 'affordability' limit on rent levels, as tenants on limited incomes simply may not be able to
pay higher rents—and the provision of housing benefit has not been adequate to
meet fully the problems of affordability that tenants face (see further, ch 8.5).
Given the fact that there is a practical ceiling on rents that can be set, many share
the view that there need to be fiscal incentives to regenerate the private rented
sector:

... **some incentive is needed ... to bridge the gap between the yield from investing in the private rented sector and the returns available elsewhere. This could be
done either through the tax system or by means of an initial grant.** (Joseph
Rowntree Foundation Housing Research Summary , December 1993, *op. cit.*)

**Second, there must be greater and more predictable degrees of liquidity than in
the past, so that landlords can be certain of the circumstances in which they can
get vacant possession and realise the value of their assets.** (Crook, *Private
Rented Housing, op. cit.*, p 104) Again, the liquidity of rental housing has been
improved by the changes in the Housing Act 1988, particularly with the easier
recovery of possession with the assured shorthold tenancy. Nevertheless, property is inherently illiquid compared to other forms of investment and this is a
matter of great concern to institutional investors in particular. Many are now
advocating that a new investment vehicle should be established along the lines
of a unit trust in residential property which would help liquidity problems and
would be more tax efficient for investors that do not pay tax (see, for example,
Joseph Rowntree Foundation Housing Research Findings No. 95, July 1993).

Third, there must be stability in the new legal framework. (Crook, *Private
Rented Housing, op. cit.*, p 104)   After the 1980 Housing Act, many investors
were deterred from using the protected shorthold by the Labour Party's assertions that, if elected, it would give security to these tenants. Investors need to be
confident that stricter controls will not be reintroduced.

**Fourth, the reputation of private renting as an investment needs to be sound.
This means laying to rest the ghost of Rachmanism. If landlordism is seen as a
repugnant form of investment many people, particularly financial institutions,
will not invest, even if the returns are good ...** (Crook, *Private Rented Housing,
op. cit.*, p 104)   The major problem remains that renting property does not generally produce sufficiently competitive returns. Many share the view expressed
by Crook *et al., The Business Expansion Scheme and Rented Housing, op. cit.*, p 36:

[unless] the housing finance system is reformed to create a 'level playing field' between renting and owning private housing, a lasting revival of the privately rented sector is unlikely to occur. In the absence of the abolition of the subsidies currently provided to home owners, some kind of subsidy will be required to maintain the new investment in the private rented sector that the BES has stimulated.

(In a similar vein, see Hills, *Thirty-nine steps to Housing Finance Reform*, 1991; Rowntree Inquiry into British Housing, *op. cit.*; Kemp, The ghost of Rachman, *op. cit.*; Gibb, Munro, *Housing Finance in the UK*, 1991, esp. ch 11; Oxley, Smith, *Private Rented Housing in the European Community*, European Housing Research Working Paper Series No. 3, June 1993; Joseph Rowntree Foundation Housing Research Summary, December 1993, *op. cit.*).

6.3 THE LOCAL AUTHORITY SECTOR

6.3.1 Legislative Controls in the Local Authority Sector

Prior to 1980, the local authority tenant enjoyed none of the statutory security of tenure offered to the private sector tenant by the Rent Act 1977. This is not to say that local authorities threw their tenants on to the street as the whim took them, but that there was no statutory system of protection. The 1980 Act, in most cases, merely codified existing practice and required a change in council procedures. There was nothing very radical about the Tenants' Charter—it did not, for instance, impose tenant involvement in decision-making.

The principal aim of the Tenants' Charter as it was initially propounded in the Housing Act 1980 was to give rights to the previously unprotected council tenant—*Harrison v Hammersmith and Fulham LBC* [1981] 2 All ER 588. Whereas private sector protection stemmed from the critical housing shortage during and after World War I, the 1980 Act had the social purpose of extending rights similar to those already granted to private sector tenants to public sector tenants— *Harrison, op. cit.*, at 597; see generally, Swenarton, *Homes Fit for Heroes*, 1981. The private sector legislation was founded on a reaction to a housing crisis and was never primarily intended as a grant of rights, although subsequent tenant protection legislation might have had that purpose, while the Housing Act 1980 set out to give tenants rights. Therefore, the restrictive approach adopted by and in relation to the Rent Act 1977 and the Housing Act 1988 in attributing protected status to private sector tenants, based on the historical roots of that legislation, is not as evident in the local authority sector.

The Tenants' Charter is now to be found in the Housing Act 1985. It gives protection to the 'secure tenant'. The secure tenant is accorded a variety of rights: amongst others, he cannot be evicted other than by court order (Housing Act 1985, s 81) and, before a court order will be given, a ground for possession must be shown to exist (Housing Act 1985, s 84, Sch 2); in addition, the secure tenant may have the

Right To Buy and the right of succession. The protection offered to secure tenants is dealt with in subsequent chapters.

6.3.2 The Operation of the Housing Act 1985—The Meaning of Secure Tenancy

The basic conditions for protection are set out in the Housing Act 1985, ss 79-81.

s 79(1) A tenancy under which a dwelling-house is let as a separate dwelling is a secure tenancy at any time when the conditions described in sections 80 and 81 as the landlord condition and the tenant condition are satisfied.

(2) Subsection (1) has effect subject to—

(a) the exceptions in Schedule 1 (tenancies which are not secure tenancies),

(b) sections 89(3) and (4) and 90(3) and (4) (tenancies ceasing to be secure after death of tenant), and

(c) sections 91(2) and 93(2) (tenancies ceasing to be secure in consequence of assignment or subletting).

(3) The provisions of this Part apply in relation to a licence to occupy a dwelling-house (whether or not granted for a consideration) as they apply in relation to a tenancy.

(4) Subsection (3) does not apply to a licence granted as a temporary expedient to a person who entered the dwelling-house or any other land as a trespasser (whether or not, before the grant of that licence, another licence to occupy that or another dwelling-house had been granted to him).

s 80(1) The landlord condition is that the interest of the landlord belongs to one of the following authorities or bodies—

a local authority,

a new town corporation,

a housing action trust

an urban development corporation,

the Development Board for Rural Wales, or

a housing co-operative to which this section applies.

. . .

(3) If a co-operative housing association ceases to be registered, it shall, within the period of 21 days beginning with the date on which it ceases to be registered, notify each of its tenants who thereby becomes a secure tenant, in writing, that he has become a secure tenant.

(4) This section applies to a housing co-operative within the meaning of section 27B (agreements under certain superseded provisions) where the dwelling-house is comprised in a housing co-operative agreement within the meaning of that section.

s 81   The tenant condition is that the tenant is an individual and occupies the

dwelling-house as his only or principal home; or, where the tenancy is a joint tenancy, that each of the joint tenants is an individual and at least one of them occupies the dwelling-house as his only or principal home.

The landlord condition will be dealt with in 6.3.2.2, but as a matter of style, references to local authorities in this book will often include new town corporations, although their differences are also highlighted on occasion. The vast majority of public sector lets, however, are made by local authorities and so the focus of analysis with respect to the Housing Act 1985 is on council housing.

If a tenant falls within ss 79 and 81 and is not excluded by any of the paragraphs in Sch 1, then he is secure and cannot contract out of that security—*R v Worthing BC, ex parte Bruce, op. cit.*, and *Barton v Fincham* [1921] 2 KB 291. The elements of s 79 are as follows:

1   The Landlord (s 80: see 6.3.2.2) and Tenant (s 81: see 6.3.2.1) Conditions must be satisfied;
2   There must be a 'tenancy';
3   The tenancy must be of a 'dwelling-house';
4   The dwelling-house has to have been 'let' as 'a separate dwelling'.

These concepts have their roots in the Rent Act 1977—*Westminster CC v Clarke, op. cit.*, at 700–01.

6.3.2.1 The Tenant Condition

The tenant condition in s 81 is complex. As *Camden LBC v Shortlife Community Housing Ltd* (1993) 25 HLR 330, makes clear, to qualify as secure, the tenant must be an individual or, in the case of joint tenants, several individuals. Further, the dwelling-house must be the only or principal home of the tenant. This is a question of fact. Where a secure tenant is excluded due to difficulties in the relationship with a partner, then the Matrimonial Homes Act 1983, s 1(6), continues that secure tenancy through a spouse's occupancy. However, once the parties divorce or if they were only ever cohabiting, then s 1(6) is redundant—*Metropolitan Properties v Cronan* (1982) 44 P & CR 1; *cf. Davis v Johnson* [1979] AC 264; see further ch 9.8. Where the tenant has two homes, it is still possible that the council dwelling will be his principal one. In *Governors of the Peabody Donation v Grant* (1982) 6 HLR 43, the daughter, seeking to succeed under what is now the Housing Act 1985, s 87, proved that she resided at her father's flat because she spent a good proportion of every week living there and she kept clothes and books there, despite her father having filled in a census form which did not include her as resident. On the other hand, in *R v Worthing BC, ex parte Bruce* [1994] 24 EG 149, where the tenant at all material times had a bungalow adapted to his disability as well as his council flat, the Court of Appeal held that it was reasonable to conclude that the council flat was not his only or principal home, although the case turned on other matters and the issue was not directly addressed.

(a) Dwelling House　Dwelling-house is defined in s 112. It includes a house and part of a house, the latter term encompassing a flat, and even land let with the dwelling-house, 'unless the land is agricultural land (as defined in the General Rate Act 1967, s 26(3)(a)) exceeding two acres'—s 112(2).

(b) A Separate Dwelling　The Housing Act 1985 requires that the dwelling-house be let as *a* separate dwelling, but there is no equivalent to the Housing Act 1988, s 3. The inter-relationship between shared accommodation, non-exclusive occupation/possession and licences is, therefore, relevant in the public sector. Under the Housing Act 1980, it had been held that to be a secure tenant, it did not matter that the occupier held under a licence (Housing Act 1980, s 48), but that he must, under the licence, have exclusive possession of essential living rooms in a separate dwelling house which provided facilities for living, sleeping and cooking, although the bathroom and lavatory might be common to other occupiers—*Family Housing Association v Miah* (1982) 5 HLR 94; *Kensington and Chelsea Royal Borough v Hayden* (1985) 17 HLR 114.

(c) Tenancy　Section 79(1) requires a 'tenancy' before security of tenure will be conferred. However, at first sight, s 79(3) eschews completely the private sector distinction between leases and licences.

s 79(3) The provisions of this Part apply in relation to a licence to occupy a dwelling-house (whether or not granted for a consideration) as they apply in relation to a tenancy.

Different interpretations of the scope of s 79(3), though, have developed. Confusion arose because s 79 Housing Act 1985, which is in slightly different terms to its predecessor, Housing Act 1980, s 48, was passed shortly after *Street v Mountford, op. cit.* The Court of Appeal decided in *Family Housing Association v Jones* [1990] 1 All ER 385 at 393 that, combining *Street* with the changes in language from s 48 of the 1980 Act, s 79, even conferred a secure tenancy on licensees without exclusive possession. The House of Lords in *Westminster CC v Clarke, op. cit.*, however, held that a secure tenant under the Housing Act 1985 must have exclusive possession of essential living rooms, overruling *Family Housing Association v Jones, op. cit.* The House of Lords took both a black letter law approach to s 79 (*op. cit.*, at 701J–702A) and a policy-oriented, purposive approach (*op. cit.*, at 702G–703A) to reach this result.

What is clear from *Clarke*, therefore, is that in order to be a secure tenant, the occupier must have exclusive possession, whether as a tenant or as a licensee. It does not necessarily follow from *Clarke*, however, that a licensee with exclusive possession will always be a secure tenant within s 79(3). It might be, for example, that as a matter of policy it is determined that certain categories of licence are not to be secure within s 79(3), even though they give exclusive possession. Having regard to all the housing duties of local authorities, including providing temporary accommodation for homeless applicants under the Housing Act 1985, s 65(3) while they find permanent accommodation of their own, it may be that to carry out these functions effectively, the council needs to be able to grant a non-secure right of residence, despite the fact that the occupier has exclusive possession. This general policy objective can be seen in the Housing Act 1985, Sch 1, para 4, which excludes from the protection of ss 79-81 certain temporary lets to homeless applicants.

para 4(1) A tenancy granted in pursuance of–
      (a) section 63 (duty to house pending inquiries in case of apparent priority need),
      (b) section 65(3) (duty to house temporarily person found to have priority need but to have become homeless intentionally), or
      (c) section 68(1) (duty to house pending determination whether conditions for referral of application are satisfied),
    is not a secure tenancy before the expiry of the period of twelve months beginning with the date specified in sub-paragraph (2), unless before the expiry of that period the tenant is notified by the landlord that the tenancy is to be regarded as a secure tenancy.

However, the occasions when a local authority has to house homeless applicants go beyond the exceptions set out in Sch 1, para 4(1)(a)–(c). If para 4 does not apply, can a local authority grant a licence with exclusive possession which, nevertheless, is non-secure so as best to be able to manage all of its housing functions? The result would be that in the appropriate context, a council could evict such an occupier without reference to the 1985 Act's security of tenure provisions. In *Ogwr BC v Dykes* [1989] 2 All ER 880, the Court of Appeal was dealing with a licence with exclusive possession granted in pursuance of the Housing Act 1985, s 65(3) and so Sch 1, para 4 was applicable. Nevertheless, Purchas LJ was prepared to hold that even where there was exclusive possession, a licence might still objectively be found to exist, but no security of tenure would flow therefrom.

If all that is disclosed is the granting of exclusive possession for a fixed term for payment of a rental fee, then, in the absence of any feature indicating to the contrary, the intention of the parties as expressed by their agreement must be to create a tenancy. If, however, the context in which the right to exclusive occupation is granted specifically and definitively negatives an intention to create a tenancy, then some other interest appropriate to the intention established by that context will be created. (*op. cit.*, at 886, *per* Purchas LJ)

Since Purchas LJ was seeking to give Ogwr BC the right to grant non-secure occupation, the right must be to grant a licence with exclusive possession outside the scope of s 79(3). However, *Ogwr* was overruled by the Court of Appeal in *City of Westminster v Clarke*, (1991), 23 HLR 506. When *Clarke* went to the House of Lords (*sub nom. Westminster CC v Clarke, op. cit.*), their lordships reversed the Court of

Appeal's decision, but *Ogwr* was not cited. As was seen in ch 4, the House of Lords focused on Clarke's non-exclusive possession of the room in the hostel, not on any intention to be gleaned from the context of the grant. Lord Templeman, who had given the leading judgment in *Street*, was prepared to find as a matter of policy, though, that the local authority needed to be able to grant non-secure occupation in order to better manage all of its housing functions, but only because it was found that Clarke did not have exclusive possession of his room. Thus, as things stand, there is no general, non-statutory power to grant non-secure occupation agreements if they are to confer exclusive possession. Further, it is hard to envisage a situation, post-*Street*, in which an occupier with exclusive possession will be held to be a licensee rather than a tenant—unless, perhaps, the context of the local authority grant of temporary accommodation were to bring the arrangement within the exceptional categories discussed by Lord Templeman in *Street*, even though he made no specific reference to this situation as being an exception.

Regardless of s 79, *Street* and *Clarke*, however, should local authorities as a matter of policy have the power to grant occupation agreements which give exclusive possession without security of tenure? The context would be with respect to housing pending decisions on homelessness—as was seen in ch 5, the courts have generally been very unwilling to give rights to applicants seeking housing under the homelessness provisions. Purchas LJ, *obiter*, in *Ogwr* was prepared to allow local authorities a general power to grant non-secure residence agreements if the context so permitted. Arguably, if the situation had presented itself to Lord Templeman in *Clarke*, his policy arguments relating to local authorities' functions could be extended to cover the case where the occupier did have exclusive possession. Even where Sch 1, para 4 does not apply, there may be an argument that a local authority can grant a non-secure occupancy with exclusive possession so that it can fulfil all of its housing obligations, and which, because of the context, is neither construed as a lease under *Street* nor as a 'secure tenancy' under s 79(3).

Local authorities can avoid giving secure licences by interposing a private company between themselves and the occupier, subject to any argument about sham and pretence—*Camden LBC v Shortlife Community Housing Ltd, op. cit.* Further, even if there is a licence that would fit within s 79(3), s 79(4) may exclude it from the guarantees given to secure tenants.

s 79(4) Subsection (3) does not apply to a licence granted as a temporary expedient to a person who entered the dwelling-house or any other land as a trespasser (whether or not, before the grant of that licence, another licence to occupy that or another dwelling-house had been granted to him).

The licence must have been granted in consequence of entering the dwelling-house, or any other land for that matter, as a trespasser; there must be a causal connection. In addition, s 79(4) is only an exception to s 79(3). If a lease is granted to an erstwhile trespasser, then a secure tenancy is created. Thus, local authorities must ensure that the agreement with the trespasser for a 'licence' does not, in fact, create a lease under *Street v Mountford* principles.

6.3.2.2 The Landlord Condition

As well as satisfying the intricacies of s 79 itself, the occupation must satisfy the landlord condition. The landlord condition is that the tenancy is granted by one of the listed bodies in s 80. As well as local authorities themselves, new town corporations, housing action trusts, urban development corporations, the Development Board for Rural Wales and certain housing co-operatives (see s 80(3) and (4), above) are qualifying landlords. Joint authorities are also included under s 4.

s 4(b) 'new town corporation' means a development corporation or the Commission for the New Towns;

(d) 'urban development corporation' means an urban development corporation established under Part XVI of the Local Government, Planning and Land Act 1980;

(e) 'local authority' means a county, district or London borough council, the Common Council of the City of London or the Council of the Isles of Scilly, . . . , and in [section] . . . 80(1), [and] paragraph 2(1) of Schedule 1 . . . includes . . . the Broads Authority and a joint authority established by Part IV of the Local Government Act 1985.

Whether the landlord condition is satisfied is usually a very straightforward question (*cf. Camden v Shortlife, op. cit.*) and needs no further elaboration.

6.3.2.3 Excluded Categories

Even if the tenant satisfies ss 79-81, he will still fail to be secure if one of the exclusionary paragraphs in Sch 1 Housing Act 1985 is applicable.

(a) Long Leases   Under Sch 1, para 1 long tenancies cannot be secure. Long tenancies are defined in s 115 to exclude leases for over 21 years or those granted under the RTB, even if for a shorter period.

(b) Employment-related Tenancies   The Housing Act 1985, Sch 1 does not give a secure tenancy to someone granted his lease as a result of his job with the local authority or other prescribed body. As such, the tenant has none of the rights associated with a secure tenancy. If the aim was merely to allow for ease of termination of the lease when employment ceased, then it might have been better to provide a specific ground for eviction (see Ch.11 below).

para 2(1) A tenancy is not a secure tenancy if the tenant is an employee of the landlord or of–
a local authority,
a new town corporation,

a housing action trust
an urban development corporation,
the Development Board for Rural Wales, or
the governors of an aided school,
and his contract of employment requires him to occupy the dwelling-house for the better performance of his duties.

(2) A tenancy is not a secure tenancy if the tenant is a member of a police force and the dwelling-house is provided for him free of rent and rates in pursuance of regulations made under section 33 of the Police Act 1964 (general regulations as to government, administration and conditions of service of police forces).

(3) A tenancy is not a secure tenancy if the tenant is an employee of a fire authority (within the meaning of the Fire Services Acts 1947 to 1959) and–
   (a) his contract of employment requires him to live in close proximity to a particular fire station, and
   (b) the dwelling-house was let to him by the authority in consequence of that requirement.

(4) A tenancy is not a secure tenancy if–
   (a) within the period of three years immediately preceding the grant the conditions mentioned in sub-paragraph (1), (2) or (3) have been satisfied with respect to a tenancy of the dwelling-house, and
   (b) before the grant the landlord notified the tenant in writing of the circumstances in which this exception applies and that in its opinion the proposed tenancy would fall within this exception,
   until the periods during which those conditions are not satisfied with respect to the tenancy amount in aggregate to more than three years.

(5) In this paragraph 'contract of employment' means a contract of service or apprenticeship, whether express or implied and (if express) whether oral or in writing.

The usual category of employee-tenant who will be caught by para 2 is the caretaker on the council estate or in the tower block who has been given his tenancy, as per his contract of employment, 'for the better performance of his duties'. An employee of the local authority or other body who is a council tenant will still have security, therefore, if he can prove that the tenancy was not granted 'for the better performance of his duties or if his residence therein is not expressly or impliedly a term of his contract. Unfortunately, from the point of view of the tenant, if a secure tenancy was originally granted and subsequently a change in employment status means that residence there became a term of his new contract of employment for the better performance of his duties, then the tenant loses his security. In *Elvidge v Coventry CC* (1994) 26 HLR 281, the Court of Appeal decided that para 2(1) had a continuing effect throughout the lifetime of the lease and had to be satisfied at all times. Comparison was made with the case of a fireman with a secure tenancy whose contract changed, for para 2(3)(b) requires that the letting was originally made once and for all time as a consequence of his employment—see Hoffman LJ at 283. On the other hand, if it is not an express term of the contract of employment that the tenant occupy the dwelling-house for the better performance of his duties, the House of Lords held in *Hughes v LB of Greenwich* (1994) 26 HLR 99, that there must be a compelling reason for deeming it to be implied. In *Hughes*, a headmaster's contract did not require him to live in school-provided accommodation and it was not essential for the better performance of his duties; the school provided a facility, it did not impose an obligation, and so he was a secure tenant. Under para 2(1) there are two steps: it must be a requirement of his contract of employment, express or implied, that he live there *and* it must be for the better performance of his duties. Further, the House of Lords held that the Rent Act distinction between service occupiers (licensees) and service tenants was wholly inapplicable to dwelling-houses let under the Housing Act 1985 because of s 79(3).

Para 2(4) is not an employment-related denial of security, but rather a denial in the interests of housing management. It allows a local authority to protect, for a maximum of three years, its stock of properties which it has set aside for potential employees. As long as it gives the tenant notice that this is a property normally used for employees covered by sub-paras (1), (2) or (3), then no security will be conferred. There is no requirement that this tenant be an employee.

(c) Shortlife Tenancies of Properties Acquired for Development   Sch 1, para 3 is meant to allow a local authority to let temporarily, on non-secure terms, a property acquired for the purposes of development.

para 3(1) A tenancy is not a secure tenancy if the dwelling-house is on land which has been acquired for development and the dwelling-house is used by the landlord, pending development of the land, as temporary housing accommodation.

(2) In this paragraph 'development' has the meaning given by section 55 of the Town and Country Planning Act 1990 (general definition of development for purposes of that Act).

The development in question must fall within the definition of the Town and Country Planning Act 1990, s 55.

Even if a secure tenancy is granted of land where development is now planned, the tenant can be evicted under Grounds 10 and 10A as long as suitable alternative accommodation is available; the overlap between the provisions of Schs 1 and 2, though, is not precise.

(d) Short Term Tenancies for Homeless Applicants   Local authorities often have to supply accommodation to homeless people while a decision is taken about their long term housing needs. Sch 1, para 4 provides a means by which to grant non-secure tenancies. (See also 6.3.2.1, above)

para 4(1) A tenancy granted in pursuance of–
  (a) section 63 (duty to house pending inquiries in case of apparent priority need),
  (b) section 65(3) (duty to house temporarily person found to have priority need but to have become homeless intentionally), or
  (c) section 68(1) (duty to house pending determination whether conditions for referral of application are satisfied),
  is not a secure tenancy before the expiry of the period of twelve months beginning with the date specified in sub-paragraph (2), unless before the expiry of that period the tenant is notified by the landlord that the tenancy is to be regarded as a secure tenancy.
  (2) The date referred to in sub-paragraph (1) is the date on which the tenant received the notification required by section 64(1) (notification of decision on question of homelessness or threatened homelessness) or, if he received a notification under section 68(3) (notification of which authority has duty to house), the date on which he received that notification.

The provision is intended to cover the case of short term provision of housing to applicants under the Housing Act 1985, Part III while decisions are taken. If the local authority unreasonably delays its decision beyond twelve months, however, then the tenant will become secure.

(e) Short Term Properties for Those Taking up Employment   If a local authority serves notice on granting a tenancy that it is subject to Sch 1, para 5, then it will not be secure during its first twelve months. The aim is to assist those people moving into the area to take up employment.

para 5(1) A tenancy is not a secure tenancy before the expiry of one year from the grant if–
  (a) the person to whom the tenancy was granted was not, immediately before the grant, resident in the district in which the dwelling-house is situated,
  (b) before the grant of the tenancy, he obtained employment, or an offer of employment, in the district or its surrounding area,
  (c) the tenancy was granted to him for the purpose of meeting his need for temporary accommodation in the district or its surrounding area in order to work there, and of enabling him to find permanent accommodation there, and
  (d) the landlord notified him in writing of the circumstances in which this exception applies and that in its opinion the proposed tenancy would fall within this exception;
  unless before the expiry of that year the tenant has been notified by the landlord that the tenancy is to be regarded as a secure tenancy.
  (2) In this paragraph –
  'district' means district of a local housing authority; and

'surrounding area', in relation to a district, means the area consisting of each district that adjoins it.

(f) Temporary Housing Leased from the Private Sector   Where the local authority takes a lease, or licence (*Tower Hamlets LBC v Miah*, [1992] 2 WLR 261) of a dwelling-house from a lessor which cannot grant secure tenancies to use as temporary accommodation for its own tenants, then such leases as the local authority grants will not be secure (Sch 1, para 6):

para 6 A tenancy is not a secure tenancy if–
>   (a) **the dwelling-house has been leased to the landlord with vacant possession for use as temporary housing accommodation,**
>   (b) **the terms on which it has been leased include provision for the lessor to obtain vacant possession from the landlord on the expiry of a specified period or when required by the lessor,**
>   (c) **the lessor is not a body which is capable of granting secure tenancies, and**
>   (d) **the landlord has no interest in the dwelling-house other than under the lease in question or as a mortgagee.**

This provision is of use to local authorities trying to meet its housing obligations in conjunction with either private landlords or housing associations: in *Tower Hamlets LBC v Abdi* (1993) 25 HLR 80, Mann LJ said, at 83,

[Private] leased accommodation . . . has to a great extent supplanted bed and breakfast accommodation as temporary accommodation for the homeless. It is a means by which local housing authorities can obtain the temporary use of private sector accommodation for the homeless.

At its peak in 1991, local authorities placed over 12,000 households in bed and breakfast accommodation, but that was reduced to a mere 5,000 by 1993 through use of dwellings leased from private sector landlords—see Wilcox, *Housing Finance Review 1994/95*, 1994, Table 74. Thus, para 6 has effected an improvement in the conditions of homeless households. However, it should be noted that para 6 would also permit a private landlord to grant wholly unprotected tenancies which can be terminated at will by using the local authority as its intermediate tenant; the individual occupying the dwelling house would be neither a 1985 Act secure tenant, nor a 1988 Act assured tenant.

(g) Short Term Lets While Works are Effected   It will be rare for this provision to be used, for it only affects leases granted to persons while works are effected on their normal residences and such persons were not secure tenants in their normal residences. Schedule 1, para 7 provides:

para 7 A tenancy is not a secure tenancy if–
>   (a) **the dwelling-house has been made available for occupation by the tenant (or a predecessor in title of his) while works are carried out on the dwelling-house which he previously occupied as his home, and**

(b) the tenant or predecessor was not a secure tenant of that other dwelling-house at the time when he ceased to occupy it as his home.

(h) Tenancies Relating to Specific Businesses   Where the lease is of premises used as either an agricultural holding, or as licensed premises, or as business premises within the 1954 Act, then no secure tenancy is created.

(i) Student Lets   Schedule 1, para 10 looks complex, but its effect is that students on designated courses can only obtain a secure tenancy if the initial lease 'is granted for the purpose of enabling the tenant to attend a designated course at an educational establishment' and they remain a tenant for six months after their courses finish.

(j) Almshouses   Where a housing association is a charity, its leases of alms-houses may not give rise to secure tenancies, as long as it succeeds in granting a licence rather than a lease (Sch 1, para 12):

para 12 A licence to occupy a dwelling-house is not a secure tenancy if–
    (a) the dwelling-house is an almshouse, and
    (b) the licence was granted by or on behalf of a charity which–
        (i) is authorised under its trusts to maintain the dwelling-house as an almshouse, and
        (ii) has no power under its trusts to grant a tenancy of the dwelling-house;
    and in this paragraph 'almshouse' means any premises maintained as an almshouse, whether they are called an almshouse or not; and 'trusts', in relation to a charity, means the provisions establishing it as a charity and regulating its purposes and administration, whether those provisions take effect by way of trust or not.

In any of the above situations, for example if a lease has been granted to a local authority to enable it to grant shortlife tenancies pending development (Sch 1, para 3), the lessor will not be subject to the statutory repairing obligations usually implied into residential leases of up to seven years by Landlord and Tenant Act 1985, s 11 (Landlord and Tenant Act 1985, Sch 1, para 4).

Finally, it should be noted that if the Tenants' Choice scheme had been successful, tenancies granted in the relevant properties would not have been secure—Housing Act 1988, s 101. Tenants' Choice provisions were intended to pass entire council estates into the private sector, but council tenants were unwilling to vote in favour of the transfers—see ch 10.6.

6.3.3 The Impact of the Housing Act 1985

The Tenants' Charter, originally found in the Housing Act 1980, in many ways mirrored good local authority practice that had existed before its passage. In creating a legal regime of protection and security, however, the 1980 Act had to provide a definition of which local authority lets would be within its ambit. The definition, as now found in the Housing Act 1985, ss 79–81, is liberal, reflecting the underlying theme that the aim was to give legal rights to council tenants—*Harrison v Hammersmith and Fulham LBC, op. cit.* Nevertheless, given the diverse range of functions which a local authority still has to fulfil, then a general power to grant non-secure occupation in the appropriate context may prove necessary.

6.4 THE COMMERCIAL PROPERTY SECTOR

6.4.1 Legislative Controls in the Commercial Property Sector

As with the private residential sector, commercial lettings were largely unregulated until the early part of this century. The primary focus of legislative control since then has been the protection of goodwill—either through providing compensation when goodwill is lost or through providing the right to remain in the business premises—and compensating the tenant for the cost of certain improvements that he has carried out on the premises. The immediate impetus for the first major regulation was, as in the private residential sector, the shortage of premises following the First World War. This shortage put landlords in a position where they could either force tenants to leave without giving them a chance to stay on fair terms or put the rents of existing tenants up to unconscionable levels, which tenants would pay in order to stay in the property (see *Select Committee on Business Premises*, 1920). While recognizing the need for some tenant protection, the Select Committee also noted that in order to avoid discouraging new building (which would be to the tenant's disadvantage in the long term), intervention should be kept to a minimum.

The early legislation was contained in Part I of the Landlord and Tenant Act 1927. This enabled tenants to obtain compensation at the end of their tenancy for the cost of certain improvements that they had carried out to the premises and for the loss of goodwill. The aim was to prevent the landlord from unfairly profiting from the tenant's business:

the mischief at which this part of the Act [the goodwill provisions] was aimed, and that also is true of the part which deals with compensation for improvements, was to deal with the case of a landlord acquiring through the activities of his tenant, either by improving the property or by creating in the property, and adherent to the property, a goodwill of which the landlord would take the benefit when the lease came to an end. It was obviously thought unjust by the legislature that the landlord should obtain that type of unearned increment on the termination of a lease . . . (*per* Lord Greene MR, *Stuchbery v General Accident Fire and Life Assurance Corp Ltd* [1949] 2 KB 256 at 264)

In practice, however, this was an extremely limited goal and offered very little tenant protection. It did not generally provide tenants with what they most wanted, security. In addition, the compensation provisions were limited. Compensation for loss of goodwill was only available if the tenant could show that as a result of carrying on his business for at least five years he had increased the letting value of the premises. But this only gave the tenant compensation when he could show what became known as 'adherent goodwill', that is goodwill adhering to the premises rather than to the business. As the following case extract shows, this is only one aspect of goodwill:

A division of the elements of goodwill . . . appears in Mr Merlin's book as the 'cat, rat and dog' basis. The cat prefers the old home to the person who keeps it, and stays in the old home though the person who has kept the house leaves. The cat represents that part of the customers who continue to go to the old shop, though the old shopkeeper has gone; the probability of their custom may be regarded as an additional value given to the premises by the tenant's trading. The dog represents that part of the customers who follow the person rather than the place; these the tenant may take away with him if he does not go too far. There remains a class of customer who may neither follow the place nor the person, but drift away elsewhere. They are neither a benefit to the landlord nor the tenant, and have been called the 'rat' for no particular reason except to keep the epigram in the animal kingdom . . . It is obvious that the division of the customers into 'cat, rat and dog' must vary enormously in different cases and different circumstances. The 'dog' class will increase with the attractiveness and new accessibility of the tenant; the 'cat' class with the advantage of the site; all sorts of variations may affect the 'rat'. (*per* Scrutton LJ, *Whiteman Smith Motor Co v Chaplin* [1934] 2 KB 35 at 42)

In order to be entitled to compensation on leaving, the tenant therefore had to show that the landlord's rent on the premises had increased beyond the mere site value, to include an amount for the 'cat' element of goodwill—the goodwill that would attach itself to any new business set up on the old premises. This would be difficult for the tenant to prove. In addition, he would be unable to claim compensation if the landlord was not going to gain from this adherent goodwill—if, for example, the landlord intended to demolish the property. However, *if* the tenant was able to prove adherent goodwill, he may also have been able to establish a case for renewal. This is because, having established adherent goodwill, if he could then prove that the compensation for loss of it would not cover the actual loss of goodwill that he would suffer through removal (that is, if he could establish that he would lose 'the rats' as well as the 'cats'), *then* he may be able to claim a renewal of the lease for up to fourteen years.

When the Leasehold Committee reported in 1949 and 1950, it noted the unsatisfactory nature of these provisions. They were both unnecessarily complicated and failed to protect the tenant's primary concern, security. The importance of security to the business tenant was noted in the Interim Report:

A tenant with a flourishing business, or with a business which is only beginning to get on its feet, necessarily feels qualms about the results of moving. This is particularly true of retail and other traders, whose customers get used to shopping with them in a certain place but may well not all remain loyal to the extent of seeking them out in another street or even some distance away in the same street. But it applies with almost equal force to manufacturers and other businesses employing a skilled or trained labour force. Removal even within a relatively small area may involve losing valued workers, and consequent loss of production: it may interrupt carefully-organised arrangements for the supply of components, disposal of by-products, etc. (Leasehold Committee, *Interim Report on Tenure and Rents of Business Premises*, 1949, Cmd 7706, at para 34)

In the Final Report, the Committee referred to the difficult exercise of balancing the tenant's security interests against management concerns of the landlord:

[The tenants] should not have such a degree of security as will protect the bad tenant or perpetuate the inefficient business; or will prevent the due expansion of existing businesses or the setting up of new ones; or will in other ways promote stagnation and interfere with redevelopment or other desirable change. (Leasehold Committee, *Final Report*, 1950, Cmd 7982. at para 143)

The Committee then considered the principles that should guide legislative change in this area. The idea of retaining the principle of compensation but improving the formula for its assessment was rejected as it did not sufficiently protect the tenant's commercial interests; by having to move premises he may lose more than goodwill, there were other inconveniences and expenses involved in displacement. Preferring then to allow the tenant to claim renewal, the difficulty was to determine the basis of any renewal. The principle to guide renewal claims was

150 . . . upon the broad ground that refusal to renew would cause a substantial diminution in the value of the business as a going concern instead of being confined to loss of goodwill, or—in the case of non-profit-making concerns—that it would cause a substantial increase in costs or loss of efficiency.
151 Security of tenure is not to be at the expense of the landlord and is not to subsidise the inefficient business. It follows that the terms of renewal, and particularly the rent, should not be out of line with those which other efficient businesses might be expected to pay for similar premises. The tenant entitled to renewal should therefore be required to pay a fair market rental. (*Final Report, op. cit.*, at paras 150-1)

No general legislation followed and three years later there was a further report. In this, the government accepted the approach of extending greater security to business tenants but rejected the details of the scheme that had been proposed earlier. The alternative scheme put forward formed the basis of the Landlord and Tenant Act 1954, Part II, which, with some later amendments, still governs renewal of business leases:

43 . . . the landlord of business premises, when an existing tenancy comes to an end, should have the right to resume possession himself if he requires the premises for the purpose of his own business or for the purpose of a scheme of redevelopment. If, however, he does not require the premises for himself for one of these purposes, he is entitled as landlord to a fair contemporary market rent for the premises—neither more nor less: and if the sitting tenant is willing and able to pay that rent and to enter in to other reasonable terms of tenancy, then the sitting tenant has a greater right than any alternative tenant to the tenancy on those terms. Unless, therefore, he is in substantial breach of his covenants, or is otherwise an unsatisfactory tenant, or has declined an offer of suitable alternative accommodation, or has failed to exercise a reasonable contractual option for renewal of his tenancy, the sitting tenant ought to be entitled to obtain a renewed tenancy without proof of 'adherent goodwill'. (By 'sitting tenant' is meant a tenant who is in occupation. No special consideration is due at the end of his tenancy to a tenant who has sublet and does not occupy; in such a case, it is the occupying sub-tenant who should be able to look for security of tenure.)

44 . . . Such a scheme would be in general conformity with the present normal practice of good landlords. The landlord's legitimate interests would be fully preserved, while the sitting tenant who wished to continue in the premises could not be forced to outbid the fair market rent as the price of doing so . . .

49 The Government consider that the tenant is entitled to compensation only if his failure to obtain a renewal is in no way attributable to anything done or omitted to be done by himself. In other words, the right to compensation should be limited to those cases where the tenant has sought renewal but the landlord has succeeded in getting possession for the purposes of his own business or of redevelopment, and should not extend to cases where the tenant's failure to obtain renewal has been due to the fact that he is in breach of his covenants or is otherwise an unsatisfactory tenant, or has declined an offer of suitable alternative accommodation, or has failed to exercise a reasonable contractual option for renewal of his tenancy. *(Government Policy on Leasehold Property in England and Wales*, 1953, Cmd 8713)

This statement sets out the framework of the Landlord and Tenant Act 1954, Part II. When the tenant's lease comes to an end the tenant can continue to occupy unless the lease is terminated in accordance with the provisions of the Act. The tenant also has the right to renew his lease unless he is a bad tenant, is offered suitable alternative accommodation or the premises are required for landlord estate management reasons. In the latter situation the tenant should be compensated for his disturbance under a rough and ready measure of his loss of goodwill.

The business tenant is thus given a similar 'protected' status to the residential tenant. While the business tenant is protected by having the right to stay in occupation at the end of his lease and to apply for renewal, the residential tenant is protected by simply staying in occupation. Neither tenant can be evicted unless the landlord is able to prove either grounds for possession or for non-renewal, and there is a considerable degree of similarity in the grounds for recovery (see ch 11). The business tenant's protection is not, however, personal to him:

It is a piece of property which he can assign or dispose of to a third person, provided that it was not prohibited by the terms of the contract. (*per* Lord Denning MR, *Cheryl Investments v Saldanha* [1978] 1 WLR 1329 at 1335)

There is also a difference in the approach to protected status—in both the public and private residential sectors the landlord is unable to recover possession without obtaining a court order, so the tenant can simply sit tight and obtain protection from his *status* as an occupier. Under the business tenancy code, the tenant must take action, either by himself serving a notice for a new lease or by serving a counter-notice in response to the landlord serving a notice to quit in order to be able to remain in occupation.

The government remains committed to the fundamental aim of the 1954 Act, to provide business tenants with security without otherwise protecting them from market forces. The belief in free market regulation is reflected in the fact that it is now possible for parties to 'contract out' of the Act. When the Act was first introduced, lettings of less than three months were excluded from Part II of the Act but all other commercial lettings were covered. In 1969 the Law Commission took the view that this was unduly restrictive:

There are many cases where the landlord would be willing to let on a temporary basis and a tenant would be willing to accept such a tenancy. This may happen, for example, when the landlord has obtained possession and intends to sell, demolish or reconstruct the property but is not ready to do so immediately . . . The permissible period of three months as the maximum for tenancies outside the Act will often be too short to be of practical use . . . We also accept that there may be cases where a tenant is willing, for good reasons, to accept a tenancy for more than six months without rights under the Act. (Law Commission, *Report on the Landlord and Tenant Act 1954 Part II*, Law Com. No. 17, 1969, paras 32–33)

As a result, the Act was amended so that lettings not exceeding six months were excluded and it was possible for the parties to a longer lease to obtain a court order excluding the lease from the Act (see further below).

It is interesting to compare this approach with the one that has been adopted in Australia. In Australia there is no general statutory regulation of commercial lettings, but in some States legislation has been introduced recently in order to protect small retail tenants from market forces. In each case, the legislation was enacted following fears that the inequality of bargaining power in negotiating leases of units in regional shopping centres was such that tenants were having unfair leases imposed on them. The legislation is directed to small retailers (excluding those with premises with a floor area exceeding one thousand square metres). While the details of the legislation varies between States, there are several common areas of control: requiring the landlord to disclose certain information to the tenant and to provide a copy of the lease, and giving the tenant a 'cooling off period'. If not complied with, the tenant may be able to end the lease. The legislation also gives the tenant the right to at least a five-year lease and rent review clauses are controlled (see further, ch 8). Warranties are also implied into the lease, for example, a warranty not to cause, and to take reasonable efforts to prevent, disruption to trading within the centre. Contracting out of the legislative controls is prohibited, as would be expected with provisions introduced to correct imbalances in the market (see further, Redfern and Cassidy, *Australian Tenancy Practice and Precedents*, 1987, [4 190]-[4 245]; Bradbrook, Croft, *Commercial Tenancy Law in Australia*, 1990, chs 23–6).

6.4.2 The Operation of the Landlord and Tenant Act 1954, Part II

6.4.2.1 Tenancies to which Part II of the 1954 Act applies

Section 23 of the Landlord and Tenant Act 1954 provides:

s 23(1) . . . this part of this Act applies to any tenancy where the property comprised in the tenancy is or includes premises which are occupied by the tenant and are so occupied for the purposes of a business carried on by him or for those and other purposes.

(2) In this Part of this Act the expression 'business' includes a trade, profession or employment and includes any activity carried on by a body of persons, whether corporate or unincorporate.

(3) . . . the expression 'the holding', in relation to a tenancy to which this Part of this Act applies, means the property comprised in the tenancy, there being excluded any part thereof which is so occupied neither by the tenant nor by a person employed by the tenant and so employed for the purposes of a business by reason of which the tenancy is one to which this Part of this Act applies.

(4) Where the tenant is carrying on a business, in all or any part of the property comprised in a tenancy, in breach of a prohibition (however expressed) of use for business purposes which subsists under the terms of the tenancy and extends to the whole of that property, this Part of this Act shall not apply to the tenancy unless the immediate landlord or his predecessor in title has consented to the breach or the immediate landlord has acquiesced therein.

In this subsection the reference to a prohibition of use for business purposes does not include a prohibition of use for the purposes of a specified business, or of use for purposes of any but a specified business, but save as aforesaid includes a prohibition of use for the purposes of some one or more only of the classes of business specified in the definition of that expression in subsection (2) of this section.

(a) There must be a lease   As with private sector residential property, in order for the occupant to be protected there must be a lease. Licences are excluded: *Shell-*

Mex & BP Ltd v Manchester Garages [1971] 1 WLR 612. However, unlike the residential sector, the word 'lease' does not include tenancies at will, whether created by operation of law (*Wheeler v Mercer, op. cit.*) or by express agreement between the parties (*Hagee (London) Ltd v AB Erikson and Larson* [1976] QB 209). In the *Wheeler* case, Lord Morton commented that it would be

surprising if the legislature had intended to bring within the scope of the Act a relationship so personal and so fleeting as a tenancy at will. (at 428)

As mentioned earlier, it can be difficult to determine whether a relationship is a periodic tenancy, a tenancy at will or a licence. In the *Hagee* case, the court said that it would look closely at an agreement purporting to be a tenancy at will to see if it was a cloak for a periodic tenancy (*op. cit.*, at 215 and 217), and in *Javad v Aqil* [1991] 1 All ER 243, Nicholls LJ commented at 245:

Given that a periodic tenancy can exist where the period is very short indeed, a layman could be forgiven for being surprised to find that the distinction between a periodic tenancy and a tenancy at will can be all-important for the purposes of the statutory protection afforded to business tenancies.

In a recent Law Commission paper, the suggestion that renewal rights should be extended to include licensees and tenants at will was discussed and dismissed:

The temporary nature of the interest granted either by a tenancy at will or by a licence is not likely to satisfy someone wanting to occupy business premises for any length of time, and we consider that the differences between such an interest and an ordinary tenancy or lease will be readily apparent, so that a prospective tenant will not enter into such an arrangement inadvertently. . . . The inclusion of tenancies at will and licences within the Act would clearly have a major effect on the balance between landlord and tenant which we wish to maintain as it is. (Law Commission, *Business Tenancies, A Periodic Review of the Landlord and Tenant Act 1954 Part II*, Law Com. No. 208, 1992, paras 3.13–3.14)

The basis for exclusion therefore appears to be the temporary nature of such interests. Yet some excluded arrangements may be of a long term nature, for example, the concessionaire operating under a licence arrangement within a department store or a kiosk in a hotel foyer. These traders will not usually have exclusive possession and cannot therefore have leases. The consequence is that the goodwill they build up in the store cannot be protected. In South Australia, the retail tenancy legislation applies to licences as well as to tenancies.

(b) There must be a letting of premises 'Premises' has been taken to include not only buildings but also land without buildings—*Bracey v Read* [1963] 1 Ch 88. In *Land Reclamation Co v Basildon District Council* [1979] 1 WLR 767, a waste disposal company gained access to its depot along a road over which it had a right of way by 'lease' and claimed that it had renewal rights under the 1954 Act. The Court of Appeal held that the wording of the Act was not appropriate to include a right of way or other incorporeal hereditament. As the Law Commission recog-

nizes, there are cases (and the *Land Reclamation* case is one example) where the renewal of such a lease is just as important to protect the goodwill and future of a business as the renewal of a normal lease of business premises. Nevertheless, the Law Commission rejected any extension of the Act as there appeared to be few difficulties caused in practice (Law Com. No. 208, *op. cit.*, paras 3.2–3.4).

(c) The tenant must occupy the premises   As with the private residential code, the aim is to ensure that only those tenants who are occupying the premises for a particular purpose will be protected. The issue of occupation is, however, more complex in the case of business use as the tenant may not personally be on-site carrying out the business but have employees and others doing so or may be generally supervising activities there. The case law has had to address the question of whether it is sufficient to be in control of the business operations on the premises or whether an element of actual physical occupation is necessary. In *Lee-Verhulst Ltd v Harwood Trust* [1973] QB 204, the tenant let twenty furnished apartments. The sole director of the company lived on site and provided a range of services to the occupants, including the employment of two chambermaids. This was held by the Court of Appeal to be sufficient to constitute occupation, Sachs LJ commenting that the word 'occupied' should be given 'its natural and ordinary meaning in the context of the subject matter of [the 1954] Act' (at 213). In *Graysim Holdings Ltd v P & O Property Holdings Ltd* [1994] 1 WLR 992 ([1994] Conv 470), the tenant had a lease of a market hall, fitted it out with wooden stalls and each stallholder secured his own unit with a padlock and key. The tenant employed a superintendent who had an office in the hall and opened and closed the market, controlled the heating system and generally kept an eye on things. The Court of Appeal held that there was a sufficient degree of presence and manifestation of control to constitute occupation. Ultimately, the question of occupation turns on factors such as the extent of physical occupation of the tenant on the site, the amount of control exercised by the tenant and the range of services provided.

The Act contains special provisions relating to occupation by beneficiaries, partnerships and companies (ss 41, 41A, 42). Where the property is let to trustees, occupation by beneficiaries of the trust will count as occupation by the trustees:

s 41(1) **Where a tenancy is held on trust, occupation by all or any of the beneficiaries under the trust, and the carrying on of a business by all or any of the beneficiaries, shall be treated for the purposes of section twenty-three of this Act as equivalent to occupation or the carrying on of a business by the tenant; and in relation to a tenancy to which this Part of this Act applies by virtue of the foregoing provisions of this subsection—**

   (a) **references (however expressed) in this Part of this Act and in the Ninth Schedule to this Act to the business of, or to carrying on of business, use, occupation or enjoyment by, the tenant shall be construed as including references to the business of, or to carrying on of business, use, occupation or enjoyment by, the beneficiaries or beneficiary;**

(b) the reference in paragraph (d) of subsection (1) of section thirty-four of this Act to the tenant shall be construed as including the beneficiaries or beneficiary; and

(c) a change in the persons of the trustees shall not be treated as a change in the person of the tenant.

(2) Where the landlord's interest is held on trust the references in paragraph (g) of subsection (1) of section thirty of this Act to the landlord shall be construed as including references to the beneficiaries under the trust or any of them; but, except in the case of a trust arising under a will or on the intestacy of any person, the reference in subsection (2) of that section to the creation of the interest therein mentioned shall be construed as including the creation of the trust.

Similarly, it is not necessary for all members of a partnership who own the lease as joint tenants to occupy the premises for business purposes in order for those who do so to have rights of renewal under the 1954 Act:

s 41A(1) The following provisions of this section shall apply where—

(a) a tenancy is held jointly by two or more persons (in this section referred to as the joint tenants); and

(b) the property comprised in the tenancy is or includes premises occupied for the purposes of a business; and

(c) the business (or some other business) was at some time during the existence of the tenancy carried on in partnership by all the persons who were then the joint tenants or by those and other persons and the joint tenants' interest in the premises was then partnership property; and

(d) the business is carried on (whether alone or in partnership with other persons) by one or some only of the joint tenants and no part of the property comprised in the tenancy is occupied, in right of the tenancy, for the purposes of a business carried on (whether alone or in partnership with other persons) by the other or others.

(2) In the following provisions of this section those of the joint tenants who for the time being carry on the business are referred to as the business tenants and the others as the other joint tenants.

(3) Any notice given by the business tenants which, had it been given by all the joint tenants, would have been—

(a) a tenant's request for a new tenancy made in accordance with section 26 of this Act; or

(b) a notice under subsection (1) or subsection (2) of section 27 of this Act; shall be treated as such if it states that it is given by virtue of this section and sets out the facts by virtue of which the persons giving it are the business tenants; and references in those sections and in section 24A of this Act to the tenant shall be construed accordingly.

(4) A notice given by the landlord to the business tenants which, had it been given to all the joint tenants, would have been a notice under section 25 of this Act shall be treated as such a notice, and references in that

section the tenant shall be construed accordingly.

(5) An application under section 24(1) of this Act for a new tenancy may, instead of being made by all the joint tenants, be made by the business tenants alone; and where it is so made—

(a) this Part of this Act shall have effect, in relation to it, as if the references therein to the tenant included references to the business tenants alone; and

(b) the business tenants shall be liable, to the exclusion of the other joint tenants, for the payment of rent and the discharge of any other obligation under the current tenancy for any rental period beginning after the date specified in the landlord's notice under section 25 of this Act or, as the case may be, beginning on or after the date specified in their request for a new tenancy.

(6) Where the court makes an order under section 29(1) of this Act for the grant of a new tenancy on an application made by the business tenants it may order the grant to be made to them or to them jointly with the persons carrying on the business in partnership with them, and may order the grant to be made subject to the satisfaction, within a time specified by the order, of such conditions as to guarantors, sureties or otherwise as appear to the court equitable, having regard to the omission of the other joint tenants from the persons who will be the tenant under the new tenancy.

(7) The business tenants shall be entitled to recover any amount payable by way of compensation under section 37 . . .

Occupation by members of the same group of companies as the tenant company will also suffice to give rights under the 1954 Act to the tenant company:

s 42(1) For the purposes of this section two bodies corporate shall be taken to be members of a group if and only if one is a subsidiary of the other or both are subsidiaries of a third body corporate.

In this subsection 'subsidiary' has the meaning given by section 736 of the Companies Act 1985.

(2) Where a tenancy is held by a member of a group, occupation by another member of the group, and the carrying on of a business by another member of the group, shall be treated for the purposes of section twenty-three of this Act as equivalent to occupation or the carrying on of a business by the member of the group holding the tenancy; and in relation to a tenancy to which this Part of this Act applies by virtue of the foregoing provisions of this subsection—

(a) references (however expressed) in this Part of this Act and in the Ninth Schedule to this Act to the business of or to use occupation or enjoyment by the tenant shall be construed as including references to the business of or to use occupation or enjoyment by the said other member;

(b) the reference in paragraph (d) of subsection (1) of section thirty four of this Act to the tenant shall be construed as including the said other member; and

(c) an assignment of the tenancy from one member of the group to another shall not be treated as a change in the person of the tenant.

(3) Where the landlord's interest is held by a member of a group—

(a) the reference in paragraph (g) of subsection (1) of section 30 of this Act to intended occupation by the landlord for the purposes of a business to be carried on by him shall be construed as including intended occupation by any member of the group for the purposes of a business to be carried on by that member; and

(b) the reference in subsection (2) of that section to the purchase or creation of any interest shall be construed as a reference to a purchase from or creation by a person other than a member of the group.

One of the recognized defects of the present legislation is, however, that the Act does not go far enough in giving recognition to the differing ways in which the landlord or tenant might organize his business affairs. So, for example, a tenant cannot renew his tenancy if he is an individual but it is his company that trades from the premises. The Law Commission has recommended extending the concept of the landlord's and tenant's identities to enable the right to renew to be available to those who in substance, if not in strict form, use the premises for business purposes (Law Com. No. 208, *op. cit.*, paras 2.2–2.13).

(d) Occupation must be for business purposes The word 'business' has been given a very wide meaning, to include not only profit making businesses and professions but also a lawn tennis club (*Addiscombe Garden Estates Ltd v Crabbe* [1958] 1 QB 513) and the letting of apartments (*Lee-Verhulst Ltd v Harwood Trust, op. cit.; Linden v Department of Health and Social Security* [1986] 1 All ER 691).

(e) The tenancy must not be excluded

(i) Excluded classes of tenancies. Some types of business tenancies are excluded from Part II by s 43:

1 Agricultural holdings. These are covered by a separate code of protection (s 43(1)(a)).

2 Mining leases (s 43(1)(b)).

3 Tenancies of on-licensed premises. Leases of premises for the sale of intoxicating liquor to be consumed on the premises (public houses) were excluded from the Act until mid-1989 but are now included—Landlord and Tenant (Licensed Premises) Act 1990. Even before this change, some on-licensed premises were included in the 1954 Act where a substantial proportion of the business consisted of something other than the sale of intoxicating liquor, for example, a hotel. The inclusion of public houses in the 1954 Act was part of a wider reform of the beer industry following a report of the Monopolies and Mergers Commission on beer supplies—taken together with other changes, it is intended to increase the tenant's independence from brewer landlords.

4 Service tenancies, i.e. tenancies granted by reason that the tenant was the holder of an office, appointment or employment from the grantor and lasting only so long as the office, appointment or employment continues:

s 43(2) This Part of this Act does not apply to a tenancy granted by reason that the tenant was the holder of an office, appointment or employment from the grantor thereof and continuing only so long as the tenant holds the office, appointment or employment, or terminable by the grantor on the tenant's ceasing to hold it, or coming to an end at a time fixed by reference to the time at which the tenant ceases to hold it:

Provided that this subsection shall not have effect in relation to a tenancy granted after the commencement of this Act unless the tenancy was granted by an instrument in writing which expressed the purpose for which the tenancy was granted.

(ii) Short term tenancies. Section 43(3) excludes tenancies for a term certain not exceeding six months. If the tenancy itself permits renewal or extension beyond six months or if the tenant (and/or a predecessor in business) has in fact occupied the premises for twelve months, then the tenancy will be within the Act:

s 43(3) This Part of this Act does not apply to a tenancy granted for a term certain not exceeding six months unless—
(a) the tenancy contains provision for renewing the term or for extending it beyond six months from its beginning; or
(b) the tenant has been in occupation for a period which, together with any period during which any predecessor in the carrying on of the business carried on by the tenant was in occupation, exceeds twelve months.

(iii) Mixed residential/business user. If the premises are used partly for residential and partly for business use, for example living accommodation over a shop, they will still be within Part II of the 1954 Act. If, however, the premises are used mainly for residential purposes and the business use is incidental, Part II will not apply to the tenancy:

It is only if the [business] activity is part of the reason for, part of his aim and object in occupying the house that . . . section [23] will apply. *(per* Geoffrey Lane LJ, *Cheryl Investments v Saldanha, op. cit.,* at 1339; and see Murdoch, *Residential Use and the 1954 Act,* (1993) 17 EG 101)

(iv) Contracting out. It is possible for the parties to a lease for a term of years certain to agree that the lease shall be excluded from the renewal provisions of the Act (s 38(4)). In *Nicholls v Kinsey* [1994] 16 EG 145, it was held that contracting out is not possible where the lease is for 12 months and thereafter from year to year.

s 38(4) The court may–
(a) on the joint application of the persons who will be the landlord and the

tenant in relation to a tenancy to be granted for a term of years certain which will be a tenancy to which this Part of this Act applies, authorise an agreement excluding in relation to that tenancy the provisions of sections 24 to 28 of this Act; and

(b) on the joint application of the persons who are the landlord and the tenant in relation to a tenancy to which this Part of this Act applies, authorise an agreement for the surrender of the tenancy on such date or in such circumstances as may be specified in the agreement and on such terms (if any) as may be so specified;

if the agreement is contained in or endorsed on the instrument creating the tenancy or such other instrument as the court may specify; and an agreement contained in or endorsed on an instrument in pursuance of an authorisation given under the subsection shall be valid notwithstanding anything in the preceding provisions of this section.

In order to contract out, a court order must be obtained on the joint application of both parties. The original intention underlying the need to obtain a court order was that this would act as a safeguard to the tenant. In practice, the existing court application route does not generally involve a full examination of the circumstances of the case and so it provides little protection to the tenant from possible abuse by the landlord of his dominant position. As Lord Denning MR observed in *Hagee (London) Ltd v AB Erikson and Larson, op. cit.*, at 215:

We are told that the court invariably approves such an agreement when it is made by business people, properly advised by their lawyers. The court has no materials on which to refuse it.

In 1989, only 15 per cent of 24,000 applications failed and these are suspected to be mainly due to technical failures. The Law Commission has proposed that instead of obtaining a court order, the parties should be able to endorse an agreement to this effect on the tenancy agreement without going to court. To ensure the tenant is aware of what he is giving up there would be a prescribed form explaining his rights to him and the consequences of giving them up (Law Com. No. 208, *op. cit.*, para 2.20).

Apart from the s 38(4) court order, any other agreement is void

in so far as it purports to preclude the tenant from making an application or request under this Part of this Act or provides for the termination or the surrender of the tenancy in the event of his making such an application or request or for the imposition of any penalty or disability on the tenant in that event. (s 38(1))

6.4.2.2 The Protection available to Business Tenants

Under the Landlord and Tenant Act 1954, Part II, the tenant of business premises is given various forms of protection.

(a) The tenancy can not be terminated other than in accordance with the provisions of the Act (s 24)   If neither party takes any action on the contractual lease expiring, it will simply continue on the same terms. During this continuation tenancy, the original tenant will cease to be liable under privity of contract (unless the contract was expressly drafted to include any statutory extension of the term). In *City of London Corporation v Fell* [1993] 4 All ER 968, Lord Templeman said at 971:

Wilde Sapte [the original tenant] are not contractually bound to pay the landlords any rent for period after 24 March 1986 [the contractual term date] because Wilde Sapte only contracted to pay rent until that date. If Wilde Sapte are liable to the landlords after that date, that liability must have been imposed by the 1954 Act. That Act does not expressly impose any liability on anybody except the landlords and the occupying tenant . . . The Act was intended and expressed to protect occupying tenants against their landlords, not to impose liability on former tenants who ceased to have any interest in the property before or after the 1954 Act.

If the tenant wishes to bring the tenancy to an end, he can do so by serving a notice to quit (s 24):

s 24(1) A tenancy to which this Part of this Act applies shall not come to an end unless terminated in accordance with the provisions of this Part of this Act; and, subject to the provisions of section twenty-nine of this Act, the tenant under such a tenancy may apply to the court for a new tenancy—
  (a) if the landlord has given notice under section 25 of this Act to terminate the tenancy, or
  (b) if the tenant has made a request for a new tenancy in accordance with section twenty-six of this Act.
  (2) The last foregoing subsection shall not prevent the coming to an end of a tenancy by notice to quit given by the tenant, by surrender or forfeiture, or by the forfeiture of a superior tenancy unless—
  (a) in the case of a notice to quit, the notice was given before the tenant had been in occupation in right of the tenancy for one month; or
  (b) in the case of an instrument of surrender, the instrument was executed before, or was executed in pursuance of an agreement made before, the tenant had been in occupation in right of the tenancy for one month.
  (3) Notwithstanding anything in subsection (1) of this section,—
  (a) where a tenancy to which this Part of this Act applies ceases to be such a tenancy, it shall not come to an end by reason only of the cesser, but if it was granted for a term of years certain and has been continued by subsection (1) of this section then (without prejudice to the termination thereof in accordance with any terms of the tenancy) it may be terminated by not less than three nor more than six months' notice in writing given by the landlord to the tenant;
  (b) where, at a time when a tenancy is not one to which this Part of this

Act applies, the landlord gives notice to quit, the operation of the notice shall not be affected by reason that the tenancy becomes one to which this Part of this Act applies after the giving of the notice.

If the landlord wishes to bring the tenancy to an end, he must serve a notice under s 25:

s 25(1) The landlord may terminate a tenancy to which this Part of this Act applies by a notice given to the tenant in the prescribed form specifying the date at which the tenancy is to come to an end (hereinafter referred to as 'the date of termination'):

Provided that this subsection has effect subject to the provisions of Part IV of this Act as to the interim continuation of tenancies pending the disposal of applications to the court.

(2) Subject to the provisions of the next following subsection, a notice under this section shall not have effect unless it is given not more than twelve nor less than six months before the date of termination specified therein.

(3) In the case of a tenancy which apart from this Act could have been brought to an end by notice to quit given by the landlord—

(a) the date of termination specified in a notice under this section shall not be earlier than the earliest date on which apart from this Part of this Act the tenancy could have been brought to an end by notice to quit given by the landlord on the date of the giving of the notice under this section; and

(b) where apart from this Part of this Act more than six months' notice to quit would have been required to bring the tenancy to an end, the last foregoing subsection shall have effect with the substitution for twelve months of a period six months longer than the length of notice to quit which would have been required as aforesaid.

(4) In the case of any other tenancy, a notice under this section shall not specify a date of termination earlier than the date on which apart from this Part of this Act the tenancy would have come to an end by effluxion of time.

(5) A notice under this section shall not have effect unless it requires the tenant, within two months after the giving of the notice, to notify the landlord in writing whether or not, at the date of termination, the tenant will be willing to give up possession of the property comprised in the tenancy.

(6) A notice under this section shall not have effect unless it states whether the landlord would oppose an application to the court under this Part of this Act for the grant of a new tenancy and, if so, also states on which of the grounds mentioned in section thirty of this Act he would do so.

The service of a s 25 notice is strictly regulated: the landlord must give between twelve and six months' notice, expiring on or after the contractual term date, and the notice must be in a prescribed form. In effect, the s 25 notice operates either as a way of the landlord seeking to end the tenancy or of triggering the renewal procedure contained in the Act. For this reason, the notice must also state whether the landlord would oppose an application for a new tenancy and, if so, his grounds of opposition. It must also require the tenant, within two months after the giving of the notice, to notify the landlord in writing whether he would be willing to give up the tenancy. If the tenant fails to do so, his existing tenancy will come to an end on the date specified in the s 25 notice. The effect of this is that if the tenant is happy to leave the premises when the notice expires, he will not serve a counter-notice on the landlord and the lease will come to an end. If, however, the tenant wishes to stay in possession, he must serve the counter-notice within the strictly prescribed time-scale or else he loses his right to do so. In addition, the tenant must apply to the court for a new tenancy between two and four months after being served with the s 25 notice (s 29(3)):

s 29(1) Subject to the provisions of this Act, on an application under subsection (1) of section twenty-four of this Act for a new tenancy the court shall make an order for the grant of a tenancy comprising such property, at such rent and on such other terms, as are hereinafter provided.

(2) Where such an application is made in consequence of a notice given by the landlord under section twenty-five of this Act, it shall not be entertained unless the tenant has duly notified the landlord that he will not be willing at the date of termination to give up possession of the property comprised in the tenancy.

(3) No application under subsection (1) of section twenty-four of this Act shall be entertained unless it is made not less than two nor more than four months after the giving of the landlord's notice under section twenty-five of this Act or, as the case may be, after the making of the tenant's request for a new tenancy.

In practice, these strict time limits provide a procedural nightmare for tenants and their professional advisers, fuelling numerous negligence claims against advisers who forget to serve the notices in time. In addition, the tenant's counter-notice tends to be served as a matter of routine as the tenant loses nothing by stating that it does not intend to vacate—the Law Commission has therefore recently recommended the abolition of the requirement to serve a counter-notice (Law Com. No. 208, *op. cit.*, para 2.39).

(b) At the end of the tenancy the tenant can apply for a new lease (s 26) If the landlord has not served a s 25 notice, the tenant may be able to initiate the renewal procedure by serving a request for a new tenancy under s 26:

s 26(1) A tenant's request for a new tenancy may be made where the tenancy under which he holds for the time being (hereinafter referred to as 'the current tenancy') is a tenancy granted for a term of years certain exceeding one year, whether or not continued by section twenty-four of this Act, or granted for a term of years certain and thereafter from year to year.

(2) A tenant's request for a new tenancy shall be for a tenancy beginning with such date, not more than twelve nor less than six months after the making of the request, as may be specified therein:

Provided that the said date shall not be earlier than the date on which apart from this Act the current tenancy would come to an end by effluxion of time or could be brought to an end by notice to quit given by the tenant.

(3) A tenant's request for a new tenancy shall not have effect unless it is made by notice in the prescribed form given to the landlord and sets out the tenant's proposals as to the property to be comprised in the new tenancy (being either the whole or part of the property comprised in the current tenancy), as to the rent to be payable under the new tenancy and as to the other terms of the new tenancy.

(4) A tenant's request for a new tenancy shall not be made if the landlord has already given notice under the last foregoing section to terminate the current tenancy, or if the tenant has already given notice to quit or notice under the next following section; and no such notice shall be given by the landlord or the tenant after the making by the tenant of a request for a new tenancy.

(5) Where the tenant makes a request for a new tenancy in accordance with the foregoing provisions of this section, the current tenancy shall, subject to the provisions of subsection (2) of section thirty-six of this Act and the provisions of Part IV of this Act as to the interim continuation of tenancies, terminate immediately before the date specified in the request for the beginning of the new tenancy.

(6) Within two months of the making of a tenant's request for a new tenancy the landlord may give notice to the tenant that he will oppose an application to the court for the grant of a new tenancy, and any such notice shall state on which of the grounds mentioned in section thirty of this Act the landlord will oppose the application.

The s 26 procedure is only available to a tenant holding under 'a term of years certain exceeding one year or granted for a term of years certain and thereafter from year to year'. The reason why a periodic tenant is unable to serve a request is because most periodic tenancies are short term and temporary and it would be inappropriate for the tenant to be able to apply for a longer-term interest. In any event, as the Law Commission noted in 1969

a periodic tenancy of its nature continues indefinitely until it is terminated. If the landlord serves notice under section 25 to terminate the tenancy, a weekly or monthly tenant has the same right as other tenants under section 24(1)(a) to apply for a new tenancy. (Law Com. No. 17, *op. cit.*, at para 53)

In practice, the tenant is usually content to continue to occupy under the terms of the old lease (particularly if this is at a favourable rent), but there may be reasons why the tenant would wish to apply for a new tenancy. This could be where the tenant wishes to have more security for his business interests than he has under a continuation tenancy.

Again there are strict requirements regulating the service of the notice. It must be in a prescribed form and ask for the new tenancy to begin not more than twelve nor less than six months from the making of the request, the request cannot be for the tenancy to begin before the current tenancy is set to expire, and the request must set out the tenant's proposals for terms of the new tenancy. Within two months of the tenant's request the landlord may give notice to the tenant that he will oppose the application and must give his grounds of opposition. The purpose behind the landlord's counter-notice is to enable the tenant to know his position. The tenant must apply to the court for a new tenancy between two and four months after serving the s 26 request (s 29(3)).

(c) If the landlord does not oppose a new lease or if the court does not uphold the landlord's ground(s) of opposition, the tenant is entitled to a new lease In practice, the terms of the new lease will usually be agreed between the parties, and the new lease takes effect from the date agreed:

s 28   **Where the landlord and tenant agree for the grant to the tenant of a future tenancy of the holding, or of the holding with other land, on terms and from a date specified in the agreement, the current tenancy shall continue until that date but no longer, and shall not be a tenancy to which this Part of this Act applies.**

However, because the tenant loses his renewal rights unless he makes a court application within the prescribed time-scale, it is routine for the tenant to apply to the court and for the hearing to be adjourned indefinitely. In 1989, there were 19,472 applications to the county court but most were made as a precautionary measure and orders granting a new tenancy were only made in 4,109 cases (*Judicial Statistics: Annual Report 1989*, Cm 1154). The Law Commission recognized that this involves an unnecessary wastage of court resources and recommended that the parties should be able to agree an extension to the time limits, and thus to extend the period within which an application to the court can be made (Law Com. No. 208, *op. cit.*, at para 2.59). This measure should reduce the number of applications made as a precautionary step.

The basis upon which the court must determine the terms of the new tenancy are set out in ss 32-35 of the Act. The new tenancy will usually be of those parts of the property that the tenant actually occupies (the 'holding', ss 32, 23(3)).

s 32(1) **Subject to the following provisions of this section, an order under section twenty-nine of this Act for the grant of a new tenancy shall be an order for the grant of a new tenancy of the holding; and in the absence of agreement between the landlord and the tenant as to the property which constitutes the holding the court shall in the order designate that property by reference to the circumstances existing at the date of the order.**

(1A) **Where the court, by virtue of paragraph (b) of section 31A(1) of this Act, makes an order under section 29 of this Act for the grant of a new tenancy in a case where the tenant is willing to accept a tenancy of part of the** holding, the order shall be an order for the grant of a new tenancy of that part only.

(2) The foregoing provisions of this section shall not apply in a case where the property comprised in the current tenancy includes other property besides the holding and the landlord requires any new tenancy ordered to be granted under section twenty-nine of this Act to be a tenancy of the whole of the property comprised in the current tenancy; but in any such case—

(a) any order under the said section twenty-nine for the grant of a new tenancy shall be an order for the grant of a new tenancy of the whole of the property comprised in the current tenancy, and

(b) references in the following provisions of this Part of this Act to the holding shall be construed as references to the whole of that property.

(3) Where the current tenancy includes rights enjoyed by the tenant in connection with the holding, those rights shall be included in a tenancy ordered to be granted under section twenty-nine of this Act except as otherwise agreed between the landlord and the tenant or, in default of such agreement, determined by the court.

The duration of the new lease will be such as the court considers reasonable in all the circumstances, up to a maximum of fourteen years (s 33).

s 33　Where on an application under this Part of this Act the court makes an order for the grant of a new tenancy, the new tenancy shall be such tenancy as may be agreed between the landlord and the tenant, or, in default of such an agreement, shall be such a tenancy as may be determined by the court to be reasonable in all the circumstances, being, if it is a tenancy for a term of years certain, a tenancy for a term not exceeding fourteen years, and shall begin on the coming to an end of the current tenancy.

By consent, the court can order a longer term such as the twenty year term ordered in *Janes (Gowns) Ltd v Harlow Development Corporation* (1979) 253 EG 799. The Law Commission lists criticisms of this limitation:

a 14-year term might be inappropriately short if the preceding lease had been much longer, it did not conveniently divide into 5- or 3- year periods for rent review purposes and, in fixing the new rent, precise comparables might be difficult to find because 14-year terms were now seldom granted by agreement. (Law Com. No. 208, *op. cit.*, para 2.76)

In the event, only minimal change was recommended by the Law Commission, to permit a fifteen-year maximum to accord better with modern rent review patterns.

The rent for the new tenancy is to be based on open market rental values based on the formula set out in s 34:

s 34(1) The rent payable under a tenancy granted by order of the court . . . shall be such as may be agreed between the landlord and the tenant or as, in default of such agreement, may be determined by the court to be that at which, having regard to the terms of the tenancy (other than those relating to rent), the holding might reasonably be expected to be let in the open market by a willing lessor, there being disregarded—

(a) any effect on rent of the fact that the tenant has or his predecessors in title have been in occupation of the holding,

(b) any goodwill attached to the holding by reason of the carrying on thereat of the business of the tenant (whether by him or by a predecessor of his in that business),

(c) any effect on rent of an improvement to which this paragraph applies,

(d) in the case of a holding comprising licensed premises, any addition to its value attributable to the licence, if it appears to the court that having regard to the terms of the current tenancy and any other relevant circumstances the benefit of the licence belongs to the tenant.

(2) Paragraph (c) of the foregoing subsection applies to any improvement carried out by a person who at the time it was carried out was the tenant, but only if it was carried out otherwise than in pursuance of an obligation to his immediate landlord, and either it was carried out during the current tenancy or the following conditions are satisfied, that is to say,—

(a) that it was completed not more than twenty-one years before the application for the new tenancy was made; and

(b) that the holding or any part of it affected by the improvement has at all times since the completion of the improvement been comprised in tenancies of the description specified in section 23(1) of this Act; and

(c) that at the termination of each of those tenancies the tenant did not quit.

(3) Where the rent is determined by the court the court may, if it thinks fit, further determine that the terms of the tenancy shall include such provision for varying the rent as may be specified in the determination.

The intention of s 34 is that the court should decide what is the open market rent for the particular premises, but disregard factors that are personal to the tenant that would inflate that figure. So, for example, the fact that the particular tenant already in occupation would pay more than other tenants in order to avoid being disturbed and losing the goodwill that it has build up there would be ignored. It is also possible for the court to include a rent review clause in the new lease—until this was permitted by an amendment in 1969, the tendency was for courts to only grant renewals for short terms in order to avoid hardship to the landlords.

The remaining terms of the tenancy are determined by reference to s 35:

s 35   The terms of a tenancy . . . (other than terms as to the duration thereof and as to the rent payable thereunder) shall be such as may be agreed between the landlord and the tenant or as, in default of such agreement, may be determined by the court; and in determining those terms the court shall have regard to the terms of the current tenancy and to all relevant circumstances.

In deciding the new terms the courts have been anxious not to allow the tenant's business interests to be worsened. This is illustrated in *Gold v Brighton Corporation* [1956] 3 All ER 442, where the landlord was seeking on renewal to prevent the tenant from selling second-hand clothes without the landlord's consent. The Court of Appeal refused this as it would damage the tenant's existing business. Denning LJ said at 443:

The Landlord and Tenant Act 1954 plainly intends to protect the tenant in respect of his business . . . In as much as the tenant is to be protected in respect of his business, the terms of the new tenancy should be such as to enable him to carry on his business as it is. They should not prevent him from carrying on an important part of it. At any rate, if he is to be prevented from using the premises in the future in a way in which he has used them in the past, it is for the landlord to justify the restriction and there ought to be strong and cogent evidence for this purpose.

As for the tenant's argument that the user clause should be the same as that in the former lease (wider than the tenant's actual business), Denning LJ rejected this, stating at 444:

The object of the Act is to protect a tenant in respect of his business, and not to put a saleable asset into his hands.

A more difficult and controversial issue has been the extent to which the landlord should be able to 'modernise' the lease, where the changes have no direct effect upon the tenant's business. This arose in *O'May v City of London Real Property Co Ltd* [1983] 2 AC 726, where the landlord argued that the new lease should be a 'clear lease'. Under the old tenancy, the landlord bore the cost of servicing the building. The landlord's proposal was that the fixed rental be reduced in return for the tenant accepting the risk of fluctuation in service charge costs. The tenant preferred to have a higher, but certain, fixed rent. Under both proposals the landlord would be responsible for carrying out maintenance, repairs and running the building, but under the clear lease proposal the cost of these services would be borne by the tenant.

Lord Hailsham stated the principle upon which the court was to determine the new terms at 740–1:

. . . I do believe that the court must begin by considering the terms of the current tenancy, that the burden of persuading the court to impose a change in those terms against the will of either party must rest on the party proposing the change, and that the change proposed must, in the circumstances of the case, be fair and reasonable, and should take into account, amongst other things, the comparatively weak negotiating position of a sitting tenant requiring renewal, particularly in conditions of scarcity, and the general purpose of the Act which is to protect the business interests of the tenant so far as they are affected . . . by the approaching termination of the current lease, in particular as regards his security of tenure . . . .

There must, in my view, be a good reason based in the absence of agreement

on essential fairness for the court to impose a new term not in the current lease by either party on the other against his will.

This did not, however, mean that it would never be possible to update a lease:

The words 'have regard to' [in s 35] . . . impose an onus upon a party seeking to introduce new, or substituted, or modified terms, to justify the change, with reasons appearing sufficient to the court . . . If such reasons are shown, then the court . . . may consider giving effect to them: there is certainly no intention . . . to freeze, or . . . to 'petrify' the terms of the lease. In some cases, especially where the lease is an old one, many of its terms will be out of date, or unsuitable in relation to the new term to be granted. (*per* Lord Wilberforce at 747)

On the facts, the landlord was unable to obtain a 'clear lease'. Indeed, the remarks of Lord Wilberforce, while directed to the issue of renewal, do seem to challenge more widely the fairness of the 'net rent' or clear concept of institutional leases:

The character of the two parties' interests in the land—the landlord's an indefinite one by freehold, the tenants' limited one over a comparatively short period, even though capable of renewal if the tenant so wishes, is such as to call for the assumption of long term risks by the former . . . Transference of these rights to the leaseholders, accompanied, as is inevitable, by separation of control, creates a risk disproportionate to their interest. If it is reasonable for the landlord to wish to get rid of these risks in exchange for a fixed payment (reduction in rent) it must be equally, or indeed more, reasonable for the tenants to wish, against receipt of that reduction, to avoid assuming it. The tenants are being asked to bear all the risks of property management, a business which they have not chosen, being management by others in the interests of those others. (at 749)

The fact that the particular lease at issue in *O'May* was for only five years makes these observations much more significant than would be the case in a more standard twenty-five-year lease where the tenant's interest is not so limited. Given, however, that under the 1954 Act the court can only grant a lease of up to fourteen years, it may generally be difficult for landlords to modernize leases on renewal.

Views differ on whether this should be the case. If the aim of the Act is to provide the tenant with security without otherwise protecting him from market forces, it seems to follow that the landlord should be able to obtain a lease conforming with contemporary market practice. The Law Commission recognized this argument in 1987 when it stated that the *O'May* decision, setting out the limits on the court's power to modernize leases on renewal, merited re-consideration (Law Commission, *Landlord and Tenant: Reform of the Law*, Law Com. No. 162, 1987, at para 4.56). By 1992, the Law Commission took a different approach, considering that the *O'May* case provides the 'necessary combination of stability and flexibility'.

Sections 32–35 have been criticized as leaving too much freedom to the judges to determine the new terms:

The current provisions are too uncertain, poorly drafted and lack sufficient detail. The inconvenient absence of guidance, coupled with the high degree of discretion foisted upon the courts, produces a system that defies coherency and predictability. (Haley, *Business tenancies and interventionism: the relegation of policy?*, (1993) 13 LS 225 at p 240)

There is little evidence, however, to support that this view is shared within the business community and, on the whole, the Act is felt to be satisfactory.

(d) After the service of a section 25 or 26 notice, the landlord is able to apply for an interim rent to be payable (s 24A) The aim of s 24A is to enable the landlord to have the rent increased from that payable under the existing tenancy without having to wait for the new tenancy to be granted (or for the tenant to leave):

s 24A(1) The landlord of a tenancy to which this Part of this Act applies may,—
    (a) if he has given notice under section 25 of this Act to terminate the tenancy; or
    (b) if the tenant has made a request for a new tenancy in accordance with section 26 of this Act;
    apply to the court to determine a rent which it would be reasonable for the tenant to pay while the tenancy continues by virtue of section 24 of this Act, and the court may determine a rent accordingly.
  (2) A rent determined in proceedings under this section shall be deemed to be the rent payable under the tenancy from the date on which the proceedings were commenced or the date specified in the landlord's notice or the tenant's request, whichever is the later.
  (3) In determining a rent under this section the court shall have regard to the rent payable under the terms of the tenancy, but otherwise subsections (1) and (2) of section 34 of this Act shall apply to the determination as they would apply to the determination of a rent under that section if a new tenancy from year to year of the whole of the property comprised in the tenancy were granted to the tenant by order of the court.

In setting the level of the interim rent, s 24A directs the court to have regard to the current rent and to assume a tenancy from year to year. In practice, this means that in a rising property market the interim rent will generally be lower than the rent that will be payable under the new tenancy—both because of the reference to a yearly tenancy and also because the comparison with the existing rent is designed to see if the tenant should be 'cushioned' against a sharp and sudden increase in the rent. The Law Commission has recommended that in cases where the tenant is certain to be able to renew the lease and there is no reason for the interim rent being at a discount from the full market figure, the interim rent should be the same as that payable at the beginning of the new tenancy (Law Com. No. 208, *op. cit.*, para 2.70). Indeed, to allow the tenant in such a situation to continue in occupation at something less than the current market rent runs contrary to the policy of the Act. In a falling property market, the new rent may well be lower than the existing rent and so it might be in the tenant's interests to apply for an interim rent. Accordingly, the Law Commission has recommended that the tenant should be able to so apply (Law Com. No. 208, *op. cit.*, para 2.63).

(e) The landlord may be able to oppose the grant of a new tenancy on specified grounds Section 30 lists seven grounds on which the landlord may oppose the grant of a new tenancy. These fall into three categories: tenant default, suitable alternative accommodation being available and landlord management interests (see further, ch 11). Where the landlord is relying on tenant default, and on one management ground, he must also show that the tenant 'ought not to be granted' a new tenancy.

(f) If the tenancy is not renewed the tenant will be entitled to compensation for disturbance on quitting unless the landlord successfully opposed the grant of a new tenancy on the grounds of tenant default or the offer of suitable alternative accommodation (s 37) Lord Reid observed in *Cramas Properties v Connaught Fur* [1965] 2 All ER 382 at 385, that

the Act of 1954 for the first time introduced for business what is in effect compensation for disturbance.

The level of compensation is not, however, linked to the tenant's own disturbance. The reasons for this are set out in the Government Report of 1953:

48 [Compensation] based on disturbance or the totality of the loss which the tenant might conceivably attribute to his failure to obtain a renewal (including removal expenses and potential diminution of trading profits in alternative premises) would be very difficult to evaluate justly, would probably lead to much uncertainty and litigation, and would sometimes be an inequitably onerous burden on the landlord. . . .

50 As for the amount of compensation, it is highly desirable to provide a formula which is both simple and certain in its operation, so that both parties know that, when compensation becomes payable, there need be no dispute about the amount due under statute; it is also an advantage if, when the lease is entered into, both parties know, at any rate within broad limits, what is the probable order of magnitude of any compensation which may become due on the expiry of the lease . . . The Government therefore propose that the compensation, where payable, should be a sum equal to the rateable value of the premises in question where the tenant has been in occupation for not more than 14 years, and to a sum equal to twice that value when the tenant has been in occupation for more than 14 years. (*Government Policy on Leasehold Property in England and Wales*, 1953, *op. cit.*)

The level of compensation is, therefore, based on the rateable value of the premises and, if the tenant and any predecessor in business have been in occupation throughout the previous 14 years, the level of compensation is doubled.

s 37(1) Where on the making of an application under section twenty-four of this Act the court is precluded (whether by subsection (1) or subsection (2) of section thirty-one of this Act) from making an order for the grant of a new tenancy by reason of any of the grounds specified in paragraphs (e), (f) and (g) of subsection (1) of section thirty of this Act and not of any grounds specified in any other paragraph of that subsection or where no other ground is specified in the landlord's notice under section 25 of this Act or, as the case may be, under section 26(6) thereof, than those specified in the said paragraphs (e), (f) and (g) and either no application under the said section 24 is made or such an application is withdrawn, then, subject to the provisions of this Act, the tenant shall be entitled on quitting the holding to recover from the landlord by way of compensation an amount determined in accordance with the following provisions of this section.

(2) Subject to subsections 5A to 5E of this section the said amount shall be as follows, that is to say,–

(a) where the conditions specified in the next following subsection are satisfied it shall be the product of the appropriate multiplier and twice the rateable value of the holding,

(b) in any other case it shall be the product of the appropriate multiplier and the rateable value of the holding.

(3) The said conditions are—

(a) that, during the whole of the fourteen years immediately preceding the termination of the current tenancy, premises being or comprised in the holding have been occupied for the purposes of a business carried on by the occupier or for those and other purposes;

(b) that, if during those fourteen years there was a change in the occupier of the premises, the person who was the occupier immediately after the change was the successor to the business carried on by the person who was the occupier immediately before the change.

(4) Where the court is precluded from making an order for the grant of a new tenancy under this Part of this Act in the circumstances mentioned in subsection (1) of this section, the court shall on the application of the tenant certify that fact.

(5) [This subsection states how the rateable value is to be determined for the purposes of subsection (2)] . . .

(8) In subsection (2) of this section 'the appropriate multiplier' means such multiplier as the Secretary of State may by order made by statutory instrument prescribe and different multipliers may be so prescribed in relation to different cases.

(9) A statutory instrument containing an order under subsection (8) of this section shall be subject to annulment in pursuance of a resolution of either House of Parliament. (Details of the current multiplier can be found in Landlord and Tenant Act 1954 (Appropriate Multiplier) Order 1990, SI 1990 No. 363.)

In addition to compensation under the 1954 Act, the tenant of business premises may be entitled to compensation for improvements under the Landlord and Tenant Act 1927, Part I. The idea underlying this is that it is unfair if the tenant spends money on improving the property in ways that will enure to the benefit of the landlord at the end of the lease without receiving any compensation. As Ormrod LJ said in *Pelosi v Newcastle Arms Brewery (Nottingham) Ltd* (1982) 43 P & CR 18 at 22:

Parliament intended that a landlord whose property had been improved by a tenant so that its letting value at the end of the tenancy had been increased, should pay compensation for the benefit he had received.

The 1927 Act provides for the tenant to be paid compensation in respect of any permitted improvement carried out on the premises, either by him or his predecessors in title, and which is not 'a trade or other fixture which the tenant is by law entitled to remove' (s 1). There are certain conditions that need to be fulfilled, in particular, notifying the landlord of the proposed improvement and either obtaining his consent or having his objection overruled by the court (s 3). The court must authorize the improvement if three conditions are met:

1 That the improvement is of such a nature that it will add to the letting value of the holding at the end of the term; and
2 The improvement is reasonable and suitable having regard to the character of the holding; and
3 The improvement does not diminish the value of any other property belonging to the landlord or any superior landlord (s 3).

The amount of compensation which a tenant may claim is the residual value of the improvement from which the landlord benefits:

Landlord and Tenant Act 1927

s 1(1) . . . the sum to be paid as compensation for any improvement shall not exceed -
   (a) the net addition to the value of the holding as a whole which may be determined to be the direct result of the improvement; or
   (b) the reasonable cost of carrying out the improvement at the termination of the tenancy, subject to a deduction of an amount equal to the cost (if any) of putting the works constituting the improvement into a reasonable state of repair, except so far as such cost is covered by the liability of the tenant under any covenant or agreement as to the repair of the premises.
   (2) In determining the amount of such net addition as aforesaid, regard shall be had to the purposes for which it is intended that the premises shall be used after the termination of the tenancy, and if it is shown that it is intended to demolish or to make structural alterations in the premises or any part thereof or to use the premises for a different purpose, regard shall be had to the effect of such demolition, alteration or change of user on the additional value to the improvement, and to the length of time likely to

elapse between the termination of the tenancy and the demolition, alteration or change of user.

Certain limitations are placed upon the right to compensation for improvements by s 2:

s 2(1) A tenant shall not be entitled to compensation under this Part of this Act—
    (a) in respect of any improvement made before the commencement of this Act; or
    (b) in respect of any improvement made in pursuance of a statutory obligation, or of any improvement which the tenant or his predecessors in title were under an obligation to make in pursuance of a contract entered into, whether before or after the passing of this Act, for valuable consideration, including a building lease; or
    (c) in respect of any improvement made less than three years before the termination of the tenancy; or
    (d) if within two months after the making of the claim under section one, subsection (1), of this Act the landlord serves on the tenant notice that he is willing and able to grant to the tenant, or obtain the grant to him of, a renewal of the tenancy at such rent and for such term as, failing agreement, the tribunal may consider reasonable; and, where such a notice is so served and the tenant does not within one month from the service of the notice send to the landlord an acceptance in writing of the offer, the tenant shall be deemed to have declined the offer.
  (2) Where an offer of the renewal of a tenancy by the landlord under this section is accepted by the tenant, the rent fixed by the tribunal shall be the rent which in the opinion of the tribunal a willing lessee other than the tenant would agree to give and a willing lessor would agree to accept for the premises, having regard to the terms of the lease, but irrespective of the value attributable to the improvement in respect of which compensation would have been payable.
  (3) The tribunal in determining the compensation for an improvement shall in reduction of the tenant's claim take into consideration any benefits which the tenant or his predecessors in title may have received from the landlord or his predecessors in title in consideration expressly or impliedly of the improvement.

In 1989, the Law Commission recommended abolition of the scheme of compensation for improvements (Law Commission, *Landlord and Tenant Law: Compensation for Tenant's Improvements*, Law Com. No. 178, 1989). The government has since confirmed its intention to abolish compensation for improvements but no legislation has yet been introduced (see Department of the Environment, Press Release No. 434, 19 July 1994). The reasons for the proposed abolition are based around the complexity of the procedure for invoking claims and the fact that it has little practical use. The objections are not, however, altogether convincing and many of them point towards there being a strong case for a simplification of the law rather than abolition (see Haley, *Business Leases: Termination and Renewal*, 1991, ch 11).

There is a certain degree of careful tactical manipulation in the exercise of the 1954 Act rights. For example, in a falling property market, it may be in the land-lord's interests to continue the existing tenancy as long as possible (at an histori-cally high rent) rather than serve a s 25 notice and trigger a renewal of the tenancy at current market values. On tactics, see Langleben, Newnham, *The 1954 Act: the change in tactics*, (1993) 11 EG 120.

6.5 AGRICULTURAL LAND

6.5.1 Legislative Controls in the Agricultural Sector

Until the late nineteenth century agricultural tenancies were governed largely by custom and common law. While in general this meant giving effect to the terms of the tenancy agreement, certain terms would be implied so as to impose cer-tain duties upon the tenant, such as a covenant to manage and cultivate the land in a good and husbandlike manner (*Powely v Walker* (1793) 5 Term Rep 373). The result was a situation in which a landlord had a number of remedies against the tenant but the tenant had very limited rights. Most tenancies were terminable by six months' notice, leaving the tenant in a precarious position. The problems generated by this are discussed by Atiyah:

... agricultural leases were usually annual leases so that the tenant had no secu-rity of tenure, nor had he any adequate incentive to invest in his farm. As an annual tenant he had no right, on termination of the lease, to compensation for improvements or fixtures, except in some places where certain customary rights were preserved. The tenant's legal position derived from the basic ideas of free-dom of contract which had, by this time, become so firmly established. The land-lord could not be made to pay compensation for improvements because he was under no obligation to pay for benefits conferred upon him without his consent. If the tenant chose to invest in the land, knowing of his limited security of tenure, it had to be 'assumed' that he knew what he was doing, and that he expected to derive an adequate return from the investment, even allowing for his limited tenure. There seems no doubt that during the last thirty years of the nineteenth century these factors were a serious inhibition on adequate investment in agri-culture, although perhaps not so much as was once thought. In the seventeenth and eighteenth centuries, the system had, on the whole, encouraged investment and enterprise, rather than the reverse, because most of the investment capital had come from the owners, and not the farmers. But in the late nineteenth cen-tury, the owners were becoming more reluctant to invest in agricultural improve-ments, and they were themselves gradually losing their social and political roots in the landed estates themselves. (Atiyah, *The Rise and Fall of Freedom of Contract*, 1979, p 634)

The tenant's position began to be improved when the Agricultural Holdings (England) Act 1875 introduced a form of compensation on quitting and gave the tenant the right to remove fixtures in limited circumstances. This approach was strengthened in 1883, with a prohibition on contracting out of the compensation provisions and an extension of the notice period required to one year. As Atiyah notes, this early legislation may well have been in response to the general agricultural depression of the 1880s caused by a series of bad harvests and cheap imports (Atiyah, *op. cit.*, p 746). The position of the tenant gradually improved with a series of statutes in the early part of the twentieth century, until in 1947 the tenant was given security of tenure. This security remains in the current law for existing leases, but leases entered into after 1 September 1995 will be subject to much less regulation (see proposed reform of agricultural tenancy laws referred to in the Queen's Speech, 16 November 1994, and see 6.5.2.3 below).

6.5.2 The Operation of the Agricultural Holdings Act 1986

6.5.2.1 Tenancies to which the Agricultural Holdings Act 1986 applies

(a) There must be an Agricultural Holding Section 1 of the Agricultural Holdings Act 1986 provides:

s 1(1) In this Act 'agricultural holding' means the aggregate of the land (whether agricultural land or not) comprised in a contract of tenancy which is a contract for an agricultural tenancy, not being a contract under which the land is let to the tenant during his continuance in any office, appointment or employment held under the landlord.

(2) For the purposes of this section, a contract of tenancy relating to any land is a contract for an agricultural tenancy if, having regard to—

(a) the terms of the tenancy,

(b) the actual or contemplated use of the land at the time of the conclusion of the contract and subsequently, and

(c) any other relevant circumstances,

the whole of the land comprised in the contract, subject to such exceptions only as do not substantially affect the character of the tenancy, is let for use as agricultural land.

(3) A change in user of the land concerned subsequent to the conclusion of a contract of tenancy which involves any breach of the terms of the tenancy shall be disregarded for the purpose of determining whether a contract which was not originally a contract for an agricultural tenancy has subsequently become one unless it is effected with the landlord's permission, consent or acquiescence.

(4) In this Act 'agricultural land' means—

(a) land used for agriculture which is so used for the purposes of a trade or business, and

(b) any other land which, by virtue of a designation under section 109(1) of the Agriculture Act 1947, is agricultural land within the meaning of that Act.

Various points should be noted about this definition:

(i) The land must be used for agriculture. Agriculture is widely defined in s 96 of the Act as including

horticulture, fruit growing, seed growing, dairy farming and livestock breeding and keeping, the use of land as grazing land, meadow land, osier land, market gardens and nursery grounds, and the use of land for woodlands where that use is ancillary to the farming of land for other agricultural purposes.

This is not intended to be an exhaustive definition. So, for example, land used for cereal production (which is not listed) can be an agricultural holding. Livestock includes

any creature kept for the production of food, wool, skins or fur or for the purpose of its use in the farming of land or the carrying on in relation to land of any agricultural activity.

This would exclude, for example, animals that are reared for sport or entertainment. So, in *Belmont Farm Ltd v Minister of Housing and Local Government* (1962) 13 P & CR 417, it was held that the breeding and keeping of horses for show-jumping was not 'agriculture'.

(ii) Mixed agricultural use and non-agricultural use. The effect of s 1(2) is that non-agricultural use will not disqualify a tenancy from being an agricultural holding so long as it does not substantially affect the character of the tenancy:

One must look at the substance of the matter and see whether as a matter of substance the land comprised in the tenancy, taken as a whole, is an agricultural holding. If it is, then the whole of it is entitled to the protection of the Act. If it is not, then none of it is so entitled. (*per* Jenkins LJ, *Howkins v Jardine* [1951] 1 KB 614 at 628)

Although *Howkins* was a case decided under the 1948 Act (which was differently worded), it is felt that s 1 of the 1986 Act incorporates this test (see *Lester v Ridd* [1989] 1 All ER 1111 at 1113, 1114; *Short v Greeves* [1988] 1 EGLR 1; *Brown v Tiernan* (1993) 65 P & CR 324).

(iii) The land must be so used 'for the purposes of trade or business'. It does not matter that the trade or business is not itself agricultural. So in *Rutherford v Maurer* [1962] 1 QB 16, the Court of Appeal held that a five acre field that was used for grazing horses that were used in a riding school was within the Act (grazing is listed in s 96), even though the business itself was not an agricultural business.

It may well be that if the tenancy is not within the 1986 Act, it is protected under the business tenancy code.

(b) There must be a 'contract of tenancy'

s 1(5) In this Act 'contract of tenancy' means a letting of land, or agreement for letting land, for a term of years or from year to year; and for the purposes of this definition a letting of land, or an agreement for letting land, which, by virtue of subsection (6) of section 149 of the Law of Property Act 1925, takes effect as such a letting of land or agreement for letting land as is mentioned in that subsection shall be deemed to be a letting of land or, as the case may be, an agreement for letting land, for a term of years.

The whole scheme of protection under the 1986 Act is based around the notion of a yearly tenancy—as seen below (6.5.2.2), security of tenure is provided by limiting the effectiveness of a notice to quit served to end the tenancy:

s 2(1) An agreement to which this section applies shall take effect, with the necessary modifications, as if it were an agreement for the letting of land for a tenancy from year to year unless the agreement was approved by the Minister before it was entered into.

(2) Subject to subsection (3) below, this section applies to an agreement under which–

(a) any land is let to a person for use as agricultural land for an interest less than a tenancy from year to year, or

(b) a person is granted a licence to occupy land for use as agricultural land, if the circumstances are such that if his interest were a tenancy from year to year he would in respect of that land be the tenant of an agricultural holding.

(3) This section does not apply to an agreement for the letting of land, or the granting of a licence to occupy land–

(a) made (whether or not it expressly so provides) in contemplation of the use of the land only for grazing or mowing (or both) during some specified period of the year, or

(b) by a person whose interest in the land is less than a tenancy from year to year and has not taken effect as such a tenancy by virtue of this section.

(4) Any dispute arising as to the operation of this section in relation to any agreement shall be determined by arbitration under this Act.

s 3(1) Subject to section 5 below, a tenancy of an agricultural holding for a term of two years or more shall, instead of terminating on the term date, continue (as from that date) as a tenancy from year to year, but otherwise on the terms of the original tenancy so far as applicable, unless–

(a) not less than one year nor more than two years before the term date a written notice has been given by either party to the other of his intention to terminate the tenancy, or

(b) section 4 below applies [where tenant dies before term date].

(2) A notice given under subsection (1) above shall be deemed, for the purposes of this Act, to be a notice to quit.

(3) This section does not apply to a tenancy which, by virtue of subsection (6)

of section 149 of the Law of Property Act 1925, takes effect as such a term
of years as is mentioned in that subsection.

(4) In this section 'term date', in relation to a tenancy granted for a term of
years, means the date fixed for the expiry of that term.

It is therefore necessary to consider how this operates in relation to particular
kinds of tenancy:

(i) The periodic tenancy.   As this will, in any event, only be terminated by service of a notice to quit this fits easily into the scheme of the legislation. By s 25 at
least twelve months' notice must be given. Section 1(5) clearly brings annual tenancies within the Act, and by s 2 a tenancy granted 'for an interest less than a tenancy from year to year' is to take effect 'as if it were an agreement for the letting of
land for a tenancy from year to year' (unless prior Ministry approval has been
obtained). Thus, short term lettings are converted into yearly tenancies with protection. It has also been held that a letting for exactly one year is within s 2 and so
is converted into a tenancy from year to year: *Bernays v Prosser* [1963] 2 QB 592.
This contrasts with business lettings which can be granted for a fixed period of up
to six months without protection.

(ii) Fixed-term lettings.   Those for less than a year will, as above, be converted
into yearly tenancies. By s 3 tenancies for a 'term of two years or more shall,
instead of terminating on the term date, continue (as from that date) as a tenancy
from year to year'. To end the tenancy prior to the transition into a yearly tenancy
requires service of a notice not less than one year nor more than two years before
the date fixed for the expiry of the term. This notice is treated as a notice to quit
(even though at common law a fixed term tenancy ends without service of a
notice to quit) and so will in any event be subject to the statutory restrictions on
termination.

(iii) Licences may be within the Act.   Section 2(2)(b) provides that a person
'granted a licence to occupy land for use as agricultural land' will be treated as
having a tenancy from year to year 'if the circumstances are such that if his interest were a tenancy from year to year he would in respect of that land be the tenant
of an agricultural holding'. In order to be within this there must be an agreement
for valuable consideration and not, for example, a merely gratuitous licence
(*Goldsack v Shore* [1950] 1 All ER 276). In addition, according to Lord Diplock in
Bahamas International Trust Co Ltd v Threadgold [1974] 1 WLR 1514 at 1527,

. . . the right of occupation for agricultural purposes must be an exclusive right
under which the grantee is entitled to prevent the grantor and any other person
authorised by the grantor from making use of the land, at any rate for agricultural
purposes, during the period of the grant. The application of section 2(1) of the Act
to licences to occupy land for use as agricultural land was, in my view, correctly
stated by Davies LJ in *Harrison-Broadley v Smith* [1964] 1 WLR 456, 470, where he
said:

'. . . there cannot be such a licence without a right of exclusive occupation during the currency of the licence in the licensee as against the licensor for that purpose'.

In theory, this contrasts with the private residential sector and the business sector where licences are excluded from the protective legislation. The need for 'exclusivity' in the terms discussed by Lord Diplock does, however, suggest that the kinds of arrangements that would be converted by s 2 would, in any event, usually be regarded as leases following *Street v Mountford* [1985] 2 All ER 289. This view is supported by *Ashdale Land & Property Co Ltd v Manners* [1992] 2 EGLR 5, where the parties had tried to enter into an arrangement outside the Act by entering into a licence 'for not more than three years'. The 1986 Act permits the parties to apply for Ministry approval for an agreement to be excluded from the definition of 'agricultural holding'. Approval can be given for a tenancy of less than from year to year and for a licence of any duration (s 2). Where such approval is given the agreement will not take effect as a tenancy from year to year. Maddocks J held, however, that the arrangement in this case was in substance a tenancy and not a licence, and so was within s 3 (see above), and the approval ineffective. In his judgment, Maddocks J referred to the earlier case of *McCarthy v Bence* [1990] 1 EGLR 1, where Dillon LJ had said at 3:

If exclusive occupation is, as held in *Street v Mountford*, the hallmark of a tenancy and a licence under section 2(2)(b) also requires exclusive occupation, as held in the *Bahamas* case, it would seem that the licence is itself a tenancy, and there is nothing for section 2(2)(b) of the 1986 Act to bite on. The explanation of that may be that the wording used in section 2(2)(b) goes back well before *Street v Mountford* to the Agricultural Holdings Act 1948 and has not been updated in recognition of *Street v Mountford*. Another explanation may be that the wording of section 2(2)(b) is intended to catch licences to use land for grazing or mowing (or both) which are not, by being limited to some specified period of the year, excluded from section 2 by subsection (3) thereof.

Commenting on this in *Ashdale Land*, Maddocks J said, *op. cit.*, at 8:

It may well be that prior to *Street v Mountford* the scope for a licence which would otherwise escape was considered to be wider. In the light of *Street v Mountford* it still exists, albeit only in a more restricted class of case. Dillon LJ gave one example—the grazing licence.

Thus, the same observation can be made as of the public sector, that although in theory certain kinds of licences are protected there are very few arrangements that would be brought within the legislation as a result of this provision—most arrangements displaying the necessary degree of exclusivity would now probably be categorised as leases. There have, however, been examples of post-*Street* cases treated as licences within s 2—presumably where the licence was taken to be within Lord Templeman's exceptional categories. In *Gold v Jacques Amand*

Ltd (1991) 63 P & CR 1, the occupant erected a building on land as part of a somewhat vague and complex commercial arrangement. The Vice-Chancellor found that there was a licence within s 2—he was neither a trespasser, nor a tenant. The focus of the decision was, however, on the issue of whether there was 'value given' in return for the occupancy and not on exclusivity.

(iv) Tenancy at will.   It is unclear whether the Agricultural Holdings Act 1986 applies to tenancies at will (see *Colchester BC v Smith* [1991] 2 All ER 29 at 48-52, first instance, where the point was not decided).

(c) The tenancy must not be excluded   Certain categories of tenancy are excluded from protection:

(i)   Tenancies to office holders (see s 1(1) above).   The effect of this exception is that where, for example, a landlord appoints a manager to run the farm and pays him for this, the manager will not have a protected agricultural holding.

(ii)   Tenancies granted with Ministry approval.   It is possible to exclude certain agreements if Ministry approval is first obtained. This can be granted in two situations:

1   Section 2—as mentioned above, Ministry approval can be given for a tenancy less than from year to year and for a licence of any duration. Consent does not need to be given for the particular terms of the letting, the policy being that the Minister is only addressing the issue of security of tenure in respect of particular land (*Epsom and Ewell Borough Council v Bell (C) Tadworth* [1983] 1 WLR 379). An agreement excluded by the Ministry is outside the definition of an agricultural holding.

2   Section 5—the Minister is able to give prior consent to the grant of a tenancy of an agricultural holding for a term of not less than two and not more than five years. If consent is given, then at the expiry of the fixed term the tenancy will not be converted into a tenancy from year to year and so the tenant will not have security of tenure. The tenancy will still be within the definition of 'agricultural holding' and so the other provisions of the Act will still apply, such as the provisions for compensation on quitting (see below, 6.5.2.2). The provision was introduced in 1984 to encourage more letting of agricultural land in line with the recommendations of the Northfield Committee, *Report to the Committee of Inquiry into the Acquisition and Occupancy of Agricultural Land*, 1979, Cmnd 7599. As with business tenancies, an application for exclusion under s 5 must be agreed between landlord and tenant.

There are no statutory criteria for approvals but the policy underlying the exercise of the Minister's discretion under these sections was set out in a Joint Announcement of the Agricultural Departments:

5 . . . The policy is to limit approval to those cases where it would be unreasonable to expect the landlord to let his land on a full agricultural tenancy. In general this applies to temporary situations but there are longer-term circumstances

where because the over-riding use of the land is non-agricultural a full agricultural tenancy would not be appropriate . . .

(a) *Land for Development*

Wherever possible, normal agricultural tenancies are encouraged for land on which development is pending, with the landlord's position being adequately protected by the provisions of the agricultural holdings legislation. However, when land is likely to go out of use within five to seven years . . . the compensation payable by the landlord on termination of a full agricultural tenancy could exceed the amount of rent paid. In these circumstances approval of a short-term letting or licence would normally be justified.

(b) *Re-organization and Transitional Arrangements*

There are a number of instances in which it is desirable to make a temporary arrangement for the cultivation of the land. Therefore, according to individual circumstances, approval may be given for a short-term letting or licence for up to five years in the situations outlined below. A further application involving the same parties on the same land can only be approved if there has been a material alteration in the circumstances:

  (i) If the landowner is planning the amalgamation or regrouping of the holding; or

 (ii) if he wishes to enable a prospective purchaser to work the land before completion of sale; or

(iii) if a landlord wishes to make temporary arrangements pending a decision on the future use of the land, eg sale or letting of the land, or a tenant has died and the landlord wishes to make temporary arrangements before re-letting or selling;

(iv) where the landlord wishes to give a tenant who is not an established or experienced tenant a period of trial before concluding a full tenancy; or

 (v) where there is a definite intention that the landlord's son or daughter will take over a vacant holding within five years.

(c) *Specialist Cropping*

Approval may be given to a short-term letting or licence in cases where a farmer wishes to let land to a specialist grower for a single crop requiring 'clean land', eg potatoes, carrots, brassicas, beans, bulbs. Consent may also be given for the growing of a crop, not normally grown on the holding, to be grown as a cleaner crop. A consent will normally be for one year only unless the specialist crop requires a longer period.

(d) *Allotments*

If allotment land is temporarily surplus to requirements approval will normally be given to a short-term letting or licence.

Operational Requirements on Government and Other Land

Approval may also be given to a short-term letting or licence where some agricultural use of the land is possible and desirable but a full agricultural tenancy is ruled out by operational or training requirements which affect the use of the land (this applies particularly, but not exclusively, to land owned by MoD).

6 Within this broad framework each case is decided according to the individual circumstances. It should be pointed out that the categories outlined above are not definitive. (Approval of Short Term Lettings and Licences: Joint Announcement

by the Agricultural Departments: 10 August 1989; extracted in Rodgers, *Agricultural Law*, 1991, pp 384–5)

This displays a much more structured and paternalistic approach than is displayed by the courts towards business tenancies in granting orders under the Landlord and Tenant Act 1954, s 38(4). There are signs that the practice of obtaining Ministry consent is increasing, rising from 1,364 consents in the year ending February 1990, to 1,495 for the year ending February 1992 (Cardwell, *Arable farming in the Short Term*, [1993] Conv 138 at p 141).

(iii) Grazing or Mowing.   Section 2(3)(a) provides that a tenancy or licence to occupy agricultural land does not take effect as an annual tenancy if it is

made (whether or not it expressly so provides) in contemplation of the use of the land only for grazing or mowing (or both) during some specified period of the year.

To fall within this exception the letting must be for less than a year and it has been held that a letting for 364 days is therefore excluded from being converted to an annual tenancy (*Reid v Dawson* [1955] 1 QB 214).

(iv) Fixed term lettings between twelve and 24 months (*Gladstone v Bower* lettings). Lettings of a fixed term between twelve and 24 months are agricultural holdings within the Act. Tenants do not, however, gain secure status. This is because the Act operates by restricting the operation of a notice to quit. Yearly tenancies, tenancies for less than from year to year (s 2) and tenancies for two or more years (s 3) are all treated as annual tenancies which must be determined by notice to quit. Fixed-term lettings of between twelve and 24 months are not converted by any of these sections into annual tenancies and so fall outside the security provisions. This was decided by Diplock J in *Gladstone v Bower* [1959] 3 All ER 475 (and confirmed by the Court of Appeal, [1960] 3 All ER 353), who commented that it was probably the result of a Parliamentary oversight. The use of such lettings as a way of avoiding security is very common and the Northfield Committee recommended that the gap should be closed. The later Acts have failed to do so.

There has also been some doubt over whether such lettings are, nevertheless, for a 'term of years'—if they are they will be within the definition of agricultural holding and thus unable to gain protection under the business tenancy code of protection instead. This has now been confirmed by the Court of Appeal in *EWP Ltd v Moore* [1992] 1 All ER 880, Bingham LJ commenting at 892:

The attention of Parliament has been clearly drawn to the apparent anomaly that agricultural business tenants for terms between one and two years alone lack the security granted by the 1954 Act and (now) the 1986 Act. Yet despite abundant opportunities Parliament has not acted to cure the anomaly, which cannot have escaped the attention of departmental lawyers and administrators. The inference

must be either that this apparent anomaly is not regarded as such or that it is regarded as a desirable or tolerable anomaly.

The tenant will therefore have no security but will be entitled to compensation on quitting for improvements and tenant right matters (see below, 6.5.2.2).

(v) Contracting out.   Some sections of the legislation expressly permit the parties to 'contract out' of the provisions. Where, however, the statute is silent on this possibility, the parties will not be free to do so if public policy dictates that the statute should override the agreement of the parties. In *Johnson v Moreton* [1980] AC 37, the tenant had covenanted not to serve a counter-notice on the landlord, and this inability to serve a counter-notice would have the effect of denying the tenant security of tenure. The House of Lords held that this covenant was unenforceable. To allow the parties to effectively contract out of statutory protection was against the public interest and the protective policies evinced in the legislation.

6.5.2.2 The Protection Available to Tenants of Agricultural Holdings

The value of an agricultural tenancy was greatly enhanced by the introduction of security of tenure in 1947. In the agricultural sector, security of tenure works by providing that the tenancy will, on expiry, continue as a tenancy from year to year. This yearly tenancy is terminable by notice to quit, but the circumstances in which the landlord can serve an effective notice to quit are restricted. If a notice to quit is served by the landlord, the tenant is given the right to contest this notice in certain cases. He does this by serving a counter-notice within one month and the notice to quit cannot then have effect unless the landlord applies for, and obtains, the consent of the Agricultural Land Tribunal to its operation. In order for the landlord to obtain consent he must show that one of the grounds for consent in s 27(3) is satisfied. These grounds are based mainly around the proposed land use under the landlord's management. So, for example, one ground is that 'the carrying out of the purpose for which the landlord proposes to terminate the tenancy is desirable in the interests of good husbandry . . .' (s 27(3)(a)). There is, however, one much more open-ended ground which places a large degree of discretion in the Tribunal: 'that greater hardship would be caused by withholding than by giving consent to the operation of the notice' (s 27(3)(e)). Even if the landlord is able to establish one of these grounds, the Agricultural Land Tribunal must still withhold consent if it is satisfied that a 'fair and reasonable landlord would not insist on possession' (s 27(2)).

The tenant's right to serve a counter-notice is, however, excluded where the landlord is relying on a ground in the 1986 Act, Sch 3, Part I (s 26(2)). This does not mean that a tenant cannot challenge the notice in any way, for example, by referring the accuracy of reasons given to arbitration, but he is unable to require the landlord to obtain the consent of the Agricultural Land Tribunal. The effect is that the notice to quit will, in these circumstances, operate automatically to end the tenancy.

The reasons given in Sch 3 are varied and although Scammell and Densham refer to them as the 'Seven Deadly Sins' they are not all based on tenant default, nor indeed are there now only seven grounds—the justification for continuing to use this phrase is 'since it is now familiar to many practitioners. It is a convenient and evocative shorthand description of the notices in question' (Scammell and Densham, *Law of Agricultural Holdings*, 7th edn, 1989, p 162).

. . . [Stated] in very general terms they cover situations in which possession of the land is required by the landlord for a different permitted use, or the tenant has in some way misbehaved as such, and the relevant fact is asserted in the notice to quit. (*per* Lord Russell, *Johnson v Moreton* [1980] AC 37 at 70)

The tenant default grounds include bad husbandry, non-payment of rent and other unremedied breach. In practice, one of the most important and useful grounds to the landlord was Case G, Part I, Sch 3, whereby notice could be given within three months of the death of the tenant, or of the sole surviving tenant. The usefulness of this was, however, greatly diminished when succession rights were introduced in 1976, enabling close relatives of a deceased tenant to succeed to his tenancy so long as they are 'suitable' and 'eligible' to take on the tenancy. This could happen twice in relation to any tenancy (*cf*. the succession rights under the Rent Act 1977). When the Northfield Committee reported in 1979, it felt that succession rights had acted as a disincentive to landlords to let farmland and therefore recommended that there should be further restrictions on the scheme. In 1986 these restrictions were implemented. It is now only possible for a successor to succeed to 'one commercial unit' and tenant farmers are able to nominate someone to succeed on reaching 65, thus encouraging voluntary retirement. These amendments only apply to pre-July 1984 tenancies; succession rights were abolished for most new tenancies after July 1984 (see also, ch 9.9). These restrictions on succession rights were, in fact, negotiated as part of a compromise package between the Country Landowners' Association (on behalf of landlords) and the National Farmers Union (on behalf of tenants). In return for accepting the restrictions, a new rent formula was agreed, by which the rent of an agricultural holding is revised every three years.

This system of security differs materially from that available to other business tenants. On the one hand, it offers the agricultural tenant less long term security, in that he is unable to apply for a new fixed term lease and only continues in occupation under a yearly tenancy. As with the business tenancy code, it is necessary for the tenant to comply with a strict statutory procedure in order to obtain protection. On the other hand, if a landlord is relying for termination on one of the landlord management grounds under the 1954 Landlord and Tenant Act, and is able to prove the ground, recovery is mandatory. Under the agricultural code, the landlord's ability to recover may depend not only on proving the relevant ground but also upon reasonableness. In addition, there is no equivalent in the agricultural code to s 30(1)(f) and (g) of the 1954 Act, which allows recovery where the landlord wishes to carry out works of reconstruction or demolition, or wishes to occupy the premises himself for business purposes. Under the housing legislation most (but not all) of the landlord management grounds for possession also give an automatic right to possession. Again by way of contrast, under the business tenancy and housing codes, tenant default generally gives only a discretionary ground for recovery whereas under the agricultural code, a proven tenant default ground will end the tenancy without any consideration being given to the issue of 'reasonableness'. These differences are presumably accounted for by the public interest in efficient farming.

As the tenant was being given security of tenure, a rent review procedure was also introduced in 1948. This was to be a fairly informal procedure, with the determination of the new rent to be referred to arbitration if the parties were unable to agree the new rent. Initially, the arbitrator was simply directed to determine the 'rent properly payable'. This produced considerable variation in the results and, in an attempt to introduce some consistency into awards, a market formula was adopted in 1958—the idea being that tenants should have security of tenure but not be shielded from paying market rents. The effect of this was, however, to depress the amount of farm land available for letting. When land became available for letting, there was strong competition for it and high rents could be commanded by landlords. This rent was unrelated to the true value of the land and the level of productivity that it could sustain. Inevitably, this also had an impact on the level of rent awarded by arbitrators on review. This caused great tenant dissatisfaction and led to the deal referred to earlier between the National Farmers Union and the Country Landowners' Association, the former agreeing to accept the restrictions on succession rights in return for a new rent formula. This new formula was introduced in 1984 and aimed to remove the scarcity value from rent valuations and to take account of the productive capacity of the farm and its profitability (Agricultural Holdings Act 1986, Sch 2, para 2). In looking at rents currently paid for comparable tenancies, the arbitrator is to disregard scarcity and the possible existence of a 'marriage factor' ('any element in the rent due to the fact that the tenant or a person tendering for a comparable holding occupies land in its vicinity conveniently capable of occupation with the holding'). This is similar to one of the objectives underlying the fair rent system in the 1977 private sector housing legislation (see further, Ch 8.4.1 and Ch 8.3.2). There are some signs, however, that the new formula is not working satisfactorily (see Law Com. No. 162, *op. cit.*, para 4.64).

If the tenant leaves the holding he is, as with business tenancies, entitled to compensation. The compensation provisions are, however, much more extensive than those applicable to business tenancies. With business tenancies, the tenant may be entitled to flat-rate compensation for non-renewal under Part II of the 1954 Act and, occasionally (but rarely in practice), to compensation for improvements under the Landlord and Tenant Act, 1927. Agricultural tenants are able to claim much more by way of compensation for what is known as 'tenant right' matters, with the aim of compensating the outgoing tenant for work done on the land for which he will not reap the benefit. As Yates and Hawkins point out,

There are no analogous provisions for business tenancies, where the outgoing tenant can only look to a purchaser of his business for the payment of work in hand or stock in trade at a valuation. (Yates and Hawkins, *Landlord and Tenant Law*, 2nd edn, 1986, p 801)

There are various heads of compensation:

1 Compensation for Tenant Right Matters: at the end of the tenancy the tenant may be able to recover the value of growing or harvested crops and produce grown in the last year of his tenancy which he has no right to sell or remove (s 65, Part II, Sch 8). He can also recover the reasonable costs of his acts of husbandry, such as sowing seeds. The amount that the tenant can recover is based on the 'value of the improvement or matter to an incoming tenant'.

2 Compensation for improvements: provided that the tenant has complied with certain requirements he is entitled to compensation for improvements that he has carried out (s 64). These improvements are divided into three categories. First, long term improvements, such as planting orchards or providing underground tanks, for which the landlord's written consent is required prior to execution (s 67(1), Part I, Sch 7). Secondly, other long term improvements, such as the erection of buildings or reclamation of waste land, for which the landlord's consent is obtained or, if refused, the Agricultural Land Tribunal's consent is given (s 67(1)(3), Part II, Sch 7). For improvements in either of these categories the amount of compensation is based on the increase in value of the holding, 'having regard to the character and situation of the holding and the average requirements of tenants reasonably skilled in husbandry' (s 66(1)). Thirdly, short term improvements, such as applying artificial manure, for which no consent is required (s 66(2), Part I, Sch 8). These are improvements which will benefit an incoming tenant by putting the land in good condition but will be of limited duration. The amount of compensation is then based on the value of the improvement to an incoming tenant.

3 compensation for disturbance: if the tenant quits after being given notice and is not in default he is entitled to compensation (ss 60, 61). The basis of compensation differs from that in the business tenancy code which, as we have seen, is a flat-rate compensation. The agricultural tenant is entitled to compensation based on

the amount of loss or expense directly attributable to the quitting of the holding which is unavoidably incurred by the tenant upon or in connection with the

sale or removal of his household goods, implements of husbandry, fixtures, farm produce or farm stock. (s 60(5))

The linkage to actual loss is, however, subject to upper and lower ceilings. The minimum compensation payable is one year's rent (irrespective of actual loss) and the upper limit is two years' rent.

There may also be an additional right to compensation of four times the annual rent of the holding to assist with the re-organisation of his affairs (s 60(4)). This is only available in a few cases, the most common being when

the landlord serves an ordinary 12 months' notice and does not specifically rely on any ground or give any reason at all and the tenant accepts it, or where the landlord serves a case B notice, eg where he wants the land back for development purposes. (Yates and Hawkins, *op. cit.*, at p 810)

4 Compensation for high farming: if the tenant has increased the value of the holding by adopting a more beneficial system of farming than is required by his tenancy agreement, or, if none, than is practised on comparable holdings (s 70). The idea underlying this is to encourage good forms of husbandry.

In order to claim compensation under the above heads, there are certain procedural formalities that need to be complied with. In addition to the consent requirements referred to above, it is necessary to give prescribed forms of notice. It is not possible to contract out of the compensation provisions, save as expressly allowed in the Act (s 78(1)).

6.5.2.3 Reform of Agricultural Tenancy—Policy and Law

The detailed controls in the Agricultural Holdings Act 1986 are considered to play a major part in inhibiting the supply of agricultural land to rent—contributing to the decline of the proportion of agricultural land which is tenanted from 90 per cent in 1910 to 36 per cent in 1991 (*cf.* security of tenure and rent control being perceived as contributing to the decline of the private residential rental sector). To revitalize this sector the government has issued proposals for reform which will be implemented during the Parliamentary session 1994-95 (see MAFF, *Agricultural Tenancy Law—Proposals for Reform*, February 1991; MAFF, *Reform of Agricultural Holdings Legislation: Detailed Proposals*, September 1992; MAFF, *News Release, Agricultural Tenancy Law Reform*, 6 October 1993).

The three guiding principles of the reform are–
1 To deregulate and simplify the existing legislation;
2 To encourage letting of land; and
3 To provide an enduring framework which can accommodate change.

The proposals are of 'a far reaching nature which . . . [will] represent the most radical revision of the agricultural legislation since 1948' (Rodgers, *op. cit.*, p 9). The main strands of the proposed reform are–

(a) A new category of 'Farm Business Tenancy'   In order to 'encourage innovation and diversification which will be to the advantage of the rural economy', a new category of farm business tenancy will apply to future lettings—the existing regime will continue to apply to existing tenancies. While these holdings must include agricultural land uses, non-agricultural uses are possible so long as they are 'ancillary to the agricultural activity and carried out by the same person'. Examples would be shops mainly selling produce from the holding, and bed and breakfast. Under the existing regime, s 1(2) requires a greater emphasis on a dominant agricultural use.

(b) Free market negotiation of terms   The parties are to be free to negotiate their own terms of the tenancy. There will be only three mandatory provisions:
 (i) full compensation for improvements that tenants make to the value of the holding, based on the increase in the value of the holding at the end of the lease—at present a different valuation basis is used for short term improvements and tenant right matters, but this is felt to add unnecessary complexity;
 (ii) unilateral recourse to simplified arbitration to settle disputes about compensation, a faster and simpler route than recourse to courts; and
 (iii) clear signposting of the end of tenancies, with at least a year's notice to be given when a tenancy is about to run out, anything less being considered inadequate for agricultural tenancies. There will be no minimum notice provisions, however, for fixed term tenancies of two years or less or for periodic tenancies for periods of less than a year.

(c) Fall-back provisions   Where the tenancy agreement is silent on certain issues there will be fall-back provisions that apply. These will cover such matters as the frequency (three-yearly) and basis (open market value) of rent reviews.

(d) No security of tenure or minimum term   Although the government recognises that short term lettings are appropriate only for certain situations, such as grazing or mowing agreements, and are not appropriate for full tenancies, it is not proposed that there should be a minimum tenancy length. Nor will there be a right to remain or renew at the end of the tenancy. This will remove the need for the current arrangements for obtaining Ministry approval to exclude short term lettings.

The tenor of these reforms resembles the policy underlying the 1988 reforms of the private residential sector—the emphasis is on non-intervention, with the parties free to agree such fundamental provisions as the length of the term and amount of the rent. There is even less security for agricultural tenants than for residential tenants, although the proposals are comparable with the assured shorthold.

Whether these changes will be sufficient to revive the tenanted sector is unclear. Even within the present regime, landowners appear to be making increasing use of short term letting arrangements designed to avoid conferring security (through Ministry consent and *Gladstone v Bower* agreements)—65 per cent of lettings made in the year to 31 October 1993 were on short term lettings of these types (see Kerr, *Farm Business Tenancies: New Farms and Land 1995–97*, Royal Institution of Chartered Surveyors, 1994, at para 5.2). Deregulation is likely to accelerate this trend. These short term lets are likely to encourage tenants to maximize profits in the short term, rather than enhancing the long term fertility of the land. It has been suggested that more should be done to promote long term tenancies, in particular to assist protection of the environment. Legal measures are not the only tool to achieve this: environmental, fiscal and grant legislation may be equally, if not more, important.

Further, as with the private residential sector, it is probably wrong to attribute the decline in the agricultural tenanted sector to statutory protection alone:

Other factors must be, for example, landowners' desire to preserve the substantial tax advantages enjoyed if they farm on their own account, the more so since full Inheritance Tax relief may now be available; and also the perceived merits of retaining flexibility. (Cardwell, *op. cit.*, p 138, footnotes omitted)

Indeed, whereas full (100 per cent) inheritance tax relief is available for owner occupied land, only 50 per cent relief is available for tenanted land and a report produced by RICS in 1994 refers to wide recognition that the two particular issues that have deterred owners from letting are the threat of land nationalisation and the unfavourable tax treatment of tenanted land (Kerr, *op. cit.*, at para 3.4; and see Annex on 1995 changes).

6.6 AVOIDING STATUTORY PROTECTION

Each sector contains a code designed to protect certain categories of tenant by conferring, *inter alia*, a degree of security on the tenant. Fear of being unable to evict bad tenants without great trouble and expense and the desire to be certain of being able to recover vacant possession of the property have caused landlords frequently to structure occupancy arrangements so as to avoid the effects of statutory controls. This occurs at various levels.

First, it may be possible for the land owner to achieve the same commercial result without triggering the legislative provisions. In the agricultural sector, for instance, the owner of farmland will often be able to secure the farming of the land without having to grant a lease to a tenant farmer, thereby avoiding the protective provisions of the agricultural tenancy legislation. This can be done by entering into partnerships, share farming and other forms of joint venture (see Rodgers, *op. cit.*, at p 2)—a report in 1990 found that 25 per cent of tenanted agricultural land was farmed under 'unconventional tenancies' in order to avoid creating protected tenancies (Agricultural Land Tenure in England and Wales, Royal Institution of Chartered Surveyors, 1990, referred to in Kerr, *op. cit.*, para 3.3).

Secondly, the landlord may take advantage of statutory exceptions which will avoid the full impact of the legislation. In the case of commercial tenancies, this can be done by obtaining a court order under the Landlord and Tenant Act 1954, s 38(4) excluding the tenancy from ss 24–28 of the Act. Similarly, under the Agricultural Holdings Act 1986, it is possible for certain tenancies to be excluded with Ministry approval (ss 2 and 5). In the private residential sector, while it is not possible to contract out of the effects of the legislation, the landlord can let property on an assured shorthold tenancy—which gives a mandatory ground for repossession at the end of the fixed term and, effectively, no limits on rent.

Thirdly, landlords may employ artificial methods of avoiding legislative control. This has occurred most commonly in the private residential sector where, unlike in the commercial sector, there is no authorised means for contracting out. One example is the way that owners have granted occupiers licences rather than leases—even where *de facto* the occupiers enjoy exclusive possession. Where the licence is genuine it will not attract statutory control but the difficulties come in determining when the arrangement is genuine, as seen in ch 4. Somewhat surprisingly, in the early 1980s, the Environment Committee received evidence that in some parts of the country virtually all new lettings were outside the then Rent Act 1977 (House of Commons Environment Committee, *The Private Rented Housing Sector*, Vol 1, 1981/2, para 23), some genuinely and some through 'evasion'. Such widespread exclusion from the legislation was 'a significant departure from the intention of the . . . legislation' (*op. cit.*, at p xxxii; and *cf.* the high proportion of furnished lettings during the 1980s that were unregulated—see 6.2.3 above).

7

Property Management

7.1 INTRODUCTION: MANAGING THE RELATIONSHIP

Within the tenancy relationship, the way in which the property is managed will affect both parties to the relationship. For the tenant, property management will affect the manner in which the tenant is able to enjoy the property—whether as a home or as a business. Perhaps the most obvious aspect of property management is maintaining the condition of the property, but other things may be equally important to the tenant, particularly in a multi-occupied property. So, for example, the commercial success of a tenant of a retail unit in a shopping centre will be dependent upon good advertising of the centre, signposting, heating, cleaning, ensuring a good tenant mix, security and so on.

For the landlord good property management is important to maintain rental income and increase the capital value of the reversion, especially in the commercial sector.

Property management is very closely linked with property investment: it is very largely about the day-to-day administration of such investments, and is instrumental in realising the aspirations of the investor, ie, income growth, capital appreciation or the release of development potential.
. . .

The best rents and rent increases will only be obtained if the tenants of the property are happy with the appearance and condition of the building, its location, and above all with the day-to-day running of the property. (Arnison, Bibby, Mulquiney, *Commercial Property Management*, 1990, xx, xxi)

Not all aspects of property management are regulated by the tenancy relationship itself. So, for example, ensuring that there is a good mix of tenants in a shopping centre is achieved primarily through matters external to the lease. The lease can set out what the tenant is allowed to use the property for, but the variety of tenants, the attractiveness of the tenants to the shopping public and the number of units occupied will be dependent upon the strength of the economy and property market at any time, and upon the allocation policy of the landlord (see ch 5). Similarly, prompt and efficient rent collection may have an effect on the value of the reversionary interest, but will have as much to do with the choice of managing agents and efficient management systems being in place as upon the terms of the lease.

7.2 CONDITION, REPAIRS AND IMPROVEMENTS

7.2.1 Introduction

The condition of rented premises necessarily has an impact on the repairing obligations of the parties. The question of what constitutes a repair and what is, on the other hand, an improvement, often seems to be another of those purely academic niceties, though it should be remembered that for the party under a repairing obligation it can represent a financial cost measured in tens of thousands of pounds. Improvements to a building can be necessitated by its initial condition. True improvements to a fit and well maintained building are different and raise different sorts of issues to those presented by problems to do with the condition of the premises and the scope of repairing covenants. Nevertheless, in practice, there is a large degree of overlap between the condition of the premises, the repairing obligations and improvements.

[If] the only defect in the door was that it did not perform its primary function of keeping out the rain, and the door was otherwise undamaged and in a condition which it or its predecessors had been at the time of the letting, then it seems to me . . . this cannot amount to a defect for the purpose of a repairing covenant even though, as it seems to me in layman's terms, that a door which does not keep out the rain is a defective door, and one which is in need of some form of repair or modification or replacement. (*Stent v Monmouth* DC (1987) 54 P & CR 193 at 209, *per* Stocker LJ, cited at *n*17, para 3.9, Law Commission Consultation Paper, *Landlord and Tenant: Responsibility for State and Condition of Property*, Law Com. No. 123, 1992)

This section cannot hope to cover the whole of the law and context pertaining to the state of housing and other premises in England and Wales—whole books have been devoted to just one leasehold sector. The aim is to raise the most important issues and to discuss how the law seeks to meet the problems that exist. The condition of leasehold property in England and Wales will be considered first, next, repairing covenants will be examined, including issues of enforcement (although the doctrine of waste receives only perfunctory consideration), and, finally, the rules regarding improvements made to the premises will be reviewed; the aim is to analyse those various topics across all the sectors, residential, commercial and agricultural, rather than study the rules for each sector separately, thereby avoiding one possible cause of repetition. The overlap between condition, repairs and improvements, though, means that certain issues will recur throughout the chapter. It should be seen as evidence that matters to do with the state and quality of the stock of buildings in England and Wales do not neatly fit into the pigeonholes that the law has created in this area. However, before looking at the substance of those matters, two overarching problems need to be raised: the nature of the leasehold interests and the imposition of repairing duties, and the special difficulties relating to premises in multiple occupation.

7.2.1.1 Leasehold Interests

Part of the general problem with leasehold repairing covenants is that the tenant may be obliged to carry out the repairs or pay the landlord's costs and obtain no benefit whatsoever. Most repairing covenants require the tenant to deliver up the premises in suitable repair: thus, at the end of the lease any contractual repairing obligation will benefit the landlord but not the tenant. The wasting nature of a lease is highlighted by this disincentive to repair and improve the property, where the beneficiary of such works will be the landlord/freeholder.

Before 1875, the relations of the parties to a tenancy of agricultural land were governed principally by common law . . . Improving the land and farming profitability require forward planning, and the insecurity of tenants at common law was clearly a disincentive to long term improvement of buildings and land, as a tenant could find his interest terminated at any time without any prospect of reaping the reward of his labours. (Rodgers, *Agricultural Law*, 1991, at p 2)

To combat the built-in disincentive, statute has intervened in certain cases either to impose the repairing obligation on the landlord (see the Landlord and Tenant Act 1985), or to provide for compensation for the tenant for improvements (see the Agricultural Holdings Act 1986), or, in the extreme case, to pass the freehold to the tenant (Leasehold Reform Act 1967; Landlord and Tenant Act 1987; and the Leasehold Reform, Housing and Urban Development Act 1993).

7.2.1.2 Multiple Occupation

Multiple occupation affects residential tenants, whether they be renting in the public or private sectors or holding on long leaseholds, and commercial tenants in office blocks or retail units such as shopping centres. The major problems where there is multiple occupation are to do with management and the allocation of responsibility and liability.

Common and frequent problems were excessive delay in repairing; responding to requests for information; the level of service charges; the quality of service, and the unexpected bills; and difficulties in enforcing lessors obligations. (Hawkins, *The Nugee Committee Report—The Management of Privately Owned Blocks of Flats*, [1986] Conv 12 at p 13. See also, *Commonhold*, 1990, Cm 1346, at para 2.5)

It is pointed out that in the case of a flat it very often happens, as it did in the present case, that the landlord does not undertake to repair the inside of the flat, and it will be observed that the practice is not for intending tenants of flats to send a surveyor to examine the building, since a surveyor could not make a proper examination of the structure in a case where other flats are in the possession of other tenants. Further, it is to be noted that, if the building is structurally in bad repair, the tenant under an ordinary tenancy of a flat has no power to rebuild or reconstruct the premises. To do that he would have to go into flats which belong to other tenants and to attempt to do work on the premises which he has no power to do. (*Cruse v Mount* [1933] Ch 278 at 283 *per* Maugham J)

The potential areas of dispute between the landlord and the tenants are similar in the residential and commercial sectors because the problem is to do with the sharing of one property with party walls and common areas such as, for example, stairs, entrance areas and communal gardens. Whether the tenant is a long leaseholder in a Mayfair mansion block, a single parent in a council tower block in an inner city, a single person in a university town bedsit or a firm of solicitors in the City, there is the same problem of not having full control of the premises *cf.* Dixon and Pottinger, *Flats as a Way of Life: Flat Management Companies in England and Wales*, 1994. Subject to statutory intervention (see 7.6 below), this may be reflected in having no control over the appointment of managing agents nor over the size of bills for repair or renovation—see *Report of the Committee of Inquiry on the Management of Privately Owned Blocks of Flats*, the Nugee Committee Report 1985, at paras 5.11–5.12.

5.11 No less than 88 per cent of respondents said that their blocks had a managing agent or management company. In 34 per cent of these cases the agent or company was said to be owned or controlled by the landlord and in 17 per cent by the residents. The management fee was a flat charge in 28 per cent of cases and a percentage of the total service charge in 48 per cent of cases. Almost 80 per cent of respondents considered that a statutory right of challenge to the appointment of agents would be either 'an advantage' or 'a great advantage' in reducing management problems.
5.12 Almost two-thirds of respondents said that they had recently been faced with substantial bills or charges for repairs or renovations to their blocks. Almost three quarters of those respondents who had substantial charges said that they had experienced major problems—presumably mainly financial—as a result.

For different reasons, both tenants and landlords or their agents felt that 'a 'sinking fund', from which major repairs or maintenance works can be financed out of regular contributions' would be an advantage as long as its ownership was clearly set out in statute—Nugee Committee Report, *op. cit.*, at paras 5.13 and 5.24; *cf.* s 42 Landlord and Tenant Act 1987 and Thomas, North, *et al.*, *The Landlord and Tenant Act 1987: Awareness, Experience and Impact*, 1991, at pp 46 *et seq.* Given the substantial cost of repairs or improvements in multi-occupied properties, especially in the ageing stock of privately owned blocks of flats, a sinking fund to which te͟ could contribute annually in a planned manner, could be a useful means of av͟ ing disputes, although younger tenants who intend to move on soon may be rel͟ tant to pay towards major capital items (see Dixon and Pottinger, *op. cit.*)

More generally, in many cases, the lack of direct control over the premises has been compounded by tenants in the worst properties in multiple occupation having no power in practice to force the landlord to bring the property up to an acceptable standard of fitness—enforcement actions through the courts are beyond the means of the tenants. The fundamental problem for tenants in that situation is that there is nowhere better to go which they can afford. Unfortunately, as the Campaign for Bedsit Rights showed in their 1993 study, *Houses in Multiple Occupation: Policy and Practice in the 1990s*, on average, over three people die and 68 people are injured in fires in this type of property each week—(see also, the *Guardian* p 5, 8 October 1994; Campbell, *After the Scarborough Affair*, ROOF, November/December 1994, p 17). There were 2 million such tenants living in properties which were unfit and were not safe to live in and the cost of repairing would have been, then, £14,000 per property.

From the mid-1980s onwards there has been consideration of the idea of commonholds—these are freehold developments 'of two or more 'units' which share services and facilities and so require a system for communal management, and for the ownership of any common parts' (Commonhold, 1990, *op. cit.*, para 3.1).

The most obvious example of a commonhold is that of a block of flats where, at present, the flats would be owned on a long-leasehold basis. But there would be nothing in the commonhold legislation to prevent commonholds from being established for non-residential purposes . . . The system might equally be adopted for commercial or mixed-use developments, and the units do not have to be horizontally divided (*i.e.* like flats). Thus, it could also be used for housing or industrial estates, or even shopping precincts with flats or offices above. Equally, it could be applied to agricultural buildings and surrounding farmland. (*Commonhold*, 1990, *op. cit.*, para 3.2)

One of the driving forces behind the move to adopt this new form of tenure was that it would improve upon standards of maintenance for common areas in dwellings in multiple occupation.

There is also concern about the problems faced by many long-leaseholders in ensuring that the common services are properly provided, that their buildings are adequately maintained, and that all these things are done at reasonable cost to them. While there are already extensive provisions in the Landlord and Tenant Acts 1985 and 1987 designed to deal with these problems, a provision which would enable long-leaseholders once and for all to get rid of their landlord, without having to establish a serious record of bad management, and to obtain control of their affairs under a purpose-built, democratic system is seen by many as a more attractive solution. (Commonhold, 1990, *op. cit.*, para 4.14)

Throughout this section, there is a sense in which the law and practice have grown up simply because no one was prepared to devise a more radical but better approach to dealing with the problems caused by premises which are not suitable to either the landlord, the tenant or, indeed, both parties.

7.2.2 The Condition of Property in Britain

The state of Britain's housing stock is nothing short of a national scandal. The scale of unfitness and serious disrepair in the homes of this country is now such that present housing policies are completely unable to halt the present rapid decline in standards. On the contrary, capital spending on housing has for the past decade or more borne a substantial part of overall reductions in public expenditure. Current programmes of demolition, rehabilitation and improvement are unable to do more than scratch the surface of the problem and local housing authorities are starved of the financial resources with which to improve them. (Luba, *Repairs: Tenants' Rights*, 2nd edn, 1991, at p 1)

The same sort of information for commercial premises or agricultural holdings is not readily available, but it is hard not to believe that serious disrepair and dilapidation are not present, although there would not be as much pressure on the finite stock as there is in the residential sector. The housing stock is deteriorating, with nearly 1.5 million homes unfit according to the *English House Condition Survey: 1991* (Department of the Environment, 1993; see also Lloyd and Walentowicz, *Changing Standards*, ROOF, September/October 1993, p 8). Although the position has improved greatly since the 1950s, when nearly 5 million dwellings lacked amenities, that is, a fixed bath or shower, the number is still depressingly high—only 62,000 had no bath or shower in a separate bathroom, but 869,000 had a poorly located bathroom, usually directly off a bedroom or kitchen (*English House Condition Survey: 1991*, at para 5.5, 1993). Worse, the condition of housing is becoming relatively poorer. Luba (*op. cit.*, p 2) suggests that 40,000 properties a year become unfit for human habitation and that to deal with the problem by replacing bad housing with good will take anywhere between 500 and 1,000 years at present rebuilding rates. The National Housing Forum's report, *Papering Over the Cracks*, 1994, found that 5.1 million homes were either unfit for human habitation or in urgent need of repair. The Standing Conference on Public Health, *Housing, Homelessness and Health*, 1994, found that the cost to the NHS of people having to live in this poor housing was £2 billion each year.

Part of the problem is to do with the age of the housing stock and design faults over the years (see Luba, *op. cit.*, at pp 3–6).

Houses built before 1914 account for approximately one-third of the housing stock and as they approach their hundredth anniversary they are coming to the

Table 7.1

Age of building	% unfit	Number unfit (000)	Total stock (000)
pre-1850	17.9	105	585
1850–1899	16.1	471	2,919
1900–1918	13.5	228	1,692
1919–1944	8.4	327	3,891
1945–1964	5.3	225	4,231
post-1964	2.2	142	6,407

Source: Table A7.1, *English House Condition Survey, 1991*, (1993)

end of their usefulness unless expensive renovation work is carried out. Between the wars, central government tried to improve housing standards by adopting minimum quality thresholds below which no subsidy would be given to a local authority for that property. Although most housing built from 1919 to 1945 was of a good standard, some properties where cavity walls were used are now experiencing serious deterioration as the internal wall-ties corrode. As might have been expected after World War II when 450,000 houses were destroyed or rendered uninhabitable (Malpass and Murie, *Housing Policy and Practice*, 4th edn, 1994, pp 64 *et seq*.), Government and builders alike in the late 1940s and 1950s experimented with new building methods. Where traditional methods were adhered to and the 1944 Dudley Report's recommended minimum standards were followed, good quality homes were built that still constitute some of the best council housing available. However, with the election of the Conservative government in 1951 on a platform of building more houses at a time when the balance of payments was causing some concern, the only way to achieve the number of new houses promised in the manifesto was to cut costs by reducing standards of size and materials (Malpass and Murie, 1994, *op. cit.*, pp 74–5). There was a great deal of prefabricated reinforced concrete used, some forms of which have been shown to be defective (Luba, *op. cit.*, p 4). The 1960s are most closely associated with high rise tower blocks, built with factory produced components and receiving additional central government subsidy to encourage local authorities to erect them. They have proved to be extremely short-lived, with local authorities having to demolish them because of all their defects (see, for example, the *Guardian* p 4, 29 March 1993).

Particularly serious problems exist on some of the [estates] that were built in the fifties and sixties using industrialized techniques. Some of this housing began to exhibit major problems after a few years due to inadequate design and materials and poor planning, construction and maintenance. The physical conditions of some of these [estates], many of which are high rise and high density, are exacerbated by

their lack of 'defensible space', by vandalism, by boarded up apartments that have deteriorated so much that they are unlettable, and by other symptoms of a complex combination of physical and social pathologies. (van Vliet, *International Handbook of Housing Policies and Practices*, 1990, p 94)

The age of so many properties and the poor standard of many of the newer houses means that the condition of housing in England and Wales is such that mere repairing covenants entered into by landlord and tenant will probably never be adequate to meet the problem. Furthermore, unless more funds become available for repairs in all residential sectors, then the rate of disrepair will continue to grow. The change in definitions of unfitness means that the *English House Condition Survey: 1991, op. cit.*, statistics cannot be directly compared with earlier Surveys, but even the Department of the Environment had to conclude with regard to the 1991 figures that 'in statistical terms, the reduction [in unfitness] is barely significant'—and that is before regard is had to fit properties needing repair (Lloyd and Walentowicz, *op. cit.*, p 8). The precise cost of repair cannot be agreed, but figures ranging in the billions of pounds have been suggested (see Luba, *op. cit.*, pp 6–7; Association of District Councils, the *Guardian* p 6, 10 September 1993; National Housing Forum Report, *op. cit.*, 1994; Wilcox, *Housing Finance Review, 1994–95*, p 122; *cf English House Condition Survey: 1991, op. cit.*, Ch 6 and Appendix E). Such amounts would require the government to approve a larger Public Sector Borrowing Requirement or an increase in taxation. A whole series of previous actions by the government makes a change of approach along those lines seem unlikely, though. During the 1980s, central government cut back on the percentage of accumulated receipts from council house sales that local authorities could use towards the capitalized costs associated with the maintenance and improvement of its own properties, at the same time as it withdrew funding from the Housing Investment Programme (HIP) and as the better local authority properties were being sold under the Right to Buy. *Papering Over the Cracks, op. cit.*, found a reduction of over £1 billion in funds for housing renewal between 1983 and 1995. Moreover, the practical effect of these policies towards HIPs was that local authorities in the inner cities, which had least by way of council house sales' receipts but which had the greatest disrepair problems, had least funds to meet their needs (see Malpass and Murie, 1994, *op. cit.*, pp 111–13).

Mandatory grants for improvements were also subject to cut backs. Part VIII of the Local Government and Housing Act 1989 provided for a new system of grants available to tenants, landlords (but not local authority landlords) and owner-occupiers. It divided grants into mandatory and discretionary, but it made both types means-tested (s 109; and see s 110 on grants claimable by landlords). Evidence gleaned from experience with social security benefits suggests that means-tests put people off claiming that to which they are entitled. The new scheme came into force in April 1990, but the failure by people to come forward and claim it has led to a government review—the *Guardian*2 p 19, 18 February 1994. On another tack, at the same time as the government imposed VAT on fuel bills, it was prepared to consider making homes less energy-efficient in order to cut the costs of the house building industry (the *Guardian* p 4, 29 March 1993). In the end, the Department of the Environment imposed higher standards of house building from 1995 against Department of Trade and Industry pressure to dereg-ulate (the *Guardian* p 10, 16 July 1994).

The lack of any long-term policy towards the condition of housing in England and Wales means that the problem is not tackled and the situation continues to drift along. The fact that there is a crude housing surplus, in that there are more dwellings than households, misses the fact that several of these properties are not in a suitable condition to be used; many of the homes that were repossessed following the economic recession of the early 1990s could not be managed under the Housing Association as Managing Agents Scheme because they were not of a suitable standard (the *Guardian* p 27, 8 September 1993). To paraphrase Aneurin Bevan, the number of homes may not be as important as the quality of those homes (See Foot, *Aneurin Bevan, 1945-60*, vol 2, at p 82 (1973), cited in Malpass and Murie, *op. cit.*, p 75).

7.2.2.1 Who Lives in Poor Housing

The poor housing conditions affect certain groups disproportionately. Up until 1991, the private rented sector always had the worst housing (see The Joseph Rowntree Foundation Inquiry into British Housing, Second Report, 1991, at p 10; Malpass and Murie, *op. cit.*, p 5). The *English House Condition Survey: 1991, op. cit.*, indicated that while this sector still had the greatest proportion of unfit dwellings (para 7.22), it had shown the greatest improvement, while housing association properties had deteriorated most significantly (see *English House Condition Survey: 1991, op. cit.*, Table A7.7). Lloyd and Walentowicz (*op. cit.*, p 8) argue, though, that this dramatic change may simply reflect the fact that housing associations have taken over some of those worst properties since the last Survey in 1986 (see *English House Condition Survey: 1991, op. cit.*, paras 7.31–7.32). On the other hand, the government's policy of trying to encourage housing associa-tions to take over the role of principal provider of social rented housing has meant that some have acquired large housing estates the running of which is beyond their experience and which are not suitable for the families who are taken on as tenants—the result has been poor management and high levels of vandalism (the *Guardian* p 5, 21 April 1993).

It is elderly tenants, single people, those on low incomes and those with larger households who have the worst conditions and they constitute a large propor-tion of housing association and private sector tenants (van Vliet, *op. cit.*, pp 94 *et seq.*). These groups suffer deprivation in many aspects of their lives, but housing features substantially (see Harrison, *Inside the Inner City*, 2nd edn, 1984). Taking, for example, large families, they self-evidently would suffer from overcrowding. The fact that local authorities have not been able to build much by way of new housing since 1979 and that larger houses proved to be popular purchases under the Right To Buy, means that large families are stuck in their overcrowded homes with little hope of relief. Over half a million households were deemed to be over-crowded—LRC Housing Update, p 4, ROOF, January/February 1994. The elderly in poor housing are often not in a position to carry out repairs or improvements to their homes. Australian experience cannot be directly compared with the position in England and Wales, but certain features are universal (see van Vliet, *op. cit.*, pp 743 *et seq.*). First, the elderly have often been in their homes for many years and the deterioration in the standard of that accommodation has resulted from their increasing incapacity either to perform or afford repairs. Secondly, as a proportion of their incomes, housing costs are much greater for elderly tenants, leaving less for maintenance and improvement. Finally, elderly people make up a disproportionate percentage of private sector tenants, where the position is that landlords are less likely to have a structured system for carrying out regular repairs than a local authority landlord would. The last group to be considered, children, have generally seen an improvement in conditions in the 1980s, but a substantial number, especially the 16 per cent who live in households where no adult is in employment, are now living in properties which are in some way unsuitable (Dorling, *Children in Need*, ROOF, September/October 1993, p 12; the *Guardian* p 18, 23 April 1993). Seventeen thousand children under five, for exam-ple, live in homes which lack exclusive access to a bath, shower or inside lavatory. Fifteen thousand children under five now live in homes where their family has to share accommodation with other households. Ten thousand children under five live in non-permanent accommodation. Where the head of household is a single parent, the likelihood of poor conditions for their children is even greater. If it is accepted that poor housing is damaging to the development of the child (see van Vliet, *op. cit.*, p 95; Kellmer-Pringle, *The Needs of Children*, 1980, pp 107 *et seq.*), then the need for a coherent national policy to tackle bad conditions is even more self-evident and essential.

There are various ways that central government can seek to improve housing conditions in England and Wales. Laws may seek to impose standards for land-lords or tenants. One way forward might be to license landlords as performing to an acceptable standard, with local authority Environmental Health Officers checking to see if a property was fit before it could be let—Rowntree Inquiry, *op. cit.*, at p 77. Financial encouragements also have a part to play; the Dutch govern-ment has prioritized subsidy schemes for dwelling improvements (see van Vliet, *op. cit.*, p 172). On the other hand, some properties are so bad that they have to be demolished and local authority powers in that regard also impinge on policies to do with the condition of housing.

The main form of financial encouragement is now found in the Local Government and Housing Act 1989, Part VIII.

s 101(2) In this Part—

    (a) a grant relating to the improvement or repair of a dwelling or to the provision of dwellings by the conversion of a house or other building is referred to as a 'renovation grant'; and

    (b) a grant relating to the improvement or repair of the common parts of a building is referred to as a 'common parts grant'; and

    ...

    (d) a grant for the improvement or repair of a house in multiple occupation or for the provision of a house in multiple occupation by the conversion of a house or other building is referred to as an 'HMO grant'.

The grants are aimed primarily at owners of the freehold or a long leasehold, but tenants can apply for renovation grants where the tenancy agreement requires them to carry out the relevant works (Local Government and Housing Act 1989, s 104). The grant is mandatory where:

(i)   the premises are unfit for human habitation (s 112, 1989 Act); and

(ii) under s 113, 1989 Act, where a landlord (excluding, under s 101(3), 1989 Act, public sector landlords) has been told to comply with a notice under the Housing Act 1985:

    s 189   (repair notice requiring works to render premises fit for human habitation);

    s 190   (repair notice where premises are fit but in a state of disrepair); or

    s 352   (notice requiring works to render premises fit for a number of occupants).

However, even where it is mandatory, it is still to be means-tested—Local Government and Housing Act 1989, s 109, adopting the measures proposed in the 1987 White Paper on Housing, Cm 214, paras 2.14 *et seq.*, esp. para 2.18. Means-testing traditionally deters potential applicants from making claims even when they would be entitled. Moreover, the regulations for assessing income do not take into account mortgage outgoings, making the grants less accessible (see SI 1990 No. 1189, as amended, Sch 3). Figures suggest that since the new scheme came into force in June 1990, the amount approved for renovations has increased and that the amount per grant has been increased, but that this may be because there are fewer successful applications. The pre-1989 scheme under the Housing Act 1985, Part XV is not directly comparable with that under the Local Government and Housing Act 1989, Part VIII but the following data, culled from the Housing and Construction Statistics, Tables 2.16, 2.17 and 2.21 March Quarter 1994, would seem to support the view that the new scheme under the 1989 Act did initially make more funding available, although fewer people were successful in obtaining grants and assistance—see also, Wilcox, *Housing Finance Review 1994/95*, 1994, pp 125–6.

Table 7.2 Approvals under the Housing Act 1985 for the year 1989: Table 2.16

Year	Conversion & improvement		Repairs		Intermediate	
	Dwellings	Amount	Dwellings	Amount	Dwellings	Amount
1989	52,400	£211.4m	34200	£99.5m	11,300	£29.8m

Table 7.3 Approvals for renovation grants under the Local Government and Housing Act 1989 for the year 1992: Table 2.17

Year	Mandatory		Discretionary	
	Grants	Amount	Grants	Amount
1993	35,277	£346.7m	4,944	£21.3m

Final payments, rather than approvals, for HMO and Common Parts Grants under the 1989 Act for the year 1993 are recorded in Table 2.21, but only about £14m was paid out and, thus, its significance is minimal in any comparison of the position pre- and post-1990.

A Department of the Environment consultation paper in 1993 suggested that the means-test for grants ought to be tightened and that the refunds to local authorities which administer the scheme ought to be reduced. The grants are helpful in combatting disrepair, but without a more concerted effort from central government in the shape of additional funding and by way of a policy of seeking to enforce standards, then they will have little impact (*cf.* the *Guardian*2 p 21, 8 October 1993). Grants to individuals cannot be expected to lead to the renovation of all the defective premises in England and Wales, rather some centralized programme to improve the stock as a whole has to be implemented given Luba's (*op. cit.*, at p 3) comments on the scandalous nature of the condition of that housing stock.

7.2.2.2 Grants, Closures and Demolitions

Financial packages, once again to individuals, have also featured as part of central government's plans where inherent defects in house building techniques have had a bearing on the condition of properties. The non-traditional building methods used in the 1950s, as was pointed out above, included using Prefabricated Reinforced Concrete. This material proved inadequate for its purpose in certain circumstances, in particular, where the Airey system of construction had been used (see Luba, *op. cit.*, p 4). Most of these defective PRC properties were owned by local authorities, but rather than establish a scheme whereby a general solution could be sought to the problems of all those living in such dwellings, the government provided relief only for those who purchased under the Right To Buy. Under the Housing Defects Act 1984 (now consolidated as the Housing Act 1985, Part XVI), owner-occupiers who had bought from public sector landlords (1985 Act, s 531) could either receive a grant to cover the cost of most of the repairs (90 per cent—1985 Act, s 543(2)) or they could sell the property back to the local authority for 95 per cent of its value, ignoring the defects (1985 Act, s 550). The Act made no provision for financial assistance to local authorities, who still own most of the properties built by these techniques, to allow repairs to council stock (Luba, *op. cit.*, p 4). Once again, maybe as part of some overall sub-text of making local authority landlordism unattractive, both to the local authorities who have to bear the costs and to their tenants who, due to the financial constraints on the local authority, cannot have their defective premises repaired, central government has failed to devise a policy to remedy defects in the housing stock; instead it has sought to protect one particular type of occupier. The general condition of housing has been ignored, but the longer that a tenure-blind, adequately funded system of financial assistance for renovation is not put in place, the greater the eventual bill will be.

Where the condition of property has deteriorated past a certain point, then closure and demolition are the only solutions. In the 1960s around 70,000 homes per year were demolished and even in 1977/78 a figure of 45,000 homes was still achieved (Rowntree Inquiry, *op. cit.*, pp 26–7). During the 1980s there was a steady decline in the number of demolitions and closures of unfit buildings, until in the 1990s the figure was only just above 2,000 (Housing and Construction Statistics, Table 2.28 March Quarter 1993). The Rowntree Inquiry estimated that at that rate, new houses would have to last 2,700 years, which may explain why the number of closed unfit buildings made fit has risen consistently during the same period, although the dramatic rise since 1990 may have more to do with the stricter definition of unfitness in the first place under amendments introduced by the Local Government and Housing Act 1989.

7.2.2.3 Summary

Since the condition of the housing stock and the schemes introduced to remedy the position have been considered, it is now necessary to examine how the law might be used to improve matters. After looking at covenants of habitability and repairing covenants, however, it will be necessary to consider how and when demolition orders can be imposed if earlier measures have failed.

7.2.3 Covenant of Habitability

The reason for considering the covenant of habitability is to see whether preventing the letting of unfit buildings, as defined in either the Landlord and Tenant Act 1985 or the Housing Act 1985, as amended, would force landlords to improve the quality of their premises.

[If] we want to decrease the relative prevalence of sub-standard rental housing in metropolitan areas, we should seek enactment and enforcement of laws that extend the warranty of habitability in a decisive manner. (Law Com. No. 123, *op. cit.*, at para 4.14, citing Hirsch, 'Landlord-tenant Relations Law', in Burrows and Veljanovski, *The Economic Approach to Law*, 1981)

At common law there are few occasions when a covenant of habitability will be implied into a lease. In *Smith v Marrable* (1843) 152 ER 693, the court held that a covenant of habitability would be imposed only for furnished accommodation. The rule was extended to include situations where the lease is granted during the course of the erection of the premises in *Perry v Sharon Development Co. Ltd* [1937] 4 All ER 390 at 395. However, there is no general duty to let the premises in a habitable condition in English law—*Hart v Windsor* (1844) 152 ER 1114. The situations when the covenant will be implied in the lease do not even include the renting of a flat where, unlike the position if a house were about to be rented, the tenant will not have an opportunity to inspect the premises as a whole before moving in—*Cruse v Mount* [1933] Ch 278. The effect of this limitation on the landlord's obligations is revealed in the decision in *Quick v Taff Ely BC* [1985] 3 All ER 321, where a house was let that suffered from damp, severe condensation and mould growth. The Court of Appeal rejected the tenant's claim for specific performance of the implied covenant to repair and damages for breach thereof, holding that there was no obligation under the lease that the property be let in a fit condition—see also *Habinteg Housing Association v James* [1994] New Property Cases 132. Furthermore, in *Post Office v Aquarius Properties Ltd* [1987] 1 All ER 1055, a commercial case, the basement of an almost new office building let in water up to ankle-deep for several years. Again, the Court of Appeal held that the lease had no implied covenant that the premises would be let in 'a satisfactory state for their intended purpose' (*per* Ralph Gibson LJ at 1063). The courts were willing to hold that if the landlord designed and built the property, as a local authority might have done in earlier years, then a duty of care would be owed to the tenant that it be let in a reasonably safe condition, but this is not the same as a leasehold covenant of habitability (*Rimmer v Liverpool Corporation* [1985] QB 1 at 16, *per* Stephenson LJ).

   In limited situations statute imposes a covenant of habitability under s 8 Landlord and Tenant Act 1985.

s 8(1) In a contract to which this section applies for the letting of a house [or part thereof] for human habitation there is implied, notwithstanding any stipulation to the contrary–

    (a) a condition that the house is fit for human habitation at the commencement of the tenancy, and

    (b) an undertaking that the house will be kept by the landlord fit for human habitation during the tenancy.

    . . .

  (3) This section applies to a contract if–

    (a) the rent does not exceed the figure applicable in accordance with subsection (4), and

    (b) the letting is not on such terms as to the tenant's responsibility as are mentioned in subsection (5).

  (4) The rent limit for the application of this section is shown by the following Table, by reference to the date of the making of the contract and the situation of the premises:

Date of Making the Contract	*Rent Limit*
Before 31st July 1923	In London: £40 p.a.
	Elsewhere: £26 p.a. or £16 p.a. [depending on whether the population of the borough or urban district was above 50,000 at the date of the last published census]
31st July 1923–6th July 1957	In London: £40 p.a.
	Elsewhere: £26 p.a.
On or after 6th July 1957	In London: £80 p.a.
	Elsewhere: £52 p.a.

  (5) This section does not apply where a house is let for a term of three years or more . . . upon terms that the tenant puts the premises into a condition reasonably fit for human habitation.

The first thing to note is how absurdly low the rent limits have been set if a property is to qualify. If s 8 is to have any role in improving the standard of residential properties let in England and Wales, then these figures need to be increased (Campbell, *Legal Eye*, ROOF, May/June 1991, p 15). Given, though, that the property falls within the limits imposed in s 8, the standard of fitness is set out in the Landlord and Tenant Act 1985, s 10 which is not the same as the much more precise and rigorous test of habitability found in the Housing Act 1985, s 604(1) (as amended by the Local Government and Housing Act 1989, Sch 9, para 83).

s 10 In determining for the purposes of this Act whether a house is unfit for human habitation, regard shall be had to its condition in respect of the following matters—

    repair,

    stability,

    freedom from damp,

> internal arrangement,
> natural lighting,
> ventilation,
> water supply,
> drainage and sanitary conveniences,
> facilities for the preparation and cooking of food and for the disposal of
> waste water;
> and the house shall be regarded as unfit for human habitation if, and only
> if, it is so far defective in one or more of those matters that it is not reason-
> ably suitable for occupation in that condition.

While it is relatively obvious to see what s 8 covers, described by Atkin LJ in *Morgan
v Liverpool Corporation* [1927] 2 KB 131, as a condition threatening the life, limb or
health of the occupier, it should be noted that the standard of fitness test is to be
applied to the house or part of the house, that is the demised premises, not to any
common parts for example. Dangerous stairs that are used by all the tenants to get
to their respective flats will not give rise to an action under Landlord and Tenant Act
1985, s 8. One argument in favour of harmonizing s 10 with the Housing Act 1985,
s 604(1) is that common parts would then be brought within the scope of s 8. Given
the generally non-interventionist approach taken to commercial leases, it is anomalous to note that the Offices, Shops and Railway Premises Act 1963, s 42 does
require the person receiving the rack rent to maintain the common parts.

The only other constraint on the effectiveness of s 8 is the decision in *Buswell v
Goodwin* [1971] 1 WLR 92, that the obligation thereunder is subject to the
premises being capable of being made fit at a reasonable expense to the landlord.
The consequence seems to be, anomalous as it might appear, that if the landlord
allows the premises to reach a level of unfitness that would require major
expense to rectify, then the property can be let, or continue to be let, without
regard to s 8. However, with the rent limitations in s 8, the provision is, for all
intents and purposes, redundant anyway.

The Law Commission queried whether there ought to be an implied covenant
that the property be fit for its intended purpose.

**To put and keep the demised property, and all parts of it, in such state and condi-
tion that it may safely, hygienically and satisfactorily be used, and continue in
the immediate future to be used, for its intended purpose with an appropriate
degree of convenience and comfort for the occupants.** (Law Com. No. 123, *op. cit.*,
para 5.7)

The idea is considered below, but the effect would be to impose a covenant of
habitability, forcing the landlord to let the premises in a fit condition—*cf.* Smith,
Repairing Obligations: A Case Against Radical Reform, [1994] Conv 186.

In the agricultural sector, the position is slightly different (see generally,
Rodgers, *Agricultural Law*, 1991, Ch 4). Habitability is part of a wider concern for

'fixed equipment'. The Agricultural Holdings Act 1986, s 11 defines fixed equipment to include any building or structure fixed to the land. The tenant-farmer can go to the agricultural land tribunal for an order requiring the landlord to, *inter alia*, repair any fixed equipment as might prove necessary to enable the tenant to comply with any statutory regulations (see Rodgers, *op. cit.*, pp 68 *et seq.*). In certain circumstances, this might include forcing the landlord to repair the residential premises included in the let, but the primary purpose of s 11 is with respect to fixed equipment used for agricultural purposes. Furthermore, s 11 of the 1986 Act is extremely cumbersome to put into effect. The only interference with commercial leases with regard to habitability, or rather usability, is to do with giving courts the power to vary the terms of the lease to allow the premise to be put or kept in a fit condition to carry on the proposed business (see Law Com. No. 123, *op. cit.*, para 2.64). The situation where such powers might have to be exercised is with respect to common parts under the Factories Act 1961, s 28 and Offices, Shops and Railway Premises Act 1963, s 16 (*Cf.*, Law Com. No. 123, *op. cit.*, para 4.16).

Habitability, however, is principally an issue for the residential sector. The English law on the subject is extremely limited, but the importance of such a covenant in maintaining the overall condition of the housing stock has been explored in several other jurisdictions, notably the United States. The Second Restatement of the Law of Property, Landlord and Tenant, §5.1 (American Law Institute, 1976) sets out the covenant as follows:

Except to the extent the parties to a lease validly agree otherwise, there is a breach of the landlord's obligations if the parties contemplate that the leased property will be used for residential purposes and on the date the lease is made and continuously thereafter until the date the tenant is entitled to possession, the leased property, without fault of the tenant, is not suitable for residential use.

In such a case, the tenant may either terminate the lease and recover damages or affirm the lease and recover damages, seek an abatement of the rent, use rent monies to remedy the unsuitable condition and even withhold the rent altogether (see the comment in the Restatement at p 170). The Restatement reflects the decisions taken in many state courts. The clearest enunciation of the position in the Restatement is found in *Reste Realty Corporation v Cooper* 251 A.2d 268 at 274 *per* Francis J, (1969).

[Any] act or omission of the landlord or of anyone who lets under authority or legal right for the landlord, or of someone having superior title to that of the landlord, which renders the premises substantially unsuitable for the purpose for which they are leased, or which seriously interferes with the beneficial enjoyment of the premises, is a breach of the covenant of quiet enjoyment and constitutes a constructive eviction of the tenant. (Cited in Law Com. No. 123, *op. cit.*, para 4.14; see also ch 3, and Cunningham et al., *The Law of Property*, 2nd edn, 1984, §6.33)

In Australia, the Poverty Commission's Second Main Report, *Law and Poverty in Australia*, 1975, proposed that there should be

a statutory obligation imposed on the landlord, notwithstanding any contrary provision in the lease, to provide premises fit for human habitation at the commencement of the tenancy . . . (at pp 63–4)

Queensland, South Australia and Victoria passed statutes incorporating such a provision (see Sackville and Neave, Property Law: Cases and Materials, 5th edn, 1994, pp 680–1). In France, Art.1719(2) of the *Code Civil* provides that it is the nature of residential leases to require the landlord to supply and maintain the premises in a condition fit for human habitation (Law Com. No. 123, *op. cit.*, para 4.13). In Scotland there is an implied warranty that the premises are fit for the purpose for which they are let (Royal Institution of Chartered Surveyors, *International Leasing Structures*, 1993, Paper No. 26, p 57).

There are several justifications for a covenant of habitability. The common law position reflected in the English law was based on the principle of *caveat emptor*. It was up to the tenant to inspect the premises before entering into a lease. Such a view of the landlord and tenant relationship is, according to US case law, founded on a principally agrarian economy which no longer exists.

The common law rule absolving the lessor of all obligation to repair originated in the early Middle Ages. Such a rule was perhaps well suited to an agrarian economy; the land was more important than whatever small living structure was included in the leasehold, and the tenant farmer was fully capable of making repairs himself. These historical facts were the basis on which the common law constructed its rule; they also provided the necessary prerequisites for its application. (*Javins v First National Realty Corporation*, 428 F.2d 1071 at 1077 (1970), footnotes omitted; the covenant of habitability was extended to commercial leases in *Davidow v Inwood North Professional Group*, 747 SW 2d 373. See also, Restatement, *op. cit.*, at pp 169 *et seq*.)

In urban areas there is a shortage of affordable, good quality housing so that tenants are forced to accept whatever is available—even if there was a choice for tenants, however, there is no easy way that someone seeking to rent a flat in a houseful of flats can adequately inspect his own potential dwelling or all the other dwellings in the house. The standard of the other flats may well impinge on the condition of the demised premises. Furthermore, *caveat emptor*, is no longer absolute even in commercial law, and some US judges have likened the covenant of habitability to consumer protection legislation—the premises should be fit for the purpose for which they were let, that is, a living unit.

Our approach to the common law of landlord and tenant ought to be aided by principles derived from the consumer protection cases referred to above. In a lease contract, a tenant seeks to purchase from his landlord shelter for a specified

period of time. The landlord sells housing as a commercial businessman and has much greater opportunity, incentive and capacity to inspect and maintain the condition of his building. Moreover, the tenant must rely upon the skill and *bona fides* of his landlord at least as much as a car buyer must rely upon the car manufacturer. In dealing with major problems, such as heating, plumbing, electrical or structural defects, the tenant's position corresponds precisely with 'the ordinary consumer who cannot be expected to have the knowledge or capacity or even the opportunity to make adequate inspection of mechanical instrumentalities, like automobiles, and to decide for himself whether they are reasonably fit for the designed purpose.' *Henningsen v. Bloomfield Motors, Inc.*, 161 A.2d 69 at 78 (1960). (Wright CJ, in *Javins, op. cit.*, at 1079, footnotes omitted; see also Tobriner J, in *Green v Superior Court of San Francisco*, 10 Cal.3d 616 (1974), cited in Law Com. No. 123, *op. cit.*, para 4.13; Glendon, *The Transformation of American Landlord-Tenant Law*, (1982), 23 Boston Col. L R 503 at p 525).

Nevertheless, the covenant of habitability has been criticised. Meyers (*The Covenant of Habitability and the American Law Institute*, (1975) 27 Stan L Rev 879 at p 881) argued that §5.1 of the Restatement was based on the unsupported premise that powerless, poor tenants were being exploited by rich landlords who could well afford to carry out any necessary repairs. Meyers showed that many US landlords were not at all rich—he emphasised less, though, the tenants' relative poverty. Looking at the variety of landlord-types in England and Wales identified by Allen and McDowell, *Landlords and Property*, 1989, Meyers' generalization would find some support, but many landlords are financially strong. On the other hand, while Meyers' argument is not wholly sound, several points he makes carry weight against the eventual effectiveness of the covenant of habitability. Private sector landlords are generally aiming to make a profit on their investment in the property to be let. If the cost of bringing the premises up to a standard where they might be considered fit for human habitation is so high that not even a market rent would provide a reasonable return, then the landlord will allow the premises to remain empty thereby reducing the stock of available housing. Meyers' argument (pp 889–90) is that even those premises which can be brought up to standard economically will be put beyond the reach of the poorest tenants because the landlord will be able to charge higher rents. Even if the landlord can improve the property without having to raise rents, the profit margins on the premises will be reduced, discouraging continued involvement or further investment in the low-rent sector (Meyers pp 890–1). The implicit suggestion is that the poorest tenants should only have substandard housing. Meyers could be answered by either restricting the levels of rent that can be charged, although that might contribute to a reduction in the number of private sector tenancies, or by providing a welfare benefit to meet the housing costs of those otherwise unable to afford a dwelling. Meyers' analysis of the likely behaviour of landlords of unfit housing is probably accurate, but his opinion that §5.1 of the Restatement should, thus, be rejected cannot be supported. Where Meyers carries more weight is when he argues that if there is to be a redistribution of wealth to the poorest tenants, it should not be from the landlords alone.

And if the rationale [for §5.1] depends on redistributive justice, still another question arises: Why are landlords singled out as the class from whom wealth should be taken for redistribution to the poor? Even if landlords as a class are rich, so are entrepreneurs in other businesses, and they are not often the subject of wealth redistribution schemes. The nonwaivable duty of habitability would seem to be a welfare proposal that ought to be financed not by one class of citizens but by all taxpayers under a progressive income tax. (p 881, n10)

Despite the considerable improvement since 1945, the condition of housing in England and Wales is so poor that only concerted central government action can halt its decline. Age and non-traditional building methods will result in continued poor standards which tenants and landlords lack the means to remedy.

Tenants have very little leverage to enforce demands for better housing. Various impediments to competition in the rental housing market, such as racial and class discrimination and standardized form leases, mean that landlords place tenants in a take it or leave it situation. The increasingly severe shortage of adequate housing further increases the landlord's bargaining power and escalates the need for maintaining and improving the existing stock. Finally, the findings by various studies of the social impact of bad housing has led to the realization that poor housing is detrimental to the whole society, not merely to the unlucky ones who must suffer the daily indignity of living in a slum. (*Javins, op. cit.*, 1079–80, footnotes omitted)

Only if the government can make the letting of fit housing an economically attractive venture, either through tax concessions or grants, will private sector landlordism gain the greater share of the rental market that the Conservative Government in the early 1990s favoured.

7.2.4 Repairs

Repairing obligations in a lease, express or implied, may impose burdens on the landlord or the tenant. The landlord and tenant will have differing objectives with regard to repairs. The law, however, is concerned first to delimit the scope of repairs, then to allocate the burden of the repairing obligation and, finally, to establish liability for the cost of repairs and enforcement mechanisms.

Repair is the major item of expenditure likely to be incurred on a building during its lifetime. The function of repair clauses in modern leases is twofold: to identify the operational repairing responsibilities of landlord and tenant and to apportion the financial liability. (Hill and Redman, *Law of Landlord and Tenant*, 18th edn, vol 3, §G General Precedents)

This section will briefly consider the interests of the parties with respect to repairs before moving on to examine those facets of the law.

Both landlord and tenant will be concerned about the condition of the property let. Their interests are, however, motivated by different considerations. For the tenant, his use and enjoyment of the property will be affected by the state of repair. In commercial lettings, the state of repair may also have an effect on the success of his business—if the premises are in a poor condition, then customers will not be attracted. Whereas the residential tenant is primarily interested in obtaining a lease in order to acquire a home, the commercial tenant, being on a more equal footing with the landlord, will see the condition of the property itself as part of the commercial success of his venture. A tenant of a new building would be wary of accepting a full repairing covenant lest some inherent defect in design or work-manship leaves the property unusable (see Ross, *Drafting and Negotiating Commercial Leases*, 3rd edn, 1989, paras 8.15–8.15:4). Negotiations between a commercial landlord and tenant would evidence a desire on both parties to maximize their potential profits, minimize their liabilities, but simultaneously to protect their respective investments through appropriately worded repairing covenants. Generally, the landlord's concern, no matter what the sector, is less direct and, in part, is linked to the maintenance of the value of his reversionary interest in the property. The private sector landlord has a reputation for being unconcerned with the physical condition of the property, but this is clearly not justified in every case and will vary in part according to the landlord-type (see Allen and McDowell, *op. cit.*). Local authority and housing association landlords are perceived to be more interested in tenant welfare, but some councils also developed a reputation for inefficiency and repairs were carried out only after some delay—as a result, the Housing and Building Control Act 1984 amended the then Housing Act 1980 (see now Housing Act 1985, s 96) to allow tenants in certain cases to employ outside contractors to carry out repairs where the local authority did not do so in a reasonable time. While housing associations catered for their tenants well when they were relatively small-scale operations, with their increased role it may be that delays will soon start to arise—it is noticeable that the *English House Condition Survey: 1991, op. cit.*, found that housing associations showed the greatest increase in the number of unfit properties since the 1986 survey. With commercial lettings, the landlord may want to see that the property is in good repair to ensure the success of the development. The more successful the development, the more likely it will be that tenants will be found to afford the rent. Connected with the issue of a guaranteed flow of rent, commercial landlords, especially where they are institutional investors, aim to impose 'clear leases', that is, leases where the financial burden of any obligation falls on the tenant (see Lord Hailsham LC in *O'May v City of London Real Property Co. Ltd* [1982] 2 AC 726 at 737). The effect is that in the commercial sector, tenants have limited interests in the property, but bear almost all the costs. Agricultural leases raise much the same issues.

7.2.4.1 What is a repair?

Allocation of responsibility for repairs will be considered in the next section, but while discussing the meaning of repair, references to tenants being under a duty should be read to include landlords where statute has so imposed the repairing obligation—at common law the responsibility would depend on the terms of the lease and it would usually be imposed on the tenant. The problem with the meaning of repair is not so much finding a definition as applying the various judicial interpretations to the particular facts of any case. Repair seems to be a term that is synonymous in all rental sectors. Ross, (*op. cit.*, para 8.1 *et seq.*) starts off his section on repairing covenants with respect to commercial leases with quotations from cases to do with residential leases. The Law Commission took a similar line.

'Repair' has a dictionary definition of 'to restore to good condition by renewal or replacement of decayed or damaged parts, or by refixing what has given way; to mend'. It has been judicially defined similarly. '[The word] connotes the idea of making good damage so as to leave the subject so far as possible as though it had not been damaged. It involves renewal of subsidiary parts; it does not involve renewal of the whole. Time must be taken into account; an old article is not to be made new; but so far as repair can make good, or protect against the ravages of time and the elements, it must be undertaken'. (Para.2.19, Law Com. 123, *op. cit.*, citing *Anstruther-Gough-Calthorpe v McOscar* [1924] 1 KB 716 at 734 *per* Atkin LJ: all other footnotes excluded)

As will be seen, the application of the test seems on occasion to be irrational, but there is an idea that at some time in the past the premises were in a better state of repair and that they have deteriorated since then. It is not a repair, for example, if it is, by way of contrast, an improvement on an always existing state of affairs. In *Post Office v Aquarius Properties Ltd* [1987] 1 All ER 1055, esp. at 1063-5, weak areas of concrete allowed water into the basement to a depth of about six inches, but no damage resulted. For a variety of reasons, the Court of Appeal held that remedying this defect would not amount to a repair because there was no damage; there had been no deterioration from a previously better condition.

Thus under a covenant simply to repair, a landlord might find himself unable to compel a tenant to rectify a discovered defect which, while seriously affecting the capital and letting value of the premises, had not yet manifested itself in physical damage. (Tromans, *Commercial Leases*, 1987, p 88)

The true test is, as the cases show, that it is always a question of degree whether that which the tenant is asked to do can properly be described as a repair, or whether on the contrary it would involve giving back to the landlord a wholly different thing from that which he demised. (*Ravenseft Properties Ltd v Davstone (Holdings) Ltd* [1979] 1 All ER 929, *per* Forbes J at 937)

A more fundamental argument put forward by the defendant [landlord] was that the landlord's covenant to repair did not extend to inherent defects in the building. This argument was also rejected by His Honour Judge Bowsher QC who held, relying upon the judgment of Fry J in *Saner v Bilton*, (1878) 7 Ch D 815, 821, that the test of what is good repair is to be judged having regard to the class to which the property belongs and not to that property itself alone. So the flat was to be put into a state of repair appropriate to a basement flat in London. Had there been no damp proofing in the basement, there would have been nothing for the defendant to repair; however there was damp proofing provided and the defendants were therefore under a duty to put it and keep it in repair. (*Luckhurst v Manyfield Ltd*, unreported, 30 July 1992: see *The Scope and Specific Enforceability of Covenants to Repair*, Building Law Monthly, vol 10:1, 1993, p 3)

The most extreme case of a true repair, though, is that where the premises burn down a day before the lease is due to expire. According to *Matthey v Curling* [1922] 2 AC 180, subject to the landlord granting access to the tenant with the repairing obligation, the latter may have to rebuild the premises within a reasonable time, even though the lease will by then have expired.

7.2.4.2 What must be repaired?

There is the additional question as to what a party under a repairing obligation is obliged to repair. There is little difficulty where the case concerns the lease of a detached house or the whole of a freestanding commercial unit, but more detailed descriptions of the scope of any repairing obligation are necessary where houses or retail units, for instance, are in multiple occupation. If the lease refers to repairing the interior, there is no way of knowing whether it simply excludes the exterior parts, the exterior parts and any structural walls, or whether it is meant to cover just the interior decorative finishes (Ross, *op. cit.*, paras 8.4–8.7). Generally speaking, at common law, the exterior parts of any building in multiple occupation are within the demise of the tenant whose premises they abut. For the sake of efficient management, however, it would make more sense to impose the burden on the landlord, by statute if necessary and regardless of whether it is a residential, commercial or agricultural lease, for he would have ease of access to the common parts and to all the exterior. The scope of any obligation in a property in multiple occupation is also complicated where there is a defect in a common internal wall or a common floor/ceiling. Such issues are considered below when looking at the responsibility for any repairing obligation.

7.2.4.3 What is the standard of repair?

The question of what is a repair is bound up with the question of the standard of any repair.

A covenant simply to 'repair' means to keep the property in substantial repair. Commonly covenants require 'good repair', 'habitable repair' or 'tenantable repair'. These expressions seem to bear the same meaning. 'Good tenantable repair' has been defined: 'such repair as, having regard to the age, character and locality of the house, would make it reasonably fit for the occupation of a reasonably minded tenant of the class who would be likely to take it'. A covenant to repair must be construed by reference to the condition of the property at the date of the letting, although it is to be construed as imposing not only a duty to keep the property in repair, but also to put it into repair. (Law Com. No. 123, *op. cit.*, para 2.27—footnotes omitted)

The cases on which the Law Commission drew for its explanation of the standard of repair arose from residential leases—*Proudfoot v Hart* (1890) 25 QBD 42, and *Walker v Hatton* (1842) 10 M & W 249. Nevertheless, the same test is applied to commercial tenancies, too. The only problem with this transplant is the reference to the class of tenant, which had some relevance in the nineteenth century with respect to residential leases, but has a somewhat uncertain meaning in relation to current commercial leases.

Would the class be defined by reference to the size and financial strength of the likely tenant, or by reference to the type of business? These questions await a definitive answer by the courts, but the landlord who wishes to achieve a greater degree of control over the standard of repair work could do so by stipulating that repairs are to be carried out to specifications provided by the landlord, or to the satisfaction of the landlord or his surveyor. (Tromans, 1987, *op. cit.*, p 94)

In determining the appropriate standard, the courts are to have regard to the 'age, character and locality' of the dwelling. However, while an old and dilapidated building will not generally merit as extensive repairs as other premises, a repairing obligation is never redundant or obsolete.

We must bear in mind that while the age and the nature of the building can qualify the meaning of the covenant, they can never relieve the [tenant] from his obligation. If he chooses to undertake to keep in good condition an old house, he is bound to do it, whatever be the means necessary for him to employ in so doing. He can never say: 'The house was old, so old that it relieved me from my covenant to keep it in good condition'. (*Lurcott v Wakely and Wheeler* [1911] 1 KB 905 at 916, *per* Fletcher Moulton LJ; *cf. Post Office v Aquarius Properties Ltd, op. cit.*)

Tenants may also find themselves unclear as to the extent of the obligation due to changes in the locality—areas may be gentrified or may deteriorate very rapidly in the type of boom-bust economy experienced in the late 1980s and the 1990s, but according to *Anstruther-Gough-Calthorpe v McOscar, op. cit.*, changes in the neighbourhood are not directly pertinent.

The standard also has to be assessed by reference to the condition, that is, the age and nature, of the property at the date of the letting. This requirement reflects the definition of repair, in that the tenant is not normally expected to return to the landlord something of a higher standard than was initially let. However, while it would seem at first sight to be wholly appropriate to determine the extent of any repairing obligation by reference to the standard of the dwelling at the date it was let to the tenant, this may not reflect the true nature of the relationship and may introduce illusory safeguards for the tenant.

First, it is never possible to do more than 'have regard' to the age and nature of the property; there is no hard and fast rule. If, when the lease starts, the property is dilapidated, that does not necessarily render any repairing obligation nugatory. On the other hand, if the lease is lengthy some natural deterioration is allowable, so one does not look exclusively at the condition of the property when the lease was granted. Secondly, no account is taken of changes in the meantime to the surrounding neighbourhood, which may make the earlier standard of repair wholly inappropriate. Thirdly, this construction of repairing covenants can lead to misunderstanding and inconvenience when property is sub-let. The head lease and the sub-lease may contain identical repairing covenants, which would appear to be appropriate when the mesne landlord wants to pass on to the sub-tenant the duties imposed on him by the head lease. However, the two covenants may be interpreted differently merely because of the different dates on which the lease and the sub-lease were granted [*Walker v Hatton, op. cit.*], so that the mesne landlord is unintentionally left with some duty to repair. Fourthly, and more fundamentally, if the property is let for a specified period so that it may be used throughout for a particular purpose, the state at the date of the letting may be seen as less relevant than whether it allows the objective to be achieved. Fifthly, the requirements of a reasonably minded class of tenant likely to take the property are also to be judged as at the commencement of the lease. In relation to commercial property with a company tenant, it is not clear whether this refers to the size and financial standing of a likely tenant, the type of business they would conduct, the way they would conduct it or to these and other factors. (Law Com. No. 123, *op. cit.*, para 3.15; footnotes omitted)

The standard as set out in *Proudfoot v Hart, op. cit.*, and *Walker v Hatton, op. cit.*, has regard to several variable factors which may or may not be relevant to any given letting or to any particular type of lease. One specific situation which would seem to contradict the general rule is that an express duty on the tenant to keep the premises in repair will oblige the latter to put premises into repair that have been let in a state of disrepair—the condition at the date of the letting is thereby rendered irrelevant (*Proudfoot v Hart, op. cit.*).

7.2.4.4 Repairs Contrasted

Before considering the allocation of the repairing obligation, some cases have arisen on a regular basis where the question turns on what is or is not a repair.

(a) Renewal   Repair and renewal have on occasion been confused.

Repair is restoration by renewal or replacement of subsidiary parts of a whole. Renewal, as distinguished from repair, is reconstruction of the entirety, meaning by the entirety not necessarily the whole, but substantially the whole. (*Lurcott v Wakely and Wheeler, op. cit.,* at 924, *per* Buckley LJ)

On the other hand, renewal of different subsidiary parts during the course of the lease may amount to an effective reconstruction of the entirety. Where the lease calls for 'renewal', as opposed to just repair, then the obligation is wider. In *Credit Suisse v Beegas Nominees Ltd* [1994] 4 All ER 803 (Morgan, [1994] Conv 145; see Leyland, *Repairing Covenants: Renew Held To Go Beyond Mere Repair,* [1993] 10 PR 462) the lease required the landlord to

maintain, repair, amend, renew, cleanse, repaint and redecorate and otherwise keep in good and tenantable condition the structure of the building and in particular the roof, foundation and walls thereof . . . (*op. cit.,* at 810)

The tenant was liable for a proportionate share of all the landlord's costs associated with performance of that obligation. The aluminium cladding on the walls had always leaked and had been a bone of contention throughout the lease. The necessary work went beyond a mere repair, but the question was whether the landlord was obliged under the duty to 'renew' in the lease to fix this defect. Lindsay J (*op. cit.,* at 826) held that each word had to be given its full meaning and, thus, the landlord was bound to fix the defect. In *New England Properties plc v Portsmouth New Shops Ltd* [1993] 23 EG 130, a badly designed roof had to be completely replaced. The court was prepared to hold that the landlord's express obligation in the lease to renew would have given rise to liability if it had not already found that the replacement of the roof was a repair within the traditional test.

(b) Inherent Defects   Inherent defects have proved problematic in both the residential and commercial sectors. The reason is that inherent defects tend to be more expensive to remedy when compared to the usual day-to-day costs of maintenance repairs. In Scotland, on the other hand, a distinction is drawn under repairing covenants between what would be understood as mere maintenance and the wider meaning attributed to repairing obligations in England— only day-to-day maintenance will be treated as a 'repair' in Scotland (RICS, *International Leasing Structures, op. cit.,* p 57). The test in England, however, turns not on the underlying cause of the problem, but on what the party obliged to carry out 'repairs', usually the tenant, is being requested to do. In *Post Office v Aquarius Properties Ltd, op. cit.,* at 1063, Ralph Gibson LJ, referring to *Quick, op. cit.,* at 324, said that it was irrelevant whether a defect was caused by design fault, poor workmanship or deliberate parsimony; the question in English law is simply whether remedying the defect falls within the scope of the repairing

obligation. If an inherent defect causes no damage, then there is no responsibility to remedy it at all.

It is not possible to hold that the wetting of the basement floor, or the presence of the water on the floor, coupled with the inconvenience caused thereby to the tenant, constitutes damage to the premises demised. There is, accordingly, no disrepair proved in this case and therefore no liability under the tenant's covenant to repair has arisen. (*Post Office v Aquarius Properties, op. cit., per* Ralph Gibson LJ at 1063)

Where an inherent defect in the premises gives rise to damage, the tenant may have to repair the damage but not remedy the inherent defect, because that would go beyond putting right deterioration that arose after the granting of the lease—*Lister v Lane and Nesham* [1893] 2 QB 212 at 216. However, if the inherent defect that causes the damage is not remedied, then the damage will recur and the tenant will be constantly carrying out short-term repairs. If, though, remedying the inherent defect is the sole means of effecting the 'repair' to the damage, the tenant may be obliged to deal with the root cause of the problem—*Quick v Taff Ely BC op. cit., per* Neill LJ at 329, (dealing, in that case, with the landlord's repairing duties). In *Ravenseft Properties Ltd v Davstone (Holdings) Ltd, op. cit.*, the tenant had to spend £55,000 replacing external cladding to remedy the inherent defect in the original fixing system: Forbes J held that in certain circumstances remedying an inherent defect could fall within a tenant's repairing obligation, but that each case must be viewed on its facts since it is a question of degree as to whether what the tenant is being obliged to do or fund 'can properly be described as a repair' (at 937). Subsequent cases, for example, have drawn attention to the cost of remedying the defect as against the value of the premises and the cost of building a replacement (see also, *Elmcroft Developments Ltd v Tankersley-Sawyer* (1984) 15 HLR 63; *New England Properties, op. cit.*). While the decision is not that radical a departure from the earlier position set out in *Lister, op. cit.*, it does question the fundamental principle of repairing obligations, that the tenant should not be required to deliver up to the landlord something different from that which was demised.

Finally, while so far the focus has been on the tenant's responsibility to fix inherent defects under a repairing obligation, if a property has just been built it may be more appropriate to impose that responsibility on the landlord who commissioned the work. Such considerations are discussed in the next section on allocating the repairing obligation.

(c) Improvements   Connected with inherent defects, repairs are sometimes difficult to distinguish from improvements. The law relating to improvements themselves is considered below, but here it is necessary to examine how the courts have dealt with the overlap with repairs.

As a matter of principle, someone who has a duty to repair property is not obliged
to improve it. Accordingly, a landlord who covenanted to repair a house, the outside walls of which had no damp proof course, was not obliged to insert one—
Pembery v Lamdin [1940] 2 All ER 434. (Law Com. No. 123, *op. cit.*, at para 2.22)

The difficulties of construction arise where an inherent defect can be fixed by an
improvement which would also deal with the damage arising from the defect
(see *Post Office v Aquarius, op. cit.*, and *McDougall v Easington DC* [1989] 1 EGLR
93 at 96, cited in Law Com. No. 123, *op. cit.*, para 3.7).

Furthermore, normally the duty to repair will not require the tenant to
improve the premises. However, in the commercial sector in particular, statute
may impose standards if premises are to continue to be used for specific purposes (see also 7.3, below). Therefore, under the Factories Act 1961, s 169 either
party can go to the county court to have the lease modified to allow work to be
carried out so that the premises might conform with the Act or any rules made
thereunder. The Offices, Shops and Railway Premises Act 1963, s 73, and Fire
Precautions Act 1971, s 28 allow modification and apportionment of consequent
expenses. The 1963 Act reads:

s 73(1) A person who, by reason of the terms of an agreement or lease relating to
any premises, is prevented from therein carrying out or doing any structural or other alterations or other thing whose carrying out or doing is requisite in order to secure compliance with a provision of this Act or of
regulations thereunder which is, or will become, applicable to the
premises, . . . , may apply to the county court within whose jurisdiction
the premises are situate, and the court may make such an order setting
aside or modifying any terms of the agreement or lease as the court considers just and equitable in the circumstances of the case.

(2) Where the carrying out or doing in any premises of any structural or other
alterations or other thing whose carrying out or doing is requisite as mentioned in the foregoing subsection involves a person having an interest in
the premises in expense or in increased expense, and he alleges that the
whole or part of the expense or, as the case may be, the increase ought to
be borne by some other person having an interest in the premises, the
first-mentioned person may apply to the county court within whose jurisdiction the premises are situate, and the court, having regard to the terms
of any agreement or lease relating to the premises, may by order give
such directions with respect to the persons by whom the expense or
increase is to be borne, and in what proportions it is to be borne by them
and, if need be, for modification of the terms of any such agreement or
lease so far as concerns rent payable in respect of the premises as the
court considers just and equitable in the circumstances of the case.
(Words in subs (1) omitted by SI 1976 No. 2005)

Such a judicial modification of the lease does not directly affect any repairing
obligation, but it-is yet another example of how work to maintain the quality of

the premises can be effected. The limits of leasehold repairing obligations do not necessarily reflect a true picture of the law pertaining to the condition of rented premises.

(d) Summary The meaning of repairs is not straightforward, but, more importantly, a repairing obligation may not fully reflect the desires of landlord or tenant as to maintaining the condition of the premises. It is little short of ridiculous in practical terms that the party under a repairing obligation has no duty to fix an inherent defect and that 'patching up' damage caused by this defect is an adequate response. Indeed, unless there is damage to the structure or fabric of the premises there is no duty to do anything (see *Post Office v Aquarius, op. cit.*, and *Quick v Taff Ely, op. cit.*). The Law Commission in its 1992 Consultation Paper No. 123, *op. cit.*, suggested that consideration ought to be given to replacing the duty to repair with a different form of obligation towards the condition of the property. Given that the tenant will have taken on the lease for a purpose, either residential, commercial or agricultural, it is not unfair to impose an obligation that the property be maintained at a standard where it is fit for its intended use, akin to §5.1 Restatement of the Law of Property 2d (*op. cit.*). This duty to maintain was formulated (see para 5.7, Law Com. No. 123, *op. cit.*) in the following terms.

To put and keep the demised property, and all parts of it, in such state and condition that it may safely, hygienically and satisfactorily be used, and continue in the immediate future to be used, for its intended purpose with an appropriate degree of convenience and comfort for the occupants.

The Commission accepted that because this proposed duty was drafted in such wide terms that necessary practical limits would have to be established (Law Com. No. 123, *op. cit.*, paras 5.10, *et seq*). Apart from the case where it is not practically possible to carry out the necessary work, other exceptions would have to be created where the original purpose no longer applies. The proposed duty to maintain is based on a known purpose of use at the date of the letting and it is that which governs the extent of the duty to maintain. If the purpose changes or becomes redundant, then the duty to maintain would have to be varied, too. However, such a reform of the law would put an end to arguments as to whether the scope of repairing obligations extended to include condensation so bad that bedding and clothes became mildewed and rotten and the house was uninhabitable in the winter (*Quick v Taff Ely, op. cit.*, at 323). Such a house would not be fit for its purpose and only work carried out under the proposed duty to maintain would return it to a standard where it could be reckoned as part of the working housing stock.

7.2.4.5 Allocating the Repairing Obligation

The law relating to repairing obligations depends on the terms of the lease, whether they be express or implied and, if implied, whether that be by the courts or by statute. In addition to leasehold covenants, there are also obligations relating to the wider duties pertaining to the condition of the premises in certain limited circumstances. The law is in need of reform and the Law Commission (Law Com. No. 123, *op. cit.*, para 3.1) set out some of the issues to be borne in mind during study of this topic.

(b) *Responsibility* The allocation of responsibility is not always satisfactory. The present arrangements may leave some work entirely out of account, not requiring either party to the lease to be concerned, or they may in practice place responsibility where it was probably not intended to lie. Although we are primarily concerned in this Paper with relations between landlords and tenants, it is necessary to take account of the public interest in the satisfactory maintenance of buildings which may in most cases be thought to require that someone be responsible;

(c) *Other property* Where the property let to the tenant is dependent on other property belonging to the landlord for its security or for necessary services, the nature and extent of the landlord's duties relating to that other property are unclear, and, to the extent that the tenant may not satisfactorily receive the services, unsatisfactory;

(d) *Enforcement* There may be no practical prospect of enforcement of some of the obligations imposed. If the aim of imposing duties to repair and maintain property is to ensure that the work be done, there is a case for reconsidering the present limits on the sanctions imposed, which often have the effect of ensuring that less compensation is payable for the breach of the duty than would be necessary to put matters right;

(e) *Lack of clarity* One of the reasons for confusion in this area of the law is the accretion of rules which overlap. The duties imposed by the law of waste, which frequently duplicate the contractual obligations of tenants provide one example. Legislation addressing repairing obligations between landlord and tenant has proliferated; the difficulty of ascertaining the rules governing any particular situation can make them less effective.

The extent of any reform, however, is still not decided. The Law Commission proposed both limited and radical changes to the present system in its 1992 Consultation Paper (Law Com. No. 123, *op. cit.*; *cf.* Smith, *Repairing Obligations, op. cit.*, at p 190)

The law relating to repairing obligations is not consistent and there is no uniform system of allocating those repairing obligations across the various rental sectors. The starting point for any consideration of repairing duties is the express terms of the lease, although other terms may be implied by the courts or statute. Looking at the various rental sectors, it is apparent that there is wide variation in the extent of intervention by the courts or statute. Before considering how repairing obligations are allocated, therefore, regard should be had to the reasons behind the intervention in the terms of the lease. The lease itself establishes a proprietal relationship, but repairing covenants are more contractual in nature—given the unequal bargaining power of the parties in the residential sector, though, if a *laissez-faire* attitude were adopted, then poor tenants would suffer harsh terms. The result has been an attempt to regulate the market.

Intervention in the free market between landlord and tenant is not new. Over 100 years ago, [Pollock] wrote, 'The truth is . . . that the law of landlord and tenant has never, at least under any usual conditions, been a law of free contract'. . . . Experience suggests that the bargaining power of the two parties to any particular lease is frequently uneven . . . The advantage may sometimes lie with the landlord and sometimes with the tenant. The imbalance may result from the nature or identity of the parties, the current state of the market or the monopolistic position of the landlord. (Law Com. No. 123, *op. cit.*, at paras 4.8 and 4.9; see also *Javins, op. cit.*, at 1079)

Arguments that governments took a protectionist role towards tenants are rejected by some commentators, however.

Government policies affecting housing, which supposedly serve the common good, systematically operate to reinforce the profitability of the housing sector and of the business community. Such improvement in housing as has occurred historically has come about only when it has served the interests of private capital, or when pressures from below (both political and economic) have forced it to occur. (Achtenburg and Marcuse, writing about the United States, cited in Malpass and Murie, 1994, *op. cit.*, at p 4)

More interestingly, however, some commentators challenge the effectiveness of repairing codes, questioning their value to tenants.

[Most] policy makers involved in housing code enforcement are themselves unsure whether code enforcement is a good thing. They are not convinced that strict enforcement of even an ideal code will really benefit the tenants whom the code is intended to 'protect'. They fear that landlords who are required to improve their properties to code standards will simply pass on the added costs to their tenants by increasing rents or that they will abandon the properties entirely, thereby depriving the tenants of even sub-code accommodations. Thus, 'effective' code enforcement may simply require the poor to allocate an additional share of their meagre budgets to the purchase of housing services when the poor themselves would prefer to purchase more food or entertainment or automobiles. (Ackerman, *Regulating Slum Housing Markets on Behalf of the Poor: Of Housing Codes, Housing Subsidies and Income Redistribution Policy,* (1971) 80 Yale LJ 1093 at p 1095)

Against this background, the differing policies on intervention in the various sectors must be judged.

The commercial sector best exemplifies the emphasis on the express terms of the lease, with covenants being drafted to favour either landlord or tenant, depending on the state of the rental market, but with nothing being left to the courts if at all possible—a *laissez-faire* approach. When landlords are in the ascendant, all repairing obligations will be imposed on the tenant (the Full Repairing and Insuring Lease—fri), although if a tenant is obliged to assume very extensive repairing obligations, then an argument might be put at the rent review for a reduction in the rent as a consequence (Ross, *op. cit.*, para 8.10); in *Norwich Union Life Insurance Soc. v British Railways Board* [1987] 2 EGLR 137, the rent was discounted by 27.5 per cent to reflect the onerous repairing obligation. Even where the premises are in multiple occupation, the landlord will usually accept responsibility for carrying out the repairs for administrative convenience, but pass on the costs to the tenant (the Full Recovery Lease). Moreover, regardless of the state of the market, institutional investors will only grant clear leases by which the tenant assumes liability for all repairing obligations. Thus, in England and Wales the commercial sector can be seen to attract least intervention and the market operates in such a way that the tenant almost always bears the cost of any repairs. The position in other countries as regards commercial leases, by contrast, is not as harsh to the tenant. In France, for example, the position has developed differently and the tenant can generally refuse a fri lease—RICS, *International Leasing Structures, op. cit.*, at para 3.2.7.

On the other hand, as will be discussed below, subject to contrary agreement, agricultural leases in England and Wales currently have several model clauses read into them by statutory instrument. This is a fundamentally different approach to that pertaining in the commercial sector. However, the Ministry of Agriculture, Food and Fisheries has stated that it wishes to deregulate agricultural tenancies (compare, MAFF, *Reform of Agricultural Holdings Legislation: Detailed Proposals*, September 1992, para 24 with MAFF, *News Release, Agricultural Tenancy Law Reform*, 6 October 1993). These changes are to be enacted in 1995 for new tenancies; all new 'farm business tenancies' will be deregulated. Residential leases are for the most part subject to statutory guarantees and those with a housing association landlord benefit from yet other measures established by government. However, leases in all sectors are open to judicial intervention as the courts are free to imply terms into the lease, although there is no general repairing obligation at common law.

(a) Implied Terms: the Common Law Fundamentals   One area that has given rise to much litigation concerns the scope of implied repairing obligations in English law. Initially such obligations were implied only where the landlord lets premises to the tenant to which access can only be gained via property retained by the landlord, such as common stairs leading to a flat.

A lessor who lets a room to a tenant and provides a common staircase which the tenant must use must come under an implied contractual obligation to keep the access in a reasonably safe condition, otherwise the tenant cannot enjoy the use of the rooms which he has contracted to take. (*Dunster v Hollis* [1918] 2 KB 795 at 802, *per* Lush J)

In *Liverpool CC v Irwin* [1976] 2 All ER 39, for instance, the House of Lords held that there should be implied a duty on the part of the landlord to take reasonable care to maintain in reasonable repair the common parts of a building and, possibly, all essential facilities. The court would imply terms in order to establish the true nature of the contract where the parties had not fully stated the terms. However, doubt was expressed by Lord Wilberforce as to whether the duty would be imposed on the landlord in every sort of case, although he expressly approved of the landlord having the duty to maintain a common area where the building was in multiple occupation on the grounds that it would facilitate greater efficiency in the management of that type of premises. A commercial case subsequent to *Irwin*, has adopted Lord Wilberforce's reasoning on when terms should be implied: in *Duke of Westminster v Guild* [1985] QB 688, however, the court refused to imply a covenant to maintain a drain on the grounds that the lease had already attempted to allocate repairing responsibilities. On another tack, however, in *Barrett v Lounova (1982) Ltd* [1990] 1 QB 348, the Court of Appeal was prepared to hold that where the lease imposes an express obligation on the tenant to keep the interior in repair, it was proper to imply a similar obligation on the landlord in relation to the exterior; indeed, it was the only option that made business sense as without such an obligation on the landlord, the tenant was unable to perform his obligation.

The courts have adopted two principal and principled approaches to implying terms into the lease—see Crabb, *'Usual Covenants' in Leases: A Misnomer*, [1992] Conv 18. Terms may be implied by law or on the basis of the specific facts. The distinction is that a term implied by law is not dependent on the presumed intent of the parties, whereas if it is to be implied on the facts then it must be one that both parties would have agreed to at the time of the contract—the latter is sometimes known as the business efficacy or officious bystander test (*Liverpool CC v Irwin*, *op. cit.*, at 47). One of the accepted justifications for implying a term in law is that the contract is of a defined type and the contract itself implicitly requires the term. The test is one of necessity, rather than reasonableness, according to Lord Wilberforce in *Liverpool CC v Irwin*, *op. cit.*, at 44; see also, *Shell UK Ltd v Lostock Garage Ltd* [1977] 1 All ER 481 *per* Lord Denning MR at 487–8, and *McAuley v Bristol CC* [1992] 1 QB 134 at 146–7. Thus, since the contract between the landlord of a property in multiple occupation with common areas (*Irwin*, *op. cit.*) and his tenants is one of those of a defined type, unless the lease has been drafted in some peculiar fashion, it will have all necessary terms implied. Whether the 'defined types' extend beyond leases of properties in multiple occupation is not certain, but the courts have been more willing of late to imply terms—see *Barrett v Lounova, op. cit.; McAuley, op. cit.;* and *King v South Northamptonshire DC* (1992) 24 HLR 284. If the term is not necessary, then only if both parties would have agreed to its inclusion at the time of the lease when asked by the 'officious bystander' will it be implied into the lease—*cf. Habinteg Housing Association v James, op. cit.*

The courts have on occasion imposed responsibility on tenants as well as on landlords as a result of implied covenants, based on the same principles— *McAuley, op. cit.* A tenant is obliged to use the premises in a tenant-like manner (*Warren v Keen* [1954] 1 QB 15 at 20, *per* Denning LJ) and, if the lease is for one year or greater duration, then he must keep the premises wind and watertight (*Wedd v Porter* [1916] 2 KB 91 at 100). *Warren v Keen* held, however, that the latter obligation did not extend to weekly tenants because of the high cost of mainte- nance by comparison with the weekly rent and because of the insecure nature of the tenancy. It is arguable that the Court of Appeal in *Warren v Keen* were over- protective towards the tenant, especially now that market rents are chargeable (such that the maintenance costs are not so wildly disproportionate) and that even the private sector residential tenant still retains a modicum of security under the Housing Act 1988. In New South Wales, for instance, the Residential Tenancies Tribunal Act 1986, s 84(1)(b) implies a covenant into every lease for the tenant to keep the premises in good and tenantable repair. There is also the anomaly that if a tenant expressly agrees to keep the property in repair and at the start of the lease it is in a state of disrepair, then he is obliged to put it right (*Proudfoot v Hart, op. cit.*).

(b) Statutorily Implied Terms   The major source of intervention in leases in rela- tion to repairs, though, has come from statute.

(i) Landlord and Tenant Act 1985.   In the residential sector, the Landlord and Tenant Act 1985 (as amended) creates duties for the landlord whether the land- lord be a local authority, a housing association or from the private sector.

s 11(1) In a lease to which this section applies (as to which, see sections 13 and 14) there is implied a covenant by the lessor—
   (a) to keep in repair the structure and exterior of the dwelling-house (including drains, gutters and external pipes),
   (b) to keep in repair and proper working order the installations in the dwelling-house for the supply of water, gas and electricity and for san- itation (including basins, sinks, baths and sanitary conveniences, but not other fixtures, fittings and appliances for making use of the supply of water, gas or electricity), and
   (c) to keep in repair and proper working order the installations in the dwelling-house for space heating and heating water.
   (1A) If a lease to which this section applies is a lease of a dwelling-house which forms part only of a building, then, subject to subsection (1B), the covenant implied by subsection (1) shall have effect as if—

    (a) the reference in paragraph (a) of that subsection to the dwelling-house included a reference to any part of the building in which the lessor has an estate or interest; and

    (b) any reference in paragraphs (b) and (c) of that subsection to an installation in the dwelling-house included a reference to an installation which, directly or indirectly, serves the dwelling-house and which either–

        (i) forms part of any part of a building in which the lessor has an estate or interest; or

        (ii) is owned by the lessor or under his control.

(1B) Nothing in subsection (1A) shall be construed as requiring the lessor to carry out any works or repairs unless the disrepair (or failure to maintain in working order) is such as to affect the lessee's enjoyment of the dwelling-house or of any common parts, as defined in section 60(1) of the Landlord and Tenant Act 1987, which the lessee, as such, is entitled to use.

(2) The covenant implied by subsection (1) ('the lessor's repairing covenant') shall not be construed as requiring the lessor—

    (a) to carry out works or repairs for which the lessee is liable by virtue of his duty to use the premises in a tenant-like manner, or would be so liable but for an express covenant on his part,

    (b) to rebuild or reinstate the premises in the case of destruction or damage by fire, or by tempest, flood or other inevitable accident, or

    (c) to keep in repair or maintain anything which the lessee is entitled to remove from the dwelling-house.

(3) In determining the standard of repair required by the lessor's repairing covenant, regard shall be had to the age, character and prospective life of the dwelling-house and the locality in which it is situated.

(3A) In any case where–

    (a) the lessor's repairing covenant has effect as mentioned in subsection (1A), and

    (b) in order to comply with the covenant the lessor needs to carry out works or repairs otherwise than in, or to an installation in, the dwelling-house, and

    (c) the lessor does not have a sufficient right in the part of the building or the installation concerned to enable him to carry out the required works or repairs, then, in any proceedings relating to a failure to comply with the lessor's repairing covenant, so far as it requires the lessor to carry out the works or repairs in question, it shall be a defence for the lessor to prove that he used all reasonable endeavours to obtain, but was unable to obtain, such rights as would be adequate to enable him to carry out the works or repairs.

(4) A covenant by the lessee for the repair of the premises is of no effect so far as it relates to the matters mentioned in subsection (1)(a) to (c), except so far as it imposes on the lessee any of the requirements mentioned in subsection (2)(a) or (c).

(5) The reference in subsection (4) to a covenant by the lessee for the repair of the premises includes a covenant—
(a) to put in repair or deliver up in repair,
(b) to paint, point or render,
(c) to pay money in lieu of repairs by the lessee, or
(d) to pay money on account of repairs by the lessor.
(6) In a case in which the lessor's repairing covenant is implied there is also implied a covenant by the lessee that the lessor, or any person authorised by him in writing, may at reasonable times of the day and on giving 24 hours' notice in writing to the occupier, enter the premises comprised in the lease for the purpose of viewing their condition and state of repair.

According to s 13, s 11 applies to a lease of a dwelling-house granted on or after 24 October 1961 for a term of less than seven years; s 12 prohibits contracting out of the s 11 obligations, although the county court with the consent of both parties can exclude or modify the terms implied by s 11. The effect is that subject to s 13, a lease, but not a licence, of residential property imposes on the landlord several repairing duties (for detailed commentary, see Hoath, *Public Housing Law*, 1989, Ch 12; and Luba, *op. cit.*, pp 18-28).

The main issue with s 11 is the breadth of its remit. It requires the landlord to keep in repair the 'structure and exterior of the dwelling-house'. Under the doctrine in *Proudfoot v Hart, op. cit.*, the landlord is, thus, under an obligation to put the premises into repair if they are not so at the commencement of the lease. It has been held that wallplaster is part of the exterior and structure—*Hussein v Mehlman* [1992] 32 EG 59. Likewise, windows—*Boswell v Crucible Steel of America* [1925] 1 KB 119, *Hastie v City of Edinburgh* 1981 SLT 61. Moreover, partition walls in converted flats will be part of the structure and exterior (*Green v Eales* (1841) 2 QB 225 at 237, 114 ER 88 at 93, *per* Lord Denman CJ):

The external parts of premises are those which form the inclosure of them, and beyond which no part of them extends: and it is immaterial whether those parts are exposed to the atmosphere, or rest upon and adjoin some other building which forms no part of the premises let.

Paths providing access to the dwelling house which are within the demise form part of the exterior (*Brown v Liverpool Corporation* [1969] 3 All ER 1345). Installations, as opposed to the structure and exterior, have to be kept in repair and proper working order. Where a house had no working space heaters at the commencement of the lease, *Hussein v Mehlman, op. cit.*, held that the landlord was in breach of s 11(1)(c) until some were installed. Regrettably, a landlord is not obliged to take preventative measures, such as lagging pipes and insulating lofts (note comments in *Hussein v Mehlman, op. cit.*, about the Court of Appeals' decision in *Wycombe AHA v Barnett* (1982) 5 HLR 84). Any damage caused to the structure, the exterior or an installation by reason of failure to take preventative measures will give rise to liability on the part of the landlord under s 11.

The position is even more complex where the tenant rents a flat in a dwelling in multiple occupation, but especially so if it is in a tower block. The problem is that the Act has been held to apply solely to the structure, exterior and installations of that particular flat. Thus, the tenant of a flat in the middle of a tower block, for instance, used not to be able to complain if the roof leaked causing damage to the interior decoration of his flat or if the communal central heating boiler situated outside his own flat broke down—*Campden Hill Towers v Gardner* [1977] QB 823. For tenancies starting on or after 15 January 1989, however, s 11 has been amended. Under s 11(1A) and (1B), added by Housing Act 1988, s 116, where the enjoyment of a flat in a dwelling in multiple occupation is affected by disrepair or failure to maintain an installation in proper working order, it is of no consequence that the disrepair is to another part or that the installation is situated in another part of the building in which the landlord has an interest or estate. The landlord is liable to the tenant so long as the effect is felt in the tenant's demise. Leases created on or after 15 January 1989 also oblige the landlord to keep the common parts in good repair.

The Landlord and Tenant Act 1985 is subject to several exceptions. There is the general rule, taken from the common law, that the landlord must know of the need to repair and that a reasonable time must have elapsed since the landlord acquired such knowledge so that he can set any repairs in motion (*Morris v Liverpool CC* (1988) 20 HLR 498, and *Hughes v Liverpool CC*, The Times, 30 March 1988; *cf. British Telecom plc v Sun Life Assurance Society plc* [1994] 43 EG 158, where duty 'to . . . keep in complete good and substantial repair and condition the demised premises . . . ' was not a repairing duty, but left the defendant in breach as soon as any deterioration occurred). There is no need for the landlord to have been informed by the tenant: the fact that a council worker, not even from the housing department, knew of the disrepair was sufficient to impute notice to the local authority landlord in *Dinefwr BC v Jones* (1987) 19 HLR 445. The only exception to the rule that the landlord has to be given notice of the disrepair is where that disrepair is to part of the premises retained by the landlord, such as common areas, for example, stairs or communal basements. Furthermore, as discussed above at 7.2.4.3, the person with the repairing obligation can take account of the age, nature and character of the premises at the start of the tenancy when assessing the level of repair necessary; if the repairing costs are too high in relation to the value of the property, then the landlord's obligation is waived—*Patel v Newham LBC* [1979] JPL 303. Section 32(2) Landlord and Tenant Act 1985, sets out that s 11 does not affect commercial tenancies, while s 14(3) excludes agricultural tenancies and s 14(5) exempts the Crown as landlord from s 11 liabilities. Finally, section 14(4) excludes certain types of tenant from protection.

s 14(4) Section 11 does not apply to a lease granted on or after 3rd October 1980
to—
a local authority,
a new town corporation,
an urban development corporation,
the Development Board for Rural Wales,
a registered housing association,
a co-operative housing association,
an educational institution or other body specified, or of a class specified,
by regulations under section 8 of the Rent Act 1977 or paragraph 8 of
Schedule 1 to the Housing Act 1988 (bodies making student lettings), or
a housing action trust established under Part III of the Housing Act 1988.

The aim would seem to be to confine the obligations to those landlords with tenants who are individuals rather than institutions.

Section 11 is a measure which, in part, has the effect of redistributing wealth from the richer landlords to the poorer tenants. Whether it is part of landlord and tenant law to impose such a system of indirect welfare is open to debate, but the direct interest the landlord has in the reversion makes him the best choice for carrying out structural repairs. Where the leases are short, and especially where the tenant rents only part of the entirety in which the landlord has an interest or estate, then the landlord may be the only one who can effect the necessary repairs to the whole of the structure or exterior, to the common parts or to communal installations—*cf. John Trenberth Ltd v National Westminster Bank Ltd* (1979) 39 P & CR 104. The landlord may also be in a position to claim a grant for the work.

(ii) Defective Premises Act 1972.   While s 11 Landlord and Tenant Act 1985 was designed to introduce repairing obligations into leases, tenants can sometimes benefit from the obligations set out in s 4 Defective Premises Act 1972.

s 4(1) Where the premises are let under a tenancy which puts on the landlord an
obligation to the tenant for the maintenance or repair of the premises, the
landlord owes to all persons who might reasonably be expected to be
affected by defects in the state of the premises a duty to take such care as is
reasonable in all the circumstances to see that they are reasonably safe from
personal injury or from damage to their property caused by a relevant defect.
        . . .
    (4) Where premises are let under a tenancy which expressly or impliedly gives
the landlord the right to enter the premises to carry out any description of
maintenance or repair of the premises, then, as from the time when he first
is, or by notice or otherwise can put himself, in a position to exercise the
right and so long as he is or can put himself in that position, he shall be
treated for the purposes of subsections (1) to (3) above (but for no other
purpose) as if he were under an obligation to the tenant for that description
of maintenance or repair of the premises; but the landlord shall not owe the

tenant any duty by virtue of this subsection in respect of any defect in the state of the premises arising from, or continuing because of, a failure to carry out an obligation expressly imposed on the tenant by the tenancy.

The provision in s 4 of the 1972 Act is not as specific as the Landlord and Tenant Act 1985, s 11, but it is not limited by any requirement to give notice to the landlord. Moreover, the generality of s 4 may be of assistance to any tenant suing for injury or damage when the Landlord and Tenant Act 1985 would not cover the particular issue. However, in *McAuley v Bristol CC, op. cit.*, the Court of Appeal held that what is now s 11 would not extend to cover the repair of a step in the garden that did not form part of a means of access to the dwelling. As a result, the Defective Premises Act 1972, s 4(1) could not provide a remedy when the plaintiff-tenant broke her ankle due to that step, since the injury did not arise from 'a "relevant defect", that is to say, a defect which constitutes a failure to carry out the repairing obligation'.

Subsection (4) extends the basis of liability by treating the landlord as being under an obligation to repair, when in fact he is not. The extension is made when the landlord is given a right to enter 'to carry out any description of maintenance or repair' but the extension of liability is not general. The landlord, when he is given a right to enter to carry out 'any description of maintenance or repair' is to be treated as if he were under an obligation to the tenant 'for that description of maintenance or repair,' not all and any description of maintenance or repair. (*McAuley, op. cit.*, per Ralph Gibson LJ at 145)

On the basis that the tenancy agreement set out the full extent of the tenant's obligations, the Court of Appeal was prepared to hold under the business efficacy test that there was an implied obligation on the landlord at common law to carry out repairs in the garden, even though such would not be within the scope of the Landlord and Tenant Act 1985, s 11. Given this implied right, the local authority were liable to the plaintiff under s 4(4) of the 1972 Act.

As stated, s 4 is limited to injury or damage arising from a failure to carry out a repair for which the landlord was liable. Thus, since remedying a problem with condensation in and of itself is not a 'repair' according to *Quick v Taff Ely BC, op. cit.*, nor does it give rise to s 4 liability. Nevertheless, there could be liability under the Defective Premises Act 1972, s 1. If the dwelling was built or provided for the landlord, such as a local authority, and if the condensation is due to a design fault or the use of poor quality materials, then s 1 of the 1972 Act imposes liability (see Luba, *op. cit.*, pp 114–15):

s 1(1) A person taking on work for or in connection with the provision of a dwelling (whether the dwelling is provided by the erection or by the conversion or enlargement of a building) owes a duty—
(a) if the building is provided to the order of any person to that person; and

(b) without prejudice to paragraph (a) above, to every person who acquires an interest (whether legal or equitable) in the dwelling;

to see that the work which he takes on is done in a workmanlike or, as the case may be, professional manner, with proper materials and so that as regards that work the dwelling will be fit for human habitation when completed.

. . .

(4) A person who—

(a) in the course of a business which consists of or includes providing or arranging for the provision of dwellings or installation in dwellings; or

(b) in the exercise of a power of making such provision or arrangements conferred by or by virtue of any enactment;

arranges for another to take on work for or in connection with the provision of a dwelling shall be treated for the purposes of this section as included among the persons who have taken on the work.

In *Alexander v Mercouris* [1979] 3 All ER 305, the Court of Appeal held that s 1 only applied to work begun after 1 January 1974.

(iii) The Tenants' Guarantee. Housing Association tenants benefit from all the foregoing provisions, but additionally there are certain other repairing expectations demanded of housing association landlords because of their social welfare objectives.

An association's performance will also be judged, in particular by the tenants, on the standard of its maintenance service, especially in terms of the speed and quality of repairs undertaken. Maintenance has often been viewed as the 'cinderella' of the housing service, yet as the housing stock grows older, it will rightly gain in prominence. Many associations have enjoyed the benefits of a relatively youthful housing stock and have contained maintenance spending within set allowance levels. However, analysis of housing association accounts undertaken by the NFHA shows that this position is no longer sustainable and associations will face similar constraints on repair expenditure as those faced by local authorities. (Cope, *Housing Associations: Policy and Practice*, 1990, p 208)

The Tenants' Guarantee (Housing Corporation Circular 29/91; see also, Housing Corporation 1994 Consultation Document, including a revised Tenants' Guarantee) states that the tenancy agreement must clearly set out the landlord's statutory obligations and define the contractual responsibility for internal decorations and repairs (§C7d). The main obligations with regard to maintenance and repair as laid down by this Guarantee are found in §E.

§E1 Registered housing associations must meet their statutory and contractual obligations to keep their housing property fit for human habitation.

§E2 They should inspect their property to ensure that they meet these obligations, and can plan effectively, and make financial provisions for, long term maintenance.

§E3   Associations should provide tenants with information in clear terms on:

a   who is responsible for which repairs, including the statutory position (eg. under ss 11–14 Landlord and Tenant Act 1985)

b   methods for reporting the need for repairs. These should give tenants open and easy access to their landlords;

c   how long it should take for defined categories of repairs to be carried out, taking into account the importance to tenants of speed of response;
...

e   what tenants can do if the association fails to meet its repairing obligations, including the right to be paid for carrying out the repair themselves or to contact the local authority Environmental Health Officer;

f   their policy for planned maintenance, including cyclical decorations of external and common parts; and

g   their policy for improvements, including the provision of alternative or temporary accommodation, disturbance payments, compensation, and the effect on rents.

(The revised Tenants' Guarantee, op. cit., makes several changes. Amongst others, specific time limits are set for carrying out repairs of emergency, urgent and routine characters—§E4 and E5; the duty to plan is now framed in terms of keeping properties lettable, not simply up to the expected standard of repair for the present tenant—§E2)

The importance of the Guarantee is not in the way it allocates repairing obligations, for that is in line with statute and any contractually agreed provision, but rather the duty to provide clear information on those obligations and the implicit duty to have planned programmes of repairs and improvements; throughout §E, the tenants' rights are to the fore—*cf.* the Housing Act 1985, ss 104 and 105.

(iv) Agricultural Holdings Act 1986.   Repairing obligations in the agricultural sector are more balanced, reflecting the greater equality between landlord and tenant. Indeed, even the limited intervention that presently occurs will be abolished under the reform of agricultural tenancy law instituted by the Ministry of Agriculture, Food and Fisheries in 1991. As the law stands, the Agricultural Holdings Act 1986, s 11 allows the tenant to go to the agricultural land tribunal to obtain a notice to require the landlord to provide fixed equipment and, subject to contrary provisions in the lease, model repairing clauses with regard to any fixed equipment, promulgated by the Secretary of State under s 7 after consultation with the various bodies representing agricultural landlords and tenants, shall be read in to that lease. Thus, regulations imply model repairing clauses into the lease, but the landlord and tenant can contract out of them.

s 7(1) The Minister may, after consultation with such bodies of persons as appear to him to represent the interests of landlords and tenants of agricultural holdings, make regulations prescribing terms as to the maintenance, repair and insurance of fixed equipment (in this Act referred to as 'the model clauses').

(2) Regulations under this section may make provision for any matter arising under them to be determined by arbitration under this Act.

(3) The model clauses shall be deemed to be incorporated in every contract of tenancy of an agricultural holding except in so far as they would impose on one of the parties to an agreement in writing a liability which under the agreement is imposed on the other.

Although the parties can contract out, under s 8 of the 1986 Act one of the parties can subsequently seek arbitration on whether the lease should be varied to bring it back in line with the model clauses.

s 8(1) This section applies where an agreement in writing relating to a tenancy of an agricultural holding effects substantial modifications in the operation of regulations under section 7 above.

(2) Where this section applies, then . . . the landlord or tenant of the holding may, if he has requested the other to vary the terms of the tenancy as to the maintenance, repair and insurance of fixed equipment so as to bring them into conformity with the model clauses but no agreement has been reached on the request, refer those terms of the tenancy to arbitration under this Act.

(3) On any reference under this section the arbitrator shall consider whether (disregarding the rent payable for the holding) the terms referred to arbitration are justifiable having regard to the circumstances of the holding and of the landlord and the tenant, and, if he determines that they are not so justifiable, he may by his award vary them in such manner as appears to him reasonable and just between the landlord and tenant.

(4) Where it appears to the arbitrator on any reference under this section that by reason of any provision included in his award it is equitable that the rent of the holding should be varied, he may vary the rent accordingly.

(5) The award of an arbitrator under this section shall have effect as if the terms and provisions specified and made in the award were contained in an agreement in writing entered into by the landlord and the tenant and having effect (by way of variation of the agreement previously in force in respect of the tenancy) as from the making of the award or, if the award so provides, from such later date as may be specified in it.

To that extent, the principle of freedom of contract in agricultural tenancies has been limited. Apart from the ramifications of s 8, though, there are other problems to do with opt-outs in writing. The case of *Burden v Hannaford* [1955] 3 All ER 401, concerned a written lease which exempted the tenant from having to repair fences and hedges (*cf.* Agriculture (Maintenance, Repair and Insurance of Fixed Equipment) Regulations 1973, Schedule, paras 5(1) and 9, SI 1973 No. 1473, as amended by SI 1988 No. 281—hereinafter, the 1973 Regulations). The Court of Appeal held that the model clauses applied to the lease except in so far as the particular clause excluded the tenant's liability, but that no corresponding duty to repair hedges and fences could be implied into the lease to burden the landlord. The result was that neither party was liable to repair hedges or fences—*cf. Barrett v Lounova (1982) Ltd, op. cit.*

The rules on repairs in the agricultural sector are specific to 'fixed equipment'. Fixed equipment is defined in the 1986 Act, s 96 to include 'any building or structure affixed to the land and any works on, in or under the land'; it also includes things grown for reasons other than to use after severance from the land, such as, for example, a line of trees planted to protect crops or buildings. The most important aspect of fixed equipment with respect to repairing obligations, however, is in relation to buildings provided for the tenant to live in and those provided to do with the running of the farm, such as a milking shed.

The model clauses provide agricultural leases with implied obligations, covering, in part, duties to repair and replace. Part I of the Schedule to the Agriculture (Maintenance, Repair and Insurance of Fixed Equipment) Regulations 1973 (SI 1973 No 1473, as amended), imposes liability on the landlord for structural repairs, although in some cases the landlord can seek a contribution from the tenant of half the costs.

para 1(1) To execute all repairs and replacements to the under-mentioned parts of the farmhouse, cottages and farm buildings, namely: roofs, including chimney stacks, chimney pots, eaves-guttering and downpipes, main walls and exterior walls, howsoever constructed, including walls and fences of open and covered yards and garden walls, together with any interior repair or decoration made necessary as a result of structural defect to such roofs or walls, floors, floor joists, ceiling joists and timbers, exterior and interior staircases and fixed ladders (including banisters or handrails) of the farmhouse and cottages, and doors, windows and skylights, including the frames of such doors, windows and skylights (but excepting glass or glass substitute, sashcords, locks and fastenings): provided that in the case of repairs and replacements to floor-boards, interior staircases and fixed ladders (including banisters or handrails), doors and windows and opening skylights (including frames), eaves-guttering and downpipes, the landlord may recover one-half of the reasonable cost thereof from the tenant.

(2) To execute all repairs and replacements to underground water supply pipes, wells, bore-holes and reservoirs and all underground installations connected therewith and to sewage disposal systems, including septic tanks, filtering media and cesspools (but excluding covers and tops).

(3) Except as provided by paragraph 8, to replace anything mentioned in paragraph 5(1) which has worn out or otherwise become incapable of further repair unless the tenant is himself liable to replace it under paragraph 6.

para 2(1) (a) To keep the farmhouse, cottages and farm buildings insured to their full value against loss or damage by fire; and

(b) as often as the farmhouse, cottages and farm buildings or any, or any part, of them shall be destroyed or damaged by fire, to execute all works of repair or replacement thereto necessary to make good damage by fire and to cause all money received in respect of such destruction or damage by virtue of such insurance to be laid out in the execution of such works.

(2) The proviso to paragraph 1(1) shall not apply to works falling within sub-paragraph (1)(b) of this paragraph.

para 3(1) As often as may be necessary in order to prevent deterioration, and in any case at intervals of not more than five years, properly to paint with at least two coats of a suitable quality or properly and adequately to gas-tar, creosote or otherwise effectively treat with a preservative material all outside wood and ironwork of the farmhouse, cottages and farm buildings, the inside wood and ironwork of all external outward opening doors and windows of farm buildings (but not of the farmhouse or cottages), and the interior structural steelwork of open-sided farm buildings which have been previously painted, gas-tarred, creosoted or otherwise treated with preservative material or which it is necessary in order to prevent deterioration of the same so to paint, gas-tar, creosote or treat with preservative material: provided that in respect of doors, windows, eaves-guttering and downpipes the landlord may recover one-half of the reasonable cost of such work from the tenant, but if any such work to any of those items is completed before the commencement of the fifth year of the tenancy the sum which the landlord may so recover from the tenant shall be restricted to an amount equal to the aggregate of one-tenth part of such reasonable cost in respect of each year that has elapsed between the commencement of the tenancy and the completion of such work.

(2) In the last foregoing sub-paragraph 'open-sided' means having the whole or the greater part of at least one side or end permanently open, apart from roof supports, if any.

para 4(1) The landlord shall be under no liability–
  (a) to execute repairs or replacements or to insure buildings or fixtures which are the property of the tenant, or
  (b) subject to paragraph 2(1)(b), to execute repairs or replacements rendered necessary by the wilful act or the negligence of the tenant or any members of his household or his employees.

The specificity contrasts sharply the Landlord and Tenant Act 1985, s 11 which, by s 14(3) of the 1985 Act, does not apply to agricultural leases. A so far unanswered question would arise if the element of the structure that was in disrepair was not listed in the regulations. The length of the list of items covered, however, renders the question somewhat moot.

The tenant's principal responsibility under the model clauses is found in the 1973 Regulations, Sch, para 5(1). It is a duty, *inter alia*, to keep in repair non-structural features of the fixed property within the demise.

para 5(1) To repair and to keep and leave clean and in good tenantable repair, order and condition the farmhouse, cottages and farm buildings together with all fixtures and fittings, boilers, ranges and grates, drains, sewers, gulleys, grease-traps, manholes and inspection chambers, electrical supply systems and fittings, water supply systems and fittings in so far as they are situated above ground, including pipes, tanks, cisterns, sanitary fittings, drinking troughs and pumping equipment, hydraulic rams (whether situated above or below ground), fences, hedges, field walls, stiles, gates and posts, cattle grids, bridges, culverts, ponds, watercourses, sluices, ditches, roads and yards in and upon the holding, or which during the tenancy may be erected or provided thereon.

(2) To repair or replace all removable covers to manholes, to inspection chambers and to sewage disposal systems.

(3) To keep clean and in good working order all roof valleys, eves-guttering and downpipes, wells, septic tanks, cesspools and sewage disposal systems.

(4) To use carefully so as to protect from wilful, reckless or negligent damage all items for the repair or replacement of which the landlord is responsible under paragraph 1; and also to report in writing immediately to the landlord any damage, however caused, to items for the repair or replacement of which the landlord is responsible.

para 6 Subject to paragraph 2(1)(b)—

(1) to replace or repair and, upon replacement or repair, adequately to paint, gas-tar, creosote or otherwise treat with effective preservative material as may be proper, all items of fixed equipment, and to do any work, where such replacement, repair or work is rendered necessary by the wilful act or negligence of the tenant or any members of his household or his employees; and

(2) to replace anything mentioned in paragraph 5(1) which has worn out or otherwise become incapable of repair if its condition has been brought about by or is substantially due to the tenant's failure to repair it.

para 7 As often as may be necessary, and in any case at intervals of not more than seven years, properly to clean, colour, whiten, paper, paint, limewash or otherwise treat with materials of suitable quality the inside of the farmhouse, cottages and farm buildings, including the interior of outward opening doors and windows of the farmhouse and cottages, which have been previously so treated and in the last year of the tenancy to limewash the inside of all buildings which previously have been limewashed.

para 8(1) Notwithstanding the general liability of the landlord for repairs and replacements, to renew all broken or cracked tiles or slates and to replace all slipped tiles or slates from time to time as the damage occurs, but so that the cost shall not exceed £100 in any one year of the tenancy.

(2) This paragraph shall not have effect so as to render a tenant liable for the cost of any renewals or replacement of tiles in excess of £25 which have been carried out by the landlord prior to 24th March 1988.

If the model clauses are incorporated, the tenant 'expressly' covenants to leave the premises in good tenantable repair. Even if at the date of the letting the premises were in a state of disrepair, the tenant has to return them to the landlord in repair. Furthermore, since the tenant has also covenanted under para 5(1) to keep the premises in repair, under the rule in *Proudfoot v Hart, op. cit.*, he is again obliged to return it to the landlord in repair (*cf. Post Office v Aquarius, op. cit.*, and *Evans v Jones* [1955] 2 All ER 118, esp. at 123).

Agricultural tenancies would be an example of limited freedom of contract, but for s 8 of the 1986 Act. The relative equality of landlord and tenant justifies the ability to draft contracts covering repairs with liability being allocated as the parties see fit. The model clauses are there simply to prevent a vacuum. However, the right of either party to seek arbitration to reimpose the model clauses where the lease excludes them, indicates that a more interventionist role was envisaged in the agricultural sector—although for the new proposed farm business tenancies, there will be no model clauses.

(v) Statutorily implied terms in the commercial sector. Statutorily implied repairing obligations in the commercial sector are much rarer. The position is much more of a patchwork than in the other sectors. Defective Premises Act 1972, s 4 considered in (ii) above, obliges a landlord who is under a repairing obligation to take reasonable care to ensure that any failure to repair does not cause physical injury or property damage to anyone who might be affected by such failure. The Act can be relied upon by a tenant in appropriate circumstances—*Smith v Bradford MC* (1982) 44 P & CR 171. On the other hand, a tenant of commercial property may be liable for the state of the premises under the Health and Safety at Work Act 1974 if he is also an employer. Other statutes place more specific duties on the parties. The Factories Act 1961, s 28(1) and the Offices, Shops and Railway Premises Act 1963, s 16(1) require that floors, passages and stairs must be properly maintained—see Law Com. No. 123, *op. cit.*, para 2.63. Nevertheless, the commercial sector displays most strongly a desire to leave the terms of the lease entirely to the parties. Given the strength of commercial landlords in negotiating leases, the practice is that, although landlords may accept the repairing responsibility under the lease, especially in multi-occupied property, they will employ managing agents to supervise the condition of the property and the landlord will pass on all costs to the tenant. In this way, the landlords pass the 'hassle' on to someone else and recover the costs of doing so.

(c) Tort Law Responsibility   Apart from implied covenants specific to the various sectors, there are also some general obligations imposed on parties under

tort law. *Liverpool CC v Irwin, op. cit.*, was a decision based on the law of negligence. Builder-landlords may also owe a duty in negligence to those using the building, including tenants—*Rimmer v Liverpool CC, op. cit.* Both cases come from the residential sector, but ought to be equally applicable in the agricultural and commercial sectors.

(d) Inherent Defects and the Allocation of Responsibility   So far, this section has focused on how the lease, the common law and statutes have allocated the repairing obligations. Several areas of law are still unclear, especially where the issue is to do with inherent defects in the property, a problem that cuts across all sectors. There are a variety of ways to deal with what may be a very expensive problem to remedy. The traditional understanding of the scope of repairing obligations between landlord and tenant is inadequate to deal with rectifying inherent defects. The 1970 Law Commission Paper, *Civil Liability of Vendors and Lessors for Defective Premises* (Law Com. No. 40, para 54; cited in Law Com. No. 123, *op. cit.*, para 2.25) recommended the following text.

A person who disposes of premises, knowing at the material time or at any time thereafter while he retains possession of the premises that there are defects in the state of the premises, owes a duty to all persons who might reasonably be expected to be affected by those defects to take reasonable care to see that they are reasonably safe from personal injury or from damage to their property caused by any of those defects.

The provision was believed to be too controversial and was not included in the Bill put before Parliament which went on to become the Defective Premises Act 1972. If it had been implemented, though, landlords would have been obliged to fix all defects that might have caused physical injury or property damage. The judge in *Credit Suisse* (*op. cit.*, at 826) found that a landlord's express covenant to keep the premises in good and tenantable condition did require the inherent defect to be fixed and that the tenant was then liable for a share of the costs (*op. cit.*, at 833). As Leyland points out (*op. cit.*, at p 464), that a landlord should have to fix inherent defects is not inappropriate, but that a tenant with a mere 25-year lease should have to bear the cost of putting right an inherent defect would seem unfair—see also Lindsay J's comments, *Credit Suisse, op. cit.*, at 818. Such an allocation of responsibility, generally, to landlords makes sense, especially when the landlord may be in the best position to inspect and carry out repairs to property in multiple occupation—although the landlord is presently under no obligation even to tell the tenant of any defect of which he is aware. In the residential sectors, the relative poverty of the tenant would mean that the landlord would have to bear the whole cost; however, there would seem to be nothing to stop commercial landlords building any cost into a specific reimbursement provision or by increasing any service charges, despite the consequences seen in *Credit Suisse, op. cit.*—see also, Smith, *Repairing Obligations, op. cit.*

An inherent defect will often result from a defect in design or construction, which if negligent, may give rise to a cause of action at common law. It is, however, difficult for a tenant who is liable to repair this defect to recover the cost of doing so. He cannot do so by an action in contract, as there is no contractual relationship between the tenant and the development team (subject to collateral warranties, discussed below). Nor will it be easy for the tenant to succeed in a tort action. While *Anns v Merton LBC* [1977] 2 All ER 462, and subsequent cases in the 1980s, provided the possibility of recovering in negligence against architects, builders and developers for pure economic loss, more recent decisions, such as *D & F Estates Ltd v Church Commissioners for England* [1989] AC 177, and *Murphy v Brentwood DC* [1990] 2 All ER 908, have held that one can only sue at common law in tort for personal injury and property damage. Moreover, such damage, in the leasehold context, cannot be to the actual property leased. Thus, a tenant could only sue architects, builders and developers for personal injury resulting from their negligence or for damage to property other than the premises demised. It is arguable that the tenant of a unit within a larger building could sue if the defect was outside that part of the premises which he had rented, but there is a strong likelihood that the courts would deny such a claim having regard to cases like *Murphy, op. cit.* Where the landlord is the builder or developer, then the tenant may be able to sue in tort—*Rimmer v Liverpool CC, op. cit.* Indeed, if the defendant is a social landlord, cases have suggested that that status alone imposes a greater duty in tort—*Siney v Dublin Corporation* [1980] IR 400 (S.Ct), *Rimmer v Liverpool CC, op. cit., cf. McNerney v Lambeth LBC* (1989) 21 HLR 188. The tenant of a new building may therefore seek to obtain a contractual duty of care from members of the building team (architects, builders and designers) or a promise from the landlord to seek compensation in contract from the building team (Ross, *op. cit.*, para 8.15:4; Tromans, 1987, *op. cit.*, p 93). In practice, such a duty of care deed will never be entered into with a later tenant—and even the original/first tenant is likely only to be able to negotiate such a collateral warranty if he is taking a lease of the whole, or a substantial part, of the building. In addition, there is an argument that if a tenant is liable for the cost of fixing any inherent defect, then any right of action that the landlord might have had against builders and others ought to be subrogated to the tenant, although this might require an extension of existing principles (see Tromans, 1987, *op. cit.*, p 93).

Other jurisdictions have seen alternative approaches to inherent defects. The most extreme case is found in Italy.

If the property is subject to serious defects which substantially reduce its fitness for the agreed use, and the tenant was not aware of them or they were not easily recognizable, he may rescind the contract or require a rent reduction. The [landlord] must pay compensation for the property's defects. He cannot escape liability by restriction of liability clauses. (RICS, *International Leasing Structures, op. cit.*, p 34)

In France, however, the tenant takes out an insurance policy for ten years, the standard length of a commercial lease, to cover the need to remedy any inherent defects; the longer length of most English commercial leases may mean that premiums would be higher, especially since some inherent defects can take fifteen to twenty years to manifest themselves (Atkins Committee, NEDO, Latent Defects in Buildings: An Analysis of Insurance Possibilities, 1985).

(e) Allocation of Responsibility and Properties in Multiple Occupation A second issue that cuts across all sectors is management of properties in multiple occupation. The problems pertaining to this situation are not limited to repairs, but it is sufficiently pressing a feature as to be recognized as a forceful ground for reform of the law. The present position is that the landlord will often assume responsibility for repairs when a property is in multiple occupation, but in the commercial sector at least, the tenant will cover all costs either through paying a share of the final bill or through service charges. Apart from the fact that generally the landlord will be the only person with a right to repair common areas, having one person responsible for all repairs, other than those to do with the interior of each of the individual properties let, prevents inter-tenant disputes as to the extent (and thus cost) of the works necessary. However, poor management of properties in multiple occupation has led the government to intervene. Part II of the Landlord and Tenant Act 1987 permits two or more tenants to seek the replacement of the managing agent where there has been a continuing failure to perform his duties—ss 21 and 24. Although this seems a very powerful tool, it only applies when the situation has deteriorated seriously and, in practice, the cost of obtaining an order has proved prohibitive. Furthermore, appointment of a manager is perceived as a mere stop-gap on the way to the tenants obtaining the freehold under the 1987 Act—below at 7.2.5; Thomas *et al., op. cit.*, para 4.8. Part I, Chapter VI of the Leasehold Reform, Housing and Urban Development Act 1993, amends the Landlord and Tenant Act 1987, Part III bringing more tenants within its scope— Part III of the 1987 Act gives tenants the right to acquire the landlord's interest when he is in serious breach of the obligation to repair. In addition, Chapter VI of the 1993 Act enables the Secretary of State to approve codes of practice governing the management of residential property, whether it be let on a lease or a licence—s 87(8), (9). Under the Leasehold Reform, Housing and Urban Development Act 1993, s 87(1):

s 87(1) The Secretary of State may, if he considers it appropriate to do so, by order,
   (a) approve any code of practice—
      (i) which appears to him to be designed to promote desirable practices in relation to any matter or matters directly or indirectly concerned with the management of residential property by relevant persons . . .

Such codes will be drafted by bodies such as the Royal Institution of Chartered Surveyors. The codes can include provisions on the resolution of disputes between tenants and landlords or their managing agents, competitive tendering for works in connection with the property and the administration of trusts to control tenants' service charge payments—s 87(6)(b). It is intended that the codes will drive up standards of management and maintenance and encourage dialogue with tenants. To that end, breach of any code does not of itself give rise to a cause of action, but the code may be put before any court as evidence of good practice—s 87(7).

The government's interest in commonhold also springs in part from a desire to deal with management problems, including repairs, when a property is in multiple occupation.

The insurance, repair and reserve fund obligations of the commonhold association are regarded as such an important aspect of the proper management of commonholds that, with limited exceptions, they could not be altered by the promoter or the unit owners.

There is also concern about the problems faced by many long-leaseholders in ensuring that the common services are properly provided, that their buildings are adequately maintained and that all these things are done at reasonable cost to them. While there are already extensive provisions in the Landlord and Tenant Acts 1985 and 1987 designed to deal with these problems, a provision which would enable long-leaseholders once for all to get rid of their landlord, without having to establish a serious record of bad management, and to obtain control of their affairs under a purpose-built, democratic system is seen by many as a more attractive solution. (*Commonhold*, 1990, *op. cit.*, at paras 3.10 and 4.14)

Properties in multiple occupation are also problematic when it comes to enforcing repairing obligations even if they have been satisfactorily allocated. That aspect of the issue is considered below in the next section.

(*f) Waste*   The final topic with regard to the allocation of repairing obligations is that of waste. In any sector, a tenant for a term of years may be liable for the tort of permissive waste. The problem is that the issue is not the subject of frequent litigation and one of the very few recent cases, *Mancetter Development Ltd v Garmanson Ltd* [1986] 1 All ER 449, left open whether an action will lie in the tort of waste if the landlord can sue in contract under any relevant covenant. If liability still exists today, then a tenant will be under a duty not to allow damage to occur to the premises (see Evans and Smith, *The Law of Landlord and Tenant*, 4th edn, 1993, pp 147–9).

7.2.5 Enforcing Standards

Although the parties might well know who is responsible for carrying out the necessary repair or upholding standards in other respects, two questions still remain. Who is liable for the associated costs and how can liability be enforced? Enforcing those obligations has proved difficult and there is a variety of means available. The aim of this section is to examine the traditional ways of enforcing the obligations before turning to alternatives that might not be as direct, but may be just as effective. Of course, since the question is one of enforcing standards rather than merely repairing obligations, it may be that in some cases the only possible response is to demolish the premises.

Before considering the various means of enforcement, the purpose of enforcement should be considered. The reason is simply that codes to do with standards and repairs are designed to preserve the finite stock of premises for as long a period as possible. As Hill and Redman, *op. cit.*, make clear (paras 365 *et seq.*), the cost of repairs is generally the biggest expense arising during the course of a tenancy. Enforcement mechanisms can prove necessary where the party liable is financially stretched, for large repair bills can be incurred with little or no warning.

As soon as issues of enforcement arise, though, the separate but related issue of liability for the financial costs of the repair also have to be addressed. Generally speaking, the obligation is imposed on the weaker party unless statute or the common law has intervened. In the residential sector, statutes impose obligations on the landlord, partly in order to effect a redistribution of wealth.

Comprehensive code enforcement is considered here as a program which may, under certain conditions, redistribute income from the landlord class to the generally poorer tenant class. If a slum dweller has been paying $80 a month for a rat-infested apartment and is still paying $80 after the landlord is forced by the code authorities to take effective steps toward rat prevention, the tenant has received something for nothing, while the landlord has paid out cash and received no additional returns. . . Thus, once our society has determined that the poor tenant class has an unfair share of the national income, comprehensive code enforcement is one of the programs which may significantly contribute to righting the balance. (Ackerman, *op. cit.*, at pp 1096–7)

7.2.5.1 The Traditional/Common Law Remedies

It should be noted that the traditional remedies differ depending on whether the complainant is the landlord or the tenant. Where the landlord is suing the tenant for breach of a repairing covenant he may seek damages or, given that a right of re-entry has been reserved, he may seek to evict the tenant, subject to statutory guarantees of security of tenure. Where the tenant is suing the landlord, once again damages are available, but the tenant might also seek specific performance, a remedy that may not be available to landlords in corresponding circumstances. Further, the tenant might be able to appoint a manager or receiver and may even be able to repudiate the contract.

(a) Financial Compensation Where a tenant is suing the landlord for breach of the repairing covenant, damages can also be claimed for any injury to the tenant's property that the landlord causes in effecting the repairs. Damages, though, are not a fully effective remedy except in the simplest of cases where the monies awarded by the court can effect the necessary repairs. On the other hand, the Landlord and Tenant Act 1927, s 18(1) limits the measure of damages a landlord can receive from a defaulting tenant: the calculation is based on the amount by which the value of the reversion is diminished as a result of the breach, although an agreement in the lease to expend a set amount each year on repairs is not affected by s 18—*Moss Empires Ltd v Olympia (Liverpool) Ltd* [1939] AC 544. The problem is that the section may be based on a false policy premise when applied to long leases.

Where a property is let on a long lease at a ground rent, the value of the reversion, which may not fall in for, say, 50–100 years, will depend little, if at all, on the state of repair of the buildings. Let us suppose that they are allowed to fall into such disrepair that it is no longer an attractive proposition, or even no longer possible, to use them. The tenant has failed to comply with his duty to repair, but—effectively—is not obliged to pay damages. The situation may become such that the landlord's only remedy is to forfeit the lease, but he then recovers premises which are in no fit state to use as intended. If the fear is that landlords will unreasonably persecute tenants with trifling demands for damages in the course of a long lease, a restriction on proceedings may be more appropriate than a limit on damages. Or, if the policy adopted were to be that landlords had no proper interest in the physical state of the property while a lease has a substantial time to run, the logical approach would be to ban obligations imposed on tenants, rather than allowing obligations but removing the sanctions from them. (Law Com. No. 123, *op. cit.*, para 3.31)

The landlord's ability to recover, amongst other things, damages is further restricted in certain cases by the Leasehold Property (Repairs) Act 1938. While originally restricted to lettings of small houses, it now applies to all properties (except those held on agricultural leases) where the leasehold term was initially for a period of seven years or more and at least three years still remain to run, unless the tenant's repairing covenant required him to cleanse the premises (*Starrokate Ltd v Burry* (1982) 265 EG 871) or to put them into repair upon taking possession (s 3). The 1938 Act prevents a landlord in the circumstances just described from enforcing a remedy for breach of a covenant to repair unless, at least one month before the commencement of the action, he served a notice under Law of Property Act 1925, s 146 indicating the breach. This notice also gives the tenant 28 days to serve a counter-notice, the effect of which is that the landlord must then seek leave to continue his action for damages or re-entry or forfeiture. The Leasehold Property (Repairs) Act 1938, s 1(5) states that leave will only be given if the landlord proves on the balance of probabilities (*Associated British Ports v C.H. Bailey plc* [1990] 2 AC 703) one of five grounds:

1   That the immediate effecting of the repair is necessary to prevent a substantial diminution in the value of the reversion or such diminution has already occurred;

2   That immediate repairs are needed to comply with any statute, court order or requirement of any authority established by statute;

3   Where the tenant is not in occupation of the whole of the premises, that remedying the defect is necessary in the interests of the occupier;

4   That current costs would be relatively small by comparison with the costs if there were to be a delay; or

5   It is otherwise just and equitable in the circumstances.

Watson (*Breach of Tenant's Repairing Covenants and the Self-Help Clause*, [1993] 11 PR 429) argues that the 1938 Act and the 1927 Act, s 18, however, can be avoided by expressly claiming in the lease, not that the cost of carrying out the repairs should be recoverable 'as damages by action', but by seeking to recover the costs as a 'debt recoverable in the same manner as rent in arrear' (and see Tromans, 1987, *op. cit.*, p 100). A debt, being liquidated damages, is not caught by the 1938 Act and this approach has been upheld in *Colchester Estates (Cardiff) v Carlton Industries plc* [1984] 2 All ER 601 (Watson, *op. cit.*, p 432). Although it might seem that the landlord is thereby evading a statutory protection for tenants, the 28 day delay that serving notice imposes might in some cases exacerbate the state of disrepair—nevertheless, an amendment of the 1938 Act so that it effectively met the mischief it was intended to deal with would be preferable.

In the agricultural sector, the landlord has a right to compensation for dilapidation or general deterioration upon termination, akin to a form of damages for failure to maintain or follow the rules of good husbandry (see Rodgers, *Agricultural Law, op. cit.*, pp 199 *et seq.*). The landlord's claim may be under the specific terms of the lease, but statute has also intervened through what is now the Agricultural Holdings Act 1986, ss 71 and 72. Section 71 looks at the effect of specific breaches of the rules of good husbandry, such as failure to maintain buildings or the productivity of fields (*Evans v Jones* [1955] 2 All ER 118); s 72 is concerned with the general deterioration of the holding.

(b) Specific Performance   However, where the landlord is in breach, the tenant will be more interested in forcing the landlord to fulfil his obligations through specific performance or mandatory injunction (*Luckhurst v Manyfield Ltd, op. cit.*: see *The Scope and Specific Enforceability of Covenants to Repair*, Building Law Monthly,

vol 10:1, 1993, p 3). In exceptionally severe cases where the tenant's enjoyment of the premises is seriously interfered with, even an interim injunction might issue— see Lord Diplock in *American Cyanamid v Ethicon* [1975] AC 396 and *Locabail International Finance Ltd v Agroexport* [1986] 1 All ER 901. However, because the tenant is seeking a mandatory injunction, that is, he is attempting to force the landlord to carry out certain works, there are further hurdles to satisfy. These include there being imminent danger of further injury to the tenant, that the threat to the tenant outweighs the cost of the work and that the order can be precisely phrased as to the work necessary and the time limit for its performance—*Redland Bricks Ltd v Morris* [1970] AC 652. There is jurisdiction to grant specific performance in equity and under the Landlord and Tenant Act 1985, s 17(1). *Jeune v Queen's Cross Ltd* [1974] Ch 97, laid down the rules for specific performance in equity.

The rule has now become settled that the court will order specific performance of an agreement to build if–
  (i) the building work is sufficiently defined by the contract, *e.g.* by reference to detailed plans;
 (ii) the plaintiff has a substantial interest in the performance of the contract of such a nature that damages would not compensate him for the defendant's failure to build; and
(iii) the defendant is in possession of the land so that the plaintiff cannot employ another person to build without committing a trespass. (*op. cit.*, at 99–100)

Financial cost is not an interest to be taken into account by the courts. The party liable cannot say it would be too expensive—in *Francis v Cowcliffe Ltd* (1976) 33 P & CR 368, the court ordered the landlord to install and maintain lifts. The Landlord and Tenant Act 1985, s 17 provides as follows:

s 17(1) In proceedings in which a tenant of a dwelling alleges a breach on the part of his landlord of a repairing covenant relating to any part of the premises in which the dwelling is comprised, the court may order specific performance of the covenant whether or not the breach relates to a part of the premises let to the tenant and notwithstanding any equitable rule restricting the scope of the remedy, whether on the basis of a lack of mutuality or otherwise.
       . . .
  (2) (d) 'repairing covenant' means a covenant to repair, maintain, renew, construct or replace any property.

As can be seen, where a tenant falls within the remit of the Landlord and Tenant Act 1985, it will be much easier to obtain specific performance. Further, under s 17 a tenant can obtain specific performance for the landlord to carry out repairs to the common parts of the building, not just to his own premises.

At first glance, specific performance and the like would seem to be the tenant's perfect remedy—it is not clear whether the old rule in *Hill v Barclay* (1810) 33 ER 1037, that a landlord could not seek specific performance against a tenant has been overruled. However, where the tenant has to use the equitable jurisdiction then the old rules concerning coming to Equity with clean hands and the court being able to supervise the works (*cf. Gordon v Selico Co. Ltd* [1986] 1 EGLR 71) still apply. Section 17 is probably not so restricted, but the remedy is still discretionary.

(c) Re-entry and Repudiation In extreme cases disrepair can bring an end to the lease. The landlord will usually have reserved a right of re-entry for disrepair and all the statutory codes on security of tenure allow for eviction in the case of disrepair. The tenant, however, would also seem to have a right to accept the landlord's repudiation of the lease in the event of a landlord persistently failing to carry out his repairing obligation—*Hussein v Mehlman, op. cit.*

7.2.5.2 New Statutory Remedies

In certain cases the tenant can also apply to the court for the appointment of a receiver or manager. Under the Supreme Court Act 1981, s 37(1) an application can be made to the courts for the appointment of a receiver, where it is just and convenient so to do, to carry out some of the functions of a landlord—it can be used where the landlord's repairing obligations have not been fulfilled. The remedy is available in the agricultural and commercial sectors and in the residential sector except with respect to local authority landlords—*Parker v Camden LBC* [1985] 2 All ER 141. The Housing Act 1985, s 21 vests all management functions in the local authority such that it is not appropriate for the court to appoint a receiver under the Supreme Court Act 1981. Receivers can collect rents and service charges and apply them to the carrying out of repairs where the landlord is not traceable or where he has persistently failed to carry out repairing obligations and resists the application—*Hart v Emelkirk Ltd* [1983] 1 WLR 1289; *Blawdziewicz v Diodon Establishment* (1988) 35 EG 83. Part II of the Landlord and Tenant Act 1987 provides in s 24 for the appointment of a manager where

1 It is not a lease under Part II of the Landlord and Tenant Act 1954— s 21(7);
2 There are two or more flats in a block—s 21(2);
3 The landlord is neither resident, nor a housing association or trust, nor a local authority—s 21(3) and s 58;
4 The landlord has been previously served with a s 22 notice by the tenant advising him that the tenant intends to bring an action under s 24 unless the defects are remedied (if this is possible); and
5 The landlord is in breach of an obligation owed to the tenant, the breach is of a continuing nature and it is just and convenient in the circumstances to appoint a manager—s 24(2).

The order under s 24 can be registered under the Land Registration Act 1925 and the Land Charges Act 1972 to prevent the landlord simply selling on his interest to some third party—s 24(8). Part II of the 1987 Act provides yet another remedy for a tenant whose premises have fallen into and remain in disrepair by the fault of the landlord. However, experience shows that the Part II remedy may not be as effective as had been hoped—see Thomas, North *et al.*, *op. cit.*, para 4.8 and Table 5.1.

The party to a long lease of a flat can also seek to vary that lease under Part IV of the Landlord and Tenant Act 1987, as amended. One ground is that the lease is so inadequate that there is not satisfactory provision for repair or maintenance— s 35(2)(a). Another ground is that the service charge, where appropriate, would be inadequate to cover the costs of repairs—s 35(4)(c), as amended by the Leasehold Reform, Housing and Urban Development Act 1993, s 86 (on service charges generally, see 7.6, below). Variation received a mixed response from tenants in the Thomas *et al.*, study, *op. cit.* para 4.7 and Ch 5.

7.2.5.3 Self-help Remedies

Before considering some remedies specific to certain types of lease, certain self-help rules need to be examined. As was pointed out above, the tenant's principal aim is to have the landlord fulfil his repairing obligation. That is why specific performance or the appointment of a receiver or manager are more useful than a mere claim for damages. Specific performance and the appointment of a receiver or manager, though, require the tenant to go to court. However, subject to clear wording excluding the right in the lease (*Gilbert-Ash (Northern) Ltd v Modern Engineering (Bristol)* [1974] AC 689; *Connaught Restaurants Ltd v Indoor Leisure Ltd* [1994] 4 All ER 834), the common law allows a tenant to carry out the repair and then set-off the cost against future rent payments—*Lee-Parker v Izzet* [1971] 1 WLR 1688. If the landlord then seeks to forfeit the lease in order to recover the shortfall in rent, the tenant will have the perfect defence—the monies were expended in performing the landlord's own repairing obligations which the rent is, in part, supposed to cover. The American Restatement Property 2d, §11.2, *op. cit.*, provides the tenant with a similar right.

If the tenant is entitled to apply his rent to eliminate the landlord's default, the tenant, after proper notice to the landlord, may deduct from his rent reasonable costs in eliminating the default.

The American Restatement, Property 2d, reflects the rationale behind the common law applied in English courts.

Given that some tenants would not be able to afford to pay for repairs and then reclaim the cost out of future rent, *Asco Developments & Newman v Lowes, Lewis and Gordon* (1978) 248 EG 683, held that a tenant could accumulate arrears and then use the rent payments saved to pay for the repair. If the landlord seeks to distrain for the arrears accumulated while the tenant is 'saving' to pay for the repairs, *Eller v Grovecrest Investments Ltd* [1994] 4 All ER 845, holds that set-off is a good defence against distraint. However, it would be wise to separate out the rent payments saved from any general household monies, lest the court find the claim for a set-off is not justified and the tenant then has to pay off the arrears—*Haringey LBC v Stewart*, (1991) 23 HLR 557.

There is also a form of statutory compensation for local authority tenants found in the Housing Act 1985, s 96, as amended by the Leasehold Reform, Housing and Urban Development Act 1993, s 121. Whereas the original s 96, which consolidated the Housing and Building Control Act 1984, s 28, referred to a right to carry out repairs, the new version speaks of a right to have repairs carried out.

s 96(1) The Secretary of State may make regulations for entitling secure tenants whose landlords are local housing authorities, subject to and in accordance with the regulations, to have qualifying repairs carried out, at their landlords' expense, to the dwelling-houses of which they are such tenants.

(2) The regulations may make all or any of the following provisions, namely—

(a) provision that, where a secure tenant makes an application to his landlord for a qualifying repair to be carried out, the landlord shall issue a repair notice—

(i) specifying the nature of the repair, the listed contractor by whom the repair is to be carried out and the last day of any prescribed period; and

(ii) containing such other particulars as may be prescribed;

(b) provision that, if the contractor specified in a repair notice fails to carry out the repair within a prescribed period, the landlord shall issue a further repair notice specifying such other listed contractor as the tenant may require; and

(c) provision that, if the contractor specified in a repair notice fails to carry out the repair within a prescribed period, the landlord shall pay to the tenant such sum by way of compensation as may be determined by or under the regulations.

(3) The regulations may also make such procedural, incidental, supplementary and transitional provisions as may appear to the Secretary of State necessary or expedient, and may in particular—

(a) require a landlord to take such steps as may be prescribed to make its secure tenants aware of the provisions of the regulations;

(b) require a landlord to maintain a list of contractors who are prepared to carry out repairs for which it is responsible under the regulations;

(c) provide that, where a landlord issues a repair notice, it shall give to the tenant a copy of the notice and the prescribed particulars of at least two other listed contractors who are competent to carry out the repair;

(d) provide for questions arising under the regulations to be determined by the county court; and

(e) enable the landlord to set off against any compensation payable under the regulations any sums owed to it by the tenant.

(4) Nothing in subsection (2) or (3) shall be taken as prejudicing the generality of subsection (1).

(5) Regulations under this section—

(a) may make different provision with respect to different cases or descriptions of case, including different provision for different areas, and

(b) shall be made by statutory instrument which shall be subject to annulment in pursuance of a resolution of either House of Parliament.

(6) In this section—

'listed contractor', in relation to a landlord, means any contractor (which may include the landlord) who is specified in the landlord's list of contractors;

'qualifying repair', in relation to a dwelling-house, means any repair of a prescribed description which the landlord is obliged by a repairing covenant to carry out;

'repairing covenant', in relation to a dwelling-house, means a covenant, whether express or implied, obliging the landlord to keep in repair the dwelling-house or any part of the dwelling- house;

and for the purposes of this subsection a prescribed description may be framed by reference to any circumstances whatever.

The former s 96 allowed the tenant to claim back as compensation the cost of any repairs he had completed for which the local authority landlord had been liable and which it had not effected after notice. The repayment provisions were complex. A similar rule for housing association tenants, found in §C6(d) of the Tenants' Guarantee, *op. cit.*, appeared remarkably simple. Where the housing association failed to carry out its repairing obligations (see §E of the Tenants' Guarantee), the tenant had 'the right to carry out repairs and have the cost refunded in certain circumstances'. However, clause 5(3) of the NFHA's Model Assured Tenancy Agreement (1994 version) incorporated the regulations about repayments promulgated under the Housing Act 1985, s 96. The new provision for local authority tenants, s 96 as amended by the Leasehold Reform, Housing and Urban Development Act 1993, s 121, is based on the idea of 'listed contractors' always carrying out council repairs, although s 96(6) states that the local authority may be one of the listed contractors specified as certified to carry out such works. A tenant needing a repair to be carried out should inform the local authority landlord which will then issue a repair notice specifying the work necessary, the accredited contractor who is to perform the repair and the period within which the work ought to be effected; set times for various works are laid down in the Schedule to the Secure Tenants of Local Housing Authorities (Right to Repair) Regulations 1994, SI 1994 No. 133. If the work is not carried out within that period, then the tenant can claim compensation for the delay from the landlord (Right to Repair Regulations, *op. cit.*, regs. 7 and 8), although the latter can set off compensation against any monies owed to it by the tenant, for example, rent arrears. However, the overall theme of the new s 96 is that local authority tenants can have repairs carried out at their landlord's expense, and there is nothing to prevent the Secretary of State's regulations allowing tenants to organize the repair in certain circumstances and then seeking repayment—s 96(1) and (4) (A similar system for housing association tenants was initially proposed in the revised Draft Tenants' Guarantee, 1994, §§C7(e) and E4—*cf.* National Federation of Housing Associations' Formal Response, *op. cit.*, which rejected this approach. The revised Tenants' Guarantee retains only the right to compensation in the event of delay—§C6(e).) Further, the common law right to set-off repair costs against rent is not excluded by s 96 statutory compensation; s 96 provides a much more straightforward remedy—Envis, *Compensation and the Right to Repair*, (1994) 138 Sol. J.504.

Landlords and tenants in the agricultural sector have a special code to protect them, although set-off and specific performance, the tenant's two most effective remedies for when dealing with disrepair, are also available. The model regulations include enforcement provisions. Where the tenant is required to perform repairs, the landlord has a right under those regulations, after notice, to carry out the repairs and have reasonable costs reimbursed.

Agriculture (Maintenance, Repair and Insurance of Fixed Equipment) Regulations 1973 (SI 1973 No 1473), **Schedule, Part I,**
para 4(2) If the tenant does not start work on the repairs or replacements for which he is liable under paragraphs 5, 6, 7 and 8 within two months, or if he fails to complete them within three months of receiving from the landlord a written notice (not being a notice to remedy breach of tenancy agreement by doing work of repair, maintenance or replacement in a form prescribed under section 19(1) and (3) of the Agriculture (Miscellaneous Provisions) Act 1963) specifying the necessary repairs or replacements and calling on him to execute them the landlord may enter and execute such repairs or replacements and recover the reasonable cost from the tenant forthwith.
(3)(a) If the tenant wishes to contest his liability to execute any repairs or replacements specified in a notice served upon him by the landlord under the last foregoing sub-paragraph he shall within one month serve a counter-notice in writing upon the landlord specifying the grounds on which and the items of repair or replacement in respect of which he denies liability and requiring the question of liability in respect thereof to be determined by arbitration under the Act.
(b) Upon service of the counter-notice on the landlord, the operation of the notice (including the running of time thereunder) shall be

suspended, in so far as it relates to the items specified in the counter-notice, until the termination of an arbitration determining the question of liability in respect of those items.

(c) In this sub-paragraph, 'termination', in relation to an arbitration, means the date on which the arbitrator's award is delivered to the tenant.

An agricultural tenant has a more specific right with respect to breaches by the landlord of repairing obligations.

Schedule, Part II
para 12(1) If the landlord fails to execute repairs other than repairs to an underground waterpipe which are his liability within three months of receiving from the tenant a written notice specifying the necessary repairs and calling on him to execute them, the tenant may execute such repairs and, except to the extent to which under the terms of Part I hereof the tenant is liable to bear the cost, recover (subject to the landlords's rights to require arbitration under sub-paragraph (5) below) the reasonable cost from the landlord forthwith.

(2) If the landlord fails to execute any repairs which are his liability to an underground waterpipe within one week of receiving from the tenant a written notice specifying the necessary repairs and calling on him to execute them, the tenant may execute such repairs and, except to the extent to which under the terms of Part I hereof the tenant is liable to bear the cost, recover (subject to the landlord's rights to require arbitration under sub-paragraph (5) below) the reasonable cost from the landlord upon the expiry of a period of one month from the execution of the repairs.

(3) Subject to sub-paragraph (4) below, if the landlord fails to execute any replacements which are his liability within three months of receiving from the tenant a written notice specifying the necessary replacements and calling on him to execute them, the tenant may execute such replacements and, except to the extent to which under the terms of Part I hereof the tenant is liable to bear the cost, recover (subject to the landlord's rights to require arbitration under sub-paragraph (5) below) the reasonable cost from the landlord forthwith.

(4) The tenant shall not be entitled to recover, in respect of the aggregate of the replacements executed by him after being specified in a notice given in pursuance of sub-paragraph (3) above, in any year of the tenancy any sum in excess of whichever of the following sums is hereinafter specified in relation to the replacements so executed, that is to say—
  . . .
  (b) in relation to replacements executed in any year of the tenancy terminating after 24th March 1988, a sum equal to the rent of the holding for that year or £2,000, whichever is the smaller.

(5) (a) If the landlord wishes to contest his liability to execute any repairs or replacements specified in a notice served upon him by the tenant under sub-paragraph (1), (2) or (3) above he shall within one month of the service of that notice serve a counter-notice in writing upon the tenant specifying the grounds on which and the items of repair or replacement in respect of which he denies liability and requiring the question of liability in respect thereof to be determined under the Act.

(b) Upon service of a counter-notice on the tenant which relates to a notice served on the landlord under sub-paragraph (1) or (3) above, the operation of the notice so served upon sub-paragraph (1) or (3) (including the running of time thereunder) shall be suspended, in so far as it relates to the items specified in the unter-notice, until the termination of an arbitration determining the question of liability in respect of those items.

(c) Upon service of a counter-notice on the tenant which relates to a notice served on the landlord under sub-paragraph (2) above, the tenant's right under that sub-paragraph to recover the reasonable cost of the repairs specified in the counter-notice shall not arise unless the question of liability to execute those repairs is first determined by arbitration in favour of the tenant, and shall thereupon arise from the termination of the arbitration.

(d) In this sub-paragraph 'termination' in relation to an arbitration means the date on which the arbitrator's award is delivered to the landlord. (Substituted by SI 1988 No. 281, reg. 2)

Given that the new specified sum is £2,000, rather than the previous figure of a mere £500, the regulations provide a useful additional means of having the repair or replacement carried out when dealing with agricultural leases. Nevertheless, the right to go to arbitration to challenge the duty to repair must have a significant impact on the speed with which repairs are carried out and costs met. It is unlikely that the government will extend these provisions to do with agriculture to other sectors, especially now that the similar system in the original s 96 Housing Act 1985 has been amended by the Leasehold Reform, Housing and Urban Development Act 1993, s 121. However, it provides an interesting model for dealing with breaches of obligation where the landlord and the tenant are in a near equal position to carry out the repairs.

7.2.5.4 Withholding Rent

What a tenant from any sector cannot do in England is simply withhold rent if the landlord fails to fulfil his repairing obligations—*Camden Nominees v Forcey* [1940] Ch 352, and *R v Parnell* (1881) 14 Cox CC 508. Whereas set-off is compensation for costs incurred, withholding rent is an act of protest and leverage. The position is not the same in the United States.

§11.3—If the tenant is entitled to withhold the rent, the tenant, after proper notice to the landlord, may place in [a special account set up for the purpose] the rent thereafter becoming due until the default is eliminated or the lease terminates, whichever first occurs. (ALI Restatement Property 2d, *op. cit.*)

The tenant is entitled to withhold rent if the landlord's failure falls within one of the provisions in earlier sections of the Restatement, such as the repairing covenants found in §§5.4(2)(d) and 5.5(4). The rationale for §11.3 is explained as follows:

In the modern urban community, the indigent tenant may find himself forced to live in conditions dangerous to his life, health or safety, despite any promises to repair, housing codes, or implied warranties of habitability which may exist for his benefit. The traditional remedy of constructive eviction which requires him to abandon the premises and look elsewhere for housing is often too costly for the indigent tenant and the available housing is often similarly substandard. [Other parts of the Restatement] . . . give the tenant in various situations the right to stay where he is and put pressure on the landlord by withholding the rent until the landlord eliminates the default that gives rise to the tenant's right to withhold the rent. (ALI Restatement Property 2d, *op. cit.*, vol 1, at p 375)

The analysis of the tenant's position is accurate, but the remedy of rent withholding in order to put pressure on the landlord to carry out the repair is exceedingly indirect when compared to set-off. There is no guarantee that the landlord will effect the repair just because the tenant stops paying rent, although it does put him under an awful lot of pressure. The only situation where rent withholding may score over set-off is where the entire estate is in need of repair and individual tenants' rents would never cover the cost. A rent strike by all the tenants on the estate might galvanize the landlord into dealing with the grievance: as, for instance, in the Glasgow Rent Strike of 1915, but that might have turned on the need to prevent domestic disturbances during World War I (Damer, 'Striking Out on Red Clyde', in Grant, *Built to Last*, 1992, pp 35 *et seq.*). There is also now the risk that a rent strike may be construed as a repudiatory breach by the tenants, enabling the landlord to end the tenancy—*Hussein v Mehlman, op. cit.* Rent withholding seems at a superficial level to be a useful additional remedy, but when it comes to repairing obligations it is inferior to other available means.

7.2.5.5 Remedies in Public Law

Alongside private law remedies, there exist a series of remedies for disrepair and poor conditions that rely on public law. These measures are not restricted to houses let to tenants, but apply to owner-occupied dwellings, as well; the statutory intervention is based on the condition of the property, not the nature of the tenure. Housing law and policy for England and Wales stem from the concern for public sanitation in the mid-nineteenth century, when the issue was not so much municipal ownership as local government monitoring of housing standards and conditions. It is hardly surprising, then, that public health legislation should provide remedies for dealing with poor conditions and disrepair.

The world's leading industrial nation was by the 1840s also the location of some of the world's worst slums. It was clear that capitalism generated extremes not only of wealth and comfort, but also of poverty and deprivation. But in what sense, and for whom, was this a problem? Was it a situation which required state intervention in defiance of property rights and the conventional wisdom? The slums were obviously a problem for the people who lived there, but that fact alone was unlikely to bring about attempts to improve their circumstances, although the danger of their misery and disaffection manifesting itself in rebellion or revolution was sufficient to unsettle the ruling class.

Perhaps a more important factor in the developing definition and recognition of the urban problem was that the lack of adequate sanitation represented a real threat to the health of all classes.

. . .

Public housing, as we understand it today, was not even on the horizon [in the mid-nineteenth century]; it was considered neither necessary nor desirable in the *laissez-faire* society. Economic theory which asserted that the market, free of restraints, would provide, popular attachment to the notion of private property, and the vested interests of the property owners who comprised the personnel of the local state, all militated against municipal housebuilding. However, the *regulation* of standards of provision of privately-owned housing did gain slow acceptance as an adjunct of sanitary policy. (Malpass and Murie, 1994, *op. cit.*, at pp 26 and 32)

Before considering the two varieties of public enforcement, there is a hybrid provision under which a tenant can directly enforce public health standards through a criminal action. The Environmental Protection Act 1990, s 82 allows anyone aggrieved by a statutory nuisance to go to the magistrates' court for an abatement order—see, for example, §E3(d), revised Tenants' Guarantee, *op. cit*. The order will prevent any future repetition of this nuisance and will require the person responsible, which might be a local authority, to do any necessary work. Such work can be extensive, as was seen in *Birmingham DC v Kelly* (1985) 17 HLR 572, where the landlord had to re-wire the house, install gas central heating and secondary double glazing, insulate the roof and fill the cavity walls. The court can also fine the perpetrator of the nuisance and can order compensation to be paid to the aggrieved party.

(a) Unfitness Public agencies, most notably local authority Environmental Health Officers (EHOs), are also involved in upholding housing standards. Statutory intervention is found in the Housing Act 1985 (as amended) and in the Environmental Protection Act 1990. The Housing Act 1985, s 605 requires local authorities to carry out annual reviews of the properties in their area and to determine what action should be taken with respect to properties that are unfit.

s 605(1) The local housing authority shall at least once in each year consider the housing conditions in their district with a view to determining what action to take in performance of their functions under—

(a) Part VI (repair notices);

(b) Part IX (slum clearance);

(c) Part XI (houses in multiple occupation);

(d) Part VII of the Local Government and Housing Act 1989 (renewal areas); and

(e) Part VIII of that Act (grants towards cost of improvements and repairs *etc.*).

The statutory definition of unfitness is found in Housing Act 1985, s 604, as substituted by the Local Government and Housing Act 1989, Sch 9, para 83 (see also *English House Condition Survey: 1991, op. cit.*, Ch 7). The definition is not the same as the common law definition used with respect to Landlord and Tenant Act 1985, s 8, discussed previously.

s 604(1) Subject to subsection (2) below, a dwelling-house is fit for human habitation for the purposes of this Act unless, in the opinion of the local housing authority, it fails to meet one or more of the requirements in paragraphs (a) to (i) below and, by reason of that failure, is not reasonably suitable for occupation,–

(a) it is structurally stable;

(b) it is free from serious disrepair;

(c) it is free from dampness prejudicial to the health of the occupants (if any);

(d) it has adequate provision for lighting, heating and ventilation;

(e) it has an adequate piped supply of wholesome water;

(f) there are satisfactory facilities in the dwelling-house for the preparation and cooking of food, including a sink with a satisfactory supply of hot and cold water;

(g) it has a suitably located water-closet for the exclusive use of the occupants (if any);

(h) it has, for the exclusive use of the occupants (if any), a suitably located fixed bath or shower and wash-hand basin each of which is provided with a satisfactory supply of hot and cold water; and

(i) it has an effective system for the draining of foul, waste and surface water;

and any reference to a dwelling-house being unfit for human habitation shall be construed accordingly.

(2) Whether or not a dwelling-house which is a flat satisfies the requirements in subsection (1), it is unfit for human habitation for the purposes of this Act if, in the opinion of the local housing authority, the building or a part of the building outside the flat fails to meet one or more of the requirements in paragraphs (a) to (e) below and, by reason of that failure, the flat is not reasonably suitable for occupation,—

    (a) the building or part is structurally stable;

    (b) it is free from serious disrepair;

    (c) it is free from dampness;

    (d) it has adequate provision for ventilation; and

    (e) it has an effective system for the draining of foul, waste and surface water.

(3) Subsection (1) applies in relation to a house in multiple occupation with the substitution of a reference to the house for any reference to a dwelling-house.

(4) Subsection (2) applies in relation to a flat in multiple occupation with the substitution for any reference to a dwelling-house which is a flat of a reference to the flat in multiple occupation.

Thus, there are nine criteria of statutory unfitness. The local authority must have found that one of those nine conditions existed, such as the dwelling being structurally unstable, and that by reason of that condition the dwelling is statutorily unfit for human habitation. If the dwelling house is a flat or a HMO, then the condition of the common parts can render the flat or HMO unfit, but it must be noted that the condition of the common parts *per se* will not render a dwelling unfit unless, also, that condition results in the dwelling-house itself not being fit for occupation.

The test for unfitness is substantially different to that used before 1990 (see *English House Condition Survey: 1991, op. cit.*, pp 133–4). The 1991 Survey found that nearly 1.5 million dwellings were unfit out of a total of just under 20 million (*op. cit.*, at para 7.4 and Table A7.1). Each of the nine grounds constitutes in its own right a finding of unfitness and the graph, 'Unfit Dwellings 1991', indicates the number of dwellings that failed each test, with s 604(1)(d) being subdivided into its constituent elements—as such, totalling up each bar would give a figure higher than 1.5 million (based on data in Figure 7.1 of the 1991 Survey, *op. cit.*, p 60; see Figure 7.1: Unfit Dwellings 1991, (figures in thousands) following page.

The age of the dwelling had an effect on the ground for unfitness, serious disrepair and damp being a problem in pre-1919 properties, and internal facilities giving rise to failure in the newer dwellings (*English House Condition Survey: 1991, op. cit.*, para 7.6). It should also be noted that serious disrepair and damp are much more prevalent in private sector stock (*English House Condition Survey: 1991, op. cit.*, para 7.7). Given that breach of each individual ground in s 604(1) would qualify a dwelling to be deemed unfit, the extent and severity of deterioration in the housing stock can also be measured in terms of how many grounds each dwelling fails upon. Over half the unfit dwellings failed on only one ground, with almost another quarter failing on only two (*English House Condition Survey: 1991, op. cit.*, para 7.8). Thus, while 7.6 per cent of the housing stock is unfit, remedying the defects may not in some cases be an overwhelming task.

Figure 7.1: Unfit dwellings 1991

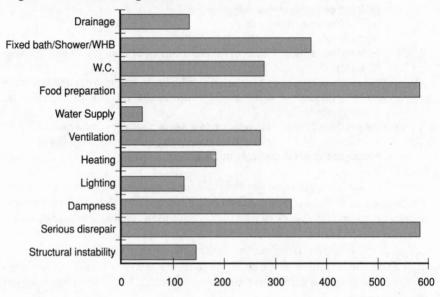

Section 604(1) dates in its current format from 1990 and it differs from its earlier incarnations. The local authority's opinion is now paramount in assessing unfitness, although it is appealable. Regard will be had, though, to earlier case law interpreting the terms used in s 604. The question of what constitutes unfitness is not necessarily one of great dilapidation requiring an expensive series of repairs, nor even of something that threatens the health or safety of the tenant (*Salford CC v McNally* [1976] AC 379). In *Summers v Salford Corporation* [1943] 1 All ER 68, the House of Lords found a house to be unfit for lack of proper ventilation where a defective sash cord prevented a window from opening. Moreover, unfitness may be found where a repairing covenant would not cover the situation. In *Quick v Taff Ely, op. cit.,* at 323, the Court of Appeal found that there had been no breach of the council's implied repairing obligation on the following facts.

The evidence shows that there was severe condensation on the walls, windows and metal surfaces in all the rooms of the house. Water had frequently to be wiped off the walls; paper peeled off the walls and ceilings, woodwork rotted, particularly inside and behind the fitted cupboards in the kitchen. Fungus or mould growth appeared in places and particularly in the two back bedrooms there was a persistent and offensive smell of damp. . . The moisture of the condensation was then absorbed by the atmosphere and transferred to bedding, clothes and other fabrics which became mildewed and rotten. . . There was evidence which the judge accepted that a three piece suite in the living room was ruined by damp so that it smelt and rotted and had to be thrown out . . . I would

conclude that, by modern standards, the house was in winter, when, of course, the condensation was worst, virtually unfit for human habitation.

Under s 604(1)(c) it would, however, qualify as unfit if the damp was prejudicial to the health of the occupants—it might also be 'prejudicial to health' under s 79 Environmental Protection Act 1990, discussed below. *The English House Condition Survey 1991* found that almost 20 per cent of the housing stock, particularly the pre-1919 dwellings, suffers from some form of damp (*op. cit.*, para 6.23 and Figure 7.2). That a major problem relating to such a large proportion of the housing stock should not be within the remit of repairing obligations emphasises the need for unfitness standards as exemplified by s 604.

If the local authority find there is unfitness, then they are obliged to make one of the following orders, and there is no requirement that the expense be reasonable—see Arden's *Introduction* to (1982) 3 HLR.

Housing Act 1985,

s 190A(1) A local housing authority shall not be under a duty to serve a repair notice under subsection (1) or, as the case may be, subsection (1A) of section 189 if, at the same time as they satisfy themselves as mentioned in the subsection in question, they determine—

    (a) that the premises concerned form part of a building which would be a qualifying building in relation to a group repair scheme; and

    (b) that, within the period of twelve months beginning at that time, they expect to prepare a group repair scheme in respect of the qualifying building (in this section referred to as a 'relevant scheme');

but where, having so determined, the authority do serve such a notice, they may do so with respect only to those works which, in their opinion, will not be carried out to the premises concerned in pursuance of the relevant scheme.

  (2) Subject to subsection (3), subsection (1) shall apply in relation to the premises concerned from the time referred to in subsection (1) until the date on which the works specified in a relevant scheme are completed to the authority's satisfaction (as certified under section 130(1) of the Local Government and Housing Act 1989).

s 604A(1) In deciding for the purposes of sections 189, 264, 265 and 289 whether the most satisfactory course of action, in respect of any dwelling-house, house in multiple occupation or building, is, if applicable,—

    (a) serving [a repair] notice under subsection (1) of section 189; or

    (b) serving [a repair] notice under subsection (1A) of that section; or

    (c) making a closing order under subsection (1) of section 264; or

    (d) making a closing order under subsection (2) of that section with respect to the whole or a part of the building concerned; or

    (e) making a demolition order under subsection (1) of section 265; or

    (f) making a demolition order under subsection (2) of that section; or

(g) declaring the area in which the dwelling-house, house in multiple occupation or building is situated to be a clearance area in accordance with section 289;

the local housing authority shall have regard to such guidance as may from time to time be given by the Secretary of State.

[The rest of s 604A deals with the Secretary of State's guidance.]

The landlord has a right of appeal from any decision of the local authority as to the appropriate order to be granted. The tenant should seek a repair notice in most cases under s 189(1) (subject only to the s 190A 'defence'), lest an order be made for the dwelling-house's demolition or closure. The local authority, primarily, have to serve the repair notice under s 189 on the person having control of the premises.

s 189(1) Subject to subsection (1A) where the local housing authority are satisfied that a dwelling-house or house in multiple occupation is unfit for human habitation, they shall serve a repair notice on the person having control of the dwelling-house or house in multiple occupation if they are satisfied, in accordance with section 604A, that serving a notice under this subsection is the most satisfactory course of action.

(1A) Where the local housing authority are satisfied that either a dwelling-house which is a flat or a flat in multiple occupation is unfit for human habitation by virtue of section 604(2), they shall serve a repair notice on the person having control of the part of the building in question if they are satisfied, in accordance with section 604A, that serving a notice under this subsection is the most satisfactory course of action.

(1B) In the case of a house in multiple occupation, a repair notice may be served on the person managing the house instead of on the person having control; and where a notice is so served, then, subject to section 191, the person managing the house shall be regarded as the person having control of it for the purposes of the provisions of this Part following that section.

(2) A repair notice under this section shall—
  (a) require the person on whom it is served to execute the works specified in the notice (which may be works of repair or improvement or both) and to begin those works not later than such reasonable date, being not earlier than the twenty-eighth day after the notice is served, as is specified in the notice and to complete those works within such reasonable time as is so specified, and
  (b) state that in the opinion of the authority the works specified in the notice will render the dwelling-house or, as the case may be, house in multiple occupation fit for human habitation.

(3) The authority, in addition to serving the notice
  (a) on the person having control of the dwelling-house or part of the building concerned or
  (b) on the person having control of or, as the case may be, on the person managing the house in multiple occupation which is concerned

shall serve a copy of the notice on any other person having an interest in the dwelling-house or part of the building or house concerned, whether as free-holder, mortgagee, or lessee.

(4) The notice becomes operative, if no appeal is brought, on the expiration of 21 days from the date of the service of the notice and is final and con-clusive as to matters which could have been raised on an appeal.

(5) A repair notice under this section which has become operative is a local land charge.

(6) This section has effect subject to section 190A.

The Housing Act 1985, s 189 has been amended and repealed with savings under the Housing Act 1988 and the Local Government and Housing Act 1989. The changes, in part, allow the notice to be served on the person managing a house in multiple occu-pation rather than the person having control. However, according to Ormandy, *More Than Safety in Numbers*, ROOF, September/October 1993, p 19, the local authorities have not done enough to protect those living in houses in multiple occu-pation, that is, principally bedsits—*cf.* Mawrey, *Controlling Control Orders*, (1994) 138 Sol Jo.598. The notice must contain details of the prescribed work, which may go beyond mere repairs, the expected starting date (no sooner than 28 days after the date of service of the notice) and the completion date. If the person on whom the notice is served fails to carry out the works in the prescribed time, then the local authority can step in and perform instead under s 193. Where a landlord deliberately fails to carry out the required works, then criminal liability may arise under s 198A.

Table 7.4 Housing action 1982–1992

	Demolished	Closed	Total	Made fit
1982/83	13354	2665	16019	6563
1983/84	8663	2437	11100	7317
1984/85	6980	2771	9751	7795
1985/86	6731	1873	8604	6073
1986/87	5181	1563	6744	5077
1987/88	4585	1748	6333	5040
1988/89	3238	1999	5237	6203
1989/90	4519	1394	5913	5812
1990/91	2465	887	3352	9295
1991/92	1332	890	2222	22326
1992/93	1363	625	1988	29733

Source: Based on information in *Housing and Construction Studies, March Qtr 1994*, Table 2.28. Note: Figures for 1990/91, 1991/92 and 1992/93 use Local Government and Housing Act 1989 definition of unfitness

Of course, sometimes the only option for the tenant is to be rehoused (see *Quick v Taff Ely, op. cit.*, where the local authority rehoused a tenant because of damp), whereupon closure (s 264) and demolition (s 265) orders will be sought along with a termination of tenancy decree from the county court under the Housing Act 1985, s 317. If the whole area is bad, then a clearance order may be made under s 289. The trend, however, seems to be away from closure and demolition towards repair, as Table 7.4 on the previous page indicates with total closures and demolitions shrinking to just 1,988 in 1992/93 compared to 29,733 dwellings made fit.

Continuing to make properties fit, though, requires funding and if the government continues its withdrawal of financial support, then demolition may become prevalent again—Moran, Housing Chair of the Association of Metropolitan Authorities, the *Guardian*2 p 22, 14 January 1994.

Even where a property is not statutorily unfit, the local authority has a discretion under s 190 to serve a repair notice.

s 190(1) Subject to subsection (1B) where the local housing authority–

> (a) are satisfied that a dwelling-house or house in multiple occupation is in such a state of disrepair that, although not unfit for human habitation, substantial repairs are necessary to bring it up to a reasonable standard, having regard to its age, character and locality, or
>
> (b) are satisfied whether on a representation made by an occupying tenant or otherwise that a dwelling-house or house in multiple occupation is in such a state of disrepair that, although not unfit for human habitation, its condition is such as to interfere materially with the personal comfort of the occupying tenant, or in the case of a house in multiple occupation, the persons occupying it (whether as tenants or licensees)
>
> they may serve a repair notice on the person having control of the dwelling-house or house in multiple occupation.

The aim is to keep in good repair the nation's housing stock and to protect tenants—*Hillbank Properties v Hackney LBC* [1978] QB 998 at 1009.

Before moving on to consider the public health laws applicable to the standard of housing, there is one general point that affects both unfitness laws and most of the provisions of the Environmental Health Act 1990. The fact that they are publicly enforced by the local authority prevents their use in favour of council tenants where the dwelling is within the local authority landlord's area. The unfitness provisions and the public health laws can be enforced against private sector landlords, housing associations and against local authority landlords where the dwelling is within the boundaries of another local authority—*R v Cardiff CC, ex parte Cross* (1982) 6 HLR 1 at 12. However, a council tenant within the local authority landlord's own area can only use the Environmental

Protection Act 1990, s 82, considered previously, of the public remedies. The logic that a local authority cannot be plaintiff and defendant in the same action should not deprive council tenants of the rights to decent housing found in the unfitness and public health provisions. The privatisation of council estates does provide this one guaranteed benefit, that the tenants can enforce these provisions against their new landlords through a notice or order served by their former landlord, the local authority. However, it should be possible through some legal fiction or, preferably, a reform in the enforcement procedures to allow council tenants to enforce against their local authority landlord.

(b) Public Health   The Public Health Act 1936 was replaced by ss 79-82 Environmental Protection Act 1990 on 1 January 1991. The 1990 Act standards are not necessarily connected to the unfitness criteria in the 1985 Act—*Salford CC v McNally* [1976] AC 379. The 1990 Act can be used by both residential and commercial tenants.

s 79(1) Subject to subsections (2) to (6) below, the following matters constitute 'statutory nuisances' for the purposes of this Part, that is to say—
  (a) any premises in such a state as to be prejudicial to health or a nuisance;
  (b) smoke emitted from premises so as to be prejudicial to health or a nuisance;
  (c) fumes or gases emitted from premises so as to be prejudicial to health or a nuisance;
  (d) any dust, steam, smell or other effluvia arising on industrial, trade or business premises and being prejudicial to health or a nuisance;
  (e) any accumulation or deposit which is prejudicial to health or a nuisance;
  (f) any animal kept in such a place or manner as to be prejudicial to health or a nuisance;
  (g) noise emitted from premises so as to be prejudicial to health or a nuisance;
  (h) any other matter declared by any enactment to be a statutory nuisance;
  and it shall be the duty of every local authority to cause its area to be inspected from time to time to detect any statutory nuisances which ought to be dealt with under section 80 below and, where a complaint of a statutory nuisance is made to it by a person living within its area, to take such steps as are reasonably practicable to investigate the complaint.

The principal ground for people seeking action under the 1990 Act is that the problem is a nuisance or that it is prejudicial to health. The House of Lords' decision in *NCB v Neath BC* [1976] 2 All ER 478 severely restricted the effectiveness of what is now s 79 by limiting nuisance to what would be either a public or private nuisance at common law. The great disadvantage instituted by this judgment is that where the problem exists in the tenant's own dwelling, he cannot complain of the nuisance—it must emanate from some external source. Only if it is prejudicial to health, that is, according to s 79(7), it is 'injurious, or likely to cause injury, to health' and not merely uncomfortable, will a tenant with a problem coming from his own property be able to seek the council's assistance under the 1990 Act.

If a property is found to violate s 79, then the local authority shall serve an abatement notice under s 80, requiring the nuisance to be abated and any necessary works to be executed or steps to be taken. If it is urgent that the works be carried out, then the local authority notice can inform the relevant person that it will execute the works in nine days and seek compensation—Building Act 1984, s 76 as amended by the 1990 Act. Failure to carry out a 1990 Act abatement notice will result in a fine which will continue to be levied at a daily rate until the necessary action is undertaken. Apart, of course, from the case where the tenant lives in a council property in the local authority's own area, these public health remedies provide a useful supplement to repairing obligations when coupled with the unfitness provisions of the Housing Act 1985. Indeed Tiplady, *Recent Developments in the Law of Landlord and Tenant: The American Experience*, (1981) 44 MLR 129 at p 140 (cited at para 4.22, Law Com. No. 123, *op. cit.*) felt that leasehold repairing covenants failed to prevent serious deterioration and that public remedies were superior.

7.2.6 Summary

The Law Commission Consultation Paper considered several reform options in detail (Law Com. No. 123, *op. cit.*, at pp 51 *et seq.*). The three that mirror the criticisms flowing from earlier comments in this chapter relate to the meaning of repair (paras 5.37 *et seq.*), the restrictions on fitness for human habitation guarantees (paras 5.53 *et seq.*) and the difficulties of enforcement (paras 5.60 *et seq.*). Nevertheless, some of the Law Commission's ideas do not go far enough and would not meet the very real fact that the cost of fixing defective premises may be prohibitive—*cf.* Smith, *Repairing Obligations, op. cit.* The following ideas for reform stem from the arguments presented earlier in this chapter.

The restrictive and uncertain definition of repairs causes wasteful litigation. Merely trying to redefine repairs, though, to include more types of problem is insufficient. Sometimes, where the cause of the damage is an inherent defect, the leasehold obligation may simply require the landlord or tenant to patch over the problem rather than remedy the underlying flaw. A change, as already suggested, to an obligation to keep the premises fit for the intended purpose would be an improvement, though it may not meet the difficulty of the situation where a temporary fix puts off the need for a long term cure. Where the source of the problem is an inherent defect, the only effective measure would be for statute to require landlords to insure against the repair costs—where appropriate, the tenant could be obliged to defray the expenses which, after a suitably long period, maybe fifteen years from the date of completion of the building, could start to reduce. The insurance companies could be subrogated in any action against architects, developers or builders, but the rectifying of the problem with the premises would not be delayed by lengthy court actions.

There are three necessary changes in the law relating to fitness of habitation. First, the definition of unfitness should be harmonized on the Housing Act 1985, s 604. The fact that cases under the Landlord and Tenant Act 1985, s 8 use a different interpretation of unfitness is confusing and unnecessary. Secondly, the rent limits on the Landlord and Tenant Act 1985, s 8 need to be raised, as was recognised by the Court of Appeal in *Quick v Taff Ely, op. cit.*, at 324. Finally, all council tenants need to be able to make use of the rights accorded in relation to unfitness in the Housing Act 1985.

Enforcement of obligations also needs to be streamlined, so that lengthy court actions do not allow premises to deteriorate even further. Specific performance is the best remedy because it achieves the initial aim of the repairing obligation and it should be available to either party. Damages are a useful secondary remedy, especially when the cost of the repair has been borne by the party not under the obligation, but both landlord and tenant, for different reasons, should place a priority on a properly maintained property. For the same reason, set-off is better than a right to withhold rent in order to put pressure on a landlord who is not fulfilling his repairing obligations. As mentioned, council tenants must also be given a means by which to seek the enforcement of unfitness and public health measures.

Other reforms are necessary, too, but if the above were implemented, then the standard of all properties would be easier to uphold.

7.2.7 Improvements

In this context, the issue is whether the tenant has the right to improve the property and the financial consequences of any such improvements. However, alongside these legal aspects, reference should also be made to the system of improvement grants and local authority improvement programmes. Although subject to cuts in the 1980s, the housing stock is preserved to some extent by the various grants available to improve properties that would otherwise be coming to the end of their useful lives—see van Vliet, *op. cit.*, at pp 99–100. Nevertheless, current government strategy towards the funding of improvements generally and, in particular, in the largest residential rental sector, local authority housing, is unclear. The government seems to favour Estate Action schemes, where resources are focussed on radically improving one or two council estates at the expense of general improvements to the local authority's entire housing stock. It leaves local authority landlords unable to take on long-term projects with any certainty that central government funding will be available for the entire period of the project.

Councils are given no guarantees about the level of spending they will be allowed beyond the current year. If [a local authority] signed up [a] multi-million pound contract for Estate Action and its overall spending allocation dropped next year or the year after, the Council might end up unable to do anything other than the Estate Action schemes.

...

[In 1994-95], £373 million of borrowing will be allocated by Estate Action and another £70 million in other Department of the Environment special programmes like converting flats over shops and giving tenants cash payments to buy a private home. This leaves £1038 million for mainstream housing investment programme (HIP) allocations—that is, approval for the council to borrow money for capital work. Ministers decide how 60 per cent of this £1038 million is divided up among the authorities, with 40 per cent allocated according to a needs-based formula. Flexibility is needed to take account of local circumstances, but the discretion given to ministers allows them to impose their political priorities on authorities. Councils have been penalised with reduced allocations for building new homes or refusals to give land free to housing associations.
Even if they succeed in jumping through the hoops, the money available is inadequate. Local authorities have a backlog of work that would cost £8.5 billion to put right, according to the Audit Commission. Council spending [in 1994-95] will be £500 million less than [in 1993-94] because of a £150 million cut in HIP and an estimated £400 million drop in what can be spent from the receipts from council house sales. (*The Guardian* 2 p 19, 17 December 1993)

Further, given that from 1994/95 on, Estate Action will be set against the Single Regeneration Budget which has to cover, amongst other things, the costs associated with Derelict Land Grant and urban development corporations, then central government commitment to Estate Action cannot be relied upon—Wilcox, *Housing Finance Review 1994/95*, 1994, at pp 19 and 159; The Government's Expenditure Plans: Department of the Environment, 1994–95 to 1996–97, Cm 2507, Figures 46 and 85, paras 6.41–6.43, 1994.

7.2.7.1 The Right to Improve

While there may be a right to improve, there can never be an obligation to improve, save in the case of building leases. The tenant has a limited interest in the property and, traditionally, only has to return what has been given, not something better—in one sense, leases are a form of hire contract with the tenant offering up rent in return for the use of certain facilities (Law Com. No. 123, *op. cit.*, para 3.6). However, where the tenant has a long term interest in a property, either through a long lease or through security of tenure guarantees, then he may be willing to invest in order to improve the property and, concomitantly, his own experience of living in or working there. On the other hand, before a tenant can carry out improvements, there are various legal hurdles to be surmounted. For instance, if a tenant makes alterations to the fabric or to the interior of a building, then an action may lie at the hands of the landlord for the tort of waste— *Mancetter Developments, op. cit.* Yet, given the lack of clarity with regard to the tort of waste, this ought to be a minor concern. More pertinent is the Landlord and Tenant Act 1927, s 19(2), which applies to all but agricultural leases. Where the landlord's permission must be sought before improvements can be effected (a 'qualified covenant'), s 19(2) states it must not be unreasonably withheld (a 'fully qualified covenant'),

but this proviso shall not preclude the right to require as a condition of such [permission] the payment of a reasonable sum in respect of any damage to or diminution in the value of the premises or any neighbouring premises belonging to the landlord, and of any legal or other expenses properly incurred in connection with such [permission] nor, in the case of an improvement which does not add to the letting value of the holding, does it preclude the right to require as a condition of such [permission], where such a requirement would be reasonable, an undertaking on the part of the tenant to reinstate the premises in the condition in which they were before the improvement was executed.

Even in the case where central heating is installed, which ought to enhance the value of the letting, it might be that a landlord could seek payment of a reasonable sum for the damage to the floorboards and walls incurred during installation. Where permission is sought under a commercial lease, the tenant's improvement might only be appropriate for the type of business carried on by that tenant and, thus, the second limb of the proviso to s 19(2) may apply, requiring the tenant to reinstate the premises before surrender. In the residential sector, council tenants are subject to a similar regime under the Housing Act 1985, ss 97, 98 and 99, while housing association tenants within the Tenants' Guarantee, *op. cit.*, are similarly constrained in §C6(c).

7.2.7.2 The Right to Compensation for Improvements

Given that an improvement may be carried out by the tenant, the question arises as to compensation for and other financial consequences of that work. While each sector has its own particular system, there are some general principles to be discerned which flow out of a consideration of policy toward tenant farmers' improvements, *inter alia*, in the late nineteenth century.

But in the 1870s Palmerston was dead and a new generation was in power. And the new generation was not afraid of some redistribution of wealth from

landlords to tenants, if that was what was involved in interference with tenancy agreements. To Joseph Chamberlain, for example, the rich already owned far too much of the nation's wealth, and any minor redistributive effect which the legislation might have, would not, for that reason, have made it unwelcome. Not that such redistribution was openly advocated, or indeed, perhaps generally understood to be the result of legislative intervention. To many, legislation to give the tenant farmer . . . compensation for improvements, was simply a matter of fairness. Even if the landlord did not consent to the improvements, what did that matter so long as the improvement was real enough and genuine enough to raise the rental value of the land to an incoming tenant? As the nature of the agricultural lease was tending anyhow to become more of an investment than a social relationship, improvements to the land without the landlord's consent seemed no less justifiable than (say) ploughing back a proportion of company profits into further investments without the shareholders' consent. (Atiyah, *The Rise and Fall of Freedom of Contract*, 1979, p 636)

That such an analysis is not universal can be garnered from the fact that no equivalent right to compensation was developed in commercial leases in France, although in Italy, if effected with the landlord's consent, the value of the improvement is compensable (see RICS, *International Leasing Structures, op. cit.*, at paras 3.2.9 and 5.2.9). In England, Landlord and Tenant Act 1927, s 1, provides that given that certain requirements are met, commercial tenants are entitled to compensation at the termination of the lease. The landlord will be liable to compensate the tenant for the increase in the letting value of the premises at the date of the termination of the lease, not at the date of the improvement. The Law Commission recommended the abolition of this little used right to compensation in 1989 (*Compensation for Tenants' Improvements*, Law Com. No. 178), but no repeal has yet been passed—see Haley, *Compensation for Tenants' Improvements*, (1991) 11 Leg. Stud. 119; and ch 6.4.2.2. The Department of the Environment has accepted the Law Commission's proposals, but it has also acknowledged the need for primary legislation to implement this change; in the meantime, the 1927 Act's compensation scheme remains in place—Department of the Environment Press Release No. 434, 19 July 1994. Furthermore, tenants' improvements are to be ignored on rent review, although the law surrounding this common sense attitude is complex—see ch 8 and Ross, *op. cit.*, paras 6.34 *et seq.* Finally, however, a tenant can take away any trade fixtures at the termination of the lease.

Council tenants' right to carry out improvements is subject to the landlord's consent, but, if given, then there is a system for compensating the tenant. Since 1980, local authorities have had the power under what is now the Housing Act 1985, s 100 to compensate the tenant.

s 100(1) Where a secure tenant has made an improvement and–
          (a) the work on the improvement was begun on or after 3rd October
          1980,

  (b) the landlord, or a predecessor in title of the landlord, has given its
written consent to the improvement or is treated as having given its
consent, and

  (c) the improvement has materially added to the price which the
dwelling-house may be expected to fetch if sold on the open market,
or the rent which the landlord may be expected to be able to charge
on letting the dwelling-house,

the landlord may, at or after the end of the tenancy, make to the tenant
(or his personal representatives) such payment in respect of the
improvement as the landlord considers to be appropriate.

 (2) The amount which a landlord may pay under this section in respect of an
improvement shall not exceed the cost, or likely cost, of the improvement after deducting the amount of any improvement grant, intermediate grant, special grant, repairs grant or common parts grant under Part
XV in respect of the improvement.

(2A) In subsection (2)—

  (a) the reference to an improvement grant under Part XV includes a reference to a renovation grant, disabled facilities grant or HMO grant
under Part VIII of the Local Government and Housing Act 1989; and

  (b) the reference to a common parts grant under Part XV includes a reference to a common parts grant under the said Part VIII.

However, following s 122 Leasehold Reform, Housing and Urban Development
Act 1993, which inserted a new s 99A into the 1985 Act, local authorities are now
under a duty to compensate a qualifying person (Housing Act 1985, s 99B) for any
improvements in line with regulations made by the Secretary of State. There is
some attempt to maintain standards in that s 99A(3)(a) states that the regulations
may prohibit compensation payments where the improvement is not of a prescribed description. There is also power to set a maximum limit on the level of
compensation under s 99A(4). The revised Tenants' Guarantee, *op. cit.*, adopts a
similar approach in §C6(d), despite the fact that the NFHA objected to some of
the detail of the scheme—National Federation of Housing Associations' Formal
Response, *op. cit.*

Council tenants are also protected under the Housing Act 1985 from rent
increases on account of the increase in value of the property resulting from an
improvement effected by the tenant at his own full or partial cost.

s 101(2) In determining, at any time while the improving tenant or his qualifying
successor is a secure tenant of the dwelling-house, whether or to what
extent to increase the rent, the landlord shall treat the improvement as
justifying only such part of an increase which would otherwise be attributable to the improvement as corresponds to the part of the cost which
was not borne by the tenant (and accordingly as not justifying an
increase if he bore the whole cost).

The most elaborate structure to provide for compensation is found in the agricultural sector. That is due to the nature of agricultural leases. Whereas in the residential sector, the lease is taken on to provide a home for the tenant and anyone normally resident with him, and the level of quality is usually determined by the rent the tenant can afford at the outset, and a commercial lease is entered into in order to provide the most appropriate 'shell' for the business' work, the very essence of an agricultural lease is that the tenant will improve the quality, and, thus, the value of the demise itself, that is, the farm. Indeed, compensation for special system farming recognizes that the tenant has instituted a more beneficial system of farming than is required by the lease or practised by other comparable farms (Agricultural Holdings Act 1986, s 70). Compensation schemes have been in place since 1875 and are now to be found in the Agricultural Holdings Act 1986 (Rodgers, *Agricultural Law, op. cit.*, pp 2–3). The reform planned for the agricultural sector recognizes as one of its principal aims the need to continue the compensation scheme for improvements—MAFF *News Release 337/93*, p 2, 6 October 1993. Thus, agricultural tenants will continue to receive compensation payments for both short-term and long-term improvements, although the precise mechanisms will be altered. Short-term improvements are presently governed by the Agricultural Holdings Act 1986, s 64(1) and Sch 8 along with Part I of the Schedule to the Agriculture (Calculation of Value for Compensation) Regulations 1978 (SI 1978 No. 809, as amended), Sch, Part I. Short-term improvements benefit only the incoming tenant. Long-term improvements, that is, those improvements not benefitting just the incoming tenant, are dealt with principally in the Agricultural Holdings Act 1986, Sch 7. There are other specific improvements, such as special system farming (1986 Act, s 70) and tenant right (s 65)—see also, ch 6.5.2.2 and 6.5.2.3.

Overall, there is no coherent policy towards improvements in the various rental sectors. There is statutory intervention in agricultural leases to reflect the essence of the tenant's interest in the very demise, while statutory compensation exists for council tenants because of the inequality of bargaining power. The lack of a provision for private sector and housing association tenants can only reflect a desire to allow market forces to operate freely.

7.3 USER

As part of the general management of the property, it is usual to have some kind of restriction in the lease on what the tenant is allowed to use the premises for. This is known as a user restriction. Independently of this restriction, there will be other factors that affect the way in which the premises can be used: planning restrictions, the law on nuisance and restrictions in any superior title.

With residential property it is common for the lease to state that the property can be used 'as a single private dwelling only'. Most leases contain general prohibitions on use for 'immoral or illegal purposes', or use that causes a nuisance, annoyance or disturbance to neighbours (see also, ch 11.4.2).

With commercial leases of individual properties, the user clauses will be directed at protecting the landlord's financial interest in the property (see Yates and Hawkins, *Landlord and Tenant Law*, 2nd edn, 1986, p 123). Where the lease is of one unit in a larger development, the user provisions will be geared to securing that the development as a whole works efficiently since, for example, in a shopping complex, both the landlord and the tenant will normally wish to ensure that there are no competing businesses in the immediate vicinity within the development and to maintain a balance of different retail outlets. For a discussion of other purposes that may be served by a user clause, see Law Commission, *Covenants Restricting Dispositions, Alterations and Change of User*, Law Com No. 141, 1985, paras 4.37–4.44.

7.3.1 Width and Variation of User Clauses

If the user clause is narrowly drawn, permitting a very limited range of uses of the property, this will enable the landlord to exercise tight management control over the premises. In a shopping complex, for example, the landlord may need to narrowly restrict user clauses so that he can ensure that all of the shoppers' needs are met. For instance, the shopper will expect a greengrocer, a butcher, a baker, a video store *etc.* Unless the tenant is confined to a particular use, there is a risk that he may simply abandon a low profit use in favour of a more profitable one. A narrow clause will, however, have an adverse effect upon the rent which the landlord is able to receive upon review (unless there is a wider hypothetical user clause assumed for the purposes of reviewing the rent; see ch 8): see *Plinth Property Investments Ltd v Mott, Hay and Anderson* (1978) 38 P & CR 361, where the rent was £89,200 per annum with user limited to civil engineering business, and £130,455 per annum without such a restriction. From the tenant's point of view, a wide user clause is advantageous in that it gives him a range of permitted uses and will make the lease easier to assign. It will also, however, generally result in higher levels of rent being awarded on review.

There are various ways in which the user clause may be drafted. It may be absolute, making no provision for the user clause to be changed in the future, for example, 'not to use the premises otherwise than as a single private dwelling-house'. The Law Commission felt that landlords might have legitimate management reasons for imposing absolute user covenants and rejected the suggestion that such covenants should no longer be allowed (see Law Com. No. 141, *op. cit.*, esp. at para 4.44). Alternatively, the user covenant may be qualified, for example, 'not to use the premises otherwise than as an office without the consent of the landlord'. Or it may be fully qualified, requiring the tenant to obtain consent for a change of use, but also providing that the landlord may not withhold his consent unreasonably. An example of a fully qualified covenant is found in *Costain Property Developments Ltd v Finlay & Co Ltd* (1988) 57 P & CR 345:

[The tenant is] . . . not without the previous consent of the landlord (such consent not to be unreasonably withheld in the case of a retail use within the meaning of Class I of the . . . Use Classes Order 1972 . . . which is consistent with the principles of good estate management and which does not in the reasonable opinion of the landlord adversely affect . . . the interests of the landlord or other tenants of the development . . .) to use . . . the demised premises other than for the purposes of retail sale of tobacco confectionery . . . newspapers magazines fancy goods . . . (etc).

There are several situations in which a tenant may wish to change the user clause—for example, if his own business interests change so that they would no longer be within the permitted use, or if he wishes to assign the lease to a tenant intending to use the premises for different purposes. However, unless the provision is fully qualified the landlord can refuse consent on any ground. This differs from the approach with both alienation and improvement clauses, where statute provides that in the case of a qualified covenant 'consent is not to be unreasonably withheld' (Landlord and Tenant Act 1927, s 19(1)(a) and (2); see ch 9 (alienation) 7.2.7.1 above (improvements)). In relation to user clauses, s 19(3) Landlord and Tenant Act 1927 provides:

s 19(3) In all leases . . . containing a covenant condition or agreement against the alteration of the user of the demised premises, without licence or consent, such covenant condition or agreement shall, if the alteration does not involve any structural alteration of the premises, be deemed, notwithstanding any express provision to the contrary, to be subject to a proviso that no fine or sum of money in the nature of a fine, whether by way of increase of rent or otherwise, shall be payable for or in respect of such licence or consent; but this proviso does not preclude the right of the landlord to require payment of a reasonable sum in respect of any damage to or diminution in the value of the premises or any neighbouring premises belonging to him and of any legal or other expenses incurred in connection with such licence or consent.

Where a dispute as to the reasonableness of any such sum has been determined by a court of competent jurisdiction, the landlord shall be bound to grant the licence or consent on payment of the sum so determined to be reasonable.

This section does not apply to agricultural leases or mining leases (s 19(4)).

The effect is that, in the case of qualified covenants, the landlord has no incentive to consent to a request for a change of use—he is under no legal obligation to act reasonably, and has no commercial incentive to consent as he cannot charge a premium or a higher rent for doing so, even though the change in use might actually make the lease more valuable to the tenant. If the tenant is also seeking consent for alterations, as will frequently happen when he is seeking to change the use of the premises, then the restriction in s 19(3) on asking for money from the tenant does not apply. Qualified covenants can be misleading—the reference to consent suggests that consent can be obtained, yet, as previously mentioned, consent does not have to be given. The Law Commission have, therefore, recommended that it should no longer be possible to have qualified user covenants— the covenant must be either absolute or fully qualified (see Law Com. No. 141, *op. cit.*).

Where the lease contains a fully qualified user provision, it is thought that, in order to determine whether or not the landlord is acting reasonably, similar principles will apply as in the case of alienation clauses (Woodfall, *Landlord and Tenant*, Vol 1, para 11.195; *Tollbench Ltd v Plymouth City Council* [1988] 1 EGLR 79; *Sood v Barker* [1991] 23 EG 112; see ch 9.3.2.3). In considering whether or not the landlord has acted reasonably in refusing consent to change use, the court will look to the purpose for which the original user covenant was imposed and whether the landlord, in refusing consent, was seeking to further that purpose or was seeking a collateral advantage: see *Anglia Building Society v Sheffield City Council* (1982) 266 EG 311.

There are other miscellaneous statutory provisions that may enable the tenant to change the use of the premises. The Housing Act 1985, s 610 is designed to facilitate the conversion of large houses into two or more dwellings. Where the conversion is prohibited or restricted, for example, by the terms of a lease, the section enables the county court to approve a modification either:

1 If changes in the character of the neighbourhood make it difficult to let as a single dwelling and it would be easier to let as converted units; or
2 If planning permission has been granted for its use when converted.

There is also power under the Law of Property Act 1925, s 84 to apply to the Land Tribunal for an obsolete restrictive covenant to be modified when the original lease was for more than 40 years and at least 25 years of the term have expired. The covenant can be discharged or modified where, *inter alia*, the covenant has been made obsolete by changes in the character of the property, the neighbourhood, or other circumstances.

7.3.2 User Clauses Restricting Trade

Certain industries have the practice of using 'tied' leases—leases of public houses may contain a tie requiring the tenant to purchase specified beers and drinks from the landlord; similarly leases of service stations may require the tenant to purchase petrol supplies from the landlord. If found to be in restraint of trade, these provisions will be illegal and unenforceable, although they will generally be severable from the rest of the lease. There is some uncertainty as to whether or not the doctrine of restraint of trade applies to trading restrictions in leases. The House of Lords, in *Esso Petroleum Co Ltd v Harper's Garage (Stourport) Ltd* [1968] AC 269, stated that the doctrine does not apply to restrictive covenants in leases, on the grounds that the tenant is not giving up a previously enjoyed freedom and, so, is not being restrained:

A person buying or leasing land had no previous right to be there at all, let alone to trade there and when he takes possession of that land subject to a negative restrictive covenant, he gives up no right or freedom which he previously had ... (*per* Lord Reid at 298; also see Lord Pearce at 325, and Lord Wilberforce at 333. *Cf.* the position in Australia: the case of *Quadramain Pty Ltd v Sevastopol Investments Pty Ltd* (1976) 133 CLR 390 followed the reasoning of the House of Lords in *Esso* and precipitated a change in the trade practices legislation to make clear that the legislation applied to leases: see ss 4H, 47 Trade Practices Act 1974 (Commonwealth). The Australian legislation regulates covenants affecting competition and 'exclusive dealing' (*cf.* ties), see Bradbrook and Croft, *Commercial Tenancy Law in Australia,* 1990, ch 12)

Given that the doctrine is based on protecting the public interest, it is hard to accept that the restraint of trade doctrine is incapable of applying to leases (see Treitel, *The Law of Contract,* 8th edn, 1991, pp 420–2). If the doctrine does apply, then whether a covenant is in restraint of trade will depend on whether the restraint is reasonable as between the parties and with reference to the public interest (*Nordenfelt v Maxim Nordenfelt Guns and Ammunition Co* [1894] AC 535; *Lobb (Alec) (Garages) Ltd v Total Oil GB Ltd* [1985] 1 All ER 303). In the case of leases, most restrictions are likely to be found to be reasonable.

There is also a risk that user clauses restricting competing businesses, or restricting the tenant's ability to deal with the landlord's competitors, might offend European Community competition rules where the effect of the clause, taken together with similar clauses in other leases from the same landlord, is to affect trade between Member States (see Treaty of Rome Articles 85 (anti-competitive agreement) and 86 (abuse of dominant position); *Inntrepeneur Estates Ltd v Mason* [1993] 45 EG 130; *Inntrepeneur Estates (GL) Ltd v Boyes* [1993] 47 EG 140; Roxburgh [1994] Prop Rev 41; Frazer [1994] Conv 150). The issue normally arises in the context of a network of similar agreements, such as 'standard' leases from a brewery landlord, and a provision in an individual lease will not generally have sufficient effect on trade between Member States. Failure to comply with Articles 85 and 86 may lead to unenforceability of the offending provisions (although they may be severed from the rest of the lease), fines and liability in damages. Issues can also arise under UK competition law, although the impact of the Restrictive Trade Practices Act 1976 has been much blunted by *Re Ravenseft Properties Application* [1978] QB 52.

In the case of tied leases, at least historically, the landlord has been involved in the tenancy relationship primarily as a means of securing outlets for its products. The return on the property investment was obtained not only through rent, but also through the product sales, such as the number of barrels sold. In *Caerns Motor Services Ltd v Texaco Ltd, Geedes v Texaco Ltd* [1994] 1 WLR 1249, a case involving leases of petrol stations with solus agreements for the tenants to sell only petroleum products and fuel supplied by the landlord, evidence was given as to the difference in rental income with and without the tie. The lease of one site was at a rent of £12,000 per annum, the rental value without the tie was £63,500 per annum. Similar ratios were presented for the other leases with ties. Tied leases also tended to be relatively short term arrangements—in the *Caerns Motor Services* case, *op. cit.*, the leases were for three years. This is less true nowadays, particularly in the case of the brewing industry. The change followed the report of the Monopolies and Mergers Commission on the supply of beer which led to controls on tied leases of public houses and allowed only partial ties (see Monopolies and Mergers Commission, *Supply of Beer*, Cm 651, 1989; Supply of Beer (Loan Ties, Licensed Premises and Wholesale Prices) Order 1989, SI 1989 No. 2558; Supply of Beer (Tied Estate) Order 1989, SI 1989 No. 2390). The result has been that the breweries now see their property holdings as commercial interests in their own right and they have turned to more conventional leasing structures, including long leases, market based rents and upwards only rent reviews.

7.4 INSURANCE

In the case of short, rack rent leases it is the landlord who will invariably insure the property because of what he stands to lose if there is no insurance. The lease may make no reference to insurance. With longer leases, the lease will normally include some fairly complex provisions relating to insurance. These provisions will need to cover such things as how much the property is to be insured for (market value, or the cost of rebuilding with modern materials, or the cost of exact reinstatement) and what risks are to be insured against (fire, storm, flood etc.). If the property is destroyed, both the landlord and the tenant potentially lose something of value. The lease will, therefore, need to state who is responsible for taking out insurance on the property. In addition, the lease should make provision for several other related issues that will be important should the property in fact be damaged or destroyed, such as, who is liable to rebuild the property and whether the tenant continues to be liable for rent during the period for which the property is unusable.

7.4.1 Responsibility and Liability for Insurance

The question of who should insure the property involves two separate issues: who is responsible for effecting the insurance, and who pays for the cost of the insurance (liability). With clear leases, the cost of the insurance is borne by the tenant, either by the tenant taking out the insurance (a full repairing and insuring lease) or, more usually, by the landlord insuring the property and recouping the cost of doing so from the tenant via the service charge (a full recovery lease). Where it is the landlord who effects the insurance at the tenant's expense, there is no obligation to 'shop around' for the cheapest insurance (*Bandar Property Holdings Ltd v J S Darwen (Successors) Ltd* [1968] 2 All ER 305; see also *Havenridge Ltd v Boston Dyers Ltd* [1994] EG 111).

Where the tenant has a lease of part of a building, the insurance will be taken out by the landlord as it is impractical for individual tenants to take out buildings insurance for only part of a building. In multi-occupied buildings, the landlord will also usually be the person responsible for repairs. If the building is damaged by fire, it is the landlord who is liable to repair or rebuild. In this way, responsibility for insurance mirrors the provisions for repair—the landlord will be responsible for external and structural repairs, and will also be the party who insures the building against the risk of damage. The *cost* of both items will, however, generally be shared amongst all the tenants of the building.

The issue is not so straightforward with leases of an entire building. Often, the lease will make the tenant liable to repair the building and, it can be argued, the responsibility for insurance should follow the responsibility for repair. If the building is destroyed by fire, the tenant is liable to rebuild under the repairing covenant and so needs to be sure that there will be insurance monies available for this purpose. On the other hand, the landlord may feel it unwise to rely simply upon the covenant of the tenant, and likewise desires the comfort of being in control of the insurance and making sure that the monies will in fact be available. Irrespective of the merits of the tenant's case for effecting the insurance, the norm, in practice, is now for the landlord to take control of insuring the property. There are ways in which the tenant can seek to secure some further protection, to make sure, *inter alia*, that the insurance is, in fact, taken out. If the lease requires the insurance to be taken out in the 'joint names' of the landlord and tenant, then both parties will be notified when the policy is due for renewal, and any insurance monies paid out will be paid into the joint names of the landlord and tenant, giving the tenant a say in the reinstatement of the building. Joint names insurance will also prevent the insurers from exercising rights of subrogation against the tenant where the tenant has caused the damage (but note that even where the insurance is in the landlord's name alone, insurers may not be able to exercise rights of subrogation against the tenant when he has contributed to the premium: *Mark Rowlands Ltd v Berni Inns Ltd* [1986] QB 211, and see Ross, *op. cit.*, para 10.18). Joint names insurance is not possible in the case of a multi-tenanted building, nor will the landlord always agree to it even if the lease is of an entire building. In this event, the tenant can still ask for his name to be noted on the policy. The effect of being noted on the policy is, again, that the insurers cannot sue the tenant by subrogation (*Petrofina (UK) Ltd v Magnaload Ltd* [1984] 1 QB 127) and should also mean that if the policy does lapse then the tenant will be notified (see Ross, *op. cit.*, para 10.19).

7.4.2 Application of the Insurance Proceeds

In the event of the building being damaged by any of the insured risks, the insurance monies will normally be spent on reinstating the premises. If, however, they are not so spent for some reason, several difficult issues arise, especially where the insurance is not in joint names and so the tenant does not automatically receive any of the insurance proceeds.

When insurance is the responsibility of the landlord, a well drafted lease will usually provide that the landlord must spend the insurance proceeds on reinstating the building. What happens if there is no such covenant in the lease? This occurred in *Mumford Hotels Ltd v Wheler* [1964] 1 Ch 117. The lease provided that the landlord was to insure the property and the tenant was to pay the cost of insurance to the landlord. The leased hotel was destroyed by fire and the insurance monies were paid to the landlord, but the landlord refused to reinstate the hotel and was not under a contractual obligation to do so. The tenant succeeded in its claim that the insurance proceeds must be spent on reinstating the property. Harman LJ rejected the idea that such a reinstatement obligation could be contractually implied but, rather, based his decision on the idea that where a tenant is paying for the insurance, the landlord has some kind of quasi-fiduciary obligation:

... Mrs. Wheler's [the landlord's] obligation to insure, done as it was at the tenant's expense, was an obligation intended to enure for the benefit of both parties, and ... Mrs. Wheler cannot simply put the money in her pocket and disregard the company's [the tenant's] claim. (at 126–7)

Later, in *Vural Ltd v Security Archives Ltd* (1989) 60 P & CR 258, Knox J implied that this obligation could arise equally from an implied contractual obligation as from a proprietary obligation, but again reached the view that rights under the insurance policy must be exercised 'in such a way as to preserve the tenant's interest in what he has paid for' (at 273).

The tenant may also have rights under the Fires Prevention (Metropolis) Act 1774, s 83. Notwithstanding the title of the Act, it applies throughout England and

Wales. Section 83 provides that 'any person or persons' 'interested in' a building can request the insurance company to 'cause the insurance money to be laid out and expended, as far as the same will go, towards rebuilding, reinstating, or rebuilding' the property. The Act is fairly limited in its application, for example, covering only fire insurance and not other insured risks, but, when applicable, will enable the tenant (or landlord) to ask for the insurance monies to be spent on rebuilding.

Rebuilding is not always possible; the issue then is who is entitled to the insurance proceeds. In *Re King, decd.* [1963] 1 Ch 459, it was not possible to rebuild after a fire, initially because of building restrictions and later because the land was compulsorily purchased. The insurance had been taken out by the tenant in the joint names of the landlord and tenant and the proceeds were paid into a joint account. The Court of Appeal held that the proceeds belonged solely to the tenant. However, Lord Denning MR's dissent on this point is more generally regarded as correct. Lord Denning MR placed great weight on the insurance being in joint names, and felt that the money 'should be divided proportionately to the interests of landlord and tenant in the property' (at 486). Proportionate division was ordered in *Beacon Carpets Ltd v Kirby* (1984) 48 P & CR 445, where the parties had both accepted that the premises would not be rebuilt as the tenants had found new premises. The Court of Appeal held that the monies were to be shared between landlord and tenant in proportions that reflected their respective interests in the building immediately before it was destroyed. *Re King* was distinguished on the grounds that rebuilding had in that case been made impossible and that in *Re King* the repairing obligation had been the tenant's, whereas in *Beacon Carpets* it was the landlord who had an obligation to reinstate (Browne-Wilkinson LJ at 454). Neither of these distinguishing features is particularly persuasive. While each case turns on its own particular facts, the trend of these cases is that where the tenant has borne the cost of insurance both parties should be seen as having some interest in the proceeds.

7.5 ESTATE MANAGEMENT

In the case of multi-occupied property, good estate management is important for the prosperity of the development, both for tenants and for landlords. Estate management goes beyond ensuring that the fabric of the property is well maintained. This is particularly true in shopping complexes. While some of the factors that will affect the success of the development are external to the lease and management policies (such as the proximity to car park facilities, transport routes, and prime shopping areas), the success of the development will also depend upon good estate management. As shopping trends change it may, for example, be necessary to refurbish and renovate the centre at intervals to remain attractive to the shopping public. In order to maintain the attractiveness of a complex, it will be necessary to ensure that entrance ways are kept clear, external surfaces are not covered with posters and graffiti, access routes are clean and so on. A well drafted lease will contain covenants to regulate tenant behaviour, such as:

. . . not to affix upon any part of the exterior of the demised premises or in any windows a signboard, poster, facia, placard or advertisement except as may previously have been approved by the lessors. (as in *Bristol and West Building Society v Marks and Spencer plc* [1991] 2 EGLR 57)

To keep the display windows, if any, of the demised unit dressed and illuminated in a suitable manner in keeping with a good class shopping centre unless prevented by matters or circumstances beyond the tenant's reasonable control and to keep the windows of those parts of the demised unit which are used for storage purposes obscured to the satisfaction of the landlord. (as in *F W Woolworth plc v Charlwood Alliance Properties Ltd* [1987] 1 EGLR 53)

In addition to specific leasehold covenants it is common to reserve general powers to make management regulations from time to time which can deal with every day matters of management, such as refuse collection.

Good estate management also requires a careful letting policy. It will be important to secure a good mix of tenants and to ensure that any voids are filled as quickly as possible. Surveys of shopping habits have found that the range of shops available within a shopping mall is a very important factor in determining where consumers choose to shop, second only to the importance of its location (see Ford, *Breathing New Life into Ailing Shopping Centres*, [1994] 4 PR 116, at p 117). Critical to the success of most shopping complexes will be the presence of an anchor tenant—in *Transworld Land Co Ltd v J Sainsbury plc*, [1990] 2 EGLR 255, Sainsbury's was the anchor tenant in a shopping centre that was no longer a prime site. When Sainsbury's closed its store, the trade of the other retail units in the centre fell off by up to 50 per cent.

To secure the vitality of a centre, it is also common to impose a covenant requiring a tenant to keep the shop open during normal business hours (but this general wording will not require it to open on a Sunday unless the lease specifically requires Sunday opening, Sunday Trading Act 1994, s 3). Such a covenant will be broken by a store closing down altogether, as well as by a store failing to open during the required hours. Although a store that closes would still remain liable for rent even in the absence of such a covenant, the advantage of such a covenant is that the landlord may be able to claim damages for breach of covenant, in addition to the rent. Actions for breach of such covenants were involved in *Transworld Land Co Ltd v J Sainsbury plc, op. cit.*; *F W Woolworth plc v Charlwood Alliance Properties Ltd, op. cit.*; and *Costain Property Developments Ltd v Finlay & Co Ltd* (1988) 57 P & CR 345. Closure of a store in breach of this covenant may have a substantial impact on the development. This is shown by the findings in the *Costain* case following the closure of Finlays, a 'well known multiple retailer of confectionery, newspapers and journals, stationery and (at that time) tobacco' (at 346). After the Finlays store had closed, the reversioners tried to sell the reversionary interests in the whole development:

(a) **The fact that the Finlays shop was closed had a detrimental effect upon the attractiveness of the Centre in the eyes of shoppers, of prospective assignees of shops, and of investors . . .**
(d) **The fact that the shop was closed greatly reduced, and perhaps eliminated, for the vendors the possibility that an institution would bid.**
(e) **The fact that the shop was closed also reduced the attractiveness of the freehold investment to a property company.**
(f) **It is more likely than not that if the shop had been open, a bid higher than £4.35 million [the price paid] would have been received from GPE [the purchaser of the reversionary interests] or from some other property company or from an institution.** (*per* Bernstein QC at 353)

During the marketing of the Centre to potential investors, there were a number of other stores also on the market, but, even so, the drop in the value of the reversionary interests caused by the closure of the Finlays store alone was found to be £180,000. The landlord may also suffer non-financial loss if a large store closes; in *Braddon Towers v International Stores Ltd* [1987] 1 EGLR 209, it was accepted that the landlord would suffer damage to its reputation as a developer/landlord by having an unsuccessful centre in its portfolio (at 211). It is not only the landlord who will suffer loss from the closure of an anchor store. Smaller retailers in the precinct may be heavily dependent for their customers on shoppers drawn into the centre by the anchor store. Local residents will also be affected, as in *Braddon Towers* where they signed a petition to try to stop the shop being closed. When an anchor store threatens to close, what is often wanted by the landlord, other tenants and local residents, is an injunction to stop the store from closing. However, even where the proposed closure is in clear breach of the lease, the courts are unable to grant an injunction and can only award damages: *F W Woolworth Plc v Charlwood Alliance Properties Ltd, op. cit.*; *Braddon Towers v International Stores Ltd, op. cit.*

7.6 SERVICE CHARGES

As we have seen, there are various situations in which the landlord is responsible for repair while tenants are expected to bear the cost of the repairs. The landlord will recover the costs from the tenants through a service charge, which will cover not only repairing costs but other management costs, such as cleaning and heating of common parts, external decoration, the employment of managing agents and caretakers, and the cost of building insurance. In a full recovery (clear) lease, the aim of the service charge provisions will be to ensure that the costs of property management are passed onto the tenant so that the landlord receives a 'clear rent'. Service charges are used in commercial lettings where the landlord has property management costs; such as multi-tenanted office blocks, shopping centres and business parks. Even if the units are freestanding they may share common services such as landscaping of the grounds, lighting and maintenance of communal roads. Service charges may also be used in residential lettings, particularly with flats which share common parts, whether rented or sold on long leases. The service charge cannot, however, include the recovery of costs in respect of items for which the landlord has been made responsible by statute: *Campden Hill Towers Ltd v Gardner* [1977] QB 823 at 832.

The entitlement of the landlord to a service charge will depend upon the terms of the contract. The service charge provisions will need to set out what services the landlord can recover payment for, how this is to be paid, and how each tenant's share of the total cost is to be allocated. The clause may either state in general terms that the tenant is to pay a *fair proportion* of the landlord's expenditure, or set out a formula for working out that share. The formula might, for example, provide for the tenant to pay a fixed percentage of the total expenditure, the percentage being based on the proportion that the floor area let to the tenant bears in relation to the floor area of the whole development (see Ross, *op. cit.*, at paras 11.8–11.11 for the advantages and disadvantages of different approaches, and see *Pole Properties Ltd v Feinberg* (1981) 43 P & CR 121, where the Court of Appeal, in an unorthodox decision, varied the fixed proportion that a tenant was liable to pay after the acquisition of further property by the landlord meant the tenant's fixed share was no longer a 'fair and reasonable' proportion).

The service charge will often provide for a 'sinking fund' to cover the costs of major items of expenditure that will be needed at irregular intervals, such as the cost of re-roofing or replacing boilers and lifts. The landlord may even be building up a fund for eventual replacement of the building itself (see Ross, *op. cit.*, para 11.21). The idea of the sinking fund is that the landlord anticipates future expense and, through the service charge, builds up a reserve to draw on, spreading the cost of major capital items over a number of years. Whether or not a sinking fund can legitimately be called part of the clear lease has been challenged. It is argued that making financial provision for major equipment and rebuilding goes beyond the concept of 'servicing and maintaining':

The 'clear lease' is an income concept. The building is provided (for profit) by a developer usually acting in conjunction with a funding institution. The rent paid by the tenant is the return for the landlord (whether he is the developer or institution or a subsequent purchaser) on his capital investment. The tenant pays for the use (i.e. occupation) of the landlord's capital (i.e. the building): he is not expected to replace it. Looked at in this way, it is no more incompatible with a clear lease that the landlord should himself meet the cost of e.g. design defects inherent in the building than that the landlord should accept depreciation in the

relative value of the building itself as it ages. (Hill and Redman, *Law of Landlord and Tenant*, 18th edn, vol 3, G[378])

The width of the service charge concept in English leases is said to contribute significantly to the strength of the United Kingdom property market in attracting institutional investment.

The division between responsibility for property management and liability for the costs of property management creates tensions with the recovery of service charge payments. A study on the impact of the Landlord and Tenant Act 1987 describes service charges and the issue of accounting and consultation as 'incendiary issues' (Thomas *et al.*, *op. cit.*, para 4.2). Similarly, the Nugee Committee found dissatisfaction with service charges (The Nugee Committee Report, *op. cit.*, paras 5.1, 5.6, 5.35).

One area of contention lies in the fact that, although the tenant is frequently obliged to pay for all services provided, there is often no corresponding obligation on the landlord to provide anything beyond essential services. Frequently the lease will impose an obligation on the landlord to provide certain essential services, with an option (but no obligation) to provide other services—beyond essential services the landlord wishes to be free to choose what work is needed and when it should be done (see Ross, *op. cit.*, paras 11.14, 11.17). The courts will not generally be willing to impose a contractual obligation on the landlord to perform the services, even if the lease provides for the tenant to pay the landlord's expenses in performing these additional services: *Sleafer v Lambeth Borough Council* [1960] 1 QB 43, *Duke of Westminster v Guild* [1985] QB 688 (although exceptionally they may do so: *Barnes v City of London Real Property Co* [1918] 2 Ch 18, *Edmonton Corpn v W M Knowles & Son Ltd* (1961) 60 LGR 124). In some cases this can lead to the landlord not providing an adequate range of services. In other situations it can lead to 'over-servicing'. The study on the 1987 Act reported many tenants feeling that managing agents were making money out of them,

providing too many services that were not required by the tenants—landscaping, re-roofing and 'over-decorating' the common parts of the building . . . (Thomas *et al.*, *op. cit.*, para 4.2).

A further question relates to how much the landlord can charge for services. As the landlord has control of property management, there is a danger that he will provide a very high level of services, using highly priced contractors who have to be paid for by the tenants. In the commercial sector this is again a matter for contractual negotiation. The tenants will generally be liable for all costs incurred by the landlord in the provision of services, unless they can negotiate for them to be 'reasonable costs' for 'reasonably required' services. Nevertheless, in *Finchbourne v Rodrigues* [1976] 3 All ER 581 (a residential case), the Court of Appeal was prepared to imply a term that the service charges must be 'fair and reasonable':

It cannot be supposed that the plaintiffs were entitled to be as extravagant as they chose in the standards of repair, the appointment of porters etc . . . [T]he parties cannot have intended that the landlords should have an unfettered discretion to adopt the highest conceivable standard and to charge the tenant with it. (*per* Cairns LJ at 587)

In *Pole Properties Ltd v Feinberg, op. cit.*, the Court of Appeal changed the charging system from one based on floor space which bore no relation to heating use, to one which they considered 'fair and reasonable' and which related to the use the tenant made of the central heating. These cases are likely to be narrowly confined as courts are generally reluctant to imply such terms into contracts. In *Havenridge Ltd v Boston Dyers Ltd, op. cit.*, Evans LJ was reluctant to treat *Finchbourne v Rodrigues* as a precedent and, in the case before him, he rejected the argument that reimbursement of insurance premiums 'properly expend[ed]' in 'some insurance office of repute' was limited to the amount of 'reasonable premiums':

The suggested implication of 'reasonably' or 'reasonable' is neither necessary nor was it clearly intended, though left unexpressed, by the parties to these contracts. (*Havenridge Ltd v Boston Dyers Ltd, op. cit.*, at 113)

Nevertheless, the Court of Appeal did accept that the tenant would be protected from having to pay wholly extravagant or outlandish claims. While the landlord did not have to show that the amount claimed was 'reasonable', the tenant only had to reimburse the landlord for premiums which reflected the 'going rate' in the market place:

The limitation [on the tenant's obligation to indemnify the landlord] . . . can best be expressed by saying that the landlord cannot recover in excess of the premium which he has paid and agreed to pay in the ordinary course of business as between the insurer and himself. If the transaction was arranged otherwise than in the normal course of business, for whatever reason, then it can be said that the premium was not properly paid, having regard to the commercial nature of the leases in question, or, equally, it can be supposed that the both parties would have agreed with the officious bystander that the tenant should not be liable for a premium which had not been arranged in that way. (*per* Evans LJ, *Havenridge Ltd v Boston Dyers Ltd, op cit.*, at 113)

In the residential sector, there are various controls on service charges, first introduced in the Housing Finance Act 1972. The Landlord and Tenant Act 1985, s 19, originally limited to flats but extended to 'dwellings' by the Landlord and Tenant Act 1987, limits service charge recovery to costs that are 'reasonably incurred':

s 19(1) Relevant costs shall be taken into account in determining the amount of a service charge payable for a period—
       (a) only to the extent that they are reasonably incurred, and

    (b) where they are incurred on the provision of services or the carrying out of works, only if the services or works are of a reasonable standard;

and the amount payable shall be limited accordingly.

(2) Where a service charge is payable before the relevant costs are incurred, no greater amount than is reasonable is so payable, and after the relevant costs have been incurred any necessary adjustment shall be made by repayment, reduction or subsequent charges or otherwise.

'Relevant costs' and 'service charge' are defined in s 18:

s 18(1) . . . 'service charge' means an amount payable by a tenant of a dwelling as part of or in addition to the rent—
    (a) which is payable, directly or indirectly, for services, repairs, maintenance or insurance or the landlord's costs of management, and
    (b) the whole or part of which varies or may vary according to the relevant costs.

(2) The relevant costs are the costs or estimated costs incurred or to be incurred by or on behalf of the landlord, or a superior landlord, in connection with the matters for which the service charge is payable.

(3) For this purpose—
    (a) 'costs' includes overheads, and
    (b) costs are relevant costs in relation to a service charge whether they are incurred, or to be incurred, in the period for which the service charge is payable or in an earlier or later period.

This provision does not apply to public sector tenants unless their lease is for more than 21 years (s 26, and see also ch 12.5.1.5). Where the lease permits the landlord to charge the tenants for the cost of 'improvements', this is not caught by the 'reasonableness' test as improvements go beyond servicing etc. and are not therefore covered by the statutory wording (*Sutton (Hastoe) Housing Association v Williams* (1988) 20 HLR 321).

Notwithstanding the legislation, many residential tenants remain dissatisfied over service charges—being charged too much for poor quality services, and finding it difficult to challenge service charge demands (Thomas *et al.*, *op. cit.*, para 4.2).

Another difficulty stemming from the division of responsibility and liability is that tenants feel excluded from management decisions. The Landlord and Tenant Act 1985 has gone some way towards redressing this in the residential context. If the work will cost more than £1,000 or £50 times the number of dwellings, whichever is the greater, the landlord must obtain at least two estimates, one of them from a person wholly unconnected with the landlord. The tenants (or their association, if any) must be given notice of the work and allowed one month to make 'observations' which the landlord 'shall have regard to' (s 20, as amended by Landlord and Tenant Act 1987 and SI 1988 No. 1285). Some local authorities have gone further and have provided advisory panels that are available for council long leaseholders to consult (see Kelly, *The Long Good Buy*, ROOF, September/October 1994, pp 34 *et seq*.). In addition, the tenant is entitled to a written summary of the costs (s 21) and to inspect accounts and supporting vouchers (s 22). Failure to comply with these sections is a criminal offence (s 25). Notwithstanding these provisions, many tenants feel that their views are simply ignored and that they are then powerless (Thomas *et al*., *op. cit.*, at para 4.3).

In commercial leases there is usually provision for certification of accounts by an accountant or surveyor, but there is seldom any formal requirement for consultation with the tenants.

7.7 COMPULSORY COMPETITIVE TENDERING

The 1980s saw the enforced contracting out of many public sector services as central government sought to cut public service costs and to try and improve services through competition—see the Local Government Act 1988. The success of Compulsory Competitive Tendering (CCT) has been questioned in a report prepared for a local government trade union which suggests that savings made in carrying out certain council functions may be outweighed by monitoring costs and that the standard of service may also fall—Local Government Information Unit and Unison, *CCT on the Record*, 1994; *cf.* Inskip, *Big Fish to Fry*, ROOF, July/August 1994, p 11. Nevertheless, given Conservative government policy toward local government, it was inevitable that CCT would eventually be required in local authority housing management (Driscoll, *The Leasehold Reform, Housing and Urban Development Act 1993: The Public Sector Housing Provisions*, (1994) 57 MLR 788 at pp 795–6). The voluntary delegation of management functions was permitted under the Housing Act 1985, s 27, subject to Ministerial consent which would only be forthcoming where the Minister was satisfied that there was tenant approval for the plans. The government's determination to introduce CCT to housing management can be gleaned from the fact that it is even to be imposed in Northern Ireland where the Northern Ireland Housing Executive was one of the Province's few success stories of the past twenty years—the threat of CCT for housing services in Northern Ireland even managed to unite the SDLP and the Ulster Unionists (Pollock, *Irish Eyes Unsmiling*, ROOF, November/December 1993, p 28).

The essence of CCT is to be found in the Leasehold Reform, Housing and Urban Development Act 1993, s 131, although the detail will be provided for in regulations—Local Government Act 1988 (Competition) (Defined Activities) (Housing Management) Order 1994 (SI 1994 No. 1671); see also, Department of the Environment, *CCT and Housing Management*, 1993. Where the Secretary of State makes an order deeming management functions under the Housing Act

1985, s 27 as amended, to be defined activity for the purposes of the Local Government Act 1988, then such functional works will be put out to tender—the only constraint is found in the Housing Act 1985, s 27AA, inserted by the Leasehold Reform, Housing and Urban Development Act 1993, s 131 which requires the local authority to consult with the tenants affected, although there is no power of veto for those tenants; the fear is that tenants would reject CCT since private managers are likely to result in increased costs for the tenants. Local authorities in England will have to put out housing management services to tender by 1996—SI 1994 No. 1671, s 4. Management functions are widely defined in s 27 of the 1985 Act, as amended by s 129 of the 1993 Act.

s 27(6) References in this section to the management functions of a local housing
authority in relation to houses or land—
(a) do not include such functions as may be prescribed by regulations
made by the Secretary of State, but
(b) subject to that, include functions conferred by any statutory provision
and the powers and duties of the authority as holder of an estate or
interest in the houses or land in question.

However, it is not so much the further residualization of local authorities in the residential sector through CCT, so much as the diminution of the tenants' right to be consulted by reason of CCT that is most relevant to a consideration of the landlord and tenant relationship. Consultation is a feature of the next section.

7.8 INFORMATION, CONSULTATION, PARTICIPATION AND MANAGEMENT

Good practice would suggest that landlords and tenants ought to keep each other abreast of proposed future activities. Indeed, the Royal Institution of Chartered Surveyors' James Report, annexed to the Nugee Report (*op. cit.*; see also, Hawkins, *The Nugee Committee Report—The Management of Privately-Owned Blocks of Flats, op. cit.*), stated that where there was good communication, there tended to be fewer management difficulties in relation to long leases. Nevertheless, communications between landlord and tenant are often poor and seldom formally required by the lease—see Thomas *et al., op. cit.*, para 4.1.

In the commercial sector there may often be a good working relationship between the tenants and the landlord or managing agent, but it is almost unheard of to provide for consultation formally in the lease. Local authorities and housing associations are the only residential landlords with general information duties, but the Landlord and Tenant Acts 1985 (ss 1–7) and 1987 (Part VI) provide for some information to be supplied to tenants within their scope, and that would include private sector tenants, including those with long leases—the obligation is simply to supply information, though. The Landlord and Tenant Act

1985 allows any tenant to seek the name of the landlord and if the landlord's interest is assigned, then the new landlord has to inform the tenant by the next due-day for rent. Section 4 obliges the landlord to supply a rent book containing his name and address to all tenants who have a 'right to occupy premises as a residence in consideration of a rent payable weekly'. Part VI of the Landlord and Tenant Act 1987 requires the landlord to provide the tenant with a name and address in the United Kingdom for service of notices and failure so to do may render the tenant not liable for rent or service charges until these statutory requirements are satisfied—*cf.* Thomas *et al., op. cit.,* at para 4.1. In the public sector, however, there has been compulsory provision of information and consultation since the 1980 Housing Act—see Johnston Birchall, 'Council Tenants: Sovereign Consumers or Pawns in the Game?', in Johnston Birchall, *Housing Policy in the 1990s,* 1992, at pp 163 *et seq.* The major provisions are now found in the Housing Act 1985 ss 27, 27A, 27AA, 103, 104, Sch 2 Pt.V and Sch 3A, dealing respectively with management agreements, including CCT, variation of the terms of the lease, the landlord's repairing obligations and consultation when privatizing estates either with or without sitting tenants. Section 27A provides a strong example of consultation requirements and reveals the continuing nature of consultation with respect to management agreements.

s 27A(1) A local housing authority who propose to enter into a management agreement shall make such arrangements as they consider appropriate to enable the tenants of the houses to which the proposal relates—
    (a) to be informed of the following details of the proposal, namely—
        (i) the terms of the agreement (including in particular the standards of service to be required under the agreement),
        (ii) the identity of the person who is to be manager under the agreement, and
        (iii) such other details (if any) as may be prescribed by regulations made by the Secretary of State, and
    (b) to make known to the authority within a specified period their views as to the proposal;
and the authority shall, before making any decision with respect to the proposal, consider any representations made to them in accordance with those arrangements.
    (2) A local housing authority who have made a management agreement shall—
    (a) during the continuance of the agreement, maintain such arrangements as they consider appropriate to enable the tenants of the houses to which the agreement relates to make known to the authority their views as to the standards of service for the time being achieved by the manager, and
    (b) before making any decision with respect to the enforcement of the standards of service required by the agreement, consider any representations made to them in accordance with those arrangements.

(3) Arrangements made or maintained under subsection (1) or (2) above
shall

   (a) include provision for securing that the authority's responses to any
   representations made to them in accordance with the arrangements
   are made known to the tenants concerned, and

   (b) comply with such requirements as may be prescribed by regulations
   made by the Secretary of State.

While the list of 1985 Act sections dealing with consultation may seem comprehensive, s 105(2) of the 1985 Act holds that matters to do with rent and other
charges, other than their collection, are not part of management for the purposes
of s 27. On the other hand, the courts in *R v Secretary of State for Social Services, ex
parte Association of Metropolitan Authorities* [1986] 1 All ER 164, have held that
consultation must be real in the sense that the advice to be given by tenants must
be based on adequate information provided with sufficient time to allow those
tenants to frame their response. Further, if tenants give advice as part of the consultation process, then the local authority landlord must consider it. It should be
noted, however, that the obligation is to consult with tenants, not with any particular tenant body, and that tenants have no veto—before the 1993 Act, the
Minister would only give consent to voluntary tendering under s 27 if a majority
of tenants approved (Driscoll 1994, *op. cit.*, p 794). The Rowntree Inquiry, *op. cit.*,
at p 76, argued for even greater tenant involvement in the running of council
estates to compensate for the anonymous and monopolistic nature of the landlord and tenant relationship in the local authority sector. Under s 27 Housing Act
1985, tenants can co-operatively take over some management decisions as part
of a management agreement, but it is also possible for them to have greater control under co-operative ownership schemes, discussed below. In conclusion, as
Hood has argued (*Question Time*, ROOF, November/December 1993, p 11), the
move to CCT, with the limited guarantees on consultation in the Leasehold
Reform, Housing and Urban Development Act 1993, ss 130 and 131 (substituting
and inserting ss 27A and 27AA in the Housing Act 1985), unfortunately, will
inevitably reduce tenant involvement in decision making. The benefits of competition are to take priority over tenant involvement.

New housing association tenancies are within the private sector regime found
in the Housing Act 1988. Nevertheless, §§F and G of the Tenants' Guarantee (*op.
cit.*) exhort and encourage housing associations to inform and consult with their
tenants on a variety of matters pertaining to management of the properties and
to take their views into account (see also, Cope, *Housing Associations: Policy and
Practice*, 1990, pp 212–17). Going further than what is required under local
authority consultation, §F1 even provides for consultation on '(c) the extent and
cost of services paid for out of the tenants' service charges' (*cf.* Housing Act 1985,
s 105(2) above).

In France, there was an attempt to institute national, regional and building-wide collective bargaining between landlords and tenants under the *Loi Quillot* (*Loi n# 82–526 du 22 juin 1982*, repealed and replaced by *Loi n# 86–1290 du 23 decembre 1986*, which was itself heavily amended by *Loi n# 89–462 du 6 juillet 1989*; see also, De Moor, *Landlord and Tenant in French Law: A Recent Statute*, (1983) 3 OJLS 425). In *Titre III*, the *Loi Quillot* established a system to allow landlords' and tenants' associations to reach collective agreements aimed at improving the specific leases struck by landlords and tenants while respecting the economic and legal balance of those leases (*Art. 44*). The *Loi Quillot* was repealed by *Art. 55 Loi n# 86-1290*, but the *Commissions des Rapports Locatifs* (Rental Agreement Commissions) were replaced in each *Département* by a *Commission Départementale de Conciliation* (*Art. 24*: Regional Conciliation Commissions). The new Regional Conciliation Commissions were meant to deal with rent reviews (*Art. 21*) and leasehold terms (*Arts. 30 and 31*). *Art. 41* established a national *Commission de Concertation* as well. The elements of collective bargaining seen in the *Loi Quillot* were not replicated in the 1986 statute which retreated from the interventionism of the former statute. The 1989 statute, however, while repealing *Art. 24* of the 1986 statute, reinstated the Rental Agreement Commissions under *Art. 41* of the 1986 statute and the idea of collective agreements in the rental sector was rehabilitated (see *Arts. 31* and *32* of the 1989 statute). The approach of the *Loi Quillot* had recognized that there is a need for an overall housing policy and that the rental sector needs to be opened up to collective agreements if it is to meet the needs of landlords, tenants and the government. The contrast between the *Loi Quillot* and English law illustrates the lack of vision manifested by successive governments toward meeting housing need through the concerted efforts of all interested parties.

7.8.1 Tenant Co-operatives

It is unusual to find any form of tenant co-operative in the commercial sector (see Adams, *Shopping Centres: Tenants Associations in Centres*, [1988] 15 EG 24). However, in the local authority sector true tenant co-operatives have emerged. The tenant involvement may come about from a perceived need for the improvement of the council estate from those living there. Given the size of council housing stock, it is easy to understand that the local authority landlord may well seem very remote and disinterested. In those circumstances, tenants have the greatest interest in and are best placed for seeking a solution to management problems. It is not surprising, then, that tenant co-operatives develop (see Cameron and Frew, *Beyond the Ballot*, ROOF, May/June 1991, p 14; and the *Guardian* p 21, 30 July 1993).

There are several different methods of establishing a tenant co-operative. As already mentioned, under s 27 Housing Act 1985 (as amended), the local authority can enter into management agreements with another person and that person might be a tenant group.

s 27(1) A local housing authority may, with the approval of the Secretary of State, agree that another person shall exercise as agent of the authority in relation to—

(a) such of the authority's houses as are specified in the agreement, and

(b) any other land so specified which is held for a related purpose,

such of the authority's management functions as are so specified.

(2) In this Act 'management agreement' and 'manager', in relation to such an agreement, mean an agreement under this section and the person with whom the agreement is made.

(3) A management agreement shall set out the terms on which the authority's functions are exercisable by the manager and shall contain such provisions as may be prescribed by regulations made by the Secretary of State.

(4) A management agreement may, where the manager is a body or association, provide that the manager's functions under the agreement may be performed by a committee or sub-committee, or by an officer, of the body or association.

Such agreements can only be made after the appropriate s 27A consultation with affected tenants has taken place, but where a tenants' organization is bidding for the contract, it is to be assumed that such support as is necessary will be forthcoming. Section 27AB, inserted by s 132(1) Leasehold Reform, Housing and Urban Development Act 1993, deals with management agreements with tenant management organizations (defined by regulation). It imposes a different regime to that instituted by s 27A, but tenant management organizations (TMOs) will turn out to be the preferred option, given that the local authority is obliged to provide financial and other forms of direct support for their efforts and can be required to enter into an agreement in prescribed circumstances. TMOs are not subject to CCT and can also hire their own staff, who may well be former council housing department workers—McIntosh, *By-pass or No-Through Road*, ROOF, May/June 1994, p 10.

s 27AB(1) The Secretary of State may make regulations for imposing requirements on a local housing authority in any case where a tenant management organisation serves written notice on the authority proposing that the authority should enter into a management agreement with that organization.

(2) The regulations may make provision requiring the authority—

(a) to provide or finance the provision of such office accommodation and facilities, and such training, as the organization reasonably requires for the purpose of pursuing the proposal;

(b) to arrange for such feasibility studies with respect to the proposal as may be determined by or under the regulations to be conducted by such persons as may be so determined;

(c) to arrange for such ballots or polls with respect to the proposal as may be determined by or under the regulations to be conducted of such persons as may be so determined; and

(d) in such circumstances as may be prescribed by the regulations (which shall include the organization becoming registered if it has not already done so), to enter into a management agreement with the organisation.

(3) The regulations may make provision with respect to any management agreement which is to be entered into in pursuance of the regulations—

(a) for determining the houses and land to which the agreement should relate, and the amounts which should be paid under the agreement to the organisation;

...

(7) Except as otherwise provided by regulations under this section—

(a) a local housing authority shall not enter into a management agreement with a tenant management organization otherwise than in pursuance of the regulations; and

(b) the provisions of the regulations shall apply in relation to the entering into of such an agreement with such an organization in place of—

(i) the provisions of section 27A (consultation with respect to management agreements),

(ii) in the case of secure tenants, the provisions of section 105 (consultation on matters of housing management), and

(iii) in the case of an organisation which is associated with the authority, the provisions of section 33 of the Local Government Act 1988 (restrictions on contracts with local authority companies).

The TMO process will be long, with two feasibility studies and two ballots of affected tenants—Driscoll 1994, *op. cit.*, at pp 794–5. Nevertheless, it is difficult to conceive of a situation where a tenants' organization will not register as a TMO if it wishes to take on management functions under a s 27 agreement; the government has made £5 million a year available in grants for TMOs—Zipfel, *Farming Out the Management*, ROOF, March/April 1994, p 12 and McIntosh, 1994, *op. cit.* Section 132(2) Leasehold Reform, Housing and Urban Development Act 1993 repealed s 27C Housing Act 1985 which s 27AB is meant to replace. Section 27C allowed housing associations of which at least half the members were affected tenants to enter into management agreements or to acquire local authority houses and land at a specified price. The new s 27AB only covers management agreements, but regulations are likely to impose a greater obligation to hand over management functions than existed under s 27C where the local authority were only obliged to take the tenant association's proposal into account. It seems likely that where council estates remain within local authority ownership, that

management agreements with tenant groups will form part of a general decen-
tralization of services; TMOs are preferable to CCT for tenants and for local
authority housing staff—see ch 10.5 and McIntosh, 1994, *op. cit.*

Under s 27 and s 27AB the tenants will remain secure tenants for the
purposes of the Housing Act 1985, since the 'other person' and the tenant management organization take on only management functions while the local
authority remains the landlord. Only if the tenants seek to establish a co-ownership scheme will they lose secure status. According to Hoath, 1989, *op. cit.*, at
pp 315–18, however, co-ownership schemes, as opposed to management agreements, have proved unpopular because the rents tended to rise making them
unattractive to poor tenants while richer tenants could always buy outright
under the Right To Buy.

7.9 RESOLVING DISPUTES IN THE RELATIONSHIP

Disputes concerning the terms governing the relationship will occasionally arise.
As has been seen (see ch 3.10 and ch 5), where an applicant for housing seeks to
challenge the local authority's decision, then judicial review may be the only
means available—see also, Law Commission, *Administrative Law: Judicial
Review and Statutory Appeals*, Law Com. No. 226, 1994. It may be that an applicant could also seek to challenge a decision of a landlord in any sector under the
Sex Discrimination Act 1975 or the Race Relations Act 1976. However, the focus
of this section is to consider dispute resolution during the existence of the landlord and tenant relationship.

In the local authority sector, some disputes concerning council maladministration might be dealt with by the local ombudsman (see also, the Housing
Associations' Tenants' Ombudsman and an association's tenant's right to refer any
complaint to him—revised Tenants' Guarantee, §C8(e)). In the commercial sector,
the lease may well be drafted with an arbitration clause, subjecting disputes to the
provisions of the Arbitration Acts 1950 and 1979; in addition, the Department of
Trade and Industry started consulting on further reform of this legislation in 1994,
although its specific impact on commercial leases will be limited. Although appeal
is possible to the High Court or Court of Appeal from an arbitrator's decision, the
grounds are limited. The benefits of appointing an arbitrator are that he may well
have expert knowledge of the problem before him, such as the proper value of a
commercial lease in a particular area. On the other hand, there is a fear among
commercial tenants that arbitrators might favour landlords and, given that both
parties will probably have legal representation before the arbitrator, arbitration can
prove to be expensive—see the Department of the Environment's Consultation
Paper of 27 May 1993, paras 3.3 *et seq.* In the alternative, Burton, *Retail Rents—Fair
and Free Market?*, 1992, suggested that the Lands Tribunal rather than an arbitrator

should carry out this review task for commercial leases, but that tribunal is formalistic and may prove to be too expensive—Department of the Environment's Consultation Paper, *op. cit.*, para 3.13; the use of a different tribunal, for instance, a Rent Assessment Committee, is not ruled out, however. A Code of Practice on proper practice in these matters for commercial leases is to be issued by the government and consultation is to take place with interested parties on a streamlined, cost-effective procedure for small business tenants—Department of the Environment Press Release No. 434, 19 July 1994. It should be noted, though, that agricultural tenancies use arbitrators and the Agricultural Lands Tribunal to deal successfully with many disputes in the relationship. The proper utilization of arbitrators and tribunals can prove to be effective.

Many conflicts, however, have to be taken to the courts which can be expensive and time-consuming, especially for a private tenant, whether of a periodic tenancy or of a fixed term long lease—the Nugee Committee Report 1985, *op. cit.*, paras 7.7.3 and 7.7.4 (see also, Hawkins, *op. cit.*; Thomas *et al., op. cit.*, para 6.3). The survey of the Landlord and Tenant Act 1987 by Thomas *et al., op. cit.*, at pp 82 *et seq.*, found that tenants would not use the courts because of the effort involved, the delays in getting a decision and, overwhelmingly, the cost of proceedings. Where the problem concerns the interpretation of the terms of the lease or of a statute, though, then the courts are possibly best placed to carry out this task, even in the commercial sector. The Nugee Committee Report, *op. cit.*, recommended that for disputes between residential long leaseholders and their landlord or managing agent, all actions should start off in the county court, as housing cases tend to do at present, but that a case might be referred to a legally qualified assessor who would operate like the small claims court, although representation would not be frowned upon—paras 7.7.6.–7.7.10. Thomas *et al., op. cit.*, at p 85, found a desire amongst tenants for a specialist housing court/tribunal or an ombudsman. However, the *Civil Justice Review*, Cm 394, 1988, rejected that approach on the ground that the important consequences of housing actions required a wholly judicial context—para 721(iv) and Recommendation 77. It should be noted, on the other hand, that the Agricultural Lands Tribunal successfully hears disputes on security of tenure under the Agricultural Holdings Act 1986, s 26 and, since several dispute resolution functions are already carried out by Rent Assessment Committees in a much cheaper and speedier fashion than by the courts (Department of the Environment's Consultation Paper, *op. cit.*, at para 3.13), then whether their role could extend to other tasks currently performed by the courts is open to investigation, despite the views of the *Civil Justice Review*.

Rent Assessment Committees have the advantage that they are generally chaired by a lawyer, but with expert advice from non-lawyers, including valuers. Originally established under the Rent Act 1965, Rent Assessment Committees are best known for their work in fixing fair and reasonable rents under the Rent Act 1977, s 70 and the Housing Act 1980, s 72:

s 72(1) Rent tribunals, as constituted for the purposes of the 1977 Act, are hereby
abolished.
(2) As from the commencement of this section the functions which, under the
1977 Act, are conferred on rent tribunals shall be carried out by rent
assessment committees.
(3) A rent assessment committee shall, when constituted to carry out functions so conferred, be known as a rent tribunal.
[Winner, I believe, of some award for gobbledygook in 1980]

That work is continued in their responsibility for determining market rents
under the Housing Act 1988, ss 14–14B and 22. However, as Prichard points out
(*A Local Property Tribunal?* (1991) 141 NLJ 973; *New Jurisdictions for Rent
Assessment Committees?* [1991] Conv 447), they have a diverse set of responsibilities. They are also responsible under the Housing Act 1988, s 6 for the fixing of
terms of statutory periodic tenancies. Furthermore, they have a wide range of
duties with respect to leasehold enfranchisement.

Leasehold Reform, Housing and Urban Development Act 1993
s 75(1) Where a scheme under section 19 of the Leasehold Reform Act 1967
(estate management schemes in connection with enfranchisement under
that Act) includes, in pursuance of subsection (6) of that section, provision for enabling the termination or variation of the scheme, or the exclusion of part of the area of the scheme, by or with the approval of the High
Court, that provision shall have effect:–
(a) as if any reference to the High Court were a reference to a leasehold
valuation tribunal, and
(b) with such modifications (if any) as are necessary in consequence of
paragraph (a).
(2) A scheme under that section may be varied by or with the approval of a
leasehold valuation tribunal for the purpose of, or in connection with,
extending the scheme to property within the area of the scheme in which
the landlord's interest may be acquired as mentioned in section 69(1)(a)
above.
(3) Where any such scheme has been varied in accordance with subsection
(2) above, section 19 of that Act shall apply as if the variation had been
effected under provisions included in the scheme in pursuance of subsection (6) of that section (and accordingly the scheme may be further varied
under provisions so included).
(4) Any application made under or by virtue of this section to a leasehold valuation tribunal shall comply with such requirements (if any) as to the
form of, or the particulars to be contained in, any such application as the
Secretary of State may by regulations prescribe.
(5) In this section any reference to a leasehold valuation tribunal is a reference to such a rent assessment committee as is mentioned in section
142(2) of the Housing Act 1980 (leasehold valuation tribunals).

The 1993 Act is but one example of a role for Rent Assessment Committees (known for this purpose as Leasehold Valuation Tribunals) with respect to leasehold enfranchisement. Section 75 is of note because it has granted to the Rent Assessment Committee functions previously carried out by the High Court which would have been much slower and a lot more expensive. The final function of the Committees is to recognize tenants' associations under s 29 Landlord and Tenant Act 1985.

Prichard, *op. cit.*, considered extending these functions even further on the ground that the traditional work of the Committees, fixing rents, was becoming less important now that the market, under the Housing Act 1988, was to determine the proper rent.

[The] settling of market rents for assured periodic and assured shorthold tenancies . . . appears unlikely ever to generate anything approaching the volume of [work that the determination of fair rents for protected tenancies used to], and while housing association tenancies may for the time being still engender some applications in respect of assured tenancies, private sector tenants holding for the most part under shorthold leases are quickly and painfully learning that querying rents leads most often to a speedy termination of the lettings. (Prichard, [1991] Conv. 447 at pp 447–8)

The Rent Assessment Committee would, according to Prichard's plan (1991b, *op. cit.*, at pp 451–2), carry out all the functions under ss 32–36 Landlord and Tenant Act 1954 in place of the county court with respect to commercial leases; this goes beyond mere rent assessment. They would not deal with non-renewal of leases under s 30, however, where the adversarial nature of the proceedings is better suited to a court. Nevertheless, Prichard's arguments commend themselves because, as stated above, contrary to the traditional arbitration procedure, a valuer and a lawyer would be involved in any determination by a Rent Assessment Committee. Prichard did not consider whether Committees should have any role in determining rents in the local authority sector. In the past it would have been inappropriate, since rent fixing was a function of government subsidy (see ch 8). However, as fewer and fewer councils receive government support for housing needs, it may be that Rent Assessment Committees could have a role in any challenge to local authority rent rises rather than tenants having to resort to judicial review. Before the Housing Act 1988, the Rent Assessment Committees were engaged in reviewing non-market rents, so they have the appropriate experience.

In New South Wales, the concept of a 'housing court' has been taken even further—Wilkinson, *Conveyancer's Notebook*, [1992] Conv.141; Lang, *Residential Tenancies: Law and Practice, New South Wales*, 2nd edn, 1990. Established under the Residential Tenancies Act 1987, s 80, the Residential Tenancies Tribunal of New South Wales has jurisdiction over most leasehold disputes—ss 3 and 83(1). Dispute resolution requires the tribunal to undertake mediation between the parties wherever possible—s 109. The Tribunal has exclusive and non-exclusive jurisdiction to determine most issues to do with the terms of the lease—Lang, *op. cit.*, pp 146 *et seq*. It is quick and eschews the use of lawyers. However, its effectiveness is as much based on the simplicity of the comprehensive standard form lease as it is on the fact that it is a tribunal rather than a court. It would not be enough to establish a 'housing court', or even a 'tenancy court' covering commercial or agricultural tenancies, in England and Wales if a speedier and cheaper review procedure is to be established. Leases in the various sectors in England and Wales tend to be similar but not identical, and there is centuries of case law making fine distinctions between certain terms that the ordinary person would not distinguish. If a cheap, speedy and informal 'housing court' is to be established, then a comprehensive and exhaustive new 'law of tenancies' would have first to be established by statute.

Housing matters alone, not including issues arising in non-residential leases, are so wide in concept that it may be false simplicity to attempt to create a single tribunal/court to deal with them all. Beyond rent, eviction and establishing the terms of the lease, allocation and entitlement to Housing Benefit are just as important for landlord and tenant alike. Furthermore, some of those issues have political and economic ramifications which render courts less than optimal for taking decisions—in the case of allocating council housing, the task is so much a question of balance and of sharing out scarce resources based on a variety of criteria, that review of the local authority's decision, rather than a direct appeal, is probably best. The government's proposal to set up an independent appeal to deal with the new allocation system whereby applicants become entitled to one year's temporary accommodation is designed to resolve questions as to whether there was no suitable accommodation and whether it was reasonable; however, given that suitability and reasonableness are relative terms dependent on the general standard of available accommodation in the local authority area, then political and economic factors will infuence any decision, such that review may still be better—the *Guardian* p 2, 19 July 1994.

On the other hand, whether judicial review and the whole panoply of other decisions currently undertaken by courts could be transferred to tribunals which combine speed, ease of use and multi-disciplinary expertise, is debateable. As Lang, *op. cit.*, p 4, makes clear, however, the move to a more informal system in New South Wales was based on a housing crisis for landlords and tenants, a situation not too dissimilar from that experienced in Britain.

8

Rent

8.1 THE FUNCTION OF RENT

Most leases will include an obligation to pay rent, although the reservation of rent is not essential to create a lease (see *Ashburn Anstalt v Arnold* [1988] 2 All ER 147 at 154).

Rent is properly called 'rent-service', terminology which illustrates the fact that landlord and tenant law has feudal origins. Thus, the payment of rent was the form of service which the tenant owed to his feudal lord. Payment for use of the land could take a variety of forms, not only monetary:

. . . **it may as well be in delivery of hens, capons, roses, spurs, bowes, shafts, horses, hawks, pepper, cummin, wheat or other profit that lieth in render, office, attendance, and such like: as in payment of money.** (Coke, *A Commentarie upon Littleton*, 1670, at 142a)

Nowadays, however, rent is seen as being a contractual and commercial payment, as representing the exchange value of the commodity:

The medieval concept of rent as a service rendered by the tenant to the landlord has been displaced by the modern concept of a payment which a tenant is bound by his contract to pay to the landlord for the use of his land. (*United Scientific Holdings Ltd v Burnley Borough Council* [1977] 2 All ER 62, *per* Lord Diplock at 76)

While it is not necessary to pay rent in order to have a lease, in both the Rent Act 1977 and the Housing Act 1988, tenancies at no rent, or at a low rent, will fall outside the scope of statutory protection (Rent Act 1977, s 5; Housing Act 1988, s 1, Sch 1, paras 3, 3A, 3B). Furthermore, the rent must be payable in money, although there is an argument that the provision of services may count *if and only if* the services are quantified in money terms (see *Hornsby v Maynard* [1925] 1 KB 514; *Bostock v Bryant* (1990) 61 P & CR 23; discussed by Lee [1991] Conv 270). In the public sector, there is no equivalent provision that rent must be paid (although a police officer provided with accommodation free of rent and rates under the Police Act 1964 will not have a secure tenancy (Housing Act 1985,

Sch 1, para 2)). Under both the agricultural and business tenancy codes there is no necessity for rent to be paid in order for the lease to be protected.

Rent represents, in part, a return on the landlord's investment in the property—it is a form of compensation for the land and building demised. The landlord will usually have incurred various costs in making the property available for renting. Often there will be capital outlay—such as the initial purchase price of the property and, if the purchase was financed by borrowing, the landlord will also be having to meet the cost of loan repayments. Sometimes, of course, there will not be any initial capital outlay, as where land is inherited. In addition, there are various running costs: the costs of maintenance and upgrading; servicing the property; the employment of managing agents, caretakers and so on. Indeed, a Canadian report found that about 38 per cent of the costs incurred in the provision of private sector rental housing were current costs unrelated to the provision or maintenance of capital (Cragg, *Rent Control Report,* at p 51, Table 2).

The importance of property being a 'good' investment will vary according to the type of landlord involved. For social landlords, the property is not primarily seen as an investment. For most landlords of commercial property, however, the property will be an investment and the level of return is therefore important. The return will be seen not only in terms of the amount of rent receivable (the income), but also in terms of the capital growth:

Most forms of investment ultimately come back to the question of income . . .
The capital value of land or property (which is just another way of saying 'the price') is thus generally related to the income it produces or could produce (we will ignore housing for the moment, where the considerations are rather different). The buyer of a revenue-producing property investment—a tenanted office block, say—is effectively paying a capital sum today in return for the right to receive a stream of income in the future.

If the property is freehold, he has the right to the income in perpetuity, though it will not necessarily remain the same. The investor hopes the income will increase, though at some point the building may become obsolete and the income will decrease or cease altogether as tenants choose more modern properties instead. At this point the owner will need to lay out further funds to refurbish or redevelop it so that he still has a building for which a tenant is prepared to pay rent.

The yield on a property is usually defined as the initial return—in the form of income—that an investor receives on the money he lays out to buy a property . . .

Why should an investor accept a return of only 6% on the property at a time when he might get a perfectly safe return of, say, 10% on a fixed-interest government stock: a gilt edged security?

The answer, of course, is that he expects the rent income from the property to grow as the general level of rents rises, whereas the interest income from the gilt-edged security will remain exactly the same throughout its life. It is worth accepting a lower yield today in return for the expectation of a rising income in the future.

But the income is not the whole story. If the rents from the office block rise, not only does the owner get a higher income. The capital value of his investment (the price somebody would be prepared to pay for it in the market) should rise as well. (Brett, *Property and Money*, 1990, pp 11–12)

In the commercial sector, the institutional lease, with provision for periodic uplift of the rent, is structured so that it provides long term income growth and this, as Brett's analysis shows, will also lead to a growth in the capital value. Investors in the private residential sector also seek a return on their investment through a combination of rental income and capital growth. Indeed, in this sector the income return (the rent) has generally been low in comparison with the returns available from other forms of investment, but, in the past, there has been growth in the capital value of the property well above the general level of inflation.

In the private residential sector it has been argued that rent control (before 1988), coupled with security of tenure, has reduced both income and capital growth:

Rent controls reduce both types of return because the rental income is directly reduced, while security of tenure holds down the asset return to the landlord since occupied dwellings sell for less than vacant properties and landlords are less able to remove tenants to get higher rents. (Gibb and Munro, *Housing Finance in the UK*, 1991, p 210)

The effect of rent control on the supply of housing will be discussed further below (8.4.3).

Rent also functions to ration fixed resources:

[Why] should rents be paid?
The answer lies in the word 'rationing'. If some useful commodity is fixed in supply, then it becomes important in both an economic and a business sense to use that commodity as fully and effectively as possible. If no rents were charged for the use of land or buildings, these commodities might be used by people who derive relatively little advantage from them to the exclusion of people who can use them most beneficially. The high rent asked for land near the centre of a city prices it out of the agricultural market and limits that land to business use, for which it is best suited. Without the rent payment, it might be used as a farm, greatly disrupting the business activities of the city. Economic rent rations a fixed resource by excluding all potential users except the one who derives maximum benefit from that resource. Very broadly, all market prices are rationing devices and economic rent is an important special type. (Smith, *Housing: The Social and Economic Elements*, 1970, cited in Partington, *Landlord and Tenant*, 2nd edn, 1980, p 241)

There might be arguments about 'who can use' residential tenancies 'most beneficially', but there can be little doubt that the rationing function is evident in the commercial property market. Prime properties, in good locations, will command the highest rents. Properties in less popular locations, constructed to lower standards, and let on less favourable terms, will command lower rents.

Smith's economic analysis proceeds on the assumption that a 'market price' will be charged. However, in the residential sector it has not always been felt appropriate to use rent as a means of rationing property. From 1915 to 1988 there was some form of rent control in relation to most private sector housing. Allowing landlords to charge a market rent prices housing beyond the means of the poorer sections of the community. Rent control was therefore imposed as a means of artificially suppressing the amount of rent that could be charged for a property, in order to maintain supplies of affordable housing. The disadvantage of this is, of course, that while destroying the rationing function of rent, it has also detracted from the investment value of rented housing and has, arguably, reduced the supply of suitable accommodation for rental. The Housing Act 1988 represents an attempt to balance the interests of investors with the need for affordable housing: the transition to market rents is intended to restore the attractiveness of rented property as an investment and thus to increase supply; but, to avoid the socially divisive effect of rent's rationing function, welfare payments are available to those otherwise unable to afford market rents. The use of housing benefit to finance market rents, though, is not an open-ended guarantee. Unreasonably high rents may not be met by housing benefit, local authorities agreeing only to pay a sum in line with the general rent for that area (see further 8.5.1).

In the case of social landlords, rent has a somewhat different function. While it provides a return on investment, the social objectives of the landlords are such that the aim of rent is neither to maximize the investment return nor to ration the property. Instead, the rent is probably best seen as a way of being able to cover the maintenance and management costs of the council housing stock. Within their financial arrangements, local authorities have to establish a Housing Revenue Account (HRA), into which rent and any government subsidy is paid, and out of which housing costs are to be met. The position has changed somewhat since 1979 and the election of the first Thatcher administration. As government subsidies have been withdrawn, local authorities have been forced to decide between increased rents or reduced services. Moreover, since the Local Government and Housing Act 1989, the local authority HRA has had to cover the cost of housing benefit, meaning that rents from better-off tenants have to be raised to meet the welfare payments of their poorer neighbours. Housing associations have also seen a reduction in their subsidies, requiring higher rents. Furthermore, the government has encouraged housing associations to seek loans from private financial institutions. The cost of these loans has, in practice, to be financed from rents and the fact that housing associations are now private sector landlords means that they can charge market rents to meet the cost of borrowing. These market rents, however, have to be tempered by the need 'to set and maintain . . . rents at levels which are within the reach of those in low paid employment' (The Tenants' Guarantee, §D2 issued by the Housing Corporation under the Housing Associations Act 1985, s 36A; Housing Corporation Circular 28 and 29/91).

8.2 FIXING THE RENT LEVEL

In both the commercial and private residential sectors, rents can be set at a market level. Some landlords may, of course, be less anxious to maximise the rental income than others—for example, subject to the financial constraints discussed above, many housing associations will seek to provide housing affordable to low income groups rather than charge market rents.

The rent obtainable is dependent on the strength of the property market and the demand for property of the particular type and in that location. In the strong commercial property market of the late 1980s, rents in the region of £50 per square foot were achievable for prime properties in Central London. During the recession of the early 1990s, rents in Central London plummeted to perhaps £30 per square foot, there were high vacancy rates and, in addition, a landlord often had to offer various incentive packages to prospective tenants. These incentives could include rent free periods (the tenant not having to pay any rent for, say, the first two or three years of the lease), the landlord carrying out the initial fitting out works at its cost (that is, fitting out the property with partitions, etc., for the tenant's particular requirements) and agreeing to five-yearly break clauses which only the tenant could trigger (giving the tenant the option to end the lease before the expiry of the fixed term). In return, landlords often required 'confidentiality clauses', whereby the tenant agreed not to disclose the details of the deal. The reason for confidentiality clauses was to hide the 'generosity' of the terms agreed, lest they should become public knowledge and prejudice the landlord's position in negotiations with other prospective tenants, or affect the level of 'comparables' for rent review purposes (see 8.3.2.1).

In relation to the private residential sector, the 1990 Private Renters Survey (Rauta and Pickering, *Private Renting in England 1990*, 1992) explored the factors that most closely explain variations in rent levels:

The factors with a significant effect on rent level in 1990 were as follows: whether or not the tenancy was an Assured Shorthold, whether or not it was in Greater London, whether or not it was a 'no security' letting [for example, a licence or holiday letting], whether or not it was a post-1988 Assured tenancy, the number of bedrooms, whether it was furnished or unfurnished, whether it was in a house or some other kind of building, whether or not it was accessible to the general public [for example, employment related accommodation, student lettings] and

whether or not it was a Regulated tenancy [under the 1977 Act] with registered
rent. 'No security' tenancies, those in a house (for example, a bedsitter), those
not accessible to the public and Regulated tenancies with registered rents all
tended to have lower rents; with the other factors the association with rent level
was positive.

Two changes stand out [from the previous survey in 1988]: that being in
Greater London or not had assumed a significance in 1990 which it did not have
in 1988 and that rent levels in 1990 were very much dependent on whether or not
the tenancy was one of the new types introduced in 1989 (and negatively with
whether or not it was a 'no security' letting). The second is not surprising, given
very much higher average rents for the new tenancies than for other types of letting. The first may perhaps be explained by the fact that in 1990 a very high proportion of lettings were Shorthold or Assured, for which the difference in rent
between Greater London and elsewhere was greater than that for Regulated tenancies, many of which had disappeared between 1988 and 1990. In 1990, the
average weekly rent for the new Assured tenancies was 88% higher in Greater
London than elsewhere and that for Assured Shorthold tenancies 86% higher.
Registered rents for Regulated tenancies were only 36% higher in Greater
London on average and unregistered rents for Regulated tenancies 66% higher.
(p 32)

Housing associations have also witnessed a revolution with regard to rents
since 1988. The Housing Act of that year placed housing associations firmly in
the private sector in terms of the legal protection offered on lettings. The corollary was that housing associations could charge market rents on these new lets.
As has been mentioned, the Tenants' Guarantee, *op. cit.*, exhorts housing associations to set rents affordable to those on low wages, but the combination of
reduced subsidies and private institutional loans make this objective difficult to
achieve. Prior to 1988, housing associations had been in a similar position to
local authorities. The Housing Finance Act 1972 had applied fair rents (that is,
generally, rents significantly lower than market rents) to housing associations'
properties; however, it was the subsidy system established by the Housing Act
1974 that made this financially possible, given the small size of most housing
associations and the concomitant inability to utilize rent pooling as local authorities did. The major element in this subsidy system was Housing Association
Grant (HAG). HAG was a capital grant to cover building and conversion costs.
Having deducted an amount for management and maintenance from the fair
rents received from all properties, the remaining sum was available to finance a
mortgage for new works—HAG made up the difference between the loan so
available and the capital costs of building and conversion (see Gibb and Munro,
op. cit., pp 113 *et seq.*). Housing associations were only going to be able to charge
fair rents if such a shortfall subsidy system existed. However, the position is now
that HAG is being cut, and anyone granted a tenancy after 15 January 1989 can be
charged a market rent, leading to the absurd consequence that neighbours with

identical properties can have substantially different rents (*cf.* Campbell, *Rules Made to be Broken*, ROOF, May/June 1994, p 15). Figures prepared by the London Research Centre (see ROOF, May/June 1991, Housing Update, pp 5–6) reveal that, between 1980 and 1989, housing association registered fair rents rose 116 per cent, over 50 per cent faster than the Retail Price Index for the same period. In 1990 alone, housing association rents for assured tenancies rose 10–22 per cent faster than dwellings let by the same association on pre-1989 fair rent leases. However, there is a wide disparity in rent levels between different housing associations. Peabody, for instance, saw its average rents rise from £37.72 per week in 1991/92 to £65.90 in 1992/93 (assured rents), whereas Merseyside Improved Homes had an increase from £25.86 (1991/92) to £28.11 (1992/93)—Fast Facts, ROOF, March/April 1994, p 13. In some areas the new rents are twice what the local council is charging (Joseph Rowntree Foundation Inquiry into British Housing, Second Report, 1991, at p 24). This situation can be particularly anomalous where the housing association takes over the running of an ex-council estate—existing tenants are protected, but their new neighbours will be paying rents to meet the cost of additional loans financed through private institutions (Brimacombe, *A Divided Rule*, ROOF, May/June 1991, pp 32 *et seq.*). The National Federation of Housing Associations predict steep rises in housing association rents. Rents will have to rise by 28 per cent by 1995 to compensate for the government's decision to limit central government contribution to 62 per cent of the cost of new housing (the *Guardian* p 4, 23 August 1993). With the government proposing to cut HAG from 71 per cent of costs in 1993 to a mere 55 per cent by 1996, the prospects can only be further substantial increases for housing association rents (see the *Guardian* p 6, 22 April 1993; p 4, 4 August 1994).

Social housing in the rest of Europe and North America has developed along slightly different lines and has faced other challenges. In the Federal Republic of Germany, rents in the social sector are set by reference to the current costs, that is administration charges, repairs and interest repayments on loans. However, that figure is then reduced in line with the amount of subsidy received from the *Länder*/municipalities (van Vliet, *International Handbook of Housing Policies and Practices*, 1990, p 139). While this approach may lead to cheap rents on some older properties, it may also mean that neighbouring houses which were built at different times have wildly differing rents. Moreover, to encourage private investment in social housing, landlords are not subject to income, property or business taxes. In the Netherlands, the government sets standard building and land costs which are fully subsidised by payment to the developer—any costs on items above the standardised levels have to be met by the tenant through rent. The overall effect is to keep rents low. The US Federal authorities in the 1970s moved from a tenant-centred subsidy system, to one which made up the difference to the landlord between a fair market rent for the dwelling and:

1 What was actually paid by the tenant; or

2 If (1) was less than 30 per cent of the tenant's income, then the difference between 30 per cent of the tenant's income and the fair market rent (see van Vliet, *op. cit.*, at pp 359–60).

Given that it guarantees a fair market rent to the landlord, this method encourages private sector investment, but it is overly bureaucratic. However, none of these methods is entirely appropriate to housing associations in the United Kingdom and no direct transplant could be put into effect. Nevertheless, rent-fixing for housing associations is undergoing a period of change; greater emphasis is to be placed on private institutional finance and landlords are meant to be charging market rents at the same time as bearing in mind the low income of the tenant—a point which will be taken up again below.

Residential rent-fixing for local authorities has also undergone a dramatic change since the early 1970s, and especially so since 1980 (see also, Goodlad and Gibb, *Housing and Social Justice*, 1994 at pp 33 *et seq.*). Rent-fixing in the local authority sector operates at the macro- and micro-level. Most of the subsequent discussion focusses on the macro-level, in which central government seeks to influence local authority determination of its overall rents. At the micro-level, the local authorities are not subject to any of the private sector controls on rent increases. Under the Housing Act 1985, s 24, the local authority can make such reasonable charges as it determines and must review such charges regularly. This apparent freedom, however, is illusory because of the control that central government exerts through subsidies.

Immediately after World War I and throughout the 1920s at least, council housing was of a significantly higher standard than that previously available to the working classes. The housing built following World War II was even more spacious (see Swenarton, *Homes Fit for Heroes*, 1981, p 137; Malpass and Murie, *Housing Policy and Practice*, 4th edn, 1994, pp 74 *et seq.*). Given the high standard of housing, local authorities felt justified in charging high rents based on pooled, historic costs, but using central subsidies to reduce those rents generally, leaving council housing accessible only to the better-off members of the working class. The Conservative Governments of the 1950s sought to change this approach so as to cut the size of the subsidy, but the method adopted was very indirect. Prior to the 1956 Housing Subsidies Act, local authorities were obliged to make a contribution to the HRA from the general rate fund in set amounts; the Act removed this strict obligation. The hope was that many local authorities would not make this payment from the general rate fund and the lesser sums paid into the HRA would mean that more had to be raised by rents. Poorer tenants would be protected by means-tested rent rebates (encouraged by central government since the 1930s). Nevertheless, despite these changes to force rents up, only 40 per cent of local authorities had rebate schemes in place by 1964 (Malpass and Murie, 1994, *op. cit.*, p 81). It was the Housing Finance Act of 1972 that made such rebates compulsory through a national scheme. At the same time, though, the Act tried to move the public sector from 'reasonable' council rents to 'fair' rents through detailed and intricate mechanisms. The system of fair rents, which it was agreed would be higher than most council rents, had been imposed on the private sector in the Rent Act 1965. The 1972 Act, however, as well as placing a greater financial burden on council tenants (both present and future), contained a new subsidy system which effectively removed local authority discretion in setting rents. From the point of view of councils, whatever housing costs they incurred which were not met by the centrally determined and limited subsidy, they would have to pay for through increasing the rents. From the point of view of central government, as rents rose to the new fair rent level, even less subsidy would be needed—indeed, the 1972 Act envisaged rents eventually covering the cost of the rebates to poorer tenants and even profits being created within the Housing Revenue Account. The Act predictably led to confrontation from the Opposition at both national and local level. The Labour Party in Parliament argued that fair rents were designed to make a profit for private landlords, but that council housing was not run on the same commercial lines. In addition, it was argued that there was little justification for raising rents and making most council tenants then claim a rebate when one could avoid such bureaucracy by setting affordable rents. At the local level several councils resisted the implementation of the Act, the most famous being Clay Cross whose councillors were prosecuted under the 1972 Act (see Malpass, *Reshaping Housing Policy*, 1990, pp 116–21). In the end however, the Act was repealed by the incoming Labour Government of 1974-79, but it did lead to the establishment of a supposedly fundamental review of housing finance between 1974 and 1977. The 1977 Green Paper (Housing Policy: A Consultative Document, Cmnd 6851, 1977) was not as radical as had been anticipated and, while sticking firmly to 'reasonable rents', accepted the need for a deficit subsidy system akin to that in the Housing Finance Act 1972. The resulting Housing Bill 1979 fell with the Labour Government and a Conservative Government was ushered in whose philosophies rejected general subsidies throughout the welfare state. In 1979 all local authorities were in receipt of central government subsidy for council housing. The 1980s saw a withering away of council house subsidies but without the direct confrontation caused by the 1972 Act; nevertheless, the long term problems envisaged in the 1970s have come to pass. Those criticisms are considered below after discussion of the rules now shaping local authority rent setting.

A new system of fixing local authority rents at the macro-level was set up in the Housing Act 1980 and, with some modifications, is now to be found in the Local Government and Housing Act 1989. It provided central government with leverage to force rent rises by the device of 'notional Housing Revenue Accounts'. The

1980 Act established a formula for calculating subsidy which came into effect in 1981:

$$\text{Subsidy} = BA + HCD - LCD$$

where

1 BA was the base amount, that is, the actual level of subsidy received the previous year;

2 HCD was the housing costs differential, that is, the amount by which a local authority's expenditure would notionally exceed the previous year's figure—expenditure included management and maintenance costs, loan charges on pre-1981 loans and 75 per cent of such charges on loans incurred after 1981;

3 LCD was the local contribution differential, that is the notional amount by which the local authority's income would exceed the previous year's—the main element of a local authority's income was the rent paid by tenants.

(See Malpass, *op. cit.*, at pp 136 *et seq.*, esp. at p 139, and Malpass and Murie, 1994, *op. cit.*, at pp 200 *et seq.*)

The beauty of the scheme from the point of view of central government was that it did not directly dictate any rent rises. Central government merely calculated a notional subsidy, upon which actual subsidy was then based, and this notional subsidy was premised on a notional rent rise which a local authority was free to impose or not—of course, if it did not impose the rent rise, then it would have less money in the HRA for management and maintenance costs. In 1981–82, the Secretary of State for the Environment assumed a notional rent rise of £2.95 per week, coupled with a 9 per cent increase in management and maintenance costs. 1982–83 saw a notional rent rise of £2.50 per week. However, as indicated, local authorities were free to impose the full notional increase or not and figures reveal that average rent rises bore only a loose correlation to the government's notional increase:

[Between] April 1980 and April 1983 rents rose by 82 per cent in cash terms. Taking the government's first term as a whole [1979–83], average unrebated council rents in England and Wales rose by 119 per cent, during a period when the retail price index rose by only 55 per cent. Increases in the real level of rents were concentrated in 1981–82 and in 1982–83, but subsequently increases were in line with the rate of inflation . . . (Malpass, *op. cit.*, pp 140–1)

After such large increases in just two years it is little wonder that the size of the central government subsidy fell rapidly—at 1987–88 values, it fell from £1,224m in 1981–82 to only £336m in 1983–84 after the first two years of the new system. Indeed, most local authorities were no longer receiving a subsidy by the mid-1980s. The corollary was, of course, that central government no longer had any leverage on rents in non-subsidized local authorities. (The Local Government, Planning and Land Act 1980 had introduced changes into the calculation of Rate Support Grant. Since there was at the time a Rate Fund Contribution to the HRA, rents could be affected by this legislation, too. However, after its initial implementation in 1981–82, the changes introduced by the Local Government,

Planning and Land Act 1980 fell into disuse, probably because it had greatest impact in terms of the size of rent increases in District Councils which were mainly Conservative.)

The rent fixing mechanisms in the Housing Act 1980 incorporated the objectives seen in the Housing Finance Act 1972—a deficit subsidy which would lead to profitable HRAs that were intended eventually to cover the cost of local means-tested rebates. However, because there was no explicit attempt to impose fair rents, it did not lead to the confrontation seen in the 1970s. Nevertheless, the deficit subsidy allowed central government to force through quite dramatic rent rises until a local authority no longer required any subsidy— according to the Rowntree Inquiry (*op. cit.*, at p 47), average council rents rose in England during the 1980s by about 53 per cent. At the general level, therefore, it would appear that the Conservatives achieved their ends, but Rowntree's research further revealed that while rent rose 123 per cent in one London Borough during the decade, in another it only went up by 13 per cent. Such disparities call into question the fairness of the system. Furthermore, it had a built-in design fault in that as rents rose local authorities were ever less dependent on central government and so, since the Local Government, Planning and Land Act 1980 was not used with respect to rent levels after 1981, there was a need for reform if leverage on rent rises was to be maintained.

The new legislation is found in Parts IV and VI Local Government and Housing Act 1989. The 1989 Act retained notional HRAs and the deficit subsidy, but, in simple terms, redefined the HRA in order to create a need for central government subsidy where, for the most part, local authorities were no longer receiving one. Further, from the end of World War I onwards, local authorities had been able to transfer money raised through the local property tax, the rates, into the HRA to defray costs and, thus, keep rents down. The 1980 Housing Act had permitted councils to make a profit on their HRAs which could be paid into the General Rate Fund, reducing rates' bills. The 1989 Act introduced the concept of the 'ring-fenced' HRA, with no contribution from or to the General Rate Fund being allowed (see Sch 4; see also, the *Guardian* 2 p 21, 15 October 1993). For most local authorities, the restriction on contributing from the General Rate Fund to the HRA was of little consequence, but for some London Boroughs it could have had a serious impact if the government had not altered other aspects of housing finance at the same time—Camden LBC, for instance, would have been faced with a rent rise of 183 per cent if it had simply been prohibited from subsidizing rents with rates (see Malpass, *op. cit.*, p 169). In 1993–94 rent increases imposed by local authorities were higher than the rate of inflation (Fast Facts, ROOF, September/October 1993, p 13).

The present system of centrally orchestrated rent-fixing cannot be understood apart from the changes instituted with regard to capital receipts (Part IV). Local authorities had received a considerable amount of capital monies during the

1980s as a result of council house sales—£33 billion according to the Rowntree Inquiry, *op. cit.*, p 70. While this money had never been wholly at the local authorities' disposal, they had been able to pay for capitalized repairs out of it. The new rules regarding capital receipts have two consequences: first, since 75 per cent has to be used to redeem outstanding debts (see s 59), it should mean that the element of rent required to cover interest on these loans should be reduced; on the other hand, less of the capital receipts will now be available to cover repairs and refurbishment (see s 40), placing an extra burden on rents. The new system for calculating subsidy has the potential to force up rents to unprecedented levels (see ss 79 *et seq.*).

It is to be observed that the method of calculating the formula for determining a Housing Revenue Account subsidy gives the Secretary of State a very wide discretion. By [s80(1)] the subsidy is to be calculated 'with such formulae as the Secretary of State may from time to time determine.' Then by subsection (3) it is provided that in determining a formula the Secretary of State may include variables framed in whatever way he considers appropriate by reference to amounts actually credited or debited in a particular authority's Housing Revenue Account in that or previous years; by notional credits or debits on such assumptions as he may determine whether or not they are likely to be borne out by events; or by such other relevant matters as he thinks fit . . . Put shortly, it is in my judgment well within that discretion to accept or reject any particular items of income or expenditure, whether actually or notionally incurred, provided that it does not produce an absurd result. (*per* Farquharson LJ in *R v Secretary of State for the Environment, ex parte Greenwich LBC* (1990) 22 HLR 543 at 546 and 552)

Furthermore, the 1989 version of housing subsidy from central government now includes an amount to cover the rent element of housing benefit paid to local authority tenants who meet the rules for receiving this means-tested benefit— about 66 per cent of local authority tenants receive some housing benefit to help meet their rent, so all local authorities will now receive subsidy, even if it is only to cover this item (Sch 4).

This change to include housing benefit costs in housing subsidy shows a confusion in the mind of the Conservative Government about housing costs, rents, subsidies and welfare payments. The Conservatives in office, since the 1950s at least, had had a preference for subsidizing poor tenants (a personal subsidy) rather than council houses (a general subsidy). However, it had recognized that a means-tested benefit to assist with rent is part of the welfare state and should be dealt with by the Department of Social Security and not be paid for through rent. The 1989 Act's version of housing subsidy, by incorporating what is essentially a welfare cost into the HRA, has shown that this Conservative Government has no rent policy for local authority housing, but rather that it has a subsidy policy designed to reduce central government costs; a rent policy would lay down guidelines as to the appropriate level of rent for council houses, whereas the only policy displayed throughout the 1980s was to force rents higher and reduce the amount of subsidy central government had to provide. With housing benefit for council tenants included since 1984 in the housing subsidy, a reduction in that subsidy would force local authorities to raise rents to meet their housing benefit obligations. Inasmuch as from the mid-1980s onwards most local authorities had received little or no subsidy, raising enough from rents to cover management and maintenance costs, now all will receive some subsidy to cover the cost of their tenants who claim housing benefit to assist with their rent. To encourage rent rises, therefore, central government can once again simply reduce subsidy and rents will have to go up so that the richer tenants can pay for the housing benefit of their poorer neighbours. Rent, however, ought to cover the cost of housing, not fund welfare benefits. Nor can local authorities use the General Rate Fund to subsidize rents any more. Given the size of the housing benefit bill, there could be long term rent rises in store for richer tenants who will, thus, find it cheaper to turn to owner-occupation through the Right To Buy. (For more detail, see Malpass, *op. cit.*, ch 8)

Rents have been rising faster than incomes since 1988 according to Muellbauer (*The Great British Housing Disaster and Economic Policy*, 1990, at p 13), and experts in the field are, almost without exception, certain that rents will continue this trend for the foreseeable future (see Dwelly, *Housing at the Crossroads*, ROOF, January/February 1993, pp 22 *et seq.*; Fast Facts, ROOF, September/October 1993, *op. cit.*). In conclusion on the 1989 Act, given the conflicting tensions already considered in the setting of rents by housing associations, it would be better for the government to lay down the general level of rent that should be charged by local authorities for council housing, especially since two-thirds of tenants already need housing benefit to cover the cost. It would be more efficient either to reduce rents so that fewer tenants needed to place a burden on the bureaucracy of the housing benefit system, or to provide a general housing subsidy, free from welfare elements, to keep the cost of everyone's rent down. Indeed, Joseph Rowntree Foundation Housing Research Findings No. 109, 1994, found that rent increases in the social sector of 10 per cent would reduce the country's Gross Domestic Product, increase the Retail Price Index, lead to an increase of over 25,000 in the number of unemployed persons and cost the Exchequer approximately £100 millon.

Alternative policies have been suggested by the Labour Party and in Rowntree's Inquiry. Prior to the 1992 election, Labour suggested that local authority rents should be set by reference to average earnings in the area. What housing costs could not be met by such rental income would be covered by subsidy (A Welcome Home, September 1991, p 14). The details of the scheme were not spelt out, but the approach reveals a completely different philosophy to social housing, based on housing need rather than financial cost—put simply, the Labour proposal obviously has more merit from the point of view of providing a policy for rents rather than merely subsidies, but it fails to show whence the extra funds for the subsidy would emanate. What is clear is that government finance in general and the level of rents are inextricably entwined (see Farquharson LJ, *Ex parte Greenwich, op. cit.*, at 549) and while Labour's plan would reduce the housing benefit cost, thereby saving the Exchequer, reasonable rents would require a larger central government subsidy. If more money would have to be channelled to social housing, then a change in the social philosophy/ideology, and hence social objectives, would have to be manifested. The Rowntree Inquiry (*op. cit.*, pp 47 *et seq.*) recommended that all rents in all sectors be set at 4 per cent of the capital value of the property, with additional fixed amounts for management, maintenance and major repairs. The Inquiry accepted that this change would lead to much higher rents in all sectors, possibly 125 per cent higher, forcing even more tenants on to housing benefit (*op. cit.*, pp 51 and 53). Thus, Rowntree proposed phasing in the 4 per cent capital values over ten years in the social sector. The justification for 4 per cent capital value rents is that such a rate of return would encourage private investors to put money into the private rented sector and that unless social sector rents also rose by a similar amount, it would lead to those properties being seen as welfare housing. However, this argument ignores the different objectives of private and social landlords—local authorities, for instance, only need to break even in their HRAs, even after the 1989 Act. Moreover, it ought to be remembered that council tenants earn a lot less on average than those who are owner-occupiers and so 4 per cent capital rents are unrealistic. While the Rowntree proposals promote greater consistency and bring an air of simplicity to rent fixing, the issues are much more complex in British housing.

8.3 VARIATION OF THE RENT DURING A TENANCY

Over the term of a lease, the economic value of the land will usually change. This can happen because the land value itself is diminished, for example, through the extraction of minerals. More commonly, it will change due to the effects of inflation. In addition to this general change in monetary values, there may well be changes more specific to the property. Property values as a whole may rise or fall independently of general monetary trends. And there may be factors peculiar to the particular property that mean its value changes out-of-line with other properties. The opening of a shopping centre next to the let premises may, for example, cause its value to rise dramatically. Conversely, the closure of an adjacent car-park or the opening a shopping complex at the other side of town may cause the value of the property to plummet.

To reflect the change in the economic value of the land, it is common for a landlord to seek an increase in the rent at regular intervals. In the private residential sector, his power to do so was heavily circumscribed until the passage of the Housing Act 1988, as was his ability to set the initial rent at as high a level as he wanted (see further on rent control 8.4).

In the local authority sector, the public law nature of the relationship between landlord and tenant is to the fore. Council tenants have always been liable to increases in their rent and local authorities were exempted from the legislative restrictions placed upon the private residential sector. Central government had to allow rent increases if it were to be able to vary subsidy. Apart from the administratively impossible method of reaching an *ad hoc* agreement with each tenant to increase the rent, the common law only allowed landlords to implement increases where there was a clause to that effect in the lease (which in practice there usually was) or upon giving notice to quit:

At common law, in the absence of agreement, the landlord cannot increase the rent except by giving a notice to quit. He must first determine the tenancy and then get the tenant to agree to pay the increase. Many tenants are frightened by a notice to quit. They do not know what is behind it. To save their feelings, the Greater London Council have inserted [a condition] so as to enable them to increase the rent without giving notice to quit. In these days money diminishes in value continually. As it diminishes, it is only reasonable that landlords should be able to increase the rent without going through the form of a notice to quit. (*GLC v Connolly* [1970] 1 All ER 870 at 874, *per* Lord Denning MR).

Legislation now provides additional means to local authorities to raise rents. Under the Housing Act 1985, s 24(1) local authorities are entitled to make such 'reasonable charges as they may determine' and under subsection (2) they may from time to time makes such changes 'as circumstances may require', but

[in] exercising their functions under this section, a local housing authority shall have regard in particular to the principle that the rents of houses of any class or description should bear broadly the same proportion to private sector rents as the rents of houses of any other class or description. (s 24(3), inserted by the Local Government and Housing Act 1989, s 162)

The effect of this new subsection is that if the cost of renting a house in the private sector is twice as much as renting a flat in that sector, then 'broadly the same' ratio ought to apply to local authority rents. Additionally, a three-bedroomed semi on a better estate ought to have a higher rent than one in a poorer area.

These vague and minor limitations on local discretion have to be seen in the context of central government's overarching power to manipulate rents through 'notional HRAs'. Moreover, this context highlights the political nature of setting and raising rents in the council sector, where market forces have little or no influence on the political machinations of government, both central and local.

It was a matter of real concern that the divisional court, exercising the power of judicial review, was increasingly . . . being used for political purposes superficially dressed up as points of law . . . The impropriety of coming to court when political capital was sought to be made could not be over stressed. It was perhaps even worse when public servants were or felt constrained to file affidavits which demonstrated a political purpose. (*R v GLC, ex parte Royal Borough of Kensington and Chelsea*, The Times, 7 April 1982, *per* McNeill J)

If the council made an increase to produce £600,000 before March, 1973, they would be forbidden to raise the rents in the following October. The council therefore decided a few hours before the [Housing Finance Act 1972] came into force, to raise the rent of an uninhabited house in Dorrien Walk to £18,000 a week . . . The last rent was £30.84 a month. (*Backhouse v Lambeth LBC*, The Times, 14 October 1972, *per* Melford-Stevenson J)

In the commercial sector, the landlord has always been free to include provisions for variation of the rent within the lease. Since the 1988 Housing Act, this is now also possible in the private residential sector (before then, any provision for review was subject to the possiblity of rent control; see further at 8.4 below).

Where the parties to the landlord and tenant relationship are able to provide for rent variation within the lease, free from political control, there are a number of general questions that need to be asked about the objectives of the rent review:

1 Should the variation in rent be related to general changes in the purchasing power of money, or tied more specifically to fluctuations in the property market or, more specifically still, related to the particular property?
2 Should the aim of rent variation be to maximize the landlord's profits from the land or to enable both parties to share the risk of changes in value? The answer to this will affect whether rent can go down on review or only be increased.
3 Should the objective on variation of rent be the same as for the fixing of the initial rent, or should regard be had to the fact that the tenant already has an estate in the property? Should the tenant be given the advantage of rent concessions that would be available on a new letting, or the landlord the advantage of any premium that would be paid on a new letting?

There are many different approaches to rent review that could be adopted. In this country, the most common method of rent variation in commercial leases is to provide for revaluation of the let property at periodic intervals, the valuation being referred to an independent third party in the event of disagreement (see further 8.3.2.1). The object of this would therefore seem to be to provide a periodic change in the rent to reflect not general monetary trends but very specifically to reflect the then current market rent for the particular property. The sophistication of these rent review clauses, and the expense of operating them, makes them unsuitable for general use in residential leases where simpler methods of review are used. It is interesting, however, that these kinds of clauses are not popular in commercial property markets elsewhere. Outside the United Kingdom, other forms of review, in particular indexation, are much more commonly used. The explanation for the popularity of the market rent review here lies in the historical dominance of institutional landlords in the United Kingdom commercial property market and their concern with certain long term income growth. (For a comparative study of rent provisions internationally, see Royal Institution of Chartered Surveyors, *International Leasing Structures*, Paper Number 26, May 1993).

Before considering the market rent review clause in more detail we shall look at some alternative methods of rent review.

8.3.1 Methods of Rent Review

8.3.1.1 Step-up or Differential Rents

The lease may provide for a simple and pre-determined rent revision at periodic intervals. This form of rent increase is not very popular as there is no flexibility built into it—it is a very crude attempt to provide for increases and ignores the effects of changes in the pace of inflation or factors special to the let property. Nevertheless, it is a relatively simple and inexpensive method of rent review. It may therefore be chosen where the annual rental of the premises is a low ground rent—for example, in a 99-year lease purchased with a substantial capital sum the initial rent may be £100 per annum, to be increased at 33 year intervals by £100.

8.3.1.2 Turnover or Equity Rents

When the rent is based on turnover, it varies in line with the income from the let premises, either by reference to the tenant's business turnover at the premises (the turnover rent) or by reference to the rents received by the tenant in subletting the property (the equity rent). Turnover and equity rents are clearly appropriate in different situations. The turnover rent is most often found in relation to retail outlets where the rent is related to the level of sales made by the tenant. Equity rents might be used where the property is an investment and the freeholder has shared in the development process, for example, where the freeholder is a local authority which has helped in assembling land together for commercial development and receives a share of the rents received by the tenant developer.

The focus of our discussion will be upon turnover rents as these relate to the occupational tenant.

Early provisions for rent variation were based upon the same kind of ideas as the turnover rent and took the form of 'produce rents', where the rent was dependent on the value of produce yielded from the land. In *Walsh v Lonsdale* (1882) 21 ChD 9, there was a variable rent of thirty shillings per loom run in a weaving mill—the tenant had to run at least 540 looms (thus ensuring the landlord a minimum guaranteed rent) and the rent would increase with every additional loom to reflect the increase in output. Nowadays the turnover rent will usually be based upon the gross sales or takings of the tenant, but may also be coupled with a minimum base rent figure representing a portion of the market rent of the premises. Thus, a lease of a retail unit in a shopping complex might provide that the tenant has to pay a fixed rent, representing 80 per cent of the market rent, plus 3 per cent of gross profits. A landlord who finds a property hard to let may agree to put more emphasis on the profit element and demand less of a base rent figure; the landlord of an easy to let complex may seek base rental figures approaching 100 per cent of the market rent.

Turnover rents lend themselves to developments where some kind of partnership exists between landlord and tenant. For the landlord, the fact that he will share in the tenant's business fortunes (both successes and slumps) will be an incentive to actively promote the tenant's business. In a shopping centre, the landlord will therefore benefit from adopting high management standards, refurbishing the centre when it becomes out-dated, promoting the complex widely and ensuring a good tenant mix. The landlord's management policies will therefore contribute to the returns he receives on the property let. He will also be able to get a more immediate return on investment than is available from rent variation based on periodic revaluation, where it may be several years before the next review date. The tenant, too, will clearly benefit from a well managed environment. In addition, the linkage between rent payable and turnover means that the tenant is sheltered during times of recession; if business is poor the rent will be correspondingly lower. Conversely, during times of good trading conditions, the rent payable will be high.

Turnover rents have not, however, proved popular in this country. There are certain problems inherent to turnover rents (see below), but the fundamental constraint has been the reluctance of institutional investors to depart from the notion of upwards only reviews and to be willing to share in the risk of the enterprise (see Walsh, *Shopping centres: why are turnover rents not more popular?*, (1988) 13 EG 20; Hawkings, *Shopping centres—turnover rents on the increase*, (1990) 38 EG 28). Where a turnover rent is used, there may be other changes to the lease structure in order to shelter the landlord from an 'under-performing' tenant:

With a turnover lease the landlord is potentially disadvantaged if a trader is under-performing (and perhaps only paying a base rental), yet under the Landlord and Tenant Act 1954 the tenant has a right to renew the lease. Turnover leases are generally, therefore, contracted out of the security of tenure provisions of the 1954 Act, to preclude the tenant's right to renew.

Similarly critical is the length of lease, which is generally agreed in the market to be for 10 years or at least subject to a break at that time. A 25-year lease is too long a period for a landlord to suffer an under-performing tenant. (Bennet and Rigby, *A Closer look at the turnover lease*, The Property Week, 15 July 1993)

In the United States, Australia and New Zealand, turnover rents are widely used in 'percentage leases', particularly for retail operations. These will normally provide for a minimum fixed rent related to the size of the premises, plus a percentage of gross sales or receipts (some, however, may be based on net rather than gross figures). In Australia, the rent for retail property is likely to be based on between 4 and 10 per cent of turnover, depending on the type of store and its location. For an anchor tenant, the percentage is likely to be lower, say, 1–3 per cent. In relation to agricultural land, there may be a sharecropping agreement whereby the tenant farmer agrees to pay for his use of the land by giving the landowner a percentage of the profits of the harvest.

It is necessary to give careful consideration to the drafting of turnover rent provisions. While it might be agreed in principle that the tenant has to pay, say, 3 per cent of gross takings, this does need to be much more carefully defined when it comes to the documentation. What items will count as takings? The kind of difficulties that arise include how to treat refunds made to customers, inter-branch stock transfers, taxes paid by customers (akin to British value added tax), discounts given to staff and so on. Even with careful drafting of the inclusion and exclusion provisions, it will be difficult to anticipate all potential difficulties. In Victoria, Australia, the Retail Tenancies Act 1986 lists a number of items that cannot constitute 'turnover', including, *inter alia*, discounts reasonably and properly allowed to any customer in the usual course of business; the value of trade-ins purchased from customers; uncollected credit accounts written off by the tenant; refunds on the return of merchandise; delivery charges; and taxes on the purchase price of goods and services.

There are further problems with turnover rents. Given that the effect of percentage leases (particularly if no minimum 'safety-net' rent is provided) is to make the landlord's receipts dependent upon the level of the tenant's activity, American courts have held that the tenant is under an implied covenant to occupy the premises and use best efforts in the operation of his business (see, for example, *Stoddard v Illinois Improv. & Ballast Co* 113 NE 913 (1916)). It would clearly be unjust if the tenant were able to leave the premises vacant or to convert the premises to non-income producing activities, such as storage, and thus deprive the landlord of rent. As well as affecting the rent receivable from the particular tenant, vacant or underused units could also have an adverse effect on trading within the complex as a whole. A well drafted lease would normally contain express use and occupancy covenants requiring the tenant to occupy the premises and to carry on the specified business throughout the agreed term.

There is also the problem of accounting and honesty. For the tenant, the provision of detailed accounts will be burdensome and may also generate concerns lest the accounts should fall into the hands of competitors. For the landlord, it is clearly critical to have an accurate record of the tenant's trading levels; a task becoming easier, though still burdensome, with the growth in electronic check outs and computing. Usually a clause will provide for periodic accounting but in the absence of this the American courts have imposed a duty on the tenant to maintain accurate books and records and to allow the landlord to have reasonable access to them. The Australian retail premises legislation provides for regular accounting and disclosure by tenants, coupled with duties of confidentiality on the landlord's part.

For problems with turnover rents, see Hecht, *Variable Rental Provision in Long Term Ground Leases*, 72 Col L Rev 625 (1972), pp 665–70. See further on the American aspects: 58 ALR 3d 384; Note, *The Percentage Lease—Its Functions and Drafting Problems*, 61 Harv L Rev 317 (1948). Generally, see Clarke and Adams, *Rent Reviews and Variable Rents*, 3rd edn, 1990, ch 21.

8.3.1.3 Sliding Scale Rent (Indexation)

This is where the rent varies by reference to an independent index, normally a consumer price index (in this country, the Retail Prices Index is generally used). Many of the early attempts at rent variation were done on this basis. Indexation has certain advantages: the rent can be increased at regular intervals (potentially at every payment date), indexation of rents is fairly easy to operate and is far cheaper than the now-standard revaluation type of review as indexation does not entail the expense of referring determination of the rent to a third party.

Nevertheless, there are draw-backs. The major disadvantange is the lack of suitable indexes to be used as the base. Consumer price indexes do not reflect fluctuations in the value of real property, only general monetary trends. In times of a buoyant property market this means that the landlord will be under-compensated for the use of the land; in times of recession in property values, the tenant may be paying well over the market rent. A tenant paying rent above the market level will find it difficult to assign the lease other than by paying a reverse premium (a capital sum paid by the tenant to the assignee, reflecting the fact that the assignee is taking on a commitment to pay rent above the market level). There are, however, no suitable property based indexes to be used as an alternative. Further, indexation ignores any local factors, such as the decrease in a retail unit's value caused by the opening of a rival store or the introduction of a one-way system. A variation on standard indexation is to link the review to items that are perceived to reflect changes in business costs, such as labour costs (see the American cases of *Rich v Don-Rich Trousers Corp* 343 NYS 2d 684 (1973) where a clause linked to the increased wages of elevator operators was upheld; and *Pittsburgh Allied Fabricators, Inc v Haber* 271 A 2d 217 (1970) where an option to renew at the same rental subject to 'adjustment for increase in taxes, water, sewage and/or maintenance costs' was held enforceable).

Indexation is not commonly used in this country but is used more frequently in other jurisdictions, such as some of the American States (where it is known as linkage rent) and on the Continent. In Italy, for example, rents are typically reviewed annually by reference to an index (not to exceed 75 per cent of the corresponding increase in the Italian consumer price index). In Portugal, rent reviews are conducted by reference to a government cost of living index. In France, indexation operates as a ceiling on the permitted level of increase: landlords are entitled to review the rent at three year intervals, with a maximum increase calculated by reference to the official index of construction costs (unless the landlord can prove an increase of more than 10 per cent in the value of the leased property since the last review). In these jurisdictions occupational leases are, however, usually much shorter than the almost standard 25 year occupational lease in the United Kingdom, generally being for periods of up to ten years maximum, and often much shorter. Generally on European lease structures, see Shone, *EC leasehold regimes: a comparison*, (1992) 91 EG 92; Ryland, *EC Leasing practices*, (1992) 26 EG 110; RICS, *International Leasing Structures, op. cit.*

8.3.1.4 Unilateral Increase

A simple form of rent review is for the lease to provide for the rent to be unilaterally increased by the landlord serving a notice stating what the new rent will be. While this is clearly a very simple and inexpensive form of rent review, it could easily be exploited by landlords in the absence of any ceiling on rent levels. In one case, Glidewell LJ felt that such a provision would not be valid: 'The tenancy agreement itself cannot give a landlord the power to alter a rent unilaterally', *Dresden Estates Ltd v Collinson* (1988) 55 P & CR 47 at 53. No explanation of this comment was given, however, and it is hard to see what doctrinal objection he was basing it on. Indeed, in the case of *Greater London Council v Connolly, op. cit.*, this kind of clause was upheld. In this case the terms of local authority tenancies provided that the rent was 'liable to be increased or decreased on notice being given'. The provision in the GLC lease reflected a power granted by Parliament in statute (then, the Housing Act 1957, ss 111 and 113; now see the Housing Act 1985, s 24) and power to vary the rent merely reflected the fact that central government could reduce its subsidy to the local authority landlord. As such, the landlord needed the right to increase the rent. The tenants were given three months notice of an increase in rent. The Court of Appeal saw no objection to this provision, so long as 'reasonable notice' of the increase was given (as it was on the facts):

**. . . this rent was sufficiently certain, even though the amount of it was depen-
dent, in a sense, on the whim of the landlords.** (*per* Lord Denning MR at 875 and see
Lord Pearson at 877)

The tenants' argument in the *Connolly* case centred on claims that the provisions were 'uncertain'. The true challenge to these clauses, however, would seem to be based not on uncertainty but unconscionability. In an American case, the challenge was presented on this basis, but the clause was still upheld. In *Witmer v Exxon Corp* 434 A 2d 1222 (1981), a clause in leases of petrol stations provided that landlord could increase the rent by no more than one cent per gallon (rent was based on the number of gallons delivered) and if the tenant objected he could end the lease. The tenants argued, *inter alia*, that the provision was 'unconscionable'. Kaufmann J did not think that the terms were unreasonably favourable to the landlord:

**Exxon was not free under the clause to raise appellants' rents at its whim, but
could do so only once during the lease term and to a maximum of one cent per
gallon. Appellants were thus assured of a maximum rental for their lease terms.**
(at 1228)

The fact that there was a ceiling on the increase in *Witmer* was, therefore, important in upholding the clause.

What would happen here if unilateral increases became commonplace in the residential market with no ceilings imposed? In *Connolly, op. cit.*, there had been no suggestion that the actual increase was extortionate. English courts have always resisted any general doctrine of 'unconscionability' in contract and intervention is generally confined to situations where there is both procedural irregularity ('victimization') and unfairness in the terms of the contract itself ('contractual imbalance'). It could be argued that the inequality of bargaining power inherent in most residential tenancies provides the necessary element of victimization, and the clause itself the necessary element of substantive unfairness. It is hard to accept, however, that the insertion of the clause *in itself* is unfair. After all, the landlord could ask for a very reasonable increase. It is unlikely that such clauses will be struck down unless the courts are willing to adopt a much wider notion of unconscionability than hitherto.

8.3.2 The Modern Rent Review Clause in Commercial Leases

In the United Kingdom commercial property market there is now an almost standard approach to rent review. This works by resetting the rent at periodic intervals throughout the lease to a level that reflects market rents current at the time of review.

The same approach is followed in relation to agricultural holdings. Rents not settled between the parties are referred to arbitration, but here there is a statutory formula which directs the arbitrator to take into account 'all relevant factors' including the terms of the tenancy, the character and situation of the holding, its productive and related earning capacities, and the current level of rents for comparable lettings (see Sch 2, Agricultural Holdings Act 1986). The intention is that the rent should be closely related to the productive and earning capacity of the holding. Within this formula there is a notion of rent control, in that there are certain factors that the arbitrator is directed to disregard when looking at comparable lettings. In particular, he is directed to disregard the impact of scarcity value (*cf.* the notion of scarcity in the residential sector, 8.4.1 below). In so far as these statutory disregards represent an attempt to break t he link between rent reviews and the free market, the agricultural review machinery is perhaps more appropriately to be considered as a form of rent control rather than market based review. The current reform of agricultural tenancy law will, however, move away from rent control. The provisions in the 1986 Act are considered overly complex and, in place of them, parties will be free to agree their own rent review mechanisms within the lease. In default of such agreement, there will be fall-back arrangements whereby the parties to a 'farm business tenancy' can call for review at not less than three year intervals. Rent will then be reviewed on an open market basis (see MAFF, *Agricultural Tenancy Law—Proposals for Reform*, February 1991, para 13; MAFF, *Reform of Agricultural Holdings Legislation: Detailed Proposals*, September 1992, paras 37–45; MAFF, *News Release, Agricultural Tenancy Law Reform*, 6 October 1993).

8.3.2.1 Operation of the Modern Rent Review Clause

With non-agricultural commercial property, the frequency and basis of review is a matter for agreement between the parties. While review clauses vary enormously in detail it is possible to identify common features. There have also been standard precedents published, the best known of which are the precedents produced jointly by the Royal Institution of Chartered Surveyors (RICS) and the Law Society (reproduced in Clarke and Adams, *op. cit.*, at pp 655-69).

Periods of review   Early clauses tended to contain provision for review every seven, ten or fourteen years. Now the standard review period is five years—a shorter period becomes cumbersome, a longer period means that the landlord does not get adequate uplift.

Machinery for review   A common pattern gives the parties the opportunity to agree the new rent between themselves and, failing agreement, for the matter to be referred to an independent person acting as either an arbitrator or an expert. The basic difference between an expert and an arbitrator is that the expert gives his opinion qua expert in that field, his decision binds the parties contractually and there may be no right to appeal, whereas the arbitrator seeks to resolve the dispute by judicial enquiry governed by the Arbitration Acts 1950-1979 and there is a right of appeal from his decision. For a fuller discussion of this distinction, see Ross, *Drafting and Negotiating Commercial Leases*, 3rd edn, 1989, at pp 145–52; Clarke and Adams, *op. cit.*, ch 6.

Formula for review   A common basis is the 'open market rent formula', that is that the new rent should be the best annual rent reasonably obtainable for the demised premises if let on the open market with vacant possession by a willing landlord to a willing tenant for a specified term (*cf.* Housing Act 1988, s 14, see 8.3.3.1 below; Landlord and Tenant Act 1954, s 34 (the formula for setting rent on a new tenancy to be granted under the Act, but, note, the s 34 wording is not entirely satisfactory, see Clarke and Adams, *op. cit.*, pp 391–2)).

The idea behind this approach is to restore the original bargain between the parties to the lease, taking account not only of inflation but also of matters peculiar to this tenancy of this property:

The objective of variable rents can be more precisely identified as a method to maintain so far as possible the original bargain struck between the parties, a bargain that would otherwise be radically transformed by the impact of inflation . . .

If a periodic attempt is made to maintain and restore the original bargain between lessor and lessee it is not only the fall in the value of money by inflation that can be taken into account, for the bargain was made in relation to a particular property, the intrinsic value of which might also have altered and fluctuations in its market value may differ from the rate of inflation. (Clarke and Adams, *op. cit.*, pp 6–7)

For the tenant, the inclusion of rent review provisions enables him to negotiate for a longer lease than would otherwise have been possible:

Tenants who are anxious for security of tenure require a term of reasonable duration, often two years or more. Landlords, on the other hand, are unwilling to grant such leases unless they contain rent revision clauses which will enable the rent to be raised at regular intervals to what is then the fair market rent of the

property demised. Accordingly, it has become the practice for all long leases to contain a rent revision clause providing for a revision of the rent every so many years . . . Both the landlord and the tenant recognize the obvious, viz. that such clauses are fair and reasonable for each of them . . . It is for the benefit of the tenant because without such a clause he would never get the long lease which he requires . . . It is for the benefit of the landlord because it ensures that for the duration of the lease he will receive a fair rent instead of a rent far below the market value of the property which he demises. (*per* Lord Salmon, *United Scientific Holdings Ltd v Burnley BC, op. cit.*, at 86–7)

The first quotation speaks of restoration of the original bargain, the next suggests that the objective is to provide the landlord with a fair rent for the property, not one considerably below the market value, which it would be if left unadjusted. In effect, the review process is intended to restore the original contractual balance. In practice, however, the standard clause typically fails to fulfil these objectives. Instead of restoring the original bargain and restoring 'fairness', the clause tends to overcompensate the landlord. This result is not a necessary consequence of this approach to rent review but reflects the negotiating strength enjoyed by institutional landlords until recently. This can be illustrated by looking at particular features of review clauses.

The hypothetical lease   While the general objective of review clauses can be briefly stated, it is necessary to make detailed provision in the lease as to how this will be implemented. The parties are seeking to agree on a market rent—but of what? Of the property? But then what sort of lease would the property be let on? The assumptions made about the terms of the lease will clearly affect the level of the market rent.

The drafting of the clause Although, generally, a particular property has a market value, it does not, without more, have a market rent. What does have a market rent is *a leasehold interest in that property*, the duration, terms and conditions of which are defined. The most common type of rent review clause therefore requires the parties to assume that certain property (usually the property which is the subject of the existing lease) is being let in the open market on a particular date (usually referred to as the review date), on a lease for a specified duration and containing specified terms and conditions (usually bearing some relationship to the duration, and terms and conditions, of the existing lease), and to agree upon the yearly rent which a hypothetical tenant in the market would pay for that lease. If they cannot agree, a third party will determine that rent for them. The lease then usually provides for the rent reserved by the existing lease to be increased to that figure. The draftsman of such a rent review clause will be well advised to work closely with his client's surveyor . . . (Ross, *op. cit.*, para 6.2)

As can be seen from this extract, the rent will not necessarily be fixed with reference to the particular lease of the particular property. In addition, it is normal for a review to take certain factors into account (the 'assumptions') and to discount other factors (the 'disregards'). Some of these assumptions and disregards will be artificial and will not reflect the actual lease under review.

Any person practising nowadays in the field of landlord and tenant will at once think of a number of questions as to the meaning of these artless phrases [market rent for the demised premises with vacant possession]; for example; in what state are the premises assumed to stand—as they in fact are at the date of review, in proper repair, or in some other, and what, state? For what term are the premises assumed to be available—for 21 years or some other term? On what conditions are the premises offered for letting . . . on the 'usual' covenants, on the covenants in the Underlease, or on some other, and if so, what covenants? (*Sterling Land Office Developments Ltd v Lloyds Bank plc* (1984) 271 EG 894, *per* Harman J at 894)

All assumptions and disregards are false to the extent that they require the parties to imagine something on rent review which is not the case in reality. It is very hard to predict the valuation consequences of certain assumptions—for example, in *Trust House Forte Albany Hotels Ltd v Daejan Investments Ltd* (1980) 256 EG 915, a lease of the Strand Palace Hotel had an assumption that part of the hotel (that was in fact used as a hotel) was 'actually let for or available for shopping and retail purposes'. Did this mean that you also had to assume that it had planning permission for this use and had been physically adapted for this use? It was held that it should be assumed that there were no legal hurdles to the stated use (that is, for example, that planning permission exists) but not that the premises had been physically adapted for the assumed use.

Due to the uncertain economic and valuation consequences of assumptions and disregards, the general rule is that it is inadvisable for the hypothetical lease to differ from the actual lease more than is necessary:

There is, I think, a presumption that the hypothesis upon which the rent should be fixed upon a review should bear as close a resemblance to reality as possible. (*Norwich Union Life Insurance Society v Trustee Savings Bank Central Board* [1986] 1 EGLR 136, *per* Hoffman J at 137)

An additional reason for the hypothetical lease to mirror as closely as possible the actual lease (and that assumptions and disregards should be kept to a minimum) is that, if the aim is to restore the initial bargain, and thus fairness, then the tenant should pay the rent on the basis of what he actually has.

However, even if the generally accepted objective of review is to restore the original contractual balance, a review of the actual lease will not necessarily achieve this. This can be seen by looking at the assumptions that need to be made about the length of the lease on review. In the case of a lease originally granted for 25 years, with the rent being reviewed after twenty years, that is, with only five years left to run, what assumption should be made about the term of the lease? To assume, on review, that the lease is for 25 years (the original bargain) may mean the tenant has to pay a far higher rent towards the end of the term than would otherwise be payable for the residue of the lease. This seems unfair to the tenant. But to assume that the lease has only five years to run (the actual lease on review) could significantly reduce the rent below the 'market rent', and thus reduce the attractiveness of commercial property as an investment medium. Which best approaches the objective of restoring contractual balance? In practice a compromise position is often adopted which assumes that the term on review is the unexpired residue subject to a minimum (for example, for 'a term of ten years or the residue then unexpired, whichever is the longer').

Another illustration of the difficulty of agreeing what the assumptions and disregards should be on review is deciding what assumptions should be made about the availability of letting incentives. During slumps in the property market tenants may be offered considerable inducements by a landlord to enter into a lease. Should these incentives be taken into account on review? In *99 Bishopsgate v Prudential Assurance* (1985) 273 EG 984, the rent was being reviewed for a thirty-floor office block. The Court of Appeal held that the rent on review should be drastically reduced, on the grounds that a hypothetical tenant in the market at the review date would have been able to negotiate a sixteen-month rent-free period because he would not personally occupy the whole building, but would have to arrange underlettings and allow his prospective underlessees a further rent-free period while they carried out their fitting out works. Since that decision, many leases have contained clauses requiring fitting-out inducements to be disregarded, the argument for this being that the inducements are 'one-off' initial concessions made to enable the tenant to fit out the premises to his particular requirements and that this should not be used at future reviews when the tenant is in possession (such a disregard is found in the RICS/Law Society *Model Forms*). In addition to fitting-out inducements, rent-free periods are also given as an incentive to take the lease. There is less agreement on whether these rent-free periods should be disregarded on review. Landlords often insert clauses seeking *all* inducements to be disregarded on review. Ross disagrees with this approach, arguing that inducements should be taken into account on review as they form an important part of comparing rents for other similar properties, which is part of the review process, and to remove them from consideration would present valuation difficulties and be unfair to the tenant (*op. cit.*, at para 6.20:3).

It is, therefore, often difficult to see what assumptions and disregards should be made in order to restore the contractual balance. Additionally, landlords often seek to 'improve' the terms of a hypothetical lease, that is, to build in assumptions that do not reflect the actual terms and will lead to a higher rent being payable. 'Improvements' are often made in relation to the user assumptions. If the lease contains a narrow user clause ('to be used only as a grocers') this will lower the rent—fewer tenants will want the property and those who do will want an allowance for the restricted use clause. Conversely, generous use provisions ('to be used for retail purposes') will raise the rent and make the property more easy to let. In practice, therefore, a landlord may try to put an onerous clause into the lease, but to assume a more generous one on review. This can make a big valuation difference: in *Plinth Property Investments Ltd v Mott, Hay and Anderson* (1979) 38 P & CR 361, the full market rent was £130,455 without any use restriction, but limited to use as a civil engineering business it was £89,200. Is it fair to assume a wider user clause on review than is found in the actual lease?

Upwards only review   The idea of restoring the original contractual balance, of reflecting the market value at review, suggests that the rent should be capable of going up or down. In practice, most rent reviews tend to be upwards only, so the rent will never fall below that being paid already. This means that if rental values have in fact fallen between the date of the last review and the date of the present review, the tenant is left paying historically high rents which do not reflect current economic conditions. This occurred commonly after the rapid rise in City rentals during the late 1980s followed by the severe decline in property values in the early 1990s.

This property slump brought with it challenges to the upwards only nature of review clauses. For tenants, the effect of such clauses is harsh during recessionary periods. Indeed, this has now been judicially recognized. In *Boots the Chemists Ltd v Pinkland Ltd* [1992] 28 EG 118, Boots were applying for a new tenancy under Part II of the Landlord and Tenant Act 1954. The general presumption in these cases is that the terms of the new tenancy should be the same as those of the current tenancy unless the party seeking a change can show that the change is fair and reasonable in the circumstances (s 35; *O'May v City of London Real Property Co Ltd* [1983] 2 AC 726). However, s 34(3) permits the court to include a rent review clause even though the original lease did not contain provisions for review. In the *Boots* case, it was agreed that the new lease should contain provision for rent review but there was a dispute over whether this should be an upwards only review. Thompson J said:

Over the last forty years there has been a more or less constant bull market in rents. In any bull market there are always bear phases, and I have no means of knowing whether the decline in rental values over the past two years is merely a bear phase in the continuing bull market or whether it is the beginning of a new bear market, indicating that the long-running bull market has now come to an

end. In order to do that which is fair and reasonable to the parties it seems to me that it would be appropriate to incorporate in the new Boots lease provision for the rent to be reviewed downwards as well as upwards. I come to that conclusion for this reason. If it be the case that we are now in the incipient stages of a prolonged bear market then present-day rents will seem exorbitant later in this decade and in the beginning of the next century. As a consequence, fixed rents, or rents which can only be revised upwards, will wreak the same sort of injustice upon tenants as that which has been suffered by landlords in previous decades when leases contained no provision for rent review at all. On the other hand, if the present period of decline in rental values is merely an aberration in a continuing bull market, the landlords will in no way be prejudiced by the inclusion of a provision for the rents to be reviewed downwards as well as upwards. I therefore so hold. (at 119)

There have been other cases in which judges have been prepared to insert two-way clauses on the renewal of a lease. In *Janes (Gowns) Ltd v Harlow Development Corporation* (1979) 253 EG 799, Judge Finlay felt that the clause should provide for review in either direction having heard evidence that the development of a neighbouring centre might well have a detrimental effect on the rent of the shop (see also, *Forbouys plc v Newport Borough Council* (1994) 24 EG 156, Morgan J ordering a two-way clause as this would be 'fair to both parties; at reviews, the rent to be determined will largely depend on prevailing market conditions' (at 157)).

Up-or-down review clauses have an impact on the investment value of the property. This was recognized by Judge Diamond in *Blythewood Plant Hire Ltd v Spiers Ltd* (1992) 48 EG 117, refusing to insert a two-way clause and stating that

A clause in this form would have the result that the landlord's interest would become more difficult to market. It would therefore have an immediate impact on the value of the landlord's interest. On the other hand, the evidence suggested that a tenant would not pay substantially more rent for an upward/downward clause as such a clause is likely to be of little immediate benefit to the tenant. (at 117)

However, in *Abdul Amarjee v Barrowfen Properties Ltd* (Correspondence (1993) 08 EG 39), the judge did award a higher rent to reflect the inclusion of an upward/downward clause.

During the recession, there was pressure for institutional landlords to reconsider the standard insistence on upwards only reviews (see the unsuccessful private member's bill, Upwards-only Rent Review Clauses (Abolition) Bill 1993/4). Few landlords were willing to depart from the upwards only review patterns, but many met tenant concerns in other ways by, for example, providing the opportunity to end the lease after a few years or by agreeing to cap the rental increase on the first review. Concerns about the impact of upwards only review clauses were aired in the Department of the Environment's Consultation Paper on Commercial Property Leases, 27 May 1993, but, in the event, the government rejected the idea of prohibiting the use of such clauses and, instead, recommended the adoption of a 'Code of Practice which draws attention not only to the implications of upwards rent review clauses but encourages flexibility on other terms' (Press Release, 19 July 1994). A Code of Practice is unlikely to have a significant effect on standard lease terms.

Comparability The aim on review is to assess the market rent for the hypothetical lease. In standard economic market analysis this would mean looking at the excess of demand or supply and expected future inflation over the period of review. In practice, surveyors and valuers have assessed market value by looking to 'comparables'—newly agreed rents of comparable premises. This is a highly subjective process as no two properties are identical. In addition, this method does not take account of zero rents from empty and unlet premises.

Adopting the yardstick of comparability also assumes the existence of an effective market—but for this to exist there needs to be full information on the market. The increasing use of confidentiality clauses, imposed particularly in the case of 'generous' lettings, again distorts the process of determining the market rent and has been heavily criticized because of the fact that it is an obstacle to a perfect market (see the Department of the Environment's Consultation Paper, *op. cit.*). It is also opposed by tenants who see confidentiality clauses as a form of landlord protectionism.

8.3.2.2 Disadvantages of the Modern Rent Review Clause

While this form of rent review has become the norm, it does have disadvantages. The procedure is time-consuming and may be expensive. Parties will often need to appoint professionals to assist in the valuation exercise and if the review cannot be settled by agreement, and frequently it cannot, the costs will increase still further with the reference to a third party.

The three features examined above (the hypothetical lease, upwards only review, and comparability), in combination, tend to increase the rent at review beyond the true market rent for the leasehold interest in the premises. A tenant paying an inflated rent will find it difficult to assign his leasehold interest and, in order to do so, may have to pay a premium to the purchaser (a 'reverse premium').

The Law Commission has asked whether the parties should be free to agree rents higher than the market rent. It concluded that there were no reasons to intervene to protect the parties (both are normally professionally advised), although there may be wider social interests in restricting rent to market levels to mitigate the inflationary effects of increased business overheads caused by the rent review process (see Law Commission, *Landlord and Tenant Law: Reform of the Law*, Law Com. No. 162, 1987, at paras 4.60–4.62).

The inflationary effect of the review process has been highlighted in a study of the retail sector which shows the rise in rents of retail outlets between 1984 and 1988 as being more than double the increase in retail sales and consumer expenditure. These rent increases have crippled many businesses and been a major factor in the failure of many others. Yet such increases are not the outcome of the operation of market forces—during a recession rents on review should fall (as did rents on new lettings), but this seldom happens in practice. Instead these steep rises flow from the standard features of institutional leases (upwards only review, long terms) and represent a core type of inflation largely unrecognised by economists and yet presenting a serious underlying problem for the British economy in general, and the retail sector in particular (see Burton, *Retail Rents, Fair and Free Market?*, 1992; and see 8.4.4).

8.3.2.3 Interpretation of Rent Review Clauses

A further disadvantage of the modern rent review clause is the amount of litigation disputing the interpretation of review clauses, spawned by the complexity of review clauses and the sums of money involved. The problem with the hypothetical lease appproach is that it becomes very hard to define exactly what it is that is being assessed. The cases reveal enormous tension between a literal construction of contractual terms and a purposive construction that will have regard to the commercial objectives of the review clause. This is illustrated by the *Arthur Young* saga.

In the *Arthur Young* case (*National Westminster Bank plc v Arthur Young McClelland Moores & Co* [1985] 1 EGLR 61), the review clause was worded in such a way that it could be interpreted on a literal reading of the words used as requiring an assumption to be made when reviewing the rent that there would be no future reviews, even though the lease did clearly provide for future reviews. The effect of such an assumption would be to inflate the rent on each review. In the actual case the rent would be 20.5 per cent higher than the market rent would be without such an assumption. The relevant part of the clause read that the rent was to be reviewed '[subject] to the provisions of this . . . lease other than the rent hereby reserved.' The aim of the wording was to exclude on review consideration of the actual rent then being paid. On a literal view, however, it could be taken as requiring the reviewer to disregard *all* of the provisions relating to rent, and thus to ignore the fact that there would be future reviews of rent. This literal approach was taken by Walton J.

The *Arthur Young* decision sent shock waves through the commercial property world. Since then, there has been a series of cases stressing the need to adopt a 'commercial' approach to the construction of review clauses. Guidelines on construction enunciated by the Vice-Chancellor in *British Gas Corporation v Universities Superannuation Scheme Ltd* [1986] 1 All ER 978, stress the need to give effect to the underlying commercial purpose of a rent review clause. This was again a case where a literal reading of the words used would require the reviewer to disregard *all* of the provisions relating to rent on review. Whilst admitting this was the only construction that the words literally bore, the Vice-Chancellor said that such a result offended common sense. In determining how to construe the clause, it was necessary therefore to look at the underlying purpose of the review provisions:

The purpose is to reflect the changes in the value of money and real increases in the value of the property during a long term. Such being the purpose, in the absence of special circumstances it would . . . be wayward to impute to the parties an intention that the landlord should get a rent which was additionally inflated by a factor which has no reference either to changes in the value of money or in the value of property but is referable to a factor which has no existence as between the actual landlord and the actual tenant, ie. the additional rent which could be obtained if there were no provisions for rent review. Of course, the lease may be expressed in words so clear that there is no room for giving effect to such underlying purpose. Again, there may be special surrounding circumstances which indicate that the parties did intend to reach such an unusual bargain. But in the absence of such clear words or surrounding circumstances . . . the lease should be construed so as to give effect to the basic purpose of the rent review clause and not so as to confer on the landlord a windfall benefit which he could never obtain on the market if he were actually letting the premises at the review date, viz. a letting on terms which contain provisions for rent review at a rent appropriate to a letting which did not contain such a provision. (at 980–1)

It is now well established that the court should have regard to the reality and commercial purpose of rent review in cases where the wording of the clause is ambiguous. Nevertheless, there is a constant stream of litigation raising new difficulties in drafting and interpretation: see, for example, the Court of Appeal's decision in *Co-operative Wholesale Society Ltd v National Westminster Bank plc*; *Broadgate Square plc v Lehman Brothers Ltd*; *Scottish Amicable Life Assurance Society v Middleton and Others* [1995] O1 EG 111; *Prudential Nominees Ltd v Greenham Trading* [1994] EGCS 184, stressing the need to take account of the purpose of rent review when interpreting review clauses.

8.3.3 Rent Review in the Residential Sector

8.3.3.1 Private Sector

Until 1988 most residential lettings were regulated by the Rent Act 1977 with its system of 'fair rents' (see 8.4.1 below). There was, therefore, very little scope for the parties to agree contractually how the rent would be varied—any such provisions could effectively be avoided by a regulated tenant applying for registration of a fair

Figure 8.1 Rent Review in Assured Periodic Tenancy

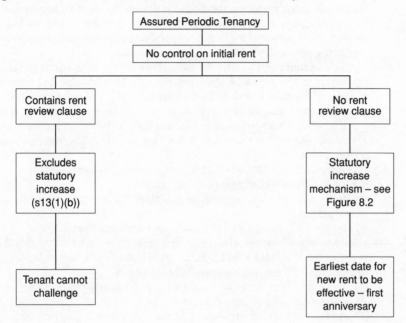

rent. Since the introduction of the Housing Act 1988, however, it is now possible for the parties to include rent review provisions within the lease. Even in the absence of such contractual agreement, there is a statutory procedure for rent variation aimed at enabling the landlord to recover the market rental for the premises.

The policy underlying the Housing Act 1988 is to permit the parties to agree the rent and any provision for reviewing it. Exactly how the provisions operate depends on the kind of tenancy involved.

In relation to periodic assured tenancies, any rent review mechanism built into the lease will govern all rent variations—see Figure 8.1.

If there is no contractual provision for changing the rent level, the landlord can take advantage of the statutory increase mechanism set out in s 13 of the Act.

s 13(1) This section applies to–
    (a) a statutory periodic tenancy other than one which, by virtue of paragraph 11 or paragraph 12 in Part I of Schedule 1 to this Act, cannot for the time being be an assured tenancy; and
    (b) any other periodic tenancy which is an assured tenancy, other than one in relation to which there is a provision, for the time being binding on the tenant, under which the rent for a particular period of the tenancy will or may be greater than the rent for an earlier period.

(2) For the purpose of securing an increase in the rent under a tenancy to which this section applies, the landlord may serve on the tenant a notice in the prescribed form proposing a new rent to take effect at the beginning of a new period of the tenancy specified in the notice, being a period beginning not earlier than—

(a) the minimum period after the date of the service of the notice; and

(b) except in the case of a statutory periodic tenancy, the first anniversary of the date on which the first period of the tenancy began; and

(c) if the rent under the tenancy has previously been increased by virtue of a notice under this subsection or a determination under section 14 below, the first anniversary of the date on which the increased rent took effect.

(3) The minimum period referred to in subsection (2) above is—

(a) in the case of a yearly tenancy, six months;

(b) in the case of a tenancy where the period is less than a month, one month; and

(c) in any other case, a period equal to the period of the tenancy.

(4) Where a notice is served under subsection (2) above, a new rent specified in the notice shall take effect as mentioned in the notice unless, before the beginning of the new period specified in the notice,—

(a) the tenant by an application in the prescribed form refers the notice to a rent assessment committee; or

(b) the landlord and the tenant agree on a variation of the rent which is different from that proposed in the notice or agree that the rent should not be varied.

(5) Nothing in this section (or in section 14 below) affects the right of the landlord and the tenant under an assured tenancy to vary by agreement any term of the tenancy (including a term relating to rent).

s 14(1) Where, under subsection (4)(a) of section 13 above, a tenant refers to a rent assessment committee a notice under subsection (2) of that section, the committee shall determine the rent at which, subject to subsections (2) and (4) below, the committee consider that the dwelling-house concerned might reasonably be expected to be let in the open market by a willing landlord under an assured tenancy—

(a) which is a periodic tenancy having the same periods as those of the tenancy to which the notice relates;

(b) which begins at the beginning of the new period specified in the notice;

(c) the terms of which (other than relating to the amount of the rent) are the same as those of the tenancy to which the notice relates; and

(d) in respect of which the same notices, if any, have been given under any of Grounds 1 to 5 of Schedule 2 to this Act, as have been given (or have effect as if given) in relation to the tenancy to which the notice relates.

(2) In making a determination under this section, there shall be disregarded—

   (a) any effect on the rent attributable to the granting of a tenancy to a sitting tenant;

   (b) any increase in the value of the dwelling-house attributable to a relevant improvement carried out by a person who at the time it was carried out was the tenant, if the improvement—

     (i) was carried out otherwise than in pursuance of an obligation to his immediate landlord, or

     (ii) was carried out pursuant to an obligation to his immediate landlord being an obligation which did not relate to the specific improvement concerned but arose by reference to consent given to the carrying out of that improvement; and

   (c) any reduction in the value of the dwelling-house attributable to a failure by the tenant to comply with any terms of the tenancy.

(3) For the purposes of subsection (2)(b) above, in relation to a notice which is referred by a tenant as mentioned in subsection (1) above, an improvement is a relevant improvement if either it was carried out during the tenancy to which the notice relates or the following conditions are satisfied, namely—

   (a) that it was carried out not more than twenty-one years before the date of service of the notice; and

   (b) that, at all times during the period beginning when the improvement was carried out and ending on the date of service of the notice, the dwelling-house has been let under an assured tenancy; and

   (c) that, on the coming to an end of an assured tenancy at any time during that period, the tenant (or, in the case of joint tenants, at least one of them) did not quit.

(3A) In making a determination under this section in any case where under Part I of the Local Government Finance Act 1992 the landlord or a superior landlord is liable to pay council tax in respect of a hereditament ('the relevant hereditament') of which the dwelling-house forms part, the rent assessment committee shall have regard to the amount of council tax which, as at the date on which the notice under section 13(2) above was served, was set by the billing authority—

   (a) for the financial year in which that notice was served, and

   (b) for the category of dwellings within which the relevant hereditament fell on that date,

but any discount or other reduction affecting the amount of council tax payable shall be disregarded.

(3B) In subsection (3A) above—

   (a) 'hereditament' means a dwelling within the meaning of Part I of the Local Government Finance Act 1992,

   (b) 'billing authority' has the same meaning as in that Part of the Act, and

   (c) 'category of dwellings' has the same meaning as in section 30(1) and (2) of that Act.

(4) In this section 'rent' does not include any service charge, within the meaning of section 18 of the Landlord and Tenant Act 1985, but, subject to that, includes any sums payable by the tenant to the landlord on account of the use of furniture, in respect of council tax or for any of the matters referred to in subsection (1)(a) of that section, whether or not those sums are separate from the sums payable for the occupation of the dwelling-house concerned or are payable under separate agreements.

(5) Where any rates in respect of the dwelling-house concerned are borne by the landlord or a superior landlord, the rent assessment committee shall make their determination under this section as if the rates were not so borne.

Figure 8.2 Statutory Increase Mechanism: s 13 Housing Act 1988

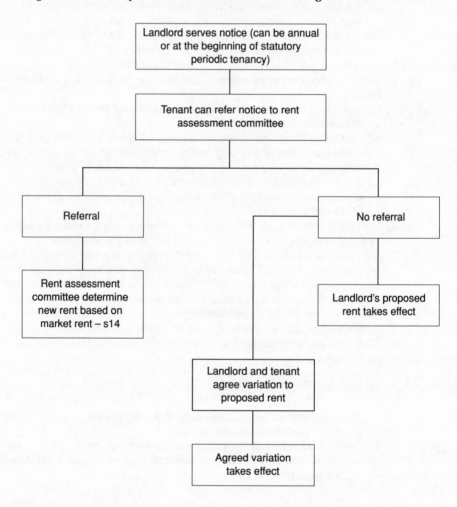

How the statutory increase mechanism works is shown in Figure 8.2. The parties are given the option of agreeing the rent increase between themselves—either by the tenant accepting the landlord's proposals as to the new rent or by reaching mutual agreement. Failing this the tenant can apply to the Rent Assessment Committee (RAC) which must consider the rent at which the 'dwelling-house concerned might reasonably be expected to be let in the open market by a willing landlord under an assured tenancy' (Housing Act 1988, s 14(1)). In reaching its decision the RAC must take account of the terms of the tenancy and the level of security the tenant has and disregard the effect of any improvements carried out by the tenant, the fact that there is a sitting tenant and any reductions in value due to breaches by the tenant. In effect, this formula is seeking a market rent in a similar way to that common in commercial rent reviews.

During a fixed term assured tenancy, the statutory mechanism for changing the rent level cannot operate—the only way that the rent can be varied during the fixed term is by the inclusion of rent review provisions within the tenancy agreement. This is shown by Figure 8.3, next page. At the expiry of the fixed term, a statutory periodic tenancy arises under the Housing Act 1988, s 5(2) and any rent review provisions contractually agreed for the fixed term tenancy will continue to apply (unless these terms have been varied by using s 6; see ch 11.2.5.2). If, however, there were no contractually agreed review provisions, the s 13 statutory increase mechanism can be invoked during the statutory periodic tenancy.

The thrust of the Housing Act 1988 is, therefore, to encourage the parties to either include review procedures within the letting agreement or to use the statutory mechanism for increase. Either way, rents are likely to follow market rents closely. The Housing Act 1988 represents a marked change in the attitude towards private sector tenancies. Before the Act, review clauses were exceptional in this sector.

What method of review will be appropriate for residential lettings? It is clear that the periodic revaluation method used in commercial lettings is inappropriate—it is expensive to operate, too slow to respond to market changes (important in the shorter lets found in the residential sector) and too complex. Review procedures need to be far simpler and cheaper to operate in the residential sector. Various forms of clause have been proposed, of varying complexity: indexation linked to the Retail Prices Index (see *Precedents for the Conveyancer*, Vol 1, 5–99); agreement between the parties, failing which the issue is referred to a valuer (see *Precedents for the Conveyancer*, Vol 1, 5–100 and 5–104); and landlord's unilateral notice of increase (see *Precedents for the Conveyancer*, Vol 1, 5–103; see further Clarke and Adams, *op. cit.*, ch 17; Clarke, *Rent Reviews in Residential Tenancies*, [1989] Conv 111).

Figure 8.3 Rent Review: Fixed Term and Statutory Periodic Tenancy

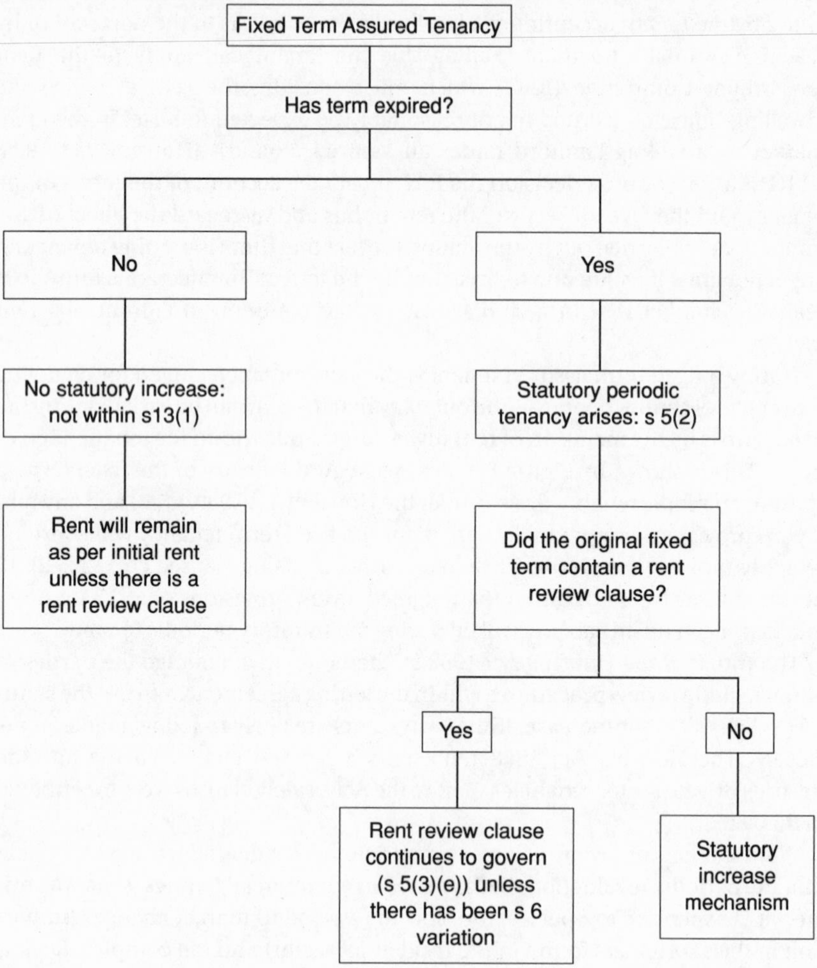

```
                    ┌──────────────────────────────┐
                    │   Fixed Term Assured Tenancy  │
                    └──────────────────────────────┘
                                   │
                    ┌──────────────────────────────┐
                    │       Has term expired?       │
                    └──────────────────────────────┘
                                   │
              ┌────────────────────┴────────────────────┐
     ┌─────────────────┐                      ┌─────────────────┐
     │       No        │                      │       Yes       │
     └─────────────────┘                      └─────────────────┘
              │                                        │
     ┌─────────────────┐                      ┌─────────────────┐
     │ No statutory     │                     │  Statutory periodic │
     │ increase:        │                     │  tenancy arises: s 5(2) │
     │ not within s13(1)│                     └─────────────────┘
     └─────────────────┘                               │
     ┌─────────────────┐                      ┌─────────────────┐
     │ Rent will remain │                     │ Did the original fixed │
     │ as per initial rent │                  │ term contain a rent │
     │ unless there is a │                    │ review clause?     │
     │ rent review clause │                   └─────────────────┘
     └─────────────────┘                               │
                                        ┌──────────────┴──────────────┐
                                  ┌───────────┐              ┌───────────┐
                                  │    Yes    │              │    No     │
                                  └───────────┘              └───────────┘
                                        │                          │
                              ┌───────────────────┐      ┌──────────────┐
                              │ Rent review clause │     │  Statutory    │
                              │ continues to govern │    │  increase     │
                              │ (s 5(3)(e)) unless  │    │  mechanism    │
                              │ there has been s 6  │    └──────────────┘
                              │ variation           │
                              └───────────────────┘
```

8.3.3.2 Local Authority Sector

Local authority landlords have always had the power to change the rent level—
see now, the Housing Act 1985, s 25. Having decided to increase the rent, the local
authority must then give notice of the change to the tenant in line with either a
provision in the lease (see *Connolly, op. cit.*) or Housing Act 1985, ss 102 and 103.

Although the tenant does not have to 'agree' the rent increase before it takes effect, there are various ways in which the increase can be challenged. As well as judicial review of the council's decision, to be considered below, a challenge can be made through an audit or the Commissioner for Local Administration (ombudsman). The auditor, either as part of a general or extraordinary audit (Local Government Finance Act 1982, Part III), can seek a declaration that the rent set is 'contrary to law'; for instance, if the new rent would be inadequate to prevent a debit in the HRA (see Local Government and Finance Act 1989, s 76). An extraordinary audit may be held at the behest of a local government elector for the relevant area. Further, a local government elector for the relevant area can ask the auditor to review the local authority's accounts and can challenge the auditor's decision in the High Court or county court. The Ombudsman can investigate a case of maladministration by the local authority in relation to a tenant's rent (Local Government Act 1974, as amended by Local Government and Housing Act 1989). However, the usual route to challenge the local authority's rent fixing is through judicial review, although it should be noted that the success rate has been minimal—there have been only two successful challenges and one of them was in the peculiar case of *Backhouse, op. cit.* Following *O'Reilly v Mackman* [1982] 3 All ER 1124, *per* Lord Diplock at 1134, a person seeking to challenge a local authority over its determination of the rent must use judicial review. However, if challenging the validity of the rent forms part of a defendant's case, then he may raise such a defence in any sort of proceedings and is not prohibited from so doing even though the limitation period for seeking review has passed (the *Wandsworth v Winder* Saga: *Wandsworth LBC v Winder* [1985] 1 AC 461; *London Borough of Wandsworth v Winder (No. 2)* (1987) 19 HLR 204 Ch; (1988) 20 HLR 400 CA; and see ch 3.10). Judicial review tests the validity of the local authority's decision against the *Wednesbury* principles:

[It] is true to say that if a decision on a competent matter is so unreasonable that no reasonable authority could have come to it, then the courts can interfere. (*Associated Provincial Picture Houses v Wednesbury Corporation* [1948] 1 KB 223, *per* Lord Greene MR at 230)

A decision will be unreasonable, according to Lord Greene MR,

if a person entrusted with a discretion (a) fails to call to his attention matters which he is bound to consider, or (b) if he does not exclude from his consideration matters which are irrelevant to what he has to consider, or (c) if a decision is so absurd that no reasonable person 'would ever dream that it lay within the powers of the authority'. (*Winder (No. 2)* (1987) 19 HLR 204, *per* Mervyn Davies J at 208–9)

A decision will not be unreasonable simply because the local authority failed to take account of a matter which it was open to consider; the matter must be compulsory, in the sense that although statute neither prescribes nor prohibits it, a reasonable local authority would take it into account (*Winder (No. 2)* (1988) 20 HLR 400 at 406). The Court of Appeal's reasoning in *Winder (No. 2)* is tautologous, but it allows the courts to remain outside the political arena and to grant local authorities a broad discretion in the setting of and raising of rents. In *Luby v Newcastle under Lyme Corporation* [1964] 2 QB 64, cited in *Hemsted v Lees and Norwich CC* (1986) 18 HLR 424 at 428–9, the Divisional Court held it was not part of its role to substitute its own decision for that of the council.

In determining the rent structure to be applied . . ., the local authority is applying what is, in effect, a social policy upon which reasonable men may hold different views . . . It is in my view quite impossible for this court to say that this choice, which is one of social policy, is one which no reasonable man could have made, and is therefore *ultra vires*, any more than it could be said that the opposite choice would have been *ultra vires*. (*Luby, op. cit., per* Diplock LJ at 72)

Forbes J in *R v Secretary of State for Health and Social Security, ex parte City of Sheffield* (1986) 18 HLR 6 at 20, went further, stating that courts ought to

hesitate long before deciding that in the field of policy a local authority had failed to take into account something material or taken into account something that was immaterial . . .

However in *R v London Borough of Ealing, ex parte Jennifer Lewis* (1992) 24 HLR 484, the Court of Appeal set limits on the scope of that discretion. The case concerned the question of what might legitimately be included as items of expenditure within the HRA for the purposes of the Local Government and Housing Act 1989. Sch 4 provides:

Part II, Debits to the Account
Item 1
The expenditure of the authority for the year in respect of the repair, maintenance, supervision and management of houses and other property within the account, . . .
If the Secretary of State so directs, this item shall include, or not include, such expenditure as may be determined under the direction.

In *Ex parte Jennifer Lewis*, the local authority had increased the rent and had included as a debit to the HRA the salaries of staff who assessed whether a person qualified as homeless under Part III of the Housing Act 1985, who ran the Housing Advisory Service and who acted as wardens in sheltered accommodation for the elderly. No-one disputed that some of their salaries could be classified as relating to the 'management of houses and other property', the question was how many aspects of their jobs satisfied that criterion, given that it ought to be accorded a broad interpretation (*Shelley v London County Council* [1948] 1 KB

274). Woolf LJ, the most liberal member of the bench, accepted that the courts should be loath to interfere with a political decision and gave reasons as to why judicial review should be secondary to an audit.

In general, I have no doubt that it is inappropriate and undesirable for a court on an application for judicial review to become involved in the detail as to how individual authorities draw up their respective HRAs. If the court were to become so involved it would lead to an undesirable increase in litigation which could interfere, as this case threatens to interfere, with the budgetary process of an authority. In general it is preferable to leave the supervision in the hands of the Secretary of State and the district auditor and for the courts, if they are to become involved, to defer that involvement until the matter has been canvassed before other bodies. If this is not done, problems may arise because in relation to the auditing process which is conducted under the Local Government Finance Act 1982, the Secretary of State has the power to sanction an item in an account although it appears to the auditor when carrying out the audit that the item is contrary to law. Furthermore, on an application to the court by the auditor where it appears to the auditor that an item of account is contrary to law, the court's power to grant a declaration is limited 'if the court is satisfied that for example the person authorising an expenditure acted reasonably.' The undesirability of the court becoming involved is underlined where the consequences of possible illegality involve calculations which the court is not in a position to make and where the amount at issue is small. (at 494)

However, Lloyd LJ set out the limits of the local authority's discretion as it applies with respect to Sch 4:

(iv) The fact that the Secretary of State has a limited discretion in relation to Item 1 shows that there are items of expenditure which, on the true construction of the statutory language, may fall on the borderline. Local authorities have a discretion to include or exclude such items, subject to any direction by the Secretary of State. But this is the limit of the local authority's discretion.

(v) Whether any particular item of expenditure falls within Item 1 is a question of fact. Whether it is capable of falling within Item 1 is a question of law. (at 486)

Local authorities have no discretion to include an item not within the statute or to exclude one within it. On this view, where the discretion lies is with items that could, at the periphery, fall within the Act—in that case, the courts will not interfere with a council's decision. *Luby* and Lloyd LJ's comments in *Lewis* are compatible, for the courts have never been averse to ruling on the interpretation of precise terms of statutes, while it is loath to become involved in political in-fighting on matters not expressly dealt with in the statute.

To grant declaratory relief without quashing the precept would have been wholly without point save perhaps in giving some politician a catch phrase and he would not add judicial authority to that end, nor could it be a legitimate exercise of

judicial authority. (*R v GLC, ex parte Kensington and Chelsea*, The Times, 7 April 1982, *per* McNeill J)

The successful challenge in *Lewis*, the first in twenty years, reflects the 'ring-fencing' of the HRA and the duty of local authorities to ensure that no extraneous items now come into the Account as defined in the 1989 Act. Lloyd LJ was at pains to point out throughout his judgment that previous practice as to what was a legitimate expense on the HRA had little or no bearing on the interpretation of the 1989 Act. More successful challenges on the wording of Sch 4 cannot be ruled out.

Local authorities are a special case when it comes to varying the rent. Given the interplay of rent and subsidy, Parliament had to grant special powers to local authorities to increase the rent—such decisions are subject to review by the courts, but they have, so far, largely avoided involvement by deeming the decision on rent levels to be a political question and outside the judicial remit unless the decision is *ultra vires* or absurd. Market forces have little or no influence on local authority rents. Nevertheless, a rent of £18,000 per week in *Backhouse, op. cit.*, was in no way *Wednesbury* reasonable!

8.3.4 Judicial Variation of Leasehold Terms?

In the absence of any provision for an increase in rent, is there anything a landlord can do if he is locked into a lease with a rent now considerably below market rent? In a private residential assured tenancy, the landlord can now invoke the statutory increase mechanism in the Housing Act 1988, s 13. There is no comparable statutory provision for commercial lettings.

Imagine a 99-year lease entered into in 1920 (when rent review clauses were exceptional) and which provided for an annual rental of £3,000. Given the huge increases in rental figures since then, the true market level would now be many times greater. To restrict the landlord to recovering rent at 1920 levels seems unfair as the landlord is being undercompensated for the use of his land at great advantage to the tenant.

From time to time there have been judges and academics who have argued that the courts have power to alter contract terms when there has been such a change in circumstances that the strict terms operate harshly. Support for this approach can be drawn from the cases of *Staffordshire Area Health Authority v South Staffordshire Waterworks Co* [1978] 1 WLR 1387 and *Pole Properties v Feinberg* (1981) 43 P & CR 121. In the *Staffordshire* case, an agreement had been entered into to supply water at a fixed price. By 1975 the cost of supply had risen to over eighteen times the contract price and the supply company purported to end the agreement by notice. Even though the contract was expressed to be binding 'at all times hereafter', the Court of Appeal held it was able to end the agreement 'on reasonable notice'. Lord Denning MR's judgment drew heavily on the language of contractual frustration:

Here we have in the present case a striking of a long term obligation entered into 50 years ago . . . Is it right that the hospital should go on forever only paying the old rate of 50 years ago?
. . . here the situation has changed so radically since the contract was made 50 years ago that the term of the contract 'at all times hereafter' ceases to bind. (at 1398)

The case did, though, turn on a question of construction inapplicable to fixed term leases, and Lord Denning MR's wide remarks have generally been taken as unrepresentative of judicial opinion.

In the *Pole Properties* case, *op. cit.*, a lease provided for the tenant to pay two-sevenths of the cost of fuel, a rate calculated by reference to the floor area of the tenant's flat in relation to the whole building. When an additional building was added the tenant argued that two-sevenths was now a disproportionate share of the total cost and the Court of Appeal agreed with this, Lord Denning MR saying that as the situation had radically changed, the terms of the lease no longer applied and the court would do what was fair and reasonable in the all the circumstances.

It is, however, very unlikely that a landlord would be able to get a revision of the rent payable in a lease in the circumstances envisaged earlier. Lord Denning cannot be said to be representative of judicial opinion and the courts have repeatedly stressed that frustration cannot be used to strike down an improvident bargain. Nor have the courts been willing to develop other ways to re-open long term contracts that have become imbalanced over time. In *British Movietonews Ltd v London and District Cinemas* [1952] AC 166, Lord Simon said at 185:

The parties to an executory contract are often faced, in the course of carrying it out, with a turn of events which they did not at all anticipate—a wholly abnormal rise or fall in prices, a sudden depreciation of currency, an unexpected obstacle to the execution, or the like. Yet this does not in itself affect the bargain which they have made. (See also *Davis Contractors Ltd v Fareham DC* [1956] 2 All ER 145, where the vastly increased cost of performing a building contract did not excuse the contractors.)

Frustration has been argued in cases analogous to long term leases with no rent review provisions, namely where the original lease was granted for a fixed rent and contained an option to renew. In *Bracknell Development Corporation v Greenlees Lennerds Ltd* (1981) 260 EG 501, the original 21-year lease contained an option to renew 'at a full and fair market rent'. Counsel for the landlord argued that the new lease should contain provisions for periodic review of the rent, the effect of inflation making a fixed rent so unfair that the doctrine of frustration would apply. This was rejected. However unfair the lease may be over time it is, therefore, very unlikely that the landlord will be able to obtain any relief.

Generally on rent review see the excellent book by Clarke and Adams, *op. cit.*; and see Bernstein and Reynolds, *Handbook of Rent Review*. For particular problems with drafting review clauses, see Ross, *op. cit.*, ch 6.

8.4 RENT CONTROL

Unlike many commodities, there is an absolute limit on the amount of land that is available. The natural supply of land is further limited by other policies, in particular the restrictions placed on new development by planning controls. This limited supply does, of course, tend to increase the level of rents receivable from land. Whether or not landlords should be free to benefit from this raises complex political issues.

On the one hand, there are those who argue that rent is effectively a transfer of wealth from one class of society to another:

Ricardo . . . developed . . . the idea that rent derived from the scarcity of land, and the varying fertility of differing parcels of land. Rent is, in effect, the surplus produce arising from better quality land, compared with the produce derived from land which is just profitable enough to cultivate. As population grew . . . more and more land had to be taken into cultivation which formerly had been left to waste, as too unprofitable to cultivate. This inevitably created higher rents, since it enlarged the gap between the productivity of the more fertile land and that which it now became profitable to cultivate. This . . . theory threw into much sharper relief the nature of rent as a sort of tax paid by the major section of the community to the landowners; it also stressed the inevitability of this tax being increased as population increased. As the supply of land could not be increased, the landowners were, in effect, monopolists. . . . Far from being the natural reward for labour and enterprise, property now seemed a way of obtaining increased returns by the mere growth of population. (Atiyah, *The Rise and Fall of Freedom of Contract*, 1979, p 317)

This argument is, of course, equally applicable to modern society as it was to an agrarian economy. Land for housing and for industry is similarly limited in supply. The legitimacy of the 'unearned' nature of rental income has been challenged by Marxists:

. . . capital is joined by landed property, which acts as a barrier to average profit and transfers a portion of surplus-value to a class that neither works itself, nor directly exploits labour, nor can find morally edifying rationalizations, as in the case of interest-bearing capital, eg risk and sacrifice of lending capital to others. (Marx, *Capital*, vol 3, p 829)

Seen in this light it may be seen as politically justifiable to impose controls on the level of rents receivable by land owners. This has not, however, been the prevalent philosophy adopted in this country. Property rights have been seen as fundamental and any interference with them must be specially justified. Nevertheless, as is seen in the next section, there has been almost continuous rent control of some sort this century in relation to the residential sector, the interference with the owner's property rights being justified by reference to the fundamental human need for affordable housing. The clash of market policies and the need to make a finite resource more readily available to the general public has forced successive governments to interfere in order to balance out the needs of landlord and tenant (see Atiyah, 1979, *op. cit.*, pp 636–7).

8.4.1 Rent Control in the Private Residential Sector—Fair Rents

Rent control in the private residential sector began in 1915 in response to the political necessity of preventing landlords from exploiting the wartime shortages. The justification for rent control has always been based around this notion of housing shortage: while there is an excess of demand over supply of affordable housing, it has been felt necessary to impose rent controls to ensure that housing remains accessible to the majority of the population. In the absence of control it is felt that prices would rise beyond the means of low income families. This approach has also been heavily challenged. There are other ways of making housing affordable, apart from imposing what is effectively a tax upon landlords as a group to subsidise tenants as a group. One obvious way is to allow the free market to regulate prices and to provide welfare support to those tenants in need, a much more carefully targeted approach (see 8.5). Another way is to increase the size of the public sector housing stock and to subsidise rents in this sector, to meet the basic housing needs, leaving the private sector free of control. Nevertheless, until recently the government retained rent control in some form, even though it was initially introduced as only a temporary measure in 1915.

The 1915 control took an extreme form: rents for most houses were frozen at the level operative at the outbreak of war. After the war, some concessions were made to meet increasing maintenance costs. Thus, there were permitted increases provided that the premises were kept 'in a reasonable state of repair'. During the 1920s and 1930s some measures of decontrol were introduced. In 1939 there was a further control introduced applying to all but the highest value properties; followed in 1957 by some decontrol of more expensive properties. All of the measures of control up to this point in time related the rent receivable to an historic rent payable at some time in the past, with certain permitted increases. There was, thus, no systematic consistency as to the level of rents payable for similar properties:

Of three identical houses in the same road, one may be let at ten shillings a week under the old control [pre-1939 control], the second at fifteen under the new control [the 1939 control], while the rent of the third, let for the first time since the war, may be 25 shillings or more. (Paish, Essay 4, *The Economics of Rent Restriction* (first published 1950), in Hayek *et al., Verdict on Rent Control,* 1972, p 48)

In 1965 there was a change in approach from one of control to regulation, with the introduction of the concept of 'fair rents'. Some properties may still today be regulated by these fair rent provisions. The Rent Act of 1965 (later consolidated in the Rent Acts 1968 and 1977) set up the machinery for either party to a regulated tenancy (or both) to apply to the local Rent Officer for the determination of a 'fair rent' for the property. The idea behind the fair rent was that in setting the level, the Rent Officer could take account of all relevant factors (other than personal circumstances), such as the age, character, state of the property, its location and the terms of the tenancy. The Rent Act 1977, s 70(1) (as amended by Housing and Planning Act 1986, ss 17(2), 24(3), Sch 12, Part I) provides:

s 70(1)	In determining . . . what rent is or would be a fair rent under a regulated tenancy of a dwelling-house, regard shall be had to all the circumstances (other than personal circumstances) and in particular to—

   (a) the age, character, locality and state of repair of the dwelling-house, and

   (b) if any furniture is provided for use under the tenancy, the quantity, quality and condition of the furniture, and

   (c) any premium, or sum in the nature of a premium, which has been or may be lawfully required or received on the grant, renewal, continuance or assignment of the tenancy.

Certain matters are, however, to be disregarded, including:

s 70(3)	(a) any disrepair or other defect attributable to a failure by the tenant under the regulated tenancy or any predecessor in title of his to comply with any terms thereof;

   (b) any improvement carried out, otherwise than in pursuance of the terms of the tenancy, by the tenant under the regulated tenancy or a predecessor in title of his; . . .

   (e) if any furniture is provided for use under the regulated tenancy, any improvement to the furniture by the tenant under the regulated tenancy or a predecessor in title of his or, as the case may be, any deterioration in the condition of the furniture due to any ill-treatment by the tenant, or any person residing or lodging with him, or any sub-tenant of his. (as amended by Housing and Planning Act 1980, s 152, Sch 25)

In practice, many tenants who have occupied property for substantial periods of time will have carried out numerous alterations to the property, such as putting in new kitchens, heating systems and so on. Section 70(3)(b) directs that the impact of such improvements are to be disregarded when assessing the fair rent, but in practice, the extent of such improvements may make it difficult to put a value on the property unimproved, especially if there are few comparable unimproved properties in the area.

The most important disregard is, however, the effect that a housing shortage has on rental levels (the 'scarcity value'). This is set out in the Rent Act 1977, s 70(2):

s 70(2) For the purposes of the determination it shall be assumed that the number of persons seeking to become tenants of similar dwelling-houses in the locality on the terms (other than those relating to rent) of the regulated tenancy is not substantially greater than the number of such dwelling-houses in the locality which are available for letting on such terms.

The aim of this instruction to disregard scarcity values is set out in the judgment of Lord Widgery CJ in *Metropolitan Property Holdings Ltd v Finegold* [1975] 1 WLR 349:

It seems to me that what parliament is saying is this. If the house has inherent amenities and advantages, by all means let them be reflected in the rent under subsection (1); but if the market rent would be influenced simply by the fact that in the locality there is a shortage, and in the locality rents are being forced up beyond the market figure, then that element of market rent must not be included when the fair rent is being considered. Parliament, I am sure, is not seeking to deprive the landlord of a proper return on the inherent value and quality of his investment in the house, but parliament is undoubtedly seeking to deprive a landlord of a wholly unmeritorious increase in rent which has come about simply because there is a scarcity of houses in the district and thus an excess of demand over supply. (at 352)

On this view, a 'fair rent' is a market rent less any element attributable to scarcity. In economic terms, however, there are two difficulties with this. First, it is an almost impossible task to know what portion of a rent is attributable to this somewhat nebulous 'scarcity factor'. In practice, Rent Officers had to rely on their own opinions and local knowledge rather than any 'hard and fast' evidence submitted to them (see the Francis Committee, *Report of the Committee on the Rent Acts*, Cmnd 4609, 1971, at pp 57-61; see also Watchman, *Fair Rents and Market Scarcity* [1985] Conv 199). On average, the registered fair rent was about 20 per cent lower than related market rents (the Francis Committee at p 62). Secondly, under the fair rent regime, there was no reliable evidence as to what free market rental levels would be:

In the course of time . . . as more rents became registered, the primacy of the market rent less scarcity test for determining a fair rent was displaced by the 'registered comparables test'. This requires a comparison with comparable registered fair rents which will have a built in scarcity deduction. In 1974 Lord Reid uttered a subsequently oft-quoted dictum to the effect that 'In my view this section [ie. the present section 70] leaves it open to the rent officer or committee to adopt any method or methods of ascertaining a fair rent provided that they do not use any method which is unlawful or unreasonable. The most obvious and direct method is to have regard to registered rents of comparable houses in the area.' (*Mason v Skilling* [1974] 1 WLR 1437, 1439). (Davey, *A Farewell to Fair Rents?*, [1992] JSW&FL 497 at p 502)

As this quotation shows, under the Rent Act 1977, registered rents for comparable properties were themselves used as evidence of what was a fair rent, market rent less scarity. The implementation of the Housing Act 1988 has, however, led to more properties being let on market rents. Combined with this, the property slump has brought more rental property into the market and reduced scarcity. It can, therefore, be argued that if there is no longer scarcity, the fair rent can, in appropriate cases, be based on market rents for comparable properties which are let on assured tenancies, not on registered rents. This argument has been judicially accepted, the principles for determining a fair rent being set out by Harrison J in *Spath Holme Ltd v Greater Manchester and Lancashire Rent Assessment Committee*, The Times, 13 July 1994:

1 A 'fair rent' under section 70 of the Rent Act 1977 was a market rent adjusted for the scarcity element under section 70(2) and disregarding the personal circumstances mentioned in section 70(1) and the matters specified in section 70(3);
2 There were various methods of assessing fair rent, including the use of comparable registered fair rents and the use of comparable assured tenancy rents;
3 The method or methods adopted by a rent assessment committee might vary according to the particular circumstances of each case;
4 The committee had to consider, and have regard to the method or methods suggested to them by the parties;
5 In deciding which method to adopt, the committee had to take into account relevant considerations and give adequate reasons for its choice of method;
6 Subject to compliance with those requirements, the committee was free to adopt the method which appeared to it, on the evidence, to be the most appropriate method provided it was not one which was unlawful or unreasonable.
It followed that a rent assessment committee was not bound to use assured tenancy comparators, although that method might be expected to be used increasingly in the future in the same way as registered fair rent comparators were used increasingly following the advent of the rent Acts.

The reduction in scarcity of housing has led to rises in registered fair rents—often in the region of 25 to 50 per cent.

While market rents on assured tenancies may be used as comparables in situations of no scarcity, it is often very difficult to know whether or not there *is* a scarcity of housing—it is not simply a question of asking how many houses are available for renting, but the rent demanded, the length of council and housing association waiting lists, the terms of other lettings, and so on, will all be very material (see Roberts, *Legal Action*, November 1993, p 17). Yet even if scarcity has not been eliminated, market rents can still be adopted as a guide to fair rents provided that they are adjusted to take account of scarcity (*BTE Ltd v The Merseyside and Cheshire Rent Assessment Committee* (1992) 24 HLR 514; *Spath Holme, op. cit.*).

Difficulty in valuing the scarcity factor might suggest that in reality fair rents had more to do with abstract notions of fairness and justice than with modern economics. Indeed, there are signs that the judiciary perceived fairness in this sense to be important:

A fair rent should be fair to the landlord as well as fair to the tenant and it can be regarded as fair to the landlord that he should receive a fair return on his capital. (*Mason v Skilling, op. cit., per* Lord Reid at 1440)

However, the idea that fairness was to do with reasonableness or affordability appears to have been dispelled by *BTE Ltd v The Merseyside and Cheshire Rent Assessment Committee, op. cit.* In this case, the Rent Assessment Committee had taken the view that even given the absence of scarcity 'there was still a paucity of accommodation available at *reasonable* rents' (emphasis added). Hutchison J held, however, that the appropriate test

in a climate where there was no scarcity of comparable rented accommodation, was, what was the fair market rent? It is nothing to the point, having made a finding about the level of fair market rents, to go on to say that fair market rents do not represent reasonable rents. (at 518)

The effect of the *BTE* decision was to reject the view that 'fair rent = reasonable/ affordable rent'; instead, the *BTE* decision appears to be that 'no scarcity, fair rent = market rent'. Nevertheless, it has been argued that even following *BTE*, the notion of 'fairness' should still be relevant so that even if all of the relevant s 70 factors have been considered, the determination should still take account of what is 'fair' (Prichard, *Fair rents and market rents*, (1992) 142 NLJ 965; Davey, *op. cit.*; and see *Aspley Hall Estate Ltd v Nottingham Rent Officers* (1992) 29 EG 130, where the East Midlands Rent Assessment Panel (chaired by Professor Prichard!) stated that

they were inclined to the view that under the authority of *Mason v Skilling* they would still have to take into account and mitigate any clear unfairness that might appear of an application of the 'market rent less scarcity' formula. (at 131))

The notion of scarcity also appears in the rent review provisions for agricultural holdings. In calculating the 'rent properly payable', the arbitrator must take into account the rent payable on 'comparable lettings' but must disregard, *inter alia*, any element of the rents which is due to an 'appreciable scarcity of compa-

rable holdings available for letting' on similar terms to the subject holding, compared with the number of persons seeking to become tenants of such holdings
(Agricultural Holdings Act 1986, Sch 2, para 1(3)(a)). The concern underlying this
provision was that the shortage of agricultural land available for renting was forcing the rent of new lettings above the level the land could support.

The guidance given to valuers on comparables looks just as difficult to apply as
the RAC's find the concept of scarcity is difficult under the Rent Act 1977:

**3.1.12 'appreciable scarcity'—the disregard only has to be quantified if there is
'appreciable scarcity'. The word 'appreciable' must mean that the scarcity is
capable of being appreciated, that is identified and therefore valued. It is not
enough that the valuer has a vague notion that supply and demand are in balance
or imbalance.
3.1.13 'scarcity'—this may have to be distinguished from rarity. Thus there will
be always a shortage of Grade 1 arable farms or of well-equipped dairy farms
with above average milk quota. This is rarity and is a very different matter from
scarcity.
3.1.14 In quantifying the amount of the scarcity disregard the valuer must decide
as a matter of skill and judgement what rent the comparable would command if
there was a balance between supply and demand. The difference between that
figure and the passing rent is the amount of the disregard.** (GUIDANCE NOTES
For Valuers Acting in reviews of Rent at Arbitration under the Agricultural Holdings
Act 1986, Royal Institution of Chartered Surveyors)

In the residential sector, once a fair rent was registered this set the 'contractual
rent limit' and any excess over this would be irrecoverable from the tenant—
although the registration could be reviewed every two years or following a
change material to the circumstances of the letting (Rent Act 1977, s 67, as
amended by Housing Act 1980, s 60). If no rent was registered, the landlord could
alter the rent payable during the contractual tenancy—but only by written agreement that set out the tenant's right to apply for a fair rent (Rent Act 1977, s 51).

While 'fair rents' are commonly perceived as a way of keeping rent levels
down, many rents did in fact rise very substantially after the implementation of
the 1965 Act. After all, we have seen that the previous control artificially held
rents at historic rent levels. Donnison explains this further:

Unlike rent *control*, which is designed to freeze a market, thus eventually depriving its prices of any systematic or constructive meaning, rent *regulation* is
designed to recreate a market in which the over-all pattern of prices responds to
changes in supply and demand, while the local impact of severe, and abnormal
scarcities is kept within bounds. The general scarcity of housing throughout
London being greater than the general scarcity throughout Birmingham, the
whole pattern of rents should be higher in London than in Birmingham, just as
Birmingham's rents will be generally higher than Oldham's, where the general
level of scarcity is less severe still. But *within* each of these cities, differences in
rents should represent differences in the value of the accommodation offered.

The hardships such a change will inflict upon some tenants must be mitigated by governments through housing allowances or other means, not by reductions in rent.

The first task of those responsible for regulating rents is to bring down some of the highest to a level that is rationally related to those that are freely determined in the open market. The second task . . . must be to help raise controlled rents to the same rational levels . . . (Donnison, *The Government of Housing*, 1967, at pp 266–7)

Whenever rent control places a ceiling on rents receivable there will be landlords who, in a strong market, seek to avoid it. One way is, of course, to avoid the grant of a protected tenancy (see chs 4,6). An alternative is to seek the payment of 'key money', that is a lump sum paid at the beginning of the tenancy, in addition to the permitted rent. Such premiums were therefore prohibited under the Rent Act 1977 (s 119). The Act also prohibited other avoidance devices such as payment of an excessive price for furniture (s 123), payments on assignment (s 120) and substantial pre-payments of rent (s 126).

8.4.2 Abandonment of Private Residential Rent Control

The Housing Act 1988 effectively decontrols rents in the private residential sector. The belief of the government when implementing the Act was that such decontrol was necessary in order to revitalize the private sector and encourage more investment. In relation to assured tenancies, there is no external control over rent levels. The only external influence is through the s 13 review procedure, but the aim of this is not to limit rents, but instead to set rents at a market level. In relation to assured shortholds, there is some form of control but this is extremely limited in its impact. An assured shorthold tenant may apply to the RAC to determine the rent

which, in the committee's opinion, the landlord might reasonably be expected to obtain. (Housing Act 1988, s 22)

However, the RAC cannot make a determination

unless they consider–
(a) that there is a sufficient number of similar dwelling-houses in the locality let on assured tenancies (whether shorthold or not); and
(b) that the rent payable under the assured shorthold tenancy in question is *significantly higher* than the rent which the landlord might reasonably be expected to obtain under the tenancy, having regard to the level of rents payable [for similar tenancies in the locality]. (Housing Act 1988, s 22(3), emphasis added)

It is unlikely that many applications will be made: shorthold tenants do not have security beyond the fixed term and this may deter them from risking upsetting the landlord. Even if they do apply, it will take a lot to convince the RAC that the rent is significantly higher than market rents—and the landlord can always point to the fact that the tenant was willing to pay as a sign that this was a market rent.

Ironically there is some evidence that tenants who do apply have been encouraged to do so by their landlord because the tenant is in receipt of housing benefit and the local authority are refusing to pay benefit above the rent officer's determination of a market rent . . . In other words, the section 22 mechanism is being used as an informal appeal against the rent officer's determination of market rent for housing benefit subsidy purposes. (Davey, *op. cit.*, p 508)

8.4.3 Theory and Practice of Private Residential Rent Control

Rent control has been a feature of housing policy in many countries. Some forms of rent control are based on the linking of the permitted level of rent to historic rent levels, as in the pre-1965 control in this country and as in Ireland, where it was successfully subjected to constitutional challenge in the case of *Blake v The Attorney General* [1982] IR 117 (see below). It was also commonly found in early rent control measures in many US States. The so-called 'Second Generation' rent controls in the United States are not as rigid—while the base rent is still fixed by reference to the rent existing at a set date prior to the introduction of rent control (often six months) and on which date a normal housing market existed (an attempt to avoid the price distortion caused by shortages), certain increases will be allowed. Often these increases can reflect a fair return on the investment or annual percentage increases (which may be at a fixed rate or linked to a consumer price index). In addition, certain 'cost pass-throughs' may be allowed to reflect, for example, the increased costs of maintenance or property taxes. Some States in the United States have made these permitted rent increases conditional upon substantial compliance with building codes (thus providing the landlord with an incentive to maintain properly the property).

Other models are based on regulatory regimes, like that in the British fair rent legislation. In Ireland, the change in law that followed the *Blake* case introduced administrative assessment of rents based on what was deemed

just and proper . . . having regard to the nature, character and location of the dwelling, the other terms of the tenancy, the means of the landlord and the tenant, the date of purchase of the dwelling by the landlord and the amount paid by him therefor, the length of the landlord's occupancy of the dwelling and the number and ages of the tenant's family residing in the dwelling. (Housing (Private Rented Dwellings) Act 1982, s 13(2) as amended by Housing (Private Rented Dwellings) (Amendment) Act 1983)

For a discussion on how these factors apply, see *Daniel Quirke v Folio Homes Ltd* [1988] ILRM 496. This model is unusual in the extent to which it directs consideration to be given to personal factors, such as the means of the parties and the purchase cost of the landlord's investment.

Rent control is seldom universal within a country. Many models do not apply to more expensive housing, presumably because it is only at the lower end of the market that people need to be ensured access to shelter. If this is the basis of the exclusion, however, one wonders why the exclusion is usually focused on only the very top end of the housing market and rent control is applied to housing that is far from basic. In America, there have been exclusions in relation to buildings with a small number of units and newly constructed housing.

There have also been some attempts to target rent control on those in need, rather than applying it to tenants generally. In New York, a rent control ordinance exempted senior citizens with an income under $4,500 from authorized increases. When this was challenged, the New York Court of Appeals upheld it on the basis that the exemption was a

classification ... [having] substantial relation to a legitimate public purpose, ... the prevention of severe hardship to aging needy citizens resulting from shortage of low and moderately priced housing accommodations. (*Parrino v Lindsay* 29 NYS 2d 30 (1971) at 35)

However, a similar provision has been held to be unconstitutional by the Supreme Court of New Jersey on the grounds that the landlords and other tenants should not be forced to subsidise senior citizens (*Helmsley v Ft Lee* 78 NJ 200 (1978)).

Rent control and regulation has therefore been a feature of housing policy in many countries for most of this century. This is somewhat surprising given the fact that most economists are highly critical of the economic effects of rent control. The arguments against control are based on both theoretical and practical grounds. The principal effects of rent control are said to be:

1 That rent control has an adverse effect on the quantity of housing stock available for renting. In terms of new stock, as it is uneconomic to build only to receive a controlled rent, central government has to be willing to underwrite some of those costs in order to encourage house building. As for existing stock, the low yield from residential property encourages landlords to disinvest.

   While there is inevitably substance in this argument, it must be noted that the decline during this century in the private residential sector in this country is attributable to a wide range of causes, only one of which is rent control.

2 That rent control has an adverse effect on the condition of the housing stock. Balchin refers to this process of deterioration noted by economists:

Rented housing ... consists of a combination of services. It is not just accommodation, but includes such items as repairs and maintenance, decoration,

and possibly cleaning, lighting and heating—all being supplied at a price
which in total constitutes rent. When rents are controlled below their market
level, the landlord's profit will be reduced or eliminated if he continues to provide services in full. He will consequently reduce the supply of services in an
attempt to maintain profitability. (Balchin, *Housing Policy*, 2nd edn, 1989, at
p 115, referring to the views of Frankena, *Alternative Models of Rent Control*, (1975)
Urban Studies 12, and Moorhouse, *Optimal Housing Maintenance under Rent Control*,
(1972) 39 Southern Econ Journal 93)

Because of this effect of rent control, some jurisdictions permit landlords to
charge higher rents if they can show that their properties are properly maintained.

3 That rent control encourages 'winkling' (the payment of cash sums to
   'encourage' tenants paying controlled rents to vacate) and harassment, so
   that the property can then be sold with vacant possession (for controls on this,
   see ch 11.5).
4 That rent control leads to an excessive demand for housing with the result
   that, as price can not be used as the basis for allocating property, other discriminatory allocation practices may be used (for controls on discriminatory
   allocation, see ch 5).
5 That rent control discourages mobility of labour. Those living in secure low-
   cost accommodation are reluctant to give it up, even if this means losing
   employment opportunities available elsewhere.
6 That rent control encourages the landlords to find ways to evade control.

As to the theoretical objections:

1 Rent control is said to be unfair, in that it involves a haphazard redistribution
   of wealth—there is no evidence that in general tenants are poor and landlords
   rich.
2 Rent control tends to place the cost of housing subsidy on landlords rather
   than taxpayers as a whole—this is unfair.
3 Rent control is a violation of individual rights (see below).

Notwithstanding the force of these arguments, there are some who still maintain
that some form of rent control or regulation is necessary in order to protect the
vulnerable in society and to ensure that housing is affordable. This is the view
propounded in the Rowntree Inquiry, *op. cit*. The Inquiry puts forward proposals
for all residential rents (irrespective of sector and landlord type) to be linked to a
formula based on the capital value of the property (as previously mentioned). In
broad outline, the proposal is that rents should represent 4 per cent of the capital
value of the property, plus certain allowances for management, maintenance
and major repairs. This would protect tenants who do not have the option of
going elsewhere and also place a limit on the amount that has to be paid out in
housing benefit. There would be certain exceptions to this, for example, it would
not apply to furnished lettings ('there is an acute need for 'easy access' housing

. . . we would be worried that any return to rent regulation might deter those (mostly small-time) landlords'). But the general approach is governed by two principles:

—we wanted a universal formula for fixing rents which would create fairness based on consistency between tenants of all kinds (not only those in different sectors but also within these sectors);
—at the same time we wanted to achieve levels of rent which would give a reasonable return on invested capital, and thereby attract substantial private sector investment into rented housing. Rents at such levels would encourage the letting of empty and under-occupied property; they would also increase incentives for existing landlords both to modernise unsatisfactory housing and to re-let properties that become vacant rather than selling these into owner-occupation. (Rowntree Inquiry, *op. cit.*, p 47)

The proposal would not, however, by itself, meet these objectives. A 4 per cent rate of return may not be sufficiently high to attract large-scale investors. Indeed, some reports suggest that net returns of more than 10 per cent are required to attract new investment (see Joseph Rowntree Foundation, Housing Research Findings No. 90, May 1993). The Inquiry therefore suggests that tax exemption or capital allowances should also be available for new lettings. An additional problem with the proposal is that the 4 per cent figure would actually represent substantial rent increases in the social sector, and therefore raise problems of affordability; it would therefore be necessary to phase in the increases over a long period (as previously mentioned; see further, Rowntree Inquiry, *op. cit.*, pp 46-63).

For more detailed criticism of the economic effects of rent control, see Hayek *et al., Verdict on Rent Control*, 1972; Hayek *et al., Rent Control, A Popular Paradox*, 1975; Albon and Stafford, *Rent Control*, 1987; Lee, *Rent Control—The Economic Impact of Social Legislation*, (1992) 12 OJLS 543. For a contrary view, see Note, *Reassessing Rent Control: Its Economic Impact in a Gentrifying Housing Market*, (1988) 101 Harv L Rev 1835.

8.4.4 Rent Control and the Commercial Sector

In relation to the commercial property sector, there has always been a policy of non-intervention in rents. It is felt that market forces should be allowed to decide rent levels without any interference—rent freezing, index-linking, statutory ceilings, fixed percentage increases and so on are not therefore appropriate. If controls were introduced, they would have the effect of keeping rents artificially low and distorting the market, thus discouraging any new investment and creating a shortage of business premises. In addition, there is not the same 'affordability problem' with commercial tenants as with residential tenants—rent increases (so long as not way out of line) can always be passed on to the consumer through pricing of the business' goods and services. The only time there has been any form of intervention in the commercial sector was during the early 1970s when a rent freeze was imposed for two-and-a-half years as part of the government's counter-inflationary measures.

The ability of the 'price mechanism' to efficiently control the market, and the ability of commercial tenants to pay, has, however, been seriously questioned. Professor Burton's study illustrates that rents under the standard system of review are 'impervious to market forces'. He does, however, reject rent controls as the solution:

One option that may be considered by a UK government confronted by both a core inflation problem and the requirements of ERM membership, is that of implementing a system of commercial property rent controls. But this would simply ape the disease. The real agenda is to make the commercial property leasing market work more efficiently according to market principles.

This study recommends the following measures for public policy consideration and action, grounded on basic principles of economic policy evaluation.

(a) Statutory replacement of the RICS-based system.

The present system for rent review dispute resolution could be replaced by an *enlargement of the functions of the Lands Tribunal* . . .

(b) Improvement of the transparency of the market.

There is a good case in economic analysis for improving the transparency of this market, currently obscured by confidentiality clauses. The most important step would be the *compulsory registration of all terms of UK commercial property leases* with the Land Registry . . .

(c) The restoration of economic principles in valuation.

The Lands Tribunal should be under the obligation, in determining disputes at rent review concerning the open market valuation of leased commercial property, to have *full regard to the economic principles appropriate* to the matter, including the general state of excess demand/supply in the market, the expected rate of inflation over the review period horizon, and market factors pertaining in the locality of the property . . .

(d) The correction of 'contractual failure'.

Most public policy debate is locked into a discussion of the imperfections of market and government 'solutions' to economic and social problems. This dichotomy gives rise to the long-standing 'market failure versus government failure' dispute in political economy. It has only recently been realised that there is a third, underlying source of economic difficulty arising from what is termed 'contractual failure'. This occurs where particular forms of contract have been evolved under long-standing legal processes and doctrines that are no longer appropriate to the economic environment in which they now exist.

This study recommends *the immediate voiding of all upwards-only rent-review clauses*. They are inconsistent with the obligation to produce an open market

valuation, and contradict the explicit purpose of rent reviews as giving effect to open market forces. (Burton, *op. cit.*, pp 82–3)

Professor Burton's study is highly critical of the standard form rent review clause, which is upwards only. Prohibiting upwards only review, and following the other principles he refers to, would not seek to suppress rents below a market level, but would rather seek to encourage rents on commercial properties to reflect full market conditions. While this form of intervention would not, therefore, be rent control as such, it would still limit the freedom of the contracting parties to agree upon the mechanisms for reviewing rent. As seen earlier, however (8.3.2.1 above), the government has opted not to intervene in this manner but has, instead, proposed the adoption of a Code of Practice on rent review.

In Australia, some limited rent controls have recently been introduced in the commercial sector. These controls apply only to leases of retail premises and were implemented to redress the inequality of bargaining power that existed between landlords and tenants in shopping centre developments. In Victoria the controls, contained in the Retail Tenancies Act 1986, are aimed at small retailers (premises with a floor area of less than 1,000 square metres), as it was found that large retailers did not suffer from the same inequality of bargaining power. The legislation makes void upwards only rent review clauses (although it has been argued that this provision can easily be avoided—see the views referred to in Bradbrook, Croft, *Commercial Tenancy Law in Australia*, 1990, at p 362). It also makes void provisions that link the rent level to any Consumer Price Index—again on the philosophy that any provision that automatically requires a rent increase should be void. This has been said to be misguided as a means of tenant protection—some tenants would prefer to have rents adjusted in a way that is likely to be reflected in the rise in their own retail prices.

There is also close control of turnover rents. While there is no comprehensive definition of 'turnover', the Act does set out a number of charges and payments that do not constitute 'turnover', the object of this being:

to ensure that the turnover figures used for the rent calculation accurately reflect the true financial position of the tenant, and to prevent the fixing of an artificially high rent by taking into account matters which the legislature has determined do not constitute genuine receipts and profits. (Bradbrook, Croft, *op. cit.*, p 363)

8.4.5 Rent Control and Property Rights

The absence of a written constitution in Britain prevents rent control measures being challenged by landlords on constitutional grounds. Such challenges have occurred in other jurisdictions.

In the Irish case of *Blake v The Attorney General, op. cit.,* landlords challenged the constitutional status of legislation which restricted rents recoverable on the lettings of dwelling houses, restricted the right to recover possession of dwellings at the end of a tenancy, and imposed repairing obligations on the landlord. The relevant legislation applied not to all dwellings, but only to those below certain rateable values (a common feature of housing legislation). The legislation had a devastating effect on property values. McWilliam J at first instance stated:

Evidence, which has not been contested, has been given by valuers with regard to the various controlled dwellings which are owned by the plaintiffs and it shows the extent of the reduction in the value of the landlords' interests in those premises. It appears that the landlord of No 32 Haroldville Avenue would sustain an annual loss of £35 if she were to carry out the appropriate repairs and mainte- nance and that, accordingly, the sale value has been almost eliminated. In the other instances the respective rents obtainable in the open market are estimated at approximately 9, 10, 11, 13, 14, 17 and 19 times greater than the controlled rents. In these cases it has been estimated that the sale value has been reduced 8,10,12 and, in one case, 17 times.

   ... It is clear that, in certain circumstances, the effect of the provisions control- ling rents and restricting the right of a landlord to obtain possession can have the effect of preventing a landlord from obtaining in the foreseeable future any bene- fit at all from his property; and that, in all instances, it must prevent him from enjoying the normal benefits which he would have were there no restrictions. (at 122)

The landlords argued that the legislation was an unjust attack on their property rights, not justified by principles of social justice and the exigencies of the com- mon good, and was therefore unconstitutional as violating the provisions of the Constitution.

   Both the first instance judge and the Supreme Court found that the legislation was unconstitutional:

[It] is apparent that in this legislation rent control is applied only to some houses and dwellings and not others; that the basis for the selection is not related to the needs of the tenants, to the financial or economic resources of the landlords, or to any established social necessity; and that, since the legislation is now not limited in duration, it is not associated with any particular temporary or emergency situ- ation.

   Such legislation, to escape the description of being unfair and unjust, would require some adequate compensatory factor for those whose rights are so arbi- trarily and detrimentally affected ...

   [All] owners whose rents are controlled are restricted in their income to the amount of the basic rent and to such lawful additions as may be related to increases in rates and to a percentage of actual expenditure on maintenance, repair or improvement. This absence of any power to review such rents, irrespec- tive of changes in conditions, is in itself a circumstance of inherent injustice which cannot be ignored. When this is coupled with the absence of any provision for compensating the owners whose rental incomes are thus permanently frozen, regardless of the significant diminution in the value of money, the conclusion that injustice has been done is inevitable.

In the opinion of the Court, the provisions of Part II of the Act of 1960 (as amended) [the rent restricting provisions] restrict the property rights of one group of citizens for the benefit of another group. This is done, without compensation and without regard to the financial capacity or the financial needs of either group, in legislation which provides no limitation of the period of restriction, gives no opportunity for review and allows no modification of the operation of the restriction. It is, therefore, both unfair and arbitrary. These provisions constitute an unjust attack on the property rights of landlords of controlled dwellings and are, therefore, contrary to the provisions of Article 40, s 3, subs.2, of the Constitution. (per O'Higgins CJ at 138–40)

In the United States, there have been numerous constitutional challenges to rent control ordinances, meeting with little success. Early rent control measures in the US were challenged for violating the due process clauses of the Constitution but the courts generally found that they were justified, initially on the grounds that they were only temporary emergency measures (*Block v Hirsch* 256 US 135 (1921)). As the schemes continued beyond the immediate aftermath of the war years it was argued by landlords that the restrictions were no longer justified as temporary responses to emergency conditions, but the courts felt that the continuing housing shortages meant that the regulations were rationally related to legitimate State goals and were therefore constitutional (see *Hutton Park Gardens v Town Council* 350 A2d 1 (1975)).

More recently, challenges have focused on the 'Takings' clause of the Constitution which provides that 'private property [shall not] . . . be taken for public use, without just compensation' (the Fifth Amendment, applied to the States through the Fourteenth Amendment (*Chicago, Burlington and Quincy RR v Chicago* 166 US 226 at 233–4 (1897)). The Supreme Court has been reluctant to entertain challenges under the Takings Clause to general housing rent control ordinances (see *Pennell v City of San Jose* 485 US 1 (1988), where the Supreme Court affirmed the constitutionality in principle of price controls, including rent controls).

In the specific context of mobile home legislation, challenges may meet with more success. Mobile home parks represent an important sector of the US housing market, particularly within certain States. Mobile home owners are, however, particularly vulnerable. Homes are generally owned by the occupants on a pitch rented from the park owner. While in theory 'mobile', the homes are, practically speaking, immobile. The body deteriorates so that movement becomes risky and expensive. In addition, tight planning controls mean that few sites are available for rent. In recent years, a number of States have found it necessary to enact legislation to protect the home owners, the measure tending to be a package of rent control combined with restrictions on eviction and restrictions on the freedom of park owners to select new tenants.

There have been several challenges to these measures, culminating in a Supreme Court decision, *Yee v City of Escondido, California* 112 S Ct 1522 (1992). Justice O'Connor, delivering the opinion of the Court, identified two classes of Takings challenges:

1 Physical Takings—where the government authorises a physical occupation of property (or actually takes title). This generally requires compensation; and
2 Regulatory takings–

> **where the government merely regulates the use of property, compensation is required only if considerations such as the purpose of the regulation or the extent to which it deprives the owner of the economic use of the property suggest that the regulation has unfairly singled out the property owner to bear a burden that should be borne by the public as a whole.** (at 1526)

The park owners in *Yee* were arguing that the ordinance was within the first limb because the rent restriction caused an increase in the capital value of the home, and the inability to evict tenants resulted in the home owners having a 'right to occupy a pad at below-market rent indefinitely'. In addition, on sale of the home, the owner would realise the increase in capital value, so there would effectively have been a transfer of wealth from the landlord to whoever was the owner at the time of the imposition of control. These factors are peculiar to mobile homes—in the usual housing situation the tenant has no capital value in the home and the wealth transfer in terms of income is from landlord to the incumbent tenant *and all future tenants*. The Court rejected the argument that there had been a physical taking as there was no physical occupation of the land, but seemed more open to the possibility that there was a regulatory taking (at 1528 and 1530). This, however, had not been properly argued. To decide if there is a regulatory taking 'necessarily entails complex factual assessments of the purposes and economic effects of government actions' (at 1526).

For further reading, see Harle, *Challenging rent control: strategies for attack*, 34 UCLA Law Review 149 (1986-87); Note, *The Constitutionality of rent control restrictions on property owners' dominion interests*, 100 Harv L Rev 1067 (1987).

8.5 MEETING RENT THROUGH WELFARE PAYMENTS

8.5.1 Market Rents and Welfare Payments

Given that rent control was driven by the need to ensure affordable housing was available to those on low incomes, the government recognised that the transition to market rents would raise problems of affordability. The gap, in theory, is met by the availability of welfare payments (Fast Facts, ROOF, November/December 1993, p 15; Fast Facts, ROOF, July/August 1994, p 17).

A similar need was faced in the Federal Republic of Germany in the 1960s. With the abolition of rent control, the federal government introduced a housing allowance. The number of claimants rose from 400,000 in 1965 to 1.5 million in 1984 (see van Vliet, *op. cit.*, p 136; Joseph Rowntree Foundation Housing Research Findings No. 131, November 1994).

However, the existence of a means-tested benefit, such as housing benefit, should not be taken to guarantee that this subsidy will be adequate to fill the gap between rent and income.

The attempt to reduce poverty by multiplying inexpensive means-tested schemes has been largely self-defeating. The result has been to create a Welfare State of such bewildering complexity that comparatively few working-class people on low incomes could possibly find out what they might be entitled to, or how to apply and to whom, for all of the benefits for which they might in theory be entitled.

The whole system is becoming increasingly irrational. Large numbers of people dependent on social security for an income are reduced to desperate poverty. Meanwhile the Government spends larger and larger sums of money on advertising campaigns to guide possible claimants through the maze of schemes, qualifying conditions, exceptions, application forms, means-tests etc., which the attempt to run the Welfare State on the cheap has generated. (Kincaid, *Poverty and Equality in Britain*, 1975, pp 11–12—and still applicable)

It is estimated that between 25 and 30 per cent of those potentially eligible for housing benefit do not claim it.

The government's attempt to make rented housing affordable while, through the Housing Act 1988, encouraging private sector investors looking for a commercial return has had drastic results for those tenants not able to afford a market rent, as welfare payments have proved insufficient.

The welfare system, moreover, does not ensure access to housing. Landlords may refuse to let property to people on housing benefit. Benefit is often paid late by local authorities and in some instances private tenants have been evicted for rent arrears due to the delays in benefit payment (Luba, Madge and McConnell, *Defending Possession Proceedings*, 2nd edn, 1989). Some landlords in the private sector do, however, recognise the benefit of a guaranteed rent which housing benefit provides (see the *Guardian* p 3, 24 August 1992).

A further difficulty is that there may be a shortfall between the amount of housing benefit payable and the contractually agreed rent—Walentowicz, *Double Trouble on the Benefit Front*, ROOF, May/June 1994, p 11. At one level, the move to market rents should not mean that there will be a shortfall to be met by the tenant—the rent should be met through benefit payments. Housing benefit is based on the 'eligible rent'—*prima facie* the rent paid by the tenant to the landlord. However, the Government's White Paper on Housing expressed concern that the deregulation of rents might lead to some landlords charging excessively high rents to benefit recipients at the expense of the taxpayer (*Housing: The Government's Proposal*, 1987, Cm 214, paras 1.21 and 3.18). To meet these concerns rent officers are required to look at the rents of all new assured tenancies. By the Housing Benefit (General) Regulations 1987 (SI 1987 No. 1971), reg 11(2)(c) the local authority *may* reduce the eligible rent if they consider the rent payable for the dwelling is 'unreasonably high by comparison with the rent payable in respect of suitable alternative accommodation elsewhere' (see *R v Sefton BC, ex parte Cunningham* (1991) 23 HLR 534). Since April 1989, local authorities have been under an obligation to refer all private sector applications for housing benefit to rent officers to see if the rent is appropriate—for local authority tenants, see Moore, *The Taxman Wants Your Bedroom*, ROOF, November/December 1994, p 12. The reason for this provision is, in the words of Schiemann LJ in *R v Housing Benefit Review Board of the London Borough of Brent, ex parte Connery* [1990] 2 All ER 353, that

It is clear that if there were no limit as to the amount of rent allowance, a person who was entitled to rent allowance in respect of 100% of his rent would be less inclined to bargain with his landlord for a lower rent than would the rest of the population who have to meet their rent bills out of their own pocket. (at 355)

See also the comments of Sir Thomas Bingham MR in *R v Housing Benefit Review Board for East Devon DC, ex parte Gibson and Gibson* (1993) 25 HLR 487.

The amount of the deduction will be that which the authority consider 'appropriate having regard in particular to the cost of suitable alternative accommodation elsewhere' (Regulation 11(2)). This means that if the local authority considers the rent to be unreasonably high, then it has a discretion to reduce the benefit payable—and in deciding whether to make any reduction it has been held that the local authority can take its own financial position into account (see *ex parte Connery, op. cit.*). If it does decide to make a reduction, it cannot reduce the eligible rent beyond the cost of suitable alternative accommodation. The tenant will, however, clearly remain bound to the landlord to meet the contractual rent even though the housing benefit awarded is not sufficient to cover this.

Some categories of persons are sheltered from this reduction. People over 60, those who are incapable of working, or those who have children can only suffer reduction 'if suitable cheaper alternative accommodation is available *and* the authority considers that, taking into account the relevant factors, it is reasonable to expect the claimant to move from his present accommodation' (reg 11(3); see *ex parte Gibson and Gibson, op. cit.*). In *R v Manchester City Council, ex parte Baragrove Properties Ltd* (1991) 23 HLR 337, landlords had targeted people within these categories as tenants. Eighty-three per cent of the tenants were vulnerable and the rents were significantly higher than market rents—up to five times the market level. The local authority felt the landlords had deliberately targeted these tenants so as to charge high rents which the council would be bound to pay. The Court of Appeal held that the local authority were entitled by reg 7(b) to withdraw housing benefit from tenants of landlords involved in such an arrangement. The aim of reg 7 is to prevent landlords from abusing the housing benefit system to obtain higher rent. Regulation 7 provides:

The following persons shall be treated as if they were not liable to make payments in respect of a dwelling . . .
(b) a person whose liability to make payments in respect of the dwelling appears to the appropriate authority to have been created to take advantage of the housing benefit scheme . . .
See also *R v Solihull Metropolitan B.C. ex parte Simpson* (1994) 26 HLR 370.

The ability of local authorities to reduce or withdraw housing benefit if rents are unreasonably high, or if landlords have deliberately targeted vulnerable categories of tenant and imposed high rents, does, of course, leave tenants in a vulnerable position. Those on low incomes and in receipt of housing benefit (and not in priority need for local authority housing) may find it hard to find a landlord willing to house them—they are therefore in a weak position to object to the rents being asked. Yet if the local authority considers the rent is unreasonably high the tenants will find that there will be a shortfall between benefits and the contractual rent.

Figures reveal that about 40 per cent of referrals to the rent officer by local authorities result in a reduction in the amount of rent eligible for the purposes of housing benefit. The average reduction is around 20 per cent (*Housing and Construction Statistics*, March Quarter 1994, Table 2.31). These not inconsiderable figures indicate the attempts by private landlords to use the housing benefit scheme to obtain large rents—the *Guardian* p 8, 30 June 1994; the *Guardian* 2 p 19, 13 May 1994; p 21, 26 August 1994). However, the result of the rent officers' intervention is consequent increased poverty for the tenants, who have to find the shortfall between the contractual rent and their housing benefit from their other meagre resources.

8.5.2 Social Landlords and Welfare Payments

As might be expected, tenants of local authorities and housing associations tend to be poorer than the rest of society (see Table 2.6, ch 2). Many of the more affluent local authority and housing association tenants exercised the Right To Buy.

Thus, the increase in rents during the 1980s has left a very large proportion of
social sector tenants on housing benefit. In the social rented sector approaching
two-thirds of tenants claim some housing benefit (van Vliet, *op. cit.*, p 93; Joseph
Rowntree Foundation Housing Research Findings No. 131, November 1994 see
Table 8.1, Figure 8.4).

Table 8.1 Percentage of tenants receiving housing benefit

Council tenants	66%
H. A. tenants	51%
Private tenants	49%
All tenants	60%

Figure 8.4 Percentage of tenants receiving housing benefit graph

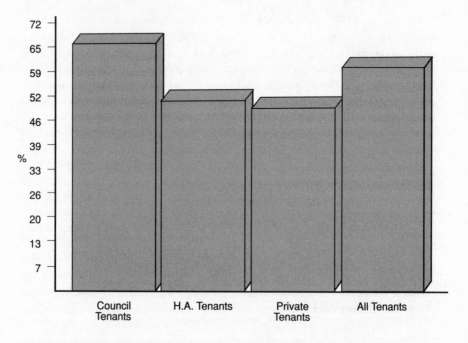

Between 1989 and 1993 average rent went up from less than £25 to £47 a week.
In London in 1992, rents went up at four times the rate of inflation, forcing 10,000
families into claiming benefit (the *Guardian* p 23, 30 April 1993). The National
Federation of Housing Associations has indicated that the proposed cut in HAG
to 55 per cent of costs by 1996 will leave 85 per cent of its tenants on housing benefit (see the *Guardian* p 6, 22 April 1993; p 21, 23 April 1993). The government has

forced through measures which have led to substantial rent rises and it has cut back on housing subsidy, but it has simultaneously 'bank rolled' these constraints on local authority expenditure and finance through the welfare state—by 1986 the housing benefit bill had reached £4 billion. It was only sensible from the government's perspective, therefore, to include the cost of housing benefit as an element of the HRA in the 1989 Local Government and Housing Act, even though it is not a housing cost. If central government was truly to control housing costs, then it had to limit housing benefit payments, an objective which it could not achieve while it was trying to force up rents. The effect had been simply to replace a general subsidy to local authorities with a subsidy to 66 per cent of tenants (almost as general). According to Harloe (in van Vliet, *op. cit.*, pp 112–13) for every £1 increase in rent, an extra 40p had to be paid out in benefits. By placing housing benefit within the HRA, however, the increased cost of housing benefit can, in part, be funded through rent increases for those remaining tenants who are not eligible for housing benefit—Fast Facts, ROOF, September/October 1994, p 17. However, it is a self-defeating process, with rent rises making more tenants eligible for housing benefit and making owner-occupation more attractive to the wealthier tenant. At some stage, the process must grind to a halt as there will not be enough unrebated rent coming in to cover costs—Petch and Carter, *Lilley Goes Pink*, ROOF, March/April 1994, p 15; the *Guardian* 2 p 21, 30 July 1993.

8.6 GUARANTEEING THE RENT

The value of a letting to a landlord is, of course, highly dependent on the ability of the tenant to perform his obligations, in particular, as to payment of rent. For this reason, as we have seen, the landlord would prefer a tenant of strong covenant. As the original tenant remains liable to the landlord throughout the term of the lease even after he has disposed of his interest in the property (see ch 9), he is effectively guaranteeing the payment of rent to the landlord. Similarly, the landlord will frequently require later tenants to enter into direct covenants with the landlord so that they will also remain liable throughout the term of the lease. There are other ways in which the landlord will also seek to improve the likelihood of performance.

8.6.1 References

It is fairly standard practice in both the commercial property sector and the private residential sector for the landlord to take up references on the tenant prior to the letting. The reference will seek information on the financial standing of the tenant and on whether he is likely to be a good and reliable tenant in other ways. The revised Tenants' Guarantee states that housing associations should not require references as a condition of tenancy.

8.6.2 Guarantees

The landlord may require a guarantor to join in the lease so as to guarantee the due performance of the tenant's obligations. This is most likely to occur with commercial lettings, but may also be required in the case of residential lettings.

In a commercial setting, a guarantor is most likely to be required if the tenant is an individual, or a newly formed company, or does not have a large paid up capital or a track record of operating at a sufficiently high level of profit to give adequate cover for the rent, or if it is an overseas company. In practice, the guarantor is often the parent company or an associated company.

Extent of guarantor's liability   The obligations of a guarantor will last throughout the term of the lease—so it will not only apply to cover the original tenant (with whom he presumably has some kind of relationship), but will apply to any assignees who may be totally unknown to the guarantor, unless expressly limited. So, if he acts as guarantor for T1, an associated company, he will remain liable if T1 assigns to T2 and it is T2 who is in default. This happened in *Junction Estate Ltd v Cope* (1974) 27 P & CR 59, where the guarantors were the directors of T1 and were required to make payments on the default of T2. If, however, the contractual lease ends but is continued under the business tenancy code (Landlord and Tenant Act 1954), the guarantor will not remain liable during the statutory extension unless the covenant was so drafted (see *Junction Estate Ltd v Cope, op. cit.; A Plesser & Co Ltd v Davis* (1983) 267 EG 1039).

The guarantor will also be liable not only to pay the initial rent reserved, but also for any increased rent payable as a result of rent review. For example, in *Torminster Properties Ltd v Green* [1983] 2 All ER 457, property was let to C Ltd at a rent of £7,100 per annum, with G and K acting as guarantors. The rent review date was 24 June 1978. C Ltd was wound up in November 1978 and the lease was surrendered in April 1979. The rent review was only settled in January 1980 at £13,500 per annum, but G and K were held liable to pay this substantially increased amount of rent between the time when C Ltd stopped paying and surrender (a guarantor's liability ending on surrender as to future liabilities).

These are very extensive liabilities for a guarantor to undertake. As they are contractual, they can be narrowed down by agreement by, for example, the landlord agreeing to release the guarantor from his obligations when the lease is assigned or when an acceptable substitute guarantor is provided (see further Ross, *op. cit.*, pp 58–67).

8.6.3 Rent Deposit

A landlord may also require the payment of a rent deposit prior to the letting. This is intended to provide security to the landlord to cover possible default by the tenant, and can be drawn against to cover things such as non-payment of rent, breakages and so on. It is common in both the private residential and commercial sectors.

In the residential sector, the requirement to pay a deposit makes it difficult for those on low incomes to gain access to rental accommodation, as they are unable to pay the up-front lump sum required. In relation to Rent Act regulated tenancies, landlords could only require the payment of a deposit representing one-sixth of the annual rental and it had to be reasonable in relation to the potential liability in respect of which it was paid (Rent Act 1977, s 128(1)(c), introduced by Housing Act 1980, s 79). Under the Housing Act 1988 there is no such limitation, although it is usual to require only the payment of four weeks rent as a deposit. The guidance issued to housing associations strongly discourages this practice of taking deposits:

§ B3.5 Associations should not deter low income applicants by requiring more rent in advance than that required to cover the first rental period. Returnable deposits should never be required for unfurnished tenancies, and should be kept as low as possible even when furniture is provided. Associations should never charge premiums for assured tenancies covered by this Guidance. (Tenants' Guarantee, *op. cit.*)

Persons in receipt of welfare benefits are not allowed to claim the deposit as a welfare payment, which creates additional hurdles for them in trying to find a home. Landlords are already reluctant to take on tenants in receipt of housing benefit because of the delays that are commonplace in its payment—the tenant's inability to put up a deposit makes it even harder to find accommodation. For this reason, a number of deposit guarantee schemes have been established by local groups. These schemes aim to help persons in housing need gain access to housing and the scheme may provide for a Deposit Bond to be issued under the scheme instead of the tenant having to pay a deposit. In the event of the landlord suffering loss once the tenant has left the accommodation, he is able to claim against the Bond.

With commercial lettings, it is common to enter into some form of rent deposit deed which will set out how the money is be held (for example, in a joint names interest bearing bank account) and the circumstances in which the landlord can draw on the account.

In the residential sector, however, it is not common to formally regulate how the deposit is held and rent deposits are a frequent cause of acrimony between landlord and tenant. Tenants frequently have great difficulty in recovering the deposit at the end of a tenancy—there are no statutory controls on how the money must be held, the tenant usually receives no interest earned by the deposit, and the landlord will often claim at the end of the tenancy that the tenant is in default (for example, in failing to leave the premises in good condition) and that he is therefore justified in retaining the deposit. For the tenant, the only recourse is to the courts.

The difficulties that tenants have faced in seeking to recover rent deposits have led to calls for an independent body to hold them, to ensure speedy recovery at the end of the tenancy. Such a scheme exists in several States in Australia in relation to residential lettings. In New South Wales, for example, the landlord is required to hand the security deposit to the Rental Bond Board. The legislation limits the amount that can be taken as a security bond to four weeks' rent in the case of furnished premises and six weeks' rent in the case of unfurnished premises. The interest on the bond is paid neither to the landlord nor the tenant, but is used for the upkeep of the Board, to subsidize schemes assisting persons in building their own homes, and to finance a tenancy advisory service. At the end of the lease the tenant applies to the Board for repayment of the bond. In South Australia a similar scheme has been established for retail lettings (see further Sackville and Neave, *Property Law Cases and Materials*, 5th edn, 1994, pp 725–7, paras [9.154]-[9.156]; Redfern and Cassidy, *Australian Tenancy Practice and Precedents*, paras 2548-2553). Several US States also have legislation regulating the use of a security deposit during the tenancy, requiring interest to be paid to the tenant and establishing procedures for the return of the deposit at the end of the tenancy (see Schoshinski, *American Law of Landlord and Tenant*, 1980, paras 6.31–6.43).

On English law, see National Consumer Council, *Rental Deposits, Resolving Disputes between Landlords and Tenants*, February 1990; Law Commission, *Landlord and Tenant, Distress for Rent*, Com. No. 194, 1991, paras 5.18, 5.36–5.39; [1992] Conv 308.

8.6.4 Late Payment Charges

Commercial leases generally provide for interest to be payable by the tenant if any rent, or other sums due under the lease, are paid late. This provides the tenant with an incentive to make prompt payment, and compensates the landlord for loss of use of the money if payment is late.

In the United States, a different form of late payment charge is often used in residential tenancies, setting the level of payment at a fixed amount rather than a percentage rate. There is a risk that this may be struck down as a 'penalty' clause. In order to be upheld the fixed amount must represent a good faith estimate of, and bear a reasonable relationship to, the loss that is likely to incur by reason of the late payment (see 5 *Corbin on Contracts* para 1059 (1974)). In *Burstein v Liberty Bell Village* 293 A2d 238 (1972) (New Jersey), the court felt that a charge of $5 if rent was in arrears for five days, and $1 penalty for each additional day that the rent was unpaid, was excessive and unenforceable.

8.7 REMEDIES FOR NON-PAYMENT OTHER THAN EVICTION

Eviction for rent arrears will be considered in ch 11. In all sectors, tenants in arrears can be evicted, even if they qualify for statutory protection. However, alternatives to eviction for rent arrears exist and are utilised, partly because of the huge social costs associated with eviction in the residential sector which are not balanced by any guaranteed benefit; there is nothing to say that the next tenant will be any better positioned to pay the rent. In the commercial sector, eviction is unlikely to lead to the arrears being paid and the loss of business premises may lead the tenant into bankruptcy or receivership, where the landlord will be just another unsecured creditor. Thus, alternatives have been adopted which seek to guarantee the recovery of the arrears and, in some cases, the future rent.

8.7.1 Damages

An action for damages can be brought, that is, an ordinary civil claim for breach of covenant. Even if judgment is given, however, it may prove difficult to enforce. One way is by an attachment of earnings order but this is only good so long as the defendant tenant is in work and if he remains in the same job—if he starts working for a new employer, a new attachment of earnings order is required (see also Law Com. No. 194, *op. cit.*).

8.7.2 Distress for Rent

Distress for rent is one of the means by which a landlord can recover rent arrears. It is an ancient remedy which generally gives the landlord a right as soon as rent is overdue to enter the tenanted property and to seize and hold goods found there, irrespective of who owns them, until the rent is paid. Since 1689 the landlord has also been entitled to sell the goods to recoup the rent due. Distress is almost always available to the landlord on premises when rent is in arrears as it is an automatic right arising from the obligation to pay rent. (Law Com. No. 194, *op. cit.*, para 1)

The use of the remedy is governed by a set of complex and anachronistic rules. It can, for example, only be carried out between sunrise and sunset. There are also rules governing which goods can be taken and which are privileged (for further detail, see Law Com. No. 194, *op. cit.*, Part II and Appendix D). It should be noted, though, that these limitations, and the generally low value of second-hand goods, make distress in the residential sector, even for local authorities, more of a 'short, sharp shock' than an effective means of recovering even a substantial portion of the arrears (see Hoath, *Council Housing*, 1982, p 146; and *Public Sector Housing Law*, 1989, p 244; see also, Codd, *Limiting Distress*, (1994) 138 Sol.Jo. 524).

The remedy is now heavily criticized. In 1968 it was described by Lord Denning MR as 'an archaic remedy which has largely fallen into disuse' (see *Abingdon RDC v O'Gorman* [1968] 3 All ER 79 at 82). Since this statement there has, however, been an appreciable growth in the use of the remedy. It is seldom used by private residential landlords—in large part because in the case of a dwelling house let on an assured tenancy (and a protected tenancy under the Rent Act 1977) the leave of the county court is required before distress can be levied (Housing Act 1988, s 19; Rent Act 1977, s 147). The landlord may therefore just as soon seek a possession order rather than a warrant for distress. In the case of commercial and public sector lettings, however, there is no need for prior judicial authorisation and distress is commonly used. It should be noted, nonetheless, that Shelter's 1978 survey, *In Distress with Rent*, found that over a third of councils using distress employed private bailiffs who were not 'sensitive to welfare considerations' (Hoath, 1982, *op. cit.*, p 146). One firm of bailiffs offering its services to local authorities provided the following instructive description of its qualifications:

We are of the opinion that the majority of tenants in arrears have the money to pay the rent but prefer to pay the gas, electricity, HP, etc before rent. The reason being that they will pay whoever presses them hardest and they know that the gas and electricity boards will not hesitate to cut off the supply of power if their bills are not paid . . . Our staff are fully trained and experienced certified Bailiffs who in their line of duty dealing with debtors act as social workers, marriage guidance councillors (*sic*) and legal advisors (*sic*) (Fielding, *Finding New Ways to Beat the Bailiff*, ROOF, May/June 1984, p 24).

For landlords, however, distress is often seen as an attractive remedy. It is quick and cheap, although it is subject to set-off—in *Eller v Grovecrest* [1994] 4 All ER 845, it was held that the tenant could set off potential damages for nuisance and breach of covenant for quiet enjoyment against a claim for distress for rent withheld in protest at the landlord's breaches. In most cases the mere threat of distress is sufficient to induce payment of the arrears: the Certificated Bailiffs' Association for England and Wales gave evidence to the Law

Commission that only 2 per cent of warrants actually lead to removal and sale, and the Chartered Institute of Public Finance and Accountancy said that the threat of distress alone is sufficient to make tenants pay in about 90 per cent of cases of arrears where local authorities use distress. Consumer and housing groups, though, have pointed out that this increases other forms of indebtedness. It is not usually a case of tenants not being willing to pay, but of genuine financial hardship. Paying the arrears is simply at the price of greater indebtedness to other creditors.

The Law Commission has recommended the abolition of distress as a remedy, as has occurred in many American and Australian jurisdictions. The objections to it are set out in Part III of their report:

3.2 We see distress for rent as wrong in principle because it offers an extra-judicial debt enforcement remedy in circumstances which are, because of its intrinsic nature, the way in which it arises and the manner of its exercise, unjust to the debtors, to other creditors and to third parties. The characteristics of distress for rent which contribute to this are:

(a) priority given to landlords over other creditors;

(b) vulnerability of third parties' goods;

(c) harshness which is caused by the limited opportunity for the tenant to challenge the landlord's claim, the scope for the rules of distress to be abused, the unexpected intrusion into the tenant's property and the possibility of the sale of the goods at an undervalue;

(d) disregard of the tenant's circumstances which demonstrates its general lack of recognition of a modern approach to debt enforcement. (Law Com. No. 194, *op. cit.*)

These objections were considered to apply to all sectors, notwithstanding arguments that the democratic controls on local authorities make them exercise distress responsibly and that the humiliation suffered from the intrusion is far less for commercial tenants than residential tenants.

8.7.3 Landlord's Lien

In many US States, the landlord's claim for rent can be protected by a statutory or contractual lien on the personal belongings of the tenant. The main difference between this and the common law remedy of distress is that the lien attaches at the beginning of the tenancy or at the time the property is brought onto the premises (see, further, Schoshinski, *op. cit.*, paras 6.22–6.23).

8.7.4 Benefits Advice

Given the complexity surrounding the welfare state benefits, especially housing benefit with its means-test, it is little wonder that some tenants are evicted for rent arrears because they did not know of their entitlement or were not given the appropriate amount (the *Guardian* pp 12–13, 30 December 1992). It would be economically sensible to send in the welfare rights experts before the bailiffs. Better still, the system of rebating rents could be made less complex by the government. (See Audit Commission, *Housing the Homeless: the Local Authority Role*, 1989, pp 30–1.)

8.7.5 Harassment of Rent Defaulters

Hoath, 1989 (*op. cit.*), gives examples from the public sector of how defaulting tenants have been embarrassed by the council in order to encourage them to pay off their arrears:

Some rather more unorthodox methods of collecting rent arrears have been considered by individual authorities, such as the use of 'shame vans' [I.e. vans which advertise the fact that they are involved in collecting arrears: see, eg., ROOF, July 1977, p 105; The Times, June 22, 1978]. (*op. cit.*, at p 245; footnotes included in square brackets)

It is hard to believe that private sector landlords have not also tried such shaming tactics. The tenant in such circumstances might gain relief through the Protection from Eviction Act 1977 (see ch 11) and Administration of Justice Act 1970, s 40. It is an offence under the Administration of Justice Act 1970 for any person

with the object of coercing another person to pay money claimed from the other as a debt due under a contract to harass . . . the other with demands for payment which, in respect of their frequency or the manner or occasion of making any such demand, *or of any threat or publicity by which any demand is accompanied*, are calculated to subject him or members of his family or household to alarm, distress *or humiliation*. (s.40(1); italics supplied; see *Antonelli v Manley*, 15 October 1993, unreported, where a prosecution of a managing agent under this section failed because it could not be proven that there had been multiple demands)

8.7.6 Suspension of Possession Order

Sometimes landlords bring an eviction action, only to suspend any repossession order while the tenant keeps up payment of the present rent plus a sum to cover arrears. Since failure to maintain payment may lead to a warrant of possession being issued, this option will be considered in ch 11.2.5.3 with eviction, although it should be noted that this is one of the most effective means of meeting the tenant's housing needs while answering the landlord's commercial need for a secure rent.

9

Change of Tenant

9.1 GENERAL INTRODUCTION

Chapter 5 discussed the matters that are considered when parties are entering into a landlord and tenant relationship. In many cases, the likelihood of the tenant being a 'good tenant', in terms of his ability to pay the rent and perform the other contractual obligations, will be a critical factor for the landlord. Given the care which the landlord may have taken in selecting the tenant, he will generally wish to have control should the tenant wish to dispose of, or share, his interest in some way. The tenant may wish to alienate his interest for a variety of reasons. It may be that the tenant has outgrown the property—whether through business expansion or an increase in the size of his family—and needs to move to a larger property. On the other hand, it may be that the premises are now too big for the tenant's needs and that the tenant is no longer able to support the financial cost of these premises. In this event, he could reduce his costs either by moving to cheaper premises or by taking in someone to share the costs. In addition, the tenant may need to raise money and offer the lease as security to the lender—a mortgage or charge of the premises will also count as a form of alienation.

Assignment   This is where the tenant transfers his leasehold interest to a new tenant. Following the assignment the tenant ceases to have a proprietary interest in the premises.

Landlord
|
Assignor—original tenant ⎯⎯⎯→ Assignee—the new tenant

If the assignor tenant was the original tenant, he will generally continue to be liable to the landlord under the leasehold covenants because of his contractual relationship with the landlord (see further 9.6.1). The assignee will be liable to the landlord to perform the leasehold covenants because of the doctrine of privity of estate (see further 9.6.2).

Subletting   This entails the tenant granting a sub-lease (or underlease) to the sub-tenant (or underlessee) for a term shorter than his own lease, and becoming a mesne landlord. In effect, the tenant carves a further proprietary interest for the sub-tenant out of his own estate.

Figure 9.1

In this situation, the tenant continues to have a leasehold estate in the property and to be liable to the landlord under the headlease. The sub-tenant is liable to his own landlord (the tenant/mesne landlord), not to the head landlord. If the tenant attempts to sublet the entire premises for the entire unexpired term of his own lease, this will count as an assignment (*Langford v Selmes* (1857) 3 K & J 220; *Milmo v Carreras* [1946] KB 306 at 310).

Taking in lodger/licensee   As with subletting, taking in a lodger does not result in a change of tenant. Lodgers, who only have a licence (*Street v Mountford* [1985] 2 All ER 289), do not affect the relationship between landlord and tenant at all.

9.2 THE RIGHT TO ALIENATE

Under the common law, if there is no provision to the contrary in the lease, the tenant is able to dispose of his interest in any way or carve new interests out of his own. In practice, however, this right is often restricted. The immediately following section will look at general issues in drafting alienation clauses, to be followed by a look at more specific controls and practices in each sector.

9.2.1 Drafting Alienation Covenants

As with user covenants (ch 7.3.1), an alienation covenant can take different forms. There are four aspects to alienation covenants.

9.2.1.1 Defining the Prohibited Form of Alienation

Alienation covenants may be concerned only with preventing one particular form of alienation. It may be, for example, that the landlord only wishes to protect the relationship of privity with this particular tenant and is not concerned about who is in occupation of the property. If so, the covenant would only restrict assignment, while permitting subletting and other forms of sharing occupation. Often, however, the prohibition is more extensive and places some form of restriction on assignment, underletting and sharing or parting with possession or occupation. A restriction on 'sharing occupation' would prevent the tenant from creating sharing licences.

9.2.1.2 Alienation of Whole Or Part

If the covenant applies to dealings with the *whole*, it will not be breached by a disposition of only *part* of the premises. If it is desired to restrict dealings with *part* as well, the clause must, therefore, specifically state this. It is unusual for a landlord to permit an *assignment* of part only of the premises—otherwise it could mean the landlord having to deal with several tenants and as a general rule, the greater the number of interests in the property, the greater the administrative and management burdens. There may be less objection to an underletting of part of the premises—particularly if the premises can be readily divided into separate parts. In a retail centre, for example, a large store may take a letting of two units which are joined to form a larger store. Should the tenant later want to underlet, there is unlikely to be any objection to it being restored to the original two separate units. Where underletting of part is permitted, it is often specified in the lease which particular parts can be sublet. In an office block, for example, underletting of whole floors may be allowed, but not underlettings of part of a floor.

9.2.1.3 Absolute, Qualified Or Fully Qualified Covenant

An absolute covenant is one which totally prohibits alienation. In the case of short term residential leases, the tenant's right to alienate is often severely restricted, and may be totally prohibited: the tenant who wants to get out will, however, normally be able to end the lease by serving the appropriate notice (see ch 11.2.1) and therefore has little need of alienation rights. Although a fixed-term tenant will be tied in for the length of the term if there is no right to alienate, the term will generally be fairly short, six months to a year. In commercial leases, too, there will usually be some form of restriction on the tenant's right to alienate—having carefully selected the tenant, the landlord will want some control over who the tenant's successor is. However, notwithstanding the landlord's desire to

control future occupation of the property, it is unusual for there to be a total prohibition on any dealing with the property by the tenant. Given the fact that most
commercial leases are for long periods, such an absolute restriction would be
unacceptable to most tenants. The type of situation in which a commercial lease
might contain an absolute prohibition is where the property has been let on a
short term basis to a particular person on concessionary terms.

A qualified covenant is one which permits alienation with the consent of the
landlord. A fully qualified covenant is one which permits alienation with the consent of the landlord and further provides that consent is not to be unreasonably
withheld. The qualified covenant is misleading—it suggests that consent may be
given and yet the landlord is under no obligation to give it. For this reason, qualified covenants are converted by the Landlord and Tenant Act 1927, s 19(1), into
fully qualified covenants:

s 19(1) **In all leases whether made before or after the commencement of this Act
containing a covenant condition or agreement against assigning, underletting, charging or parting with the possession of demised premises or
any part thereof without licence or consent, such covenant condition or
agreement shall, notwithstanding any express provision to the contrary,
be deemed to be subject–**

(a) **to a proviso to the effect that such licence or consent is not to be
unreasonably withheld, but this proviso does not preclude the right of
the landlord to require payment of a reasonable sum in respect of any
legal or other expenses incurred in connection with such licence or
consent; and**

(b) **(if the lease is for more than forty years, and is made in consideration
wholly or partially of the erection, or the substantial improvement,
addition or alteration of buildings, and the lessor is not a Government
department or local authority, or a statutory or public utility company) to a proviso to the effect that in the case of any assignment,
under-letting, charging or parting with the possession (whether by
the holders of the lease or any under-tenant whether immediate or
not) effected more than seven years before the end of the term no
consent or licence shall be required, if notice in writing of the transaction is given to the lessor within six months after the transaction is
effected.**

The section does not apply to leases of agricultural holdings, and para (b) does
not apply to mining leases (s 19(4)). The effect is that in all leases to which
s 19(1) applies, a qualified covenant becomes one in which the landlord's consent is not to be unreasonably withheld. When it is reasonable for the landlord
to refuse consent to a proposed disposition by the tenant is considered below—
see 9.3.2.

In 1985, the Law Commission explored whether absolute covenants should
continue to be allowed, noting the restriction this placed on tenant's rights:

4.15 ... we start from the position that a basic incident of the tenant's rights of property is that he should be able to dispose of the property by assignment, subletting or otherwise. (Law Commission, *Covenants Restricting Dispositions, Alterations and Change of User*, Law Com. No. 141, 1985) [An alternative premise would have been to say that a tenant has no rights, save those conferred on him by the landlord on such terms as the landlord wishes (see the dissenting view in footnote 37A to para 4.31)]

On this view, any inroad on this basic freedom must be justified. In the event, the Law Commission felt that in future it should only be possible to have fully qualified alienation covenants and not absolute covenants—subject to exceptions. The exceptions would be those

classes of case in which the identity of the tenant and the existence of trust and confidence between the parties are of great importance to the landlord; and in which ... tenants have for very many years not expected to be free to assign their tenancies. (Law Com. No. 141, *op. cit.*, para 7.2)

Absolute covenants would continue to be allowed for dealings with part; agricultural leases; short leases (capable of being ended within one year of their commencement) except protected business leases; leases giving mandatory grounds for possession; and 'special lettings', including concessionary lettings. No legislation has yet followed on from this recommendation. Given the vast number of exceptional categories and no evidence of hardship currently being caused by the use of absolute alienation covenants, it is, perhaps, best left unimplemented.

9.2.1.4 Attaching Conditions to Consent

Where a landlord is willing in principle to consent to a proposed disposition, he may nevertheless wish to attach conditions to it. If there is a fully qualified covenant (whether within the lease or by statute), then any conditions attached must be reasonable (see Landlord and Tenant Act 1988, s 1(4)). In the public sector, consent to a subletting of part cannot be made subject to conditions (Housing Act 1985, s 94(5)).

Assignment　Following an assignment, an assignor-tenant ceases to be in a relationship of privity of estate with the landlord. This means that he ceases to be liable for future performance of the leasehold covenants—unless, that is, he continues to be in a contractual relationship with the landlord. The original tenant continues to be liable in contract (subject to the reform of original liability). In commercial cases, the landlord will often require a proposed assignee to enter into a direct covenant with the landlord as a condition of his consent. By this covenant, the assignee agrees to pay the rent and observe the leasehold covenants for the residue of the term. The effect is to create a relationship of contract between the landlord and the assignee, giving the assignee an incentive to find a responsible successor should he, in turn, dispose of the lease as he will remain liable on the covenant. The landlord may also require the proposed assignee to provide guarantors, who will also enter into covenants with the landlord.

Underletting   As with proposed assignments, the landlord may require a proposed underlessee to enter into a direct covenant with the landlord and to provide guarantors. The direct covenant will enable the landlord to take speedy enforcement action for breach of the underlease, rather than having to rely on the tenant to do so. In addition, the landlord is likely to want to approve the form of the underlease. There are various ways in which the tenant may drop out of the picture, leaving the landlord with the undertenant as his tenant. One instance would be if the tenant's lease is forfeited for insolvency, and the subtenant obtains relief against forfeiture against the head landlord (see 9.7 below; see also Ross, *Drafting and Negotiating Commercial Leases*, 3rd edn, 1989, para 7.1.2, note 17). Given the possibility that he may take over the underlease, the landlord will want to ensure that it is on acceptable terms—especially as to rent. The landlord will also be concerned to make sure that the undertenant is not permitted to do anything that would cause a breach of his own superior lease (if any). It is not uncommon to require that a s 38 order is obtained in respect of the proposed underlease, ensuring that the undertenant does not get rights of renewal under the Landlord and Tenant Act 1954; see ch 6.4.2.1(e).

9.2.2 Alienation Clauses in Commercial Leases

The particular form that an alienation clause takes will depend upon a variety of factors: the length of the lease (the longer it is, the more disposition powers the tenant will want); the type of premises (how easily they can be sub-divided, etc.); and the relative bargaining powers of the parties. Generally, the wider the alienation clause, the higher the rent will be, both initially and on review.

Alienation clauses can be of considerable length. The following is an extract of *part* of an alienation clause used in a lease of a whole office building, incorporating many of the considerations mentioned earlier:

The Tenant Covenants
1.1 Not to hold on trust for another or (save pursuant to a transaction permitted by and effected in accordance with the provisions of this Lease) to part with the possession of the whole or any part of the Premises or permit another to occupy the whole or any part of the Premises . . .
1.2 Not to assign or charge part only of the Premises
1.3 Not to underlet part only of the Premises
    1.3.1 except by way of an underlease comprising the whole of the lettable space on any floor or floors of the Premises (other than the ground floor)

1.3.2 so that the number of separate occupations . . . at any time exceeds [four]

1.3.3 except by way of an underlease including provisions upon terms approved by the Landlord (such approval not to be unreasonably with-held or delayed) for the payment of a service charge in respect of (inter alia) the repair maintenance and rebuilding of all structural parts of the Premises and any other part or parts of the Premises used or capable of being used by any occupier in common with others

1.3.4 unless prior to the grant of such underlease and to occupation being taken

1.3.4.1 an Order has been obtained from the High Court or the relevant County Court authorizing the exclusion of Sections 24 to 28 of the 1954 Act from the operation of such underlease . . .

1.4 Without prejudice to the foregoing provisions of this Clause not to underlet part only of the Premises without the prior consent of the Landlord such con-sent not to be unreasonably withheld or delayed

1.5 Not to assign underlet or charge the whole of the Premises without the prior consent of the Landlord such consent not to be unreasonably withheld or delayed

1.6 Prior to any permitted assignment to procure that the assignee enters into direct covenants with the Landlord to perform and observe all the Tenant's covenant and all other provisions contained or referred to in this Lease dur-ing the residue of the Term . . .

[The clause also contains provision for an assignment to a company to be guaranteed by directors (or others). There is substantial regulation of the terms of any permitted underlease, to include ensuring that it is let at whichever is the higher of a market rent and a rent proportionate to that payable under the Lease, and that the rent is review-able in an upward only direction. The undertenant is required to enter into a direct covenant with the landlord, and the tenant is required to enforce the terms of the underlease. (Kindly provided by Brecher and Co, Solicitors.)]

If the tenant is assigning the lease, there may well be a premium payable by the assignee. This is particularly likely where the current rent under the lease is less than the market rent—as the assignee is acquiring an asset at less than market value the tenant will be able to charge a premium. In a recessionary market, how-ever, it may well be that the rent that the tenant is currently paying is, in fact, higher than prevailing rents (the consequence of upwards only rent review clauses). In this case, the tenant may have to pay a premium to the assignee in order to be able to dispose of the lease (a reverse premium).

Landlords may wish to realise the premium value of the lease for themselves should the tenant wish to dispose of the lease. In this case, the landlord may insert a surrender-back clause into the lease. This works by requiring the tenant to offer to surrender the lease to the landlord—only if the landlord refuses the offer can the tenant then proceed to dispose of the lease. These clauses have generated difficulty with protected business leases—an agreement to surrender is void under the Landlord and Tenant Act 1954, s 38(1), as it, in effect, prevents the 'tenant from making an application or request' for renewal under the Act. The tenant may therefore be left in a position where the agreement to surrender is void and yet the tenant is still not free to dispose of the premises in any other way (see *Allnatt London Properties Ltd v Newton* [1984] 1 All ER 423; see Ross, *op. cit.*, para 7.7.6).

9.2.3 Alienation and Public Sector Tenancies

9.2.3.1 General Restrictions

Secure tenants have the right under the Housing Act 1985, s 93(1)(a) to take in lodgers regardless of the local authority landlord's views, although the premises must not become overcrowded. The dramatic increases in council rents in the last decade may well have led to more tenants exercising this right.

The right to assign the tenancy is, however, removed (Housing Act 1985, s 91(1)). Even if the tenancy agreement purports to permit assignment, this is overridden by the statutory prohibition (*City of London Corporation v Bown* (1989) 22 HLR 32 at 37). The only exceptions to this are:

1 Where the assignment is by way of exchange (see 9.2.3.2);
2 Where the assignment is made pursuant to a property adjustment order in matrimonial proceedings under the Matrimonial Causes Act 1973, s 24 (see 9.8); or
3 The assignment is to someone who would have had a statutory right of succession had the tenant died immediately before the assignment (see 9.9; s 91(3)).

[Note: different rules apply to fixed-term secure tenancies granted before 5 November 1982: Housing Act 1985, s 91(2).]

The fact that a secure tenancy is non-assignable (subject to the exceptions) has led to the Court of Appeal classifying it, at least during statutory continuation under s 86 (see ch 11.2.5.2), as a personal right and not a right of property (*City of London Corporation v Bown, op. cit*; see 9.9).

The right to sublet is also restricted. Subletting of the whole will result in the tenancy ceasing to be secure (Housing Act 1985, s 93(2); see 9.4). There is a right, however, subject to consent from the local authority landlord, to sublet part only of the premises (Housing Act 1985, s 93(1)(b); see 9.3.1). Similar restrictions on assignment and underletting relate to public sector tenancies which are not secure—the aim being to prevent tenants not in occupation, and hence not secure, from assigning etc. to persons who might become secure tenants (Housing Act 1985, s 95).

These limited rights of alienation reflect the fact that council housing is seen to be for people in need. If the tenant could assign or sublet the whole dwelling, there would be no guarantee that the new assignee or sub-tenant would be in as great a need for such housing as the person at the head of the council's waiting list. Given that a family house might be under-used once children leave home but that the original secure tenant or succeeding spouse cannot be evicted for undercrowding (Housing Act 1985, Sch 2, Pt.III, Ground 16), then the right to sublet part of the premises may enable better use to be made of the property.

9.2.3.2 Permitted Transfers and Exchanges

There may be reasons for a public sector tenant to move from one local authority property to another. A tenant may want to move to be closer to a job or to be nearer family, while the local authority may want the tenant to leave in order to end under-occupation of scarce housing resources. Such a move may take place by either exchange or transfer: an exchange, in essence, involves swapping with another tenant; a transfer involves moving into an empty council property, so there is no assignment/swap of the tenancy in the old property. The Housing Act 1985 allows for the assignment of a secure tenancy to effect an exchange.

Granting a tenant a transfer to a better property will usually be at the expense of the applicant at the top of the waiting list. In some ways, therefore, a transfer can be seen as a reward for being a good tenant—the unknown applicant on the waiting list will then be given the tenant's former dwelling. There is a question, however, about how far councils should balance a good record against housing need. Hoath, *Public Housing Law*, 1989, p 41, suggests that some local authorities use a points scheme for transfers in the same way as for applicants on the waiting list.

Exchanges are more formal. A council tenant can effect an exchange with any other tenant, whether in the same local authority or outside it, and even with a housing association tenant. The exchange might be facilitated through the National Mobility Scheme or the London Area Mobility Scheme, bodies that were set up to allocate council housing to people from outside the locality. There is also the Tenants' Exchange Scheme, a computerized database of council tenants seeking exchanges established by the Department of the Environment. The Secretary of State for the Environment may provide grants or loans to assist with any move under the Local Government and Housing Act 1989, s 168. However the tenants make contact, it is essential that the exchange be effected with the consent of the landlord(s). Indeed, it is possible for the exchange to take place upon both tenants surrendering their leases and the landlord(s) then granting new ones. However, there is special provision in the Housing Act 1985 to permit exchange by way of assignment. Section 92, as amended by the Local Government and Housing Act 1989, s 163, provides a process in subsections (1), (2) and (2A).

s 92(1) It is a term of every secure tenancy that the tenant may, with the written consent of the landlord, assign the tenancy to another secure tenant who satisfies the condition in subsection (2) or to an assured tenant who satisfies the conditions in subsection (2A).

   (2) The condition is that the other secure tenant has the written consent of his landlord to an assignment of his tenancy either to the first-mentioned tenant or to another secure tenant who satisfies the condition in this subsection.

   (2A) The conditions to be satisfied with respect to an assured tenant are—
      (a) that the landlord under his assured tenancy is either the Housing Corporation, Housing for Wales, a registered housing association or a housing trust which is a charity; and
      (b) that he intends to assign his assured tenancy to the secure tenant referred to in subsection (1) or to another secure tenant who satisfies the condition in subsection (2)

Section 92 allows for chains of exchanges, but only with local authority tenants; subsection (2A)(b) would not allow an assured housing association tenant moving into a council property by way of an exchange with a secure tenant to pass on housing association property to another housing association tenant. A variety of reasons can be given under Sch 3 for refusing consent. Apart from the obvious, such as that either tenant has lost or is about to lose possession of his dwelling without there being any suitable alternative accommodation necessarily available, consent can be refused if the exchange would lead to undercrowding or overcrowding, or to a person without special needs ending up in accommodation designed for people with special needs. Ground 10, added by the Housing and Planning Act 1986, allows for refusal where there is a s 27 management agreement where the manager is a housing association of which at least half the members are tenants of the dwelling-houses and the assignee refuses to become a member. However, consent cannot be refused for any other reason, including, for instance, a previous bad record as a tenant, no matter how reasonable. Housing association tenants are given similar rights in the Tenants' Guarantee (Housing Corporation Circular 29/91, 1991, issued in accordance with the Housing Act 1985, s 36A). Under §A, housing associations are to participate in exchange schemes to facilitate tenant mobility, while §C.6(a) gives tenants the right to exchange tenancies with other associations, New Towns or local authorities.

9.2.4 Alienation and Private Sector Tenancies

In some assured tenancies, statute implies a limited right to alienate (s 15 Housing Act 1988). The effect of the statute is best considered by looking at different tenancy situations.

9.2.4.1 Assured Periodic Tenancies

The limited right to alienate is set out in s 15(1):

s 15(1) Subject to subsection (3) below, it shall be an implied term of every assured tenancy which is a periodic tenancy that, except with the consent of the landlord, the tenant shall not—
   (a) assign the tenancy (in whole or part); or
   (b) sub-let or part with possession of the whole or any part of the dwelling-house let on the tenancy.
   ...
   (3) In the case of a periodic tenancy which is not a statutory periodic tenancy or an assured periodic tenancy arising under Schedule 10 to the Local Government and Housing Act 1989 subsection (1) above does not apply if—
   (a) there is a provision (whether contained in the tenancy or not) under which the tenant is prohibited (whether absolutely or conditionally) from assigning or sub-letting or parting with possession or is permitted (whether absolutely or conditionally) to assign, sub-let or part with possession; or
   (b) a premium is required to be paid on the grant or renewal of the tenancy.

Although this is expressed as a qualified covenant, it is in fact an illusory right to alienate as the Landlord and Tenant Act 1927, s 19 is expressly excluded (s 15(2)). The effect is that the landlord can withhold consent for any reason—or no reason.

This illusory right to alienate applies to the following tenancies: an assured periodic tenancy with no alienation clause and for which no premium is required to be paid on grant or renewal; a statutory periodic tenancy which arises at the end of a fixed term assured tenancy by Housing Act 1988, s 5 (see ch 11.2.5.2); and a periodic tenancy arising at the end of a long lease at a low rent by the Local Government and Housing Act 1989, Sch 10 (see ch 12.2).

If an assured periodic tenancy contains an alienation clause, this will govern (s 15(3)(a)). If the express covenant is qualified, it will be converted into a fully qualified one by the Landlord and Tenant Act 1927, s 19(1).

In the case of housing associations, the Tenants' Guarantee, *op. cit.*, suggests that the rights given to housing association tenants should mirror those of public sector secure tenants. Paragraph C states:

§C6 Associations are expected to give their assured tenants additional contractual rights within the terms of the tenancy agreement, which should include:
   ...
   (b) the right to take in lodgers, or to sublet part of their accommodation, (provided it does not cause overcrowding and that the sub-letting attracts no

security of tenure) subject to the association's permission which should not be unreasonably withheld;

...

§C7 In addition the tenancy agreement should:

...

(b) permit assignment of the tenancy only:
   by order of the courts under the Matrimonial Causes Act, or
   by way of exchange . . . [see 9.2.3.2]

(Associations may also wish to grant a right of assignment to a person who would be entitled to succeed to the tenancy on the death of the tenant, subject to the landlord's consent which should not be unreasonably withheld) (notes omitted)

9.2.4.2 Other Tenancies

There is no specific control on alienation clauses for non-assured periodic tenancies or during fixed term tenancies (apart from the general provisions, such as Landlord and Tenant Act 1927, s 19(1)). The ability of the tenant to dispose of his interest therefore depends on whether there are any restrictions in the lease.

Long residential leases will not usually contain restrictions on the right to alienate.

9.2.5 Alienation and Agricultural Leases

In agricultural leases, it is usual for the tenant to have limited ability to alienate. As seen in ch 5.3.5, either party has power to request a written agreement containing matters set out in Sch 1 (Agricultural Holdings Act 1986, s 6). One of these is a 'covenant by the tenant not to assign, sublet or part with possession of the holding or any part of it without the landlord's consent in writing' (para 9). The statutory covenant does not prevent the tenant from *sharing* possession (for example, by a share farming contract), but many negotiated covenants will prohibit sharing.

It should also be noted that Landlord and Tenant Act 1927, s 19(1), does not apply to agricultural leases. The reason why agricultural leases have tended to be treated differently is because of the 'importance to the landlord of the character and ability of the tenant' (Law Com. No. 141, *op. cit.*, at para 6.6). The Law Commission felt that qualified covenants in agricultural leases should be fully qualified but that there was still a case for permitting absolute covenants.

9.3 OBTAINING CONSENT

In many leases it is therefore possible for the tenant to dispose of an interest in the lease with the landlord's consent, and such consent is not to be unreasonably withheld. There are special rules relating to consent to alienation in the public sector, but general principles apply to the other sectors.

9.3.1 Subletting in the Public Sector

In the case of public sector secure tenancies, there are special principles which regulate when the landlord can refuse consent to a subletting of part (for rules on assignment and subletting of the whole, see 9.2.3 above).

Consent to a subletting of part cannot be unreasonably withheld and the burden of proof is on the local authority landlord to prove that the withholding is reasonable (Housing Act 1985, s 94(2)).

s 94(3) In determining [the question of reasonableness] . . . the following matters, if shown by the landlord, are among those to be taken into account–
   (a) that the consent would lead to overcrowding of the dwelling-house within the meaning of Part X (overcrowding);
   (b) that the landlord proposes to carry out works in the dwelling-house, or on the building of which it forms part, and that the proposed works will affect the accommodation likely to be used by the sub-tenant who would reside in the dwelling-house as a result of the consent.
   (4) Consent may be validly given notwithstanding that it follows, instead of preceding, the action requiring it.
   (5) Consent cannot be given subject to a condition (and if purporting to be given subject to a condition shall be treated as given unconditionally).
   (6) Where the tenant has applied in writing for consent, then–
   (a) if the landlord refused to give consent, it shall give the tenant a written statement of the reasons why consent was refused, and
   (b) if the landlord neither gives nor refuses to give consent within a reasonable time, consent shall be taken to have been withheld.

9.3.2 Obtaining Consent in other Sectors

In other cases, the question of when it is reasonable for the landlord to refuse the tenant's request for consent to deal with the property is regulated by common law and statute. In practice, when the tenant is seeking to dispose of an interest in the property, he will approach the landlord with his request. Often this will be coupled with a request for consent for change of use and a licence for alterations where the proposed disponee needs to make a different use of the premises. The landlord will usually ask for information about the proposed dealing and may require references and so on to be provided. On what grounds is the landlord able to refuse the tenant's application?

9.3.2.1 Cannot Charge a Premium

The landlord is not permitted to charge a premium as the price for giving consent to a disposition. The Law of Property Act 1925, s 144, which applies to all types of leases with restrictions on alienation, provides:

s 144 **In all leases containing a covenant, condition, or agreement against assigning, underletting, or parting with the possession, or disposing of the land or property leased without licence or consent, such covenant, condition, or agreement shall, unless the lease contains an express provision to the contrary, be deemed to be subject to a proviso to the effect that no fine or sum of money in the nature of a fine shall be payable for or in respect of such licence or consent; but this proviso does not preclude the right to require the payment of a reasonable sum in respect of any legal or other expense incurred in relation to such licence or consent.**

Section 144 can, however, be excluded by the lease. By its wording, s 144 does not apply to leases containing absolute prohibitions on alienation. With absolute covenants the landlord is therefore free to withhold consent or to charge a premium for granting consent. In relation to qualified and fully qualified covenants, the combined effect of s 144 and of the Landlord and Tenant Act 1927, s 19 is that the landlord cannot charge a premium for giving consent and cannot unreasonably withhold consent. In any event, it may be that s 144 is unnecessary as charging a premium would probably be construed as unreasonably withholding consent: see Law Com. No. 141, *op. cit.*, para 3.9; *Greene v Church Commissioners* [1974] 1 Ch 467 *per* Lord Denning MR at 477, Sir Eric Sachs at 479.

9.3.2.2 Must Not Act in Discriminatory Manner

It is unlawful to withhold consent on the grounds of colour, race, nationality, ethnic or national origins (Race Relations Act 1976, s 24). There is one minor exception in the case of 'small premises' where the disponee would be in close contact to the landlord or a near relative of his. Similar restrictions exist for discrimination on the grounds of sex: Sex Discrimination Act 1975, s 31.

9.3.2.3 Must Act Reasonably

The question of reasonableness is one of fact, depending on the particular circumstances. The relevant principles were set out in the judgment of Balcombe LJ in *International Drilling Fluids Ltd v Louisville Investments (Uxbridge) Ltd* [1986] 1 Ch 513 at 519–21:

(1) **The purpose of a covenant against assignment without the consent of the landlord, such consent not to be unreasonably withheld, is to protect the lessor**

from having his premises used or occupied in an undesirable way, or by an undesirable tenant or assignee: *per* Smith LJ in *Bates v Donaldson* [1896] 2 QB 241 at 247, approved by all the members of the Court of Appeal in *Houlder Brothers & Co Ltd v Gibbs* [1925] Ch 575.

(2) As a corollary to the first proposition, a landlord is not entitled to refuse his consent to an assignment on grounds which have nothing whatever to do with the relationship of landlord and tenant in regard to the subject matter of the lease: see *Houlder Brothers & Co Ltd v Gibbs*, a decision which (despite some criticism) is binding on this court: *Bickel v Duke of Westminster* [1977] QB 517. A recent example of a case where the landlord's consent was unreasonably withheld because the refusal was designed to achieve a collateral purpose unconnected with the terms of the lease is *Bromley Park Garden Estates Ltd v Moss* [1982] 1 WLR 1019. [In this case there were separate lettings of a restaurant and a flat above it. The landlord refused consent to assign the flat as he wanted the tenant to leave so that he could relet both as a single unit. This was held unreasonable—although it made sense in estate management terms, the single letting was not an object which the covenant had been designed to achieve.]

(3) The onus of proving that consent has been unreasonably withheld is on the tenant: see *Shanly v Ward* (1913) 29 TLR 714 and *Pimms Ltd v Tallow Chandlers Company* [1964] 2 QB 547 at 564.

[This is no longer the case: see s 1(6)(c) Landlord and Tenant Act 1988; 9.3.2.4 below.]

(4) It is not necessary for the landlord to prove that the conclusions which led him to refuse consent were justified, if they were conclusions which might be reached by a reasonable man in the circumstances: *Pimms Ltd v Tallow Chandlers Company*, *op. cit.*

(5) It may be reasonable for the landlord to refuse his consent to an assignment on the ground of the purpose for which the proposed assignee intends to use the premises, even though that purpose is not forbidden by the lease: see *Bates v Donaldson*, *op. cit.*, at 244.

(6) There is a divergence of authority on the question, in considering whether the landlord's refusal of consent is reasonable, whether it is permissible to have regard to the consequences to the tenant if consent to the proposed assignment is withheld . . .

[After reviewing the authorities Balcombe LJ concluded that] while a landlord need usually only consider his own relevant interests, there may be cases where there is such a disproportion between the benefit to the landlord and the detriment to the tenant if the landlord withholds his consent to an assignment that it is unreasonable for the landlord to refuse consent.

(7) Subject to the propositions set out above, it is in each case a question of fact, depending upon all the circumstances, whether the landlord's consent to an assignment is being unreasonably withheld: see *Bickel v Duke of Westminster*, *op. cit.*, at 524 and *West Layton Ltd v Ford* [1979] QB 593 at 604, 606–607.

The tenants in *International Drilling Fluids*, *op. cit.*, were seeking consent to assign the lease of a two-storey office building to a company for use as serviced office accommodation (the offices being made available to businesses for temporary use, fully furnished and with office services such as typists and receptionists). The tenants had used the premises as offices but had vacated the premises before asking for consent to assign. The tenants were themselves assignees but had entered into a direct covenant with the landlord. Even if the assignment proceeded, therefore, the landlords could still look to the tenants and the original tenant for payment of sums due under the lease. The main reason for the landlord's refusal of consent was that the 'investment value of [the reversion] . . . would be detrimentally affected by the proposed use'. The Court of Appeal agreed with the first instance judge that any such loss would be only a 'paper loss' as there was no intention to sell the reversion. It was also influenced by the fact that if the landlord was justified in refusing consent solely by looking at its own interests and not looking to the impact of a refusal on the tenant, it would make certain leases effectively non-assignable. This would be so if the tenant was a government department—no proposed assignee (unless another government department) would provide as strong a covenant and so, it could be argued, the reversion would be less valuable if an assignment were allowed; but to refuse any such assignment would be grossly unfair. On the particular facts, the Court of Appeal held that consent had been unreasonably refused.

The question of whether a refusal is reasonable has to be judged at the time when consent is refused—no account can be taken of later events: *CIN Properties Ltd v Gill* [1993] 37 EG 152.

Numerous examples can be given of when it is reasonable to refuse consent, and when it is unreasonable:

Reasonable refusal In *Olympia & York Canary Wharf Ltd v Oil Property Investments Ltd* [1994] 29 EG 121, the current tenant was in severe financial difficulties and the original tenant was having to pay the rent. The rent payable was over one million pounds per annum, settled at the last review, but the market rent had fallen to only £450,000 per annum as a result of the slump in the property market. This made it impossible for the current tenant to assign the lease— and if a buyer could be found it would mean paying a reverse premium of at least four million pounds. As a way around this, the current tenant proposed to re-assign the lease to the original tenant so that it could operate a break clause that was personal to the original tenant, and so end the lease. Not surprisingly, the landlord refused consent to the assignment—given the prevailing market, the landlord would lose rent of around £3.6 million per annum and the value of its reversion would be reduced by £6 million. The Court of Appeal held that this was a reasonable refusal. The break clause had been specifically drafted so that only the original tenant could exercise it—to allow the re-assignment would negate the true intention of this clause.

Other examples are given by the Law Commission:

3.61 ... Withholding consent has been held *reasonable*;
when the references of the proposed assignee were unsatisfactory [*Shanly v Ward, op. cit.*];
when the property would be used by the assignee for trade competition detrimental to other premises of the landlord [*Premier Confectionery (London) Co Ltd v London Commercial Sale Rooms Ltd* [1933] Ch 904];
when the intention of the assignee was to use their bargaining position in order to force the landlord to let them participate in a redevelopment scheme at the end of the term [*Pimms Ltd v Tallow Chandlers Company, op. cit.*];
when the assignee would acquire statutory protection under the Rent Acts [*Lee v K Carter Ltd* [1949] 1 KB 85; *Swanson v Forton* [1949] Ch 143; *Dollar v Winston* [1950] Ch 236; *Brann v Westminster Anglo-Continental Investment Co Ltd* (1975) 240 EG 927], or a statutory right under the Leasehold Reform Act [*Norfolk Capital Group Ltd v Kitway* [1977] QB 506; *Bickel v Duke of Westminster, op. cit.*], which the assignor could not claim or did not want. (Law Com. No. 141, *op. cit.*)

Unreasonable Refusal   Examples of *unreasonable* withholding are also given by the Law Commission:

3.61 ... Withholding consent has been held *unreasonable*:
when the landlord wanted to recover the premises for himself [*Bates v Donaldson, op. cit.*];
when the would-be assignee was a tenant of other property of the landlord and planned to vacate the other property which would be hard to re-let [*Houlder Brothers & Co Ltd v Gibbs, op. cit.*];
when the landlord said he would consent to a sub-letting only if the proposed sub-tenant made a direct covenant with the head landlord to pay him rent under the head tenancy (which was greater than the rent under the sub-tenancy) [*Balfour v Kensington Gardens Mansions Ltd* (1932) 49 TLR 29] (Law Com. No. 141, *op. cit.*).

If the landlord has restricted his ability to withhold consent, he will be bound by these restrictions. In *Moat v Martin* [1950] 1 KB 175, the lease provided that 'consent will not be withheld in the case of a respectable and responsible person'. It was held that if the proposed assignee was respectable and responsible, consent could not be withheld even though there might be other good reasons for refusing consent. Following the Landlord and Tenant Act 1988 (see 9.3.2.4 below), the landlord will be liable for damages if he refuses consent for an assignment to an assignee falling within these limits (s 1(5); see Ross, *op. cit.*, para 7.6, note 15).

9.3.2.4 Duty to Decide within Reasonable Time and to Give Reasons

Until 1988, one of the problems that tenants faced was that landlords would often 'sit on' requests for consent, fail to deal with them expeditiously and fail to give any reasons for a refusal. Delay and refusal could cause considerable loss to tenants. The Landlord and Tenant Act 1988 was passed in an attempt to remedy this. The Act applies to tenancies containing alienation clauses which are fully qualified (whether fully qualified by the lease or by statute). When the tenant makes a written application for consent, the landlord:

s 1(3) . . . owes a duty to the tenant within a reasonable time–
  (a) to give consent, except in a case where it is reasonable not to give consent,
  (b) to serve on the tenant written notice of his decision whether or not to give consent specifying in addition–
    (i) if the consent is given subject to conditions, the conditions,
    (ii) if the consent is withheld, the reasons for withholding it . . .
    . . .
  (6) It is for the person who owed a duty under subsection (3) above–
  (a) if he gave consent and the question arises whether he gave it within a reasonable time, to show that he did,
  (b) if he gave consent subject to any condition and the question arises whether the condition was a reasonable condition, to show that it was,
  (c) if he did not give consent and the question arises whether it was reasonable for him not to do so, to show that it was reasonable,
  and, if the question arises whether he served notice under that subsection within a reasonable time, to show that he did.

The landlord is also under a duty to pass on the request to any other person whose consent must be given, such as a superior or inferior landlord (s 2(1)). Similar provisions apply where the tenant has sublet the property and his subtenant is seeking consent but also needs the consent of the tenant's landlord (s 3). The Act does not apply to secure tenancies (s 5(3)), as to which see 9.3.1 above.

The duty to give reasons does not require the landlord to justify as a matter of fact the matters upon which he replies: *Air India v Balabel* [1993] 30 EG 90. Any breach of a duty in the Act 'may be made the subject of civil proceedings in like manner as any other claim in tort for breach of statutory duty' (s 4).

9.3.2.5 The Effect of A Wrongful Refusal of Consent

Under the common law, if the landlord unreasonably withheld consent, it was held that he was not liable for damages for breach of contract: *Sear v House Property and Investment Society* [1880] 16 Ch D 387; *Rendall v Roberts & Stacey* [1960] 175 EG 265. If the tenant considered that consent was being unreasonably withheld, the tenant would have two options. He could simply go ahead with the proposed transaction. This was risky—if it turned out to be the case that the refusal of consent was reasonable, the tenant would be liable for breach and the landlord might be able to forfeit the lease. Alternatively, the tenant could seek a declaration that consent was being unreasonably withheld—this could be slow and, in the meantime, the proposed disponee could lose interest. The 1988 Act, however, now enables the tenant to claim damages (see *Dong Bang Minerva (UK) Ltd v Davina Ltd* [1995] 05 EG 162).

9.4 DISPOSITION IN BREACH OF AN ALIENATION CLAUSE

If the tenant fails to seek consent to a disposition, he will be in breach of covenant, even if consent could not have been reasonably withheld: *Eastern Telegraph Co v Dent* [1899] 1 QB 835; *Barrow v Isaacs & Son* [1891] 1 QB 417; *Creery v Summersell and Flowerdew & Co Ltd* [1949] Ch 751. If the tenant does dispose in breach of the clause, the landlord can claim for damages to his reversion and bring an action for forfeiture (assuming the lease contains a forfeiture clause and that the breach has not been waived; see ch 11.2.3). If the tenancy is assured, the landlord has a discretionary ground for possession (Housing Act 1988, Sch 2, Ground 12).

In the public sector unlawful disposition will lead to the landlord being entitled to recover possession: the idea underlying controls on dispositions in the public sector is to ensure that it is the local authority that remains in control of allocating housing, and this goal cannot be circumvented by tenant dispositions. In the case of a subletting of part without the landlord's consent, this will entail a breach of the tenancy giving the landlord a discretionary ground for possession (Housing Act 1985, Sch 2, Part 1, Ground 1). With a subletting of the whole, the tenancy itself will cease to be secure:

Housing Act 1985
s 93(2) **If the tenant under a secure tenancy parts with the possession of the dwelling-house or sublets the whole of it (or sublets first part of it and then the remainder), the tenancy ceases to be a secure tenancy and cannot subsequently become a secure tenancy.**

This subsection refers also to a 'parting with possession'. To part with possession it is necessary to part with legal possession (*Stening v Abrahams* [1931] 1 Ch 470)—and this phrase normally includes an 'assignment' (*Marks v Warren* [1979] 1 All ER 29). In the case of the exceptional assignments permitted by s 91(3) it is clear that, notwithstanding s 93(2), the assignee in this case is a secure tenant (see the combined effects of ss 87–92). It would seem, therefore, that s 93(2) should be read as if it said 'parts with possession other than by assignment'. In the case of a purported assignment not within any of the permitted exceptions, the assignment is ineffectual (*City of London Corporation v Bown, op. cit.*, at 38-9)—the assignor tenant ceases to be a secure tenant as he will no longer satisfy the tenant condition (not being in occupation) and the new occupier has no tenancy.

In the case of agricultural leases, breach of an alienation clause will give the landlord a right to take possession proceedings under the Agricultural Holdings Act 1986, Sch 3, Case E (see *Troop v Gibson* [1986] 1 EGLR 1).

9.5 FORMALITIES AND ALIENATION

In order for a lease to be validly assigned, the assignment must be by deed (Law of Property Act 1925, s 52(1)). This is so even though the lease itself may be created orally if for not more than three years (*Crago v Julian* [1992] 1 All ER 744). If there is a purported oral assignment, this will be of no effect. If the purported assignment is in writing, but not by deed, then it will take effect as an equitable assignment.

In order to create a sub-lease, the same rules apply as for the creation of the head-lease (see ch 5.2.1).

In commercial cases, where the landlord's consent is required for a dealing, the consent will often be contained in a deed called a Licence to Assign/Sublet. This deed will deal not only with the issue of consent but will also contain a covenant by the assignee/sub-tenant (if required) to observe the leasehold covenants, and will cover the consent and conditions attached to any attendant change of use or alterations to the property.

9.6 ENFORCING COVENANTS AFTER ASSIGNMENT

In this chapter, the focus is upon a change of tenant. When looking at the enforcement of leasehold covenants, many of the same principles apply following a change of landlord as to a change of tenant. The position of landlords post-assignment will be discussed in ch 10.

9.6.1 Liability of the Original Tenant

9.6.1.1 Original Tenant Liability

As the original parties to a lease are in a contractual relationship they will remain liable for performance of the leasehold covenants throughout the term of the lease, unless this liability has been limited by the contract itself. This result stems from normal principles of contract law but there are proposals to limit original tenant liability in relation to future leases (see 9.6.1.2). The effect of original liability is that even after the tenant has assigned the lease and no longer has any interest in the property, he will be liable for breach of any covenants by the assignee. In practice, with a rack rent lease, it is the liability for rent that tends to be most commonly enforced against the original tenant. Although original liability exists with all leases, it is in the commercial sector that original tenants are most often sued. Short residential leases are seldom assigned, and, if they are, the landlord would generally end the lease if the rent is not being paid by the assignee. With long residential leases, original liability may be a problem but, as the rent is generally only a ground rent, it is only in the case of major repairs that it will be worth pursuing the original tenant. With commercial leases, there is no incentive for the landlord to forfeit the lease if he can simply look to the original tenant for payment, particularly in a market where the property will be hard to re-let. Furthermore, the original tenant's liability is direct and primary and the landlord does not have to exhaust possible remedies against other persons before claiming from the original tenant (*Baynton v Morgan* (1888) 22 QBD 74; *Norwich Union Life Insurance Ltd v Low Profile Fashions Ltd* (1991) 64 P & CR 187). During recessionary periods, with a high insolvency rate, landlords frequently turn to the original tenant for payment of substantial sums of money. The tenant has an implied right of indemnity against his assignee (Law of Property Act 1925, s 77(1)(C) but only if the assignment is for valuable consideration; Land Registration Act 1925, s 24(1)(b)) and a quasi-contractual right to be re-imbursed by the current tenant (see *Moule v Garret* (1872) LR 7 Ex 101). In addition, the tenant may have an express indemnity. In practice, however, the indemnity is often worthless as the very time that the landlord will seek recovery from the original tenant is when the current tenant is insolvent.

The original tenant will be liable not only to pay amounts agreed in the original lease, but also by any amendments to it, even though he generally has no right to be consulted on any proposed variations to the lease. So, in *Centrovincial Estate plc v Bulk Storage Ltd* (1983) 46 P & CR 393, the tenant was liable to pay an increased rent which had been agreed by an assignee under the rent review procedure in the lease. Similarly, in *Selous Street Properties v Oronel Fabrics Ltd* (1984) 270 EG 643, the original tenant was liable for a rent increase which reflected the value of improvements carried out to the premises by a later assignee even though the alterations were not permitted by the original lease. As the principle of original tenant liability stems from contract law, it is arguable that it should only extend to liability envisaged by the original contract. Yates and Hawkins argue:

[If] the original tenant is to be bound by alterations or variations in the lease subsequent to assignment, it ought to be a requirement that those variations lie within the contemplation of the original contract. For the original tenant to be liable for rent increases agreed after assignment, therefore, the rent review must, on general principle, be one which the tenant had originally agreed to. It is doubtful that a review occasioned by an assignee's breach of contract falls within this

principle, and to this extent it would appear that recent decisions to the contrary are wrongly decided. (*Landlord and Tenant Law*, 2nd edn, 1986, p 162 (footnotes omitted); and see McLoughlin [1984] Conv 443)

Any guarantor of the original tenant will also be subject to continuing liability. Under the general law, the guarantor would be discharged if any variations are agreed to the lease without his consent (*Holme v Brunskill* (1878) 3 QBD 495), but, in practice, many guarantee covenants are drafted so that his liability will continue in this event.

Various arguments can be given in support of continuing liability:

1 The landlord may exercise very careful selection of the original tenant but has relatively little control over the identity of the assignee, save for being able to refuse consent to the assignment if such refusal is reasonable. The landlord should not bear the risk of the assignee selected by the original tenant being a poor tenant.
2 Continuing liability encourages the original tenant to be careful over his choice of assignee.
3 If the tenant is concerned about loss of the right to participate in future rent reviews, he can choose to sublet rather than assign.
4 The original tenant has a right of indemnity from his assignee.
5 Liability can always be limited by contract (see 9.6.1.2).

Against this, it is said that it is grossly unfair that a tenant should continue to be liable after ceasing to have any interest in the property and without there being any fault on his part. In practice, a tenant has little effective choice as to its assignee—the lease is sold to whoever the tenant is able to sell it to for a good price.

9.6.1.2 Limits on Original Tenant Liability

(a) Contractual Limitations In theory, the original tenant's liability can be limited by contract to the period for which the original tenant has an estate in the property. In 1992, some brewery landlords announced that they were abandoning original tenant liability in leases of their public houses (see *Financial Times*, 3 June 1992; *Morning Advertiser*, 20 April 1992). It is, however, still relatively unusual for this to be agreed to by the landlord. Even during the recession, with property hard to let, landlords were reluctant to agree to such limitations and preferred to offer other inducements to tenants to encourage them to take leases, such as rent-free periods and shorter leases.

It is slightly more common for the landlord to agree for a guarantor's liability to be limited to the period for which the tenant for whom he is willing to act as guarantor has an interest in the property.

(b) Release Even if the tenant is unable to negotiate for his liability to be limited

by the original lease, he may be able to negotiate for the landlord to release him upon assignment, especially if the assignee is of equal or greater financial strength.

(c) No Liability During Statutory Continuation   Unless the period of liability is extended by the wording of the lease, the original tenant's liability will cease when the contractual tenancy comes to an end (*City of London Corp v Fell* [1993] 4 All ER 968). In the *Fell* case, the original tenant, a large firm of solicitors, had assigned a ten-year lease to a company which later became insolvent. The landlord sought to argue that the original tenant remained liable even during the statutory continuation of the tenancy by the Landlord and Tenant Act 1954, s 24, but the House of Lords firmly rejected this.

In *Fell*, the term of the lease was defined as being for a set period (ten years). In some leases, however, the term will be defined to include the original grant plus any continuation or extension of it and, in this event, the contractual liability of the original tenant will extend to the statutory continuation (*City of London Corp v Fell, Herbert Duncan Ltd v Cluttons* [1993] 2 All ER 449 (CA)).

9.6.1.3 Reform of Original Tenant Liability

The injustice of continuing liability led the Law Commission to recommend changes (see Law Commission, *Landlord and Tenant, Privity of Contract and Estate*, Law Com. No. 174, 1988). In 1993, the Lord Chancellor announced that the Law Commission's proposals on original tenant liability will be implemented for future, but not existing, leases. The first principle on which the Law Commission's recommendations were based was that

a landlord or a tenant of property should not continue to enjoy rights nor be under any obligations arising from a lease once he has parted with all interest in the property. (Law Com. No. 174, *op. cit.*, para 4.1)

This principle suggests that there should be a clean break on assignment. The proposals partially achieve this end in relation to tenants. As a general rule, tenants will not remain liable after assignment. However, in cases where the lease contains an alienation covenant, the landlord may require the tenant to 'guarantee' the performance of the leasehold covenants (in whole or part) by the tenant's immediate successor. If there is a later assignment, the guarantee will cease. Where, as is usual, the covenant is fully qualified, the landlord will only be able to require such a guarantee if it is reasonable to do so (see 9.2.1.4 above). As the tenant will be acting as guarantor to the assignee, he will be released if the terms of the lease are later varied. When his own liability ceases, any guarantor of the tenant will also be released from liability. Contracting out will be prohibited.

The original tenant is often particularly aggrieved if the extent of his liability has been increased by poor estate management by the landlord, for example, by allowing substantial arrears of rent to accrue. The reforms will therefore include a statutory requirement in respect of both future and existing leases to encourage landlords to act promptly when suing for arrears of rent or service charges. Notice of any such claims against a former tenant will in future have to be served within nine months after the money becomes due. (Lord Chancellor's Department, Press Notice, 31 March 1993)

The aim of the reform is to balance fairness to the tenant against protecting the commercial interests of landlords. If the assignee is of weaker covenant than the assignor tenant, the landlord's financial interests are protected by the security of the guarantee. This does, however, raise the question of what would happen on a further assignment. If the original tenant provides a stronger covenant than the first and second assignees, the landlord will be losing the protection of this covenant on the second assignment. The Law Commission suggested that this should be a factor relevant to the reasonableness of the landlord withholding consent to the later assignment:

... when a second assignment is proposed [the landlord] may decline to give consent if the loss of the former tenant's guarantee would unreasonably leave him without sufficient protection. (Law Com. No. 174, *op. cit.*, para 4.15)

It is thought that these reforms could have a significant impact on the property market. Landlords have argued that the security of income provided by the original tenant covenant throughout the lease is essential to the property investment market, and that losing this will make property a less attractive investment medium and will detrimentally affect the return on investment. Other possible consequences of the reforms are that rents will rise on initial lettings to compensate for the loss of continuing liability; there will be closer scrutiny by landlords of proposed assignees, especially as to their ability to perform in the mid to long term; alienation clauses may be more tightly drafted, for example, permitting only one assignment; and landlords may insist on more security on assignments, in the form of guarantees and rent deposits. See also Patterson, *Investment Implications*, (1993) 29 EG 88.

During the debate on reform of continuing liability, reference is often made to the fact that in Scotland the concept of original tenant liability does not exist. There is, however, an important further difference between English and Scottish law. In Scotland, alienation clauses are generally qualified, but not fully qualified (there being no equivalent of the Landlord and Tenant Act 1927, s 19(1)). The effect is that a landlord has the right to veto any proposed assignee. The English reforms will do more to promote the free alienability of land as landlords can only veto assignments if it is reasonable to do so and the possibility of a tenant guarantee will make it harder to refuse consent lawfully.

9.6.2 The Position of the Assignee

9.6.2.1 Privity of Estate

In most contractual situations, if a contract has been entered into between A and B and one party assigns its interest under the contract, it is only the benefit of the contract that passes to the third party. The burden will remain with the original contracting party alone. Leases are, however, treated differently in this respect from other contracts. Leases are not only contracts, but also estates in land capable of lasting for very long periods and of changing ownership several times. The law has, therefore, developed the doctrine of privity of estate whereby leasehold covenants can be enforced by and against the persons who are landlord and tenant for the time being even though they are not in a contractual relationship. This is explained by Lord Templeman in *City of London Corp v Fell, op. cit.*, at 972–3:

Common law, and statute following the common law, were faced with the problem of rendering effective the obligations under a lease which might endure for a period of 999 years or more beyond the control of any covenantor. The solution was to annex to the term and the reversion the benefit and burden of covenants which touch and concern the land. The covenants having been annexed, every legal owner of the term granted by the lease and every legal owner of the reversion from time to time holds his estate with the benefit of and subject to the covenants which touch and concern the land. The system of leasehold tenure requires that the obligations in the lease shall be enforceable throughout the term, whether those obligations are affirmative or negative. The owner of a reversion must be able to enforce the positive covenants to pay rent and keep in repair against an assignee who in turn must be able to enforce any positive covenants entered into by the original landlord . . .

The effect of common law and statute on a lease is to create rights and obligations which are independent of the parallel rights and obligations of the original human covenantor who and whose heirs may fail or the parallel rights and obligations of a corporate covenantor which may be dissolved. Common law and statute achieve that effect by annexing those rights and obligations so far as they touch and concern the land to the term and to the reversion. Nourse LJ neatly summarized the position when he said in an impeccable judgment ([1993] 2 All ER 449 at 454 . . .):

'The contractual obligations which touch and concern the land having become imprinted on the estate, the tenancy is capable of existence as a species of property independently of the contract.'

The rules for enforcement of covenants post-assignment are set out in *Spencer's Case* (1583) 5 Co Rep 16a. In order for covenants to be enforceable there must be privity of estate, that is, the legal relationship of landlord and tenant, and the covenant must touch and concern the land. Provided that these two conditions are satisfied, an assignee tenant will both be liable to have covenants enforced against it by the current landlord and able to enforce the benefit of any covenants against the current landlord. Both aspects of the rule need to be examined further.

(a) Legal Relationships   The application of *Spencer's Case, op. cit.*, is said to depend upon there being a legal relationship of landlord and tenant. This would mean that the rules do not apply where either there is an assignment of an equitable lease or a purported assignment of a legal lease by writing but not by deed. In some jurisdictions it has, however, been suggested that there can be privity of estate with equitable leases—and so *Spencer's Case* would apply (see Gray, *Elements of Land Law*, 2nd edn, 1993, p 872 and footnote 16). The position with equitable assignees is discussed at 9.6.2.4 below.

(b) Covenants which touch and concern the Land   It is only covenants which 'touch and concern' the land which can be enforced under *Spencer's Case, op. cit.* In practice, most leasehold covenants do satisfy this requirement. So, for example, the landlord can enforce rent covenants and decorating covenants against the assignee tenant, and the assignee tenant can enforce a covenant to insure against the landlord. It is only personal or collateral contracts that are likely not to be covered, such as a covenant to clean the landlord's premises or a covenant requiring payment of an annual sum to a third party (*Mayho v Buckhurst* (1617) Cro. Jac. 438). In *Hua Chiao Commercial Bank Ltd v Chiaphua Industries Ltd* [1987] AC 99, the Privy Council held that a landlord's covenant to return the tenant's deposit was a merely personal obligation and did not have reference to the subject matter of the lease. The case itself involved a change of landlord, not tenant, but the principle applies equally in the converse situation.

In *P & A Swift Investments v Combined English Stores Group plc* [1988] 2 All ER 885, Lord Oliver put forward a working test for when the covenant touches and concerns the land:

(1) The covenant benefits only the reversioner for the time being, and if separated from the reversion ceases to be of benefit to the covenantee. (2) The covenant affects the nature, quality, mode of user or value of the land of the reversioner. (3) The covenant is not expressed to be personal (that is to say neither being given only to a specific reversioner nor in respect of the obligations only of a specific tenant). (4) The fact that a covenant is to pay a sum of money will not prevent it from touching and concerning the land so long as the three foregoing conditions are satisfied and the covenant is connected with something to be done on, to or in relation to the land. (at 891)

In 1988, the Law Commission recommended the abolition of the distinction between covenants which touch and concern the land and personal covenants. This change should accompany the reform of continuing liability:

. . . all the terms of the lease should be regarded as a single bargain for letting the property. When the interest of one of the parties changes hands the successor should fully take his predecessor's place as landlord or tenant, without distinguishing between different categories of covenant. (Law Com. No. 174, *op. cit.*, para 4.1)

9.6.2.2 Further Assignment

Unless the assignee has entered into a direct covenant with the landlord, he will not be liable for any breaches that occur after he has parted with his interest in the property (or for any breaches which occurred before he acquired an interest).

9.6.2.3 Liability under a Direct Covenant

As mentioned earlier, a landlord will often require an assignee to enter into a direct covenant with him as a condition of his consent to the assignment. In *Estates Gazette Ltd v Benjamin Restaurants Ltd* [1995] 1 All ER 129, the assignee had entered into a standard form of covenant 'to pay the rents reserved by the lease at the time and in the manner provided for and to observe and perform the covenants on the lessee's part and the conditions contained therein.' A surety also covenanted that the assignee would perform these obligations. After a further assignment, the assignee sought to argue that it was no longer liable. The Court of Appeal rejected this—both the assignee and the surety were liable on the covenants for the remainder of the term.

9.6.2.4 Equitable Leases and Equitable Assignments of Legal Leases

As the rule in *Spencer's Case, op. cit.*, depends upon there being privity of estate, there may be problems enforcing covenants where there is only an equitable relationship between the landlord and the tenant. It seems there will be no difficulty in the assignee tenant being able to enforce covenants against the landlord (*Manchester Brewery v Coombs* [1901] 2 Ch 608). This ties in with general contract law, under which the *benefit* of a contract can be assigned. An equitable assignment will thus pass the benefit of all covenants to the assignee. The problem lies with the burden, that is, the liability of the assignee tenant to be sued by the landlord.

The case of *Purchase v Lichfield Brewery* [1915] 1 KB 184 has generated a lot of difficulty. In this case, Purchase had entered into an agreement for lease with the tenant. This equitable lease was then assigned to Lichfield by way of mortgage. The issue in the case was whether Lichfield could be held liable for non-payment of rent. Lush J held it could not. The implication of this decision is that an assignee of an equitable lease cannot be sued on covenants in the lease.

There are, however, various ways of challenging this result. First, it may be that *Purchase* is not of general application and is confined to its special facts, in particular, that the assignee was a mortgagee and had not entered into possession. Secondly, it is felt to be wrong in principle that the assignee tenant can sue the landlord but cannot be sued by the landlord. Smith suggests that the assignee tenant might be liable under the doctrine of mutual benefit and burden (see Smith, *The Running of Covenants in Equitable Leases and Equitable Assignments of Legal Leases*, [1978] CLJ 98 at pp 110 and 118). Thirdly, in *Boyer v Warby* [1953] 1 QB 234, Denning LJ mounted a brave argument that *Purchase* was simply wrong and that the rules should be the same in equity as at law:

> . . . since the fusion of law and equity . . . the distinction between agreements under hand and covenants under seal has been largely obliterated. There is no valid reason nowadays why the doctrine of covenants running with the land—or with the reversion—should not apply equally to agreements under hand as to covenants under seal; and I think we should so hold, not only in the case of agreements for more than three years which need the intervention of equity to protect them, but also in the case of agreements for three years or less which do not. (at 245)

As Gray observes, this is generally felt to be a maverick view (Gray, 1993, *op. cit.*, p 872). The Judicature Act 1873 fused the administration of law and equity but not the rules themselves. Fourthly, Smith suggests that when the assignee tenant enters possession and starts to pay rent, there should be an implied contract between the assignee and the landlord which will be upon essentially the same terms as the assignor's lease (Smith, 1978, *op. cit.*, pp 105–8 and 117–18).

The decision in *Purchase* will not affect the running of negative covenants under the doctrine in *Tulk v Moxhay* (1848) 2 Ph 774. Often, however, it is the positive covenants to pay rent etc. that will be in issue. In addition, even though the covenants themselves may not be binding on the equitable assignee, the landlord may, in the event of a 'breach', be able to re-enter and forfeit the lease if it contains a forfeiture clause (see Gray, 1993, *op. cit.*, p 871).

Whichever approach is adopted, there can be little doubt that, in principle, the assignee tenant should be bound by the covenants in the lease (see also Maudsley and Burn's, *Land Law Cases and Materials*, 6th edn, 1992, p 521).

For further discussion on the enforceability of covenants after assignment, see Smith, 1978, *op. cit.*; Gordon, *The Burden and Benefit of the Rules of Assignment*, [1987] Conv 103; Thornton, *Enforceability of Leasehold Covenants*, (1991) 11 LS 47.

9.7 THE POSITION OF SUBTENANTS

In this section, the term 'head tenancy' will be used to refer to the lease between the landlord and the tenant, and 'subtenancy' to the lease between the tenant and the subtenant. Two particular issues may be important to the subtenant: whether the subtenancy ends if the head tenancy is brought to an end, and whether the subtenant has protected status.

Under the common law, the general position is that if the head tenancy fails, then so will the subtenancy. In the case of the head tenancy being forfeited (see ch 11.2.3) the subtenancy would also come to an end (*Great Western Railway v Smith* (1876) 2 Ch D 235 at 253; *Viscount Chelsea v Hutchinson* [1994] 43 EG 153). However, the subtenant has a right to apply for relief from forfeiture:

Law of Property Act 1925

s 146(4)　Where a lessor is proceeding by action or otherwise to enforce a right of re-entry or forfeiture under any covenant, proviso, or stipulation in a lease, or for non-payment of rent, the court may, on application by any person claiming as under-lessee any estate or interest in the property comprised in the lease or any part thereof, either in the lessor's action (if any) or in any action brought by such person for that purpose, make an order vesting, for the whole term of the lease or any less term, the property comprised in the lease or any part thereof in any person entitled as under-lessee to any estate or interest in such property upon such conditions as to execution of any deed or other document, payment of rent, costs, expenses, damages, compensation, giving security, or otherwise, as the court in the circumstances of each case may think fit, but in no case shall any such under-lessee be entitled to require a lease to be granted to him for any longer term than he had under his original sublease.

The terms of any relief given are at the discretion of the court (*Ewart v Fryer* [1901] 1 Ch 499) and any term granted will be a new term, not a reinstated term.

Where, however, it is the tenant who ends the head tenancy by surrender, the subtenancy is not affected (Law of Property Act 1925, s 139; *Mellor v Watkins* (1874) LR 9 QB 400). It has been suggested that the same principle applies when the tenant ends the head tenancy by serving a notice to quit (Woodfall, *Landlord and Tenant*, Vol 1, paras 16.079, 17.200) but Woodfall argues elsewhere (Vol 2, at para 21.157) that ending a lease by notice to quit is a quite different process than ending a lease by surrender and it is doubtful if the subtenancy would continue in this event. Later Court of Appeal authority supports this view—in *Pennell v Payne* [1995] 06 EG 152, it was held that the landlord will not be bound by an unlawful subletting when the tenant serves a notice to quit on the landlord. Although the case concerned an unlawful subletting, the judgment would appear to apply more generally to any subletting, lawful or otherwise.

The question of whether or not a subtenant has protected status will depend upon general rules applicable to that sector (see ch 6).

In the public sector, a subtenant cannot be a secure tenant as the landlord condition is not satisfied (Housing Act 1985, s 80(1)). He is unlikely to be an 'assured tenant' under the Housing Act 1988 as there will, generally, be a 'resident landlord' on a subletting of part. The head tenancy will cease to be a secure tenancy if there is a subletting of the whole (Housing Act 1985, s 93(1)(b)). The basic common law rule will apply on the termination of the head tenancy, so the subtenancy will fall with it (*Acme Housing Association and Royal Borough of Kensington and Chelsea v Chevska*, Legal Action 17 (June 1987), cited in Hoath, *Public Housing Law*, 1989, at p 214, note 24). If the head tenancy is surrendered, the subtenancy will bind the local authority and the part sublet may be a secure tenancy subject to complying with the 'separate dwelling' requirement (Housing Act 1985, s 79; *Basingstoke and Deane BC v Paice*, The Times, CA, 3 April 1995).

In the private sector, on a subletting of the whole, the head tenancy will not be assured as the tenant will not be in occupation (Housing Act 1988, s 1). The subtenant may, however, be an 'assured tenant' so long as the conditions in s 1 are met ('tenancy' and 'tenant' include 'sub-tenancy' and 'sub-tenant', s 45). Should the head tenancy be ended, the subtenancy will continue to be assured, so long as the head landlord (who now becomes the immediate landlord) is not within any of the categories of landlord unable to grant an assured tenancy, such as the Crown or a local authority.

Housing Act 1988
s 18(1) If at any time–
    (a) a dwelling-house is for the time being lawfully let on an assured tenancy; and
    (b) the landlord under the assured tenancy is himself a tenant under a superior tenancy; and
    (c) the superior tenancy comes to an end, then, subject to subsection (2) below, the assured tenancy shall continue in existence as a tenancy held of the person whose interest would, apart from the continuance of the assured tenancy, entitle him to actual possession of the dwelling-house at that time.
  (2) Subsection (1) above does not apply to an assured tenancy if the interest which, by virtue of that subsection, would become that of the landlord, is such that, by virtue of Schedule 1 to this Act, the tenancy could not be an assured tenancy.

Section 18 is relatively straightforward, unlike its predecessor, Rent Act 1977, s 137, which was notoriously complex (see Evans and Smith, *The Law of Landlord and Tenant*, 4th edn, 1993, at pp 281–3). If there is a subletting of part, the subtenant will not be an assured tenant if there is a resident landlord. The tenant is not prevented from being an assured tenant simply because some of the accommodation is shared:

Housing Act 1988
s 4(1) Where the tenant of a dwelling-house has sublet a part but not the whole of the dwelling-house, then, as against his landlord or any superior

landlord, no part of the dwelling-house shall be treated as excluded from being a dwelling-house let on an assured tenancy by reason only that the terms on which any persons claiming under the tenant holds any part of the dwelling-house include the use of accommodation in common with other persons.

In the commercial sector, if there is a lawful subletting of the whole of business premises, the tenant will not have renewal rights under the Landlord and Tenant Act 1954 as he is no longer in occupation of the premises (s 23(1)). However, the subtenant may have renewal rights if the conditions in s 23 are satisfied ('tenancy' includes a 'sub-tenancy', s 69), although many subtenancies in practice have these rights excluded by court order (s 38(4)). On a subletting of part, both the tenant and subtenant can have rights of renewal in relation to the part they occupy.

9.8 PREMISES AS THE FAMILY HOME

In the event of a family breakdown, there is no general policy of seeking to pre-serve tenanted property as the family home. In some situations the law does work to protect the family home, even though the tenant (or one of joint tenants) has left and the home may be under-occupied. Yet there are many situations in which the 'deserving, deserted' partner is unable to stay in the family home. The impact of a family breakdown will depend on whether the couple were married, and whether the tenancy is in the name of only one partner, or of both.

In the public sector, Hoath says that it is standard practice to grant a joint ten-ancy when the occupants are married, but that some local authorities are less willing to do so with cohabitees (1989, *op. cit.*, p 250). The revised Draft Tenants' Guarantee, 1994, issued by the Housing Corporation, recommended that hous-ing associations should use joint tenancies 'in the case of married and unmarried couples, including those of the same gender' (§C3). The National Federation of Housing Associations' Formal Response (p.4) expressed concern about this as

a vulnerable sole tenant could be disadvantaged if required to share the tenancy with a partner. Associations catering for specified groups (for example, women) could find themselves in grave difficulties if obliged to extend joint tenancies to partners not belonging to the targeted group.

The preference of the National Federation of Housing Associations is for associa-tions to be given the discretion to choose the appropriateness of sole or joint ten-ancies on an individual basis—the earlier recommendation on granting joint tenancies was omitted from the final version of the revised Tenants' Guarantee.

In the case of a joint tenancy, if one tenant leaves the other will still be able to occupy the property and both tenants remain liable for payment of rent, etc. The departure of one tenant will not affect the protected status of a tenancy:

Housing Act 1988

s 1(1) A tenancy under which a dwelling-house is let as a separate dwelling is for the purposes of this Act an assured tenancy if and so long as—

. . .

   (b) . . . at least one of the joint tenants occupies the dwelling-house as his only or principal home . . . . (*Cf.* Housing Act 1985, s 81 for secure tenancies.)

The departing joint tenant will still, technically, be entitled to co-occupy the home (*Bull v Bull* [1953] 3 WLR 326) and for this reason the remaining tenant may seek to have the tenancy transferred to him/her by way of assignment. Assuming that the departing tenant is amenable to this, the ability of the parties to assign a periodic assured tenancy will depend, in the private sector, upon the terms of any alienation covenant in the lease and, if none, upon getting the landlord to consent. In the public sector, a secure tenancy can be assigned

Housing Act 1985

s 91(3) (c) to a person who would be qualified to succeed the tenant if the tenant died immediately before the assignment

(that is, to either a spouse or a member of the tenant's family who was living with the tenant for twelve months ending on the assignment and, in either event, occupying the house as the principal home—unless the tenant was already a successor to the tenancy, s 87, and see 9.9 below).

This will enable a transfer to a cohabitee so long as the assignment takes place before the tenant leaves (the twelve-month residence ending on the assignment).

If, however, the departing joint tenant is not happy for the former partner to take over the tenancy, or, indeed, to remain a tenant at all in the property, there are ways in which (s)he can prevent this happening. If the joint tenancy is a periodic tenancy (as will generally be the case in the public sector), the departing tenant can simply end the tenancy by serving a notice to quit (see *Hammersmith LBC v Monk* [1992] 1 All ER 1). Unless the landlord is happy to grant a new tenancy to the remaining partner (and in the public sector this will also depend upon its allocation procedures), the deserted partner will be left without a home. There have been suggestions of collusion between local authorities and the departing joint tenant, so that provided the departing tenant serves a notice to quit, (s)he will be rehoused in a smaller unit and the local authority will recover possession of a larger, under-occupied, family property—indeed, this occurred in *Crawley BC v Ure* (The Times, 23 February 1995). Alternatively, the departing joint tenant may simply stop paying the rent without telling the former partner. Unless the remaining joint tenant is aware of the need to pay rent, rent arrears may quickly build up, giving the landlord a ground for possession (see ch 11.4.1). If the couple are (or were) married, the spouse or former spouse is able to apply for suspension or postponement of the possession order (Housing Act 1985, s 85(5); Housing Act 1988, s 9(5)—see ch 11.2.5.3 on suspension of possession orders generally). A cohabitee, though, has no right to apply for a possession order to be suspended or postponed. If there has already been a suspended possession order made in respect of a *secure* tenancy, any further breach will immediately put an end to the tenancy (*Thompson v Elmbridge Borough Council* (1987) 19 HLR 526) and, again, this will leave the remaining tenant with no right to stay in the home.

A transfer can be made to the remaining tenant, even against the will of the departing tenant, in two situations. First, if the couple were married and obtain a decree of divorce, nullity or judicial separation, the court has power to order a transfer of a regulated/secure/assured tenancy under the Matrimonial Homes Act 1983, s 7 and Sch 1, so long as the property has at some time been the matrimonial home (s 1(10), *Hall v King* (1987) 19 HLR 440) and the spouse seeking the transfer has not remarried (Sch 1, para 7):

Matrimonial Homes Act 1983, Sch 1, Part I,
para 1(1) Where one spouse is entitled, either in his or her own right or jointly with the other spouse, to occupy a dwelling house by virtue of—
     (a) a protected tenancy or statutory tenancy within the meaning of the Rent Act 1977, or
     . . .
     (c) a secure tenancy within the meaning of section 79 of the Housing Act 1985, or
     (d) an assured tenancy or assured agricultural occupancy, within the meaning of Part 1 of the Housing Act 1988,
    then, on granting a decree of divorce, a decree of nullity of marriage or a decree of judicial separation, or at any time thereafter (whether, in the case of a decree of divorce or nullity of marriage, before or after the decree is made absolute), the court by which the decree is granted may make an order under Part II below.
  1(2) References in this Schedule to a spouse being entitled to occupy a dwelling house by virtue of a protected, statutory or secure tenancy or an assured tenancy or assured agricultural occupancy, apply whether that entitlement is in his or her own right, or jointly with the other spouse.

Part II
para 2(1) Where a spouse is entitled to occupy the dwelling house by virtue of a protected tenancy within the meaning of the Rent Act 1977, or a secure tenancy within the meaning of the Housing Act 1985 or an assured tenancy or assured agricultural occupancy within the meaning of Part I of the Housing Act 1988, the court may by order direct that, as from such date as may be specified in the order, there shall, by virtue of the order and without further assurance, be transferred to, and vested in, the other spouse—

(a) the estate or interest which the spouse so entitled had in the
dwelling house immediately before that date by virtue of the lease
or agreement creating the tenancy . . .

As the transfer takes effect 'by virtue of the order', the alienation provisions
within the tenancy are not relevant to the efficacy of the transfer. A similar, but
not identical, jurisdiction exists to transfer 'property' on divorce etc. in the
Matrimonial Causes Act 1973, ss 24, 25—unlike the 1983 Act, this would extend to
cover 'non-secure' and 'non-assured' tenancies. While it might be argued that a
'secure tenancy' is not a 'property right' (see *City of London Corporation v Bown*,
op. cit.; and 9.9 below) and so can not be transferred under s 24, the specific reference to s 24 in the context of permitted assignments of secure tenancies
(Housing Act 1985, s 91(3)(b)) must mean that secure tenancies can be transferred by s 24. In a similar vein, while there is an argument that private sector tenancies can only be transferred by s 24 if assignment is permitted under the lease
(see Bromley and Lowe, *Bromley's Family Law*, 8th edn, 1992, p 637), this would
again seem to be an unnecessary restriction on the statutory objective and the
statutory power must be taken to override any limitations in the lease. No comparable powers exist for the court to order a transfer of the tenancy where the
occupiers are unmarried cohabitees.

The second situation in which the court may order a transfer of the tenancy is
where there are children involved. This power is contained in the Children Act
1989, Sch 1, para 1(2)(d) and (e), formerly the Guardianship of Minors Act 1971,
s 11B. The court can make an 'order requiring either parent to transfer [property]
to the other parent for the benefit of the child'. The transfer need not be shown to
be for the financial benefit of the child, 'benefit' is a word of wide import and will
include *welfare* benefit (*K v K* [1992] 1 WLR 530). The criteria which the court is to
use in the exercise of its discretion are set out in the Children Act 1989, Sch 1, para
4(1):

. . . the court shall have regard to all the circumstances of the case including the
following matters, that is to say–
(a) the income, earning capacity, property and other financial resources
    which the mother or father of the child has or is likely to have in the fore-
    seeable future;
(b) the financial needs, obligations and responsibilities which the mother or
    father of the child has or is likely to have in the foreseeable future;
(c) the financial needs of the child;
(d) the income, earning capacity (if any), property and other financial
    resources of the child;
(e) any physical or mental disability of the child.

In *K v K* the power was used to order the father to transfer his rights in a joint tenancy of council property to the mother. It seems, however, that it might not be
possible to use the power if the proposed transfer is not a permitted assignment

within the tenancy (see Law Commission, *Domestic Violence and Occupation of the Family Home*, Law Com. No. 207, 1992, para 6.5). Again, however, it could be argued that this specific statutory power should be taken to override any limitations in the lease so as not to defeat the statutory objective.

If there is a sole tenancy some different considerations arise. As in the case of a joint tenancy, the departing tenant may be willing to assign the tenancy to the former partner—his ability to do so will depend upon the same factors discussed earlier. The jurisdiction to order a transfer of the tenancy under the Matrimonial Homes Act 1983, the Matrimonial Causes Act 1973 and the Children Act 1989 will also be available. Where these powers do not arise (for instance, no divorce, no children), the remaining partner may be in a weak position. If it is the sole tenant who has left there will no longer be a protected tenancy as the tenant no longer occupies the house 'as his only or principal home' (as required for protection in both public and private sectors—Housing Act 1985, s 81, Housing Act 1988, s 1(1)(b)) and the landlord may be able to end the tenancy without needing to prove a ground for possession. The position of married couples is stronger. Under the Matrimonial Homes Act 1983 the remaining spouse has a statutory right of occupation which can be treated as being occupation by the tenant (s 1(6)) and a right to pay rent, etc., as if it were being paid by the tenant (s 1(5)). Again, this right exists only if the property has at some time been used as the matrimonial home (s 1(10)). While this gives the remaining spouse protection *vis-à-vis* the landlord, (s)he is not protected against a vengeful departing spouse who could simply end the tenancy. There will also be a problem if the transfer of the tenancy is not ordered upon divorce—after the divorce has become absolute the occupation of the remaining former spouse will cease to be seen as occupation by the tenant under s 1(6) as they are no longer married. The result is that the tenancy will cease to be protected as there is no longer a *tenant* in occupation, the court has no jurisdiction to order a transfer under Sch 1 and the landlord can end the tenancy.

On a family breakdown, it may be difficult to resolve the family's housing needs without court order in view of the way that the homelessness legislation operates (see ch 5). In *K v K, op. cit.*, although the mother had been granted care and custody of the children and no longer wanted the father to live with them, the father refused to leave the home because he was concerned that if he left 'voluntarily' he would not get rehoused by the local authority. The mother had similar reasons for not walking out with the children. Had the mother left, the local authority would find itself with a severely under-occupied property and no ground to recover possession—a bad use of limited resources. Hoath suggests that local authorities could put pressure on the tenant by legitimately increasing the rent in the case of under-occupation (1989, *op. cit.*, p 268)—see the Housing Act 1985, s 24.

The Law Commission have examined some of the shortcomings in this area—but fail to tackle the issues raised by the *Monk* and *Elmbridge* cases whereby the action of the former partner can defeat any legislative goal of preserving the family home. The Law Commission recommended that there should be a power to transfer tenancies between cohabitees, as exists for married couples in the 1983 Matrimonial Homes Act (Law Com. No. 207, *op. cit.*, para 6.6) as

this would remove the present discrimination against cohabitants . . . ; would give the courts wider powers to ensure that children were properly housed; and would assist local authorities in discharging their responsibilities to people who would otherwise be homeless or be stranded for a long period of time in unsuitable accommodation while awaiting rehousing. (para 6.2)

It also recommends the adoption of statutory criteria to guide the courts, which would apply to both married and unmarried couples (at paras 6.8-6.9), and the ability to order the payment of compensation by the transferee to the transferor in appropriate cases (at para 6.12).

9.9 STATUTORY SUCCESSION ON DEATH

A lease is, in one sense, a chattel real. As such, the remainder of the term can pass on death. In the case of a long leasehold with 80 years unexpired, a child could inherit that when the parents died. In the case of short term residential leases, the contractual tenancy can generally be terminated on notice and so the transmission on death of a bare contractual tenancy is of little importance. Instead, what is important is to determine the effect of the tenant's death on the protected status of the tenancy. Under the Rent Act 1977, once the contractual term of the tenancy had ended, the tenancy was continued by the statute. A protected tenant was merely given a personal right to occupy after expiry of the contractual term, a 'status of irremovability' (see ch 3.11). On the death of the tenant, the personal right would end—and so there was nothing to pass in the tenant's estate. The Act did, however, also give certain rights of succession. The regime under the Housing Act 1988 is very different. An assured tenant under this Act has a right in rem, not a merely personal right. This means that, on his death, an assured tenant can pass the tenancy to his estate by intestacy or by will. To prevent the tenancy continuing indefinitely, the protected status of the tenant can be brought to an end—the landlord is given a right to end the tenancy within twelve months of the tenant's death (Housing Act 1988, Sch 2, Ground 7). Rights of succession are, however, given to the tenant's spouse (see below). In the public sector, it was held by the Court of Appeal in *City of London Corporation v Bown, op. cit.,* that a secure tenancy is a mere personal right (at 38–9) and not a right of property. The context of the case was whether the tenancy could form part of the estate of the bankrupt tenant and it was held that it could not. On this particular point the law has been altered by an amendment to the insolvency legislation, which provides that assured, protected and secure tenancies can all be vested in the bankrupt's estate upon service of notice (Housing Act 1988, s 117, inserting s 283(3A) and 308A into the Insolvency Act 1986). The interest of *Bown* here, however, is in the finding that the secure tenancy was not property. The Court of Appeal was influenced by the fact that the right to buy (see ch 12) cannot be exercised by a trustee in bankruptcy, as he is not in occupation, and by the fact that a secure tenancy is incapable of assignment. However, as seen earlier, a secure tenant does have certain rights of alienation, rights which are suggestive of property ownership. Also, the Housing Act 1985, s 89(3), suggests that the secure tenancy is a right in rem which vests in the tenant's estate on his death. The subsection then removes security from such a vested tenancy unless there is a person qualified to succeed to the tenancy (s 87) or the tenancy vested under the matrimonial legislation. Whichever view is correct, it is clear that the tenancy will generally cease to be secure on the tenant's death, subject to succession rights.

Secure tenants of local authorities may pass their secure tenancy on death under the Housing Act 1985, s 87, with all concomitant rights, including the Right To Buy—*Harrow LBC v Tonge* (1992) 25 HLR 99.

s 87 A person is qualified to succeed the tenant under a secure tenancy if he occupies the dwelling-house as his only or principal home at the time of the tenant's death and either–

(a) he is the tenant's spouse, or

(b) he is another member of the tenant's family and has resided with the tenant throughout the period of twelve months ending with the tenant's death;

unless, in either case, the tenant was himself a successor, as defined in section 88.

The proviso limits the right to just one statutory succession on death. The successor must have occupied the dwelling-house as his only or principal home at the date of the secure tenant's death. However, there is no need for non-spouse members of the family to have occupied the particular dwelling-house for the previous twelve months. The requirement is that they have resided with the tenant for twelve months, but they could have moved into the particular council property the day before the secure tenant died—*Waltham Forest LBC v Thomas* [1992] 3 All ER 244 at 246, where Lord Templeman's judgment takes a generous view of s 87:

The effect of s 87 is to ensure that a qualified member of the tenant's family who has made his home with the tenant shall not lose his home when the tenant dies but shall succeed to that home and to the secure tenancy which protected both the tenant and the successor while the tenant was alive and which shall continue to protect the successor after the death of the tenant . . . In the present case, the respondents have been unable to suggest why the appellant should lose his home as well as brother by reason of the death of his brother.

Primacy under s 87 is given to the spouse, but other members of the family can qualify given that they meet the additional requirement of having resided with the deceased secure tenant for the twelve months prior to death. The Housing Act 1985, s 113 defines members of the family to include people living together as husband and wife. Thus, cohabitees are not treated as favourably as spouses in the local authority sector.

In the private sector, the Housing Act 1988, s 17, provides for succession to assured tenancies and simplifies the law from that which existed (and still exists for leases granted before 15 January 1989) under the Rent Act 1977 (for the earlier law, see Evans and Smith, *op. cit.*, pp 272–4).

s 17(1) In any case where
    (a) the sole tenant under an assured periodic tenancy dies, and
    (b) immediately before the death, the tenant's spouse was occupying the dwelling-house as his or her only or principal home, and
    (c) the tenant was not himself a successor, as defined in subsection (2) or subsection (3) below,
    then, on the death, the tenancy vests by virtue of this section in the spouse (and, accordingly, does not devolve under the tenant's will or intestacy).
(2) For the purposes of this section, a tenant is a successor in relation to a tenancy if–
    (a) the tenancy became vested in him either by virtue of this section or under the will or intestacy of a previous tenant; or
    (b) at some time before the tenant's death the tenancy was a joint tenancy held by himself and one or more other persons and, prior to his death, he became the sole tenant by survivorship; or
    (c) he became entitled to the tenancy as mentioned in section 39(5) below.
(3) For the purposes of this section, a tenant is also a successor in relation to a tenancy (in this subsection referred to as 'the new tenancy') which was granted to him (alone or jointly with others) if–
    (a) at some time before the grant of the new tenancy, he was, by virtue of subsection (2) above, a successor in relation to an earlier tenancy of the same or substantially the same dwelling-house as is let under the new tenancy; and
    (b) at all times since he became such a successor he has been a tenant (alone or jointly with others) of the dwelling-house which is let under the new tenancy or of a dwelling-house which is substantially the same as that dwelling-house.
(4) For the purposes of this section, a person who was living with the tenant as his or her wife or husband shall be treated as the tenant's spouse.
(5) If, on the death of the tenant, there is, by virtue of subsection (4) above, more than one person who fulfils the condition in subsection (1)(b) above, such one of them as may be decided by agreement or, in default of

agreement, by the county court shall be treated as the tenant's spouse for the purposes of this section.

Section 17 again provides for a single succession to someone living in the dwelling-house as his or her only or principal home, but this time the right is limited to spouses. However, subsection (4) holds that those living together as husband and wife shall be treated as a spouse. Nevertheless, for both the private and public sectors it would now seem that living together as husband and wife will be an easier test to satisfy than was the case under the Rent Act 1977 (cf. *Dyson Holdings Ltd v Fox* [1976] QB 503; *Helby v Rafferty* [1979] 1 WLR 13; *Chios Property Investment Co v Lopez* (1987) 20 HLR 120). In the public sector, members of the family, other than those living together as husband and wife, are a parent, grandparent, child, grandchild, brother, sister, uncle, aunt, nephew and niece, whether the relationship be by marriage or the half-blood and illegitimate children are to be treated as the legitimate child of the mother and the reputed father (Housing Act 1985, s 113). It does not include mere social relationships where one person cares for another as if that other were a relative, such as a parent or sibling—*Carega Properties SA v Sharratt* [1979] 2 All ER 1084, where 'Bunny' caring for 'Aunt Nora', a woman 50 years his senior, did not succeed. Further, homosexual relationships do not qualify either as those living together as husband and wife or even as members of the family—*Harrogate BC v Simpson* (1986) 2 FLR 91. In the revised Tenants' Guarantee, *op. cit.*, §C7 there is a recommendation that housing associations should consider granting a right of succession to a member of the tenant's family or to a same-sex partner

who had been living with the tenant for the year before the tenant's death and had been looking after the tenant, or had accepted responsibility for the tenant's dependants, or who would be made homeless if reqired to vacate the accommodation.

While accepting this suggestion, the NFHA's Formal Response to the draft revision pointed out that with the various levels of rights accorded, some statutory and some contractual, and with a residual right to devise the tenancy by will where there is no statutory successor, a clearer, more exhaustive provision on succession would be needed. As it stands, §C7 may lead to protracted litigation.

Before 1984, any consideration of statutory succession would have spent some time looking at the position in the agricultural sector, where two successions upon death were permitted to properly qualified successors. This was a highly developed system reflecting the fact that the lease was not simply a means of providing a dwelling for the tenant, but also the tenant's business. Thus, a lease granted before 12 July 1984 could, and, indeed, still can, be passed on upon the retirement of the tenant at 65. However, the Agricultural Holdings Act 1984 abolished all succession rights for new leases created after 11 July 1984. Whereas a residential tenant wants the premises for his home until he moves out or dies and a commercial tenant will either never die (if it is a company, for example) or will have to assign the lease to a new party, a farm is more than a home. The agricultural tenant uses the leased property itself to make his living, but it may well also be the family home. Once the tenant is too old to farm the land, he will want to retire and pass it on to a member of the family who can continue to farm it—the provisions regarding succession on retirement require that the successor, *inter alia*, be a close relative and that in the past seven years he has made his livelihood out of farming the holding. The right to succeed on retirement reflected the way of life of the farming community. On the other hand:

The existence of two-generation succession rights has been criticized as a disincentive to landlords, and a factor contributing to the accelerated decline of the tenanted sector of agricultural land. The Agricultural Holdings Act 1984 consequently amended [the scheme established under Part II of the Agriculture (Miscellaneous Provisions) Act 1976] in two ways:
(1) Section 2 of the 1984 Act abolished succession rights for all new tenancies granted on or after 12 July 1984 . . . . Abolition was agreed as part of a package deal between the National Farmers Union and the Country Landowners' Association on which the 1984 Act was based, the *quid pro quo* being reform of the rent valuation provisions.
(2) The 1984 Act also enacted modifications to the scheme following suggestions by the Northfield Report [Cmnd 7599, paras 626–31] in 1979. The latter suggested there could be a maximum area of land to which a successor could succeed, and that stricter rules on 'eligibility' and 'suitability' for succession should be introduced, so as to encourage efficiency. Transfer to eligible successors prior to death [through succession on retirement] should also be encouraged. (Rodgers, *Agricultural Law*, 1991, p 151)

To have two sets of rules for agricultural leases, with the application of which particular set depending solely on the date of the grant, does not make sense, although leases with succession rights are very slowly dying out. Furthermore, the complete abolition of succession rights does not encourage long term planning by an older farmer nor the involvement of families in the farming business—the reform has ensured that the 'family farm' will be confined to the owner-occupied sector. The right to two statutory successions was probably excessive, but it may be that the baby was thrown out with the bath water.

10

Change of Landlord

10.1 GENERAL INTRODUCTION

Just as the tenant may wish to dispose of his interest in the property, so the land-lord may wish to sell his reversion, or there may be an involuntary disposition on his death or insolvency. However, whereas the landlord will normally restrict the tenant's power to alienate the property, in particular to provide the landlord with a way of vetting the assignee, it is unusual for the tenant to have any control over a disposition by a landlord. In the public sector, however, there are various meth-ods by which there may be a bulk disposition of the housing stock to a new land-lord and for each of these methods there are consultation procedures to be followed to take account of tenants' views.

10.2 LIABILITY AFTER ASSIGNMENT

If there is a change of landlord, the new landlord will generally step into the shoes of the old landlord, assuming the ability to enforce the tenant's covenants and the liability to perform the landlord's covenants. The principles that operate are similar to those discussed in relation to a change of tenant in ch 9.6.

10.2.1 Liability of the Original Landlord

As the original parties to the lease are in a contractual relationship, they will remain liable for performance of the leasehold covenants throughout the term of the lease, unless this liability has been limited by the contract itself. The effect of this is that even after the landlord has assigned the reversion and no longer has any interest in the property, he will be liable for breach of any covenants by the new reversioner. There is no statutory indemnity from the new reversioner when a landlord assigns the reversion and, accordingly, the landlord should take an express indemnity for his own protection (contrast the positions for tenants, see ch 9.6.1.1). In practice, original landlord liability presents few problems and cer-tainly does not generate the same claims of injustice as original tenant liability.

In part, this is because landlords generally undertake far fewer obligations than the tenant and it is rare for a landlord to be sued by the tenant for post assignment breaches (see Law Commission, *Privity of Contract and Estate*, Law Com. No. 174, 1988, para 4.16). It may also be that many landlords restrict their liability either by the terms of the covenant (so that they are liable only so long as they are landlord) or by getting the tenant to release them from liability on assignment (Spencer-Silver, *Landlord's continuing liability*, (1993) 32 EG 69).

Although original landlord liability is to be reformed, along with the reforms on original tenant liability, the reform is to be much less radical. The first principle upon which the Law Commission based its report was that

a landlord or a tenant of property should not continue to enjoy rights nor be under any obligations arising from a lease once he has parted with all interest in the property. (Law Com. No. 174, *op. cit,*. at para 4.1)

In relation to landlord covenants, this principle is by no means followed through in the recommendations. Because the tenant does not have the right to give or withhold consent on an assignment of the landlord's reversion, it was said that the proposals for landlord liability could not mirror those adopted for tenant liability—the starting point could not be to discharge the landlord's liability upon assignment because the tenant would not have a way of ensuring that in appropriate cases there would remain continuing landlord liability after an assignment by being able to require a guarantee from the assignor landlord (Law Com. No. 174, *op. cit.*, para 4.16; contrast the landlord's position on tenant assignment, see ch 9.6.1.3). Instead, the assignment of the landlord's interest will not automatically have any effect upon liability. The landlord will remain liable unless he serves a prescribed notice on the tenant claiming release. The tenant will then have four weeks to serve a written objection. If there are no objections, the landlord will be released upon assignment. However, if the tenant does object to the landlord being released from liability, the landlord will have to apply to the court and establish that it is reasonable for him to be released. If the landlord is not released, he remains liable throughout the remainder of the term, not just until the next assignment (although the landlord can apply again for a release on a later assignment). According to the draft Bill annexed to the Law Commission report, there would seem to be no reason why the landlord could not define his liability in the lease as being limited to the period for which he is landlord (but see contrasting argument of Spencer-Silver, *op. cit.*).

10.2.2 The Position of the New Reversioner

In the case of an assignment of the reversion, there are statutory rules laid down in the Law of Property Act 1925, ss 141 and 142, relating to the passing of covenants.

Passing the benefit, that is, the ability to enforce covenants against the tenant, is dealt with by s 141. This provides:

s 141(1) Rent reserved by a lease, and the benefit of every covenant or provision therein contained, having reference to the subject-matter thereof, and on the lessee's part to be observed or performed, and every condition of re-entry and other condition therein contained, shall be annexed and incident to and shall go with the reversionary estate in the land, or in any part thereof, immediately expectant on the term granted by the lease, notwithstanding severance of that reversionary estate, and without prejudice to any liability affecting a covenantor or his estate.

When the new reversioner acquires the benefit of the covenants, the old landlord loses any rights of action, even if the breaches were committed before the assignment (*In re King* [1963] Ch 459 at 488, 497).

The liability of the new reversioner is dealt with in s 142, which provides:

s 142(1) The obligation under a condition or of a covenant entered into by a lessor with reference to the subject-matter of the lease shall, if and as far as the lessor has power to bind the reversionary estate immediately expectant on the term granted by the lease, be annexed and incident to and shall go with that reversionary estate, or the several parts thereof, notwithstanding severance of that reversionary estate, and may be taken advantage of and enforced by the person in whom the term is from time to time vested by conveyance, devolution in law, or otherwise; and, if and as far as the lessor has power to bind the person from time to time entitled to that reversionary estate, the obligation aforesaid may be taken advantage of and entered against any person so entitled . . .

(2) . . . This section takes effect without prejudice to any liability affecting a covenantor or his estate.

The effect of these sections is that the new reversioner both is able to enforce all tenant covenants, and is bound by all landlord covenants, so long as they have 'reference to the subject matter of the lease'. This phrase is construed in the same manner as the reference to covenants which 'touch and concern' the land, discussed in ch 9.6.2.1(b). On the tenant's part, covenants to pay rent and decorate will touch and concern the land. On the landlord's part, covenants to insure, repair, and give quiet enjoyment all touch and concern the land. However, in *Hua Chiao Commercial Bank Ltd v Chiaphua Industries Ltd* [1987] AC 99, the Privy Council held that a landlord's covenant to return the tenant's deposit was a merely personal obligation and did not have reference to the subject matter of the lease. The effect in this case was that the tenant was unable to get the deposit returned—the new reversioner was not bound by the covenant to return it and the old landlord was insolvent. In *Caerns Motor Services Ltd v Texaco Ltd, Geedes v Texaco Ltd* [1994] 1 WLR 1249, the reversions of petrol station leases were assigned and the tenants argued that the new landlord could not enforce the covenants requiring the tenants exclusively to buy petroleum products and motor fuel from the landlord. Part of their argument was that these were personal covenants, to which the identity of the landlord was of vital importance. Various factors supported this view:

> The success of the entire business depends on marketability of products, an intensely competitive business. There is a commercial relationship with the landlord here which depends on their acting with integrity and fair play. It is important, thirdly, that Texaco [the original landlord] are not a one-man band, but a large organisation and so their standard terms will not be oppressive. Fourthly, there is no covenant by the landlords that their products are of good quality so the tenant is left to rely on the integrity of Texaco. Fifthly, there is no power to select which products the tenant takes so long as the landlord markets the products. They have to take their whole supply from the landlord and they have to stay open 24 hours a day. When you put all that together, it shows that the supplier has powers of life and death over the tenant. (*per* Judge Paul Baker QC at 1264)

Nevertheless, the judge was influenced by an earlier case involving a brewery tie, *Clegg v Hands* (1890) 44 ChD 503. In *Clegg v Hands*, the Court of Appeal had found that a tie in a lease of a public house did 'touch and concern the land':

> It relates to the mode of enjoyment of a public house. The thing demised is a public-house, and the covenant compels the covenantee to buy the beer of the covenantor and his assigns.
> In my opinion, it touches and concerns the demised premises; it affects the mode of enjoyment of the premises, and therefore it runs with the reversion. (*per* Lopes LJ at 523)

In *Caerns Motors*, the solus agreements were similarly held to be enforceable by the new landlord.

The Law Commission report recommended that this distinction between personal covenants and covenants which touch and concern the land be abandoned (Law Com. No. 174, *op. cit.*, para 4.1). Depending on how the legislation is framed, it is likely that parties who wish to enter into a covenant which will be binding only between them, and not between successors, will still be able to do so by ensuring that the personal covenant is expressed to be enforceable only while the parties both own an interest in the property.

10.2.3 The Ability to Enforce Guarantees

A landlord will often have required the tenant to provide a guarantor to give security for the payment of the rent and performance of the other leasehold obligations. The guarantor will usually be in a contractual relationship with the person who was landlord at the time the tenant he is guaranteeing acquired an interest in the property. The contractual promise will either be contained in the lease itself (if guaranteeing the original tenant) or in a Licence to Assign. If the landlord then sells the reversion, is the new reversioner able to enforce the benefit of this guarantee contract? The Law of Property Act 1925, s 141 does not cover this situation as it refers only to covenants 'on the *lessee's* part to be observed and performed', not third party promises (*P & A Swift Investments v Combined English Stores Group plc* [1988] 2 All ER 885 at 888). It is possible for the landlord to expressly assign the benefit of the guarantee to the new reversioner, but this does not always happen. In *P & A Swift Investments, op. cit.*, the House of Lords held that the new reversioner was, in any event, able to enforce the guarantee. They reached this result by relying on the common law rule under which the benefit of a covenant will run with the land if the assignee has a legal estate and the covenant is one which touches and concerns the land. The House of Lords rejected the argument that a surety covenant is 'purely collateral'and does not affect the value of the land. Adopting the view of Browne-Wilkinson VC in *Kumar v Dunning* [1987] 2 All ER 801, Lord Oliver said:

It has been said that the surety's obligation is simply that of paying money and, of course, in a sense that is true if one looks only at the remedy which the landlord has against him in the event of default by the tenant. But . . . I do not think that this is a complete analysis. The tenant covenants that he will do or refrain from doing certain things which undoubtedly touch and concern the land. A surety covenants that those things shall be done or not done as the case may be . . . The content of the primary obligation is, as it seems to me, exactly the same and if that of the tenant touches and concerns the land that of the surety must, as it seems to me, equally do so. (at 890)

Similarly, in *Coronation Street Industrial Properties Ltd v Ingall Industries plc* [1989] 1 All ER 979, a guarantor had covenanted that if the tenant went into liquidation and the lease was disclaimed the surety would 'accept from the Lessor a Lease of the Demised Premises' for the unexpired residue and on the same terms and conditions as the tenant's lease. The House of Lords held that this was a covenant which ran with the land and was enforceable by the new reversioner.

10.2.4 Equitable Leases and Equitable Assignments of Legal Leases

On a change of tenant there may be difficulties in enforcing a covenant against an equitable tenant (see ch 9.6.2.4). These problems do not arise with a change of landlord. Both ss 141 and 142 of the Law of Property Act 1925 apply equally to equitable leases as legal leases, and so the rules discussed earlier will mean that the new reversioner is both subject to, and takes the benefit of, all covenants which have reference to the subject matter of the lease.

10.3 FORMALITIES ON A CHANGE OF LANDLORD

An assignment of the reversion needs to be by deed in order to convey the legal estate (Law of Property Act 1925, s 52).

Where the property assigned includes a dwelling, the Landlord and Tenant Act 1985, s 3 requires the new landlord to give written notice to the tenant of the assignment and of his name and address. This notice must be given 'not later than the next day on which rent is payable under the tenancy or, if that is within two months of the assignment, the end of that period of two months'. Failure to give this notice without reasonable excuse is a criminal offence (s 3(3)). The assignor landlord is also given an incentive to ensure that notice is given, either by the new landlord or by himself, as until written notice is given, the assignor landlord:

s 3(3A) . . . shall be liable to the tenant in respect of any breach of any covenant, condition or agreement under the tenancy . . . in like manner as if the interest assigned were still vested in him; and where the new landlord is also liable to the tenant in respect of any such breach occurring within that period, he and the old landlord shall be jointly and severally liable in respect of it.

10.4 CHANGE OF LANDLORD IN THE PUBLIC SECTOR

Around 1.5 million homes have been sold under the Right To Buy since 1980 (the *Guardian* p 31, 11 September 1993; Wilcox, *Housing Finance Review 1994/95*, 1994, Table 17). However, with the recession in the housing market that started in the late 1980s, the numbers of sales started to dwindle. Those who could afford to buy had already bought. Those left in council accommodation either wanted to remain tenants or could not afford to buy. The government introduced the Rent To Mortgage scheme in the Leasehold Reform, Housing and Urban Development Act 1993 in order to revive the move towards greater owner-occupation, but the Housing Act 1988 had already created means by which to take whole council estates out of local authority control. Parts III and IV of the 1988 Act had established Housing Action Trusts (HATs) and the inaccurately named Tenants' Choice procedure, by which tenants could vote for a new landlord, respectively. The government justified these new measures on the need for more investment, for improvement in housing conditions and on tenant dissatisfaction (1987 White Paper on Housing, Cm 214, Chapters 5 and 6). Both schemes should be seen, however, as part of a concerted effort to privatize council housing and residualize the role of the local authority in the provision of housing. Although local authorities had been able to transfer their housing stock voluntarily in the past, the 1988 Act meant that a local authority's housing stock could be compulsorily transferred either to a HAT at the instigation of the Secretary of State, or to a housing association or private sector landlord, subject, though, to tenant disapproval. Voluntary transfer by local authorities and Tenants' Choice have now been complemented by the Compulsory Competitive Tendering procedures which will see housing services contracted out to non-council bodies.

So far there have only been a few HATs created, and their future impact on the ownership of council housing is unclear. The number of properties voluntarily transferred to housing associations and other bodies by local authorities in England declined in the early 1990s, but has since started to revive—whether the government favours such a revival is debateable having regard to the restrictive provisions in the Leasehold Reform, Housing and Urban Development Act 1993, ss 133–136 (see 10.5, below). Table 10.1 shows the number of properties voluntarily transferred by local authorities between 1989 and 1993.

Table 10.1 Voluntary Transfers by Local Authorities

| | To housing associations | | To other | |
	Total	Of which tenanted	Total	Of which tenanted
1989	13,765	13,424	247	—
1990	30,420	29,987	8,029	8,029
1991	20,017	19,913	1	—
1992	17,869	17,837	9	—
1993	23,919	23,388	41	—

Source: Housing and Construction Statistics, September 1992, March 1993 and March 1994 Qtrs, Table 2.12

Nevertheless, since December 1988, £1,216.4 million has been received through large scale voluntary transfers alone. All bar one of these transfers was made to a housing association, although in several instances the housing association was specifically created to take over the transferred properties (see Table 10.2).

10.5 VOLUNTARY TRANSFER

The Joseph Rowntree Foundation Inquiry into British Housing, Second Report, 1991, found that local authority housing stock effectively only changed hands when the local authority divested itself of its holdings through voluntary transfer (at p 23). Tenants' Choice and HATs have had very limited impact by comparison. Under the Housing Act 1985, ss 32 and 43, the local authority needs ministerial consent for any voluntary disposal. The Department of the Environment in deciding whether to give approval looks to see that the local authority does not have too

Table 10.2

Local authority	Date of transfer	Number of dwellings	Average cost per dwelling (£)	Gross receipts (£m)	% Vote in favour—s 106A and Sch 3A 1985 Act
Chiltern	December 1988	4,650	6,926	32.9	85
Sevenoaks	March 1989	6,526	10,037	65.5	85
Newbury	November 1989	7,053	6,664	47.0	82
Swale	March 1990	7,352	7,501	55.2	54
Broadland	April 1990	3,721	6,739	25.1	53
North Beds.	June 1990	7,472	8,605	64.3	72
Medina	July 1990	2,825	9,858	27.9	69
Rochester	July 1990	8,029	9,590	77.0	60
South Wight	July 1990	2,119	10,776	22.8	91
Mid-Sussex	November 1990	4,426	9,984	44.2	77
East Dorset	December 1990	2,245	9,620	21.6	84
Tonbridge & Malling	January 1991	6,382	8,524	54.4	71
Ryedale	February 1991	3,353	8,436	28.3	82
South Bucks.	March 1991	3,319	10,244	34.0	75
Christchurch	March 1991	1,621	9,144	15.4	54
Suffolk Coastal	May 1991	5,272	6,508	34.0	57
Tunbridge Wells	January 1992	5,519	10,221	58.1	60
Bromley	April 1992	12,393	9,489	117.6	55

cont. overleaf

Table 10.2 *cont.*

Local authority	Date of transfer	Number of dwellings	Average cost per dwelling (£)	Gross receipts (£m)	% Vote in favour— s 106A and Sch 3A 1985 Act
Surrey Heath	January 1993	2,885	9,962	28.7	71
Breckland	March 1993	6,781	8,879	60.2	62
East Cambs.	March 1993	4,266	7,384	31.5	70
Hambleton	April 1993	4,268	7,873	33.5	66
West Dorset	May 1993	5,279	7,629	40.3	65
Havant	January 1994	3,561	9,893	35.2	51
Epsom & Ewell	February 1994	1,740	11,665	20.3	53
Hart	March 1994	2,408	9,593	23.1	76
South Shropshire	March 1994	1,500	9,400	14.1	70
Leominster	March 1994	1,832	8,460	15.5	87
South Ribble	March 1994	3,445	9,097	32.3	78
Hertsmere	March 1994	6,284	8,688	56.4	78/76 (two HAs)
Cherwell	April 1994	1,920	n/a	n/a	35
Basingstoke & Deane	April 1994	9,392	n/a	n/a	52/53 (two HAs)
		Total 149,478	Avg £8,804	Total £1,216.4m	Avg 69%

Source: ROOF, May/June 1994, p 13 (footnotes omitted) and Wilcox, *op. cit.,* Tables 54(a) and (b)

much control over the body to which the stock is being transferred—the current limit is 20 per cent of the new landlord body. Nor should the new landlord have too much housing stock in the same area—there is no intention to replace one large, mostly anonymous landlord with another (Housing Act 1985, ss 34(4A) and 43(3A); Legal Action, September 1991, p 15). While housing associations have traditionally been the new landlord, the rise of local housing companies as an alternative looks likely to continue—Wilcox, *op. cit.*, pp 25–7; Wilcox *et al.*, *Local Housing Companies: New Opportunities for Council Housing*, 1993.

The future of Large Scale Voluntary Transfers is somewhat unclear. They are one way that local authorities can receive capital monies which can, in part, be invested in new stock. Nevertheless, as was discussed in ch 8, central government has built the housing benefit costs of local authority tenants into the Housing Revenue Account. Thus, surpluses in rent can be offset against the housing benefit costs of those council tenants in receipt thereof. However, when the local authority transfers the properties to a new landlord, this saving on housing benefit costs is lost to the Treasury. Therefore, the Leasehold Reform, Housing and Urban Development Act 1993, ss 133–136 provide for limits on transfers by local authorities and require a 20 per cent one-off levy on the transfer price to be paid to the Treasury—see Driscoll, *The Leasehold Reform, Housing and Urban Development Act 1993: The Public Sector Housing Provisions*, (1994) 57 MLR 788 at pp 791–3; Wilcox, *op. cit.*, pp 23 *et seq.*

Depending upon whether the local authority is seeking to dispose of the properties with or without the tenants, there are different procedures (see Hoath, *Public Housing Law*, 1989, pp 369 *et seq.*). Where the purchaser is to obtain vacant possession of the properties, which the Housing and Construction Statistics cited above would suggest is rarely the case, it will be to effect a redevelopment of those properties. In those circumstances, the court will order the eviction of the tenants under Ground 10A (Housing Act 1985, s 84(2)(b) and Sch 2, Pts II, IV and V) to enable the transfer to go ahead, provided that it is satisfied that suitable alternative accommodation is available for the tenants and that the local authority will dispose of the properties in accordance with the redevelopment scheme within a reasonable time of obtaining possession. The local authority will also have had to consult any affected tenants and consider their views before applying to obtain ministerial consent for the redevelopment scheme (Housing Act 1985, Sch 2, Pt V). The Minister must also have regard to these comments, as well as having regard to the level of control the local authority seeks to retain with respect to the properties of which it is seeking to dispose. Although the transferee will carry out the redevelopment, it is for the local authority to obtain ministerial consent for the transfer of its housing stock based on the redevelopment plans.

Usually, though, the local authority will voluntarily dispose of the properties with the tenants still resident. Under the Housing Act 1985, s 106A special consultation duties are imposed on local authorities if they are to obtain ministerial consent. Since the new landlord will not satisfy the 'landlord condition' of the Housing Act 1985, ss 79 and 80, the tenants will lose their 'secure' status, although the Right To Buy is preserved under ss 171A–171H. Their views have to be considered carefully and Sch 3A prohibits the Minister from giving approval for the disposal if a majority of tenants oppose it. Where the disposal receives approval, the purchaser, however, will become landlord of all the properties, even those where the tenants wished to remain with the local authority.

Voluntary transfer does not provide tenants with the rights envisaged for those affected by Tenants' Choice or HATs with regard to consultation and consent to the transfer. Indeed, there have been allegations of malpractice with respect to one attempt by a local authority to transfer all of its stock (the *Guardian* 2 p 21, 12 November 1993). Nevertheless, since most large-scale transfers are to housing associations, the likelihood is that the existing, transferred tenants will be for the most part protected by their new landlords once the transfer has gone through (see the Tenants' Guarantee, issued under the Housing Act 1985, s 36A, Housing Corporation Circular 29/91, 1991; *cf.* Exford, *West Kent Row Reverberates*, ROOF, November/ December 1994, p 9).

Alongside voluntary transfer there will run in parallel both Compulsory Competitive Tendering (CCT) and Tenant Management Organizations (TMOs), in that the result in all three cases is that some organization other than the local authority provides housing services—see ch 7.8.1 and Local Government Act 1988 (Competition) (Defined Activities) (Housing Management) Order 1994 (SI 1994 No. 1671). Where the local authority contracts out the management of entire estates to non-council bodies, probably housing associations or TMOs, then, at first sight, there will be little difference from voluntary transfer: however, CCT and TMO leave the local authority as landlord and, thus, the tenants remain secure under the Housing Act 1985. CCT is less popular amongst housing association managers because the tenants do not have to vote in favour of the contract, whereas their approval is necessary for voluntary transfer (compare the Housing Act 1985, s 27AA and Sch 3A). Tenants fear, with some justification, that rents will rise after voluntary transfer or contracting out and are likely to favour TMO (Dwelly, *Tender Moments*, and Brimacombe, *A Divided Rule*, ROOF, May/June 1991, pp 19 and 32; Zipfel, *Farming Out the Management*, ROOF, March/April 1994, p 12; McIntosh, *By-pass or No-Through Road*, ROOF, May/June 1994, p 10). Further, housing associations are wary of taking on the management of run down estates without additional government funding—'It's a dangerous route for associations to promise tenants they will get blood out of a stone' (Dwelly, *No Sign of Movement*, ROOF, November/December 1992, p 24; see also, Dwelly, *Tender Moments, op. cit.*, p 19). It would seem that local authorities are prepared to provide financial support to the transferee when a voluntary transfer is effected—Wilcox, *op. cit.*, pp 23 *et seq.*, and Table 54.

The conclusion may be that in the end, however, the management of housing is not the cause of tenant dissatisfaction and that voluntary transfer and CCT, nor even TMO, are not, therefore, the solution. Malpass and Murie (*Housing Policy and Practice*, 4th edn, 1994, pp 308–10) found that other factors, such as size of household, whether the household was unemployed, how recently the tenant had moved in and, most importantly, the condition of the housing, affected tenant satisfaction in a comparative study of housing association and council tenants.

What this suggests is that most forms of dissatisfaction are not easily resolved by 'better management'. Better repairs and major improvement programmes could be expected to reduce dissatisfaction. But for housing associations some features of their stock are likely to remain sources of dissatisfaction, however well managed. In these cases, dissatisfaction would derive from the property, irrespective of who the landlord was. (Malpass and Murie, 1994, *op. cit.*, p 309)

If the new owners under voluntary transfer or new managers under CCT/TMO cannot raise enough money through the existing rent to improve the estate, then the new 'managing landlord' will turn out to be just the same as the old one (Dwelly, *No Sign of Movement, op. cit.*, p 24; Exford, *op. cit.*; McIntosh, 1994, *op. cit.*).

10.6 HOUSING ACTION TRUSTS AND TENANTS' CHOICE

10.6.1 General Introduction

By comparison with voluntary transfer, HATs and Tenants' Choice have proved to be ineffective. There have been few transfers of local authority housing stock to housing associations or private sector landlords under either scheme. Both are meant to be used on rundown estates or areas, with HATs being imposed on those with the worst problems. However, both require tenants' approval which has not generally been forthcoming, although HATs have fared better more recently.

HATs were expressly modelled on Urban Development Corporations (1987 White Paper on Housing, *op. cit.*, paras 6.2 and 6.3) which had been created to deal with derelict industrial estates, whereas Tenants' Choice seems to treat local authorities as if they were New Towns. The New Towns Act 1946 allowed for the establishment of government appointed agencies to plan, develop and run new towns created for a specific purpose.

All the new towns were concerned with meeting housing need, but in different contexts. Thus, the new towns of the 1940s were conceived in the context of congestion and overspill from London and those of the 1960s with regional policy and economic growth. (Malpass and Murie, 3rd edn, 1990, *op. cit.*, p 142)

However, by the 1980s the role of these New Town agencies had become anomalous. The agencies appointed to develop the new town were only accountable to central government, not the local population. Until 1986, New Town housing was transferred to local authorities once the development stage had been completed. The precursor to Tenants' Choice with respect to local authority landlords is seen in government policy towards unaccountable New Town agencies, which were never intended to have had a role in the long-term management of housing.

Following a ballot, the Secretary of State, in 1989, approved the transfer of about 7,000 dwellings in Runcorn to five housing associations. Plans for a similar transfer in Telford were strongly opposed locally, and were not carried through. . . . The government's stated objective was to secure the disposal of remaining new town housing . . . and for tenants to be given a choice over who their new landlord should be. (Malpass and Murie, 3rd edn, 1990, *op. cit.*, p 143).

Where the landlord is unaccountable to its tenants or the wider population and it has been established for a specific purpose, which has now been fulfilled, there seem to be good policy reasons for transferring the properties to a more accessible and responsive landlord. However, to then adopt the same policy with respect to an elected body, for which housing management functions have been part of its role since at least the 1920s, shows that Tenants' Choice is not the only factor motivating government legislation in this area—local authority residualization is also furthered through Tenants' Choice and the 1988 Act's provisions would suggest that that seems to have been a stronger influence on government action than any attempt to improve tenants' rights.

10.6.2 Tenants Choice

The law relating to Tenants' Choice is found in the Housing Act 1988, Part IV. The basic provision is s 93.

s 93(1) This Part has effect for the purpose of conferring on any person who has been approved under section 94 below the right to acquire from a public sector landlord, subject to and in accordance with the provisions of this Part—

  (a) the fee simple estate in any buildings each of which comprises or contains one or more dwelling-houses which on the relevant date are occupied by qualifying tenants of the public sector landlord; and

  (b) the fee simple estate in any other property which is reasonably required for occupation with buildings falling within paragraph (a) above.

  (3) Subject to subsection (4) below, a secure tenant of a public sector landlord is a qualifying tenant for the purposes of this Part if (and only if) his

secure tenancy is held directly from the landlord as owner of the fee simple estate and, in relation to any acquisition or proposed acquisition under this Part, any reference in the following provisions of this Part to qualifying tenant is a reference only to a qualifying tenant of the public sector landlord from whom the acquisition is or is proposed to be made.

(4) A secure tenant is not a qualifying tenant for the purposes of this Part if—

    (a) he is obliged to give up possession of the dwelling-house in pursuance of an order of the court or will be so obliged at a date specified in such order; or

    (b) the circumstances are as set out in any of paragraphs 5 to 11 of Schedule 5 to the 1985 Act (exceptions to right to buy).

Public sector landlords include not only local authorities, but also, interestingly, new towns—s 93(2)(b). Section 94 confers on the Housing Corporation the right to approve landlords for the Tenants' Choice scheme.

s 94(1) The right conferred by this Part shall not be exercisable except by a person who is for the time being approved by the Corporation under this section; and neither a public sector landlord nor the council of a county nor any other body which the Corporation have reason to believe might not be independent of such a landlord or council may be approved under this section.

(2) For the purposes of subsection (1) above, a body shall not be regarded as independent of a public sector landlord or the council of a county if the body is or appears likely to be under the control of, or subject to influence from, such a landlord or council or particular members or officers of such a landlord or council.

The Housing Corporation issued *Tenants' Choice: Criteria for Approval and Guidance Notes for Applicants* in 1989. There are some general rules based directly on the 1988 Act to start off with, but the rest of the criteria for approval, while open to anyone (unincorporated associations, companies, individuals or groups of individuals—para 2) would seem to reveal a preference for housing associations or, at least, existing landlords with substantial holdings. On the other hand, para 6 states that the Housing Corporation must be satisfied that any acquisitions under Tenants' Choice must be consistent with the applicant's existing capacity. There are specific sections on control and accountability, financial requirements, managerial efficiency and equal opportunities. However, tenants' interests are expressly dealt with in para 8. There are general rules on the consultation process, the vote and audited accounts, but, more importantly, the acquiring landlord must promise to abide by the terms offered to tenants during the Housing Act 1988, s 102, consultation, keep rents within the reach of those in low-paid work and keep rents on similar properties consistent, follow the guidance on management issued by the Housing Corporation for Tenants' Choice landlords, and refrain from evicting tenants on the ground that the landlord wishes to demolish the dwelling. The requirements on rents are likely to dissuade all but housing associations, since commercial organisations could not make an adequate return on social rents.

Approved landlords can acquire the fee simple of council owned buildings which comprise one or more dwellings and which are occupied by qualifying tenants—part of the test as to whether a secure tenant is a qualifying tenant is that the tenant must hold his tenancy directly from the council as owner of the fee simple estate. Taking ss 93 and 96 together, though, it is the approved landlord who must make the application. Thus, the designation of this procedure as 'Tenants' Choice' is something of a misnomer; the right belongs to the potential new landlord to apply under s 96 to take over the council properties. However, there are several exceptions to the right found in ss 95, 93 and 100.

s 95(1) A building shall be excluded from an acquisition under this Part if on the relevant date–

(a) any part or parts of the building is or are occupied or intended to be occupied otherwise than for residential purposes; and

(b) the internal floor area of that part or those parts (taken together) exceeds 50 per cent. of the internal floor area of the building (taken as a whole);

and for the purposes of this subsection the internal floor area of any common parts or common facilities shall be disregarded.

(2) In the application of subsection (1) above to property falling within section 93(1)(b) above, a building or part of a building which, apart from this subsection, would not be regarded as occupied for residential purposes shall be so regarded if—

(a) it is or is intended to be occupied together with a dwelling-house and used for purposes connected with the occupation of the dwelling-house; or

(b) it is or is intended to be used for the provision of services to a dwelling-house which is comprised in a building falling within section 93(1)(a) above.

(Subsection (1) is intended to exclude caretakers' houses in school grounds, for example, but it may also catch flats above shops).

s 95(3) A building shall be excluded from an acquisition under this Part if–

(a) it contains two or more dwelling-houses which on the relevant date are occupied by secure tenants who are not qualifying tenants; and

(b) the number of dwelling-houses which on that date are occupied by such tenants exceeds 50 per cent. of the total number of dwelling-houses in the building.

(Subsection (3) excludes buildings with two or more dwellings where the secure tenant residents are not qualifying tenants within the meaning of s 93. A secure tenant will not be a qualifying tenant if there is a court order obliging him to give up possession now or on some specified date or if he is excluded from the Right To Buy under the Housing Act 1985, Sch 5, paras 5–11—see also subs (4), below, which excludes properties where the tenant is not secure, as well).

s 95(4) A dwelling-house shall be excluded from an acquisition under this Part if it is a house and it is occupied on the relevant date by–
(a) a secure tenant who is precluded from being a qualifying tenant by section 93(4)(b) above; or
(b) a tenant who is not a secure tenant.
(5) A building or other property shall be excluded from an acquisition under this Part if–
(a) it was specified in some other application made under section 96 below made before the relevant date; and
(b) that other application has not been disposed of.
(Subsection (5) seeks to prevent open competition between acquiring landlords. Once an application is being processed, then no new application may be entertained. However, where there are several potential new landlords, including the possibility of a tenant-led buy out, the Housing Corporation's *Criteria for Approval*, para 8.3, requires all acquiring landlords to informally consult tenants in the initial stages to see which has most support in order to introduce some competition and genuine choice for tenants—see Johnston Birchall, *Housing Policy in the 1990s*, 1992, at p 180.)

There are other exceptions pertaining to associated lands where those are pleasure grounds or open spaces and, more pertinently, where the tenant objects to the transfer of his particular dwelling. The latter exception will be dealt with below when looking at the consultation process.

The approved landlord must make the application in the form prescribed by s 96. It must include a plan setting out all the property sought to be acquired. The local authority is under a duty to supply the approved landlord with a list of the names, addresses and status of all the tenants and licensees in the affected properties and to give access to any necessary documentation—s 97. Subsequently, further duties are imposed on the local authority.

s 98(1) Within twelve weeks of the relevant date, the landlord shall serve on the applicant a notice stating–
(a) which (if any) of the buildings proposed to be acquired by virtue of paragraph (a) of subsection (1) of section 93 above should be excluded from the acquisition on the ground that they do not comprise or contain one or more dwelling-houses which on the relevant date were occupied by qualifying tenants;
(b) which (if any) property proposed to be acquired by virtue of paragraph (b) of that subsection should be excluded from the acquisition on the ground that it is not reasonably required for occupation with

any of the buildings proposed to be acquired by virtue of paragraph (a) of that subsection or that it is reasonably required for occupation with such of those buildings as should be excluded from the acquisition on the ground mentioned in paragraph (a) above;

(c) which (if any) property proposed to be acquired by virtue of either paragraph of that subsection should be excluded from the acquisition on the ground that its inclusion is precluded by section 95 above or that it is reasonably required for occupation with property the inclusion of which is so precluded or that it is a building which is excluded from the acquisition by virtue of section 96(2)(b) above [approved co-operative management schemes];

(d) which property (if any) the landlord desires to have included in the acquisition on the ground that it cannot otherwise be reasonably managed or maintained;

(e) which rights (if any) the landlord desires to retain over property included in the acquisition on the ground that they are necessary for the proper management or maintenance of land to be retained by the landlord;

(f) the other proposed terms of the conveyance; and

(g) such other particulars as may be prescribed.

(2) A building which is excluded from acquisition by virtue of section 95 or section 96(2)(b) above may not be included by virtue of subsection (1)(d) above.

(3) Where a notice under subsection (1) above specifies property falling within paragraph (d) of that subsection, the applicant shall have a right of access, at any reasonable time and on giving reasonable notice, to any of that property which is not subject to a tenancy.

. . .

(6) In relation to a proposed acquisition under this Part, any reference in the following provisions of this Part to the property to which the acquisition relates is a reference to the whole of the property which, in accordance with the provisions of this section, is to be acquired, disregarding the effect of any exclusion by virtue of regulations under section 100 below.

Further on again in the process, the local authority must serve on the acquiring landlord its cost analysis of the transfer in a price/disposal cost notice- s 99. It may be that the acquiring landlord will have to pay the local authority for the value of the buildings in the agreement, but if they were in a very poor state of repair then the cost of bringing them up to standard might exceed their value, resulting in the local authority having to pay the acquiring landlord to taking them off its hands.

Once the council's price notice has been served, the acquiring landlord must undertake consultation procedures with all qualifying tenants and those former tenants of flats who exercised the Right To Buy and now have long leases—s 102. Since secure tenants will lose that status and become assured private sector tenants, but with a preserved Right To Buy under the Housing Act 1985, ss 171A–171H, the consultation is important if tenants are to make the right choices. Given that the acquiring landlord will usually do so on the basis of offering an improved, if more expensive, service, the consultation process will be something of a sales-pitch by the acquiring landlord: there is nothing to stop the local authority informing tenants as well, however. There is a somewhat peculiarly weighted voting system where abstentions count in favour of the acquiring landlord. A proposal to acquire cannot go ahead if more than 50 per cent of the tenants eligible to be consulted voice their opposition or if less than 50 per cent respond to this part of the consultation process. However, if, for example, 65 per cent of eligible tenants were to vote and there was a 45:20 split against the transfer, then the acquiring landlord would still succeed since the 35 per cent who failed to vote at all are presumed to be in favour—Housing Act 1988, s 103(2). Given the way the voting procedure is weighted against local authorities, it is surprising that there have been so few Tenants' Choice transfers—883 properties in total, and see the *Guardian* 2 p 21, 12 November 1993. If a tenant opposes the transfer, then he will remain a council tenant. His property will not be part of the acquiring landlord's properties rented to individual tenants. Council houses occupied by opposing tenants will remain council property, but where the opposing tenant rents a flat, the block will be transferred, while the individual flat will be leased back to the council—ss 100 and 103.

s100(1) The Secretary of State shall make regulations imposing the following requirements in relation to any acquisition under this Part, namely

    (a) that any dwelling-house which is a house and is occupied by a tenant to whom subsection (2) below applies shall be excluded from the acquisition; and

    (b) that a lease of any dwelling-house which is a flat and is occupied by a tenant to whom subsection (2) below applies or by a tenant of a description prescribed for the purposes of this paragraph shall be granted by the applicant to the [council] landlord immediately after the acquisition.

  (2) This subsection applies–

    (a) to any qualifying tenant whose tenancy commenced before the relevant date, and

    (b) to any tenant of a description prescribed for the purposes of this subsection,

being, in either case, a tenant who, before the end of the period mentioned in section 102 below and in response to the consultation under that section, gives notice as mentioned in section 103(2) below of his wish to continue as a tenant of the landlord.

s103(1) Subject to subsection (2) below, the applicant may, within two weeks of the end of the period mentioned in section 102 above, serve on the landlord notice of his intention to proceed with the acquisition; and in that notice the applicant, in such circumstances as may be prescribed, may inform the landlord–

(a) that he wishes to enter into a prescribed covenant to make payments to the landlord on the occasion of any prescribed disposal (occurring after the date of the acquisition) of a dwelling-house comprised in the property to be acquired; and

(b) that he requires the value of that covenant to be taken into account in reducing the price which would otherwise be payable for the property to be acquired.

(2) The applicant shall not be entitled to serve a notice under subsection (1) above if, in response to the consultation under section 102 above,–

(a) less than 50 per cent. of the tenants to whom that section applies have given notice of their wishes in such manner as may be prescribed; or

(b) the number of tenants to whom that section applies who have given notice in that manner of their wish to continue as tenants of the landlord exceeds 50 per cent. of the total number of tenants to whom that section applies.

(3) In any case where a tenancy is held by two or more persons jointly, those persons shall be regarded as a single tenant for the purposes of subsection (2) above and, accordingly, any notice given in response to the consultation under section 102 above shall be of no effect for the purposes of subsection (2) above unless it is given by or on behalf of all the joint tenants.

The result is that there may well be the diversity of tenure for which the government hoped, but from the point of view of ease of management and consistency in the standard of housing, the result may not be the best. The new landlord may well have additional resources for improving the property but may also raise the rents. The local authority may use the one or two properties remaining with them for homeless applicants, transferring the original tenant to better housing, especially if it has no resources with which to match the works carried out by the acquiring landlord. And there is no way for former tenants to opt back into the local authority if the new landlord does not live up to its promises. To that extent, if CCT could be combined with some partnership with the local authority in the running of estates, then one might at last see a policy designed to improve the housing stock and efficiency and protect tenants.

The Tenants' Choice scheme has not proved to be an outstanding success if the number of transfers thereunder is used as the measure. In Westminster 820 properties were transferred, and in Merton there were a mere eight; a further 55 were transferred in Beaconsfield in February 1994. Fewer than 1,000 transfers of buildings since the 1988 Act came into force suggests that Tenants' Choice has failed. Tenants are wary of new private sector landlords, even if the local authority is a poor manager of its estates. Moreover, potential landlords are afraid of not being able to deliver all that they promise because the profit margins on social rents are so low. Tenants' Choice is likely to fall into disuse with the introduction of CCT. In the end, it is not a question of landlords, but rather of standards, and the government needs to devise laws that have the improvement of the housing stock as their principal aim, regardless of landlord or tenure. To that extent, Tenants' Choice is a diversion.

10.6.3 Housing Action Trusts

Housing Action Trusts, on the other hand, after a slow start, are picking up, partly because they are concerned with poor conditions. It was always intended that HATs would be imposed only on the most run-down estates.

[There] are some areas of local authority housing, particularly in some of the inner urban areas, where social problems and housing disrepair are so serious that in the Government's view more direct action—involving both public and private sectors—is needed to obtain improvements over a reasonable timescale. Unless major improvements can be made in the fabric and general environment of these areas it is unlikely that policies such as the right to transfer to other landlords would be successful there. (1987 White Paper on Housing, *op. cit.*, para 6.1)

Nevertheless, it was only after amendments to the government's original Bill that sufficient balancing of improvements against tenants' rights was introduced.

HATs owed more to urban development corporations than to any housing model; the [original] aim was for a trust set up by the Secretary of State and led by business people to lever private funding into the worst estates, and over three to five years repair the stock, improve the environment and introduce diversity of tenure. Tenants would have no rights at all until the end of the HAT, when they could choose a permanent landlord. The authoritarian nature of the proposal, with its denial of any ballot among tenants and of any representation on the HAT board, and its weak promise of consultation of residents, led tenants to oppose all six of the original HATs. Then, after some vigorous campaigning, and in a last-minute amendment in the House of Lords, they eventually obtained the right to ballot. Further concessions followed; a promise was exacted that councils would be given the necessary finance to buy the estates back at the end of the HAT's life, if tenants so wished. (Johnston Birchall, *op. cit.*, p 179)

So great were the apprehensions surrounding HATs that tenants voted in favour for the first time only in 1991. Transfers to HATs took place in North Hull and Waltham Forest in that year, in Liverpool in 1992 and in Tower Hamlets and Castle Vale Birmingham the year after that. A further one was established in Brent in Spring 1994. Not only did the North Hull HAT guarantee that the council would receive sufficient resources with which to reacquire the estate after the HAT had completed its work, but local councillors were members of the board of the HAT as well, emphasising the co-operation between public and private sectors. As the Rowntree Inquiry (*op. cit.*, pp 66–8) pointed out, this model of HAT has a lot in common with the Scottish Partnership Areas scheme. The Liverpool HAT had the same guarantees about returning to the local authority at the end of the HAT as the tenants in North Hull, and four tenants were members of the board—Black, *High Hopes*, ROOF, January/February 1993, p 20.

The law relating to HATs is found in Part III of the Housing Act 1988. Under s 60(1), the Secretary of State designates an area of council dwellings to be a HAT. The rest of s 60 provides, *inter alia*, that the area can be made up of two areas which need not be contiguous and need not even have the same local authority as landlord. Designation is at the discretion of the Secretary of State, having regard to various factors set out in s 60(5).

s 60(5) Without prejudice to the generality of subsection (4) above, among the matters to which the Secretary of State may have regard in deciding whether to include a particular area of land in an order under this section, are–
    (a) the extent to which the housing accommodation in the area as a whole is occupied by tenants or owner-occupiers and the extent to which it is local authority housing;
    (b) the physical state and design of the housing accommodation in the area and any need to repair or improve it;
    (c) the way in which the local authority housing in the area is being managed; and
    (d) the living conditions of those who live in the area and the social conditions and general environment of the area.

Central government's dual aim of residualizing local authority housing functions and, yet, of instituting fundamental repairs to rundown council properties is evident in s 60(5)(a) and (b).

There are consultation procedures laid down in Part III. The Secretary of State must consult with every local authority which is included within the proposed area before making the designation order. There must also be consultation with the affected tenants. This includes supplying them with the relevant information regarding the planned HAT and then balloting them.

s 61(2) Where the Secretary of State is considering a proposal to make a designation order, he shall use his best endeavours to secure that notice of the proposal is given to all tenants of houses in the area proposed to be designated who are either secure tenants or tenants of such description as may be prescribed by regulations.
    (3) After having taken the action required by subsection (2) above, the Secretary of State shall either–
    (a) make arrangements for such independent persons as appear to him to be appropriate to conduct, in such manner as seems best to them, a ballot or poll of the tenants who have been given notice of the

proposal as mentioned in that subsection with a view to establishing their opinions about the proposal to make a designation order; or

(b) if it seems appropriate to him to do so, arrange for the conduct of a ballot or poll of those tenants in such manner as appears to him best suited to establish their opinions about the proposal.

(4) If it appears from a ballot or poll conducted as mentioned in subsection (3) above that a majority of the tenants who, on that ballot or poll, express an opinion about the proposal to make the designation order are opposed to it, the Secretary of State shall not make the order proposed.

Unlike Tenants' Choice, the decision to go ahead on the HAT is based on the result of those who actually vote. Those who abstain lose their right to have any say in whether the designation order is made: abstentions are not treated as votes in favour of the HAT. By way of corollary, where the vote is in favour of the HAT, then those tenants who voted against the scheme have no right to remain with the council.

If the HAT receives tenant approval, then the minister must appoint the Trust members for the newly designated area in accordance with s 62 and Sch 7. Its finances are dealt with under Sch 8. Strangely, one might think, it is only after the tenants have voted in the HAT that it has to produce a statement of its proposals under s 64. The statement must coincide with the objects and powers of HATs set out in s 63.

s 63(1) The primary objects of a housing action trust in relation to the designated area for which it is established shall be—

(a) to secure the repair or improvement of housing accommodation for the time being held by the trust;

(b) to secure the proper and effective management and use of that housing accommodation;

(c) to encourage diversity in the interests by virtue of which housing accommodation in the area is occupied and, in the case of accommodation which is occupied under tenancies, diversity in the identity of the landlords; and

(d) generally to secure or facilitate the improvement of living conditions in the area and the social conditions and general environment of the area.

(2) Without prejudice to subsection (1) above, a housing action trust may—

(a) provide and maintain housing accommodation; and

(b) facilitate the provision of shops, advice centres and other facilities for the benefit of the community or communities who live in the designated area.

(3) For the purpose of achieving its objects and exercising the powers conferred on it by subsection (2) above, a housing action trust may—

(a) acquire, hold, manage, reclaim and dispose of land and other property;

(b) carry out building and other operations;

(c) seek to ensure the provision of water, electricity, gas, sewerage and other services; and

(d) carry on any business or undertaking;

and may generally do anything necessary or expedient for the purposes of those objects and powers or for purposes incidental thereto.

(4) For the avoidance of doubt it is hereby declared that subsection (3) above relates only to the capacity of a housing action trust as a statutory corporation; and nothing in this section authorises such a trust to disregard any enactment or rule of law.

(5) Section 71 of the Race Relations Act 1976 (local authorities: general statutory duty) shall apply to a housing action trust as it applies to a local authority.

In order, partly, to fulfil these objects, Part III provides for the transfer of local authority housing to the HAT (s 74 *et seq*.) along with a whole panoply of local authority functions, including those of the former housing authorities (s 65), planning control (ss 66 and 67), public health (s 68), highways (s 69) and even homelessness responsibilities (s 70). In ordering the transfer of the housing to the HAT, the Secretary of State must consult with all affected local authorities and inform all the secure tenants. There will also be measures on the financial aspects of the transfer which, depending on the extent of the work necessary, might require the local authority to pay monies to the HAT (s 74).

Once the HAT is established, then the landlord and tenant relationship of former council tenants is changed and even owner-occupiers and private sector tenants are affected. HATs are designed to deal with rundown council estates, but if privately rented properties are very closely connected with the council housing, then the HAT may take over those as well. Regardless, where the HAT takes over local authority functions in the designated area, then planning matters therein, for example, will be handled by the HAT for every occupier. Unlike the situation where the Tenants' Choice procedure effects a change of landlord, however, the former council tenants remain secure tenants under the Housing Act 1985 because a HAT fulfils the landlord condition. Indeed, if the HAT grants a new tenancy, this tenancy is secure, too. Furthermore, where a HAT wishes to dispose of some of the former council dwellings, it must give first refusal to local authorities in its designated area—ss 84 and 84A, as amended by s 125 Leasehold Reform, Housing and Urban Development Act 1993. Rents should also remain in line with those that the former local authority landlord would have charged, at least until any improvements have been effected.

s 85(1) A housing action trust may make such reasonable charges as it may determine for the tenancy or occupation of housing accommodation for the time being held by it.

(2) A housing action trust shall from time to time review rents and make such changes, either of rents generally or of particular rents, as circumstances may require.

Section 85 mirrors the Housing Act 1985, s 24, which governs local authority rent-fixing.

At the end of the HAT's work, it must be dissolved. Long-term housing management is not within the remit of HATs. The dissolution provisions are found in s 88. The HAT must use its best endeavours to bring its objects to fulfilment as soon as possible and then the Secretary of State, upon the HAT submitting proposals for its dissolution and the transfer of the properties, can order its winding up. If a housing association or private landlord takes over, then, subject to a preserved Right To Buy, the tenants will become 'assured' rather than 'secure'. Tenants, though, are requiring central government to guarantee that the local authority will be given sufficient finance to buy back the properties at the end of the HAT before they will approve its establishment under the s 61 ballot.

HATs are now seen as the only way for a council to ensure that its worst estates are upgraded. The restrictions on expenditure imposed by central government on local authorities mean that large scale improvements cannot be carried out within normal budgets. The government, however, was prepared to inject £115 million into HATs for the three financial years 1991/92 to 1993/94—The Government's Expenditure Plans: Department of the Environment, 1994–95 to 1996–97, Cm 2507, Figure 75 and paras 6.48–6.50, 1994. It was proposed to pump a further £88.2 million in 1994-95, with another £90 million in each of the two subsequent years, but through the Single Regeneration Budget—Figure 46, Government Expenditure Plans, 1994, *op. cit*. While those may seem to be substantial sums, the cost of repairing the 67 tower blocks transferred to the HAT in Liverpool alone was estimated to be £128 million—Black, 1993, *op. cit.*, at p 20. Finally, if the government is so concerned about the dilapidated state of many of the council estates that it is prepared to transfer them into the hands of an appointed board, it seems strange that it is prepared to ignore the much worse condition of housing found in the private sector—see *English House Condition Survey: 1991*, 1993, at pp 50 *et seq*. A true housing policy that was aimed at bringing housing in general up to the appropriate standard would allow HATs to take control of all rented dwellings in a designated area and to direct repair works for owner-occupied housing in disrepair as well. What Part III of the Housing Act 1988 offers is an attempt to lever tenants out of local authority control on a promise of better housing—so far it is only tenant pressure on government through the s 61 ballot that has ensured that local authorities will have the funding to be able to buy back the council estates upon the dissolution of the HAT.

Greater diversity in the rented sector is being pushed through in a variety of ways. With local authority budgets being restricted, there will inevitably be pressure to agree to voluntary transfers and, in appropriate cases, HATs. CCT is also being imposed. The traditional view of local authority landlordism is, therefore, undergoing radical change. Thus, the object must be to guarantee tenants rights, and not just the Right To Buy, under the various transfer schemes in place. In addition, given the condition of housing in Britain, a more generally applicable scheme than HATs needs to be introduced.

11

Ending the Relationship

11.1 EVICTION

The landlord and tenant relationship can end amicably with the term coming to an end or with the landlord or tenant giving notice. The tenant might also become an owner-occupier through enfranchisement or the Right To Buy (see ch 12). However, this section on eviction will concentrate on the tenant's right to remain in the property in the face of the landlord's desire to be rid of him. It should be recognized, though, that whilst eviction might evince a hostile intention, it can also be a device for rehousing. For example, a secure tenant of a local authority can only be removed from his housing against his will in accordance with the Housing Act 1985, s 84 and Sch 2. Thus, if a local authority wish to refurbish a council house, they must 'evict' the tenant under Ground 10 of Sch 2, but, at the same time, provide suitable alternative accommodation. Eviction from one property need not mean the end of the landlord and tenant relationship.

Nevertheless, the typical grounds for eviction, of rent arrears and 'annoying the neighbours', reflect an undesired termination of the relationship from the point of view of the tenant. Even in these circumstances, however, eviction can also be seen as part of the allocation process. If one tenant has failed to fulfil the bargain struck in the granting of the lease, then the landlord may wish to reallocate the premises to another tenant whom he believes to be a better prospect. In Japan the allocation aspect of eviction was taken one stage further. A tenant of welfare housing would have to quit his tenancy if his income exceeded a prescribed level and find new accommodation in the ordinary housing market (van Vliet, *International Handbook of Housing Policies and Practices*, 1990, pp 681–3). The British attitude has been, though, that eviction is a remedy of last resort, both from the practical point of view that it is difficult to be sure that any new tenant will be any better and from the legal perspective that limits on eviction reflect a strong belief in the social good of security of tenure.

In England, protecting the tenant's rights has been achieved through statutory protection, whereas much the same result has been achieved in the United

States through developments in case law as well as statute. In 1968, for instance, the DC Circuit Court held it to be unlawful to fail to renew a tenant's lease in retaliation for the tenant complaining about the landlord's breaches of the housing code—*Edwards v Habib*, 397 F 2d 687 (1968). In addition, some States in the United States have introduced 'just cause' eviction statutes. Such statutes only allow a landlord to evict a tenant for one of the grounds listed in the statute, akin to the English system. Commentators in the United States have criticized these statutes on the ground that the tenant can give notice to quit as and when he feels like, but that the landlord can only do so for just cause—Rabin, *The Revolution in Residential Landlord-Tenant Law: Causes and Consequences*, 69 Cornell L Rev 517 at pp 534 *et seq.* (1984). Given the dearth of affordable rented housing, however, it is unlikely that a tenant would give up a property unless the circumstances became untenable. Another criticism of the just cause statutes and of security of tenure laws generally, though, carries more weight. Rabin, *op. cit.*, at n.92, argues that the difficulty of removing undesirable tenants may put off better, more responsible tenants; security of tenure affects the other tenants who have to live in the same multi-occupation premises as problem tenants as much as landlords. Whilst the shortage of rented housing would suggest that such issues play only a small part in choosing accommodation, it may be relevant to an understanding of the popularity of the Right To Buy in the local authority sector, where those who could afford to took the first steps toward moving off the council estates by becoming owner-occupiers.

Security of tenure protects periodic tenants by restricting the efficacy of notices to quit. Where a fixed term lease comes to an end, then some guarantee of renewal is necessary if eviction is not to take place by default. In France, where the normal residential lease is a fixed term for three or six years, Articles 10 and 15 of *Loi n# 89-462 du 6 juillet 1989* (see also, De Moor, *Landlord and Tenant in French Law: A Recent Statute*, (1983) 3 OJLS 425 at 428–9) provide for a right of renewal. In England in the private residential sector, an assured tenant with a fixed term is protected not by renewal but by a periodic tenancy arising at the end of the fixed term (Housing Act 1988, s 5(2) and (3); see also the Landlord and Tenant Act 1954, s 3, continuation of long residential leases, and the Housing Act 1985, s 86, continuation of fixed term secure tenancies). Commercial tenants, who often have fixed term leases, are protected by having a right to apply for a new tenancy (Landlord and Tenant Act 1954, ss 24 and 26). The Landlord and Tenant Act 1954, s 29, provides for a right of renewal subject to some exceptions (all of which will be considered below) unless the statutory guarantee has been excluded—s 38(4) of the 1954 Act allows for the exclusion of the right of renewal by the parties with the authorization of the court. The restrictions on renewal are effectively grounds for eviction and will be treated as such.

However, for the moment, whether eviction or non-renewal is the question, the issue is the balancing of the tenant's right to a home or business premises as against the landlord's right to use his property as he sees fit. In Germany, apart from breach of a term of the tenancy agreement, the German residential landlord's only ground for eviction is that he needs the property for himself (van Vliet, *op. cit.*, p 139). In the United States, on the other hand, the landlord's right to use the property as he sees fit has been termed the owners' liberty interest, but it has been contrasted with their economic interest. The United States courts have been prepared to override the residential tenant's security of tenure if the owner wished to occupy the premises. Any restriction on this right has generally been deemed unconstitutional—*Polednak v Rent Control Board*, 494 NE 2d 1025 at 1028 (1986), cited in Note, *The Constitutionality of Rent Control Restrictions on Property Owners' Dominion Interests*, 100 Harv L Rev 1067 at p 1082 (1987). However, where the landlord is merely trying to uphold his economic interests, the courts have been more circumspect in challenging the tenant—*Gilbert v City of Cambridge*, 745 F Supp. 42 (1990), 932 F2d 51 (1991); *Levald Inc. v City of Palm Desert*, 998 F 2d 680 (1993). The courts see any interference with the landlord's dominion as a potential 'taking' of the property by the State contrary to the Fifth and Fourteenth Amendments—'nor shall private property be taken for public use, without just compensation'. What is rarely voiced, is the view that tenants who pay rent have rights in the property as well, which are reinforced by the security of tenure guarantees. The approach of protecting the tenant's occupancy interests at the expense of the landlord's economic interests can be fully justified, if it is accepted that laws relating to housing ought to give primacy to securing a dwelling for an occupant over financial gain for the property owner. *Loi n# 89-462*, Art.15, though, allows the landlord to terminate the tenancy in order to occupy the premises himself or to sell them, presumably at a profit (although see Art.15 II). In English law, private landlords who wish to use their properties as a home, subject to the lease and notice, can evict tenants—Housing Act 1988, s 7 and Sch 2, Ground 1. It may be argued, though, that what ought to be prohibited in any system of security of tenure is the eviction of any tenant so that a new tenant can be taken on at a higher rent, on the ground that that would, from certain perspectives, place too high a regard on the landlord's economic interests. The law relating to eviction is another example of where housing is recognised as more than just a consumable, such that simple market forces have to be constrained (see ch 12.7.2.1).

11.2 GENERAL RULES ON TERMINATION OF LEASES

Before looking at the grounds for eviction contained in the protective codes, the general rules on termination of leases will be outlined.

11.2.1 Periodic tenancies

At common law a periodic tenancy is ended by serving a notice to quit. The length of notice needed depends upon the period of the tenancy (and any relevant statutory provisions). Ignoring statutory requirements, the length of notice required will usually be the period of the tenancy, given so as to expire at the end of a completed period (but see Cooke, *Notices to Quit for the Monthly Tenant* [1992] Conv 263 where it is argued that a lunar month should suffice for a monthly tenancy even though the period of the tenancy is a calendar month). So, for example, a quarterly tenancy will be ended by one quarter's notice, ending at the end of a completed quarter. Yearly tenancies are treated differently, requiring only a half years notice, ending at the end of a completed year. These notice provisions can be varied by contract. (See also ch 6 for the effect of contractual restrictions on the right of a party to end a periodic tenancy.) In the case of a joint periodic tenancy, an effective notice to quit can be served by only one of the joint tenants: *Hammersmith and Fulham LBC v Monk* [1992] 1 All ER 1 (and see ch 3.1).

11.2.2 Fixed Term Leases

Leases for a fixed term generally end by effluxion of time, without any need to serve a notice to quit. It may be ended sooner by merger (where the lease and reversion become vested in the same person), if the parties agree to a surrender of the lease, or if the lease contains a break clause giving one party the right to bring the lease to an end at set points during the lease. Break clauses became more common during the recession—landlords were reluctant to depart from the standard long lease of fifteen or 25 years and tenants were unwilling to assume obligations for such a long period. The break clause was therefore a compromise giving the tenant an option to break after, say, five years—often timed to coincide with the first rent review so that the tenant can elect to leave if the new rent is too high. If there is a joint tenancy all tenants must act together to surrender the tenancy or to operate a break clause: *Hounslow LBC v Pilling* [1994] 1 All ER 432; *Hammersmith LBC v Monk, op. cit.*, at 9 (the difference between this and serving a notice to quit being that the latter is non-renewal of a contract whereas surrender/break is ending an existing contract and therefore requires the consent of all contracting parties).

11.2.3 Forfeiture

A lease may also end early if the tenant is in breach and the landlord elects to forfeit the lease. The law on forfeiture is complex. In its Report on Forfeiture the Law Commission described the law as:

... a body of rules which, besides being unnecessarily complicated, is no longer coherent and may give rise to injustice. (Law Commission, *Forfeiture of Tenancies*, Law Com. No. 142, 1985, para 1.3)

What follows is an outline only (for more detail, see Pawlowski, *The Forfeiture of Leases*, 1993).

The right to forfeit will only arise if the tenant is in breach of a condition (relatively unusual) or if the tenant is in breach of covenant and the lease contains a 'right of re-entry' (a forfeiture clause). It is standard practice for a lease to contain a forfeiture clause, allowing the landlord to forfeit if the tenant is in breach of any of the leasehold covenants. In theory, it would similarly be possible for the tenant to be given the right to end the lease following a breach by the landlord but this is extremely rare (see Law Com. No. 142, *op. cit.*, at para 1.4).

Even when the tenant is in breach and the right to forfeit arises, the lease is not automatically ended. The right of re-entry simply gives the landlord the option of forfeiture. If the tenant has breached the lease by, for example, assigning the lease to a new tenant without the landlord's consent, the landlord may choose to continue the lease if he is happy with the new tenant. If the landlord wishes to end the lease, he will do so either by bringing possession proceedings or by peaceably repossessing the property (respectively referred to as 'constructive' and 'actual' entry by the Law Commission, Law Com. No. 142, *op. cit.*). If the landlord does wish to pursue this course it is important that he does not in the meantime do any unequivocal act which recognises the continuing existence of the lease as this will waive his right to forfeit. Waiver occurs only when the landlord or his agent is aware of facts giving rise to the breach—but can occur quite unintentionally as, for example, when the landlord's managing agent sees a new tenant in occupation and the landlord's office accepts payment of rent without this information having been passed onto it (for an example of unintentional waiver, see *Central Estates Ltd v Woolgar (No 2)* [1972] 3 All ER 610). This may be hard on the landlord—as recognised by the Law Commission in recommending that the landlord should only lose the right to end the lease

if his conduct is such that a reasonable tenant would believe, and the actual tenant does in fact believe, that he will not seek a termination order. (Law Com. No. 142, *op. cit.*, para 3.35 and Part VI)

If the lease is forfeited, it is brought to an end. This can have severe consequences for the tenant—it means the loss of possession of premises which may be a home or business site, but can also result in large financial loss where the lease was purchased for a capital sum or the tenant's interest has a premium value (for example, where the current rent is less than the market rent). There are other personal and financial costs associated with the need for relocation. The costs to the tenant may be out of all proportion with the landlord's loss caused by breach. In addition, with the loss of the tenant's interest all interests derived from it will also fall, such as subtenancies and mortgages over the lease.

In view of these consequences, the courts have always tended to lean against forfeiture, notwithstanding the fact that the landlord's strict contractual rights entitle him to forfeit even when forfeiture appears unconscionable. There are several areas in which this tendency to restrict and monitor forfeiture can be seen—the general thrust being that the lease should not be forfeited where the landlord has suffered no irreparable damage or where that damage is disproportionately small compared to the loss that will be suffered by the tenant. As mentioned earlier, the law on forfeiture is highly complex—in part because the law on forfeiture for non-payment of rent has developed separately from the law on forfeiture for breach of other covenants, but also because the law is overlaid by statutory interventions, some of which only apply to forfeiture by legal proceedings and not peaceable re-entry and some of which apply differently to actions commenced in different courts.

Nevertheless certain trends can be seen.

11.2.3.1 Notifying the Tenant of Breach and Giving an Opportunity to Remedy the Breach

In relation to breach of covenants other than for non-payment of rent, the Law of Property Act 1925, s 146 requires the landlord to notify the tenant of the breach and to give an opportunity to remedy the breach or make compensation before forfeiting the lease:

s 146(1) A right of re-entry or forfeiture under any proviso or stipulation in a lease for a breach of any covenant or condition in the lease shall not be enforceable, by action or otherwise, unless and until the lessor serves on the lessee a notice–
(a) specifying the particular breach complained of; and
(b) if the breach is capable of remedy, requiring the lessee to remedy the breach; and
(c) in any case, requiring the lessee to make compensation in money for the breach;
and the lessee fails, within a reasonable time thereafter, to remedy the

breach, if it is capable of remedy, and to make reasonable compensation in money, to the satisfaction of the lessor, for the breach.

The object of this notice procedure was set out by Slade LJ in *Expert Clothing Service & Sales Ltd v Hillgate House* [1986] Ch 340 at 351:

In a case where the breach is 'capable of remedy' within the meaning of the section, the principal object of the notice procedure provided for by section 146(1), as I read it, is to afford the lessee two opportunities before the lessor actually proceeds to enforce his right of re-entry, namely (1) the opportunity to remedy the breach within a reasonable time after service of the notice, and (2) the opportunity to apply to the court for relief from forfeiture [see below]. In a case where the breach is not 'capable of remedy' there is clearly no point in affording the first of these two opportunities; the object of the notice procedure is thus simply to give the lessee the opportunity to apply for relief.

Later he adds,

An important purpose of the section 146 procedure is to give even tenants who have hitherto lacked the will or the means to comply with their obligations one last chance to summon up that will or find the necessary means before the landlord re-enters. (at 358).

The phrase 'capable of remedy' has caused the courts some difficulty. In one sense, no breach can ever truly be remedied in that the breach itself has occurred (see Harman J in *Hoffman v Fineberg* [1949] Ch 245 at 253). Nevertheless, the intent of s 146 is to prevent the landlord from forfeiting where the breach can be put right without any harm being caused to the landlord:

... the concept of capability of remedy for the purpose of section 146 must surely be directed to the question whether the harm that has been done to the landlord by the relevant breach is for practicable purposes capable of being retrieved. (*per* Slade LJ, *Expert Clothing Service & Sales Ltd v Hillgate House, op. cit.*, at 355)

In trying to work out what this means the courts have drawn distinctions between different types of covenants. Thus, a negative covenant is unlikely to be capable of remedy—particularly if it is regarded as a once and for all breach. In *Rugby School (Governors) v Tannahill* [1935] 1 KB 87, the premises were used as a brothel in breach of a covenant not to use them for illegal or immoral purposes. In holding the breach incapable of remedy, Greer LJ said that the

result of committing the breach would be known all over the neighbourhood and seriously affect the value of the premises. Even a money payment together with the cessation of the improper use of the house could not be a remedy. (at 91)

Similarly, in *Scala House & District Property Co Ltd v Forbes* [1974] QB 575, the Court of Appeal held that the breach of a covenant not to assign, underlet or part with possession was not a breach capable of remedy. In a different context—that of compliance with covenants so as to trigger an option to renew—it has been doubted whether it is always the case that breach of a negative covenant cannot be undone. In *Bass Ltd v Morton Ltd* [1988] 1 Ch 493, Bingham LJ felt that this was too formalistic—an unlawful subletting could be brought to an end, undertakings given and compensation made without any continuing damage to the landlord (at 541; see also the comments of Harman J in *Van Haarlam v Kasner* [1992] 36 EG 135 at 142, where he suggested that trivial breaches of negative covenants may be remediable; see also Browne-Wilkinson VC in *Billson v Residential Apartments Ltd* [1991] 3 WLR 264 at 274, (CA)).

In contrast, the breach of a positive covenant, such as a covenant to decorate or build, can generally be remedied by the required act being done—even if this is after the time prescribed by the covenant (see Slade LJ, *Expert Clothing Service & Sales Ltd v Hillgate House, op. cit.*, at 355).

The importance of the distinction between positive and negative covenants must not, however, be overplayed. As Kerr LJ pointed out in *Bass Ltd v Morton Ltd, op. cit.*, the distinction does not go to the 'substance of the rights and obligations of the parties, but merely to the form of the notices which must be given pursuant to the section' (at 527). A tenant who has breached an irremediable negative covenant may still be able to keep the lease if he is granted relief against forfeiture (see below). However, if the tenant does remedy the breach and pay compensation within a reasonable time prescribed by the s 146 notice, the landlord is not able to forfeit the lease—in this sense the distinction is substantive.

Section 146 applies to most leases and covenants apart from covenants for the payment of rent (s 146 (11); for limited exceptions see s 146(8) and (9)). The section cannot be contracted out of (s 146(12)) and any provision in a lease which has the same effect as a forfeiture clause will be treated as such even though the landlord appears to have secured a way of ending the lease for breach without it technically being a forfeiture (see *Clarke (Richard & Co) v Widnall* [1976] 1 WLR 845; *Plymouth Corporation v Harvey* [1971] 1 WLR 549; s 146(7)).

s 146(7) For the purposes of this section a lease limited to continue only as long as the lessee abstains from committing a breach of covenant shall be and take effect as a lease to continue for any longer term for which it could subsist, but determinable by a proviso for re-entry on such a breach.

11.2.3.2 Relief Against Forfeiture

In view of the harsh results of forfeiture, equity intervened early on to grant the tenant relief from forfeiture in certain situations. These situations were initially limited to instances when the tenant was prevented from strict compliance with the contractual provisions through unavoidable accident, fraud, surprise or ignorance which did not constitute wilful neglect or misconduct (see *Eaton v*

Lyon (1798) 3 Ves Jun 691; and contrast the denial of any jurisdiction to relieve against forfeiture in relation to contracts not involving property rights, see ch 3.2.1.2). This was part of equity's general jurisdiction to intervene in order to prevent unconscionable insistence on strict legal rights, seen also in the development of the equity of redemption in mortgages (see generally, Meagher *et al.*, *Equity Doctrines and Remedies*, 3rd edn, 1992, ch 18 esp. [1805]–[1815]). This equitable jurisdiction was soon supplemented by statutory powers to relieve against forfeiture, the development being traced by Lord Templeman in *Billson v Residential Apartments Ltd* [1992] 2 WLR 15 (HL):

Before the intervention of Parliament, if a landlord forfeited by entering into possession or by issuing and serving a writ for possession, equity could relieve the tenant against forfeiture but only in cases under the general principles of equity whereby a party may be relieved from the consequences of fraud, accident or mistake or in cases where the breach of covenant entitling the landlord to forfeit was a breach of the covenant for payment of rent . . .

In 1881 Parliament interfered to supplement equity and to enable any tenant to be relieved from forfeiture. The need for such intervention was and is manifest because otherwise a tenant who had paid a large premium for a 999 year lease at a low rent could lose his asset by a breach of covenant which was remediable or which caused the landlord no damage. The forfeiture of any lease, however short, may unjustly enrich the landlord at the expense of the tenant. In creating a power to relieve against forfeiture for breach of covenant Parliament protected the landlord by conferring on the court a wide discretion to grant relief on terms or to refuse relief altogether. In practice this discretion is exercised with the object of ensuring that the landlord is not substantially prejudiced or damaged by the revival of the lease . . . (at 18–19)

The statutory power to grant relief is now contained in of the Law of Property Act 1925, s 146(2):

s 146(2) Where a lessor is proceeding, by action or otherwise, to enforce such a right of re-entry or forfeiture, the lessee may, in the lessor's action, if any, or in any action brought by himself, apply to the court for relief; and the court may grant or refuse relief, as the court, having regard to the proceedings and conduct of the parties under the foregoing provision of this section, and to all the other circumstances, thinks fit; and in case of relief may grant it on such terms, if any, as to costs, expenses, damages, compensation, penalty, or otherwise, including the granting of an injunction to restrain any like breach in the future, as the court, in the circumstances of each case, thinks fit.

This subsection enables the tenant to apply for relief when the landlord 'is proceeding' to forfeit the lease. This has been interpreted by the House of Lords in *Billson v Residential Apartments Ltd*, (HL) *op. cit.*, as enabling the tenant to apply any time after the service of a s 146 notice up until the point when the landlord has forfeited the lease by issuing and serving a writ for possession, recovered judgment and entered into possession pursuant to that judgment. The tenant is also able to apply for relief when the landlord has forfeited by peaceable re-entry and not by court order, the absence of a time limit being balanced by the fact that delay on the part of the tenant in applying for relief will be taken account of in deciding whether or not to grant relief.

In *Hyman v Rose* [1912] AC 623, Earl Loreburn LC stressed that the court is given a free discretion to consider all the circumstances and the conduct of the parties:

[When] the Act is so express to provide a wide discretion, meaning, no doubt, to prevent one man from forfeiting what in fair dealing belongs to someone else, by taking advantage of a breach from which he is not commensurately and irreparably damaged, it is not advisable to lay down any rigid rules for guiding that discretion. (at 631, commenting on s 14(2) of the Conveyancing Act 1881 which was replaced by s 146(2) of the Law of Property Act 1925)

Since then the courts have maintained that this discretion should remain unfettered. In many cases the courts adopt the approach put forward by Lord Wilberforce in *Shiloh Spinners Ltd v Harding* [1973] AC 691, even though he was then addressing the equitable jurisdiction to relieve and not the statutory jurisdiction:

[It] remains true today that equity expects men to carry out their bargains and will not let them buy their way out by uncovenanted payment. But it is consistent with these principles that we should reaffirm the right of courts of equity in appropriate and limited cases to relieve against forfeiture for breach of covenant or condition where the primary object of the bargain is to secure a stated result which can effectively be obtained when the matter comes before the court, and where the forfeiture provision is added by way of security for the production of that result.
The word 'appropriate' involves consideration of the conduct of the applicant for relief, in particular whether his default was wilful, of the gravity of the breaches, and of the disparity between the value of the property of which forfeiture is claimed as compared with the damage caused by the breach. (at 723)

When the breach has been remedied relief will generally be given, unless there are some exceptional circumstances:

... for example, if the breaches have been gross and wilful or it appears that the tenant is not likely to comply with his obligations in the future. (*per* Slade LJ, *Cremin v Barjack Properties Ltd* [1985] 1 EGLR 30 at 32)

In practice, however, the courts seem to be most influenced by proportionality—whether the harm that would be suffered by the tenant through forfeiture is disproportionate to the harm occasioned to the landlord through the breach (see, for example, *Central Estates Ltd v Woolgar (No 2)* [1972] 3 All ER 610 at 615), and whether the landlord's gain if no relief is granted is out of proportion to the harm he has suffered. In *Southern Depot Co Ltd v British Railways Board* [1990] 2 EGLR 39, Morritt J was faced with three breaches of covenant, two of which were wilful. Nevertheless, unlike in the exercise of the equitable jurisdiction, the wilfulness was only one factor amongst many. Under the equitable jurisdiction, relief can only be given for a deliberate and wilful breach in exceptional circumstances (see Lord Wilberforce, *Shiloh Spinners Ltd v Harding, op. cit.*, at 725). Morritt J preferred to focus not on wilfulness but on proportionality—the essential question was

whether the damage sustained by [the landlord] . . . is proportionate to the advantage it will obtain if no relief is granted and, if not, whether in all the circumstances it is just that [the landlord] . . . should retain that advantage' (at 44)

On the facts, relief was given—otherwise the landlord would obtain an advantage worth not less than £1.4 million from breaches which had caused it no lasting damage.

This approach restricts the situations in which relief will be denied, so long as the tenant is willing and able to pay for past errors. Lasting damage is rare—most breaches can be made good through payment. Perhaps the two main instances where lasting damage remains are breach of an alienation covenant (although even then it may sometimes be possible to make good, see Bingham LJ in *Bass Ltd v Morton Ltd, op. cit.*) and breach of a covenant against immoral user where 'stigma' may linger and affect the property for some time. Even then, however, the courts have been willing to give relief where the stigma will be short-lived. In *Ropemaker Properties Ltd v Noonhaven Ltd* [1989] 34 EG 39, there was a 'grave breach', use of the premises for prostitution. Millet J said that where there has been immoral user it

will . . . be in only the rarest and most exceptional circumstances that the court will grant relief . . . particularly where the breach of covenant has been both wilful and serious. (at 56)

Nevertheless, on the facts relief was granted taking account, *inter alia*, of the fact that the lease had substantial value, loss of the lease would cause substantial financial loss to the tenant 'out of all proportion to their offence or to any conceivable damage caused' to the landlord and give an 'adventitious profit' to the landlord and that the immoral user had ended and was unlikely to recur. See also *van Haarlam v Kasner, op. cit.*

Another factor that will be relevant to the court is whether third party rights are involved, as where the landlord has relet the property following forfeiture. The general approach has been to focus on the landlord's conduct and to be more willing to grant relief where the landlord acted hastily in reletting the property—

the issue of a third party being a relevant factor in considering whether or not to grant relief (see, for example, *Bhojwani v Kingsley Investment Trust Ltd* [1992] 39 EG 138). There are, however, conflicting approaches. In *Fuller v Judy Properties Ltd* (1991) 64 P & CR 176, the Court of Appeal granted relief but did not allow this to affect the third party—the third party involvement being relevant not so much for the question of whether relief should be given but whether the 'revived lease' should bind the third party. The end result in *Fuller* was that the new third party tenant was in possession and the old (relieved) tenant was in the position of immediate reversioner on the new lease (for a criticism, see [1992] Conv 343).

In the case of non-payment of rent the tenant is effectively entitled to relief if he pays all rent arrears and costs, even if he has a persistent record of late payment and arrears. This result stems from a variety of equitable and statutory jurisdictions: see *Howard v Fanshawe* [1895] 2 Ch 581; Common Law Procedure Act 1852, ss 210, 212; County Courts Act 1984, ss 138, 139(2); Supreme Court Act 1981, s 38(1). In some ways this is surprising. The tenant may have an appalling record of payment but so long as he pays the arrears (in some cases even after the landlord has regained possession, see Common Law Procedure Act 1852, s 210) he can keep the lease. The right to forfeit is seen as simply a means of securing payment of the money.

As all derivative interests, such as underleases and mortgages, also fall with the tenant's lease, there are provisions to enable owners of derivative interests to apply for relief: see s 146(4); Tromans, *Forfeiture of Leases: Relief for Underlessees and Holders of Other Derivative Interests* [1986] Conv 187; and see ch 9.7.

11.2.3.3 Procedural Requirements

In the case of forfeiture for breach of repairing covenants it may be necessary to obtain a court order before forfeiting. This is because of the effect of the Leasehold Property (Repairs) Act 1938. A landlord seeking to forfeit for breach of repairing covenant where the lease was initially for seven years or more and has at least three years left unexpired must include in his s 146 notice advice to the tenant of his right to serve a counter-notice within 28 days. If the tenant does serve such a counter-notice claiming the protection of the statute, the landlord is unable to bring proceedings in respect of the repairing covenant without leave of the court. Leave will not be given unless the landlord proves on the balance of probabilities (*Associated British Ports v Bailey plc* [1990] 2 AC 703) one of five grounds:
(a) That the immediate remedying of the breach is necessary to prevent a substantial diminution in the value of the reversion, or that such diminution has already occurred;
(b) That immediate repairs are needed to comply with any statute, court order or requirement of any authority established by statute;

(c) Where the tenant is not in occupation of the whole of the premises, that remedying the breach is necessary in the interests of the occupier;

(d) That current costs would be relatively small by comparison with the costs if there were to be a delay; or

(e) It is otherwise just and equitable in the circumstances (s 1(5)).

The Act does not apply to agricultural leases but otherwise covers both residential and commercial leases. The purpose of the Act was to prevent landlords from harassing tenants with long lists of dilapidations which may not be very material but which would generate a great deal of uncertainty for tenants who could not be sure that landlords would not proceed to forfeit the lease:

In practice many a tenant lost his lease or submitted to an increased rent or substantial expenditure rather than face the expense and uncertainty of a forfeiture action. (*per* Lord Templeman, *Associated British Ports v Bailey plc, op. cit.*, at 709; see also Vinelott J, *Hamilton v Martell Ltd* [1984] 1 Ch 266 at 278)

The effect of the Act is to ensure that a landlord can only pursue a remedy for breach of the repairing covenant if the repair is necessary in the sense of one of the five grounds (in the *Associated British Ports* case, the tenants were being asked to repair a dry dock at a cost of £600,000 even though it would probably never be used for ship repair again). Even if one these grounds is proven the tenant may still apply for relief in the subsequent forfeiture proceedings. On the 1938 Act see also ch 7.2.5.1(a); Smith, *A Review of the Operation of the Leasehold Property (Repairs) Act 1938* [1986] Conv 85.

A similar and overlapping provision exists in relation to internal decorative repairs. By the Law of Property Act 1925, s 147, the tenant is able to apply for relief when the landlord has served a s 146 notice relating to internal decorative repairs. If the court 'is satisfied that the notice is unreasonable' 'having regard to all the circumstances of the case (including in particular the length of the lessee's term or interest remaining unexpired)' it may relieve the tenant of liability for the repairs. The section does not cover, *inter alia*, repairs necessary or proper for getting the property into a sanitary condition or structural repairs (s 147(2)(ii)) or any statutory liability to keep the house 'reasonably fit for human habitation' (s 147(2)(iii)). The section covers all leases, of any length.

In order for the landlord to forfeit a residential lease, it is necessary to obtain a court order. The Protection from Eviction Act 1977, s 2 states:

s 2 Where any premises are let as a dwelling on a lease which is subject to a right of re-entry or forfeiture it shall not be lawful to enforce that right otherwise than by proceedings in the court whilst any person is lawfully residing in the premises or part of them.

Apart from these situations, there is no requirement for the landlord to forfeit by legal proceedings. If the landlord chooses to forfeit by peaceable re-entry this is, in practice, usually effected out of business hours—to avoid an offence under the Criminal Law Act 1977. This Act makes it an offence to use or threaten violence without lawful authority for the purposes of securing entry into any premises where, to the knowledge of the entrant, there is someone present who is opposed to the entry (s 6(1)). Hence in the *Billson* case, *op. cit.*, the landlord's agents re-entered the premises at 6 a.m., changed the locks and put up notices stating that the lease had been forfeited. The availability of such a self-help remedy is at odds with most modern trends. In the *Billson* case the House of Lords had to decide whether a tenant was able to apply for relief where the landlord had peaceably re-entered. With what was arguably a straining of the language in s 146(2) (to read 'is proceeding' as including 'proceeds'), the House of Lords overturned a controversial Court of Appeal decision and held that the tenant did have the right to apply for relief. In reaching this decision their Lordships were heavily influenced by the desire to reduce the incentive for landlords to pursue 'the dubious and dangerous method of determining the lease by re-entering the premises' (*per* Lord Templeman, *Billson, op. cit.*, at 20 (HL)). The dislike of self-help remedies was well expressed by Nicholls LJ in his dissenting judgement in the Court of Appeal:

Nor can it be right to encourage law-abiding citizens to embark on a course which is a sure recipe for violence . . .The policy of the law is to discourage self-help when confrontation and a breach of the peace are likely to follow. If a tenant, who is in breach of covenant, will not quit but persists in carrying on his business despite the landlord's right of re-entry, the proper course for a responsible landlord is to invoke the due process of the law and seek an order for possession from the court. (*op. cit.*, at 290 (CA))

Against this, it has to be said that peaceable re-entry is fast and effective (see also the arguments supporting the remedy of distress for rent, ch 8.7.2) and will be especially attractive where the tenant has abandoned the premises and is therefore unlikely to seek relief. For a general discussion of self-help remedies in property law, see Clarke, *Property Law* (1992) 45 CLP 81.

In ch 3.2.1.2 it was noted that the ability to grant relief from forfeiture has been judicially confined to contracts involving proprietary rights, although the reasoning for this is not convincing. It is clear, however, that the ability to end a contract for breach is not confined to leases and it could therefore be argued that the law relating to forfeiture of leases represents the application of more general principles of contract law (see Bradbrook, Croft, *Commercial Tenancy Law in Australia,* 1990, pp 295–7). In *Clark Ltd v Dupre Ltd* [1992] Ch 297 forfeiture was seen as an application of the law on repudiation of contracts:

. . . Whenever there has been a breach of covenant, for example a repairing covenant, which has not been remedied within the time specified in the notice, the landlord is treating the tenant's breach as repudiatory and, by serving pro-

ceedings claiming forfeiture of the lease, is accepting that repudiation. (Thomas Morison QC at 309)

The significance of this argument is that:

[if] forfeiture is but an example of the determination of an agreement in accordance with the principles of the law of contract, re-entry is not to be regarded as some ancient rite deriving its significance from the medieval mysteries of landlord and tenant law; it is merely one kind of unequivocal act exercising the landlord's option to determine the lease, and is essential (to the exclusion of other modes of exercising the option) only if the lease so provides. (Bradbrook, Croft, *op. cit.*, p 297)

Support for this is given in the Australian case of *Progressive Mailing House Pty Ltd v Tabali Pty Ltd* (1985) 57 ALR 609, where Mason J said that

re-entry is essential only where the parties stipulate that advantage shall not be taken of a forfeiture except by an entry upon the land. (at 618)

Thus it might be possible for a landlord to reserve power to effect forfeiture by, for example, simply serving notice on the tenant (in cases not regulated by statute). In practice, however, leases are not drafted in this way—even if they were, the landlord would still have to serve a s 146 notice before forfeiting and the tenant would be able to apply for relief (see reference to 'action or otherwise' in s 146(2)). It would also be an undesirable development given the dislike of self-help remedies.

Forfeiture occurs as soon as the landlord re-enters. In the case of forfeiture by court order the forfeiture occurs as soon as the writ or summons is served. If relief is given the forfeiture is undone. The effect is that, from the time of forfeiture, the tenant is no longer bound by the covenants in the tenancy, including the covenant to pay rent. If, however, the tenant remains in occupation he will be liable to pay either 'mesne profits', which are based on the current rental value of the property, or, if relief is granted, rent. This suspension of the lease has been criticised by the Law Commission—it made sense in past days when re-entry was usually peaceable and tenant's were seldom granted relief but nowadays forfeiture is often effected by court order and relief is more common (see Law Com. No. 142, *op. cit.*, paras 3.2–3.10. For general comment on Law Com. No. 142, *op. cit.*, see Smith, *Reform of the Law of Forfeiture*, [1986] Conv 165).

Instead of forfeiture, the Law Commission propose a scheme of termination orders. Under this scheme, court proceedings would always be necessary to end a tenancy (unless the tenant consents to termination or where the tenant has abandoned the premises) and the tenancy continues in force until the court orders termination (see Law Com. No. 142, *op. cit.*, paras 3.2–3.10). The court would have power to make an absolute order to end the tenancy, a remedial order which will end the lease only if the tenant fails to take prescribed remedial action by a date specified or to make no order. An absolute order will be made only where the serious nature of the tenant's breaches and/or their frequency means that the tenant 'is so unsatisfactory a tenant that he ought not in all the circumstances to remain tenant of the property' (para 3.46). A tenant is not deemed to be automatically satisfactory if all past breaches have been remedied—the landlord should, at the court's discretion, be able to end the lease of a tenant with a record of persistent breaches. In combination this represents a significant change from the present law—the proposal focuses on whether the tenant is unsatisfactory, not on proportionality and deliberateness. In the majority of cases it is anticipated that a remedial order will be made.

Given the historic link between relief and the unconscionability of the landlord's conduct, it does seem more appropriate to base relief on the tenant's characteristics as a tenant rather than on whether the tenant will lose disproportionately from the forfeiture. A landlord may have good management reasons for wishing to forfeit the lease of a tenant who has a bad record of payment but would not be able to do so under the present law if all arrears have been paid, even though the leasehold contract reserves the power to do so if the rent falls into arrears. In these circumstances it would not seem unconscionable to allow the landlord to end the lease in accordance with the contract—under the proposed law he would not, however, be enforcing a contractual right of forfeiture but a statutory right of termination. If proportionality is disregarded, however, it may mean that the landlord does get a windfall at the tenant's expense—a windfall not necessarily bearing any relation to the damage suffered by the landlord (see, for example, what would have resulted in *Southern Depot Co Ltd v British Railways Board, op. cit.*, had relief been refused). In *Darlington BC v Denmark Chemists Ltd* [1993] 1 EGLR 62, the tenant sought to turn this reasoning into an unjust enrichment argument and claimed that compensation should be paid if the court upheld the forfeiture. The 125-year lease contained a covenant to build a pharmacy and a surgery on the site. The tenant built the pharmacy at a cost of £90,000 but did not build the surgery. The Court of Appeal refused to grant relief from forfeiture and also rejected the unjust enrichment argument, stating that there was not necessarily enrichment (the landlord may have no use for a pharmacy), nor, if there was, was it unjust. The idea of requiring the landlord to make compensation to the tenant in this situation was considered but rejected by the Law Commission—on the grounds that this would add yet more complexity. It was also noted that in this situation the lease will usually be assignable and the tenant can realize the value of the lease through an assignment, which is made possible if a remedial order is used.

Under the termination order scheme there would be no need to serve a notice on the tenant before commencing termination proceedings, other than in cases involving want of repair (*cf.* the Leasehold Property (Repairs) Act 1938 and the Law of Property Act 1925, s 147). An optional notice procedure would be available if the landlord was primarily seeking remedy of the breach rather than for the lease to be ended.

A major change proposed in the 1985 Report (Law Com. No. 142, *op. cit.*) was for a tenant termination scheme to be available, similar to the landlord termination scheme outline above. It was felt that both landlord and tenant should have similar weapons in their armoury. The tenant termination order could be coupled also with a right to damages to compensate the tenant for losses suffered as a consequence of having to move (see Part XVII). When the Law Commission produced its draft Bill the tenant termination scheme was not included, priority being given to enacting the less controversial landlord termination order scheme (Law Commission, *Termination of Tenancies Bill*, Law Com. No. 221, 1994). It may be that the common law will be able to develop to fill this gap by permitting the tenant to bring a lease to an end by accepting a repudiatory breach of the landlord (see *Hussein v Mehlman* [1992] 2 EGLR 87, ch 3.2.2.1). The development of repudiatory breach is, however, controversial and given the strength of the case for a tenant termination order scheme put in the earlier Law Commission report, it is regrettable that it is not being actively pursued.

11.2.4 Repudiation and Frustration

Hussein v Mehlman, op. cit., is the only recent English authority recognising that a lease can be ended by repudiation. In Canada and Australia there are several cases accepting that a lease can be ended in this manner: see, for example, *Highway Properties Ltd v Kelly, Douglas & Co Ltd* (1971) 17 DLR (3d) 710; *Progressive Mailing House Pty Ltd v Tabali Pty Ltd, op. cit.*, (and see ch 3.2.2.1). A repudiatory act is one which shows an intention no longer to be bound by the contract:

... a contract may be repudiated if one party renounces his liabilities under it—if he evinces an intention no longer to be bound by the contract ... or shows that he intends to fulfill the contract only in a manner substantially inconsistent with his obligations and not in any other way ... (*Shevill v Builders Licensing Board* (1982) 149 CLR 620 at 625–6, Gibbs CJ)

An isolated breach of covenant may therefore not be a repudiatory breach, even though it may be a breach which would give rise to a right to forfeit. In the cases, the following breaches have been said to be repudiatory: serious breach of the landlord's statutory obligation to repair in the Landlord and Tenant Act 1985, s 11 (*Hussein v Mehlman, op. cit.*); abandonment of the premises with no intention to return (*Highway Properties Ltd v Kelly, Douglas & Co Ltd, op. cit.*); intentional non-payment of rent over a significant period (*Progressive Mailing House Pty Ltd v Tabali Pty Ltd, op. cit.*; *Wood Factory Pty Ltd v Kiritos Pty Ltd* [1985] 2 NSWLR 105; *Nai Pty Ltd v Hassoun Nominees Pty Ltd* [1985–1986] Aust and NZ

Conv Rep 349); and subletting in breach of the lease (*Nai, op. cit.*). Being consistently late in paying rent, without more, is not enough (*Shevill v Builders Licensing Board, op. cit.*).

Hussein v Mehlman, op. cit., illustrates how repudiation can be developed to provide an effective remedy to a tenant, entitling him to walk away from the lease with no further rent liability. If the tenant seeks rehousing from the local authority there is a risk that they may treat the tenant as intentionally homeless if he has 'chosen' to accept a repudiatory breach (although the severity of the breach may mean that is not 'reasonable for him to continue to occupy'— Housing Act 1985, ss 58(2A), 65(3); see ch 5.1.4.1(b)(iii)).

Where, as is more commonly the case, it is the tenant who has committed a repudiatory act we run into the question of how the contractual doctrine of repudiation interacts with traditional landlord and tenant law. If the same act can give rise to a right to forfeit or a repudiatory breach, and the landlord is free to elect to treat it is a repudiatory breach, this may give him a way of ending the lease without giving the tenant any right to relief. However the Law of Property Act 1925, s 146(7) (11.2.3.1, above) might be interpreted to mean that acceptance of a repudiatory breach would be treated as if it were a 'proviso for re-entry on such breach', bringing repudiatory breach within s 146 and giving the tenant a right to apply for relief. Under landlord and tenant law, the tenant is able to apply for relief and, as seen earlier, relief will generally be given when the breach has been remedied. It would be undesirable, and contrary to equitable principles developed over many years, for repudiation to be used to circumvent controls designed to protect tenants from unconscionable behaviour by landlords. See also ch 3.2.2.4, and see Harpum, *Leases as Contracts*, [1993] CLJ 212 at 214.

Following *National Carriers Ltd v Panalpina (Northern) Ltd* [1981] 1 All ER 161, it is clear that a lease can also be ended by frustration, but seldom will be.

11.2.5 Statutory Restrictions on Ending Protected Tenancies

Tenant protection statutes operate by augmenting or restricting the common law rules on termination, either by restricting the landlord's right to end a contractual tenancy or by providing for the tenant to have a new tenancy (either by having a right to renew or by giving a statutory or periodic tenancy in place of the contractual tenancy which has been terminated).

11.2.5.1 Protected Residential Periodic Tenancies

A periodic tenancy will usually be ended by the landlord (or tenant) serving a notice to quit. However, in the case of a private sector periodic assured tenancy, s 5 Housing Act 1988 states that the landlord can only end the tenancy by court

order and the 'service of a notice to quit shall be of no effect'. A court order will
only be granted if a statutory ground for possession exists. Some of the statutory
grounds for possession are mandatory, for example, possession on the ground
that the tenant owes three month's rent (Housing Act 1988, Sch 2, Ground 8).
Other grounds are discretionary and the court may only order possession where
it considers it reasonable to do so, as, for example, where the tenant is persistently late in paying rent (Housing Act 1988, Sch 2, Ground 11; see 11.4 below on
grounds for possession). Similar provisions exist in relation to public sector periodic tenancies: Housing Act 1985, ss 82, 84.

11.2.5.2 Protected Residential Fixed Term Tenancies

If a tenant has a private sector assured tenancy for a fixed term, the landlord is
only able to forfeit the lease during that fixed term if not only the right to forfeit
exists at common law but also one of certain specified grounds for possession
exists under the Housing Act 1988. The available grounds are mostly, but not
exclusively, based on tenant default, see s 7(6), (7). At the end of the fixed term,
instead of expiring by effluxion of time as would be the case at common law, a
statutory periodic assured tenancy comes into existence (Housing Act 1988, s 5).
The terms of this periodic tenancy will be the same as those of the expired fixed
term tenancy, excluding any break clause, and the periods of the tenancy will be
'the same as those for which rent was last payable under the fixed term tenancy'
(Housing Act 1988, s 5(3)(d),(e)). Within twelve months of the fixed term tenancy
expiring, either party may serve a notice on the other proposing different terms
and a variation in the rent to take account of these different terms (Housing Act
1988, s 6). There is also provision for the notice to be referred to a rent assessment
committee if the parties are unable to agree on the proposed terms. This statutory periodic tenancy can then only be ended in the same way as other periodic
assured tenancies.

There are similar provisions in the public sector. The way in which a secure
tenant is protected against forfeiture operates in a different manner, but the
effect is that the tenancy cannot be forfeited unless a statutory ground for possession exists: Housing Act 1985, s 82, 86. The terms of the periodic tenancy arising at the end of the fixed term can be varied by the procedure set out in the
Housing Act 1985, ss 102, 103 (see ch 5.3.7).

11.2.5.3 Protected Residential Tenancies and Court Orders for Possession

The scheme under both the private and public sector legislation ensures that a
protected tenancy can only be brought to an end by court order (Housing Act
1988, ss 5 (assured tenancy), 21 (assured shorthold tenancy); Housing Act 1985,

s 82 (secure tenancy)). The court order will only be granted if a statutory ground for possession exists.

The requirement of a court order is intended to provide additional protection to the occupant—to ensure that he does not unnecessarily and unknowingly surrender any rights that he has. In 1993, an accelerated possession procedure was introduced enabling a landlord seeking possession on certain mandatory grounds to obtain an order for possession by paper without the parties having to attend court (a procedure described as 'another . . . nail in the coffin of private tenants' rights' by Sue Waller, Camden Federation of Private Tenants, quoted in Jew, *Law and Order in Private Rented Housing: Tackling Harassment and Illegal Eviction*, 1994, at p 6). This accelerated procedure applies to possession proceedings under Ground 1 (landlord occupation), Ground 3 (winter lets), Ground 4 (student vacation lets), and Ground 5 (minister of religion); County Court (Amendment No. 3) Rules 1993; see 11.3 below for an explanation of the grounds).

Where the landlord is relying on a non-discretionary ground for possession (Grounds 9-11 in the public sector; Housing Act 1988, Sch 2, Part 1 and assured shorthold tenancies in the private sector), the court will grant an absolute order for possession if the ground is established. The order for possession can be postponed, but only for a short period.

Housing Act 1980
s 89 . . . the giving up of possession shall not be postponed (whether by the order or any variation, suspension or stay of execution) to a date later than fourteen days after the making of the order, unless it appears to the court that exceptional hardship would be caused by requiring possession to be given up by that date; and shall not in any event be postponed to a date later than six weeks after the making of the order.

In *Bain & Co v Church Commissioners* (1988) 21 HLR 29, Harman J stated that he found this restriction on the court's powers 'astonishing' and held that s 89 only applied to the county court, not to the High Court or Court of Appeal. Most housing cases will be in the county court.

In the private sector, if an absolute order for possession is made, it is unclear precisely when the tenancy ends or what the status of the occupier is during the period between the order and the date that possession is given up. *American Economic Laundry, Ld v Little* [1951] 1 KB 400, suggested that the tenancy ends when the order is made and thereafter the occupier has only a limited interest granted by 'the indulgence of the court' (Jenkins LJ at 407). Other cases suggest that the occupier is a trespasser, see *Landau v Stone* [1980] 2 All ER 539 at 545. However, in *Haniff v Robinson* (1994) 26 HLR 386, a case decided under the Rent Act 1977, the Court of Appeal held that after the possession order was made, the occupier continued to be a statutory tenant, but his rights as statutory tenant were curtailed. Certainly, the right to succeed to the tenancy will not be exercisable after a possession order is made (*American Economic Laundry, Ld v Little, op. cit.*), but the protection afforded by the Protection from Eviction Act 1977, s 3 not to be evicted other than by court proceedings, is still available (*Haniff v Robinson, op. cit.*) In the public sector the Housing Act 1985, s 82(2) states that where a possession order is given 'the tenancy ends on the date on which the tenant is to give up possession in pursuance of the order'.

Where the landlord is relying on a discretionary ground for possession, the court has much wider powers. Possession can only be ordered if the court considers it 'reasonable' to make the order. There is also power to postpone the proceedings for such period or periods as the court thinks fit (Housing Act 1988, s 9(1); Housing Act 1985, s 85(1)).

If the court decides to grant a possession order, it may still 'at any time before the execution of such an order' either

(a) **stay or suspend execution of the order, or**
(b) **postpone the date of possession,**
    for such period or periods as the court thinks just. (Housing Act 1988, s 9(2); almost identical wording is used in Housing Act 1985, s 85(2))

If the possession order is suspended or postponed, it should usually be made a conditional order:

[The] court, unless it considers that to do so would cause exceptional hardship to the tenant or would otherwise be unreasonable, shall impose conditions with regard to payment by the tenant of arrears of rent (if any) and rent or payments in respect of occupation after the termination of the tenancy (mesne profits) and may impose such other conditions as it thinks fit. (Housing Act 1988, s 9(3); *cf.* Housing Act 1985, s 85(3))

This works in a similar way to the jurisdiction to grant relief from forfeiture (see 11.2.3.2, above), in that the tenant may be given a last chance to put things right and so to keep the tenancy. If the tenant complies with these conditions, the court may, if it thinks fit, rescind the order for possession (Housing Act 1988, s 9(4); Housing Act 1985, s 85(4)).

If the tenant fails to comply with the conditions attached to the possession order, the landlord can apply for a warrant of possession. Nevertheless, it seems that the tenant is still able to appeal to the court for a further suspension, which could be given if, for example, the tenant had not paid rent arrears due to an innocent mistake: see *R v Ilkeston County Court, ex parte Kruza* (1985) 17 HLR 539. Indeed, in some situations, the court may set aside an possession order even though it has already been executed: *Governors of the Peabody Donation Fund v Hay* (1987) 19 HLR 145; *Hammersmith and Fulham London Borough Council v Hill*, The Times, CA, 25 April 1994.

Given the court's power to further suspend a conditional possession order, it could be that the tenant continues to have a tenancy until possession is executed, even though he is in breach of the conditions attached to the suspended possession order. This was held to be the case in *Sherrin v Brand* [1956] 1 QB 403. The Court of Appeal held that even though a statutory tenant had breached a condition of a suspended possession order, there nevertheless remained a statutory tenancy capable of transmission on the tenant's death. *Sherrin* was a private sector case decided under the statutory tenancy regime of earlier Rent Acts but there is no reason for thinking that Housing Act assured tenancies would not similarly continue until possession is actually executed. In the public sector a different result has been reached. In *Thompson v Elmbridge Borough Council* (1987) 19 HLR 526, the tenant failed to pay arrears as required by the condition attached to a suspended possession order. The Court of Appeal held that the tenancy had come to an end as soon as the rent was unpaid.

[Once] the defendant in proceedings of this kind where there is a suspended order for possession, ceases to comply with the conditions of the order, namely 'the punctual payment of the current rent and arrears', and there is a breach of the terms of the order, the tenancy, whatever it may be, from that moment comes to an end. (*per* Russell LJ at 531. See also *Leicester CC v Aldwinkle* (1992) 24 HLR 40)

In distinguishing *Sherrin*, the court attached significance to the Housing Act 1985, s 82(2) which states that where a possession order is given 'the tenancy ends on the date on which the tenant is to give up possession in pursuance of the order'. No comparable provision is found in the private sector legislation. This does, however, raise difficult questions about the status of the occupier. The consequence of *Thompson* appears to be that the occupant ceases to be a tenant as soon as the conditions attached to a suspended possession order are breached. Given that the tenancy is at an end, the occupier is presumably a trespasser liable to pay mesne profits, with none of the rights of a secure tenant. In *R v London Borough of Newham, ex parte Campbell* (1994) 26 HLR 183, the judge (Sir Louis Blom-Cooper QC) referred to such occupation as unlawful (at 188). If the occupier then obtains a further suspension, it would seem that his status as a secure tenant revives (see Hoath, *Public Sector Housing Law*, 1989, p 205). For criticism of *Thompson*, see Driscoll, *Rent Arrears, Suspended Possession Orders and the Rights of Secure Tenants*, (1988) 51 MLR 371.

11.2.5.4 Protected Business Tenants

In the case of a protected business tenancy, forfeiture aside (Landlord and Tenant Act 1954, s 24(2)), the landlord can only end the tenancy by serving a notice under Landlord and Tenant Act 1954, s 25. The tenant is given 'security' by being able to apply for a new tenancy which can only be opposed by the landlord on certain grounds (see the Landlord and Tenant Act 1954, ss 24, 26 and 30).

11.2.5.5 Protected Agricultural Tenants

In the agricultural sector, the landlord ends the tenancy by serving a notice to quit. On the expiry of a fixed term lease, the lease will continue as a yearly tenancy which can be ended by the landlord serving a notice to quit. Where the tenant is given 'security', this operates by enabling the tenant to challenge the notice. In order for the notice to quit to be effective, the landlord will need the consent of the Agricultural Land Tribunal, which can only be given on certain grounds (Agricultural Holdings Act 1986, s 27). Following the implementation of the proposals for reform of agricultural tenancy law (see ch 6.5.2.3), tenants will have to be given at least one year's notice of the end of the tenancy but will not have security beyond that.

11.2.5.6 Minimum Notice Requirements for Protected Tenants

In the case of certain categories of tenants, there are minimum notice provisions provided by various statutes. Residential tenants must generally be given at least four weeks' notice (Protection from Eviction Act 1977, s 5, see 11.2.6 below). A protected business tenant must be given between six and twelve months' notice to quit (Landlord and Tenant Act 1954, s 25(2)—occasionally longer, see subs(3)). A protected agricultural tenant must be given at least twelve months' notice (Agricultural Holdings Act 1986, s 25(1)).

11.2.5.7 Informing Protected Tenants of their Rights

Where the tenant has an assured tenancy under the Housing Act 1988, the tenancy can only be ended by court order (s 5). Before the landlord can obtain a court order he must serve a notice under the Housing Act 1988, s 8.

s 8(1) The court shall not entertain proceedings for possession of a dwelling-house let on an assured tenancy unless—
  (a) the landlord, or in the case of joint landlords, at least one of them has served on the tenant a notice in accordance with this section and the proceedings are begun within the time limits stated in the notice in accordance with subsections (3) and (4) below; or
  (b) the court considers it just and equitable to dispense with the requirement of such a notice.
  (2) The court shall not make an order for possession on any of the grounds in Schedule 2 to this Act unless that ground and particulars of it are specified in the notice under this section; but the grounds specified in such a notice may be altered or added to with the leave of the court.
  (3) A notice under this section is one in the prescribed form informing the tenant that—

(a) the landlord intends to begin proceedings for possession of the dwelling-house on one or more of the grounds specified in the notice; and

(b) those proceedings will not begin earlier than a date specified in the notice which . . . shall not be earlier than the expiry of the period of two weeks from the date of service of the notice; and

(c) those proceedings will not begin later than twelve months from the date of service of the notice.

. . .

(5) The court may not exercise the power conferred by subsection (1)(b) above if the landlord seeks to recover possession on Ground 8 in Schedule 2 to this Act. (For the prescribed form of notices, see Assured Tenancies and Agricultural Occupancies (Forms) Regulations, SI 1988 No. 2203, as amended by SI 1989 No. 146, SI 1990 No. 1532 and SI 1993 No. 654)

In the public sector, there are similar provisions—a secure tenancy can only be ended by court order (Housing Act 1985, s 82), and the court can only entertain proceedings if the tenant has been served with a prescribed form of notice, or a form 'substantially to the same effect' (Housing Act 1985, s 83; Secure Tenancies (Notices) Regulations 1987, SI 1987 No. 755). In the commercial sector, the landlord can only end a protected business tenancy by serving a notice in a prescribed form, or in a form 'substantially to the like effect', a form which advises the tenant of his rights under the 1954 Act (Landlord and Tenant Act 1954, s 25; Landlord and Tenant Act 1954 Part II (Notices) Regulations 1983, SI 1983 No. 133, Form 1; as amended by the Landlord and Tenant Act 1954 Part II (Notices) (Amendment) Regulations 1989, SI 1989 No. 1548).

What is important about these notices is that they can provide advice to the tenant about his position and about any rights that he might have. So long as the notice served is in substance the same as the prescribed notice, it will be effective. If the notice contains a minor inaccuracy that could not mislead the tenant, it will still be valid (*Tegerdine v Brooks* [1977] 36 P & CR 261 esp. at 266; *Morrow v Nadeem* [1986] 1 WLR 1381—both cases concerning s 25 notices). In *Mountain v Hastings* (1993) 25 HLR 427, the landlord was seeking possession of an assured tenancy on several grounds. The s 8 notice served on the tenant listed the grounds relied on, but did not give the full text of each ground as was required by the prescribed form of notice (see Assured Tenancies and Agricultural Occupancies (Forms) Regulations 1988). The Court of Appeal held that the notice was defective. It was not, however, defective simply because it failed to give the full text of the ground. The notice would be valid if it was in the prescribed form or one to 'substantially . . . the same effect'. It would, therefore, still be a good notice if it conveyed the substance of the ground:

[The] ground in Schedule 2 may validly be 'specified in the notice' . . . in words different from those in which the ground is set out in the schedule, provided that the words used set out fully the substance of the ground so that the notice is adequate to achieve the legislative purpose of the provision. That purpose, in my judgment, is to give to the tenant the information which the provision requires to be given in the notice to enable the tenant to consider what she should do and, with or without advice, to do that which is in her power and which will best protect her against the loss of her home. (*per* Ralph Gibson LJ at 433)

The problem with the particular notice was that it did not convey the substance of one of the grounds being relied on. The relevant ground, Ground 8, would only lead to recovery of possession if the rent was unpaid for three months at the date of service of the notice *and* at the date of the hearing. This was not mentioned in the s 8 notice that had been served, and this meant that the notice was not 'substantially to the like effect as the notice in the prescribed form' (at 435; see also the public sector case of *Torridge District Council v Jones* (1985) 18 HLR 107 esp. at 113, 114).

11.2.6 Statutory Notice Requirements—Protected and Unprotected Tenants

The common law rules are also augmented in some cases where the tenant does not have 'assured' or 'protected' status. Thus, a periodic residential tenancy (whether protected or not) cannot be brought to an end by less than four weeks' notice, unless all parties agree to treat a short notice to quit as valid (*Hounslow London BC v Pilling, op. cit.*, at 438-9). The Protection from Eviction Act 1977, s 5(1) provides that a notice to quit a dwelling given by a landlord or a tenant shall not be valid unless—

(a) it is in writing and contains such information as may be prescribed, and
(b) it is given not less than 4 weeks before the date on which it is to take effect.

Subsection (1A) applies the same notice requirements to a 'periodic licence to occupy premises as a dwelling'. In *Norris v Checksfield* [1991] 4 All ER 327, Woolf LJ described the periodic licence as 'a new animal' (at 332). The Court of Appeal had some difficulty in working out what a periodic licence was, but found that a licence for the period of employment was not periodic (unhindered by the problems of terms for uncertain periods that apply to leases, see *Prudential Assurance Company Limited v London Residuary Body* [1992] 3 All ER 504; ch 4.4.1)

The subsection . . . confines its operation to those licences which continue for a series of periods until terminated by a notice. The analogy is with weekly, monthly, or quarterly tenancies. (at 333)

The aim of s 5 is to give the other party time to make alternative arrangements (find a new tenant or a new home). Where it is the landlord/licensor who gives notice, the notice must contain information advising the tenant/licensee that the owner must get a court order before the tenant/licensee can be lawfully evicted and that he may have a right to remain (see Notices to Quit etc. (Prescribed Information) Regulations 1988, SI 1988 No. 2201). The section does not apply where no notice to quit is necessary, for example, on the expiry of a fixed term lease (but, as seen in 11.2.5.2 above, if this is an assured fixed term tenancy, an assured periodic tenancy may arise at the end of the fixed term). In *Norris v Checksfield, op. cit.*, the Court of Appeal said it did not apply to a licence for the period of employment—this licence could be ended without notice on the termination of the employment.

Section 5 does not apply to 'excluded' tenancies or licences entered into on or after 15 January 1989. Excluded tenancies are defined in s 3A of the Act. It excludes tenancies and licences which involve sharing accommodation with the landlord/licensor and which is the landlord's/licensor's only or principal home (subs (2)—the resident landlord exception). Subsection (3) extends the resident landlord exception to sharing with a member of the landlord's/licensor's family so long as the landlord/licensor has his only or principal home in the same building (provided the building is not a purpose-built block of flats). This exception, introduced in 1988, was part of the government's programme of removing controls on resident landlords, and may also reflect concern that in the case of resident landlords a breakdown in the tenancy relationship may require early termination (see *Rose v Curtin*, 18 February 1993, *Lexis*, where the Court of Appeal confirmed that a weekly excluded tenancy could be ended by only one week's notice: '. . . there may well be cases in which a tenant will be only too pleased to rid himself of an obligation to occupy premises which have for any reason become uncongenial . . .').

Also excluded are tenancies or licences 'granted as a temporary expedient to a person who entered the premises . . . as a trespasser' (subs (6)); those granted 'for a holiday only' (subs (7)(a)); and those granted 'otherwise than for money or money's worth' (subs (7)(b)). Hostel accommodation let by certain categories of landlord is also excluded (subs (8)).

If the tenant/licensee refuses to leave then, even when a valid notice to quit has been served or a fixed term lease has expired, the landlord cannot recover possession of a dwelling without first obtaining a court order (Protection from Eviction Act 1977, s 3). During the period after service of the notice to quit and before obtaining the court order, the status of the occupier is unclear. In *London Borough of Hammersmith v Harrison* [1981] 2 All ER 588, Waller LJ felt that he was not a trespasser, licensee or tenant at sufferance; instead, he was best described as an ex-tenant (at 601). This view appears to be at odds with that expressed in *Haniff v Robinson, op. cit.*, which held that a statutory tenant continues to be a statutory tenant (but with limited rights) even after a possession order has been made. Section 3 continues to provide protection to the occupier until 'there has actually been execution [of possession] in the ordinary way by the court's bailiff'

(Haniff v Robinson, op. cit., at 392). Section 3 does not apply to excluded tenancies or licences (as defined above) or to 'statutorily protected' tenancies. These are defined in s 8(1) and include Rent Act protected tenancies and Housing Act assured tenancies—but in these cases, as we have seen, the separate protective legislation requires a court order to end in the tenancy in any event. If the landlord ignores s 3 and evicts the tenant without a court order, the eviction is unlawful and opens the landlord up to criminal prosecution and potentially large liability for civil damages (see 11.5 below).

The effect of s 3 is that even if a tenant has no right to remain in the premises he cannot be evicted before the landlord has obtained a court order. Where a tenant is seeking to be rehoused by the local authority this creates a difficulty. If the tenant leaves before the landlord has obtained a possession order, will he be treated as intentionally homeless and therefore not entitled to permanent rehousing? (See Housing Act 1985, s 65(3), ch 5.1.4.1(b)(iii) for local authority duties towards the homeless.) The Code of Guidance issued under the Housing Act 1985, s 71 states:

Local authorities should not require tenants to fight a possession action where the landlord has a certain prospect of success, such as an action for recovery of property let on an assured shorthold tenancy, on the ground that the fixed term of the tenancy has ended. (Homelessness Code of Guidance for Local Authorities, 3rd edn, para 10.12)

Similarly, in *Din v Wandsworth Borough Council* [1983] 1 AC 657, Lord Lowry said:

It . . . seems unacceptable that anyone should have to cling to accommodation and defend hopeless cases of ejectment for tactical reasons and thus be compelled by the law to misuse court procedure lest his claim to a house be irretrievably prejudiced. (at 679, 680. See also *R v Newham LBC, ex parte Ugbo*, (1994) 26 HLR 263, esp. at 266)

Yet in *R v London Borough of Croydon ex parte Jarvis* (1994) 26 HLR 194, an assured shorthold tenant had been served with a possession notice by her landlord but was told that the local authority would not consider her claim for housing until the landlord had obtained a court order. The judge (A. Collins QC) held that even though this approach had been deprecated by the Code of Guidance and by the House of Lords in *Din*, it was not unlawful. The local authority had reasons—there was a pressing demand for housing for homeless persons and the extra weeks of not having to house Mrs Jarvis would make a significant difference to the public purse. Nevertheless it seems wrong that a tenant faced with certain eviction should have to endure the additional stress, costs and delay of a court action.

11.3 MOBILE HOMES AND AGRICULTURAL TENANCIES

Before considering the mainstream provisions on security of tenure, some special cases will be examined. Mobile home owners, for instance, are in a very peculiar situation (see Niner, *Mobile Homes Survey: Final Report of the Department of the Environment*, 1992). Whilst they own their caravans, the site on which they park them is rented. The rules on eviction, therefore, relate to the right to secure the services provided by a mobile homes park. The Mobile Homes Act 1983 requires park owners to go to court for a termination order. Whilst the Act affords three principal grounds for eviction, Niner's survey (*op. cit.*, paras 582 *et seq.*) found that the threat of eviction was rare.

583. The reasons given for asking residents to leave were wide-ranging, with no single reason predominating. They were: condition of the mobile home, non-payment of pitch rent, breach of park rules and mobile homes not being used as main residence (all accounting for two cases each); and problems over sales commission, being a 'bad' tenant and overcrowding each accounting for one tenant.
584. Only 14 respondents (3%) said that the park owner had ever tried to get them to leave the park. Of the 14, five had been asked to leave because of the age and/or condition of their home. Two said that they had been offered money to leave so that the park owner could replace their home with a new unit. Four of the five had refused to move and had heard no more about it. One was speaking of a previous home [he had owned], and had had to remove it following court action.

The rules relating to eviction are implied into all agreements under s 2 of the 1983 Act. The first ground, as might be expected, provides that breach of the agreement with the park owner will permit the latter to terminate, so long as the court deem it to be reasonable—1983 Act, Sch 1, Part I, para 4. The second ground has more to do with the dearth of mobile home sites and the need to utilize them as efficiently as possible. A mobile home owner can be evicted from the site if he is not occupying the home as his only or main residence—1983 Act, Sch 1, Part I, para 5. The final ground, though, raises some questions concerning the obligations of owner-occupiers.

Mobile Homes Act 1983, Sch 1, Part I
para 6(1) The owner shall be entitled to terminate the agreement at the end of a relevant period if, on the application of the owner, the court is satisfied that, having regard to its age and condition, the mobile home—
(a) is having a detrimental effect on the amenity of the site; or
(b) is likely to have such an effect before the end of the next relevant period.
(2) In sub-paragraph (1) above 'relevant period' means the period of five years beginning with the commencement of the agreement and each succeeding period of five years.

Unless the mobile home owner maintains his property to an appropriate standard, then he can be asked to move on. There is no equivalent power to force an owner-occupier of a house to maintain his property, though, as will be seen, a tenant may be evicted if the property he rents falls into disrepair. The analogy with a house owner is not quite absolute, since mobile homes can be moved off the park. Nevertheless, unless the house owner's property is in an area about to be demolished, one cannot force him to maintain his property. The mobile home owner's interest in his home is, thus, made subject to the amenity of the site as a whole. The 1983 Act does, however, show that there is nothing inherently inappropriate in forcing owner-occupiers to keep their properties in repair.

Whilst the landlord and tenant relationship in the agricultural sector may be terminated for reasons also found in the residential and commercial sectors, there are some grounds peculiar to the nature of a farming lease. Security of tenure in the agricultural sector was only introduced in the Agriculture Act 1947—see Rodgers, *Agricultural Law*, 1991, at p 3, and see ch 6.5.2.3. There are two types of termination process found now in the Agricultural Holdings Act 1986—there are those situations where a general notice to quit is served under s 26(1) (general in the sense of there being no Sch 3 case listed) and those where the notice to quit relies on one of the Cases for Possession in Sch 3. Procedurally, agricultural evictions are different too, in that even if the landlord serves a general notice, the tenant has to serve a counter-notice under s 26(1)(b) if he is to receive the benefit of the security of tenure guarantees—if no counter-notice is served, the landlord can evict without having to prove before the Agricultural Land Tribunal that one of the grounds therefor has been satisfied. On the other hand, if the landlord relies on one of the Sch 3 Cases, then the only challenge a tenant can make is under the common law for ambiguity or through the 1986 Act's arbitration procedure—Rodgers, *Agricultural Law, op. cit.*, at p 101.

s 26(1) Where—
   (a) notice to quit an agricultural holding or part of an agricultural holding
       is given to the tenant, and
   (b) not later than one month from the giving of the notice to quit the ten-
       ant serves on the landlord a counter-notice in writing requiring that
       this subsection shall apply to the notice to quit,
   then, subject to subsection (2) below, the notice to quit shall not have
   effect unless, on an application by the landlord, the Tribunal consent to
   its operation.
   (2) Subsection (1) above shall not apply in any of the Cases set out in Part I of
       Schedule 3 to this Act; and in this Act 'Case A', 'Case B' (and so on) refer
       severally to the Cases set out and so named in that Part of that Schedule.
   (3) Part II of that Schedule shall have effect in relation to the Cases there
       specified.

The procedural niceties of evictions in the agricultural sector do not need to be examined here (see Rodgers, *Agricultural Law, op. cit.*), but certain grounds in s 27 and Sch 3 of the 1986 Act specific to the nature of a farming lease are worthy of consideration in their own right as highlighting the nature of the agricultural landlord and tenant relationship.

s 27(1) Subject to subsection (2) below, the Tribunal shall consent under section 26 above to the operation of [a general] notice to quit an agricultural holding or part of an agricultural holding if, but only if, they are satisfied as to one or more of the matters mentioned in subsection (3) below, being a matter or matters specified by the landlord in his application for their consent.

(2) Even if they are satisfied as mentioned in subsection (1) above, the Tribunal shall withhold consent under section 26 above to the operation of the notice to quit if in all the circumstances it appears to them that a fair and reasonable landlord would not insist on possession.

(3) The matters referred to in subsection (1) above are—
  (a) that the carrying out of the purpose for which the landlord proposes to terminate the tenancy is desirable in the interests of good husbandry as respects the land to which the notice relates, treated as a separate unit;
  (b) that the carrying out of the purpose is desirable in the interests of sound management of the estate of which the land to which the notice relates forms part or which that land constitutes;
  (c) that the carrying out of the purpose is desirable for the purposes of agricultural research, education, experiment or demonstration, or for the purposes of the enactments relating to smallholdings;
  (d) that the carrying out of the purpose is desirable for the purposes of the enactments relating to allotments;
  (e) that greater hardship would be caused by withholding than by giving consent to the operation of the notice;
  (f) that the landlord proposes to terminate the tenancy for the purpose of the land's being used for a use, other than for agriculture, not falling within Case B.

There are two steps to the tribunal deciding to order eviction under s 27 in response to a general notice. First, it must find that one of the subsection (3) grounds is proven and then, under s 27(2), that it is not a case where 'a fair and reasonable landlord would not insist on possession'.

Section 27(3)(a) should be contrasted with Case C in Sch 3 which deals with Certificates of Bad Husbandry.

Case C Not more than six months before the giving of the notice to quit, the Tribunal granted a certificate under paragraph 9 of Part II of this Schedule that the tenant of the holding was not fulfilling his responsibilities to farm in accordance with the rules of good husbandry, and that fact is stated in the notice.

The different procedures relating to s 27(3)(a) and Sch 3, Part I Case C are not of concern, what is relevant is that it has been thought fit to require the tenant not only to occupy the premises in a fit and proper manner, as with any tenancy, but also to carry on his business according to certain standards. There is no equivalent requirement implied into commercial leases. Section 27(3)(a) requires the Agricultural Land Tribunal to consider whether the landlord would make a better job of running the farmland leased under the tenancy. Mere bad husbandry by the tenant is not enough for s 27(3)(a), the landlord must come up with an improved system for farming that particular unit of land—according to *Davies v Price* [1958] 1WLR 434, the landlord cannot show better use of the land by reference to any amalgamation of the land leased and his own neighbouring farmland. Where the tenant is farming the land badly, the landlord can apply to the Agricultural Land Tribunal for a Certificate of Bad Husbandry and then seek his eviction under Case C. Whilst s 27(3)(a) focusses on the landlord's future action, Case C looks at the tenant's past practice. Both provisions though, look not at the property interest granted by the lease, but at the commercial benefit to be gained from the land let. No commercial sector lease would look at whether the tenant was carrying on his business in the best possible way. On the other hand, the way the premises are left in the commercial sector has only a minimal effect on the reletting value, whilst bad farming methods can leave the farmland almost irremediably worthless if not corrected. Furthermore, in addition to commercial matters, Case C has regard to environmental concerns under Sch 3, Part II, para 9, Agricultural Holdings Act 1986.

para 9(1) For the purposes of Case C the landlord of an agricultural holding may apply to the Tribunal for a certificate that the tenant is not fulfilling his responsibilities to farm in accordance with the rules of good husbandry; and the Tribunal, if satisfied that the tenant is not fulfilling his said responsibilities, shall grant such a certificate.

(2) In determining whether to grant a certificate under this paragraph the Tribunal shall disregard any practice adopted by the tenant in pursuance of any provision of the contract of tenancy, or of any other agreement with the landlord, which indicates (in whatever terms) that its object is the furtherance of one or more of the following purposes, namely–

(a) the conservation of flora or fauna or of geological or physiographical features of special interest;

(b) the protection of buildings or other objects of archaeological, architectural or historic interest;

(c) the conservation or enhancement of the natural beauty or amenity of the countryside or the promotion of its enjoyment by the public.

The agricultural sector has a wider view of the nature of the landlord and tenant relationship than a mere contract to provide a residence or a place to carry on a business. This is evident from the statutory grounds for bringing that relationship to an end. If, generally, the lease is to be seen as embracing more than just a proprietary interest in land, taking into account, for instance, the tenant's interest in his 'home', then in the agricultural sector it should be recognised that the lease gives the tenant his livelihood. Unlike the commercial sector where the lease provides the tenant with a place to carry out his livelihood, the thing leased in the agricultural sector is the tenant's very livelihood.

Returning to the specifically agricultural grounds for eviction in the 1986 Act, another provision, closely related in purpose to s 27(3)(a) and Case C, is s 27(3)(b), which deals with a tenant's failure to exercise sound management. Indeed, in *Greaves v Mitchell* (1971) 222 EG 1395, it was held that the same facts might give rise to an eviction under either subparagraph (a) or (b). Section 27(3)(b) allows the landlord, however, to show that there would be better management if the farmland leased were to be conjoined with other land owned by the landlord; thus, it can be used to amalgamate two neighbouring farms—*Evans v Roper* [1960] 1 WLR 814.

Section 27(3)(c) is also peculiar, though of limited interest, in that it allows for termination of the lease in the interests of agricultural research, education, experiment or demonstration. The final major ground, though, for repossession that is specific to the agricultural sector is one that might easily translate to the commercial and residential sectors and which might prove very useful there. The traditional approach in the commercial sector is for the lease to reserve to the landlord a right of re-entry upon the tenant's insolvency: statute then imposes restrictions upon this right. Case F of Sch 3 Agricultural Holdings Act 1986, however, implies into every lease the right to serve a notice to quit if the tenant becomes insolvent.

Case F At the date of the giving of the notice to quit the tenant was a person who had become insolvent, and it is stated in the notice that it is given by reason of the said matter.

Insolvency is defined widely in the Agricultural Holdings Act 1986, s 96. The only way a tenant can challenge a Case F notice is to prove that the notice itself is bad or that he is not in fact bankrupt. It is, thus, simple for an agricultural landlord to evict an insolvent tenant. In the commercial sector, insolvency is not in itself a ground for non-renewal, although it will almost invariably lead to breach of a leasehold obligation (Landlord and Tenant Act 1954, s 30(1)(c)) which is a ground. Insolvency will normally give rise to a right to forfeit but forfeiture is not straightforward, especially when sub-tenants and mortgagees have interests derived from the lease (Ross, *Drafting and Negotiating Commercial Leases*, 3rd edn, 1989, p 291, and see 11.2.3.2 above). The difference in practice in the two sectors may reflect different attitudes toward farming and other enterprises and, indeed, a fundamental difference in the nature of what is leased. With a business, it may be better to let it remain trading in the hope that it can be taken over with the goodwill that comes from having established premises, whereas in the agricultural sector the farmland remains when a new tenant is taken on.

The final element of termination in the agricultural sector worthy of comment, concerns the tenant's entitlement to removal costs. Compensation for disturbance is dealt with under the Agricultural Holdings Act 1986, ss 60–63. It comes in two forms, basic and additional. Both require that the tenant's lease is terminated as a consequence of the landlord's notice to quit. Basic compensation, one year's rent or the tenant's actual losses up to a maximum of two years' rent, is not available where the landlord's notice cannot be challenged under s 26 because he is relying on Sch 3, Cases C, D, E, F or G. Thus, if the tenant has been served with a Certificate of Bad Husbandry (Case C), no compensation will be available. Where the notice to quit is based on Cases A, B or H or on s 27(3)(a)–(c), then basic compensation can be sought, but additional compensation, equivalent to four years' rent, will be unavailable. Basic compensation can cover the costs associated with leaving the farm, thereby forcing the landlord to meet the tenant's expenses associated with the termination of the tenancy (see also ch 6).

The government's proposed reforms of agricultural tenancies (MAFF, *Agricultural Tenancy Law—Proposals for Reform*, February 1991; MAFF, *Reform of Agricultural Holdings Legislation: Detailed Proposals*, September 1992; MAFF, *News Release, Agricultural Tenancy Law Reform*, 6 October 1993) will wholly deregulate protection from eviction, leaving everything to the parties to negotiate in the lease. Disturbance payments would similarly be left to the parties. The only statutory intervention would be to guarantee at least one year's notice, subject to a right of re-entry written into the lease. The tenant would still be entitled to compensation for improvements, though. This attitude towards tenant farmers treats their interest in the property solely as commercial. It is likely to encourage the move to owning farms rather than renting them, although the intention of government is to revitalize the rental sector. Whether such an approach could ever be tried in the residential sector is unlikely—one year's notice on each side is too generous in most cases, but, more importantly, the imbalance in bargaining position between landlord and tenant would make 'freedom of contract' simply the landlord's freedom to act as he pleases. It should be noted, however, that one of the reasons for giving agricultural tenants greater rights in the nineteenth century was to improve standards of farming—taking away those rights may well kill off the rented sector rather than revive it as the government hopes (Atiyah, *The Rise and Fall of Freedom of Contract*, 1979, pp 634 *et seq*.).

The lack of security of tenure to the tenant farmer, on the one hand, and the strict settlements restricting the powers of the landlord, on the other, were seen by many [economists] as creating a classic situation of market failure. Investment which would be favourable from a social point of view was not being made because it was not sufficiently profitable either to the landlord or to the tenant. In economic theory, it can be argued that such economic failures should not occur.

Landlords and tenants ought to perceive their interests, and if security of tenure is necessary to enable them both to benefit from profitable investment, it ought to follow that they would freely negotiate a lease with sufficient security of tenure to enable the investment to take place. In practice, however, this just did not happen. (at pp 636–7, footnotes omitted)

11.4 RESIDENTIAL AND COMMERCIAL EVICTION

The procedures for eviction of protected tenants vary, sometimes significantly, in the commercial and residential sectors, and even between public and private in the residential sector. However, there is a great overlap between the actual prescribed grounds for eviction or non-renewal. This section will examine those grounds. The detailed consideration of the statutory procedures for eviction and non-renewal is beyond the scope of this book—see the Local Government Act 1972, s 233, the Housing Act 1985, ss 82, 83 and 86, Secure Tenancies (Notice) Regulations SI 1987 No. 755; Housing Act 1988, s 8, Assured Tenancies and Agricultural Occupancies (Forms) Regulations SI 1988 No. 2203, as amended by SI 1989 No. 146, SI 1990 No. 1532, SI 1993 No. 654; and the Landlord and Tenant Act 1954, ss 24–28, Landlord and Tenant Act 1954 Part II (Notices) (Amendment) Regulations SI 1989 No. 1548 and Landlord and Tenant Act 1954 Part II (Notices) Regulations SI 1983 No. 133: and see, Hoath 1989, *op. cit.*, pp 189–91; Evans and Smith, *The Law of Landlord and Tenant*, 4th edn, 1993, pp 309–10; Bridge, *Residential Leases*, 1994, pp 54 *et seq.* and 236–7, and Ross, *op. cit.*, at pp 310–20.

In the residential sector the general rules for possession proceedings require the landlord to serve a notice informing the tenant of intended proceedings and specifying the ground for eviction (Housing Act 1985, s 83; Housing Act 1988, s 8). In the public sector, the Housing Act 1985, s 84(1) states that the court cannot grant a possession order except for one of the grounds set out in Sch 2.

s 84(1) The court shall not make an order for the possession of a dwelling-house let under a secure tenancy except on one or more of the grounds set out in Schedule 2.

    (2) The court shall not make an order for possession–
        (a) on the grounds set out in Part I of that Schedule (grounds 1 to 8), unless it considers it reasonable to make the order,
        (b) on the grounds set out in Part II of that Schedule (grounds 9 to 11), unless it is satisfied that suitable accommodation will be available for the tenant when the order takes effect,
        (c) on the grounds set out in Part III of that Schedule (grounds 12 to 16), unless it both considers it reasonable to make the order and is satisfied that suitable accommodation will be available for the tenant when the order takes effect;

>   and Part IV of that Schedule has effect for determining whether suitable
>   accommodation will be available for a tenant.
>   (3) The court shall not make such an order on any of those grounds unless the
>   ground is specified in the notice in pursuance of which proceedings for
>   possession are begun; but the grounds so specified may be altered or
>   added to with the leave of the court.

Section 84(2) imposes general constraints on the court in the granting of the various orders. Grounds 1–8 and 12–16 are subject to a requirement of reasonableness. The only general point about s 84 reasonableness is that the court must look at the case as a whole, including matters not directly to do with the grounds for eviction. In *Enfield LBC v McKeon* [1986] 2 All ER 730, for instance, the court had regard to the fact that the tenant was in the process of exercising the Right To Buy. However, the court is not to substitute its own ideas of what ought to have been done in practice if the council's request for a possession order is reasonable—*Sheffield CC v Green* [1993] EGCS 185. It is not unreasonable, however, that the tenant will become homeless as a result of the eviction—*Lee-Steere v Jennings* (1988) 20 HLR 1.

In the private residential sector some grounds for eviction are mandatory and some are discretionary. The Housing Act 1988, s 7 states:

> s 7(1) The court shall not make an order for possession of a dwelling-house let
>   on an assured tenancy except on one or more of the grounds set out in
>   Schedule 2 to this Act; but nothing in this Part of this Act relates to pro-
>   ceedings for possession of such a dwelling-house which are brought by a
>   mortgagee, within the meaning of the Law of Property Act 1925, who has
>   lent money on the security of the assured tenancy.
>   (2)   The following provisions of this section shall have effect, subject to sec-
>   tion 8 below, in relation to proceedings for the recovery of possession of a
>   dwelling-house let on an assured tenancy.
>   (3)   If the court is satisfied that any of the grounds in Part I of Schedule 2 to
>   this Act is established then, subject to subsections (5A) and (6) below, the
>   court shall make an order for possession.
>   (4)   If the court is satisfied that any of the grounds in Part II of Schedule 2 to
>   this Act is established, then, subject to subsections (5A) and (6) below, the
>   court may make an order for possession if it considers it reasonable to do
>   so.

Subsection (5A) restricts the grounds available to the landlord of a periodic tenancy arising at the end of a long residential lease under Schedule 10 of the Local Government and Housing Act 1989. Subsection (6) restricts the right of the landlord to forfeit during a fixed term lease so that forfeiture is only possible on certain grounds.

The question of reasonableness is one of fact and the court must take account of all relevant circumstances in a 'broad, common sense' way (Lord Greene MR, *Cumming v Danson* [1942] 2 All ER 653 at 655).

In the commercial sector there are seven grounds upon which the landlord can oppose a new tenancy (Landlord and Tenant Act 1954, s 30(1) (a)–(g)). If the landlord is able to establish any of these grounds the court 'shall not make an order for the grant of a new tenancy' (Landlord and Tenant Act 1954, s 31(1)). The mandatory aspect of this section is balanced by the fact that some of the grounds themselves contain an element of discretion—the tenant 'ought not to be granted a new tenancy' ((a), (b), (c) and (e); and see *Hurstfell Ltd v Leicester Square Property Ltd* [1988] 2 EGLR 105; *Betty's Cafes Ltd v Phillips Furnishing Stores Ltd* [1957] Ch 67 at 82).

It should further be noted that all of the statutory codes on eviction contain the general ground that possession may be ordered for any breach of a term of the lease (Landlord and Tenant Act 1954, s 30(1)(c); Housing Act 1985, Sch 2, Ground 1; Housing Act 1988, Sch 2, Ground 12, which expressly does not apply to non-payment of rent). Thus, the lease should be the starting point for any considera-tion of whether the tenant may be evicted. For instance, if the lease prohibits the keeping of pets, the landlord does not have to prove that the pet is a nuisance or annoyance to neighbours (Housing Act 1985, Sch 2, Ground 2 and Housing Act 1988, Sch 2, Ground 14), merely that a pet is being kept contrary to the terms of the lease—*Sheffield CC v Green, op. cit.*. Furthermore, as Hoath pointed out in *Council Housing*, 1982, at pp 22 and 36 (though, sadly, not in *Public Housing Law*, 1989), leases can contain some very strange clauses. Students of landlord and tenant law should be eternally indebted to him for the following:

- '[The] tenant shall see that the bath is used only for the purpose for which it is intended.'
- '[No] breeding of animals may take place without consent from the Housing Officer.'
- There was also the 'Dog Passport', where council tenants wishing to keep a dog had to register it with the local authority annually and produce a photograph of the dog for that very purpose.

It would be interesting to know what a court would deem to be an unreasonable 'other use' of the bath for which eviction would be justified. And a court would have to put itself through jurisprudential contortions if the tenant was so rash as to keep rabbits.

Whilst housing association lets are governed by the Housing Act 1988, the National Federation of Housing Associations' model assured tenancy agree-ment, in line with the perceived social role of housing associations, states that housing associations should always give four weeks' notice and that only a lim-ited number of grounds should be available when seeking repossession. Further, some of those grounds mirror provisions in the Housing Act 1985, once more highlighting the housing associations' social role akin to local authorities and its mixed private and public status. Clause 4(2) of the model agreement states that the housing association will only seek eviction for the following reasons:

- rent arrears under Ground 10 (but not Grounds 8 or 11);
- breach of some other term of the lease under Ground 12;
- causing damage to or failing to look after the building or its common parts under Ground 13;
- nuisance or annoyance to neighbours under Ground 14;
- where the tenancy has passed on the death of the original tenant by will or intestacy, but subject to statutory succession—Ground 7; and
- suitable alternative accommodation is available to the tenant (Ground 9) and the housing association needs the premises because
  (i)   it wishes to carry out repairs
  (ii) the property is designed to be suitable for someone with special needs, such a person has need of it and the tenant no longer does
  (iii) the tenant is a successor other than a spouse who succeeded on the death of the original tenant and the premises are under-occupied.
  (Sub-paragraphs (i) to (iii) are the equivalent of Grounds found in Sch 2 Housing Act 1985.)

The structure of this analysis of grounds for eviction follows, for the most part, the order laid down in the Housing Act 1985.

11.4.1 Eviction and Arrears

Principally, this section is to do with eviction for rent arrears, but in the property slump and general recession of the late 1980s and 1990s several landlords lost their properties through mortgage arrears with consequences for their tenants.

Since rent is such a fundamental element of every lease, non-payment should be expected to lead to eviction. However, even where the tenant has true arrears due to his own fault, eviction should be a 'weapon' of last resort. The landlord will incur costs evicting the tenant and in finding a new tenant. Moreover, there is no guarantee that this new tenant will be any more reliable than the one just evicted (see Culyer, cited in Partington, *Landlord and Tenant*, 2nd edn, 1980, at pp 517-19). On the other hand, there is no point 'investing' in a tenant who over a long period has shown himself to be irresponsible with regard to payment of the rent. One solution used regularly in the local authority sector is to seek eviction, but obtain a suspended order for possession which does not come into effect whilst the tenant pays the rent and a contribution to the arrears. If the tenant defaults, the landlord already has a possession notice which can be activated immediately by applying for a warrant for possession, unless the former seeks a further suspension—Housing Act 1985, ss 82 and 85; *Thompson v Elmbridge BC, op. cit.*, and 11.2.5.3 above.

Turning to the law, there are special rules relating to forfeiture for non-payment of rent—see 11.2.3.2 above. The simplest rules on security of tenure regarding arrears of rent apply to local authority leases. Ground 1 of Sch 2 to the Housing Act 1985 is as follows.

Ground 1 [subject to reasonableness] – Rent lawfully due from the tenant has not been paid or an obligation of the tenancy has been broken or not performed.

This is subject to the general common law rule found in *Bird v Hildage* [1948] 1 KB 91, that if the tenant pays off the arrears before the hearing then the court cannot issue an order for possession. At common law, persistent late payment is not a ground for eviction. It is likely that even if the tenant only paid off the arrears during the course of the hearing, that it would be 's 84(2) unreasonable' to order the tenant's eviction. Other factors going to reasonableness with respect to rent arrears would be, according to *Woodspring DC v Taylor* (1982) 4 HLR 95, the tenant's previous record of rent payments and the cause of the arrears. The fact that tenants are making 'arrears direct' payments from any state welfare benefit would also suggest that eviction would be unreasonable—Social Security (Claims and Payments) Regulations 1987 (SI 1987 No. 1968, reg. 35 and Sch 9, para 2).

In the private residential sector, the position is more complex. The equivalent to Ground 1 of the 1985 Act is the Housing Act 1988, Sch 2, Ground 10. Ground 10 is a discretionary ground and implicitly incorporates some element of reasonableness.

Ground 10 [subject to reasonableness] – Some rent lawfully due from the tenant–
(a) is unpaid on the date on which the proceedings for possession are begun; and
(b) except where subsection (1)(b) of section 8 of this Act applies, was in arrears at the date of the service of the notice under that section relating to those proceedings.
(s 8(1)(b) deals with the case where it is just and reasonable to dispense with the service of notice).

However, a tenant's rent payment record can lead to eviction, in theory, in two other situations, although housing association landlords have forsaken these extra grounds in the model tenancy agreement drafted by the National Federation of Housing Associations, *op. cit.* For private landlords, Ground 11, also discretionary, seeks to reverse, in part, *Bird v Hildage, op. cit.*

Ground 11 [subject to reasonableness] – Whether or not any rent is in arrears on the date on which proceedings for possession are begun, the tenant has persistently delayed paying rent which has become lawfully due.

It is to be assumed that the landlord served notice when arrears were due and that prior to the proceedings commencing the tenant has paid them off.

Ground 11 allows a private sector landlord to continue with the action because the tenant is a bad risk. The provision has been borrowed from the commercial sector. Section 30(1)(b) of the Landlord and Tenant Act 1954, dealing with grounds for non-renewal of a lease, provides as follows:

s 30(1) (b) that the tenant ought not to be granted a new tenancy in view of his persistent delay in paying rent which has become due.

The case law under the 1954 Act will, *mutatis mutandis*, apply to 1988 Act cases. Persistent has been taken to refer to the frequency and duration of earlier delays in the payment of rent and the difficulty the landlord faced in obtaining the arrears—*Hopcutt v Carver* (1969) 209 EG 1069. The tenant in the commercial sector has a defence of 'good reason'; there is no reason to believe that this will not be applied in the private residential sector, too. A prime candidate for triggering the defence would be delays in the payment of the tenant's Housing Benefit (housing benefit issues with respect to eviction are considered below).

The Housing Act 1988, Sch 2 also provides for a rent arrears based eviction in Ground 8.

Ground 8 [mandatory] – Both at the date of the service of the notice under section 8 of this Act relating to the proceedings for possession and at the date of the hearing—
(a) if rent is payable weekly or fortnightly, at least thirteen weeks' rent is unpaid;
(b) if rent is payable monthly, at least three months' rent is unpaid;
(c) if rent is payable quarterly, at least one quarter's rent is more than three months in arrears; and
(d) if rent is payable yearly, at least three months' rent is more than three months in arrears;
and for the purpose of this ground 'rent' means rent lawfully due from the tenant.

While no one would doubt that three months of arrears would justify possession proceedings, it is difficult to see what Ground 8 adds to Ground 10 other than that it is a mandatory ground for ordering repossession. Hickman criticizes Ground 8 in *The Housing Act 1988—Four Years On*, (1993) 143 NLJ 1271 at p 1272. His views are that the only situation where it might be effective is if the reason for the three months of arrears is that there has been a delay in the payment of the tenant's housing benefit. Under Ground 10, eviction is discretionary and the court would be loath to so order if the tenant's arrears were due to a benefit failure: however, Ground 8 is mandatory. Nevertheless, it is hardly an appropriate use of the statutory power.

Housing benefit delays have contributed significantly to problems of arrears in both the private and public residential sectors: even to the extent of the housing department of a London local authority taking action against some of its tenants because the housing benefit department did not make the required payments for over a year—the *Guardian* 2, pp 12 and 13, 30 December 1992. The Audit Commission and the National Audit Office both found that bureaucratic delays in the administration of housing benefit led to increased rent arrears—see Joseph Rowntree Foundation Inquiry into British Housing, Second Report, 1991, p 20. A 1990 survey of those seeking advice on housing found that housing benefit related arrears were a major problem—for more detail, see Sharp, *Slow Coach to Eviction*, ROOF, May/June 1991, at p 12. Despite the statutory requirement in the housing benefit laws to make an interim payment after fourteen days if no final decision has been reached, the survey found a case where a woman received no housing benefit for six months from the date of making her claim. In her case, the housing benefit met all the accumulated arrears. The Commons Public Accounts Committee found that Nottingham, Lambeth, Haringey, Brent, Barnet and Harrow were the worst offenders when it came to delays in paying housing benefit in a survey of how housing associations had fared in terms of accumulated rent arrears; the Metropolitan Housing Trust was owed some £400,000 in rent arrears due to delays in processing housing benefit claims (Housing Corporation: Financial Management of Housing Associations, Twentieth Report of the Committee of Public Accounts, May 1994). Where there are delays in paying housing benefit, landlords, both private and housing association, have found that issuing proceedings for arrears to regain possession often spurs the local authority, who administer payment of the benefit, into taking action—the *Guardian* 2, pp 12 and 13, 30 December 1992. What would be funny if the circumstances were not so tragic, is that if tenants are evicted for housing benefit related arrears, they will probably qualify as unintentionally homeless and place an even larger financial burden on the local authority who administer the payment of housing benefit on behalf of the DSS; *cf.* Campbell, *Rules Made to be Broken*, ROOF, May/June 1994, p 15.

Furthermore, though, rent officers now have to decide whether private sector rents are too high when a claim is made for housing benefit. Under s 121 Housing Act 1988, the Secretary of State has made regulations requiring rent officers to determine the reasonable rent for each property.

Rent Officers (Additional Functions) Order 1990 (SI 1990 No. 428)
Sch 1 Determinations
para 1(1) The rent officer shall determine whether, in his opinion, the rent payable under the tenancy of the dwelling at the relevant time is significantly higher than the rent which the landlord might reasonably have been expected to obtain under the tenancy at that time, having regard to the level of rent under similar tenancies of similar dwellings in the locality (or as similar as regards tenancy, dwelling and locality as is reasonably practicable), but on the assumption that no one who would have been entitled to housing benefit had sought or is seeking the tenancy.

(2) If the rent officer determines under sub-paragraph (1) that the rent is significantly higher, the rent officer shall also determine the rent which the landlord might reasonably have been expected to obtain under the tenancy at the relevant time, having regard to the same matter and on the same assumption as in sub-paragraph (1).

para 2(1) The rent officer shall determine whether the dwelling, at the relevant time, exceeds the size criteria for the occupiers.

(2) If the rent officer determines that the dwelling exceeds the size criteria, the rent officer shall also determine the rent which a landlord might reasonably have been expected to obtain, at the relevant time, for a tenancy which is similar to the tenancy of the dwelling, on the same terms (other than the term relating to the amount of rent) and of a dwelling which is in the same locality as the dwelling, but which—
(a) accords with the size criteria for the occupiers,
(b) is in a reasonable state of repair, and
(c) corresponds in other respects, in the rent officer's opinion, as closely as is reasonably practicable to the dwelling.

Under Sch 2, there are rules regarding the number of bedrooms and living rooms required to satisfy the 'size criteria', having regard to the overall size of the family and the number of adults and children. It may be that a rent officer will set the reasonable rent at less than the landlord's figure, leaving the tenant to meet the difference from very low wages or from other state benefits (see also, ch 8.5).

The final aspect of arrears and eviction relates not to tenants and rent, but to landlords defaulting on mortgage payments. The Rowntree Inquiry, *op. cit.*, p 16, noted that at the nadir of the housing slump over twice as many people were homeless for mortgage arrears as for rent arrears. However, the issue here is tenants being evicted because their landlords are subject to repossession proceedings by the mortgagees. This is permitted in the private residential sector under Ground 2.

Ground 2 [mandatory]
The dwelling-house is subject to a mortgage granted before the beginning of the tenancy and –
(a) the mortgagee is entitled to exercise a power of sale conferred on him by the mortgage or by section 101 of the Law of Property Act 1925; and
(b) the mortgagee requires possession of the dwelling-house for the purpose of disposing of it with vacant possession in exercise of that power; and
(c) either notice was given as mentioned in Ground 1 above or the court is satisfied that it is just and equitable to dispense with the requirement of notice; and for the purposes of this ground 'mortgage' includes a charge and 'mortgagee' shall be construed accordingly.

Since November 1993, mortgagees have had to give fourteen days' notice of possession to the occupier, that is, the tenant, but it does not prevent the court making the mandatory repossession order (contrast the four weeks' notice required by the Protection from Eviction Act 1977, s 5). It merely gives the tenant due warning of his impending homelessness. The essence of Ground 2 is that the mortgagee, usually a building society or bank, needs to evict the tenant to sell the property and recoup its loan. To succeed under Ground 2, the landlord must have given a Ground 1 notice not later than the beginning of the tenancy, unless the court is prepared to find it is just and equitable to dispense with this notice in writing. A landlord serves a Ground 1 notice where the premises were his principal or only home at some time before the beginning of the tenancy or where he may want the premises as his only or principal home at some time in the future. Therefore, Ground 2 is limited to the case of the owner-occupier, or intending owner-occupier, who has now let his premises and who had a mortgage thereon prior to the granting of the lease. It would not cover the case where the landlord lets out several properties none of which were occupied by him prior to the tenancy, nor the case where the lease pre-dates the mortgage on the property. In *Britannia Building Society v Earl* [1990] 2 All ER 469, decided under the similar provision in Rent Act 1977, Sch 15, the Court of Appeal had to consider the case where the mortgage prohibited the granting of a lease without the consent of the mortgagee (the typical case), yet the landlord/mortgagor had let the premises without such consent. The landlord then fell into arrears on his mortgage and the building society sought to repossess the property. The tenants tried to rely on their status of irremovability under the Rent Act 1977, but the court held that whilst the landlord was bound by the tenant's interest, the building society with its prior interest was not bound—at 475, quoting *Quennell v Maltby*, [1979] 1 All ER 568 at 572. The tenant, despite all the statutory protection in the 1977 Act, has no greater rights than the landlord who has defaulted on his mortgage and who is in breach of its terms by taking on, undeclared, the tenant.

In conclusion, rent arrears should in appropriate circumstances lead to eviction and, for that reason, there are specific grounds in each sector. In addition, since payment of rent will be a term of the lease, arrears will be caught by the general ground as well, except, that is, in the private residential sector.

Housing Act 1988, Sch 2
Ground 12 [subject to reasonableness]
Any obligation of the tenancy (other than one related to the payment of rent) has been broken or not performed.

With three specific grounds for eviction based on rent arrears, another was probably seen as overkill. Nevertheless, Ground 12 does prevent the landlord and tenant agreeing a customized clause in the lease dealing with eviction for non-payment of rent.

11.4.2 Nuisance and Annoyance

Both private and public residential sector laws allow, in very similar terms, for eviction where the tenant is a nuisance or annoyance to neighbours.

Housing Act 1988, Sch 2
Ground 14 [subject to reasonableness]
The tenant or any other person residing in the dwelling-house has been guilty of conduct which is a nuisance or annoyance to adjoining occupiers, or has been convicted of using the dwelling-house or allowing the dwelling-house to be used for immoral or illegal purposes.

Housing Act 1985, Sch 2 Part I
Ground 2 [subject to reasonableness]
The tenant or a person residing in the dwelling-house has been guilty of conduct which is a nuisance or annoyance to neighbours, or has been convicted of using the dwelling-house or allowing it to be used for immoral or illegal purposes.

'Adjoining' in the 1988 Act has been held not to be limited to contiguous properties, but neighbours in a more general sense are included—*Cobstone Investments Ltd v Maxim* [1985] QB 140, decided under Case 2, Sch 15 Rent Act 1977. The use of such provisions can be controversial for good and ill. At one level, these provisions are aimed at so-called 'problem families'. However, Popplestone showed in 1979 that problem families were often the victims rather than the cause of the problems (*Difficult Tenants: Who Are They and What To Do About Them*, cited in Partington, *op. cit.*, at p 520; see also, Hughes, Karn and Lickiss, *Neighbour Disputes: Social Landlords and the Law*, [1994] JSW&FL 201):

Behind complaints about neighbouring tenants often lie a host of other grievances that have not been dealt with. They often stem from the lack of choice available to council tenants over the question of who to live next to . . . Also, tenants are often obliged to live in housing patently inadequate for their needs. In the course of the research we came across complaints which stemmed from the stressful conditions brought about by physical densities as well as the high child population of some estates. Few estates cater adequately for the needs of young or teenage children. Families living in stressful circumstances at very high densities cannot be expected to tolerate disruptive families. This is the nub of many of the intractable problems. Unsatisfactory tenants are often the scapegoats for intolerable conditions. (Popplestone at p 520)

The nuisance and annoyance ground has proved to be useful, however, in evicting tenants who have subjected their neighbours to racial harassment (*Islington LBC v Isherwood*, Legal Action, June 1987, 19; the *Guardian* 2—Society pp 6–7, 12 October 1994), although many local authorities now include a specific anti-racism provision in the lease—the *Guardian* p 3, 19 August 1993. The National Federation of Housing Associations' model tenancy agreement, *op. cit.*, goes further and includes in Clause 4(2)(iv) a specific rule that the tenant might be evicted if he is responsible for harassment of other tenants on the grounds of race, colour, sex or disability. Furthermore, it is an express term of the model agreement that the tenant is obliged not to commit any form of harassment on the grounds of race, colour, religion, sex, sexual orientation or disability—Clause 3(5); see also, §C11, revised Tenants' Guarantee.

Whilst the landlord has the power to evict for nuisance and annoyance, he cannot be forced to act at the instigation of neighbouring tenants—*O'Leary v Islington LBC* (1983) 9 HLR 81. However, a tenant has the right to quiet enjoyment of the property and if the landlord could be shown to be responsible for the other tenant's acts, then the annoyed tenant might be able to sue for breach of covenant. Normally, a landlord will not be responsible for the other tenant's acts, but if the landlord was negligent in its allocation procedures and took on as a tenant someone likely to disrupt the lives of the neighbours, then, dependent on the landlord's knowledge, a case of breach of the covenant for quiet enjoyment could be made out—see Brimacombe, *Weed Out the Undesirables*, ROOF, p 24, November/December 1993, and *Hilton v James Smith & Sons (Norwood)* (1979) 251 EG 1063.

11.4.3 Deterioration in Condition

The legislation applying to residential leases and to commercial leases provides for eviction or non-renewal where the property deteriorates during the tenancy as a result of the tenant's acts or omissions.

Housing Act 1988, Sch 2
Ground 13 [subject to reasonableness]
The condition of the dwelling-house or any of the common parts has deteriorated owing to acts of waste by, or the neglect or default of, the tenant or any other person residing in the dwelling-house and, in the case of an act of waste by, or the neglect or default of, a person lodging with the tenant or a sub-tenant of his, the tenant has not taken such steps as he ought reasonably to have taken for the removal of the lodger or sub-tenant.

For the purposes of this ground, 'common parts' means any part of a building comprising the dwelling-house and any other premises which the tenant is entitled under the terms of the tenancy to use in common with the occupiers of other dwelling-houses in which the landlord has an estate or interest.

Ground 15 [subject to reasonableness]
The condition of any furniture provided for use under the tenancy has, in the opinion of the court, deteriorated owing to ill-treatment by the tenant or any other person residing in the dwelling-house and, in the case of ill-treatment by a person lodging with the tenant or by a sub-tenant of his, the tenant has not taken

such steps as he ought reasonably to have taken for the removal of the lodger or sub-tenant.

Housing Act 1985, Sch 2, Part I

Ground 3 [subject to reasonableness]

The condition of the dwelling-house or of any of the common parts has deteriorated owing to acts of waste by, or the neglect or default of, the tenant or a person residing in the dwelling-house and, in the case of an act of waste by, or the neglect or default of, a person lodging with the tenant or a sub-tenant of his, the tenant has not taken such steps as he ought reasonably to have taken for the removal of the lodger or sub-tenant.

Ground 4 [subject to reasonableness]

The condition of furniture provided by the landlord for use under the tenancy, or for use in the common parts, has deteriorated owing to ill-treatment by the tenant or a person residing in the dwelling-house and, in the case of ill-treatment by a person lodging with the tenant or a sub-tenant of his, the tenant has not taken such steps as he ought reasonably to have taken for the removal of the lodger or sub-tenant.

Landlord and Tenant Act 1954

s 30(1) The grounds on which a landlord may oppose an application under subsection (1) of section twenty-four of this Act are such of the following grounds . . . , that is to say:

    (a) where under the current tenancy the tenant has any obligations as respects the repair and maintenance of the holding, that the tenant ought not to be granted a new tenancy in view of the state of repair of the holding, being a state resulting from the tenant's failure to comply with the said obligations; . . .

    (c) that the tenant ought not to be granted a new tenancy in view of other substantial breaches by him of his obligations under the current tenancy, or for any other reason connected with the tenant's use or management of the holding;

The 1985 and 1988 Acts are remarkably similar in their wording. Apart from the reference to damage to the common parts in Ground 13, the 1988 Act mirrors the provisions of the Rent Act 1977. The cases under the old law indicate that as well as if he actually caused the damage, the tenant may be liable if the damage is allowed to remain whilst the tenant does not repair it when he is so obliged—*cf.* Landlord and Tenant Act 1985; *Liverpool CC v Irwin* [1976] 2 All ER 39. In one Court of Appeal case mentioned in Evans and Smith, *op. cit.,* at p 261, allowing a garden to become totally overgrown was sufficient to leave the tenant liable—*Holloway v Povey* (1984) 271 EG 195. Nevertheless, under the 1985 and 1988 Acts the court must find it reasonable to grant a possession order on the facts.

The provision for non-renewal of the lease in the Landlord and Tenant Act 1954, s 30(1)(a) is slightly different. It focusses on the tenant's failure to carry out his repairing obligations under the lease and the resulting disrepair of the prop-

erty. It was held by Ormerod LJ in *Lyons v Central Commercial Properties Ltd*
[1958] 2 All ER 767, that there is a discretion which would allow the court to look
at matters beyond the specific repairing obligation and the extent of any disrepair. Commonly, the repairing obligation will be on the landlord and a failure by
the tenant to contribute towards the cost through the service charge would lead
to a breach within s 30(1)(c).

As well as a commercial landlord being able to refuse renewal if the premises fall
into disrepair as a result of a s 30(1) reason, if he has reserved a right of re-entry
under the lease for similar reasons, as well as having to comply with the Law of
Property Act 1925, s 146 he may also have to prove that the provisions of the
Leasehold Property (Repairs) Act 1938 have been met, discussed above at 11.2.3.3.

11.4.4 Tenancy Induced by False Statements

Strangely, only the Housing Act 1985 allows for eviction on this ground.

Ground 5 [subject to reasonableness]
**The tenant is the person, or one of the persons, to whom the tenancy was granted
and the landlord was induced to grant the tenancy by a false statement made
knowingly or recklessly by the tenant.**

It may be that the type of false statement that might induce a tenancy in the private residential or commercial sector, such as that the tenant had a guaranteed
source of income, would eventually lead to arrears and eviction on that ground.
Given that local authorities are responsible for the homeless, then there is a
wider scope for the lies that might induce a tenancy—see also, the Housing Act
1985, s 74. Nevertheless, housing associations with their increasing role in the
provision of social rented housing and their sometimes strict qualification rules
might also want to evict for this sort of reason. Ground 5 is in part a housing management ground, but it is subject to the reasonableness test.

Although none of the other sectors have comparable grounds for recovery, it
may be possible to end the tenancy in any event under the general law for misrepresentation. In *Killick v Roberts* [1991] 1 WLR 1146 ((1992) 51 CLJ 21; [1992]
Conv 269), a lease was rescinded on the grounds of fraudulent misrepresentation
by the tenant. The landlord intended to 'winter let' the premises (but did not
serve a notice to take advantage of the Rent Act 1977 equivalent of Ground 3, see
11.4.14, below). Before the letting, the tenant had falsely told the landlord that he
was having a house built elsewhere that would be completed before the end of
the winter. In this case, the contractual tenancy had already expired by the time
of the court hearing and the Court of Appeal confirmed that even a statutory
(non-contractual) tenancy under the Rent Act 1977 could be rescinded for the
fraudulent misrepresentation.

A lease can also be rescinded by the tenant for a misrepresentation by the landlord: see *Laurence v Lexcourt Holdings Ltd* [1978] 1 WLR 1128 (misrepresentation that planning permission for office use existed for the premises let). If this approach is followed it would seem possible for a landlord to seek rescission of tenancies on the grounds, for example, that the tenant has misrepresented his financial status or the number (and ages) of the intended occupants of the premises if these factors were material to the landlord in letting the property to this particular tenant.

11.4.5 Premiums

Housing Act 1985, Sch 2
Ground 6 [subject to reasonableness]
The tenancy was assigned to the tenant, or to a predecessor in title of his who is a member of his family and is residing in the dwelling-house, by an assignment made by virtue of section 92 (assignments by way of exchange) and a premium was paid either in connection with that assignment or the assignment which the tenant or predecessor himself made by virtue of that section.

In this paragraph 'premium' means any fine or other like sum and any other pecuniary consideration in addition to rent.

Again, this provision is peculiar to the 1985 Act. There is more justification here, however, for exchanges take place predominantly within the local authority sector, although, on occasion, a council tenant may need to swap with a housing association or private sector tenant. The tenant can be evicted whether he paid or received the premium and regardless of who proposed its payment, but Ground 6 is subject to the reasonableness test.

11.4.6 Employment Related Tenancies

The Housing Acts 1985 and 1988 provide special rules for the case where the lease is related to the tenant's, or prospective tenant's, employment.

Housing Act 1985, Sch 2
Ground 7 [subject to reasonableness]
The dwelling-house forms part of, or is within the curtilage of, a building which, or so much of it as is held by the landlord, is held mainly for purposes other than housing purposes and consists mainly of accommodation other than housing accommodation, and—
(a) the dwelling-house was let to the tenant or a predecessor in title of his in consequence of the tenant or predecessor being in the employment of the landlord, or of–
    a local authority,

a new town corporation,
a housing action trust
an urban development corporation,
the Development Board for Rural Wales, or
the governors of an aided school,
and
(b) the tenant or a person residing in the dwelling-house has been guilty of conduct such that, having regard to the purpose for which the building is used, it
   would not be right for him to continue in occupation of the dwelling-house.

Ground 12 [subject to reasonableness and suitable alternative accommodation]
The dwelling-house forms part of, or is within the curtilage of, a building which,
or so much of it as is held by the landlord, is held mainly for purposes other than
housing purposes and consists mainly of accommodation other than housing
accommodation, or is situated in a cemetery, and–
(a) the dwelling-house was let to the tenant or a predecessor in title of his in consequence of the tenant or predecessor being in the employment of the landlord or of–
      a local authority,
      a new town corporation,
      a housing action trust
      an urban development corporation,
      the Development Board for Rural Wales, or
      the governors of an aided school,
and that employment has ceased, and
(b) the landlord reasonably requires the dwelling-house for occupation as a residence for some person either engaged in the employment of the landlord, or
   of such a body, or with whom a contract for such employment has been
   entered into conditional on housing being provided.

One of the 1988 Act's provisions (as amended by the National Health Service
and Community Care Act 1990, s 60, Sch 8, Part III, para 10) is of a more general
nature than those found in the 1985 Act.

Ground 16 [subject to reasonableness]—
The dwelling-house was let to the tenant in consequence of his employment by
the landlord seeking possession or a previous landlord under the tenancy and the
tenant has ceased to be in that employment.
   For the purposes of this ground, at a time when the landlord is or was the
Secretary of State, employment by a health service body, as defined in section
60(7) of the National Health Service and Community Care Act 1990, shall be
regarded as employment by the Secretary of State.

However, the 1988 Act also has a very specific ground for properties used by ministers of religion.

Ground 5 [mandatory]
The dwelling-house is held for the purpose of being available for occupation by a

minister of religion as a residence from which to perform the duties of his office and–

(a) not later than the beginning of the tenancy the landlord gave notice in writing to the tenant that possession might be recovered on this ground; and

(b) the court is satisfied that the dwelling-house is required for occupation by a minister of religion as such a residence.

The Grounds set out in the Housing Act 1985 differ slightly in operation as well as in their precise terms. Whilst Ground 7 requires the court to find that eviction would be reasonable, under Ground 12 eviction must be reasonable and there must be suitable alternative accommodation available to the tenant as well. The concept of suitable alternative accommodation will be considered below at 11.4.8. Ground 7 allows for eviction where the tenant's property is part of a building or is within the curtilage of a building used principally for non-housing purposes, the tenant obtained the lease in consequence of his employment by the landlord or one of the other named bodies and he has now behaved in a manner inconsistent with the purpose for which the building as a whole is principally used. Since the building as a whole is to be used mainly for non-housing purposes, then this Ground has no application to caretakers of blocks of flats, given, of course, that they were found to be secure tenants despite Sch 1, para 2 (see ch 6, above). However, it would catch the caretaker of a school who was found to be a child sex abuser (*cf.* Sch 1, para 2(1)). The question is what sort of conduct is going to be inappropriate to the main purpose of the building in most cases. Furthermore, since there has to be a building used for non-housing purposes, it would not apply to a cemetery worker with a property in the grounds, nor a park keeper. In such a case, Ground 12 would be the only means of obtaining possession. Once again there must be a building which is used for non-housing purposes or, to deal with the problem indicated above, the property must be in a cemetery. Eviction is possible under Ground 12 if the tenant or predecessor in title obtained the lease through his employment by the landlord or other named body, that employment has ceased and the new, replacement employee's contract states that his new job is conditional on housing being provided. Grounds 12 and 7 overlap in that the inappropriate conduct might be sufficient to justify dismissal from the employment; for instance, if a pyromaniac fire station caretaker were to burn down the town hall. The only other point to note is that both Grounds only apply where the building is used mainly for non-housing purposes—they have no application to blocks of flats or council estates in general, although in most cases tenants whose employment relates to such housing will not be secure under Sch 1, para 2(1).

Ground 16 of the Housing Act 1988 is of a more general nature. The tenancy must have been let originally in consequence of the tenant being employed by the landlord or his predecessor in title and that employment has now ceased. There are no rules about the nature of the property, nor about the new employee's contract of employment referring to the tenancy. Nevertheless, the court has a discretion as to whether to grant possession, and, therefore, the eviction must be at least reasonable. Ground 5, on the other hand, is mandatory if the tenant has been given notice in advance of the tenancy—see the Housing Act 1988, Sch 2, Part IV. It allows the landlord to regain possession if the property is necessary for a minister of religion as a residence from which to carry out his functions. Not a Ground, however, that will be oft-litigated, one would imagine.

11.4.7 Temporary Accommodation During Repairs

This Ground is peculiar to local authority sector lettings.

Housing Act 1985, Sch 2
Ground 8 [subject to reasonableness]
The dwelling-house was made available for occupation by the tenant (or a predecessor in title of his) whilst works were carried out on the dwelling-house which he previously occupied as his only or principal home and—
(a) the tenant (or predecessor) was a secure tenant of the other dwelling-house at the time when he ceased to occupy it as his home,
(b) the tenant (or predecessor) accepted the tenancy of the dwelling-house of which possession is sought on the understanding that he would give up occupation when, on completion of the works, the other dwelling-house was again available for occupation by him under a secure tenancy, and
(c) the works have been completed and the other dwelling-house is so available.

Its purpose is to allow a local authority to return its tenants to their original homes once repairs or improvements have been carried out. The change of accommodation is intended to be temporary from the start. However, since it is within the first group of 1985 Act Grounds, the eviction must be reasonable as well. Thus, if the repairs take an excessively long time, it may not be reasonable to return the tenants to their original dwelling. There is no equivalent ground under the Housing Act 1988, so a housing association which moved an assured tenant out whilst it carried out repairs or improvements to the original premises could not necessarily return the tenant to those original premises if he had become an assured tenant of the substitute premises. The only way round this impasse might be to evict the tenant under Ground 9 of the 1988 Act and provide suitable alternative accommodation on an assured shorthold tenancy. According to the Tenants' Guarantee (Housing Corporation Circular 29/91; see also, Housing Corporation 1994 Consultation Document, including a revised Draft Tenants' Guarantee) housing associations are only to grant assured shorthold tenancies in exceptional circumstances and with the approval of the Housing Corporation—§C3. Since keeping the premises in repair is an obligation imposed upon the landlord in the National Federation of Housing Associations' model tenancy agreement, the Housing Corporation should allow the granting of an assured shorthold where the accommodation is intended to be temporary whilst works are executed on the tenant's original premises.

11.4.8 Suitable Alternative Accommodation (SAA)

SAA is relevant to repossession proceedings in the public and private residential and the commercial sectors. Under the Housing Act 1985, it forms a pertinent consideration for the court for all the Grounds from, and including, 9 onwards—there must be SAA if repossession is to be ordered. Under the Housing Act 1988 and the Landlord and Tenant Act 1954, SAA on its own will allow the landlord to evict the tenant from his present premises. SAA is a much considered phrase.

In the 1985 Act, SAA must be available when considering whether to evict under any of Grounds laid out in Parts II and III of Sch 2. Under Part II Grounds, the court will only order repossession if SAA is made available to the tenant, whilst under Part III, there must be SAA and it must be reasonable to evict. Part IV of Sch 2 partially defines SAA—*Enfield LBC v French* (1984) 17 HLR 211 at 215 and 218–19.

Housing Act 1985, Sch 2, Part IV

para 1 For the purposes of section 84(2)(b) and (c) (case in which court is not to make an order for possession unless satisfied that suitable accommodation will be available), accommodation is suitable if it consists of premises–

(a) which are to be let as a separate dwelling under a secure tenancy, or

(b) which are to be let as a separate dwelling under a protected tenancy, not being a tenancy under which the landlord might recover possession under one of the Cases in Part II of Schedule 15 to the Rent Act 1977 (cases where court must order possession), or

(c) which are to be let as a separate dwelling under an assured tenancy which is neither an assured shorthold tenancy, within the meaning of Part I of the Housing Act 1988, nor a tenancy under which the landlord might recover possession under any of Grounds 1 to 5 in Schedule 2 to that Act

and, in the opinion of the court, the accommodation is reasonably suitable to the needs of the tenant and his family.

para 2 In determining whether the accommodation is reasonably suitable to the needs of the tenant and his family, regard shall be had to—

(a) the nature of the accommodation which it is the practice of the landlord to allocate to persons with similar needs;

(b) the distance of the accommodation available from the place of work or education of the tenant and of any members of his family;

(c) its distance from the home of any member of the tenant's family if proximity to it is essential to that member's or the tenant's well-being;

(d) the needs (as regards extent of accommodation) and means of the tenant and his family;

(e) the terms on which the accommodation is available and the terms of the secure tenancy;

(f) if furniture was provided by the landlord for use under the secure tenancy, whether furniture is to be provided for use in the other accommodation, and if so the nature of the furniture to be provided.

para 3   Where possession of a dwelling-house is sought on ground 9 (overcrowding such as to render occupier guilty of offence), other accommodation may be reasonably suitable to the needs of the tenant and his family notwithstanding that the permitted number of persons for that accommodation, as defined in section 326(3) (overcrowding: the space standard), is less than the number of persons living in the dwelling-house of which possession is sought.

para 4(1)   A certificate of the appropriate local housing authority that they will provide suitable accommodation for the tenant by a date specified in the certificate is conclusive evidence that suitable accommodation will be available for him by that date.

(2)   The appropriate local housing authority is the authority for the district in which the dwelling-house of which possession is sought is situated.

(3)   This paragraph does not apply where the landlord is a local housing authority.

It is apparent from paragraph 1 that the SAA need not be in the local authority sector. The only limitation as regards private sector lets, is that the lease must not be subject to a mandatory ground for eviction following notice under the Rent Act 1977 or Housing Act 1988. Paragraph 2 lists some of the factors to which the court ought to have regard. They are very similar to those relevant to cases under the Rent Act 1977 or the Housing Act 1988 and so a more detailed analysis is set out below. Where the private sector legislation and the Housing Act 1985 differ is in the fact that in assessing suitability, no regard is to be had to the character of the property from which the local authority tenant is evicted as regards the property in which he is to be rehoused. The effect is that a tenant can be moved from a very pleasant council house to a flat in a tower block so long as the flat meets all the other paragraph 2 criteria. It should be noted, though, that subparagraph (a) does require the court to have regard to the 'nature of the accommodation which it is the practice of the landlord to allocate to persons with similar needs'. The final point on SAA in the local authority sector concerns the situation where there is a joint tenancy but some of the tenants have moved out. Following *Hammersmith and Fulham LBC v Monk, op. cit.*, it ought to be the case that since the contractual nature of the tenancy is determinative, that the new accommodation should be suitable for all joint tenants, not just those resident at the date of eviction. However, practice seems to be that only the resident tenants need be offered SAA.

SAA is an independent discretionary ground for eviction under the Housing Act 1988. Whilst private landlords may evict whenever there is SAA, subject to the court's overriding discretion, housing association landlords voluntarily limit themselves to using Ground 9 where there is a need for vacant possession to carry out repairs or improvements, where the premises are designed for and are needed by a person with special needs and the present tenant has no such need, and where there is undercrowding—National Federation of Housing Associations' model tenancy agreement, *op. cit.*, and see, *Trustees of the Dame Margaret Hungerford Charity v Beazely* (1994) 26 HLR 269. Subject to those self-imposed limitations, housing associations must satisfy the general requirements of Ground 9 like any other landlord of an assured tenant.

Housing Act 1988, Sch 2
Ground 9 [subject to reasonableness]
Suitable alternative accommodation is available for the tenant or will be available for him when the order for possession takes effect.

Ground 9 mirrors for the most part the Rent Act 1977, Sch 15, Part IV. The 1988 Act imposes on the landlord the additional obligation that he meet the tenant's reasonable removal expenses—s 11. The 1988 Act lists some of the matters to be taken into account in Sch 2, Part III. Since Ground 9 is discretionary, however, the court is free to take other matters into account.

Housing Act 1988, Sch 2, Part III
para 1 For the purposes of Ground 9 above, a certificate of the local housing authority for the district in which the dwelling-house in question is situated, certifying that the authority will provide suitable alternative accommodation for the tenant by a date specified in the certificate, shall be conclusive evidence that suitable alternative accommodation will be available for him by that date.

para 2 Where no such certificate as is mentioned in paragraph 1 above is produced to the court, accommodation shall be deemed to be suitable for the purposes of Ground 9 above if it consists of either—
   (a) premises which are to be let as a separate dwelling such that they will then be let on an assured tenancy, other than—
      (i) a tenancy in respect of which notice is given not later than the beginning of the tenancy that possession might be recovered on any of Grounds 1 to 5 above, or
      (ii) an assured shorthold tenancy, within the meaning of Chapter II of Part I of this Act, or
   (b) premises to be let as a separate dwelling on terms which will, in the opinion of the court, afford to the tenant security of tenure reasonably equivalent to the security afforded by Chapter I of Part I of this Act in the case of an assured tenancy of a kind mentioned in sub-paragraph (a) above,

and, in the opinion of the court, the accommodation fulfils the relevant conditions as defined in paragraph 3 below.

para 3(1) For the purposes of paragraph 2 above, the relevant conditions are that the accommodation is reasonably suitable to the needs of the tenant and his family as regards proximity to place of work, and either—

(a) similar as regards rental and extent to the accommodation afforded by dwelling-houses provided in the neighbourhood by any local housing authority for persons whose needs as regards extent are, in the opinion of the court, similar to those of the tenant and of his family; or

(b) reasonably suitable to the means of the tenant and to the needs of the tenant and his family as regards extent and character; and

that if any furniture was provided for use under the assured tenancy in question, furniture is provided for use in the accommodation which is either similar to that so provided or is reasonably suitable to the needs of the tenant and his family.

(2) For the purposes of sub-paragraph (1)(a) above, a certificate of a local housing authority stating—

(a) the extent of the accommodation afforded by dwelling-houses provided by the authority to meet the needs of tenants with families of such number as may be specified in the certificate, and

(b) the amount of the rent charged by the authority for dwelling-houses affording accommodation of that extent, shall be conclusive evidence of the facts so stated.

para 4   Accommodation shall not be deemed to be suitable to the needs of the tenant and his family if the result of their occupation of the accommodation would be that it would be an overcrowded dwelling-house for the purposes of Part X of the Housing Act 1985.

para 5   Any document purporting to be a certificate of a local housing authority named therein issued for the purposes of this Part of this Schedule and to be signed by the proper officer of that authority shall be received in evidence and, unless the contrary is shown, shall be deemed to be such a certificate without further proof.

para 6   In this Part of this Schedule 'local housing authority' and 'district', in relation to such an authority, have the same meaning as in the Housing Act 1985.

It is worth noting that despite a concerted policy since 1979, which was reinforced in the Government's White Paper on Housing, 1987 (Cm 214), to residualize the role of the local authority as a provider of housing, paragraph 1 states that a local authority certificate will be treated as conclusive proof that the private sector landlord has satisfied his duty to provide SAA. Where no such certificate exists, the court has to find either that the tenant will move into an assured tenancy where none of the first five mandatory grounds for eviction exists nor that it is an assured shorthold, or that he will have equivalent security of tenure. In addition, the new premises must satisfy certain qualitative criteria and must not leave the family in statutorily overcrowded conditions.

Suitability has often been contested in the courts where the judge must also find that the eviction is reasonable within his general discretion. The fact that the new accommodation would not take the tenant's furniture was held to render it unsuitable in *McIntyre v Hardcastle* [1948] 2 KB 82, and where the tenant had children, the absence of a garden was similarly fatal to the landlord's claim—*De Markozoff v Craig* (1949) 93 Sol.Jo.693. *Dawncar Investments Ltd v Plews* (1993) 25 HLR 639, dealt with the issue of how far environmental factors should be taken into account under what would now be the Housing Act 1988, Sch 2, Part III, para 3(1)(a) and (b). The tenant leased a flat in the quiet, 'leafy environs' of Hampstead Heath in London. The landlord offered her and her child a flat in Kilburn which was internally superior to her present accommodation. The Court of Appeal accepted the trial judge's decision that for environmental reasons it was not suitable.

I would be very unhappy for a woman like Miss Plews, having to live in 42 Iverson Road because of the noise, traffic, heavy lorries, proximity of railway lines, general roughness of the area and of the inhabitants. (at 640)

The Court of Appeal seems to have blurred the distinction between an objective assessment of the environment of the two premises and the tenant's own personal interests. There is nothing wrong under paragraph 3 in looking at the neighbourhood of the two properties, but *Siddiqui v Rashid*, [1980] 3 All ER 184, held that a loss of culture could not be taken into account. Further, though, the Court of Appeal in *Dawncar Investments, op. cit.*, did make it clear that whether the claim for suitability is based on subparagraph (a) or (b), environmental issues were of equal relevance—(b) might expressly refer to character, but the judge had to assess the overall reasonableness of the eviction under (a), including environmental factors.

As well as the Land Compensation Act 1973, described below, the Housing Act 1988, s 11(1) provides for compensation to be paid to the tenant by the landlord.

s 11(1)   Where a court makes an order for the possession of a dwelling-house let on an assured tenancy on Ground 6 or Ground 9 in Schedule 2 to this Act (but not on any other ground), the landlord shall pay the tenant a sum equal to the reasonable expenses likely to be incurred by the tenant in removing from the dwelling-house.

Since the landlord is forcing the move under both Grounds 6 (demolition, *etc.*, see 11.4.10 below) and 9, it seems only fair that he should meet the reasonable expenses.

In the commercial sector, the landlord can oppose the grant of a new tenancy of the existing premises by offering the tenant SAA.

Landlord and Tenant Act 1954

s 30(1) The grounds on which a landlord may oppose an application under sub-section (1) of section twenty-four of this Act are such of the following grounds, that is to say:

. . .

(d) that the landlord has offered and is willing to provide or secure the provision of alternative accommodation for the tenant, that the terms on which the alternative accommodation is available are reasonable having regard to the terms of the current tenancy and to all other relevant circumstances, and that the accommodation and the time at which it will be available are suitable for the tenant's requirements (including the requirement to preserve goodwill) having regard to the nature and class of his business and to the situation and extent of, and facilities afforded by, the holding.

Such SAA may simply amount to a smaller part of the original premises—*Lawrence v Carter* (1956) 167 EG 222. It is very similar in terminology to the Rent Act 1977 and the Housing Act 1988, but the residential cases are unlikely to be of much assistance—suitability as a home is a very different concept from suitability for a business (see Woodfall, *Landlord and Tenant*, vol 2, at para 22.103). The only additional feature of note is that the preservation of the goodwill of the present business must be taken into account in assessing the suitability of the new premises. In most cases, therefore, the new accommodation should be close to the old premises and should try to maintain the situation, extent of, and facilities afforded by those original premises. In this sector, however, the tenant is not entitled to any expenses or compensation when the failure to renew is for Ground (d). It might be arguable that the expenses of moving would be 'other relevant circumstances' to be taken into account in considering whether the alternative accommodation is suitable, but there are no cases on this point. The explanation as to why compensation is not available in this instance but is for non-renewal on some other grounds seems to be that compensation should not be given where there is tenant default—and failure to take up other accommodation is associated with fault (see *Government Policy on Leasehold Property in England and Wales*, Cmd 8713, 1953, para 49). Unless relocation and removal expenses are taken account of in determining whether the alternative accommodation is suitable then it seems wrong to deny compensation and against the spirit of the legislation.

11.4.9 Over- and Undercrowding

Whilst SAA is a separate ground in the private residential and commercial sectors, overcrowding and the so-called undercrowding are peculiar to the local authority sector. However, the mixed nature of housing associations, being both private and public, led the National Federation of Housing Associations to include in its model tenancy agreement, *op. cit.*, a similar express clause on undercrowding. Further, given that landlords in the private sector can evict assured tenants for breach of a term of the tenancy, Clause 3(13) of the National Federation of Housing Associations' model tenancy agreement stipulates the maximum number of people who can reside at the premises. Thus, in effect, local authority and housing association landlords can evict for over- and undercrowding.

Overcrowding is dealt with in Ground 9 of the 1985 Act. It represents the first of the true housing management grounds for eviction although Ground 8 which allows for eviction from temporary housing provided to the tenant whilst his original premises are repaired or improved must also be included in this group.

Housing Act 1985, Sch 2
Ground 9 [subject to SAA]
The dwelling-house is overcrowded, within the meaning of Part X, in such circumstances as to render the occupier guilty of an offence.

Reasonableness is not an issue under Ground 9. The only issue is whether there is, or will be, suitable alternative accommodation available for the tenant at the termination of the present lease. Local authorities can thus obtain an order for eviction of a tenant from overcrowded premises as soon as SAA is available. In deciding what is suitable, regard should be had to Part IV, Sch 2 Housing Act 1985.

para 3 Where possession of a dwelling-house is sought on ground 9 (overcrowding such as to render occupier guilty of offence), other accommodation may be reasonably suitable to the needs of the tenant and his family notwithstanding that the permitted number of persons for that accommodation, as defined in section 326(3) (overcrowding: the space standard), is less than the number of persons living in the dwelling-house of which possession is sought.

The underlying purpose of paragraph 3 is to make sure that the new accommodation does not have to accommodate any lodgers or sub-tenants (Housing Act 1985, ss 93 and 94) from the original dwelling. The local authority only has to provide SAA for the tenant and his family, as defined in s 113.

Undercrowding is dealt with in Ground 16 of the 1985 Act. Not only must there be SAA as for Ground 9, but it must be reasonable to evict as well. There are a myriad of internal conditions placed on the exercise of Ground 16, too.

Ground 16 [subject to reasonableness and SAA]
The accommodation afforded by the dwelling-house is more extensive than is reasonably required by the tenant and–
(a) the tenancy vested in the tenant by virtue of section 89 (succession to periodic tenancy), the tenant being qualified to succeed by virtue of section 87(b) (members of family other than spouse), and
(b) notice of the proceedings for possession was served under section 83 more than six months but less than twelve months after the date of the previous tenant's death.
The matters to be taken into account by the court in determining whether it is reasonable to make an order on this ground include–
(a) the age of the tenant,
(b) the period during which the tenant has occupied the dwelling-house as his only or principal home, and
(c) any financial or other support given by the tenant to the previous tenant.

This Ground can not be used against the original tenant, nor against the spouse of the original tenant who statutorily succeeded to the secure tenancy on the spouse's death (cf. Moore, *The Taxman Wants Your Bedroom*, ROOF, November/December 1994, p 12). Local authorities and increasingly housing associations, too, have waiting lists designed to match the prospective tenant to the appropriate property. The shortage of housing means that it is inefficient to leave a large family property under-occupied. Ground 16 allows the local authority to move the secure tenant into SAA where it is reasonable to do so and then allocate the property to an applicant needing a property of that size. Nevertheless, efficient use of property is given a lower priority than protecting the original tenant's interest in his home and the emotional attachment of the spouse on that tenant's death. Even members of the family might not be evicted where their age, length of residence or support to the deceased original tenant would render it unreasonable; and the local authority only has a limited period of time during which it can serve the s 83 notice. To that extent, Ground 16 recognizes that the lease provides more than merely four walls and a roof and that the tenant might have a psychological attachment to the dwelling which overrides the need for efficient allocation procedures.

11.4.10 Demolition, Reconstruction and Works and the Tenancy

All three pieces of legislation provide for eviction where the landlord intends to demolish or carry out works on the premises.

Housing Act 1985, Sch 2 Part II
Ground 10 [subject to SAA]
The landlord intends, within a reasonable time of obtaining possession of the dwelling-house–

(a) to demolish or reconstruct the building or part of the building comprising the dwelling-house, or

(b) to carry out work on that building or on land let together with, and thus treated as part of, the dwelling-house,

and cannot reasonably do so without obtaining possession of the dwelling-house.

Ground 10A [subject to SAA]

The dwelling-house is in an area which is the subject of a redevelopment scheme approved by the Secretary of State or the Corporation in accordance with Part V of this Schedule and the landlord intends within a reasonable time of obtaining possession to dispose of the dwelling-house in accordance with the scheme.

or

Part of the dwelling-house is in such an area and the landlord intends within a reasonable time of obtaining possession to dispose of that part in accordance with the scheme and for that purpose reasonably requires possession of the dwelling-house.

Housing Act 1988, Sch 2 Part I

Ground 6 [mandatory]

The landlord who is seeking possession or, if that landlord is a registered housing association or charitable housing trust, a superior landlord intends to demolish or reconstruct the whole or a substantial part of the dwelling-house or to carry out substantial works on the dwelling-house or any part thereof or any building of which it forms part and the following conditions are fulfilled–

(a) the intended work cannot reasonably be carried out without the tenant giving up possession of the dwelling-house because–

  (i) the tenant is not willing to agree to such a variation of the terms of the tenancy as would give such access and other facilities as would permit the intended work to be carried out, or

 (ii) the nature of the intended work is such that no such variation is practicable, or

(iii) the tenant is not willing to accept an assured tenancy of such part only of the dwelling-house (in this sub-paragraph referred to as 'the reduced part') as would leave in the possession of his landlord so much of the dwelling-house as would be reasonable to enable the intended work to be carried out and, where appropriate, as would give such access and other facilities over the reduced part as would permit the intended work to be carried out, or

 (iv) the nature of the intended work is such that such a tenancy is not practicable; and

(b) either the landlord seeking possession acquired his interest in the dwelling-house before the grant of the tenancy or that interest was in existence at the time of that grant and neither that landlord (or, in the case of joint landlords, any of them) nor any other person who, alone or jointly with others, has acquired that interest since that time acquired it for money or money's worth; and

(c) the assured tenancy on which the dwelling-house is let did not come into being by virtue of any provision of Schedule 1 to the Rent Act 1977, as amended by Part I of Schedule 4 to this Act or, as the case may be, section 4 of the Rent (Agriculture) Act 1976, as amended by Part II of that Schedule.

For the purposes of this ground, if, immediately before the grant of the tenancy, the tenant to whom it was granted or, if it was granted to joint tenants, any of them was the tenant or one of the joint tenants of the dwelling-house concerned under an earlier assured tenancy or, as the case may be, under a tenancy to which Schedule 10 to the Local Government and Housing Act 1989 applied, any reference in paragraph (b) above to the grant of the tenancy is a reference to the grant of that earlier assured tenancy or, as the case may be, to the grant of the tenancy to which the said Schedule 10 applied.

For the purposes of this ground 'registered housing association' has the same meaning as in the Housing Associations Act 1985 and 'charitable housing trust' means a housing trust, within the meaning of that Act, which is a charity, within the meaning of the Charities Act 1993.

For the purposes of this ground, every acquisition under Part IV of this Act shall be taken to be an acquisition for money or money's worth; and in any case where–

(i) the tenancy (in this paragraph referred to as 'the current tenancy') was granted to a person (alone or jointly with others) who, immediately before it was granted, was a tenant under a tenancy of a different dwelling-house (in this paragraph referred to as 'the earlier tenancy'), and

(ii) the landlord under the current tenancy is the person who, immediately before that tenancy was granted, was the landlord under the earlier tenancy, and

(iii) the condition in paragraph (b) above could not have been fulfilled with respect to the earlier tenancy by virtue of an acquisition under Part IV of this Act (including one taken to be such an acquisition by virtue of the previous operation of this paragraph),

the acquisition of the landlord's interest under the current tenancy shall be taken to have been under that Part and the landlord shall be taken to have acquired that interest after the grant of the current tenancy.

Landlord and Tenant Act 1954

s 30(1) The grounds on which a landlord may oppose an application under subsection (1) of section twenty-four of this Act are such of the following grounds . . . , that is to say:

. . .

(f) that on the termination of the current tenancy the landlord intends to demolish or reconstruct the premises comprised in the holding or a substantial part of those premises or to carry out substantial work of construction on the holding or part thereof and that he could not reasonably do so without obtaining possession of the holding

It should also be noted that under the National Federation of Housing Associations model tenancy agreement, *op. cit.*, housing associations are permitted to evict the tenant where the landlord makes available SAA so that the premises can be obtained with vacant possession in order for the works to be carried out.

Grounds 10 and 10A of the 1985 Act are subject to the requirement that the local authority also makes available SAA. Ground 10 is very similar to the Landlord and Tenant Act 1954, s 30. Although Ground 10 is in the second group of Sch 2 Grounds which are subject only to the SAA requirement, it expressly imposes a reasonableness test, although from the landlord's perspective. Nevertheless, the tenant's interests must be one of the factors thrown in to the balance. As such, whereas the character of the tenant's original property is irrelevant to any assessment of suitability under the Housing Act 1985, a court should have regard to such issues under this requirement that eviction should only take place if the works can only reasonably be effected with vacant possession—self-evidently, demolition of the whole can only be reasonably carried out once the tenant has been evicted.

Where the local authority needs to demolish or carry out works on a property, though, it may evict the tenant under Ground 10 given that at the date of the hearing it can show that it has an intention to demolish or carry out the specified works within a reasonable time of obtaining possession and that it could not reasonably demolish or carry out the works without obtaining possession— *Wansbeck DC v Morley,* (1988), 20 HLR 247 at 255–7. Ground 10A is appropriate where the local authority are going to sell the dwelling-house to a private firm for the latter to demolish or carry out the works. This redevelopment scheme must be approved by the Secretary of State in accordance with Sch 2, Part V Housing Act 1985. Part V requires that the developer consult with affected secure tenants and take into account their views before applying to the Secretary of State for approval. The Secretary of State must have regard to the following matters:

Housing Act 1985, Sch 2 Part V
para 3(1) In considering whether to give his approval to a scheme or variation the Secretary of State shall take into account, in particular—
   (a) the effect of the scheme on the extent and character of housing accommodation in the neighbourhood,
   (b) over what period of time it is proposed that the disposal and redevelopment will take place in accordance with the scheme, and
   (c) to what extent the scheme includes provision for housing provided under the scheme to be sold or let to existing tenants or persons nominated by the landlord;
   and he shall take into account any representations made to him and, so far as they are brought to his notice, any representations made to the landlord.
   (2) The landlord shall give to the Secretary of State such information as to the representations made to it, and other relevant matters, as the Secretary of State may require.

If a tenant is evicted under Ground 10 or 10A, then he is entitled to compensation under the Land Compensation Act 1973, s 29, as amended, for loss of his home. Even if the tenant leaves voluntarily in circumstances where Grounds 10 or 10A might apply, then the local authority has a discretion as to whether to grant a compensation payment—1973 Act, s 32(7B). However, he may not be entitled to a disturbance payment under the 1973 Act, s 37, because the tenant may not be treated as having any interest in the land which the landlord would acquire on the termination of the tenancy—*Newey v Liverpool CC* (1982) 14 HLR 73; *cf. R v Islington LBC ex parte Knight* [1984] 1 All ER 154; and *Bulgar v Knowsley BC* Legal Action, June 1989, at p 25.

Schedule 2, Ground 6 is one of the mandatory grounds under 1988 Act. Given that the 'landlord seeking possession' complies with s 8, the court cannot refuse possession if Ground 6 is made out. Ground 6 is a new provision, not found in the 1977 Act. Although much longer than either the 1985 or 1954 Act, its purpose is still to allow a landlord to evict a tenant where vacant possession is necessary so that works may be carried out on the dwelling house or that it might be demolished. The National Federation of Housing Associations' model tenancy agreement does not list Ground 6 in Clause 4 as one of the grounds housing associations might use to evict a tenant. However, Clause 4(2)(vi)(a) states that a housing association landlord can evict under Ground 9 (suitable alternative accommodation) if the reason is so that works might be performed on the dwelling house. The paragraph (b) purchaser's exception has no application to a landlord who acquired the reversion either by will or intestacy or where no consideration passed. However, a landlord who acquired the dwelling houses under the Tenants' Choice provisions of Part IV, Housing Act 1988, is always subject to the paragraph (b) purchaser's exception. The exception for purchasers is in part justified on the basis that the tenant's right was pre-existing, but that would not explain why a landlord who inherits the property or receives it without giving consideration should not also be bound. It is possible that Ground 6 represents an attempt to prevent asset stripping.

Under general 1988 Act rules, Ground 6 can only be used against a periodic tenant—s 7(6). The assured fixed-term tenant can remain in the property until the expiry date in the lease passes. As mentioned earlier, a landlord forcing a tenant to move under Ground 6 may have to pay the tenant's expenses.

Commercial landlords, like their residential counterparts, need to be able to manage the holding. In some cases this will entail demolition or major works being carried out. The forerunner of the 1985 and 1988 Acts' provisions for residential sector lettings is to be found in the Landlord and Tenant Act 1954, s 30(1)(f). Some of the common terms have received substantial comment and the courts in residential cases will, in all likelihood, follow such analyses—see, for example, *Cerex Jewels Ltd v Peachey Property Corporation Ltd* (1986) 279 EG 971. For instance, the House of Lords in *Betty's Cafés Ltd v Phillips Furnishings Stores*

Ltd [1959] AC 20, approved the view that intention connoted not only a desire that the demolition or works would be effected, but also that there was a reasonable prospect of them actually being carried out. Thus, it will be necessary to show that adequate funds are available for the enterprise (*DAF Motoring Centre (Gosport) Ltd v Hatfield and Wheeler Ltd* (1982) 263 EG 976) and that where planning permission is required, the landlord ought to have obtained it by the date of the hearing, although his case can succeed without it if it is likely to be granted. Such an intention can be proven if the landlord shows that he intends to re-let the premises on a building lease—*Reohorn v Barry Corporation* [1956] 2 All ER 742, *Spook Erection Ltd v British Railways Board* [1989] QB 300; *cf.* Housing Act 1985, Ground 10A. However, the landlord's motive for carrying out the demolition, reconstruction or works of construction is irrelevant—*Turner v Wandsworth LBC* [1994] EGCS 30. In recognition of the loss of goodwill and expense of moving the tenant is entitled to flat-rate compensation geared to the rateable value of the premises if the lease is not renewed (Landlord and Tenant Act 1954, s 37). Compensation is also available for other heads of non-renewal not based on tenant fault: (e) uneconomic subletting and (g) own occupation.

All three statutes talk of demolishing or reconstructing or carrying out works on the whole or part of the building. In the commercial sector the terms have been held to be disjunctive—*Turner v Wandsworth LBC, op. cit.* Demolition speaks for itself, but reconstruction implies, in some sense, rebuilding, possibly after a partial demolition: construction means that something new is being built for the first time or something is being added on to a pre-existing structure—*Cook v Mott* (1961) 178 EG 637. Mere refurbishment may not suffice, therefore. Moreover, the demolition, reconstruction or works must, under the 1954 Act, be carried out on the holding itself. Ross, *op. cit.*, at p 332 n1, argues that an intention to perform works on common parts of the building not comprised in the demise would not permit non-renewal under s 30(1)(f). The 1985 Act also speaks of works being carried out on the building or part thereof comprising the dwelling house. The 1988 Act avoids this problem by providing that the works need only be 'on the dwelling-house or any part thereof or any building of which it forms part'. In the commercial sector, unless the lease demises the roof or other common parts to the tenant, then works being carried out thereon will not justify non-renewal under s 30(1)(f) because they will not be being performed on the holding. Further, non-renewal of the lease is only justified where the works cannot reasonably be carried out whilst the tenant is in possession. Under s 31A, inserted by the Law of Property Act 1969, s 7, a tenant can frustrate the landlord's aim of not renewing the lease by agreeing to give the landlord access or by using only a part of the premises during the works. Section 31A only applies where the landlord makes out his case under s 30(1)(f).

Demolition, reconstruction and works of construction are necessary to preserve the stock of housing and business premises. Where necessary, therefore, the landlord ought to be able to evict in order to carry out the task. Case law on this topic should be readily interchangeable between the various sectors.

11.4.11 Allocation and Management of Special Needs Housing

For both local authorities and housing associations, the dearth of specialised housing for people with special needs means that whatever exists cannot be wasted. Therefore, the Housing Act 1985, Sch 2 and the National Federation of Housing Associations' Model Tenancy Agreement, *op. cit.*, both provide grounds to evict tenants for the better use of such housing by people with special needs. Under the 1985 Act, these Grounds fall in the third group where the local authority landlord has to prove, as well as the actual ground, that the eviction would be reasonable and that there is SAA available for the tenant.

Ground 13 [subject to reasonableness and SAA]
The dwelling-house has features which are substantially different from those of ordinary dwelling-houses and which are designed to make it suitable for occupation by a physically disabled person who requires accommodation of a kind provided by the dwelling-house and–
(a) there is no longer such a person residing in the dwelling-house, and
(b) the landlord requires it for occupation (whether alone or with members of his family) by such a person.

Ground 15 [subject to reasonableness and SAA]
The dwelling-house is one of a group of dwelling-houses which it is the practice of the landlord to let for occupation by persons with special needs and–
(a) a social service or special facility is provided in close proximity to the group of dwelling-houses in order to assist persons with those special needs,
(b) there is no longer a person with those special needs residing in the dwelling-house, and
(c) the landlord requires the dwelling-house for occupation (whether alone or with members of his family) by a person who has those special needs.

Ground 13 relates specifically to housing for physically disabled people. The differences between this dwelling house and the general local authority housing have to be substantial and they have to have been designed for their purpose. A feature which would prove to be useful but which was not 'designed', would not meet this test. Ground 15 is aimed at sheltered accommodation with a warden or other form of social service. If there is no longer a person in the dwelling house with those special needs and, as with Ground 13, there is a person with those needs requiring the premises, the local authority can evict the present incumbent.

Housing associations which have let the dwelling house on an assured tenancy can at law evict for any of the grounds in the Housing Act 1988, Sch 2.

However, the National Federation of Housing Associations' Model Tenancy Agreement restricts housing associations to using the statutory grounds in the circumstances set out in clause 4(2). One such circumstance mirrors Grounds 13 and 15 of the 1985 Act.

Clause 4(2)(vi) SAA is available to the Tenant [in accordance with Ground 9 of the 1988 Act], provided that in addition the Association can show:
...
(b) that the Premises are needed for someone who requires the special amenities or services provided and the Tenant no longer does so . . .

The clause is narrower in its scope than Ground 14 Housing Act 1985. Ground 14 of the 1985 Act still applies to all housing association tenancies granted before the coming in to force of the Housing Act 1988.

Housing Act 1985, **Sch 2 Ground 14**
The landlord is a housing association or housing trust which lets dwelling-houses only for occupation (whether alone or with others) by persons whose circumstances (other than merely financial circumstances) make it especially difficult for them to satisfy their need for housing, and–
(a) either there is no longer such a person residing in the dwelling-house or the tenant has received from a local housing authority an offer of accommodation in premises which are to be let as a separate dwelling under a secure tenancy,
and
(b) the landlord requires the dwelling-house for occupation (whether alone or with members of his family) by such a person.

It should also be remembered that charitable housing associations have a separate ground for possession under the 1985 Act which might be useful in these circumstances, as long as the tenancy was granted before the 1988 Act came in to force

Ground 11
The landlord is a charity and the tenant's continued occupation of the dwelling-house would conflict with the objects of the charity.

With housing associations now granting assured tenancies, there is a need for a special statutory provision to be inserted in the 1988 Act so as to allow them to manage their special needs properties. As it is, tenants and the housing association landlord have to rely on the non-statutory model tenancy agreement. The change of status of housing association lets from public to private did not alter the housing association landlord's management needs with respect to their special needs properties and a Housing Act 1985, Ground 14 equivalent should be implemented for assured housing association tenants.

11.4.12 The Landlord's Own Need to Occupy the Property

Local authorities and housing associations have no need to occupy for themselves the property they have let, but a private or commercial landlord may well need to move in to the demised premises. Security of tenure laws in the United States which prevented re-occupation of the property by the landlord have been deemed unconstitutional—see generally, Note, *The Constitutionality of Rent Control Restrictions on Property Owners' Dominion Interests, op. cit.*

Although the Housing Act 1988 recognises the landlord's priority, the rules that need to be satisfied if the landlord is to make this priority effective are complex. Furthermore, in some circumstances they are wider than a mere ground for re-occupation.

Ground 1 [mandatory]
Not later than the beginning of the tenancy the landlord gave notice in writing to the tenant that possession might be recovered on this ground or the court is of the opinion that it is just and equitable to dispense with the requirement of notice and (in either case)–
(a) at some time before the beginning of the tenancy, the landlord who is seeking possession or, in the case of joint landlords seeking possession, at least one of them occupied the dwelling-house as his only or principal home; or
(b) the landlord who is seeking possession or, in the case of joint landlords seeking possession, at least one of them requires the dwelling-house as his or his spouse's only or principal home and neither the landlord (or, in the case of joint landlords, any one of them) nor any other person who, as landlord, derived title under the landlord who gave the notice mentioned above acquired the reversion on the tenancy for money or money's worth.

Ground 1 is a mandatory ground, so the court must grant possession if the landlord or one of the joint landlords has fulfilled all the conditions. Notice of possible Ground 1 repossession must have been given by a landlord in writing, unless the court feels it just and equitable to dispense with notice. Given proper notice was given, then either the landlord must have occupied the premises as his principal or only home at some time before the tenancy was granted or the landlord or his successor landlord, who received the property without giving money or money's worth, needs the property for himself or his spouse. Paragraph (a) might include the landlord who many years ago squatted in the premises; it would definitely include the landlord who occupied the premises under a licence many years ago. Moreover, paragraph (a) would allow the landlord who had previously been in occupation of the premises as his only or principal home to evict a tenant in order to sell the property with vacant possession (*cf. Lipton v Whitworth* (1994) 26 HLR 293). The only justification for supporting the landlord's economic interests over the tenant's right to a home is that the landlord must have warned the tenant of the possibility of the tenant's eviction under Ground 1 when he gave the written notice. Paragraph (b) is more straightforward: the landlord needs the property as a principal or only home for himself or his spouse—*Lohen v Hilton* [1994] EGCS 83. There is no need for prior occupation, so it would allow for the situation where the landlord had bought the premises as a retirement home for the future—*viz.* Cases 11 and 12 of the Rent Act 1977. Where Ground 1 is deficient, according to Hickman, *op. cit.*, is that it does not meet the case of the voluntary successor-in-title who wishes to sell the property with vacant possession. Only the landlord who is seeking possession who previously occupied the premises as his only or principal home can evict the tenant in order to sell; other landlords have to need the premises as their principal or only home. Hickman fails to consider the case of the spouse or child of the landlord who inherits the property and becomes landlord—such a spouse or child will, in all likelihood, have occupied the premises as his principal or only home some time previously. The question is whether priority should be given to the successor-in-title over the tenant who is using the property as a home, not just to make a profit.

In the commercial sector, non-renewal can be opposed under s 30(1)(g).

Landlord and Tenant Act 1954

s 30(1) The grounds on which a landlord may oppose an application under subsection (1) of section twenty-four of this Act are such of the following grounds . . . , that is to say:

. . .

(g) subject as hereinafter provided, that on the termination of the current tenancy the landlord intends to occupy the holding for the purposes, or partly for the purposes, of a business to be carried on by him therein, or as his residence.

(2) The landlord shall not be entitled to oppose an application on the ground specified in paragraph (g) of the last foregoing subsection if the interest of the landlord, or an interest which has merged in that interest and but for the merger would be the interest of the landlord, was purchased or created after the beginning of the period of five years which ends with the termination of the current tenancy, and at all times since the purchase or creation thereof the holding has been comprised in a tenancy or successive tenancies of the description specified in subsection (1) of section twenty-three of this Act.

(3) Where the landlord has a controlling interest in a company any business to be carried on by the company shall be treated for the purposes of subsection (1)(g) of this section as a business to be carried on by him.

For the purposes of this subsection, a person has a controlling interest in a company if and only if either–

(a) he is a member of it and able, without the consent of any other person, to appoint or remove the holders of at least a majority of the directorships; or

(b) he holds more than one-half of its equity share capital, there being disregarded any shares held by him in a fiduciary capacity or as nominee for another person;

and in this subsection 'company' and 'share' have the meanings assigned to them by section 455(1) of the Companies Act 1948 and 'equity share capital' the meaning assigned to it by section 154(5) of that Act.

Paragraph (g) requires that the landlord has an intention to occupy the premises to carry on a business or to reside there. Intention here bears the same meaning as under paragraph (f), that is, that there is not only a desire to occupy, but that there is a reasonable likelihood that it will come to fruition in the form of the landlord carrying on a business or, in the alternative, residing there. Letting a manager run the business is sufficient—*Skeet v Powell-Sneddon* [1988] 2 EGLR 112. Under subsection (3), a business carried on by a company in which the landlord has a controlling interest shall be enough for subsection 1(g). By s 42(3), where the landlord is member of a group of companies, intended occupation by any other member of that group will also satisfy (g). The section would not apply, however. where the landlord is a company and the business is to be carried on by the individual who controls it, or who controls another company in the group. The Law Commission have recommended that it should apply in this situation (Law Commission, *Business Tenancies: A Periodic Review of the Landlord and Tenant Act 1954 Pt II*, 1992, Law Com. No. 208, at para 2.10). It seems, furthermore, that following *Willis v Association of the Universities of the British Commonwealth* [1965] 1 QB 140, the landlord must intend to occupy for more than a *de minimis* period, but six months might suffice. Subsection (2) prevents the landlord from using paragraph (g) to oppose renewal where his interest was created or was purchased by him within the five years preceding the termination of the current business tenancy—*Artemiou v Procopiou* [1966] 1 QB 878. The Law Commission have recommended that this limitation also apply to cases in which a landlord seeks possession in order that a company in which he has a controlling interest may occupy the premises (*op. cit.*, para 2.11). Thus, the landlord who purchases the reversion within the last five years of the tenancy cannot justify non-renewal on the basis that he wishes to occupy the premises to carry on his own business. This provision may be unduly restrictive for the good of business. Where there is a takeover of a business, the purchaser may intend to expand the business in to the premises let, but would not be able to oppose renewal under s 30(2). Compensation for disturbance is available to a commercial tenant (Landlord and Tenant Act 1954, s 37) but there is no right to compensation or expenses for the residential tenant (in this instance, the residential tenant will have had prior notice of the risk of losing possession).

11.4.13 Death of the Tenant

Under the Housing Act 1988, s 17, discussed in ch 9.9, a periodic tenancy can be passed on the assured tenant's death by statute to the widow/widower or to a person who lived with the assured tenant as husband and wife. If there is no such person, then it may devolve by will or intestacy. However, in such a case, the mandatory Ground 7 is available to the landlord.

Housing Act 1988, Sch 2
Ground 7 [mandatory]
The tenancy is a periodic tenancy (including a statutory periodic tenancy) which has devolved under the will or intestacy of the former tenant and the proceedings for the recovery of possession are begun not later than twelve months after the death of the former tenant or, if the court so directs, after the date on which, in the opinion of the court, the landlord or, in the case of joint landlords, any one of them became aware of the former tenant's death.

For the purposes of this ground, the acceptance by the landlord of rent from a new tenant after the death of the former tenant shall not be regarded as creating a new periodic tenancy, unless the landlord agrees in writing to a change (as compared with the tenancy before the death) in the amount of the rent, the period of the tenancy, the premises which are let or any other term of the tenancy.

The special rule about acceptance of rent from the inheriting tenant is to prevent any implied grant of tenancy unless the landlord 'agrees in writing to a change (as compared with the tenancy before the death) in the amount of the rent, the period of the tenancy, the premises which are let or any other term of the tenancy'.

11.4.14 Winter Lets

Housing Act 1988, Sch 2
Ground 3 [mandatory]
The tenancy is a fixed term tenancy for a term not exceeding eight months and—
(a) not later than the beginning of the tenancy the landlord gave notice in writing to the tenant that possession might be recovered on this ground; and
(b) at some time within the period of twelve months ending with the beginning of the tenancy, the dwelling-house was occupied under a right to occupy it for a holiday.

Private sector residential landlords of properties in holiday resorts need to be able to let the premises out during the winter but then be secure in the knowledge that the tenant can be evicted before the lucrative holiday season starts. The justification for mandatory eviction to further landlords economic interests is that the tenant took on the premises knowing his position due to the notice in writing.

11.4.15 Vacation Lets of Student Accommodation

Housing Act 1988, Sch 2

Ground 4 [mandatory]

The tenancy is a fixed term tenancy for a term not exceeding twelve months and—

(a) not later than the beginning of the tenancy the landlord gave notice in writing to the tenant that possession might be recovered on this ground; and

(b) at some time within the period of twelve months ending with the beginning of the tenancy, the dwelling-house was let on a tenancy falling within paragraph 8 of Schedule 1 to this Act.

This ground allows private sector residential landlords to let out on a short term accommodation normally let to students. Thus, during the summer vacation a university might let out one of its properties giving notice that it might be repossessed under this ground.

11.4.16 Uneconomic Subletting

Whereas an argument can be made out that the landlord's economic interests should not take priority over the tenant's interest in the premises as a home in the residential sector, such arguments are not as strong where the tenant merely uses the property to carry on a business in the commercial sector. Thus, the Landlord and Tenant Act 1954, s 30(1)(e) allows for non-renewal in limited circumstances where the landlord could make greater profits.

s 30(1) The grounds on which a landlord may oppose an application under subsection (1) of section twenty-four of this Act are such of the following grounds . . ., that is to say:

. . .

(e) where the current tenancy was created by the sub-letting of part only of the property comprised in a superior tenancy and the landlord is the owner of an interest in reversion expectant on the termination of that superior tenancy, that the aggregate of the rents reasonably obtainable on separate lettings of the holding and the remainder of that property would be substantially less than the rent reasonably obtainable on a letting of that property as a whole, that on the termination of the current tenancy the landlord requires possession of the holding for the purpose of letting or otherwise disposing of the said property as a whole, and that in view thereof the tenant ought not to be granted a new tenancy;

The provision is very narrowly drafted according to Ross, *op. cit.*, pp 328–9. Tromans, *Commercial Leases*, 1987, pp 181–2, claims it is a little used ground. It allows a superior landlord, at the discretion of the court, to refuse renewal of a lease of part of the holding to a sub-tenant. However, the superior landlord has to prove that the rental value of the separate sub-leases is less than the return available if the property was let as a whole and it is only the return on rent, and no other matter under the lease, that is relevant. Nevertheless, if the superior landlord can prove this ground, then there is nothing to stop him selling the property rather than re-letting it.

11.4.17 Assured Shorthold Tenancies

The grounds discussed so far apply either to commercial tenancies within the Landlord and Tenant Act 1954, secure tenants under the Housing Act 1985 or assured tenants under the Housing Act 1988. Assured shorthold tenants under the 1988 Act have practically no rights at all by comparison. In 1990, about 30 per cent of all the tenancies under the 1988 Act were assured shortholds (Jew, *op. cit.*, p 78); in 1992, 70 per cent of all new lettings managed by members of the Association of Residential Letting Agents were assured shortholds (Joseph Rowntree Foundation, Housing Research Findings No. 90, May 1993).

If the lease is a properly drafted assured shorthold tenancy under the Housing Act 1988, ss 20 and 21, then, as well as the grounds listed above that apply to assured tenancies, the landlord can evict once the initial fixed-term lease of at least six months has terminated as long as he has given two months' notice that he requires possession. If, however, the assured shorthold is not in the prescribed form, then the landlord loses all the benefits of ss 20 and 21—*Panyai & Pyrkos v Roberts* (1993) 25 HLR 421; see also, Campbell, *All's Well that Ends Well*, ROOF, September/October 1994, p 15.

s 21(1) Without prejudice to any right of the landlord under an assured shorthold tenancy to recover possession of the dwelling-house let on the tenancy in accordance with Chapter I above, on or after the coming to an end of an assured shorthold tenancy which was a fixed term tenancy, a court shall make an order for possession of the dwelling-house if it is satisfied–

    (a) that the assured shorthold tenancy has come to an end and no further assured tenancy (whether shorthold or not) is for the time being in existence, other than an assured shorthold periodic tenancy (whether statutory or not), and

    (b) the landlord or, in the case of joint landlords, at least one of them has given to the tenant not less than two months' notice stating that he requires possession of the dwelling-house.

  (2) A notice under paragraph (b) of subsection (1) above may be given before or on the day on which the tenancy comes to an end; and that subsection shall have effect notwithstanding that on the coming to an end of the fixed term tenancy a statutory periodic tenancy arises.

(3) Where a court makes an order for possession of a dwelling-house by virtue of subsection (1) above, any statutory periodic tenancy which has arisen on the coming to an end of the assured shorthold tenancy shall end (without further notice and regardless of the period) on the day on which the order takes effect.

(4) Without prejudice to any such right as is referred to in subsection (1) above, a court shall make an order for possession of a dwelling-house let on an assured shorthold tenancy which is a periodic tenancy if the court is satisfied—

(a) that the landlord or, in the case of joint landlords, at least one of them has given to the tenant a notice stating that, after a date specified in the notice, being the last day of a period of the tenancy and not earlier than two months after the date the notice was given, possession of the dwelling-house is required by virtue of this section; and

(b) that the date specified in the notice under paragraph (a) above is not earlier than the earliest day on which, apart from section 5(1) above, the tenancy could be brought to an end by a notice to quit given by the landlord on the same date as the notice under paragraph (a) above.

The two months' notice can be given before the expiry of the assured shorthold. The court must grant possession if the notice has been properly given; there is no prescribed form under s 21 and *Panyai & Pyrkos v Roberts, op. cit.*, held that the s 8 form used for assured tenancies should not be foisted on to s 21. Given the ease with which a landlord can evict an assured shorthold tenant, it is likely that many landlords will opt for this form of lease if ease of repossession is one of their main priorities.

11.4.18 Summary

The various sources of law that deal with eviction in the different sectors have many similarities. The reason is that landlords in all sectors have much the same needs. They need to be able to rid themselves of bad tenants and they need to be able to manage the properties they let out. The different sorts of landlord mean that the detailed provisions to effect those needs vary. Given that security of tenure is accepted as a social good, then the types of grounds for eviction or non-renewal discussed merely balances the interests of the two parties. However, where the tenant has security of tenure, it may be that the landlord cannot evict lawfully. In some cases landlords resort to unlawful means and harassment.

11.5 UNLAWFUL EVICTION AND HARASSMENT

In the earlier part of this chapter we saw the procedure which a landlord needs to follow in order to bring a residential lease to an end (generally four weeks notice, and obtaining a court order). Where a tenancy relationship has broken down, the landlord may try to get rid of the tenant more quickly and more cheaply by, for example, removing the tenant's possessions and changing the locks.

Harassment can take a variety of forms. A research project by the Campaign for Bedsit Rights lists some:

An examination of reported cases—those which have reached the courts, and they are only a fraction of actual incidents—reveals that harassment and illegal eviction takes many forms. It can be subtle or direct, involving physical or mental violence, cruelty and intimidation. It includes such acts as;
- refusing to allow tenants access to parts of their letting such as the bathroom or kitchen or only allowing access at restricted times
- stopping tenants from having guests or visitors
- constant visits by the landlord or landlord's agent without warning and at unsociable hours
- offering the tenant money to leave
- threatening the tenant
- entering the tenant's home without permission
- allowing the property to get into such a bad state of repair that it is uncomfortable or dangerous to stay there
- starting building works and leaving them unfinished or sending in builders without notice or at unreasonable times
- removing or restricting services such as hot water or heating or failing to pay bills so that services are cut off
- harassment because of the tenant's race, sex or sexuality
- forcing the tenant to sign agreements which reduce their rights
- theft of the tenant's belongings.

(Jew, *op. cit.*, p 14)

The landlord's conduct may well constitute a civil offence under the general law, such as trespass, breach of the covenant of quiet enjoyment, and nuisance (and, in the commercial sector, the general law will still be the appropriate channel for an aggrieved tenant to follow). Until the early 1960s there was no legislation specifically directed to controlling such abuses.

In the early 1960s, the problems of harassment came to the political fore. The 1957 Rent Act had introduced a measure of decontrol, some housing being decontrolled immediately but other housing becoming decontrolled when the sitting tenant left, known as 'creeping decontrol'. One result of this was that landlords now had an incentive to get rid of sitting tenants so that they could be replaced by tenants paying a higher rent. Peter Kemp writes:

In the late 1950s and early 1960s, stories began to appear in the local press about intimidation of tenants, evictions and homelessness. What transformed the situation, however, was the storm of publicity surrounding the west London landlord Peter Rachman. His nefarious activities came to light in the wake of the Profumo scandal in 1963. It turned out that one of the call girls involved in the Profumo 'sex and security' scandal had earlier been Rachman's mistress. The addition of slum landlordism to the already potent media cocktail of sex and national security allowed the press to inject new life into the Profumo affair. (Kemp, 'The ghost of Rachman', in Grant, *Built to Last?*, 1992, ch 14, p 113).

Rachman, at the height of his involvement in housing, owned around 1,000 tenancies. He tended to buy up the short ends of long leases of houses which were occupied by controlled tenants paying low rents. Most houses were in bad repair. He would then buy out the controlled tenants and replace them with higher paying tenants, often immigrants who were finding it difficult to get homes in a time of housing shortage. The method of getting tenants to leave was not always so generous, he turned to other less-acceptable ways of persuading tenants to leave. But whilst Rachman has come 'to symbolize the unacceptable face of private landlordism in Britain' (Kemp, *op. cit.*, p 114), harassment was not a key part of his methods, his 'success' was in the policy of letting slum housing for high rents. For further information on Rachman, see Nelken, *The Limits of the Legal Process, A Study of Landlords, Law and Crime* 1983, ch 1, pp 1–5.

When the Labour government came to power in October 1964 following the Rachman affair they had a mandate to offer urgent assistance to tenants. This they did by passing the Protection from Eviction Act 1964 which made it an offence to evict a tenant without first obtaining a court order. A year later this was replaced by Part III of the Rent Act 1965, making illegal eviction and harassment into criminal offences. The current provisions are now contained in the Protection from Eviction Act 1977 (as amended by the Housing Act 1988). By s 1(2) it is an offence to unlawfully deprive a residential occupier of his occupation of premises. The kind of conduct caught by this section is excluding the occupant from the premises by changing the locks without either having served a proper notice or obtaining a court order. By s 1(3) it is an offence to harass the residential occupier by disturbing him or withdrawing services if this is likely to cause the occupant to leave or not pursue a right or remedy in respect of the premises. This would cover, for example, persistently turning off the gas and electricity supplies to the premises in the hope that this will deter the tenant from reporting the landlord to the local environmental health office or causing the tenant to leave. Further details of both offences are given below.

Although the 1960s legislation was a response—in part—to the Rachman scandal, the activities constrained by the legislation do not really affect Rachman-style landlords. These more commercial landlords seldom resort to illegal tactics. The main public outcry over Rachman related to his charging exorbitant rents for slum property—since the Housing Act 1988 with the transition to market rents this is a perfectly legitimate activity. The only landlord malpractices to be treated as criminal following the Rachman scandal were unlawful eviction and harassment and not, for example, profiteering or winkling (tempting the tenant to leave by financial inducement; see Nelken, *op. cit., passim*).

The result is that the legislation most affects small landlords. There are several reasons why this is so:

1 Small landlords are more likely to be personally involved with the tenants. Any tenancy dispute is therefore likely to affect personal relationships and lead to acrimony. The Milner-Holland Committee found that abuse was concentrated in 'stress areas' where there was overcrowding, multi-occupation and small-time landlords. The abuse took a variety of forms:

> Most of the cases seem to occur in some of the worst multi-occupied property in London and demonstrate how uncomfortable it can be to live under such conditions. Many different types of property are involved but the picture that emerges most clearly is of two rooms with a shared W.C. in an obsolete house in the County of London. Crowded into these two rooms are a young manual worker, his wife and children, paying a high rent . . .The landlord bears little resemblance to the 'big businessman' or 'slick operator' stereotypes—instead he is in a small way of business, perhaps sub-letting part of his own home and living in close proximity to the tenant, in conditions which exacerbate all disagreements. Against this background the fact that over half of the abuses took place in decontrolled property from which the tenant could, instead, legally have been given four weeks notice to quit, becomes more comprehensible. It becomes possible to envisage in these housing conditions not only an illegal eviction, the 'beating up' of a tenant, the theft of his possessions by the landlord, and the placing of dead rats or snakes in his accommodation, but also such petty and vindictive actions as turning off water, electricity or gas, changing a door lock and refusing the tenant a key, making excessive noise at night with the intention of keeping the tenant awake, refusing admittance to the tenant's visitors, and turning a tenant out of his home because he had complained to the Public Health Department about the condition of the dwelling.(Milner-Holland Report of the Committee on Housing in Greater London,1965, Cmnd 2605, App III at pp 267–8)

2 Whereas for commercial landlords the letting is important for its financial return in the form of rental income and long-term capital growth, small landlords often let for very different reasons. Paley's survey of densely populated areas in England and Wales found that only 7 per cent of resident landlords viewed their property mainly as a financial investment (or liability) whilst 92 per cent saw it mainly as a home (Paley, *Attitudes to Letting in 1976*, 1978, at p 9). In view of the different motivation for letting the property, small landlords are less likely to be tolerant of tenant misbehaviour.

3 Small landlords are less likely to pre-vet tenants thoroughly and therefore more likely to take on undesirable tenants and to encounter difficulties with rent payments. Jew, *op. cit.*, found that the most common cause of harassment and illegal eviction was rent arrears, often caused by delays in housing benefit payment or restrictions in the level of benefit. Similar findings were reached by Shelter in 1990 (Burrows, Hunter, *Forced Out, A Shelter Publication on Harassment and Illegal Eviction*, 1990).

4   Nelken's study shows that small landlords often have unrealistic expectations
    of the tenancy relationship:

> Differences amongst landlords in economic resources and political pull are
> also relevant in other respects to the way the law was framed and operated.
> Although the direct influence of large landlords on the *passage* of legislation
> was inconsiderable, these differences amongst landlords are of crucial impor-
> tance to explaining why the type of landlords drawn into the criminal process
> have so much in common with the usual criminal court fodder of the legal sys-
> tem. In Paley's sample around seventy per cent of resident and non-resident
> individual landlords in London were either skilled workers or were lower in
> the social scale and my evidence is that those landlords who felt the sharp end
> of the criminal law were the less successful members of these groups, in addi-
> tion to the fact that the large majority were from immigrant backgrounds.
> Conflicts of expectation and understanding between landlords with these
> backgrounds, their tenants and the officials responsible for enforcing the law
> were a material contribution to the likelihood of them harassing their tenants
> and help to explain why so many of these landlords in turn felt harassed by
> their tenants and by the officials who were supposed to reconcile the parties.
> (Nelkin, *op. cit.*, pp 12–13)

5   If the tenant refuses to leave, small landlords are less likely to rely on legal
    means of repossession. Jew, *op. cit.*, found that landlord ignorance of the law
    was a very significant factor in harassment cases. In addition, the legal reme-
    dies are time consuming and expensive. In *Nwokorie v Mason* (1994) 26 HLR
    60, for example, the court acknowledged that it could take up to six months to
    recover possession even though the tenant had no security (28 days notice to
    quit, a period awaiting a court hearing, and a period up to three months
    before possession is given according to the court order).

Whilst harassment is most likely to occur with small landlords, certain tenant
groups are also more vulnerable than others. A survey in 1990 found that tenants
with no security were most likely to suffer from attempts to make them leave (18
per cent of tenants in this group; Rauta and Pickering, *Private Renting in England
1990*, 1992, Table 7.12 at p 51). This is similar to the observations made by the
Milner-Holland Committee *op. cit*. Single parents were the most likely group to
suffer harassment (Rauta and Pickering, *op. cit*, Table 7.13 at p 52) but tenants on
low incomes or from black or racial minorities were also more likely to be victims
(Jew, *op. cit.*, p 91).

11.5.1 The Offences of Unlawful Eviction and Harassment

The offences of unlawful eviction and harassment are set out in the Protection
from Eviction Act 1977, s 1:

s 1(2) [the offence of unlawful eviction]: If any person unlawfully deprives the residential occupier of any premises of his occupation of the premises or any part thereof, or attempts to do so, he shall be guilty of an offence unless he proves that he believed, and had reasonable cause to believe, that the residential occupier had ceased to reside in the premises.

(3) [the offence of harassment]: If any person with intent to cause the residential occupier of any premises–

(a) to give up the occupation of the premises or any part thereof; or

(b) to refrain from exercising any right or pursuing any remedy in respect of the premises or part thereof;

does acts likely to interfere with the peace or comfort of the residential occupier or members of his household, or persistently withdraws or withholds services reasonably required for the occupation of the premises as a residence, he shall be guilty of an offence.

(3A) Subject to subsection (3B) below, the landlord of a residential occupier or an agent of the landlord shall be guilty of an offence if–

(a) he does acts likely to interfere with the peace or comfort of the residential occupier or members of his household, or

(b) he persistently withdraws or withholds services reasonably required for the occupation of the premises in question as a residence,

and (in either case) he knows, or has reasonable cause to believe, that the conduct is likely to cause the residential occupier to give up the occupation of the whole or part of the premises or to refrain from exercising any right or pursuing any remedy in respect of the whole or part of the premises.

(3B) A person shall not be guilty of an offence under subsection (3A) above if he proves that he had reasonable grounds for doing the acts or withdrawing or withholding the services in question.

(3C) In subsection (3A) above 'landlord', in relation to a residential occupier of any premises, means the person who, but for—

(a) the residential occupier's right to remain in occupation of the premises, or

(b) a restriction on the person's right to recover possession of the premises, would be entitled to occupation of the premises and any superior landlord under whom that person derives title.

Both subsections apply to protect 'residential occupiers'. This is defined in s 1(1):

s 1(1) In this section 'residential occupier', in relation to any premises, means a person occupying the premises as a residence, whether under a contract or by virtue of any enactment or rule of law giving him the right to remain in occupation or restricting the right of any other person to recover possession of the premises.

The sections therefore cover not only tenants but also licensees. It is not only the landlord himself who may be prosecuted for harassment—under subs(3A) his agent may also be guilty and under subs(3) 'any person' with intent can commit the offence. By s 1(2) it will be an offence not only to evict an occupier whose licence or tenancy is continuing but also a tenant whose tenancy has come to an end but who has not been served with any necessary court order under s 3 of the Act (see 11.2.6).

Subsections 1(3)(A–C) were added by the 1988 Housing Act and apply only to acts committed after 15 January 1989. Under subs(3) it is necessary for the prosecutor to prove that there was a specific intent to cause the occupier to leave or to refrain from exercising a right or pursuing a remedy. This intent would often be difficult to prove and the new offence in subs(3)(A-C) removes the need to prove intent. The anti-harassment provisions were strengthened by the Housing Act 1988 to meet fears that the deregulation of the private sector would lead to higher levels of harassment. Notwithstanding the removal of the need to prove intent there has been no significant change in the number of prosecutions being brought (see Jew, *op. cit.*, pp 80–4).

In order to commit the offence of harassment it is not necessary that the act complained of must also be actionable under the civil law. Thus, the offence of harassment may be committed if the landlord refuses to let the occupier have a replacement key (having lost the original) even though this is not necessarily in breach of contract (or otherwise a civil wrong): *R v Yuthiwattana* (1984) 80 Cr App R 55; *R v Burke* [1990] 2 All ER 385.

Although these subsections clearly criminalise unlawful eviction and harassment, they have not been wholly effective in either punishing offenders or sending out a message to the community that interfering with residential occupation is wrong. In some cases, few would dispute that the landlord has behaved wrongfully. In *Afzal Mohammed Madarbakus* (1992) 13 Cr.App.R.(S) 542, the landlord's son had, on separate occasions, told two tenants to leave. Both tenants claimed that they were entitled to four weeks' notice. In both cases, the son returned later with 'heavies', who physically abused the tenants and forcefully drove them from the premises. The son was sentenced to twelve months' imprisonment. In cases which do not involve physical violence, though, the conduct is less obviously wrongful. Often the tenant is not without fault—he may be in serious rent arrears, pursuing a disreputable lifestyle, or abusing the landlord's property. In some cases the landlord might have the option of lawfully terminating the tenancy, but if he does so this will be time-consuming and expensive. In other instances, it may be difficult for the landlord to prove a ground for possession against a protected tenant and then the only option is unlawful eviction or harassment. It is not always clear therefore that the landlord has greater 'moral blame' for what transpires than the tenant. In addition, tenancy disputes are often perceived as being civil matters—for resolution between the two parties and not involving a wrong against society, in many ways akin to past attitudes to domestic violence (see Jew, *op. cit.*, p 17). There is also a belief held by some that the landlord as property owner is entitled to exercise dominion over his property and to exclude undesirable occupiers. The ambiguous response to the criminality of unlawful eviction and harassment has had a marked effect upon the interpretation of the law and its enforcement.

Both subsections refer to the offences being committed only if the occupier (unlawful eviction) is deprived of his occupation (or an attempt is made to do this) or (harassment) is likely to give up occupation. It would be expected that 'occupation' would have the same meaning in the two subsections. In *R v Yuthiwattana, op. cit.*, the Court of Appeal said that for the purposes of unlawful eviction it was necessary to show 'eviction', but this might include deprivation for a period. 'Locking-out' cases—where the occupier is denied access on one or more isolated occasions and for shorter periods—are more likely to come within the definition of harassment than unlawful eviction. However, in *Schon v London Borough of Camden* (1986) 18 HLR 341, it was held that the offence of harassment was not committed when the tenant was forced out for two weeks. Hill comments that it is undesirable for different interpretations to be adopted within the same section (*Section 1 of the Protection from Eviction Act 1977: The Meaning of 'Occupation'* [1987] Conv 265) but the *Schon* case may simply reflect the court's perception of the morality of the landlord's conduct. In this case the landlord was installing a bathroom above the tenant's flat and needed to strengthen the floor of the bathroom. This could be done either with access from the tenant's flat (the landlord's preferred option) or from above. The tenant was offered alternative accommodation for the expected two-week period of the works but turned it down. The landlord went ahead and did the work from above but the ceiling of the tenant's flat collapsed. Glidewell LJ held that it had not been proved that the landlord intended to cause her to give up occupation of the premises—adopting the same meaning of 'occupation' as used in the Rent Act 1977 for determining who is in occupation for the purposes of being a protected tenant. Under this, a tenant remains in occupation if physically absent for a period but intending to return, for example, if the tenant had moved out whilst having works done through her own choice to her flat. The landlord's conduct in *Schon* does not seem unreasonable—he had offered substitute accommodation. Had the landlord gone about things differently, and caused the tenant to give up occupation for the same intended two-week period but by sending the 'heavies' in, it is tempting to ask whether the court would not then have found the offence of harassment committed.

Whilst the police are able to prosecute s 1 offences, s 6 also gives local authorities the power to bring prosecutions. Many local authorities have Tenancy Relations Officers whose job includes dealing with harassment and illegal eviction complaints, although there is considerable variation amongst authorities as to the level of resources dedicated to anti-harassment work (see Jew, *op. cit.*, ch 2). In practice, it is local authorities that have taken the most active role in law enforcement. Nevertheless, very few complaints proceed through to prosecution:

Role of Local Authorities Under Protection From Eviction Act 1977
7. The 1988 Act makes no changes to s 6 of the 1977 Act, under which local authorities ... generally have the power to institute proceedings for offences of harassment and illegal eviction. It is important that local authorities should know and use their powers under the Act. The police consider that the responsibility for bringing prosecutions lies with local authorities, and they do not normally intervene unless physical violence is involved. In the past the number of prosecutions brought each year under the Act has been low (some 100 a year for the years 1983-88) and the level of fines for successful prosecutions has also been low, notwithstanding the high penalties that can be imposed for an offence under s 1. This may have discouraged authorities from instituting proceedings ...
The framing of charges
8. Prosecutions may also have failed in the past because the charges as framed did not convey to the court the real nature of the alleged offence. For example, a single action in isolation may appear defensible, and only when the cumulative effect of the defendant's actions is clear does the true nature of the activity become apparent. Care therefore needs to be taken in framing charges. (Joint Circular from the Department of the Environment and Welsh Office, Circular 3/89, *Housing Act 1988: Protection of Residential Occupiers*)

The very small numbers of prosecutions for harassment and illegal eviction does not reflect the true scale of the problem. The survey by Rauta and Pickering, *op. cit.*, found that 9 per cent of private renters had suffered from harassment, but this was not defined in the technical legal sense:

Nine per cent of all tenants said that some [attempt to make them leave] ... had been made. Only 2 per cent said that the landlord had tried to persuade them to sign a less favourable agreement than the one they had; one half of these said that they had complied. One per cent of tenants said that they had been offered money to leave and 2 per cent that the landlord had tried to evict them by other methods. Seven per cent said that the landlord had made them feel uncomfortable or made them want to leave. (Rauta and Pickering, *op. cit.*, at p 50)

Why do so few of these offenders get prosecuted?
1 Whilst tenant surveys show this high level of harassment, the proportion of cases that actually get reported is much less—Jew, *op. cit.*, suggests that as much as 80 per cent of harassment and unlawful eviction is unreported. Such a high degree of under-reporting is due to several factors: fear of landlord reprisal; ignorance of the availability of legal channels for complaint (many landlords and tenants sharing the view that the landlord does have the right to behave in this way), and, if there is alternative accommodation, it is easier to simply get away from the acrimonious situation and not pursue past wrongs. Under-reporting seems to be highest amongst certain (vulnerable) groups—tenants

with no security and single parents. Whilst Rauta and Pickering's survey, *op. cit.*, showed tenants with no security as most likely to suffer from attempts to make them leave, Jew, *op. cit.*, indicated that assured and assured shorthold tenants were the most likely to report harassment and unlawful eviction. The explanation of this discrepancy is

probably a reflection of the fact that people with such severely limited security of tenure are very unlikely to exercise their right to seek the help of the local authority regarding harassment, as they can be evicted from their homes very quickly and legally. (Jew, *op. cit.*, p 33)

Similarly, Rauta and Pickering's survey showed that single parents are the most likely group to suffer harassment, whereas Jew found that most likely group to report harassment was single men (with no children).

2 There is a low prosecution rate for reported offences. Many local authorities pursue harassment complaints without resorting to prosecution of the landlord, for example, by sending a warning letter or issuing a caution. This is often found to be effective in preventing further harassment (see Jew, *op. cit.*, p 61). It is also often difficult to prosecute because of the high standard of proof required by criminal courts and the reluctance of tenants to act as witnesses through fear of reprisals, mistrust of the judicial system, the length of time it takes for cases to reach the courts (between six months and two years), the fact that tenants move away during this time and because tenants see no benefit for them in prosecuting (even though criminal conviction would help in any civil claim; see Jew, *op. cit.*, p 68).

3 There is a low conviction rate. In 1990 there were only 181 prosecutions and only 106 guilty verdicts (Jew, *op. cit.*, pp 83–4).

4 Penalties given tend to be low. Of those found guilty in 1990, three were given an immediate custodial sentence and 77 were fined—only seven of these being fined more than £500 (the maximum fine in the magistrates court is £5,000: in the Crown Court it is unlimited). Jew, *op. cit.*, describes the level of fines and sentences as derisory: 'They are sending a message to private landlords that crime can pay' (p 92). The low level of sentences suggests that magistrates do not regard harassment and illegal eviction as a serious offence.

11.5.2 Civil Remedies for Illegal Eviction and Harassment

11.5.2.1 General Law

From the tenant's perspective the criminal law may avenge a perceived injustice but it does little to help his plight. An occupier threatened with eviction or enduring repeated harassment is more likely to want to pursue a civil action and obtain an injunction, restraining the landlord's conduct or allowing the tenant to re-enter his home (see, for example, *Warder v Cooper* [1970] 1 Ch 495; *Drane v Evangelou* [1978] 1 WLR 455). The landlord's behaviour may involve trespass, trespass to goods if any possessions are deliberately interfered with (Torts (Interference with Goods) Act 1977), nuisance, breach of the covenant of quiet enjoyment or assault. In *McCall v Abelesz* [1976] QB 585, it was argued that breach of the Protection from Eviction Act 1977, s 1 would found civil liability as well as being a criminal offence but the Court of Appeal rejected this.

The occupier may also seek damages under the general law. The general principle for damages in tort actions is that the plaintiff be compensated for his loss. This will include general damages for the loss of the right to occupy and for distress, inconvenience and hardship caused by the eviction (see *Millington v Duffy* (1984) 17 HLR 232) and special damages. The evicted tenant may therefore be able to recover living out expenses after eviction and the cost of items taken from the property *(Ramdath v Daley* (1993) 25 HLR 273), and the return of any premium paid. In addition, it may be possible to recover exemplary and aggravated damages. These two measures of damages have frequently been confused by judges but they are intended to serve different purposes:

Aggravated damages are awarded to compensate the plaintiff for injury to his proper feelings of dignity and pride and for aggravation generally, whereas exemplary damages are awarded in order to punish the defendant (Nourse LJ, *Ramdath v Daley, op. cit.*, at 277)

Aggravated damages of £1,000 were awarded in *Nwokorie v Mason, op. cit.*, for conduct that was calculated to cause humiliation and shame and to be thoroughly offensive to the occupant's feelings (see also *McMillan v Singh* (1984) 17 HLR 120; *Jones v Miah* (1992) 24 HLR 578). Although Lord Devlin in *Rookes v Barnard* [1964] AC 1129, regarded aggravated damages as being compensatory, they can only be given when the defendant's motive or conduct aggravated the injury to the plaintiff. There is therefore a punitive element to them as well (see Law Commission, *Aggravated, Exemplary and Restitutionary Damages*, Consultation Paper No. 132, 1993, esp. paras 3.24–3.32). It is also possible to award exemplary damages following wrongful eviction. Again, although punitive damages cannot generally be awarded for a civil wrong there are certain exceptional categories and wrongful eviction cases can come within the second category admitted by Lord Devlin in *Rookes v Barnard*:

Where a defendant with a cynical disregard for a plaintiff's rights has calculated that the money to be made out of his wrong doing will probably exceed the damages at risk, it is necessary for the law to show that it cannot be broken with impunity . . . Exemplary damages can properly be awarded whenever it is necessary to teach a wrongdoer that tort does not pay. (*op. cit.*, at 1227)

It is clear that this can cover wrongful eviction:

How, it may be asked, about the late Mr Rachman, who is alleged to have used hired bullies to intimidate statutory tenants by violence or threats of violence into giving vacant possession of their residences and so placing a valuable asset in the hands of the landlord? My answer must be that if this is not a cynical calculation of profit and cold-blooded disregard of a plaintiff's rights, I do not know what is. (*per* Lord Hailsham LC, *Cassell & Co Ltd v Broome* [1972] AC 1027 at 1079)

In order to recover exemplary damages, though, the tenants must be able to show that the landlord knew that what he was doing was against the law or that he had a reckless disregard as to whether what he intended to do was legal or illegal, and a decision to carry on doing it because the prospects of material advantage outweigh the prospects of material loss (*Cassell v Broome, op. cit.*, at 1079). In *Ramdath v Daley, op. cit.*, it was not possible to award exemplary damages against the landlord's agent because it had not been shown that the agent had sufficient (financial) interest to come within this category. In *Drane v Evangelou, op. cit.*, the evicted tenant was awarded £1,000 exemplary damages for the 'monstrous behaviour' of the landlord 'to teach the landlord a lesson' (*per* Lord Denning MR, although Lawton LJ and Goff LJ seem to categorize the award as aggravated damages). Even if the tenant has not been a 'model tenant' and has not behaved with propriety, this cannot be taken account of so as to reduce the damages: *McMillan v Singh, op. cit.* Where exemplary damages are given it is not therefore strictly to compensate the evicted occupant but to make a statement about the landlord's conduct—this may be to confuse the function of the civil and criminal law, especially as the landlord may be separately prosecuted under the Protection from Eviction Act 1977 (although the availability of exemplary damages may help balance the low prosecution rate; see Law Commission, Consultation Paper No. 132, *op. cit.*, for a discussion of the justification for the award of exemplary damages, esp. Part V). Where the action is framed in contract for breach of the covenant of quiet enjoyment, it is not possible to claim exemplary damages or damages for injured feelings and mental distress (*Bratchett v Beaney* [1992] 3 All ER 910).

11.5.2.2 Statutory Damages under Sections 27 and 28 Housing Act 1988

When the plans to partially deregulate the private rented sector were announced in the late 1980s, tenant bodies voiced fears that this would lead to high levels of harassment and illegal eviction, with landlords seeking to replace Rent Act regulated tenants (paying a fair rent) with Housing Act tenants paying a market rent and with little security of tenure (under the assured shorthold). To counter these fears the criminal offences were strengthened (removing the need to prove intent) and a new civil remedy was created. This civil remedy aimed to deprive the landlord of financial gain arising from the eviction, to act as a deterrent to landlords and give substantial damages to tenants (for example, £31,000 in *Tagro v Cafane* [1991] 2 All ER 235; £35,000 in *Canlin and Gray v Berkshire Holdings* September 1990, Legal Action, p 10; and £20,278 in *Chappel v Panchall* December 1991, Legal Action, p 19).

Section 27 Housing Act 1988 provides for liability if a landlord unlawfully deprives a residential occupier of his occupation of the whole or part of any premises (or attempts to do so) or harasses the occupier causing the occupier to leave:

s 27(1) This section applies if, at any time after 9th June 1988, a landlord (in this section referred to as 'the landlord in default') or any person acting on behalf of the landlord in default unlawfully deprives the residential occupier of any premises of his occupation of the whole or part of the premises.

(2) This section also applies if, at any time after 9th June 1988, a landlord (in this section referred to as 'the landlord in default') or any person acting on behalf of the landlord in default—

(a) attempts unlawfully to deprive the residential occupier of any premises of his occupation of the whole or part of the premises, or

(b) knowing or having reasonable cause to believe that the conduct is likely to cause the residential occupier of any premises—

(i) to give up his occupation of the premises or any part thereof, or

(ii) to refrain from exercising any right or pursuing any remedy in respect of the premises or any part thereof,

does acts likely to interfere with the peace or comfort of the residential occupier or members of his household, or persistently withdraws or withholds services reasonably required for the occupation of the premises as a residence, and, as a result, the residential occupier gives up his occupation of the premises as a residence.

(3) Subject to the following provisions of this section, where this section applies, the landlord in default shall, by virtue of this section, be liable to pay to the former residential occupier, in respect of his loss of the right to occupy the premises in question as his residence, damages assessed on the basis set out in section 28 below.

Section 28 sets out the appropriate measure of damages where a claim is brought under s 27. It is essentially a comparison of the value of the property with and without the interest of the evicted occupier:

s 28(1) The basis for the assessment of damages referred to in section 27 (3) above is the difference in value, determined as at the time immediately before the residential occupier ceased to occupy the premises in question as his residence, between—

(a) the value of the interest of the landlord in default determined on the assumption that the residential occupier continues to have the same right to occupy the premises as before that time; and

(b) the value of that interest determined on the assumption that the residential occupier has ceased to have that right.
(2) In relation to any premises, any reference in this section to the interest of
the landlord in default is a reference to his interest in the building in which
the premises in question are comprised (whether or not that building contains any other premises) together with its curtilage.

Three important assumptions are made in making this comparative valuation
(s 28(3)):
1 That the landlord is selling his interest on the open market to a willing buyer.
2 That neither the residential occupier nor any member of his family wishes to
   buy.
3 That it is unlawful to carry out any 'substantial development' of any of the land
   in which the landlord's interest exists or demolish the whole or part of the
   building on that land. This excludes, to the landlord's advantage, the possibility that the land could now be turned to commercial office use, for example. It
   would not, however, exclude developments covered by the general development order (see s 28(6)). In practice, this provision is a compromise between
   the aim of depriving landlords of all financial gain and the possibility of damages being awarded out of all proportion to the tenant's loss.

The basis of damages awarded under s 28 represents a considerable shift from
the normal compensation-based approach to damages. The measure of damages is the benefit which the defendant has obtained from his unlawful act; it is
not criminal legislation (*Jones v Miah, op. cit.*) and is best viewed as restitutionary
(see Law Commission Consultation Paper No. 132, *op. cit.*, para 7.5). The clear
aim of this is to ensure that the landlord stands to gain nothing from his wrong
conduct and therefore has no incentive to throw the occupier out without following the correct procedures. The result if he does so is likely to be a windfall
gain to the former occupant.

In practice, s 28 is proving difficult for the courts to apply. It is necessary to
work out the value of the immediate landlord's interest in the whole building
(assuming he—and not a superior landlord—is the landlord at fault) with the
occupier present and the value without the occupier in. This is a notoriously difficult valuation exercise, especially if the building has many occupants, and the
courts have frequently been handicapped by the poor quality of valuation evidence produced:

The difficulty here is formidable, since none of the four professional valuers who
were called to give evidence gave the judge any assistance at all. This may have
been because of the ineptitude of these four individual valuers, or it may have
been because the habits of thought of valuers trained in the processes of valuing
interests in land are so different from the habits of thought of lawyers who seek to
apply the formula under section 28 that there is no meeting of minds, and the valuers can never bring their mind to understand what the calculation is that the

lawyers are wanting them to make. (*per* Dillon LJ, *Jones v Miah, op. cit.*, at 588; see also *Tagro v Cafane, op. cit.*, where one side failed to produce valuation evidence; *Nwokorie v Mason, op. cit.*)

The formula has also led to disagreement within cases—in *Jones v Miah, op. cit.*, Dillon LJ would have awarded £5,750 for statutory damages, Nourse and Legatt LJJ would have given £8,000.

Where damages are awarded under this section, any general damages, aggravated and exemplary damages must be set off against them as it should not be possible to recover twice over for the same 'loss'—see *Nwokorie v Mason, op. cit.* In *Nwokorie v Mason*, Dillon LJ also held that s 27(5) requires aggravated damages to be set-off against the statutory damages, but Bridge (*Damages for Eviction: Confusion Compounded*, [1994] Conv 411 at p 414) argues that aggravated damages should be additional to statutory damages, on the basis that 'landlords resigned to be hung for a sheep as well as a lamb, would otherwise have no incentive to evict with minimum force'. Consequential damage, such as damage to goods, can be recovered in addition.

The landlord will not be liable if the occupier is reinstated before the proceedings are finally disposed of (s 27(6)). In practice, there will often be a reluctance on the occupier's part to return to the premises, especially as it seems that the occupier has a choice between accepting reinstatement or refusing reinstatement and pursuing a claim for damages (*Tagro v Cafane, op. cit.*). If, however, the offer to reinstate was made before the proceedings are begun, the court may reduce the damages if it was unreasonable of the occupier to refuse the offer (s 27(7)). If the occupier is reinstated he may still be able to claim damages under the general law: *McCormack v Namjou* [1990] CLY 1725 (where a substantial award was given in the form of general, aggravated and exemplary damages). The landlord will have a defence if he believes that the residential occupier has ceased to reside in the premises or, where liability arises by virtue of the doing of acts or withdrawal of services, the landlord had reasonable grounds for acting in the way in which he or she did (s 27(8)). The court may also reduce the damages by taking account of the conduct of the occupant (s 27(7))—he is often far from innocent.

11.5.3 Other remedies

In cases of severe harassment, the local authority may be able to resort to other measures. In *R v Secretary of State for the Environment ex parte Royal Borough of Kensington and Chelsea* (1987) 19 HLR 161, Taylor J confirmed that a local authority may, in extreme cases, be able to compulsorily purchase the property. The relevant powers of compulsory purchase are found in ss 9 and 17 of the Housing Act 1985. So far as is relevant, the sections provide:

s 9(1) A local housing authority may provide housing accommodation . . .
      (b) by acquiring houses.

s 17(1) A local housing authority may for the purposes of this Part - . . .
      (b) acquire houses, or buildings, which may be suitable as houses,
         together with any land occupied with the houses or buildings.
    (3) Land may be acquired by a local housing authority for the purposes of
       this Part by agreement, or they may be authorised by the Secretary of
       State to acquire it compulsorily.

In *ex parte Kensington and Chelsea, op. cit.*, a compulsory purchase order was
made in respect of five houses where the tenants had complained of harassment
and intimidation. The landlord objected and the Secretary of State ordered a
public inquiry. In relation to the issue of whether evidence of harassment was
relevant to the inquiry Taylor J said:

In my judgment, if there is, in any case, evidence of such harassment, intimidation or other grave conduct by a landlord as to vitiate the provision of proper
housing accommodation by depriving it of the essential incident of quiet enjoyment, then it would be open to the Secretary of State to confirm a Compulsory
Purchase Order under Part II of the Act. If, by reason of the landlord's conduct, a
tenant is put in bodily fear, is harassed, threatened with eviction or exclusion, if
essential services are not maintained, or if the tenant's property is invaded and
he is verbally abused, it would be a callous misuse of language to say that he was
being provided with proper housing accommodation. Of course, it must be a matter for the Secretary of State to judge, on the evidence, whether such conduct is
proved, and whether it is of such gravity as to justify an order. This he cannot do
unless the Inspector receives and reports such evidence as is relevant to that
issue. (at 170; see also Joint Circular from the Department of the Environment and
Welsh Office, Circular 3/89, *Housing Act 1988: Protection of Residential Occupiers*,
para 27).

11.5.4 The Effectiveness of the Law

Given the high level of harassment found in the Rauta and Pickering survey, *op.
cit.*, it seems that the law is not very effective in deterring harassment; over two-
thirds of the authorities in Jew's survey, *op. cit.*, who expressed an opinion considered that the current anti-harassment and illegal eviction laws were not an
adequate deterrent (p 86). A clear duty placed on local authorities to investigate
and pursue all complaints would help harassment be treated as a more serious
offence. The 1988 Housing Act does not appear to have led to any decrease in
harassment, indeed there are signs of a slight increase:

The local authorities in our survey reported that Assured Shorthold tenancies,
market rents, excluded tenancies and Housing Benefit restrictions—all central

provisions of the 1988 Act—were factors to an increase or no significant change in harassment levels. (Jew, *op. cit.*, p 79)

Although damages awarded may be higher, there is no evidence that more tenants are bringing civil actions—and the cuts in legal aid mean that fewer tenants can afford to bring legal action. Fears are expressed that the situation may worsen with easier, 'paper-only' repossession of assured shorthold and certain other assured tenancies (introduced in 1993); changes to laws on squatting making recovery of premises easier (and occupiers ignorant of their rights may not challenge the owners assertions that they are squatters); and a recovery in the housing market meaning that more landlords will want to sell with vacant possession.

11.6 DISCLAIMER ON TENANT INSOLVENCY

This chapter has focused mainly on the landlord's ability to end the tenancy relationship against the will of the tenant. It is possible for the tenant to end the relationship by serving notice to quit, surrendering the lease, operating a break clause, and occasionally by accepting a repudiatory breach. The tenant's insolvency may also trigger the end of the relationship.

When the lease is at a market rent, tenant insolvency will usually give the landlord the right to forfeit. If the property is likely to be hard to relet, as during property slumps, and the tenant is not the original tenant, then by choosing not to forfeit the landlord keeps the lease in train and may be able to recover rent and service charges from former tenants.

The tenant's trustee in bankruptcy may also be able to end the relationship. On insolvency, the lease will usually vest in the trustee in bankruptcy and the trustee becomes liable for rent and compliance with the leasehold covenants (in cases of corporate insolvency, the lease does not automatically vest in the liquidator). The trustee in bankruptcy has power to disclaim 'onerous property', including leases (see Insolvency Act 1986, ss 315–321 (individuals), Insolvency Act 1986, ss 178–182 (companies)). The effect of a disclaimer will vary according to whether or not the insolvent tenant was the original tenant. Section 315 Insolvency Act 1986 provides:

s 315(1) Subject as follows, the trustee may, by the giving of the prescribed notice, disclaim any onerous property and may do so notwithstanding that he has taken possession of it, endeavoured to sell it or otherwise exercised rights of ownership in relation to it.

(2) The following is onerous property for the purposes of this section, that is to say—

(a) any unprofitable contract, and

(b) any other property comprised in the bankrupt's estate which is unsaleable or not readily saleable, or is such that it may give rise to a liability to pay money or perform any other onerous act.

> (3) A disclaimer under this section–
> (a) operates so as to determine, as from the date of the disclaimer, the rights, interests and liabilities of the bankrupt and his estate in or in respect of the property disclaimed, and
> (b) discharges the trustee from all personal liability in respect of that property as from the commencement of his trusteeship,
> but does not, except so far as is necessary for the purpose of releasing the bankrupt, the bankrupt's estate and the trustee from any liability, affect the rights or liabilities of any other person. (See s 178 for parallel provision for companies.)

The effect of this is that where the insolvent tenant is the original tenant and the lease has not been assigned, the lease comes to an end on disclaimer and any surety of the tenant is also discharged from liability (*Stacey v Hill* [1901] 1 KB 660). If the insolvent tenant is an assignee, then the lease continues to exist following disclaimer—all the disclaimer does is to extinguish the liability of the bankrupt assignee to pay rent:

> [Where] the disclaimed lease was vested in an assignee, the lease was described by Uthwatt J in *In re Thompson & Cottrell's Contract* [1943] Ch 97, 100, as being 'something like a dormant volcano. It may break out into active operation at any time.' The activating event is the making of a vesting order. (*per* Megarry VC, *Warnford Investments Ltd v Duckworth* [1979] 1 Ch 127 at 135)

In *Hindcastle v Barbara Attenborough Associates* [1994] 4 All ER 129, Millet LJ acknowledged the somewhat peculiar status of the lease in a commercial liquidation for which no vesting order had been made—the lease is ownerless and yet still exists in some sense.

> [As] between the lessor and the bankrupt assignee, the lease is *deemed* to have been surrendered; as between the lessor and the original lessee and his surety, it is not deemed to have been surrendered. (at 134)

Where it is an assignee who becomes insolvent, the original tenant remains liable for unpaid rent under the lease (past and future): *Hill v East and West India Dock Co* 9 App Cas 448, *Warnford Investments Ltd v Duckworth, op. cit.* Any surety of the original tenant is also liable (*Hindcastle v Barbara Attenborough Associates, op. cit.*), as is any intermediate assignee who is in a direct contractual relationship with the landlord. The liability of the insolvent assignee to indemnify them is, however, extinguished (*Hindcastle v Barbara Attenborough Associates, op. cit.*).

12

Changing the Tenant's Interest

12.1 INTRODUCTION

This chapter examines various rights that have been given to tenants to change the nature of the tenancy relationship. The relationship may change by reason of the tenants taking a more active part in management of the property through the formation of tenant management organizations in the public sector—see, in part, ch 7.8.1 and ch 10.5. In other cases, tenants have been given, either individually or collectively, the right to enfranchise, that is, to acquire the freehold from the landlord.

Although most legislation on enfranchisement is of recent origin there have been movements supporting enfranchisement for over 100 years, the first Bill being presented (unsuccessfully) in 1884. Enfranchisement has been consistently opposed by landlords on the grounds that it interferes with freedom of contract and property. In the public sector, resistance has also formed part of the central versus local government struggle with claims that it is an undue interference with locally determined policies and priorities.

The first major piece of legislation on enfranchisement was the Leasehold Reform Act 1967 which applied to tenants of long leasehold houses paying a low rent and gave them the right to buy the freehold or extend their leases in return for compensation. Long leaseholders of flats were given the collective right to purchase the freehold at market value under the Leasehold Reform, Housing and Urban Development Act 1993, or individually to extend their leases. There are also limited rights to enfranchise contained in the Landlord and Tenant Act 1987. In the public sector, council tenants who are renting property on a periodic basis were given the right to buy the freehold at a substantial discount from market value by the Housing Act 1980.

It is only in the public sector that general enfranchisement rights have been given to persons renting property. In the private sector, these rights have only been available to tenants of long leases at a low rent, although the more limited rights under the 1987 Act apply to some renters.

No comparable rights exist in the commercial or agricultural sectors. The primary force behind the enfranchisement laws has been the government's desire to further extend home ownership, a concern clearly inapplicable to the commercial and agricultural sectors. In addition, in the private residential sector, the reforms attempted to rectify perceived injustices in the system of long leasehold tenure and to alleviate management difficulties in multi-occupied property. In the public sector, the Right to Buy has been an important part of the government's wider political goals. The Right to Buy has proven to be attractive to the electorate and its popularity has also helped to implement the aim of reducing the state's role in housing provision. Capital receipts from council house sales form an important part of public expenditure planning.

The fact that it has been felt politically desirable to give enfranchisement rights does cast shadows on the ability of leasehold law to adequately protect certain classes of people. While there is no doubt of the need for a revived private residential rental sector, Sir George Young, as housing minister, stated that the 1993 Act aimed to 'move away from leasehold as a form of tenure' (Standing Committee B, second sitting, 12 November 1992, p 73).

Similarly, the government's desire to move away from public sector renting is well known. To that extent, while the end result is the same in the public and private sectors, in that the tenant becomes owner-occupier (although, it should be noted, those who enfranchise flats become long-leaseholders), the philosophy behind the Right To Buy in the public sector is wholly different from enfranchisement in the private sector. Thus, different issues arise in relation to the specific laws and the policies and results in the two sectors. These differences reveal themselves in the approach taken to the Right To Buy and private enfranchisement in this chapter.

12.2 CONTINUING RIGHTS OF OCCUPATION FOR LONG LEASEHOLDERS

Until 1954, tenants of long leases would face the loss of their home at the end of the lease as they had no right to remain. In addition, they would often be faced with expensive claims for dilapidations to put the house back into repair.

The early case for enfranchisement was heavily based upon the effect that the 'building lease' had on housing standards and conditions. Under the building lease, the tenant is granted a lease, generally for 99 years, at a ground rent and undertakes to build a house on the site and to deliver it up in good repair at the end of the lease. The Royal Commission on the Housing of Working Classes (1884–5) supported enfranchisement on the grounds that it would lead to an improvement in housing for the working classes. The building lease system was considered conducive to bad building and led to a deterioration in property towards the end of the lease due to lack of incentive for the occupier to keep it in repair. A few years later the Select Committee on Town Holdings (1889), while accepting these arguments, was against general enfranchisement for fear that it would discourage new development and so lead to a decline in housing provision for the working classes. The Select Committee were also concerned that it would make good estate management difficult. The quality, character and general amenity level of many estates was felt to have been preserved by the active management policies pursued by the landlord. It was feared that the loss of such a common policy on management through diversity in ownership would lead to a deterioration in the standards of such estates. This fear has been repeated on many occasions since.

During the twentieth century, concern over housing conditions diminished as other mechanisms were put in place to monitor this, such as the development of planning laws and the strengthening of public health laws. The growth in public sector housing—from less than one per cent of all housing stock in 1914 to 32 per cent in 1979—also ensured a supply of accessible, reasonable quality housing.

By the middle of this century there was increasing concern over the position of the tenant on the expiry of his lease, but in 1950 the Leasehold Committee did not accept the view that long leases were based on inequality and injustice, although it was felt that Rent Act protection should be extended to ground lessees (*Leasehold Committee Final Report*, 1950, Cmd 7982). By 1953 it was the practical difficulties that would follow enfranchisement that stood in its way (prohibitive costs to tenants, management of large estates and so on; see *Government Policy on Leasehold Property in England and Wales*, 1953, Cmd 8713). Instead, it was felt that what long leaseholders really needed was security of tenure rather than freehold ownership—it would therefore be sufficient to protect their right of occupation, rather than give a new right of ownership. In consequence, the Landlord and Tenant Act 1954 was passed. Part I of the 1954 Act conferred on tenants of long leases at a low rent a right to remain at the end of the contractual term and entitled them to a statutory tenancy within the Rent Acts. The 1954 Act is now being gradually phased out and replaced by the Local Government and Housing Act 1989, Sch 10 (see 1989 Act, s 186). The approach followed under the 1989 Act is essentially the same as the earlier legislation.

12.2.1 Qualifying for Protection

In relation to tenancies entered into before 1 April 1990, and to which the 1954 Act will apply until 1999, the following conditions have to be met:

12.2.1.1 There must be a Long Tenancy

That is a tenancy granted for a term of years exceeding 21 years (s 2(4), see also s 2(7)). Twenty-one years is taken as the basic guide to what is a long lease for most enfranchisement laws, not just the 1954 Act. The significance of this period is felt to be that it distinguishes between a person who is simply renting property and one who has purchased a 'major interest' in the property. The Act will also apply to a periodic tenancy at a low rent if it follows on from a tenancy which was a long tenancy (s 19).

12.2.1.2 The Tenancy must be at a Low Rent (s 2(5))

The aim was that the 1954 Act would apply to tenancies which would otherwise be within the statutory protection afforded by the Rent Acts, but were excluded because they were at a low rent (see ch 6). To be a low rent, it must be less than two-thirds of the rateable value of the house excluding payments for maintenance, insurance, repairs, rates and services (s 2(4), (5) and (7), as amended).

12.2.1.3 The Tenant must satisfy the 'Qualifying Condition' set out in s 2(1)

s 2(1) . . . that is to say that the circumstances (as respects the property comprised in the tenancy, the use of that property, and all other relevant matters) are such that on the coming to an end of the tenancy at that time the tenant would, if the tenancy had not been one at a low rent, be entitled by virtue of the [Rent Act] to retain possession of the whole or part of the property comprised in the tenancy.

The intention behind this was referred to by Lord Denning MR in *Herbert v Byrne* [1964] 1 WLR 519:

You are to look at the position at the end of the lease, and ask yourself whether the leaseholder would have been protected if it had not been a long lease at a low rent, but a short lease at a rack rent. If the leaseholder would have qualified under the old Rent Acts for protection on the expiry of such a short lease, he qualifies now, under the Act of 1954, for protection on the expiry of the long lease. There is, however, this difference—in determining whether he qualifies or not, you do not look at the terms of the old long lease itself as you would look at the terms of a short lease, . . . but you look at the state of affairs as it actually existed at the end of the long lease. That is made clear by section 22(3) of the Act of 1954. (at 525)

This means that there must be a tenancy of a separate dwelling occupied by the tenant as his residence, both at the contractual term date and at the time that the landlord serves an effective notice to end it (ss 2(1), 4(1)).

12.2.2 Continuing or Ending the Tenancy

If the tenant wants to end the tenancy, he can do so by serving one month's notice, which can end on or after the term date (s 5). If the tenant does not end the tenancy, it will simply continue on the same terms and at the same rent until the landlord takes some action to end the tenancy (s 3). The landlord can end the tenancy either on the term date or at a later date by giving not more than twelve, nor less than six, months' notice (s 4(2)).

The landlord has two options:

1   To seek to recover possession on grounds set out in s 12. Available grounds are:

(a) that the landlord proposes to demolish or reconstruct the whole or a substantial part of the premises for the purposes of redevelopment. This ground is only available where the landlord is one of certain public bodies (see Leasehold Reform Act 1967, ss 38(1), 28(5));

(b) grounds which correspond to the discretionary grounds for possession under the Rent Act 1977, that is Cases 1 to 9 in Sch 15 to the Rent Act 1977 (1954 Act, Sch 3). Several of these grounds are similar to the discretionary grounds for possession in Part II, Sch 2, Housing Act 1988 (discussed in ch 11). Rent Act 1977 grounds for possession are discussed in Yates and Hawkins, *Landlord and Tenant Law*, 2nd edn, 1986, pp 449–57.

2   To serve a notice proposing a statutory tenancy and stating the proposed property to be included, the rent and who shall carry out specified internal repairs (ss 4(5)(a), 7). If the parties are unable to agree terms they can be settled by court order (s 7(2)) and, unlike s 35 of the 1954 Act which applies to renewal of business leases, there is no statutory guidance on the matters to be considered (see *Etablissement Commercial Kamira v Schiazzano* [1984] 3 WLR 95). If such a tenancy then comes into existence, it can only be determined in accordance with the Rent Act 1977.

It is not possible to contract out of the Act (s 17).

12.2.3 Sch 10, Local Government and Housing Act 1989

In relation to tenancies entered into on or after 1 April 1990, it is Sch 10 of the Local Government and Housing Act 1989 which applies and not Part I of the 1954 Act (Local Government and Housing Act 1989, s 186). The 1989 Act will also affect tenancies entered into before this date and still in existence on 15 January 1999— as from the beginning of 1999, it will be the 1989 Act, Sch 10 which applies on termination and not the 1954 Act (s 186(3)).

Schedule 10 applies to the same types of tenancies as Part I of the 1954 Act.

There must be a long tenancy of a dwelling house at a low rent. 'Long' means more than 21 years (para 2(3)) and a tenancy at a low rent is one for which:

1 No rent is payable;
2 If entered into on or after 1 April 1990, the maximum rent is £1,000 a year or less if the property is in Greater London or £250 a year or less elsewhere (para 4(b));
3 If entered into before 1 April 1990, the maximum rent is less than two-thirds of the rateable value of the house.

The qualifying condition is

that the circumstances (as respects the property let under the tenancy, the use of that property and all other relevant matters) are such that, if the tenancy were not at a low rent, it would at that time be an assured tenancy within the meaning of Part I of the Housing Act 1988. (para 1(1))

The scheme of protection is also similar to that found in the 1954 Act, but applying the assured tenancy regime of the Housing Act 1988 in place of the statutory tenancy of the Rent Act 1977. In outline, the landlord is given three options on the expiry of a long lease:

1 The tenant can continue in possession under the terms of the original tenancy (para 3).
2 The landlord can seek to recover possession on grounds set out in para 5(1) of Sch 10. Available grounds are:
   (a) Housing Act 1988, Sch 2, Ground 6 (demolition or reconstruction, but see para 5(2), Sch 10) and the discretionary grounds for possession in Sch 2 to the Housing Act 1988 (except Ground 16 (employment related accommodation));
   (b) the landlord proposes to demolish or reconstruct the whole or a substantial part of the premises for redevelopment. This is again only available to certain public bodies (para 5(4));
   (c) the landlord reasonably requires the premises for occupation as a residence for himself or a specified member of his family (but see para 5(5) if the landlord's interest was acquired after 1966).
3 The landlord may serve a notice proposing an assured monthly periodic tenancy (para 4(5)(a)). If such a tenancy then comes into existence, it can only be determined in accordance with the Housing Act 1988.

12.3 ENFRANCHISEMENT OF LONG LEASEHOLD HOUSES— THE LEASEHOLD REFORM ACT 1967

Although Part I of the Landlord and Tenant Act 1954 gave the tenant a degree of security, the fact that the landlord was able to recover possession on certain grounds and to receive a rack rent in the meantime meant that it soon became apparent that this measure did not succeed in relieving the injustice to tenants at the expiry of their leases. By the mid-1960s enfranchisement was becoming an urgent political issue. Large areas of South Wales had been developed in the late eighteenth century under the building lease system. As these leases were now nearing the end of their terms the harshness of the long leasehold system was more evident. Tenants on some estates were able to extend their leases on a voluntary basis on reasonable terms whereas other landlords were taking a much more commercial approach. By 1966 the government was persuaded that tenants of long leases should be given the right to enfranchise and the principle underlying the Leasehold Reform Act 1967 was that 'the land belongs in equity to the landowner and the house belongs in equity to the occupying leaseholder' (*Leasehold Reform in England and Wales*, 1966, Cmnd 2916, para 4).

The Leasehold Reform Act 1967 gave tenants of non-expensive houses held on long leases at a low rent the right to acquire the freehold of the premises by enfranchisement or the right to an extended lease, expiring 50 years after the date of expiry of the existing lease.

The legislation did not extend to flats allegedly because 'different considerations of equity apply and there would be many practical difficulties in providing for enfranchisement of flats' (*Leasehold Reform in England and Wales, op. cit.*, para 8). It is hard to discern what the 'different considerations of equity' are for long leasehold flats. Although the flat owner has not built the property as in the building lease, he has effectively paid for its construction through the premium and his moral claim must be as strong as that of the house owner. While there are admittedly 'practical difficulties' with enfranchisement of flats (not least, that enfranchisement rights must be collective, see 12.4), this does not explain why the right to extend the lease could not be given to flat owners. A more significant fact was probably that enfranchisement of flats was simply not then an issue on the political agenda.

12.3.1 Qualifying Conditions

In order for the Act to apply various conditions must be satisfied:

12.3.1.1 The Tenant must Occupy a House

The 1967 Act only applies to 'houses' (s 1(1)). Determining whether a property is a house is not always straightforward. Section 2 states that it:

s 2(1) . . . includes any building designed or adapted for living in and reasonably so called, notwithstanding that the building is not structurally detached, or was or is not solely designed or adapted for living in, or is divided horizontally into flats or maisonettes; and

(a) where a building is divided horizontally, the flats or other units into which it is so divided are not separate 'houses', though the building as a whole may be; and

(b) where a building is divided vertically the building as a whole is not a 'house' though any of the units into which it is divided may be.

(2) References in this Part of this Act do not apply to a house which is not structurally detached and of which a material part lies above or below a part of the structure not comprised in the house.

Difficulties arise in relation to divided buildings. Terraced houses will individually be houses. A block of flats will, as a whole, count as a house but the individual units will not. The reasons for this somewhat complex approach is to prevent interdependent premises from qualifying as this would raise the difficult issues of enforcing repairing obligations and so on.

The primary purpose of [s 2(2) is] . . . the exclusion from the operation of the Act of houses in respect of which the inability of one freehold owner to enforce positive obligations against successors in title of the other would be likely to prejudice the enjoyment of the house or another part of the structure. (*per* Nourse LJ, *Duke of Westminster v Birrane* [1995] 3 WLR 270 at 276)

A part would be 'material' for the purposes of subsection (2) if enfranchisement of it would cause difficulties, in particular due to problems of enforcement of positive covenants against successors to another freehold owner. Thus, in *Duke of Westminster v Birrane, op. cit.*, a house could not be enfranchised when the basement of the house lay below another property.

In interpreting the word 'house', the courts have been anxious to promote the policy of the legislation, to enable resident tenants to enfranchise. Accordingly, mixed use premises have been held within the Act so long as the building 'can reasonably be called a house' even though it could also reasonably be called something else (Lord Roskill, *Tandon v Trustees of Spurgeon's Homes* [1982] AC 755 at 767; see also [1982] Conv 378). This is so even though the premises may also come within the business tenancy code in Part II of the Landlord and Tenant Act 1954.

Certain premises surrounding the house can also be included in the enfranchisement claim: s 2(3) states that there will be included

any garage, outhouse, garden, yard, and appurtenances which at the relevant time are let to him with the house and are occupied with and used for the purposes of the house.

In *Methuen-Campbell v Walters* [1979] 2 WLR 113, though, a paddock at the end of the garden could not be included in the tenant's claim.

12.3.1.2 The House must be within Certain Rateable Value Limits

When initially enacted, the 1967 Act did not extend to housing with high rateable values. At first the limit was a maximum rateable value of £200, or £400 if in Greater London (s 1(4)). These limits were raised by somewhat complex provisions in 1974 (see s 1(5), (6)) to bring most housing within the Act. The Leasehold Reform, Housing and Urban Development Act 1993 removes all rateable value limits under the 1967 Act in relation to the tenant's right to enfranchise (but not in relation to the right to an extended lease, Leasehold Reform, Housing and Urban Development Act 1993, s 63).

12.3.1.3 There must be a Long Lease

A lease for a term of years certain exceeding 21 years will be a long lease (s 3) and certain other tenancies are also treated as long leases, such as certain leases granted under the right to buy provisions of the Housing Act 1985, s 173.

12.3.1.4 The Lease must be at a Low Rent (s 1(1)(b))

This will usually mean that the rent must not exceed two-thirds of the rateable value, excluding payments for repairs, maintenance and insurance (s 4(1)(b); see also s 4(1)(c)).

An alternative low rent test was introduced by the 1993 Act, inserting a new s 4A into the 1967 Act. In order to be a low rent:

1 If granted before 1 April 1963, the aggregate rent in the initial year must not have exceeded two-thirds of the letting value (this same test applied under the 1967 Act to leases, other than building leases, granted between 1939 and 1963);
2 If granted before 1 April 1990 (but after 1 April 1963), the aggregate rent in the initial year must not be more than two-thirds of the rateable value of the property on the day the lease began;
3 If granted on or after 1 April 1990, the aggregate rent in the initial year must be not more than £1,000 if the property is in Greater London or £250 elsewhere.

12.3.1.5 The Residency Test

The tenant must occupy the house as his only or main residence (whether or not he uses it also for other purposes—s 1(2)) and must have been so occupying it 'for the last three years or for periods amounting to three years in the last ten years' (s 1(1)(b)). When initially enacted, five years' occupation was required. Whether or not a tenant is occupying a house as his residence is a question of fact and degree (*Poland v Earl Cadogan* [1980] 3 All ER 544 at 549). The tenant of an agricultural holding does not have rights under the Act (s 1(3)(b)); nor is a company or other artificial person able to satisfy the residency test (s 37(5)).

12.3.1.6 The House must not be Exempt

Certain properties cannot be enfranchised because of the identity of the landlord, for example National Trust properties (s 32; see also s 33 for Crown property). Where the tenancy was entered into after 1 November 1993 there are
further exempted properties: houses let by charitable housing trusts (s 1(3A)
1967 Act) and certain 'great houses' (s 32A).

12.3.2 The Price of Enfranchisement

The price that the tenant has to pay to enfranchise or to extend his lease has
proven highly controversial. Section 1 of the Act states that the tenant has a right
to acquire *on fair terms*. The compensation provisions of the 1967 Act followed
through the premise underlying the legislation, that the house belonged in
equity to the tenant. Given that this premise was itself questioned by many, it is
inevitable that many saw the compensation provisions as totally inadequate.

On enfranchisement the price payable was the open market value of the reversion on the assumption that the tenant had exercised his statutory right to extend
the lease for 50 years and (after amendment in 1969) that the tenant was not buying or seeking to buy.

> s 9(1) . . . the price payable for a house and premises . . . shall be the amount
> which at the relevant time the house and premises, if sold in the open mar-
> ket by a willing seller (with the tenant and members of his family who
> reside in the house not buying or seeking to buy), might be expected to
> realise on the following assumptions:
> (a) on the assumption that the vendor was selling for an estate in fee sim-
> ple, subject to the tenancy but on the assumption that this Part of this
> Act conferred no right to acquire the freehold; and if the tenancy has
> not been extended under this Part of this Act, on the assumption that
> (subject to the landlord's [redevelopment] rights under section 17
> below) it was to be so extended.

The value of the landlord's interest is therefore broadly based on the capitalized
value of the ground rents during the tenancy and the presumed extended term,
with the right to possess deferred until the expiry of the extended lease. The overall effect was that the tenant was deemed to have already paid for the house and
so only had to pay for the site value and no element of the 'marriage value'. It is
important to understand this concept of marriage value. The sum of the freeholder's interest (subject to the lease) and the leaseholder's interest is less than
vacant possession value. When a leaseholder acquires the freehold he gains the
additional value released by the merger of the freeholder's and the leaseholder's
interests. This is known as the marriage value.

Let us take a simple illustration of a house that would be worth £100,000 with vacant possession. The value of the existing tenancy with fifty years unexpired is, say, £60,000. The value of the freeholder's reversion is £10,000. The marriage value would be—

$$£100,000 - (£10,000 + £60,000) = £30,000$$

It is only by the landlord's and the tenant's interests coming together (marrying) that this sum can be released. Under the 1967 formula, the fact that this sum is released to the tenant on enfranchisement is ignored for valuation purposes, that is, the reversion is valued without taking account of any special bids that the tenant purchaser would make, the 'sale' is assumed to be to a third party who would not be able to benefit from marriage value.

The effect of the 1967 formula was that a tenant with a lease nearing the end of its term could acquire the freehold for a relatively small sum and then sell the premises at their market value: the Act was felt by many to result in undeserved windfall profits for the former tenant. An extreme example was a tenant who had paid a low price for a lease before the 1967 Act (and, therefore, without the prospect of enfranchisement), bought the freehold at 28 per cent of its proper value and sold it less than a year later for a profit of 636 per cent (£116,000 profit; see *James v United Kingdom* (1986) 8 EHRR 123 at paras 18, 29).

When the Leasehold Reform Act was extended in 1974 to include some houses with a higher rateable value, a different basis of valuation was applied to properties newly brought within the legislation. The price payable was the amount that the freehold would fetch on the open market on the assumption that at the end of the tenancy the tenant had the right to remain in possession of the house under the 1954 Act (or Local Government and Housing Act 1989, Sch 10). This was intended to give the landlord a more favourable figure. In addition, the tenant could now be viewed as a competitor bidder and so the purchase price should reflect the fact that he is a special purchaser who would pay more in order to be able to unlock the marriage value (see *Norfolk v Trinity College, Cambridge* (1976) 32 P & CR 147):

s 9(1A) The price payable for a house and premises . . . shall be the amount which at the relevant time the house and premises, if sold in the open market by a willing seller, might be expected to realise on the following assumptions:

   (a) on the assumption that the vendor was selling for an estate in fee simple, subject to the tenancy, but on the assumption that this Part of this Act conferred no right to acquire the freehold or an extended lease and, where the tenancy has been extended under this Part of this Act, that the tenancy will terminate on the original term date;

   (b) on the assumption that at the end of the tenancy the tenant has the right to remain in possession of the house and premises . . . under the provisions of Part I of the Landlord and Tenant Act 1954;

(c) on the assumption that the tenant has no liability to carry out any repairs, maintenance or redecorations under the terms of the tenancy or Part I of the Landlord and Tenant Act 1954;

(d) on the assumption that the price be diminished by the extent to which the value of the house and premises has been increased by any improvement carried out by the tenant or his predecessors in title at their own expense.

Under both the 1967 and 1974 methods of valuation the tenant must additionally pay the landlord's reasonable costs, both legal and valuation fees.

As mentioned earlier, the Leasehold Reform, Housing and Urban Development Act 1993 extended the scope of the 1967 Act by removing the upper value limits and introducing an alternative low rent test in relation to the right to acquire the freehold to all houses (see 1993 Act, Part I, Chapter III). Where the tenant is able to enfranchise by virtue of these amendments, the valuation base in the 1967 Act is to be in accordance with the 1974 approach subject to the following amendments:

1 To require the tenant to pay at least half of the marriage value (s 9(1C)(a), 1967 Act).

2 There would be no assumption that the tenant has security of tenure at the end of the lease (1967 Act, s 9(1C)). The result is that any rights under Part I of the 1954 Act will not be presumed. As most expensive houses are excluded from the 1954 Act, most tenants will pay a price without any recognition of a moral right to occupy the property.

3 The landlord may be entitled to 'injurious affection' payments. This is to compensate him for damage to the value of other interests which he has which is caused by the sale of this property. Injurious affection is a concept that has been used in relation to compensation for compulsory purchase in planning law (see Purdoe, Young and Rowan, *Planning Law and Procedure*, 1989, pp 460–7) and was introduced into enfranchisement by the 1993 Act (becoming the 1967 Act, s 9A). The freeholder therefore receives compensation for any reduction—caused by the sale—in the value of other land he owns and compensation for any loss of rights in such other land (for example, where the sale prevents a development partly on retained land).

These amendments bring the valuation provisions for expensive housing into line with the market value approach adopted for enfranchisement of flats under the 1993 Act (see below). The compensation provisions under both Acts will be discussed generally below (12.7.2.2).

12.3.3 The Right to an Extended Lease

As an alternative to enfranchisement, the tenant is able to acquire an extended lease which will be for 50 years from the expiry of the existing lease and on corresponding terms (ss 14 and 15). After the original term date the rent will be a ground rent in the sense that it shall represent the letting value of the site (without including anything for the value of the buildings on the site) for the uses to which the house and premises have been put since the commencement of the existing tenancy. (Leasehold Reform Act 1967, s 15(2)(a)).

Few tenants chose to extend the lease rather than to buy the freehold. It is a much less attractive right and can only be exercised once. Thereafter, the tenant has no right to either further renewal or to protection under Part I of the 1954 Act.

12.3.4 Landlord's Overriding Rights

The landlord is able to resist the tenant's claim to extend the lease if he wishes to

resume possession of the property on the ground that for purposes of redevelopment he proposes to demolish or reconstruct the whole or a substantial part of the house and premises. (Leasehold Reform Act 1967, s 17(1))

If the lease has already been extended, the landlord can claim possession on this ground at any time 'not earlier than twelve months before the original term date'. The landlord is also able to resist a claim for enfranchisement or an extended lease if he wishes to

resume possession on the ground that it or part of it is or will be reasonably required by him for occupation as the only or main residence of the landlord or of a person who is at the time of the application an adult member of the landlord's family. (Leasehold Reform Act 1967, s 18)

This right is only available to landlords who acquired their interest on or before 18 February 1966. If the landlord is able to resume possession on either of these grounds, compensation is payable to the tenant.

The parties are not able to contract out of the Act (Leasehold Reform Act 1967, s 23).

12.3.5 Estate Management Schemes

In order to meet the fears that enfranchisement would make good estate management difficult, the Act enabled the landlord to apply (within certain time limits—now expired) for an estate management scheme to be approved by the court (The 1967 Act, s 19). Schemes are essentially a means to enable landlords to continue to enforce covenants against the owners of enfranchised property and so to retain powers of management in respect of the property.

12.4 ENFRANCHISEMENT OF FLATS

Enfranchisement of flats has always been a much more difficult issue than enfranchisement of houses as it raises particular difficulties stemming from the interdependency of the units and the collectivity of interests. An individual tenant cannot buy the freehold of an individual flat—the freehold subsists in relation to the whole building and individual flats can only be owned on a leasehold basis. Any 'enfranchisement' must, therefore, be of the whole building. Even after 'enfranchisement', the landlord/tenant relationship remains, it is simply that the purchasing tenants will be collectively in control of the landlord. There are likely to be continuing difficulties in managing the property as any collective of people will have differing views on standards of repair, etc. In addition, it will often be the case that not all tenants participate in the enfranchisement process—any unsatisfactory lease structures will then remain and there may be friction between the tenant controlled landlord and the non-participating tenants.

12.4.1 Landlord and Tenant Act 1987

The limited rights to enfranchise contained in the Landlord and Tenant Act 1987 formed part of the response to the problems of management highlighted by the Nugee Report in 1985 (*Report of the Committee of Enquiry on the Management of Privately Owned Blocks of Flats*, 1985; see Hawkins [1986] Conv 12 and ch 7).

Some of the problems identified by the Nugee Committee—such as poor communications, lack of say in the appointment of managing agents, and inadequate information being provided—can be cured by the tenants taking control of the management. The 1987 Act as a whole was directed towards strengthening the tenant's hand in management. There were also two provisions enabling the tenants to acquire the freehold to the block. The first, contained in Part I, gives the tenants a right of first refusal whenever the landlord intends to dispose of the premises. The second, contained in Part III, enables the tenants to compulsorily acquire the landlord's interest when the landlord is in serious breach of his management obligations—for general commentaries on the Act, see Percival (1988) 51 MLR 97; Rodgers, *Residential Flats—A New Deal?* [1988] Conv 122.

12.4.1.1 The Right of First Refusal (Part I)

Before making a 'relevant disposal' of premises within Part I of the Act, the landlord must offer them to qualifying tenants (s 1). There are several phrases that need defining:

(a) Qualifying tenant (s 3)   Most residential tenants of long leases qualify. Whereas the 1967 and 1993 Acts apply *only* to tenants of long leases, short term tenants also qualify under the 1987 Act so long as they are not within one of the excluded categories. Excluded from being a qualiying tenant are protected short-hold tenants (within the Housing Act 1980, s 52, the predecessor to assured shortholds); tenants with employment related accommodation; assured tenants and assured agricultural tenants (within the Housing Act 1988); business tenants; and tenants who have more than two flats in the premises.

(b) Relevant disposal (s 4)   Relevant disposal is broadly defined as being a 'disposal by the landlord of any estate or interest (whether legal or equitable) in any such premises, including the disposal of any such estate or interest in any common parts of any such premises' (s 4(1)). There is, however, a long list of exceptions contained in subs (2) so that, for example, a gift to a member of the landlord's family or a disposal to an associated company, will not be a relevant disposal. There are several ways a landlord can evade the Act, disposing of the property in a way that does not trigger Part I, for example, by selling shares in the company which owns the property rather than by selling the property itself (for other methods, see Thomas *et al.*, *The Landlord and Tenant Act 1987: Awareness, Experience and Impact*, 1991, pp 70–3).

(c) Premises (s 1)   Section 1 states:

s 1(2) Subject to subsections (3) and (4), this part applies to premises if—
    (a) they consist of the whole or part of a building; and
    (b) they contain two or more flats held by qualifying tenants; and
    (c) the number of flats held by such tenants exceeds 50 per cent of the total number of flats contained in the premises.
  (3) This Part does not apply to premises falling within subsection (2) if—
    (a) any part or parts of the premises is or are occupied or intended to be occupied otherwise than for residential purposes; and
    (b) the internal floor area of that part or those parts (taken together) exceeds 50 per cent of the internal floor area of the premises (taken as a whole); and for the purposes of this subsection the internal floor area of any common parts shall be disregarded.

These conditions are more favourable to the tenants than those under the Leasehold Reform, Housing and Urban Development Act 1993 (requiring two-thirds of the flats to be held by qualifying tenants, one-half of the participating tenants to be resident, and no more than 10 per cent of the floor space to be for non-residential use). The reason given for permitting more premises to qualify under the 1987 Act is that the disposal is voluntary whereas under the 1993 Act the disposal may be against the landlord's wishes.

(d) Exempt/Resident Landlords   Certain landlords are exempted from the legislation, for example, a local authority or a charitable housing trust (s 58(1)). In
addition, premises owned by a resident landlord are exempted—the landlord
being resident if the premises are not purpose-built, he has occupied a flat in the
premises as his only or principal residence for at least twelve months and the
building contains two or more flats (s 58(2)).

(e) The Disposal Procedure   A landlord intending to make a relevant disposal
must first offer the premises to the qualifying tenants. He does this by serving a
notice on the tenants in a prescribed form including the main terms of the proposed disposal, especially the price (s 5). The tenants are then given two months
to state whether they wish to accept the offer. At least 50 per cent of the qualifying
tenants must participate (the 'requisite majority', s 5(6)). If the tenants accept the
offer, the landlord is not permitted to dispose of the property to anyone other
than the purchaser nominated by the tenants within a prescribed time (see s 6(1),
(2))—this is to give the tenants time to proceed with the purchase. If the qualifying tenants do not accept the offer, the landlord is free to dispose of the property
during a twelve-month period beginning on the expiry of the notice, so long as
the disposal is not on more favourable terms than offered to the qualifying tenants (s 7(1)). If the landlord does wish to sell for a lower price, he must first go
back to the tenants to see if they wish to proceed at the lower price. The tenants
are also free to respond to the landlord's offer by serving a counter-notice, setting
out alternative proposals to which the landlord must respond (s 7).

(f) Enforcement Provisions   If the landlord does make a disposal in breach of the
provisions in the Act the tenants can require the new landlord to provide details
of the terms of the disposal and to compel the new landlord to transfer the property to their nominated purchaser on identical terms (ss 12 and 13). In order to
avoid continuing uncertainty as to the purchaser's title, the request for details
must be within two months of the requisite majority of qualifying tenants receiving notice that the disposal has taken place (s 11(2)).

12.4.1.2 The Right of Compulsory Acquisition (Part III)

The right to apply for a compulsory acquisition order is only available either when
the landlord has failed to discharge his obligations relating to repair, maintenance,
insurance or management of the premises and the situation is likely to continue or
when a manager, appointed under Part II of the Act, has been acting for the preceding three years (s 29(2), (3) as amended by the Leasehold Reform, Housing and
Urban Development Act 1993, s 85; and see ch 7.2.4.5(e)). This provision is directed
to blocks held predominantly on long leases. Section 25(3) requires:

**s 25(3) (a) where the premises contain less than four flats, that all of the flats are
          let by the landlord on long leases;**

(b) where the premises contain more than three but less than ten flats, that all, or all but one, of the flats are so let; and

(c) where the premises contain ten or more flats, that at least 90 per cent of the flats are so let.

As with Part I, the right does not apply to premises with more than 50 per cent non-residential use, or where the premises are held by an exempt or resident landlord (s 25(4), (5)).

The premises must consist of the whole or part of a building and contain at least two flats held by qualifying tenants. Qualifying tenants here have a different meaning than in Part I. In order to qualify the tenant must have a long lease (generally, one exceeding 21 years—s 59(3)) and must not be the tenant of more than two flats (see s 26).

When initially enacted, 50 per cent of the qualifying tenants were able to exercise the right but this was amended by the Leasehold Reform, Housing and Urban Development Act 1993 to require 'not less than two-thirds' (s 85, amending the Landlord and Tenant Act 1987, s 27(4)). This is in line with the general approach of the 1993 legislation requiring substantial support from the tenants in order to justify the compulsory acquisition of the landlord's interest. Given that in order for Part III rights to be exercised the landlord has to have seriously neglected his responsibilities as a property owner, this is a questionable requirement.

The price payable on compulsory acquisition is either that agreed between the parties or

an amount equal to the amount which, in their opinion, that interest might be expected to realise if sold on the open market by a willing seller on the appropriate terms and on the assumption that none of the tenants of the landlord of any premises comprised in those premises was buying or seeking to buy that interest. (s 31(2))

12.4.1.3 Impact of the 1987 Act

A study of the 1987 Act in operation found that there was a marked lack of awareness of the Act and its provisions and implications (Thomas, North *et al.*, *op. cit.*). In relation to the right of first refusal various difficulties were encountered in exercising the right:

1 The lack of interest of some of the residents living in the block effectually penalizes those who do want to buy the freehold to the flats;

2 It was difficult to raise sufficient money;

3 It was difficult to meet the statutory deadlines;

4 The venture was stressful and time consuming.

The rights of first refusal in the 1987 Act have also proved easy to evade and to have very little effective penalty for non-compliance. Many of these problems stem from the fact that collective action is required by the tenants and that tight deadlines are imposed for responding to the landlord.

Similarly, although none of those in the survey had direct experience of using the compulsory acquisition right in Part III, comments were received that it should not be necessary to have collective purchase (now, not less than two-thirds).

The Act is generally acknowledged to have been poorly thought through, the Vice Chancellor commenting that it is 'an ill-drafted, complicated and confused Act' (*Denetower Ltd v Toop* [1991] 3 All ER 661 at 668; see also Smith, *A Nasty Measure—Part I of the Landlord and Tenant Act 1987*, (1992) 12 LS 42; Joseph Rowntree Housing Research Findings No. 106, January 1994).

12.4.2 Leasehold Reform, Housing and Urban Development Act 1993

During the 1980s pressure built up for something of more general application to be done about long leases of flats. The Nugee Report of 1985 highlighted the management problems that exist. Tenants and other interested bodies became increasingly concerned over the diminishing asset problem: at about the mid-point of a 99-year lease and often earlier, the leasehold interest ceases to increase its value, or even to maintain its value, against other property values. The tenant will then find it difficult to sell the lease, in part because lenders are reluctant to accept a mortgage over a leasehold interest which is of diminishing value. During the 1980s the early long leasehold flats were reaching this critical stage in the lease's life and the unfairness of the leasehold system became more visible. In addition, enfranchisement was an important part of the government's plan to extend home ownership. For further criticisms of long leasehold tenure, see *Leasehold—Time for a Change*, Building Societies Association, 1984; Neo, *Problems of Private Flat Ownership in England and Wales—Is Strata Title the Solution?*, RICS, 1990.

Part I of The Leasehold Reform, Housing and Urban Development Act 1993 gives tenants of long leasehold flats the collective right to enfranchise at market value, or the individual right to extend their leases by 90 years at market value.

12.4.2.1 The Collective Right to Enfranchise

The procedure for enfranchisement is complex. In part, this is an inevitable consequence of granting rights collectively, but it is also the result of an effective lobbying campaign during the progress of the Act on behalf of landlords opposed to the principle of compulsory enfranchisement.

(a) Does the Tenant qualify? The tests for qualification are shown diagrammatically in Figure 12.1 (see p 662). In order to qualify:

(i) There must be a long lease (s 7). Generally, this means that the lease must have been originally granted for more than 21 years, but some additional leases will qualify, such as leases granted in pursuance of the right to buy under the Housing Act 1985 (see s 7).

(ii) There must be a lease at a low rent (s 8). In order to be a lease at a low rent, the aggregate rent in the initial year must:

1 If granted before 1 April 1963, not have exceeded two-thirds of the letting value;

2 If granted before 1 April 1990 (but after 1 April 1963), not be more than two-thirds of the rateable value of the flat on the day the lease began; and

3 If granted on or after 1 April 1990, not be more than £1,000 if the flat is in Greater London or £250 elsewhere.

Amounts payable for services, repair, maintenance or insurance do not count as rent for this purpose.

(iii) It must not be a business lease. That is, it must not be one to which Part II of the Landlord and Tenant Act 1954 applies (ss 5(2)(a) and 101).

(iv) A person who would otherwise be a qualifying tenant of three or more flats cannot be a qualifying tenant of any (s 5(5)). Associated companies are considered to be the same person.

The purpose of this restriction is to prevent someone from buying interests in several flats in order to enfranchise. Enfranchisement is a right directed to residents, not investors.

(b) Do the Premises qualify? Working out whether the Act applies to particular premises also requires running through a series of tests, shown in Figure 12.2 (see p 663).

(i) The premises must be 'a self-contained building or part of a building' (s 3(1)(a)). In order to satisfy this, the building must either be detached or it must be capable of being divided vertically into a part that could be redeveloped independently of the remainder of the building and services provided without causing significant interruption for occupiers of the remainder of the building.

(ii) There must be two or more flats held by qualifying tenants (s 3(1)(b)).

(iii) At least two-thirds of the flats must be held by qualifying tenants (s 3(1)(c)).

(iv) No more than 10 per cent of the floorspace can be used for non-residential purposes (s 4(1)). This means that for every one unit of commercial space there will need to be at least nine units of residential space for the building to qualify and so premises consisting of shops with a row of flats above will not be enfranchisable as of right. The Government was concerned to ensure that residential leaseholders do not, in effect, become managers of commercial property and so the legislation applies to property that is predominantly residential. If there were a higher percentage of commercial use permitted, it would also make the cost of enfranchising extremely expensive for tenants—as it is, even one commercial

Figure 12.1 Does the Tenant Qualify?

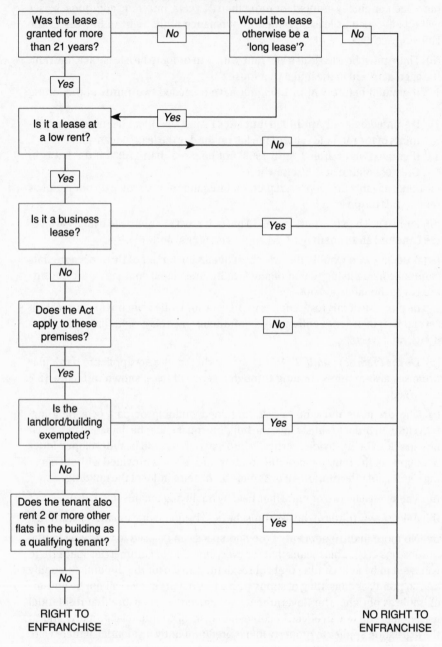

Figure 12.2 Does the Act apply to these Premises?

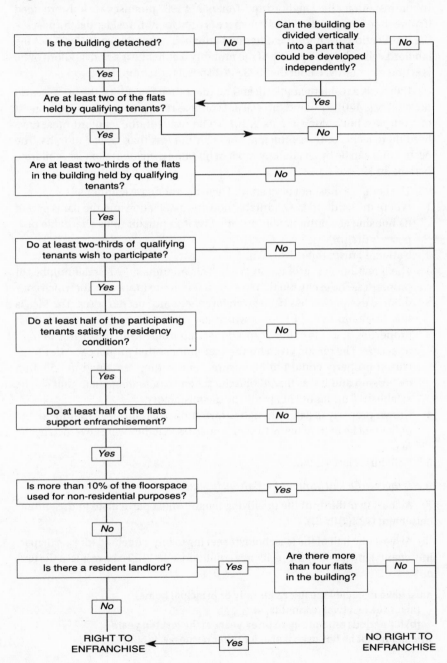

Is the building detached? — No — Can the building be divided vertically into a part that could be developed independently? — No

Yes

Are at least two of the flats held by qualifying tenants? ← Yes

Yes — No

Are at least two-thirds of the flats in the building held by qualifying tenants? — No

Yes

Do at least two-thirds of qualifying tenants wish to participate? — No

Yes

Do at least half of the participating tenants satisfy the residency condition? — No

Yes

Do at least half of the flats support enfranchisement? — No

Yes

Is more than 10% of the floorspace used for non-residential purposes? — Yes

No

Is there a resident landlord? — Yes — Are there more than four flats in the building? — No

No

RIGHT TO ENFRANCHISE ← Yes

NO RIGHT TO ENFRANCHISE

unit can greatly increase the cost of enfranchising and may make it prohibitive. In contrast, under the Landlord and Tenant Act 1987 premises are only excluded if more than 50 per cent of the floorspace is used for non-residential purposes—the justification given for the differing figure being that under the 1987 Act the landlord will only be disposing of the property if either he is a bad landlord or he is acting voluntarily. Under the 1993 Act disposals are compulsory.

(v) If there is a resident landlord, and no more than four units, the premises do not qualify (s 4(4)). The landlord will not count as resident if the premises consist of a purpose built block of flats (s 10). To be resident, the landlord must have lived there as his only or principal home for not less than twelve months. The occupation can be by an adult member of his family, including spouse, children, parents and in-laws.

(vi) The landlord must not be exempt. There are various exemptions:
1   Where the landlord is a charitable housing association and the flat is part of its housing accommodation provided by it in pursuit of its charitable purposes (s 5(2)(b));
2   National Trust properties (s 95);
3   The 'great houses' exemption (s 31). This exempts only a small number of properties. The exclusion is drafted by reference to properties for which conditional exemption has been given for inheritance tax purposes. The idea is that it should exempt houses which are comparable with National Trust properties in terms of quality, national importance and the degree of public access. The reason given for the exemption is that proper care of enfranchised property could not be ensured unless they remained in common ownership and it was feared that the schemes of management that can be established under the Act would be unsatisfactory.
4   Crown property (s 94). Although Crown property is formally exempted, the policy will be to treat many Crown properties as if they were governed by the Act.
5   Cathedral closes (s 96).

(c) Is there sufficient Support for Enfranchisement?

(i) At least two-thirds of the qualifying tenants must participate in the enfranchisement (s 13(2)(b)(i)).

(ii) At least one half of the leaseholders seeking to buy a freehold (the participating tenants) must satisfy the residency condition (s 13(2)). To be resident the tenant

must have occupied the flat as his only or principal home–
    (a) for the last twelve months, or
    (b) for periods amounting to three years in the last ten years,
whether or not he has used it also for other purposes. (s 6(2))

This is a less stringent test than under the 1967 Act (which requires three years' residency) and was selected in the light of evidence from the Consumers Association that there is a fairly rapid turnover of flat dwellers and to impose a long residency requirement would render many ineligible. It is not necessary for this occupation to have been under a qualifying lease (s 6(3)(b)). Thus someone who has lived in a flat owned by his parents and who has recently inherited a long lease, or a former secure tenant who has exercised the Right To Buy, will be able to participate.

Although companies and artificial persons may be qualifying tenants, they cannot satisfy the residency condition.

(iii) At least one-half of all the flats must support enfranchisement (s 13(2)(b)(ii)). This is to ensure that a minority (which the two-thirds qualifying, two-thirds participating requirements could theoretically produce) is not able to enfranchise against the will of the majority.

(d) *The Property to be Enfranchised*   Where the requisite number of qualifying tenants choose to enfranchise, they must nominate a purchaser, which will usually be a company. The question of which property can be acquired is not straightforward. Let us assume that the tenants live in a block of twelve flats with one commercial shop unit, a communal garden and a physically separate row of garages, two of which are allocated to the shop and the remainder let to residential tenants under their flat leases. In this situation, the nominee purchaser can claim the freehold to:

1   'The relevant premises' (the block of flats);
2   'Appurtenant property', that is 'any garage, outhouse, garden, yard, or appurtenances belonging to, or usually enjoyed with, the flat' (s 1(7)—the garages which are let to the residential tenants);
3   Property which the tenant 'is entitled under the terms of the lease of the flat to use in common with the occupiers of other premises' (s 1(3)(b)—the communal garden).

Although the nominee purchaser is entitled to claim the freehold to all of these properties, the claim can be made for only some of the property (s 1(5)).

If there is an intermediate lease between the freehold and the qualifying tenant, the nominee purchaser must buy the leasehold interest between the leases of qualifying tenants and the freeholder (s 2). This does not apply, however, when the intermediate lessor is a public sector landlord letting on secure tenancies.

While the nominee purchaser has no right to claim appurtenant property or shared property which is not held by qualifying tenants, in our example, the garages used by the shop, the freeholder may require the nominee purchaser to acquire property additional to that specified in the purchaser's initial notice.

This is so if the property

(a) **would for all practical purposes cease to be of use and benefit to [the land-lord], or**
(b) **would cease to be capable of being reasonably managed or maintained by him.** (s 18(4))

This will prevent the landlord from being left with a commercially redundant property.

In addition, the freeholder has a right to leaseback certain units (s 36 and Sch 9, Parts II and III). Schedule 9, Part II states that any flats in the premises let on secure tenancies by a local authority or let by a housing association freeholder to a tenant who is neither a secure tenant nor a qualifying tenant *must* be leased back to the local authority or housing association. Neither the nominee purchaser nor the freeholder have an option. The idea behind this is to ensure that secure tenants renting from local authorities and tenants of housing associations will continue to have the same landlord.

Schedule 9, Part III provides that where the property includes non-residential parts and/or flats not let on long leases, the freeholder will have the right to lease-back all or some of these parts. The leaseback will be for 999 years at a peppercorn rent. This will enable the landlord to continue to manage any commercial or rental units he wishes to.

The freeholder may be able to prevent enfranchisement if he intends to redevelop the premises. This only applies in a narrow set of circumstances, where not less than two-thirds of all the long leases are due to terminate within the period of five years and the landlord intends to demolish, reconstruct or carry out substantial works of construction on the whole or a substantial part of the premises (s 23).

(e) The Price of Enfranchisement   Whereas the 1967 Act was widely acknowledged to be confiscatory in effect, the intention was that the 1993 Act would have a fairer system of compensation for the landlord, based on normal valuation practice. The provisions for calculating the cost of enfranchisement are set out in Sch 6. Working out how much is to be paid is complex and there are differing views as to how, in particular, the marriage value should be arrived at—the chairman of the first Leasehold Valuation Tribunal decision to look at this stated that they approached the task with 'some trepidation' (Lady Fox, *Waitt v Morris* [1994] 39 EG 140 at 141). What follows is a simplified account of the provisions (for a more detailed analysis, see Clarke, *Leasehold Enfranchisement*, 1994, chs 18–21). The price of enfranchisement is the aggregate of four elements:

(i) The open market value of the freeholder's interest.   This is effectively the price at which the freeholder could sell his interest to a third party.

Leasehold Reform, Housing and Urban Development Act 1993, Sch 6
para 3 . . . the value of the freeholder's interest in the specified premises is the amount which at the valuation date that interest might be expected to

realise if sold on the open market by a willing seller (with neither the nominee purchaser nor any participating tenant buying or seeking to buy) . . .

It is assumed that the freehold is being sold subject to existing leases and that there is no right to enfranchise or extend leases. The 'special bid' that tenants would make to purchase is ignored at this stage.

The overall intention is therefore for the reversion to be valued on normal valuation principles, looking to the value of rents passing, the reversionary value when leases expire and any security rights of tenants.

(ii) At least 50 per cent of the 'marriage value'.   Marriage value has been referred to earlier (see 12.3.2). In the case of collective enfranchisement, it is a misnomer as there is no 'marriage' after enfranchisement, as the tenants' interests do not merge with the freehold. Here the so-called marriage value comes from the fact that the participating tenants are, after enfranchisement, collectively in control and so able to grant themselves longer leases without having to pay for them.

It is defined in Sch 6, para 4(2):

Sch 6

para 4(2) The marriage value is any increase in the aggregate value of the freehold and every intermediate leasehold interest in the specified premises, when regarded as being (in consequence of their being acquired by the nominee purchaser) interests under the control of the participating tenants, as compared with the aggregate value of those interests when held by the person from whom they are to be so acquired, being an increase in value–

(a) which is attributable to the potential ability of the participating tenants, once those interests have been so acquired, to have new leases granted to them without payment of any premium and without restriction as to length of term, and

(b) which, if those interests were being sold to the nominee purchaser on the open market by willing sellers, the nominee purchaser would have to agree to share with the sellers in order to reach agreement as to price.

The freeholder is to receive at least half of this:

Sch 6

para 4(1) . . . the freeholder's share of the marriage value is–

(a) such proportion of that amount as is determined by agreement between the reversioner and the nominee purchaser or, in default of agreement, as is determined by a leasehold valuation tribunal to be the proportion which in its opinion would have been determined by an agreement made at the valuation date between the parties on a sale on the open market by a willing seller, or

(b) 50 per cent of that amount,
whichever is the greater.

In theory, the 'at least 50 per cent' approach is intended to reflect market practice, but this is hard to accept. If it reflects market practice, why include subparagraph (b)? The same result would be achieved without it. In addition, if the
market would give the landlord a lower share of the marriage value, why should
the tenant have to pay more?

A simple illustration of how this works was provided by the then housing minister, Sir George Young:

*Property: a block with 10 flats on leases with 50 years unexpired, ground rents of £60
per annum:*

Open market value of lease of each flat	£160,000
Aggregate value of leasehold interests	£1,600,000
Open market value of freeholder's reversion	£30,000
Vacant possession value of block	£2,000,000
Marriage Value	
(£2,000,000 – (£1,600,000 + £30,000))	£370,000
Collective cost to tenants	
(reversion + at least half marriage value) ,	minimum £215,000
(£30,000 + at least £185,000)	
Average minimum cost per tenant assuming full participation	*minimum £21,500*

In practice there will often not be full participation, nor is there any provision
in the Act as to how the price of enfranchisement is to be shared by the participating tenants. In addition to the £21,500 in the example given, the tenants may
have to compensate the landlord for injurious affection and to pay his costs, see
below.

(iii) Injurious Affection Payments.   The price will also include sums for 'injurious affection' (Sch 6, para 5), a phrase explained earlier (12.3.2) in relation to the
1993 amendments to the Leasehold Reform Act 1967.

(iv) The Landlord's Costs (s 33).   The nominee purchaser also has to pay the
landlord's reasonable professional costs.

12.4.2.2 The Right to an Extended Lease

As an alternative to collective enfranchisement, an individual tenant may have a
right to an extended lease (see the 1993 Act, Part I, Chapter II). This right is available if the tenant is a qualifying tenant of the flat (s 39, see above 12.4.2.1(a)). In
outline this means that he must have a long lease at a low rent, but there is no
restriction on the total number of flats he can own (but he will only be able to satisfy the residency condition for one).

The residency condition for lease extension requires the tenant to have occupied the flat as his only or principal home for the last three years, or for three out
of the last ten years (s 39(2)). There is no need for the premises as a whole to qualify. Extension will be by surrender of the unexpired portion of the lease followed
by the grant of a new one, which would expire ninety years after the expiry date of

the present lease and will be at a peppercorn rent (s 56). Apart from that, the new lease will be on identical terms. A renewed lease can be extended again by the same procedure (s 59).

The landlord is given the right to apply to the court for possession of such an extended lease on the grounds that he wishes to redevelop the property. The ground can only be exercised by application to a court within either twelve months of the expiry date of the original lease or within five years of the expiry date of the renewed lease (s 61). If possession is given, the landlord may have to pay compensation under Sch 14. The price to be paid for such a lease, and the procedure to be adopted for its acquisition, follow similar principles to those for collective enfranchisement.

When the Bill was first introduced, this right to a lease extension was only available to tenants who would not otherwise qualify for enfranchisement, the aim being to give primacy to enfranchisement. Wider availability of the right was resisted on the grounds that tenants might prefer lease extension to enfranchisement. The right is now available to all tenants qualifying under s 39 and those expected preferences are likely to be realised: lease extension will be a much simpler process as there is no need for the premises as a whole to qualify and no need to co-ordinate a collection of tenants. It will also solve the diminishing asset problem faced by tenants.

12.4.2.3 Estate Management Schemes

The Leasehold Reform, Housing and Urban Development Act 1993, Part I, Chapter IV, enables a landlord to apply for a scheme of management in respect of property which is likely to be enfranchised. This includes property which might be enfranchised as a result of the removal of the upper value limits under the Leasehold Reform Act 1967, as well as property that can be enfranchised under the 1993 Act. The provisions work in the same manner as those contained in s 19 of the 1967 Act (12.3.5)—but are simplified and the responsibility for approval of schemes is transferred from the High Court to the leasehold valuation tribunal.

12.5 THE RIGHT TO BUY AND RENT TO MORTGAGE

'a bulwark against bolshevism' (Sir Harold Belman, cited in Boddy, *The Building Societies*, 1980, at p 23)

The awkward fact, of course, is that modern capitalism subsidized by the state has been able to extend home ownership and realistic aspirations to it, to a steadily increasing proportion of the working class, while the same forces have so undermined any proto-socialist potential in council housing that it has become increasingly unpopular, expensive and generally indefensible . . . Putting it quite crudely and acknowledging the many poor working class home owners, the distinction between tenants and owners symbolises in Britain, more closely than any other indicator, the difference between the 'haves' and the 'have-nots' not only in society as a whole but *within* the working class. (Ginsburg, *Home Ownership and Socialism in Britain: A Bulwark Against Bolshevism*, (1983) 3:1 *Critical Social Policy* 34)

The Right To Buy (RTB) can be seen as merely another example of leasehold enfranchisement alongside the Leasehold Reform Act 1967 and the Leasehold Reform, Housing and Urban Development Act 1993. However, there are different issues of policy behind enfranchisement in the local authority and housing association sectors and that in the private residential sector under the 1967 and 1993 Acts. One major difference is that the RTB is aimed at periodic tenants, not long leaseholders. However, the differences are more fundamental and go to the root of overall housing policy in Britain.

[Home] ownership is offered to the proletariat so that if ever they contemplate overthrowing the existing order there would be, in addition to their chains, a house to lose. Choice utterances on the theme are Neville Chamberlain's, "every spadeful of manure dug in, every fruit tree planted', converted a potential revolutionary into a citizen' or Henry Brooke's, 'a home owner can get his roots down and get his roses planted—ownership and responsibility go hand in hand'. The encouragement of working-class owner-occupation is, at least, partly motivated by the desire to subvert revolutionary and militant activity and, in this, the ruling class must be taken at their (often enough repeated) word. Given the history of British social policy, it would be astonishing if the extension of owner-occupation through council house sales was not divisive in intent. (Jacobs, *The Sale of Council Houses: Does It Matter?*, (1981) 4:3 *Critical Social Policy* 35, pp 41–2; footnotes omitted)

Although in the immediate aftermath of World War II the sale of council houses was frowned upon, councils were given the general discretion to sell their housing with ministerial consent from 1951 onwards; indeed, in 1978, the last full year of Labour government before the RTB was introduced, 28,000 properties were sold—Jacobs, 1981, *op. cit.*, p 37. Before 1980, Birmingham City Council had a policy of selling off its council stock, subject to some limitations to protect its holdings of specialized properties, such as housing for elderly people and some types of four-bedroom houses—Malpass and Murie, *Housing Policy and Practice*, 3rd edn, 1990, p 271; see also 4th edn, 1994, pp 297 *et seq*. This sale of council houses did not reflect any housing policy by Birmingham council, rather it was based on political and economic ideology: nevertheless, the choice of housing to exclude in the early stages did indicate that the distribution of a scarce resource could take precedence over sales in the appropriate circumstances— Malpass and Murie, 1990, *op. cit.* However, the Housing Act 1980 created for the first time an obligation to sell—see ss 1–27 of the 1980 Act. The result has been the largest ever transfer of public assets into the private sector—council house sales contributed almost as much in terms of capital receipts as the whole of the rest of the government's privatisation programme put together (Joseph Rowntree Foundation Inquiry into British Housing, Second Report, 1991, at p 71). A third of the increase in owner-occupation in the 1980s was due to the RTB—Audit Commission, *Developing Local Authority Housing Strategies*, para 10 (1992).

Selling council houses was the most substantial element in the privatisation policies of the Thatcher government, a privatisation which has benefitted ordinary working families rather than the wealthy or those able to shift their investment portfolios around. In the [period up to 1992] some one and a half million public sector dwellings have been sold. Most of these have been under the right to buy introduced in the Housing Act 1980.

Those who have bought have mostly bought good houses at cheap (discounted) prices, and in general they have benefitted from house price inflation. In some cases, they have bought because it is cheaper to buy than to rent. Rising interest rates have probably had less impact on those who bought under the right to buy than on those who bought at market prices elsewhere. However, the impact of recession and job losses is felt by this group as much as any other.

Evaluating council house sales [from 1980 to 1992] is complex. The policy has not operated in a vacuum. It has formed part of a general reshaping of housing policy. (Forrest and Murie, 'The Right to Buy', in Grant, *Built to Last*, 1992, p 139)

The Conservative election victory of 1979 was partly built on the Right To Buy and even in the mid-1990s the Conservative administration still believed in the superiority of owner-occupation, as evidenced by the Rent To Mortgage scheme found in the Leasehold Reform, Housing and Urban Development Act 1993. The Labour Party, after initially opposing the RTB, found that such opposition was a vote loser and changed its policy to be broadly in favour of the RTB. Critical analysis comes, therefore, from academics, especially those on the left. Jacobs, *op. cit.*, focused his attention on the non-socialist nature of council housing *per se*. However, the article raises questions that go to the root of the RTB scheme and policy. The RTB was, first, meant to offer tenants a choice they would not otherwise have to become home owners, it was to extend the property owning democracy and, secondly, there was some idea that owner-occupiers were more likely to vote Conservative; owner-occupation was seen as a bulwark against bolshevism. However, on the second point this simplistic analysis was questioned by Jacobs, partly on the basis that the Peoples' Republic of China encouraged owner-occupation and the former West Germany, the leading industrial democracy in Europe, had only a third of its homes in owner-occupation as late as 1968 (*cf.* van Vliet, *International Handbook of Housing Policies and Practices*, 1990, at p 129—in 1982, 60 per cent of West Germans were rental dwellers, although there was a policy of promoting owner-occupation).

While undoubtedly powerful vested interests are behind the primacy of owner-occupation within the housing market, the financial advantages overall are not altogether clear and the explanation for its growth is as much ideological as it is financial. Among its ideological benefits, the association between council housing and socialism has helped keep Tory principles safe from the seduction of welfarism during the boom years of public sector expansion. More importantly, it has helped avoid too close a scrutiny of the nature of the public sector so that, for instance, in the 1960s, high rise housing could be passed off as a means of solving pressing housing problems rather than being an expression of, in Dunleavy's words [Protest and quiescence in urban politics, in Harloe, *Urban Change and Conflict*, 1977, p 175]:

'the monopoly power of a small number of construction companies within the public housing apparatus and the powerlessness of council tenants excluded from any control over their housing.'

While the left concentrates on defending the 'socialist' public sector, interest rates from monies raised on the private market consume housing budgets, the large building firms prosper and local housing departments continue to sift the 'deserving' from the 'undeserving' among council tenants. (Jacobs, 1981, *op. cit.*, p 37)

In the view of left-wing commentators, the major issue was the total lack of an overall housing policy, socialist or otherwise, coupled with the Conservative and Labour myth that council house dwellers were socialist and owner-occupiers were Tory. To left-wing commentators, the RTB, therefore, was not the beginning of the end of socialist housing—it never had been socialist and had, in fact, always favoured the better-off working class (Malpass and Murie, 1994, *op. cit.*, pp 61–3). Conversely,

[at] a local level in Britain, too, it is not always true that the more conservative an area, the greater the preponderance of owner occupiers. We have already mentioned Coventry's very high level of working class owner occupation in a city famous for wage militancy and its shop stewards movement. Coventry has four parliamentary constituencies, of which three returned Labour MPs in 1979 and one a Tory. Yet the constituency with the highest proportion of owner-occupiers voted Labour. Even in Dennis Skinner's Bolsover constituency where two thirds of the vote went to Labour, owner-occupiers outnumber council tenants. At the extremes of course, tenure and electoral preference go hand in hand, but in general housing tenure is reflected in voting even less clearly than trade union membership, and 35 per cent of trade unionists voted Tory in 1979! (Ginsburg, *op. cit.*, at p 47)

Cowling and Smith, *Home Ownership, Socialism and Realistic Socialist Policy*, (1984) 3:3 *Critical Social Policy* 64, went so far as to argue that universal owner-occupation could well form the platform of a socialist housing policy and might be better than the current system of mixed tenures.

It needs also to be understood that to the working class it is equally a matter of relative indifference whether their housing is provided by private rented, public rented or owner-occupied property. What is of concern to them is that they receive decent housing, at the most advantageous terms possible, at minimum political cost. (Jacobs, *op. cit.*, p 41)

What is clear, though, is that when considered carefully, owner-occupation does not provide a bulwark against Bolshevism and council housing is not a hotbed of revolutionary socialism. The ideological foundations of the RTB are not empirically well founded, therefore, in this one aspect at least—later in this chapter the question of the RTB and 'choice' will be examined, but in the wider context of 'loss and benefit' caused by the RTB legislation.

To understand fully the nature of the change brought about by the RTB in the local authority and, to a lesser extent, the housing association sectors, however, some idea of the size of the transfer effected by the legislation is necessary. At the peak of council house sales in England and Wales in 1982, almost 200,000 properties were transferred into the private sector through the RTB. Overall, approximately a fifth of council housing stock has been sold since 1980. In recent years, the figures have fallen as many of those wealthy enough to buy have already bought and the better properties have already been transferred. (See Table 12.1 (OO = owner-occupier). Source: Housing and Construction Statistics, various years)

Table 12.1 Sale of dwellings in England and Wales 1980–93

	LA to OO		New town to OO		HA to OO
		Formerly tenant		Formerly tenant	
1980	81416		4223		
1981	102720	97053	3801	3196	7233
1982	202045	196913	5312	4475	17417
1983	138406	133698	4832	3741	16359
1984	103175	98241	4281	2909	12493
1985	92290	87803	3085	2118	9498
1986	88146	84650	2400	2084	10437
1987	98769	96389	3071	2738	7557
1988	147188	144086	4630	4614	8154
1989	160786	157111	4824	4819	6769
1990	105553	101431	1608	1575	6033
1991	58495	55563	893	765	5687
1992	47782	44830	286	273	4252
1993	9208	8698	59	59	2820
Total	1,435,979	1,306,466	43,305	33,366	114,709

The volume of sales shows steady growth from 1980–82 as the first flush of interest in the RTB reached its peak. The increase in sales from 1987–89 was probably due to the rise in rents and the boom in house prices at that time. The decline since then, however, is a reflection of the fact that house prices generally are falling, turning home ownership into a less enticing form of investment, the better properties have all been sold off and the remaining tenants are not necessarily able from a financial standpoint to exercise the RTB even with a discount. It should also be noted that almost three-quarters of the properties sold have been houses, despite the favourable discount given on the sale of flats. As will be seen, those purchasers of flats have found it very difficult to sell them subsequently, a factor which many potential purchasers may have taken into account in deciding not to use the RTB. The government's Rent To Mortgage scheme is intended to continue the move to owner-occupation amongst those council tenants who cannot afford the RTB, but the slow down in sales is not solely to do with the lower income levels of many of the remaining tenants.

12.5.1 The Law Relating to the Right To Buy

This case raises party politics . . . It is about the sale of council houses. The local authorities own a great number of council houses. They have built them for the purpose of housing those in need . . . Parliament has passed the Housing Act 1980. It gives council tenants the right to buy their houses at a big discount. Sometimes at half price. Some local councils think this is undesirable. It means that the houses are taken out of their housing stock. They are no longer available for the young marrieds and others who are desperately in need of accommodation. (*Norwich CC v Secretary of State for the Environment* [1982] 1 All ER 737, *per* Lord Denning MR at 739)

The RTB was introduced by the Housing Act 1980. It is now found in much the same form in Part V of the Housing Act 1985, although the ancillary right to a mortgage from the local authority, *inter alia*, was abolished by s 107 Leasehold Reform, Housing and Urban Development Act 1993. Given, however, that due to central government pressure, local authorities charged higher rates of interest than building societies, the passing of the right to a mortgage will not be greatly mourned—the *Guardian* p 30, 30 January 1993.

12.5.1.1 The Right

The Housing Act 1985 provides that a secure tenant can purchase the freehold of a house, or, if the local authority is itself a leaseholder or the property is a flat, a lease for 125 years or for five days fewer than the council's own lease, subject to modification by ministerial order under s 171.

Housing Act 1985

s 118(1) A secure tenant has the right to buy, that is to say, the right, in the circumstances and subject to the conditions and exceptions stated in the following provisions of this Part—

    (a) if the dwelling-house is a house and the landlord owns the freehold, to acquire the freehold of the dwelling-house;

    (b) if the landlord does not own the freehold or if the dwelling-house is a flat (whether or not the landlord owns the freehold), to be granted a lease of the dwelling-house.

    (2) Where a secure tenancy is a joint tenancy then, whether or not each of the joint tenants occupies the dwelling-house as his only or principal home, the right to buy belongs jointly to all of them or to such one or more of them as may be agreed between them; but such an agreement is not valid unless the person or at least one of the persons to whom the right to buy is to belong occupies the dwelling-house as his only or principal home.

Housing Act 1985, Sch 6, Pt. III

para 11 A lease shall be for the appropriate term defined in paragraph 12 (but subject to sub-paragraph (3) of that paragraph) and at a rent not exceeding £10 per annum, and the following provisions have effect with respect to the other terms of the lease.

The appropriate term

para 12(1) If at the time the grant is made the landlord's interest in the dwelling-house is not less than a lease for a term of which more than 125 years and five days are unexpired, the appropriate term is a term of not less than 125 years.

    (2) In any other case the appropriate term is a term expiring five days before the term of the landlord's lease of the dwelling-house (or, as the case may require, five days before the first date on which the term of any lease under which the landlord holds any part of the dwelling-house) is to expire.

    (3) If the dwelling-house is a flat contained in a building which also contains one or more other flats and the landlord has, since 8th August 1980, granted a lease of one or more of them for the appropriate term, the lease of the dwelling-house may be for a term expiring at the end of the term for which the other lease (or one of the other leases) was granted.

The effect of Sch 6, Part III, para 12(3) is that the purchaser of a flat in a building or on an estate (for example, of maisonettes) will obtain a lease where the length is determined by reference to the remaining length of lease granted to the first purchaser in the building or on the estate under the RTB. For example, if on a council estate made up of a mixture of houses, one-bedroomed flats and maisonettes, one of the maisonettes was sold on a 125-year lease under the RTB in 1987, a tenant buying a flat or maisonette in 1995 would only obtain a lease for 117 years.

The Housing (Extension of Right to Buy) Order 1987, SI 1987 No. 1732, (as modified by the Housing (Extension of Right to Buy) Order 1990, SI 1990 No. 179, arts. 2, 3, and Schedule, para 2), allows the tenant of a house to obtain the freehold even where the local authority landlord has only a lease, as long as the superior landlord is specified in para 2 and that authority has the freehold:

art 3(2) This article applies to an interest held by–
        a local authority,
        a new town corporation,
        an urban development corporation,
        the Development Board for Rural Wales,
        the Housing Corporation, or
        a registered housing association, other than one excepted from the right to buy by Schedule 5, paragraph 1 (charities), 2 (co-operatives) or 3 (associations which have not received grant),
    which is immediately superior to the interest of the landlord or to another interest to which this article applies.

On the other hand, there are cases where the property does not come within the RTB—Housing Act 1985, s 120. The minimum length of lease to be granted with respect to a house is 21 years and to a flat is 50 years, with the length to be established at the date of the tenant's notice claiming the RTB; if the local authority's interest is insufficient to grant these minimum terms, then the RTB cannot be exercised—Sch 5, para 4. Furthermore, dwelling houses which are part of a group which have features designed for either physically disabled, mentally disordered or elderly tenants cannot be bought under the RTB—Sch 5, paras 7–11.

12.5.1.2 House or Flat?

The principal distinction in the Housing Act 1985 is between the secure tenant who buys a freehold house and the one who buys a leasehold flat, but there are difficult cases concerning surrounding land let with the dwelling house, such as a garage or parking space away from the dwelling house. The house-flat distinction is based on whether the dwelling is divided, if at all, horizontally or vertically from neighbouring properties.

s 183(1) The following provisions apply to the interpretation of 'house', 'flat' and 'dwelling-house' when used in this Part.
    (2) A dwelling-house is a house if, and only if, it (or so much of it as does not

consist of land included by virtue of section 184) is a structure reasonably so called; so that–

(a) where a building is divided horizontally, the flats or other units into
which it is divided are not houses;

(b) where a building is divided vertically, the units into which it is
divided may be houses;

(c) where a building is not structurally detached, it is not a house if a
material part of it lies above or below the remainder of the structure.

(3) A dwelling-house which is not a house is a flat.

s 184(1) For the purpose of this Part land let together with a dwelling-house shall
be treated as part of the dwelling-house, unless the land is agricultural
land (within the meaning set out in section 26(3)(a) of the General Rate
Act 1967) exceeding two acres.

(2) There shall be treated as included in a dwelling-house any land which is
not within subsection (1) but is or has been used for the purpose of the
dwelling-house if—

(a) the tenant, by a written notice served on the landlord at any time
before he exercises the right to buy or the right to acquire on rent to
mortgage terms, requires the land to be included in the dwelling-
house, and

(b) it is reasonable in all the circumstances for the land to be so included.

(3) A notice under subsection (2) may be withdrawn by a written notice
served on the landlord at any time before the tenant exercises the right
to buy or the right to acquire on rent to mortgage terms.

(4) Where a notice under subsection (2) is served or withdrawn after the service of the notice under section 125 (landlord's notice of purchase price,
etc.), the parties shall, as soon as practicable after the service or withdrawal, take all such steps (whether by way of amending, withdrawing
or re-serving any notice or extending any period or otherwise) as may be
requisite for the purpose of securing that all parties are, as nearly as may
be, in the same position as they would have been in if the notice under
subsection (2) had been served or withdrawn before the service of the
notice under section 125.

12.5.1.3 Who Has the Right to Buy?

Under ss 118 and 119 Housing Act 1985, a secure tenant of two years' standing
may exercise the RTB. Where the entire council estate has been sold to either a
private landlord or a housing association, the tenant will no longer be secure
under the Housing Act 1985 because the 'landlord condition' under ss 79 and 80
will no longer be satisfied. However, subject to registration the former secure
tenant's RTB is preserved under ss 171A-171H and Sch 9A (see 12.5.3).

s 119(1) The right to buy does not arise unless the period which, in accordance

with Schedule 4, is to be taken into account for the purposes of this section is at least two years.

(2) Where the secure tenancy is a joint tenancy the condition in subsection
(1) need be satisfied with respect to one only of the joint tenants.

Schedule 4 allows for the aggregation of various periods as a 'public sector tenant' in order to satisfy the requirement of two years of secure tenancy. 'Public
sector tenant' is defined in Sch 4, para 6.

Meaning of 'public sector tenant'
para 6(1) In this Schedule a 'public sector tenant' means a tenant under a public
sector tenancy.

(2) For the purposes of this Schedule, a tenancy, other than a long tenancy, under which a dwelling-house was let as a separate dwelling was
a public sector tenancy at any time when the conditions described
below as the landlord condition and the tenant condition were satisfied.

(3) The provisions of this Schedule apply in relation to a licence to occupy
a dwelling-house (whether or not granted for a consideration) as they
apply in relation to a tenancy.

(4) Sub-paragraph (3) does not apply to a licence granted as a temporary
expedient to a person who entered the dwelling-house or any other
land as a trespasser (whether or not, before the grant of that licence,
another licence to occupy that or another dwelling-house had been
granted to him).

Subparagraph (2), *inter alia*, allows a tenant to include periods as a council tenant, or tenant of some other public sector authority, before the legal status of
secure tenant was introduced in the Housing Act 1980. The landlord and tenant
conditions referred to in subparagraph (2) are dealt with in paras 7–10. As well as
a local authority, new town corporations, housing action trusts, urban development corporations, registered housing associations, the Housing Corporation
and any other landlord specified by the Minister in regulations under Sch 4 all
satisfy the landlord condition. The tenant condition, extended from the standard
s 81 definition by para 10, can be satisfied by any joint tenant, by the spouse of
the current tenant (whether the spouse is still living or now deceased) and by the
deceased parent of the current tenant in certain circumstances—Sch 4, paras
2–4.

Periods occupying accommodation subject to public sector tenancy
para 2   A period qualifies under this paragraph if it is a period during which,
before the relevant time–

(a) the secure tenant, or

(b) his spouse (if they are living together at the relevant time), or

(c) a deceased spouse of his (if they were living together at the time of
the death),

was a public sector tenant or was the spouse of a public sector tenant and occupied as his only or principal home the dwelling-house of which the spouse was such a tenant.

para 3   For the purposes of paragraph 2 a person who, as a joint tenant under a public sector tenancy, occupied a dwelling-house as his only or principal home shall be treated as having been the public sector tenant under that tenancy.

para 4(1) This paragraph applies where the public sector tenant of a dwelling-house died or otherwise ceased to be a public sector tenant of the dwelling-house, and thereupon a child of his who occupied the dwelling-house as his only or principal home (the 'new tenant') became the public sector tenant of the dwelling-house (whether under the same or under another public sector tenancy).

   (2) A period during which the new tenant, since reaching the age of 16, occupied as his only or principal home a dwelling-house of which a parent of his was the public sector tenant or one of joint tenants under a public sector tenancy, being either–
      (a) the period at the end of which he became the public sector tenant, or
      (b) an earlier period ending two years or less before the period mentioned in paragraph (a) or before another period within this paragraph,
      shall be treated for the purposes of paragraph 2 as a period during which he was a public sector tenant.

   (3) For the purposes of this paragraph two persons shall be treated as parent and child if they would be so treated under section 186(2) (members of a person's family; relationships other than those of the whole blood).

No matter how long the period of secure tenancy, a tenant who obtained his dwelling house as a result of his employment cannot exercise the RTB—Sch 5, para 5.

Dwelling-houses let in connection with employment
para 5(1) The right to buy does not arise if the dwelling-house–
      (a) forms part of, or is within the curtilage of, a building which, or so much of it as is held by the landlord, is held mainly for purposes other than housing purposes and consists mainly of accommodation other than housing accommodation, or is situated in a cemetery, and
      (b) was let to the tenant or a predecessor in title of his in consequence of the tenant or predecessor being in the employment of the landlord or of–
         a local authority,
         a new town corporation,

a housing action trust,
the Development Board for Rural Wales,
an urban development corporation, or
the governors of an aided school.

(2) In sub-paragraph (1)(a) 'housing purposes' means the purposes for
which dwelling-houses are held by local housing authorities under Part
II (provision of housing) or purposes corresponding to those purposes.

Caretakers of schools or fire stations are caught by this provision, unless the
dwelling house is situated some distance from the 'building which . . . is held
mainly for purposes other than housing purposes' and so is not within the curtilage—*Dyer v Dorset CC* [1988] 3 WLR 213. Further, it is for the local authority to
prove that the dwelling-house was let to the tenant 'in consequence' of his
employment—see generally *Hughes v LB of Greenwich* (1994) 26 HLR 99.

In addition, the Housing Act 1985, s 121 also prohibits sale under the RTB
where there is a possession order against the secure tenant and where a secure
tenant is bankrupt.

Even if there is no possession order, s 138(2) permits the local authority to
leave uncompleted the grant of either the freehold or the lease

[if] the tenant has failed to pay the rent or any other payment due from him as a
tenant for a period of four weeks after it had been lawfully demanded from him,
[the landlord is not bound to comply with subsection (1)] while the whole or part
of that payment remains outstanding. (s 138(2))

Under the Housing Act 1985, s 123 a secure tenant may nominate up to three
resident members of his family who are not joint tenants to share the RTB with
him. If so nominated, and the secure tenant dies, then the nominated members
of the family can enforce the RTB—*Harrow LBC v Tonge* (1993) 25 HLR 99.

12.5.1.4 The Discount

The secure tenant buys his dwelling house at a discount which is determined by
the length of his secure tenancy and by whether he is purchasing a house or a flat.
Originally, the same discount rates applied to both houses and flats, but with the
disproportionately poor take-up of flats a preferential discount had to be introduced. Before 1986, fewer than 20,000 flats were sold compared to 500,000
houses, whereas with the increased discount there were, in 1994, 165,000 flat
purchasers out of almost 1.5 million sales—see Birch, *Flat Broke*, ROOF
November/December 1993, p 19, and the *Guardian* p 34, 2 July 1994.

The original justification for discounting prices for council house sales (prior to
the right to buy) derived from the lower value of properties in the private rented
sector with sitting tenants as opposed to vacant possession. The link to length of
tenancy came later, and the discount rate has become no more than a balancing

act between providing sufficient incentive to maintain sales and generating a certain level of capital receipts. (Forrest and Murie, 'The Right to Buy', *op. cit.*, p 141)

This policy was continued in the practice of the RTB, but there was also some concept that the tenant's prior rent payments were to be taken into account when calculating what should be paid—thus, the discount is dependent on the number of years of prior secure tenancy.

The valuation of the dwelling house is based on its vacant-possession price.

s 126(1) **The price payable for a dwelling-house on a conveyance or grant in pursuance of this Part is–**

    (a) **the amount which under section 127 is to be taken as its value at the relevant time, less**

    (b) **the discount to which the purchaser is entitled under this Part.**

  (2) **References in this Part to the purchase price include references to the consideration for the grant of a lease.**

s 127(1) **The value of a dwelling-house at the relevant time shall be taken to be the price which at that time it would realise if sold on the open market by a willing vendor–**

    (a) **on the assumptions stated for a conveyance in subsection (2) and for a grant in subsection (3),**

    (b) **disregarding any improvements made by any of the persons specified in subsection (4) and any failure by any of those persons to keep the dwelling-house in good internal repair, and**

    (c) **on the assumption that any service charges or improvement contributions payable will not be less than the amounts to be expected in accordance with the estimates contained in the landlord's notice under section 125.**

  (2) **For a conveyance the assumptions are -**

    (a) **that the vendor was selling for an estate in fee simple with vacant possession,**

    (b) **that neither the tenant nor a member of his family residing with him wanted to buy, and**

    (c) **that the dwelling-house was to be conveyed with the same rights and subject to the same burdens as it would be in pursuance of this Part.**

  (3) **For the grant of a lease the assumptions are–**

    (a **that the vendor was granting a lease with vacant possession for the appropriate term defined in paragraph 12 of Schedule 6 (but subject to sub-paragraph (3) of that paragraph),**

    (b) **that neither the tenant nor a member of his family residing with him wanted to take the lease,**

    (c) **that the ground rent would not exceed £10 per annum, and**

    (d) **that the grant was to be made with the same rights and subject to the same burdens as it would be in pursuance of this Part.**

  (4) **The persons referred to in subsection (1)(b) are–**

    (a) **the secure tenant,**

(b) any person who under the same tenancy was a secure tenant before
him, and

(c) any member of his family who, immediately before the secure tenancy was granted, was a secure tenant of the same dwelling-house
under another tenancy,

but do not include, in a case where the secure tenant's tenancy has at
any time been assigned by virtue of section 92 (assignments by way of
exchange), a person who under that tenancy was a secure tenant before
the assignment.

As well as ignoring the fact that there is a sitting tenant in calculating the sale
price, s 127(1)(b) requires the valuer to disregard any improvements made by the
secure tenant and any failure to keep the premises in good internal repair. Given
that many council houses are in a poor condition and that owner-occupiers (as
tenants exercising the RTB will become) generally fail to maintain their properties, it might have been worthwhile to prevent the exercise of the RTB until the
premises were in good repair—see *English House Condition Survey: 1991*, 1993,
at p 66.

The two rates of discount for houses and flats, respectively, are provided for in
s 129.

s 129(1) Subject to the following provisions of this Part, a person exercising the
right to buy is entitled to a discount of a percentage calculated by reference to the period which is to be taken into account in accordance with
Schedule 4 (qualifying period for right to buy and discount).

(2) The discount is, subject to any order under subsection (2A)–

(a) in the case of a house, 32 per cent. plus one per cent. for each complete year by which the qualifying period exceeds two years, up to a
maximum of 60 per cent.;

(b) in the case of a flat, 44 per cent. plus two per cent. for each complete
year by which the qualifying period exceeds two years, up to a maximum of 70 per cent.

(2A) The Secretary of State may by order made with the consent of the
Treasury provide that, in such cases as may be specified in the order–

(a) the minimum percentage discount,

(b) the percentage increase for each complete year of the qualifying
period after the first two, or

(c) the maximum percentage discount,

shall be such percentage, higher than that specified in subsection (2), as
may be specified in the order.

(2B) An order—

(a) may make different provision with respect to different cases or
descriptions of case,

(b) may contain such incidental, supplementary or transitional provisions as appear to the Secretary of State to be necessary or expedient, and

(c) shall be made by statutory instrument and shall not be made unless a draft of it has been laid before and approved by resolution of each House of Parliament.

(3) Where joint tenants exercise the right to buy, Schedule 4 shall be construed as if for the secure tenant there were substituted that one of the joint tenants whose substitution will produce the largest discount.

Given that a secure tenant has to have at least two years' residence in order to qualify for the RTB in the first place, the calculation for each type of dwelling is as follows:

House Discount =   30 per cent + 1 per cent for each year's residence as a secure tenant up to a maximum of 60 per cent (i.e. after 30 years' residence).

Flat Discount =   40 per cent + 2 per cent for each year's residence as a secure tenant up to a maximum of 70 per cent (i.e. after 15 years' residence).

Furthermore, the maximum discount is £50,000, even if the amount calculated by reference to the percentage would be greater (SI 1989 No. 513). Any previous discount with respect to any other relevant RTB purchase received by a tenant, his spouse or deceased spouse will also reduce the amount of discount now available, although this will be rare—s 130. In addition, the discount cannot reduce the value of the dwelling house below its base cost value, based, normally, on the amounts spent by the local authority on the property in the last eight years.

s 131(1) Except where the Secretary of State so determines, the discount shall not reduce the price below the amount which, in accordance with a determination made by him, is to be taken as representing so much of the costs incurred in respect of the dwelling-house as, in accordance with the determination—

(a) is to be treated as incurred at or after the beginning of that period of account of the landlord in which falls the date which is eight years, or such other period of time as may be specified in an order made by the Secretary of State, earlier than the relevant time, and

(b) is to be treated as relevant for the purposes of this subsection;

and if the price before discount is below that amount, there shall be no discount.

(1A) In subsection (1)(a) above 'period of account', in relation to any costs, means the period for which the landlord made up those of its accounts in which account is taken of those costs.

(2) The discount shall not in any case reduce the price by more than such sum as the Secretary of State may by order prescribe.

(3) An order or determination under this section may make different provision for different cases or descriptions of case, including different provision for different areas.

(4) An order under this section shall be made by statutory instrument which shall be subject to annulment in pursuance of a resolution of either House of Parliament.

The effect of s 131 is that purchasers of newer properties will obtain very little discount. Subsection (3) is intended to allow the Secretary of State to fix different maximum discounts by reference to area—it is an acknowledgement that house prices vary throughout the country and that £50,000 may represent only a small proportion of the value of a house in the south-east, especially London. So far, the Secretary of State has not exercised his discretion under s 131(3).

To prevent tenants cashing in on the discount by immediately reselling the dwelling house for its true value, the discount will have to be repaid, in whole or in part, if a non-exempt resale occurs within a specified period. To enforce the repayment rules in the Housing Act 1985, however, the local authority must have included a covenant to that effect in the conveyance of the freehold or the lease which establishes 'a charge on the dwelling-house, taking effect as if it had been created by deed expressed to be by way of legal mortgage'—ss 155 and 156.

s 155(1) A conveyance of the freehold or grant of a lease in pursuance of this Part shall contain (unless, in the case of a conveyance or grant in pursuance of the right to buy, there is no discount) a covenant binding on the secure tenant and his successors in title to the following effect.

(2) In the case of a conveyance or grant in pursuance of the right to buy, the covenant shall be to pay to the landlord on demand, if within a period of three years there is a relevant disposal which is not an exempted disposal (but if there is more than one such disposal, then only on the first of them), the discount to which the secure tenant was entitled, reduced by one third for each complete year which has elapsed after the conveyance or grant and before the disposal.

(3) In the case of a conveyance or grant in pursuance of the right to acquire on rent to mortgage terms, the covenant shall be to pay to the landlord on demand, if within the period of three years commencing with the making of the initial payment there is a relevant disposal which is not an exempted disposal (but if there is more than one such disposal, then only on the first of them), the discount (if any) to which the tenant was entitled on the making of—

(a) the initial payment,

(b) any interim payment made before the disposal, or

(c) the final payment if so made,

reduced, in each case, by one-third for each complete year which has elapsed after the making of the initial payment and before the disposal. (Under subs(3A), the tenant will benefit in the calculation of the three years from any operative notice of delay under s 153A—see 12.5.1.6)

Thus, under s 155 (as amended by the Housing Act 1988 and the Leasehold Reform, Housing and Urban Development Act 1993), any relevant disposal within a year of the conveyance or grant under the RTB will require the repayment of the entire discount; between one year and two years afterwards and the repayment is two-thirds of the discount; from two years after the grant or conveyance under the RTB but before the third anniversary and one-third of the discount is repayable. Relevant disposals are defined in the Housing Act 1985, ss 159 and 163, with exempt disposals defined in ss 160 and 161. Any subsequent transfer (not 'conveyance', since upon any conveyance under the RTB, the title to the land becomes registered by virtue of the Housing Act 1985, s 154) of the freehold, assignment of the leasehold or grant of a new lease for over 21 years at more than a rack rent (which includes the grant of an option to lease) shall be a relevant disposal unless exempt. Exempt disposals, which do not require the discount to be repaid, are defined in s 160:

s 160(1) A disposal is an exempted disposal for the purposes of this Part if–

    (a) it is a disposal of the whole of the dwelling-house and a further conveyance of the freehold or an assignment of the lease and the person or each of the persons to whom it is made is a qualifying person (as defined in subsection (2));

    (b) it is a vesting of the whole of the dwelling-house in a person taking under a will or on an intestacy;

    (c) it is a disposal of the whole of the dwelling-house in pursuance of an order made under section 24 of the Matrimonial Causes Act 1973 (property adjustment orders in connection with matrimonial proceedings) or section 2 of the Inheritance (Provision for Family and Dependants) Act 1975 (orders as to financial provision to be made from estate);

    (d) it is a compulsory disposal (as defined in section 161); or

    (e) it is a disposal of property consisting of land included in the dwelling-house by virtue of section 184 (land let with or used for the purposes of the dwelling-house).

    (2) For the purposes of subsection (1)(a), a person is a qualifying person in relation to a disposal if–

    (a) he is the person, or one of the persons, by whom the disposal is made,

    (b) he is the spouse or a former spouse of that person, or one of those persons, or

    (c) he is a member of the family of that person, or one of those persons, and has resided with him throughout the period of twelve months ending with the disposal.

s 161   In this Part a 'compulsory disposal' means a disposal of property which is acquired compulsorily, or is acquired by a person who has made or would have made, or for whom another person has made or would have made, a compulsory purchase order authorising its compulsory purchase for the purposes for which it is acquired.

Even if the first disposal is exempt, any subsequent transfer within three years of the exercising of the RTB will still be caught by s 155 unless s 162 applies (exempt disposals under s 160(1)(d) and (e)).

12.5.1.5 Terms of the Transfer

No attempt is made here to give a comprehensive account of all the terms of the standard transfer under the RTB, whether it be a conveyance or lease. The objective is to point out only what is peculiar to a sale under the RTB which reflects the nature of former landlord and tenant relationship of the vendor and purchaser. One such term, the covenant for discount repayment has just been dealt with. Many of the other provisions are found in the Housing Act 1985, Sch 6. For instance, all charges (however created or arising) on the dwelling house are not binding on the former tenant, except for tenants' incumbrances and rentcharges—Sch 6, Parts I and IV, paras 7, 20 and 21. However, restrictive covenants, rights of way, passage of water, access to light and support, *inter alia*, are preserved for the benefit of the tenant and for the benefit of any third party— Sch 6, Part I.

para 2(1) The conveyance or grant shall, by virtue of this Schedule, have the effect . . .

para 4   The conveyance or grant shall include such provisions (if any) as the landlord may require to secure that the tenant is bound by, or to indemnify the landlord against breaches of, restrictive covenants (that is to say, covenants or agreements restrictive of the use of any land or premises) which affect the dwelling-house otherwise than by virtue of the secure tenancy or an agreement collateral to it and are enforceable for the benefit of other property.

Sch 6, Part II deals with terms to be implied into every conveyance of the freehold. The Law of Property Act 1925, s 63 is specifically applied to the conveyance except in certain circumstances and the former tenant takes subject to

burdens (other than burdens created by the conveyance) in respect of the upkeep or regulation for the benefit of any locality of any land, building, structure, works, ways or watercourses. (para 9(1)(b))

The grant of a lease under the RTB, however, gives rise to a large number of implied terms under Sch 6. Part III thereof is devoted solely to clauses that are to be included in any grant. Ground rent, as we have already seen, cannot exceed ten pounds per annum—Sch 6, Part III, para 11. The most detailed provisions in Part III, though, relate to repairs and their costs.

Sch 6, Part III
para 14(1) This paragraph applies where the dwelling-house is a flat.
**   (2) There are implied covenants by the landlord–**

(a) to keep in repair the structure and exterior of the dwelling-house and of the building in which it is situated (including drains, gutters and external pipes) and to make good any defect affecting that structure;

(b) to keep in repair any other property over or in respect of which the tenant has rights by virtue of this Schedule;

(c) to ensure, so far as practicable, that services which are to be provided by the landlord and to which the tenant is entitled (whether by himself or in common with others) are maintained at a reasonable level and to keep in repair any installation connected with the provision of those services;

(3) There is an implied covenant that the landlord shall rebuild or reinstate the dwelling-house and the building in which it is situated in the case of destruction or damage by fire, tempest, flood or any other cause against the risk of which it is normal practice to insure.

(3A) Sub-paragraphs (2) and (3) have effect subject to paragraph 15(3) (certain obligations not to be imposed, where landlord's title is leasehold, by reason of provisions of superior lease).

(4) The county court may, by order made with the consent of the parties, authorise the inclusion in the lease or in an agreement collateral to it of provisions excluding or modifying the obligations of the landlord under the covenants implied by this paragraph, if it appears to the court that it is reasonable to do so.

para 15(1) This paragraph applies where the landlord's interest in the dwelling-house is leasehold.

(2) There is implied a covenant by the landlord to pay the rent reserved by the landlord's lease and, except in so far as they fall to be discharged by the tenant, to discharge its obligations under the covenants contained in that lease.

(3) A covenant implied by virtue of paragraph 14 (implied covenants where dwelling-house is a flat) shall not impose on the landlord an obligation which the landlord is not entitled to discharge under the provisions of the landlord's lease or a superior lease.

(4) Where the landlord's lease or a superior lease, or an agreement collateral to the landlord's lease or a superior lease, contains a covenant by a person imposing obligations which, but for sub-paragraph (3), would be imposed by a covenant implied by virtue of paragraph 14, there is implied a covenant by the landlord to use its best endeavours to secure that that person's obligations under the first-mentioned covenant are discharged.

para 16 Unless otherwise agreed between the landlord and tenant, there is implied a covenant by the tenant–

(a) where the dwelling-house is a house, to keep the dwelling-house in good repair (including decorative repair);

(b) where the dwelling-house is a flat, to keep the interior of the dwelling-house in such repair.

Paragraph 14(2)(a) removes any doubt as to the allocation of the repairing burden following cases such as *Ravenseft Properties v Davstone (Holdings)* [1980] QB 12, and *Campden Hill Towers v Gardner* [1977] QB 823, both dealt with in ch 7.

Schedule 6 also provides for the recouping of expenses by the local authority in connection with repairs and improvements. Once five years have expired since the exercise of the RTB, the landlord of the long leasehold flat can require the tenant to pay a reasonable contribution towards the landlord's costs—para 16A(1). Within the first five years, though, the local authority can only normally obtain from the former tenant costs as they are stipulated in the response notice under s 125, as supplemented by ss 125A and 125B, plus inflation—inflation is calculated in accordance with the formula found in the Housing (Right to Buy) (Service Charges) Order 1986, SI 1986 No. 2195, reg 3. Where the work or improvement was listed in the s 125 notice, then the long leasehold tenant is required to pay only the stipulated cost plus inflation (paras 16B(2) and 16C(3)): where the repair was not specified, then the tenant is only liable for the estimated annual average amount for works of repair (para 16B(3)), and if an improvement was not listed, then the tenant has no liability whatsoever (para 16C(2)).

para 16B(1) Where a lease of a flat requires the tenant to pay service charges in respect of repairs (including works for the making good of structural defects), his liability in respect of costs incurred in the initial period of the lease is restricted as follows.

(2) He is not required to pay in respect of works itemised in the estimates contained in the landlord's notice under section 125 any more than the amount shown as his estimated contribution in respect of that item, together with an inflation allowance.

(3) He is not required to pay in respect of works not so itemised at a rate exceeding–

(a) as regards parts of the initial period falling within the reference period for the purposes of the estimates contained in the landlord's notice under section 125, the estimated annual average amount shown in the estimates;

(b) as regards parts of the initial period not falling within that reference period, the average rate produced by averaging over the reference period all works for which estimates are contained in the notice;

together, in each case, with an inflation allowance.

(4) The initial period of the lease for the purposes of this paragraph begins with the grant of the lease and ends five years after the grant, except that—

(a) if the lease includes provision for service charges to be payable in respect of costs incurred in a period before the grant of the lease, the initial period begins with the beginning of that period;

(b) if the lease provides for service charges to be calculated by reference to a specified annual period, the initial period continues until the end of the fifth such period beginning after the grant of the lease.

para 16C(1) Where a lease of a flat requires the tenant to pay improvement contributions, his liability in respect of costs incurred in the initial period of the lease is restricted as follows.

(2) He is not required to make any payment in respect of works for which no estimate was given in the landlord's notice under section 125.

(3) He is not required to pay in respect of works for which an estimate was given in that notice any more than the amount shown as his estimated contribution in respect of that item, together with an inflation allowance.

(4) The initial period of the lease for the purposes of this paragraph begins with the grant of the lease and ends five years after the grant, except that—

(a) if the lease includes provision for improvement contributions to be payable in respect of costs incurred in a period before the grant of the lease, the initial period begins with the beginning of that period;

(b) if the lease provides for improvement contributions to be calculated by reference to a specified annual period, the initial period continues until the end of the fifth such period beginning after the grant of the lease.

The long leasehold tenant may obtain a loan from the local authority landlord by virtue of the Housing Act 1985, ss 450A–450C in order to meet these costs.

The final type of provision to be discussed that can be inserted in a sale under the RTB concerns restrictive covenants against further disposals and rights of preemption for the local authority. Such clauses can only be inserted when the property sold under the RTB is in certain areas, for instance, National Parks, areas of outstanding natural beauty or designated rural areas—for example, SI 1990 No. 1282 covers parts of Devon. Ordinarily, the local authority cannot insert a clause into the conveyance or grant to ensure that the property comes back into the public sector on first resale. The justification for the restrictive covenant or right of preemption is that housing in the designated areas is generally scarce and expensive and so low-cost rented dwellings need to be preserved as an essential resource for local people or those working in the region. Even the exceptions to the rule reinforce this approach.

Housing Act 1985
s 157(1)   Where in pursuance of this Part a conveyance or grant is executed by a local authority, the Development Board for Rural Wales or a housing association ('the landlord') of a dwelling-house situated in–

(a) a National Park,

(b) an area designated under section 87 of the National Parks and Access to the Countryside Act 1949 as an area of outstanding natural beauty, or

(c) an area designated by order of the Secretary of State as a rural area,

the conveyance or grant may contain a covenant limiting the freedom of the tenant (including any successor in title of his and any person deriving title under him or such a successor) to dispose of the dwelling-house in the manner specified below.

(2) The limitation is, subject to subsection (4), that until such time (if any) as may be notified in writing by the landlord to the tenant or a successor in title of his

(a) there will be no relevant disposal which is not an exempted disposal without the written consent of the landlord; but that consent shall not be withheld if the disposal is to a person satisfying the condition stated in subsection (3); and

(b) there will be no disposal by way of tenancy or licence without the written consent of the landlord unless the disposal is to a person satisfying that condition or by a person whose only or principal home is and, throughout the duration of the tenancy or licence, remains the dwelling-house.

(3) The condition is that the person to whom the disposal is made (or, if it is made to more than one person, at least one of them) has, throughout the period of three years immediately preceding the application for consent or, in the case of a disposal by way of tenancy or licence, preceding the disposal—

(a) had his place of work in a region designated by order of the Secretary of State which, or part of which, is comprised in the National Park or area, or

(b) had his only or principal home in such a region;

or has had the one in part or parts of that period and the other in the remainder; but the region need not have been the same throughout the period.

(4) If the Secretary of State or, where the landlord is a housing association, the Corporation, consents, the limitation specified in subsection (2) may be replaced by the following limitation, that is to say, that until the end of the period of ten years beginning with the conveyance or grant there will be no relevant disposal which is not an exempted disposal, unless in relation to that or a previous such disposal—

(a) the tenant (or his successor in title or the person deriving title under him or his successor) has offered to reconvey the dwelling-house, or as the case may be surrender the lease, to the landlord for such consideration as is mentioned in section 158, and

(b) the landlord has refused the offer or has failed to accept it within one month after it was made.

...

(6) A disposal in breach of such a covenant as is mentioned in subsection (1) is void and, so far as it relates to disposals by way of tenancy or licence, such a covenant may be enforced by the landlord as if–
   (a) the landlord were possessed of land adjacent to the house concerned; and
   (b) the covenant were expressed to be made for the benefit of such adjacent land.

The restrictive covenant against resales or granting tenancies or licences is open-ended. Even the original purchaser's successors in title are bound to seek permission from the local authority, unless the relevant disposal is an exempted one (ss 159-162). The only exemption is for prospective purchasers, tenants or licensees who have worked or lived in the designated region for at least three years preceding the application for consent. The right of preemption is only binding for ten years and such a clause can only be inserted with the Secretary of State's consent. The procedure for calculating the price at which the local authority has to re-purchase under any right of preemption is laid down under s 158 as being 'such amount as may be agreed between the parties or determined by the district valuer as being the amount which is to be taken as the value of the dwelling-house at the time the offer is made'. The value is based on the open market value if sold by a willing vendor, assuming the vendor repays any discounts repayable for early disposal (s 158(2)). It should be noted that in no other circumstance can the local authority seek to try and regain the dwelling house for the public sector upon the RTB purchaser's resale. The RTB is part of an overall scheme to reduce local authority involvement in the provision of housing.

12.5.1.6 Methods of Enforcing the RTB

When the RTB was first introduced in the Housing Act 1980, several Labour local authorities were opposed to it. There were allegations that some local authorities were seeking to frustrate the purpose of the RTB—for example, by threatening to move difficult neighbours in next door to put the tenants off wanting to buy. Admittedly, some local authorities took a long time to process applications under the RTB, but it should be noted, first, that local authority budgets, including those to pay for staff to process claims, such as surveyors, were being cut back in the 1980s and, secondly, that when estates had been built, it had never been anticipated that individual dwelling houses would be sold off requiring detailed outlines of the property. Where there is delay, though, the applicant tenant has several rights and the Secretary of State has a general power of intervention.

Under the Housing Act 1985, s 138(3) the tenant's right can be enforced by injunction in the County Court. Moreover, since the duty to sell the dwelling house is owed to the tenant as an individual, following *Harrison v Hammersmith and Fulham LBC* [1981] 1 WLR 650, and *Wandsworth LBC v Winder* [1985] AC 461, the tenant ought to be able to enforce and seek damages in a civil action for breach of the statutory duty owed to him, again in the county court—s 181.

An alternative remedy is open to the tenant without there being any need to go to court where the council delays in the processing of the application. The effect of this remedy is that after a set period during which the council fails to answer the tenant's notices, the tenant can deduct rent paid from the eventual purchase price.

Housing Act 1985

s 153A(1) Where a secure tenant has claimed to exercise the right to buy, he may serve on his landlord a notice (in this section referred to as an 'initial notice of delay') in any of the following cases, namely,–

(a) where the landlord has failed to serve a notice under section 124 within the period appropriate under subsection (2) of that section;

(b) where the tenant's right to buy has been established and the landlord has failed to serve a notice under section 125 within the period appropriate under subsection (1) of that section; or

. . .

(e) where the tenant considers that delays on the part of the landlord are preventing him from exercising expeditiously his right to buy or his right to acquire on rent to mortgage terms;

and where an initial notice of delay specifies either of the cases in paragraphs (a) and (b), any reference in this section or section 153B to the default date is a reference to the end of the period referred to in the paragraph in question or, if it is later, the day appointed for the coming into force of section 124 of the Housing Act 1988.

(2) An initial notice of delay–

(a) shall specify the most recent action of which the tenant is aware which has been taken by the landlord pursuant to this Part of this Act; and

(b) shall specify a period (in this section referred to as 'the response period'), not being less than one month, beginning on the date of service of the notice, within which the service by the landlord of a counter notice under subsection (3) will have the effect of cancelling the initial notice of delay.

(3) Within the response period specified in an initial notice of delay or at any time thereafter, the landlord may serve on the tenant a counter notice in either of the following circumstances—

(a) if the tenant's notice specifies either of the cases in paragraphs (a) and (b) of subsection (1) and the landlord has served, or is serving together with the counter notice, the required notice under section 124 or section 125, as the case may be; or

(b) if the initial notice specifies the case in subsection (1)(e) and there is no action under this Part which, at the beginning of the response period, it was for the landlord to take in order to allow the tenant expeditiously to exercise his right to buy or his right to acquire on rent to mortgage terms and which remains to be taken at the time of service of the counter notice.

(4) A counter notice under subsection (3) shall specify the circumstances by virtue of which it is served.

(5) At any time when—

(a) the response period specified in an initial notice of delay has expired, and

(b) the landlord has not served a counter notice under subsection (3),

the tenant may serve on the landlord a notice (in this section and section 153B referred to as an 'operative notice of delay') which shall state that section 153B will apply to payments of rent made by the tenant on or after the default date or, if the initial notice of delay specified the case in subsection (1)(e), the date of the service of the notice.

(6) If, after a tenant has served an initial notice of delay, a counter notice has been served under subsection (3), then, whether or not the tenant has also served an operative notice of delay, if any of the cases in subsection (1) again arises, the tenant may serve a further initial notice of delay and the provisions of this section shall apply again accordingly.

If the landlord, after an initial notice of delay and an operative notice of delay, fails to complete within twelve months of the default date, then a notional 50 per cent is added to the rent paid in and deducted from the purchase price— s 153B(3)(b) and (4).

Finally, the Secretary of State also has the power under the Housing Act 1985 to intervene and take over sales under the RTB where the local authority appear to be defeating the purpose of the legislation. He may act after complaints from applicants under the RTB.

s 164(1) The Secretary of State may use his powers under this section where it appears to him that tenants generally, a tenant or tenants of a particular landlord, or tenants of a description of landlords, have or may have difficulty in exercising effectively and expeditiously the right to buy or the right to acquire on rent to mortgage terms.

(2) The powers may be exercised only after he has given the landlord or landlords notice in writing of his intention to do so and while the notice is in force.

(3) Such a notice shall be deemed to be given 72 hours after it has been sent.

(4) Where a notice under this section has been given to a landlord or landlords, no step taken by the landlord or any of the landlords while the notice is in force or before it was given has any effect in relation to the exercise by a secure tenant of the right to buy or the right to acquire on rent to mortgage terms, except in so far as the notice otherwise provides.

(5) While a notice under this section is in force the Secretary of State may do all such things as appear to him necessary or expedient to enable secure tenants of the landlord or landlords to which the notice was given to exercise the right to buy and the right to acquire on rent to mortgage terms; and he is not bound to take the steps which the landlord would have been bound to take under this Part.

Where the Secretary of State does exercise powers under s 164, then ultimately he can transfer the freehold or grant a long lease to any applicant tenant. Indeed, the Secretary of State's general powers in this area are extremely extensive—ss 165–170. The Secretary of State intervened in Norwich in 1981 after the council were accused of excessive delays, of overpricing their houses and of including onerous covenants in the conveyances and grants—see generally, Malpass and Murie, 1994, *op. cit.*, pp 252 *et seq.* The local authority sought judicial review—*Norwich CC v Secretary of State for the Environment* [1982] 1 All ER 737. While it was found that the Norwich CC acted in good faith, it was held that the Secretary of State had the right to intervene, subject to scrutiny by the courts.

Local self-government is such an important part of our constitution that, to my mind, the courts should be vigilant to see that this power of central government is not exceeded or misused. Wherever the wording of the Act permits, the courts should read into it a provision that the 'default power' should not be exercised except in accordance with the rules of natural justice. Apart from this, the very decision of the minister himself is open to judicial review. If the minister does not act in good faith, or if he acts on extraneous considerations which ought not to influence him, or if he misdirects himself in fact or law, the court will in a proper case intervene and set his order aside ... Also, if the minister assumes to interfere with a decision of the local authority to which they came quite reasonably and sensibly, the court may intervene to stop the minister ... But if the decision of the local authority is unreasonable, then the minister may be justified in interfering. (*per* Lord Denning MR at 745)

Given the Secretary of State's wide powers to intervene, it will be rare that his order can be challenged unless the local authority's own actions could not be said to be unreasonable or lacking sense. However, disputes in this field tend to reflect party politics and are best sorted out through negotiation away from courts of law.

12.5.2 The Law Relating to Rent to Mortgage Schemes

The Leasehold Reform, Housing and Urban Development Act 1993, s 107 repealed the right to be granted a shared ownership lease under the Housing Act 1985, ss 143–151. Under the shared ownership scheme, the tenant would buy a proportion of the interest in the property and pay proportionate rent on the remainder of the interest. He could buy up the remaining interest (a practice known as 'staircasing') as he found himself financially able so to do—see Hoath, 1989, *op. cit.*, pp 350 *et seq.* Transitional provisions preserve the original ss 143–147 for the sake of extant shared ownership leases—SI 1993 No. 2134, art. 4, Sch 1, para 4(1). Shared ownership leases are replaced by a new right to acquire on rent to mortgage terms—Leasehold Reform, Housing and Urban Development Act 1993, ss 108–120, amending or inserting, *inter alia*, ss 143–151B Housing Act 1985; Driscoll, *Leasehold Reform, Housing and Urban Development Act 1993: The Public Sector Housing Provisions*, (1994) 57 MLR 788, pp 790–1. Rent To Mortgage (RTM) represents the government's new thrust to extend home ownership. In essence, the tenant's current rent payments are converted to mortgage repayments and whatever the value of mortgage that those mortgage repayments would redeem, that is the share of the property the tenant initially purchases. The tenant can subsequently increase the repayments and increase his share in the property or, on sale or death, the landlord's remaining share can be redeemed out of the sale price. There are many criticisms of this new scheme and its eventual effectiveness is seriously doubted, all of which will be considered below. For the present, the law relating to the RTM scheme, which is exceedingly complex, needs to be examined.

To qualify for the RTM scheme, the tenant or tenants must satisfy all the basic conditions for the RTB and not fall within any of the s 121 exclusions—s 143 Housing Act 1985, as amended (see 12.5.1.3). There are two additional conditions for qualifying tenants wishing to exercise their right to acquire on RTM terms. The first is contained in s 143A and bars anyone from acquiring on RTM terms who within the period beginning twelve months before the day on which he exercises the right to acquire on RTM terms was entitled to housing benefit or put in a claim therefor. While s 143A appears straightforward, it is arguable that a tenant who did not claim housing benefit, but who was technically entitled to it would be excluded under s 143A.

Housing Act 1985
s 143A(1) The right to acquire on rent to mortgage terms cannot be exercised if–
　　　　　(a) it has been determined that the tenant is or was entitled to housing benefit in respect of any part of the relevant period, or
　　　　　(b) a claim for housing benefit in respect of any part of that period has been made (or is treated as having been made) by or on behalf of the tenant and has not been determined or withdrawn.
　　　(2) In this section 'the relevant period' means the period—
　　　　　(a) beginning twelve months before the day on which the tenant claims to exercise the right to acquire on rent to mortgage terms, and
　　　　　(b) ending with the day on which the conveyance or grant is executed in pursuance of that right.

The second additional qualifying condition is contained in s 143B and is not at all straightforward. The effect of s 143B is that any tenant whose rent is more than 80 per cent of the mortgage payment on a mortgage that would buy the dwelling house outright is excluded from the RTM scheme—on the grounds that such a tenant ought to purchase under the RTB.

s 143B(1) The right to acquire on rent to mortgage terms cannot be exercised if the minimum initial payment in respect of the dwelling-house exceeds the maximum initial payment in respect of it.

(2) The maximum initial payment in respect of a dwelling-house is 80 per cent of the price which would be payable if the tenant were exercising the right to buy.

(3) Where, in the case of a dwelling-house which is a house, the weekly rent at the relevant time did not exceed the relevant amount, the minimum initial payment shall be determined by the formula—

$$P = R \times M$$

where—

P = the minimum initial payment;

R = the amount of the weekly rent at the relevant time;

M = the multiplier which at that time was for the time being declared by the Secretary of State for the purposes of this subsection.

(4) Where, in the case of a dwelling-house which is a house, the weekly rent at the relevant time exceeded the relevant amount, the minimum initial payment shall be determined by the formula—

$$P = Q + (E \times M)$$

where—

P = the minimum initial payment;

Q = the qualifying maximum for the year of assessment which included the relevant time;

E = the amount by which the weekly rent at that time exceeded the relevant amount;

M = the multiplier which at that time was for the time being declared by the Secretary of State for the purposes of this subsection.

(5) The minimum initial payment in respect of a dwelling-house which is a flat is 80 per cent of the amount which would be the minimum initial payment in respect of the dwelling-house if it were a house.

(6) The relevant amount and multipliers for the time being declared for the purposes of this section shall be such that, in the case of a dwelling-house which is a house, they will produce a minimum initial payment equal to the capital sum which, in the opinion of the Secretary of State, could be raised on a 25 year repayment mortgage in the case of which the net amount of the monthly mortgage payments was equal to the rent at the relevant time calculated on a monthly basis.

(7) For the purposes of subsection (6) the Secretary of State shall assume—

(a) that the interest rate applicable throughout the 25 year term were the standard national rate for the time being declared by the Secretary of State under paragraph 2 of Schedule 16 (local authority mortgage interest rates); and

(b) that the monthly mortgage payments represented payments of capital and interest only.

(8) In this section—

'net amount', in relation to monthly mortgage payments, means the amount of such payments after deduction of tax under section 369 of the Income and Corporation Taxes Act 1988 (mortgage interest payable under deduction of tax);

'qualifying maximum' means the qualifying maximum defined in section 367(5) of that Act (limit on relief for interest on certain loans);

'relevant amount' means the amount which at the relevant time was for the time being declared by the Secretary of State for the purposes of this section;

'relevant time' means the time of the service of the landlord's notice under section 146 (landlord's notice admitting or denying right);

'rent' means rent payable under the secure tenancy, but excluding any element which is expressed to be payable for services, repairs, maintenance or insurance or the landlord's costs of management.

The manner of carrying out this basic principle is very complicated. Section 143B defines 'maximum' and 'minimum' initial payments. The maximum initial payment is, for a house, 80 per cent 'of the price which would be payable if the tenant were exercising the right to buy' (s 143B(2)), that is, after his discount has been deducted. The minimum initial payment is different depending on whether the dwelling is a house or a flat, and formulae set out in s 143B(3) and (4) (which relate to a house) show how to calculate the minimum initial payment for the property, by reference to the weekly rent and a multiplier set by the Secretary of State. The aim of the minimum initial payment formulae is to produce the capital sum which the rental payment would equate to in mortgage terms—if the minimum initial payment produced by these formulae is greater than the maximum initial payment for that property, then the RTM cannot be exercised (s 143B(1)).

The minimum initial payment for a flat is 80 per cent of the minimum initial payment if it were a house; since the maximum initial payment is based on the discounted value of the dwelling house if the tenant were exercising the RTB and since the discount on a flat falls away more steeply than a house, it is necessary to set the minimum initial payment for a flat lower than for a house—the figure of 80 per cent is arbitrary (and a tad confusing given that the same percentage is used in relation to calculating the maximum initial payment).

As well as providing a bar on exercising the right to acquire on RTM terms, s 143B also provides the formulae for calculating what share of the dwelling house the tenant will purchase initially.

The procedure for exercising RTM involves the tenant serving notice on the landlord stating the amount he intends to pay, which must be not less than the minimum initial payment and not more than the maximum initial payment (s 146A).

The tenant having served notice under s 146A, the landlord must then serve a notice under s 147, as substituted, setting out the landlord's share and the amount of the initial discount, calculated in accordance with the new s 148. Section 148, put simply, states that the landlord's share shall be the amount remaining after the tenant's initial payment has been deducted from the full price, expressed as a percentage: the initial discount is full discount reduced in proportion to the fraction of the full price that the initial payment represents. Thus, the tenant's rent (at minimum) is turned into mortgage repayments and whatever sum those repayments would redeem on a 25-year mortgage, that is the tenant's share of the property, the remainder being the landlord's share.

For the typical tenant, who has been living in council accommodation for 20 years with their house worth £42,000, taking a right-to-buy discount of 50 per cent, the price comes down to £21,000. The weekly rent of, say, £30, is then converted into a 25-year mortgage of £16,000 – which allows the tenant to buy 75 per cent of the equity in their home. (the *Guardian* Weekend p 41, 22 January 1994)

The specific law relating to the tenant acquiring the freehold or long leasehold of the dwelling house on RTM terms is found in ss 150, 151, 151A and 151B and Schs 6 and 6A. The tenant acquires the property on RTM terms with a mortgage in favour of the local authority landlord to secure the landlord's share. Under s 151, the conveyance or grant must comply with Sch 6, as with any purchase under the RTB, as amended—the major difference is that a new para 16E is inserted to reduce *pro rata* the tenant's contribution to the service charge for repairs or improvement costs in line with the percentage of the property that is the landlord's share. A new Sch 6A is inserted, setting out the terms of the conveyance or grant that are specific to those purchasers acquiring on RTM terms— s 151A, Sch 6A and s 151B have to be read together. Para 1 of Sch 6A requires a covenant to be included in the conveyance to ensure that if the dwelling house is disposed of or the purchaser or as the case may be, the last surviving purchaser, acquiring on RTM terms dies, then the landlord's share should be redeemed, either immediately or within one year of a 'relevant death'—unless it is an exempt disposal.

Housing Act 1985, Sch 6A
para 1(1) The conveyance or grant shall contain a covenant binding on the secure tenant and his successors in title to make to the landlord, immediately after–
    (a) the making of a relevant disposal which is not an excluded disposal, or

(b) the expiry of the period of one year beginning with a relevant death,

(whichever first occurs), a final payment, that is to say, a payment of the amount required to redeem the landlord's share.

(2) A disposal is an excluded disposal for the purposes of this paragraph if–

   (a) it is a further conveyance of the freehold or an assignment of the lease and the person or each of the persons to whom it is made is, or is the spouse of, the person or one of the persons by whom it is made;

   (b) it is a vesting in a person taking under a will or intestacy; or

   (c) it is a disposal in pursuance of an order under section 24 of the Matrimonial Causes Act 1973 (property adjustment orders in connection with matrimonial proceedings) or section 2 of the Inheritance (Provision for Family and Dependants) Act 1975 (orders as to financial provision to be made from estate),

and (in any case) an interest to which this paragraph applies subsists immediately after the disposal.

(3) In this paragraph 'relevant death' means the death of a person who immediately before his death was the person or, as the case may be, the last remaining person entitled to an interest to which this paragraph applies.

(4) A beneficial interest in the dwelling-house is an interest to which this paragraph applies if the person entitled to it is—

   (a) the secure tenant or, as the case may be, one of the secure tenants, or

   (b) a qualifying person (defined in para 12).

While the provision relating to a relevant disposal is sensible, the rule as it pertains to a relevant death may seem somewhat harsh. However, sub-paras (2)(b) and (4) exclude the case where the disposal is by way of will or intestacy and an interest belonging to a secure tenant or a qualifying spouse or qualifying resident subsists immediately after the disposal (it will not be a relevant death under sub-para (3) if a qualifying spouse or qualifying resident takes under the will or intestacy—sub-para (4)). Para 12 applies to interests

(4) . . . if the person entitled to it is the secure tenant or, as the case may be, one of the secure tenants.

(5) References in this Schedule to the secure tenant are references to the secure tenant or tenants to whom the conveyance or grant is made and references to the secure tenant or, as the case may be, one of the secure tenants shall be construed accordingly.

Under Sch 6A, para 12(2) and (3), qualifying spouse and resident are defined as:

para 12(2) A person is a qualifying spouse for the purposes of this Schedule if–

   (a) he is entitled to a beneficial interest in the dwelling-house immediately after the time when there ceases to be an interest to which this paragraph applies [see above, sub-paras (4) and (5)];

(b) he is occupying the dwelling-house as his only or principal home immediately before that time; and

(c) he is the spouse or surviving spouse of the person who immediately before that time was entitled to the interest to which this paragraph applies or, as the case may be, the last remaining such interest, or is the surviving spouse of a person who immediately before his death was entitled to such an interest;

and any reference in this paragraph to the spouse or surviving spouse of a person includes a reference to a former spouse or surviving former spouse of that person.

(3) A person is a qualifying resident for the purposes of this Schedule if–

(a) he is entitled to a beneficial interest in the dwelling-house immediately after the time when there ceases to be an interest to which this paragraph applies;

(b) he is occupying the dwelling-house as his only or principal home immediately before that time;

(c) he has resided throughout the period of twelve months ending with that time–

(i) with the person who immediately before that time was entitled to the interest to which this paragraph applies or, as the case may be, the last remaining such interest, or

(ii) with two or more persons in succession each of whom was throughout the period of residence with him entitled to such an interest; and

(d) he is not a qualifying spouse.

Sch 6A, paras 1 and 12 apply to slightly different categories of interest (compare sub-para (4) of each paragraph). Their combined effect, however, is that a spouse or person living with the secure tenant who was acquiring on RTM terms for the twelve months prior to death will satisfy the exception in para 1(2) and the landlord's share will not have to be redeemed until the next relevant disposal or relevant death.

The Sch 6A covenant protecting the landlord's share takes effect as a mortgage and has priority over all subsequent charges other than the mortgage granted to the secure tenant in order to acquire under the RTM scheme—s 151B(2). However, s 151B(3), (4) and (6) provide for exceptions to the priority for the landlord's share where the subsequent charge is for a loan granted by an approved organisation (subs (5)) for 'approved purposes':

Housing Act 1985
s 151B(6) The approved purposes for the purposes of this section are–

(a) to enable the tenant to make an interim or final payment,

(b) to enable the tenant to defray, or to defray on his behalf, any of the following–

(i) the cost of any works to the dwelling-house,

(ii) any service charge payable in respect of the dwelling-house for works, whether or not to the dwelling-house, and

(iii) any service charge or other amount payable in respect of the dwelling-house for insurance, whether or not of the dwelling-house, and

(c) to enable the tenant to discharge, or to discharge on his behalf, any of the following–

(i) much as is still outstanding of any advance or further advance which ranks in priority to the mortgage,

(ii) any arrears of interest on such an advance or further advance, and

(iii) any costs and expenses incurred in enforcing payment of any such interest, or repayment (in whole or in part) of any such advance or further advance.

Thus, subject to the local authority consenting in writing to the postponement of the mortgage in its favour, only if a subsequent loan is for a purpose in subs (6) will it take priority. Those purposes include, however, any further advance in order that the tenant shall increase his share in the property or even buy out the landlord altogether with a final payment. Under Sch 6A, a final or interim payment can be made at any time—paras 2, 6 and 8. There are complicated formulae for calculating the value of the landlord's share and any discount for such final or interim payment in paras 3 and 7, as well as more general considerations in paras 4 and 5. The overall effect of those provisions is that no final discount should reduce the total price paid for the property below what would have been paid if there had been a single transaction under the RTB—see Housing Act 1985, ss 130 and 131.

A further advance will also take priority over the mortgage granted to protect the landlord's share under s 151B(6), if it is to meet the cost of works or service charges for works or insurance. Finally, an advance related to the discharging of the initial advance or arrears connected therewith, will also have priority. While there is little prospect of an approved lending institution granting a further advance for any purpose outside s 151B(6), subs (6) is wide enough to cover most reasons for seeking a further mortgage.

The law relating to acquiring on RTM terms has been dealt with in detail because it is so new and there are few indications of how it is working in practice. It is an attempt to apply the concepts of the RTB to a situation where the tenant is buying the property over an extended period, rather than in one single payment to the local authority. The rules governing the landlord's continuing interest in the property and the discounts to be granted as the former tenant buys additional tranches seem complicated, but their effect is simply that all the normal RTB rules apply, reduced *pro rata*.

12.5.3 Housing Associations and the RTB

In some respects the law relating to the RTB and housing associations is of only historical interest. New assured housing association tenants are not within the Housing Act 1985's RTB scheme. However, while RTB is not generally available for housing association tenants, some categories of tenant will have the RTB on the same terms as local authority tenants. The law relating to housing association tenants has to be read on top of the law pertaining to local authority tenants. The categories of housing association tenant with the RTB are:

1   Housing association tenants who continue to have secure tenancies, that is, who were granted tenancies before 15 January 1989 and who are not excluded by Sch 5. There are additional grounds, specific to housing association tenants, for exclusion from the RTB (Sch 5). Excluded are tenants of charitable housing associations, tenants of co-operative housing associations and those of housing associations which have never received government funding, particularly Housing Association Grant:

Housing Act 1985, Sch 5
para 1.3 **The right to buy does not arise if the landlord is a housing association which at no time received a grant under–**
> **any enactment mentioned in paragraph 2 of Schedule 1 to the Housing Associations Act 1985 (grants under enactments super-
seded by the Housing Act 1974),**
> **section 31 of the Housing Act 1974 (management grants),**
> **section 41 of the Housing Associations Act 1985 (housing associa-
tion grants),**
> **section 54 of that Act (revenue deficit grants),**
> **section 55 of that Act (hostel deficit grants),**
> **section 58(2) of that Act (grants by local authorities)**
> **section 50 of the Housing Act 1988 (housing association grants
[HAG]), or**
> **section 51 of that Act (revenue deficit grants).**

2   Housing association tenants who were formerly secure tenants and who, through a change of landlord, are now assured tenants. Their RTB is preserved by ss 171A-171C.

By s 171A(1) the RTB is preserved

> **where a person ceases to be a secure tenant of a dwelling-house by reason of the disposal by the landlord of an interest in the dwelling-house to a person who is not an authority or body within section 80 (the landlord condition for secure tenancies).**

The section does not apply where the RTB could not have been exercised against the former landlord, for example, where the former landlord was a charity (see

Sch 5, para 1), or in cases excluded by the Secretary of State (s 171A(3)). The tenant must also continue to occupy the dwelling-house as his only or principal home (s 171B(1)) and must be a qualifying tenant, the categories of which are set out in s 171B to include:

(a) **the former secure tenant, or in the case of a joint tenancy, each of them;**
(b) **a qualifying successor . . . [as defined in subsection (4) as including (a) a member of the former secure tenant's family who either (i) succeeded to the tenancy on the tenant's death, or (ii) had the tenancy assigned to him; or (b) a person to whom the tenancy was transferred on a family breakdown (under s 24 Matrimonial Causes Act 1973, or Sch 1 to the Matrimonial Homes Act 1983—see ch 9.8); and**
(c) **a person to whom a tenancy of a dwelling-house is granted jointly with a person who has the preserved right to buy in relation to that dwelling-house.**

The RTB will also be preserved if there is a change of dwelling

(whether the new dwelling-house is entirely different or partly or substantially the same as the previous dwelling-house) and the landlord is the same person as the landlord of the previous dwelling-house or, where that landlord was a company, is a connected company. (s 171B(6))

The preserved RTB may be modified by the Secretary of State (s 171C).

Cope, *Housing Associations: Policy and Practice*, 1990, pp 273–4, considers that this preservation of the RTB may cause problems both in terms of private investment and in terms of tenant mobility, as housing associations would not want to move a tenant with the preserved RTB into a newer property because of the limits on the minimum price inserted by the Housing Act 1988 into the Housing Act 1985, Sch 5A. Given the very few housing association properties that have been sold, however, these concerns seem to be exaggerated. The number of properties transferred by housing associations to owner-occupiers between 1981 and 1993 was just over 114,000.

In addition, there are special schemes for some housing association tenants who do not have the RTB, which provide alternative methods of moving into the owner-occupied sector. The Housing and Building Control Act 1984 introduced the Home Ownership for Tenants of Charitable Housing Associations (HOTCHA) scheme. Tenants of charitable housing associations in receipt of government funding could receive a cheque equal to the discount that they would have received if exercising the RTB, in order to permit them to buy a dwelling on the open market—for more detail, see Cope, *op. cit.*, pp 274–5. HOTCHA was superseded by the Tenants' Incentive Scheme (TIS) which is available to any tenant of a housing association property who does not possess or retain the RTB; thus, assured tenants can take advantage of the TIS—see Cope, *op. cit.*, pp 275–6. The Housing Corporation makes money available to housing associations to fund the subsidy; the former tenant finds a property to buy, which then releases his present housing association property for someone seeking to rent. Indeed, the new property can be anywhere in the world—the *Guardian* p 21, 12 November 1993.

12.6 ALIENATION AND ENFRANCHISEMENT

Some residential leases contain qualified restrictions on the tenant's ability to dispose of his interest, requiring the landlord's consent prior to any disposition, such consent not to be unreasonably withheld (see ch 9). If the lease potentially qualifies for enfranchisement depending on the status of the particular tenant, as with long leases, is this something the landlord can take account of when considering whether to consent to a proposed disposition? This is most likely to arise with leases in the high quality bracket of the housing market, especially in the traditional London estates.

A number of cases have arisen under the 1967 Leasehold Reform Act as to whether it would be unreasonable to refuse consent to an assignment from a tenant unable to take advantage of the enfranchisement provisions to a tenant who potentially could make an enfranchisement claim. In *Bickel v Duke of Westminster* [1977] 1 QB 517, the Court of Appeal decided that given the potential prejudice to the landlord's interest that could result from such as assignment it was not unreasonable to withhold consent. Here the proposed assignment was from a non-resident tenant to a resident sub-tenant. Waller LJ commented:

[The] proposed assignment would be pregnant with future possibilities because the present lessees are not in a position to enfranchise their leasehold interest. If, however, this assignment were permitted, then the assignee would be in a position to enfranchise his leasehold interest. In my opinion, this clearly affects the property which is the subject matter of the lease and the relationship between the landlord and the tenant, and accordingly, . . . the landlord was entitled to refuse consent . . . (at 528; see also *Welch v Birrane* (1974) 29 P & CR 102; *Norfolk Capital Group Ltd v Kitway Ltd* [1977] 1 QB 506)

It is less clear whether a similar result would follow in relation to the proposed assignment of a flat under the 1993 Act. The prejudice to the landlord under the 1993 Act is much less, given that there is a more adequate basis of compensation. In addition, the prejudice is less direct. While an individual might be able to get a lease extension, an individual acting alone cannot enfranchise. Under the 1967 Act, a non-resident individual or a company could not enfranchise and an assignment to a resident tenant could therefore lead to an enfranchisement claim where no possibility of such existed before. Under the 1993 Act a non-resident individual or company (the assignor in our example) may already count as one of the qualifying tenants. Assignment to a resident tenant will not therefore affect the number of qualifying tenants; it would however add to the requisite proportion of *resident* participating tenants needed to enfranchise (50 per cent). An assignment to a resident individual will not of itself be sufficient for enfranchisement, it depends on the mix of other owners within the building. It does therefore seem less likely that refusing consent to an assignee of a flat on this ground will be reasonable (see also the views of Clarke, 1994, *op. cit.*, pp 148–9).

12.7 ENFRANCHISEMENT AND EXPROPRIATION OF PROPERTY

Enfranchisement has been consistently opposed on the grounds that it interferes with the sanctity of contract and property rights. That it does so cannot be disputed. But neither of these principles is indefeasible.

12.7.1 Freedom of Contract

Opponents to enfranchisement state that as a lease is a freely negotiated contract both parties should be bound by it. There are, however, many examples of legislative intervention in contractual relations in the public interest and, in particular, of intervention in order to strengthen the position of a person in his home (as, for example, the court's power to postpone possession proceedings brought by a mortgagee of a dwelling house under the Administration of Justice Act 1970, s 36 and the Rent Acts).

Furthermore, it is questionable whether there is freedom of contract for the tenant-purchaser. The form of tenure in the purchase of a flat is not optional. Landlords are able to use their 'quasi-monopolistic' position to insist upon particular forms of tenure and length of lease being granted.

12.7.2 Freedom of Property

12.7.2.1 Are Property Rights Sacrosanct?

The absence of a written constitution in England and Wales means that there is no legal ground to challenge enfranchisement as being an unconstitutional interference with property rights. Nevertheless, appeal is made to more general notions of rights and it is claimed that enfranchisement violates the fundamental rights of property.

Again, however, there is little doubt that there are circumstances in which it is recognised to be legitimate in pursuit of some public or social goal to compulsorily acquire property from others as, for example, in the nationalisation of the shipbuilding industry. The legitimacy of enfranchisement was challenged by the

Duke of Westminster before the European Court of Human Rights. The trustees
for the Duke argued that the Leasehold Reform Act 1967 violated his property
rights secured by the European Convention on Human Rights (1950). Article 1 of
Protocol No. 1 to the Convention provides:

**Every natural or legal person is entitled to the peaceful enjoyment of his posses-
sions. No one shall be deprived of his possessions except in the public interest
and subject to the conditions provided for by law and by the general principles of
international law.**

Between April 1979 and November 1983, eighty tenants had enfranchised their
interests, causing losses to the trustees of the Duke of Westminster of about £2.5
million. Furthermore, several of these tenants later sold on the newly acquired
freehold at a substantial profit. One argument relied upon by the trustees was
that enfranchisement could not be in the 'public interest' as the property was not
to be used for the community generally but for an individual's private benefit.
The European Court of Human Rights rejected this: the phrase 'public interest'
could include transfer from one individual to another where it was in pursuance
of legitimate social policies. The aim of eliminating what was perceived to be a
social injustice in an area of prime social need (housing) was within this:

**The taking of property in pursuance of a policy calculated to enhance social jus-
tice within the community can properly be described as being 'in the public interest'. In particular, the fairness of a system of law governing the contractual or
property rights of private parties is a matter of public concern and therefore legislative measures intended to bring about such fairness are capable of being 'in
the public interest', even if they involve the compulsory transfer of property from
one individual to another.** (*James v United Kingdom, op. cit.,* at para 41)

It was also argued that to apply a 'blanket solution' approach, applying the
same rule to all cases, infringed the 'principle of proportionality' (that is, that
there must be a reasonable relationship of proportionality between the means
employed and the aim sought to be realised). The European Court of Human
Rights observed that the compensation provisions would lead to anomalies with
tenants who purchased end-of-term leases making 'windfall profits' (at para 69).
Both the principle of enfranchisement and the compensation provisions were,
however, within the State's 'margin of appreciation'. Under the Convention,
States are given a 'margin of appreciation' to determine the appropriate action to
remedy a perceived problem. This is necessary as the national authorities are
better placed with their direct knowledge of their society and its needs to appreciate what is in the 'public interest' (see especially paras 46–50 of the *James* case,
op. cit.).

In the United States of America there have been several challenges to legislation which allegedly deprives owners of property. The constitutional basis for
these challenges lies in 'The Takings Clause', the Fifth Amendment of the US

Constitution which provides that 'private property [shall not] . . . be taken for public use, without just compensation'. The Takings Clause applies to the States through the Fourteenth Amendment (*Chicago, Burlington and Quincy RR v Chicago* 166 US 226 (1897) at 233–4). In some cases, the challenge has been to legislation which gives rights to compulsorily acquire another's property (*cf.* enfranchisement).

In Hawaii, legislation was passed to seek to reduce the high concentration of land ownership in a few persons. Forty-seven per cent of the land was in the hands of only 72 landowners. These landowners leased land to tenants rather than selling on a fee simple basis. In 1967 the Land Reform Act was passed enabling tenants collectively (at least 25 tenants or half the lots in the tract, whichever is the fewer) to apply for land to be 'condemned'. A public hearing would then be held to determine whether acquisition by the State would 'effectuate the public purposes' of the Act and, if so, the State could acquire the land at full market value and sell the fee simple title to tenants. In order to prove that this was not an unconstitutional 'taking', it had to be shown that there was a 'justifying public purpose', even though compensation was being paid (see *Thompson v Consolidated Gas Corp* 300 US 55 (1984) at 80). The Supreme Court held the Act constitutional:

The people of Hawaii have attempted, much as the settlers of the original 13 Colonies did, to reduce the perceived social and economic evils of a land oligopoly traceable to their monarchs. The land oligopoly has, according to the Hawaii Legislature, created artificial deterrents to the normal functioning of the State's residential land market and forced thousands of individual homeowners to lease, rather than buy, the land underneath their homes . . .
Redistribution of fees simple to correct deficiencies in the market determined by the state legislature to be attributable to land oligopoly is a rational exercise of the eminent domain power. [footnotes omitted] (*Hawaii Housing Authority v Midkiff* 104 S.Ct 2321 (1984) at 2330)

It was also argued that because the transfer was to a private individual it could not be a public purpose (*cf. James*). The Supreme Court also rejected this claim:

The Court long ago rejected any literal requirement that condemned property be put into use for the general public. 'It is not essential that the entire community, nor even any considerable portion, . . . directly enjoy or participate in any improvement in order [for it] to constitute a public use' *Rindge Co.* v *Los Angeles*, **262 US, at 707 . . . As the unique way titles were held in Hawaii skewed the land market, exercise of the power of eminent domain was justified. The Act advances it purposes without the State's taking actual possession of the land.** (*Midkiff. op. cit.*, at 2331)

The issue has also arisen in relation to rights of first refusal granted to mobile home owners, similar to the rights contained in Part I of the Landlord and Tenant Act 1987. These rights have, however, been held to be unconstitutional. Mobile home owners have been perceived to be in a particularly weak bargaining position in relation to park owners, in part due to the fact that while in theory 'mobile', most mobile homes are in practice immobile because of their limited life and the difficulties and expense of transportation to other sites. In response, various rights have been given to mobile home owners, ranging from limits on rent increases and evictions through to rights of first refusal when the park owner wishes to sell the site for an alternative use. In California a mobile home rent control ordinance gave tenants a statutory right of first refusal on the mobile-home park, the purpose being to afford 'mobile home residents a measure of control over their own living situations' (cf. the purpose underlying the Landlord and Tenant Act 1987). Park owners challenged the ordinance and, in contrast to the result in the *James* and *Hawaii* cases, this was found to be unconstitutional by the Californian Court of Appeal.

The ability to sell and transfer property is a fundamental aspect of property ownership. Property consists mainly of three powers: possession, use and disposition . . . This part of the ordinance simply appropriates an owner's right to sell his property to persons of his choice. [The] City has thus 'extinguish[ed] a fundamental attribute of ownership in violation of federal and state constitutions'. (*per* Kaufman J, *Gregory v City of San Juan Capistrano* 191 Cal Rep 47 (App. 1983) at 58)

The *Gregory* case is an isolated decision and is thought by some to be an anomaly. The ordinance in issue in that case worked in a similar manner to Part I of the Landlord and Tenant Act 1987, giving tenants the right to buy on terms proposed by the landlord. The court in *Gregory* regarded the right to sell to a person of one's choice as a fundamental right. To deny this right to the owner was a taking, 'a naked taking of preemptive rights'.

It may also be that the decision is explicable on the basis that the professed purpose of the Act was to give the tenants 'control over their own living standards' (quaere, not in the public interest) whereas a provision designed 'to preserve affordable housing' would be a public purpose (see Ertel, *Vermont's Efforts to Protect Mobile Home Park Tenants: Is there a Taking?*, (1992) 16 Vermont L Rev.1027, at pp 1051–4).

Some other States have given mobile home owners somewhat lesser rights. So, for example, in Vermont the home owners must be notified of a proposed sale and are granted a period in which, if the tenants wish to purchase, the park owner must negotiate with them in good faith. After that period, if there is no agreement, the park owner is free to sell elsewhere. This is less likely to violate the Takings Clause as it is only a partial restraint on alienation (see further Ertel, *op. cit.*).

Challenges have also been brought in cases where rental tenants are resisting the landlord's attempt to redevelop the property as condominium units. In America, most blocks of flats were developed not for sale (whether on long leasehold or otherwise) but for rental. As condominium developments have become increasingly popular since the 1960s (see 12.9), the focus has not been on the conversion to condominium development against the landlord's will (as with enfranchisement in England) but on protecting existing rental tenants in the rush to convert. Indeed, condominium conversion has gathered such a pace that there have been legislative attempts to curb conversion in order to restrict the displacement of local citizens and the depletion of low and moderate income housing stock. The form of protection varies, from requiring notice to be given through to tenant purchase provisions.

Some programs require that landlords offer a bona fide building-wide tenant organisation the right of first refusal for the entire building; others require that each tenant be offered an option to buy his or her unit. Still other programs require that a certain percentage of tenants approve conversion or agree to purchase their units before conversion will be permitted. (Judson, *Defining Property Rights: The Constitutionality of Protecting Tenants from Condominium Conversions*, (1983) 18 Harv CR-CL LR 179, at p 196; footnotes omitted)

The constitutional challenge brought by landlords against these provisions is based not on claims of an improper expropriation of property but on a claim that there is an interference with the owner's right to dispose of property: that it permanently restricts property use, resulting in a transfer of certain property interests from the owner to the tenant and that it infringes on an owner's right to exclude tenants from occupancy. Whereas in England, the 'home security' interest of the long leasehold tenant has been used to claim a positive form of protection (a right to buy the freehold), the rental tenants in America have sought to rely on a similar security interest to claim a negative form of protection, restricting the right of the owner to convert to condominium.

The special interest in the home is an important element in justifying both enfranchisement laws and other tenant protection legislation. All the major pieces of enfranchisement legislation in England and Wales are restricted to *residential* leases. The 1967 Act contains a residency test and the 1993 Act requires at least half of the participating tenants to be resident. The Right To Buy legislation only applies to a person occupying a dwelling house as his only or principal home. This focus on enfranchising the home has not always been seen as integral to arguments for enfranchisement. Before 1950, twenty different Enfranchisement Bills had been put forward, but only one restricted the right to enfranchise to residential tenants. There is, however, a much stronger justification for interfering with property rights where the home is involved. Professor Honoré, in his Hamlyn lectures in 1982, referred to a 'psychological interest' in the home, the emotional attachment to a particular home and its environment, friends and so on (see Honoré, *The Quest for Security: Employees, Tenants, Wives*, The Hamlyn Lectures, 1982). This psychological interest weighs more heavily than an interest in property that is purely financial. Where, as is usually the case, the landlord's interest is primarily an investment he will be adequately protected if he receives a fair substitute for his source of wealth. Not all landlords, however, own property for pure investment reasons. In relation to the private sector landlords of the great London estates, there is also a psychological interest in the property: it is not only a source of wealth but a family inheritance and an estate over which they exercise a kind of 'biblical stewardship'. For public sector landlords the housing stock is not primarily a source of wealth but a means of fulfilling their social housing responsibilities, including obligations towards the homeless.

Yet, in all of the instances where rights to enfranchise have been given there have been additional reasons for enfranchisement beyond the psychological interest. With long leases there has been an attempt to alleviate management difficulties, to rectify a perceived injustice and to give the tenant of a diminished lease a marketable asset. The Right To Buy cannot not be seen in isolation from the government's economic and housing policies: while there is a property principle at stake in that landlords are compulsorily required to transfer freeholds this is very much subsidiary to the wider political issues.

When assessing whether enfranchisement is justifiable it is necessary to weigh the landlord's interest in continued investment in this particular property against the tenant's psychological interest in his home and the other reasons supporting enfranchisement. So long as the landlord receives full and adequate compensation intervention can be justified.

12.7.2.2 Compensation to Landlords versus Affordability to Tenants

The RTB is founded on the discount which has a variety of impacts in the sale of council houses. However, it cannot be understood in isolation and is discussed further at 12.8.2.

In the private sector, the compensation provisions are an extremely important part of the legislation. To justify compulsory acquisition of property there must be adequate levels of compensation.

The compensation provisions of the Leasehold Reform Act 1967 followed through the premise underlying the legislation (that the house belonged in equity to the tenant) and the tenant only had to pay a relatively low price to enfranchise. The position under the Leasehold Reform, Housing and Urban Development Act 1993 is very different and the tenants must pay not only market value for the reversion but also at least 50 per cent of the marriage value. If enfranchisement occurs during the early years of a long lease the different formulae in the 1967 and 1993 Acts will produce similar results. The differences emerge as the length of the lease shortens—as it does, so the value of the freeholder's reversion and the marriage value both rise. Under the original 1967 formula the tenant effectively paid only site value. This could mean substantial windfall profits for the tenant who enfranchised near the end of a lease. Under the 1993 Act approach, the tenant enfranchising near the end of a lease will have to pay a very substantial sum, approaching the vacant possession value of the property.

The market value approach is generally considered to be the correct one. Under this the landlord receives capital monies that compensate for the lost investment and provide him with an alternative source of wealth. The payment of a share of marriage value in addition to the market value of the reversion reflects the special bid of the tenants which is felt to be an important part of pricing a product. It also reduces the level of windfall profits that a tenant can make by enfranchising and then selling in order to realize the balance of the marriage value.

There is, however, an alternative view if one approaches the question with affordability in mind. It could be said that the landlord is adequately compensated if he receives a sum equivalent to the value of his investment in the property, that is the open market value of the reversion. Marriage value is additional to this and while it might seem unfair for the tenant potentially to obtain the windfall of realising the full marriage value on a subsequent sale it may be a necessary tool to achieve wider policy objectives. To require the tenant to pay marriage value in addition to paying the market price for the reversion makes the property less affordable to the tenants. This means that fewer tenants will enfranchise and the wider goal of extending home ownership will be missed. There are parallels that can be drawn with the public sector where the 'the discount rate has become no more than a balancing act between providing sufficient incentive to maintain sales and generating a certain level of capital receipts' (Forrest and Murie, 'The Right to Buy', *op. cit.*, at p 141). A similar 'discounting of marriage value' may be necessary in the private sector in order that a sufficient number of tenants will find enfranchisement affordable.

12.8 ARE ENFRANCHISEMENT ACTS EFFECTIVE?

12.8.1 Internal Effects—Are the Rights Exercised?

The right to enfranchise houses has been well used. Under the RTB, as was shown above, it is houses that have been bought rather than flats. The Landlord and Tenant Act 1987 has not, however, been a success and the Leasehold Reform, Housing and Urban Development Act 1993 may well share a similar fate along with the RTM scheme. Many of the difficulties that have been encountered in exercising the rights under the 1987 Act will also exist in relation to collective enfranchisement claims under the 1993 Act. Whereas under the 1967 Leasehold Reform Act only one property is at issue, the 1993 Act depends upon a certain proportion of tenants within a block satisfying the criteria laid down. In aggregate, these criteria will make it hard for enfranchising tenants to reach the requisite majority.

12.8.2 External Effects of the Acts

Judging the efficacy of the various enfranchisement Acts requires a consideration of the goals they set out to achieve. The problem with an evaluation of the RTB and RTM is that there are various contexts applicable; the relationship between the local authority and the purchasing tenant, between the local authority and prospective tenants and between the local authority and central government. The answer to the question 'Is it right to buy?' depends on who is asking.

The first contrast to be made is between purchasing tenants, non-purchasing tenants and prospective tenants. For the purchasing tenant, there would appear to be little to lose. They obtain their home at a discount and can sell and reap the full profit after a mere three years. Surveys show, furthermore, that it is the skilled working class tenant who was best placed to benefit from the RTB—see Kerr, *The Right To Buy*, 1989, at p 28, cited in Malpass and Murie, 1994, *op. cit.*, p 301.

It has long been established practice for local authorities to grade their tenants, in the Cullingworth Committee's phrase, 'according to moral desert' so that 'moral rectitude, social conformity, clean living and a 'clear' rent book . . . seem(ed) to be essential qualifications for eligibility – at least for new houses'. Thus, those in a position to benefit from council house sales will almost exclusively be drawn from the 'respectable' working class, determined not only by their ability to afford the purchase price but also, they would have been allocated the most desirable council property. In effect, they are being rewarded twice in now being offered the best houses at bargain prices. (Jacobs, *op. cit.*, p 44: footnotes omitted)

Put negatively, those who do not buy are the youngest and oldest, the unemployed, female-headed households, lone parent families, and those in the lowest paid and unskilled sectors. And in most areas, there is a coincidence between those groups with least bargaining power in the labour market and those in the least desirable parts of the council stock—flats and maisonettes and houses on the least popular estates. (Forrest and Murie, 'The Right To Buy', *op. cit.*, at p 145)

The government's policy of allowing secure tenants to buy at a discount provided certain tenants with a bargain. The best quality housing was sold off to some tenants who might well have been financially able to buy on the open market and it removed one more good quality home from the council's stock for transfer, exchange or allocation. On the other hand, though, not all former secure tenants could have afforded such good quality housing on the open market.

The age composition of purchaser households would probably exclude some from receiving mortgages of the necessary size. In some cases, age and income factors would probably prevent purchasers from becoming owners through any other process. This factor is a 'consequence' of the lending policies of local authorities, building societies and other agencies. To this extent some purchasers are excluded. Council house purchase may offer the only possibility of changing tenure and at the same time maintaining housing facilities, and providing the new opportunities associated with owning. It may be argued, however, that a package of housing services of this type is available to few. Rather than extending a choice to a deprived group, council house sales may be seen as having added to the privilege of a highly selected group. The characteristics of purchaser households suggested that a continuation of the policy of council house sales would have had the effect of 'creaming off' a distinct group and reducing the social diversity in council-owned dwellings. (Malpass and Murie, 1994, *op. cit.*, pp 299–300)

For those tenants who could not afford to exercise the RTB, as well as the likelihood that an older, larger, better quality house is no longer available to transfer into, the sales would also add to the need to raise rents. Local authorities have very little debt left on their older properties and, given the policy of pooled rents, there is, therefore, a proportionate increase in the local authority's remaining debt for all remaining tenants. It must be admitted, however, that the sale of older properties has a very limited effect by comparison with other causes of raised rents.

Furthermore, as has been seen above, the government did not allow local authorities to use capital receipts to build new dwelling houses to replace what was sold—*cf.* the *Guardian* 2—Society p 8, 5 October 1994. Thus, given that around 1.5 million homes have been sold under the RTB, there are 1.5 million households seeking low cost social housing that no longer exists. Over a long time frame, the number of households seeking new accommodation will come to equal or exceed the number of properties sold under the RTB.

Any assessment of the social effects of the sale of council houses involves more than the households who bought as sitting tenants. The longer-term effect of sale is to increase the stock of dwellings allocated through market processes and to reduce those allocated through bureaucratic and needs-related processes. (Malpass and Murie, 1994, *op. cit.*, p 301)

The effect is that for those in greatest need, the homeless and those in poor quality council housing, there is only the rump of a financially constrained public sector in which to house them.

However, there are some pitfalls to beware even for purchasing tenants. Those former secure tenants who bought flats, for instance, are finding it very hard to sell their properties—Kelly, *The Long Good Buy*, ROOF, September/October 1994, p 34. Some former tenants in the London Borough of Wandsworth have seen the value of their flats fall 90 per cent in a mere three years—the *Guardian* p 6, 18 January 1994 and the *Guardian* 2 p 21, 22 April 1994. The problem is that lending institutions are unwilling to grant mortgages to potential purchasers because of the high maintenance costs that might be associated with the properties, especially if they are in high rise dwellings around 25 years old—the *Guardian* p 31, 11 November 1993; the *Guardian* Weekend p 64, 27 March 1993. Indeed, 'high rise' need not be that high—the Northern Rock and Cheltenham and Gloucester building societies impose restrictions on the granting of mortgages once the property has four storeys.

'We have consistently been concerned about high rise flats as mortgage securities. We informed the [Department of the Environment] in 1987 that we did not agree with their proposals to relaunch the right to buy with the emphasis on flat tenants.' This is the verdict of one leading lender on the leasehold crisis, and it is a view shared by a significant number of its competitors. (Birch, 1993, *op. cit.*, at p 20)

So serious is the problem, that the government is considering allowing the local authority to buy back the property given that the former tenant then buys another local authority property—the *Guardian* p 8, 29 April 1994; p 34, 2 July 1994. Other conditions exist, but the essence of the scheme is that the local authority take back a property that is expensive to maintain and loses a better property because the government encouraged people to buy and the lending institutions were free with their money in the late 1980s.

Furthermore, it should be noted that for all purchasers under the RTB, even if the mortgage repayments are similar in cost to the old weekly rent, the new owner now has to meet the costs of capital upkeep. Where the purchased dwelling house is a flat on an estate or in a tower block, then general repairs and improvements can cost the new owner several thousand pounds. The government is again concerned and is considering issuing a code of practice on service charges.

If purchasing tenants generally can find the RTB brings problems as well as benefits, those secure tenants acquiring on RTM terms are even worse placed. They are unable to afford a mortgage for the entire price less discount, otherwise they would purchase under the more favourable RTB scheme, yet they are encouraged to take on a mortgage equal to their former rent and additionally bear the cost of insurance and repairs or improvements in order to obtain a mere proportionate share. If they sell the property, then in many cases they have to buy out the landlord's share there and then from the proceeds leaving them little with which to purchase a new property on the open market. The Bradford and Bingley Building Society described the RTM scheme as a non-event—Birch, *op. cit.*, at p 20. Considering the exclusions, especially of those on housing benefit under the Housing Act 1985, s 143A, there is little hope for a large take-up by tenants—see the *Guardian* p 35, 15 March 1991; p 31, 9 May 1992; p 6, 22 July 1992; p 30, 1 August 1992; p 4, 14 October 1993; and p 32, 16 October 1993: during the first six months of the operation of the RTM scheme, only two tenants in England

and Wales had taken up the offer—the *Guardian* p 6, 17 October 1994; see also, the *Guardian* p 15, 25 November 1994.

Enfranchisement in the local authority sector including both the RTB and the RTM scheme, is potentially good news for the purchasing tenant, but even in that case the additional costs can make it a poisoned chalice. As for non-purchasing tenants and for those on the waiting list or homeless, the sale *per se* is not a direct source of any problem, since the purchasing tenant would have remained in the dwelling house if he had not bought, but in the long run the amount of social housing available has been reduced.

As regards central and local government, local authorities obviously lose part of their stock, generally the better quality properties with little debt and lower than average maintenance costs. Central government has one less house to subsidize. Thus, it looks as though central government obtains all the benefits of a sale and the local authority loses out. However, the local authority does receive a lump-sum payment that can be set-off against debt—on an even playing field, this might even allow for a reduction in rent, but other policies of central government have led to a continuous ratchet effect, forcing up rents until local authorities as a whole make a profit on council housing by comparison with what central government dispenses through ring-fenced subsidy (see ch 8). Nevertheless, local authorities do receive some compensation. The local authority no longer has to maintain the property, but it is likely to be a low maintenance property that is sold and the reduction in costs may be insignificant if it is just a few properties sold on a large estate.

When a tenant takes out a mortgage he or she is allowed tax relief on the interest payments and hence the Exchequer loses potential tax revenues . . . The RTB purchaser enjoys other benefits from the tax treatment of owner-occupation, particularly the lack of any capital gains tax . . . when the dwelling is eventually sold. There is a major element of uncertainty in attempting to estimate the size of tax losses from the RTB in that the future market behaviour of this new generation of house buyers is unpredictable. Some may use this first house purchase as a stepping-stone into the private housing market and become eligible for successive injections of tax relief. Others may choose to stay in the house they have bought, in which case the tax losses will be smaller . . . Against these losses, the Exchequer will benefit to the extent that it no longer has to support the costs of providing a dwelling in the public sector . . .

A final consideration is the support given through the benefit system to owners and tenants. Whereas many tenants would have their rent paid through the housing benefit system in old age, older owners, who own outright, typically receive very little support from the benefit system . . . Therefore, as the purchasers under the RTB scheme become older, they may be entitled to less public expenditure than they would have received as tenants. It is not clear whether the tax losses or potential benefit gains should be expected to dominate overall. (Gibb and Munro, *Housing Finance in the UK*, 1991, at pp 143–4)

Thus, the RTB is a mixed blessing at best for all affected parties. The lack of an overall housing policy that would consider the housing needs of all households, existing and potential, leaves the RTB confusing 'freedom of choice' with mere licence (in its non-technical sense)—the Housing Act 1980 introduced the RTB to give tenants the 'freedom' to choose to become owner-occupiers, but there is no real freedom since housing subsidies have been weighted in favour of owner-occupation and council housing has been subject to a policy of government attrition. Freedom to choose would allow for a real choice between owner-occupation and remaning a council tenant, but tenants have merely been given licence to become owner-occupiers if they can afford it.

Moreover, experience in other jurisdictions suggests that moves towards almost total reliance on owner-occupation can disproportionately distort the overall housing market. In Canada, little was ever done to provide subsidized, public housing, reliance being placed almost entirely on the private sector and the mortgage providers.

This focus on starts and near total reliance on the private market has been the subject of continuing criticism, but little has changed. In 1964 a major housing-policy review stated that 'housing performance under the National Housing Act had been production oriented rather than distribution oriented, a quantitative operation qualitatively devoid of broad social objectives and economically inaccessible to many Canadians'. The 1968 Federal Task Force on Housing and Urban Development found 'ample evidence of imperfection within the existing market mechanism' and noted that housing 'is a universal need, yet the private market on which Canadians have relied is anything but universal in its present scope and application'. A 1972 study of low-income housing policy noted that 'production goals are adopted on the assumption that all Canadians will be decently housed if a sufficient number of units are produced so that there is one adequate dwelling for every Canadian family'. The size, type, location, price and tenure were left largely to the market and local regulations, with low-income households dependent on the filtering process [ie the trickle-down effect]. The 1972 study concluded that filtering had not worked. (van Vliet, *op. cit.*, at p 300; references omitted)

Australia embarked on a de-municipalization programme of transforming public sector tenants into owner-occupiers decades before the Housing Act 1980, although the initial motivation came from willing State authorities rather than tenants exercising a right to buy. With that caveat, the Australian experience reflects more closely and may predict more clearly the effects of the RTB.

[A] notable feature of Australian public housing policy has been its promotion of home ownership for low-income public tenants. Reflecting the dominance of conservative federal and state governments, various [Commonwealth State Housing Agreements] from the mid-1950s to the early 1980s have progressively allowed the State Housing Commissions to sell off their public housing stock to existing tenants. In Victoria, the state where the policy was most aggressively pursued, 51.5 percent of the metropolitan housing stock had been sold by 1981. In Australia the scale of conversion from public rental stock to private owner occupancy has been considerably greater, occurred earlier and was certainly less politically and academically debated than were the privatization policies occurring in Great Britain, the United States and some other European countries. Because of the privatizing of so much of the public housing stock, state housing authorities in Australia have created many of the negative outcomes predicted by researchers in those overseas countries that more recently embarked on a similar policy. Much high-quality and better-located stock has been sold, leaving behind a residual of low-status, often high-rise, dwellings. Moreover, public authorities . . . are hard pressed to find the public funds to meet the increasing demand for rental rebates to the predominantly welfare tenants left in the wake of privatization. (Burke, Newton and Wulff in van Vliet, *op. cit.*, pp 730–1)

The Australian response, once the full effect of these problems had been perceived, was set out in the Commonwealth State Housing Agreement of 1984. As Burke, Newton and Wulff show (van Vliet, *op. cit.*, p 731), it still promoted home ownership for even low income families, but the following safeguards were also established:

1 Each dwelling sold had to be replaced in order to maintain the public housing stock.
2 The groups of people eligible for public housing was extended to include the young, single homeless.
3 Market rents were abandoned in favour of historic cost rents, while rental rebate schemes remained in place.
4 There was to be an effort to build new public housing stock to meet the growing demand; new housing units were built, but demand still outstripped supply.

There is a stark contrast with British policy in the face of the same problems but with less experience of the consequences.

The most interesting facet of HOTCHA and the TIS, however, is that the government was willing to provide cash to tenants to permit them to purchase a house on the open market (incidentally helping the building industry during the recession). Given the shortage of affordable rented accommodation, that local authority tenants were only given the right to buy their own home shows that the RTB had as much to do with residualizing the role of local authorities in the provision of accommodation as it had to do with giving choice to tenants.

In the private sector, the 1967 Act seems to have been largely effective within its own aims. The fears of a deterioration in the quality of estates have not materialized, in part because of the introduction of estate management schemes whereby the landlord can apply for a scheme to be established enabling him to retain powers of management over houses to be enfranchised.

As mentioned earlier, there has been very poor take up of the rights under the 1987 Act. Even if this were not the case, there must be questions over how far enfranchisement can go towards solving problems of management in blocks of flats. Some of the problems identified by the Nugee Committee—such as poor communications, lack of say in the appointment of managing agents, and inadequate information being provided—can be cured by the tenants taking control of the management, but it is not always necessary to buy the freehold in order to set up a management company. Indeed, in a recent survey it was found that only 54 per cent of flat management companies owned the freehold and in the other cases, where relations were good with the freeholder and leases were well drafted, it was not felt that freehold ownership would have a significant impact on management. Freehold ownership was still considered important, however, for dealing with the wasting asset problem (see Dixon and Pottinger, *Flats as a Way of Life: Flat Management Companies in England and Wales*, 1994; summarized in Joseph Rowntree Foundation, Housing Research Findings No. 124, September 1994). Further, even with tenant controlled management, many problems would remain and are inherent to communal living as tenants will inevitably have different incomes and different views on which repairs to give priority to and the appropriate standards of repair. The Nugee report itself questioned the impact that self-management would have: '. . . while the surveys indicated that resident owned blocks had a lower incidence of management problems, the transfer of ownership would not of itself solve all such problems' (para 7.9.13).

The same comments can be made of the 1993 Act in so far as it was seeking to cure problems of management. Further, the Nugee Committee reported that the incidence and severity of management problems was much greater in older, mixed tenure blocks of flats than in newer purpose-built blocks. Yet although there is a greater problem to be cured, it is less likely that tenants will chose to enfranchise in these blocks—partly because the existence of mixed tenure means that it will be harder to reach the requisite number of qualifying tenants with long leases and also because tenants are less likely to want to assume management of a block with a history of disrepair.

Given the practical difficulties in exercising rights under the 1993 Act—the logistical problems of co-ordinating a large number of tenants and the expense—it is also doubtful how far the Act will achieve its primary object of extending home ownership (see also, Bright, *Enfranchisement—A Fair Deal for All or for None?*, [1994] Conv 211).

12.9 THE DEMISE OF THE LONG LEASE?

Many of the problems of enfranchising flats arise from the unsatisfactory nature of the long leasehold system, which would remain notwithstanding enfranchisement. All enfranchisement does is to change the identity of the landlord. This does give greater opportunity for also changing management systems but the

Nugee Report traced several of the problems to badly drafted leases which set up unsuitable and inefficient management structures. Examples given were the failure to make any provision for sinking funds for long term renewal or to impose any service obligations on the landlord. Post-enfranchisement, the participating tenants—the new 'landlord'—may agree to amend their own leases (but will not necessarily do so), but cannot impose change on non-participating tenants and renters in the block.

The focus throughout recent years has been on the introduction of commonhold legislation and on implementing a modified version of the Law Commission's proposals on enforcing freehold covenants. For details see *Commonhold—Freehold Flats and Freehold Ownership of other Interdependent Buildings*, Cm 179, July 1987; *Commonhold, A Consultation Paper*, 1990, Cm 1346; Law Commission, *Transfer of Land—The Law of Positive and Restrictive Covenants*, Law Com. No. 127, 1984

Commonhold is to be a totally new form of tenure to meet the problems raised by common ownership of land, similar to the strata title schemes of Australia and New Zealand and the condominium scheme in America. The detail of commonhold is still to be finalized, but the Lord Chancellor's department explanatory leaflet on commonhold states:

A *commonhold* is a freehold development consisting of two or more separate properties, or *units*, which share services and facilities (such as lifts, corridors, an entrance hallway and stairs, dustbin areas, and the like) and so need a system for the communal management and ownership of the common parts . . .

The idea behind the Government's commonhold scheme is to provide owners in multi-occupier developments with the freehold interest in their units and, at the same time, furnish them with a system for the efficient management of the development (the *commonhold*) as a whole.

This will be achieved by the creation of commonhold associations and the imposition of a statutory framework of rights and obligations between unit owners, and also between the owners and their commonhold association.

Commonhold ownership would be available for both residential and commercial premises.

Various questions were left open for debate in the commonhold scheme (see *Commonhold: A Consultation Paper*, 1990, *op. cit.*, Part IV):

1 Should there be a provision for the compulsory conversion of residential leasehold developments to commonhold without the agreement of all interested parties (para 4.1)? Compulsion was only considered in relation to residential property because of the 'special importance to people of their own homes, and of their right to own and control them'. Much of the discussion in the Consultation Paper has now been superseded by the enfranchisement provisions and any commonhold proposals brought forward will presumably follow the approach of the 1993 Act and admit compulsory conversion to

commonhold where the requisite majority of tenants so decide. In other jurisdictions, the collective ownership schemes have been implemented without
compulsion. The situations are, however, very different. In England and
Wales there is a significant (and unique) amount of long leasehold property
and any conversion to commonhold will mean that the landlord loses all long
term investment value in the building. In America, most blocks of flats were
developed for rental on a short-medium term basis. Long-leasehold sales
were not usual. Once condominiums became popular landlords saw the
attraction of selling on a condominium basis rather than continuing to rent.
Compulsion was therefore not necessary in order to promote condominium
ownership:

**There have been two primary catalysts for conversions. First, demand for
condominium housing has grown, causing a concomitant increase in the profitability of conversion. Second, stagnation of tenant income levels and regulation of rental housing have caused a decrease in the profitability of rental
housing. These two economic factors make conversion increasingly attractive
to the landlord. Several factors create the growing demand for condominium
housing. They include changing demographics, tax advantages of home ownership, changing housing preferences, and the escalation of construction
costs.** (Judson, *op. cit.*, pp 184–5)

2   Should there be a rule against the granting of long leases of commonhold
    units? Again, this question was left open, but some of the discussion in the
    Consultation Paper suggests that there is considerable support for the demise
    of the long leasehold sector:

**4.54 In the first place, one of the central purposes of the commonhold scheme
is to replace the existing system of long leases and, in particular, to avoid the
problem of dwindling lease terms. It hardly seems appropriate to perpetuate
that problem within a system designed to get rid of it . . .**
**4.57 . . . One of the central purposes of the commonhold scheme is to abolish
the third-party ground landlord who has limited direct continuing interest in
the day-to-day management of the property . . .**
**4.59 Quite apart from the issues of principle involved in the question of ban-
ning long leases, there would be a considerable advantage in terms of simplification of the legislation. There would no longer be any need for the provision
for enforcing service charges against long-leaseholders.**

Elsewhere in the Paper the question is posed whether there should be a rule
that no future residential long-leasehold developments should be allowed (para
4.7). The response is that the market should be allowed to choose between commonhold and long leasehold. Given a choice between the two tenures there is little doubt that unit purchasers will seek commonhold.

Annex

AGRICULTURAL TENANCIES BILL 1995

Throughout this book reference has been made to the proposed MAFF reforms for the agricultural tenancy sector. The substance of this reform was well documented in advance of the Bill being presented to Parliament and the basic scheme of the Bill remains as referred to in the various government announcements. At the time of writing, the Bill is still proceeding through the various Parliamentary stages but it is not anticipated that there will be any substantial changes. The commencement date is planned for 1 September 1995 and the Bill will not apply to tenancies entered into before that date.

The intention behind the Agricultural Tenancies Bill is to deregulate agricultural lettings in order to reverse the decline in the size of the tenanted sector and to permit greater diversification in land use. There is widespread support within the agricultural industry for these reforms—the Bill has the backing of the National Farmers Union, the Country Landowners' Association, the Tenant Farmers' Association and the National Federation of Young Farmers' Clubs. One of the central planks of the reform is the removal of security of tenure, perceived as necessary if farm owners are to be willing to let a farm:

Principal [among the reasons for the decline in the proportion of land let on protected tenancies] is the maze of restrictive tenancy legislation, and the security of tenure provision in particular. These represent a major disincentive to any landowners who might otherwise consider letting their land. The supply of new full tenancies has slowed to the merest trickle. (Earl Howe, Hansard, HL Deb, 28 November 1994, vol 559, cols 486–7)

In addition, the Bill provides that (in the absence of contractual provision for rent review) either party can seek a rent review every three years, the tenant is entitled to compensation for improvements on quitting the letting and any disputes can be referred to arbitration. Beyond this, the terms of the tenancy are left to be agreed between the parties.

The Bill will apply to a 'farm business tenancy', defined in clause 1:

cl 1(1) A tenancy is a 'farm business tenancy' for the purposes of this Act if—
   (a) it meets the business conditions together with either the agricultural condition or the notice conditions, and
   (b) it is not a tenancy which, by virtue of section 2 of this Act, cannot be a farm business tenancy.

(2) The business conditions are—
    (a) that all or part of the land comprised in the tenancy is farmed for the purposes of a trade or business, and
    (b) that, since the beginning of the tenancy, all or part of the land so comprised has been so farmed.

(3) The agricultural condition is that, having regard to—
    (a) the terms of the tenancy,
    (b) the use of the land comprised in the tenancy,
    (c) the nature of any commercial activities carried on on that land, and
    (d) any other relevant circumstances,
the character of the tenancy is primarily or wholly agricultural.

(4) The notice conditions are—
    (a) that, on or before the relevant day, the landlord and the tenant each gave the other a written notice—
        (i) identifying (by name or otherwise) the land to be comprised in the tenancy or proposed tenancy, and
        (ii) containing a statement to the effect that the person giving the notice intends that the tenancy or proposed tenancy is to be, and remain, a farm business tenancy, and
    (b) that, at the beginning of the tenancy, having regard to the terms of the tenancy and any other relevant circumstances, the character of the tenancy was primarily or wholly agricultural.

(5) In subsection (4) above 'the relevant day' means whichever is the earlier of the following—
    (a) the day on which the parties enter into any instrument creating the tenancy, other than an agreement to enter into a tenancy on a future date, or
    (b) the beginning of the tenancy.

(6) The written notice referred to in subsection (4) above must not be included in any instrument creating the tenancy.

(7) If in any proceedings—
    (a) any question arises as to whether a tenancy was a farm business tenancy at any time, and
    (b) it is proved that all or part of the land comprised in the tenancy was farmed for the purposes of a trade or business at that time,
it shall be presumed, unless the contrary is proved, that all or part of the land so comprised has been so farmed since the beginning of the tenancy.

(8) Any use of land in breach of the terms of the tenancy, any commercial activities carried on in breach of those terms, and any cessation of such activities in breach of those terms, shall be disregarded in determining whether at any time the tenancy meets the business conditions or the agriculture condition, unless the landlord or his predecessor in title has consented to the breach or the landlord has acquiesced in the breach.

Section 2 excludes tenancies entered into before the commencement of the Act and tenancies created under the statutory succession provisions of the 1986 Act, the intention being that existing tenants should not lose their security under the 1986 Act.

In order to be a farm business tenancy, the letting must satisfy the business condition test, that at least part of the land is farmed for the purposes of a trade or business. In addition it must satisfy either the agriculture condition or the notice conditions. It is expected that most lettings will take advantage of the notice conditions—all this requires is that the specified notice is given before the tenancy and that *at the beginning of the tenancy* the character of the tenancy was primarily or wholly agricultural. The effect of this is that after the commencement of the tenancy there could be a substantial change in the land use and yet the tenancy will remain a farm business tenancy (and largely unregulated) so long only that part of the land is farmed commercially. Where no notice is served, however, the letting will only remain a farm business tenancy so long as the character of the tenancy is primarily or wholly agricultural. Later diversification in land use to more commercial and non-agricultural activity could result in a 'no-notice' letting becoming subject to Part II of the Landlord and Tenant Act 1954 with rights of renewal for the tenant.

'Agriculture' is defined in the same way as under the 1986 Agricultural Holdings Act (clause 37; see ch 6.5.2.1). The opposition sought to modernise this as the present definition does not specifially refer to many contemporary land uses, such as arable land, land set-aside under the Common Agricultural Policy, or energy crops (such as miscanthus and biomass). The government felt that the present definition is adequate as it is not exclusive (agriculture 'includes' the listed activities). It was accepted, though, that there might be a case for updating the definition for all purposes (and not just for the 1995 Act) in the future.

There are no formality requirements for farm business tenancies aside from the requirement to give notice in order to take advantage of the option of ensuring that the farm business tenancy will remain such notwithstanding any later change in use (the notice conditions). The lettings will be subject to the general formality requirements if the lease is for more than three years (see ch 5.2.1) but, if for a shorter period, a written or oral lease is capable of being a farm business tenancy. Nor will there be any prescription of minimum length of leases or model clauses, although industry groups are preparing model forms of tenancy that can be used on a voluntary basis.

The biggest change from the present regime is the removal of security of tenure. Whereas agricultural tenants under the Agricultural Holdings Act 1986 often have what is effectively lifetime security of tenure (and lettings granted prior to 12 July 1984 additionally could be secure for two further generations under the succession rules), tenants under the new regime will have no security beyond their contractual term—although they must be given twelve months' notice if the lease is for more than two years.

cl 5(1) A farm business tenancy for a term of more than two years shall, instead of terminating on the term date, continue (as from that date) as a tenancy from year to year, but otherwise on the terms of the original tenancy so far as applicable, unless at least twelve months but less than twenty-four months before the term date a written notice has been given by either party to the other of his intention to terminate the tenancy.

(2) In subsection (1) above 'the term date', in relation to a fixed term tenancy, means the date fixed for the expiry of the term.

. . .

(4) This section has effect notwithstanding any agreement to the contrary.

cl 6(1) Where a farm business tenancy is a tenancy from year to year, a notice to quit the holding or part of the holding shall (notwithstanding any provision to the contrary in the tenancy) be invalid unless—

(a) it is in writing,

(b) it is to take effect at the end of a year of the tenancy, and

(c) it is given at least twelve months but less than twenty-four months before the date on which it is to take effect

(2) Where, by virtue of section 5(1) of this Act, a farm business tenancy for a term of more than two years is to continue (as from the term date) as a tenancy from year to year, a notice to quit which complies with subsection (1) above and which is to take effect on the first anniversary of the term date shall not be invalid merely because it is given before the term date; and in this subsection 'the term date' has the meaning given by section 5(2) of this Act.

The reason for denying security of tenure to tenant farmers is policy-based, in that the government perceive that this is essential if more farmland is to be let, and that it is essential to secure more lettings of agricultural land in order to permit new entrants to the farming world. The belief is that under the 1986 Act landowners are reluctant to let land for fear that the letting might tie that land up for a lifetime—hence the popularity of *Gladstone v Bower* type lettings and short-term lettings excluded from protection by Ministerial consent (see ch 6.5 and 6.6). This is understandable given the much lower value of tenanted agricultural land than agricultural land with vacant possession, tenanted land being worth only around two-thirds of the value of vacant possession land (see Country Landowners' Association, *Land Statistics 1993*, Tables 1 and 2.4).

There are, however, various concerns over this policy of removing security. First, it is not clear that the new Bill will in fact lead to a shift from owner-occupation to tenanted land. Although it is difficult to predict whether such a shift will occur, the recent announcement that 100 per cent inheritance tax relief will be available to owners of tenanted land removes a further, and substantial, disincentive to letting. This change will apply in relation to land let on or after 1 September 1995 (see Inland Revenue Press Release, 27 January 1995). There was a widely held belief that the fiscal disadvantages of letting resulted in much land being owner occupied (see Kerr, *Farm Business Tenancies: New Farms and Land 1995–97*, Royal Institution of Chartered Surveyors, 1994, at para 3.4) and it may be that the removal of the fiscal disincentive will have more impact on letting policy than the reform of tenancy law itself. Secondly, there is concern that the changes will lead to short-term lettings. With occupancy guaranteed only for short periods tenant farmers will have no incentive to preserve the long-term interests of the land and to adopt sustainable farming techniques. In addition, it may be hard for tenant farmers to borrow money to finance improvements to the land. To refute these fears, reference was made at Committee stage in the House of Lords to the survey by Kerr, *op.cit.*, as supporting the view that over a two year period after the introduction of the Bill there is likely to be one million acres of new tenanted land, more than half of which will be let on 10 to 15 year tenancies (see Earl Howe, Hansard, HL Deb, 28 November 1994, vol 559, col 527; Lord Northbourne, Hansard, HL Deb, 28 November 1994, vol 559, col 498). The same survey was also used, however, to support the opposition concern that the Bill will lead to short-term lettings of only five years (see Lord Carter, Hansard, HL Deb, 28 November 1994, vol 559, col 492). These conflicting views of the Kerr survey illustrate the difficulties in interpreting survey results. The explanation for the divergent interpretation of the results lies in whether one looks to the land area of the expected new farm business lettings (only 34 per cent of the acreage would be on five year lets, the rest being for longer periods), or at the number of holdings let (57 per cent of units let would be for five years). There is also a view that bare land units (which are not equipped for farming by the owner) are most likely to be let to existing farmers who seek to achieve economies of scale, whereas new entrants to farming are more likely to seek equipped farms. Of the expected new lettings, only 26 per cent of the units would be equipped farms (see generally Table A3, Kerr, *op.cit.*). A further point to note on the survey is that RICS requested information on expected lettings for 'five years or more' and did not ask for views on shorter lettings. The overall conclusion reached by Kerr was that

nearly 900,000 acres will be let through chartered surveyors for 5 years or more under a farm business tenancy. This would comprise 1,166 equipped farms and 3,315 blocks of bare land. (Kerr, *op.cit*, at para 2.8)

The fears over the impact of the Bill are expressed in the following statement from the Farmers' Union of Wales, one of the few industry groups to oppose the Bill:

With short term lets, tenants would face constant uncertainty, unable to plan ahead.

Looking into the 'crystal ball', FUW believes that the established farmer would gain, resulting in fewer farmers, larger holdings, and little hope for the young

farmer/new entrant, to gain access to the industry. Banks could not support an entrant to the industry who only had a short-term agreement.

There is a danger that, with short-term lets, onerous terms could be imposed. There is also a danger that entrants would accept any terms in their desperation to enter the industry (as witnessed by the high number of applicants for Council holdings).

If it were possible to let farms and land on a short-term basis, then we fear that land could be exploited for short-term gain, but would result in long-term detriment to the land. This might well have repercussions for the environment and the countryside in general. (quoted by Lord Geraint, Hansard, HL Deb, 28 November 1994, vol 559, col 522)

A third concern expressed was that removing security of tenure ignores the fact that for many farmers the land is not only a source of income but his family home, when the tenancy comes to an end, the farmer and his family may well may be left without a home.

The rent under a farm business tenancy is also to be a matter of free market negotiation. There is no control on initial rent fixing and the parties are free to agree a rent review mechanism by which the rent is to be varied by a specified amount or in accordance with an objective formula which does not preclude a reduction (clause 9). This prevents an upwards only review clause from being effective. If there is no such rent review mechanism in the lease, either party can request the rent to be reviewed by arbitration at three yearly intervals (clause 10). The arbitrator can increase or reduce the rent payable (clause 13(1)) on an open market basis:

cl 13(1) On any reference made in pursuance of a statutory review notice, the arbitrator shall determine the rent properly payable in respect of the holding at the review date and accordingly shall, with effect from that date, increase or reduce the rent previously payable or direct that it shall continue unchanged.

(2) For the purposes of subsection (1) above, the rent properly payable in respect of a holding is the rent at which the holding might reasonably be expected to be let on the open market by a willing landlord to a willing tenant, taking into account (subject to subsections (3) and (4) below) all relevant factors, including (in every case) the terms of the tenancy (including those which are relevant for the purposes of section 10(4) to (6) of this Act, but not those relating to the criteria by reference to which any new rent is to be determined).

(3) The arbitrator shall disregard any increase in the rental value of the holding which is due to tenant's improvements other than—

(a) any tenant's improvement provided under an obligation which was imposed on the tenant by the terms of his tenancy or any previous tenancy and which arose on or before the beginning of the tenancy in question,

(b) any tenant's improvement to the extent that any allowance or benefit has been made or given by the landlord in consideration of its provision, and

(c) any tenant's improvement to the extent that the tenant has received any compensation from the landlord in respect of it.

(4) The arbitrator—

(a) shall disregard any effect on the rent of the fact that the tenant who is party to the arbitration is in occupation of the holding, and

(b) shall not fix the rent at a lower amount by reason of any dilapidation or deterioration of, or damage to, buildings or land caused or permitted by the tenant.

While open market rent is intended to encourage more letting of land, fears have been expressed that it will drive rents up to uneconomic levels—in order to get a farm a new entrant will agree to high rents that cannot be supported from the land, and high initial rents will also impact upon the rents set by arbitrators. The government feel that the arbitrators will, however, have regard to the character and situation of a holding and its productive capacity when setting the rent as part of the 'relevant factors' in clause 13(2) (see Hansard, HL Deb, 12 December 1994, vol 559, col 1188).

The tenant will be entitled to compensation for improvements on quitting the holding, provided that the improvement is not removed from the holding (clause 16) and that the landlord has given written consent to the improvement (clause 17). The landlord's consent can be given either in response to an individual request or in the tenancy agreement itself. Although, therefore, there is no statutory right to compensation for tenant right matters (growing crops, *etc.*, see ch 6.5.2.2), the landlord and the tenant may agree in a written tenancy agreement that there will be compensation for tenant right: the opposition fears that the bargaining strength of landlords is such that they will contract out of tenant right compensation (see Hansard, HL Deb, 13 December 1994, vol 559, cols 1228–9). During the tenancy there is no requirement for the landlord to give consent but the tenant is able to refer the issue to arbitration if the landlord refuses consent and the arbitrator

shall consider whether, having regard to the terms of the tenancy and any other relevant circumstances (including the circumstances of the tenant and the landlord), it is reasonable for the tenant to provide the proposed tenant's improvement. (clause 19(4))

The definition of an improvement is given in clause 15:

cl 15 For the purposes of this Part of this Act a 'tenant's improvement', in relation to any farm business tenancy, means—

(a) any physical improvement which is made on the holding by the tenant by his own effort or wholly or partly at his own expense, or

(b) any intangible advantage which—

(i) is obtained for the holding by the tenant by his own effort or wholly or partly at his own expense, and

(ii) becomes attached to the holding,

and references to the provision of a tenant's improvement are references to the making by the tenant of any physical improvement falling within paragraph (a) above or the obtaining by the tenant of any intangible advantage falling within paragraph (b) above.

Tenant's improvements include not only physical improvements but also intangible benefits, which could include goodwill so long as the tenant had first obtained the landlord's written consent to this counting as an improvement. So, a tenant farmer who has diversified into offering bed and breakfast accommodation can claim compensation on quitting for the goodwill attached to the commercial element, but only if he has obtained the landlord's consent to this 'improvement'—a curious idea.

There are special provisions that apply to planning permission obtained by the tenant farmer for development on the land:

cl 18(1) A tenant shall not be entitled to compensation under section 16 of this Act in respect of a tenant's improvement which consists of planning permission unless—

(a) the landlord has given his consent in writing to the making of the application for planning permission,

(b) that consent is expressed to be given for the purpose—

(i) of enabling a specified physical improvement falling within paragraph (a) of section 15 of this Act lawfully to be provided by the tenant, or

(ii) of enabling the tenant lawfully to effect a specified change of use, and

(c) on the termination of the tenancy, the specified physical improvement has not been completed or the specified change of use has not been effected.

(2) Any such consent may be given either unconditionally or on condition that the tenant agrees to a specified variation in the terms of the tenancy.

(3) The variation referred to in subsection (2) above must be related to the physical improvement or change of use in question.

Unlike with other tenant improvements, the obtaining of the landlord's consent for the planning application cannot be referred to arbitration.

The amount of compensation is the 'an amount equal to the increase attributable to the improvement in the value of the holding at the termination of the tenancy' (clause 20(1)), with discount for any allowance made by the landlord to the tenant (clause 20(2)) and any public grant paid to the tenant (clause 20(3)). Where the improvement consists of unimplemented planning permission the amount of compensation is 'an amount equal to the increase attributable to the fact that the relevant development is authorised by the planning permission in the value of the holding at the termination of the tenancy' (clause 21(1)).

The idea underlying the compensation provisions is, as under the 1986 Act, that the tenant should receive compensation for value that he has added to the landlord's interest at his own expense or effort. The right to compensation provides the tenant with an incentive to make improvements to the land and the system under the 1995 Bill is simpler than in the 1986 Act. In addition, unlike the 1986 Act, these compensation provisions will override any agreement to the contrary (clause 26) and so it will not be possible for the level of compensation to be written down. Nevertheless, concerns have been voiced that because the tenant must obtain the landlord's written consent to the improvement, the landlord may unreasonably withhold consent. This is most likely to arise when the tenant is improving in order to diversify beyond traditional agricultural land use. Although it is always possible for the tenant to refer the refusal to arbitration, the costs of doing so may be prohibitive.

Disputes that arise in relation to farm business tenancies can either be referred to a third party under a provision in the lease agreement or referred to an arbitrator (clauses 28, 29).

Bibliography

Access to Local Authority and Housing Association Tenancies: see, Department of the Environment

Ackerman, *Regulating Slum Housing Markets on Behalf of the Poor: Of Housing Codes, Housing Subsidies and Income Redistribution Policy*, (1971) 80 Yale LJ 1093

Adams, *Shopping Centres: Tenants' Associations in Centres*, [1988] 15 EG 24

Albon and Stafford, *Rent Control*, 1987

Allen and McDowell, *Landlords and Property*, 1989

Anstey and Freedman, *A standard form of business lease*, (1991) 24 LS Gaz. 27

Arden, *Bashing the Homeless*, ROOF, March/April 1982, p 13

Arden, *Homeless Persons*, 1988

Argent, *A Worthwhile Price To Pay*, ROOF, November/December 1994, p 14

Arnison, Bibby and Mulquiney, *Commercial Property Management*, 1990

Atiyah, *The Rise and Fall of Freedom of Contract*, 1979

Atiyah, *Essays on Contract*, 1988

Atkins Committee, NEDO, Latent Defects in Buildings: An Analysis of Insurance Possibilities, 1985

Audit Commission, *Housing the Homeless: the Local Authority Role*, 1989

Audit Commission, *Developing Local Authority Housing Strategies*, 1992

Baar, *The Right to Sell the "Im"mobile Manufactured Home in its Rent Controlled Space in the "Im"mobile Home Park: valid regulation or unconstitutional taking?*, (1992) 24 The Urban Lawyer 157

Balchin, *Housing Policy*, 2nd edn, 1989

Ball, *Housing Policy and Economic Power*, 1983

Battersby, *Contractual and estoppel licences as proprietary interests in land*, [1991] Conv 36

Battle, *How to Bridge the Funding Gap*, ROOF, July/August 1994, p 9

Bennet and Rigby, *A Closer look at the turnover lease*, The Property Week, 15 July 1993

Berger, *The New Residential Tenancy Law—Are Landlords Public Utilities?*, (1981) 60 Neb L Rev 707

Bernstein and Lewis, *UK lease structures in the melting pot*, (1992) 45 EG 108

Bernstein and Reynolds, *Handbook of Rent Review*

Birch, *Flat Broke*, ROOF, November/December 1993, p 18

Birch, *For the Defence*, ROOF, July/August 1994, p 30

Birch, Dwelly and Kemp, *The Point of Low Return*, ROOF, March/April 1993, p 22

Black, *High Hopes*, ROOF, January/February 1993, p 20

Black, *Waking Up To Racism*, ROOF January/February 1994, p 20

Blake, *Playing the New Numbers Game*, ROOF, July/August 1993, p 9

Blake, *The Right to Act*, ROOF, September/October 1993, p 27

Blake, *Housing's High Noon*, ROOF, January/February 1994, p 23

Blake, *Homeless All At Sea*, ROOF, May/June 1994, p 26

Blake, *Whose Future Is It Anyway?*, ROOF, September/October 1994, p 20

Boddy, *The Building Societies*, 1980

Borrie, *Think Tank Rolls into Action*, ROOF, May/June 1994, p 8

Bowley, 'Housing and the State', 1945, in Malpass and Murie, (eds) *Housing Policy and Practice*, 4th edn, 1994

Bradbrook and Croft, *Commercial Tenancy Law in Australia*, 1990

Brett, *Property and Money*, 1990

Bridge, *Residential Leases*, 1994

Bridge, *Damages for Eviction: Confusion Compounded*, [1994] Conv 411

Briggs, *Licences: Back to Basics*, [1981] Conv 212

Briggs, *Contractual Licences: A Reply*, [1983] Conv 285

Bright, *Beyond Sham and Into Pretence*, (1991) 11 OJLS 136

Bright, *Protecting multiple occupancy—Brady revisited*, (1992) 142 NLJ 575

Bright, *Uncertainty in leases—Is it a Vice?*, (1993) 13 LS 38

Bright, *Enfranchisement—A Fair Deal for All or for None?*, [1994] Conv 211

Brimacombe, *A Divided Rule*, ROOF, May/June 1991, p 32

Brimacombe, *Weed Out the Undesirables*, ROOF, November/December 1993, p 24

Bromley and Lowe, *Bromley's Family Law*, 8th edn, 1992

Building Societies Association, *Leasehold—Time for a Change*, 1984

Burnett, *A Social History of Housing 1815–1970*, 2nd edn, 1985

Burns, *Notes*, ROOF, September/October 1994, p 8

Burrows and Hunter, *Forced Out, A Shelter Publication on Harassment and Illegal Eviction*, 1990

Burrows and Walentowicz, *Homes Cost Less than Homelessness*, 1992

Burton, *Retail Rents, Fair and Free Market?*, 1992

Butler, Carlisle and Lloyd, *Homelessness in the 1990s: Local Authority Practice*, 1994

Calvert, *Social Security Law*, 1978

Cameron and Frew, *Beyond the Ballot*, ROOF, May/June 1991, p 14

Campaign for Bedsit Rights, *Houses in Multiple Occupation: Policy and Practice in the 1990s*, 1993

Campaign for the Homeless and Rootless (CHAR), *Reassessing Priorities*, 1993

Campaign for the Homeless and Rootless (CHAR), *Acting in Isolation*, 1994

Campbell, *Legal Eye*, ROOF, May/June 1991, p 15

Campbell, *Three's a Crowd*, ROOF, May/June 1993, p 13

Campbell, *New Borders to Cross*, ROOF, July/August 1993, p 11

Campbell, *Legal Eye: Cathy Comes Back*, ROOF, March/April 1994, p 14

Campbell, *Rules Made to be Broken*, ROOF, May/June 1994

Campbell, *All's Well that Ends Well*, ROOF, September/October 1994

Campbell, *After the Scarborough Affair*, ROOF, November/December 1994, p 17

Cardwell, *Arable farming in the Short Term*, [1993] Conv 138

Carver, 'Houses for Canadians', 1948, in van Vliet (ed.) *International Handbook of Housing Policies and Practices*, 1990

Cheshire and Burn, *Modern Law of Real Property*, 15th edn, 1994

Chitty on Contracts, 27th edn, 1994

Civil Justice Review, *Report of the Review Body on Civil Justice*, Cm 394, 1988

Clapham, 'A Woman of Her Time', in Grant (ed.), *Built To Last*, 1992

Clarke, *Rent Reviews in Residential Tenancies*, [1989] Conv 111

Clarke, *Property Law*, (1992) 45 CLP 81

Clarke, *Leasehold Enfranchisement*, 1994

Clarke and Adams, *Rent Reviews and Variable Rents*, 3rd edn, 1990

Codd, *Limiting Distress*, (1994) 138 Sol.Jo.524

Cohen, *Dialogue on Private Property*, (1954) 9 Rutgers L Rev 357

Coke, *A Commentarie upon Littleton*, 1670

Commonhold—Freehold Flats and Freehold Ownership of other Interdependent Buildings, Cm 179, 1987

Commonhold, A Consultation Paper, Cm 1346, 1990

Cooke, *Notices to Quit for the Monthly Tenant*, [1992] Conv 263

Cope, *Housing Associations: Policy and Practice*, 1990

Corbin on Contracts, 1974

Cowan, *The Public/Private Dichotomy and 'Suitable Accommodation' under s69(1) of the Housing Act 1985*, [1993] JSW&FL 236

Cowan and Fionda, (1993a) *New Angles on Homelessness*, [1993] JSW&FL 403

Cowan and Fionda, (1993b) *Cause for Offence*, ROOF, May/June 1993, p 10

Cowling and Smith, *Home Ownership, Socialism and Realistic Socialist Policy*, (1984) 3:3 *Critical Social Policy* 64

Crabb, *'Usual Covenants' in Leases: A Misnomer*, [1992] Conv 18

Croftin, *Tales of Lost Regeneration*, ROOF, November/December 1994, p 30

Crook, 'Private rented housing and the impact of deregulation', in Johnston Birchall (ed.) *Housing Policy in the 1990s*, 1992

Crook, Kemp, Anderson and Bowman, *The Business Expansion Scheme and Rented Housing*, May 1991

Cullen and McMillian, *Lease Structure Changes 1992*, Royal Institution of Chartered Surveyors, Paper Number 32, 1994

Cullingworth, *Problems of an Urban Society*, 1973

Cullingworth Report, *Council Housing: Purposes, Procedures and Priorities*, 9th Report of the Housing Management Sub-Committee on the Central Housing Advisory Committee, 1969

Cunningham, *The New Implied and Statutory Warranties of Habitability in Residential Leases: From Contract to Status*, (1979) 16 Urb L Ann 6

Cunningham *et al.*, *The Law of Property*, 2nd edn, 1984

Damer, 'Striking Out on Red Clyde', in Grant (ed.), *Built to Last*, 1992

Davey, *A Farewell to Fair Rents?*, [1992] JSW&FL 497

Davies and Molnar, *All Our Tomorrows*, National Housing Forum, 1993

De Moor, *Landlord and tenant in French law: a recent statute*, (1983) 3 OJLS 425

Department of the Environment, *English House Condition Survey: 1991*, 1993

Department of the Environment and Welsh Office (Joint Circular from the), *Housing Act 1988: Protection of Residential Occupiers*, Circular 3/89

Department of the Environment's Consultation Paper on Commercial Property Leases, 27 May 1993

Department of the Environment, *CCT and Housing Management*, 1993

Department of the Environment, *Access to Local Authority and Housing Association Tenancies: A Consultation Paper*, 1994

Dewar, *Licences and Land Law: An Alternative View*, (1986) 49 MLR 741

Dewar, *When Joint Tenants Part*, (1992) 108 LQR 375

Dixon and Pottinger, *Flats as a Way of Life: Flat Management Companies in England and Wales*, 1994

Donnison, *The Government of Housing*, 1967

Donnison and Ungerson, *Housing Policy*, 1982

Dorling, *Children in Need*, ROOF, September/October 1993, p 12

Dow, *Move On Up*, ROOF, November/December 1992, p 18

Down, Holmans and Small, *Trends in the Size of the Private Rented Sector in England*, Housing Finance No.22, May 1994, p 7

Draft Tenants' Guarantee: see, Housing Corporation

Driscoll, *Rent Arrears, Suspended Possession Orders and the Rights of Secure Tenants*, (1988) 51 MLR 371

Driscoll, *The Leasehold Reform, Housing and Urban Development Act 1993: The Public Sector Housing Provisions*, (1994) 57 MLR 788

Dwelly, *Tender Moments*, ROOF, May/June 1991, p 19

Dwelly, *Labour's Bank Job*, ROOF, November/December 1991, p 26

Dwelly, *No Sign of Movement*, ROOF, November/December 1992, p 21

Dwelly, *Housing at the Crossroads*, ROOF, January/February 1993, p 22

Dwelly, *Kilburn's High Road*, ROOF, March/April 1993, p 29

Dwelly, *Nothing Ruled Out*, ROOF, September/October 1993, p 22

Dwelly, *Eyes on the Prize*, ROOF, March/April 1994, p 20

Edmonds, *How to Score a Classic Own Goal*, ROOF, November/December 1992, p 15

Effron, *The Contractualisation of the Law of Leasehold*, (1988) 14 Monash Univ Law Rev 83

English, *Built to Last*, ROOF, November/December 1991, p 34

English House Condition Survey: 1991: see, Department of the Environment

Envis, *Compensation and the Right to Repair*, (1994) 138 Sol J 504

Ertel, *Vermont's Efforts to Protect Mobile Home Park Tenants: Is there a Taking?*, (1992) 16 Vermont L Rev 1027

Evans and Smith, *The Law of Landlord and Tenant*, 4th edn, 1993

Exford, *West Kent Row Reverberates*, ROOF, November/December 1994, p 9

Expenditure Plans 1991–92 to 1992–93, Cm 1008, 1990

Fielding, *Finding New Ways to Beat the Bailiff*, ROOF, May/June 1984, p 23

Ford, *Breathing New Life into Ailing Shopping Centres*, [1994] 4 PR 116

Forrest and Murie, 'The Right to Buy', in Grant (ed.), *Built to Last*, 1992

Francis Committee, *Report of the Committee on the Rent Acts*, Cmnd 4609, 1971

Gardner, *The Proprietary Effect of Contractual Obligations under Tulk v Moxhay and De Mattos v Gibson*, (1982) 98 LQR 279

Gauldie, *Cruel Habitations*, 1974

Gibb and Munro, *Housing Finance in the UK*, 1991

Ginsburg, *Home Ownership and Socialism in Britain: A Bulwark Against Bolshevism*, (1983) 3:1 Critical Social Policy 34

Ginsburg and Watson, 'Issues of Race and Gender Facing Housing Policy', in Johnston Birchall (ed.), *Housing Policy in the 1990s*, 1992

Glendon, *The Transformation of American Landlord–Tenant Law*, (1982) 23 Bos C LR 503

Goodlad and Gibb, *Housing and Social Justice*, 1994

Gordon, *The Burden and Benefit of the Rules of Assignment*, [1987] Conv 103

Government Policy on Leasehold Property in England and Wales, Cmd 8713, 1953

Government's Expenditure Plans (The): Department of the Environment, 1994–95 to 1996–97, Cm 2507, 1994

Government's White Paper on Housing, 1987: see, Housing: the Government's Proposals

Grant, *Built to Last*, 1992

Grant, *Don't Shoot the Messenger*, ROOF, May/June 1994, p 19

Gray, *Elements of Land Law*, 1st edn, 1987

Gray, *Property in Thin Air*, [1991] CLJ 252

Gray, *Elements of Land Law*, 2nd edn, 1993

Haley, *Business Leases: Termination and Renewal*, 1991

Haley, *Compensation for Tenants' Improvements*, (1991) 11 Leg Stud 119

Haley, *Business tenancies and interventionism: the relegation of policy?*, (1993) 13 LS 225

Hands, *The Statutory Tenancy: An Unrecognised Proprietary Interest*, [1980] Conv 351

Handy, *Discrimination in Housing*, 1994

Hanson, *How Affordable Can Social Housing Be?*, (1993) 11 EG 104

Harle, *Challenging rent control: strategies for attack*, (1986–87) 34 UCLA Law Review 149

Harloe, *Private Rented Housing in the United States and Europe*, 1985

Harpum, *Relief Against Forfeiture and the Purchaser of Land*, [1984] CLJ 134

Harpum, *Leases as Contracts*, [1993] CLJ 212

Harrison, *Inside the Inner City*, 2nd edn, 1984

Hawkings, *Shopping centres—turnover rents on the increase?*, (1990) 38 EG 28

Hawkins, *The Nugee Committee Report—The Management of Privately Owned Blocks of Flats*, [1986] Conv 12

Hayek, Friedman, Stigler, de Jouvenel, Paish, Rydenfelt and Pennace, *Verdict on Rent Control*, 1972

Hayek, Friedman *et al.*, *Rent Control: A Popular Paradox*, 1975

Hecht, *Variable Rental Provision in Long Term Ground Leases*, (1972) 72 Col L Rev 625

Henderson and Karn, *Race, Class and State Housing: Inequality and the Allocation of Public Housing in Britain*, 1987

Hendry, *Taking Back the Empties*, ROOF, September/October 1993, p 17

Hendry, *Hysterical and Exaggerated*, ROOF, May/June 1994, p 18

Hickman, *The Housing Act 1988—Four Years On*, (1993) 143 NLJ 1271

Hicks, *The Contractual Nature of Real Property Leases*, (1972) 24 Baylor LR 443

Hill, *Section 1 of the Protection from Eviction Act 1977: The Meaning of 'Occupation'*, [1987] Conv 265

Hill, *In the Land of the Rising Sums*, ROOF, November/December 1994, p 10

Hill and Redman, *Law of Landlord and Tenant*, 18th edn

Hills, *Thirty-nine steps to Housing Finance Reform*, 1991

Hills, *Unravelling Housing Finance*, 1991

Hoath, *Rent Books: The Law, Its Uses and Abuses*, [1978–9] JSWL 3

Hoath, *Council Housing*, 1982

Hoath, *Public Sector Housing Law*, 1989

Holdsworth, *History of English Law*, 3rd edn, 1923

Holman, *Housing Policy in Britain*, 1987

Homelessness Code of Guidance for Local Authorities

Honoré, *The Quest for Security: Employees, Tenants, Wives*, The Hamlyn Lectures, 1982

Hood, *Question Time*, ROOF, November/December 1993, p 11

House of Commons Environment Committee, *The Private Rented Housing Sector*, 1981/2

Housing Corporation, *Tenants' Choice: Criteria for Approval and Guidance Notes for Applicants*, 1989

Housing Corporation: Financial Management of Housing Associations, Twentieth Report of the Committee of Public Accounts, May 1994

Housing Corporation, Tenants' Guarantee: Guidance on the Management of Accommodation Let on Assured Tenancies by Registered Housing Associations (Housing Corporation Circulars 28 and 29/91)

Housing Corporation, 1994 Consultation Document, including a revised Draft Tenants' Guarantee: Guidance on the Management of Accommodation Let on Assured Tenancies by Registered Housing Associations

Housing Corporation, Tenants' Guarantee: Guidance on the Management of Accommodation Let on Assured Tenancies by Registered Housing Associations (revised Tenants' Guarantee); now, Housing Corporation Circular 36/94

Housing Policy: A Consultative Document, Cmnd 6851, 1977

Housing: The Government's Proposals, Cm 214, 1987

Hughes, Karn and Lickiss, *Neighbour Disputes: Social Landlords and the Law*, [1994] JSW&FL 201

Inskip, *Big Fish to Fry*, ROOF, July/August 1994, p 11

Jacobs, *The Sale of Council Houses: Does It Matter?*, (1981) 1:2 *Critical Social Policy* 35

Jacobs, *Race, Empire and the Welfare State: Council Housing and Racism*, (1986) 13 *Critical Social Policy* 6

Jew, *Law and Order in Private Rented Housing: Tackling Harassment and Illegal Eviction*, 1994

Johnson, *Untold Tales of the City*, ROOF, September/October 1994, p 13

Johnston Birchall (ed.), 'Council Tenants: Sovereign Consumers or Pawns in the Game?', in Johnston Birchall (ed.) *Housing Policy in the 1990s*, 1992

Johnston Birchall (ed.), *Housing Policy in the 1990s*, 1992

Joseph Rowntree Foundation, see, Rowntree (Joseph) Foundation

Judicial Statistics: Annual Report 1989, Cm 1154

Judson, *Defining Property Rights: The Constitutionality of Protecting Tenants from Condominium Conversions*, (1983) 18 Harv CR-CL LR 179

Karn and Sheridan, *New Homes in the 1990s*, 1994

Kellmer-Pringle, *The Needs of Children*, 2nd edn, 1980

Kelly, *Knock, Knock. Who's There?*, ROOF, November/December 1993, p 16

Kelly, *The Long Good Buy*, ROOF, September/October 1994, p 34

Kemp, 'The ghost of Rachman', in Grant (ed.), *Built to Last*, 1992, ch 14

Kemp, Anderson and Quilgars, *Single Homelessness—What Lies Behind the Numbers*, ROOF, September/October 1993, p 18

Kerr, *Farm Business Tenancies: New Farms and Land 1995–97*, Royal Institution of Chartered Surveyors, 1994

Kincaid, *Poverty and Equality in Britain*, 1975

LRC Housing Update, ROOF, May/June 1993

Labour Party, *A Welcome Home*, September 1991

Lang, *Residential Tenancies: Law and Practice, New South Wales*, 2nd edn, 1990

Langleben, Newnham, *The 1954 Act: the change in tactics*, (1993) 11 EG 120

Langstaff, 'Housing Associations: A Move to Centre Stage', in Johnston Birchall (ed), *Housing Policy in the 1990s*, 1992

Law Commission, *Report on the Landlord and Tenant Act 1954 Part II*, Law Com. No.17, 1969

Law Commission, *Transfer of Land—The Law of Positive and Restrictive Covenants*, Law Com. No.127, 1984

Law Commission, *Covenants Restricting Dispositions, Alterations and Change of User*, Law Com No.141, 1985

Law Commission, *Forfeiture of Tenancies*, Law Com. No.142, 1985

Law Commission, *Landlord and Tenant, Privity of Contract and Estate, Duration of Liability of Parties to Leases*, Working Paper No.95, 1986

Law Commission, *Distress for Rent*, Working Paper No.97, 1986

Law Commission, *Landlord and Tenant: Reform of the Law*, Law Com. No.162, 1987

Law Commission, *Landlord and Tenant: Privity of Contract and Estate*, Law Com. No.174, 1988

Law Commission, *Landlord and Tenant Law: Compensation for Tenant's Improvements*, Law Com. No.178, 1989

Law Commission, *Landlord and Tenant, Distress for Rent*, Law Com. No.194, 1991

Law Commission, *Landlord and Tenant: Responsibility for State and Condition of Property*, Consultation Paper, Law Com. No.123, 1992

Law Commission, *Domestic Violence and Occupation of the Family Home*, Law Com. No.207, 1992

Law Commission, *Business Tenancies, A Periodic Review of the Landlord and Tenant Act 1954 Part II*, Law Com. No.208, 1992

Law Commission, *Aggravated, Exemplary and Restitutionary Damages*, Consultation Paper No.132, 1993

Law Commission, *Termination of Tenancies Bill*, Law Com. No.221, 1994

Law Commission, *Administrative Law: Judicial Review and Statutory Appeals*, Law Com. No.226, 1994

Leasehold Committee, *Interim Report on Tenure and Rents of Business Premises*, Cmd 7706, 1949

Leasehold Committee, *Final Report*, Cmd 7982, 1950

Leasehold Reform in England and Wales, Cmd 2916, 1966

Leather and Murie, 'The Decline in Public Expenditure', in Malpass (ed.), *The Housing Crisis*, 1986

Lee, *Rent Control—The Economic Impact of Social Legislation*, (1992) 12 OJLS 543

Lem, *The Landlord's Duty to Mitigate Upon a Tenant's Repudiation of a Commercial Lease*, (1993) 30 RPR (2d) 33

Letall, *Mobile Homes, An Occupiers Guide*, 1988, Shelter

Leyland, *Repairing Covenants: Renew Held To Go Beyond Mere Repair*, [1993] 10 PR 462

Lloyd and Walentowicz, *Changing Standards*, ROOF, September/October 1993, p 8

Lomax, *Corporation Woes in Perspective*, ROOF, July/August 1994, p 8

Loveland, *Administrative Law, Administrative Processes and the Housing of Homeless Persons: A View from the Sharp End*, (1991) JSW&FL 4

Loveland, *The Politics, Law and Practice of 'Intentional Homelessness': 1— Housing Debt*, [1993] JSW&FL 113

Loveland, *The Politics, Law and Practice of 'Intentional Homelessness': 2— Abandonment of Existing Housing*, [1993] JSW&FL 185

Loveland, *Cathy Sod Off! The End of Homelessness Legislation*, [1994] JSW&FL 367

Luba, *Repairs: Tenants' Rights*, 2nd edn, 1991

Luba, Madge and McConnell, *Defending Possession Proceedings*, 2nd edn, 1989

Lyons, *The Meaning of 'Holiday' under the Rent Acts*, [1984] Conv 286

MAFF, *Agricultural Tenancy Law—Proposals for Reform*, February 1991

MAFF, *Reform of Agricultural Holdings Legislation: Detailed Proposals*, September 1992

MAFF, *News Release 337/93, Agricultural Tenancy Law Reform*, 6 October 1993

Malpass, *Reshaping Housing Policy*, 1990

Malpass, 'Housing Policy and the Disabling of Local Authorities', in Johnston Birchall (ed.), *Housing Policy in the 1990s*, 1992

Malpass and Means, *Implementing Housing Policy*, 1993

Malpass and Murie, *Housing Policy and Practice*, 3rd edn, 1990

Malpass and Murie, *Housing Policy and Practice*, 4th edn, 1994

Marx, *Capital*, vol 3

Maudsley and Burn, *Land Law Cases and Materials*, 6th edn, 1992

Mawrey, *Controlling Control Orders*, (1994) 138 Sol J 598

McGrath and Hunter, *Time to Get the Act Together*, ROOF, March/April 1993, p 15

McIntosh, *Tender Moments*, ROOF, March/April 1993, p 38

McIntosh, *By-pass or No-Through Road*, ROOF, May/June 1994, p 10

McIntosh and Sykes, *A Guide to Institutional Property Investment*, 1985

McManus, *Renting's Long Goodbye*, ROOF, May/June 1993, p 28

Meagher, Gummow, Lehane, *Equity Doctrines and Remedies*, 3rd edn, 1992

Megarry, *The Rent Acts*, 11th edn, 1988

Megarry and Wade, *The Law of Real Property*, 4th edn, 1975

Megarry and Wade, *The Law of Real Property*, 5th edn, 1984

Meyers, *The Covenant of Habitability and the American Law Institute*, (1975) 27 Stan L Rev 879

Miller, *The Let Down*, ROOF, March/April 1993, p 20

Miller, *Criminal Tenancies*, ROOF, November/December 1993, p 16

Milner-Holland Report of the Committee on Housing in Greater London, Cmnd 2605, 1965

Ministry of Agriculture, Fisheries and Food, see MAFF

Mitchell, *The Equitable Doctrine of Relief against Forfeiture*, (1987) 11 Sydney Law Rev 387

Monopolies and Mergers Commission, *Supply of Beer*, Cm 651, 1989

Moore, *The Taxman Wants Your Bedroom*, ROOF, November/December 1994

Moriarty, *Licences and Land Law: Legal Principles and Public Policies*, (1984) 100 LQR 376

Muellbauer, *The Great British Housing Disaster and Economic Policy*, 1990

Muellbauer, *Housing's Economic Hangover*, ROOF, May/June 1993, p 16

Murdoch, *Residential Use and the 1954 Act*, (1993) 17 EG 101

National Consumer Council, *Rental Deposits, Resolving Disputes between Landlords and Tenants*, February 1990

National Federation of Housing Associations' Model Tenancy Agreement

National Federation of Housing Associations, *Formal Response to Draft Tenants' Guarantee*, 1994

National Housing Forum, *Papering Over the Cracks*, 1994

Nelken, *The Limits of the Legal Process, A Study of Landlords, Law and Crime*, 1983

Neo, *Problems of Private Flat Ownership in England and Wales—Is Strata Title the Solution?*, Royal Institution of Chartered Surveyors, 1990

Niner, *Mobile Homes Survey: Final Report of the Department of the Environment*, 1992

Northfield Committee, *Report to the Committee of Inquiry into the Acquisition and Occupancy of Agricultural Land*, Cmnd 7599, 1979

Note, *The Percentage Lease—Its Functions and Drafting Problems*, (1948) 61 Harv L Rev 317

Note, *The Constitutionality of rent control restrictions on property owners' dominion interests*, (1987) 100 Harv L Rev 1067

Note, *Reassessing Rent Control: Its Economic Impact in a Gentrifying Housing Market*, (1988) 101 Harv L Rev 1835

Nugee Committee, *Report of the Committee of Inquiry on the Management of Privately Owned Blocks of Flats*, 1985

Ormandy, *More Than Safety in Numbers*, ROOF, September/October 1993, p 19

Oxley and Smith, *Private Rented Housing in the European Community*, European Housing Research Working Paper Series No.3, June 1993

Page, *Housing for the Have-Nots*, ROOF, July/August 1993, p 10

Paish, Essay 4, 'The Economics of Rent Restriction' (first published 1950), in Hayek *et al.* (eds), *Verdict on Rent Control*, 1972

Paley, *Attitudes to Letting in 1976*, 1978

Papering Over the Cracks: see, National Housing Forum

Partington, *Reforming Judicial Review: the Impact on Homelessness Cases*, [1994] JSW&FL 47

Partington, *Landlord and Tenant*, 2nd edn, 1980

Patterson, *Investment Implications*, (1993) 29 EG 88

Pawlowski, *Residence and the resident landlord*, (1991) 11 EG 78

Pawlowski, *The Forfeiture of Leases*, 1993

Petch and Carter, *Lilley Goes Pink*, ROOF, March/April 1994, p 15

Pollock, *Irish Eyes Unsmiling*, ROOF, November/December 1993, p 28

Popplestone, 'Difficult Tenants: Who Are They and What To Do About Them', in Partington, *Landlord and Tenant*, 2nd edn, 1980

Poverty Commission's Second Main Report, *Law and Poverty in Australia*, 1975

Precedents for the Conveyancer

Prichard, *Fair rents and market rents*, (1992) 142 NLJ 965

Prichard, (1991a), *A Local Property Tribunal?*, (1991) 141 NLJ 973

Prichard, (1991b), *New Jurisdictions for Rent Assessment Committees*, [1991] Conv 447

Prosser, *An Offer They Can Refuse*, ROOF January/February 1993, p 15

Purdoe, Young and Rowan, *Planning Law and Procedure*, 1989

Quinn and Phillips, *The Law of Landlord–Tenant: A Critical Evaluation of the Past with Guidelines for the Future*, (1969) 38 Fordham L Rev 225

Rabin, *The Revolution in Residential Landlord–Tenant Law: Causes and Consequences*, (1984) 69 Cornell LR 517

Randall, *Out for the Count*, ROOF, September/October 1993, p 9

Randolph, 'The Reprivatisation of Housing Associations', in Malpass and Means (ed.), *Implementing Housing Policy*, 1993

Rauta and Pickering, *Private Renting in England 1990*, 1992

Redfern and Cassidy, *Australian Tenancy Practice and Precedents*, 1987

Reich, *The New Property*, (1964) 73 Yale LJ 733

Revised Tenants' Guarantee: see, Housing Corporation

Richards, *The Housing (Homeless Persons) Act 1977—A Study in Policymaking*, Working Paper 22, SAUS University of Bristol, 1981

Richards, 'A Sense of Duty', in Grant (ed.), *Built to Last*, 1992

Roberts, *Legal Action*, November 1993, p 17

Robertson, *You take the high rents, and I'll take the low rents*, ROOF, November/December 1992, p 12

Robertson, *Backdoor*, ROOF, March/April 1993

Rodgers, *Residential Flats—A New Deal?*, [1988] Conv 122

Rodgers, *Agricultural Law*, 1991

Rodgers, *Share Farming, Joint Ventures and Problems of Exclusive Possession*, [1991] Conv 58

Ross, *Drafting and Negotiating Commercial Leases*, 3rd edn, 1989

Rowntree (Joseph) Foundation Inquiry into British Housing, First Report, 1985 (First Report)

Rowntree (Joseph) Foundation Inquiry into British Housing, Second Report, 1991 (Rowntree Inquiry)

Rowntree (Joseph) Foundation, Housing Research Findings No.90, May 1993

Rowntree (Joseph) Foundation, Housing Research Findings No.95, July 1993

Rowntree (Joseph) Foundation, Housing Research Findings No.102, December 1993

Rowntree (Joseph) Foundation, Housing Research Summary, December 1993

Rowntree (Joseph) Foundation, *A Competitive Economy: the Challenge for Housing Policy*, 1994

Rowntree (Joseph) Foundation, Housing Research Findings No.106, January 1994

Rowntree (Joseph) Foundation, Housing Research Findings No.109, March 1994

Rowntree (Joseph) Foundation, Housing Research Findings No.111, March 1994

Rowntree (Joseph) Foundation, Housing Research Findings No.126, September 1994

Rowntree (Joseph) Foundation, Housing Research Findings No.129, October 1994

Rowntree (Joseph) Foundation, Housing Research Findings No.131, November 1994

Royal Commission on the Housing of the Working Classes, 1885

Royal Institution of Chartered Surveyors, *International Leasing Structures*, Paper No.26, May 1993

Ryland, *EC Leasing practices*, (1992) 26 EG 110

Sackville and Neave, *Property Law: Cases and Materials*, 5th edn, 1994

Saunders, *A Nation of Home Owners*, 1990

Scammell and Densham, *Law of Agricultural Holdings*, 7th edn, 1989

Schoshinski, *American Law of Landlord and Tenant*, 1980

Scott, *Financial Institutions and the British Property Investment Market 1850–1980*, D.Phil Thesis, Oxford University, 1992

Second Restatement of the Law of Property, Landlord and Tenant (The), American Law Institute, 1976

Select Committee on Business Premises, 1920

Sharp, *Slow Coach to Eviction*, ROOF, May/June 1991, p 12

Shelter, *In Distress with Rent*, 1978

Sheppard, *Bias to the Poor*, 1984

Shone, *EC leasehold regimes: a comparison*, (1992) 11 EG 92

Singh, *Backdoor*, ROOF, March/April 1994

Smith, *The Running of Covenants in Equitable Leases and Equitable Assignments of Legal Leases*, [1978] CLJ 98

Smith, *A Review of the Operation of the Leasehold Property (Repairs) Act 1938*, [1986] Conv 85

Smith, *Reform of the Law of Forfeiture*, [1986] Conv 165

Smith, *A Nasty Measure—Part I of the Landlord and Tenant Act 1987*, (1992) 12 LS 42

Smith, *What is Wrong with Certainty in Leases?*, [1993] Conv 461

Smith, *Repairing Obligations: A Case Against Radical Reform*, [1994] Conv 186

Smith, *Backdoor*, ROOF, May/June 1994

Smith and Hill, 'An Unwelcome Home', in Grant (ed.), *Built to Last*, 1992

Sparkes, *Purchasers in Possession*, [1987] Conv 278

Sparkes, *Breaking Flat Sharing Agreements*, (1989) 5 JSWL 295

Sparkes, *Co-Tenants, Joint Tenants and Tenants in Common*, (1989) 18 Anglo-Amer L Rev 151

Sparkes, *Certainty of Leasehold Terms*, (1993) 109 LQR 93

Spencer-Silver, *Landlord's continuing liability*, (1993) 32 EG 69

Spicker, 'Victorian Values', in Grant (ed.), *Built To Last*, 1992

Standing Conference on Public Health, *Housing, Homelessness and Health*, 1994

Steele, *Unfair Shares*, ROOF, May/June 1994, p 17

Stein, *Legal Institutions*, 1984

Sternberg, *The Commercial Landlord's Duty to Mitigate Upon a Tenant's Abandonment of the Premises*, (1984–85) 5 Advocates' Q 385

Sternlieb and Hughes, *The Future of Rental Housing*, 1981

Summerskill, *Homebusters*, ROOF, September/October 1994, p 26

Sunkin, Bridges and Mészáros, *Judicial Review in Perspective*, 1993

Swenarton, *Homes Fit for Heroes*, 1981

Taylor, *Scottish Let Down*, ROOF, July/August 1993, p 17

Tee, *The Negative Nature of a Notice to Quit*, [1992] CLJ 218

Tenants' Guarantee: see, Housing Corporation

Tenants' Guarantee (Draft): see, Housing Corporation

Tenants' Guarantee (revised): see, Housing Corporation

Thomas, North, Spencer and Ward, *The Landlord and Tenant Act 1987: Awareness, Experience and Impact*, 1991

Thompson, *Licences: Questioning the Basics*, [1983] Conv 50

Thompson, *Correspondence*, [1983] Conv 471

Thornton, *Enforceability of Leasehold Covenants*, (1991) 11 LS 47

Thornton, *Who Houses? Homelessness, Local Connection and Inter-Authority Referrals under Section 67 of the Housing Act 1985*, [1994] JSW&FL 29

Todd, *Slow Train Coming*, ROOF, November/December 1992, p 16

Todd and Foxon, *Recent Private Lettings 1982–84*, 1987

Treitel, *The Law of Contract*, 8th edn, 1991

Tromans, *Forfeiture of Leases: Relief for Underlessees and Holders of Other Derivative Interests*, [1986] Conv 187

Tromans, *Commercial Leases*, 1987

van Vliet, *International Handbook of Housing Policies and Practices*, 1990

Walentowicz, *Double Trouble on the Benefit Front*, ROOF, May/June 1994, p 11

Walsh, *Shopping centres: why are turnover rents not more popular?*, (1988) 13 EG 20

Walter, *Open Door, Open Mind?*, ROOF, November/December 1994, p 20

Warburton, *Backdoor*, ROOF, September/October 1994

Watchman, *Fair Rents and Market Scarcity*, [1985] Conv 199

Watson, *Breach of Tenant's Repairing Covenants and the Self-Help Clause*, [1993] 11 PR 429

Webb, *Notices to Quit by One Joint Tenant*, [1983] Conv 211

Welcome Home (A): see, Labour Party

White, 'Business Out Of Charity', in Grant (ed.), *Built To Last*, 1992

White Paper on Local Government in England, Cmnd 4584, 1971

White Paper on Housing, Cm 214, 1987

Wilcox, *Housing Finance Review 1994/95*, 1994

Wilcox, Bramley, Ferguson, Perry and Woods, *Local Housing Companies: New Opportunities for Council Housing*, 1993

Williams, *Allies or Adversaries*, ROOF, January/February 1993, p 28

Wilkinson, *Conveyancer's Notebook*, [1992] Conv 141

Wilkinson, *Fresh Thoughts from Abroad*, [1994] Conv 428

Woodfall, *Landlord and Tenant*

Yates and Hawkins, *Landlord and Tenant Law*, 2nd edn, 1986

Zipfel, *Farming Out the Management*, ROOF, March/April 1994, p 12

INDEX